Lecture Notes in Computer Science **13694**

More information about this series at https://link.springer.com/bookseries/558

Shai Avidan · Gabriel Brostow ·
Moustapha Cissé · Giovanni Maria Farinella ·
Tal Hassner (Eds.)

Computer Vision – ECCV 2022

17th European Conference
Tel Aviv, Israel, October 23–27, 2022
Proceedings, Part XXXIV

Editors
Shai Avidan
Tel Aviv University
Tel Aviv, Israel

Gabriel Brostow
University College London
London, UK

Moustapha Cissé
Google AI
Accra, Ghana

Giovanni Maria Farinella
University of Catania
Catania, Italy

Tal Hassner
Facebook (United States)
Menlo Park, CA, USA

ISSN 0302-9743 ISSN 1611-3349 (electronic)
Lecture Notes in Computer Science
ISBN 978-3-031-19829-8 ISBN 978-3-031-19830-4 (eBook)
https://doi.org/10.1007/978-3-031-19830-4

This Springer imprint is published by the registered company Springer Nature Switzerland AG
The registered company address is: Gewerbestrasse 11, 6330 Cham, Switzerland

Foreword

Organizing the European Conference on Computer Vision (ECCV 2022) in Tel-Aviv during a global pandemic was no easy feat. The uncertainty level was extremely high, and decisions had to be postponed to the last minute. Still, we managed to plan things just in time for ECCV 2022 to be held in person. Participation in physical events is crucial to stimulating collaborations and nurturing the culture of the Computer Vision community.

There were many people who worked hard to ensure attendees enjoyed the best science at the 16th edition of ECCV. We are grateful to the Program Chairs Gabriel Brostow and Tal Hassner, who went above and beyond to ensure the ECCV reviewing process ran smoothly. The scientific program includes dozens of workshops and tutorials in addition to the main conference and we would like to thank Leonid Karlinsky and Tomer Michaeli for their hard work. Finally, special thanks to the web chairs Lorenzo Baraldi and Kosta Derpanis, who put in extra hours to transfer information fast and efficiently to the ECCV community.

We would like to express gratitude to our generous sponsors and the Industry Chairs, Dimosthenis Karatzas and Chen Sagiv, who oversaw industry relations and proposed new ways for academia-industry collaboration and technology transfer. It's great to see so much industrial interest in what we're doing!

Authors' draft versions of the papers appeared online with open access on both the Computer Vision Foundation (CVF) and the European Computer Vision Association (ECVA) websites as with previous ECCVs. Springer, the publisher of the proceedings, has arranged for archival publication. The final version of the papers is hosted by SpringerLink, with active references and supplementary materials. It benefits all potential readers that we offer both a free and citeable version for all researchers, as well as an authoritative, citeable version for SpringerLink readers. Our thanks go to Ronan Nugent from Springer, who helped us negotiate this agreement. Last but not least, we wish to thank Eric Mortensen, our publication chair, whose expertise made the process smooth.

October 2022

Rita Cucchiara
Jiří Matas
Amnon Shashua
Lihi Zelnik-Manor

Preface

Welcome to the proceedings of the European Conference on Computer Vision (ECCV 2022). This was a hybrid edition of ECCV as we made our way out of the COVID-19 pandemic. The conference received 5804 valid paper submissions, compared to 5150 submissions to ECCV 2020 (a 12.7% increase) and 2439 in ECCV 2018. 1645 submissions were accepted for publication (28%) and, of those, 157 (2.7% overall) as orals.

846 of the submissions were desk-rejected for various reasons. Many of them because they revealed author identity, thus violating the double-blind policy. This violation came in many forms: some had author names with the title, others added acknowledgments to specific grants, yet others had links to their github account where their name was visible. Tampering with the LaTeX template was another reason for automatic desk rejection.

ECCV 2022 used the traditional CMT system to manage the entire double-blind reviewing process. Authors did not know the names of the reviewers and vice versa. Each paper received at least 3 reviews (except 6 papers that received only 2 reviews), totalling more than 15,000 reviews.

Handling the review process at this scale was a significant challenge. To ensure that each submission received as fair and high-quality reviews as possible, we recruited more than 4719 reviewers (in the end, 4719 reviewers did at least one review). Similarly we recruited more than 276 area chairs (eventually, only 276 area chairs handled a batch of papers). The area chairs were selected based on their technical expertise and reputation, largely among people who served as area chairs in previous top computer vision and machine learning conferences (ECCV, ICCV, CVPR, NeurIPS, etc.).

Reviewers were similarly invited from previous conferences, and also from the pool of authors. We also encouraged experienced area chairs to suggest additional chairs and reviewers in the initial phase of recruiting. The median reviewer load was five papers per reviewer, while the average load was about four papers, because of the emergency reviewers. The area chair load was 35 papers, on average.

Conflicts of interest between authors, area chairs, and reviewers were handled largely automatically by the CMT platform, with some manual help from the Program Chairs. Reviewers were allowed to describe themselves as senior reviewer (load of 8 papers to review) or junior reviewers (load of 4 papers). Papers were matched to area chairs based on a subject-area affinity score computed in CMT and an affinity score computed by the Toronto Paper Matching System (TPMS). TPMS is based on the paper's full text. An area chair handling each submission would bid for preferred expert reviewers, and we balanced load and prevented conflicts.

The assignment of submissions to area chairs was relatively smooth, as was the assignment of submissions to reviewers. A small percentage of reviewers were not happy with their assignments in terms of subjects and self-reported expertise. This is an area for improvement, although it's interesting that many of these cases were reviewers hand-picked by AC's. We made a later round of reviewer recruiting, targeted at the list of authors of papers submitted to the conference, and had an excellent response which helped provide enough emergency reviewers. In the end, all but six papers received at least 3 reviews.

The challenges of the reviewing process are in line with past experiences at ECCV 2020. As the community grows, and the number of submissions increases, it becomes ever more challenging to recruit enough reviewers and ensure a high enough quality of reviews. Enlisting authors by default as reviewers might be one step to address this challenge.

Authors were given a week to rebut the initial reviews, and address reviewers' concerns. Each rebuttal was limited to a single pdf page with a fixed template.

The Area Chairs then led discussions with the reviewers on the merits of each submission. The goal was to reach consensus, but, ultimately, it was up to the Area Chair to make a decision. The decision was then discussed with a buddy Area Chair to make sure decisions were fair and informative. The entire process was conducted virtually with no in-person meetings taking place.

The Program Chairs were informed in cases where the Area Chairs overturned a decisive consensus reached by the reviewers, and pushed for the meta-reviews to contain details that explained the reasoning for such decisions. Obviously these were the most contentious cases, where reviewer inexperience was the most common reported factor.

Once the list of accepted papers was finalized and released, we went through the laborious process of plagiarism (including self-plagiarism) detection. A total of 4 accepted papers were rejected because of that.

Finally, we would like to thank our Technical Program Chair, Pavel Lifshits, who did tremendous work behind the scenes, and we thank the tireless CMT team.

October 2022

Gabriel Brostow
Giovanni Maria Farinella
Moustapha Cissé
Shai Avidan
Tal Hassner

Organization

General Chairs

Rita Cucchiara	University of Modena and Reggio Emilia, Italy
Jiří Matas	Czech Technical University in Prague, Czech Republic
Amnon Shashua	Hebrew University of Jerusalem, Israel
Lihi Zelnik-Manor	Technion – Israel Institute of Technology, Israel

Program Chairs

Shai Avidan	Tel-Aviv University, Israel
Gabriel Brostow	University College London, UK
Moustapha Cissé	Google AI, Ghana
Giovanni Maria Farinella	University of Catania, Italy
Tal Hassner	Facebook AI, USA

Program Technical Chair

Pavel Lifshits	Technion – Israel Institute of Technology, Israel

Workshops Chairs

Leonid Karlinsky	IBM Research, Israel
Tomer Michaeli	Technion – Israel Institute of Technology, Israel
Ko Nishino	Kyoto University, Japan

Tutorial Chairs

Thomas Pock	Graz University of Technology, Austria
Natalia Neverova	Facebook AI Research, UK

Demo Chair

Bohyung Han	Seoul National University, Korea

Social and Student Activities Chairs

Tatiana Tommasi — Italian Institute of Technology, Italy
Sagie Benaim — University of Copenhagen, Denmark

Diversity and Inclusion Chairs

Xi Yin — Facebook AI Research, USA
Bryan Russell — Adobe, USA

Communications Chairs

Lorenzo Baraldi — University of Modena and Reggio Emilia, Italy
Kosta Derpanis — York University & Samsung AI Centre Toronto, Canada

Industrial Liaison Chairs

Dimosthenis Karatzas — Universitat Autònoma de Barcelona, Spain
Chen Sagiv — SagivTech, Israel

Finance Chair

Gerard Medioni — University of Southern California & Amazon, USA

Publication Chair

Eric Mortensen — MiCROTEC, USA

Area Chairs

Lourdes Agapito — University College London, UK
Zeynep Akata — University of Tübingen, Germany
Naveed Akhtar — University of Western Australia, Australia
Karteek Alahari — Inria Grenoble Rhône-Alpes, France
Alexandre Alahi — École polytechnique fédérale de Lausanne, Switzerland
Pablo Arbelaez — Universidad de Los Andes, Columbia
Antonis A. Argyros — University of Crete & Foundation for Research and Technology-Hellas, Crete
Yuki M. Asano — University of Amsterdam, The Netherlands
Kalle Åström — Lund University, Sweden
Hadar Averbuch-Elor — Cornell University, USA

Hossein Azizpour	KTH Royal Institute of Technology, Sweden
Vineeth N. Balasubramanian	Indian Institute of Technology, Hyderabad, India
Lamberto Ballan	University of Padova, Italy
Adrien Bartoli	Université Clermont Auvergne, France
Horst Bischof	Graz University of Technology, Austria
Matthew B. Blaschko	KU Leuven, Belgium
Federica Bogo	Meta Reality Labs Research, Switzerland
Katherine Bouman	California Institute of Technology, USA
Edmond Boyer	Inria Grenoble Rhône-Alpes, France
Michael S. Brown	York University, Canada
Vittorio Caggiano	Meta AI Research, USA
Neill Campbell	University of Bath, UK
Octavia Camps	Northeastern University, USA
Duygu Ceylan	Adobe Research, USA
Ayan Chakrabarti	Google Research, USA
Tat-Jen Cham	Nanyang Technological University, Singapore
Antoni Chan	City University of Hong Kong, Hong Kong, China
Manmohan Chandraker	NEC Labs America, USA
Xinlei Chen	Facebook AI Research, USA
Xilin Chen	Institute of Computing Technology, Chinese Academy of Sciences, China
Dongdong Chen	Microsoft Cloud AI, USA
Chen Chen	University of Central Florida, USA
Ondrej Chum	Vision Recognition Group, Czech Technical University in Prague, Czech Republic
John Collomosse	Adobe Research & University of Surrey, UK
Camille Couprie	Facebook, France
David Crandall	Indiana University, USA
Daniel Cremers	Technical University of Munich, Germany
Marco Cristani	University of Verona, Italy
Canton Cristian	Facebook AI Research, USA
Dengxin Dai	ETH Zurich, Switzerland
Dima Damen	University of Bristol, UK
Kostas Daniilidis	University of Pennsylvania, USA
Trevor Darrell	University of California, Berkeley, USA
Andrew Davison	Imperial College London, UK
Tali Dekel	Weizmann Institute of Science, Israel
Alessio Del Bue	Istituto Italiano di Tecnologia, Italy
Weihong Deng	Beijing University of Posts and Telecommunications, China
Konstantinos Derpanis	Ryerson University, Canada
Carl Doersch	DeepMind, UK

Matthijs Douze	Facebook AI Research, USA
Mohamed Elhoseiny	King Abdullah University of Science and Technology, Saudi Arabia
Sergio Escalera	University of Barcelona, Spain
Yi Fang	New York University, USA
Ryan Farrell	Brigham Young University, USA
Alireza Fathi	Google, USA
Christoph Feichtenhofer	Facebook AI Research, USA
Basura Fernando	Agency for Science, Technology and Research (A*STAR), Singapore
Vittorio Ferrari	Google Research, Switzerland
Andrew W. Fitzgibbon	Graphcore, UK
David J. Fleet	University of Toronto, Canada
David Forsyth	University of Illinois at Urbana-Champaign, USA
David Fouhey	University of Michigan, USA
Katerina Fragkiadaki	Carnegie Mellon University, USA
Friedrich Fraundorfer	Graz University of Technology, Austria
Oren Freifeld	Ben-Gurion University, Israel
Thomas Funkhouser	Google Research & Princeton University, USA
Yasutaka Furukawa	Simon Fraser University, Canada
Fabio Galasso	Sapienza University of Rome, Italy
Jürgen Gall	University of Bonn, Germany
Chuang Gan	Massachusetts Institute of Technology, USA
Zhe Gan	Microsoft, USA
Animesh Garg	University of Toronto, Vector Institute, Nvidia, Canada
Efstratios Gavves	University of Amsterdam, The Netherlands
Peter Gehler	Amazon, Germany
Theo Gevers	University of Amsterdam, The Netherlands
Bernard Ghanem	King Abdullah University of Science and Technology, Saudi Arabia
Ross B. Girshick	Facebook AI Research, USA
Georgia Gkioxari	Facebook AI Research, USA
Albert Gordo	Facebook, USA
Stephen Gould	Australian National University, Australia
Venu Madhav Govindu	Indian Institute of Science, India
Kristen Grauman	Facebook AI Research & UT Austin, USA
Abhinav Gupta	Carnegie Mellon University & Facebook AI Research, USA
Mohit Gupta	University of Wisconsin-Madison, USA
Hu Han	Institute of Computing Technology, Chinese Academy of Sciences, China

Bohyung Han	Seoul National University, Korea
Tian Han	Stevens Institute of Technology, USA
Emily Hand	University of Nevada, Reno, USA
Bharath Hariharan	Cornell University, USA
Ran He	Institute of Automation, Chinese Academy of Sciences, China
Otmar Hilliges	ETH Zurich, Switzerland
Adrian Hilton	University of Surrey, UK
Minh Hoai	Stony Brook University, USA
Yedid Hoshen	Hebrew University of Jerusalem, Israel
Timothy Hospedales	University of Edinburgh, UK
Gang Hua	Wormpex AI Research, USA
Di Huang	Beihang University, China
Jing Huang	Facebook, USA
Jia-Bin Huang	Facebook, USA
Nathan Jacobs	Washington University in St. Louis, USA
C.V. Jawahar	International Institute of Information Technology, Hyderabad, India
Herve Jegou	Facebook AI Research, France
Neel Joshi	Microsoft Research, USA
Armand Joulin	Facebook AI Research, France
Frederic Jurie	University of Caen Normandie, France
Fredrik Kahl	Chalmers University of Technology, Sweden
Yannis Kalantidis	NAVER LABS Europe, France
Evangelos Kalogerakis	University of Massachusetts, Amherst, USA
Sing Bing Kang	Zillow Group, USA
Yosi Keller	Bar Ilan University, Israel
Margret Keuper	University of Mannheim, Germany
Tae-Kyun Kim	Imperial College London, UK
Benjamin Kimia	Brown University, USA
Alexander Kirillov	Facebook AI Research, USA
Kris Kitani	Carnegie Mellon University, USA
Iasonas Kokkinos	Snap Inc. & University College London, UK
Vladlen Koltun	Apple, USA
Nikos Komodakis	University of Crete, Crete
Piotr Koniusz	Australian National University, Australia
Philipp Kraehenbuehl	University of Texas at Austin, USA
Dilip Krishnan	Google, USA
Ajay Kumar	Hong Kong Polytechnic University, Hong Kong, China
Junseok Kwon	Chung-Ang University, Korea
Jean-Francois Lalonde	Université Laval, Canada

Vittorio Murino	Istituto Italiano di Tecnologia, Italy
P. J. Narayanan	International Institute of Information Technology, Hyderabad, India
Ram Nevatia	University of Southern California, USA
Natalia Neverova	Facebook AI Research, UK
Richard Newcombe	Facebook, USA
Cuong V. Nguyen	Florida International University, USA
Bingbing Ni	Shanghai Jiao Tong University, China
Juan Carlos Niebles	Salesforce & Stanford University, USA
Ko Nishino	Kyoto University, Japan
Jean-Marc Odobez	Idiap Research Institute, École polytechnique fédérale de Lausanne, Switzerland
Francesca Odone	University of Genova, Italy
Takayuki Okatani	Tohoku University & RIKEN Center for Advanced Intelligence Project, Japan
Manohar Paluri	Facebook, USA
Guan Pang	Facebook, USA
Maja Pantic	Imperial College London, UK
Sylvain Paris	Adobe Research, USA
Jaesik Park	Pohang University of Science and Technology, Korea
Hyun Soo Park	The University of Minnesota, USA
Omkar M. Parkhi	Facebook, USA
Deepak Pathak	Carnegie Mellon University, USA
Georgios Pavlakos	University of California, Berkeley, USA
Marcello Pelillo	University of Venice, Italy
Marc Pollefeys	ETH Zurich & Microsoft, Switzerland
Jean Ponce	Inria, France
Gerard Pons-Moll	University of Tübingen, Germany
Fatih Porikli	Qualcomm, USA
Victor Adrian Prisacariu	University of Oxford, UK
Petia Radeva	University of Barcelona, Spain
Ravi Ramamoorthi	University of California, San Diego, USA
Deva Ramanan	Carnegie Mellon University, USA
Vignesh Ramanathan	Facebook, USA
Nalini Ratha	State University of New York at Buffalo, USA
Tammy Riklin Raviv	Ben-Gurion University, Israel
Tobias Ritschel	University College London, UK
Emanuele Rodola	Sapienza University of Rome, Italy
Amit K. Roy-Chowdhury	University of California, Riverside, USA
Michael Rubinstein	Google, USA
Olga Russakovsky	Princeton University, USA

Mathieu Salzmann	École polytechnique fédérale de Lausanne, Switzerland
Dimitris Samaras	Stony Brook University, USA
Aswin Sankaranarayanan	Carnegie Mellon University, USA
Imari Sato	National Institute of Informatics, Japan
Yoichi Sato	University of Tokyo, Japan
Shin'ichi Satoh	National Institute of Informatics, Japan
Walter Scheirer	University of Notre Dame, USA
Bernt Schiele	Max Planck Institute for Informatics, Germany
Konrad Schindler	ETH Zurich, Switzerland
Cordelia Schmid	Inria & Google, France
Alexander Schwing	University of Illinois at Urbana-Champaign, USA
Nicu Sebe	University of Trento, Italy
Greg Shakhnarovich	Toyota Technological Institute at Chicago, USA
Eli Shechtman	Adobe Research, USA
Humphrey Shi	University of Oregon & University of Illinois at Urbana-Champaign & Picsart AI Research, USA
Jianbo Shi	University of Pennsylvania, USA
Roy Shilkrot	Massachusetts Institute of Technology, USA
Mike Zheng Shou	National University of Singapore, Singapore
Kaleem Siddiqi	McGill University, Canada
Richa Singh	Indian Institute of Technology Jodhpur, India
Greg Slabaugh	Queen Mary University of London, UK
Cees Snoek	University of Amsterdam, The Netherlands
Yale Song	Facebook AI Research, USA
Yi-Zhe Song	University of Surrey, UK
Bjorn Stenger	Rakuten Institute of Technology
Abby Stylianou	Saint Louis University, USA
Akihiro Sugimoto	National Institute of Informatics, Japan
Chen Sun	Brown University, USA
Deqing Sun	Google, USA
Kalyan Sunkavalli	Adobe Research, USA
Ying Tai	Tencent YouTu Lab, China
Ayellet Tal	Technion – Israel Institute of Technology, Israel
Ping Tan	Simon Fraser University, Canada
Siyu Tang	ETH Zurich, Switzerland
Chi-Keung Tang	Hong Kong University of Science and Technology, Hong Kong, China
Radu Timofte	University of Würzburg, Germany & ETH Zurich, Switzerland
Federico Tombari	Google, Switzerland & Technical University of Munich, Germany

James Tompkin	Brown University, USA
Lorenzo Torresani	Dartmouth College, USA
Alexander Toshev	Apple, USA
Du Tran	Facebook AI Research, USA
Anh T. Tran	VinAI, Vietnam
Zhuowen Tu	University of California, San Diego, USA
Georgios Tzimiropoulos	Queen Mary University of London, UK
Jasper Uijlings	Google Research, Switzerland
Jan C. van Gemert	Delft University of Technology, The Netherlands
Gul Varol	Ecole des Ponts ParisTech, France
Nuno Vasconcelos	University of California, San Diego, USA
Mayank Vatsa	Indian Institute of Technology Jodhpur, India
Ashok Veeraraghavan	Rice University, USA
Jakob Verbeek	Facebook AI Research, France
Carl Vondrick	Columbia University, USA
Ruiping Wang	Institute of Computing Technology, Chinese Academy of Sciences, China
Xinchao Wang	National University of Singapore, Singapore
Liwei Wang	The Chinese University of Hong Kong, Hong Kong, China
Chaohui Wang	Université Paris-Est, France
Xiaolong Wang	University of California, San Diego, USA
Christian Wolf	NAVER LABS Europe, France
Tao Xiang	University of Surrey, UK
Saining Xie	Facebook AI Research, USA
Cihang Xie	University of California, Santa Cruz, USA
Zeki Yalniz	Facebook, USA
Ming-Hsuan Yang	University of California, Merced, USA
Angela Yao	National University of Singapore, Singapore
Shaodi You	University of Amsterdam, The Netherlands
Stella X. Yu	University of California, Berkeley, USA
Junsong Yuan	State University of New York at Buffalo, USA
Stefanos Zafeiriou	Imperial College London, UK
Amir Zamir	École polytechnique fédérale de Lausanne, Switzerland
Lei Zhang	Alibaba & Hong Kong Polytechnic University, Hong Kong, China
Lei Zhang	International Digital Economy Academy (IDEA), China
Pengchuan Zhang	Meta AI, USA
Bolei Zhou	University of California, Los Angeles, USA
Yuke Zhu	University of Texas at Austin, USA

Todd Zickler	Harvard University, USA
Wangmeng Zuo	Harbin Institute of Technology, China

Technical Program Committee

Davide Abati
Soroush Abbasi Koohpayegani
Amos L. Abbott
Rameen Abdal
Rabab Abdelfattah
Sahar Abdelnabi
Hassan Abu Alhaija
Abulikemu Abuduweili
Ron Abutbul
Hanno Ackermann
Aikaterini Adam
Kamil Adamczewski
Ehsan Adeli
Vida Adeli
Donald Adjeroh
Arman Afrasiyabi
Akshay Agarwal
Sameer Agarwal
Abhinav Agarwalla
Vaibhav Aggarwal
Sara Aghajanzadeh
Susmit Agrawal
Antonio Agudo
Touqeer Ahmad
Sk Miraj Ahmed
Chaitanya Ahuja
Nilesh A. Ahuja
Abhishek Aich
Shubhra Aich
Noam Aigerman
Arash Akbarinia
Peri Akiva
Derya Akkaynak
Emre Aksan
Arjun R. Akula
Yuval Alaluf
Stephan Alaniz
Paul Albert
Cenek Albl
Filippo Aleotti
Konstantinos P. Alexandridis
Motasem Alfarra
Mohsen Ali
Thiemo Alldieck
Hadi Alzayer
Liang An
Shan An
Yi An
Zhulin An
Dongsheng An
Jie An
Xiang An
Saket Anand
Cosmin Ancuti
Juan Andrade-Cetto
Alexander Andreopoulos
Bjoern Andres
Jerone T. A. Andrews
Shivangi Aneja
Anelia Angelova
Dragomir Anguelov
Rushil Anirudh
Oron Anschel
Rao Muhammad Anwer
Djamila Aouada
Evlampios Apostolidis
Srikar Appalaraju
Nikita Araslanov
Andre Araujo
Eric Arazo
Dawit Mureja Argaw
Anurag Arnab
Aditya Arora
Chetan Arora
Sunpreet S. Arora
Alexey Artemov
Muhammad Asad
Kumar Ashutosh
Sinem Aslan
Vishal Asnani
Mahmoud Assran
Amir Atapour-Abarghouei
Nikos Athanasiou
Ali Athar
ShahRukh Athar
Sara Atito
Souhaib Attaiki
Matan Atzmon
Mathieu Aubry
Nicolas Audebert
Tristan T. Aumentado-Armstrong
Melinos Averkiou
Yannis Avrithis
Stephane Ayache
Mehmet Aygün
Seyed Mehdi Ayyoubzadeh
Hossein Azizpour
George Azzopardi
Mallikarjun B. R.
Yunhao Ba
Abhishek Badki
Seung-Hwan Bae
Seung-Hwan Baek
Seungryul Baek
Piyush Nitin Bagad
Shai Bagon
Gaetan Bahl
Shikhar Bahl
Sherwin Bahmani
Haoran Bai
Lei Bai
Jiawang Bai
Haoyue Bai
Jinbin Bai
Xiang Bai
Xuyang Bai

Yang Bai
Yuanchao Bai
Ziqian Bai
Sungyong Baik
Kevin Bailly
Max Bain
Federico Baldassarre
Wele Gedara Chaminda Bandara
Biplab Banerjee
Pratyay Banerjee
Sandipan Banerjee
Jihwan Bang
Antyanta Bangunharcana
Aayush Bansal
Ankan Bansal
Siddhant Bansal
Wentao Bao
Zhipeng Bao
Amir Bar
Manel Baradad Jurjo
Lorenzo Baraldi
Danny Barash
Daniel Barath
Connelly Barnes
Ioan Andrei Bârsan
Steven Basart
Dina Bashkirova
Chaim Baskin
Peyman Bateni
Anil Batra
Sebastiano Battiato
Ardhendu Behera
Harkirat Behl
Jens Behley
Vasileios Belagiannis
Boulbaba Ben Amor
Emanuel Ben Baruch
Abdessamad Ben Hamza
Gil Ben-Artzi
Assia Benbihi
Fabian Benitez-Quiroz
Guy Ben-Yosef
Philipp Benz
Alexander W. Bergman
Urs Bergmann
Jesus Bermudez-Cameo
Stefano Berretti
Gedas Bertasius
Zachary Bessinger
Petra Bevandić
Matthew Beveridge
Lucas Beyer
Yash Bhalgat
Suvaansh Bhambri
Samarth Bharadwaj
Gaurav Bharaj
Aparna Bharati
Bharat Lal Bhatnagar
Uttaran Bhattacharya
Apratim Bhattacharyya
Brojeshwar Bhowmick
Ankan Kumar Bhunia
Ayan Kumar Bhunia
Qi Bi
Sai Bi
Michael Bi Mi
Gui-Bin Bian
Jia-Wang Bian
Shaojun Bian
Pia Bideau
Mario Bijelic
Hakan Bilen
Guillaume-Alexandre Bilodeau
Alexander Binder
Tolga Birdal
Vighnesh N. Birodkar
Sandika Biswas
Andreas Blattmann
Janusz Bobulski
Giuseppe Boccignone
Vishnu Boddeti
Navaneeth Bodla
Moritz Böhle
Aleksei Bokhovkin
Sam Bond-Taylor
Vivek Boominathan
Shubhankar Borse
Mark Boss
Andrea Bottino
Adnane Boukhayma
Fadi Boutros
Nicolas C. Boutry
Richard S. Bowen
Ivaylo Boyadzhiev
Aidan Boyd
Yuri Boykov
Aljaz Bozic
Behzad Bozorgtabar
Eric Brachmann
Samarth Brahmbhatt
Gustav Bredell
Francois Bremond
Joel Brogan
Andrew Brown
Thomas Brox
Marcus A. Brubaker
Robert-Jan Bruintjes
Yuqi Bu
Anders G. Buch
Himanshu Buckchash
Mateusz Buda
Ignas Budvytis
José M. Buenaposada
Marcel C. Bühler
Tu Bui
Adrian Bulat
Hannah Bull
Evgeny Burnaev
Andrei Bursuc
Benjamin Busam
Sergey N. Buzykanov
Wonmin Byeon
Fabian Caba
Martin Cadik
Guanyu Cai
Minjie Cai
Qing Cai
Zhongang Cai
Qi Cai
Yancheng Cai
Shen Cai
Han Cai
Jiarui Cai

Bowen Cai
Mu Cai
Qin Cai
Ruojin Cai
Weidong Cai
Weiwei Cai
Yi Cai
Yujun Cai
Zhiping Cai
Akin Caliskan
Lilian Calvet
Baris Can Cam
Necati Cihan Camgoz
Tommaso Campari
Dylan Campbell
Ziang Cao
Ang Cao
Xu Cao
Zhiwen Cao
Shengcao Cao
Song Cao
Weipeng Cao
Xiangyong Cao
Xiaochun Cao
Yue Cao
Yunhao Cao
Zhangjie Cao
Jiale Cao
Yang Cao
Jiajiong Cao
Jie Cao
Jinkun Cao
Lele Cao
Yulong Cao
Zhiguo Cao
Chen Cao
Razvan Caramalau
Marlène Careil
Gustavo Carneiro
Joao Carreira
Dan Casas
Paola Cascante-Bonilla
Angela Castillo
Francisco M. Castro
Pedro Castro
Luca Cavalli
George J. Cazenavette
Oya Celiktutan
Hakan Cevikalp
Sri Harsha C. H.
Sungmin Cha
Geonho Cha
Menglei Chai
Lucy Chai
Yuning Chai
Zenghao Chai
Anirban Chakraborty
Deep Chakraborty
Rudrasis Chakraborty
Souradeep Chakraborty
Kelvin C. K. Chan
Chee Seng Chan
Paramanand Chandramouli
Arjun Chandrasekaran
Kenneth Chaney
Dongliang Chang
Huiwen Chang
Peng Chang
Xiaojun Chang
Jia-Ren Chang
Hyung Jin Chang
Hyun Sung Chang
Ju Yong Chang
Li-Jen Chang
Qi Chang
Wei-Yi Chang
Yi Chang
Nadine Chang
Hanqing Chao
Pradyumna Chari
Dibyadip Chatterjee
Chiranjoy Chattopadhyay
Siddhartha Chaudhuri
Zhengping Che
Gal Chechik
Lianggangxu Chen
Qi Alfred Chen
Brian Chen
Bor-Chun Chen
Bo-Hao Chen
Bohong Chen
Bin Chen
Ziliang Chen
Cheng Chen
Chen Chen
Chaofeng Chen
Xi Chen
Haoyu Chen
Xuanhong Chen
Wei Chen
Qiang Chen
Shi Chen
Xianyu Chen
Chang Chen
Changhuai Chen
Hao Chen
Jie Chen
Jianbo Chen
Jingjing Chen
Jun Chen
Kejiang Chen
Mingcai Chen
Nenglun Chen
Qifeng Chen
Ruoyu Chen
Shu-Yu Chen
Weidong Chen
Weijie Chen
Weikai Chen
Xiang Chen
Xiuyi Chen
Xingyu Chen
Yaofo Chen
Yueting Chen
Yu Chen
Yunjin Chen
Yuntao Chen
Yun Chen
Zhenfang Chen
Zhuangzhuang Chen
Chu-Song Chen
Xiangyu Chen
Zhuo Chen
Chaoqi Chen
Shizhe Chen

Xiaotong Chen
Xiaozhi Chen
Dian Chen
Defang Chen
Dingfan Chen
Ding-Jie Chen
Ee Heng Chen
Tao Chen
Yixin Chen
Wei-Ting Chen
Lin Chen
Guang Chen
Guangyi Chen
Guanying Chen
Guangyao Chen
Hwann-Tzong Chen
Junwen Chen
Jiacheng Chen
Jianxu Chen
Hui Chen
Kai Chen
Kan Chen
Kevin Chen
Kuan-Wen Chen
Weihua Chen
Zhang Chen
Liang-Chieh Chen
Lele Chen
Liang Chen
Fanglin Chen
Zehui Chen
Minghui Chen
Minghao Chen
Xiaokang Chen
Qian Chen
Jun-Cheng Chen
Qi Chen
Qingcai Chen
Richard J. Chen
Runnan Chen
Rui Chen
Shuo Chen
Sentao Chen
Shaoyu Chen
Shixing Chen
Shuai Chen
Shuya Chen
Sizhe Chen
Simin Chen
Shaoxiang Chen
Zitian Chen
Tianlong Chen
Tianshui Chen
Min-Hung Chen
Xiangning Chen
Xin Chen
Xinghao Chen
Xuejin Chen
Xu Chen
Xuxi Chen
Yunlu Chen
Yanbei Chen
Yuxiao Chen
Yun-Chun Chen
Yi-Ting Chen
Yi-Wen Chen
Yinbo Chen
Yiran Chen
Yuanhong Chen
Yubei Chen
Yuefeng Chen
Yuhua Chen
Yukang Chen
Zerui Chen
Zhaoyu Chen
Zhen Chen
Zhenyu Chen
Zhi Chen
Zhiwei Chen
Zhixiang Chen
Long Chen
Bowen Cheng
Jun Cheng
Yi Cheng
Jingchun Cheng
Lechao Cheng
Xi Cheng
Yuan Cheng
Ho Kei Cheng
Kevin Ho Man Cheng
Jiacheng Cheng
Kelvin B. Cheng
Li Cheng
Mengjun Cheng
Zhen Cheng
Qingrong Cheng
Tianheng Cheng
Harry Cheng
Yihua Cheng
Yu Cheng
Ziheng Cheng
Soon Yau Cheong
Anoop Cherian
Manuela Chessa
Zhixiang Chi
Naoki Chiba
Julian Chibane
Kashyap Chitta
Tai-Yin Chiu
Hsu-kuang Chiu
Wei-Chen Chiu
Sungmin Cho
Donghyeon Cho
Hyeon Cho
Yooshin Cho
Gyusang Cho
Jang Hyun Cho
Seungju Cho
Nam Ik Cho
Sunghyun Cho
Hanbyel Cho
Jaesung Choe
Jooyoung Choi
Chiho Choi
Changwoon Choi
Jongwon Choi
Myungsub Choi
Dooseop Choi
Jonghyun Choi
Jinwoo Choi
Jun Won Choi
Min-Kook Choi
Hongsuk Choi
Janghoon Choi
Yoon-Ho Choi

Yukyung Choi
Jaegul Choo
Ayush Chopra
Siddharth Choudhary
Subhabrata Choudhury
Vasileios Choutas
Ka-Ho Chow
Pinaki Nath Chowdhury
Sammy Christen
Anders Christensen
Grigorios Chrysos
Hang Chu
Wen-Hsuan Chu
Peng Chu
Qi Chu
Ruihang Chu
Wei-Ta Chu
Yung-Yu Chuang
Sanghyuk Chun
Se Young Chun
Antonio Cinà
Ramazan Gokberk Cinbis
Javier Civera
Albert Clapés
Ronald Clark
Brian S. Clipp
Felipe Codevilla
Daniel Coelho de Castro
Niv Cohen
Forrester Cole
Maxwell D. Collins
Robert T. Collins
Marc Comino Trinidad
Runmin Cong
Wenyan Cong
Maxime Cordy
Marcella Cornia
Enric Corona
Huseyin Coskun
Luca Cosmo
Dragos Costea
Davide Cozzolino
Arun C. S. Kumar
Aiyu Cui
Qiongjie Cui
Quan Cui
Shuhao Cui
Yiming Cui
Ying Cui
Zijun Cui
Jiali Cui
Jiequan Cui
Yawen Cui
Zhen Cui
Zhaopeng Cui
Jack Culpepper
Xiaodong Cun
Ross Cutler
Adam Czajka
Ali Dabouei
Konstantinos M. Dafnis
Manuel Dahnert
Tao Dai
Yuchao Dai
Bo Dai
Mengyu Dai
Hang Dai
Haixing Dai
Peng Dai
Pingyang Dai
Qi Dai
Qiyu Dai
Yutong Dai
Naser Damer
Zhiyuan Dang
Mohamed Daoudi
Ayan Das
Abir Das
Debasmit Das
Deepayan Das
Partha Das
Sagnik Das
Soumi Das
Srijan Das
Swagatam Das
Avijit Dasgupta
Jim Davis
Adrian K. Davison
Homa Davoudi
Laura Daza
Matthias De Lange
Shalini De Mello
Marco De Nadai
Christophe De Vleeschouwer
Alp Dener
Boyang Deng
Congyue Deng
Bailin Deng
Yong Deng
Ye Deng
Zhuo Deng
Zhijie Deng
Xiaoming Deng
Jiankang Deng
Jinhong Deng
Jingjing Deng
Liang-Jian Deng
Siqi Deng
Xiang Deng
Xueqing Deng
Zhongying Deng
Karan Desai
Jean-Emmanuel Deschaud
Aniket Anand Deshmukh
Neel Dey
Helisa Dhamo
Prithviraj Dhar
Amaya Dharmasiri
Yan Di
Xing Di
Ousmane A. Dia
Haiwen Diao
Xiaolei Diao
Gonçalo José Dias Pais
Abdallah Dib
Anastasios Dimou
Changxing Ding
Henghui Ding
Guodong Ding
Yaqing Ding
Shuangrui Ding
Yuhang Ding
Yikang Ding
Shouhong Ding

Haisong Ding
Hui Ding
Jiahao Ding
Jian Ding
Jian-Jiun Ding
Shuxiao Ding
Tianyu Ding
Wenhao Ding
Yuqi Ding
Yi Ding
Yuzhen Ding
Zhengming Ding
Tan Minh Dinh
Vu Dinh
Christos Diou
Mandar Dixit
Bao Gia Doan
Khoa D. Doan
Dzung Anh Doan
Debi Prosad Dogra
Nehal Doiphode
Chengdong Dong
Bowen Dong
Zhenxing Dong
Hang Dong
Xiaoyi Dong
Haoye Dong
Jiangxin Dong
Shichao Dong
Xuan Dong
Zhen Dong
Shuting Dong
Jing Dong
Li Dong
Ming Dong
Nanqing Dong
Qiulei Dong
Runpei Dong
Siyan Dong
Tian Dong
Wei Dong
Xiaomeng Dong
Xin Dong
Xingbo Dong
Yuan Dong
Samuel Dooley
Gianfranco Doretto
Michael Dorkenwald
Keval Doshi
Zhaopeng Dou
Xiaotian Dou
Hazel Doughty
Ahmad Droby
Iddo Drori
Jie Du
Yong Du
Dawei Du
Dong Du
Ruoyi Du
Yuntao Du
Xuefeng Du
Yilun Du
Yuming Du
Radhika Dua
Haodong Duan
Jiafei Duan
Kaiwen Duan
Peiqi Duan
Ye Duan
Haoran Duan
Jiali Duan
Amanda Duarte
Abhimanyu Dubey
Shiv Ram Dubey
Florian Dubost
Lukasz Dudziak
Shivam Duggal
Justin M. Dulay
Matteo Dunnhofer
Chi Nhan Duong
Thibaut Durand
Mihai Dusmanu
Ujjal Kr Dutta
Debidatta Dwibedi
Isht Dwivedi
Sai Kumar Dwivedi
Takeharu Eda
Mark Edmonds
Alexei A. Efros
Thibaud Ehret
Max Ehrlich
Mahsa Ehsanpour
Iván Eichhardt
Farshad Einabadi
Marvin Eisenberger
Hazim Kemal Ekenel
Mohamed El Banani
Ismail Elezi
Moshe Eliasof
Alaa El-Nouby
Ian Endres
Francis Engelmann
Deniz Engin
Chanho Eom
Dave Epstein
Maria C. Escobar
Victor A. Escorcia
Carlos Esteves
Sungmin Eum
Bernard J. E. Evans
Ivan Evtimov
Fevziye Irem Eyiokur Yaman
Matteo Fabbri
Sébastien Fabbro
Gabriele Facciolo
Masud Fahim
Bin Fan
Hehe Fan
Deng-Ping Fan
Aoxiang Fan
Chen-Chen Fan
Qi Fan
Zhaoxin Fan
Haoqi Fan
Heng Fan
Hongyi Fan
Linxi Fan
Baojie Fan
Jiayuan Fan
Lei Fan
Quanfu Fan
Yonghui Fan
Yingruo Fan
Zhiwen Fan

Zicong Fan
Sean Fanello
Jiansheng Fang
Chaowei Fang
Yuming Fang
Jianwu Fang
Jin Fang
Qi Fang
Shancheng Fang
Tian Fang
Xianyong Fang
Gongfan Fang
Zhen Fang
Hui Fang
Jiemin Fang
Le Fang
Pengfei Fang
Xiaolin Fang
Yuxin Fang
Zhaoyuan Fang
Ammarah Farooq
Azade Farshad
Zhengcong Fei
Michael Felsberg
Wei Feng
Chen Feng
Fan Feng
Andrew Feng
Xin Feng
Zheyun Feng
Ruicheng Feng
Mingtao Feng
Qianyu Feng
Shangbin Feng
Chun-Mei Feng
Zunlei Feng
Zhiyong Feng
Martin Fergie
Mustansar Fiaz
Marco Fiorucci
Michael Firman
Hamed Firooz
Volker Fischer
Corneliu O. Florea
Georgios Floros
Wolfgang Foerstner
Gianni Franchi
Jean-Sebastien Franco
Simone Frintrop
Anna Fruehstueck
Changhong Fu
Chaoyou Fu
Cheng-Yang Fu
Chi-Wing Fu
Deqing Fu
Huan Fu
Jun Fu
Kexue Fu
Ying Fu
Jianlong Fu
Jingjing Fu
Qichen Fu
Tsu-Jui Fu
Xueyang Fu
Yang Fu
Yanwei Fu
Yonggan Fu
Wolfgang Fuhl
Yasuhisa Fujii
Kent Fujiwara
Marco Fumero
Takuya Funatomi
Isabel Funke
Dario Fuoli
Antonino Furnari
Matheus A. Gadelha
Akshay Gadi Patil
Adrian Galdran
Guillermo Gallego
Silvano Galliani
Orazio Gallo
Leonardo Galteri
Matteo Gamba
Yiming Gan
Sujoy Ganguly
Harald Ganster
Boyan Gao
Changxin Gao
Daiheng Gao
Difei Gao
Chen Gao
Fei Gao
Lin Gao
Wei Gao
Yiming Gao
Junyu Gao
Guangyu Ryan Gao
Haichang Gao
Hongchang Gao
Jialin Gao
Jin Gao
Jun Gao
Katelyn Gao
Mingchen Gao
Mingfei Gao
Pan Gao
Shangqian Gao
Shanghua Gao
Xitong Gao
Yunhe Gao
Zhanning Gao
Elena Garces
Nuno Cruz Garcia
Noa Garcia
Guillermo Garcia-Hernando
Isha Garg
Rahul Garg
Sourav Garg
Quentin Garrido
Stefano Gasperini
Kent Gauen
Chandan Gautam
Shivam Gautam
Paul Gay
Chunjiang Ge
Shiming Ge
Wenhang Ge
Yanhao Ge
Zheng Ge
Songwei Ge
Weifeng Ge
Yixiao Ge
Yuying Ge
Shijie Geng

Zhengyang Geng
Kyle A. Genova
Georgios Georgakis
Markos Georgopoulos
Marcel Geppert
Shabnam Ghadar
Mina Ghadimi Atigh
Deepti Ghadiyaram
Maani Ghaffari Jadidi
Sedigh Ghamari
Zahra Gharaee
Michaël Gharbi
Golnaz Ghiasi
Reza Ghoddoosian
Soumya Suvra Ghosal
Adhiraj Ghosh
Arthita Ghosh
Pallabi Ghosh
Soumyadeep Ghosh
Andrew Gilbert
Igor Gilitschenski
Jhony H. Giraldo
Andreu Girbau Xalabarder
Rohit Girdhar
Sharath Girish
Xavier Giro-i-Nieto
Raja Giryes
Thomas Gittings
Nikolaos Gkanatsios
Ioannis Gkioulekas
Abhiram Gnanasambandam
Aurele T. Gnanha
Clement L. J. C. Godard
Arushi Goel
Vidit Goel
Shubham Goel
Zan Gojcic
Aaron K. Gokaslan
Tejas Gokhale
S. Alireza Golestaneh
Thiago L. Gomes
Nuno Goncalves
Boqing Gong
Chen Gong
Yuanhao Gong
Guoqiang Gong
Jingyu Gong
Rui Gong
Yu Gong
Mingming Gong
Neil Zhenqiang Gong
Xun Gong
Yunye Gong
Yihong Gong
Cristina I. González
Nithin Gopalakrishnan Nair
Gaurav Goswami
Jianping Gou
Shreyank N. Gowda
Ankit Goyal
Helmut Grabner
Patrick L. Grady
Ben Graham
Eric Granger
Douglas R. Gray
Matej Grcić
David Griffiths
Jinjin Gu
Yun Gu
Shuyang Gu
Jianyang Gu
Fuqiang Gu
Jiatao Gu
Jindong Gu
Jiaqi Gu
Jinwei Gu
Jiaxin Gu
Geonmo Gu
Xiao Gu
Xinqian Gu
Xiuye Gu
Yuming Gu
Zhangxuan Gu
Dayan Guan
Junfeng Guan
Qingji Guan
Tianrui Guan
Shanyan Guan
Denis A. Gudovskiy
Ricardo Guerrero
Pierre-Louis Guhur
Jie Gui
Liangyan Gui
Liangke Gui
Benoit Guillard
Erhan Gundogdu
Manuel Günther
Jingcai Guo
Yuanfang Guo
Junfeng Guo
Chenqi Guo
Dan Guo
Hongji Guo
Jia Guo
Jie Guo
Minghao Guo
Shi Guo
Yanhui Guo
Yangyang Guo
Yuan-Chen Guo
Yilu Guo
Yiluan Guo
Yong Guo
Guangyu Guo
Haiyun Guo
Jinyang Guo
Jianyuan Guo
Pengsheng Guo
Pengfei Guo
Shuxuan Guo
Song Guo
Tianyu Guo
Qing Guo
Qiushan Guo
Wen Guo
Xiefan Guo
Xiaohu Guo
Xiaoqing Guo
Yufei Guo
Yuhui Guo
Yuliang Guo
Yunhui Guo
Yanwen Guo

Akshita Gupta
Ankush Gupta
Kamal Gupta
Kartik Gupta
Ritwik Gupta
Rohit Gupta
Siddharth Gururani
Fredrik K. Gustafsson
Abner Guzman Rivera
Vladimir Guzov
Matthew A. Gwilliam
Jung-Woo Ha
Marc Habermann
Isma Hadji
Christian Haene
Martin Hahner
Levente Hajder
Alexandros Haliassos
Emanuela Haller
Bumsub Ham
Abdullah J. Hamdi
Shreyas Hampali
Dongyoon Han
Chunrui Han
Dong-Jun Han
Dong-Sig Han
Guangxing Han
Zhizhong Han
Ruize Han
Jiaming Han
Jin Han
Ligong Han
Xian-Hua Han
Xiaoguang Han
Yizeng Han
Zhi Han
Zhenjun Han
Zhongyi Han
Jungong Han
Junlin Han
Kai Han
Kun Han
Sungwon Han
Songfang Han
Wei Han
Xiao Han
Xintong Han
Xinzhe Han
Yahong Han
Yan Han
Zongbo Han
Nicolai Hani
Rana Hanocka
Niklas Hanselmann
Nicklas A. Hansen
Hong Hanyu
Fusheng Hao
Yanbin Hao
Shijie Hao
Udith Haputhanthri
Mehrtash Harandi
Josh Harguess
Adam Harley
David M. Hart
Atsushi Hashimoto
Ali Hassani
Mohammed Hassanin
Yana Hasson
Joakim Bruslund Haurum
Bo He
Kun He
Chen He
Xin He
Fazhi He
Gaoqi He
Hao He
Haoyu He
Jiangpeng He
Hongliang He
Qian He
Xiangteng He
Xuming He
Yannan He
Yuhang He
Yang He
Xiangyu He
Nanjun He
Pan He
Sen He
Shengfeng He
Songtao He
Tao He
Tong He
Wei He
Xuehai He
Xiaoxiao He
Ying He
Yisheng He
Ziwen He
Peter Hedman
Felix Heide
Yacov Hel-Or
Paul Henderson
Philipp Henzler
Byeongho Heo
Jae-Pil Heo
Miran Heo
Sachini A. Herath
Stephane Herbin
Pedro Hermosilla Casajus
Monica Hernandez
Charles Herrmann
Roei Herzig
Mauricio Hess-Flores
Carlos Hinojosa
Tobias Hinz
Tsubasa Hirakawa
Chih-Hui Ho
Lam Si Tung Ho
Jennifer Hobbs
Derek Hoiem
Yannick Hold-Geoffroy
Aleksander Holynski
Cheeun Hong
Fa-Ting Hong
Hanbin Hong
Guan Zhe Hong
Danfeng Hong
Lanqing Hong
Xiaopeng Hong
Xin Hong
Jie Hong
Seungbum Hong
Cheng-Yao Hong
Seunghoon Hong

Yi Hong
Yuan Hong
Yuchen Hong
Anthony Hoogs
Maxwell C. Horton
Kazuhiro Hotta
Qibin Hou
Tingbo Hou
Junhui Hou
Ji Hou
Qiqi Hou
Rui Hou
Ruibing Hou
Zhi Hou
Henry Howard-Jenkins
Lukas Hoyer
Wei-Lin Hsiao
Chiou-Ting Hsu
Anthony Hu
Brian Hu
Yusong Hu
Hexiang Hu
Haoji Hu
Di Hu
Hengtong Hu
Haigen Hu
Lianyu Hu
Hanzhe Hu
Jie Hu
Junlin Hu
Shizhe Hu
Jian Hu
Zhiming Hu
Juhua Hu
Peng Hu
Ping Hu
Ronghang Hu
MengShun Hu
Tao Hu
Vincent Tao Hu
Xiaoling Hu
Xinting Hu
Xiaolin Hu
Xuefeng Hu
Xiaowei Hu
Yang Hu
Yueyu Hu
Zeyu Hu
Zhongyun Hu
Binh-Son Hua
Guoliang Hua
Yi Hua
Linzhi Huang
Qiusheng Huang
Bo Huang
Chen Huang
Hsin-Ping Huang
Ye Huang
Shuangping Huang
Zeng Huang
Buzhen Huang
Cong Huang
Heng Huang
Hao Huang
Qidong Huang
Huaibo Huang
Chaoqin Huang
Feihu Huang
Jiahui Huang
Jingjia Huang
Kun Huang
Lei Huang
Sheng Huang
Shuaiyi Huang
Siyu Huang
Xiaoshui Huang
Xiaoyang Huang
Yan Huang
Yihao Huang
Ying Huang
Ziling Huang
Xiaoke Huang
Yifei Huang
Haiyang Huang
Zhewei Huang
Jin Huang
Haibin Huang
Jiaxing Huang
Junjie Huang
Keli Huang
Lang Huang
Lin Huang
Luojie Huang
Mingzhen Huang
Shijia Huang
Shengyu Huang
Siyuan Huang
He Huang
Xiuyu Huang
Lianghua Huang
Yue Huang
Yaping Huang
Yuge Huang
Zehao Huang
Zeyi Huang
Zhiqi Huang
Zhongzhan Huang
Zilong Huang
Ziyuan Huang
Tianrui Hui
Zhuo Hui
Le Hui
Jing Huo
Junhwa Hur
Shehzeen S. Hussain
Chuong Minh Huynh
Seunghyun Hwang
Jaehui Hwang
Jyh-Jing Hwang
Sukjun Hwang
Soonmin Hwang
Wonjun Hwang
Rakib Hyder
Sangeek Hyun
Sarah Ibrahimi
Tomoki Ichikawa
Yerlan Idelbayev
A. S. M. Iftekhar
Masaaki Iiyama
Satoshi Ikehata
Sunghoon Im
Atul N. Ingle
Eldar Insafutdinov
Yani A. Ioannou
Radu Tudor Ionescu

Umar Iqbal
Go Irie
Muhammad Zubair Irshad
Ahmet Iscen
Berivan Isik
Ashraful Islam
Md Amirul Islam
Syed Islam
Mariko Isogawa
Vamsi Krishna K. Ithapu
Boris Ivanovic
Darshan Iyer
Sarah Jabbour
Ayush Jain
Nishant Jain
Samyak Jain
Vidit Jain
Vineet Jain
Priyank Jaini
Tomas Jakab
Mohammad A. A. K. Jalwana
Muhammad Abdullah Jamal
Hadi Jamali-Rad
Stuart James
Varun Jampani
Young Kyun Jang
YeongJun Jang
Yunseok Jang
Ronnachai Jaroensri
Bhavan Jasani
Krishna Murthy Jatavallabhula
Mojan Javaheripi
Syed A. Javed
Guillaume Jeanneret
Pranav Jeevan
Herve Jegou
Rohit Jena
Tomas Jenicek
Porter Jenkins
Simon Jenni
Hae-Gon Jeon
Sangryul Jeon
Boseung Jeong
Yoonwoo Jeong
Seong-Gyun Jeong
Jisoo Jeong
Allan D. Jepson
Ankit Jha
Sumit K. Jha
I-Hong Jhuo
Ge-Peng Ji
Chaonan Ji
Deyi Ji
Jingwei Ji
Wei Ji
Zhong Ji
Jiayi Ji
Pengliang Ji
Hui Ji
Mingi Ji
Xiaopeng Ji
Yuzhu Ji
Baoxiong Jia
Songhao Jia
Dan Jia
Shan Jia
Xiaojun Jia
Xiuyi Jia
Xu Jia
Menglin Jia
Wenqi Jia
Boyuan Jiang
Wenhao Jiang
Huaizu Jiang
Hanwen Jiang
Haiyong Jiang
Hao Jiang
Huajie Jiang
Huiqin Jiang
Haojun Jiang
Haobo Jiang
Junjun Jiang
Xingyu Jiang
Yangbangyan Jiang
Yu Jiang
Jianmin Jiang
Jiaxi Jiang
Jing Jiang
Kui Jiang
Li Jiang
Liming Jiang
Chiyu Jiang
Meirui Jiang
Chen Jiang
Peng Jiang
Tai-Xiang Jiang
Wen Jiang
Xinyang Jiang
Yifan Jiang
Yuming Jiang
Yingying Jiang
Zeren Jiang
ZhengKai Jiang
Zhenyu Jiang
Shuming Jiao
Jianbo Jiao
Licheng Jiao
Dongkwon Jin
Yeying Jin
Cheng Jin
Linyi Jin
Qing Jin
Taisong Jin
Xiao Jin
Xin Jin
Sheng Jin
Kyong Hwan Jin
Ruibing Jin
SouYoung Jin
Yueming Jin
Chenchen Jing
Longlong Jing
Taotao Jing
Yongcheng Jing
Younghyun Jo
Joakim Johnander
Jeff Johnson
Michael J. Jones
R. Kenny Jones
Rico Jonschkowski
Ameya Joshi
Sunghun Joung

Felix Juefei-Xu
Claudio R. Jung
Steffen Jung
Hari Chandana K.
Rahul Vigneswaran K.
Prajwal K. R.
Abhishek Kadian
Jhony Kaesemodel Pontes
Kumara Kahatapitiya
Anmol Kalia
Sinan Kalkan
Tarun Kalluri
Jaewon Kam
Sandesh Kamath
Meina Kan
Menelaos Kanakis
Takuhiro Kaneko
Di Kang
Guoliang Kang
Hao Kang
Jaeyeon Kang
Kyoungkook Kang
Li-Wei Kang
MinGuk Kang
Suk-Ju Kang
Zhao Kang
Yash Mukund Kant
Yueying Kao
Aupendu Kar
Konstantinos Karantzalos
Sezer Karaoglu
Navid Kardan
Sanjay Kariyappa
Leonid Karlinsky
Animesh Karnewar
Shyamgopal Karthik
Hirak J. Kashyap
Marc A. Kastner
Hirokatsu Kataoka
Angelos Katharopoulos
Hiroharu Kato
Kai Katsumata
Manuel Kaufmann
Chaitanya Kaul
Prakhar Kaushik
Yuki Kawana
Lei Ke
Lipeng Ke
Tsung-Wei Ke
Wei Ke
Petr Kellnhofer
Aniruddha Kembhavi
John Kender
Corentin Kervadec
Leonid Keselman
Daniel Keysers
Nima Khademi Kalantari
Taras Khakhulin
Samir Khaki
Muhammad Haris Khan
Qadeer Khan
Salman Khan
Subash Khanal
Vaishnavi M. Khindkar
Rawal Khirodkar
Saeed Khorram
Pirazh Khorramshahi
Kourosh Khoshelham
Ansh Khurana
Benjamin Kiefer
Jae Myung Kim
Junho Kim
Boah Kim
Hyeonseong Kim
Dong-Jin Kim
Dongwan Kim
Donghyun Kim
Doyeon Kim
Yonghyun Kim
Hyung-Il Kim
Hyunwoo Kim
Hyeongwoo Kim
Hyo Jin Kim
Hyunwoo J. Kim
Taehoon Kim
Jaeha Kim
Jiwon Kim
Jung Uk Kim
Kangyeol Kim
Eunji Kim
Daeha Kim
Dongwon Kim
Kunhee Kim
Kyungmin Kim
Junsik Kim
Min H. Kim
Namil Kim
Kookhoi Kim
Sanghyun Kim
Seongyeop Kim
Seungryong Kim
Saehoon Kim
Euyoung Kim
Guisik Kim
Sungyeon Kim
Sunnie S. Y. Kim
Taehun Kim
Tae Oh Kim
Won Hwa Kim
Seungwook Kim
YoungBin Kim
Youngeun Kim
Akisato Kimura
Furkan Osman Kınlı
Zsolt Kira
Hedvig Kjellström
Florian Kleber
Jan P. Klopp
Florian Kluger
Laurent Kneip
Byungsoo Ko
Muhammed Kocabas
A. Sophia Koepke
Kevin Koeser
Nick Kolkin
Nikos Kolotouros
Wai-Kin Adams Kong
Deying Kong
Caihua Kong
Youyong Kong
Shuyu Kong
Shu Kong
Tao Kong
Yajing Kong
Yu Kong

Zishang Kong
Theodora Kontogianni
Anton S. Konushin
Julian F. P. Kooij
Bruno Korbar
Giorgos Kordopatis-Zilos
Jari Korhonen
Adam Kortylewski
Denis Korzhenkov
Divya Kothandaraman
Suraj Kothawade
Iuliia Kotseruba
Satwik Kottur
Shashank Kotyan
Alexandros Kouris
Petros Koutras
Anna Kreshuk
Ranjay Krishna
Dilip Krishnan
Andrey Kuehlkamp
Hilde Kuehne
Jason Kuen
David Kügler
Arjan Kuijper
Anna Kukleva
Sumith Kulal
Viveka Kulharia
Akshay R. Kulkarni
Nilesh Kulkarni
Dominik Kulon
Abhinav Kumar
Akash Kumar
Suryansh Kumar
B. V. K. Vijaya Kumar
Pulkit Kumar
Ratnesh Kumar
Sateesh Kumar
Satish Kumar
Vijay Kumar B. G.
Nupur Kumari
Sudhakar Kumawat
Jogendra Nath Kundu
Hsien-Kai Kuo
Meng-Yu Jennifer Kuo
Vinod Kumar Kurmi
Yusuke Kurose
Keerthy Kusumam
Alina Kuznetsova
Henry Kvinge
Ho Man Kwan
Hyeokjun Kweon
Heeseung Kwon
Gihyun Kwon
Myung-Joon Kwon
Taesung Kwon
YoungJoong Kwon
Christos Kyrkou
Jorma Laaksonen
Yann Labbe
Zorah Laehner
Florent Lafarge
Hamid Laga
Manuel Lagunas
Shenqi Lai
Jian-Huang Lai
Zihang Lai
Mohamed I. Lakhal
Mohit Lamba
Meng Lan
Loic Landrieu
Zhiqiang Lang
Natalie Lang
Dong Lao
Yizhen Lao
Yingjie Lao
Issam Hadj Laradji
Gustav Larsson
Viktor Larsson
Zakaria Laskar
Stéphane Lathuilière
Chun Pong Lau
Rynson W. H. Lau
Hei Law
Justin Lazarow
Verica Lazova
Eric-Tuan Le
Hieu Le
Trung-Nghia Le
Mathias Lechner
Byeong-Uk Lee
Chen-Yu Lee
Che-Rung Lee
Chul Lee
Hong Joo Lee
Dongsoo Lee
Jiyoung Lee
Eugene Eu Tzuan Lee
Daeun Lee
Saehyung Lee
Jewook Lee
Hyungtae Lee
Hyunmin Lee
Jungbeom Lee
Joon-Young Lee
Jong-Seok Lee
Joonseok Lee
Junha Lee
Kibok Lee
Byung-Kwan Lee
Jangwon Lee
Jinho Lee
Jongmin Lee
Seunghyun Lee
Sohyun Lee
Minsik Lee
Dogyoon Lee
Seungmin Lee
Min Jun Lee
Sangho Lee
Sangmin Lee
Seungeun Lee
Seon-Ho Lee
Sungmin Lee
Sungho Lee
Sangyoun Lee
Vincent C. S. S. Lee
Jaeseong Lee
Yong Jae Lee
Chenyang Lei
Chenyi Lei
Jiahui Lei
Xinyu Lei
Yinjie Lei
Jiaxu Leng
Luziwei Leng

Jan E. Lenssen
Vincent Lepetit
Thomas Leung
María Leyva-Vallina
Xin Li
Yikang Li
Baoxin Li
Bin Li
Bing Li
Bowen Li
Changlin Li
Chao Li
Chongyi Li
Guanyue Li
Shuai Li
Jin Li
Dingquan Li
Dongxu Li
Yiting Li
Gang Li
Dian Li
Guohao Li
Haoang Li
Haoliang Li
Haoran Li
Hengduo Li
Huafeng Li
Xiaoming Li
Hanao Li
Hongwei Li
Ziqiang Li
Jisheng Li
Jiacheng Li
Jia Li
Jiachen Li
Jiahao Li
Jianwei Li
Jiazhi Li
Jie Li
Jing Li
Jingjing Li
Jingtao Li
Jun Li
Junxuan Li
Kai Li
Kailin Li
Kenneth Li
Kun Li
Kunpeng Li
Aoxue Li
Chenglong Li
Chenglin Li
Changsheng Li
Zhichao Li
Qiang Li
Yanyu Li
Zuoyue Li
Xiang Li
Xuelong Li
Fangda Li
Ailin Li
Liang Li
Chun-Guang Li
Daiqing Li
Dong Li
Guanbin Li
Guorong Li
Haifeng Li
Jianan Li
Jianing Li
Jiaxin Li
Ke Li
Lei Li
Lincheng Li
Liulei Li
Lujun Li
Linjie Li
Lin Li
Pengyu Li
Ping Li
Qiufu Li
Qingyong Li
Rui Li
Siyuan Li
Wei Li
Wenbin Li
Xiangyang Li
Xinyu Li
Xiujun Li
Xiu Li
Xu Li
Ya-Li Li
Yao Li
Yongjie Li
Yijun Li
Yiming Li
Yuezun Li
Yu Li
Yunheng Li
Yuqi Li
Zhe Li
Zeming Li
Zhen Li
Zhengqin Li
Zhimin Li
Jiefeng Li
Jinpeng Li
Chengze Li
Jianwu Li
Lerenhan Li
Shan Li
Suichan Li
Xiangtai Li
Yanjie Li
Yandong Li
Zhuoling Li
Zhenqiang Li
Manyi Li
Maosen Li
Ji Li
Minjun Li
Mingrui Li
Mengtian Li
Junyi Li
Nianyi Li
Bo Li
Xiao Li
Peihua Li
Peike Li
Peizhao Li
Peiliang Li
Qi Li
Ren Li
Runze Li
Shile Li

Sheng Li
Shigang Li
Shiyu Li
Shuang Li
Shasha Li
Shichao Li
Tianye Li
Yuexiang Li
Wei-Hong Li
Wanhua Li
Weihao Li
Weiming Li
Weixin Li
Wenbo Li
Wenshuo Li
Weijian Li
Yunan Li
Xirong Li
Xianhang Li
Xiaoyu Li
Xueqian Li
Xuanlin Li
Xianzhi Li
Yunqiang Li
Yanjing Li
Yansheng Li
Yawei Li
Yi Li
Yong Li
Yong-Lu Li
Yuhang Li
Yu-Jhe Li
Yuxi Li
Yunsheng Li
Yanwei Li
Zechao Li
Zejian Li
Zeju Li
Zekun Li
Zhaowen Li
Zheng Li
Zhenyu Li
Zhiheng Li
Zhi Li
Zhong Li
Zhuowei Li
Zhuowan Li
Zhuohang Li
Zizhang Li
Chen Li
Yuan-Fang Li
Dongze Lian
Xiaochen Lian
Zhouhui Lian
Long Lian
Qing Lian
Jin Lianbao
Jinxiu S. Liang
Dingkang Liang
Jiahao Liang
Jianming Liang
Jingyun Liang
Kevin J. Liang
Kaizhao Liang
Chen Liang
Jie Liang
Senwei Liang
Ding Liang
Jiajun Liang
Jian Liang
Kongming Liang
Siyuan Liang
Yuanzhi Liang
Zhengfa Liang
Mingfu Liang
Xiaodan Liang
Xuefeng Liang
Yuxuan Liang
Kang Liao
Liang Liao
Hong-Yuan Mark Liao
Wentong Liao
Haofu Liao
Yue Liao
Minghui Liao
Shengcai Liao
Ting-Hsuan Liao
Xin Liao
Yinghong Liao
Teck Yian Lim
Che-Tsung Lin
Chung-Ching Lin
Chen-Hsuan Lin
Cheng Lin
Chuming Lin
Chunyu Lin
Dahua Lin
Wei Lin
Zheng Lin
Huaijia Lin
Jason Lin
Jierui Lin
Jiaying Lin
Jie Lin
Kai-En Lin
Kevin Lin
Guangfeng Lin
Jiehong Lin
Feng Lin
Hang Lin
Kwan-Yee Lin
Ke Lin
Luojun Lin
Qinghong Lin
Xiangbo Lin
Yi Lin
Zudi Lin
Shijie Lin
Yiqun Lin
Tzu-Heng Lin
Ming Lin
Shaohui Lin
SongNan Lin
Ji Lin
Tsung-Yu Lin
Xudong Lin
Yancong Lin
Yen-Chen Lin
Yiming Lin
Yuewei Lin
Zhiqiu Lin
Zinan Lin
Zhe Lin
David B. Lindell
Zhixin Ling

Zhan Ling
Alexander Liniger
Venice Erin B. Liong
Joey Litalien
Or Litany
Roee Litman
Ron Litman
Jim Little
Dor Litvak
Shaoteng Liu
Shuaicheng Liu
Andrew Liu
Xian Liu
Shaohui Liu
Bei Liu
Bo Liu
Yong Liu
Ming Liu
Yanbin Liu
Chenxi Liu
Daqi Liu
Di Liu
Difan Liu
Dong Liu
Dongfang Liu
Daizong Liu
Xiao Liu
Fangyi Liu
Fengbei Liu
Fenglin Liu
Bin Liu
Yuang Liu
Ao Liu
Hong Liu
Hongfu Liu
Huidong Liu
Ziyi Liu
Feng Liu
Hao Liu
Jie Liu
Jialun Liu
Jiang Liu
Jing Liu
Jingya Liu
Jiaming Liu
Jun Liu
Juncheng Liu
Jiawei Liu
Hongyu Liu
Chuanbin Liu
Haotian Liu
Lingqiao Liu
Chang Liu
Han Liu
Liu Liu
Min Liu
Yingqi Liu
Aishan Liu
Bingyu Liu
Benlin Liu
Boxiao Liu
Chenchen Liu
Chuanjian Liu
Daqing Liu
Huan Liu
Haozhe Liu
Jiaheng Liu
Wei Liu
Jingzhou Liu
Jiyuan Liu
Lingbo Liu
Nian Liu
Peiye Liu
Qiankun Liu
Shenglan Liu
Shilong Liu
Wen Liu
Wenyu Liu
Weifeng Liu
Wu Liu
Xiaolong Liu
Yang Liu
Yanwei Liu
Yingcheng Liu
Yongfei Liu
Yihao Liu
Yu Liu
Yunze Liu
Ze Liu
Zhenhua Liu
Zhenguang Liu
Lin Liu
Lihao Liu
Pengju Liu
Xinhai Liu
Yunfei Liu
Meng Liu
Minghua Liu
Mingyuan Liu
Miao Liu
Peirong Liu
Ping Liu
Qingjie Liu
Ruoshi Liu
Risheng Liu
Songtao Liu
Xing Liu
Shikun Liu
Shuming Liu
Sheng Liu
Songhua Liu
Tongliang Liu
Weibo Liu
Weide Liu
Weizhe Liu
Wenxi Liu
Weiyang Liu
Xin Liu
Xiaobin Liu
Xudong Liu
Xiaoyi Liu
Xihui Liu
Xinchen Liu
Xingtong Liu
Xinpeng Liu
Xinyu Liu
Xianpeng Liu
Xu Liu
Xingyu Liu
Yongtuo Liu
Yahui Liu
Yangxin Liu
Yaoyao Liu
Yaojie Liu
Yuliang Liu

Yongcheng Liu
Yuan Liu
Yufan Liu
Yu-Lun Liu
Yun Liu
Yunfan Liu
Yuanzhong Liu
Zhuoran Liu
Zhen Liu
Zheng Liu
Zhijian Liu
Zhisong Liu
Ziquan Liu
Ziyu Liu
Zhihua Liu
Zechun Liu
Zhaoyang Liu
Zhengzhe Liu
Stephan Liwicki
Shao-Yuan Lo
Sylvain Lobry
Suhas Lohit
Vishnu Suresh Lokhande
Vincenzo Lomonaco
Chengjiang Long
Guodong Long
Fuchen Long
Shangbang Long
Yang Long
Zijun Long
Vasco Lopes
Antonio M. Lopez
Roberto Javier Lopez-Sastre
Tobias Lorenz
Javier Lorenzo-Navarro
Yujing Lou
Qian Lou
Xiankai Lu
Changsheng Lu
Huimin Lu
Yongxi Lu
Hao Lu
Hong Lu
Jiasen Lu
Juwei Lu
Fan Lu
Guangming Lu
Jiwen Lu
Shun Lu
Tao Lu
Xiaonan Lu
Yang Lu
Yao Lu
Yongchun Lu
Zhiwu Lu
Cheng Lu
Liying Lu
Guo Lu
Xuequan Lu
Yanye Lu
Yantao Lu
Yuhang Lu
Fujun Luan
Jonathon Luiten
Jovita Lukasik
Alan Lukezic
Jonathan Samuel Lumentut
Mayank Lunayach
Ao Luo
Canjie Luo
Chong Luo
Xu Luo
Grace Luo
Jun Luo
Katie Z. Luo
Tao Luo
Cheng Luo
Fangzhou Luo
Gen Luo
Lei Luo
Sihui Luo
Weixin Luo
Yan Luo
Xiaoyan Luo
Yong Luo
Yadan Luo
Hao Luo
Ruotian Luo
Mi Luo
Tiange Luo
Wenjie Luo
Wenhan Luo
Xiao Luo
Zhiming Luo
Zhipeng Luo
Zhengyi Luo
Diogo C. Luvizon
Zhaoyang Lv
Gengyu Lyu
Lingjuan Lyu
Jun Lyu
Yuanyuan Lyu
Youwei Lyu
Yueming Lyu
Bingpeng Ma
Chao Ma
Chongyang Ma
Congbo Ma
Chih-Yao Ma
Fan Ma
Lin Ma
Haoyu Ma
Hengbo Ma
Jianqi Ma
Jiawei Ma
Jiayi Ma
Kede Ma
Kai Ma
Lingni Ma
Lei Ma
Xu Ma
Ning Ma
Benteng Ma
Cheng Ma
Andy J. Ma
Long Ma
Zhanyu Ma
Zhiheng Ma
Qianli Ma
Shiqiang Ma
Sizhuo Ma
Shiqing Ma
Xiaolong Ma
Xinzhu Ma

Gautam B. Machiraju
Spandan Madan
Mathew Magimai-Doss
Luca Magri
Behrooz Mahasseni
Upal Mahbub
Siddharth Mahendran
Paridhi Maheshwari
Rishabh Maheshwary
Mohammed Mahmoud
Shishira R. R. Maiya
Sylwia Majchrowska
Arjun Majumdar
Puspita Majumdar
Orchid Majumder
Sagnik Majumder
Ilya Makarov
Farkhod F. Makhmudkhujaev
Yasushi Makihara
Ankur Mali
Mateusz Malinowski
Utkarsh Mall
Srikanth Malla
Clement Mallet
Dimitrios Mallis
Yunze Man
Dipu Manandhar
Massimiliano Mancini
Murari Mandal
Raunak Manekar
Karttikeya Mangalam
Puneet Mangla
Fabian Manhardt
Sivabalan Manivasagam
Fahim Mannan
Chengzhi Mao
Hanzi Mao
Jiayuan Mao
Junhua Mao
Zhiyuan Mao
Jiageng Mao
Yunyao Mao
Zhendong Mao
Alberto Marchisio
Diego Marcos
Riccardo Marin
Aram Markosyan
Renaud Marlet
Ricardo Marques
Miquel Martí i Rabadán
Diego Martin Arroyo
Niki Martinel
Brais Martinez
Julieta Martinez
Marc Masana
Tomohiro Mashita
Timothée Masquelier
Minesh Mathew
Tetsu Matsukawa
Marwan Mattar
Bruce A. Maxwell
Christoph Mayer
Mantas Mazeika
Pratik Mazumder
Scott McCloskey
Steven McDonagh
Ishit Mehta
Jie Mei
Kangfu Mei
Jieru Mei
Xiaoguang Mei
Givi Meishvili
Luke Melas-Kyriazi
Iaroslav Melekhov
Andres Mendez-Vazquez
Heydi Mendez-Vazquez
Matias Mendieta
Ricardo A. Mendoza-León
Chenlin Meng
Depu Meng
Rang Meng
Zibo Meng
Qingjie Meng
Qier Meng
Yanda Meng
Zihang Meng
Thomas Mensink
Fabian Mentzer
Christopher Metzler
Gregory P. Meyer
Vasileios Mezaris
Liang Mi
Lu Mi
Bo Miao
Changtao Miao
Zichen Miao
Qiguang Miao
Xin Miao
Zhongqi Miao
Frank Michel
Simone Milani
Ben Mildenhall
Roy V. Miles
Juhong Min
Kyle Min
Hyun-Seok Min
Weiqing Min
Yuecong Min
Zhixiang Min
Qi Ming
David Minnen
Aymen Mir
Deepak Mishra
Anand Mishra
Shlok K. Mishra
Niluthpol Mithun
Gaurav Mittal
Trisha Mittal
Daisuke Miyazaki
Kaichun Mo
Hong Mo
Zhipeng Mo
Davide Modolo
Abduallah A. Mohamed
Mohamed Afham Mohamed Aflal
Ron Mokady
Pavlo Molchanov
Davide Moltisanti
Liliane Momeni
Gianluca Monaci
Pascal Monasse
Ajoy Mondal
Tom Monnier

Aron Monszpart
Gyeongsik Moon
Suhong Moon
Taesup Moon
Sean Moran
Daniel Moreira
Pietro Morerio
Alexandre Morgand
Lia Morra
Ali Mosleh
Inbar Mosseri
Sayed Mohammad Mostafavi Isfahani
Saman Motamed
Ramy A. Mounir
Fangzhou Mu
Jiteng Mu
Norman Mu
Yasuhiro Mukaigawa
Ryan Mukherjee
Tanmoy Mukherjee
Yusuke Mukuta
Ravi Teja Mullapudi
Lea Müller
Matthias Müller
Martin Mundt
Nils Murrugarra-Llerena
Damien Muselet
Armin Mustafa
Muhammad Ferjad Naeem
Sauradip Nag
Hajime Nagahara
Pravin Nagar
Rajendra Nagar
Naveen Shankar Nagaraja
Varun Nagaraja
Tushar Nagarajan
Seungjun Nah
Gaku Nakano
Yuta Nakashima
Giljoo Nam
Seonghyeon Nam
Liangliang Nan
Yuesong Nan
Yeshwanth Napolean
Dinesh Reddy Narapureddy
Medhini Narasimhan
Supreeth Narasimhaswamy
Sriram Narayanan
Erickson R. Nascimento
Varun Nasery
K. L. Navaneet
Pablo Navarrete Michelini
Shant Navasardyan
Shah Nawaz
Nihal Nayak
Farhood Negin
Lukáš Neumann
Alejandro Newell
Evonne Ng
Kam Woh Ng
Tony Ng
Anh Nguyen
Tuan Anh Nguyen
Cuong Cao Nguyen
Ngoc Cuong Nguyen
Thanh Nguyen
Khoi Nguyen
Phi Le Nguyen
Phong Ha Nguyen
Tam Nguyen
Truong Nguyen
Anh Tuan Nguyen
Rang Nguyen
Thao Thi Phuong Nguyen
Van Nguyen Nguyen
Zhen-Liang Ni
Yao Ni
Shijie Nie
Xuecheng Nie
Yongwei Nie
Weizhi Nie
Ying Nie
Yinyu Nie
Kshitij N. Nikhal
Simon Niklaus
Xuefei Ning
Jifeng Ning
Yotam Nitzan
Di Niu
Shuaicheng Niu
Li Niu
Wei Niu
Yulei Niu
Zhenxing Niu
Albert No
Shohei Nobuhara
Nicoletta Noceti
Junhyug Noh
Sotiris Nousias
Slawomir Nowaczyk
Ewa M. Nowara
Valsamis Ntouskos
Gilberto Ochoa-Ruiz
Ferda Ofli
Jihyong Oh
Sangyun Oh
Youngtaek Oh
Hiroki Ohashi
Takahiro Okabe
Kemal Oksuz
Fumio Okura
Daniel Olmeda Reino
Matthew Olson
Carl Olsson
Roy Or-El
Alessandro Ortis
Guillermo Ortiz-Jimenez
Magnus Oskarsson
Ahmed A. A. Osman
Martin R. Oswald
Mayu Otani
Naima Otberdout
Cheng Ouyang
Jiahong Ouyang
Wanli Ouyang
Andrew Owens
Poojan B. Oza
Mete Ozay
A. Cengiz Oztireli
Gautam Pai
Tomas Pajdla
Umapada Pal

Simone Palazzo
Luca Palmieri
Bowen Pan
Hao Pan
Lili Pan
Tai-Yu Pan
Liang Pan
Chengwei Pan
Yingwei Pan
Xuran Pan
Jinshan Pan
Xinyu Pan
Liyuan Pan
Xingang Pan
Xingjia Pan
Zhihong Pan
Zizheng Pan
Priyadarshini Panda
Rameswar Panda
Rohit Pandey
Kaiyue Pang
Bo Pang
Guansong Pang
Jiangmiao Pang
Meng Pang
Tianyu Pang
Ziqi Pang
Omiros Pantazis
Andreas Panteli
Maja Pantic
Marina Paolanti
Joao P. Papa
Samuele Papa
Mike Papadakis
Dim P. Papadopoulos
George Papandreou
Constantin Pape
Toufiq Parag
Chethan Parameshwara
Shaifali Parashar
Alejandro Pardo
Rishubh Parihar
Sarah Parisot
JaeYoo Park
Gyeong-Moon Park
Hyojin Park
Hyoungseob Park
Jongchan Park
Jae Sung Park
Kiru Park
Chunghyun Park
Kwanyong Park
Sunghyun Park
Sungrae Park
Seongsik Park
Sanghyun Park
Sungjune Park
Taesung Park
Gaurav Parmar
Paritosh Parmar
Alvaro Parra
Despoina Paschalidou
Or Patashnik
Shivansh Patel
Pushpak Pati
Prashant W. Patil
Vaishakh Patil
Suvam Patra
Jay Patravali
Badri Narayana Patro
Angshuman Paul
Sudipta Paul
Rémi Pautrat
Nick E. Pears
Adithya Pediredla
Wenjie Pei
Shmuel Peleg
Latha Pemula
Bo Peng
Houwen Peng
Yue Peng
Liangzu Peng
Baoyun Peng
Jun Peng
Pai Peng
Sida Peng
Xi Peng
Yuxin Peng
Songyou Peng
Wei Peng
Weiqi Peng
Wen-Hsiao Peng
Pramuditha Perera
Juan C. Perez
Eduardo Pérez Pellitero
Juan-Manuel Perez-Rua
Federico Pernici
Marco Pesavento
Stavros Petridis
Ilya A. Petrov
Vladan Petrovic
Mathis Petrovich
Suzanne Petryk
Hieu Pham
Quang Pham
Khoi Pham
Tung Pham
Huy Phan
Stephen Phillips
Cheng Perng Phoo
David Picard
Marco Piccirilli
Georg Pichler
A. J. Piergiovanni
Vipin Pillai
Silvia L. Pintea
Giovanni Pintore
Robinson Piramuthu
Fiora Pirri
Theodoros Pissas
Fabio Pizzati
Benjamin Planche
Bryan Plummer
Matteo Poggi
Ashwini Pokle
Georgy E. Ponimatkin
Adrian Popescu
Stefan Popov
Nikola Popović
Ronald Poppe
Angelo Porrello
Michael Potter
Charalambos Poullis
Hadi Pouransari
Omid Poursaeed

Shraman Pramanick
Mantini Pranav
Dilip K. Prasad
Meghshyam Prasad
B. H. Pawan Prasad
Shitala Prasad
Prateek Prasanna
Ekta Prashnani
Derek S. Prijatelj
Luke Y. Prince
Véronique Prinet
Victor Adrian Prisacariu
James Pritts
Thomas Probst
Sergey Prokudin
Rita Pucci
Chi-Man Pun
Matthew Purri
Haozhi Qi
Lu Qi
Lei Qi
Xianbiao Qi
Yonggang Qi
Yuankai Qi
Siyuan Qi
Guocheng Qian
Hangwei Qian
Qi Qian
Deheng Qian
Shengsheng Qian
Wen Qian
Rui Qian
Yiming Qian
Shengju Qian
Shengyi Qian
Xuelin Qian
Zhenxing Qian
Nan Qiao
Xiaotian Qiao
Jing Qin
Can Qin
Siyang Qin
Hongwei Qin
Jie Qin
Minghai Qin
Yipeng Qin
Yongqiang Qin
Wenda Qin
Xuebin Qin
Yuzhe Qin
Yao Qin
Zhenyue Qin
Zhiwu Qing
Heqian Qiu
Jiayan Qiu
Jielin Qiu
Yue Qiu
Jiaxiong Qiu
Zhongxi Qiu
Shi Qiu
Zhaofan Qiu
Zhongnan Qu
Yanyun Qu
Kha Gia Quach
Yuhui Quan
Ruijie Quan
Mike Rabbat
Rahul Shekhar Rade
Filip Radenovic
Gorjan Radevski
Bogdan Raducanu
Francesco Ragusa
Shafin Rahman
Md Mahfuzur Rahman Siddiquee
Hossein Rahmani
Kiran Raja
Sivaramakrishnan Rajaraman
Jathushan Rajasegaran
Adnan Siraj Rakin
Michaël Ramamonjisoa
Chirag A. Raman
Shanmuganathan Raman
Vignesh Ramanathan
Vasili Ramanishka
Vikram V. Ramaswamy
Merey Ramazanova
Jason Rambach
Sai Saketh Rambhatla
Clément Rambour
Ashwin Ramesh Babu
Adín Ramírez Rivera
Arianna Rampini
Haoxi Ran
Aakanksha Rana
Aayush Jung Bahadur Rana
Kanchana N. Ranasinghe
Aneesh Rangnekar
Samrudhdhi B. Rangrej
Harsh Rangwani
Viresh Ranjan
Anyi Rao
Yongming Rao
Carolina Raposo
Michalis Raptis
Amir Rasouli
Vivek Rathod
Adepu Ravi Sankar
Avinash Ravichandran
Bharadwaj Ravichandran
Dripta S. Raychaudhuri
Adria Recasens
Simon Reiß
Davis Rempe
Daxuan Ren
Jiawei Ren
Jimmy Ren
Sucheng Ren
Dayong Ren
Zhile Ren
Dongwei Ren
Qibing Ren
Pengfei Ren
Zhenwen Ren
Xuqian Ren
Yixuan Ren
Zhongzheng Ren
Ambareesh Revanur
Hamed Rezazadegan Tavakoli
Rafael S. Rezende
Wonjong Rhee
Alexander Richard

Christian Richardt
Stephan R. Richter
Benjamin Riggan
Dominik Rivoir
Mamshad Nayeem Rizve
Joshua D. Robinson
Joseph Robinson
Chris Rockwell
Ranga Rodrigo
Andres C. Rodriguez
Carlos Rodriguez-Pardo
Marcus Rohrbach
Gemma Roig
Yu Rong
David A. Ross
Mohammad Rostami
Edward Rosten
Karsten Roth
Anirban Roy
Debaditya Roy
Shuvendu Roy
Ahana Roy Choudhury
Aruni Roy Chowdhury
Denys Rozumnyi
Shulan Ruan
Wenjie Ruan
Patrick Ruhkamp
Danila Rukhovich
Anian Ruoss
Chris Russell
Dan Ruta
Dawid Damian Rymarczyk
DongHun Ryu
Hyeonggon Ryu
Kwonyoung Ryu
Balasubramanian S.
Alexandre Sablayrolles
Mohammad Sabokrou
Arka Sadhu
Aniruddha Saha
Oindrila Saha
Pritish Sahu
Aneeshan Sain
Nirat Saini
Saurabh Saini
Takeshi Saitoh
Christos Sakaridis
Fumihiko Sakaue
Dimitrios Sakkos
Ken Sakurada
Parikshit V. Sakurikar
Rohit Saluja
Nermin Samet
Leo Sampaio Ferraz Ribeiro
Jorge Sanchez
Enrique Sanchez
Shengtian Sang
Anush Sankaran
Soubhik Sanyal
Nikolaos Sarafianos
Vishwanath Saragadam
István Sárándi
Saquib Sarfraz
Mert Bulent Sariyildiz
Anindya Sarkar
Pritam Sarkar
Paul-Edouard Sarlin
Hiroshi Sasaki
Takami Sato
Torsten Sattler
Ravi Kumar Satzoda
Axel Sauer
Stefano Savian
Artem Savkin
Manolis Savva
Gerald Schaefer
Simone Schaub-Meyer
Yoni Schirris
Samuel Schulter
Katja Schwarz
Jesse Scott
Sinisa Segvic
Constantin Marc Seibold
Lorenzo Seidenari
Matan Sela
Fadime Sener
Paul Hongsuck Seo
Kwanggyoon Seo
Hongje Seong
Dario Serez
Francesco Setti
Bryan Seybold
Mohamad Shahbazi
Shima Shahfar
Xinxin Shan
Caifeng Shan
Dandan Shan
Shawn Shan
Wei Shang
Jinghuan Shang
Jiaxiang Shang
Lei Shang
Sukrit Shankar
Ken Shao
Rui Shao
Jie Shao
Mingwen Shao
Aashish Sharma
Gaurav Sharma
Vivek Sharma
Abhishek Sharma
Yoli Shavit
Shashank Shekhar
Sumit Shekhar
Zhijie Shen
Fengyi Shen
Furao Shen
Jialie Shen
Jingjing Shen
Ziyi Shen
Linlin Shen
Guangyu Shen
Biluo Shen
Falong Shen
Jiajun Shen
Qiu Shen
Qiuhong Shen
Shuai Shen
Wang Shen
Yiqing Shen
Yunhang Shen
Siqi Shen
Bin Shen
Tianwei Shen

Xi Shen
Yilin Shen
Yuming Shen
Yucong Shen
Zhiqiang Shen
Lu Sheng
Yichen Sheng
Shivanand Venkanna Sheshappanavar
Shelly Sheynin
Baifeng Shi
Ruoxi Shi
Botian Shi
Hailin Shi
Jia Shi
Jing Shi
Shaoshuai Shi
Baoguang Shi
Boxin Shi
Hengcan Shi
Tianyang Shi
Xiaodan Shi
Yongjie Shi
Zhensheng Shi
Yinghuan Shi
Weiqi Shi
Wu Shi
Xuepeng Shi
Xiaoshuang Shi
Yujiao Shi
Zenglin Shi
Zhenmei Shi
Takashi Shibata
Meng-Li Shih
Yichang Shih
Hyunjung Shim
Dongseok Shim
Soshi Shimada
Inkyu Shin
Jinwoo Shin
Seungjoo Shin
Seungjae Shin
Koichi Shinoda
Suprosanna Shit
Palaiahnakote Shivakumara
Eli Shlizerman
Gaurav Shrivastava
Xiao Shu
Xiangbo Shu
Xiujun Shu
Yang Shu
Tianmin Shu
Jun Shu
Zhixin Shu
Bing Shuai
Maria Shugrina
Ivan Shugurov
Satya Narayan Shukla
Pranjay Shyam
Jianlou Si
Yawar Siddiqui
Alberto Signoroni
Pedro Silva
Jae-Young Sim
Oriane Siméoni
Martin Simon
Andrea Simonelli
Abhishek Singh
Ashish Singh
Dinesh Singh
Gurkirt Singh
Krishna Kumar Singh
Mannat Singh
Pravendra Singh
Rajat Vikram Singh
Utkarsh Singhal
Dipika Singhania
Vasu Singla
Harsh Sinha
Sudipta Sinha
Josef Sivic
Elena Sizikova
Geri Skenderi
Ivan Skorokhodov
Dmitriy Smirnov
Cameron Y. Smith
James S. Smith
Patrick Snape
Mattia Soldan
Hyeongseok Son
Sanghyun Son
Chuanbiao Song
Chen Song
Chunfeng Song
Dan Song
Dongjin Song
Hwanjun Song
Guoxian Song
Jiaming Song
Jie Song
Liangchen Song
Ran Song
Luchuan Song
Xibin Song
Li Song
Fenglong Song
Guoli Song
Guanglu Song
Zhenbo Song
Lin Song
Xinhang Song
Yang Song
Yibing Song
Rajiv Soundararajan
Hossein Souri
Cristovao Sousa
Riccardo Spezialetti
Leonidas Spinoulas
Michael W. Spratling
Deepak Sridhar
Srinath Sridhar
Gaurang Sriramanan
Vinkle Kumar Srivastav
Themos Stafylakis
Serban Stan
Anastasis Stathopoulos
Markus Steinberger
Jan Steinbrener
Sinisa Stekovic
Alexandros Stergiou
Gleb Sterkin
Rainer Stiefelhagen
Pierre Stock

Ombretta Strafforello
Julian Straub
Yannick Strümpler
Joerg Stueckler
Hang Su
Weijie Su
Jong-Chyi Su
Bing Su
Haisheng Su
Jinming Su
Yiyang Su
Yukun Su
Yuxin Su
Zhuo Su
Zhaoqi Su
Xiu Su
Yu-Chuan Su
Zhixun Su
Arulkumar Subramaniam
Akshayvarun Subramanya
A. Subramanyam
Swathikiran Sudhakaran
Yusuke Sugano
Masanori Suganuma
Yumin Suh
Yang Sui
Baochen Sun
Cheng Sun
Long Sun
Guolei Sun
Haoliang Sun
Haomiao Sun
He Sun
Hanqing Sun
Hao Sun
Lichao Sun
Jiachen Sun
Jiaming Sun
Jian Sun
Jin Sun
Jennifer J. Sun
Tiancheng Sun
Libo Sun
Peize Sun
Qianru Sun
Shanlin Sun
Yu Sun
Zhun Sun
Che Sun
Lin Sun
Tao Sun
Yiyou Sun
Chunyi Sun
Chong Sun
Weiwei Sun
Weixuan Sun
Xiuyu Sun
Yanan Sun
Zeren Sun
Zhaodong Sun
Zhiqing Sun
Minhyuk Sung
Jinli Suo
Simon Suo
Abhijit Suprem
Anshuman Suri
Saksham Suri
Joshua M. Susskind
Roman Suvorov
Gurumurthy Swaminathan
Robin Swanson
Paul Swoboda
Tabish A. Syed
Richard Szeliski
Fariborz Taherkhani
Yu-Wing Tai
Keita Takahashi
Walter Talbott
Gary Tam
Masato Tamura
Feitong Tan
Fuwen Tan
Shuhan Tan
Andong Tan
Bin Tan
Cheng Tan
Jianchao Tan
Lei Tan
Mingxing Tan
Xin Tan
Zichang Tan
Zhentao Tan
Kenichiro Tanaka
Masayuki Tanaka
Yushun Tang
Hao Tang
Jingqun Tang
Jinhui Tang
Kaihua Tang
Luming Tang
Lv Tang
Sheyang Tang
Shitao Tang
Siliang Tang
Shixiang Tang
Yansong Tang
Keke Tang
Chang Tang
Chenwei Tang
Jie Tang
Junshu Tang
Ming Tang
Peng Tang
Xu Tang
Yao Tang
Chen Tang
Fan Tang
Haoran Tang
Shengeng Tang
Yehui Tang
Zhipeng Tang
Ugo Tanielian
Chaofan Tao
Jiale Tao
Junli Tao
Renshuai Tao
An Tao
Guanhong Tao
Zhiqiang Tao
Makarand Tapaswi
Jean-Philippe G. Tarel
Juan J. Tarrio
Enzo Tartaglione
Keisuke Tateno
Zachary Teed

Ajinkya B. Tejankar
Bugra Tekin
Purva Tendulkar
Damien Teney
Minggui Teng
Chris Tensmeyer
Andrew Beng Jin Teoh
Philipp Terhörst
Kartik Thakral
Nupur Thakur
Kevin Thandiackal
Spyridon Thermos
Diego Thomas
William Thong
Yuesong Tian
Guanzhong Tian
Lin Tian
Shiqi Tian
Kai Tian
Meng Tian
Tai-Peng Tian
Zhuotao Tian
Shangxuan Tian
Tian Tian
Yapeng Tian
Yu Tian
Yuxin Tian
Leslie Ching Ow Tiong
Praveen Tirupattur
Garvita Tiwari
George Toderici
Antoine Toisoul
Aysim Toker
Tatiana Tommasi
Zhan Tong
Alessio Tonioni
Alessandro Torcinovich
Fabio Tosi
Matteo Toso
Hugo Touvron
Quan Hung Tran
Son Tran
Hung Tran
Ngoc-Trung Tran
Vinh Tran
Phong Tran
Giovanni Trappolini
Edith Tretschk
Subarna Tripathi
Shubhendu Trivedi
Eduard Trulls
Prune Truong
Thanh-Dat Truong
Tomasz Trzcinski
Sam Tsai
Yi-Hsuan Tsai
Ethan Tseng
Yu-Chee Tseng
Shahar Tsiper
Stavros Tsogkas
Shikui Tu
Zhigang Tu
Zhengzhong Tu
Richard Tucker
Sergey Tulyakov
Cigdem Turan
Daniyar Turmukhambetov
Victor G. Turrisi da Costa
Bartlomiej Twardowski
Christopher D. Twigg
Radim Tylecek
Mostofa Rafid Uddin
Md. Zasim Uddin
Kohei Uehara
Nicolas Ugrinovic
Youngjung Uh
Norimichi Ukita
Anwaar Ulhaq
Devesh Upadhyay
Paul Upchurch
Yoshitaka Ushiku
Yuzuko Utsumi
Mikaela Angelina Uy
Mohit Vaishnav
Pratik Vaishnavi
Jeya Maria Jose Valanarasu
Matias A. Valdenegro Toro
Diego Valsesia
Wouter Van Gansbeke
Nanne van Noord
Simon Vandenhende
Farshid Varno
Cristina Vasconcelos
Francisco Vasconcelos
Alex Vasilescu
Subeesh Vasu
Arun Balajee Vasudevan
Kanav Vats
Vaibhav S. Vavilala
Sagar Vaze
Javier Vazquez-Corral
Andrea Vedaldi
Olga Veksler
Andreas Velten
Sai H. Vemprala
Raviteja Vemulapalli
Shashanka Venkataramanan
Dor Verbin
Luisa Verdoliva
Manisha Verma
Yashaswi Verma
Constantin Vertan
Eli Verwimp
Deepak Vijaykeerthy
Pablo Villanueva
Ruben Villegas
Markus Vincze
Vibhav Vineet
Minh P. Vo
Huy V. Vo
Duc Minh Vo
Tomas Vojir
Igor Vozniak
Nicholas Vretos
Vibashan VS
Tuan-Anh Vu
Thang Vu
Mårten Wadenbäck
Neal Wadhwa
Aaron T. Walsman
Steven Walton
Jin Wan
Alvin Wan
Jia Wan

Jun Wan
Xiaoyue Wan
Fang Wan
Guowei Wan
Renjie Wan
Zhiqiang Wan
Ziyu Wan
Bastian Wandt
Dongdong Wang
Limin Wang
Haiyang Wang
Xiaobing Wang
Angtian Wang
Angelina Wang
Bing Wang
Bo Wang
Boyu Wang
Binghui Wang
Chen Wang
Chien-Yi Wang
Congli Wang
Qi Wang
Chengrui Wang
Rui Wang
Yiqun Wang
Cong Wang
Wenjing Wang
Dongkai Wang
Di Wang
Xiaogang Wang
Kai Wang
Zhizhong Wang
Fangjinhua Wang
Feng Wang
Hang Wang
Gaoang Wang
Guoqing Wang
Guangcong Wang
Guangzhi Wang
Hanqing Wang
Hao Wang
Haohan Wang
Haoran Wang
Hong Wang
Haotao Wang
Hu Wang
Huan Wang
Hua Wang
Hui-Po Wang
Hengli Wang
Hanyu Wang
Hongxing Wang
Jingwen Wang
Jialiang Wang
Jian Wang
Jianyi Wang
Jiashun Wang
Jiahao Wang
Tsun-Hsuan Wang
Xiaoqian Wang
Jinqiao Wang
Jun Wang
Jianzong Wang
Kaihong Wang
Ke Wang
Lei Wang
Lingjing Wang
Linnan Wang
Lin Wang
Liansheng Wang
Mengjiao Wang
Manning Wang
Nannan Wang
Peihao Wang
Jiayun Wang
Pu Wang
Qiang Wang
Qiufeng Wang
Qilong Wang
Qiangchang Wang
Qin Wang
Qing Wang
Ruocheng Wang
Ruibin Wang
Ruisheng Wang
Ruizhe Wang
Runqi Wang
Runzhong Wang
Wenxuan Wang
Sen Wang
Shangfei Wang
Shaofei Wang
Shijie Wang
Shiqi Wang
Zhibo Wang
Song Wang
Xinjiang Wang
Tai Wang
Tao Wang
Teng Wang
Xiang Wang
Tianren Wang
Tiantian Wang
Tianyi Wang
Fengjiao Wang
Wei Wang
Miaohui Wang
Suchen Wang
Siyue Wang
Yaoming Wang
Xiao Wang
Ze Wang
Biao Wang
Chaofei Wang
Dong Wang
Gu Wang
Guangrun Wang
Guangming Wang
Guo-Hua Wang
Haoqing Wang
Hesheng Wang
Huafeng Wang
Jinghua Wang
Jingdong Wang
Jingjing Wang
Jingya Wang
Jingkang Wang
Jiakai Wang
Junke Wang
Kuo Wang
Lichen Wang
Lizhi Wang
Longguang Wang
Mang Wang
Mei Wang

Min Wang
Peng-Shuai Wang
Run Wang
Shaoru Wang
Shuhui Wang
Tan Wang
Tiancai Wang
Tianqi Wang
Wenhai Wang
Wenzhe Wang
Xiaobo Wang
Xiudong Wang
Xu Wang
Yajie Wang
Yan Wang
Yuan-Gen Wang
Yingqian Wang
Yizhi Wang
Yulin Wang
Yu Wang
Yujie Wang
Yunhe Wang
Yuxi Wang
Yaowei Wang
Yiwei Wang
Zezheng Wang
Hongzhi Wang
Zhiqiang Wang
Ziteng Wang
Ziwei Wang
Zheng Wang
Zhenyu Wang
Binglu Wang
Zhongdao Wang
Ce Wang
Weining Wang
Weiyao Wang
Wenbin Wang
Wenguan Wang
Guangting Wang
Haolin Wang
Haiyan Wang
Huiyu Wang
Naiyan Wang
Jingbo Wang
Jinpeng Wang
Jiaqi Wang
Liyuan Wang
Lizhen Wang
Ning Wang
Wenqian Wang
Sheng-Yu Wang
Weimin Wang
Xiaohan Wang
Yifan Wang
Yi Wang
Yongtao Wang
Yizhou Wang
Zhuo Wang
Zhe Wang
Xudong Wang
Xiaofang Wang
Xinggang Wang
Xiaosen Wang
Xiaosong Wang
Xiaoyang Wang
Lijun Wang
Xinlong Wang
Xuan Wang
Xue Wang
Yangang Wang
Yaohui Wang
Yu-Chiang Frank Wang
Yida Wang
Yilin Wang
Yi Ru Wang
Yali Wang
Yinglong Wang
Yufu Wang
Yujiang Wang
Yuwang Wang
Yuting Wang
Yang Wang
Yu-Xiong Wang
Yixu Wang
Ziqi Wang
Zhicheng Wang
Zeyu Wang
Zhaowen Wang
Zhenyi Wang
Zhenzhi Wang
Zhijie Wang
Zhiyong Wang
Zhongling Wang
Zhuowei Wang
Zian Wang
Zifu Wang
Zihao Wang
Zirui Wang
Ziyan Wang
Wenxiao Wang
Zhen Wang
Zhepeng Wang
Zi Wang
Zihao W. Wang
Steven L. Waslander
Olivia Watkins
Daniel Watson
Silvan Weder
Dongyoon Wee
Dongming Wei
Tianyi Wei
Jia Wei
Dong Wei
Fangyun Wei
Longhui Wei
Mingqiang Wei
Xinyue Wei
Chen Wei
Donglai Wei
Pengxu Wei
Xing Wei
Xiu-Shen Wei
Wenqi Wei
Guoqiang Wei
Wei Wei
XingKui Wei
Xian Wei
Xingxing Wei
Yake Wei
Yuxiang Wei
Yi Wei
Luca Weihs
Michael Weinmann
Martin Weinmann

Congcong Wen
Chuan Wen
Jie Wen
Sijia Wen
Song Wen
Chao Wen
Xiang Wen
Zeyi Wen
Xin Wen
Yilin Wen
Yijia Weng
Shuchen Weng
Junwu Weng
Wenming Weng
Renliang Weng
Zhenyu Weng
Xinshuo Weng
Nicholas J. Westlake
Gordon Wetzstein
Lena M. Widin Klasén
Rick Wildes
Bryan M. Williams
Williem Williem
Ole Winther
Scott Wisdom
Alex Wong
Chau-Wai Wong
Kwan-Yee K. Wong
Yongkang Wong
Scott Workman
Marcel Worring
Michael Wray
Safwan Wshah
Xiang Wu
Aming Wu
Chongruo Wu
Cho-Ying Wu
Chunpeng Wu
Chenyan Wu
Ziyi Wu
Fuxiang Wu
Gang Wu
Haiping Wu
Huisi Wu
Jane Wu
Jialian Wu
Jing Wu
Jinjian Wu
Jianlong Wu
Xian Wu
Lifang Wu
Lifan Wu
Minye Wu
Qianyi Wu
Rongliang Wu
Rui Wu
Shiqian Wu
Shuzhe Wu
Shangzhe Wu
Tsung-Han Wu
Tz-Ying Wu
Ting-Wei Wu
Jiannan Wu
Zhiliang Wu
Yu Wu
Chenyun Wu
Dayan Wu
Dongxian Wu
Fei Wu
Hefeng Wu
Jianxin Wu
Weibin Wu
Wenxuan Wu
Wenhao Wu
Xiao Wu
Yicheng Wu
Yuanwei Wu
Yu-Huan Wu
Zhenxin Wu
Zhenyu Wu
Wei Wu
Peng Wu
Xiaohe Wu
Xindi Wu
Xinxing Wu
Xinyi Wu
Xingjiao Wu
Xiongwei Wu
Yangzheng Wu
Yanzhao Wu
Yawen Wu
Yong Wu
Yi Wu
Ying Nian Wu
Zhenyao Wu
Zhonghua Wu
Zongze Wu
Zuxuan Wu
Stefanie Wuhrer
Teng Xi
Jianing Xi
Fei Xia
Haifeng Xia
Menghan Xia
Yuanqing Xia
Zhihua Xia
Xiaobo Xia
Weihao Xia
Shihong Xia
Yan Xia
Yong Xia
Zhaoyang Xia
Zhihao Xia
Chuhua Xian
Yongqin Xian
Wangmeng Xiang
Fanbo Xiang
Tiange Xiang
Tao Xiang
Liuyu Xiang
Xiaoyu Xiang
Zhiyu Xiang
Aoran Xiao
Chunxia Xiao
Fanyi Xiao
Jimin Xiao
Jun Xiao
Taihong Xiao
Anqi Xiao
Junfei Xiao
Jing Xiao
Liang Xiao
Yang Xiao
Yuting Xiao
Yijun Xiao

Yao Xiao
Zeyu Xiao
Zhisheng Xiao
Zihao Xiao
Binhui Xie
Christopher Xie
Haozhe Xie
Jin Xie
Guo-Sen Xie
Hongtao Xie
Ming-Kun Xie
Tingting Xie
Chaohao Xie
Weicheng Xie
Xudong Xie
Jiyang Xie
Xiaohua Xie
Yuan Xie
Zhenyu Xie
Ning Xie
Xianghui Xie
Xiufeng Xie
You Xie
Yutong Xie
Fuyong Xing
Yifan Xing
Zhen Xing
Yuanjun Xiong
Jinhui Xiong
Weihua Xiong
Hongkai Xiong
Zhitong Xiong
Yuanhao Xiong
Yunyang Xiong
Yuwen Xiong
Zhiwei Xiong
Yuliang Xiu
An Xu
Chang Xu
Chenliang Xu
Chengming Xu
Chenshu Xu
Xiang Xu
Huijuan Xu
Zhe Xu
Jie Xu
Jingyi Xu
Jiarui Xu
Yinghao Xu
Kele Xu
Ke Xu
Li Xu
Linchuan Xu
Linning Xu
Mengde Xu
Mengmeng Frost Xu
Min Xu
Mingye Xu
Jun Xu
Ning Xu
Peng Xu
Runsheng Xu
Sheng Xu
Wenqiang Xu
Xiaogang Xu
Renzhe Xu
Kaidi Xu
Yi Xu
Chi Xu
Qiuling Xu
Baobei Xu
Feng Xu
Haohang Xu
Haofei Xu
Lan Xu
Mingze Xu
Songcen Xu
Weipeng Xu
Wenjia Xu
Wenju Xu
Xiangyu Xu
Xin Xu
Yinshuang Xu
Yixing Xu
Yuting Xu
Yanyu Xu
Zhenbo Xu
Zhiliang Xu
Zhiyuan Xu
Xiaohao Xu
Yanwu Xu
Yan Xu
Yiran Xu
Yifan Xu
Yufei Xu
Yong Xu
Zichuan Xu
Zenglin Xu
Zexiang Xu
Zhan Xu
Zheng Xu
Zhiwei Xu
Ziyue Xu
Shiyu Xuan
Hanyu Xuan
Fei Xue
Jianru Xue
Mingfu Xue
Qinghan Xue
Tianfan Xue
Chao Xue
Chuhui Xue
Nan Xue
Zhou Xue
Xiangyang Xue
Yuan Xue
Abhay Yadav
Ravindra Yadav
Kota Yamaguchi
Toshihiko Yamasaki
Kohei Yamashita
Chaochao Yan
Feng Yan
Kun Yan
Qingsen Yan
Qixin Yan
Rui Yan
Siming Yan
Xinchen Yan
Yaping Yan
Bin Yan
Qingan Yan
Shen Yan
Shipeng Yan
Xu Yan

Yan Yan
Yichao Yan
Zhaoyi Yan
Zike Yan
Zhiqiang Yan
Hongliang Yan
Zizheng Yan
Jiewen Yang
Anqi Joyce Yang
Shan Yang
Anqi Yang
Antoine Yang
Bo Yang
Baoyao Yang
Chenhongyi Yang
Dingkang Yang
De-Nian Yang
Dong Yang
David Yang
Fan Yang
Fengyu Yang
Fengting Yang
Fei Yang
Gengshan Yang
Heng Yang
Han Yang
Huan Yang
Yibo Yang
Jiancheng Yang
Jihan Yang
Jiawei Yang
Jiayu Yang
Jie Yang
Jinfa Yang
Jingkang Yang
Jinyu Yang
Cheng-Fu Yang
Ji Yang
Jianyu Yang
Kailun Yang
Tian Yang
Luyu Yang
Liang Yang
Li Yang
Michael Ying Yang
Yang Yang
Muli Yang
Le Yang
Qiushi Yang
Ren Yang
Ruihan Yang
Shuang Yang
Siyuan Yang
Su Yang
Shiqi Yang
Taojiannan Yang
Tianyu Yang
Lei Yang
Wanzhao Yang
Shuai Yang
William Yang
Wei Yang
Xiaofeng Yang
Xiaoshan Yang
Xin Yang
Xuan Yang
Xu Yang
Xingyi Yang
Xitong Yang
Jing Yang
Yanchao Yang
Wenming Yang
Yujiu Yang
Herb Yang
Jianfei Yang
Jinhui Yang
Chuanguang Yang
Guanglei Yang
Haitao Yang
Kewei Yang
Linlin Yang
Lijin Yang
Longrong Yang
Meng Yang
MingKun Yang
Sibei Yang
Shicai Yang
Tong Yang
Wen Yang
Xi Yang
Xiaolong Yang
Xue Yang
Yubin Yang
Ze Yang
Ziyi Yang
Yi Yang
Linjie Yang
Yuzhe Yang
Yiding Yang
Zhenpei Yang
Zhaohui Yang
Zhengyuan Yang
Zhibo Yang
Zongxin Yang
Hantao Yao
Mingde Yao
Rui Yao
Taiping Yao
Ting Yao
Cong Yao
Qingsong Yao
Quanming Yao
Xu Yao
Yuan Yao
Yao Yao
Yazhou Yao
Jiawen Yao
Shunyu Yao
Pew-Thian Yap
Sudhir Yarram
Rajeev Yasarla
Peng Ye
Botao Ye
Mao Ye
Fei Ye
Hanrong Ye
Jingwen Ye
Jinwei Ye
Jiarong Ye
Mang Ye
Meng Ye
Qi Ye
Qian Ye
Qixiang Ye
Junjie Ye

Sheng Ye
Nanyang Ye
Yufei Ye
Xiaoqing Ye
Ruolin Ye
Yousef Yeganeh
Chun-Hsiao Yeh
Raymond A. Yeh
Yu-Ying Yeh
Kai Yi
Chang Yi
Renjiao Yi
Xinping Yi
Peng Yi
Alper Yilmaz
Junho Yim
Hui Yin
Bangjie Yin
Jia-Li Yin
Miao Yin
Wenzhe Yin
Xuwang Yin
Ming Yin
Yu Yin
Aoxiong Yin
Kangxue Yin
Tianwei Yin
Wei Yin
Xianghua Ying
Rio Yokota
Tatsuya Yokota
Naoto Yokoya
Ryo Yonetani
Ki Yoon Yoo
Jinsu Yoo
Sunjae Yoon
Jae Shin Yoon
Jihun Yoon
Sung-Hoon Yoon
Ryota Yoshihashi
Yusuke Yoshiyasu
Chenyu You
Haoran You
Haoxuan You
Yang You
Quanzeng You
Tackgeun You
Kaichao You
Shan You
Xinge You
Yurong You
Baosheng Yu
Bei Yu
Haichao Yu
Hao Yu
Chaohui Yu
Fisher Yu
Jin-Gang Yu
Jiyang Yu
Jason J. Yu
Jiashuo Yu
Hong-Xing Yu
Lei Yu
Mulin Yu
Ning Yu
Peilin Yu
Qi Yu
Qian Yu
Rui Yu
Shuzhi Yu
Gang Yu
Tan Yu
Weijiang Yu
Xin Yu
Bingyao Yu
Ye Yu
Hanchao Yu
Yingchen Yu
Tao Yu
Xiaotian Yu
Qing Yu
Houjian Yu
Changqian Yu
Jing Yu
Jun Yu
Shujian Yu
Xiang Yu
Zhaofei Yu
Zhenbo Yu
Yinfeng Yu
Zhuoran Yu
Zitong Yu
Bo Yuan
Jiangbo Yuan
Liangzhe Yuan
Weihao Yuan
Jianbo Yuan
Xiaoyun Yuan
Ye Yuan
Li Yuan
Geng Yuan
Jialin Yuan
Maoxun Yuan
Peng Yuan
Xin Yuan
Yuan Yuan
Yuhui Yuan
Yixuan Yuan
Zheng Yuan
Mehmet Kerim Yücel
Kaiyu Yue
Haixiao Yue
Heeseung Yun
Sangdoo Yun
Tian Yun
Mahmut Yurt
Ekim Yurtsever
Ahmet Yüzügüler
Edouard Yvinec
Eloi Zablocki
Christopher Zach
Muhammad Zaigham Zaheer
Pierluigi Zama Ramirez
Yuhang Zang
Pietro Zanuttigh
Alexey Zaytsev
Bernhard Zeisl
Haitian Zeng
Pengpeng Zeng
Jiabei Zeng
Runhao Zeng
Wei Zeng
Yawen Zeng
Yi Zeng

Yiming Zeng
Tieyong Zeng
Huanqiang Zeng
Dan Zeng
Yu Zeng
Wei Zhai
Yuanhao Zhai
Fangneng Zhan
Kun Zhan
Xiong Zhang
Jingdong Zhang
Jiangning Zhang
Zhilu Zhang
Gengwei Zhang
Dongsu Zhang
Hui Zhang
Binjie Zhang
Bo Zhang
Tianhao Zhang
Cecilia Zhang
Jing Zhang
Chaoning Zhang
Chenxu Zhang
Chi Zhang
Chris Zhang
Yabin Zhang
Zhao Zhang
Rufeng Zhang
Chaoyi Zhang
Zheng Zhang
Da Zhang
Yi Zhang
Edward Zhang
Xin Zhang
Feifei Zhang
Feilong Zhang
Yuqi Zhang
GuiXuan Zhang
Hanlin Zhang
Hanwang Zhang
Hanzhen Zhang
Haotian Zhang
He Zhang
Haokui Zhang
Hongyuan Zhang
Hengrui Zhang
Hongming Zhang
Mingfang Zhang
Jianpeng Zhang
Jiaming Zhang
Jichao Zhang
Jie Zhang
Jingfeng Zhang
Jingyi Zhang
Jinnian Zhang
David Junhao Zhang
Junjie Zhang
Junzhe Zhang
Jiawan Zhang
Jingyang Zhang
Kai Zhang
Lei Zhang
Lihua Zhang
Lu Zhang
Miao Zhang
Minjia Zhang
Mingjin Zhang
Qi Zhang
Qian Zhang
Qilong Zhang
Qiming Zhang
Qiang Zhang
Richard Zhang
Ruimao Zhang
Ruisi Zhang
Ruixin Zhang
Runze Zhang
Qilin Zhang
Shan Zhang
Shanshan Zhang
Xi Sheryl Zhang
Song-Hai Zhang
Chongyang Zhang
Kaihao Zhang
Songyang Zhang
Shu Zhang
Siwei Zhang
Shujian Zhang
Tianyun Zhang
Tong Zhang
Tao Zhang
Wenwei Zhang
Wenqiang Zhang
Wen Zhang
Xiaolin Zhang
Xingchen Zhang
Xingxuan Zhang
Xiuming Zhang
Xiaoshuai Zhang
Xuanmeng Zhang
Xuanyang Zhang
Xucong Zhang
Xingxing Zhang
Xikun Zhang
Xiaohan Zhang
Yahui Zhang
Yunhua Zhang
Yan Zhang
Yanghao Zhang
Yifei Zhang
Yifan Zhang
Yi-Fan Zhang
Yihao Zhang
Yingliang Zhang
Youshan Zhang
Yulun Zhang
Yushu Zhang
Yixiao Zhang
Yide Zhang
Zhongwen Zhang
Bowen Zhang
Chen-Lin Zhang
Zehua Zhang
Zekun Zhang
Zeyu Zhang
Xiaowei Zhang
Yifeng Zhang
Cheng Zhang
Hongguang Zhang
Yuexi Zhang
Fa Zhang
Guofeng Zhang
Hao Zhang
Haofeng Zhang
Hongwen Zhang

Hua Zhang
Jiaxin Zhang
Zhenyu Zhang
Jian Zhang
Jianfeng Zhang
Jiao Zhang
Jiakai Zhang
Lefei Zhang
Le Zhang
Mi Zhang
Min Zhang
Ning Zhang
Pan Zhang
Pu Zhang
Qing Zhang
Renrui Zhang
Shifeng Zhang
Shuo Zhang
Shaoxiong Zhang
Weizhong Zhang
Xi Zhang
Xiaomei Zhang
Xinyu Zhang
Yin Zhang
Zicheng Zhang
Zihao Zhang
Ziqi Zhang
Zhaoxiang Zhang
Zhen Zhang
Zhipeng Zhang
Zhixing Zhang
Zhizheng Zhang
Jiawei Zhang
Zhong Zhang
Pingping Zhang
Yixin Zhang
Kui Zhang
Lingzhi Zhang
Huaiwen Zhang
Quanshi Zhang
Zhoutong Zhang
Yuhang Zhang
Yuting Zhang
Zhang Zhang
Ziming Zhang
Zhizhong Zhang
Qilong Zhangli
Bingyin Zhao
Bin Zhao
Chenglong Zhao
Lei Zhao
Feng Zhao
Gangming Zhao
Haiyan Zhao
Hao Zhao
Handong Zhao
Hengshuang Zhao
Yinan Zhao
Jiaojiao Zhao
Jiaqi Zhao
Jing Zhao
Kaili Zhao
Haojie Zhao
Yucheng Zhao
Longjiao Zhao
Long Zhao
Qingsong Zhao
Qingyu Zhao
Rui Zhao
Rui-Wei Zhao
Sicheng Zhao
Shuang Zhao
Siyan Zhao
Zelin Zhao
Shiyu Zhao
Wang Zhao
Tiesong Zhao
Qian Zhao
Wangbo Zhao
Xi-Le Zhao
Xu Zhao
Yajie Zhao
Yang Zhao
Ying Zhao
Yin Zhao
Yizhou Zhao
Yunhan Zhao
Yuyang Zhao
Yue Zhao
Yuzhi Zhao
Bowen Zhao
Pu Zhao
Bingchen Zhao
Borui Zhao
Fuqiang Zhao
Hanbin Zhao
Jian Zhao
Mingyang Zhao
Na Zhao
Rongchang Zhao
Ruiqi Zhao
Shuai Zhao
Wenda Zhao
Wenliang Zhao
Xiangyun Zhao
Yifan Zhao
Yaping Zhao
Zhou Zhao
He Zhao
Jie Zhao
Xibin Zhao
Xiaoqi Zhao
Zhengyu Zhao
Jin Zhe
Chuanxia Zheng
Huan Zheng
Hao Zheng
Jia Zheng
Jian-Qing Zheng
Shuai Zheng
Meng Zheng
Mingkai Zheng
Qian Zheng
Qi Zheng
Wu Zheng
Yinqiang Zheng
Yufeng Zheng
Yutong Zheng
Yalin Zheng
Yu Zheng
Feng Zheng
Zhaoheng Zheng
Haitian Zheng
Kang Zheng
Bolun Zheng

Haiyong Zheng
Mingwu Zheng
Sipeng Zheng
Tu Zheng
Wenzhao Zheng
Xiawu Zheng
Yinglin Zheng
Zhuo Zheng
Zilong Zheng
Kecheng Zheng
Zerong Zheng
Shuaifeng Zhi
Tiancheng Zhi
Jia-Xing Zhong
Yiwu Zhong
Fangwei Zhong
Zhihang Zhong
Yaoyao Zhong
Yiran Zhong
Zhun Zhong
Zichun Zhong
Bo Zhou
Boyao Zhou
Brady Zhou
Mo Zhou
Chunluan Zhou
Dingfu Zhou
Fan Zhou
Jingkai Zhou
Honglu Zhou
Jiaming Zhou
Jiahuan Zhou
Jun Zhou
Kaiyang Zhou
Keyang Zhou
Kuangqi Zhou
Lei Zhou
Lihua Zhou
Man Zhou
Mingyi Zhou
Mingyuan Zhou
Ning Zhou
Peng Zhou
Penghao Zhou
Qianyi Zhou
Shuigeng Zhou
Shangchen Zhou
Huayi Zhou
Zhize Zhou
Sanping Zhou
Qin Zhou
Tao Zhou
Wenbo Zhou
Xiangdong Zhou
Xiao-Yun Zhou
Xiao Zhou
Yang Zhou
Yipin Zhou
Zhenyu Zhou
Hao Zhou
Chu Zhou
Daquan Zhou
Da-Wei Zhou
Hang Zhou
Kang Zhou
Qianyu Zhou
Sheng Zhou
Wenhui Zhou
Xingyi Zhou
Yan-Jie Zhou
Yiyi Zhou
Yu Zhou
Yuan Zhou
Yuqian Zhou
Yuxuan Zhou
Zixiang Zhou
Wengang Zhou
Shuchang Zhou
Tianfei Zhou
Yichao Zhou
Alex Zhu
Chenchen Zhu
Deyao Zhu
Xiatian Zhu
Guibo Zhu
Haidong Zhu
Hao Zhu
Hongzi Zhu
Rui Zhu
Jing Zhu
Jianke Zhu
Junchen Zhu
Lei Zhu
Lingyu Zhu
Luyang Zhu
Menglong Zhu
Peihao Zhu
Hui Zhu
Xiaofeng Zhu
Tyler (Lixuan) Zhu
Wentao Zhu
Xiangyu Zhu
Xinqi Zhu
Xinxin Zhu
Xinliang Zhu
Yangguang Zhu
Yichen Zhu
Yixin Zhu
Yanjun Zhu
Yousong Zhu
Yuhao Zhu
Ye Zhu
Feng Zhu
Zhen Zhu
Fangrui Zhu
Jinjing Zhu
Linchao Zhu
Pengfei Zhu
Sijie Zhu
Xiaobin Zhu
Xiaoguang Zhu
Zezhou Zhu
Zhenyao Zhu
Kai Zhu
Pengkai Zhu
Bingbing Zhuang
Chengyuan Zhuang
Liansheng Zhuang
Peiye Zhuang
Yixin Zhuang
Yihong Zhuang
Junbao Zhuo
Andrea Ziani
Bartosz Zieliński
Primo Zingaretti

Nikolaos Zioulis
Andrew Zisserman
Yael Ziv
Liu Ziyin
Xingxing Zou
Danping Zou
Qi Zou
Shihao Zou
Xueyan Zou
Yang Zou
Yuliang Zou
Zihang Zou
Chuhang Zou
Dongqing Zou
Xu Zou
Zhiming Zou
Maria A. Zuluaga
Xinxin Zuo
Zhiwen Zuo
Reyer Zwiggelaar

Contents – Part XXXIV

Interpretable Open-Set Domain Adaptation via Angular Margin Separation

Xinhao Li[1], Jingjing Li[1,2](✉), Zhekai Du[1], Lei Zhu[3], and Wen Li[1]

[1] University of Electronic Science and Technology of China, Chengdu, China
[2] Institute of Electronic and Information Engineering of UESTC in Guangdong, Dongguan, China
lijin117@yeah.net
[3] Shandong Normal University, Jinan, China

Abstract. Open-set Domain Adaptation (OSDA) aims to recognize classes in the target domain that are seen in the source domain while rejecting other unseen target-exclusive classes into an unknown class, which ignores the diversity of the latter and is therefore incapable of their interpretation. The recently-proposed Semantic Recovery OSDA (SR-OSDA) brings in semantic attributes and attacks the challenge via partial alignment and visual-semantic projection, marking the first step towards interpretable OSDA. Following that line, in this work, we propose a representation learning framework termed Angular Margin Separation (AMS) that unveils the power of discriminative and robust representation for both open-set domain adaptation and cross-domain semantic recovery. Our core idea is to exploit an additive angular margin with regularization for both robust feature fine-tuning and discriminative joint feature alignment, which turns out advantageous to learning an accurate and less biased visual-semantic projection. Further, we propose a post-training re-projection that boosts the performance of seen classes interpretation without deterioration on unseen classes. Verified by extensive experiments, AMS achieves a notable improvement over the existing SR-OSDA baseline, with an average 7.6% increment in semantic recovery accuracy of unseen classes in multiple transfer tasks. Our code is available at AMS.

Keywords: Open-set domain adaptation · Zero-shot learning

1 Introduction

The advent of deep neural network (DNN) [15] and corresponding deep learning algorithms [17] has enabled computer vision unprecedented development and wide application in real-world production. However, meanwhile, some common

---

Supplementary Information The online version contains supplementary material available at https://doi.org/10.1007/978-3-031-19830-4_1.

S. Avidan et al. (Eds.): ECCV 2022, LNCS 13694, pp. 1–18, 2022.
https://doi.org/10.1007/978-3-031-19830-4_1

assumptions adopted by conventional machine learning frameworks, such as the i.i.d assumption and the closed world assumption, have gradually hindered the data-driven large-scale deep learning models, bringing two potential challenges in real-world applications [5,6,49]. First, the distribution of target data faced in deployment may be quite different from that of the well-labeled source data, and it is often too costly and even infeasible to collect adequate annotations for the new data distribution. Second, the real world is an open world, with new classes unseen during training possibly emerging at any time, and failure to carefully handle them could lead to fatal consequences, e.g., for self-driving vehicles.

Under such demands, open-set domain adaptation (OSDA) [3,25,31,38] has been widely studied, bridging the domain gap between a well-labeled source domain and an unlabeled target domain while rejecting all target-exclusive classes into one unknown class. However, few existing methods pay attention to the inter-class difference among different unknown classes, and none of them is capable of their interpretation. Although such deficiencies may not violate the task of OSDA by definition, they are essentially suboptimal for many real-world scenarios, where the unknown classes are diverse and their interpretation could be important for human intervention and model evolution. To overcome this limitation, semantic recovery domain adaptation (SR-OSDA) [13] has been recently proposed, which introduces semantic attributes to interpret the unseen novelties. On top of OSDA, SR-OSDA additionally learns a projection from visual features to their corresponding semantic attributes on seen classes in hope that it could also be applicable to the unseen classes. Besides, SR-OSDA purposefully differentiates between target data detected unknown to avoid interpreting them as one naive unknown class. Nevertheless, SR-OSDA, at its budding phase with only a prospective yet general objective, still has large room to improve.

Extensive studies have shown the significance of representation learning [1,9,21,34] for visual tasks, and we argue that the same is true for SR-OSDA. In this paper, we investigate the power of discriminative and robust representation for both open-set domain adaptation and cross-domain semantic recovery. Specifically, we first exploit an additive angular margin in visual space to fine-tune the pre-trained model on the source domain to learn representation suitable for cross-domain novelty detection and seen class recognition. Afterwards, we resort to additive angular margin again on the visual-semantic joint representation to facilitate compact alignment of seen classes and discriminative separation of unseen classes, which proves effective for both seen class recognition and distinct interpretation of diverse unseen classes. Finally, we propose a post-training re-projection to efficiently boost semantic recovery for seen classes without deterioration on unseen classes. We can summarize our contributions as follows:

- We unveil the power of discriminative and robust representation for SR-OSDA by exploiting an additive angular margin in both the fine-tuning phase and the training phase, which proves advantageous to both open-set domain adaptation and cross-domain semantic recovery.

- We propose a post-training re-projection with minimal cost to further boost semantic recovery on seen classes in the target domain without deterioration on unseen classes.
- Verified by extensive experiments, our proposed AMS achieves a notable improvement over the existing SR-OSDA framework, with an average increment of 7.6% in semantic recovery accuracy of unseen classes, and various improvements on other evaluation metrics in multiple transfer tasks.

2 Related Work

Open-Set Domain Adaptation. Open-set domain adaptation (OSDA) [3,12, 25,31,38] is recognized as a more practical form of domain adaptation [7,18,19, 22,42]. Confronted with the domain gap between a well-labeled source domain and an unlabeled target domain, OSDA not only needs to recognize the classes in the target domain that are seen in the source domain but also to detect the target-domain-exclusive classes as an unknown (unseen) class. Despite much progress achieved, few works consider the intrinsic diversity of the unknown classes, and none can provide interpretation for them, which in fact could be critical for human intervention or even the evolution of the model. Motivated by such deficiency, semantic-recovery domain adaptation (SR-OSDA) [13] was recently proposed to leverage attributes [16] to recover the semantics of unseen classes and thus realize their interpretation. In this work, we follow the recent SR-OSDA and interpret target unseen classes by semantic attributes.

Zero-Shot Learning. Zero-shot learning (ZSL) [33,45] aims to enable the machine to recognize classes with no training samples via side information [16,43]. ZSL methods are typically taxonomized by two criteria: (i) inductive ZSL vs. transductive ZSL, and (ii) classical ZSL vs. generalized ZSL (GZSL). Inductive ZSL only has access to the samples and side information of seen classes for training, while transductive ZSL [24,40] can further access the unlabeled samples or side information of the unseen classes. Classical ZSL assumes the sole presence of unseen classes in testing, while GZSL [4,20,41,44] needs to handle both. Since SR-OSDA has access to labeled samples and semantic attributes of seen classes as well as unlabeled samples from unseen classes, and needs to deal with both in inference, it is more similar to transductive GZSL. However, there are two distinct differences worth noting: (i) ZSL does not consider domain gap, and (ii) transductive ZSL typically assumes that the range of unseen classes is known, and thus often uses the semantic attributes of unseen classes with techniques like dictionary learning [48] and matrix factorization [46] to enhance classification. In contrast, SR-OSDA does not assume the range of unseen classes as prior knowledge and aims to recover the semantics of any unseen classes as accurately as possible. Therefore, the semantic attributes of unseen classes are only for evaluation and cannot be used in any form to proactively enhance performance.

3 Method

3.1 Problem Setup

We use $x \in \mathcal{X} \subset \mathbb{R}^p$, $y \in \mathcal{Y}$, and $a \in \mathcal{A} \subset \mathbb{R}^m$ to denote samples, labels, and semantic attributes. Let P, Q be the source and target distribution defined on $\mathcal{X} \times \mathcal{Y}$. In SR-OSDA, the source domain $\mathcal{D}_s$ consists of N_s labeled samples with semantic attribute prototypes $\{x_s^i, y_s^i, a_s^i\}_{i=1}^{N_s}$ with $x_s^i \in \mathcal{X}_s \subset \mathbb{R}^{p\times N_s}$, $y_s^i \in \mathcal{Y}_s$, and $a_s^i \in \mathcal{A}_s \subset \mathcal{R}^{m\times N_s}$ drawn i.i.d from P. The target domain $\mathcal{D}_t$ consists of N_t unlabeled samples $\{x_t^i\}_{i=1}^{N_t}$ with x_t^i drawn i.i.d from Q. Owing to domain gap, $p(x_s) \neq q(x_t)$. The source domain is associated with a set of seen classes $\mathcal{Y}_s = \{1, ..., |C_s|\}$, which is a subset of classes in target domain $\mathcal{Y}_t = \mathcal{Y}_s \cup \{|C_s| + 1, ...|C_s| + |C_t|\}$. In the m-dimensional semantic space, each class is associated with one semantic attribute prototype. Therefore, $\mathcal{A}_s = \{A_1, ..., A_{|C_s|}\}$ and $\mathcal{A}_t = \mathcal{A}_s \cup \{A_{|C_s|+1}, ..., A_{|C_s|+|C_t|}\}$. Our goal is two-fold: (i) to learn a target prediction function $h_t : x_t \rightarrow y_t$ that correctly classifies the $|C_s|$ known classes and rejects the other classes into an general unseen class, (ii) to learn a visual-semantic projection $\phi_t : x_t \rightarrow a_t$ that recovers the interpretable semantic attributes of target data.

Algorithm 1. The complete procedure of AMS.

Training Procedure
for epoch=1 to T_1 **do**
  Fine-tune f, g_s with Eq. (3).
end for
for epoch=1 to T_2 **do**
  Separate target samples from seen and unseen classes with Eq. (4).
  Pseudo-label target samples from unseen classes with Eq. (8).
  Train f, g, ϕ with Eq. (10).
end for
Use $h = g \circ f$ to classify target samples into seen and unseen classes.
Learn W on target samples from seen classes with Eq. (11).
Inference Procedure
Use $h = g \circ f$ to classify target samples into seen and unseen classes.
Recovery attributes of seen and unseen target samples with W and ϕ, respectively.

3.2 Framework Overview

When designing a method for SR-OSDA, we face two main challenges: seen/unseen separation, and class differentiation. Primarily, the solving of SR-OSDA largely relies upon the correct separation of seen and unseen classes. If not, samples from seen and unseen classes would be forcefully aligned, leading to severe negative transfer [23]. Besides, diverse seen and unseen classes should be differentiated so that their recognition and semantic recovery would not be

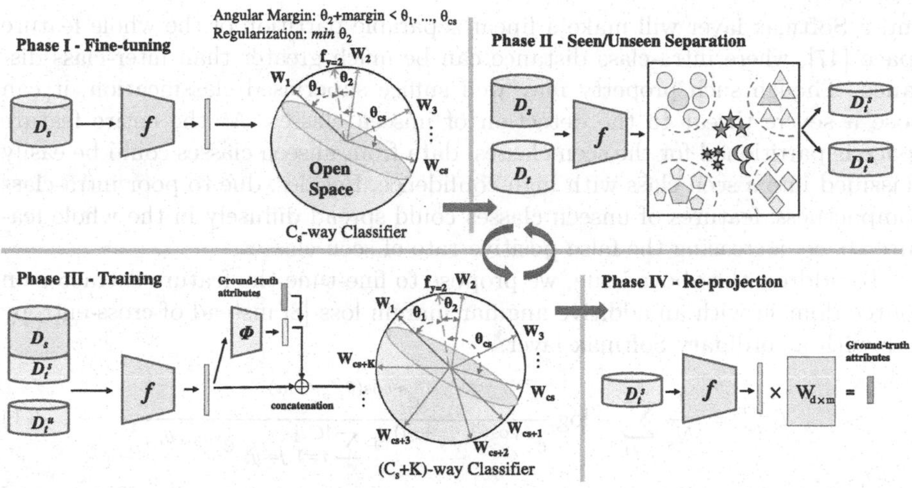

Fig. 1. Illustration of our proposed AMS. Phase I: Fine-tune the pre-trained feature extractor f on the seen classes of source domain with additive angular margin and angular regularization to enable highly discriminative representation of seen classes and leave out open space for future outliers. Phase II: Seen/Unseen separation: Separate target samples into seen and unseen classes based on feature distance and have them pseudo-labeled. Phase III: Train the model on both domains by applying additive angular margin and angular regularization on joint visual-semantic representation. The extra K channels in the classifier work under the maximum-response correspondence (MRC) strategy to differentiate diverse unseen classes. We alternate between Phase II and III to acquire higher accuracy of pseudo-labels. Phase IV: Learn a regularized linear projection W on target samples detected from seen classes to corresponding ground-truth attributes to further boost their semantic recovery. Best viewed in color. (Color figure online)

confused. In our proposed framework AMS (Fig. 1), we leverage a kind of angular-discriminative and robust representation to tackle both challenges in four phases. In phase I, we aim to learn discriminative representation of seen classes robust to anomalies, which is expected to benefit the seen/unseen separation in phase II. In phase III, we again resort to such representation to potently differentiate diverse seen and unseen classes. Lastly, in phase IV, we seek to further promote the interpretation of target seen classes by learning a visual-semantic re-projection. Details on each of the four phases are presented sequentially in Sect. 3.3–3.6, and the overall procedure is shown in Algorithm 1.

3.3 Discriminative and Robust Fine-Tuning

As analyzed in Sect. 3.2, the detection of unseen classes lies the foundation of SR-OSDA. Distance-based outlier detection [2,29] has proven effective for detecting visual outliers from unseen classes based on the distance between representations. However, representation learned via the classical combination of CNN and a Softmax layer will make a linear separable partition of the whole feature space [47], where intra-class distance can be much greater than inter-class distance. Though such property may well suffice supervised classification, it can pose a severe threat to the detection of unseen classes. As the entire feature space is partitioned for the seen classes, data from unseen classes could be easily classified into a seen class with high confidence. Besides, due to poor intra-class compactness, features of unseen classes could spread diffusely in the whole feature space, increasing the false positive rate of seen classes.

To address the above issue, we propose to fine-tune the feature extractor on source domain with an additive angular margin loss [8] instead of cross-entropy loss with an ordinary Softmax layer:

$$\mathcal{L}_{src}^{Arc} = \frac{1}{N_s}\sum_{i=1}^{N_s} -\log \frac{e^{s\cdot\cos(\theta_{i,y_s^i}+m)}}{e^{s\cdot\cos(\theta_{i,y_s^i}+m)} + \sum_{j=1,j\neq y_s^i}^{|C_s|} e^{s\cdot\cos\theta_{i,j}}}, \tag{1}$$

where m is the additive angular margin penalty, s is a re-scaling factor, and $\theta_{i,j} = \arccos \frac{W_j^\top f(x_s^i)}{\|W_j\|\cdot\|f(x_s^i)\|}$ is the angle between the i-th source feature extracted by the feature extractor $f : \mathcal{X} \to \mathbb{R}^d$ and the weights of the j-th neuron of the $|C_s|$-way classifier $g_s : \mathbb{R}^d \to \mathbb{R}^{|C_s|}$. Note that we fix $b_j = 0$ as in [8]. This objective guides the model to learn highly angular-discriminative representation of seen classes on a hypersphere.

However, Eq. (1) still leads to features that are approximately linearly separable and form a partition of the entire feature space, particularly when m is relatively small, which is not robust in the presence of anomalies. For instance, the decision boundary for class one in a binary case is $\cos(\theta_1 + m) > \cos\theta_2$, which can be rewritten as $\cos\theta_1 \cdot \cos m - \sin\theta_1 \cdot \sin m > \cos\theta_2$. When m is set to a small value such as 0.05 or 0.1, $\sin m \approx 0$, and therefore the decision boundary is approximately linearly separable: $(\frac{W_1^\top}{\|W_1\|\cdot\|f(x)\|} \cdot \cos m - \frac{W_2^\top}{\|W_2\|\cdot\|f(x)\|})f(x) > 0$. Although a larger m brings in more non-linearity, it increases optimization difficulty and causes convergence problems. Thus, m is often set small in practice [8]. Inspired by [47] that regularizes training by distance to class prototypes, we propose a regularization term for the angle between the learned representation and corresponding classifier weight to learn intra-class compact and angular discriminative features with non-linear decision boundaries, making room for the future unseen classes:

$$\mathcal{L}_{src}^{reg} = \sum_{i=1}^{N_s} -\cos\theta_{i,y_s^i}. \tag{2}$$

Therefore, the overall objective of our fine-tuning phase is:

$$\min_{f,g_s} \mathcal{L}_{src} = \mathcal{L}_{src}^{Arc} + \mathcal{L}_{src}^{reg}. \tag{3}$$

3.4 Seen/Unseen Separation

Thanks to the angular regularization above, the decision boundary is less overfitting to seen classes, leaving out an open space, wherein unseen classes are tightly bounded and stay farther away from all seen classes. Besides, experimental evidence in metric-based few-shot learning shows that optimizing prototype-based metrics could facilitate class-discriminative features when generalizing to unseen classes [28,39]. Therefore, the features of unseen classes are expected to have better clustering properties (see Appendix for experimental evidence). In such a desirable feature space, we define the probability of a target sample x_t^i belonging to a seen class as $p(y_t^i = c|x_t^i) = \frac{e^{-d(x_t^i, \mu_s^c)}}{\sum_{c'} e^{-d(x_t^i, \mu_s^{c'})}}$, where μ_s^c is the feature centroid of the c-th known class in the source domain, and d is cosine distance. The target sample is then pseudo-labeled by $\hat{y}_t^i = \arg\max_{c'} p(y_t^i = c'|x_t^i)$ with confidence $p_t^i = \max_{c'} p(y_t^i = c'|x_t^i)$. Next, we adopt a class-wise threshold to re-pseudo-label each target sample x_t^i to ensure more balanced results:

$$\hat{y}_t^i = \begin{cases} \hat{y}_t^i & \text{if } p_t^i > \bar{p}_t^{\hat{y}_t^i} \\ |C_s| + 1 & \text{otherwise} \end{cases}, \tag{4}$$

where $\bar{p}_t^{\hat{y}_t^i}$ is the average confidence of target samples pseudo-labeled as class $\hat{y}_t^i$, and $|C_s| + 1$ means a general unseen class. Afterwards, we use K-means to cluster the detected unknown samples into K clusters, and then use K-means again with the $|C_s| + K$ centroids as initialization to refine pseudo-labels for one time. To this end, all target samples are pseudo-labeled by $\hat{y} \in \{1, ..., |C_s| + K\}$ with corresponding centroids $R = \{R_1, ..., R_{|C_s|+K}\} \subset \mathbb{R}^{d \times (|C_s|+K)}$, and are separated into a seen set $\mathcal{D}_t^s$ and unseen set $\mathcal{D}_t^u$.

3.5 Alignment and Separation with Angular Margin

With all target samples pseudo-labeled, the focus now becomes aligning source and target features from the same seen class to boost recognition and separating the detected target features from unseen classes to avoid negative transfer. Meanwhile, the diversity of unseen classes should be preserved and their intrinsic difference should even be accentuated to facilitate discriminative and diverse semantic recovery results. To achieve this goal, [13] deployed center loss:

$$\mathcal{L}_c = \frac{1}{N_1} \sum_{i=1}^{N_1} \sum_{c=1}^{|C_s|+K} (\mathbb{I}_{[y^i=c]} d(f(x_{s/t}^i), R_c) - \frac{\mathbb{I}_{[y^i \neq c]}}{|C_s| + K - 1} d(f(x_{s/t}^i), R_c)), \tag{5}$$

where $N_1 = N_s + N_t$, d is cosine distance, $\mathbb{I}$ is the indicator function, and y_i is ground-truth label and pseudo-label for source and target samples respectively. However, we argue that there are mainly two defects: (i) Eq. (5) requires features of different classes to be far away from each other, but does not demarcate a margin that specifies how far is enough, which could be less efficient in optimization, (ii) Eq. (5) only ensures the discriminativeness of visual representation, and thus could not guarantee the visual-semantic joint representation, which is more informative for recognition, is still discriminative enough.

To tackle the above issues, we again resort to additive angular margin loss with angular prototype regularization in the joint visual-semantic feature space:

$$\mathcal{L}_{Arc} = \frac{1}{N_2} \sum_{i=1}^{N_2} - \log \frac{e^{s \cdot \cos(\theta_{i,y_i}+m)}}{e^{s \cdot \cos(\theta_{i,y_i}+m)} + \sum_{j=1, j \neq y_i}^{|C_s|+K} e^{s \cdot \cos \theta_{i,j}}}. \tag{6}$$

Despite with a similar formulation to Eq. (1) at first glance, there are some substantial differences. First, instead of deploying a $(|C_s|+1)$-way classifier, we use a $(|C_s|+K)$-way classifier $g : \mathcal{R}^d \rightarrow \mathcal{R}^{C_s+K}$ for the more discriminative recognition of seen classes and diverse unseen classes. Second, the features now become the visual-semantic joint features. For labeled source samples $F_s = \{f(x_s^i) \oplus a_s^i, f(x_s^i) \oplus \tilde{a}_s^i\}$ for $x_s^i \in \mathcal{D}_s$, for target samples pseudo-labeled as seen classes $F_t^s = \{f(x_t^i) \oplus \hat{a}_t^i, f(x_t^i) \oplus \tilde{a}_t^i\}$ for $x_t^i \in \mathcal{D}_t^s$, and target samples pseudo-labeled as unseen classes $F_t^u = \{f(x_t^i) \oplus \tilde{a}_t^i\}$ for $x_t^i \in \mathcal{D}_t^u$, where a, $\hat{a}$ denotes ground-truth, pseudo-labeled attributes, $\tilde{a}$ denotes attributes predicted by the visual-semantic projector $\phi : \mathbb{R}^d \rightarrow \mathbb{R}^m$, and $\oplus$ denotes feature concatenation. Thus, the joint feature set is $F = F_s \cup F_t^s \cup F_t^u$ with cardinality N_2, and $\theta_{i,j} = \arccos \frac{W_j^\top f_i}{\|W_j\| \cdot \|f_i\|}$. Similarly, the angular prototype regularization forms as:

$$\mathcal{L}_{reg} = \sum_{i=1}^{N_2} - \cos \theta_{i,y_i}. \tag{7}$$

It is worth noting that for training classifier g, the pseudo-labeling of target samples detected from unseen classes is non-trivial. After using K-means discussed in Sect. 3.4, the target samples detected from unseen classes are pseudo-labeled as $\hat{y}_{unseen}^i \in \{|C_s|+1, ..., |C_s|+K\}$, which seems plausible for training the classifier neurons corresponding to K unseen class clusters. However, since there is no guarantee that the same unseen cluster label generated by K-means in different iterations has the same semantic meaning, directly using such pseudo-labels could lead to inconsistent correspondence between samples and classifier neurons, increasing the difficulty of optimization. To address such problem, we propose a straightforward strategy termed **maximum-response correspondence (MRC)** to decide the pseudo-label $\mathring{y}_{unseen}^i$ of each x_{unseen}^i for training the classifier g:

$$\mathring{y}_{unseen}^i = \begin{cases} \hat{y}_{unseen}^i & \text{if current epoch=1} \\ \arg\max_{c \in C_u} p(y = c | x_{unseen}^i; \theta) & \text{otherwise} \end{cases}, \tag{8}$$

where $C_u = \{|C_s|+1, ..., |C_s|+K\}$ and θ denotes the parameters of the classifier.

With angular margin and regularization deployed, the learned representation is naturally more suitable for semantic recovery, since the joint visual-semantic representation is forced to be intra-class compact and inter-class separated, which means the input of the visual-semantic projection ϕ, i.e., visual features, as well as the output, i.e., semantic features, are both learned in a similar manner, savoring a mutual-reinforcing advantage. Hence, we can simply adopt the same binary cross-entropy objective as [13] but can observe much better results:

$$\min_{f,\phi} \mathcal{L}_A = \frac{1}{N_s + N_t^s} \sum_{x^i \in \mathcal{D}_s \cup \mathcal{D}_t^s} \mathcal{L}_{bce}(\hat{a}^i, a^i), \tag{9}$$

where N_s, N_t^s denotes the number of source and target samples detected from seen classes respectively, $\hat{a}^i = \sum_j W_{ij}\phi(f(x^j))$, and W is the propagator matrix [35,51] based on visual similarity.

Therefore, the objective of our training phase becomes:

$$\min_{f,g,\phi} \mathcal{L}_{AS} = \lambda_1 \mathcal{L}_c + \lambda_2(\mathcal{L}_{Arc} + \mathcal{L}_{reg}) + \lambda_3 \mathcal{L}_A, \tag{10}$$

and we alternate between phase II and III in every training epoch to constantly reinforce model performance.

3.6 Attribute Re-projection for Seen Classes

For visual-semantic projection, early works in ZSL typically resort to linear projection with regularization [14,36], while neural network-based projectors [26,50] are getting increasingly popular for their non-linearity and learnable representation. In SR-OSDA, the advantages of a neural-network-based projector trained end-to-end are conspicuous, as complementary signals back-propagated from both semantic and visual modalities can directly update the feature, making it more suitable for projecting to semantic space.

However, we note that in Eq. (9), the better generalizability to unseen classes of ϕ comes at the sacrifice of seen classes, since the propagated attribute vector is different from its original prediction. To address this issue, we propose to deploy an efficient attribute re-projection after training, in which we learn a regularized linear mapping from the visual representation of target seen classes to corresponding pseudo attributes:

$$\min_{W} \mathcal{L}(Wf(X_t^s), \hat{A}_t^s) + \Omega(W), \tag{11}$$

where $f(X_t^s) \in \mathbb{R}^{d \times N_t^s}$ is the feature matrix of target samples recognized as from seen classes by g, $\hat{A}_t^s$ is the corresponding pseudo attribute matrix, $W \in \mathbb{R}^{m \times d}$ is the projection matrix, and Ω is a certain regularization. For simplicity, we apply squared loss for Eq. (11) with a closed-form solution [36]. There are mainly two merits of such re-projection. First, X_t^s is based on the final classification result, which is expected to be more accurate. The projection matrix W can now exert its full power to project $f(X_t^s)$ to $\hat{A}_t^s$ as accurately as possible, and thus is expected to perform better than ϕ on seen classes. Second, unlike a neural-network-based projector that takes a long training time, W has a closed-form solution and can be solved instantly. Therefore, after the model is trained and used to separate target data into seen X_t^s and unseen X_t^u, we use W and ϕ to recover attributes for X_t^s and X_t^u respectively.

4 Experiments

4.1 Setup

Datasets. We evaluate our method on the two datasets curated by [13] for the SR-OSDA problem. (1) **D2AwA** is collected from the shared 17 classes of "real image" (R) and "painting" (P) domains of the DomainNet [32] dataset and the AwA2 [45] dataset. Following alphabetic order, the first 10 classes are chosen as shared seen classes, and the other 7 classes as unseen classes. (2) **I2AwA** [53] consists of the 3D2 (I) dataset and the AwA2 dataset. Since the 3D2 dataset only has 40 classes, it is used as the source domain, while the AwA2 dataset with 10 more classes serves as the target domain. We use the binary attributes of AwA2 as semantic description to evaluate our method, and only the ground-truth attributes of seen categories are available throughout training.

Evaluation Metrics. Following the standard evaluation protocols in OSDA and ZSL, for the open-set recognition aspect, we evaluate the per-class average accuracy of seen (known) classes OS^*, the accuracy of unseen (unknown) class recognition $OS^\diamond$, and their harmonic mean $H_1 = \frac{2 \times OS^* \times OS^\diamond}{OS^* + OS^\diamond}$; for the semantic recovery aspect, we first determine if a sample is from seen or unseen classes based on the recognition result, and then make inference based on the matching of recovered semantic attributes with class semantic attribute prototypes in the corresponding range (C_s or C_u) by cosine similarity, and evaluate the per-class average accuracy of seen class recovery S, unseen class recovery U, and their harmonic mean $H_2 = \frac{2 \times S \times U}{S + U}$.

Implementation Details. We use ResNet-50 [11] pre-trained on ImageNet [37] as backbone. For fair comparison, we adopt the same network architecture for feature encoder, attribute projector, and classifier as [13]. If not specified, we set K to the ground-truth unseen cluster number, as we experimentally notice the performance is not sensitive to its value in a certain range. We set $m = 0.05$, $s = 30$, $\lambda_1 = 0.1$, $\lambda_2 = 0.1$, and $\lambda_3 = 1$ in all experiments. Since [13] has not released code at the time of our work, we report our reproduced results in this paper. Please refer to the Appendix for more details as well as openness analysis, qualitative study, and parameter analysis.

Table 1. Open-set domain adaptation accuracy (%) on D2AwA and I2AwA.

Tasks	A→P			A→R			P→A			P→R			R→A			R→P			I→A		
Method	OS^*	$OS^\diamond$	H_1	OS^*	$OS^\diamond$	H_1	OS^*	$OS^\diamond$	H_1	OS^*	$OS^\diamond$	H_1	OS^*	$OS^\diamond$	H_1	OS^*	$OS^\diamond$	H_1	OS^*	$OS^\diamond$	H_1
Source-only	63.5	0.0	0.0	86.1	0.0	0.0	92.5	0.0	0.0	86.8	0.0	0.0	96.2	0.0	0.0	68.3	0.0	0.0	76.2	0.0	0.0
OSBP [38]†	49.6	10.8	17.7	74.2	13.6	23.0	76.0	9.1	16.3	63.3	6.9	12.4	90.1	13.7	23.8	55.9	10.6	17.8	67.6	7.5	13.5
STA [25]†	60.1	33.0	42.6	85.5	10.8	19.2	90.2	5.7	10.7	82.8	7.4	13.58	88.5	7.2	13.3	66.9	13.5	22.5	51.5	45.5	48.3
AOD [10]†	50.7	9.5	16.0	78.4	12.7	21.9	80.3	5.1	9.6	79.7	5.3	9.9	92.0	12.8	22.5	61.2	9.6	16.6	75.2	6.3	11.6
BCA [12]†	35.8	86.4	50.6	73.4	87.5	**79.8**	75.7	91.9	82.9	63.3	85.3	69.5	90.6	92.9	91.7	55.1	77.7	64.5	2.3	53.9	4.3
SR-OSDA [13]†	42.6	83.1	56.3	80.4	76.4	78.3	79.5	96.6	**87.2**	77.9	88.1	82.7	91.4	93.8	92.6	53.2	85.3	65.6	68.3	70.2	69.2
AMS (ours)	48.1	79.5	**59.9**	83.4	76.3	79.6	79.3	96.5	87.0	82.4	91.7	**86.8**	94.7	92.6	**93.7**	63.0	77.0	**69.3**	76.3	75.6	**75.9**

† Cited from [13]. † Reproduced with official codes. † Reproduced by us.
* Emboldened figures: the best balanced performance H_1.

Table 2. Semantic recovery accuracy (%) on D2AwA and I2AwA.

Tasks	A→P			A→R			P→A			P→R			R→A			R→P			I→A		
Method	S	U	H_2	S	U	H_2	S	U	H_2	S	U	H_2	S	U	H_2	S	U	H_2	S	U	H_2
Source-only	67.6	0.0	0.0	87.6	0.0	0.0	91.3	0.0	0.0	85.3	0.0	0.0	94.1	0.0	0.0	71.1	0.0	0.0	77.2	0.3	0.7
ABP* [52]†	68.1	0.0	0.0	87.9	0.0	0.0	91.7	0.0	0.0	83.6	0.0	0.0	94.4	0.0	0.0	70.0	0.0	0.0	79.8	0.0	0.0
TF-VAE* [30]†	70.4	0.0	0.0	88.4	0.0	0.0	85.1	0.0	0.0	79.6	0.0	0.0	96.4	0.0	0.0	72.5	0.0	0.0	62.8	0.0	0.0
ABP [52]†	64.5	6.4	11.7	86.0	5.9	11.1	84.0	24.4	37.8	81.3	12.7	21.9	93.8	16.2	27.6	67.6	7.9	14.1	78.0	13.4	22.9
TF-VAE [30]†	59.7	12.8	21.0	77.9	16.4	27.1	35.1	35.6	35.3	34.8	32.7	33.7	68.5	36.1	47.3	50.7	21.0	29.7	37.7	20.0	26.2
SR-OSDA [13]†	42.7	20.2	27.4	80.3	34.3	48.0	77.5	50.9	61.4	77.7	45.6	57.4	90.0	49.2	63.6	52.9	24.0	32.9	59.4	27.8	37.8
AMS (ours)	48.1	24.8	**32.7**	83.5	45.9	**59.1**	79.8	64.0	**71.0**	82.8	58.1	**68.3**	94.9	59.1	**72.8**	63.2	25.2	**36.0**	74.8	28.3	**41.0**

† Cited from [13]. † Reproduced by us. * Emboldened figures: the best balanced performance H_2.

4.2 Experimental Results

Open-Set Domain Adaptation Evaluation. From results in table 1 we can see that existing pure OSDA methods tend to underperform in all tasks because they often learn to automatically separate samples into seen and unseen classes via adversarial learning, which is unstable and could either accept most target samples into seen classes or reject them into unseen classes, leading to highly imbalanced performance (high OS^* or $OS^\diamond$, but low H_1). Besides, OSDA methods are not designed to work with semantic information and cannot leverage the complementary information in semantic attributes. In addition, our proposed AMS notably outperforms the SR-OSDA baseline: our accuracy on seen class (OS^*) is higher in *6 out of 7* tasks with an average improvement of *4.8%*, accuracy on unseen class ($OS^\diamond$) is higher or comparable in *4 out of 7* tasks with a notable improvement of 5.4% in I→A, and harmonic mean H_1 is higher or comparable in *all 7* tasks with an average increment of 2.9%, suggesting that we achieve *a balanced improvement* on seen and unseen recognition accuracy.

Semantic Recovery Evaluation. We compare our method with several ZSL methods as well as the recently-proposed SR-OSDA baseline on the task of semantic recovery in Table 2. ABP [52] and TF-VAE [30] are both GZSL methods that need access to semantic attributes of unseen classes, and therefore violate the SR-OSDA setting. We also report their results using only semantic attributes of seen classes as ABP* and TF-VAE*. From Table 2 we can have two observations. Firstly, the semantic recovery capability of semantic-transductive GZSL methods largely relies upon the prior knowledge of unseen classes, whereas even when given such prior knowledge they still tend to not behave well because they cannot cope with domain gap. Secondly, our proposed AMS significantly outperforms the existing SR-OSDA baseline on all metrics, with a notable average increment of *6.6%*, *7.6%*, and *7.4%* in S, U, and H_2 respectively.

4.3 Ablation Study

Fine-Tuning Phase. As is shown in Table 3, fine-tuning with additive margin loss notably increases the final $OS^\diamond$ and U of *unseen* classes by 2.2% and 5.3%, respectively. This result verifies that the model can benefit from the highly discriminative representation that is initially learned on the seen classes in source

Table 3. The evolution path of AMS (in P→R). Margin: additive angular margin. Reg: angular regularization. Multi-unseen: $|C_s + K|$-way classifier instead of $|C_s + 1|$-way. MRC: maximum-response correspondence strategy. Re-projection: regularized linear projection on detected target samples from seen classes.

Modules	Base [13]								AMS
Fine-tuning margin		✓	✓	✓	✓	✓	✓	✓	✓	✓
Fine-tuning reg			✓	✓	✓	✓	✓	✓	✓	✓
Training margin				✓	✓	✓	✓	✓	✓	✓
Training reg					✓		✓		✓	✓
Training multi-unseen						✓	✓	✓	✓	✓
Training MRC								✓	✓	✓
Post-training re-projection										✓
$OS^*(\%)$	77.9	77.8	78.3	82.6	83.7	85.7	85.8	81.8	82.4	82.4
$OS^\circ(\%)$	88.1	90.3	90.2	90.4	89.5	82.9	81.5	91.4	91.7	91.7
$H_1(\%)$	82.7	83.6	83.2	86.3	86.5	84.3	83.6	86.3	86.8	86.8
$S(\%)$	77.7	77.2	77.6	82.6	83.3	84.9	85.3	81.1	81.7	82.8
$U(\%)$	45.6	50.9	50.7	47.3	41.6	47.3	40.5	56.8	58.1	58.1
$H_2(\%)$	57.4	61.3	61.3	60.1	55.4	60.7	54.9	66.8	67.9	68.3

domain, even when such properties of representation are no longer purposefully emphasized during the entire next training phase. Further, when angular regularization is applied in fine-tuning, OS^* and S of *seen* classes are further improved by 0.5% and 0.4% respectively, which verifies that robust representation of seen classes is beneficial to their recognition and recovery in presence of outliers.

Training Phase. As is shown in Table 3, applying angular margin loss in training brings salient improvements on all evaluation metrics except for a decrease on U. This phenomenon is because to this end the classifier is set to $|C_s+1|$-way, which treats different unseen classes as one class. As a result, though recognition accuracy on seen classes and the overall unseen class benefits from the learned discriminative representation, the diverse unseen classes are forced to be aligned, leading to confused semantic recovery. Besides, if angular regularization is added at this time, there is a further decrease in U, which is caused by further pulling different unseen classes closer.

With such observation, we now turn the classifier to $|C_s + K|$-way to cope with diverse unseen classes, but still cannot see a notable improvement. This is caused by the inconsistent correspondence between clusters of unseen classes and classifier neurons in different training epochs, which hinders the knowledge learning of unseen classes. Therefore, it is not until the maximum-response correspondence (MRC) mechanism is adopted that the power of multiple unseen clusters can be truly exerted, bringing notable improvements on all metrics, and particularly, semantic recovery accuracy U of unseen classes is increased by a whopping 12.5%.

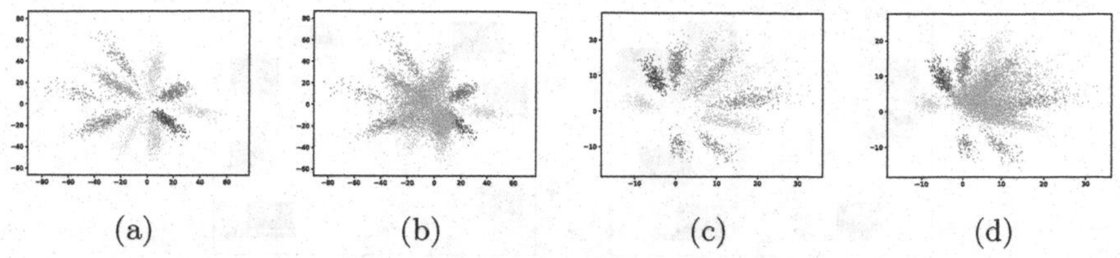

Fig. 2. Visualization of representation learned with/without the proposed fine-tuning phase. Points of bright color are from seen classes in the source domain. Gray points are from unseen classes in the target domain. Best viewed in color. (Color figure online)

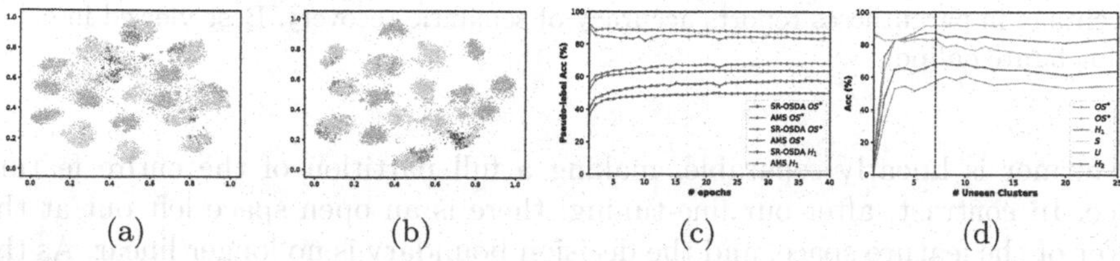

Fig. 3. Visualization of representation and relevant studies of training phase. (a), (b): Lavender and gray points are from seen and unseen classes in the target domain respectively. Points in other colors are from different seen classes in the source domain. (c): Accuracy of pseudo-labels determined by K-means (in task R→P) during training. (d): Final accuracy of recognition and semantic recovery using different number of clusters for unseen classes. Best viewed in color. (Color figure online)

To this end, we can conclude that in the training phase, for semantic recovery of unseen classes U, angular regularization is beneficial only when the classifier has *multiple* channels for unseen classes, while such classifier should work under the *MRC* mechanism.

Post-training Re-projection. Results in the last two columns in Table 3 verify the effectiveness of learning a re-projection on detected target seen classes after training, bringing an extra 1.1% increment on seen class recovery S, which is non-trivial for accuracy averaged over 10 classes with more than 10,000 images in total. Note that the only difference between the last two columns lies in their S results, since the re-projection is only learned on target samples recognized as from seen class after the training phase, and therefore will not have any effect on unseen classes as they are now completely separated.

4.4 Visual Study of Representation

Visual Representation Learned in the Fine-Tuning Phase. To better observe the property of representation learned in fine-tuning phase, we set the dimension of visual features to 2 and plot them in Fig. 2. Figure 2(a) and (c) visualize the representation of *seen* classes learned with ordinary Softmax and with our proposed fine-tuning phase in task P→R, respectively. We can see that

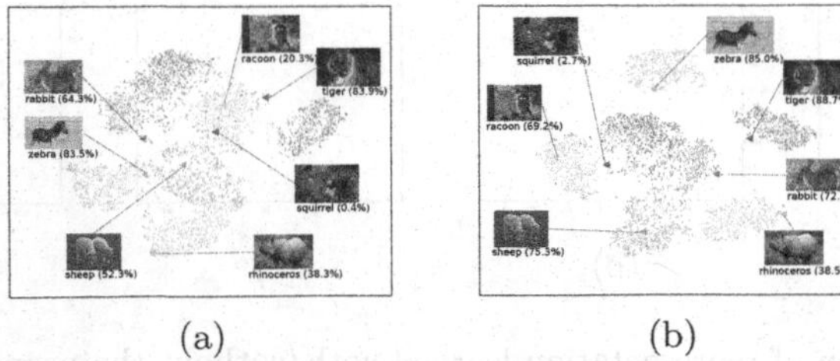

Fig. 4. Visualization of semantic representation (projected attributes). Round points in different colors are representations of target samples from different unseen classes, while triangles are their ground-truth prototypes accompanied by a typical image. The percentage in parentheses reports accuracy of semantic recovery. Best viewed in color. (Color figure online)

the former is linearly separable, making a full partition of the entire feature space. In contrast, after our fine-tuning, there is an open space left out at the center of the feature space, and the decision boundary is no longer linear. As the result, when deployed on the target domain, as is shown in Fig. 2(b), (c), in the former case, samples from *unseen* classes are misclassified into almost all *seen* classes, while in the latter case, part of samples from *unseen* classes are rejected into the vacant space at the center, and *seen* classes are less affected.

Visual Representation Learned in the Training Phase. Figure 3(a), (b) show the T-SNE [27] visualization of representation learned by the SR-OSDA framework proposed in [13] and our AMS in task P→R, respectively. We can observe that feature clusters of both *seen* and *unseen* classes are more compact, and different clusters are better separated in AMS, thanks to the angular margin and regularization. We also show the accuracy of pseudo-labels determined by K-means clustering in task R→P in Fig. 3(c) and can see that AMS achieves a better balance between seen and unseen classes, i.e., a higher H_1, which underpins the better performance of the later cross-domain alignment and recognition.

Semantic Representation Learned in the Training Phase. Figure 4(a), (b) show the T-SNE [27] visualization of semantic representation (projected attributes) of *unseen* classes in task P→R. Compared with [13], our semantic representation mainly has two merits. First, our semantic representation is more compactly clustered around corresponding semantic prototypes. For instance, our representations of zebra and tiger better enclose their prototypes, which boosts their recovery accuracy by 1.5% and 4.8%. Second, our semantic representations of different classes are more separated. For example, our representations of sheep and racoon are farther away from the prototypes of other classes, which increases their recovery accuracy by 23% and 48.9%. These phenomena verify the functionality of angular margin and regularization for semantic recovery.

How Does the Number of Clusters Affect Learning? Figure 3(d) shows the performance of AMS in task P→R when the cluster number K varies from 1 to up to 25. It can be observed that when K is very small, $OS^{\diamond}$ and U are low since the model nearly completely ignores the intrinsic diversity of unseen classes. As K grows, $OS^{\diamond}$ and U rise rapidly, resulting in more balanced H_1 and H_2. When K surpasses the ground truth, as is to the right of the dashed line in Fig. 3(d), performance on all metrics is still stable, even when K reaches more than three times that of the ground truth. This result verifies the robustness of AMS and also suggests we choose a relatively large cluster number in real-world deployment.

5 Conclusion

In this paper, we present a novel framework termed AMS for the practical semantic recovery open-set domain adaptation challenge. At the core of our conception is the widely acknowledged significance of representation learning for visual tasks. To learn discriminative visual representation robust to outliers, AMS first fine-tunes a pre-trained model on the seen classes in the source domain with an additive angular margin and angular regularization. Grounded by such learned initial representation, AMS performs cross-domain alignment on seen classes, separates unseen classes from seen ones, and accentuates the intrinsic diversity of unseen classes by resorting to additive angular margin and angular regularization again on the joint visual-semantic representation of the target domain. Further, AMS adopts an efficient post-training re-projection to boost semantic recovery of target seen classes without hurting that of unseen classes. Extensive quantitative experiments as well as various visual studies verify that AMS achieves competitive and even state-of-the-art performance.

Acknowledgements. This work was supported in part by the National Natural Science Foundation of China under Grant 62176042 and 62073059, in part by CCF-Baidu Open Fund (NO. 2021PP15002000), in part by CCF-Tencent Open Fund (NO. RAGR20210107), and in part by Guangdong Basic and Applied Basic Research Foundation (No. 2021B1515140013).

References

1. Bengio, Y., Courville, A., Vincent, P.: Representation learning: a review and new perspectives. IEEE Trans. Pattern Anal. Mach. Intell. **35**(8), 1798–1828 (2013)
2. Bucci, S., Borlino, F.C., Caputo, B., Tommasi, T.: Distance-based hyperspherical classification for multi-source open-set domain adaptation. In: Proceedings of the IEEE/CVF Winter Conference on Applications of Computer Vision, pp. 1119–1128 (2022)
3. Bucci, S., Loghmani, M.R., Tommasi, T.: On the effectiveness of image rotation for open set domain adaptation. In: Vedaldi, A., Bischof, H., Brox, T., Frahm, J.-M. (eds.) ECCV 2020. LNCS, vol. 12361, pp. 422–438. Springer, Cham (2020). https://doi.org/10.1007/978-3-030-58517-4_25
4. Chao, W.-L., Changpinyo, S., Gong, B., Sha, F.: An empirical study and analysis of generalized zero-shot learning for object recognition in the wild. In: Leibe, B., Matas, J., Sebe, N., Welling, M. (eds.) ECCV 2016. LNCS, vol. 9906, pp. 52–68. Springer, Cham (2016). https://doi.org/10.1007/978-3-319-46475-6_4

5. Chen, Y., Li, W., Sakaridis, C., Dai, D., Van Gool, L.: Domain adaptive faster R-CNN for object detection in the wild. In: Proceedings of the IEEE Conference on Computer Vision and Pattern Recognition, pp. 3339–3348 (2018)
6. Choi, J., Sharma, G., Schulter, S., Huang, J.-B.: Shuffle and attend: video domain adaptation. In: Vedaldi, A., Bischof, H., Brox, T., Frahm, J.-M. (eds.) ECCV 2020. LNCS, vol. 12357, pp. 678–695. Springer, Cham (2020). https://doi.org/10.1007/978-3-030-58610-2_40
7. Csurka, G.: Domain adaptation for visual applications: a comprehensive survey. arXiv preprint arXiv:1702.05374 (2017)
8. Deng, J., Guo, J., Xue, N., Zafeiriou, S.: ArcFace: additive angular margin loss for deep face recognition. In: Proceedings of the IEEE/CVF Conference on Computer Vision and Pattern Recognition, pp. 4690–4699 (2019)
9. Du, Z., Li, J., Lu, K., Zhu, L., Huang, Z.: Learning transferrable and interpretable representations for domain generalization. In: Proceedings of the 29th ACM International Conference on Multimedia, pp. 3340–3349 (2021)
10. Feng, Q., Kang, G., Fan, H., Yang, Y.: Attract or distract: exploit the margin of open set. In: Proceedings of the IEEE/CVF International Conference on Computer Vision, pp. 7990–7999 (2019)
11. He, K., Zhang, X., Ren, S., Sun, J.: Deep residual learning for image recognition. In: Proceedings of the IEEE Conference on Computer Vision and Pattern Recognition, pp. 770–778 (2016)
12. Jing, M., Li, J., Zhu, L., Ding, Z., Lu, K., Yang, Y.: Balanced open set domain adaptation via centroid alignment. In: Proceedings of the AAAI Conference on Artificial Intelligence, vol. 35, pp. 8013–8020 (2021)
13. Jing, T., Liu, H., Ding, Z.: Towards novel target discovery through open-set domain adaptation. In: Proceedings of the IEEE/CVF International Conference on Computer Vision, pp. 9322–9331 (2021)
14. Kodirov, E., Xiang, T., Gong, S.: Semantic autoencoder for zero-shot learning. In: Proceedings of the IEEE Conference on Computer Vision and Pattern Recognition, pp. 3174–3183 (2017)
15. Krizhevsky, A., Sutskever, I., Hinton, G.E.: ImageNet classification with deep convolutional neural networks. Advances in Neural Information Processing Systems 25 (2012)
16. Lampert, C.H., Nickisch, H., Harmeling, S.: Learning to detect unseen object classes by between-class attribute transfer. In: 2009 IEEE Conference on Computer Vision and Pattern Recognition, pp. 951–958. IEEE (2009)
17. LeCun, Y., Bengio, Y., Hinton, G.: Deep learning. Nature **521**(7553), 436–444 (2015)
18. Li, J., Chen, E., Ding, Z., Zhu, L., Lu, K., Shen, H.T.: Maximum density divergence for domain adaptation. IEEE Trans. Pattern Anal. Mach. Intell. **43**(11), 3918–3930 (2020)
19. Li, J., Du, Z., Zhu, L., Ding, Z., Lu, K., Shen, H.T.: Divergence-agnostic unsupervised domain adaptation by adversarial attacks. IEEE Trans. Pattern Anal. Mach. Intell. (2021)
20. Li, J., Jing, M., Lu, K., Ding, Z., Zhu, L., Huang, Z.: Leveraging the invariant side of generative zero-shot learning. In: Proceedings of the IEEE/CVF Conference on Computer Vision and Pattern Recognition, pp. 7402–7411 (2019)
21. Li, J., Jing, M., Zhu, L., Ding, Z., Lu, K., Yang, Y.: Learning modality-invariant latent representations for generalized zero-shot learning. In: Proceedings of the 28th ACM International Conference on Multimedia, pp. 1348–1356 (2020)

22. Li, J., Lu, K., Huang, Z., Zhu, L., Shen, H.T.: Transfer independently together: a generalized framework for domain adaptation. IEEE Trans. Cybernet. **49**(6), 2144–2155 (2018)
23. Li, X., Li, J., Zhu, L., Wang, G., Huang, Z.: Imbalanced source-free domain adaptation. In: Proceedings of the 29th ACM International Conference on Multimedia, pp. 3330–3339 (2021)
24. Li, Y., Wang, D., Hu, H., Lin, Y., Zhuang, Y.: Zero-shot recognition using dual visual-semantic mapping paths. In: Proceedings of the IEEE Conference on Computer Vision and Pattern Recognition, pp. 3279–3287 (2017)
25. Liu, H., Cao, Z., Long, M., Wang, J., Yang, Q.: Separate to adapt: open set domain adaptation via progressive separation. In: Proceedings of the IEEE/CVF Conference on Computer Vision and Pattern Recognition, pp. 2927–2936 (2019)
26. Liu, S., Long, M., Wang, J., Jordan, M.I.: Generalized zero-shot learning with deep calibration network. Advances in Neural Information Processing Systems 31 (2018)
27. Van der Maaten, L., Hinton, G.: Visualizing data using t-SNE. J. Mach. Learn. Res. **9**(11) (2008)
28. Mensink, T., Verbeek, J., Perronnin, F., Csurka, G.: Distance-based image classification: generalizing to new classes at near-zero cost. IEEE Trans. Pattern Anal. Mach. Intell. **35**(11), 2624–2637 (2013)
29. Miller, D., Sunderhauf, N., Milford, M., Dayoub, F.: Class anchor clustering: a loss for distance-based open set recognition. In: Proceedings of the IEEE/CVF Winter Conference on Applications of Computer Vision, pp. 3570–3578 (2021)
30. Narayan, S., Gupta, A., Khan, F.S., Snoek, C.G.M., Shao, L.: Latent embedding feedback and discriminative features for zero-shot classification. In: Vedaldi, A., Bischof, H., Brox, T., Frahm, J.-M. (eds.) ECCV 2020. LNCS, vol. 12367, pp. 479–495. Springer, Cham (2020). https://doi.org/10.1007/978-3-030-58542-6_29
31. Panareda Busto, P., Gall, J.: Open set domain adaptation. In: Proceedings of the IEEE International Conference on Computer Vision, pp. 754–763 (2017)
32. Peng, X., Bai, Q., Xia, X., Huang, Z., Saenko, K., Wang, B.: Moment matching for multi-source domain adaptation. In: Proceedings of the IEEE/CVF International Conference on Computer Vision, pp. 1406–1415 (2019)
33. Pourpanah, F., et al.: A review of generalized zero-shot learning methods. arXiv preprint arXiv:2011.08641 (2020)
34. Radford, A., Metz, L., Chintala, S.: Unsupervised representation learning with deep convolutional generative adversarial networks. arXiv preprint arXiv:1511.06434 (2015)
35. Rodríguez, P., Laradji, I., Drouin, A., Lacoste, A.: Embedding propagation: smoother manifold for few-shot classification. In: Vedaldi, A., Bischof, H., Brox, T., Frahm, J.-M. (eds.) ECCV 2020. LNCS, vol. 12371, pp. 121–138. Springer, Cham (2020). https://doi.org/10.1007/978-3-030-58574-7_8
36. Romera-Paredes, B., Torr, P.: An embarrassingly simple approach to zero-shot learning. In: International Conference on Machine Learning, pp. 2152–2161. PMLR (2015)
37. Russakovsky, O., et al.: ImageNet large scale visual recognition challenge. Int. J. Comput. Vision **115**(3), 211–252 (2015)
38. Saito, K., Yamamoto, S., Ushiku, Y., Harada, T.: Open set domain adaptation by backpropagation. In: Ferrari, V., Hebert, M., Sminchisescu, C., Weiss, Y. (eds.) ECCV 2018. LNCS, vol. 11209, pp. 156–171. Springer, Cham (2018). https://doi.org/10.1007/978-3-030-01228-1_10
39. Snell, J., Swersky, K., Zemel, R.: Prototypical networks for few-shot learning. Advances in Neural Information Processing Systems 30 (2017)

40. Song, J., Shen, C., Yang, Y., Liu, Y., Song, M.: Transductive unbiased embedding for zero-shot learning. In: Proceedings of the IEEE Conference on Computer Vision and Pattern Recognition, pp. 1024–1033 (2018)
41. Su, H., Li, J., Chen, Z., Zhu, L., Lu, K.: Distinguishing unseen from seen for generalized zero-shot learning. In: Proceedings of the IEEE/CVF Conference on Computer Vision and Pattern Recognition, pp. 7885–7894 (2022)
42. Wang, M., Deng, W.: Deep visual domain adaptation: a survey. Neurocomputing **312**, 135–153 (2018)
43. Wang, X., Ye, Y., Gupta, A.: Zero-shot recognition via semantic embeddings and knowledge graphs. In: Proceedings of the IEEE Conference on Computer Vision and Pattern Recognition, pp. 6857–6866 (2018)
44. Wang, Z., Gou, Y., Li, J., Zhang, Y., Yang, Y.: Region semantically aligned network for zero-shot learning. In: Proceedings of the 30th ACM International Conference on Information & Knowledge Management, pp. 2080–2090 (2021)
45. Xian, Y., Lampert, C.H., Schiele, B., Akata, Z.: Zero-shot learning—a comprehensive evaluation of the good, the bad and the ugly. IEEE Trans. Pattern Anal. Mach. Intell. **41**(9), 2251–2265 (2018)
46. Xu, X., et al.: Matrix tri-factorization with manifold regularizations for zero-shot learning. In: Proceedings of the IEEE Conference on Computer Vision and Pattern Recognition, pp. 3798–3807 (2017)
47. Yang, H.M., Zhang, X.Y., Yin, F., Liu, C.L.: Robust classification with convolutional prototype learning. In: Proceedings of the IEEE Conference on Computer Vision and Pattern Recognition, pp. 3474–3482 (2018)
48. Ye, M., Guo, Y.: Zero-shot classification with discriminative semantic representation learning. In: Proceedings of the IEEE Conference on Computer Vision and Pattern Recognition, pp. 7140–7148 (2017)
49. You, F., Li, J., Zhu, L., Chen, Z., Huang, Z.: Domain adaptive semantic segmentation without source data. In: Proceedings of the 29th ACM International Conference on Multimedia, pp. 3293–3302 (2021)
50. Zhang, L., Xiang, T., Gong, S.: Learning a deep embedding model for zero-shot learning. In: Proceedings of the IEEE Conference on Computer Vision and Pattern Recognition, pp. 2021–2030 (2017)
51. Zhou, D., Bousquet, O., Lal, T., Weston, J., Schölkopf, B.: Learning with local and global consistency. Advances in Neural Information Processing Systems 16 (2003)
52. Zhu, Y., Xie, J., Liu, B., Elgammal, A.: Learning feature-to-feature translator by alternating back-propagation for generative zero-shot learning. In: Proceedings of the IEEE/CVF International Conference on Computer Vision, pp. 9844–9854 (2019)
53. Zhuo, J., Wang, S., Cui, S., Huang, Q.: Unsupervised open domain recognition by semantic discrepancy minimization. In: Proceedings of the IEEE/CVF Conference on Computer Vision and Pattern Recognition, pp. 750–759 (2019)

TACS: Taxonomy Adaptive Cross-Domain Semantic Segmentation

Rui Gong[1(✉)], Martin Danelljan[1], Dengxin Dai[3], Danda Pani Paudel[1], Ajad Chhatkuli[1], Fisher Yu[1], and Luc Van Gool[1,2]

[1] Computer Vision Lab, ETH Zurich, Zürich, Switzerland
{gongr,martin.danelljan,paudel,ajad.chhatkuli,vangool}@vision.ee.ethz.ch, i@yf.io

[2] VISICS, ESAT/PSI, KU Leuven, Leuven, Belgium

[3] VAS, MPI for Informatics, Saarbrücken, Germany
ddai@mpi-inf.mpg.de

Abstract. Traditional domain adaptive semantic segmentation addresses the task of adapting a model to a novel target domain under limited or no additional supervision. While tackling the input domain gap, the standard domain adaptation settings assume no domain change in the output space. In semantic prediction tasks, different datasets are often labeled according to different semantic taxonomies. In many real-world settings, the target domain task requires a different taxonomy than the one imposed by the source domain. We therefore introduce the more general taxonomy adaptive cross-domain semantic segmentation (TACS) problem, allowing for inconsistent taxonomies between the two domains. We further propose an approach that jointly addresses the image-level and label-level domain adaptation. On the label-level, we employ a bilateral mixed sampling strategy to augment the target domain, and a relabelling method to unify and align the label spaces. We address the image-level domain gap by proposing an uncertainty-rectified contrastive learning method, leading to more domain-invariant and class-discriminative features. We extensively evaluate the effectiveness of our framework under different TACS settings: open taxonomy, coarse-to-fine taxonomy, and implicitly-overlapping taxonomy. Our approach outperforms the previous state-of-the-art by a large margin, while being capable of adapting to target taxonomies. Our implementation is publicly available at https://github.com/ETHRuiGong/TADA.

Keywords: Domain adaptation · Semantic segmentation · Inconsistent taxonomy

1 Introduction

Traditional unsupervised domain adaptation (UDA) approaches for semantic segmentation [7,15,20,34,35,37] typically focus on the *image level* domain gap,

Supplementary Information The online version contains supplementary material available at https://doi.org/10.1007/978-3-031-19830-4_2.

S. Avidan et al. (Eds.): ECCV 2022, LNCS 13694, pp. 19–35, 2022.
https://doi.org/10.1007/978-3-031-19830-4_2

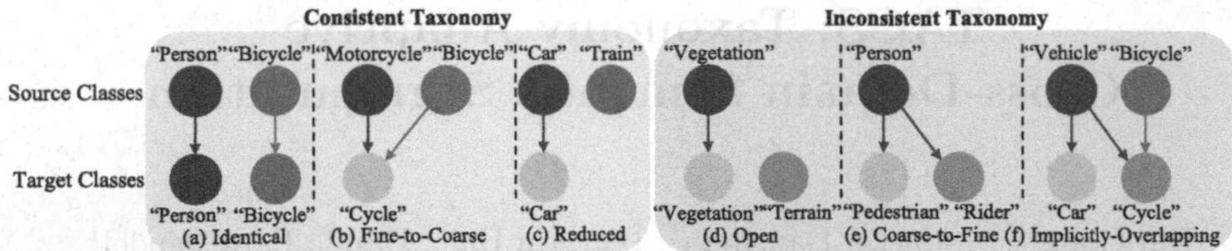

Fig. 1. Consistent *vs.* inconsistent taxonomy. In (a)–(f), the upper row shows the source domain classes, and the lower row the target domain classes. Circles represent classes while an arrow represents a mapping from a source domain class to a target domain class. (a)–(c) and (d)–(f) are examples of consistent and inconsistent taxonomies, resp. Different from other domain adaptation problems, *e.g.*, universal/partial/open-set domain adaptation [2,27,43], that only touch the consistent taxonomy or special case of open taxonomy, our TACS provides a more general problem, including the consistent taxonomy and different inconsistent taxonomies types. More detailed comparisons with other domain adaptation problems are put in Sect. 2 and Sect. S2 in the supplementary.

which can involve visual style, weather, lighting conditions, *etc.* However, these methods are restricted by the assumption of having consistent taxonomies between source and target domains, *i.e.*, each source domain class can be unambiguously mapped to one target domain class (Fig. 1(a–c)), which is often not the case. In many applications, the label spaces of the source and target domains are inconsistent, due to different scenarios or requirements, inconsistent annotation practices, or the strive towards an increasingly fine-grained taxonomy [8,19,25].

The aforementioned considerations motivate us to consider the *label level* domain gap problem. Even though recent open/universal/class-incremental domain adaptation works [18,27,43] touched upon the label level domain gap, they 1) only took image classification as test-bed, and 2) only focused on unseen classes in the target domain. However, the label level domain gap in practical scenarios is more complicated than only involving unseen classes. We therefore formulate and explore the label level domain gap problem in a more general and complete setting. We identify three typical types of label taxonomy inconsistency. i) *Open taxonomy*: some classes, *e.g.*, "terrain" in Fig. 1(d), appear in the target domain, but are unlabeled or unseen in the source domain. ii) *Coarse-to-fine taxonomy*: some classes in the source domain, *e.g.*, "person", are split into several sub-classes in the target domain, *e.g.*, "pedestrian" and "rider' (Fig. 1(e)). iii) *Implicitly-overlapping taxonomy*: for a certain class in the source domain, one or more of its sub-classes are merged into other classes in the target domain. For example, there exists a taxonomic conflict between {"vehicle", "bicycle"} in the source domain and {"car", "cycle"} in the target domain (Fig. 1(f)).

We therefore introduce a more general and challenging domain adaptation problem, namely *taxonomy adaptive cross-domain semantic segmentation* (TACS). In traditional UDA for semantic segmentation, the goal is to transfer a model learned on a labelled source domain to an unlabelled target domain, under the consistent taxonomy assumption. In contrast, TACS allows for inconsistent taxonomies between a labeled source domain and a few-shot/partially labeled target domain, where the inconsistent classes of the target domain are exemplified by a few labeled samples. Thus TACS approaches domain adaptation on both the image and label side, under the few-shot/partially labeled setting. Such task setting is realistic, but involves practical challenges. On the one hand, TACS allows methods to make full use of the labeled source domain without annotation costs in the target domain for the consistent classes. On the other hand, for the inconsistent classes the taxonomy adaptation should only require very limited supervision in the target domain, *i.e.*, only few samples should be labeled there.

We put forward the first approach for TACS, addressing both the image and label domain gaps. As to the latter, we aim to remedy the gap using pseudo-labelling techniques. First, a *bilateral mixed sampling* strategy is proposed to augment unlabeled images by mixing them with both labeled source-domain and target-domain samples. Second, we map inconsistent source domain labels with a *stochastic label mapping* strategy, which encourages a more flexible taxonomy adaptation during the earlier learning phase. Third, a *pseudo-label based relabeling* strategy is proposed to replace the inconsistent classes in the source-domain according to the model's predictions, to further enforce taxonomy adaptation during the training process. To tackle the image level domain gap, we introduce an *uncertainty-rectified contrastive learning* scheme that facilitates the learning of class-discriminative and domain-invariant features, under the uncertainty-aware guidance of predicted pseudo-labels. Our complete approach for TACS demonstrates strong results in different inconsistent taxonomy settings (*i.e.*, open, coarse-to-fine, and implicitly-overlapping). Moreover, our suggested mixed-sampling and contrastive-learning scheme outperforms current state-of-the-art methods by a large margin in the traditional UDA setting.

To summarize, our contributions are three-fold:

- A new problem – *taxonomy adaptive cross-domain semantic segmentation* (TACS) – of addressing both image and label domain gaps is proposed. It opens up a new avenue for more flexible cross-domain semantic segmentation.
- A generic solution for UDA and TACS is proposed, for which the unified mixed-sampling, pseudo-labeling and uncertainty-rectified contrastive learning scheme is presented to solve both image and label level domain gaps.
- Extensive experiments are conducted under the traditional UDA and the new TACS settings, showing the effectiveness of our approach.

2 Related Work

Domain Adaptation: The traditional unsupervised domain adaptation (UDA) [9,16,21,35,47,48] considers the case when the source and target domain share the same label space and where the target domain is unlabeled. However, this setting does not conform with many practical applications. Some recent works have therefore explored alternative settings. **Open-set/universal domain adaptation** [27,31,43] aims at recognizing the new unseen classes in the target domain together as the "unknown" class. **Class-incremental/zero-shot domain adaptation** [1,18] are proposed to recognize the new unseen classes explicitly and separately in the target domain under the source domain free setting and in the zero-shot segmentation way, resp. These works touch upon the specific case of the open taxonomy setting in TACS. However, the above works only consider the case where the unseen classes are absent in the source domain. In contrast, the open taxonomy setting in TACS also allows for the unseen classes to exist in the source domain, where they are unlabelled. Besides, the above works do not consider the coarse-to-fine and implicitly-overlapping taxonomy problems, which are covered by the more general TACS formulation. Recent **few-shot/semi-supervised domain adaptation** works [24,33,46] aim at improving the domain adaptation performance by introducing few-shot fully labeled target domain samples. However, they still assume a consistent taxonomy between the source and target domain. Moreover, all the aforementioned non-UDA works, except for [1] and [46], only touch upon the image classification task. Instead, our TACS aims at semantic segmentation, which is more challenging and raises particular interest due to its great importance in autonomous driving [23,34,35,37]. More detailed comparisons between our TACS and different domain adaptation problems are put in the supplementary.

Contrastive Learning: Recently, contrastive learning [4–6,12,13,36] was proven to be successful for unsupervised image classification. Benefiting from the strong representation learning ability, contrastive learning has been applied to different applications, including semantic segmentation [38], image translation [28], object detection [41] and domain adaptation [17]. In [17], contrastive learning is exploited to minimize the intra-class discrepancy and maximize the inter-class discrepancy for the domain adaptive image classification task. However, since the approach is designed for the image classification task, it utilizes the contrastive learning between the whole feature vectors of the different image samples, which is not directly applicable to dense prediction tasks, such as semantic segmentation. Instead, we develop a pseudo-label guided and uncertainty-rectified pixel-wise contrastive learning, to distinguish between positive and negative pixel samples to learn more robust and effective cross-domain representations.

3 Method

3.1 Problem Statement

In our taxonomy adaptive cross-domain semantic segmentation (TACS) problem, we are given the labeled source domain $\mathcal{D}_s = \{(\mathbf{x}_i^s, \mathbf{y}_i^s)\}_{i=1}^{n_s}$, where $\mathbf{x}^s \in \mathbb{R}^{H\times W\times 3}$ is the RGB color image, and $\mathbf{y}^s$ is the associated ground truth C_S-class semantic label map, $\mathbf{y}^s \in \{1, ..., C_S\}^{H\times W}$. In the target domain, we are also given a limited number of labeled samples $\mathcal{D}_t = \{(\mathbf{x}_i^t, \mathbf{y}_i^t)\}_{i=1}^{n^t}$, which we refer to as few-shot or partially labeled target domain samples. We are also given a large set of unlabeled target domain samples $\mathcal{D}_u = \{\mathbf{x}_i^u\}_{i=1}^{n^u}$. The target ground truth $\mathbf{y}^t$ follows the C_T-class semantic label map. Denoting the source and target image samples distributions as P_S and P_T, we have $\mathbf{x}^s \sim P_S$, $\mathbf{x}^t, \mathbf{x}^u \sim P_T$. The source and target image distributions are different, *i.e.*, $P_S \neq P_T$. The label set space of $\mathcal{D}_s$ and $\{\mathcal{D}_t, \mathcal{D}_u\}$ are given by $\mathcal{C}_s = \{\mathbf{c}_1^s, \mathbf{c}_2^s, ..., \mathbf{c}_{C_S}^s\}$ and $\mathcal{C}_t = \{\mathbf{c}_1^t, \mathbf{c}_2^t, ..., \mathbf{c}_{C_T}^t\}$ resp., and $\mathcal{C}_s \neq \mathcal{C}_t$. The inconsistent taxonomy subsets of $\mathcal{C}_s, \mathcal{C}_t$ are denoted as $\overline{\mathcal{C}_s}, \overline{\mathcal{C}_t}$, resp. Our goal is to train the model on $\mathcal{D}_s$, $\mathcal{D}_t$ and $\mathcal{D}_u$, and evaluate on the target domain data in the label sets space $\mathcal{C}_t$.

Inconsistent Taxonomy.[1] Specifically, we consider three different cases of inconsistent taxonomy. 1) The *open taxonomy* considers the case where new classes, unseen or unlabeled in the source domain, appear in the target domain. That is, $\exists \mathbf{c}_j^t \in \mathcal{C}_t$ such that $\mathbf{c}_i^s \cap \mathbf{c}_j^t = \varnothing, \forall \mathbf{c}_i^s \in \mathcal{C}_s$. 2) The *coarse-to-fine taxonomy* considers the case where the target domain has a *finer* taxonomy where source classes have been split into two or more target classes. That is, $\exists \mathbf{c}_i^s \in \mathcal{C}_s, \mathbf{c}_{j_1}^t \in \mathcal{C}_t, \mathbf{c}_{j_2}^t \in \mathcal{C}_t, j_1 \neq j_2$ such that $\mathbf{c}_{j_1}^t, \mathbf{c}_{j_2}^t \neq \mathbf{c}_i^s$ and $(\mathbf{c}_{j_1}^t \cup \mathbf{c}_{j_2}^t) \subseteq \mathbf{c}_i^s$. 3) The *implicitly-overlapping taxonomy* considers the case where a class in the target domain has a common part with the class in the source domain, but also owns the private part. That is, $\exists \mathbf{c}_i^s \in \mathcal{C}_s, \mathbf{c}_j^t \in \mathcal{C}_t$ such that $\mathbf{c}_j^t \not\subseteq \mathbf{c}_i^s, \mathbf{c}_i^s \cap \mathbf{c}_j^t \neq \varnothing$, and $(\mathbf{c}_j^t \setminus (\mathbf{c}_i^s \cap \mathbf{c}_j^t)) \notin \{\varnothing, \mathbf{c}_q^s, q = 1, ..., C_S\}$.

Few-shot/Partially Labeled. In TACS, the $\mathcal{D}_t$ is only few-shot/partially labeled for the inconsistent taxonomy classes, in the class-wise way. More specifically, for each of the class $\mathbf{c}_j^t \in \overline{\mathcal{C}_t}$, we have n^t-shot labeled samples $\{(\mathbf{x}_i^{t_j}, \mathbf{y}_i^{t_j})\}_{i=1}^{n^t}$, where only the class $\mathbf{c}_j^t$ is labeled in $\mathbf{y}_i^{t_j}$. When $n^t \ll n^u$, it is called few-shot labeled. When $n^t \not\ll n^u$, it is named partially-labeled. The sample and corresponding semantic map is written as $\mathbf{x}^{t_j}$ and $\mathbf{y}^{t_j}$.

Technical Challenges. The main technical challenge of TACS is to deal with both of the label-level and image-level domain gap. On the **label level**, there are two main problems: i) The inconsistent taxonomy may induce there is the *one-to-many* mapping from the source domain to the target domain classes. If we purely assign the source class of inconsistent taxonomy to one of the corresponding target class, it will generate incorrect supervision, degrading the performance of the model. However, if we instead take the inconsistent source class as unlabeled, the source domain information is not fully exploited. ii) The complete target domain label taxonomy is partially inherited from the source domain for the consistent taxonomy, and partially provided by the few-shot/partially labeled target domain. The problem of how to *unify the consistent and inconsistent taxonomy classes* for the target domain is non-trivial. The naive way is to train the model on the source domain for the consistent taxonomy classes, and on the few-shot/partially labeled target domain for the inconsistent taxonomy classes separately, in the supervised way. However, the few-shot labeled target domain samples are far fewer than the labeled source domain samples, causing the model training to be easily dominated by the consistent taxonomy classes, therefore the inconsistent taxonomy classes are possibly ignored. Meanwhile, most of the pixels in the few-shot/partially labeled target domain samples are unlabeled except for the pixels of class $\mathbf{c}_j^t$, and the arbitrarily incorrect prediction on these

[1] With a slight abuse of notation, each class, *e.g.*, $\mathbf{c}_i^s$, is also considered as a set consisting of its domain of definition. The set operations $\cap, \cup, \setminus, \subset$ thus applies to the underlying definition of the class.

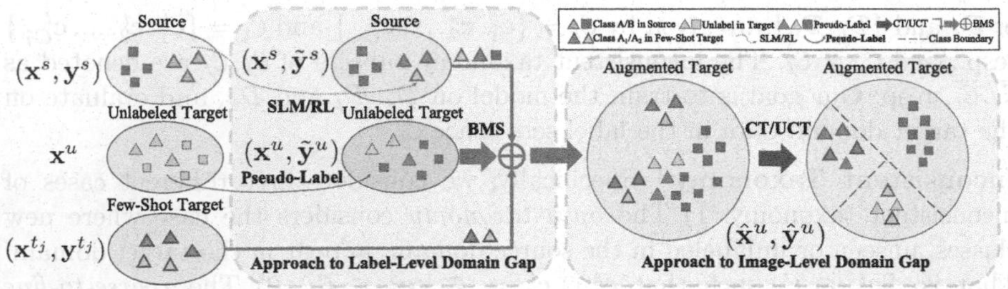

Fig. 2. Framework overview. Class A is an inconsistent taxonomy class (*e.g.*, "person") in the source domain, related to class A_1 (*e.g.*, "pedestrian") and A_2 (*e.g.*, "rider") in the target domain. Class B is a consistent taxonomy class. On the label level, SLM/RL module maps the inconsistent taxonomy class A in the source domain to the related classes A_1, A_2 in the target domain. BMS module unifies label space and augments the few-shot supervision, by randomly selecting samples from the source domain and the few-shot/partially labeled target domain and then mixing them in the unlabeled target domain. On the image level, CT/UCT module adopts the pseudo-label to distinguish the positive and negative pixel samples, and then conducts the pixel-wise contrastive learning, to learn more domain-invariant and class-discriminative features.

unlabeled parts can bring the negative effect since most of these parts belong to the consistent taxonomy classes or other inconsistent taxonomy classes. On the **image level**, the image domain distribution difference between the source and target domain, $P_S \neq P_T$, still exists in TACS.

3.2 Our Approach to the TACS Problem

Motivation. Motivated by the technical challenge i) of the label level in Sect. 3.1, the stochastic label mapping (SLM) and pseudo-label based relabeling (RL) module are proposed to solve the problem of the one-to-many mappings from the source domain to the target domain classes. Motivated by the technical challenge ii) of the label level in Sect. 3.1, the bilateral mixed sampling (BMS) module is proposed to unify the consistent and inconsistent taxonomy classes and augment the few-shot supervision for the target domain. Motivated by the technical challenge of the image level in Sect. 3.1, the contrastive learning (CT/UCT) module is proposed to train the domain-invariant but class-discriminative features.

Training Strategy. The whole framework adopts the pseudo-label based self-training strategy. Following the self-training structure of [26], there are two components of our framework, namely a student network $\mathcal{F}_\theta$ and a mean-teacher network $\mathcal{F}_{\theta'}$, which are both semantic segmentation networks. The student network $\mathcal{F}_\theta$ is used to backpropagate the gradients and update θ according to the training loss. The pseudo-labels $\tilde{\mathbf{y}}^u = \mathcal{F}_{\theta'}(\mathbf{x}^u)$ are generated by the mean-teacher network $\mathcal{F}_{\theta'}$ by feeding the unlabeled target sample $\mathbf{x}^u$. The parameters θ' are the exponential moving average of the parameters θ during the optimization process, which is proven to bring more stable training [32,34]. During inference, the mean-teacher network $\mathcal{F}_{\theta'}$ is used to output the final segmentation map.

Framework Overview. The framework overview is shown in Fig. 2. The SLM and RL modules (Sect. 3.3) are used to map inconsistent taxonomy class labels $\mathbf{y}^s$ in the source domain to target-domain class labels $\tilde{\mathbf{y}}^s$. Then in order to unify the label spaces, the source domain sample $(\mathbf{x}^s, \tilde{\mathbf{y}}^s)$ and the few-shot/partially labeled target domain sample $(\mathbf{x}^{t_j}, \mathbf{y}^{t_j})$ is cut and mixed with the unlabeled target domain sample and corresponding pseudo-label $(\mathbf{x}^u, \tilde{\mathbf{y}}^u)$, to synthesize the sample $(\hat{\mathbf{x}}^u, \hat{\mathbf{y}}^u)$ through the BMS module (Sect. 3.3). In this way, the synthesized sample $(\hat{\mathbf{x}}^u, \hat{\mathbf{y}}^u)$ is a cross-domain mixed sample and covers the consistent taxonomy class from $(\mathbf{x}^s, \tilde{\mathbf{y}}^s)$ and inconsistent taxonomy class from $(\mathbf{x}^{t_j}, \mathbf{y}^{t_j})$. The CT/UCT module (Sect. 3.4) is further utilized on the $(\hat{\mathbf{x}}^u, \hat{\mathbf{y}}^u)$ to train the domain-invariant and class-discriminative features using pixel-wise contrastive learning. All the modules are thus employed together in a single framework. Next, we detail individual components.

3.3 Approach to the Label Level Domain Gap

In order to solve the problem of *one-to-many class mappings*, the SLM and RL modules are proposed. In the initial training stage, the model is unable to distinguish the different inconsistent taxonomy classes reliably. Thus, taking the coarse-to-fine taxonomy as example, we propose the SLM module, and it stochastically assigns the source "coarse class" to different corresponding target "finer classes" to guide the model to predict the uniform distribution over the "finer classes" on the source domain samples. In this way, in the early training stage, the prediction of the model on the "finer classes" will be mainly guided by the few-shot labeled target samples. As the training goes on, with the help of the few-shot labeled target samples, the teacher network gradually has the capacity to distinguish the "finer classes". In the second stage, we then replace the SLM module with the RL module. It relabels the "coarse-class" pixel in the source domain with the "finer class" predicted by the teacher network.

Stochastic Label Mapping (SLM). We propose the SLM module, which maps the source domain classes of inconsistent taxonomy, *e.g.*, "person" in Fig. 1(e), to the corresponding target domain classes stochastically, *e.g.*, "pedestrian" and "rider" in Fig. 1(e), in the initial training stage and *in each training iteration*. Under the inconsistent taxonomy setting, there might be the one-to-many class mapping from the source domain classes to the target domain label space. Without loss of generality and for the convenience of clarification, we take the example that the corresponding classes in $\mathcal{C}_t$ of $\mathbf{c}_i^s$ include q classes $\mathbf{c}_p^t, \mathbf{c}_{p+1}^t, ..., \mathbf{c}_{p+q-1}^t$. Then the SLM module can be described as, $\tilde{\mathbf{y}}^{s(m,n)} = \text{rand}(\mathbf{c}_p^t, \mathbf{c}_{p+1}^t, ..., \mathbf{c}_{p+q-1}^t)$, where the (m, n) is the (row, column) index. The rand$(\cdot)$ represents the uniformly discrete sampling function. With the obtained new labels $\tilde{\mathbf{y}}^s$, we employ the standard cross-entropy loss, $\mathcal{L}_{slm} = CE(\mathcal{F}_\theta(\mathbf{x}_s), \tilde{\mathbf{y}}^s)$ to learn the model.

Pseudo-Label Based Relabeling (RL). As the training goes on, the model learns to distinguish the different inconsistent taxonomy classes to some extent. Instead of adopting SLM strategy at the latter part of the training, we introduce an alternative strategy. To exploit the capabilities learned by the model, we perform the pseudo-label based relabeling (RL), which relabels the pixels of inconsistent taxonomy classes in the source domain with the classes predicted by the model. Without loss of generality and for the writing convenience, we take the same example that $\mathbf{c}_i^s$ is related to $\mathbf{c}_p^t, \mathbf{c}_{p+1}^t, ..., \mathbf{c}_{p+q-1}^t$ as in SLM module. We generate predictions $\mathbf{f}^s = \mathcal{F}_{\theta'}(\mathbf{x}^s)$ by feeding the source domain sample $\mathbf{x}^s$ into the mean-teacher network $\mathcal{F}_{\theta'}$. Then the prediction $\mathbf{f}^s$ is used to relabel the source domain sample $\mathbf{x}^s$ for the inconsistent taxonomy classes $\mathbf{c}_i^s$, to generate the complete label $\tilde{\mathbf{y}}^s$ as, $\tilde{\mathbf{y}}^{s(m_i^s,n_i^s)} = \arg\max_c \mathbf{f}^{s(m_i^s,n_i^s)}$, if $\max_c \mathbf{f}^{s(m_i^s,n_i^s)} > \delta$, and $\arg\max_c \mathbf{f}^{s(m_i^s,n_i^s)} \in \{\mathbf{c}_p^t, ..., \mathbf{c}_{p+q-1}^t\}$. (m_i^s, n_i^s) is the index of the pixel corresponding to $\mathbf{c}_i^s$. The δ represents the threshold to decide whether the predicted label is used. The pseudo-label based relabeling module loss is written as $\mathcal{L}_{rl} = CE(\tilde{\mathbf{y}^s}, \mathcal{F}_\theta(\mathbf{x}^s))$. The SLM module and the RL module are used in the sequential manner during the training process, *i.e.*, initially SLM and then RL.

Bilateral Mixed Sampling (BMS). In order to *unify the consistent and inconsistent taxonomy classes* and *augment the few-shot supervision* for the target domain, we propose the bilateral mixed sampling (BMS) module, which cuts and mixes the source domain and few-shot/partially labeled target domain samples on the unlabeled target domain. Recently, the mixed sampling based data augmentation approach [11,44,45] is proven to be able to generate the synthetic data to combine the samples and corresponding labels, thus provides such a potential to unify the label space. In [34], the cross-domain mixed sampling (DACS) is shown helpful to UDA of consistent taxonomy.

Similar to DACS for UDA, we adopt the class-mixed sampling strategy for TACS. Different from DACS, which only focus on the labeled source domain and the unlabeled target domain, our BMS module conducts the class-mixed sampling in the bilateral way: 1) from labeled source domain samples $\mathbf{x}^s$ to unlabeled target domain samples $\mathbf{x}^u$; 2) from few-shot/partially labeled target domain samples $\mathbf{x}^{t_j}$ to unlabeled target domain samples $\mathbf{x}^u$. The bilateral mixed sampling mask $\mathbf{m}^s$ of $\mathbf{x}^s$ is,

$$\mathbf{m}^{s(m,n)} = \begin{cases} 1, \text{if } \tilde{\mathbf{y}}^{s(m,n)} = \mathbf{c}_r \\ 0, \text{otherwise}, \end{cases} \tag{1}$$

where the sampling class $\mathbf{c}_r$ is randomly selected from the available classes in $\tilde{\mathbf{y}}^s$. Following [34], half of all the available classes in $\tilde{\mathbf{y}}^s$ is randomly selected as the sampling class in each training iteration. Similar to $\mathbf{m}^s$, the bilateral mixed sampling mask $\mathbf{m}^{t_j}$ of $\mathbf{x}^{t_j}$ is defined. Then the augmented target domain sample and the corresponding pseudo-label $\hat{\mathbf{x}}^u$, $\hat{\mathbf{y}}^u$ are,

$$\hat{\mathbf{x}}^u = \mathbf{m}^s \odot \mathbf{x}^s + (1 - \mathbf{m}^s) \odot (\mathbf{m}^{t_j} \odot \mathbf{x}^{t_j} + (1 - \mathbf{m}^{t_j}) \odot \mathbf{x}^u), \tag{2}$$

$$\hat{\mathbf{y}}^u = \mathbf{m}^s \odot \tilde{\mathbf{y}}^s + (1 - \mathbf{m}^s) \odot (\mathbf{m}^{t_j} \odot \mathbf{y}^{t_j} + (1 - \mathbf{m}^{t_j}) \odot \tilde{\mathbf{y}}^u). \tag{3}$$

where $\odot$ denotes element-wise multiplication. On this basis, the pseudo-label based self-training loss of our BMS module is formulated as, $\mathcal{L}_{bms} = CE(\hat{\mathbf{x}}^u, \hat{\mathbf{y}}^u)$.

3.4 Approach to the Image Level Domain Gap

Besides dealing with the label-level domain gap, we also need to tackle the *image-level domain gap*. We propose a pseudo-label based contrastive learning (CT) module, and further the pseudo-label based uncertainty-rectified contrastive learning (UCT) module. They are easy to be plugged into our self-training pipeline and trained jointly with the BMS, SLM and RL modules.

Contrastive Learning (CT) for Domain Adaptation. The typical strategy of image-level adaptation is to train the domain-invariant but class-discriminative features in the cross-domain embedding space [9,10,35]. The pixels of the same class from different or same domains need to have similar features in the feature embedding space, while the pixels of different classes needs be distinguishable in the feature embedding space. This kind of distinction between features can naturally be formulated as a contrastive learning problem, where positive pairs stem from pixels of the same class, irrespective of their domain. In [38], the pixel-wise contrastive learning is proven to be helpful for semantic segmentation. However, it relies on ground truth label, which is unavailable for our unlabeled samples.

In order to exploit contrastive learning to train domain-invariant and class-discriminative features under cross-domain setting, we propose the pseudo-label based contrastive learning for domain adaptation. We employ pseudo-labels as guidance for distinguishing the positive and negative samples. The contrastive learning is conducted on the augmented target domain image sample $\hat{\mathbf{x}}^u$, and corresponding pseudo-label $\hat{\mathbf{y}}^u$ in the BMS module. Our main semantic segmentation network $\mathcal{F}_\theta$ can be decomposed into the encoder $\mathcal{E}_\theta$ and the decoder $\mathcal{M}_\theta$. The decoder is used to map the embedding space $\mathcal{V}$ to the label domain $\mathcal{Y}$. The encoder $\mathcal{E}_\theta$ maps the source image domain $\mathcal{S}$ and the target image domain $\mathcal{T}$ to the embedding space $\mathcal{V}$, *i.e.*, $\mathcal{E}_\theta : \mathcal{S}, \mathcal{T} \rightarrow \mathcal{V}$. The feature embedding corresponding to the sample $\hat{\mathbf{x}}^u$ is denoted as $\hat{\mathbf{v}}^u$, *i.e.*, $\hat{\mathbf{v}}^u = \mathcal{E}_\theta(\hat{\mathbf{x}}^u)$. Then the pseudo-label based contrastive learning module loss $\mathcal{L}_{ct}$ can be described as,

$$\mathcal{L}_{ct} = -\sum_h \sum_w \log \sum_{v^+ \in \mathcal{P}_v} \text{Contrast}(v, v^+), \tag{4}$$

$$\text{Contrast}(v, v^+) = \frac{\exp(v \cdot v^+ / \tau)}{\exp(v \cdot v^+ / \tau) + \sum_{v^- \in \mathcal{N}_v} \exp(v \cdot v^- / \tau)}, \tag{5}$$

where $v = \hat{\mathbf{v}}^{u(h,w)}$ is the feature vector of $\hat{\mathbf{v}}^u$ at the position (h, w). The positive samples in $\mathcal{P}_v$ are the feature vectors whose corresponding pixels in $\hat{\mathbf{y}}^u$ have the same class label as that of the corresponding pixel of v. The negative samples in $\mathcal{N}_v$ are the feature vectors whose corresponding pixels in $\hat{\mathbf{y}}^u$ have the different class label from that of the corresponding pixel of v. Equation (5) tries to learn similar features for the pixels of the same class, and learn discriminative features for the different class pixels, no matter whether pixels are in the same domain or not.

Uncertainty-Rectified Contrastive Learning (UCT) for Domain Adaptation. There unavoidably exist incorrect predictions in the pseudo-label $\hat{\mathbf{y}}^u$ of the unlabeled part in CT module, resulting in incorrect guidance to the contrastive module for the selection of the positive and negative samples. In order to alleviate the incorrect guidance, we propose the uncertainty-rectified contrastive learning (UCT) module based on the CT module. In our UCT module, we use the prediction uncertainty of the pseudo-label $\hat{\mathbf{y}}^u$ to rectify the contrastive learning, so that the uncertain prediction of $\hat{\mathbf{y}}^u$ has less effect on the contrastive learning. The uncertainty estimation map of $\hat{\mathbf{y}}^u$ is denoted as $\hat{\mathbf{u}}^u$, and the uncertainty measurement function is denoted as $\mathcal{U}(\cdot)$, *i.e.*, $\hat{\mathbf{u}}^u = \mathcal{U}(\hat{\mathbf{y}}^u)$. We adopt the maximum prediction probability of $\hat{\mathbf{x}}^u$ as $\mathcal{U}(\cdot)$, formulated as,

$$\hat{\mathbf{u}}^u = \max_c \mathcal{F}_{\theta'}(\hat{\mathbf{x}}^u). \tag{6}$$

Then, based on Eq. (5), the uncertainty-rectified CT loss $\mathcal{L}_{uct}$ is formulated as,

$$\mathcal{L}_{uct} = -\sum_h \sum_w \hat{\mathbf{u}}^u(v)\hat{\mathbf{u}}^u(v^+)\text{Contrast}(v, v^+), \tag{7}$$

where $\hat{\mathbf{u}}^u(v)$, $\hat{\mathbf{u}}^u(v^+)$ are the uncertainty estimation value of the pixel corresponding to v, v^+, resp.

3.5 Joint Training

With the above proposed BMS, SLM, RL and UCT modules, the total loss function is derived as,

$$\mathcal{L}_{total} = \mathcal{L}_{bms} + \lambda_1 \mathcal{L}_{slm} + \lambda_2 \mathcal{L}_{rl} + \lambda_3 \mathcal{L}_{uct} \tag{8}$$

where λ_1 and λ_2 are used to train the SLM and RL module in a sequential manner. When iteration $t < T$, $\lambda_1 = 1, \lambda_2 = 0$. When iteration $t \geq T$, $\lambda_1 = 0, \lambda_2 = 1$. T is the number of iterations to start training the RL module. λ_3 is the hyper-parameter to balance the UCT module loss and other loss, which is set as 0.01 in our work. Our model is trained end-to-end with the loss in Eq. (8).

4 Experiments

We evaluate the effectiveness of our framework under different scenarios, including the consistent and inconsistent taxonomy settings. For the consistent taxonomy, we follow the traditional UDA setting. For the inconsistent taxonomy, we build different benchmarks for TACS, including the open, coarse-to-fine and implicitly-overlapping taxonomy setting. The DeepLabv2-ResNet101 [3,14] is adopted as the segmentation network. The baselines in Table 2, 3 and 4 adopt the SOTA few-shot cross-domain semantic segmentation training strategy, *i.e.*, finetuning [46] and pseudo-label [26], to exploit the supervision from the few-shot labeled target domain. More experimental details are put in the supplementary.

4.1 Experimental Setup

UDA: Consistent Taxonomy. We adopt the UDA setting for the consistent taxonomy. The target domain is completely unlabeled. SYNTHIA [30] is used as the source domain, while Cityscapes [8] is treated as the target domain. The

Table 1. Consistent Taxonomy: SYNTHIA→Cityscapes. The mIoU are over 13 classes and 16 classes, resp. In UDA setting, we adopt the class-mixed sampling strategy in DACS to augment the target domain. *3 classes are not included when calculating mIoU over 13 classes.

Method	Road	SW	Build	Wall*	Fence*	Pole*	TL	TS	Veg	Sky	Person	Rider	Car	Bus	MC	Bike	mIoU*	mIoU
ADVENT [37]	87.0	44.1	79.7	9.6	0.6	24.3	4.8	7.2	80.1	83.6	56.4	23.7	72.7	32.6	12.8	33.7	47.6	40.8
FDA [42]	79.3	35.0	73.2	–	–	–	19.9	24.0	61.7	82.6	61.4	31.1	83.9	40.8	**38.4**	51.1	52.5	–
IAST [23]	81.9	41.5	**83.3**	17.7	4.6	32.3	30.9	28.8	83.4	85.0	65.5	30.8	**86.5**	38.2	33.1	**52.7**	57.0	49.8
DACS [34]	80.56	25.12	81.90	21.46	**2.85**	**37.20**	22.67	23.99	83.69	**90.77**	**67.61**	**38.33**	82.92	38.90	28.49	47.58	54.81	48.34
Ours (DACS+CT)	86.32	26.63	82.71	5.78	1.97	33.87	**34.60**	**40.00**	83.83	86.73	67.52	36.53	83.46	**55.23**	25.03	41.46	57.70	49.47
Ours (DACS+UCT)	**91.54**	**60.41**	82.52	**21.80**	1.48	31.66	31.59	27.95	**84.71**	88.95	66.68	35.78	81.04	42.79	28.49	45.88	**59.10**	**51.45**

Table 2. Open Taxonomy: SYNTHIA→Cityscapes. There are 13 classes labeled in the SYNTHIA dataset, and 6 new classes few-shot labeled in Cityscapes. The gray columns are the 6 new classes and mean IoU of 6 new classes in Cityscapes. "M" represents BMS module.

Method	Road	SW	Build	Wall	Fence	Pole	TL	TS	Veg	Terrain	Sky	Person	Rider	Car	Truck	Bus	Train	MC	Bike	mIoU	mIoU
Source	29.22	6.58	55.48	4.79	8.71	10.11	4.04	12.93	64.06	5.09	71.90	43.26	11.93	22.43	6.04	6.96	2.42	2.61	16.41	6.19	20.26
ADVENT [37]	75.72	24.62	74.94	0.00	0.17	18.98	11.30	16.01	76.87	**21.03**	78.91	48.24	14.20	54.97	2.54	18.38	17.58	12.22	20.90	10.20	30.97
FDA [42]	28.87	13.22	67.10	4.63	14.52	18.94	10.99	14.75	51.56	12.48	78.85	56.78	25.81	70.10	14.24	20.85	21.27	19.22	41.14	14.35	30.81
IAST [23]	70.73	29.60	75.49	6.90	0.00	1.36	36.43	25.37	66.17	7.65	83.96	60.72	19.99	82.51	0.00	39.52	0.09	27.42	23.55	2.67	34.60
DACS [34]	66.48	1.42	6.55	10.26	9.47	4.39	0.47	2.09	33.38	3.75	36.45	46.75	18.23	20.90	1.91	2.78	7.18	1.30	5.08	6.16	14.68
Ours (M)	87.59	27.18	80.98	5.99	15.74	7.13	37.09	18.51	83.68	0.08	87.46	65.89	**37.45**	86.55	24.76	40.58	37.71	**37.57**	43.44	15.24	43.44
Ours (M+CT)	86.33	32.57	82.62	9.49	12.78	5.10	**37.49**	**39.32**	82.00	0.73	**88.03**	65.70	33.09	78.92	33.55	**62.53**	**41.90**	29.83	49.35	17.26	45.86
Ours (M+UCT)	90.84	57.64	80.77	5.79	**16.67**	8.40	32.82	33.21	83.68	1.68	86.89	63.54	26.57	86.87	33.43	48.65	35.57	31.51	49.29	16.92	45.99
Ours (M+UCT+RL)	**92.64**	**58.66**	**84.21**	**20.55**	15.04	**29.47**	35.26	32.41	**84.63**	4.45	87.91	**66.16**	34.07	**87.52**	**36.37**	57.63	31.21	34.17	**52.28**	**22.85**	**49.72**
$n^t = 2975$	89.19	41.08	86.14	37.54	33.68	33.45	32.25	39.99	85.39	31.64	89.51	67.02	35.61	80.49	50.54	49.43	51.70	32.41	47.90	39.76	53.42
Oracle [39]	96.7	75.7	88.3	46.0	41.7	42.6	47.9	62.7	88.8	53.5	90.6	69.1	49.7	91.6	71.0	73.6	45.3	52.0	65.5	50.0	65.9

source domain and target domains share the same label space, where there are 16 classes in total: *road*, *sidewalk*, *building*, *wall*, *fence*, *pole*, *traffic light*, *traffic sign*, *vegetation*, *sky*, *person*, *rider*, *car*, *bus*, *motorcycle* and *bike*.

TACS: Open Taxonomy. The SYNTHIA dataset [30] is used as the source domain, and the Cityscapes dataset [8] is adopted as the target domain. In the SYNTHIA dataset, the main 13 classes are labeled: *road*, *sidewalk*, *building*, *traffic light*, *traffic sign*, *vegetation*, *sky*, *person*, *rider*, *car*, *bus*, *motorcycle* and *bike*. In the Cityscapes dataset, the 6 classes *wall*, *fence*, *pole*, *terrain*, *truck* and *train* are few-shot labeled, with 30 image samples per class.

TACS: Coarse-to-Fine Taxonomy. The GTA5 dataset [29] is utilized as the source domain, and the Cityscapes dataset [8] as the target domain. The label space of source domain is composed of *road*, *sidewalk*, *building*, *wall*, *fence*, *pole*, *traffic light*, *traffic sign*, *vegetation*, *sky*, *person*, *car*, *truck*, *bus*, *train*, *cycle*. The *vegetation* class of source domain is further divided into *vegetation* and *terrain* in the target domain, *person* in source domain is mapped to *person* and *rider* in the target domain, and *cycle* in the source domain is fine-grained labeled into *bicycle* and *motorcycle* in the target domain. In Cityscapes, each of the fine-grained 6 classes is 30-shot labeled.

TACS: Implicitly-Overlapping Taxonomy. The Synscapes dataset [40] is treated as the source domain, while the Cityscapes dataset [8] is seen as the target domain. The label space of the source domain contains the *road*, *sidewalk*,

Table 3. Coarse-to-Fine Taxonomy: GTA5→Cityscapes. There are 3 classes in the GTA5 dataset fine-grained into 6 classes in the Cityscapes dataset. The gray columns are the 6 fine-grained classes in the Cityscapes and corresponding mean IoU of these classes. "M": BMS. "*" with SLM module.

Method	Road	SW	Build	Wall	Fence	Pole	TL	TS	Veg	Terrain	Sky	Person	Rider	Car	Truck	Bus	Train	MC	Bike	mIoU	mIoU
Source	54.12	16.20	70.08	13.07	19.37	22.56	28.59	20.59	75.87	13.49	74.36	47.91	5.35	36.15	16.08	9.71	1.61	8.77	21.34	28.79	29.22
Source*	63.38	20.95	67.65	15.07	18.60	23.03	27.74	18.00	76.03	14.11	75.19	38.36	10.25	49.01	26.32	9.23	2.68	9.93	27.26	29.32	31.20
ADVENT [37]	88.91	38.93	79.18	26.22	22.65	25.45	31.24	25.42	75.22	0.03	78.91	55.76	0.00	77.76	28.22	33.19	0.55	13.02	7.15	25.20	37.25
ADVENT*	86.72	34.02	79.22	22.32	23.60	26.92	31.36	24.89	59.86	3.39	75.47	41.83	7.73	69.62	32.71	20.39	0.49	12.06	39.25	27.35	36.41
FDA [42]	90.83	45.07	81.62	28.37	31.04	32.56	34.00	29.80	83.09	6.31	72.61	60.67	10.13	82.71	29.06	51.51	0.11	15.69	45.61	36.92	43.73
FDA*	88.96	39.53	80.23	22.58	29.73	32.78	33.64	26.66	80.06	25.39	73.63	36.78	10.91	77.82	26.35	46.14	1.37	22.80	50.31	37.71	42.40
IAST [23]	83.20	37.84	82.63	36.00	21.59	32.34	43.48	44.69	84.92	36.51	88.77	59.71	28.04	84.34	32.64	38.66	2.52	31.27	35.57	46.00	47.62
IAST*	76.62	32.39	83.04	**37.52**	23.43	28.96	39.11	39.47	81.33	26.02	**89.10**	56.83	26.41	82.36	18.95	38.16	**23.03**	21.14	44.22	42.66	45.69
DACS [34]	82.93	29.50	69.67	31.58	24.87	18.17	20.71	17.43	69.69	8.54	64.06	32.17	9.78	76.99	36.40	44.26	0.00	8.64	30.39	26.54	35.57
DACS*	45.03	18.55	24.01	9.80	12.25	10.14	13.08	5.62	46.05	4.23	23.95	14.94	8.64	52.14	36.28	12.43	0.00	8.35	15.08	16.22	18.98
Ours(M)	93.60	60.14	85.64	34.57	25.27	33.67	34.67	41.84	83.03	2.67	86.96	60.15	2.34	87.25	52.06	47.66	0.00	17.81	42.53	34.76	46.94
Ours(M+SLM)	93.33	57.28	86.14	36.66	29.25	36.84	43.25	43.09	85.50	**39.17**	85.85	63.47	26.95	88.71	52.76	53.06	0.00	**41.46**	57.13	52.28	53.68
Ours(M+SLM+CT)	93.83	60.53	86.37	30.73	35.05	36.69	41.74	47.82	**85.70**	38.69	85.75	62.65	36.28	87.89	51.00	52.84	0.00	39.71	59.11	53.69	54.34
Ours(M+SLM+UCT)	**94.51**	**62.40**	87.15	29.95	35.96	37.96	44.17	52.17	84.56	34.33	84.80	65.79	37.41	**90.03**	**56.10**	52.57	0.00	40.46	59.82	53.73	55.27
Ours(M+SLM+UCT+RL)	93.97	59.71	**87.58**	29.81	**36.26**	**38.81**	**45.38**	**52.53**	85.26	35.18	87.28	**66.58**	**38.74**	89.74	55.23	**54.72**	0.00	40.72	**60.47**	**54.49**	**55.68**
$n^t = 2975$	93.65	56.25	86.48	27.37	39.02	37.59	43.73	50.49	87.08	49.25	86.38	67.71	43.83	89.40	50.98	47.01	0.09	45.42	63.96	59.54	56.09
Oracle [39]	96.7	75.7	88.3	46.0	41.7	42.6	47.9	62.7	88.8	53.5	90.6	69.1	49.7	91.6	71.0	73.6	45.3	52.0	65.5	63.1	65.9

building, *wall*, *fence*, *pole*, *traffic light*, *traffic sign*, *vegetation*, *terrain*, *sky*, *person*, *rider* and *vehicle*. The *vehicle* class in source domain can be seen as the union of the *car*, *truck*, *bus*, and *motorcycle* classes. In the target domain, each of 3 classes are few-shot labeled in 15 image samples, including the vehicle, public transport and cycle. The *vehicle* class in the target domain is the union of *car* and *truck*, the *public transport* is the union of *bus* and *train*, and *cycle* is the union of the *bicycle* and *motorcycle*.

4.2 Experimental Results

Comparison with the SOTA. In Table 1, it is shown that our proposed contrastive-learning based scheme outperforms the previous SOTA methods under the UDA setting, including the adversarial learning based ADVENT [37], the image translation based FDA [42], the self-training based IAST [23], and the data augmentation based DACS [34]. It proves the effectiveness of our contrastive learning for dealing with the domain gap on the image level. In Table 2, Table 3, and Table 4, it is shown that our proposed framework improves other SOTA methods performance by a large margin, under the open, coarse-to-fine and implicitly-overlapping taxonomy settings. It validates the proposed framework for dealing with both of the image- and label-level domain gap. In Fig. 5, we show qualitative semantic segmentation results on the target domain.

Ablation Study. The ablation study in Table 2, Table 3, and Table 4 proves that each module, BMS, SLM, RL, CT/UCT, all contributes to the final performance under open, coarse-to-fine, and implicitly-overlapping taxonomy settings. In different settings, the improvement brought by different modules are different. It is mainly because different settings in TACS touch diverse and broad aspects of inconsistent taxonomy. For example, the open taxonomy setting includes the new classes which are unseen or unlabeled in the source domain. The RL module is especially helpful to those unlabeled classes, *e.g.*, "wall" class. The SLM module

Table 4. Implicitly-Overlapping Taxonomy: Synscapes→Cityscapes. There are 3 classes (in gray) in the Cityscapes corresponding to the implicitly-overlapping taxonomy. "M": BMS. "*": with SLM.

Method	Road	SW	Build	Wall	Fence	Pole	TL	TS	Veg	Terrain	Sky	Person	Rider	Vehicle	PT	Cycle	mIoU	mIoU
Source	82.74	43.14	70.95	29.04	19.24	33.99	34.47	36.29	81.90	28.67	86.61	55.17	28.25	54.75	1.75	34.99	30.50	45.12
Source*	87.95	40.99	74.68	24.35	22.67	32.17	31.86	34.74	81.53	27.52	83.74	55.08	26.68	67.51	11.34	21.56	33.47	45.27
ADVENT [37]	92.84	54.32	82.54	31.40	25.90	37.67	38.92	40.55	85.46	35.95	87.69	58.12	29.75	73.19	2.42	3.23	26.28	48.75
ADVENT*	90.02	46.16	80.37	27.90	24.56	35.69	31.48	37.81	83.96	38.81	84.83	54.73	30.69	73.67	16.02	18.80	36.16	48.47
FDA [42]	89.45	44.66	75.82	28.3	27.91	37.89	41.09	49.91	83.78	26.17	83.50	61.24	39.37	65.35	6.32	26.56	32.74	49.21
FDA*	86.86	43.56	75.32	28.01	27.68	38.50	39.50	50.31	83.80	21.69	83.93	63.45	**42.32**	80.99	10.96	42.64	44.86	51.22
IAST [23]	91.65	54.26	81.82	31.61	28.48	35.33	42.83	46.74	85.67	41.89	89.47	57.51	32.77	75.78	31.13	50.45	52.45	54.84
IAST*	93.00	55.31	83.55	32.80	30.49	38.21	46.04	53.09	86.46	41.91	88.57	60.58	29.17	83.18	39.01	36.76	52.98	56.13
DACS [34]	89.72	61.93	57.59	28.87	26.87	33.42	41.44	41.14	84.57	41.96	86.49	57.94	25.36	59.88	2.13	19.63	27.21	47.43
DACS*	82.27	41.83	13.43	17.67	18.84	23.23	23.93	23.54	56.89	18.20	68.49	44.60	13.75	22.09	2.39	16.75	13.74	30.49
Ours(M)	91.35	59.29	**86.81**	**34.60**	32.14	43.9	49.29	55.8	83.51	**42.28**	90.44	**67.98**	37.27	83.01	16.89	**43.92**	47.94	57.40
Ours(M+SLM)	93.66	65.25	81.31	28.81	26.43	44.96	51.70	55.84	87.59	38.47	88.80	67.93	35.10	87.71	35.55	36.29	53.18	57.84
Ours(M+SLM+CT)	**95.70**	**70.24**	85.42	29.16	25.78	42.10	49.77	54.14	**87.67**	42.11	90.10	66.59	36.67	87.55	34.97	40.43	54.32	58.65
Ours(M+SLM+UCT)	92.43	66.46	82.25	32.24	**32.47**	45.37	**52.29**	**57.15**	87.20	36.48	**91.85**	65.03	37.87	88.53	41.95	38.11	56.20	59.23
Ours(M+SLM+UCT+RL)	92.47	65.40	83.21	33.33	30.87	**45.94**	49.86	55.86	87.23	39.50	91.30	66.56	39.87	**88.75**	**42.59**	39.64	**56.99**	**59.52**
$n^t = 2975$	94.62	63.90	85.13	28.52	31.03	46.46	53.44	50.16	86.98	41.21	91.00	67.61	35.04	89.98	74.72	52.85	72.52	62.04
Oracle	96.79	76.53	87.75	49.21	41.14	40.64	43.82	60.49	88.01	52.68	89.16	68.68	49.33	91.05	74.69	64.26	76.67	67.14

is significantly beneficial under the coarse-to-fine taxonomy setting since each fine class is corresponding to one coarse class unambiguously. The CT/UCT module contribution difference is mainly related to the image-level difference, *e.g.*, the style difference of SYNTHIA, GTA, Synscapes. Besides, it is shown that the UCT module is able to reach higher performance than the CT module, verifying the help of our uncertainty rectification for contrastive learning. It is also observed that the combination of SLM and other baseline methods, *e.g.*, ADVENT, FDA, IAST and DACS, does not necessarily bring the performance improvement. It is because the model prediction, when using SLM, is guided by the few-shot labeled target samples, but the baseline methods cannot effectively extract and exploit few-shot supervision with the previous SOTA few-shot cross domain semantic segmentation strategy, *i.e.*, fine-tuning [46] and pseudo-label [26]. Instead, our proposed BMS can augment and utilize the few-shot supervision effectively, guiding the model prediction when using SLM.

Partially Labeled/Oracle. In Table 2, Table 3, and Table 4, under the open, coarse-to-fine and implicitly-overlapping taxonomy settings, we report the partially labeled performance where inconsistent taxonomy classes are labeled in all the available target domain image samples, *i.e.*, $n^t = 2975$. Compared to the few-shot performance, the partially labeled performance is further improved due to more labeled samples on the target domain being available. But there is still gap to the fully supervised oracle performance on the target domain. It shows that our method serves as a strong baseline, but still provides the potential to develop stronger algorithms for the TACS problem.

Effect of Few-Shot Samples Number. In order to analyze the effect of the number of few-shot samples in the target domain for the inconsistent taxonomy adaptation performance, we take the open taxonomy setting as the example, and show the performance change with different number of few-shot samples in Fig. 3. It is shown that the inconsistent taxonomy class adaptation performance is improved, when more few-shot labeled samples are available.

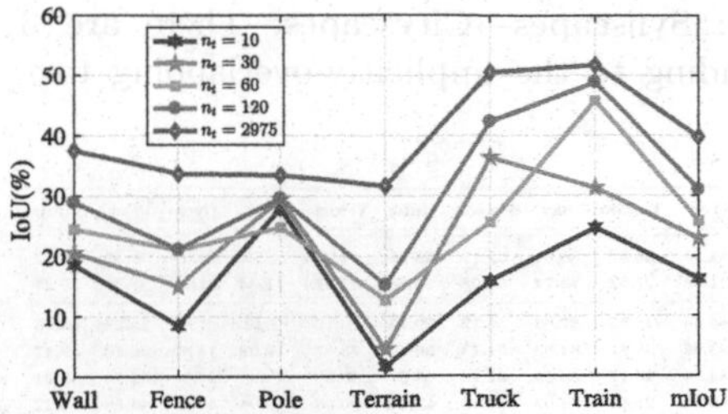

Fig. 3. Performance of inconsistent taxonomy classes under open taxonomy setting, varying n^t.

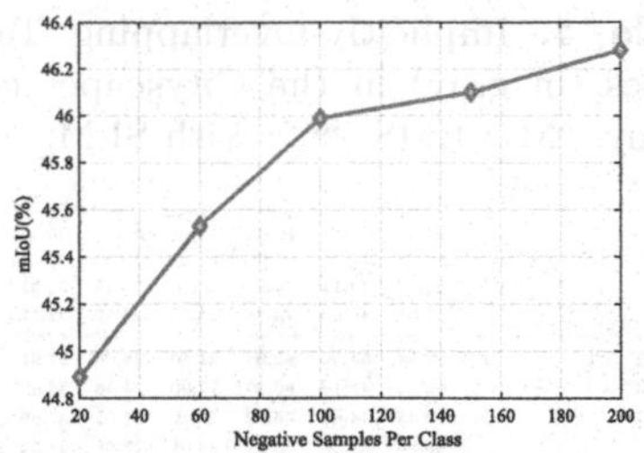

Fig. 4. Negative samples number study for contrastive learning, under M+UCT in Table 2.

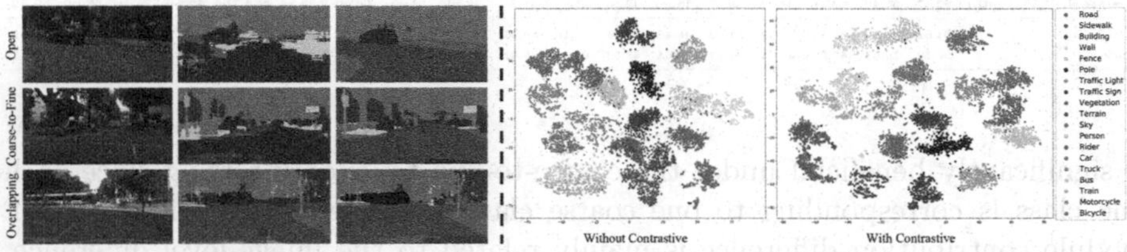

Fig. 5. Left: Qualitative results under different inconsistent taxonomy settings. Each group has the RGB image (left), the results without adaptation (middle) and adapted with our method (right). Refer to the red box region for the adaptation of the inconsistent taxonomy classes. **Right:** t-SNE visualization of the features with/without contrastive learning under the open taxonomy setting.

Contrastive Learning. In Fig. 4, the performance when varying the number of negative samples in the contrastive learning is shown. It is observed that the performance increases as more samples are taken. Balancing the performance and memory, we adopt 100 samples per class. In Fig. 5, we compare the t-SNE visualization [22] of the feature embedding of the model trained with/without UCT, taking open taxonomy setting as example. It verifies the contrastive learning is helpful to train the cross-domain invariant and class-discriminative features.

5 Conclusion

We propose the new TACS problem, allowing inconsistent taxonomies between the source and the target domain in the cross-domain semantic segmentation. Three typical types of inconsistent taxonomies are identified. To resolve TACS, the mixed-sampling, pseudo-label and contrastive learning based techniques are developed. Extensive experiments prove the effectiveness of our approach.

Acknowledgements. This project was funded by the EU Horizon 2020 research and innovation program under grant agreement No. 820434. This project was also supported by the European Lighthouse on Secure and Safe AI (ELSA) Project, a Facebook Academic Gift on Robust Perception (INFO224), and the ETH Future Computing Laboratory (EFCL). Special thanks goes to Dr. Wenguan Wang.

References

1. Bucher, M., Vu, T.H., Cord, M., Pérez, P.: Handling new target classes in semantic segmentation with domain adaptation. arXiv preprint arXiv:2004.01130 (2020)
2. Cao, Z., Ma, L., Long, M., Wang, J.: Partial adversarial domain adaptation. In: Ferrari, V., Hebert, M., Sminchisescu, C., Weiss, Y. (eds.) ECCV 2018. LNCS, vol. 11212, pp. 139–155. Springer, Cham (2018). https://doi.org/10.1007/978-3-030-01237-3_9
3. Chen, L.C., Papandreou, G., Kokkinos, I., Murphy, K., Yuille, A.L.: DeepLab: semantic image segmentation with deep convolutional nets, atrous convolution, and fully connected CRFs. TPAMI **40**(4), 834–848 (2017)
4. Chen, T., Kornblith, S., Norouzi, M., Hinton, G.: A simple framework for contrastive learning of visual representations. In: ICML (2020)
5. Chen, T., Kornblith, S., Swersky, K., Norouzi, M., Hinton, G.: Big self-supervised models are strong semi-supervised learners. In: NeurIPS (2020)
6. Chen, X., Fan, H., Girshick, R., He, K.: Improved baselines with momentum contrastive learning. arXiv preprint arXiv:2003.04297 (2020)
7. Chen, Y., Li, W., Sakaridis, C., Dai, D., Van Gool, L.: Domain adaptive faster R-CNN for object detection in the wild. In: CVPR (2018)
8. Cordts, M., et al.: The cityscapes dataset for semantic urban scene understanding. In: CVPR (2016)
9. Ganin, Y., Lempitsky, V.: Unsupervised domain adaptation by backpropagation. In: ICML (2015)
10. Ganin, Y., et al.: Domain-adversarial training of neural networks. JMLR **17**(1), 2030–2096 (2016)
11. Ghiasi, G., et al.: Simple copy-paste is a strong data augmentation method for instance segmentation. arXiv preprint arXiv:2012.07177 (2020)
12. Grill, J.B., et al.: Bootstrap your own latent: a new approach to self-supervised learning. arXiv preprint arXiv:2006.07733 (2020)
13. He, K., Fan, H., Wu, Y., Xie, S., Girshick, R.: Momentum contrast for unsupervised visual representation learning. In: CVPR (2020)
14. He, K., Zhang, X., Ren, S., Sun, J.: Deep residual learning for image recognition. In: CVPR (2016)
15. Hoffman, J., et al.: CYCADA: cycle-consistent adversarial domain adaptation. In: ICML (2018)
16. Hoffman, J., Wang, D., Yu, F., Darrell, T.: FCNs in the wild: pixel-level adversarial and constraint-based adaptation. arXiv preprint arXiv:1612.02649 (2016)
17. Kang, G., Jiang, L., Yang, Y., Hauptmann, A.G.: Contrastive adaptation network for unsupervised domain adaptation. In: CVPR (2019)
18. Kundu, J.N., Venkatesh, R.M., Venkat, N., Revanur, A., Babu, R.V.: Class-incremental domain adaptation. In: Vedaldi, A., Bischof, H., Brox, T., Frahm, J.-M. (eds.) ECCV 2020. LNCS, vol. 12358, pp. 53–69. Springer, Cham (2020). https://doi.org/10.1007/978-3-030-58601-0_4

19. Lambert, J., Liu, Z., Sener, O., Hays, J., Koltun, V.: MSeg: a composite dataset for multi-domain semantic segmentation. In: CVPR (2020)
20. Liu, Z., et al.: Open compound domain adaptation. In: CVPR (2020)
21. Long, M., Cao, Y., Wang, J., Jordan, M.: Learning transferable features with deep adaptation networks. In: ICML (2015)
22. Van der Maaten, L., Hinton, G.: Visualizing data using T-SNE. JMLR **9**(11) (2008)
23. Mei, K., Zhu, C., Zou, J., Zhang, S.: Instance adaptive self-training for unsupervised domain adaptation. In: Vedaldi, A., Bischof, H., Brox, T., Frahm, J.-M. (eds.) ECCV 2020. LNCS, vol. 12371, pp. 415–430. Springer, Cham (2020). https://doi.org/10.1007/978-3-030-58574-7_25
24. Motiian, S., Jones, Q., Iranmanesh, S.M., Doretto, G.: Few-shot adversarial domain adaptation. In: NeurIPS (2017)
25. Neuhold, G., Ollmann, T., Rota Bulo, S., Kontschieder, P.: The mapillary vistas dataset for semantic understanding of street scenes. In: ICCV (2017)
26. Olsson, V., Tranheden, W., Pinto, J., Svensson, L.: ClassMix: segmentation-based data augmentation for semi-supervised learning. In: WACV (2021)
27. Panareda Busto, P., Gall, J.: Open set domain adaptation. In: ICCV (2017)
28. Park, T., Efros, A.A., Zhang, R., Zhu, J.-Y.: Contrastive learning for unpaired image-to-image translation. In: Vedaldi, A., Bischof, H., Brox, T., Frahm, J.-M. (eds.) ECCV 2020. LNCS, vol. 12354, pp. 319–345. Springer, Cham (2020). https://doi.org/10.1007/978-3-030-58545-7_19
29. Richter, S.R., Vineet, V., Roth, S., Koltun, V.: Playing for data: ground truth from computer games. In: Leibe, B., Matas, J., Sebe, N., Welling, M. (eds.) ECCV 2016. LNCS, vol. 9906, pp. 102–118. Springer, Cham (2016). https://doi.org/10.1007/978-3-319-46475-6_7
30. Ros, G., Sellart, L., Materzynska, J., Vazquez, D., Lopez, A.M.: The synthia dataset: a large collection of synthetic images for semantic segmentation of urban scenes. In: CVPR (2016)
31. Saito, K., Yamamoto, S., Ushiku, Y., Harada, T.: Open set domain adaptation by backpropagation. In: Ferrari, V., Hebert, M., Sminchisescu, C., Weiss, Y. (eds.) ECCV 2018. LNCS, vol. 11209, pp. 156–171. Springer, Cham (2018). https://doi.org/10.1007/978-3-030-01228-1_10
32. Tarvainen, A., Valpola, H.: Mean teachers are better role models: Weight-averaged consistency targets improve semi-supervised deep learning results. In: NeurIPS (2017)
33. Teshima, T., Sato, I., Sugiyama, M.: Few-shot domain adaptation by causal mechanism transfer. In: ICML (2020)
34. Tranheden, W., Olsson, V., Pinto, J., Svensson, L.: DACS: domain adaptation via cross-domain mixed sampling. In: WACV (2021)
35. Tsai, Y.H., Hung, W.C., Schulter, S., Sohn, K., Yang, M.H., Chandraker, M.: Learning to adapt structured output space for semantic segmentation. In: CVPR (2018)
36. Van Gansbeke, W., Vandenhende, S., Georgoulis, S., Proesmans, M., Van Gool, L.: SCAN: learning to classify images without labels. In: Vedaldi, A., Bischof, H., Brox, T., Frahm, J.-M. (eds.) ECCV 2020. LNCS, vol. 12355, pp. 268–285. Springer, Cham (2020). https://doi.org/10.1007/978-3-030-58607-2_16
37. Vu, T.H., Jain, H., Bucher, M., Cord, M., Pérez, P.: ADVENT: adversarial entropy minimization for domain adaptation in semantic segmentation. In: CVPR (2019)
38. Wang, W., Zhou, T., Yu, F., Dai, J., Konukoglu, E., Van Gool, L.: Exploring cross-image pixel contrast for semantic segmentation. arXiv preprint arXiv:2101.11939 (2021)

39. Wang, Z., et al.: Alleviating semantic-level shift: a semi-supervised domain adaptation method for semantic segmentation. In: CVPR Workshops (2020)
40. Wrenninge, M., Unger, J.: Synscapes: a photorealistic synthetic dataset for street scene parsing. arXiv preprint arXiv:1810.08705 (2018)
41. Xie, E., et al.: DetCo: unsupervised contrastive learning for object detection. arXiv preprint arXiv:2102.04803 (2021)
42. Yang, Y., Soatto, S.: FDA: Fourier domain adaptation for semantic segmentation. In: CVPR (2020)
43. You, K., Long, M., Cao, Z., Wang, J., Jordan, M.I.: Universal domain adaptation. In: CVPR (2019)
44. Yun, S., Han, D., Oh, S.J., Chun, S., Choe, J., Yoo, Y.: CutMix: regularization strategy to train strong classifiers with localizable features. In: ICCV (2019)
45. Zhang, H., Cisse, M., Dauphin, Y.N., Lopez-Paz, D.: mixup: Beyond empirical risk minimization. In: ICLR (2018)
46. Zhang, J., Chen, Z., Huang, J., Lin, L., Zhang, D.: Few-shot structured domain adaptation for virtual-to-real scene parsing. In: ICCV Workshops (2019)
47. Zhang, Y., David, P., Gong, B.: Curriculum domain adaptation for semantic segmentation of urban scenes. In: ICCV (2017)
48. Zou, Y., Yu, Z., Vijaya Kumar, B.V.K., Wang, J.: Unsupervised domain adaptation for semantic segmentation via class-balanced self-training. In: Ferrari, V., Hebert, M., Sminchisescu, C., Weiss, Y. (eds.) ECCV 2018. LNCS, vol. 11207, pp. 297–313. Springer, Cham (2018). https://doi.org/10.1007/978-3-030-01219-9_18

Prototypical Contrast Adaptation for Domain Adaptive Semantic Segmentation

Zhengkai Jiang[1], Yuxi Li[1], Ceyuan Yang[2], Peng Gao[2], Yabiao Wang[1(✉)], Ying Tai[1], and Chengjie Wang[1(✉)]

[1] Tencent Youtu Lab, Shanghai, China
{zhengkjiang,caseywang,jasoncjwang}@tencent.com
[2] The Chinese University of Hong Kong, Ma Liu Shui, Hong Kong

Abstract. Unsupervised Domain Adaptation (UDA) aims to adapt the model trained on the labeled source domain to an unlabeled target domain. In this paper, we present Prototypical Contrast Adaptation (ProCA), a simple and efficient contrastive learning method for unsupervised domain adaptive semantic segmentation. Previous domain adaptation methods merely consider the alignment of the intra-class representational distributions across various domains, while the inter-class structural relationship is insufficiently explored, resulting in the aligned representations on the target domain might not be as easily discriminated as done on the source domain anymore. Instead, ProCA incorporates inter-class information into class-wise prototypes, and adopts the class-centered distribution alignment for adaptation. By considering the same class prototypes as positives and other class prototypes as negatives to achieve class-centered distribution alignment, ProCA achieves state-of-the-art performance on classical domain adaptation tasks, *i.e., GTA5 → Cityscapes and SYNTHIA → Cityscapes.* Code is available at ProCA.

Keywords: Domain adaptive semantic segmentation · Prototypical Contrast Adaptation

1 Introduction

Semantic segmentation is a fundamental computer vision task, which requires per-pixel predictions for a given image. Recently, with the development of deep neural networks (DNN) [11,14,16–18,44,46], semantic segmentation has achieved remarkable progress [2,24,49]. However, state-of-the-art methods still suffer from significant performance drops when the distribution of testing data is different from training data owing to the domain shifts problem [27,30,32]. At the same time, labeling pixel-wise large-scale semantic segmentation in the target domain is time-consuming and prohibitively expensive. Thus, Unsupervised Domain Adaptation (UDA) is a promising direction to solve such problem by

S. Avidan et al. (Eds.): ECCV 2022, LNCS 13694, pp. 36–54, 2022.
https://doi.org/10.1007/978-3-031-19830-4_3

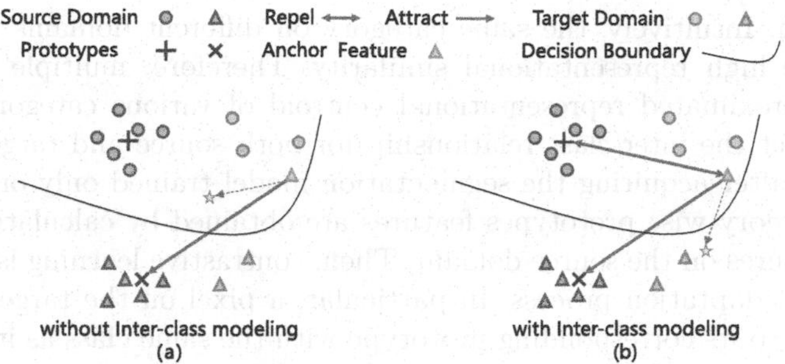

Fig. 1. Illustration of inter-class modeling. ⋆ means the adapted feature of target domain. With explicit inter-class constraints during adaptation, adapted features of target domain can appear at the right place of decision boundary.

adapting a model trained from largely labeled source domain to an unlabeled target domain without additional cost of annotations.

Several works relying on adversarial training [12,40,42] have achieved remarkable progress for UDA semantic segmentation. These methods reduce the domain discrepancy between source and target domains by minimizing a series of adversarial training losses. Specifically, it is formulated as a two-player game, where a backbone network (*i.e. ResNet-101 backbone*) serves as the feature extractor, while a discriminator identifies which domain the features are derived from. To reach equilibrium in this minmax game, it requires the backbone network to produce the domain invariant representations for generalization. Such adversarial training will result in aligned and indistinguishable feature distributions between two domains. However, even though the global feature distributions across domains become closer, it is not guaranteed that pixels attributing to different semantic categories in the target domain are well separated, leading to poor generalization ability and even inferior performance.

To tackle the issues above, some works attempt to take the category-wise information into account. The idea of encouraging high-confidence predictions is achieved by minimizing the entropy of the output [42]. The discrepancies between the outputs of two classifiers are utilized to achieve category-level alignment implicitly [27]. In addition, a fine-grained adversarial learning framework [43] is proposed to incorporate class information into domain discrimination, which helps to align features at a fine-grained level. However, prior approaches tend to apply such adversarial training in the intra-class, without considering the consistency of the representational structure between the source and target domains. Namely, to some extent, multiple categories on the target domain could be projected to a same group, which are usually well-discriminated on the source domain on the contrary. Therefore, merely considering the intra-class distributional alignment might be insufficient to make the best of the learned representations from labeled source data.

In order to fully exploit the class-level information, we propose *Prototypical Contrast Adaptation* (ProCA) for unsupervised domain adaptive semantic segmentation. Intuitively, the same category on different domains is supposed to share the high representational similarity. Therefore, multiple prototypes, *i.e.*, the approximated representational centroid of various categories are utilized to depict the inter-class relationship for both source and target domains. Specifically, after acquiring the segmentation model trained only on the source domain, category-wise prototypes features are obtained by calculating the centroids of features on the source domain. Then, contrastive learning is introduced into domain adaptation process. In particular, a pixel on the target domain is pulled closer to its corresponding prototype with the same class as its estimated pseudo-label and pushed away from other prototypes. In addition, in order to be invariant to domains, category-wise prototypes would be further updated by the current features of two domains. Besides, such prototypical contrastive adaptation scheme is applied at the feature and output level simultaneously. Based on the self-training framework, we further improve the performance with class-aware pseudo-label thresholds.

Experimental results on the domain adaptation benchmarks for semantic segmentation, *i.e., GTA5 → Cityscapes and SYNTHIA → Cityscapes* further demonstrate the effectiveness of our approach, leading to the state-of-the-art performance. Specifically, with the DeepLab-v2 networks and ResNet-101 backbone, we achieve Cityscapes [4] semantic segmentation mIoU by 56.3% and 53.0% when adapting from GTA5 [35] and SYNTHIA [36] datasets, largely outperforming previous state-of-the-arts.

We summarize the major contributions as follows:

- We propose *Prototypical Contrastive Adaptation* (*ProCA*) by explicitly introducing constraints on features of different categories for UDA problem in semantic segmentation. This is implemented by not only pulling closer to prototypes with the same class, but also pushing away from prototypes with different classes simultaneously. A multi-level variant is also designed to further improve the adaptation ability.
- Online prototypes updating scheme is introduced to improve the domain invariance and discriminant ability of class-wise prototypes.
- Combined with self-training method of class-wise adaptive thresholds, the proposed method achieves 56.3% and 52.6% mIoU when adapting GTA5 and SYNTHIA to Cityscapes, respectively, which outperforms previous state-of-the-arts by a large margin.

2 Related Works

2.1 Semantic Segmentation

Semantic segmentation is a fundamental computer vision task, which requires per-pixel predictions for a given image. Recently, with the help of convolution neural networks [24], semantic segmentation has achieved remarkable progress. Numerous approaches focus to enlarge receptive fields [2] and capture context information [49]. These methods generally require dense pixel-wise annotation datasets, such as Cityscapes [4], PASCAL VOC [6] and ADE20K [51]. Since per-pixel level annotation of large amounts of data is time-consuming and expensive, some synthetic datasets are proposed such as GTA5 [35] and SYNTHIA [36] to generate largely labeled segmentation datasets at lower cost. However, when testing models trained on the synthetic datasets on the real-world datasets, significant performance drops are observed even for state-of-the-art methods. In presence of the domain shifts, we deal with the semantic segmentation task that aims to learn a well performing model on the target domain with only the source domain supervision.

2.2 UDA for Semantic Segmentation

Existing approaches for UDA of semantic segmentation can be primarily divided into three groups, including style transfer [31], feature alignment [8,12,13,52] and self-training [1,56]. Motivated by the recent progress of unpaired image-to-image translation works [55], researches on style transfer aim to learn the mapping from virtual to realistic data [12,31]. Previous works on feature alignment minimize the discrepancy between source and target domains to obtain domain-invariant features. This can be achieved by directly minimizing the Maximum Mean Discrepancy (MMD) distances across domains over domain-specific layers [25] or using discriminator to train the model in an adversarial way to avoid generating domain-aware discriminative features [13]. There are also some works attempting to absorb class-wise information into feature alignment. The fine-grained adversarial learning framework [43] is proposed to incorporate class information into the discriminator, which helps to align feature in a class-aware manner, resulting better feature adaptation and performance. Approaches on self-training mainly focus on assigning pseudo-labels on target domain. Iterative self-training method is proposed [56] by alternatively generating pseudo-labels and retraining the model with a sampling module to deal with the category imbalanced issue. Uncertainty estimation [50] is proposed to rectify pseudo-label generation. Consistency based methods [1] have been adopted by enforcing consistency between predictions of different perturbations. In the work of [48], a prototype-based sample-wise pseudo-label correction scheme is proposed and embedded into a complicated multi-stage training framework to enhance segmentation performance. Nevertheless, the methods above neglect the explicit modeling of the relationship between clusters of different categories, on the contrary, we directly explore such constraints of different category centroids by prototypical contrastive adaptation. In this way, the categories with similar distributions on the target domain can be easier to distinguish, leading to superior performance.

2.3 Contrastive Learning

Contrastive learning [3,10,53] has lead remarkable performance in self-supervised representation learning. STC [17] uses contrastive learning to learn association embeddings for video instance segmentation task. For UDA semantic segmentation, CLST [29] attempts to leverage contrastive learning to learn finer adapted feature representation. The concurrent work SDCA [21] proposes using high-order semantic information to conduct contrast adaptation for UDA segmentation, which we found that it is not necessary. In this paper, with the aid of contrastive learning, we explicitly model the relationships of pixel-wise features between different categories and domains to obtain domain-invariant representation for unsupervised domain adaptive semantic segmentation.

3 Methodology

By minimizing the distributional distance between the source and target domains, previous approaches aim to obtain the domain-invariant representations for domain adaptation problem. However, the inter-class structural relationship is insufficiently explored. As shown in Fig. 1(a), after alignment within the intra-class across two domains, it could be much more challenging to distinguish different categories since the decision boundaries identified on source domain could hardly be maintained on the target domain. Therefore, we propose a novel *category-aware prototypical contrast adaptation* which introduces multiple prototypes to explicitly model the intra-class and inter-class relationships in a contrastive manner.

Akin to previous state-of-the-art approaches [21,43,48], a segmentation model is first trained on source domain in the supervised manner. Meanwhile, multiple prototypes are initialized to represent each category. Contrast adaptation is then adopted to constrain the inter-class relationship. Besides, prototypes are updated on both source domain and target domain to enhance the domain-invariant representations. As last, we present a modified pseudo-label generation method with class-aware adaptive thresholds for self-training, leading to new state-of-the-art performances.

3.1 Preliminaries

Given the labeled source domain images $\mathcal{D}_s = \{(\mathbf{x}_n^s, y_n^s)\}_{n=1}^{N_s}$, as well as unlabeled target images $\mathcal{D}_t = \{(\mathbf{x}_n^t)\}_{n=1}^{N_t}$, the goal of UDA of semantic segmentation is to train a model on $\mathcal{D}_s$ and $\mathcal{D}_t$; and evaluate the performance on the target domain. The segmentation model consists of a feature extractor $\mathcal{F}$ and a classifier $\mathcal{C}$, which predicts pixel-wise predictions for a given image.

Following previous works [12,21,43], the segmentation model is first trained on the labeled source domain in a supervised manner by minimizing the loss between the prediction p_n^s and the ground-truth label $Y_n^s \in \mathbb{L}^{H\times W}, \mathbb{L} = \{1, 2, \cdots, C\}$ annotated with C category labels, for a given image $x_n^s \in \mathbb{R}^{H\times W}$. We use the standard cross-entropy loss, which can be formulated as:

$$\mathcal{L}_n^{ce} = -\sum_{n=1}^{N_s}\sum_{i=1}^{H}\sum_{j=1}^{W}\sum_{c=1}^{C} y_{n,i,j,c}^s \log(p_{n,i,j,c}^s), \tag{1}$$

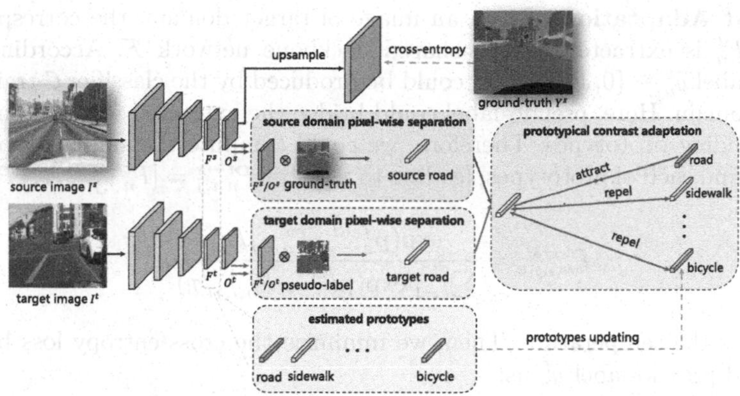

Fig. 2. The framework of proposed ProCA. For given source image I^s and target image I^t, features F^s and F^t of two domains are first obtained through a shared feature encoder $\mathcal{F}$. Then, outputs O^s and O^t are obtained by a shared classifier $\mathcal{C}$. After obtaining initialized prototypes, a pixel from two domains acts as a contrastive manner with class-aware prototypes to directly model inter-class constraints. We conduct such prototypical contrast adaption on both feature-level and output-level. At last, the initialized prototypes are also updated during training to enhance the domain-invariant representational ability.

where N_s is the number of source domain images, H and W denote the height and the width of an image, i, j are the pixel index of height and width, C is the number of categories. $p_n^s \in \mathbb{R}^{H\times W\times C}$ is the predicted probability of the image x_n^s, which is obtained by up-sampling the prediction $\mathcal{C}(\mathcal{F}(x_n^s))$. $y_n^s \in \{0,1\}^{H\times W\times C}$ is the one-hot representation of the ground-truth label Y_n^s.

3.2 Prototypical Contrast Adaptation

Here, intra-class and inter-class relations are simultaneously considered by prototypes-based contrastive learning as shown in Fig. 2. Specifically, *ProCA* contains three stages, including *prototypes initialization*, *contrast adaptation* and *prototypes updating.*

Prototypes Initialization. After obtaining the model trained on the labeled source domain, the initialized class-aware prototypes can be calculated as:

$$\mathbf{p}_c^{feat} = \frac{\sum_{n=1}^{N_s}\sum_{i=1}^{H}\sum_{j=1}^{W} F_{n,i,j}^s \mathbb{1}[Y_{n,i,j}^s = c]}{\sum_{n=1}^{N_s}\sum_{i=1}^{H}\sum_{j=1}^{W} \mathbb{1}[Y_{n,i,j}^s = c]}, \tag{2}$$

where $F_{n,i,j}^s \in \mathbb{R}^d$ is the extracted source feature vector with dimension d, c is the index of categories number C, H and W denote the height and width of the features, $\mathbb{1}[Y_{n,i,j}^s = c]$ is an indicator function, which equals to 1 if $Y_{n,i,j}^s = c$ and 0 otherwise. Prototypes could be regarded as the approximated representational centroid of various categories.

Contrast Adaptation. Given an image of target domain, the corresponding feature F_n^t is extracted by the shared backbone network $\mathcal{F}$. Accordingly, its pseudo-label $\widetilde{y}_n^t \in \{0,1\}^{H \times W \times C}$ could be produced by the classifier $\mathcal{C}$ trained on source domain. Here, pseudo-label could bridge the extracted features and their corresponding prototypes. Therefore, we could compute the similarity between features and each of prototypes, leading to a vector $P_{n,i,j}^{t \to s} = [P_{n,i,j,1}^{t \to s}, \ldots, P_{n,i,j,C}^{t \to s}]$:

$$P_{n,i,j,c}^{t \to s} = \frac{\exp(\mathbf{p}_c^{feat} \cdot F_{n,i,j}^t / \tau)}{\sum_{c=1}^{C} \exp(\mathbf{p}_c^{feat} \cdot F_{n,i,j}^t / \tau)}, \tag{3}$$

where τ is the temperature. Then, we minimize the cross entropy loss between $P_{n,i,j}^{t \to s}$ and pseudo-label $\widetilde{y}_n^t$ as:

$$\mathcal{L}_n^{t \to s} = -\sum_{i=1}^{H} \sum_{j=1}^{W} \sum_{c=1}^{C} \widetilde{y}_{n,i,j,c}^t \log P_{n,i,j,c}^{s \to t}. \tag{4}$$

The goal of such objective is to enforce the pixels belonging to the same category are supposed to share high representational similarity. In addition to the cross-domain adaptation, we also use source-source contrastive loss $\mathcal{L}_n^{s \to s}$ similarly:

$$\mathcal{L}_n^{s \to s} = -\sum_{i=1}^{H} \sum_{j=1}^{W} \sum_{c=1}^{C} y_{n,i,j,c}^s \log P_{n,i,j,c}^{s \to s}, \tag{5}$$

where y_n^s is the ground-truth one-hot source domain label, $P_{n,i,j}^{s \to s}$ is calculated similarly as Eq. 3. The final pixel-prototypes contrastive loss on feature-level is:

$$\mathcal{L}_{\text{ContraFeat}} = \sum_{n=1}^{N_t} \mathcal{L}_n^{t \to s} + \sum_{n=1}^{N_s} \mathcal{L}_n^{s \to s}. \tag{6}$$

Prototypes Updating. To enhance the domain-invariant representational ability of prototypes, we propose two schemes of prototype updating along with training to incorporate target-related information into prototypes. One is to update according to the computation of strict statistical mean of global data as:

$$\mathbf{p}_c^{feat} \leftarrow \frac{\mathbf{p}_c^{feat} n_c^{feat} + \widetilde{\mathbf{p}}_c^{feat} \widetilde{n}_c^{feat}}{n_c^{feat} + \widetilde{n}_c^{feat}}, \tag{7}$$

where n_c^{feat} represents the accumulated number of pixels belonging to category c until the last update, $\widetilde{\mathbf{p}}_c^{feat}$ represents the online estimated prototypes for category c, and $\widetilde{n}_c^{feat}$ represents the total number of pixels belonging to category c from a newly appended mini-batch during training.

In addition to source domain class-wise prototypes, we also leverage target features to update prototypes during feature adaptation process. This mixed prototypes scheme could be regarded as a bridge across two domains, which could naturally interact with each other. Thus, we further propose an alternative and more stable and robust way to directly update prototypes with a mixed domain scheme:

$$\mathbf{p}_c^{feat} \leftarrow m\mathbf{p}_c^{feat^s} + (1-m)\mathbf{p}_c^{feat^t}, \tag{8}$$

where m is a hyper-parameter, which defines a constant rate of source and target prototypes updating during training. $\mathbf{p}_c^{feat^s}$ is the estimated source prototype, and $\mathbf{p}_c^{feat^t}$ is the estimated target prototype.

Label Space Adaptation. As we mentioned before, prototypes are initialized, calculated and updated at the feature level *i.e.*, output of the backbone network $\mathcal{F}$. Apart from this, we could also apply the proposed prototypical contrast adaptation in the label space *i.e.*, the output of the classifier $\mathcal{C}$. The major difference is that the dimension of prototypes becomes the number of categories rather than the hidden channels in the feature space. Accordingly, the overall prototypical contrast adaptation losses becomes:

$$\mathcal{L}_{\text{Contra}} = \mathcal{L}_{\text{ContraFeat}} + \mathcal{L}_{\text{ContraOut}}. \tag{9}$$

3.3 Combining ProCA with Self-training

Since the proposed category-aware prototypical contrast adaptation is orthogonal to self-training based methods, we further improve the adaptation performance through the self-training strategy following previous works [21,30].

Class-Wise Adaptive Pseudo-label Thresholds. After the prototypical contrast adaptation stage, we could obtain the sorted predicted confidence set $\theta_c = [\theta_{c,1}, \theta_{c,2}, ..., \theta_{c,l_c}]$ of each category c, the length of confidence set belonging to category c can be calculated as follows:

$$\mathbf{l}_c = \sum_{n=1}^{N_t}\sum_{i=1}^{H}\sum_{j=1}^{W} \mathbb{1}[\widetilde{Y}_{n,i,j}^t = c], \tag{10}$$

where $\widetilde{Y}_{n,i,j}^t \in \mathbb{L}^{H\times W}, \mathbb{L} = \{1,2,\cdots,C\}$ is the predicted pseudo-label for the image x_n^t. Then, each class threshold of pseudo-labels can be obtained by fixed percentage of the ranked confidence sets, where the percentage is denoted as a hyper-parameter η.

In addition to above self-training strategy, there are some works [30,48,50] focusing on self-training itself improvements, like ProDA [48] which leverages prototypes to obtain accurate pseudo-label. Since our proposed ProCA mainly works during feature adaptation process, which is orthogonal to such self-training based improvements. Thus we could combine our ProCA with such self-training methods to achieve better performance, which is shown in Table 6.

Table 1. Comparison results of **GTA5 → Cityscapes**. All methods use DeepLab-v2 with ResNet-101 backbone for **fair comparison.** † means that we report the first stage self-training result of ProDA [48] for fair comparison, please see Table 3 of ProDA [48] for details.

Method	Venue	Road	Sidewalk	Building	Wall	Fence	Pole	Light	Sign	Vegetation	Terrain	Sky	Person	Rider	Car	Trunk	Bus	Train	Motorbike	Bike	mIoU	Gain
Source Only	–	53.8	15.6	69.3	28.1	18.8	27.6	34.9	18.2	82.5	27.8	71.6	59.4	35.3	44.1	25.9	37.5	0.1	28.9	24.9	37.3	+0.0
PatchAlign [41]	CVPR'19	92.3	51.9	82.1	29.2	25.1	24.5	33.8	33.0	82.4	32.8	82.2	58.6	27.2	84.3	33.4	46.3	2.2	29.5	32.3	46.5	+9.2
ADVENT [42]	CVPR'19	89.4	33.1	81.0	26.6	26.8	27.2	33.5	24.7	83.9	36.7	78.8	58.7	30.5	84.8	38.5	44.5	1.7	31.6	32.4	45.5	+8.2
BDL [22]	CVPR'19	91.0	44.7	84.2	34.6	27.6	30.2	36.0	36.0	85.0	43.6	83.0	58.6	31.6	83.3	35.3	49.7	3.3	28.8	35.6	48.5	+11.2
UIDA [32]	CVPR'20	90.6	37.1	82.6	30.1	19.1	29.5	32.4	20.6	85.7	40.5	79.7	58.7	31.1	86.3	31.5	48.3	0.0	30.2	35.8	46.3	+9.0
LTIR [19]	CVPR'20	92.9	55.0	85.3	34.2	31.1	34.9	40.7	34.0	85.2	40.1	87.1	61.0	31.1	82.5	32.3	42.9	0.3	36.4	46.1	50.2	+12.9
PIT [28]	CVPR'20	87.5	43.4	78.8	31.2	30.2	36.3	39.9	42.0	79.2	37.1	79.3	65.4	37.5	83.2	**46.0**	45.6	25.7	23.5	49.9	50.6	+13.2
LSE [38]	ECCV'20	90.2	40.0	83.5	31.9	26.4	32.6	38.7	37.5	81.0	34.2	84.6	61.6	33.4	82.5	32.8	45.9	6.7	29.1	30.6	47.5	+10.2
WeakSeg [34]	ECCV'20	91.6	47.4	84.0	30.4	28.3	31.4	37.4	35.4	83.9	38.3	83.9	61.2	28.2	83.7	28.8	41.3	8.8	24.7	46.4	48.2	+10.9
CrCDA [15]	ECCV'20	92.4	55.3	82.3	31.2	29.1	32.5	33.2	35.6	83.5	34.8	84.2	58.9	32.2	84.7	40.6	46.1	2.1	31.1	32.7	48.6	+11.3
FADA [43]	ECCV'20	92.5	47.5	85.1	37.6	**32.8**	33.4	33.8	18.4	85.3	37.7	83.5	63.2	39.7	87.5	32.9	47.8	1.6	34.9	39.5	49.2	+11.9
IAST [30]	ECCV'20	**94.1**	**58.8**	85.4	39.7	29.2	25.1	43.1	34.2	84.8	34.6	88.7	62.7	30.3	87.6	42.3	**50.3**	24.7	35.2	40.2	52.2	+14.9
ASA [54]	TIP'21	89.2	27.8	81.3	25.3	22.7	28.7	36.5	19.6	83.8	31.4	77.1	59.2	29.8	84.3	33.2	45.6	16.9	34.5	30.8	45.1	+7.8
CLAN [26]	TPAMI'21	88.7	35.5	80.3	27.5	25.0	29.3	36.4	28.1	84.5	37.0	76.6	58.4	29.7	81.2	38.8	40.9	5.6	32.9	28.8	45.5	+8.2
DACS [39]	WACV'21	89.9	39.7	**87.9**	39.7	39.5	38.5	46.4	52.8	**88.0**	**44.0**	**88.8**	67.2	35.8	84.5	45.7	50.2	0.0	27.3	34.0	52.1	+14.8
RPLL [50]	IJCV'21	90.4	31.2	85.1	36.9	25.6	37.5	**48.8**	48.5	85.3	34.8	81.1	64.4	36.8	86.3	34.9	52.2	1.7	29.0	44.6	50.3	+13.0
DAST [47]	AAAI'21	92.2	49.0	84.3	36.5	28.9	33.9	38.8	28.4	84.9	41.6	83.2	60.0	28.7	87.2	45.0	45.3	7.4	33.8	32.8	49.6	+12.3
ConTrans [20]	AAAI'21	95.3	65.1	84.6	33.2	23.7	32.8	32.7	36.9	86.0	41.0	85.6	56.1	25.9	86.3	34.5	39.1	11.5	28.3	43.0	49.6	+13.2
CIRN [7]	AAAI'21	91.5	48.7	85.2	33.1	26.0	32.3	33.8	34.6	85.1	43.6	86.9	62.2	28.5	84.6	37.9	47.6	0.0	35.0	36.0	49.1	+11.8
SDCA [21]	Arxiv'21	92.8	52.5	85.9	34.8	28.1	40.3	44.4	33.4	86.7	41.7	87.1	67.4	37.3	88.1	39.9	52.5	1.4	34.2	55.0	52.9	+15.6
PWCL [23]	Arxiv'21	93.3	54.2	83.0	25.9	28.1	37.2	41.1	39.3	83.1	38.9	78.2	61.3	36.2	84.2	35.8	54.0	18.1	26.7	47.5	50.9	+13.6
CLST [29]	Arxiv'21	92.8	53.5	86.1	39.1	28.1	28.9	43.6	39.4	84.6	35.7	88.1	63.9	38.3	86.0	41.6	50.6	0.1	30.4	51.7	51.6	+14.3
ESL [37]	CVPR'21	90.2	43.9	84.7	35.9	28.5	31.2	37.9	34.0	84.5	42.2	83.9	59.0	32.2	81.8	36.7	49.4	1.8	30.6	34.1	48.6	+11.3
MetaCorrect [9]	CVPR'21	92.8	58.1	86.2	39.7	33.1	36.3	42.0	38.6	85.5	37.8	87.6	62.8	31.7	84.8	35.7	50.3	2.0	36.8	48.0	52.1	+14.8
ProDA† [48]	CVPR'21	91.5	52.3	82.9	**42.0**	35.7	40.0	44.4	**43.2**	87.0	43.8	79.5	66.4	31.3	86.7	41.1	52.5	0.0	**45.4**	53.8	53.7	+16.4
UPLR [45]	ICCV'21	90.5	38.7	86.5	41.1	32.9	40.5	48.2	42.1	86.5	36.8	84.2	64.5	38.1	87.2	34.8	50.4	0.2	41.8	54.6	52.6	+15.3
Ours	–	91.9	48.4	87.3	41.5	31.8	**41.9**	47.9	36.7	86.5	42.3	84.7	**68.4**	**43.1**	**88.1**	39.6	48.8	**40.6**	43.6	**56.9**	**56.3**	**+19.0**

4 Experiments

Datasets and Evaluation Metrics: Following previous works [21,43], we evaluate the model in common UDA of semantic segmentation benchmarks, GTA5 [35] → Cityscapes [4] and SYNTHIA [36] → Cityscapes [4]. GTA5 is an image dataset synthesized by a photo-realistic open-world computer game. Which shares 19 classes with Cityscapes. It has 24,966 images with the resolution 1914 × 1052. SYNTHIA is a synthetic urban scene dataset. Following previous works [40], we use the subset SYNTHIA-RAND-CITYSCAPES sharing 16 common classes with Cityscapes. It contains 9400 images with the resolution 1280 × 760. Cityscapes is a dataset of real urban scenes, which is collected from 50 cities in Germany and neighboring cities. It has 2,975 training images, 500 validation images, and 1,525 test images, with the resolution 2048 × 1024. We report the results on Cityscapes validation set using the category-wise Intersection over Union (IoU). Specifically, we report the mean IoU (mIoU) of all 19 classes in GTA5 → Cityscapes setting and the 16 common categories in SYNTHIA → Cityscapes setting. In addition, since some works [26,40] only report mIoU for 13 common categories in SYNTHIA → CItyscapes setting, we also report the 13 common categories performance denoted as mIoU*.

Implementation Details. Following most previous works [12,21,43], we use the DeepLab-v2 framework [2] with ResNet-101 [11] encoder as our segmentation model for fair comparison. All models are pre-trained on ImageNet [5]. Atrous Spatial Pyramid Pooling (ASPP) [2] is inserted after the last encoder layer with dilated rates {6, 12, 18, 24}. At last, an up-sampling layer is used to obtain the

Table 2. Ablation studies of each component for GTA5 → Cityscapes. F refers to feature-level prototypical contrast adaptation; O refers to output-level prototypical contrast adaptation; Ada-ST refers to adaptive threshold self-training; MST refers to multi-scale testing. All methods use DeepLab-v2 with ResNet-101 backbone.

Source only	F	O	Ada-ST	MST	mIoU
✓					37.3
✓	✓				47.9
✓		✓			48.4
✓	✓	✓			48.8
✓			✓		43.9
✓	✓	✓	✓		55.1
✓	✓	✓	✓	✓	**56.3**

Table 3. Ablation studies of different domain alignment methods for GTA5 → Cityscapes. FADA [43] refers fine-grained adversarial training for feature-level and output-level; SDCA [21] refers semantic distribution-aware adaptation; Memory Bank refers to pixel-level bank for contrast adaptation. ProCA refers to prototypical contrast adaptation. All methods use DeepLab-v2 with ResNet-101 backbone.

Source only	FADA	SDCA	Memory Bank	ProCA	mIoU
✓					37.3
✓	✓				46.9
✓		✓			47.2
✓			✓		47.6
✓				✓	**48.8**

final per-pixel predictions with the same image size as input. We implement the proposed method with PyTorch [33] on NVIDIA Tesla V100. We apply SGD optimizer with the initial learning rate of 2.5×10^{-4}, momentum 0.9 and weight decay of 5.0×10^{-4}. We use polynomial learning rate scheduling with the power of 0.9. During prototypical contrast adaptation, the pseudo-label threshold of target domain is set to 0.9. For self-training stage. We assign pseudo-labels based on the predicted category probabilities with the adaptive thresholds. The percentage η of the number of pixels for each category is 0.6 in default.

4.1 Comparisons with State-of-the-Art Methods

In order to compare with previous state-of-the-art methods comprehensively, we include two typical methods: 1) Domain alignment methods which aim to align the distribution between source and target domains by distribution distances or adversarial training, including LITR [19], PIT [28], WeakSeg [34], CrCDA [15], FADA [43], ASA [54], CLAN [26], ConTrans [20], SDCA [21], and CIRN [7]. 2)

Table 4. Comparison results of **SYNTHIA → Cityscapes**. mIoU* denotes the mean IoU of 13 classes, which excludes the classes marked by the asterisk. All methods use DeepLab-v2 with ResNet-101 backbone for fair comparison. † means that we report the first stage self-training result of ProDA [48] for fair comparison. The result of ProDA [48] is from their released code.

Method	Venue	Road	Sidewalk	Building	Wall*	Fence*	Pole*	Light	Sign	Vegetation	Sky	Person	Rider	Car	Bus	Motorbike	Bike	mIoU	Gain	mIoU*	Gain*
Source Only	–	55.6	23.8	74.6	9.2	0.2	24.4	6.1	12.1	74.8	79.0	55.3	19.1	39.6	23.3	13.7	25.0	33.5	0.0	38.6	0.0
PatchAlign [41]	CVPR'19	82.4	38.0	78.6	–	–	–	9.9	10.5	78.2	80.5	53.5	19.6	67.0	29.5	21.6	31.3	–	–	46.5	+7.9
ADVENT [42]	CVPR'19	85.6	42.2	79.7	8.7	0.4	25.9	5.4	8.1	80.4	84.1	57.9	23.8	73.3	36.4	14.2	33.0	41.2	+7.7	48.0	+9.4
BDL [22]	CVPR'19	86.0	46.7	80.3	–	–	–	14.1	11.6	79.2	81.3	54.1	27.9	73.7	42.2	25.7	45.3	–	–	51.4	+12.8
UIDA [32]	CVPR'20	84.3	37.7	79.5	5.3	0.4	24.9	9.2	8.4	80.0	84.1	57.2	23.0	78.0	38.1	20.3	36.5	41.7	+8.2	48.9	+10.3
LTIR [19]	CVPR'20	92.6	53.2	79.2	–	–	–	1.6	7.5	78.6	84.4	52.6	20.0	82.1	34.8	14.6	39.4	–	–	49.3	+10.7
PIT [28]	CVPR'20	83.1	27.6	81.5	8.9	0.3	21.8	26.4	33.8	76.4	78.8	64.2	27.6	79.6	31.2	31.0	31.3	44.0	+10.5	51.8	+13.2
LSE [38]	ECCV'20	82.9	43.1	78.1	9.3	0.6	28.2	9.1	14.4	77.0	83.5	58.1	25.9	71.9	38.0	29.4	31.2	42.6	+9.1	49.4	+10.8
CrCDA [15]	ECCV'20	86.2	44.9	79.5	8.3	0.7	27.8	9.4	11.8	78.6	86.5	57.2	26.1	76.8	39.9	21.5	32.1	42.9	+9.4	50.0	+11.4
WeakSeg [34]	ECCV'20	92.0	53.5	80.9	11.4	0.4	21.8	3.8	6.0	81.6	84.4	60.8	24.4	80.5	39.0	26.0	41.7	44.3	+10.8	51.9	+13.3
IAST [30]	ECCV'20	81.9	41.5	83.3	17.7	**4.6**	32.3	30.9	28.8	83.4	85.0	65.5	30.8	86.5	38.2	**33.1**	52.7	49.8	+16.3	57.0	+18.4
FADA [43]	ECCV'20	84.5	40.1	83.1	4.8	0.0	34.3	20.1	27.2	84.8	84.0	53.5	22.6	85.4	43.7	26.8	27.8	45.2	+11.7	52.5	+13.9
ASA [54]	TIP'21	91.2	48.5	80.4	3.7	0.3	21.7	5.5	5.2	79.5	83.6	56.4	21.9	80.3	36.2	20.0	32.9	41.7	+8.2	49.3	+10.7
CLAN [26]	TPAMI'21	82.7	37.2	81.5	–	–	–	17.1	13.1	81.2	83.3	55.5	22.1	76.6	30.1	23.5	30.7	–	–	48.8	+10.2
DACS [39]	WACV'21	80.6	25.1	81.9	21.5	2.9	37.2	22.7	24.0	83.7	**90.8**	67.6	**38.3**	82.9	38.9	28.5	47.6	48.3	+14.8	54.8	+16.2
RPLL [50]	IJCV'21	87.6	41.9	83.1	14.7	1.7	36.2	31.3	19.9	81.6	80.6	63.0	21.8	86.2	40.7	23.6	53.1	47.9	+14.4	54.9	+16.3
CIRN [7]	AAAI'21	85.8	40.4	80.4	4.7	1.8	30.8	16.4	18.6	80.7	80.4	55.2	26.3	83.9	43.8	18.6	34.3	43.9	+10.4	51.1	+12.5
DAST [47]	AAAI'21	87.1	44.5	82.3	10.7	0.8	29.9	13.9	13.1	81.6	86.0	60.3	25.1	83.1	40.1	24.4	40.5	45.2	+11.7	52.5	+13.9
ConTrans [20]	AAAI'21	**93.3**	**54.0**	81.3	14.3	0.7	28.8	21.3	22.8	82.6	83.3	57.7	22.8	83.4	30.7	20.2	47.2	46.5	+13.0	53.9	+15.3
SDCA [21]	Arxiv'21	88.4	45.9	83.9	24.0	1.7	38.1	25.2	17.0	85.3	82.9	67.3	26.6	87.1	47.2	28.6	53.4	50.2	+16.7	56.8	+18.2
PWCL [23]	Arxiv'21	–	–	–	–	–	–	–	–	–	–	–	–	–	–	–	–	–	–	53.3	+14.7
CLST [29]	Arxiv'21	88.0	49.2	82.2	16.3	0.4	29.2	31.8	23.9	84.1	88.0	59.1	27.2	85.5	46.4	28.9	**56.5**	49.8	+16.3	57.8	+19.2
ESL [37]	CVPR'21	84.3	39.7	79.0	9.4	0.7	27.7	16.0	14.3	78.3	83.8	59.1	26.6	72.7	35.8	23.6	45.8	43.5	+10.0	50.7	+12.1
MetaCorrect [9]	CVPR'21	92.6	52.7	81.3	8.9	2.4	28.1	13.0	7.3	83.5	85.0	60.1	19.7	84.8	37.2	21.5	43.9	45.1	+11.6	52.5	+13.9
ProDA† [48]	CVPR'21	87.1	44.0	83.2	26.9	0.0	**42.0**	**45.8**	**34.2**	86.7	81.3	68.4	22.1	87.7	50.0	31.4	38.6	51.9	+18.4	58.5	+19.9
UPLR [45]	ICCV'21	79.4	34.6	83.5	19.3	2.8	35.3	32.1	26.9	78.8	79.6	66.6	30.3	86.1	36.6	19.5	56.9	48.0	+14.5	54.6	+16.0
Ours	–	90.5	52.1	**84.6**	**29.2**	3.3	40.3	37.4	27.3	**86.4**	85.9	**69.8**	28.7	**88.7**	**53.7**	14.8	54.8	**53.0**	**+19.5**	**59.6**	**+21.0**

Table 5. Ablation studies of different prototypes updating scheme for GTA5 → Cityscapes. Fixed refers to no-updating for calculated prototypes; Source means updating in a strict statistical way on in source domain as Eq. 7; Mixed refers updating in Eq. 8 in both source and target domain.

Source only	Fixed	Source	Mixed	mIoU
✓				37.3
✓	✓			47.8
✓		✓		48.3
✓			✓	**48.8**

Self-training approaches, including UIDA [32], LSE [38], IAST [30], DACS [39], RPLL [50], DAST [47], ESL [37], MetaCorrect [9], and ProDA [48].

Results on GTA5 → Cityscapes. As shown in Table 1, our approach achieves 56.3% mIoU, outperforming prior methods by a large margin. In particular, the most challenging classes stated in [21] including pole, person, rider, bike, and train, obtains the significant improvements, compared to previous work. It demonstrates our motivation that the inter-class modeling via prototypes indeed help the category recognition on the target domain, especially for the harder classes.

Results on SYNTHIA → Cityscapes. The comparisons of SYNTHIA → Cityscapes are shown in Table 4. Among all the 16 categories, we achieve the best scores on 6 categories, most of those are hard classes stated in [21], *e.g.*, person, and bike. To be specific, the proposed method achieves the mIoU score by 53.0% and 59.6% over the 16 and 13 categories respectively, which obtains the gains over the baseline by 19.5% and 21.0%.

Table 6. Ablation studies of different self-training schemes for GTA5 → Cityscapes. Naive Self-Training refers to fixed 0.9 threshold for pseudo-label generation; Adaptive Self-Training refers to adaptive pseudo-label generation, which is median of predicted confidence set of each class in default (Sect. 3.3). Prototypes-based Self-Training refers to pseudo-label generation strategy by utilizing prototypes which is proposed by ProDA [48].

ProCA	Naive	Adaptive	Prototypes-based	mIoU
✓				48.8
✓	✓			55.2
✓		✓		56.3
✓			✓	57.5

Discussion with ProDA. It should be noticeable that our proposed prototype contrastive learning method surpass a similar prototype-based method ProDA [48] on both transferring scenarios under a *fair* comparison setting. Especially, in GTA5 → Cityscapes, our adaptive method outperforms [48] by a large margin of 1.4% mIOU. This is due to the fact that ProDA only utilizes prototypes to rectify pseudo-labels or align feature in a purely sample-wise manner, which is more vulnerable to the interference from outlier or noisy samples in the target domain, while our pipeline directly depicts the class-wise relation in a sample-to-prototype manner, making the learning process more robust and friendly to cross-domain transferring.

Discussion with Other Contrastive Learning Based Methods. It should also be noticed that compared with a similar patch-wise contrastive learning method PWCL [23], our approach achieves superiority of 4.2% and 5.4% mIOU improvement on both GTA5 → Cityscapes and SYNTHIA → Cityscapes respectively. This is due to the fact that PWCL only takes patch-wise features for contrastive feature adaptation, which is coarse to depict class-wise relation and ignores the fine-grained pixel-wise distribution variation during training process, resulting in less discriminative and general representation.

Table 7. Ablation studies of different percentages determining class-wise thresholds during self-training process for GTA5 → Cityscapes. All methods use DeepLab-v2 with ResNet-101 backbone.

η (%)	30	40	50	60	70	80	90
mIoU	54.3	54.7	54.9	55.1	54.4	54.1	52.5

Table 8. Ablation studies of different contrastive adaptation choices for GTA5 → Cityscapes. $s \to s$ means Eq. 5 and $t \to s$ means Eq. 4

Source only	$s \to s$	$t \to s$	mIoU
✓			37.3
✓	✓		44.9
✓		✓	46.8
✓	✓	✓	48.8

How ProCA Helps Poor Classes Adaptation? As shown in Table 1, the performance of *train* class could not be improved by state-of-the-art pseudo-label method ProDA. This is because initialized predictions are totally wrong, thus ProDA could not estimate accurate pseudo-label for *train* class. Different from ProDA, our ProCA first corrects the *train* class predictions by push aware from others class centroids, which progressively obtain more and more accurate feature representation of *train* class. After introducing such relationship between different classes, our proposed method achieves highest *train* class performance after combining with self-training method.

4.2 Ablation Studies

Effectiveness of Each Component. We conduct ablation studies to demonstrate the effectiveness of each component. We use the ResNet-101 backbone with DeepLab-v2 segmentation for GTA5 → Cityscapes adaptation. As shown in Table 2, the source-only baseline achieves 37.3% mIoU on Cityscapes val set. Further, we achieve 48.8% mIoU score after using the proposed prototypical contrast adaptation. At last, the performance can be improved to 55.1% mIoU through self-training with class-aware adaptive thresholds. Finally, we obtain 56.3% mIoU score by multi-scale testing following FADA [43]. When directly using self-training after source-domain training, we could only obtain 43.9% mIoU, which is 11.2% mIoU lower than 55.1% mIoU score, demonstrating the effectiveness of ProCA.

Effectiveness of ProCA. To verify the effectiveness of ProCA, we implement other feature alignment methods, *e.g.*, class-wise adversarial training without inter-class modeling FADA [43], semantic-distribution modeling with category-wise information. As shown in Table 3, FADA improves the baseline to 46.9%

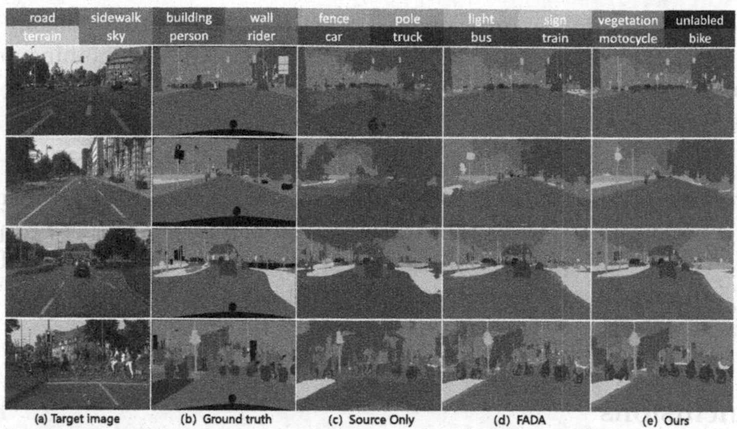

Fig. 3. Qualitative segmentation results for GTA5 → Cityscapes. From the left to right: target image, ground-truth, predictions by Source Only, FADA [43] and our proposed method are shown.

mIoU, which indicates the effectiveness of the adversarial training. SDCA [21] obtains 47.2% mIoU by considering semantic-aware feature alignment. Memory Bank obtains 47.6% mIoU by introducing pixel-wise contrastive adaptation, which already achieves better performance than FADA and SDCA. Compared with above methods, our ProCA achieves the best mIoU score 48.8%, which demonstrates the superiority of the proposed class-aware prototypical contrast adaptation than pixel-wise memory bank scheme.

Effectiveness of Mixed Updating. We conduce ablation studies to verify the effectiveness of mixed updating for prototypes. As shown in 5, a naive fixed prototype scheme only achieves 47.8% mIoU, while centroid updating way only in source domain obtains 48.3% mIoU, which has 0.5% gain compared with fixed-prototype scheme. Mixed updating scheme achieves best 48.8% mIoU score, which demonstrates the effectiveness of latest features during training.

Effectiveness of Multi-level Adaptation. We conduct ablation studies to verify the effectiveness of multi-level adaptation. The results are shown in Table 2. When only using feature-level adaptation or output-level adaptation, we achieve 47.9% mIoU and 48.4% mIoU, respectively. After combining them, we obtain the best mIoU score 48.8%, demonstrating the superiority of multi-level adaptation (Fig. 3).

Effectiveness of In-domain Contrastive Adaptation and Cross-Domain Contrastive Adaptation. We conduct experiments to study the influence of different domain choices of prototypical contrastive adaptation. The results are shown in Table 8. When only using source-to-source ProCA scheme, we could obtain 7.6% mIoU improvement. When only using cross-domain ProCA scheme, we could obtain 9.5% mIoU improvement. After combining both in-domain and cross-domain strategies, we finally obtain 48.8% mIoU, which verifies the effectiveness of the proposed method.

Effectiveness of Different Percentages for Adaptive Self-training. We conduct experiments to study the influence of different percentages of pseudo-labels generation during self-training stage. The results are shown in Table 7. Using 60% to generate pseudo-labels, ProCA achieves the best mIoU 55.1%. And larger percentages harm the performance.

5 Conclusions

In this paper, we propose ProCA, which utilizes class-wise prototypes to align features in a fine-grained manner. Apart from feature-level adaptation, output-level prototypes are also exploited to boost the adaptation performance. The proposed method achieves the state-of-the-art performance on challenging benchmarks, outperforming previous methods by a large margin. Elaborate ablative studies demonstrate the advancement of our ProCA. We hope the proposed prototypical contrast adaptation could extend to more tasks, such as object detection and instance segmentation.

References

1. Araslanov, N., Roth, S.: Self-supervised augmentation consistency for adapting semantic segmentation. In: Proceedings of the IEEE Conference on Computer Vision and Pattern Recognition, pp. 15384–15394 (2021)
2. Chen, L.C., Papandreou, G., Kokkinos, I., Murphy, K., Yuille, A.L.: DeepLab: semantic image segmentation with deep convolutional nets, Atrous convolution, and fully connected CRFs. IEEE Trans. Pattern Anal. Mach. Intell. **40**(4), 834–848 (2017)
3. Chen, T., Kornblith, S., Norouzi, M., Hinton, G.: A simple framework for contrastive learning of visual representations. In: International Conference on Machine Learning, pp. 1597–1607. PMLR (2020)
4. Cordts, M., et al.: The cityscapes dataset for semantic urban scene understanding. In: Proceedings of the IEEE Conference on Computer Vision and Pattern Recognition, pp. 3213–3223 (2016)
5. Deng, J., Dong, W., Socher, R., Li, L.J., Li, K., Fei-Fei, L.: ImageNet: a large-scale hierarchical image database. In: IEEE Conference on Computer Vision and Pattern Recognition, pp. 248–255 (2009)
6. Everingham, M., Van Gool, L., Williams, C.K., Winn, J., Zisserman, A.: The pascal visual object classes (VOC) challenge. Int. J. Comput. Vision **88**(2), 303–338 (2010)
7. Gao, L., Zhang, L., Zhang, Q.: Addressing domain gap via content invariant representation for semantic segmentation. In: Proceedings of the AAAI Conference on Artificial Intelligence, pp. 7528–7536 (2021)

8. Gu, Q., et al.: PIT: position-invariant transform for cross-FoV domain adaptation. In: Proceedings of the IEEE/CVF International Conference on Computer Vision, pp. 8761–8770 (2021)
9. Guo, X., Yang, C., Li, B., Yuan, Y.: MetaCorrection: domain-aware meta loss correction for unsupervised domain adaptation in semantic segmentation. In: Proceedings of the IEEE Conference on Computer Vision and Pattern Recognition, pp. 3927–3936 (2021)
10. He, K., Fan, H., Wu, Y., Xie, S., Girshick, R.: Momentum contrast for unsupervised visual representation learning. In: Proceedings of the IEEE Conference on Computer Vision and Pattern Recognition, pp. 9729–9738 (2020)
11. He, K., Zhang, X., Ren, S., Sun, J.: Deep residual learning for image recognition. In: Proceedings of the IEEE Conference on Computer Vision and Pattern Recognition, pp. 770–778 (2016)
12. Hoffman, J., et al.: CyCADA: cycle-consistent adversarial domain adaptation. In: International Conference on Machine Learning, pp. 1989–1998. PMLR (2018)
13. Hoffman, J., Wang, D., Yu, F., Darrell, T.: FCNs in the wild: pixel-level adversarial and constraint-based adaptation. arXiv preprint arXiv:1612.02649 (2016)
14. Huang, G., Liu, Z., Van Der Maaten, L., Weinberger, K.Q.: Densely connected convolutional networks. In: Proceedings of the IEEE Conference on Computer Vision and Pattern Recognition, pp. 4700–4708 (2017)
15. Huang, J., Lu, S., Guan, D., Zhang, X.: Contextual-relation consistent domain adaptation for semantic segmentation. In: Vedaldi, A., Bischof, H., Brox, T., Frahm, J.-M. (eds.) ECCV 2020. LNCS, vol. 12360, pp. 705–722. Springer, Cham (2020). https://doi.org/10.1007/978-3-030-58555-6_42
16. Jiang, Z., Gao, P., Guo, C., Zhang, Q., Xiang, S., Pan, C.: Video object detection with locally-weighted deformable neighbors. In: Proceedings of the AAAI Conference on Artificial Intelligence (2019)
17. Jiang, Z., et al.: STC: spatio-temporal contrastive learning for video instance segmentation. arXiv preprint arXiv:2202.03747 (2022)
18. Jiang, Z., et al.: Learning where to focus for efficient video object detection. In: Vedaldi, A., Bischof, H., Brox, T., Frahm, J.-M. (eds.) ECCV 2020. LNCS, vol. 12361, pp. 18–34. Springer, Cham (2020). https://doi.org/10.1007/978-3-030-58517-4_2
19. Kim, M., Byun, H.: Learning texture invariant representation for domain adaptation of semantic segmentation. In: Proceedings of the IEEE Conference on Computer Vision and Pattern Recognition, pp. 12975–12984 (2020)
20. Lee, S., Hyun, J., Seong, H., Kim, E.: Unsupervised domain adaptation for semantic segmentation by content transfer. arXiv preprint arXiv:2012.12545 (2020)
21. Li, S., et al.: Semantic distribution-aware contrastive adaptation for semantic segmentation. arXiv preprint arXiv:2105.05013 (2021)
22. Li, Y., Yuan, L., Vasconcelos, N.: Bidirectional learning for domain adaptation of semantic segmentation. In: Proceedings of the IEEE/CVF Conference on Computer Vision and Pattern Recognition, pp. 6936–6945 (2019)
23. Liu, W., Ferstl, D., Schulter, S., Zebedin, L., Fua, P., Leistner, C.: Domain adaptation for semantic segmentation via patch-wise contrastive learning. arXiv preprint arXiv:2104.11056 (2021)
24. Long, J., Shelhamer, E., Darrell, T.: Fully convolutional networks for semantic segmentation. In: Proceedings of the IEEE Conference on Computer Vision and Pattern Recognition, pp. 3431–3440 (2015)

25. Long, M., Cao, Y., Wang, J., Jordan, M.: Learning transferable features with deep adaptation networks. In: International Conference on Machine Learning, pp. 97–105. PMLR (2015)
26. Luo, Y., Liu, P., Zheng, L., Guan, T., Yu, J., Yang, Y.: Category-level adversarial adaptation for semantic segmentation using purified features. IEEE Trans. Pattern Anal. Mach. Intell. (2021)
27. Luo, Y., Zheng, L., Guan, T., Yu, J., Yang, Y.: Taking a closer look at domain shift: category-level adversaries for semantics consistent domain adaptation. In: Proceedings of the IEEE Conference on Computer Vision and Pattern Recognition, pp. 2507–2516 (2019)
28. Lv, F., Liang, T., Chen, X., Lin, G.: Cross-domain semantic segmentation via domain-invariant interactive relation transfer. In: Proceedings of the IEEE Conference on Computer Vision and Pattern Recognition, pp. 4334–4343 (2020)
29. Marsden, R.A., Bartler, A., Döbler, M., Yang, B.: Contrastive learning and self-training for unsupervised domain adaptation in semantic segmentation. arXiv preprint arXiv:2105.02001 (2021)
30. Mei, K., Zhu, C., Zou, J., Zhang, S.: Instance adaptive self-training for unsupervised domain adaptation. In: Vedaldi, A., Bischof, H., Brox, T., Frahm, J.-M. (eds.) ECCV 2020. LNCS, vol. 12371, pp. 415–430. Springer, Cham (2020). https://doi.org/10.1007/978-3-030-58574-7_25
31. Murez, Z., Kolouri, S., Kriegman, D., Ramamoorthi, R., Kim, K.: Image to image translation for domain adaptation. In: Proceedings of the IEEE Conference on Computer Vision and Pattern Recognition, pp. 4500–4509 (2018)
32. Pan, F., Shin, I., Rameau, F., Lee, S., Kweon, I.S.: Unsupervised intra-domain adaptation for semantic segmentation through self-supervision. In: Proceedings of the IEEE Conference on Computer Vision and Pattern Recognition, pp. 3764–3773 (2020)
33. Paszke, A., et al.: PyTorch: an imperative style, high-performance deep learning library. In: Advances in Neural Information Processing Systems, pp. 8026–8037 (2019)
34. Paul, S., Tsai, Y.-H., Schulter, S., Roy-Chowdhury, A.K., Chandraker, M.: Domain adaptive semantic segmentation using weak labels. In: Vedaldi, A., Bischof, H., Brox, T., Frahm, J.-M. (eds.) ECCV 2020. LNCS, vol. 12354, pp. 571–587. Springer, Cham (2020). https://doi.org/10.1007/978-3-030-58545-7_33
35. Richter, S.R., Vineet, V., Roth, S., Koltun, V.: Playing for data: ground truth from computer games. In: Leibe, B., Matas, J., Sebe, N., Welling, M. (eds.) ECCV 2016. LNCS, vol. 9906, pp. 102–118. Springer, Cham (2016). https://doi.org/10.1007/978-3-319-46475-6_7
36. Ros, G., Sellart, L., Materzynska, J., Vazquez, D., Lopez, A.M.: The synthia dataset: a large collection of synthetic images for semantic segmentation of urban scenes. In: Proceedings of the IEEE Conference on Computer Vision and Pattern Recognition, pp. 3234–3243 (2016)
37. Saporta, A., Vu, T.H., Cord, M., Pérez, P.: ESL: entropy-guided self-supervised learning for domain adaptation in semantic segmentation. arXiv preprint arXiv:2006.08658 (2020)
38. Subhani, M.N., Ali, M.: Learning from scale-invariant examples for domain adaptation in semantic segmentation. In: Vedaldi, A., Bischof, H., Brox, T., Frahm, J.-M. (eds.) ECCV 2020. LNCS, vol. 12367, pp. 290–306. Springer, Cham (2020). https://doi.org/10.1007/978-3-030-58542-6_18

39. Tranheden, W., Olsson, V., Pinto, J., Svensson, L.: DACS: domain adaptation via cross-domain mixed sampling. In: Proceedings of the IEEE Winter Conference on Applications of Computer Vision, pp. 1379–1389 (2021)
40. Tsai, Y.H., Hung, W.C., Schulter, S., Sohn, K., Yang, M.H., Chandraker, M.: Learning to adapt structured output space for semantic segmentation. In: Proceedings of the IEEE Conference on Computer Vision and Pattern Recognition, pp. 7472–7481 (2018)
41. Tsai, Y.H., Sohn, K., Schulter, S., Chandraker, M.: Domain adaptation for structured output via discriminative patch representations. In: Proceedings of the IEEE/CVF International Conference on Computer Vision, pp. 1456–1465 (2019)
42. Vu, T.H., Jain, H., Bucher, M., Cord, M., Pérez, P.: ADVENT: adversarial entropy minimization for domain adaptation in semantic segmentation. In: Proceedings of the IEEE Conference on Computer Vision and Pattern Recognition, pp. 2517–2526 (2019)
43. Wang, H., Shen, T., Zhang, W., Duan, L.-Y., Mei, T.: Classes matter: a fine-grained adversarial approach to cross-domain semantic segmentation. In: Vedaldi, A., Bischof, H., Brox, T., Frahm, J.-M. (eds.) ECCV 2020. LNCS, vol. 12359, pp. 642–659. Springer, Cham (2020). https://doi.org/10.1007/978-3-030-58568-6_38
44. Wang, J., et al.: Deep high-resolution representation learning for visual recognition. IEEE Trans. Pattern Anal. Mach. Intell. **43**, 3349–3364 (2020)
45. Wang, Y., Peng, J., Zhang, Z.: Uncertainty-aware pseudo label refinery for domain adaptive semantic segmentation. In: Proceedings of the IEEE/CVF International Conference on Computer Vision, pp. 9092–9101 (2021)
46. Xu, Q., et al.: DIRL: domain-invariant representation learning for generalizable semantic segmentation (2022)
47. Yu, F., Zhang, M., Dong, H., Hu, S., Dong, B., Zhang, L.: DAST: unsupervised domain adaptation in semantic segmentation based on discriminator attention and self-training. In: Proceedings of the AAAI Conference on Artificial Intelligence, pp. 10754–10762 (2021)
48. Zhang, P., Zhang, B., Zhang, T., Chen, D., Wang, Y., Wen, F.: Prototypical pseudo label denoising and target structure learning for domain adaptive semantic segmentation. In: Proceedings of the IEEE Conference on Computer Vision and Pattern Recognition, pp. 12414–12424 (2021)
49. Zhao, H., Shi, J., Qi, X., Wang, X., Jia, J.: Pyramid scene parsing network. In: Proceedings of the IEEE Conference on Computer Vision and Pattern Recognition, pp. 2881–2890 (2017)
50. Zheng, Z., Yang, Y.: Rectifying pseudo label learning via uncertainty estimation for domain adaptive semantic segmentation. Int. J. Comput. Vision **129**(4), 1106–1120 (2021)
51. Zhou, B., Zhao, H., Puig, X., Fidler, S., Barriuso, A., Torralba, A.: Scene parsing through ade20k dataset. In: Proceedings of the IEEE Conference on Computer Vision and Pattern Recognition, pp. 633–641 (2017)
52. Zhou, Q., et al.: Self-adversarial disentangling for specific domain adaptation. arXiv preprint arXiv:2108.03553 (2021)
53. Zhou, Q., Zhuang, C., Lu, X., Ma, L.: Domain adaptive semantic segmentation with regional contrastive consistency regularization. arXiv preprint arXiv:2110.05170 (2021)
54. Zhou, W., Wang, Y., Chu, J., Yang, J., Bai, X., Xu, Y.: Affinity space adaptation for semantic segmentation across domains. IEEE Trans. Image Process. **30**, 2549–2561 (2020)

55. Zhu, J.Y., Park, T., Isola, P., Efros, A.A.: Unpaired image-to-image translation using cycle-consistent adversarial networks. In: Proceedings of the IEEE International Conference on Computer Vision, pp. 2223–2232 (2017)
56. Zou, Y., Yu, Z., Vijaya Kumar, B.V.K., Wang, J.: Unsupervised domain adaptation for semantic segmentation via class-balanced self-training. In: Ferrari, V., Hebert, M., Sminchisescu, C., Weiss, Y. (eds.) ECCV 2018. LNCS, vol. 11207, pp. 297–313. Springer, Cham (2018). https://doi.org/10.1007/978-3-030-01219-9_18

RBC: Rectifying the Biased Context in Continual Semantic Segmentation

Hanbin Zhao[1], Fengyu Yang[4], Xinghe Fu[1], and Xi Li[1,2,3](✉)

[1] College of Computer Science and Technology, Zhejiang University, Hangzhou, China
{zhaohanbin,xinghefu,xilizju}@zju.edu.cn
[2] Shanghai Institute for Advanced Study, Zhejiang University, Hangzhou, China
[3] Shanghai AI Laboratory, Shanghai, China
[4] University of Michigan, Ann Arbor, USA
fredyang@umich.edu

Abstract. Recent years have witnessed a great development of Convolutional Neural Networks in semantic segmentation, where all classes of training images are simultaneously available. In practice, new images are usually made available in a consecutive manner, leading to a problem called Continual Semantic Segmentation (CSS). Typically, CSS faces the forgetting problem since previous training images are unavailable, and the semantic shift problem of the background class. Considering the semantic segmentation as a context-dependent pixel-level classification task, we explore CSS from a new perspective of context analysis in this paper. We observe that the context of old-class pixels in the new images is much more biased on new classes than that in the old images, which can sharply aggravate the old-class forgetting and new-class overfitting. To tackle the obstacle, we propose a biased-context-rectified CSS framework with a context-rectified image-duplet learning scheme and a biased-context-insensitive consistency loss. Furthermore, we propose an adaptive re-weighting class-balanced learning strategy for the biased class distribution. Our approach outperforms state-of-the-art methods by a large margin in existing CSS scenarios. Code is available in https://github.com/sntc129/RBC.

Keywords: Continual semantic segmentation · Class-incremental learning · Continual learning · Biased context

1 Introduction

Semantic segmentation is a classic pixel-level classification problem in the computer vision area, where deep learning approaches have led to marvelous effect

H. Zhao and F. Yang—The first two authors contributed equally to this paper.

Supplementary Information The online version contains supplementary material available at https://doi.org/10.1007/978-3-031-19830-4_4.

S. Avidan et al. (Eds.): ECCV 2022, LNCS 13694, pp. 55–72, 2022.
https://doi.org/10.1007/978-3-031-19830-4_4

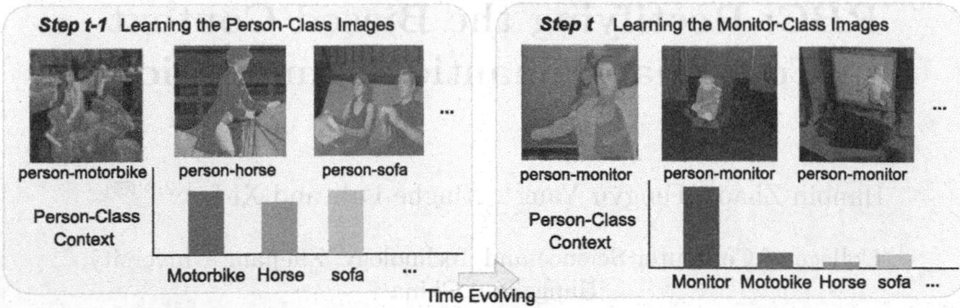

Fig. 1. Illustration of biased context correlation between the old-class and new-class pixels in the added new images. At step $t-1$, the context of *person*-class contains different types (e.g. person-horse, person-sofa) while the model learning person-class images firstly. However, the person context mainly contains person-monitor while the model learning the added *monitor*-class images at step t. Thus, a new-class-biased context for the old-class (person) pixels exists in the added new-class (monitor) images, which aggravates the old-class forgetting and new-class overfitting problem of the model.

when a large-scale pixel-wise labeled dataset is given [5,32,48,51]. However, in a more practical scenario, deep neural networks are required to learn a sequence of tasks with incremental classes and data which is known as the continual learning setup. Semantic segmentation under the setting of continual learning is referred as Continual Semantic Segmentation (CSS) [3,14,39]. The study of CSS aims at alleviating the forgetting of the network on past tasks and the overfitting on the current task without past data available.

Currently, there are two main challenges in the study of CSS problem. The first challenge is the catastrophic forgetting phenomenon in continual learning [36]. In CSS, the images for past tasks are usually unavailable while the model learning the current task, and only the pixels belonging to new semantic classes are labeled. The model tends to forget the ability to distinguish pixels belonging to old classes due to the shortage of labeled old-class data in the training stage. The second challenge is CSS-specific and called semantic shift of background class [3]. In the current task of CSS, only new-class pixels are labeled as a semantic class and other pixels including old-class pixels are labeled as background class. This semantic shift of pixel-wise labels causes the ambiguous meaning of old-class pixels during the continual learning process and brings an obstacle to the correct model prediction. Since the semantic segmentation is usually considered as a context-dependent pixel-level classification task [10], we explore CSS from the perspective of context. As shown in Fig. 1, we find out there is another CSS-specific challenge that has not drawn attention. The context of old-class pixels in the new images is much more biased on new classes than that in the old images, which can cause the sharp aggravation of old-class forgetting and new-class overfitting. We call this challenge "biased context" in CSS.

In the literature, a number of pseudo-labeling-based CSS methods [14,47] attempt to solve the first two main challenges by labeling the mislabeled pixels of old classes with the model obtained from the last learning step (as shown

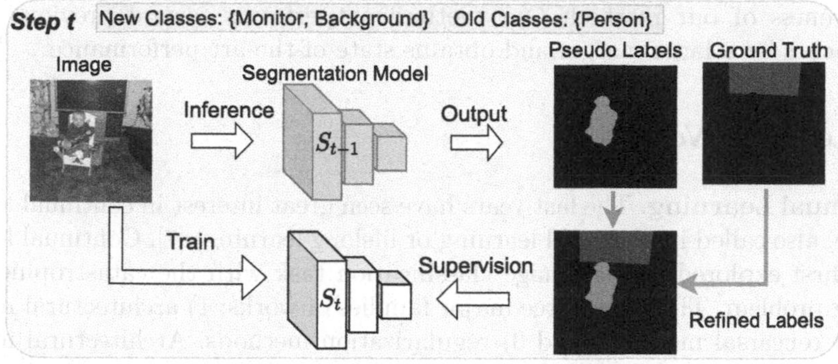

Fig. 2. Pseudo-labeling-based CSS methods. At step t, only the new-class (*monitor*) pixels in the added images are labeled and other pixels are all "background class" pixels. With the old model S_{t-1} from the last step, the mislabeled old-class pixels (*person*) can be pseudo-labeled, and then the model S_t is updated with the old-class pseudo labels and new-class ground truth labels.

in Fig. 2). However, the incrementally updated segmentation model still suffers from the biased prediction towards new classes on account of the following two observations: 1) the new images contain the new-class-biased context for the old-class pixels, and 2) the number of new-class pixels included in the new task is much larger than that of old-class pixels, which is commonly termed as an imbalanced class distribution problem.

Motivated by the observations above, we try to address the CSS from the following two aspects: 1) building a biased-context-rectified CSS learning scheme that is less sensitive to the biased context information of old-class pixels in the incremental images, and 2) developing a class-balance CSS learning strategy for the imbalanced class distribution at different learning steps. We propose a biased-context-insensitive consistency loss, which resorts to a consistency constraint on the context of old classes in an image pair. The duplet of images, consisting of the original image (containing the new-class pixels) and the corresponding erased image (erasing the new-class pixels in the original image), rectify the context of old classes with respect to new classes. Furthermore, we propose an adaptive class-balance CSS learning strategy to cope with the biased class distribution, which adaptively assigns higher weights to the old-class pixels.

Overall, the main contributions of this paper are three-fold: (1) We first consider the biased context in the CSS scenario and propose a biased-context-rectified CSS framework, which aims to avoid overfitting on new classes while not forgetting old classes. (2) We design a novel context-rectified image-duplet learning scheme and a biased-context-insensitive consistency loss that ingeniously rectifies the context of old classes with respect to new classes. To cope with the imbalanced class distribution, we propose an adaptive re-weighting class-balanced learning strategy for CSS. (3) Extensive experiments demonstrate the effectiveness of our method. Our method outperforms several previous CSS approaches by a large margin and obtains state-of-the-art performance.

2 Related Work

Continual Learning. The last years have seen great interest in continual learning (i.e. also called incremental learning or lifelong learning) [7]. Continual learning is first explored on the image classification task with the catastrophic forgetting problem. These are three major families of works: 1) architectural methods, 2) rehearsal methods, and 3) regularization methods. Architectural methods [1,2,29,33,34,54] adjust the network architecture to maintain the learned knowledge from old tasks and acquire new information from the current task. Rehearsal methods [19,31,41,46,53] replay the knowledge of old tasks when learning the new task, and the old knowledge is memorized by storing previous tasks' exemplars or the distribution of old tasks data via generative models. Regularization methods [9,13,30] alleviate forgetting by regularization loss terms enabling the updated parameters of networks to retain past knowledge. Continual learning is usually conducted under two scenarios (task-incremental or the class-incremental learning). The latter is more challenging because the task identity is unavailable at inference time. Recently, continual learning has been also explored on several other computer vision tasks, *e.g.*, incremental object detection [25], incremental video classification [52], incremental instance segmentation [17], continual semantic segmentation [3,14,16,20,27,35,37,43,47,49,56], incremental domain adaptation [11,12,28]. Our work focuses on the CSS problem which can be considered as the class-incremental learning scenario on semantic segmentation. Exploring the imbalanced class distribution problem is important for continual learning (e.g., the methods [19,46] are proposed to address the problem in classic class-incremental image classification scenario) and our work utilizes an adaptive re-weighting class-balanced learning strategy to alleviate this problem in CSS scenario.

Continual Semantic Segmentation. The forgetting problem in CSS is first considered in ILT [37] and the more challenging CSS-tailored problem (background shift) is proposed in MiB [3]. To cope with the problems, some regularization based CSS methods [14,38] utilizes a confidence-based pseudo-labeling method and a feature-based multi-scale pooling distillation scheme or employs a prototype consistency constraint at the latent space, and some replay-based CSS methods [35] utilize an extra memory to replay the data for old classes by an extra generative adversarial network or web crawling process. Semantic segmentation is a pixel-wise classification problem [6,22,24,32,40,42,44,48] and classifying a local pixel with context information is helpful for reducing the local ambiguities [21,23,45,51,55]. Our work first analyzes the effect of biased context in CSS, and we design several biased-context-rectified continual learning strategies tailored for CSS problem.

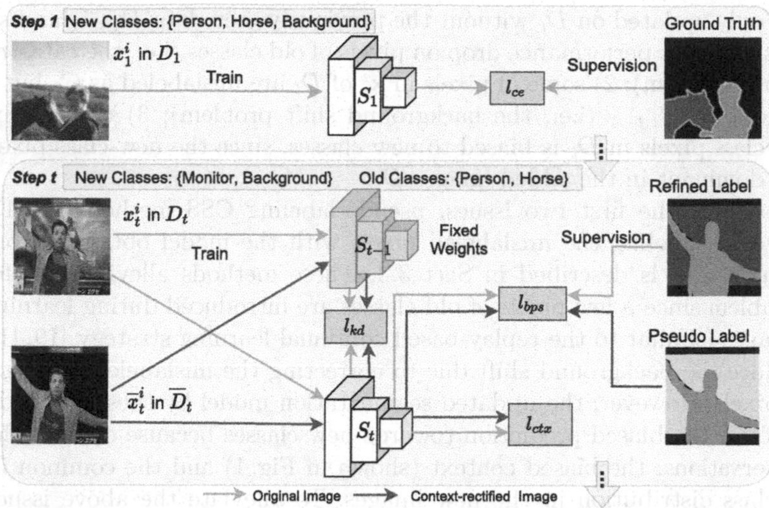

Fig. 3. Illustration of our biased-context-rectified CSS framework. At step 1, the semantic segmentation model is trained from scratch via the classic cross-entropy loss l_{ce} on D_1. At the latter steps (e.g. step t), we first obtain the context-rectified image-duplet $(D_t, \overline{D}_t)$ and update the model by our context-rectified image-duplet learning scheme with the balanced pseudo-labeling loss l_{bps} and the distillation loss l_{kd} and our biased-context-insensitive consistency loss l_{ctx}.

3 Method

3.1 CSS Problem Formulation

In a continual semantic segmentation scenario, a segmentation model learns several image segmentation tasks continually, and the image subset in each learning step contains pixels from one or several new classes [3,14,39]. We suppose the training image set for the t-th learning step is D_t that consists of a set of pairs $(\mathbf{x}_t^i, \mathbf{y}_t^i)$, where $\mathbf{x}_t^i \in \mathbb{R}^{H\times W\times 3}$ and $\mathbf{y}_t^i \in \tilde{\mathcal{Y}}_t^{H\times W}$ denote the i-th input image of size $W\times H$ and the corresponding ground truth segmentation mask, respectively. New categories C_t are introduced and required to be learnt at the t-th step. $\mathbf{y}_t^i$ only contains the labels of C_t and all other labels (e.g., old classes $C_{1:t-1}$) are collapsed into the background class C_0.

We assume a typical semantic segmentation model S with parameters Θ, which consists of an encoder-decoder backbone network F extracting a dense feature map and a convolution head G producing the segmentation score map. Classically, we utilize $S(\mathbf{x}) = G \cdot F(\mathbf{x})$ to represent the output predicted segmentation mask of $\mathbf{x}$, $S^{w,h,c}(\mathbf{x})$ denotes the prediction score (about the class c) of the pixel at the location (w, h) of $\mathbf{x}$, and $\hat{S}(\mathbf{x}) = \text{Softmax}(S(\mathbf{x}))$ denotes the output of the network. Then, S_t with parameters Θ_t is updated on D_t at the t-th step. Our goal is to obtain S_t which performs well on both previously seen classes $C_{1:t-1}$ and the current classes C_t. CSS task is faced with three dilemmas:

1) S_t is only updated on D_t without the previously seen data $D_{1:t-1}$ and suffers from a significant performance drop on pixels of old classes (i.e., the catastrophic forgetting problem); 2) some of pixels in $\mathbf{x}_t^i$ of D_t are mislabeled as C_0 but actually belong to $C_{1:t-1}$ (i.e., the background shift problem); 3) the context for the old-class pixels in D_t is biased to new classes, since the new-class pixels are usually dominant in the added images D_t.

To address the first two issues, pseudo-labeling CSS methods [14,47] are proposed by labeling the mislabeled pixels with the model obtained from the last step, which is described in Sect. 3.2. These methods alleviate the forgetting problem since a few pixels of old classes are introduced during learning the new images (similar to the replay-based continual learning strategy [19,41,46]), and reduce the background shift due to correcting the mislabeled "background class" pixels. However, the updated segmentation model by these methods still suffers from the biased prediction towards new classes because of the following two observations: the biased context (shown in Fig. 1) and the common imbalanced class distribution in the new images. To alleviate the above issues, we propose a biased-context-rectified CSS framework including a context-rectified image-duplet learning scheme and a biased-context-insensitive consistency loss in Sect. 3.3 and the illustration of our framework is shown in Fig. 3 and propose an adaptive class-balance strategy for tackle the biased class distribution in Sect. 3.4.

3.2 Pseudo-labeling-Based CSS

To alleviate the forgetting and background shift problems, pseudo-labeling-based methods [14,47] are utilized in CSS. Specifically, at the t-th learning step, we can access to S_{t-1} from the last step and correct the mislabeled "background class" pixels with S_{t-1} (as shown in Fig. 2). For each $(\mathbf{x}_t^i, \mathbf{y}_t^i)$ in D_t, the pixels belonging to the new classes C_t have ground-truth labels and some of the other pixels belonging to the old classes $C_{1:t-1}$ are mislabeled as C_0. The predictions of the old model for these mislabeled pixels $\hat{S}_{t-1}(\mathbf{x}_t^i)$ are utilized as clues if they belong to any of the old classes. After that, each $\mathbf{x}_t^i$ in D_t can have a refined segmentation label $\tilde{S}_t(\mathbf{x}_t^i)$ by combining the pseudo label $\hat{S}_{t-1}(\mathbf{x}_t^i)$ and the ground truth $\mathbf{y}_t^i$ (as shown in Fig. 2). Then the model S_t is updated by optimizing the following objective function:

$$\mathcal{L}_{total}(\Theta_t) = \frac{1}{|D_t|} \sum_{(\mathbf{x},\mathbf{y}) \in D_t} l(\mathbf{x}; \Theta_t), \tag{1}$$

where $l(\mathbf{x}; \Theta_t)$ is usually composed of a cross-entropy loss term with pseudo-labeling and a knowledge distillation term:

$$l(\mathbf{x}; \Theta_t) = l_{ps}(\mathbf{x}; \Theta_t) + \alpha l_{kd}(\mathbf{x}; \Theta_t), \tag{2}$$

where α is a hyper-parameter balancing the importance of the loss terms. $l_{ps}(\mathbf{x}; \Theta_t)$ is utilized to maintain the performance on old classes and reduce the ambiguity of old-class pixels labeled as background class at step t:

$$l_{ps}(\mathbf{x};\Theta_t) = -\frac{\beta}{WH}\sum_{w,h}^{W,H}\sum_{c\in C_{0:t}} \tilde{S}_t^{w,h,c}(\mathbf{x})\log\hat{S}_t^{w,h,c}(\mathbf{x}), \tag{3}$$

where β is the ratio of accepted old classes pixels over the total number of such pixels. $l_{kd}(\mathbf{x};\Theta_t)$ is added to the backbone network $F(\cdot)$ to retain information of the old classes:

$$l_{kd}(\mathbf{x};\Theta_t) = \|\Phi(F_t(\mathbf{x}))) - \Phi(F_{t-1}(\mathbf{x})))\|^2, \tag{4}$$

where $\|\cdot\|$ and $\Phi(F(\mathbf{x})) \in \mathbb{R}^{(H+W)\times C}$ denotes the Euclidean distance and concatenation operation, respectively. The concatenation operation function $\Phi(F(\mathbf{x}))$ is formulated as follows:

$$\Phi(F(\mathbf{x})) = \left[\frac{1}{W}\sum_{w=1}^{W} F^{:,w,:}(\mathbf{x}) \Big\| \frac{1}{H}\sum_{h=1}^{H} F^{h,:,:}(\mathbf{x})\right], \tag{5}$$

where $[\cdot\|\cdot]$ denotes concatenation over the channel axis.

3.3 Biased-Context-Rectified Framework

To alleviate the biased context correlation between the old-class and new-class pixels in CSS, we propose a biased-context-rectified framework with a context-rectified image-duplet learning scheme and a biased-context-insensitive consistency loss. Taking the t-th step as an example (shown in Fig. 1), the incrementally added images D_t mainly contain the new-class-related context for the old-class pixels, which leads to the aggravation of the old-class forgetting and new-class overfitting problems.

Context-Rectified Image-Duplet Learning. As for the new-class-related context, we observe that the contextual information of old-class pixels included in the incremental images is biased to the pixels of new classes (shown in Fig. 1). In order to continually learn a semantic segmentation model that is less sensitive to the entangled new-class-context, we firstly rectify the biased context between new classes and old classes in these new images by erasing the new-class pixels of the original image (shown in Fig. 4(a)). At the t-th step, we obtain the corresponding erased image $\overline{\mathbf{x}}_t^i$ for each new image $\mathbf{x}_t^i$ in D_t. Then an image-duplet $(\mathbf{x}_t^i, \mathbf{y}_t^i, \overline{\mathbf{x}}_t^i, \overline{\mathbf{y}}_t^i)$ is constructed from the erased image and the corresponding original image. The set of image-duplets with D_t and $\overline{D}_t$ are denoted as:

$$\begin{aligned}(D_t, \overline{D}_t) &= \left\{(\mathbf{x}_t^i, \mathbf{y}_t^i, \overline{\mathbf{x}}_t^i, \overline{\mathbf{y}}_t^i)\right\}_{i=1}^{|D_t|} \\ s.t.\ (\mathbf{x}_t^i, \mathbf{y}_t^i) &\in D_t, (\overline{\mathbf{x}}_t^i, \overline{\mathbf{y}}_t^i) \in \overline{D}_t,\end{aligned} \tag{6}$$

With the image-duplets $(D_t, \overline{D}_t)$ at the t-th step, our method updates the model S_t by optimizing the following loss function:

$$\mathcal{L}_{total}(\Theta_t) = \frac{1}{|D_t|+|\overline{D}_t|}\sum_{(\mathbf{x},\overline{\mathbf{x}})}[l_{dup}(\mathbf{x},\overline{\mathbf{x}};\Theta_t) + \gamma l_{ctx}(\mathbf{x},\overline{\mathbf{x}};\Theta_t)], \tag{7}$$

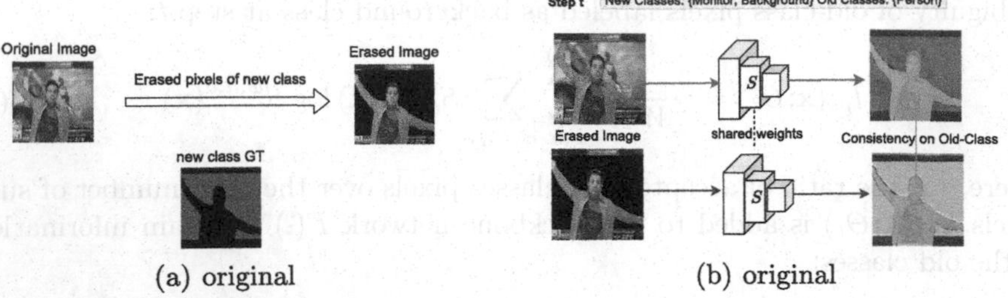

(a) original (b) original

Fig. 4. The illustration of (a): generating the context-rectified image-duplet, (b): a biased-context-insensitive consistency loss.

where γ is a hyper-parameter balancing the importance of the loss terms. The first loss term $l_{dup}(\mathbf{x}, \overline{\mathbf{x}}; \Theta_t)$ takes the similar form of Equation (2) on the original image $\mathbf{x}$ and the corresponding erased image $\overline{\mathbf{x}}$:

$$l_{dup}(\mathbf{x}, \overline{\mathbf{x}}; \Theta_t) = l(\mathbf{x}; \Theta_t) + l(\overline{\mathbf{x}}; \Theta_t), \tag{8}$$

Biased-Context-Insensitive Consistency Loss. To further address the biased context, the second loss term $l_{ctx}(\mathbf{x}, \overline{\mathbf{x}}; \Theta_t)$ is introduced and utilized to keep a biased-context-insensitive consistency between the original image $\mathbf{x}$ and the corresponding erased image $\overline{\mathbf{x}}$ (as shown in Fig. 4(b)). For the old-class pixels, the new-class-related context are included in the original image $\mathbf{x}$ and erased in the corresponding erased image $\overline{\mathbf{x}}$. For simplicity, we utilize $O(\mathbf{x})$ to represent the locations $\{(w_o^j, h_o^j)\}_{j=1}^{O(\mathbf{x})}$ of old-class pixels included in the image $\mathbf{x}$. To reduce the effect of biased context between the old-class and new-class, the prediction of the updated model S_t on the old-class pixels with the new-class-related context should be consistent with that without the new-class-related context. Then $l_{ctx}(\mathbf{x}, \overline{\mathbf{x}}; \Theta_t)$ is formulated as follows:

$$l_{ctx}(\mathbf{x}, \overline{\mathbf{x}}; \Theta_t) = \sum_{(w,h) \in O(\mathbf{x})} \sum_{c \in C_{1:t-1}} \left\| S_t^{w,h,c}(\overline{\mathbf{x}}) - S_t^{w,h,c}(\mathbf{x}) \right\|^2, \tag{9}$$

3.4 Adaptive Class-Balance CSS

As for the imbalanced class distribution problem, we observe that the number of new-class pixels included in the new images is much larger than that of pseudo-labeled old-class pixels. This class-imbalance problem usually results in the updated classifier being biased towards the new classes. To cope with the problem, we propose to adaptively assign different weights to the pixels of different classes based on the number of pixels. We optimize the biased classifier by a balanced pseudo-labeling cross-entropy loss $l_{bps}(\mathbf{x}; \Theta_t)$ with different weights.

To address the class-imbalance problem in CSS, the balanced pseudo-labeling cross-entropy loss is formulated as follows:

$$l_{bps}(\mathbf{x};\Theta_t) = -\frac{\beta}{WH}\sum_{w,h}^{W,H}\sum_{c\in C_{0:t}} \eta^{w,h}(\mathbf{x})\tilde{S}_t^{w,h,c}(\mathbf{x})\log \hat{S}_t^{w,h,c}(\mathbf{x}), \tag{10}$$

where $\eta^{w,h}(\mathbf{x})$ denotes the weight of the pixel at the location (w,h) in the image $\mathbf{x}$. $\eta^{w,h}(\mathbf{x})$ depends on the category of the pixel and the number of pixels from different classes in the image:

$$\eta^{w,h}(\mathbf{x}) = \begin{cases} 0.5 + \sigma(\frac{N^{old}(\mathbf{x})}{N^{new}(\mathbf{x})}) & (w,h)\in O(\mathbf{x}) \\ 1 & \text{otherwise,} \end{cases} \tag{11}$$

where $N^{old}(\mathbf{x})$, $N^{new}(\mathbf{x})$ and $\sigma(\cdot)$ are the number of pixels belonging to old classes $C_{1:t-1}$, the total number of pixels belonging to the new classes C_t and the sigmoid function respectively. Then $l_{dup}(\mathbf{x},\overline{\mathbf{x}};\Theta_t)$ in Eq. (8) with the balanced pseudo-labeling is formulated as follows:

$$l_{dup}(\mathbf{x},\overline{\mathbf{x}};\Theta_t) = l^{'}(\mathbf{x};\Theta_t) + l(\overline{\mathbf{x}};\Theta_t), \tag{12}$$

where $l^{'}(\mathbf{x};\Theta_t)$ is denoted as follows:

$$l^{'}(\mathbf{x};\Theta_t) = l_{bps}(\mathbf{x};\Theta_t) + \alpha l_{kd}(\mathbf{x};\Theta_t), \tag{13}$$

4 Experiments

4.1 Datasets

We follow previous CSS works [3,14,35] and utilize the commonly used semantic segmentation datasets PASCAL VOC 2012 [15] and ADE20k [57] for experiments: VOC contains 10,582 fully-annotated images for training and 1,449 for testing, over 20 foreground object classes. ADE20k is a large-scale dataset that has 20,210 training images and 2,000 testing images in 150 classes. For all datasets, we resize the images to 512×512, with a center crop and employ the random horizontal flip augmentation strategy as the practice in PLOP [14] at training time.

4.2 Experimental Setup

Continual Semantic Segmentation Setting: MiB [3] introduces two different CSS settings (*Disjoint* and *Overlapped*). In the *Disjoint* setting, the incremental new images D_t at t-th step contain pixels belonging to old and current new classes $(C_{1:t-1} \cup C_t)$, each training step contains a unique set of images, whose pixels belong to classes seen either in the current or in the previous learning steps. In the *Overlapped* setting, the new images contains the pixels belonging to old, current new and future classes $(C_{1:t-1} \cup C_t \cup C_{t+1:T})$, each step contains

Table 1. CSS results under the *Disjoint* setting on VOC-19-1, VOC-15-5 and VOC-15-1 benchmarks. † means the results from [14,38]. Best in **bold**.

Method	19-1 (2 steps)			15-5 (2 steps)			15-1 (6 steps)		
	0–19	20	*All*	0–15	16–20	*All*	0–15	16–20	*All*
FT	5.80	12.30	6.20	1.10	33.60	9.20	0.20	1.80	0.60
PI† [50]	5.40	14.10	5.90	1.30	34.10	9.50	0.00	1.80	0.40
EWC† [26]	23.20	16.00	22.90	26.70	37.70	29.40	0.30	4.30	1.30
RW† [4]	19.40	15.70	19.20	17.90	36.90	22.70	0.80	3.60	1.30
LwF† [30]	53.00	9.10	50.80	58.40	37.40	53.10	0.80	3.60	1.50
LwF-MC† [41]	63.00	13.20	60.50	67.20	41.20	60.70	4.50	7.00	5.20
ILT† [37]	69.10	16.40	66.40	63.20	39.50	57.30	3.70	5.70	4.20
MiB† [3]	69.60	25.60	67.40	71.80	43.30	64.70	46.20	12.90	37.90
SDR† [38]	69.90	37.30	68.40	73.50	47.30	67.20	59.20	12.90	48.10
PLOP† [14]	75.37	38.89	73.64	71.00	42.82	64.29	57.86	13.67	46.48
Ours	**76.43**	**45.79**	**75.01**	**75.12**	**49.71**	**69.89**	**61.68**	**19.52**	**51.60**
Joint	77.40	78.00	77.40	79.10	72.56	77.39	79.10	72.56	77.39

all the images that have at least one pixel of a novel class, with only the latter annotated. The *Overlapped* setting is usually more challenging than the *Disjoint* setting.

Evaluation Protocol: We evaluate our method under these two CSS settings on the commonly used CSS benchmarks (VOC-19-1, VOC-15-5, VOC-15-1, ADE-100-50, ADE-50-50 and ADE-100-10), where 19-1 means learning 19 then 1 class (2 learning steps), 15-5 learning 15 then 5 classes (2 steps) and 15-1 learning 15 classes followed by five times 1 class (6 steps). The benchmarks on ADE20k are 100-50 (2 steps), 50–50 (3 steps) and 100-10 (6 steps). The benchmark with higher number of steps is usually more challenging. Each method is trained on the CSS benchmark in several steps. At the last step, we follow [14,38] and report the traditional mean Intersection over Union (mIoU) for the initial classes C_1, for the incremented classes $C_{2:T}$, for all classes $C_{1:T}$ (*all*).

Training Details: We implement our models with Pytorch and use SGD for optimization. Following [3,14], we use the Deeplab-V3 [5] architecture with a ResNet-101 [18] pre-trained on ImageNet [8] as the backbone network. As for our proposed context-rectified image-duplet learning scheme, we train our model with a batch size of 24 on both Pascal VOC and ADE20k datasets. At the first CSS step, all the images are the original images since no old model is kept for pseudo-labeling and the learning rate is set to 0.01 on both VOC and ADE20k CSS benchmarks. At other CSS steps, the sample duplets are generated by the old model from the last step (half of the images in each batch are the original images and half of them are the corresponding new-class-erased images). The learning rate on VOC/ADE20k is set to 0.001/0.005. The loss weight γ of the biased-context-insensitive consistency loss term in Equation (7) is set to 0.01 for all datasets. More experimental results are included in the supplementary materials.

Table 2. CSS results under the *Overlapped* setting on VOC-19-1, VOC-15-5 and VOC-15-1 benchmarks. † means the results from [14,38]. Best in **bold**.

Method	19-1 (2 steps)			15-5 (2 steps)			15-1 (6 steps)		
	0–19	20	*All*	0–15	16–20	*All*	0–15	16–20	*All*
FT	6.80	12.90	7.10	2.10	33.10	9.80	0.20	1.80	0.60
PI† [50]	7.50	14.00	7.80	1.60	33.30	9.50	0.00	1.80	0.50
EWC† [26]	26.90	14.00	26.30	24.30	35.50	27.10	0.30	4.30	1.30
RW† [4]	23.30	14.20	22.90	16.60	34.90	21.20	0.00	5.20	1.30
LwF† [30]	51.20	8.50	49.10	58.90	36.60	53.30	1.00	3.90	1.80
LwF-MC† [41]	64.40	13.30	61.90	58.10	35.00	52.30	6.4	8.40	6.90
ILT† [37]	67.75	10.88	65.05	67.08	39.23	60.45	8.75	7.99	8.56
MiB† [3]	71.43	23.59	69.15	76.37	49.97	70.08	34.22	13.50	29.29
SDR† [38]	69.10	32.60	67.40	75.40	52.60	69.90	44.70	21.80	39.20
PLOP† [14]	75.35	37.35	73.54	75.73	51.71	70.09	65.12	21.11	54.64
Ours	**77.26**	**55.60**	**76.23**	**76.59**	**52.78**	**70.92**	**69.54**	**38.44**	**62.14**
Joint	77.40	78.00	77.40	79.10	72.56	77.39	79.10	72.56	77.39

4.3 Comparison to State-of-the-Art Methods

In this section, we evaluate the CSS performance of our proposed method on Pascal VOC and ADE20k datasets, against existing state-of-the-art methods, including PI [50], EWC [26], RW [4], LwF [30], LwF-MC [41], ILT [37], MiB [3], SDR [38] and PLOP [14]. In the tables, we also provide the results of the other two methods: the simple fine-tuning approach which trains the model on the new images with no additional constraints (denoted by "FT"), and training the model on all classes off-line (denoted by "Joint"). The former can be regarded as a lower limit and the latter as an upper limit.

Results on Pascal VOC. Table 1 and Table 2 summarizes the experimental results for the *Disjoint* and *Overlapped* settings of three VOC benchmarks respectively. Under the *Disjoint* setting, it is observed that the performance of our method consistently surpasses the other methods at the last learning step on each evaluated benchmark. On VOC-19-1, we can see that the mIOU of our method on new classes (20) is 6.90% higher than that of PLOP. On the VOC-15-1 with a large number of learning steps, our method consistently performs better than other methods. All of these results indicate the effectiveness of our method to catastrophic forgetting of past classes and overfitting on the current classes. Under the *Overlapped* setting, we can see that the performance of our method consistently outperforms that of other methods by a sizable margin on all evaluated VOC benchmarks (i.e., 19-1, 15-5 and 15-1). On VOC-19-1, the forgetting of old classes (1–19) is reduced by 1.91% while performance on new classes is greatly improved by 18.25%. On the most challenging benchmark VOC-15-1, it is worth noting that the performance of our method on all the seen classes outperforms its closest contender PLOP [14] by around 7.50%. All of these results

Table 3. CSS results under the *Overlapped* setting on ADE-100-50, ADE50-50 and ADE-100-10 benchmarks. $*$ means the results from re-production.

Method	100-50 (2 steps)			50-50 (3 steps)			100-10 (6 steps)		
	0–100	101–150	*All*	0–50	51–150	*All*	0–100	101–150	*All*
FT	0.00	22.50	7.50	13.90	12.00	12.60	0.00	2.50	9.20
ILT† [37]	18.29	14.40	17.00	3.53	12.85	9.70	0.11	3.06	1.09
MiB† [3]	40.52	17.17	32.79	45.57	21.01	29.31	38.21	11.12	29.24
PLOP* [14]	41.66	15.42	32.97	47.75	21.60	30.43	**39.42**	13.63	30.88
Ours	**42.90**	**21.49**	**35.81**	**49.59**	**26.32**	**34.18**	39.01	**21.67**	**33.27**
Joint	43.90	27.20	38.30	50.90	32.10	38.30	43.90	27.20	38.30

Table 4. Ablation experimental results on VOC-*Overlapped*-15-1.

Ablation	Method	15-1 (6 steps)		
		0–15	16–20	*All*
Ablation I	Baseline	65.12	21.11	54.64
	Baseline+double	60.23	11.95	48.73
	Baseline+duplet	**70.54**	**31.06**	**61.14**
Ablation II	Baseline+duplet	**70.54**	31.06	61.14
	Baseline+duplet+ctx	69.54	**38.44**	**62.14**
Ablation III	Baseline	65.12	21.11	54.64
	Baseline+balance	**65.35**	**24.89**	**55.72**

indicate the effectiveness of our method to catastrophic forgetting of past classes and overfitting on the current classes.

Results on ADE20k. We have also evaluated our method under the *Overlapped* setting of ADE-100-50, ADE-50-50 and ADE-100-10 benchmarks and the results are shown in Table 3. This dataset is very hard because the mIoU of the joint model is only 38.30%. On these ADE CSS benchmarks, our method improves the mIoU on new classes by a sizable margin (more than 4.5%) and shows comparable performance on previous classes with its closest contender PLOP. The overview on the performance of new classes reveals that our approach is greatly helpful to avoid the overfitting on new classes while maintaining the performance on previous classes.

4.4 Ablation Study

In this section, we first carry out ablation experiments to validate the effectiveness of the context-rectified image-duplet. Then we conduct experiments to validate our biased-context-insensitive consistency loss and adaptive class-balance strategy. All of the ablation experiments are conducted on the challenging *Overlapped* setting of the benchmark VOC-15-1.

Baseline. Our main baseline is given based on a classical pseudo-labeling-based CSS method PLOP [14], which utilizes a multi-scale pooling distillation scheme

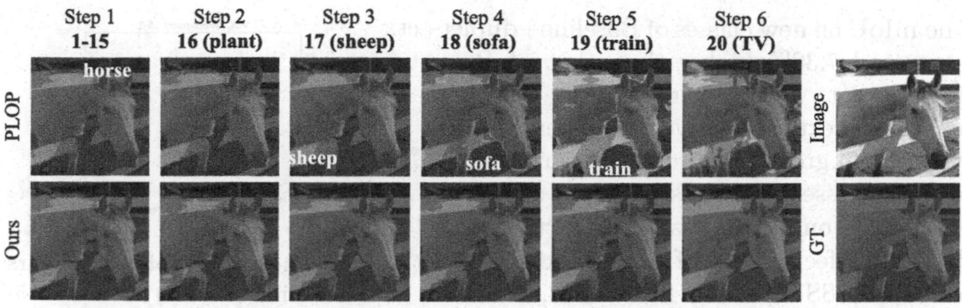

Fig. 5. Visualization of PLOP and our method at different steps under the *Overlapped* setting of VOC-15-1.

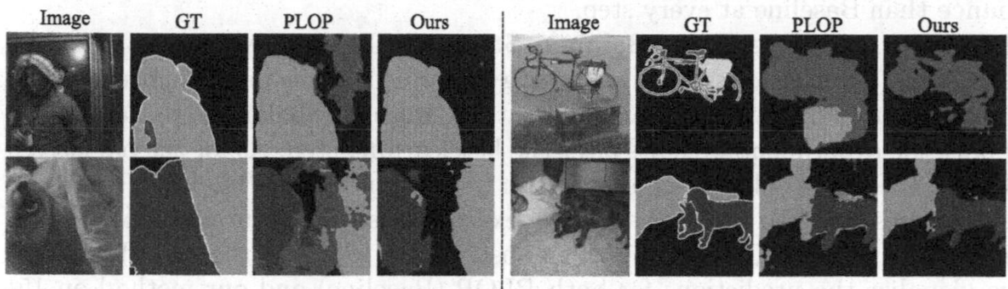

Fig. 6. The predictions of PLOP and our method for different images at the last step under the *Overlapped* setting of VOC-15-1.

to preserve the performance on previously seen classes and an entropy-based pseudo-labeling strategy on the mislabeled background class pixels to reduce the background shift.

Effect of the Context-Rectified Image-Duplet. In order to demonstrate the effectiveness of the context-rectified image-duplet, we compare the performance of "Baseline" with our image-duplet including the original image and the corresponding new-class-erased image (denoted by "Baseline+duplet"). The results are shown in Table 4. We can see that the performance of Baseline+duplet surpasses that of Baseline. In particular, the mIoU on new classes of Baseline+duplet outperforms that of Baseline by a large margin (9.95%). Moreover, we also compare Baseline+duplet with Baseline+double to reduce the influence of increasing the number of samples. In a minibatch, Baseline+duplet utilizes the original images and the corresponding erased images. Baseline+double utilizes the original images and the corresponding copied original images. As shown in Table 4, the performance of Baseline+duplet is higher than Baseline+double, which demonstrates that directly increasing the number of images can not lead to performance improvement.

Effect of Biased-Context-Insensitive Consistency Constraint. We evaluate the performance of "Baseline+duplet" with our biased-context-insensitive consistency loss (denoted by "Baseline+duplet+ctx") and Table 4 summarizes the experimental results on the *Overlapped* setting of the benchmark VOC-15-1.

The mIoU on new classes of Baseline+duplet+ctx is around 7.38% higher than that of Baseline+duplet, which demonstrates that the biased-context-insensitive consistency constraint can greatly improve the performance on new classes and is essential to avoid the overfitting on new classes. To further validate the effectiveness of our biased-context-rectified CSS learning framework, we also compare our method with Baseline and show the average mIoU curves in Fig. 7. It is observed that Ours achieves better performance than Baseline at every step.

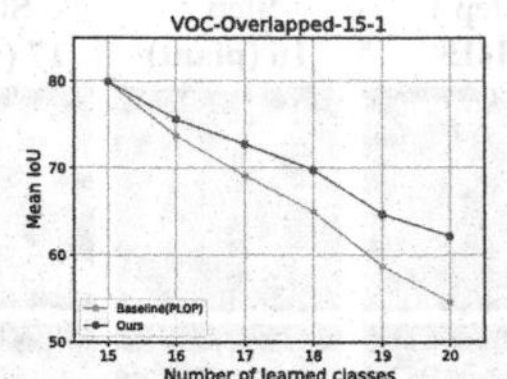

Fig. 7. The mIoU evolution of ours and Baseline (PLOP) on VOC-15-1.

Effect of Adaptive Class-Balance Strategy. To demonstrate the effectiveness of our adaptive class-balance strategy, we evaluate the performance of Baseline with our adaptive class-balance strategy (Baseline+balance). In Table 4, we report the experimental results after the last learning step. As for the old classes (0–15), Baseline+balance achieves better performance than Baseline. Regarding new classes (16–20), Baseline+balance exceeds Baseline by around 4%.

Effect of Biased Context. To demonstrate the effect of the biased context, we visualize the predictions for both PLOP (Baseline) and our method on 15-1 protocol of the benchmark VOC-*Overlapped*. As shown in Fig. 5, PLOP is more prone to overfitting on new classes (sheep, sofa, train, TV) than ours at the latter steps. Besides, we visualize the predictions of ours and PLOP for different samples at the last step in Fig. 6. Ours achieve less forgetting on old classes (person, dog, bicycle) than PLOP, illustrating that the biased context aggravates the old-class forgetting and new-class overfitting.

5 Conclusion

In this paper, we first consider the biased context problem in CSS and design a novel biased-context-rectified CSS framework for it. Firstly, our method utilizes a context-rectified image-duplet learning scheme and a biased-context-insensitive consistency loss to rectify the biased context correlation between the old-class pixels and new-class pixels, which effectively alleviates the old-class forgetting and new-class overfitting. Secondly, we propose an adaptive re-weighting class-balanced learning strategy to cope with the dynamiclly changing imbalanced class distribution in CSS. Lastly, we perform intensive evaluations of our method and other CSS methods, showing the effectiveness of our method.

Acknowledgments. This work is supported in part by National Key Research and Development Program of China under Grant 2020AAA0107400, Zhejiang Provincial Natural Science Foundation of China under Grant LR19F020004, National Natural Science Foundation of China under Grant U20A20222.

References

1. Abati, D., Tomczak, J., Blankevoort, T., Calderara, S., Cucchiara, R., Bejnordi, B.E.: Conditional channel gated networks for task-aware continual learning. In: Proceedings of the IEEE/CVF Conference on Computer Vision and Pattern Recognition, pp. 3931–3940 (2020)
2. Aljundi, R., Chakravarty, P., Tuytelaars, T.: Expert gate: lifelong learning with a network of experts. In: Proceedings of the IEEE Conference on Computer Vision and Pattern Recognition, pp. 3366–3375 (2017)
3. Cermelli, F., Mancini, M., Bulo, S.R., Ricci, E., Caputo, B.: Modeling the background for incremental learning in semantic segmentation. In: Proceedings of the IEEE/CVF Conference on Computer Vision and Pattern Recognition, pp. 9233–9242 (2020)
4. Chaudhry, A., Dokania, P.K., Ajanthan, T., Torr, P.H.S.: Riemannian walk for incremental learning: understanding forgetting and intransigence. In: Ferrari, V., Hebert, M., Sminchisescu, C., Weiss, Y. (eds.) ECCV 2018. LNCS, vol. 11215, pp. 556–572. Springer, Cham (2018). https://doi.org/10.1007/978-3-030-01252-6_33
5. Chen, L.C., Papandreou, G., Schroff, F., Adam, H.: Rethinking atrous convolution for semantic image segmentation. arXiv preprint arXiv:1706.05587 (2017)
6. Chen, L.-C., Zhu, Y., Papandreou, G., Schroff, F., Adam, H.: Encoder-decoder with atrous separable convolution for semantic image segmentation. In: Ferrari, V., Hebert, M., Sminchisescu, C., Weiss, Y. (eds.) ECCV 2018. LNCS, vol. 11211, pp. 833–851. Springer, Cham (2018). https://doi.org/10.1007/978-3-030-01234-2_49
7. Delange, M., et al.: A continual learning survey: defying forgetting in classification tasks. IEEE Trans. Pattern Anal. Mach. Intell. **44**, 3366–3385 (2021)
8. Deng, J., Dong, W., Socher, R., Li, L.J., Li, K., Fei-Fei, L.: ImageNet: a large-scale hierarchical image database. In: 2009 IEEE Conference on Computer Vision and Pattern Recognition, pp. 248–255. IEEE (2009)
9. Dhar, P., Singh, R.V., Peng, K.C., Wu, Z., Chellappa, R.: Learning without memorizing. In: Proceedings of the IEEE/CVF Conference on Computer Vision and Pattern Recognition, pp. 5138–5146 (2019)
10. Ding, H., Jiang, X., Shuai, B., Liu, A.Q., Wang, G.: Context contrasted feature and gated multi-scale aggregation for scene segmentation. In: Proceedings of the IEEE Conference on Computer Vision and Pattern Recognition, pp. 2393–2402 (2018)
11. Dong, J., Cong, Y., Sun, G., Fang, Z., Ding, Z.: Where and how to transfer: knowledge aggregation-induced transferability perception for unsupervised domain adaptation. IEEE Trans. Pattern Anal. Mach. Intell., 1 (2021). https://doi.org/10.1109/TPAMI.2021.3128560
12. Dong, J., Cong, Y., Sun, G., Zhong, B., Xu, X.: What can be transferred: unsupervised domain adaptation for endoscopic lesions segmentation. In: IEEE/CVF Conference on Computer Vision and Pattern Recognition (CVPR), pp. 4022–4031, June 2020
13. Dong, J., et al.: Federated class-incremental learning. In: Proceedings of the IEEE/CVF Conference on Computer Vision and Pattern Recognition (CVPR), pp. 10164–10173, June 2022
14. Douillard, A., Chen, Y., Dapogny, A., Cord, M.: PLOP: learning without forgetting for continual semantic segmentation. In: Proceedings of the IEEE/CVF Conference on Computer Vision and Pattern Recognition, pp. 4040–4050 (2021)

15. Everingham, M., Van Gool, L., Williams, C.K., Winn, J., Zisserman, A.: The pascal visual object classes (VOC) challenge. Int. J. Comput. Vision **88**(2), 303–338 (2010)
16. Fontanel, D., Cermelli, F., Mancini, M., Caputo, B.: Detecting anomalies in semantic segmentation with prototypes. In: Proceedings of the IEEE/CVF Conference on Computer Vision and Pattern Recognition, pp. 113–121 (2021)
17. Ganea, D.A., Boom, B., Poppe, R.: Incremental few-shot instance segmentation. In: Proceedings of the IEEE/CVF Conference on Computer Vision and Pattern Recognition, pp. 1185–1194 (2021)
18. He, K., Zhang, X., Ren, S., Sun, J.: Deep residual learning for image recognition. In: Proceedings of the IEEE Conference on Computer Vision and Pattern Recognition, pp. 770–778 (2016)
19. Hou, S., Pan, X., Loy, C.C., Wang, Z., Lin, D.: Learning a unified classifier incrementally via rebalancing. In: Proceedings of the IEEE/CVF Conference on Computer Vision and Pattern Recognition, pp. 831–839 (2019)
20. Huang, Z., et al.: Half-real half-fake distillation for class-incremental semantic segmentation. arXiv preprint arXiv:2104.00875 (2021)
21. Huang, Z., Wang, X., Huang, L., Huang, C., Wei, Y., Liu, W.: CCNet: criss-cross attention for semantic segmentation. In: Proceedings of the IEEE/CVF International Conference on Computer Vision, pp. 603–612 (2019)
22. Huang, Z., Wei, Y., Wang, X., Shi, H., Liu, W., Huang, T.S.: AlignSeg: feature-aligned segmentation networks. IEEE Trans. Pattern Anal. Mach. Intell. **44**, 550–557 (2021)
23. Ji, W., Li, X., Wei, L., Wu, F., Zhuang, Y.: Context-aware graph label propagation network for saliency detection. IEEE Trans. Image Process. **29**, 8177–8186 (2020)
24. Ji, W., Li, X., Wu, F., Pan, Z., Zhuang, Y.: Human-centric clothing segmentation via deformable semantic locality-preserving network. IEEE Trans. Circuits Syst. Video Technol. **30**(12), 4837–4848 (2019)
25. Joseph, K., Khan, S., Khan, F.S., Balasubramanian, V.N.: Towards open world object detection. In: Proceedings of the IEEE/CVF Conference on Computer Vision and Pattern Recognition, pp. 5830–5840 (2021)
26. Kirkpatrick, J., et al.: Overcoming catastrophic forgetting in neural networks. Proc. Natl. Acad. Sci. **114**(13), 3521–3526 (2017)
27. Klingner, M., Bär, A., Donn, P., Fingscheidt, T.: Class-incremental learning for semantic segmentation re-using neither old data nor old labels. In: 2020 IEEE 23rd International Conference on Intelligent Transportation Systems (ITSC), pp. 1–8. IEEE (2020)
28. Kundu, J.N., Venkatesh, R.M., Venkat, N., Revanur, A., Babu, R.V.: Class-incremental domain adaptation. In: Vedaldi, A., Bischof, H., Brox, T., Frahm, J.-M. (eds.) ECCV 2020. LNCS, vol. 12358, pp. 53–69. Springer, Cham (2020). https://doi.org/10.1007/978-3-030-58601-0_4
29. Li, X., Zhou, Y., Wu, T., Socher, R., Xiong, C.: Learn to grow: a continual structure learning framework for overcoming catastrophic forgetting. In: International Conference on Machine Learning, pp. 3925–3934. PMLR (2019)
30. Li, Z., Hoiem, D.: Learning without forgetting. IEEE Trans. Pattern Anal. Mach. Intell. **40**(12), 2935–2947 (2017)
31. Liu, Y., Su, Y., Liu, A.A., Schiele, B., Sun, Q.: Mnemonics training: multi-class incremental learning without forgetting. In: Proceedings of the IEEE/CVF conference on Computer Vision and Pattern Recognition, pp. 12245–12254 (2020)
32. Long, J., Shelhamer, E., Darrell, T.: Fully convolutional networks for semantic segmentation. In: Proceedings of the IEEE Conference on Computer Vision and Pattern Recognition, pp. 3431–3440 (2015)

33. Mallya, Arun, Davis, Dillon, Lazebnik, Svetlana: Piggyback: adapting a single network to multiple tasks by learning to mask weights. In: Ferrari, Vittorio, Hebert, Martial, Sminchisescu, Cristian, Weiss, Yair (eds.) ECCV 2018. LNCS, vol. 11208, pp. 72–88. Springer, Cham (2018). https://doi.org/10.1007/978-3-030-01225-0_5
34. Mallya, A., Lazebnik, S.: PackNet: adding multiple tasks to a single network by iterative pruning. In: Proceedings of the IEEE conference on Computer Vision and Pattern Recognition, pp. 7765–7773 (2018)
35. Maracani, A., Michieli, U., Toldo, M., Zanuttigh, P.: Recall: replay-based continual learning in semantic segmentation. In: Proceedings of the IEEE/CVF International Conference on Computer Vision, pp. 7026–7035 (2021)
36. McCloskey, M., Cohen, N.J.: Catastrophic interference in connectionist networks: the sequential learning problem. In: Psychology of Learning and Motivation, vol. 24, pp. 109–165. Elsevier (1989)
37. Michieli, U., Zanuttigh, P.: Incremental learning techniques for semantic segmentation. In: Proceedings of the IEEE/CVF International Conference on Computer Vision Workshops, p. 0 (2019)
38. Michieli, U., Zanuttigh, P.: Continual semantic segmentation via repulsion-attraction of sparse and disentangled latent representations. In: Proceedings of the IEEE/CVF Conference on Computer Vision and Pattern Recognition, pp. 1114–1124 (2021)
39. Michieli, U., Zanuttigh, P.: Knowledge distillation for incremental learning in semantic segmentation. Comput. Vis. Image Underst. **205**, 103167 (2021)
40. Pohlen, T., Hermans, A., Mathias, M., Leibe, B.: Full-resolution residual networks for semantic segmentation in street scenes. In: Proceedings of the IEEE Conference on Computer Vision and Pattern Recognition, pp. 4151–4160 (2017)
41. Rebuffi, S.A., Kolesnikov, A., Sperl, G., Lampert, C.H.: iCaRL: incremental classifier and representation learning. In: Proceedings of the IEEE Conference on Computer Vision and Pattern Recognition, pp. 2001–2010 (2017)
42. Ronneberger, O., Fischer, P., Brox, T.: U-Net: convolutional networks for biomedical image segmentation. In: Navab, N., Hornegger, J., Wells, W.M., Frangi, A.F. (eds.) MICCAI 2015. LNCS, vol. 9351, pp. 234–241. Springer, Cham (2015). https://doi.org/10.1007/978-3-319-24574-4_28
43. Stan, S., Rostami, M.: Unsupervised model adaptation for continual semantic segmentation. arXiv preprint arXiv:2009.12518 (2020)
44. Wang, J., et al.: Deep high-resolution representation learning for visual recognition. IEEE Trans. Pattern Anal. Mach. Intell. **43**, 3349–3364 (2020)
45. Wang, X., Girshick, R., Gupta, A., He, K.: Non-local neural networks. In: Proceedings of the IEEE Conference on Computer Vision and Pattern Recognition, pp. 7794–7803 (2018)
46. Wu, Y., et al.: Large scale incremental learning. In: Proceedings of the IEEE/CVF Conference on Computer Vision and Pattern Recognition, pp. 374–382 (2019)
47. Yan, S., Zhou, J., Xie, J., Zhang, S., He, X.: An EM framework for online incremental learning of semantic segmentation. In: Proceedings of the 29th ACM International Conference on Multimedia, pp. 3052–3060 (2021)
48. Yu, F., Wang, D., Shelhamer, E., Darrell, T.: Deep layer aggregation. In: Proceedings of the IEEE Conference on Computer Vision and Pattern Recognition, pp. 2403–2412 (2018)
49. Yu, L., Liu, X., van de Weijer, J.: Self-training for class-incremental semantic segmentation. arXiv preprint arXiv:2012.03362 (2020)
50. Zenke, F., Poole, B., Ganguli, S.: Continual learning through synaptic intelligence. In: International Conference on Machine Learning, pp. 3987–3995. PMLR (2017)

51. Zhang, H., et al.: Context encoding for semantic segmentation. In: Proceedings of the IEEE conference on Computer Vision and Pattern Recognition, pp. 7151–7160 (2018)
52. Zhao, H., Qin, X., Su, S., Fu, Y., Lin, Z., Li, X.: When video classification meets incremental classes. In: Proceedings of the 29th ACM International Conference on Multimedia, pp. 880–889 (2021)
53. Zhao, H., Wang, H., Fu, Y., Wu, F., Li, X.: Memory efficient class-incremental learning for image classification. IEEE Trans. Neural Netw. Learn. Syst. **33**, 5966–5977 (2021)
54. Zhao, H., et al.: What and where: learn to plug adapters via NAS for multidomain learning. IEEE Trans. Neural Netw. Learn. Syst., 1–13 (2021)
55. Zhao, H., Shi, J., Qi, X., Wang, X., Jia, J.: Pyramid scene parsing network. In: Proceedings of the IEEE Conference on Computer Vision and Pattern Recognition, pp. 2881–2890 (2017)
56. Zheng, E., Yu, Q., Li, R., Shi, P., Haake, A.: A continual learning framework for uncertainty-aware interactive image segmentation. In: Proceedings of the AAAI Conference on Artificial Intelligence, pp. 6030–6038 (2021)
57. Zhou, B., Zhao, H., Puig, X., Fidler, S., Barriuso, A., Torralba, A.: Scene parsing through ade20k dataset. In: Proceedings of the IEEE Conference on Computer Vision and Pattern Recognition, pp. 633–641 (2017)

Factorizing Knowledge in Neural Networks

Xingyi Yang, Jingwen Ye, and Xinchao Wang(✉)

National University of Singapore, Singapore, Singapore
xyang@u.nus.edu, {jingweny,xinchao}@nus.edu.sg

Abstract. In this paper, we explore a novel and ambitious knowledge-transfer task, termed Knowledge Factorization (KF). The core idea of KF lies in the modularization and assemblability of knowledge: given a pretrained network model as input, KF aims to decompose it into several factor networks, each of which handles only a dedicated task and maintains task-specific knowledge factorized from the source network. Such factor networks are task-wise disentangled and can be directly assembled, without any fine-tuning, to produce the more competent combined-task networks. In other words, the factor networks serve as Lego-brick-like building blocks, allowing us to construct customized networks in a plug-and-play manner. Specifically, each factor network comprises two modules, a common-knowledge module that is task-agnostic and shared by all factor networks, alongside with a task-specific module dedicated to the factor network itself. We introduce an information-theoretic objective, InfoMax-Bottleneck (IMB), to carry out KF by optimizing the mutual information between the learned representations and input. Experiments across various benchmarks demonstrate that, the derived factor networks yield gratifying performances on not only the dedicated tasks but also disentanglement, while enjoying much better interpretability and modularity. Moreover, the learned common-knowledge representations give rise to impressive results on transfer learning. Our code is available at https://github.com/Adamdad/KnowledgeFactor.

Keywords: Transfer learning · Knowledge factorization

1 Introduction

Over the past decade, deep neural networks (DNNs) have evolved to the *de facto* a standard approach for most if not all computer vision tasks, yielding unprecedentedly promising results. Due to the time- and resource-consuming DNN training process, many developers have generously released their pretrained models online, so that users may adopt these models in a plug-and-play manner

Supplementary Information The online version contains supplementary material available at https://doi.org/10.1007/978-3-031-19830-4_5.

S. Avidan et al. (Eds.): ECCV 2022, LNCS 13694, pp. 73–91, 2022.
https://doi.org/10.1007/978-3-031-19830-4_5

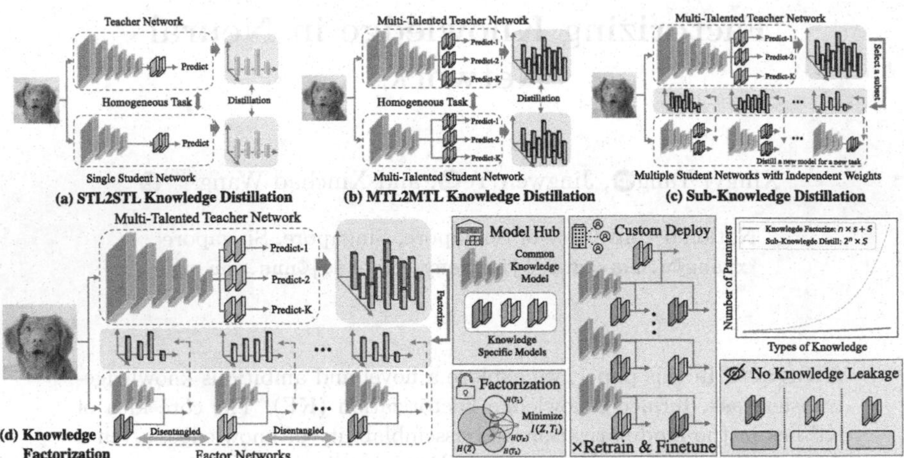

Fig. 1. Illustration of (top) 3 types of Knowledge Distillation and (bottom) our proposed Knowledge Factorization. (a) Single-Task Learning to Single-Task Learning (STL2STL) KD refers to distill a single-tasked student from a single-tasked teacher, (b) Multi-Task Learning to Multi-Task Learning (MTL2MTL) KD stands for distilling a multi-tasked student from a multi-tasked teacher and (c) Sub-Knowledge Distillation distill a subset of the teacher's knowledge to its student model.

without training from scratch. Nevertheless, pretrained DNNs often come with heavy architectures, making them extremely cumbersome to be deployed in real-world scenarios, especially resource-critical applications such as edge computing. Numerous endeavors have thus been made towards reducing the sizes of DNNs, among which one mainstream scheme is known as Knowledge Distillation (KD). The goal of KD is to "distill" knowledge from a large pre-trained model known as a teacher, to a compact model known as a student. The derived student is expected to master the expertise of the teacher yet come with a much smaller size, making it applicable to edge devices. Since the seminal work of [20], a series of KD approaches have been proposed to strengthen the performances of student models [47,51,66].

Albeit encouraging results achieved, KD has largely been treated as a black-box procedure, in which the intrinsic knowledge flow process remains opaque. Consequently, the derived student model may inherit the teacher's task-wise competence but unfortunately lacks interpretability, since it is unclear how and what knowledge has been transferred to the student. In addition, as demonstrated in Fig. 1(a) and (b), conventional KD assumes that teacher and student models master homogeneous tasks or knowledge, which greatly limits its wide applications. Even if it is allowed to distill a subset of knowledge from the teacher, shown in Fig. 1(c), the problem setup of KD, by nature, overlooks the scalability of the student. For example, given a versatile classification teacher pretrained on ImageNet, if we are to learn two students, one handling cat-dog classification and one handling cat-fish, we will have to carry out the KD twice; if, however, we are to learn all k-class classification students from a pool of $1,000$ classes, we will have to conduct KD for $\sum_{k=1}^{1000} \binom{1,000}{k} = 2^{1000}$ times, which is computational intractable.

In this paper, we introduce a novel task, termed Knowledge Factorization (KF), that alleviates the aforementioned flaws of KD at a problem-setup level. The core idea of KF regards the modularization and assemblability of knowledge: given a pretrained teacher, KF decomposes it into several *factor networks*, each of which masters one specific knowledge factorized from the teacher, while remaining disentangled with respect to others. Moreover, these factor networks are expected to be readily integratable, meaning that we may directly assemble multiple factor networks, without any fine-tuning, to produce a more competent multi-talented network. As shown in Fig. 1(d), those factor networks can be organized into a open-sourced model hub. At the same time, users could treat them as Lego-brick-like units of knowledge to build customized networks in a plug-and-play fashion, thereby lending itself to great scalability. Furthermore, the disentanglement property effectively enables the IP protection of network knowledge: since the factor networks are learned in a disentangled manner, they possess only task-specific knowledge, allowing the network owners to selectively conduct knowledge transfer without leaking knowledge of other tasks.

Admittedly, the aims of KF are unarguably ambitious, since the factor networks are, again, expected to be modularized and readily integratable, and meanwhile knowledge-wise disentangled and hence more interpretable. Notably, despite orthogonal in expertise, these factor networks will inherit the common knowledge shared by all tasks. As such, each factor network should be designed to account for both the task-agnostic commonality and its task-relevant specialization, which in turn reduces the overall parameter overhead for KF. As demonstrated in Fig. 1, given n types of knowledge, sub-KD requires an exponential number of 2^n models, each with S parameters, while KF reduces the model number to a linear scale, with one full-sized common knowledge model and n mini models, each with s parameter, where $s \ll S$.

To this end, we propose a dedicated scheme for conducting KF, that comprises two mechanisms, namely *structural factorization* and *representation factorization*.

- **Structural Factorization.** Structural factorization decomposes the teacher network into a set of factor networks with different functionalities. Each factor network comprises a shared *common-knowledge network* (CKN) and a *task-specific network* (TSN). CKN extracts task-agnostic representations to capture the commonality among tasks, whereas the TSN accounts for task-specific information. Factor networks are trained to specialize in an individual task via fusing task-agnostic and task-specific knowledge.
- **Representation Factorization.** Representation factorization disentangles the shared knowledge and task-level representations into statistically independent components. For this purpose, we introduce a novel information-theoretical objective, termed *InfoMax Bottleneck* (IMB). It maximizes the mutual information between input and the common features to encourage

the lossless information transmission in CKN. Meanwhile, IMB minimizes data-task mutual information to ensure that, the task features are only predictive for a specific task. Specifically, we derive a variational lower bound for IMB to practically optimize this loss.

By integrating both mechanisms, we demonstrate in the experiments that KF indeed achieves architecture-level and representation-level disentanglement. Different from KD that transmits holistic knowledge in a black-box manner, KF offers unique interpretability for the factor networks through the knowledge transfer. Moreover, the learned common-knowledge representations facilitate the transfer learning to unseen downstream tasks, as will be verified empirically in our experiments.

Our contribution are therefore summarized as follows

- We introduce a novel knowledge-transfer task, termed *Knowledge Factorization* (KF), which accounts for learning factor networks that are modularized and interpretable. Factor networks are expected to be readily integratable, without any retraining, to assemble multi-task networks.
- We propose an effective solution towards KF. Our approach decomposes a pretrained teacher into factor networks that are task-wise disentangled.
- We design an *InfoMax Bottleneck* objective to disentangle the representation between common knowledge and the task-specific representations, by exerting control over the mutual information between input and representations. We derive its variational bound for its numerical optimization.
- Our method achieves strong performance and disentanglement capability across various benchmarks, with better modularity and transferability.

2 Related Work

Knowledge Distillation. Knowledge distillation (KD) [20] refers to the process to transfer the knowledge from one model or an ensemble of models to a student model. KD is originally designed for model compression [5,31,36,50,55,63], but it has been found to be beneficial in other tasks like adversarial defense [46], domain adaptation [15,43], continual learning [32,67] and amalgamate the knowledge from multiple teachers [23,38,64]. Different from the common KD methods that disseminates knowledge as a whole, we factorize the knowledge of a multi-talented teacher to factor networks with disentangled representations.

Disentangled Representation Learning. It is often assumed that real-world observations should be controlled by factors. Therefore, a recent line of research argues the importance of finding disentangled variables in representation learning [4,13,35,44,48,62] while providing invariance in learning [1,14,22]. The disentanglement are usually done through adversarial learning [10,34,40,58] or variational auto-encoder [7,19,26]. In this work, we aim to disentangle the task-agnostic and task-related representation by optimizing the mutual information.

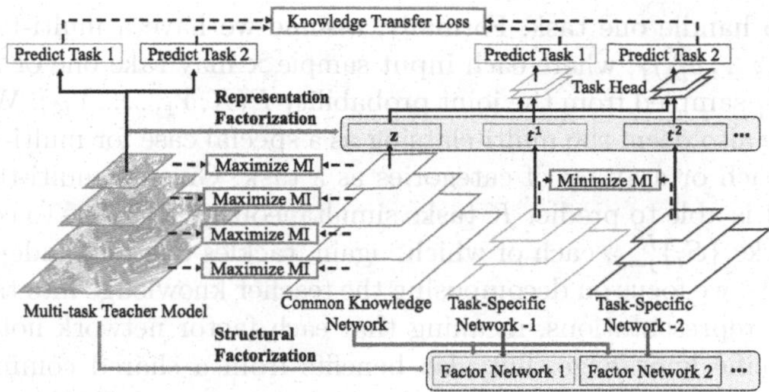

Fig. 2. The overall framework of the proposed knowledge factorization. The factor networks are trained to mimic the prediction of the teacher. The CKN learns to maximize the mutual information between input and its features, whereas the TSNs are dedicated to minimizing the task-wise mutual information.

InfoMax Principle and Information Bottleneck. As one of the foundations of machine learning, information theory has promoted a series of learning algorithms. *InfoMax* [33] is a core principle of representation learning that encourages the mutual information should be maximized between multi-views or between representation and input. This principle gave birth to the recent trend on self-supervised learning [2,21,59] and contrastive learning [9,16,17,25,45,56]. On the contrary, *Information Bottleneck* (IB) [57] aims to compress the representation while achieving realistic reconstruction results. In this study, we take a unified view of the two principles in multi-task learning. Infomax guarantees the learning of common knowledge across tasks, while IB promotes task-specific knowledge for an individual task.

Multi-task Learning. Multi-task learning (MTL) is designed to train models that handle multiple tasks by taking advantage of the common information among tasks. Some recent solutions explore on the decomposition between shared and task-specific processing [24,39,68]. Unlike conventional methods, we decompose a pre-training model into knowledge modules according to tasks.

3 Method

The essence of this work is to factorize a multi-task teacher into independent students by posing fine-grained control of the information among teacher and students. Figure 2 provides an overall sketch of our proposed KF. In what follows, we first give a definition of knowledge factorization, and then introduce the general procedure to decompose a teacher into factorized students.

3.1 Knowledge Factorization in Neural Network

We define Knowledge Factorization (KF) to be the process of subdividing a teacher network into multiple *factor networks*, each of which possesses distinctive knowledge to handle one task. Formally, assume we have a multi-task dataset $\mathcal{D} = \{(\mathbf{x}_i, y_i^1, \dots, y_i^K)\}$, where each input sample $\mathbf{x}$ may take one of K different labels $\{y^j\}_{j=1}^K$ sampled from the joint probability $P(X, Y_1, \dots, Y_K)$. With a loose definition, we also deem the multi-classing as a special case for multi-tasking, by considering each or a group of categories as a task. Given a multi-task teacher model $\mathcal{T}$ that is able to predict K tasks simultaneously, KF aims to construct K factor networks $\{\mathcal{S}_j\}_{j=1}^K$, each of which, again, tackles one task independently.

Specifically, we focus on decomposing the teacher knowledge into task-specific and common representations, meaning that each factor network not only masters task-specific knowledge, but also benefits from a shared common feature to make final predictions. To this end, we design two mechanisms to factorize knowledge: *structural factorization* to decompose the teacher network into a set of factor networks, as well as *representation factorization* to disentangle the common features from task-specific features by optimizing mutual information.

3.2 Structural Factorization

The goal of structural factorization is to endow different sub-networks with functional distinctions. Each factor networks is expected to inherit only a portion of the knowledge from the teacher, and specializes in an individual task. Specifically, a factor network $\mathcal{S}_j$ for the j-th task comprises two modular networks: a Common Knowledge Network (CKN) $\mathcal{S}_C(\cdot; \Theta_{\mathcal{S}_C})$ which is shared across all tasks, and a Task-specific Network (TSN) $\mathcal{S}_{T_j}(\cdot; \Theta_{\mathcal{S}_{T_j}})$ which is task-exclusive. $\Theta_{\mathcal{S}_C}$ and $\Theta_{\mathcal{S}_{T_j}}$ are the model parameters for CKN and TSN respectively. For each input sample, $\mathcal{S}_C$ is adopted to extract the task-agnostic feature $\mathbf{z}$:

$$\mathbf{z} = \mathcal{S}_C(\mathbf{x}; \Theta_{\mathcal{S}_C}). \tag{1}$$

On the contrary, $\mathcal{S}_{T_j}$ learns the task-related knowledge $\mathbf{t}^j$ from the input $\mathbf{x}$, which together with $\mathbf{z}$ is processed by a task head $\mathcal{H}_j$ to make the final prediction:

$$\mathbf{t}^j = \mathcal{S}_{T_j}(\mathbf{x}; \Theta_{\mathcal{S}_{T_j}}); \hat{y}_S^j = \mathcal{H}_j(\mathbf{z}, \mathbf{t}^j; \Theta_{\mathcal{H}_j}), \tag{2}$$

which constrains each factor network $\mathcal{S}_j$ to share the same common knowledge network but maintain the task-specific one to handle different tasks.

Intuitively, we expect that $\mathcal{S}_j$ only masters the knowledge about task j by using the common knowledge $\mathbf{z}$ and $\mathbf{t}^j$. We accordingly define a structure factorization objective $\mathcal{L}_{sf}^{(j)}$ to enforce each single-task factor network to imitate the teacher's prediction while minimizing the supervised loss:

$$\mathcal{L}_{sf}^{(j)} = \mathcal{L}_{\text{sup}}^{(j)} + \lambda_{\text{kt}} \mathcal{L}_{\text{kt}}^{(j)}, \tag{3}$$

where $\mathcal{L}_{\text{sup}}^{(j)}$ and $\mathcal{L}_{\text{kt}}^{(j)}$ denote the supervised loss and the knowledge transfer loss for the j-th task, respectively, and λ_{kt} is the weight coefficient. Notably, we may readily adopt various implementations for each of the loss terms here. For example, $\mathcal{L}_{\text{sup}}^{(j)}$ may take the form of L2 norm for regression and cross-entropy for classification, while $\mathcal{L}_{\text{kt}}^{(j)}$ may take the form of soft-target [20], hint-loss [51], or attention transfer [66]. More details can be found in the supplement.

Structure factorization therefore enables us to construct new combined-task models by assembling multiple networks without retraining. If, for example, a 3-category classifier is needed, we can readily integrate CKN and the corresponding 3 TSNs from the pre-defined network pool. This property, in turn, greatly improves the scalability of the model.

3.3 Representation Factorization

Apart from the functionality disentanglement, we hope that learned representations of the factor networks are statistically independent as well, so that each sub-network masters task-wise disentangled knowledge. This means task-specific features should only contain minimal information only related to a certain task, while the common representation contains as much information as possible.

To this end, we introduce the *Infomax Bottleneck* (IMB) objective to optimize the mutual information (MI) between features and input. For two random variables X, Y, MI $\mathcal{I}(X,Y)$ quantifies the "number information" that variable X tells about Y, denoted by Kullback Leibler (KL) divergence between the joint probability $p(\boldsymbol{x}, \boldsymbol{y})$ and the product of marginal distribution $p(\boldsymbol{x})p(\boldsymbol{y})$:

$$\mathcal{I}(X,Y) = D_{KL}\Big[p(\boldsymbol{x}, \boldsymbol{y})||p(\boldsymbol{x})p(\boldsymbol{y})\Big]. \tag{4}$$

In our problem, for each input sample $\mathbf{x} \sim P(X)$, we compute its common knowledge feature $\mathbf{z} \sim P(Z)$ and the task-predictive representation $\mathbf{t}^j \sim P(T_j)$. Ultimately, IMB attempts to maximize $\mathcal{I}(X, Z)$ so that common knowledge keeps as much information of the input as possible, while minimize $\mathcal{I}(X, T_j)$ so that task representations only preserve information related to the task. The representation disentanglement can then be formulated as an optimization problem:

$$\max \mathcal{I}(T_j, Y_j); \quad \text{s.t. } \mathcal{I}(X, T_j) \leq \epsilon_1, -\mathcal{I}(X, Z) \leq \epsilon_2, \tag{5}$$

where ϵ_1 and ϵ_2 are the information constraints we define. In order to solve Eq. 5, we introduce two Lagrange multiplier $\alpha > 0, \beta > 0$ to construct the function:

$$\mathcal{L}_I^{(j)} = \mathcal{I}(T_j, Y_j) + \alpha\mathcal{I}(X, Z) - \beta\mathcal{I}(X, T_j). \tag{6}$$

By maximizing the first term $\mathcal{I}(T_j, Y_j)$, we ensure that the task representation $\mathbf{t}^j$ is capable to accomplish individual task j. $\mathcal{I}(X, Z)$ term encourages the lossless transmission of information and high fidelity feature extraction for the CKN, while minimizing $\mathcal{I}(X, T_j)$ enforces the only the task-informative representation is extracted by TSN, thus de-correlate the task knowledge $\mathbf{t}^j$ with the common knowledge $\mathbf{z}$. Unlike the convectional information bottleneck (IB) principle [57], our proposed IMB attempts to maximize $\mathcal{I}(X, Z)$ [21,37,45], so that the CKN learns a general representation $\mathbf{z}$ with high fidelity.

3.4 Variational Bound for Mutual Information

Due to the difficulty of estimating mutual information for continuous variables, we derive a variational lower bound to approximate the exact IMB objective[1]:

$$\hat{\mathcal{L}}_I = \mathbb{E}_{p(\mathbf{y}_j, \mathbf{t}_j)}[\log q(\mathbf{y}_j|\mathbf{t}_j)] + \alpha(\mathbb{E}_{p(\mathbf{z},\mathbf{x})}[\log q(\mathbf{z}|\mathbf{x})] + H(Z)) - \beta\mathbb{E}_{p(\mathbf{t}_j)}\Big[D_{KL}[p(\mathbf{t}_j|\mathbf{x})||q(\mathbf{t}_j)]\Big], \tag{7}$$

[1] Due to space limitations, we only show the final formulations in the main body of this paper. The derivations can be found in the supplementary material.

where D_{KL} denotes the KL divergence between two distributions and $q(\cdot)$ denotes the variational distributions. We claim that $\mathcal{L}_I \geq \hat{\mathcal{L}}_I$, with the equality acheived if and only if $q(\mathbf{y}_j|\mathbf{t}_j) = p(\mathbf{y}_j|\mathbf{t}_j)$, $q(\mathbf{z}|\mathbf{x}) = p(\mathbf{z}|\mathbf{x})$ and $q(\mathbf{t}_j) = p(\mathbf{t}_j)$.

For better understanding, we explain the meaning of each term, specify the parametric forms of variational distribution and implementation details of Eq. 7.

Term 1. We maximize $\mathcal{I}(T_j, Y_j)$ by maximizing its lower bound $\mathbb{E}_{p(\mathbf{y}_j,\mathbf{t}_j)}[\log q(\mathbf{y}_j|\mathbf{t}_j)]$. We set $q(\mathbf{y}_j|\mathbf{t}_j)$ to Gaussian for regression tasks and the multinomial distribution for classification tasks. Under this assumption, maximizing $\mathbb{E}_{p(\mathbf{y}_j,\mathbf{t}_j)}[\log q(\mathbf{y}_j|\mathbf{t}_j)]$ is nothing more than minimizing the L2 norm or cross-entropy loss for the prediction. $q(\mathbf{y}_j|\mathbf{t}_j)$ is parameterized with another task head $\mathcal{H}_{j'}$ that takes $\mathbf{t}^j$ as input and makes the task prediction. Notably, $\mathcal{H}_{j'}$ is different from $\mathcal{H}_j$ since $\mathcal{H}_j$ takes both $\mathbf{z}$ and $\mathbf{t}^j$ as input.

Term 2. We maximize $\mathcal{I}(X, Z)$ by maximizing its lower bound $\mathbb{E}_{p(\mathbf{z},\mathbf{x})}[\log q(\mathbf{z}|\mathbf{x})] + H(Z)$. We choose $q(\mathbf{z}|\mathbf{x})$ to be an energy-based function that is parameterized by a critic function $f(\mathbf{x}, \mathbf{z}) : \mathcal{X} \times \mathcal{Z} \to \mathbb{R}$

$$q(\mathbf{z}|\mathbf{x}) = \frac{p(\mathbf{z})}{C} e^{f(\mathbf{x},\mathbf{z})}, \text{ where } C = \mathbb{E}_{p(\mathbf{z})}\left[e^{f(\mathbf{x},\mathbf{z})}\right]. \tag{8}$$

Substituting $q(\mathbf{z}|\mathbf{x})$ into the second term gives us an unnormalized lower bound:

$$\mathcal{I}(X, Z) \geq \mathbb{E}_{p(\mathbf{z},\mathbf{x})}[f(\mathbf{x}, \mathbf{z})] - \log \mathbb{E}_{p(\mathbf{x})}[C], \tag{9}$$

The same bound is also mentioned in Mutual Information Neural Estimation (MINE) [3]. Different from original MINE, in our implementation, we estimate the $\mathcal{I}(X, Z)$ through a feature-wise loss between teacher and students. With a slight abuse of notation, we refer $\mathbf{z}_{\mathcal{T}} = \mathcal{T}(\mathbf{x})_l \in \mathbb{R}^{d_{\mathcal{T}}}$ and $\mathbf{z}_{\mathcal{C}} = \mathcal{S}_{\mathcal{C}}(\mathbf{x})_l \in \mathbb{R}^{d_{\mathcal{C}}}$ as the intermediate feature vectors from teacher and CKN at the l-th layer. Given a pair of $(\mathbf{z}_{\mathcal{T}}, \mathbf{z}_{\mathcal{C}})$, f is defined as inner product of two vectors $f(\mathbf{x}, \mathbf{z}_{\mathcal{C}}) = \langle \mathbf{z}_{\mathcal{C}}, FFN(\mathbf{z}_{\mathcal{T}})\rangle$, where $FFN(\cdot) : \mathbb{R}^{d_{\mathcal{T}}} \to \mathbb{R}^{d_{\mathcal{C}}}$ is a feed-forward network to align the dimensions between $\mathbf{z}_{\mathcal{T}}$ and $\mathbf{z}_{\mathcal{C}}$.

Term 3. $\mathbb{E}_{p(\mathbf{t}_j)}\left[D_{KL}[p(\mathbf{t}_j|\mathbf{x})||q(\mathbf{t}_j)]\right]$ is the expected KL divergence between the posterior $p(\mathbf{t}_j|\mathbf{x})$ and the prior $q(\mathbf{t}_j)$, which is a upper bound for $\mathcal{I}(X, T_j)$. We minimize $\mathcal{I}(X, T_j)$ by minimizing $\mathbb{E}_{p(\mathbf{t}_j)}\left[D_{KL}[p(\mathbf{t}_j|\mathbf{x})||q(\mathbf{t}_j)]\right]$.

Following the common practice in variational inference [19,27], we set the prior $q(\mathbf{t}_j)$ as zero-mean unit-variance Gaussian. Besides, we assume the $p(\mathbf{t}_j|\mathbf{x}) = \mathcal{N}(\boldsymbol{\mu}_{t_j}, \text{diag}(\boldsymbol{\sigma}_{t_j}))$ is a Gaussian distribution. Accordingly, we compute the mean and variance for the task feature $\mathbf{t}_j$ in each forward pass:

$$\mathbf{t}_j = \mathcal{S}_{T_j}(\mathbf{x}; \Theta_{\mathcal{S}_{T_j}}); \boldsymbol{\mu}_{t_j} = \mathbb{E}[\mathbf{t}_j], \boldsymbol{\sigma}^2_{t_j} = \text{Var}[\mathbf{t}_j], \tag{10}$$

Then, the KL divergence between $p(\mathbf{t}_j|\mathbf{x})$ and $q(\mathbf{t}_j)$ can be computed as:

$$D_{KL}[p(\mathbf{t}_j|\mathbf{x})||q(\mathbf{t}_j)] = \frac{1}{2}\sum_{l=1}^{L}(1 + \log \sigma^{(l)}_{t_j} - (\mu^{(l)}_{t_j})^2 - \sigma^{(l)}_{t_j}). \tag{11}$$

The superscript denotes the l-th element of $\boldsymbol{\mu}_{t_j}$ and $\boldsymbol{\sigma}_{t_j}$.

Training. We minimize the following overall loss to achieve both structural and representation factorization between students:

$$\min_{\Theta_{S_C}, \Theta_{S_{T_j}}, \Theta_{\mathcal{H}_j}} \sum_{j=1}^{K} \mathcal{L}_{sf}^{(j)} - \lambda_{\text{I}} \mathcal{L}_{\text{I}}^{(j)}, \tag{12}$$

where λ_{I} is weighting coefficient of the IMB objective.

4 Experiments

In this section, we investigate how factorization works to promote the performance, modularity and transferability of the model. Defaultly, we set $\alpha = 1.0$ and $\beta = 1\text{e}{-3}$, $\lambda_{\text{I}} = 1$ and $\lambda_{\text{kt}} = 0.1$. Due to the space limit, more hyper-parameter settings, distillation loss, implementation details, data descriptions, and definitions of the metrics are listed in supplementary material.

4.1 Factor Networks Make Strong Task Prediction

We conduct comprehensive experiments on synthetic and real-world classification and multi-task benchmarks to investigate whether the factorized networks still maintain competitive predictive performance, especially on each subtask.

Synthetic Evaluation. We first evaluate our KF on two synthetic imagery benchmarks dSprites [41] and Shape3D [6]. Two datasets are both generated by 6 ground truth independent latent factors. We define each latent factor as a prediction target and treat both datasets as multi-label classification benchmarks. We compare our KF with 4 other baseline methods: single-task baseline, multi-task baselines, MTL2MTL KD and MTL2STL KD. Single-task baseline denotes training 6 single-task networks, while multi-task denotes that one model trained to predict all 6 tasks. MTL2MTL KD distill a multi-tasked student, whereas MTL2STL KD refers to distilling 6 single-tasked students. KF represents our results with factor networks. We train a teacher network as 6-layer CNN model. Besides, all students network encoders, including both the CKN and TSNs, are parametrized by the 3-layer CNN. We take a random train-test split of 7:3 on each dataset and report the ROC-AUC score on the test split.

Results. Figure 3 visualizes the bar plots for the ROC-AUC scores for our KF and its KD opponents on two datasets. Though all method achieves a high AUC score larger than 0.92 on both datasets, it is evident that our KF not only surpasses the multi-tasked baseline but also exceeds two distillation paradigms. In addition, it is noted that multi-tasked models generally achieves better performance than their single-task counterpart, revealing that the prediction performance benefits from learning from multiple labels on two datasets.

Real Image Classification. We further evaluate our KF on two real image classification CIFAR-10 [29] and ImageNet1K [52]. To apply factorization, we construct two *Pseudo-Multi-task Datasets* by considering the category hierarchy.

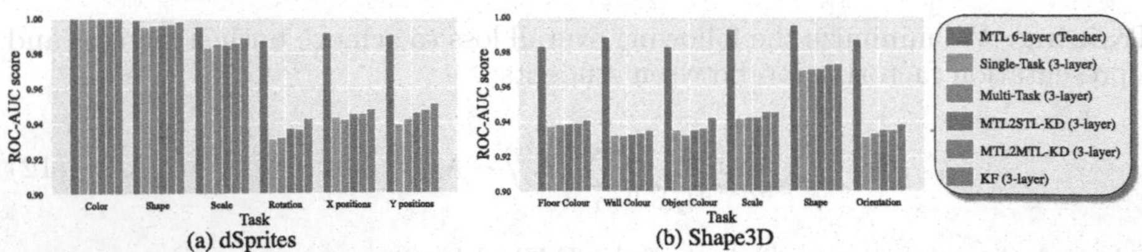

Fig. 3. Test ROC-AUC comparison on dSprites and Shape3D datasets.

Table 1. Test accuracy (%) comparison on CIFAR-10 between KD and KF. We report mean ± std over 3 runs.

Teacher:Acc	Student/CKN:Acc	1-Task KD	2-Task KD	1-Task KF	2-Task KF
ResNet-18:94.54	MBNv2:93.58	93.79 ± 0.17	92.59 ± 0.08	94.03 ± 0.23	**94.41** ± 0.05
	ResNet-18:94.54	94.72 ± 0.24	93.69 ± 0.11	95.04 ± 0.12	**95.20** ± 0.04
	WRN28-2:93.98	94.57 ± 0.13	93.71 ± 0.22	**94.86** ± 0.17	94.77 ± 0.06
WRN28-2:93.98	MBNv2:93.58	94.14 ± 0.08	94.10 ± 0.03	94.34 ± 0.14	**94.56** ± 0.10
	ResNet-18:94.54	94.75 ± 0.22	94.22 ± 0.07	95.03 ± 0.12	**95.12** ± 0.12
	WRN28-2:93.98	94.02 ± 0.07	93.31 ± 0.12	94.59 ± 0.11	**94.62** ± 0.13
WRN28-10:95.32	MBNv2:93.58	94.47 ± 0.31	94.10 ± 0.22	94.80 ± 0.15	**94.97** ± 0.15
	ResNet-18:94.54	95.28 ± 0.14	94.62 ± 0.09	**95.40** ± 0.08	95.32 ± 0.05
	WRN28-2:93.98	94.68 ± 0.14	94.11 ± 0.26	94.80 ± 0.07	**95.03** ± 0.12

Table 2. Top-1 Accuracy (%) comparison on ImageNet.

Teacher:Acc	Student/CKN:Acc	1-Task KD	1-Task KF	11-Task KF
ResNet-18:69.90	MBNv2:71.86	72.15	72.20 (+0.05)	**72.52**(+0.37)
	ResNet-18:69.90	70.53	70.26(−0.27)	**70.93**(+0.40)
ResNet-34:73.62	MBNv2:71.86	72.58	72.95(+0.37)	**73.12**(+0.54)
	ResNet-18:69.90	70.82	70.98(+0.16)	**72.13**(+1.31)
ResNet-50:76.55	MBNv2: 71.86	72.73	72.92(+0.19)	**73.15**(+0.42)
	ResNet-18:69.90	71.12	71.14(+0.02)	**72.20** (+1.08)

The 10 classes in CIFAR-10 can be divided into 6 *animal* and 4 *vehicle* categories. Similarly, ImageNet1K classes are organized using WordNet [42] synset tree, with 11 super-classes. We accordingly construct the CIFAR-10 2-task and ImageNet1K 11-task datasets, with each task considering one super-class.

On the single-task and pseudo-multi-task evaluations, we take a pretrained classifier and distill or factorize its knowledge to single-task or pseudo-multi-task students. Each pseudo-multi-task factor/distilled network only manages to predict the categories within one super-class, with the concatenated output serving as the final prediction. We include ResNet-18 [18], WideResNet28-2 (WRN28-2) [65] and WideResNet28-10 (WRN28-10) [65] as our teacher networks on CIFAR-10; MobileNetv2 (MBNv2) [53], along with ResNet-18, WRN28-2 as student or CKN backbone. On ImageNet1K evaluation, the teacher networks are selected to be ResNet-18, ResNet-34 [18] and ResNet-50 [18], with MBNv2 and ResNet-18 as student or CKN backbone. We select a lightweight backbone MBNv2x0.5 to be TSNs. MBNv2x0.5 represents the width multiplier is 0.5.

Results. Table 1 and Table 2 provide the classification accuracy comparison between single-task or pseudo-multi-tasked KD and our proposed KF over 3 runs. Though both approaches improve the baselines under the single-task setting, we note that KD fails to improve the results on the pseudo-multi-tasked evaluation. We also do not report the 11-task KD results on ImageNet because the accuracy is generally lower than 20%. Notably, we observed that the imbalanced labeling causes the deterioration in training: when one network only masters one super-class and the rest of the classes are treated as negative samples, the distilled networks are prone to make low-confident predictions in the end. In comparison, KF has a CKN shared across all tasks, which considerably alleviates the imbalance problem in conventional KD. For example, factor networks obtained by 11-Task KF improve the performance of ResNet18-KD on ImageNet over 1.08% and 1.31% when learning from ResNet-50 and ResNet-34. On other evaluations, KF consistently makes progress overall the normal KD, which suggests that the factorization of task-specific and task-agnostic benefit the performance.

Multi-task Dense Prediction. Two multi-task dense prediction datasets are also used to verify the effectiveness of KF, including NYU Depth Dataset V2 (NYUDv2) [54] and PASCAL Context [11]. NYUDv2 dataset contains indoor scene images annotated for segmentation and monocular depth estimation. We include 4 tasks in PASCAL Context, including semantic/human part segmentation, normal prediction, and saliency detection. We use the mean intersection over union (mIoU), the angle mean error (mErr) and root mean square error (rmse) are used to measure the prediction quality.

We include both the single-task and multi-task together with their STL2STL/MTL2STL/MTL2MTL distilled models as our baselines. We adopt the HRNet48 [61] and ResNet-50 DeepLabv3 as teacher and HRNet18 and ResNet-18 DeepLabv3 as student or CNK. The TSN are set to MBNv2x0.5. We use a smaller $\beta = 1\text{e}{-5}$. The networks are initialized with the ImageNet pretrained weights.

Results. We show the evaluation results on NYUDv2 and PASCAL datasets in Table 3 and Table 4. On NYUDv2, the multi-task baselines are generally better-performed than its single-task competitors. On the contrary, in the PASCAL experiments of HRNet48, ResNet18 and ResNet50, the performance of multitask baseline has largely degraded. It reveals the *negative transfer* problem in MTL that the joint optimization of multiple objective might cause the contradiction between tasks, thus leading to undesirable performance reduction.

The same problem remains when comparing MTL2MTL-KD to STL2-STL-KD in Table 4, where the MTL teacher is inferior to STL ones. Our factor networks automatically resolve this problem, because different TSNs are structurally and representationally independent. As a result, KF achieved strong student performance compared to other baselines.

Table 3. Performance comparison on the NYUDv2 dataset.

Method	Teacher	Student/CKN	Seg. (mIoU)↑	Depth (rmse)↓
Single-task	–	HRNet18	27.37	0.612
Multi-task	–	HRNet18	37.59	0.641
Single-task	–	HRNet48	48.19	0.556
Multi-task	–	HRNet48	48.92	0.578
STL2STL-KD	HRNet48	HRNet18	39.27	0.603
MTL2MTL-KD	HRNet48	HRNet18	38.02	0.604
MTL2STL-KD	HRNet48	HRNet18	39.04	0.601
Ours	HRNet48	HRNet18	**40.78**	**0.592**
Single-task	–	ResNet-18	38.07	0.652
Multi-task	–	ResNet-18	39.18	0.623
Single-task	–	ResNet-50	44.30	0.625
Multi-task	–	ResNet-50	44.78	0.602
STL2STL-KD	ResNet-50	ResNet-18	39.76	0.633
MTL2MTL-KD	ResNet-50	ResNet-18	39.98	0.623
MTL2STL-KD	ResNet-50	ResNet-18	40.60	0.621
Ours	ResNet-50	ResNet-18	**41.33**	**0.615**

Table 4. Performance comparison on the PASCAL dataset.

Method	Teacher	Student/CKN	Seg.(mIoU)↑	H.Part(mIOU)↑	Norm.(mErr)↓	Sal.(mIOU)↑
Single-task	–	HRNet18	51.18	64.10	14.54	56.08
Multi-task	–	HRNet18	54.61	62.40	14.77	66.07
Single-task	–	HRNet48	60.92	67.15	14.53	68.12
Multi-task	–	HRNet48	55.93	67.06	14.31	67.08
STL2STL-KD	HRNet48	HRNet18	52.63	64.98	14.49	60.72
MTL2MTL-KD	HRNet48	HRNet18	52.02	60.33	14.63	65.45
MTL2STL-KD	HRNet48	HRNet18	54.77	65.18	14.53	64.31
Ours	HRNet48	HRNet18	**56.65**	**66.83**	**14.44**	**67.05**
Single-task	–	ResNet-18	64.75	58.68	13.95	65.59
Multi-task	–	ResNet-18	63.48	58.17	15.12	64.50
Single-task	–	ResNet-50	70.29	61.47	14.65	66.22
Multi-task	–	ResNet-50	68.04	63.05	14.88	65.65
STL2STL-KD	ResNet-50	ResNet-18	66.10	59.43	**14.19**	66.33
MTL2MTL-KD	ResNet-50	ResNet-18	61.31	60.14	14.73	62.45
MTL2STL-KD	ResNet-50	ResNet-18	66.60	**62.33**	14.29	66.14
Ours	ResNet-50	ResNet-18	**67.18**	61.09	14.31	**66.83**

4.2 Factorization Brings Disentanglement

Given the distilled and factorized models in the previous section we measure a set of disentanglement metrics and representation similarity to confirm that the knowledge factorization captures the independent variables across tasks.

Disentanglement Evaluation Setup. We first validate the disentanglement between factor models on dSprites [41] and Shape3D [6]. We measure 4 disentanglement metrics to quantify how well the learned representations summarize the factor variables. Those metrics are disentanglement-completness-informativeness (DCI) [12], Mutual information gap (MIG) [8], FactorVAE metric [26], and Separated Attribute Predictability (SAP) score [30]. Higher means better.

We compare our KF with 3 other baseline methods: single-task baseline, multi-task baselines, and MTL2STL KD students, which has been introduced in previous section. Following the evaluation protocol in [35], we adopt the concatenation of all average-pooled task-specific representations as our final feature vector for evaluation and compute all scores on test set.

Results. Figure 4 illustrates the quantitative results of different disentanglement metrics using box plots. First, we see that multi-task learning naturally comes with disentangled representations, where MTL achieves a slightly higher score than the STL. Another observation is that knowledge transfer methods like KD and KF also help the model to find factors that are unappreciable for the teachers. The features extracted by our factor networks generally score the best, especially on the dSprites dataset, with an improvement over median of 0.47 and 0.09 on DCI and MIG scores. It is in line with our expectation that decomposing the knowledge into parts leads to disentangled representations.

Representation Similarity. We further conduct representation similarity analysis using centered kernel alignment (CKA) [28] between teacher models, distilled models and our factorized models across 4 datasets, including dSprites, Shape3D, CIFAR10 and NYUDv2. On each dataset, CKA is adopted to quantifying feature similarity among (1) MTL teacher (2) MTL2MTL-KD student (3) MTL2STL students and (4) Our CKN and TSNs. We compute linear kernel CKA between all pairs of models at the last feature layer on test set. The model architectures are described in the Appendix. The higher CKA index suggests higher correlation between two networks.

Results. Figure 5 visualizes the CKA confusion matrix between all model pairs on 4 tasks. We made the following observations. First, models mastering the same subtask has high feature similarity. Second, our factorized TSN captures more "pure" knowledge compared with MTL2STL students. On each heatmap, the bottom left region has high similarity (in darker red), suggesting that the conventional distilled models still maintains high similarity with its peers even though they are trained on dedicated tasks. In comparison, factorized TSNs achieve smaller similarities (in upper right region), again supporting our argument that factor networks capture the disentangled factors across tasks.

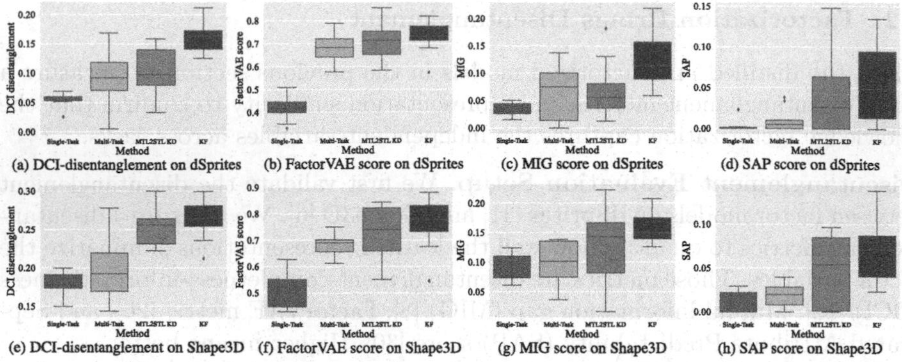

(a) DCI-disentanglement on dSprites (b) FactorVAE score on dSprites (c) MIG score on dSprites (d) SAP score on dSprites

(e) DCI-disentanglement on Shape3D (f) FactorVAE score on Shape3D (g) MIG score on Shape3D (h) SAP score on Shape3D

Fig. 4. Disentanglement Metrics comparison between (1) Single-Task Baseline, (2) Multi-Task Baseline, (3) KD, and (4) our proposed KF on dSprite (top) and Shape3D (bottom) datasets. Each experiment is repeated over 10 runs.

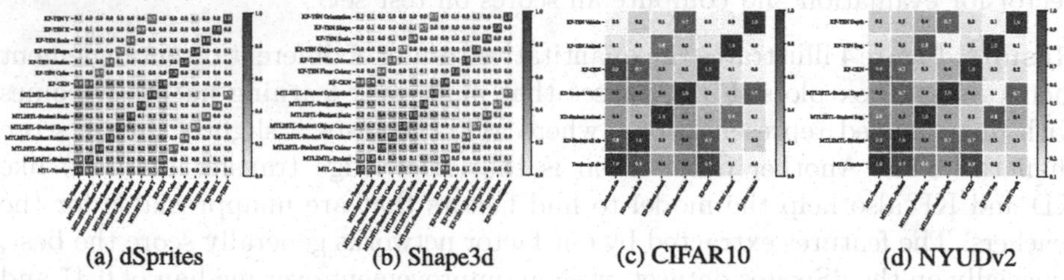

(a) dSprites (b) Shape3d (c) CIFAR10 (d) NYUDv2

Fig. 5. CKA representation similarity between distilled and factorized models.

4.3 Common Knowledge Benefits Transferring

We then finetune the factorized CKN on two downstream tasks to see if the common knowledge facilities the transfer learning to unseen domains. We train ResNet-18 networks with different initializations on Caltech-UCSD Birds (CUB-200) [60] and MIT indoor scene (Scene) [49]. The trained models are then reestablished as teachers to educate student networks like MBNv2 and ShuffleNetv2.

Results. Table 5 shows the transfer learning performance and distillation accuracy using different pretrained weights. R18 w/ImageNet-CKN refers to the ResNet-18 CKN factorized from ImageNet pretrained ResNet-18. Compared with the original pretrained weights, ImageNet-CKN achieves substantial improvement on both datasets. By reusing the finetuned ResNet-18 as teacher network, we show in Fig. 5 that CKN serves as a better role model to educate the student networks. It provides compelling evidence that common knowledge factorized from the teacher network benefits the transfer learning to other tasks.

Table 5. Finetuning performance and distillation accuracy with different pretrained weights. R18 is the short for ResNet-18.

Teacher	Student	CUB-200	Scene
–	R18 w/Rand init.	46.14	65.17
–	R18 w/ImageNet	65.28	65.19
–	R18 w/ImageNet-CKN	**69.17**	**72.37**
–	MobileNetV2 w/Rand init.	48.80	64.59
R18 w/Rand init.	MobileNetV2 w/Rand init.	54.18	66.78
R18 w/ImageNet	MobileNetV2 w/Rand init.	61.30	66.40
R18 w/ImageNet-CKN	MobileNetV2 w/Rand init.	**64.25**	**70.94**
–	ShuffleNetv2 w/Rand init.	52.51	64.39
R18 w/Rand init.	ShuffleNetv2 w/Rand init.	48.19	65.70
R18 w/ImageNet	ShuffleNetv2 w/Rand init.	59.15	66.00
R18 w/ImageNet-CKN	ShuffleNetv2 w/Rand init.	**60.69**	**68.95**

5 Conclusion

In this paper, we introduce a novel knowledge-transfer task termed *Knowledge Factorization*. Given a pretrained teacher, KF decomposes it into task-disentangled factor networks, each of which masters the task-specific and the common knowledge factorized from the teacher. Factor networks may operate independently, or be integrated to assemble multi-task networks, allowing for great scalability. We design an InfoMax Bottleneck objective to disentangle the common and task-specific representations by optimizing the mutual information between input and representations. Our method achieves strong and robust performance, and meanwhile demonstrates great disentanglement capability across various benchmarks, with better modularity and transferability.

Acknowledgement. This work is supported by NUS Advanced Research and Technology Innovation Centre (ARTIC) Project Reference ECT-RP2, and Faculty Research Committee Grant (WBS: A-0009440-00-00). Xinchao Wang is the corresponding author.

References

1. Achille, A., Soatto, S.: Emergence of invariance and disentanglement in deep representations. J. Mach. Learn. Res. **19**(1), 1947–1980 (2018)
2. Bachman, P., Hjelm, R.D., Buchwalter, W.: Learning representations by maximizing mutual information across views. arXiv preprint arXiv:1906.00910 (2019)
3. Belghazi, M.I., et al.: MINE: mutual information neural estimation. arXiv preprint arXiv:1801.04062 (2018)
4. Bengio, Y., Courville, A., Vincent, P.: Representation learning: a review and new perspectives. IEEE Trans. Pattern Anal. Mach. Intell. **35**(8), 1798–1828 (2013)

5. Buciluă, C., Caruana, R., Niculescu-Mizil, A.: Model compression. In: Proceedings of the 12th ACM SIGKDD International Conference on Knowledge Discovery and Data Mining, pp. 535–541 (2006)
6. Burgess, C., Kim, H.: 3d shapes dataset (2018). https://github.com/deepmind/3dshapes-dataset/
7. Burgess, C.P., et al.: Understanding disentangling in β-VAE. arXiv preprint arXiv:1804.03599 (2018)
8. Chen, R.T., Li, X., Grosse, R., Duvenaud, D.: Isolating sources of disentanglement in variational autoencoders. arXiv preprint arXiv:1802.04942 (2018)
9. Chen, T., Kornblith, S., Norouzi, M., Hinton, G.: A simple framework for contrastive learning of visual representations. In: International Conference on Machine Learning, pp. 1597–1607. PMLR (2020)
10. Chen, X., Duan, Y., Houthooft, R., Schulman, J., Sutskever, I., Abbeel, P.: InfoGAN: interpretable representation learning by information maximizing generative adversarial nets. In: NIPS (2016)
11. Chen, X., Mottaghi, R., Liu, X., Fidler, S., Urtasun, R., Yuille, A.: Detect what you can: detecting and representing objects using holistic models and body parts. In: Proceedings of the IEEE Conference on Computer Vision and Pattern Recognition, pp. 1971–1978 (2014)
12. Eastwood, C., Williams, C.K.: A framework for the quantitative evaluation of disentangled representations. In: International Conference on Learning Representations (2018)
13. Feng, Z., Wang, X., Ke, C., Zeng, A., Tao, D., Song, M.: Dual swap disentangling. In: Conference on Neural Information Processing Systems (2018)
14. Goodfellow, I., Lee, H., Le, Q., Saxe, A., Ng, A.: Measuring invariances in deep networks. Adv. Neural. Inf. Process. Syst. **22**, 646–654 (2009)
15. Granger, E., Kiran, M., Dolz, J., Blais-Morin, L.A., et al.: Joint progressive knowledge distillation and unsupervised domain adaptation. In: 2020 International Joint Conference on Neural Networks (IJCNN), pp. 1–8. IEEE (2020)
16. Grill, J.B., et al.: Bootstrap your own latent: a new approach to self-supervised learning. arXiv preprint arXiv:2006.07733 (2020)
17. He, K., Fan, H., Wu, Y., Xie, S., Girshick, R.: Momentum contrast for unsupervised visual representation learning. In: Proceedings of the IEEE/CVF Conference on Computer Vision and Pattern Recognition, pp. 9729–9738 (2020)
18. He, K., Zhang, X., Ren, S., Sun, J.: Deep residual learning for image recognition. In: Proceedings of the IEEE Conference on Computer Vision and Pattern Recognition, pp. 770–778 (2016)
19. Higgins, I., et al.: beta-VAE: learning basic visual concepts with a constrained variational framework (2016)
20. Hinton, G.E., Vinyals, O., Dean, J.: Distilling the knowledge in a neural network. ArXiv abs/1503.02531 (2015)
21. Hjelm, R.D., et al.: Learning deep representations by mutual information estimation and maximization. arXiv preprint arXiv:1808.06670 (2018)
22. Jaiswal, A., Wu, Y., AbdAlmageed, W., Natarajan, P.: Unsupervised adversarial invariance. arXiv preprint arXiv:1809.10083 (2018)
23. Jing, Y., Yang, Y., Wang, X., Song, M., Tao, D.: Amalgamating knowledge from heterogeneous graph neural networks. In: Proceedings of the IEEE/CVF Conference on Computer Vision and Pattern Recognition, pp. 15709–15718 (2021)

24. Kanakis, M., Bruggemann, D., Saha, S., Georgoulis, S., Obukhov, A., Van Gool, L.: Reparameterizing convolutions for incremental multi-task learning without task interference. In: Vedaldi, A., Bischof, H., Brox, T., Frahm, J.-M. (eds.) ECCV 2020. LNCS, vol. 12365, pp. 689–707. Springer, Cham (2020). https://doi.org/10.1007/978-3-030-58565-5_41
25. Khosla, P., et al.: Supervised contrastive learning. arXiv preprint arXiv:2004.11362 (2020)
26. Kim, H., Mnih, A.: Disentangling by factorising. ArXiv abs/1802.05983 (2018)
27. Kingma, D.P., Welling, M.: Auto-encoding variational bayes. arXiv preprint arXiv:1312.6114 (2013)
28. Kornblith, S., Norouzi, M., Lee, H., Hinton, G.: Similarity of neural network representations revisited. In: International Conference on Machine Learning, pp. 3519–3529. PMLR (2019)
29. Krizhevsky, A., Hinton, G., et al.: Learning multiple layers of features from tiny images (2009)
30. Kumar, A., Sattigeri, P., Balakrishnan, A.: Variational inference of disentangled latent concepts from unlabeled observations. arXiv preprint arXiv:1711.00848 (2017)
31. Li, T., Li, J., Liu, Z., Zhang, C.: Few sample knowledge distillation for efficient network compression. In: Proceedings of the IEEE/CVF Conference on Computer Vision and Pattern Recognition, pp. 14639–14647 (2020)
32. Li, Z., Hoiem, D.: Learning without forgetting. IEEE Trans. Pattern Anal. Mach. Intell. **40**(12), 2935–2947 (2017)
33. Linsker, R.: Self-organization in a perceptual network. Computer **21**(3), 105–117 (1988)
34. Liu, Y., Wang, Z., Jin, H., Wassell, I.: Multi-task adversarial network for disentangled feature learning. In: Proceedings of the IEEE Conference on Computer Vision and Pattern Recognition, pp. 3743–3751 (2018)
35. Locatello, F., et al.: Challenging common assumptions in the unsupervised learning of disentangled representations. In: International Conference on Machine Learning, pp. 4114–4124. PMLR (2019)
36. Lopes, R.G., Fenu, S., Starner, T.: Data-free knowledge distillation for deep neural networks. arXiv preprint arXiv:1710.07535 (2017)
37. Löwe, S., O'Connor, P., Veeling, B.S.: Greedy infomax for self-supervised representation learning (2019)
38. Luo, S., Wang, X., Fang, G., Hu, Y., Tao, D., Song, M.: Knowledge amalgamation from heterogeneous networks by common feature learning. In: Kraus, S. (ed.) Proceedings of the Twenty-Eighth International Joint Conference on Artificial Intelligence, IJCAI 2019, Macao, China, 10–16 August 2019, pp. 3087–3093. ijcai.org (2019). https://doi.org/10.24963/ijcai.2019/428
39. Maninis, K.K., Radosavovic, I., Kokkinos, I.: Attentive single-tasking of multiple tasks. In: Proceedings of the IEEE/CVF Conference on Computer Vision and Pattern Recognition, pp. 1851–1860 (2019)
40. Mathieu, M.F., Zhao, J.J., Zhao, J., Ramesh, A., Sprechmann, P., LeCun, Y.: Disentangling factors of variation in deep representation using adversarial training. In: Lee, D., Sugiyama, M., Luxburg, U., Guyon, I., Garnett, R. (eds.) Advances in Neural Information Processing Systems, vol. 29. Curran Associates, Inc. (2016). https://proceedings.neurips.cc/paper/2016/file/ef0917ea498b1665ad6c701057155abe-Paper.pdf
41. Matthey, L., Higgins, I., Hassabis, D., Lerchner, A.: dSprites: disentanglement testing sprites dataset (2017). https://github.com/deepmind/dsprites-dataset/

42. Miller, G.A.: WordNet: a lexical database for English. Commun. ACM **38**(11), 39–41 (1995)
43. Nguyen-Meidine, L.T., Belal, A., Kiran, M., Dolz, J., Blais-Morin, L.A., Granger, E.: Unsupervised multi-target domain adaptation through knowledge distillation. In: Proceedings of the IEEE/CVF Winter Conference on Applications of Computer Vision, pp. 1339–1347 (2021)
44. Niemeyer, M., Geiger, A.: GIRAFFE: representing scenes as compositional generative neural feature fields. In: Proceedings of the IEEE/CVF Conference on Computer Vision and Pattern Recognition, pp. 11453–11464 (2021)
45. van den Oord, A., Li, Y., Vinyals, O.: Representation learning with contrastive predictive coding. arXiv preprint arXiv:1807.03748 (2018)
46. Papernot, N., McDaniel, P., Wu, X., Jha, S., Swami, A.: Distillation as a defense to adversarial perturbations against deep neural networks. In: 2016 IEEE Symposium on Security and Privacy (SP), pp. 582–597. IEEE (2016)
47. Passalis, N., Tefas, A.: Learning deep representations with probabilistic knowledge transfer. In: Ferrari, V., Hebert, M., Sminchisescu, C., Weiss, Y. (eds.) ECCV 2018. LNCS, vol. 11215, pp. 283–299. Springer, Cham (2018). https://doi.org/10.1007/978-3-030-01252-6_17
48. Peters, J., Janzing, D., Schölkopf, B.: Elements of Causal Inference: Foundations and Learning Algorithms. The MIT Press, Cambridge (2017)
49. Quattoni, A., Torralba, A.: Recognizing indoor scenes. In: 2009 IEEE Conference on Computer Vision and Pattern Recognition, pp. 413–420. IEEE (2009)
50. Ren, S., Zhou, D., He, S., Feng, J., Wang, X.: Shunted self-attention via multi-scale token aggregation. In: Proceedings of the IEEE/CVF Conference on Computer Vision and Pattern Recognition (2022)
51. Romero, A., Ballas, N., Kahou, S.E., Chassang, A., Gatta, C., Bengio, Y.: FitNets: hints for thin deep nets. arXiv preprint arXiv:1412.6550 (2014)
52. Russakovsky, O., et al.: ImageNet large scale visual recognition challenge. Int. J. Comput. Vision **115**(3), 211–252 (2015). https://doi.org/10.1007/s11263-015-0816-y
53. Sandler, M., Howard, A., Zhu, M., Zhmoginov, A., Chen, L.C.: MobileNetV 2: inverted residuals and linear bottlenecks. In: Proceedings of the IEEE Conference on Computer Vision and Pattern Recognition, pp. 4510–4520 (2018)
54. Silberman, N., Hoiem, D., Kohli, P., Fergus, R.: Indoor segmentation and support inference from RGBD images. In: Fitzgibbon, A., Lazebnik, S., Perona, P., Sato, Y., Schmid, C. (eds.) ECCV 2012. LNCS, vol. 7576, pp. 746–760. Springer, Heidelberg (2012). https://doi.org/10.1007/978-3-642-33715-4_54
55. Sun, S., Cheng, Y., Gan, Z., Liu, J.: Patient knowledge distillation for BERT model compression. In: EMNLP (2019)
56. Tian, Y., Sun, C., Poole, B., Krishnan, D., Schmid, C., Isola, P.: What makes for good views for contrastive learning? arXiv preprint arXiv:2005.10243 (2020)
57. Tishby, N., Pereira, F.C., Bialek, W.: The information bottleneck method. arXiv preprint physics/0004057 (2000)
58. Tran, L., Yin, X., Liu, X.: Disentangled representation learning GAN for pose-invariant face recognition. In: Proceedings of the IEEE Conference on Computer Vision and Pattern Recognition, pp. 1415–1424 (2017)
59. Tschannen, M., Djolonga, J., Rubenstein, P.K., Gelly, S., Lucic, M.: On mutual information maximization for representation learning. arXiv preprint arXiv:1907.13625 (2019)

60. Wah, C., Branson, S., Welinder, P., Perona, P., Belongie, S.: The Caltech-UCSD birds-200-2011 dataset. Technical report. CNS-TR-2011-001, California Institute of Technology (2011)
61. Wang, J., et al.: Deep high-resolution representation learning for visual recognition. IEEE Trans. Pattern Anal. Mach. Intell. **43**, 3349–3364 (2020)
62. Yang, Y., Feng, Z., Song, M., Wang, X.: Factorizable graph convolutional networks. In: Conference on Neural Information Processing Systems (2020)
63. Yang, Y., Qiu, J., Song, M., Tao, D., Wang, X.: Distilling knowledge from graph convolutional networks. In: Proceedings of the IEEE/CVF Conference on Computer Vision and Pattern Recognition (2020)
64. Ye, J., Ji, Y., Wang, X., Ou, K., Tao, D., Song, M.: Student becoming the master: Knowledge amalgamation for joint scene parsing, depth estimation, and more. In: Proceedings of the IEEE/CVF Conference on Computer Vision and Pattern Recognition, pp. 2829–2838 (2019)
65. Zagoruyko, S., Komodakis, N.: Wide residual networks. arXiv preprint arXiv:1605.07146 (2016)
66. Zagoruyko, S., Komodakis, N.: Paying more attention to attention: improving the performance of convolutional neural networks via attention transfer. In: ICLR (2017). https://arxiv.org/abs/1612.03928
67. Zenke, F., Poole, B., Ganguli, S.: Continual learning through synaptic intelligence. In: International Conference on Machine Learning, pp. 3987–3995. PMLR (2017)
68. Zhang, J.O., Sax, A., Zamir, A., Guibas, L., Malik, J.: Side-tuning: a baseline for network adaptation via additive side networks. In: Vedaldi, A., Bischof, H., Brox, T., Frahm, J.-M. (eds.) ECCV 2020. LNCS, vol. 12348, pp. 698–714. Springer, Cham (2020). https://doi.org/10.1007/978-3-030-58580-8_41

Contrastive Vicinal Space for Unsupervised Domain Adaptation

Jaemin Na[1], Dongyoon Han[2], Hyung Jin Chang[3], and Wonjun Hwang[1](✉)

[1] Ajou University, Suwon, Korea
{osial46,wjhwang}@ajou.ac.kr
[2] NAVER AI Lab, Daejeon, Korea
dongyoon.han@navercorp.com
[3] University of Birmingham, Birmingham, UK
h.j.chang@bham.ac.uk

Abstract. Recent unsupervised domain adaptation methods have utilized vicinal space between the source and target domains. However, the equilibrium collapse of labels, a problem where the source labels are dominant over the target labels in the predictions of vicinal instances, has never been addressed. In this paper, we propose an instance-wise minimax strategy that minimizes the entropy of high uncertainty instances in the vicinal space to tackle the stated problem. We divide the vicinal space into two subspaces through the solution of the minimax problem: contrastive space and consensus space. In the contrastive space, inter-domain discrepancy is mitigated by constraining instances to have contrastive views and labels, and the consensus space reduces the confusion between intra-domain categories. The effectiveness of our method is demonstrated on public benchmarks, including Office-31, Office-Home, and VisDA-C, achieving state-of-the-art performances. We further show that our method outperforms the current state-of-the-art methods on PACS, which indicates that our instance-wise approach works well for multi-source domain adaptation as well. Code is available at https://github.com/NaJaeMin92/CoVi.

Keywords: Unsupervised domain adaptation · Equilibrium collapse · Contrastive Vicinal space

1 Introduction

Unsupervised domain adaptation (UDA) aims to adapt a model trained on a labeled source domain to an unlabeled target domain. One of the most important problems to solve in UDA is the domain shift [42] (*i.e.*, distribution shift) problem. The domain shift arises from the change in the data distribution between the training domain (*i.e.*, source domain) of an algorithm and the test domain encountered in a practical application (*i.e.*, target domain). Although recent

---

Supplementary Information The online version contains supplementary material available at https://doi.org/10.1007/978-3-031-19830-4_6.

S. Avidan et al. (Eds.): ECCV 2022, LNCS 13694, pp. 92–110, 2022.
https://doi.org/10.1007/978-3-031-19830-4_6

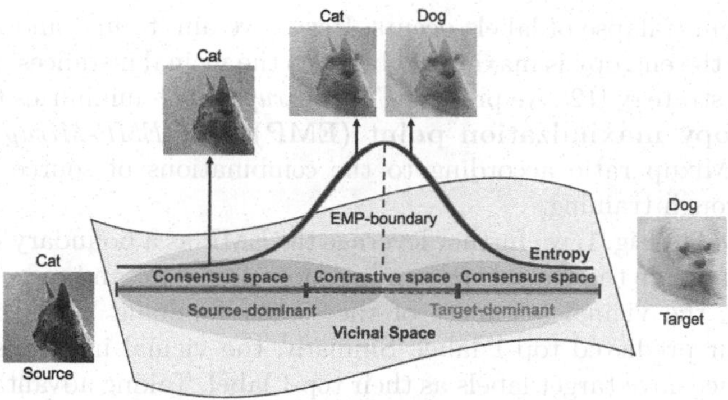

Fig. 1. Overview. Vicinal space between the source and target domains is divided into contrastive space and consensus space. Our methodology alleviates inter-domain discrepancy in the contrastive space and simultaneously resolves intra-domain categorical confusion in the consensus space.

UDA studies [33,49,54] have shown encouraging results, a large domain shift is still a significant obstacle.

One recent paradigm to address the large domain shift problem is to leverage intermediate domains between the source and target domains instead of direct domain adaptation. Recent studies [5,15] inspired by generative adversarial networks [16] (GANs) generate instances of intermediate domains to bridge the source and target domains. Moreover, [3,10] learn domain-invariant representations by borrowing only the concept of adversarial training. Meanwhile, with the development of data augmentation techniques, many approaches have emerged built on data augmentation to construct the intermediate spaces. Recent studies [33,48,51] have shown promising results by grafting Mixup augmentation [55] to the domain adaptation task. These studies use inter-domain mixup to efficiently overcome the domain shift problem by utilizing vicinal instances between the source and target domains. However, none of them consider leveraging the predictions of the vicinal instances in the perspective of self-training [24].

Self-training is the straightforward approach that uses self-predictions of a model to train itself. Semi-supervised learning methods [24,36] leverage a model's predictions on unlabeled data to obtain additional information used during training as their supervision. In particular, unsupervised domain adaptation methods [17,38,43] have shown that pseudo-label for the target domain can play an important role in alleviating the domain shift problem.

In this work, we introduce a new **Co**ntrastive **Vi**cinal space-based (CoVi) algorithm that leverages vicinal instances from the perspective of self-training [24]. In vicinal space, we observe that the source label is generally dominant over the target label before applying domain adaptation. In other words, even if vicinal instances consist of a higher proportion of target instances than source instances (*i.e.*, target-dominant instances), their one-hot predictions are more likely to be source labels (*i.e.*, source-dominant labels). We define this phenomenon as an **equilibrium collapse of labels** between vicinal instances. We also discover that the entropy of the predictions is maximum at the points where the equilibrium collapse of labels occurs. Hence, we aim to find and address the points where the entropy is maximized between the vicinal instances. Inspired by the minimax strategy [12], we present *EMP-Mixup*, which minimizes the entropy for the **entropy maximization point (EMP)**. Our *EMP-Mixup* adaptively adjusts the Mixup ratio according to the combinations of source and target instances through training.

As depicted in Fig. 1, we further leverage the EMP as a boundary (*i.e.*, EMP-boundary) to divide the vicinal space into source-dominant and target-dominant spaces. Here, the vicinal instances of the source-dominant space have source labels as their predicted top-1 label. Similarly, the vicinal instances of target-dominant space have target labels as their top-1 label. Taking advantage of these properties, we configure two specialized subspaces to reduce inter-domain and intra-domain discrepancy simultaneously.

First, we construct a **contrastive space** around the EMP-boundary to ensure that the vicinal instances have contrastive views: source-dominant and target-dominant views. Since the contrastive views share the same combination of source and target instances, they should have the same top-2 labels containing the source and target labels. In addition, under our constraints, the two contrastive views have opposite order of the first and second labels in the top-2 labels. Inspired by consistency training [1,44], we propose to impose consistency on predictions of the two contrastive views. Specifically, we mitigate inter-domain discrepancy by solving a *"swapped" prediction problem* where we predict the top-2 labels of a contrastive view from the other contrastive view.

Second, we constrain a **consensus space** outside of the contrastive space to alleviate the categorical confusion within the intra-domain. In this space, we generate target-dominant vicinal instances utilizing multiple source instances as a perturbation to a single target instance. Here, the role of the source instances is not to learn classification information of the source domain but to confuse the predictions of the target instances. We can ensure consistent and robust predictions for target instances by enforcing label consensus among the multiple target-dominant vicinal instances to a single target label.

We perform extensive ablation studies for a detailed analysis of the proposed methods. In particular, we achieve comparable performance to the recent state-of-the-art methods in standard unsupervised domain adaptation benchmarks such as Office-31 [37], Office-Home [46], and VisDA-C [35]. Furthermore, we validate the superiority of our instance-wise approach on the PACS [26] dataset for multi-source domain adaptation. Overall, we make the following contributions:

- This is the first study in UDA to leverage the vicinal space from the perspective of self-training. We shed light on the problem of the equilibrium collapse of labels in the vicinal space and propose a minimax strategy to handle it.
- We alleviate inter-domain and intra-domain confusions simultaneously by dividing the vicinal space into contrastive and consensus spaces.
- Our method achieves state-of-the-art performance and is further validated through extensive ablation studies.

2 Related Work

Unsupervised Domain Adaptation. One of the representative domain adaptation approaches [13,50] is learning a domain-invariant representation by aligning the global distribution between the source and target domains. Of particular interest, Xie *et al.* [50] presented a moving semantic transfer network that aligns labeled source centroids and pseudo-labeled target centroids to learn semantic representations for unlabeled target data. Following [6,17,33], we adopt this simple but efficient method as our baseline.

Our work is also related to the domain adaptation approaches that consider the inter-domain and intra-domain gap together. Kang *et al.* [23] proposed to minimize the intra-class discrepancy and maximize the inter-class discrepancy to perform class-aware domain alignment. Pan *et al.* [34] presented a semantic segmentation method that minimizes both inter-domain and intra-domain gaps. Unlike these methods, we introduce a practical approach that uses two specialized spaces to reduce inter-domain and intra-domain discrepancy for each.

Mixup Augmentation. Mixup [55] is a data-agnostic and straightforward augmentation using a linear interpolation between two data instances. The Mixup has been applied to various tasks and shown to improve the robustness of neural networks. The recent semi-supervised learning methods [1,2,44] efficiently utilized Mixup to leverage unlabeled data. Meanwhile, several domain adaptation methods [33,48,51] with Mixup were proposed to alleviate the domain-shift problem successfully. Xu *et al.* [51] and Wu *et al.* [48] showed promising results using inter-domain Mixup between source and target domains. Recently, Na *et al.* [33] achieved a significant performance gain by using two networks trained with two fixed Mixup ratios. Moreover, the latest studies [18,31,56] suggested adaptive Mixup techniques instead of using manually designed interpolation policies. For example, Zhu *et al.* [56] introduced a more advanced interpolation technique that seeks the Wasserstein barycenter between two instances and proposed an adaptive Mixup. Mai *et al.* [31] introduced a meta-learning-based optimization strategy for dynamically learning the interpolation policy in semi-supervised learning. However, unsupervised domain adaptation methods still count on hand-tuned or random interpolation policies. In this work, we derive the Mixup ratio according to the convex combinations of source and target instances.

Consistency Training. Consistency training is one of the promising components for leveraging unlabeled data, which enforces a model to produce similar predictions of original and perturbed instances. The recent semi-supervised learning methods [1,2,44] utilize unlabeled data by assuming that the model should output similar predictions when fed perturbed versions of the same instance. Berthelot *et al.* [2] applied augmentations several times for each unlabeled instance and averaged them to produce guessed labels. In ReMixMatch [1], Berthelot *et al.* used the model's prediction for a weakly-augmented instance as the guessed label for multiple strongly-augmented variants of the same instance. Recently, Sohn *et al.* [44] encouraged predictions from strongly-augmented instances to match pseudo-labels generated from weakly-augmented instances.

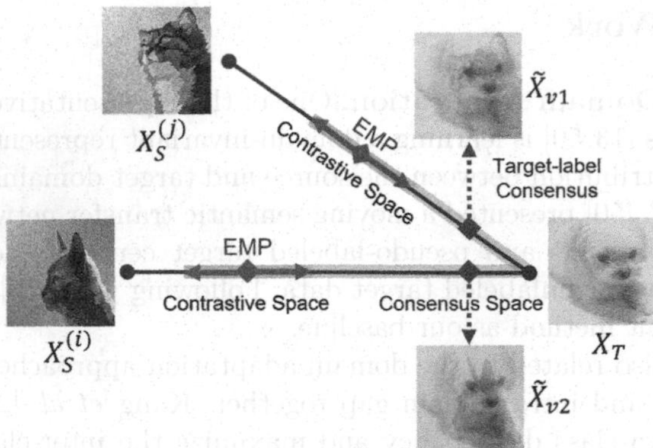

Fig. 2. Schematic illustration of CoVi. The *EMP-Mixup* finds the most confusing point (*i.e.*, EMP) among vicinal instances. CoVi then learns through top-k contrastive predictions from contrastive views in the contrastive space determined by the EMP. In the consensus space, we achieve a target-label consensus with perturbations of the source instances.

Although effective, these methods rely on augmentation techniques such as random augmentation, AutoAugment [8], RandAugment [9], and CTAugment [1]. By contrast, our method is free from these augmentation techniques and does not require carefully selected combinations of augmentations. We solely leverage mixup augmentation [55] to generate the vicinal spaces and achieve the effect of consistency training.

3 Methodology

CoVi introduces three techniques to leverage the vicinal space between the source and target domains: i) EMP-Mixup, ii) contrastive views and labels, and iii) a label-consensus. An overall depiction of CoVi is in Fig. 2.

3.1 Preliminaries

Notation. We denote a mini-batch of m-images as $\mathcal{X}$, corresponding labels as $\mathcal{Y}$, and extracted features from $\mathcal{X}$ as $\mathcal{Z}$. Specifically, $\mathcal{X}_S \subset \mathbb{R}^{m \times i}$ and $\mathcal{Y}_S \subset \{0,1\}^{m \times n}$ denote the mini-batches of source instances and their corresponding one-hot labels, respectively. Here, n denotes the number of classes and $i = c{\cdot}h{\cdot}w$, where c denotes the channel size, and h and w denote the height and width of the image instances, respectively. Similarly, the mini-batch of unlabeled target instances is $\mathcal{X}_T \subset \mathbb{R}^{m \times i}$. Our model consists of the following subcomponents: an *encoder* f_θ, a *classifier* h_θ, and an *EMP-learner* g_ϕ.

Mixup. The *Mixup* augmentation [55] based on the Vicinal Risk Minimization (VRM) [7] principle exploits virtual instances constructed with the linear interpolation of two instances. These vicinal instances can benefit unsupervised domain adaptation, which has no target domain labels. We define the inter-domain Mixup applied between the source and target domains as follows:

$$\tilde{\mathcal{X}}_\lambda = \lambda \cdot \mathcal{X}_S + (1-\lambda) \cdot \mathcal{X}_T \\ \tilde{\mathcal{Y}}_\lambda = \lambda \cdot \mathcal{Y}_S + (1-\lambda) \cdot \hat{\mathcal{Y}}_T, \tag{1}$$

where $\hat{\mathcal{Y}}_T$ denotes the pseudo labels of the target instances and $\lambda \in [0, 1]$ is the Mixup ratio. Then, the empirical risk for vicinal instances in the inter-domain Mixup is defined as follows:

$$\mathcal{R}_\lambda = \frac{1}{m} \sum_{i=1}^{m} \mathcal{H}[h(f(\tilde{\mathcal{X}}_\lambda^{(i)})), \tilde{\mathcal{Y}}_\lambda^{(i)}], \tag{2}$$

where $\mathcal{H}$ is a standard cross-entropy loss.

3.2 EMP-Mixup

In the vicinal space between the source and target domains, we make interesting observations on unsupervised domain adaptation.

Observation 1. *"The labels of the target domain are relatively recessive to the source domain labels."*

We investigate the dominance of the predicted top-1 labels between the source and target instances in vicinal instances. We find that the label dominance is balanced when the labels of both the source and target domains are provided (*i.e.*, supervised learning). In this case, the top-1 label of the vicinal instance is determined by the instance occupying a relatively larger proportion. However, in the UDA, where the label of the target domain is not given, the balance of label dominance is broken (*i.e.*, equilibrium collapse of labels). Indeed, we discover that source labels frequently represent vicinal instances even with a higher proportion of target instances than source instances.

Observation 2. *"Depending on the convex combinations of source and target instances, the label dominance is changed."*

Next, we observe that the label dominance is altered according to the convex combinations of instances. It implies that an instance-wise approach can be a key to solving the label equilibrium collapse problem. In addition, we discover that the entropy of the prediction is maximum at the point where the label dominance changes because the source and target instances become most confusing at this point (see Figs. 4 and 5).

Based on these observations, we aim to capture and mitigate the most confusing points, which vary with the combination of instances. Inspired by [12,16,32], we introduce a minimax strategy to break through the worst-case risk [12] among the vicinal instances between the source and target domains. We minimize the worst risk by finding the **entropy maximization point (EMP)** among the vicinal instances. In order to estimate the EMPs, we introduce a small network, *EMP-learner*. This network aims to generate Mixup ratios that maximize the entropy of the encoder f_θ (*e.g., ResNet*) followed by a classifier h_θ.

Given $\mathcal{X}_\mathcal{S}$ and $\mathcal{X}_\mathcal{T}$, we obtain the instance features $\mathcal{Z}_\mathcal{S} = f_\theta(\mathcal{X}_\mathcal{S})$ and $\mathcal{Z}_\mathcal{T} = f_\theta(\mathcal{X}_\mathcal{T})$ from the encoder f_θ. Then, we pass the concatenated features $\mathcal{Z}_\mathcal{S} \oplus \mathcal{Z}_\mathcal{T}$ to the *EMP-learner* g_ϕ. Then, the *EMP-learner* produces the entropy maximization ratio λ^* that maximizes the entropy of the encoder f_θ. Formally, the Mixup ratios for our *EMP-Mixup* are defined as follows:

$$\lambda^* = \underset{\lambda \in [0,1]}{\arg\max}\, \mathcal{H}[h_\theta(f_\theta(\tilde{\mathcal{X}}_\lambda))], \tag{3}$$

where $\lambda = g_\phi(\mathcal{Z}_\mathcal{S} \oplus \mathcal{Z}_\mathcal{T})$ and $\mathcal{H}$ is the entropy loss.

Finally, we design the objective function for *EMP-learner* to **maximize the entropy** as follows:

$$\mathcal{R}_\lambda(\phi) = \frac{1}{m}\sum_{i=1}^{m} \mathcal{H}[h(f(\tilde{\mathcal{X}}_\lambda^{(i)}))], \tag{4}$$

where $\mathcal{H}$ is the entropy loss. Note that we only update the parameter ϕ of the *EMP-learner*, not the parameter θ of the encoder and the classifier. With the worst-case ratio λ^*, *EMP-Mixup* **minimizes the worst-case risk** on vicinal instances as follows:

$$\mathcal{R}_{\lambda^*}(\theta) = \frac{1}{m}\sum_{i=1}^{m} \mathcal{H}[h(f(\tilde{\mathcal{X}}_{\lambda^*}^{(i)})), \tilde{\mathcal{Y}}_{\lambda^*}^{(i)}], \tag{5}$$

where $\mathcal{H}$ is the standard cross-entropy loss.

It is noteworthy that our $\lambda^* = [\lambda_1, ..., \lambda_m]$ has different optimized ratios according to the combinations of the source and target instances within a mini-batch. Finally, *EMP-Mixup* minimizes the risk of vicinal instances from the viewpoint of the worst-case risk. The overall objective functions are defined as follows:

$$\mathcal{R}_{emp} = \mathcal{R}_{\lambda^*}(\theta) - \mathcal{R}_\lambda(\phi). \tag{6}$$

3.3 Contrastive Views and Labels

Observation 3. *"The dominant/recessive labels of the vicinal instances are switched at the EMP."*

Looking back to the previous observations, the label dominance depends on the convex combination of instances, and the point of change is the EMP. In other words, with the EMP as a boundary (*i.e., EMP-boundary*), the dominant/recessive label is switched between the source and target domains. It means that vicinal instances around the *EMP-boundary* should have source and target labels as their top-2 labels.

These observations and analyses lead us to design the concepts of contrastive views and contrastive labels. Owing to the *EMP-boundary*, we can divide the

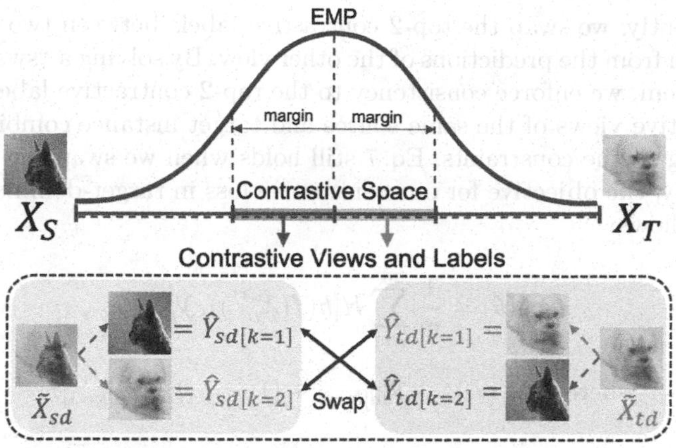

Fig. 3. Contrastive views and labels. (i) The **contrastive views** consist of a source-dominant view $\tilde{\mathcal{X}}_{sd}$ and a target-dominant view $\tilde{\mathcal{X}}_{td}$. (ii) The **contrastive labels** comprise the source-dominant label and target-recessive label from the top-2 predictions in the contrastive view $\tilde{\mathcal{X}}_{sd}$ (and vice versa).

vicinal space into source-dominant and target-dominant space, as described in Fig. 3. Specifically, we constrain the source-dominant and target-dominant spaces of the contrastive space to $\lambda^* - \omega < \lambda_{sd} < \lambda^*$ and $\lambda^* < \lambda_{td} < \lambda^* + \omega$, respectively. Here, ω is the margin of the ratio from the *EMP-boundary*, which is manually designed. Consequently, the source-dominant instances $\tilde{\mathcal{X}}_{sd}$ and target-dominant instances $\tilde{\mathcal{X}}_{td}$ have **contrastive views** of each other.

From the contrastive views, we focus on the top-2 labels for each prediction because we are only interested in the classes that correspond to the source and target instances, not the other classes. Here, we define a set of top-2 one-hot labels within a mini-batch as $\hat{\mathcal{Y}}_{[k=1]}$ and $\hat{\mathcal{Y}}_{[k=2]}$. Unlike a general Mixup that uses pure source and target labels (see Eq. 1), we directly exploit the predicted labels from vicinal instances. In this case, for example, the labels for the instances of the target-dominant space are constructed as follows:

$$\tilde{\mathcal{Y}}_{td} = \lambda_{td} \cdot \hat{\mathcal{Y}}_{td[k=1]} + (1 - \lambda_{td}) \cdot \hat{\mathcal{Y}}_{td[k=2]}. \tag{7}$$

Furthermore, we expand on this and propose a new concept of **contrastive labels.** We constrain the top-2 labels from the contrastive views as follows:

- $\hat{\mathcal{Y}}_{sd[k=1]}$ *from* $\tilde{\mathcal{X}}_{sd}$ *and* $\hat{\mathcal{Y}}_{td[k=2]}$ *from* $\tilde{\mathcal{X}}_{td}$ *must be equal, as the predictions of the source instances.*
- *Similarly,* $\hat{\mathcal{Y}}_{sd[k=2]}$ *must be equal to* $\hat{\mathcal{Y}}_{td[k=1]}$*, as for the predictions of the target instances.*

In other words, the dominant label $\hat{\mathcal{Y}}_{sd[k=1]}$ of $\tilde{\mathcal{X}}_{sd}$ and the recessive label $\hat{\mathcal{Y}}_{td[k=2]}$ of $\tilde{\mathcal{X}}_{td}$ must be the same as the source labels and vice versa. Note that our contrastive constraints are instance-level constraints that must be satisfied between any instances, regardless of the class category.

Consequently, we swap the top-2 contrastive labels between two contrastive views to learn from the predictions of the other view. By solving a "swapped" prediction problem, we enforce consistency to the top-2 contrastive labels obtained from contrastive views of the same source and target instance combinations.

According to the constraints, Eq. 7 still holds when we swap the contrastive labels. Finally, the objective for our contrastive loss in target-dominant space is defined as follows:

$$\mathcal{R}_{td}(\theta) = \frac{1}{m}\sum_{i=1}^{m} \mathcal{H}[h(f(\tilde{\mathcal{X}}_{td}^{(i)})), \hat{\mathcal{Y}}_{td}^{(i)}], \tag{8}$$

$$\text{where } \hat{\mathcal{Y}}_{td} = \lambda_{td} \cdot \hat{\mathcal{Y}}_{sd[k=2]} + (1 - \lambda_{td}) \cdot \hat{\mathcal{Y}}_{sd[k=1]}.$$

Similarly, we define $\mathcal{R}_{sd}(\theta)$ in the source-dominant space and omit it for clarity. The overall objective functions for contrastive loss are defined as follows:

$$\mathcal{R}_{ct} = \mathcal{R}_{td}(\theta) + \mathcal{R}_{sd}(\theta). \tag{9}$$

3.4 Label Consensus

Even though the confusion between the source and target instances is crucial in the contrastive space, outside of the contrastive space (*i.e.*, **consensus space**), we pay more attention to the uncertainty of predictions within the intra-domain than inter-domain instances (see Fig. 6). Here, we exploit multiple source instances to impose perturbations to target predictions rather than classification information for the source domain. It makes a model more robust to the target predictions by enforcing consistent predictions on the target instances even with the source perturbations.

We construct two randomly shuffled versions of the source instances within a mini-batch. We then apply Mixup with a single target mini-batch to obtain two different perturbed views v_1 and v_2. Here, we set the mixup ratio for the source instances sufficiently small since too strong perturbations can impair the target class semantics. We compute two softmax probabilities from the perturbed instances $\tilde{\mathcal{X}}_{v_1}$ and $\tilde{\mathcal{X}}_{v_2}$ using an encoder, followed by a classifier. Finally, we aggregate the softmax probabilities and yield a one-hot prediction $\hat{\mathcal{Y}}$.

We accomplish **target-label consensus** by assigning the label $\hat{\mathcal{Y}}$ to both versions of the perturbed target-dominant instances $\tilde{\mathcal{X}}_{v_1}$ and $\tilde{\mathcal{X}}_{v_2}$. Imposing consistency to differently perturbed instances for a single target label allows us to focus on categorical information for the target domain. The objective for label consensus on target instances can be defined as follows:

$$\mathcal{R}_{cs}(\theta) = \frac{1}{m}\sum_{i=1}^{m} [\mathcal{H}(h(f(\tilde{\mathcal{X}}_{v_1}^{(i)}), \hat{\mathcal{Y}}^{(i)})) + \mathcal{H}(h(f(\tilde{\mathcal{X}}_{v_2}^{(i)}), \hat{\mathcal{Y}}^{(i)}))], \tag{10}$$

where $\mathcal{H}$ is the cross-entropy loss.

Note that this approach is also applicable to source-dominant space, but we exclude it from the final loss as it does not significantly affect the performance.

4 Experiments

We evaluate our method on four popular benchmarks, including Office-31, Office-Home, VisDA-C, and PACS. Moreover, we validate our method in a multi-source domain adaptation scenario using the PACS dataset.

Table 1. Accuracy (%) on Office-31 for unsupervised domain adaptation (ResNet-50). The best accuracy is indicated in bold, and the second-best accuracy is underlined. * Reproduced by [6].

Method	A→W	D→W	W→D	A→D	D→A	W→A	Avg.
MSTN* (Baseline) [50]	91.3	98.9	**100.0**	90.4	72.7	65.6	86.5
DWL (CVPR'21) [49]	89.2	99.2	**100.0**	91.2	73.1	69.8	87.1
DMRL (ECCV'20) [48]	90.8±0.3	99.0±0.2	**100.0±0.0**	93.4±0.5	73.0±0.3	71.2±0.3	87.9
ILA-DA (CVPR'21) [41]	95.72	99.25	**100.0**	93.37	72.10	75.40	89.3
MCC (ECCV'20) [22]	95.5±0.2	98.6±0.1	**100.0±0.0**	94.4±0.3	72.9±0.2	74.9±0.3	89.4
GSDA (CVPR'20) [21]	95.7	99.1	**100**	94.8	73.5	74.9	89.7
SRDC (CVPR'20) [45]	95.7±0.2	99.2±0.1	**100.0±0.0**	95.8±0.2	76.7±0.3	77.1±0.1	90.8
RSDA (CVPR'20) [17]	<u>96.1±0.2</u>	<u>99.3±0.2</u>	**100.0±0.0**	<u>95.8±0.3</u>	77.4±0.8	<u>78.9±0.3</u>	91.1
FixBi (CVPR'21) [33]	<u>96.1±0.2</u>	<u>99.3±0.2</u>	**100.0±0.0**	95.0±0.4	**78.7±0.5**	**79.4±0.3**	91.4
CoVi (Ours)	**97.6±0.2**	**99.3±0.1**	**100.0±0.0**	**98.0±0.3**	<u>77.5±0.3</u>	78.4±0.3	**91.8**

- **Office-31** [37] contains 31 categories and 4,110 images in three domains: Amazon (A), Webcam (W), and DSLR (D). We verify our methodology in six domain adaptation tasks.
- **Office-Home** [46] consists of 64 categories and 15,500 images in four domains: Art (Ar), Clipart (Cl), Product (Pr), and Real-World (Rw).
- **VisDA-C** [35] is a large-scale dataset for synthetic-to-real domain adaptation across 12 categories. It contains 152,397 synthetic images for the source domain and 55,388 real-world images for the target domain.
- **PACS** [26] is organized into seven categories with 9,991 images in four domains: Photo (P), Art Painting (A), Cartoon (C), and Sketch (S).

4.1 Experimental Setups

Following the standard UDA protocol [13,14], we utilize labeled source data and unlabeled target data. We exploit ResNet-50 [19,20] for Office-31 and Office-Home, and ResNet-101 for VisDA-C. For multi-source domain adaptation, we use ResNet-18 in the PACS dataset. We use stochastic gradient descent (SGD) with a momentum of 0.9 in all experiments and follow the same learning rate schedule as in [13]. For the contrastive loss and label consensus loss, we follow the confidence masking policy of [33] that adaptively changes according to the sample mean and standard deviation across all mini-batches. Meanwhile, we design the *EMP-learner* by using four convolutional layers, regardless of the dataset. More detailed information is provided in the supplementary materials.

4.2 Comparison with the State-of-the-Art Methods

We validate our method compared with the state-of-the-art methods on three public benchmarks, including Office-31, Office-Home, and VisDA-C.

Office-31. In Table 1, we show the comparative performance on ResNet-50. We achieve an accuracy of 91.8%, which is 5.3% higher than the baseline MSTN [50], surpassing other state-of-the-art methods. Our method performs best in four out of six situations, *e.g.*, A→W, D→W, W→D, and A→D tasks. In particular, in A→W and A→D, although the performance improvement of the recent methods has stagnated, our method achieves a significant performance gain. We also attain better performance than the Mixup-based methods, *i.e.*, DMRL [48] and FixBi [33].

Office-Home. Table 2 demonstrates the comparison results on the Office-Home dataset based on ResNet-50. Our method achieves the highest accuracy in half of the tasks and is the first to break the 73% barrier. In particular, we attain over 10% higher performance from the baseline in Cl→Pr and Pr→Cl. In addition, our method outperforms MetaAlign [47], which uses meta-learning schemes, and FixBi [33], which operates two backbone networks (*i.e.*, ResNet).

Table 2. Accuracy (%) on Office-Home for unsupervised domain adaptation (ResNet-50). The best accuracy is indicated in bold, and the second-best accuracy is underlined. * Reproduced by [17].

Method	Ar→Cl	Ar→Pr	Ar→Rw	Cl→Ar	Cl→Pr	Cl→Rw	Pr→Ar	Pr→Cl	Pr→Rw	Rw→Ar	Rw→Cl	Rw→Pr	Avg.
MSTN* (Baseline) [50]	49.8	70.3	76.3	60.4	68.5	69.6	61.4	48.9	75.7	70.9	55	81.1	65.7
AADA (ECCV'20) [52]	54.0	71.3	77.5	60.8	70.8	71.2	59.1	51.8	76.9	71.0	57.4	81.8	67.0
ETD (CVPR'20) [27]	51.3	71.9	**85.7**	57.6	69.2	73.7	57.8	51.2	79.3	70.2	57.5	82.1	67.3
GSDA (CVPR'20) [21]	**61.3**	76.1	79.4	65.4	73.3	74.3	65	53.2	80	72.2	60.6	83.1	70.3
GVB-GD (CVPR'20) [10]	57	74.7	79.8	64.6	74.1	74.6	65.2	55.1	81	74.6	59.7	84.3	70.4
TCM (ICCV'21) [54]	58.6	74.4	79.6	64.5	74.0	75.1	64.6	56.2	80.9	74.6	60.7	84.7	70.7
RSDA (CVPR'20) [17]	53.2	77.7	81.3	66.4	74	76.5	67.9	53	82	75.8	57.8	85.4	70.9
SRDC (CVPR'20) [45]	52.3	76.3	81	**69.5**	76.2	78	**68.7**	53.8	81.7	76.3	57.1	85	71.3
MetaAlign (CVPR'21) [47]	59.3	76.0	80.2	65.7	74.7	75.1	65.7	56.5	81.6	74.1	61.1	85.2	71.3
FixBi (CVPR'21) [33]	58.1	77.3	80.4	67.7	79.5	**78.1**	65.8	57.9	81.7	76.4	62.9	**86.7**	72.7
CoVi (Ours)	58.5	**78.1**	80.0	68.1	**80.0**	77.0	66.4	**60.2**	**82.1**	**76.6**	**63.6**	86.5	**73.1**

Table 3. Accuracy (%) on VisDA-C for unsupervised domain adaptation (ResNet-101). The best accuracy is indicated in bold, and the second-best accuracy is underlined. * Reproduced by [6].

Method	Aero	Bicycle	Bus	Car	Horse	Knife	Motor	Person	Plant	Skate	Train	Truck	Avg.
MSTN* (Baseline) [50]	89.3	49.5	74.3	67.6	90.1	16.6	**93.6**	70.1	86.5	40.4	83.2	18.5	65.0
DMRL (ECCV'20) [48]	-	-	-	-	-	-	-	-	-	-	-	-	75.5
TCM (ICCV'21) [54]	-	-	-	-	-	-	-	-	-	-	-	-	75.8
DWL (CVPR'21) [49]	90.7	80.2	86.1	67.6	92.4	81.5	86.8	78.1	90.6	57.1	85.6	28.7	77.1
CGDM (ICCV'21) [11]	93.4	82.7	73.2	68.4	92.9	94.5	88.7	82.1	93.4	82.5	86.8	49.2	82.3
STAR (CVPR'20) [29]	95	84	84.6	73	91.6	91.8	85.9	78.4	94.4	84.7	87	42.2	82.7
CAN (CVPR'19) [23]	**97**	87.2	82.5	74.3	**97.8**	**96.2**	90.8	80.7	96.6	**96.3**	87.5	**59.9**	87.2
FixBi (CVPR'21) [33]	96.1	**87.8**	**90.5**	**90.3**	96.8	95.3	92.8	**88.7**	**97.2**	94.2	90.9	25.7	87.2
CoVi (Ours)	96.8	85.6	88.9	88.6	**97.8**	93.4	91.9	87.6	96.0	93.8	**93.6**	48.1	**88.5**

VisDA-C. In Table 3, we validate our method on a large visual domain adaptation challenge dataset with ResNet-101. Our method outperforms the state-of-the-art methods with an accuracy of 88.5%. Compared to the baseline MSTN [50], our method achieves a performance improvement of over 23%. In addition, our method shows better performance than the mixup-based DMRL [48] and FixBi [33]. We could not achieve the best accuracy across all categories due to the poor accuracy of the baseline (65.0%), yet the overall score supports the effectiveness of our method.

4.3 Ablation Studies and Discussions

Analysis of EMP. We provide visual examples of the predictions of vicinal instances using Grad-CAM [39] in Fig. 4. Grad-CAM highlights class-discriminative region in an instance; hence, we can identify the most dominant label in each vicinal instance. Now we demonstrate our crucial observations based on the EMP. First, we observe that the EMP is formed differently depending on the convex combinations of the source and target instances. Second, the dominant labels are switched between the source and target labels at the EMP. Lastly, because the EMP is the highest entropy point, Grad-CAM fails to highlight one specific category at this point adequately. We claim that this outcome is due to the uncertainty arising from the confusion between the source and target instances. Furthermore, we discover that the source and target classes are highlighted in instances on both sides of the EMP.

Equilibrium Collapse. In Fig. 5, we analyze the dominance of labels between the source and target domains. Before adaptation (*i.e.*, source-only), the equilibrium of the labels is broken by the dominant-source and recessive-target domains.

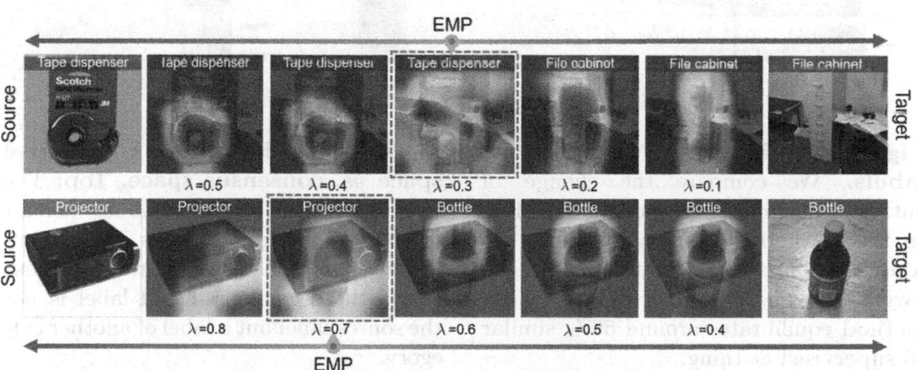

Fig. 4. Grad-CAM visualization. Our key observations in the vicinal space are as follows: (i) *EMPs* vary depending on the convex combination of instances. (ii) The *top-1* prediction is switched between the source and target labels (*e.g.*, Tape dispenser ↔ File cabinet) around the EMP. (iii) Grad-CAM highlights the same category as our *top-1* prediction as the most class-discriminative region.

In this case, even if the proportion of the target instances in the mixed-up instance is more than half (*i.e.*, target-dominant instance), the top-1 predicted label is determined by the source label (*i.e.*, source-dominant label). In other words, the EMP is formed where it is biased towards the source domain. By contrast, after applying our method, we achieve equilibrium at around 50%, which is similar to the results of the supervised learning method. Consequently, our method alleviates the equilibrium collapse so that the target-dominant instance is properly predicted as a target label rather than a source label.

Analysis of the Vicinal Space. Our method leverages the vicinal spaces by dividing them into a contrastive space and a consensus space. In Fig. 6, we observe that the *top-5* predictions of the two spaces have different characteristics. In the contrastive space, the top-2 predictions consist of the target label (*i.e.*, mobile phone) and source label (*i.e.*, backpack). In other words, the uncertainty between inter-domain categories is the most critical factor in the predictions. By contrast, in the top-2 predictions of the consensus space, the second label is not the source label but another category (*i.e.*, trash can) in the target domain that looks similar to the target label (*i.e.*, mobile phone). Hence, mitigating the intra-domain confusion of the target domain in the consensus space can be another starting point to improve performance further.

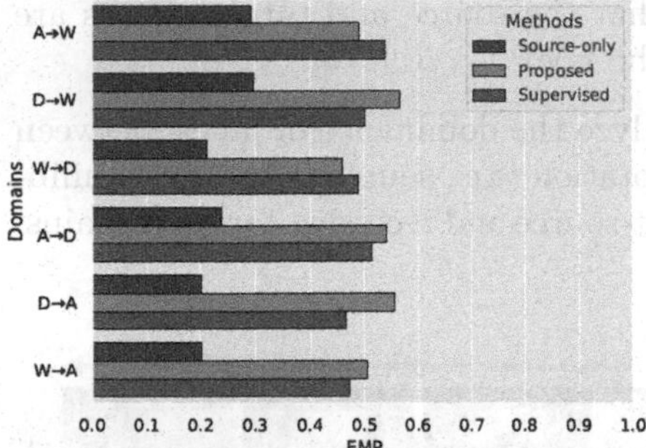

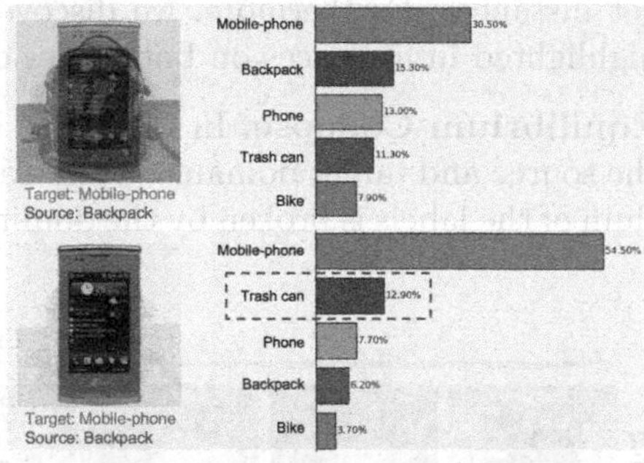

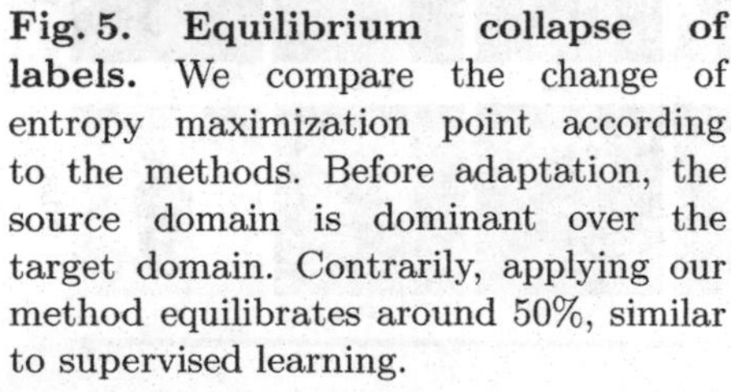

Fig. 5. Equilibrium collapse of labels. We compare the change of entropy maximization point according to the methods. Before adaptation, the source domain is dominant over the target domain. Contrarily, applying our method equilibrates around 50%, similar to supervised learning.

Fig. 6. Predictions in the contrastive space *vs.* consensus space. Top: The first and second predicted labels consist of source and target labels in the contrastive space. **Bottom:** In the consensus space, the second predicted label is not the source label but a label of another category.

Table 4. Ablation results (%) of investigating the effects of our components on Office-31.

Baseline	$\mathcal{R}_{emp}$	$\mathcal{R}_{ct}$	$\mathcal{R}_{cs}$	A→W	D→W	W→D	A→D	D→A	W→A	Avg.
✓				91.3	98.9	100.0	90.4	72.7	65.6	86.5
✓	✓			95.9	99.1	100.0	95.6	76.3	75.4	90.4
✓	✓	✓		97.1	99.2	100.0	97.2	76.4	76.4	91.1
✓	✓	✓	✓	**97.6**	**99.3**	**100.0**	**98.0**	**77.5**	**78.4**	**91.8**

Effect of the Components. We conduct ablation studies to investigate the effectiveness for each component of our method in Table 4. We observe that our *EMP-Mixup* improves the accuracy by an average of 3.9% compared to the baseline [50]. In addition, our contrastive loss shows a substantial improvement in the tasks A→W and A→D. Meanwhile, in the tasks of D→A and W→A, our label-consensus loss significantly impacts the performance gain. Overall, our proposed method improves the baseline by an average of 5.3%. This experiment verifies that each component contributes positively to performance improvement.

Multi-source Domain Adaptation. To demonstrate the generality of our instance-wise approach, we experiment with a multi-source domain adaptation task, as shown in Table 5. Our method achieves a performance improvement of over 6% on the PACS dataset compared to the baseline MSTN [50]. In terms of the average accuracy, our method shows a significant performance improvement compared to the state-of-the-art methods. In particular, our method outperforms three out of four tasks when compared with the recent methods.

Table 5. Accuracy (%) on PACS for multi-source unsupervised domain adaptation (ResNet-18). The best accuracy is indicated in bold, and the second-best accuracy is underlined. * Reproduced by ourselves.

Method	C,S,P→A	A,S,P→C	A,C,P→S	A,C,S→P	Avg.
MSTN* (Baseline) [50]	85.5	86.22	80.81	95.27	86.95
JiGen (CVPR'19) [4]	86.1	87.6	73.4	98.3	86.3
Meta-MCD (ECCV'20) [25]	87.4	86.18	78.26	97.13	87.24
CMSS (ECCV'20) [53]	88.6	90.4	82	96.9	89.5
DSON (ECCV'20) [40]	86.54	88.61	<u>86.93</u>	**99.42**	90.38
T-SVDNet (ICCV'21) [28]	<u>90.43</u>	<u>90.61</u>	85.49	98.5	<u>91.25</u>
CoVi (Ours)	**93.11**	**93.86**	**88.06**	<u>99.04</u>	**93.52**

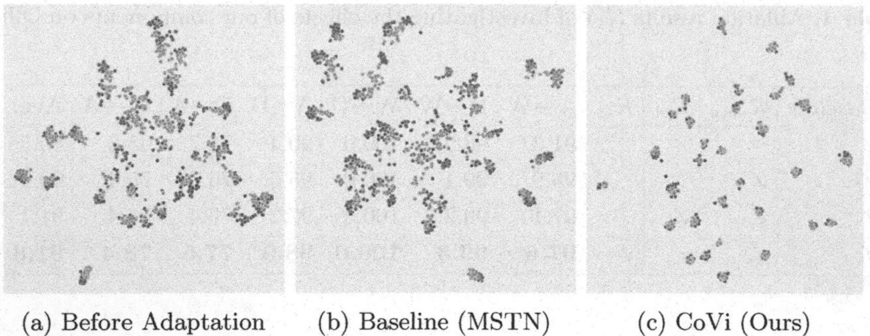

(a) Before Adaptation (b) Baseline (MSTN) (c) CoVi (Ours)

Fig. 7. t-SNE visualization. Visualization of embedded features on task A→D. Blue and orange points denote the source and target domains, respectively. (Color figure online)

Feature Visualization. We visualize the embedded features on task A→D of the Office-31 dataset using t-SNE [30] in Fig. 7. Before adaptation, the source embeddings are naturally more cohesive than that of target features because only source supervision is accessible. After applying the baseline (*i.e.*, MSTN [50]), we observe that the cohesion of the target features is improved but still fails to form tight clusters. By contrast, in our method, the target features construct compact clusters comparable to the source features. These results prove that our method works successfully in the unsupervised domain adaptation task.

5 Conclusions

In this study, we investigated the vicinal space between the source and target domains from the perspective of self-training. We raised the problem of the equilibrium collapse of labels and proposed three novel approaches. Our EMP-Mixup efficiently minimized the worst-case risk in the vicinal space. In addition, we reduce inter-domain and intra-domain confusions by dividing the vicinal space into contrastive and consensus space. The competitiveness of our approach suggests that self-predictions in vicinal space can play an important role in solving the UDA problem.

Acknowledgement. This work was partially supported by the IITP grant funded by the MSIT, Korea [2014-3-00123, 2021-0-02130] and the BK21 FOUR program (NRF-5199991014091).

References

1. Berthelot, D., et al.: ReMixMatch: semi-supervised learning with distribution alignment and augmentation anchoring. arXiv preprint arXiv:1911.09785 (2019)

2. Berthelot, D., Carlini, N., Goodfellow, I., Papernot, N., Oliver, A., Raffel, C.: MixMatch: a holistic approach to semi-supervised learning. arXiv preprint arXiv:1905.02249 (2019)
3. Bousmalis, K., Trigeorgis, G., Silberman, N., Krishnan, D., Erhan, D.: Domain separation networks. In: Advances in Neural Information Processing Systems 29, pp. 343–351 (2016)
4. Carlucci, F.M., D'Innocente, A., Bucci, S., Caputo, B., Tommasi, T.: Domain generalization by solving jigsaw puzzles. In: Proceedings of the IEEE/CVF Conference on Computer Vision and Pattern Recognition, pp. 2229–2238 (2019)
5. Chang, W.L., Wang, H.P., Peng, W.H., Chiu, W.C.: All about structure: adapting structural information across domains for boosting semantic segmentation. In: Proceedings of the IEEE/CVF Conference on Computer Vision and Pattern Recognition, pp. 1900–1909 (2019)
6. Chang, W.G., You, T., Seo, S., Kwak, S., Han, B.: Domain-specific batch normalization for unsupervised domain adaptation. In: Proceedings of the IEEE/CVF Conference on Computer Vision and Pattern Recognition, pp. 7354–7362 (2019)
7. Chapelle, O., Weston, J., Bottou, L., Vapnik, V.: Vicinal risk minimization. In: Advances in Neural Information Processing Systems, pp. 416–422 (2001)
8. Cubuk, E.D., Zoph, B., Mane, D., Vasudevan, V., Le, Q.V.: AutoAugment: learning augmentation policies from data. arXiv preprint arXiv:1805.09501 (2018)
9. Cubuk, E.D., Zoph, B., Shlens, J., Le, Q.V.: RandAugment: practical automated data augmentation with a reduced search space. In: Proceedings of the IEEE/CVF Conference on Computer Vision and Pattern Recognition Workshops, pp. 702–703 (2020)
10. Cui, S., Wang, S., Zhuo, J., Su, C., Huang, Q., Tian, Q.: Gradually vanishing bridge for adversarial domain adaptation. In: Proceedings of the IEEE/CVF Conference on Computer Vision and Pattern Recognition, pp. 12455–12464 (2020)
11. Du, Z., Li, J., Su, H., Zhu, L., Lu, K.: Cross-domain gradient discrepancy minimization for unsupervised domain adaptation. In: Proceedings of the IEEE/CVF Conference on Computer Vision and Pattern Recognition, pp. 3937–3946 (2021)
12. Fan, K.: Minimax theorems. Proc. Natl. Acad. Sci. U.S.A. **39**(1), 42 (1953)
13. Ganin, Y., Lempitsky, V.: Unsupervised domain adaptation by backpropagation. In: International Conference on Machine Learning, pp. 1180–1189. PMLR (2015)
14. Ganin, Y., et al.: Domain-adversarial training of neural networks. J. Mach. Learn. Res. **17**(1), 2096–2130 (2016)
15. Gong, R., Li, W., Chen, Y., Gool, L.V.: DLOW: domain flow for adaptation and generalization. In: Proceedings of the IEEE/CVF Conference on Computer Vision and Pattern Recognition, pp. 2477–2486 (2019)
16. Goodfellow, I., et al.: Generative adversarial nets. In: Advances in Neural Information Processing Systems 27 (2014)
17. Gu, X., Sun, J., Xu, Z.: Spherical space domain adaptation with robust pseudo-label loss. In: Proceedings of the IEEE/CVF Conference on Computer Vision and Pattern Recognition, pp. 9101–9110 (2020)
18. Guo, H., Mao, Y., Zhang, R.: MixUp as locally linear out-of-manifold regularization. In: Proceedings of the AAAI Conference on Artificial Intelligence, pp. 3714–3722 (2019)
19. He, K., Zhang, X., Ren, S., Sun, J.: Deep residual learning for image recognition. In: Proceedings of the IEEE Conference on Computer Vision and Pattern Recognition, pp. 770–778 (2016)

20. He, K., Zhang, X., Ren, S., Sun, J.: Identity mappings in deep residual networks. In: Leibe, B., Matas, J., Sebe, N., Welling, M. (eds.) ECCV 2016. LNCS, vol. 9908, pp. 630–645. Springer, Cham (2016). https://doi.org/10.1007/978-3-319-46493-0_38
21. Hu, L., Kan, M., Shan, S., Chen, X.: Unsupervised domain adaptation with hierarchical gradient synchronization. In: Proceedings of the IEEE/CVF Conference on Computer Vision and Pattern Recognition, pp. 4043–4052 (2020)
22. Jin, Y., Wang, X., Long, M., Wang, J.: Minimum class confusion for versatile domain adaptation. In: Vedaldi, A., Bischof, H., Brox, T., Frahm, J.-M. (eds.) ECCV 2020. LNCS, vol. 12366, pp. 464–480. Springer, Cham (2020). https://doi.org/10.1007/978-3-030-58589-1_28
23. Kang, G., Jiang, L., Yang, Y., Hauptmann, A.G.: Contrastive adaptation network for unsupervised domain adaptation. In: Proceedings of the IEEE/CVF Conference on Computer Vision and Pattern Recognition, pp. 4893–4902 (2019)
24. Lee, D.H., et al.: Pseudo-label: the simple and efficient semi-supervised learning method for deep neural networks. In: Workshop on Challenges in Representation Learning, ICML, p. 896 (2013)
25. Li, D., Hospedales, T.: Online meta-learning for multi-source and semi-supervised domain adaptation. In: Vedaldi, A., Bischof, H., Brox, T., Frahm, J.-M. (eds.) ECCV 2020. LNCS, vol. 12361, pp. 382–403. Springer, Cham (2020). https://doi.org/10.1007/978-3-030-58517-4_23
26. Li, D., Yang, Y., Song, Y.Z., Hospedales, T.M.: Deeper, broader and artier domain generalization. In: Proceedings of the IEEE International Conference on Computer Vision, pp. 5542–5550 (2017)
27. Li, M., Zhai, Y.M., Luo, Y.W., Ge, P.F., Ren, C.X.: Enhanced transport distance for unsupervised domain adaptation. In: Proceedings of the IEEE/CVF Conference on Computer Vision and Pattern Recognition, pp. 13936–13944 (2020)
28. Li, R., Jia, X., He, J., Chen, S., Hu, Q.: T-SVDNet: exploring high-order prototypical correlations for multi-source domain adaptation. In: Proceedings of the IEEE/CVF International Conference on Computer Vision, pp. 9991–10000 (2021)
29. Lu, Z., Yang, Y., Zhu, X., Liu, C., Song, Y.Z., Xiang, T.: Stochastic classifiers for unsupervised domain adaptation. In: Proceedings of the IEEE/CVF Conference on Computer Vision and Pattern Recognition, pp. 9111–9120 (2020)
30. Van der Maaten, L., Hinton, G.: Visualizing data using t-SNE. J. Mach. Learn. Res. **9**(11), 2579–2605 (2008)
31. Mai, Z., Hu, G., Chen, D., Shen, F., Shen, H.T.: MetaMixUp: learning adaptive interpolation policy of MixUp with metalearning. IEEE Trans. Neural Netw. Learn. Syst. **33**, 3050–3064 (2021)
32. Miyato, T., Maeda, S., Koyama, M., Ishii, S.: Virtual adversarial training: a regularization method for supervised and semi-supervised learning. IEEE Trans. Pattern Anal. Mach. Intell. **41**(8), 1979–1993 (2018)
33. Na, J., Jung, H., Chang, H.J., Hwang, W.: FixBi: bridging domain spaces for unsupervised domain adaptation. In: Proceedings of the IEEE/CVF Conference on Computer Vision and Pattern Recognition, pp. 1094–1103 (2021)
34. Pan, F., Shin, I., Rameau, F., Lee, S., Kweon, I.S.: Unsupervised intra-domain adaptation for semantic segmentation through self-supervision. In: Proceedings of the IEEE/CVF Conference on Computer Vision and Pattern Recognition, pp. 3764–3773 (2020)
35. Peng, X., Usman, B., Kaushik, N., Hoffman, J., Wang, D., Saenko, K.: VisDA: the visual domain adaptation challenge. arXiv preprint arXiv:1710.06924 (2017)

36. Pham, H., Dai, Z., Xie, Q., Le, Q.V.: Meta pseudo labels. In: Proceedings of the IEEE/CVF Conference on Computer Vision and Pattern Recognition, pp. 11557–11568 (2021)
37. Saenko, K., Kulis, B., Fritz, M., Darrell, T.: Adapting visual category models to new domains. In: Daniilidis, K., Maragos, P., Paragios, N. (eds.) ECCV 2010. LNCS, vol. 6314, pp. 213–226. Springer, Heidelberg (2010). https://doi.org/10.1007/978-3-642-15561-1_16
38. Saito, K., Ushiku, Y., Harada, T.: Asymmetric tri-training for unsupervised domain adaptation. In: International Conference on Machine Learning, pp. 2988–2997. PMLR (2017)
39. Selvaraju, R.R., Cogswell, M., Das, A., Vedantam, R., Parikh, D., Batra, D.: Grad-CAM: visual explanations from deep networks via gradient-based localization. In: Proceedings of the IEEE International Conference on Computer Vision, pp. 618–626 (2017)
40. Seo, S., Suh, Y., Kim, D., Kim, G., Han, J., Han, B.: Learning to optimize domain specific normalization for domain generalization. In: Vedaldi, A., Bischof, H., Brox, T., Frahm, J.-M. (eds.) ECCV 2020, Part XXII. LNCS, vol. 12367, pp. 68–83. Springer, Cham (2020). https://doi.org/10.1007/978-3-030-58542-6_5
41. Sharma, A., Kalluri, T., Chandraker, M.: Instance level affinity-based transfer for unsupervised domain adaptation. In: Proceedings of the IEEE/CVF Conference on Computer Vision and Pattern Recognition, pp. 5361–5371 (2021)
42. Shimodaira, H.: Improving predictive inference under covariate shift by weighting the log-likelihood function. J. Stat. Plann. Infer. **90**(2), 227–244 (2000)
43. Shin, I., Woo, S., Pan, F., Kweon, I.S.: Two-phase pseudo label densification for self-training based domain adaptation. In: Vedaldi, A., Bischof, H., Brox, T., Frahm, J.-M. (eds.) ECCV 2020. LNCS, vol. 12358, pp. 532–548. Springer, Cham (2020). https://doi.org/10.1007/978-3-030-58601-0_32
44. Sohn, K., et al.: FixMatch: simplifying semi-supervised learning with consistency and confidence. arXiv preprint arXiv:2001.07685 (2020)
45. Tang, H., Chen, K., Jia, K.: Unsupervised domain adaptation via structurally regularized deep clustering. In: Proceedings of the IEEE/CVF Conference on Computer Vision and Pattern Recognition, pp. 8725–8735 (2020)
46. Venkateswara, H., Eusebio, J., Chakraborty, S., Panchanathan, S.: Deep hashing network for unsupervised domain adaptation. In: Proceedings of the IEEE Conference on Computer Vision and Pattern Recognition, pp. 5018–5027 (2017)
47. Wei, G., Lan, C., Zeng, W., Chen, Z.: MetaAlign: coordinating domain alignment and classification for unsupervised domain adaptation. In: Proceedings of the IEEE/CVF Conference on Computer Vision and Pattern Recognition, pp. 16643–16653 (2021)
48. Wu, Y., Inkpen, D., El-Roby, A.: Dual mixup regularized learning for adversarial domain adaptation. In: Vedaldi, A., Bischof, H., Brox, T., Frahm, J.-M. (eds.) ECCV 2020. LNCS, vol. 12374, pp. 540–555. Springer, Cham (2020). https://doi.org/10.1007/978-3-030-58526-6_32
49. Xiao, N., Zhang, L.: Dynamic weighted learning for unsupervised domain adaptation. In: Proceedings of the IEEE/CVF Conference on Computer Vision and Pattern Recognition, pp. 15242–15251 (2021)
50. Xie, S., Zheng, Z., Chen, L., Chen, C.: Learning semantic representations for unsupervised domain adaptation. In: International Conference on Machine Learning, pp. 5423–5432. PMLR (2018)
51. Xu, M., et al.: Adversarial domain adaptation with domain mixup. In: Proceedings of the AAAI Conference on Artificial Intelligence, pp. 6502–6509 (2020)

52. Yang, J., Zou, H., Zhou, Y., Zeng, Z., Xie, L.: Mind the discriminability: asymmetric adversarial domain adaptation. In: Vedaldi, A., Bischof, H., Brox, T., Frahm, J.-M. (eds.) ECCV 2020. LNCS, vol. 12369, pp. 589–606. Springer, Cham (2020). https://doi.org/10.1007/978-3-030-58586-0_35
53. Yang, L., Balaji, Y., Lim, S.-N., Shrivastava, A.: Curriculum manager for source selection in multi-source domain adaptation. In: Vedaldi, A., Bischof, H., Brox, T., Frahm, J.-M. (eds.) ECCV 2020, Part XIV. LNCS, vol. 12359, pp. 608–624. Springer, Cham (2020). https://doi.org/10.1007/978-3-030-58568-6_36
54. Yue, Z., Sun, Q., Hua, X.S., Zhang, H.: Transporting causal mechanisms for unsupervised domain adaptation. In: Proceedings of the IEEE/CVF International Conference on Computer Vision, pp. 8599–8608 (2021)
55. Zhang, H., Cisse, M., Dauphin, Y.N., Lopez-Paz, D.: mixup: beyond empirical risk minimization. arXiv preprint arXiv:1710.09412 (2017)
56. Zhu, J., Shi, L., Yan, J., Zha, H.: AutoMix: mixup networks for sample interpolation via cooperative barycenter learning. In: Vedaldi, A., Bischof, H., Brox, T., Frahm, J.-M. (eds.) ECCV 2020. LNCS, vol. 12355, pp. 633–649. Springer, Cham (2020). https://doi.org/10.1007/978-3-030-58607-2_37

Cross-Modal Knowledge Transfer Without Task-Relevant Source Data

Sk Miraj Ahmed[1], Suhas Lohit[2(✉)], Kuan-Chuan Peng[2], Michael J. Jones[2], and Amit K. Roy-Chowdhury[1]

[1] University of California, Riverside, CA 92507, USA
sahme047@ucr.edu, amitrc@ece.ucr.edu

[2] Mitsubishi Electric Research Laboratories (MERL), Cambridge, MA 02139, USA
{slohit,kpeng,mjones}@merl.com
https://www.merl.com

Abstract. Cost-effective depth and infrared sensors as alternatives to usual RGB sensors are now a reality, and have some advantages over RGB in domains like autonomous navigation and remote sensing. As such, building computer vision and deep learning systems for depth and infrared data are crucial. However, large labeled datasets for these modalities are still lacking. In such cases, transferring knowledge from a neural network trained on a well-labeled large dataset in the source modality (RGB) to a neural network that works on a target modality (depth, infrared, etc.) is of great value. For reasons like memory and privacy, it may not be possible to access the source data, and knowledge transfer needs to work with only the source models. We describe an effective solution, SOCKET: SOurce-free Cross-modal KnowledgE Transfer for this challenging task of transferring knowledge from one source modality to a different target modality without access to task-relevant source data. The framework reduces the modality gap using paired task-irrelevant data, as well as by matching the mean and variance of the target features with the batch-norm statistics that are present in the source models. We show through extensive experiments that our method significantly outperforms existing source-free methods for classification tasks which do not account for the modality gap.

Keywords: Source free adaptation · Cross modal knowledge distillation · Unsupervised domain adaptation

1 Introduction

Depth sensors like Kinect and RealSense, LIDAR for measuring point clouds directly, or high resolution infra-red sensors such as from FLIR, allow for expanding the range of applications of computer vision compared to using only vis-

Supplementary Information The online version contains supplementary material available at https://doi.org/10.1007/978-3-031-19830-4_7.

S. Avidan et al. (Eds.): ECCV 2022, LNCS 13694, pp. 111–127, 2022.
https://doi.org/10.1007/978-3-031-19830-4_7

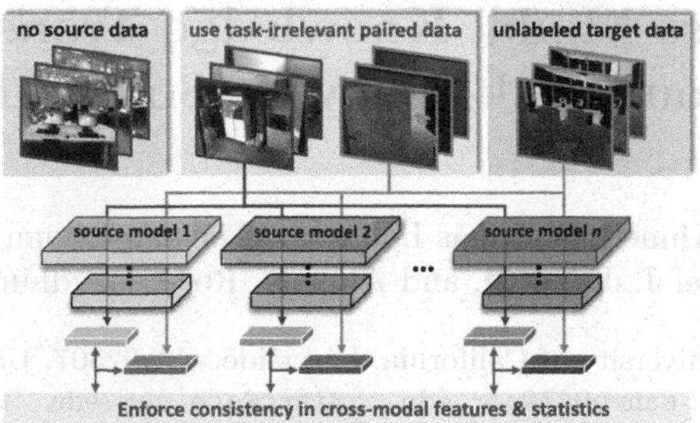

Fig. 1. SOCKET: We describe the problem of single/multi-source cross-modality knowledge transfer using no data used to train the source models. To effectively perform knowledge transfer, we minimize the modality gap by enforcing consistency of cross modal features on **task-irrelevant** paired data in feature space, and by **matching the distributions** of the unlabeled task-relevant features and the source features

ible wavelengths. Sensing depth directly can provide an approximate three-dimensional picture of the scene and thus improve the performance of applications like autonomous navigation, while sensing in the infra-red wavelengths can allow for easier pedestrian detection or better object detection in adverse atmospheric conditions like rain, fog, and smoke. These are just a few examples (Figs. 1 and 2).

Building computer vision applications using the now-straightforward supervised deep learning approach for modalities like depth and infrared needs large amounts of diverse labeled data. However, such large and diverse datasets do not exist for these modalities and the cost of building such datasets can be prohibitively high. In such cases, researchers have developed methods like knowledge distillation to transfer the knowledge from a model trained on a modality like RGB, where large amounts of labeled data are available, to the modality of interest like depth [1].

In contrast to prior work, we tackle a novel and challenging problem in the context of cross-modal knowledge transfer. We assume that we have access only to (a) the source models trained for the task of interest (TOI), and (b) unlabeled data in the target modality where we need to construct a model for the same TOI. The key aspect is that we assume we have **no access to any data in the source modality** for TOI. Such a problem setup is important in cases where memory and privacy considerations do not allow for sharing the training data from the source modality; only the trained models can be shared [2–5].

We develop **SOCKET**: **SO**urce-free **C**ross-modal **K**nowledg**E** **T**ransfer as an effective solution to this problem for bridging the gap between the source and target modalities. To this end, we show that employing an external dataset of source-target modality pairs, which are not relevant to TOI – which we call Task-Irrelevant (TI) data – can help in learning an effective target model by bringing the features of the two modalities closer. In addition to using TI data, we encourage matching the statistics of the features of the unlabeled target data – which are Task-Relevant (TR) by definition – with the statistics of the source data which are available to us from the normalization layers that are present in the trained source model.

We provide important empirical evidence showing that the modality-shift from a source modality like RGB to a target modality like depth can be much more challenging than a domain shift from one RGB dataset to another. This shows that the proposed framework is necessary to help minimize the modality gap, so as to make the knowledge transfer more effective. Based on the above ideas, we show that we can improve on existing state-of-the-art methods which were devised only for cross-domain setting in the same modality. We summarize our main contributions below:

1. We formulate a novel problem for knowledge transfer from a model trained for a source modality to a different target modality without any access to task-relevant source data and when the target data is unlabeled.
2. In order to bridge the gap between modalities, we propose a novel framework, SOCKET, for cross-modal knowledge transfer without access to source data (a) using an external task-irrelevant paired dataset, and (b) by matching the moments obtained from the normalization layers in the source models with the moments computed on the unlabeled target data.
3. Extensive experiments on multiple datasets – both for knowledge transfer from RGB to depth, and from RGB to IR, and both for single-source and multi-source cases – show that SOCKET is useful in reducing the modality gap in the feature space and produces significantly better performance (improvement of as high as 12% for some cases) over the existing source-free domain adaptation baselines which do not account for the modality difference between the source and target modalities.
4. We also show empirically that, for the datasets of interest, the problem of knowledge transfer between modalities like RGB and depth is harder than domain shifts in the same modality such as sensor changes and viewpoint shifts, considered previously in literature.

2 Related Work

Cross-Modal Distillation Methods. Cross-modal knowledge distillation (CMKD) methods aim to learn representations for a modality which does not have a large amount of labeled data from a large labeled dataset of another modality [1]. These methods have been used for a variety of practical computer vision and learning tasks [6–9]. Most of these works assume access to task-relevant paired data across modalities [1,8,10,11]. A recent line of work relaxed this assumption in the context of domain generalization, where one does not have access to the Task-Relevant paired data on the target domain but has access to them for the source domain [12]. There also exist some works regarding domain translation across modalities for better classification of indoor scenes [13–15]. However these methods consider UDA across domains, where the target domain

Table 1. We compare the proposed work SOCKET with existing problem settings in literature for knowledge transfer across different domains and modalities. The competitive settings described in this table are: (1) UDA (Unsupervised Domain Adaptation), DT (Domain Translation) [13–15,17–20] [$\mathcal{C}_1$], (2) MSDA (Multi-source domain adaptation) [21] [$\mathcal{C}_2$], (3) SFDA (Source free single source DA) [3,22–26] [$\mathcal{C}_3$], (4) MSFDA (Source free multi-source DA) [4] [$\mathcal{C}_4$], (5) CMKD (Cross modal knowledge distillation) [1,6–8] [$\mathcal{C}_5$], and (6) ZDDA (Zero shot DA) [16] [$\mathcal{C}_6$], respectively. We group citations into [$\mathcal{C}_1$] to [$\mathcal{C}_6$] based on problem settings. Only SOCKET allows cross-modal knowledge transfer from multiple sources without any access to relevant source training data for an unlabeled target dataset of a different modality

Property	Problem setting						
	UDA+DT [$\mathcal{C}_1$]	MSDA [$\mathcal{C}_2$]	SFDA [$\mathcal{C}_3$]	MSFDA [$\mathcal{C}_4$]	CMKD [$\mathcal{C}_5$]	ZDDA [$\mathcal{C}_6$]	SOCKET
Multiple sources	✗	✓	✗	✗	✗	✗	✓
No source data	✗	✗	✓	✓	✗	✗	✓
Unlabeled target data	✓	✓	✗	✓	✗	✗	✓
Different target modality	✗	✗	✗	✗	✓	✓	✓
Usage of task-irrelevant data	✗	✗	✗	✗	✗	✓	✓

has unlabeled RGB-D pairs instead of a single modality. All of the above works either utilize the Task-Relevant paired data for cross modal knowledge transfer [1], or consider cross modal paired data as a domain [12,13]. There are also works in zero-shot domain adaptation that utilize external task-irrelevant paired data [16] but need access to the source data. Our work takes steps to allow for different source and target modalities, and can perform effective knowledge transfer without access to the TR paired data between source and target.

Unsupervised Domain Adaptation Methods without Source Data. Most UDA methods that have been used for a wide variety of tasks [17–20] need access to the source data while adapting to a new target domain [21,27]. To combat the storage or privacy issue regarding the source data, a new line of work named Hypothesis Transfer Learning (HTL) [2,5] has emerged recently, where one has access only to the trained source model instead of the source data [3,4]. Here, people have explored adapting target domain data, which has limited labels [2] or no labels at all [3] in the presence of both single source [3,22,23] or multiple source models [4]. [3,26] adapts a single source model to an unlabeled target domain via information maximization and an iterative self-supervised pseudo-label based cross entropy loss. [22] ensured that the adapted source model performs well, both on source and target domains, while [23] proposed a source free domain adaptation (SFDA) method by encouraging label consistency among local target features. [24] proposed to add an extra classifier for refinement of the source decision boundary, while [25] proposed a more robust adaptation method which works well in the presence of noisy pseudo-labels. The authors in [4] proposed fusion of multiple source models with appropriate weights so as to minimize the effect of negative transfer, which we refer to as multiple source free domain adaptation (MSFDA) in Table 1. Both these methods do not work well in a regime where the unlabeled target set is from a different modality than the source. We solve this problem by modality gap reduction via feature

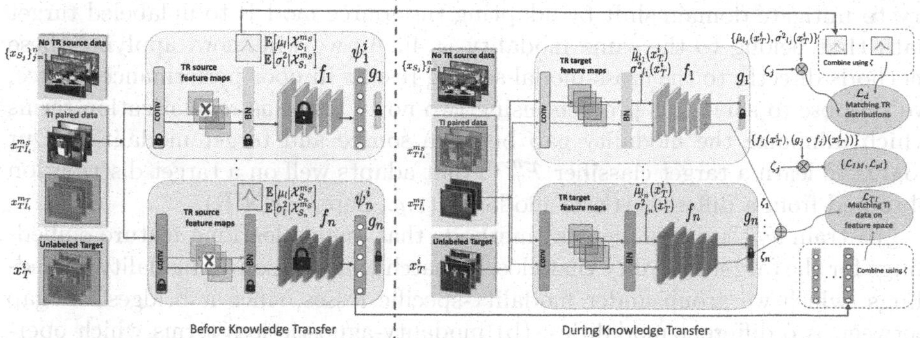

Fig. 2. SOCKET description: Our framework can be split into two parts: (i) Before Knowledge Transfer (left): We freeze the source models and pass the task-irrelevant (TI) source data through the source feature encoders to extract the TI source features. As task-relevant (TR) source feature maps are not available, we extract the stored moments of its distribution from the BN layers. (ii) During Knowledge Transfer (right): We freeze only the classification layers and feed the TI and unlabeled TR target data through the models to get batch-wise TI target features and the TR target moments, respectively, which we match with pre-extracted source features and moments to jointly train all the feature encoders along with the mixing weights, ζ_k's. The final target model is the optimal linear combination of the updated source models

matching of the task-irrelevant external data, as well as data statistics matching between the source and target modalities.

Table 1 summarizes the related work and compares them with SOCKET.

3 Problem Setup and Notation

We address the problem of source-data free cross-modality knowledge transfer by devising specialized loss functions that help reduce the gap between source and target modality features. We focus on the task of classification where both the source and target data belong to the same N classes. Let us consider that we have n source models of the same modality (*e.g.*, RGB). We denote the trained source classifiers as $\{\mathcal{F}_{S_k}^{m_S}\}_{k=1}^{n}$, where S_k denotes the k-th source model and m_S represents the modality on which the source models were trained. The source models are denoted as $\mathcal{F}_{S_k}^{m_S}$ which are trained models that map images from the source modality distribution $\mathcal{X}_{S_k}^{m_S}$ to probability distribution over the classes. $\{x_{S_k}^i, y_{S_k}^i\}_{i=1}^{n_k} \sim \mathcal{X}_{S_k}^{m_S}$ are the data on which the k-th source model was trained, n_k being the number of training data points corresponding to the k-th source. In our problem setting, at the time of knowledge transfer to the target modality, the source data are unavailable for all the sources.

We also have access to an unlabeled dataset in the target modality $\{x_T^i\}_{i=1}^{n_T} \sim \mathcal{X}_T^{m_T}$, where n_T is the number of target samples. Note that the target modality, m_T, is different from the source modality. Traditional source free UDA methods try to mitigate domain shift by adapting the source models to unlabeled target data that belong to the same modality [3,4]. As we will show, applying these methods directly to the cross-modal setting results in poor performance. Hence, we propose to solve this problem using two novel losses as regularization terms which minimize the modality gap between source and target modalities. Our goal is to learn a target classifier $\mathcal{F}_T^{m_T}$, that adapts well on a target distribution obtained from a different sensor modality (*e.g.*, depth or NIR).

To train $\mathcal{F}_T^{m_T}$, we employ (a) methods that enable learning feature embeddings for the target modality that closely match with the source modality embeddings, which we group under modality-specific losses, since it bridges the gap between two different modalities; (b) modality-agnostic loss terms which operate only on the unlabeled target data and do not take into account shift in modality.

We split each of the source models into two blocks – *feature encoder* and *classifier*. For the k-th source model, we denote these blocks as f_k and g_k, respectively. The function $f_k : \mathbb{R}^{H\times W} \to \mathbb{R}^{\eta}$ maps the input image to an η dimensional feature vector and $g_k : \mathbb{R}^{\eta} \to \mathbb{R}^{N}$ maps those features to the probability distributions over the N classes, the maximum of which is treated as the classifier prediction. We can thus write $\mathcal{F}_{S_k}^{m_S} = g_k \circ f_k$, where "$\circ$" is function composition. Since the classifier layer g_k contains the information about unseen k-th source domain distribution, following the protocol of [4], we freeze all the g_k's and train the target specific feature encoders by optimizing over all f_k's.

4 Cross-Modal Feature Alignment

Traditional source free UDA methods [3,4] use domain specific but modality-agnostic losses which do not help in reducing the feature distance between the source and target modalities. In order to train the target model, $\mathcal{F}_T^{m_T}$, with reduced modality-gap, we propose SOCKET, which uses *task-irrelevant feature matching* and *task-relevant distribution matching* which are described next.

4.1 Task-Irrelevant Feature Matching

Capturing the mapping between two modalities effectively requires lots of paired data from both modalities [28]. For our task of interest, we do not have task relevant (TR) data on the source side. As a result, it is not possible to match the target modality with the source modality by using the data from task relevant classes directly. Hence, we propose to use **Task-Irrelevant (TI) paired data** from both modalities to reduce modality gap. TI data contain only classes that are completely **disjoint** from the TR classes and can be from any external dataset. For modalities like RGB-depth and RGB-IR, we can access a large amount of paired TI data that contain classes with no privacy concerns, which are available in public datasets or can be collected using multi-modal sensors. Moreover there are many real world applications where pairwise TI data can be collected and used beyond RGB-D or RGB-IR, such as autonomous driving, adpatation of LiDAR data, medical applications [29]. We denote paired TI data as $\{x_{TI_i}^{m_S}, x_{TI_i}^{m_T}\}_{i=1}^{n_{TI}}$, where $x_{TI_i}^{m_S}$ is the i-th TI data point from source modality and $x_{TI_i}^{m_T}$ is its paired counterpart from the target modality, n_{TI} the total number of pairs. We compute our proposed loss $\mathcal{L}_{TI}$ using TI data as follows:

Step 1: We feed source modality images of the TI dataset through each of the source models to pre-compute features that are good representations of modality m_S. We denote the i-th TI source feature extracted from source j as ψ_j^i:

$$\psi_j^i = f_j(x_{TI_i}^{m_S}). \tag{1}$$

Step 2: During the knowledge transfer phase, we feed the target modality images of the TI dataset which are encouraged to match the corresponding pre-extracted source modality features. We do so by minimizing $\mathcal{L}_{TI}$ defined below with respect to the parameters in the feature encoders for the target modality:

$$\mathcal{L}_{TI} = \sum_{i=1}^{n_{TI}} \sum_{j=1}^{n} \left\| \zeta_j (\psi_j^i - f_j(x_{TI_i}^{m_T})) \right\|^2. \tag{2}$$

4.2 Task-Relevant Distribution Matching

In the task-irrelevant feature matching, we match the TI features of two modalities in the feature space. Even if this captures some class independent cross modal mapping between source and target modalities, it has no information about the *TR-class conditional cross modal mapping.* By this term we refer to the cross modal relationship between source and target, given the relevant classes. Assuming that the marginal distribution of the source features across the batches can be modeled as Gaussian, such feature statistics can be fully characterized by its mean and variance. We propose to match the feature statistics across the source and target, to reduce the modality gap further.

It might seem as though some amount of source data would be required to estimate the batch-wise mean and and variance of its feature map, but the running average statistics stored in the conventional BatchNorm (BN) layers are good enough to serve our purpose. The BN layers normalize the feature maps during the course of training to mitigate the covariate shifts [30,31]. As a result it is able to capture the channel-wise feature statistics cumulatively over all the batches, which gives rise to a rough estimate of the expected mean and variance of the batch-wise feature map, at the end of training. Let us consider that the BN layer corresponding to the l-th convolution layer ($\mathcal{B}_l$) has r_l nodes and there exist b number of such layers per source model. Then we refer to the expected batch-wise mean and variance of the l-th convolution layer of the k-th source model as $\mathbb{E}\left[\mu_l | \mathcal{X}_{S_k}^{m_S}\right] \in \mathbb{R}^{r_l}$ and $\mathbb{E}\left[\sigma_l^2 | \mathcal{X}_{S_k}^{m_S}\right] \in \mathbb{R}^{r_l}$.

Prior to the start of the knowledge transfer phase, we pre-extract the information about the source feature statistics from all of the pre-trained source models. During the knowledge transfer phase, for each iteration we calculate the batch-wise mean and variance of the feature map of target data from all the source models, linearly combine them according to the weights ζ_i and minimize the distance of this weighted combination with the weighted combination of the pre-computed source feature statistics. We calculate this loss $\mathcal{L}_d$ given by

$$\mathcal{L}_d = \sum_{l=1}^{b} \left(\left\| \sum_{j=1}^{n} \zeta_j \mathbb{E}[\mu_l | \mathcal{X}_{S_j}^{ms}] - \sum_{j=1}^{n} \zeta_j \hat{\mu}_{l_j} \right\| + \left\| \sum_{j=1}^{n} \zeta_j \mathbb{E}[\sigma_l^2 | \mathcal{X}_{S_j}^{ms}] - \sum_{j=1}^{n} \zeta_j \hat{\sigma^2}_{l_j} \right\| \right), \tag{3}$$

where $\mathbb{E}[\mu_l | \mathcal{X}_{S_j}^{ms}]$ and $\mathbb{E}[\sigma_l^2 | \mathcal{X}_{S_j}^{ms}]$ are the running mean and variance of the batchnorm layer corresponding to the l-th convolution layer of source j, which we refer as $\mathcal{B}_l^j$, and $\hat{\mu}_{l_j} = \frac{1}{n_T} \sum_{k=1}^{n_T} \mathcal{B}_l^j(x_T^k)$ and $\hat{\sigma^2}_{l_j} = \frac{1}{n_T} \sum_{k=1}^{n_T} (\mathcal{B}_l^j(x_T^k) - \hat{\mu}_{l_j})^2$ denote the mean and variance of the target output from the same batchnorm layer. The losses $\mathcal{L}_{TI}$ and $\mathcal{L}_d$ minimize the modality gap between source and target. We name the combination of these two losses as *Modality Specific Loss* $\mathcal{L}_{ms} = \lambda_{TI}\mathcal{L}_{TI} + \lambda_d \mathcal{L}_d$, where λ_{TI} and λ_d are regularization hyper-parameters.

4.3 Overall Optimization

The two proposed methods above help to reduce the modality gap between source and target without accessing task-relevant source data. In addition to them, we employ the unlabeled target data directly for knowledge transfer. Specifically, we perform *information maximization* along with minimization of a self-supervised *pseudo-label loss*, which have shown promising results in source-free UDA [3,4] where the source and target modalities are the same.

Information Maximization (IM): IM is essentially the task of performing maximization of the mutual information between distribution of the target data and its labels predicted by the source models. This mutual information is a combination of a conditional and a marginal entropy of the target label distribution.

Motivated by [4], we calculate the *conditional entropy* $\mathcal{L}_{ent}$ and the marginal entropy termed as *diversity* $\mathcal{L}_{div}$ as follows:

$$\mathcal{L}_{ent} = -\frac{1}{n_T} \left[\sum_{i=1}^{n_T} (\mathcal{F}_T^{m_T}(x_T^i)) \log(\mathcal{F}_T^{m_T}(x_T^i)) \right], \mathcal{L}_{div} = -\sum_{j=1}^{N} \bar{p}_j \log \bar{p}_j, \tag{4}$$

where $\mathcal{F}_T^{m_T}(x_T^i) = \sum_{k=1}^{n} \zeta_k \mathcal{F}_{S_k}^{m_S}(x_T^i)$, ζ_k is the weight assigned to the k-th source such that $\zeta_k \geq 0$, $\sum_{k=1}^{n} \zeta_k = 1$ and $\bar{p} = \frac{1}{n_T} \sum_{i=1}^{n_T} \left[\mathcal{F}_T^{m_T}(x_T^i) \right] \in \mathbb{R}^N$ is the empirical label distribution. The *mutual information* is calculated as $\mathcal{L}_{IM} = \mathcal{L}_{div} - \mathcal{L}_{ent}$. Maximization of $\mathcal{L}_{IM}$ (or minimization of $-\mathcal{L}_{IM}$) ensures the target labels, as predicted by the sources, more confident and diverse in nature.

Pseudo-label Loss: Maximizing $\mathcal{L}_{IM}$ helps to obtain labels that are more confident in prediction and globally diverse. However, that does not prevent mislabeling (*i.e.*, assigning wrong labels to the inputs), which leads to *confirmation bias* [32]. To alleviate this problem, we adopt a self supervised pseudo-label based cross entropy loss, inspired by [3,4] (see the supplement for the exact details about computing the self-supervised pseudo-labels.) After calculating pseudo-labels we compute the *pseudo-label cross entropy* loss $\mathcal{L}_{pl}$ as follows:

$$\mathcal{L}_{pl} = -\frac{1}{n_T}\sum_{i=1}^{n_T}\sum_{k=1}^{K} \mathbf{1}\{\hat{y}_T^i = k\} \log\left[\mathcal{F}_T^{m_T}(x_T^i)\right]_k, \tag{5}$$

where $\hat{y}_T^i$ is the pseudo-label for the i-th target data point and $\mathbf{1}\{.\}$ is an indicator function that gives value 1 when the argument is true. Our final loss is the combination of the above two losses. We call this combination *modality agnostic loss* $\mathcal{L}_{ma}$, which is expressed as $\mathcal{L}_{ma} = -\mathcal{L}_{IM} + \lambda_{pl}\mathcal{L}_{pl}$.

We calculate the overall objective function as the sum of *modality agnostic* and *modality specific* losses and optimize Eq. (6) using Algorithm 1.

$$\underset{\{f_j\}_{j=1}^n,\zeta}{\text{minimize}} \quad \mathcal{L}_{ma} + \mathcal{L}_{ms} \quad \text{s.t.} \sum_{k=1}^{n} \zeta_k = 1, \zeta_k \geq 0 \tag{6}$$

Algorithm 1: Algorithm to Solve Eq. (6)

Input: n source models trained on modality m_S $\{\mathcal{F}_{S_k}^{m_S}\}_{k=1}^n = \{g_k \circ f_k\}_{k=1}^n$, unlabeled target data $\{x_T^i\}_{i=1}^{n_T}$ from modality m_T, TI cross modal pairs $\{x_{TI_i}^{m_S}, x_{TI_i}^{m_T}\}_{i=1}^{n_{TI}}$, mixing weights $\{\zeta_k\}_{k=1}^n$, max number of epochs E, regularization parameters λ_{TI}, λ_d, number of batches B

Output: Optimal adapted feature enocoders $\{f_k^\star\}_{k=1}^n$, mixing weights $\{\zeta_k^*\}_{k=1}^n$

Initialization: Freeze final classification layers $\{g_k\}_{k=1}^n$, set $\zeta_k = \frac{1}{n}$ for all k

Calculate $\{\psi_j^i\}_{j=1}^n \; \forall i \in [1, 2 \ldots, n_{TI}]$ using Eq. (1)

Retrieve $\mathbb{E}\big[\mu_l | \mathcal{X}_{S_j}\big]$ and $\mathbb{E}\big[\sigma_l^2 | \mathcal{X}_{S_j}\big]$ for all j and l as in Section 4.2

Knowledge Transfer Phase:

for *epoch* = 1 *to* E **do**

  for *iteration* = 1 *to* B **do**

    Sample a mini batch of target data and feed it through each of the source models

    Calculate loss terms in Eq. (2), (3), (4), and (5)

    Compute overall objective from Eq. (6)

    Update parameters in $\{f_j\}_{j=1}^n$ and $\{\zeta_k\}_{k=1}^n$ by optimizing (6)

    Make ζ non-negative by setting $\zeta_k := 1/(1 + e^{-\zeta_k})$

    Normalize ζ by setting $\zeta_k := \zeta_k / \sum_{i=1}^n \zeta_i$

  end

end

Final target model $\mathcal{F}_T^{m_T} = \sum_{k=1}^n \zeta_k^\star (g_k \circ f_k^\star)$

---

5 Experiments

We first describe the datasets, baselines and experimental details we employ. Next, we show results of single and multi-source cross modal transfer which show the efficacy of our method. In Sect. 5.3 we demonstrate experimentally why source free cross modal is a much harder problem compared to cross domain knowledge transfer. We conclude this section by performing analysis on different hyperparameters.

5.1 Datasets, Baselines and Experimental Details

Datasets: To show the efficacy of our method we extensively test on publicly available cross-modal datasets. We show results on two RGB-D (RGB and Depth) datasets – SUN RGB-D [33] and DIML RGB+D [34], and the RGB-NIR Scene (RGB and Near Infrared) dataset [35]. We summarize the statistics of the datasets in Table 2. In the supplement, we provide examples from each dataset and the list of classes which we use as TI and TR data in our experiments.

1. SUN RGB-D: A scene understanding benchmark dataset which contains 10335 RGB-D image pairs of indoor scenes. The dataset has images acquired from four different sensors named *Kinect version1 (kv1)*, *Kinect version2 (kv2)*, *Intel RealSense* and *Asus Xtion*. We treat these four sensors as four different domains. Out of total 45 classes, 17 common classes are treated as TR classes and the remaining 28 classes as TI classes. To train four source models, one for each domain, we use the RGB images from the TR classes, specific to that particular domain. We treat the TR depth images from each of the domains as the target modality data.
2. DIML RGB+D: This dataset consists of more than 200 indoor/outdoor scenes. We use the smaller sample dataset instead of the full dataset, which has 1500/500 RGB-D pairs for training/testing distributed among 18 scene classes. We split the training pairs into RGB and depth, and treat those two as source and target, respectively. The synchronized RGB-D frames are captured using Kinect v2 and Zed stereo camera [36–38].
3. RGB-NIR Scene: This dataset consists of 477 images from 9 scene categories captured in RGB and Near-infrared (NIR). The images were captured using separate exposures from modified SLR cameras, using visible and NIR [35]. We perform single source knowledge transfer from RGB to NIR and vice versa for this dataset. For all the datasets, TR/TI split is done according to Table 2.

Baseline Methods: The problem statement we focus on in this paper is new and has not been considered in literature before. As such, there is no direct baseline for our method. However, the closest related works are source free cross domain knowledge transfer methods that operates under both single and multi-source cases [3,4,22–26]. SHOT [3] and DECISION [4] are the best-known works on single source and multi-source SFDA and we compare against only these two methods. Unlike SOCKET, neither of these baselines employ strategies to overcome modality differences and use only the modality-agnostic loss $\mathcal{L}_{ma}$ for training the target models. Using scene classification as the task of interest, we will show that SOCKET outperforms these baselines for cross-modal knowledge transfer with no access to task-relevant source data. We provide details about the network architecture in the supplement. We note that there a few more recent works [22–26] which have shown small improvements over SHOT, and are orthogonal to the ideas in this paper. Incorporating these improvements for SOCKET as well can be interesting and consider this future work.

Performing Knowledge Transfer: Recall that we initialize the target models with the source weights and the classifier layers are frozen. The weights in the feature encoders and source mixing weight parameters (ζ_k's) in the case of multi-source are the optimization parameters. The values of various parameters like the learning rate are given in the supplement.

Table 2. Datasets statistics

	SUN-RGBD [33]	RGB-NIR Scene [35]	DIML [34]
Number of domains	4	1	1
Domain names	kv1,kv2,Realsense,Xtion	N/A	N/A
# of TR images for source training	1264,1234,238,2512	204	527
# of TR unlabeled images	1264,1234,238,2512	204	527
Number of TI paired images	1709	153	1088
Number of TR & TI classes	17 & 28	6 & 3	6 & 12
Modalities	RGB-D	RGB-NIR	RGB-D

Table 3. Results on the SUN RGB-D dataset [33] for the task of single-source cross-modal knowledge transfer from RGB to depth modality without access to task relevant source data. The rows represent RGB domains on which the source models are trained. The columns represent the knowledge transfer results on the depth domains for three methods – *Unadapted* shows results with unadapted source, SHOT [3] and SOCKET.

Source RGB	Target depth											
	Kinect v1			Kinect v2			Realsense			Xtion		
	Unadapted	SHOT	SOCKET	Unadapted	SHOT	SOCKET	Unadapted	SHOT	SOCKET	Unadapted	SHOT	SOCKET
Kinect v1	14.8	16.7	**25.3**	14.6	20.3	**23.6**	9.0	11.9	**13.4**	7.1	15.3	**18.1**
Kinect v2	4.0	12.8	**13.6**	17.0	29.4	**35.2**	10.8	19.3	**22.8**	**10.6**	7.0	8.3
Realsense	2.0	7.9	**20.3**	7.1	18.4	**23.5**	14.7	27.4	**30.0**	5.1	9.5	**11.8**
Xtion	0.7	9.5	**14.2**	6.0	20.2	**24.2**	9.0	21.8	**23.5**	8.1	13.2	**22.2**
Average	5.4	11.7	**18.4**	11.2	22.1	**26.6**	10.9	20.1	**22.4**	7.7	11.3	**15.1**

λ_{pl} is set as 0.3 for all the experiments following [4]. For the regularization parameters λ_{TI} and λ_d of *modality specific* losses, we set them to be equal. We empirically choose those parameters in such a way so as to balance it with the *modality agnostic* losses such that no loss component overpowers the other by a large margin. Empirically we found that a range of $(0.1, 0.5)$ works best. All of the values in this range outperform the baselines and we report the best accuracies amongst those. For images from the modalities other than RGB, which are depth and NIR, we repeat the single-channel images into three-channel images, to be able to feed it through the feature encoders which are initialized from the source models trained on RGB images. We use a batch size of 32 for all of our experiments. We run our method 3 times for all experiments with 3 random seeds in PyTorch [39] and report the average accuracies over those.

5.2 Main Results

Results on the SUN RGB-D Dataset [33]: Our method is general enough to deal with any number of sources and we demonstrate both single and multi-source knowledge transfer. In Table 3, we show single source RGB to depth results for all of the four domains. Treating the unlabeled depth data of each domain as target, we adapt these using source models trained on RGB data from each of the four domains. It is easily evident from Table 3, that for the target domains Kinect V1, Kinect V2, Realsense and Xtion, SOCKET consistently outperforms the baseline by a good margin of 6.7%, 4.5%, 2.3%, and 3.8%, respectively, thus proving the efficacy of SOCKET in a source-free cross modal setting. In some of the cases SOCKET outperforms the baseline by a very large margin, as high as 12.4% (Realsense-RGB to Kinect V1-depth). We show two-source RGB to depth adaptation results in Table 4. For four domains we get six two-source combinations, each of which is used for adaptation to depth data from all four domains. We see that in this case also, on average SOCKET outperforms the baseline for all four target domains by good margins. SOCKET shows good improvement for some individual cases like (Kinect v1 + Xtion)-RGB to Kinect v1 depth – improvement of 12.2% – and (Kinect v2 + Realsense)-RGB to Kinect v2 depth –improvement of 10.4%.

Table 4. Results on the SUN RGB-D dataset [33] **for the task of multiple cross-modal knowledge transfer from RGB to depth modality without access to task relevant source data.** The rows show the six combinations of two trained source models on RGB data from four different domains. The columns represent the knowledge transfer results on the domain specific depth data for *DECISION* [4], the current SOTA for multiple source adaptation without source data, and SOCKET

Source RGB	Target depth							
	Kinect v1		Kinect v2		Realsense		Xtion	
	DECISION	SOCKET	DECISION	SOCKET	DECISION	SOCKET	DECISION	SOCKET
Kinect v1 + Kinect v2	17.9	**19.5**	34.2	**36.6**	18.8	**19.8**	14.6	**18.0**
Kinect v1 + Realsense	12.6	**18.0**	23.3	**26.8**	24.3	**24.7**	10.9	**12.2**
Kinect v1 + Xtion	11.7	**23.9**	29.6	**35.7**	20.3	**21.1**	16.7	**20.0**
Kinect v2 + Realsense	7.4	**11.7**	22.7	**33.1**	28.4	**29.4**	6.9	**9.1**
Kinect v2 + Xtion	14.8	**16.2**	27.0	**31.0**	**25.4**	25.0	11.6	**18.3**
Realsense + Xtion	8.3	**10.7**	23.1	**25.2**	30.1	**31.5**	9.5	**10.8**
Average	12.1	**16.6**	26.7	**31.4**	24.6	**25.3**	11.7	**14.7**

Table 5. Classification accuracy (%) on DIML dataset with different TI data

TI data	Unadapted	SHOT [3]	SOCKET	SOCKET
	N/A	N/A	DIML RGB+D	SUN RGB-D
RGB→Depth	26.9	41.4	**46.1**	**53.2**

Results on the DIML RGB+D Dataset [34]: We performed a single source adaptation experiment (Table 5) by restructuring the dataset according to Table 2. In Table 5, we use the TI data from both the DIML RGB+D as well as SUN RGB-D datasets in two separate columns, where the TI data of SUN RGB+D is the same that have been used for experiments related to the SUN RGB-D dataset. By doing so, we show that SOCKET can perform well even with TI data from a completely different dataset, and find that SOCKET has a gain of 4.7% and 11.8% over baseline for these two TI data settings, respectively.

Results on the RGB-NIR Scene Dataset [35]: We now show that SOCKET also outperforms baslines when the modalitiies are RGB and NIR using the RGB-NIR dataset. We follow the splits described in Table 2. We do experiments on both RGB to NIR and vice versa. The results are given in Table 6. For RGB to NIR transfer, SOCKET shows 3.5% improvement, while for NIR to RGB transfer, it shows 0.5% improvement over the competing method.

Table 6. Results on RGB-NIR dataset [35] for the task of single-source cross-modal knowledge transfer from RGB to NIR and vice versa without task-relevant source data

Setting	Method		
	Unadapted	SHOT [3]	SOCKET
RGB → NIR	84.8	86.7	**90.2**
NIR → RGB	65.2	92.2	**92.7**

Table 7. Cross modal vs cross domain knowledge transfer for SUN RGB-D dataset scene classification using SHOT [3]: (1) The first columm shows the accuracies for RGB to depth transfer within the same domain. (2) The second column is generated by transferring knowledge from one RGB domain to other three RGB domains taking the average of the accuracies

Source	Cross-modal	Cross-domain
Kinect v1	16.7	24.5
Kinect v2	29.4	39.6
Realsense	27.4	29.7
Xtion	13.2	43.1
Average	21.7	34.2

5.3 Cross Modal vs Cross Domain

In order to show the importance of the novel problem we consider, we compare the single-source knowledge transfer results on the SUN RGB-D dataset for modality change vs domain shift in Table 7. We use SHOT [3] which is a source-free UDA method for this experiment. All the domain-specific source models are trained on RGB images. For domain shift, the targets are all the RGB images of the remaining 3 domains and we report the average over them. Domain shift involves changes in sensor configuration, viewpoints, etc. For modality change, the target data are depth images from the same domain. The scenes are the same as in the RGB source, except they are captured using the depth sensor. The table clearly shows that the accuracy drops by a large margin of 12.5% when we transfer knowledge across modalities instead of domains of the same modality. This shows that a cross-modal knowledge transfer is not the same as DA and a framework like SOCKET is necessary to reduce the modality gap.

5.4 Ablation and Sensitivity Analysis

Contribution of Loss Components: In Table 8, the first row has the result with just the *modality agnostic* loss $\mathcal{L}_{ma}$, whereas second and third row shows the individual effect of our proposed *modality specific* losses along with the $\mathcal{L}_{ma}$. For all cases, SOCKET outperforms the baseline and using both losses in conjunction with $\mathcal{L}_{ma}$ yields best results.

Table 8. Ablation of contribution of our proposed novel loss components. The first accuracy column (a) corresponds to single source adaptation from RGB to depth on *kv2* domain, whereas the second column (b) shows the multi-source adaptation result from *kv1+xtion* to *kv1* domain of SUN RGB-D dataset. We show the accuracy gain over using $\mathcal{L}_{ma}$ only inside the parentheses

$\mathcal{L}_{ma}$	$\mathcal{L}_{d}$	$\mathcal{L}_{TI}$	(a) accuracy (%)	(b) accuracy (%)
✓			30.0	11.7
✓	✓		31.6 (↑1.6)	18.3 (↑6.6)
✓		✓	34.9 (↑4.9)	22.6 (↑10.9)
✓	✓	✓	**36.3** (↑6.3)	**23.9** (↑12.2)

Table 9. Left: Effect of number of TI data. We perform knowledge transfer from Kinect v1 RGB to unlabeled depth data. We use six random TI classes and vary the number of TI images per class from 0 to 60 in steps of 20. **Right: Effect of regularization hyper-parameters**. We perform Kinect v1 and Kinect v2 RGB to Kinect v1 depth transfer with varying $(\lambda_{TI}, \lambda_d)$ and tabulate the accuracy of SOCKET

Images per class	60	40	20	0
Accuracy (%)	25.0	22.5	20.3	16.7

$(\lambda_{TI}, \lambda_d)$	0.00	0.05	0.10	0.50	1.00
Kinect v1	16.1	15.0	16.6	23.4	21.0
Kinect v2	29.3	34.2	35.0	36.7	16.3

Effect of Number of TI images: We randomly chose six classes from SUN RGB-D dataset as TI data. Table 9 clearly shows that increasing per class samples of TI data results in improving the scene-classification accuracy for RGB to depth transfer on the SUN RGB-D dataset. In short, for a fixed number of TI classes, the more TI images per class, the better SOCKET performs.

Effect of Regularization Parameters: In Table 9, we observe the effect of test accuracy vs the regularization hyper-parameters for our novel losses proposed as a part of SOCKET. We keep λ_{TI} and λ_d equal to each other for values between 0 to 1. Using the value of 0 is the same as using SHOT. From the table, we see that as the value of the parameter increases the accuracy also increases up to a certain point, and then it starts decreasing.

6 Conclusion

We identify the novel and challenging problem of cross-modality knowledge transfer with no access to the task-relevant data from the source sensor modality, and only unlabeled data in the target. We propose our framework, SOCKET, which includes devising loss functions that help bridge the gap between the two modalities in the feature space. Our results for both RGB-to-depth and RGB-to-NIR experiments show that SOCKET outperforms the baselines which cannot effectively handle modality shift.

Acknowledgements. SMA, SL, KCP and MJ were supported by Mitsubishi Electric Research Laboratories. SMA and ARC were partially supported by ONR grant N00014-19-1-2264 and the NSF grants CCF-2008020 and IIS-1724341.

References

1. Gupta, S., Hoffman, J., Malik, J.: Cross modal distillation for supervision transfer. In: Proceedings of the IEEE Conference on Computer Vision and Pattern Recognition, pp. 2827–2836 (2016)
2. Ahmed, S.M., Lejbolle, A.R., Panda, R., Roy-Chowdhury, A.K.: Camera on-boarding for person re-identification using hypothesis transfer learning. In: Proceedings of the IEEE/CVF Conference on Computer Vision and Pattern Recognition, pp. 12144–12153 (2020)
3. Liang, J., Hu, D., Feng, J.: Do we really need to access the source data? source hypothesis transfer for unsupervised domain adaptation. In: International Conference on Machine Learning, PMLR, pp. 6028–6039 (2020)
4. Ahmed, S.M., Raychaudhuri, D.S., Paul, S., Oymak, S., Roy-Chowdhury, A.K.: Unsupervised multi-source domain adaptation without access to source data. In: Proceedings of the IEEE/CVF Conference on Computer Vision and Pattern Recognition, pp. 10103–10112 (2021)
5. Perrot, M., Habrard, A.: A theoretical analysis of metric hypothesis transfer learning. In: International Conference on Machine Learning, PMLR, pp. 1708–1717 (2015)
6. Thoker, F.M., Gall, J.: Cross-modal knowledge distillation for action recognition. In: 2019 IEEE International Conference on Image Processing (ICIP), pp. 6–10. IEEE (2019)
7. Dai, R., Das, S., Bremond, F.: Learning an augmented RGB representation with cross-modal knowledge distillation for action detection. In: Proceedings of the IEEE/CVF International Conference on Computer Vision, pp. 13053–13064 (2021)

8. Garcia, N.C., Bargal, S.A., Ablavsky, V., Morerio, P., Murino, V., Sclaroff, S.: Dmcl: distillation multiple choice learning for multimodal action recognition. arXiv preprint arXiv:1912.10982 (2019)
9. Wang, J., Tang, Z., Li, X., Yu, M., Fang, Q., Liu, L.: Cross-modal knowledge distillation method for automatic cued speech recognition. arXiv preprint arXiv:2106.13686 (2021)
10. Sayed, N., Brattoli, B., Ommer, B.: Cross and learn: cross-modal self-supervision. In: Brox, T., Bruhn, A., Fritz, M. (eds.) GCPR 2018. LNCS, vol. 11269, pp. 228–243. Springer, Cham (2019). https://doi.org/10.1007/978-3-030-12939-2_17
11. Hoffman, J., Gupta, S., Leong, J., Guadarrama, S., Darrell, T.: Cross-modal adaptation for RGB-d detection. In: 2016 IEEE International Conference on Robotics and Automation (ICRA), pp. 5032–5039. IEEE (2016)
12. Zhao, L., Peng, X., Chen, Y., Kapadia, M., Metaxas, D.N.: Knowledge as priors: cross-modal knowledge generalization for datasets without superior knowledge. In: Proceedings of the IEEE/CVF Conference on Computer Vision and Pattern Recognition, pp. 6528–6537 (2020)
13. Ferreri, A., Bucci, S., Tommasi, T.: Translate to adapt: RGB-d scene recognition across domains. arXiv preprint arXiv:2103.14672 (2021)
14. Du, D., Wang, L., Wang, H., Zhao, K., Wu, G.: Translate-to-recognize networks for RGB-d scene recognition. In: Proceedings of the IEEE/CVF Conference on Computer Vision and Pattern Recognition, pp. 11836–11845 (2019)
15. Ayub, A., Wagner, A.R.: Centroid based concept learning for RGB-d indoor scene classification. arXiv preprint arXiv:1911.00155 (2019)
16. Peng, K.C., Wu, Z., Ernst, J.: Zero-shot deep domain adaptation. In: Proceedings of the European Conference on Computer Vision (ECCV), pp. 764–781 (2018)
17. Hsu, H.K., et al.: Progressive domain adaptation for object detection. In: Proceedings of the IEEE/CVF Winter Conference on Applications of Computer Vision, pp. 749–757 (2020)
18. Tzeng, E., Hoffman, J., Saenko, K., Darrell, T.: Adversarial discriminative domain adaptation. In: Proceedings of the IEEE Conference on Computer Vision and Pattern Recognition, pp. 7167–7176 (2017)
19. Paul, S., Tsai, Y.-H., Schulter, S., Roy-Chowdhury, A.K., Chandraker, M.: Domain adaptive semantic segmentation using weak labels. In: Vedaldi, A., Bischof, H., Brox, T., Frahm, J.-M. (eds.) ECCV 2020. LNCS, vol. 12354, pp. 571–587. Springer, Cham (2020). https://doi.org/10.1007/978-3-030-58545-7_33
20. Hoffman, J., et al.: Cycada: cycle-consistent adversarial domain adaptation. In: International conference on machine learning, PMLR, pp. 1989–1998 (2018)
21. Peng, X., Bai, Q., Xia, X., Huang, Z., Saenko, K., Wang, B.: Moment matching for multi-source domain adaptation. In: Proceedings of the IEEE/CVF International Conference on Computer Vision, pp. 1406–1415 (2019)
22. Yang, S., Wang, Y., van de Weijer, J., Herranz, L., Jui, S.: Generalized source-free domain adaptation. In: Proceedings of the IEEE/CVF International Conference on Computer Vision, pp. 8978–8987 (2021)
23. Yang, S., Wang, Y., van de Weijer, J., Herranz, L., Jui, S.: Exploiting the intrinsic neighborhood structure for source-free domain adaptation. arXiv preprint arXiv:2110.04202 (2021)
24. Yang, S., Wang, Y., van de Weijer, J., Herranz, L., Jui, S.: Casting a bait for offline and online source-free domain adaptation. arXiv preprint arXiv:2010.12427 (2020)
25. Agarwal, P., Paudel, D.P., Zaech, J.N., Van Gool, L.: Unsupervised robust domain adaptation without source data. In: Proceedings of the IEEE/CVF Winter Conference on Applications of Computer Vision, pp. 2009–2018 (2022)

26. Liang, J., Hu, D., Wang, Y., He, R., Feng, J.: Source data-absent unsupervised domain adaptation through hypothesis transfer and labeling transfer. IEEE Trans. Pattern Anal. Mach. Intell. **44**(11), 8602–8617 (2021)
27. Ganin, Y., et al.: Domain-adversarial training of neural networks. J. Mach. Learn. Res. **17**(1), 2030–2096 (2016)
28. Bridle, J.S., Heading, A.J., MacKay, D.J.: Unsupervised classifiers, mutual information and phantom targets (1992)
29. Kutbi, M., Peng, K.C., Wu, Z.: Zero-shot deep domain adaptation with common representation learning. IEEE Trans. Pattern Anal. Mach. Intell. **44**(7), 3909–3924 (2021)
30. Ioffe, S., Normalization, C.S.B.: Accelerating deep network training by reducing internal covariate shift. arXiv preprint arXiv:1502.03167
31. Yin, H., et al.: Dreaming to distill: data-free knowledge transfer via deepinversion. In: Proceedings of the IEEE/CVF Conference on Computer Vision and Pattern Recognition, pp. 8715–8724 (2020)
32. Tarvainen, A., Valpola, H.: Mean teachers are better role models: weight-averaged consistency targets improve semi-supervised deep learning results. In: Advances in Neural Information Processing Systems, pp. 1195–1204 (2017)
33. Song, S., Lichtenberg, S.P., Xiao, J.: Sun RGB-D: a RGB-D scene understanding benchmark suite. In: Proceedings of the IEEE Conference on Computer Vision and Pattern Recognition, pp. 567–576 (2015)
34. Cho, J., Min, D., Kim, Y., Sohn, K.: Deep monocular depth estimation leveraging a large-scale outdoor stereo dataset. Expert Syst. Appl. **178**, 114877 (2021)
35. Brown, M., Süsstrunk, S.: Multi-spectral sift for scene category recognition. In: CVPR 2011, pp. 177–184. IEEE (2011)
36. Kim, Y., Ham, B., Oh, C., Sohn, K.: Structure selective depth superresolution for RGB-D cameras. IEEE Trans. Image Process. **25**(11), 5227–5238 (2016)
37. Kim, S., Min, D., Ham, B., Kim, S., Sohn, K.: Deep stereo confidence prediction for depth estimation. In: 2017 IEEE International Conference on Image Processing (ICIP), pp.992–996 IEEE (2017)
38. Kim, Y., Jung, H., Min, D., Sohn, K.: Deep monocular depth estimation via integration of global and local predictions. IEEE Trans. Image Process. **27**(8), 4131–4144 (2018)
39. Paszke, A., et al.: Pytorch: an imperative style, high-performance deep learning library. Adv. Neural Inf. Process. Syst. **32**, 8026–8037 (2019)

Online Domain Adaptation for Semantic Segmentation in Ever-Changing Conditions

Theodoros Panagiotakopoulos[1], Pier Luigi Dovesi[2], Linus Härenstam-Nielsen[3,4], and Matteo Poggi[5](✉)

[1] King, Stockholm, Sweden
[2] Univrses, Stockholm, Sweden
[3] Kudan, Tokyo, Japan
[4] Technical University of Munich, Munich, Germany
[5] University of Bologna, Bologna, Italy
m.poggi@unibo.it

Abstract. Unsupervised Domain Adaptation (UDA) aims at reducing the domain gap between training and testing data and is, in most cases, carried out in offline manner. However, domain changes may occur continuously and unpredictably during deployment (e.g. sudden weather changes). In such conditions, deep neural networks witness dramatic drops in accuracy and offline adaptation may not be enough to contrast it. In this paper, we tackle Online Domain Adaptation (OnDA) for semantic segmentation. We design a pipeline that is robust to continuous domain shifts, either gradual or sudden, and we evaluate it in the case of rainy and foggy scenarios. Our experiments show that our framework can effectively adapt to new domains during deployment, while not being affected by catastrophic forgetting of the previous domains.

1 Introduction

The task of semantic segmentation consist of assigning each pixel of an image to a specific class. With the spread of deep learning, Convolutional Neural Networks (CNNs) have been established as the state-of-the-art for tackling this kind of problem [6,7,54]. However, despite training on a large quantity of annotated images, the network predictions can often be unreliable when deployed on new scenarios, because of the *domain shift* occurring between training and deployment. For example, the shift can be due to the images being collected in very different environments (e.g., urban versus rural roads) or lighting conditions (e.g., day versus night).

T. Panagiotakopoulos and L. Härenstam-Nielsen—Part of the work carried out while at Univrses.

Supplementary Information The online version contains supplementary material available at https://doi.org/10.1007/978-3-031-19830-4_8.

S. Avidan et al. (Eds.): ECCV 2022, LNCS 13694, pp. 128–146, 2022.
https://doi.org/10.1007/978-3-031-19830-4_8

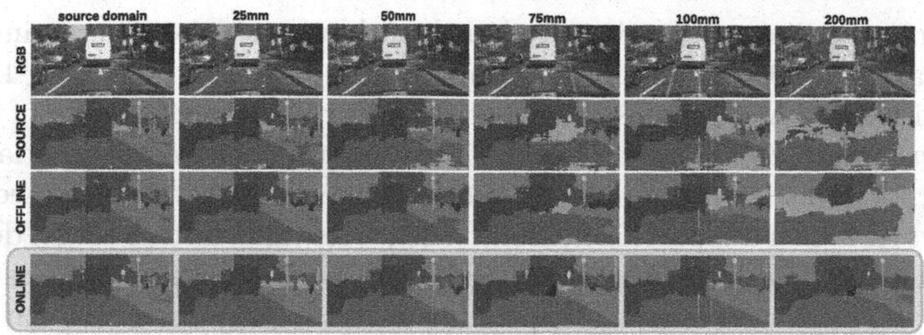

Fig. 1. OnDA framework in action. We show images with varying intensity of rain (from 0 to 200 mm). When dealing with such complicated domain shifts, both pretrained networks and offline adaptations struggle, whereas our online framework is able to adapt, without forgetting.

Consequently, Unsupervised Domain Adaptation (UDA) arose as a popular research trend to overcome the domain shift problem. It aims at shrinking the gap between a labeled set of images – the *source* domain, over which supervised training is possible – and an unlabeled one – the *target* domain, for which ground truth annotations are not available. This is performed in several ways, such as transferring the image style across the two [16,49,59], or either conditioning or normalizing the feature space [14,47]. Techniques for UDA have been extensively studied in the offline setting, thus assuming to have availability of both the source and the target domain images in advance, then proceeding by adapting a model, trained with ground truth supervision on source, to the target. However, such an assumption is often too strong to hold in the context of an actual application. We argue that domain shifts are likely to continuously arise during deployment. Some examples can be related to different cities or weather conditions, or even, at a lower level, involving different camera positioning and intrinsics.

While some domain shifts come in predictable ways (e.g., day-night cycle), some others can occur unpredictably – such as weather changes, either in a slow (e.g., rain, fog) or sudden way (e.g., storms). Leveraging the fact that environmental changes may often happen gradually, we propose an online adaptation pipeline that exploits progressive adaptation. Inspired by recent progress in Curriculum Learning applied to UDA, we expand the paradigm beyond the adaptation to an *intermediate* domain by designing a framework able to autonomously identify domain changes and adapt its self-training policy accordingly. In online settings, we seek to seamlessly find the optimal response to the current deployment domain while, crucially, we would like to proactively prepare for future scenarios. We argue that online settings need to break the dichotomy between Source and Target domain, where the Target has now to be modeled as a "domain sequence". Extensive empirical studies will highlight how the good modeling of the domain sequence is paramount for this purpose. Indeed, most of the improvements observed in specific target domains are gained "in advance", i.e. before the model has ever been exposed to that specific distribution.

To perform online adaptation, we benchmark our model on increasing intensities of rain (25, 50, 75, 100, and 200 mm of rain) and fog (750, 375, 150, and 75 m of visibility). We demonstrate that deep learning models aware of domain shift *intensity* and *direction* can exploit intermediate domains substantially better. We achieve this by introducing an active teacher-model switching mechanism that allows for higher adaptation flexibility, hence reaching farther target domains, as visible in Fig. 1. Additionally, when needed, the switching mechanism can revert the adaptation process allowing adapting back to source domain without experiencing catastrophic forgetting. Our main contributions are:

- We introduce an online progressive adaptation benchmark for UDA methods.
- We propose an approach that leverages progressive adaptation to increase performance on distant domains in an online manner.
- We demonstrate that catastrophic forgetting can be avoided by actively updating the self-training policy during adaptation and using a Replay Buffer.
- We run experiments on various simulated scenarios and, crucially, we show that models that have been previously exposed to gradual domain adaptation can acquire the ability to cope with sharp changes as well.

2 Related Work

Online Domain Adaptation is directly connected to many fields of Machine Learning, such as Transfer Learning and Continuous Learning. We now review methods that focus on reducing the domain gap, lessening the effect of catastrophic forgetting, and continuously adapting to upcoming domains.

Unsupervised Domain Adaptation. Unsupervised Domain Adaptation (UDA), is a relatively new field that has gained interest due to the rising amount of data and the limited and expensive resources needed to annotate them. Early UDA approaches focus on constructing domain invariant feature representations [14] or transferring the "style" from one domain to another, for instance, by means of the CycleGAN [59] framework. First attempts [16,49] learned this transfer in an offline manner before training, then translating images during training itself. More modern approaches [12,27,52] combine the two phases in one in an end-to-end framework. This strategy has been extended by LTIR [22], in order to learn texture-invariant features by training on source images augmented with textures coming from other real images. Often, adversarial learning has been deployed for UDA aiming at obtaining better alignment of the source and target distributions, either in features [9,14,17,47] or output [42] spaces. Later works [9,10] highlight the use of class information in adversarial learning, while Advent [44] introduces an adversarial approach to perform entropy minimization.

Self-training. Recent trends concerning UDA leverage the idea of producing *pseudo-labels* [26] for self-training over the target domain, inspired by the recent success in semi-supervised tasks [36,55]. Since these labels are noisy, designing robust strategies to reduce the effect of wrong labels is of paramount importance for this family of approaches. [61] implements this by means of a confidence-based thresholding algorithm, [32] extends this approach with an instance adaptive variant, further improving the quality of the produced pseudo-labels. Nevertheless, naive pseudo-labeling can produce unreliable confidence estimates and an increased bias towards the most common classes. To contrast this [18,60] propose approaches that balances class predictions, while [62] regularizes the model confidence. On this same track, [58] uses pseudo-labels to minimize the discrepancy between two classifiers, while [33] aims at inter-domain and intra-domain gap minimization, supported by pseudo-labels, and [3] uses shallow features to improve class boundaries. Finally, newer approaches [5,56,57] leverage *prototypes*, defined as feature-space class centroids, to produce unbiased pseudo-labels.

Source-free UDA or "model adaptation", is a topic that was introduced to assist continual learning [37]. In contrast to traditional unsupervised domain adaptation, the use of source and target samples happens separately. Therefore, the learning approach consists of two separate steps, the *task learning step* using the source data and the *adaptation step* using the target. Several approaches have been explored: [29] tries to solve the lack of source samples by deploying a generator that produces samples that resemble the source data. In contrast, [28] freezes the final layers of the network and performs self-training. Similarly [46] retrains Batch-Normalization layers through entropy minimization. To avoid forgetting source during adaptation, [30] introduces a feature alignment during adaptation. Finally, [21] uses the distance between embeddings and test-time adapting prototypes to compute the predictions. Notably, these latter [21,30] have been proposed and tested for classification tasks on toy datasets.

Curriculum Learning is a training strategy that focuses on the order in which information is exploited. As described by [1], machine learning models can learn much better when information is presented in a meaningful order. [31] developed a domain encoder to express domain distance. The target domains were then ordered based on their similarity to the source domain. Adaptation was then performed from the closest to the furthest from the source domain. [35] propose using generated foggy images as an intermediate step to adapting to real weather scenarios.

Continuous UDA. Some works tried to integrate UDA with continual learning, tackling the problem of "adapting without forgetting". Several methods employ Replay Buffers [2,24,25], ACE [50] leverages AdaIN [19] to perform style transfer while retaining previous knowledge through a task memory. [38] adapts through Contrastive Learning while constraining the gradient to reduce forgetting, and [51] uses a generator to produce the necessary data to perform adversarial training.

Despite the large body of existing literature, as raised by a contemporary work [39], current datasets and UDA methods fall short of representing and testing on realistic online scenarios, *i.e.* with incremental domain-shifts occurring continuously with the flowing of input images.

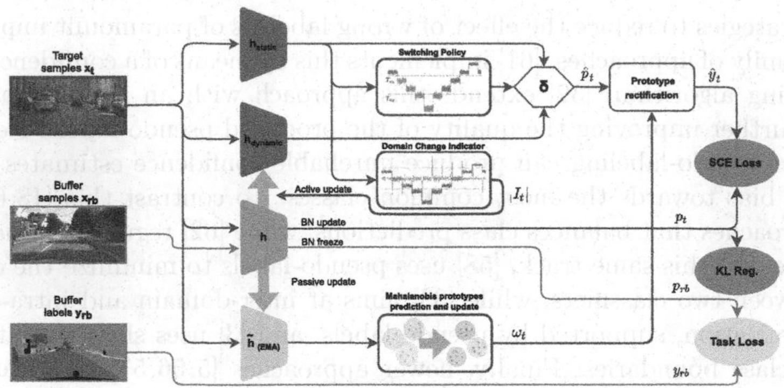

Fig. 2. Overview of our OnDA framework. It comprises Switching Policy, Domain Change Indicator, Mahalanobis prototypes prediction, and BN freezing.

3 Online Domain Adaptation

This section introduces our framework for Online Domain Adaptation (OnDA) specific to face ever-changing environments. While adopting state-of-the-art UDA strategies for prototypical self-training [48,56,62], we design a novel strategy to address online settings. We present a student-teacher approach [13] which allows for dynamic teachers orchestration by both actively updating the teacher according to the *domain change* and by strategically choosing the best teacher to employ to train the student model. Furthermore, we propose to exploit feature variance for better prototype predictions, we investigate the impact of BatchNorm during adaptation and we assess the importance of a Replay Buffer to prevent catastrophic forgetting. We present an overview of OnDA in Fig. 2.

3.1 Online Prototypical Self-training

We now introduce the design of a prototypical framework for the online setting.

Replay Buffer. First of all, in order to simulate a realistic deployment, where storing the full source dataset D_S might be infeasible, we sample a subset $D_{RB} \subseteq D_S$ as a Replay Buffer. The buffer is used for training with segmentation loss during adaptation and prevents the network from forgetting the original domain. As we will show in Sect. 4.3, even a small buffer is very helpful in the mitigation of catastrophic forgetting.

Problem Formulation. We define our network as $h = g \circ f$, where f is the feature encoder mapping images into a space of dimension K and g maps features into class labels. We denote sample-label pair from the source and Replay Buffer as (x_s, y_s) and (x_{rb}, y_{rb}) respectively. We model the target domain D_T as a sequence of Θ sub-domains, such that $D_T = (D_{T_1}, D_{T_2}, ..., D_{T_\Theta})$.

Prototypes Initialization. In online scenarios target samples appear sequentially $(x_t^{(1)}, x_t^{(2)}, ..., x_t^{(N)})$ and it is unknown from which D_{T_θ} they have been sampled. Therefore, target samples can not be used to initialize the class prototypes before the adaptation process takes place. To address this limitation, we initialize the prototypes using the source dataset and update them on the fly using target samples. Letting $h_{\text{static}} = g_{\text{static}} \circ f_{\text{static}}$ be the network fully trained on D_S before adaptation, the prototype initialization $\eta^c \in \mathbb{R}^K$ for each class c is given by:

$$\eta^c = \frac{1}{|\Lambda_{\mathbf{S}}^c|} \sum_{i=1}^{N_S} \sum_{j}^{H \times W} \left(y_s^{(i)}|_j = c \right) f_{\text{static}} \left(x_s^{(i)} \right) \Big|_j \tag{1}$$

where N_S, H, W are the number of source samples, image height and image width respectively. $|\Lambda_{\mathbf{S}}^c|$ denotes the number of pixels that belong to class c from set S, and $|\Lambda_{\mathbf{S}}| = \sum_c |\Lambda_{\mathbf{S}}^c|$. The variance $\sigma \in \mathbb{R}^K$ of each dimension k of the prototype space is then obtained through:

$$\sigma^2 = \frac{1}{|\Lambda_{\mathbf{S}}|} \sum_{i=1}^{N_S} \sum_{j}^{H \times W} f_{\text{static}} \left(x_s^{(i)} \right)^2 \Big|_j - \left(\frac{1}{|\Lambda_{\mathbf{S}}|} \sum_{i=1}^{N_S} \sum_{j}^{H \times W} f_{\text{static}} \left(x_s^{(i)} \right) \Big|_j \right)^2 . \tag{2}$$

Hence, given a target sample x_t, we obtain the prediction ω_t^c as the softmax of the variance-normalized proximity between prototypes η and the momentum encoder prediction $\tilde{f}\,(x_t)$,

$$\omega_t^c = \frac{\exp\left(- \left\| \left(\tilde{f}(x_t) - \eta^c \right) / \sigma \right\| \right)}{\sum_{c'} \exp\left(- \left\| \left(\tilde{f}\,(x_t) - \eta^{c'} \right) / \sigma \right\| \right)} \tag{3}$$

where $\tilde{h} = \tilde{g} \circ \tilde{f}$ is the momentum model of the network h. The momentum encoder $\tilde{f}$ is used to produce stable predictions compared to using the main encoder f directly and it is created by exponentially averaging the parameters of f over time. In Eq. 3, we employ a form of Mahalanobis distance, including the variances in each dimension of the feature vector. Compared to the Euclidean distance, this leads to a more accurate measure of the distance and higher overall metrics (+4.5% mIoU in the hardest target domain).

Prototypes Update. During the adaptation, the prototypes are updated online through target samples pseudo-labeling. Given a batch of N target samples B, the batch prototypes are defined as follows:

$$\hat{\eta}^c = \frac{1}{|\Lambda_{\mathbf{B}}^c|} \sum_{i=1}^{N} \sum_{j}^{H \times W} \left(\tilde{h}(x_t^{(i)}) = c \right) \tilde{f} \left(x_t^{(i)} \right) \Big|_j . \tag{4}$$

Then for all classes c where $|\Lambda_{\mathbf{B}}^c| > 0$ we update the corresponding prototype using $\eta^c \longleftarrow \lambda \eta^c + (1 - \lambda) \hat{\eta}^c$. Prototypes are used to lessen the reliance on the source label distribution. Naive pseudo-labeling will produce models that are highly biased towards the most popular and easier classes. In domain adaptation, source and target label distributions do not necessarily align. Feature distance through prototypes, on the other hand, removes class biases and produces unbiased predictions. Finally, the pseudo-label $\hat{y}_t$ for a sample x_t is computed by rectifying the model prediction using the prototype softmax output ω_t as follows:

$$\hat{y}_t = \xi(\hat{p}_t \cdot \omega_t) \tag{5}$$

where ξ is a function that transforms soft-labels to one-hot encoded hard labels. Moreover, instead of directly using the model prediction $p_t = h(x_t)$, checkpoints of the h model are used. In particular, we define:

$$\hat{p}_t = \delta h_{\text{static}}(x_t) + (1 - \delta) h_{\text{dynamic}}(x_t) \tag{6}$$

where h_{dynamic} is the last adapted model on the previous deployment domain, and $\delta \in [0, 1]$ determines the contribution of each model. In Sect. 3.3 we will describe how to guide the adaptation process by dynamically updating δ.

Overconfidence Handling. Self-training is a form of entropy minimization which means that the network will tend to become overconfident. Pseudo-labeling with thresholding strategies alone fail since confidence is no longer a reliable guideline. We utilize loss functions that can withstand overfitting to noisy labels. For this reason, two key techniques are used: confidence regularization and Symmetrical cross-entropy [48]. Given the model prediction $p_t = h(x_t)$ we apply a KL divergence regularizer [62]

$$\mathcal{L}_{\text{reg}} = -\gamma \sum_{k=1}^{K} \frac{1}{K} \log p_t. \tag{7}$$

Moreover, to mitigate the impact of noisy labels we employ Symmetrical Cross-Entropy (SCE). The pseudo-label loss is then described as follows:

$$\mathcal{L}_{\text{pseudo}} = \alpha \ell_{\text{ce}} \left(p_t, \hat{y}_t\right) + \beta \ell_{\text{ce}} \left(\hat{y}_t, p_t\right). \tag{8}$$

where ℓ_{ce} is the Cross-Entropy loss, and α and β are two weighting hyper-parameters. The complete loss function to perform learning using source and target samples is defined as follows:

$$\mathcal{L}_{\text{total}} = \mathcal{L}_{\text{task}}(x_{rb}, y_{rb}) + \mathcal{L}_{\text{pseudo}}(x_t, \hat{y}_t) + \mathcal{L}_{\text{reg}}(x_t). \tag{9}$$

Batch Normalization Switching. Batch Normalization (BN) layers [20] are employed to normalize features so as to obtain zero-mean and unit standard deviation distributions by iteratively accumulating statistics after processing any batch. Given features x_i for the i-th element of the batch, the output y_i of any BN layer is computed as $y_i = \frac{x_i - \mu_{\text{B}}}{\sigma_{\text{B}}}$ with $\mu_{\text{B}}, \sigma_{\text{B}}$ being the exponential moving average of the mean and variance of features x respectively. During online adaptation, our network processes data from two different distributions; the samples in the Replay Buffer ($\mathcal{D}_{\text{RB}}$) and those belonging to the target domain distribution ($\mathcal{D}_{T_\theta}$). This leads to cumulative statistics not being meaningful as an actual distribution, as already observed in [4,23]. Hence, we investigate two approaches to batch normalization: i) freezing BN layers when processing samples from $\mathcal{D}_{\text{RB}}$

or ii) swapping BN statistics between $\mathcal{D}_{\text{RB}}$ and $\mathcal{D}_{T_x}$. Both turn out to be beneficial in our online settings, thus we selected i) for simplicity. We provide a comparison between the BN approaches in the supplementary material.

3.2 Domain Shift Detection

An essential part of online adaptation is being able to detect the domain shifts and act accordingly. Inspired by the key role of the model confidence as a mean for measuring and minimizing domain shift [43,45], we use the confidence of h_{static} to identify domain changes as well as the "direction" of such a change. In online settings, it is indeed crucial to both recognize whether the deployment domain is changing and if the transition is leading towards a more distant domain (*forward*) or a closer domain (*backwards*), relatively to the source. Defining z_t as the confidence of h_{static} over the t-th batch, expressed as

$$z_t = \frac{1}{|\Lambda_{\mathbf{B}}|} \sum_{i=1}^{N} \sum_{j}^{H \times W} \max_c h_{\text{static}} \left(x^{(i)} \right) \Big|_{j,c} \tag{10}$$

we notice clear changes while transitioning between domains (see Fig. 2, the Domain Change Indicator, and Sect. 3 of the supplementary material). Therefore, the confidence derivative can be leveraged as an indicator of domain changes and computed using the difference between consecutive values. In order to reduce noise and have a robust representation, a shifting window of length n is used. On each new batch t, confidence values (z_t) are appended to the window, while old ones are removed (z_{t-n}). At any given time we compute the weighted average confidence of the window as $\mu_t = \frac{1}{n}\sum_{i=0}^{n} w[i] z_{t-i}$, where w is the discrete Hamming window [34] of length n. The switching indicator function can then be defined as:

$$I_t = \begin{cases} 1, & \mu_t - \mu_{t-1} > T_{\text{cd}} \\ -1, & \mu_t - \mu_{t-1} < -T_{\text{cd}} \\ 0, & \text{otherwise} \end{cases}, \ \forall\, t > n + 1. \tag{11}$$

when the window has not been filled yet ($t \leq n+1$), we set $I_t = 0$. T_{cd} is a hyperparameter that controls model sensitivity to domain changes. We then detect domain changes by examining the absolute value $|I_t| > 0$ and their direction studying its sign. In the supplementary material video, we present the behavior of the Domain Change Indicator for much more challenging scenarios, which led us to introduce a simple debouncing window to ensure robust switching.

3.3 Prior Model Switching Techniques

In this section we will focus on the prior predictions $\hat{p}$ introduced in Eq. 6. In particular, two models are used to acquire the prior: h_{static} and h_{dynamic}. h_{static} is the initial model, before any adaptation, while h_{dynamic} is the model before the adaptation to the current domain takes place. For example, in an adaptation sequence over domains $D_{T_1}, D_{T_2}, D_{T_3}$, during the first adaptation

(D_{T_1}) the dynamic and static models coincide. As the switching indicator I_t perceives that we are moving to the second domain (D_{T_2}), h_{dynamic} is updated becoming the model right after the adaptation on D_{T_1}. Similarly, for the third adaptation (on D_{T_3}), h_{dynamic} will become the model after the adaptation on D_{T_2} and before D_{T_3}. The choice of which teacher model is going to be used for the prototypes rectification heavily influence the adaptation capabilities.

In the experimental section, we will show that employing h_{dynamic} ($\delta = 0$) grants extra flexibility, allowing adaptation to *harder* (i.e. more distant) domains. On one hand, as a drawback, it performs sub-optimally while "adapting back" to previous domains and even D_S. On the other hand, h_{static} ($\delta = 1$) intrinsically limits adaptation due to its predictions guiding the self-training towards the original model. Nonetheless, it allows for better adaptation in domains closer to D_S, preventing catastrophic forgetting. We thus identify the need for a mechanism that allows for an effective switching between the two prior models, hence making δ function of μ_t, i.e. $\delta_t = Switch(\mu_t, t)$. We introduce the following policies, summarized in Fig. 3:

- *Confidence Switch (CS)*: Applies simple thresholding on the static model confidence z_t.

$$\delta_t^{\text{CS}} = \begin{cases} 1, & \mu_t > T_c \\ 0, & \mu_t \leq T_c \end{cases}, \quad t \geq 0 \tag{12}$$

- *Soft-Confidence Switch (SCS)*: Performs a *Confidence Switch* with a smooth transition through a weighted average of the models. By moving farther from the source, i.e. lower confidence, h_{dynamic} is weighted more, while, when coming back to the source, increases h_{static} contribution. We define two thresholds T_{s}, T_{d} with $T_{\text{s}} > T_{\text{d}}$ which indicate the μ_t values where h_{static} and h_{dynamic} will be solely used respectively, and we linearly interpolate between the two models when μ_t is in-between the two thresholds. That is:

$$\delta_t^{\text{SCS}} = \max\{\min\{\frac{1}{T_{\text{s}} - T_{\text{d}}}\mu_t - \frac{T_{\text{d}}}{T_{\text{s}} - T_{\text{d}}}, 1\}, 0\} \tag{13}$$

- *Confidence Derivative Switch (CDS)*: Uses the indicator function previously described in Sect. 3.2 to understand if the new domain is farther or closer from the source and selects h_{dynamic} or h_{static} accordingly.

$$\delta_t^{\text{CDS}} = \begin{cases} 1, & I_t > 0 \\ 0, & I_t < 0 \\ \delta_{t-1}^{\text{CDS}}, & I_t = 0 \end{cases}, \quad t > 0, \ \delta_0^{\text{CDS}} = 1 \tag{14}$$

- *Hybrid Switch (HS)*: Sets two thresholds T_{cA}, T_{cB} with $T_{cA} > T_{cB}$ and acts based on confidence values μ_t

$$\delta_t^{\text{HS}} = \begin{cases} 1, & \mu_t > T_{cA} \\ \delta_t^{\text{CDS}}, & T_{cB} \leq \mu_t \leq T_{cA} \\ 0, & \mu_t < T_{cB} \end{cases}, \quad t \geq 0 \tag{15}$$

The *Hybrid Switch* therefore combines *Confidence Switch* and *Confidence Derivative Switch*: it follows the former for high/low μ_t, the latter otherwise.

4 Experimental Results

The experiments are carried out on the Cityscapes [11] dataset by generating realistic synthetic rain [41]. In particular, we generate a new training set (2975 samples) and validation set (500 samples) for each rain intensity. Given a pre-trained model on the original dataset, the online adaptation process takes place by training (without labels) on the rain intensities sequentially. After each pass, the model is validated on all rain intensity validation sets. The experiments include severe rain conditions and show how gradual adaptation compares to direct – offline – adaptation.

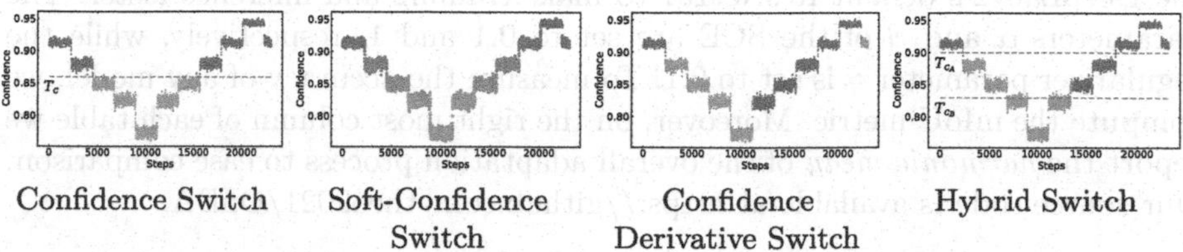

Fig. 3. Visualization of the switching policies. The dots show the static models confidence values over time and their color represents δ values: blue corresponds to $\delta = 1$, i.e. h_{static}, while orange $\delta = 0$, i.e. h_{dynamic}. The *Soft-Confidence Switch* performs a linear transition from one prior to the other and it is represented through a color gradient.

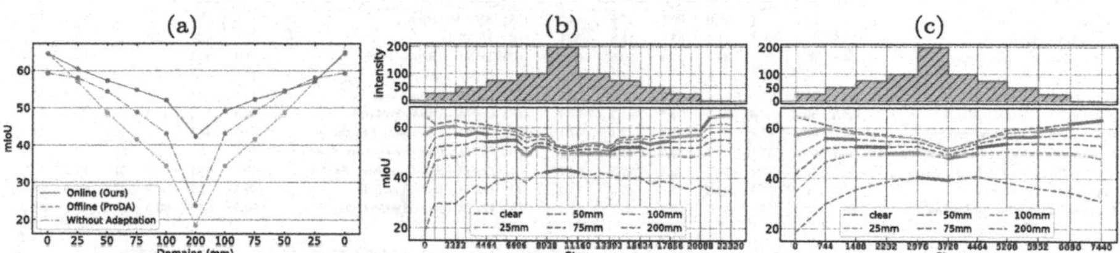

Fig. 4. Performance comparison and learning process on Increasing Storm. (a) We plot the mIoU achieved by OnDA using Hybrid Switch (blue), the offline adaptation (green) and the source model (orange), trained on *clear* weather. The offline model is trained using the source domain, and then adapted to all the rainy domains shown in the x axis at once. In (b), (c) we show for OnDA, at any given time, mIoU of the model in the currently deployed domain with bold segments. The dashed lines show mIoU over past or future domains. (Color figure online)

4.1 Baseline Scenario: Increasing Storm

As baseline scenario, we use rain intensities of 25, 50, 75, 100 and 200. Adaptation happens gradually, from low to high intensities, and then backward until *clear* weather domain, D_S, is reached again. We will refer to this adaptation sequence, where we move from source to a sequence of targets and eventually return to the source, as an *adaptation cycle*. Each domain counts about 9K frames – or 5 min at 30fps. Harder scenarios will be studied in the remainder.

Experiment Parameters. We use DeepLabv2 [8], which is a common baseline when dealing with domain adaptation on semantic segmentation. The network is although modified to use the ResNet50 [15] feature extractor instead of the DeepLabv2's default ResNet101 to make training and inference faster. The parameters α and β of the SCE are set to 0.1 and 1, respectively, while the regularizer parameter γ is set to 0.1. To measure the accuracy of any model, we compute the mIoU metric. Moreover, on the right most column of each table we report the *harmonic mean* of the overall adaptation process to ease comparison. Our source code is available at https://github.com/theo2021/OnDA.

Table 1. Domain adaptation main results. Online forward (a), backward (b), Offline (c) and Supervised (d) models are compared. Adaptation happens gradually from low (25 mm) to high (200 mm) intensities (a) and backward (b).

(a)

	Domain:	clear	25mm	50mm	75mm	100mm	200mm	h-mean
	Source Model	64.5	57.1	48.7	41.5	34.4	18.5	37.3
Online	(A) BN adaptation	64.5	58.2	51.1	44.8	39.7	27.9	44.3
	(B) TENT [46]	64.5	57.1	48.1	41.3	33.6	15.8	35.1
	(C) TENT + Replay Buffer	64.5	57.6	50.0	43.8	37.4	20.5	39.7
	(D) Online Advent	64.5	58.7	53.5	47.6	43.0	31.1	47.0
	(E) OnDA - Static Model	64.5	**60.4**	57.5	53.5	48.2	37.8	52.0
	(F) OnDA - Dynamic Model	64.5	**60.4**	**57.8**	54.7	**52.7**	41.2	54.1
	(G) OnDA - Confidence Switch	64.5	**60.4**	57.5	55.1	51.3	42.1	54.1
	(H) OnDA - Confidence Derivative Switch	64.5	**60.4**	57.1	54.3	52.0	**42.4**	54.2
	(I) OnDA - Soft-Confidence Switch	64.5	**60.4**	57.4	54.7	52.1	42.3	**54.3**
	(J) OnDA - Hybrid Switch	64.5	**60.4**	57.3	**54.8**	52.0	42.2	54.2
	(K) OnDA - Hybrid Switch One Pass	64.5	59.5	55.3	52.5	50.3	39.3	52.2

(b)

Domain:	100mm	75mm	50mm	25mm	clear	h-mean
Source Model	34.4	41.5	48.7	57.1	64.5	37.3
(A) BN adaptation	39.5	45.1	51.2	58.1	64.4	50.1
(B) TENT [46]	28.5	35.7	43.6	52.7	60.5	41.1
(C) TENT + Replay Buffer	37.3	44.1	50.3	57.7	64.3	48.9
(D) Online Advent	43.3	48.5	54.2	58.9	64.3	52.8
(E) OnDA - Static Model	47.1	50.5	52.3	56.4	**64.8**	53.6
(F) OnDA - Dynamic Model	49.8	50.1	49.9	50.3	53.3	50.6
(G) OnDA - Confidence Switch	48.3	48.8	52.7	56.0	64.6	53.5
(H) OnDA - Confidence Derivative Switch	50.1	52.5	54.4	56.6	64.7	55.2
(I) OnDA - Soft-Confidence Switch	49.3	49.7	50.1	51.8	64.2	52.5
(J) OnDA - Hybrid Switch	49.1	52.2	54.5	57.1	**64.8**	55.1
(K) OnDA - Hybrid Switch One Pass	**50.2**	**53.8**	**56.5**	**60.1**	63.2	**56.3**

(c)

	Domain:	clear	25mm	50mm	75mm	100mm	200mm	h-mean
Offline	Offline 25mm	**62.8**	**60.2**	**56.6**	51.1	45.7	26.4	46.3
	Offline 50mm	60.9	59.0	55.9	**51.3**	**46.4**	28.9	**47.3**
	Offline 75mm	58.8	57.2	53.6	48.5	43.8	27.2	45.0
	Offline 100mm	55.9	54.6	51.1	46.2	41.8	26.7	43.2
	Offline 200mm	49.2	50.7	49.7	47.6	45.0	**35.9**	45.7
	Offline All	59.3	58.1	54.4	48.8	43.1	23.7	43.4
	Offline All - Advent	50.8	51.7	49.1	45.9	41.9	30.9	43.6

(d)

	Domain:	clear	25mm	50mm	75mm	100mm	200mm	h-mean
Supervised	Supervised 25mm	63.0	62.4	61.1	58.3	56.7	44.1	56.7
	Supervised 50mm	60.4	60.6	60.4	58.2	56.9	47.4	56.9
	Supervised 75mm	56.7	58.8	58.6	57.1	56.0	48.4	55.7
	Supervised 100mm	56.5	59.0	59.9	58.3	58.0	51.8	57.1
	Supervised 200mm	48.9	52.6	54.3	54.5	54.5	51.3	52.6
	Supervised All	**64.5**	**64.1**	**63.7**	**63.0**	**62.4**	**58.2**	**62.6**

4.2 Results on Increasing Storm

Figure 4, on the left, resumes a direct comparison on the Increasing Storm scenario, between the Source model and those adapted either Offline or Online (with the Hybrid Switch). We can notice a higher mIoU achieved by our framework on any domain. Table 1 showcases more in detail all the major experiments performed, comparing Test-Time/Online Adaptation, Supervised and Offline Adaptation models in the Increasing Storm scenario. In the Offline experiments, we employ a modified version of [56] (Stage 1) which is obtained by adopting the Mahalanobis distance (Eq. 3) and active BN statistics selection Sect. 3.1, as these improvements result beneficial also in the traditional offline UDA settings. Training is performed until convergence (10 epochs) with decaying learning rate in a standard setup for both Offline and Supervised models, i.e. they have access – in advance – to the complete data, hence prototypes can be initialized using the target samples. The key comparisons are between adaptations methods, either online or offline and how adaptation compares to the fully supervised, ideal case (oracle). In sum, progressive adaptation sees a significant performance gain compared to directly adapting to a domain offline, as evident by comparing best values (in bold) achieved on each domain. We will now discuss in detail the behavior of the different methods involved in our experiments.

Online Adaptation. The simplest way to perform adaptation, is by adjusting the BatchNorm statistics (A) in an online manner. Although simple, it manages to yields significant improvements over the source model. Adaptation using TENT [46] (B) results less effective compared to simply updating BatchNorm statistics, both in forward (a) and backward (b) adaptation. Introducing the Replay Buffer (C) partially improves the results, yet not surpassing (A). Online Advent model (D), which is obtained through the use of the Replay Buffer, increases performance even further, yet resulting less performant than self-training approaches. The Static Model (obtained by fixing $\delta_t = 1$) (E) is capable of adapting and reverting to the original domain. Nevertheless, we notice that performance in adaptation can be further increased using a dynamic prior ($\delta_t = 0$) (F) – introduced in Sect. 3.3. Compared to the Static Model (E), the Dynamic Model better adapts to the most challenging domains (100 and 200 mm), motivating the need for updating the prior during adaptation. However, the Dynamic Model is more prone to forgetting: Table 1 (b), shows performance while gradually returning to the source domain, i.e. retracing domains in reverse order. The Dynamic Model (F) achieves the worst performance once returned to source domain (*clear*). This issue is solved by switching between the two priors (G-J). Among the switching policies, the Confidence Derivative (H) and Hybrid (J) perform the best, increasing adaptation performance substantially (~24% mIoU on the hardest domain). Furthermore, all policies managed to regain the initial performance before adaptation – see Table 1 (b). Finally (K) presents the adaptation capabilities of the Hybrid Switch over a 3 times faster Increasing Storm (i.e., happening within fewer frames, as shown in Fig. 4 (c)): while the forward adaptation achieves marginally lower metrics compared to (J), backward adaptation results more effective on average.

Online vs Offline Adaptation. From Table 1 (c), it is evident that Offline methods fall short against Online ones (a), proving that it is harder to adapt to the most challenging domains without intermediate adaptations. We have some evidence of this among the entries in the table. Indeed, the best Offline model results on 75 and 100 mm domains are achieved by the model adapted on 50 mm, suggesting that, sometimes, adapting to an easier domain can be even preferable compared to direct adaptation to the hardest one. Figure 4 (b, c), outlines the mIoU scores while adapting in an Online manner, on the Increasing Storm setting described so far (b) or by shortening each domain to one third of their length (c). At any time, we also plot the performance for past/future domains (dashed lines). This allows to denote that adapting to close domains (e.g. 50 mm) already increases performance to the next to come (75 mm, as we can notice from the red dashed line on the left of the bold segment), without yet observing it. Furthermore, the experiment on shorter domains yields similar performance demonstrating, the fast adaptation capabilities of the approach.

Adaptation vs Supervised Learning. Although adaptation managed to improve performance, a significant gap between adaptation and supervised learning still exists. Not surprisingly, supervised models perform quite well when fully labelled data is provided, but are always constrained to the source domain, while online adaptation methods can adjust models to new domains on-the-fly.

4.3 Experiments Under Additional Settings

In this section, we extend our evaluation by considering different rainy sequences, by studying the impact of the Replay Buffer and by generalizing our framework to different domain changes, such as increasing fog.

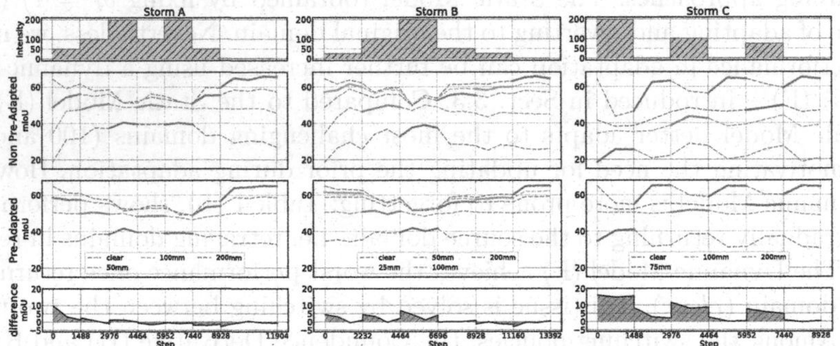

Fig. 5. Model performance during adaptation. Experiments on storms A, B & C. Comparison between starting adaptation from source (Non Pre-Adapted) and after a full *adaptation cycle* on the Increasing Storm (Pre-Adapted).

Evaluation on Different Storms. We now run experiments on different rainy scenarios to confirm our previous findings. In particular, we evaluate over three adaptation sequences. In all of them, we use the Hybrid Switch, and we compare two models. The first model is pre-trained on source (*clean* images), while the second model has already experienced a full *adaptation cycle* over the Increasing Storm (Sect. 4.1). Results are collected in Fig. 5. On top, we plot histograms describing the three storm intensities, labeled A, B and C and being respectively an *oscillatory* storm (to evaluate OnDA capability of going back and forth in harder domains), a *sudden* storm (with a more aggressive intensity growth) and a *instantaneous* storm (starting with the hardest domain and oscillating significantly). The plots below show the performance of the two models exposed to the same storm. The last row instead shows the mIoU difference between the two. Starting from storm A, we can notice how both models perform similarly and quickly adapt to each domain change. At bootstrap, the pre-adapted model results better, anyway, the non pre-adapted one quickly catches up, eventually closing the gap between the two. The same trend occurs on storm B, although the pre-adapted model results more effective during the whole "forward" pass. By looking at storm C, instead, we witness an interesting behavior. Storm C is by far the most challenging in our benchmark due to its abrupt first intensity. The non pre-adapted model fails to adapt to the 200 mm domain encountered at the very beginning, hinting once again that gradual adaptation is preferable. Indeed, the pre-adapted model can instead easily reach the same performance achieved during the Increasing Storm on just a single pass. This result proves that after an *adaptation cycle*, the model is not only able to reach again the source domain with no catastrophic forgetting, but, crucially, it also maintains a memory of the previously experienced domains. Hence, it acquires the ability to cope with more challenging and sudden domain shifts. Finally, our supplementary material contains qualitative results and refers to a video, showing OnDA in action on the Increasing Storm scenario.

Table 2. Additional experiments. (a): impact of the Replay Buffer on the Increasing Storm cycle using the Hybrid Switch. (b): comparison between Offline and Online adaptation on foggy domains. F: adaptation from *clear* to the hardest domain, B: backward adaptation (from the hardest domain back to *clear*).

(a)

Buffer	clear		25mm		50mm		75mm		100mm		200mm	
	F	B	F	B	F	B	F	B	F	B	F	B
(A) 0	64.5	57.5	60.5	55.0	57.6	53.5	54.0	50.9	50.1	49.1	41.0	-
(B) 100	64.5	63.0	60.3	56.9	56.2	54.1	54.2	51.6	51.5	**49.3**	**42.9**	-
(C) 1000	64.5	64.8	60.4	**57.1**	57.3	**54.5**	**54.8**	**52.2**	**52.0**	49.1	42.2	-
(D) All	64.5	**65.4**	**61.0**	55.9	**58.1**	54.4	53.5	51.1	51.8	49.2	41.4	-

(b)

Domain (visibility):	clear		750m		375m		150m		75m		h-mean	
	F	B	F	B	F	B	F	B	F	B	F	B
Source	**64.9**	-	60.9	-	54.7	-	39.8	-	25.2	-	43.5	-
Offline All	62.4	-	62.3	-	59.6	-	46.8	-	31.9	-	49.2	-
OnDA - Hybrid Switch	**64.9**	65.8	**63.3**	62.3	**60.7**	58.8	**51.6**	49.1	**42.1**	42.1	**55.1**	54.1

Ablation Study - Replay Buffer Size. We now study the impact of the Replay Buffer size, so far set to 1000 source samples. Table 2 (a) shows a comparison between different Replay Buffer sizes. The model manages to adapt to hard domains even in the absence of a Replay Buffer (A), this although results to a considerable drop in accuracy in the backward phase (about 10%). With a buffer of 100 (B) or 1000 images (C) catastrophic forgetting is solved, while (C) allows for going back to the source with even increased performance. Keeping the whole dataset in the buffer (D) further increases accuracy once back to source, yet not improving adaptation.

Additional Case Study - Fog. Finally, we test the proposed framework on artificially generated fog [41] on the Cityscapes training set. The dataset is randomly split into 2475 training and 500 validation samples and we adopted the same experimental set-up presented in the rain scenario. Table 2 (b) shows a comparison between Source, Offline All and OnDA. Again, our model achieves +10% mIoU on the hardest domain compared to the one adapted offline, confirming that OnDA can be successfully applied to various domain changes.

Limitations. Online training requires significant computational resources, which heavily hinder deployment in real-time applications. We believe that lighter backbones [53], efficient training paradigms [40] or selective adaptation can improve this aspect. From an experimental standpoint, we analyse domain shifts which only affects the input distribution. A larger body of test scenarios, with real data and additional gradual domain shifts would be the ideal stage to assess the performance of OnDA frameworks.

5 Summary and Conclusion

In this paper, we have presented a novel framework for Online Domain Adaptation (OnDA). While state-of-the-art offline adaptation and continuous adaptation methods can successfully tackle limited domain shift, they fall short on cases where there is a significant gap between the source and the deployment domain. In contrast, we have empirically shown that casting adaptation as an online task and gradually adapting to evolving domains are beneficial for reaching high accuracy on distant domains. We exhaustively evaluated our framework on simulated weather conditions with increasing intensity and in four different kinds of storms, highlighting the robustness of our method in comparison to offline techniques. We believe that our framework will pave the way towards tackling UDA in online manner in the real world.

Acknowledgement. The authors thank Hossein Azizpour, Hedvig Kjellström and Raoul de Charette for the helpful discussions and guidance.

References

1. Bengio, Y., Louradour, J., Collobert, R., Weston, J.: Curriculum learning. In: Proceedings of the 26th Annual International Conference on Machine Learning, ICML 2009, pp. 41–48. Association for Computing Machinery, New York (2009). https://doi.org/10.1145/1553374.1553380
2. Bobu, A., Hoffman, J., Tzeng, E., Darrell, T.: Adapting to continuously shifting domains. In: ICLR 2018 Workshop Program Chairs (2018). https://openreview.net/forum?id=BJsBjPJvf
3. Cardace, A., Zama Ramirez, P., Salti, S., Di Stefano, L.: Shallow features guide unsupervised domain adaptation for semantic segmentation at class boundaries. In: Proceedings of the IEEE/CVF Winter Conference on Applications of Computer Vision (WACV), pp. 1160–1170, January 2022
4. Chang, W.G., You, T., Seo, S., Kwak, S., Han, B.: Domain-specific batch normalization for unsupervised domain adaptation. CoRR (2019). http://arxiv.org/abs/1906.03950
5. Chen, C., et al.: Progressive feature alignment for unsupervised domain adaptation. In: Proceedings of the IEEE/CVF Conference on Computer Vision and Pattern Recognition, pp. 627–636 (2019)
6. Chen, L.-C., et al.: Naive-student: leveraging semi-supervised learning in video sequences for urban scene segmentation. In: Vedaldi, A., Bischof, H., Brox, T., Frahm, J.-M. (eds.) ECCV 2020. LNCS, vol. 12354, pp. 695–714. Springer, Cham (2020). https://doi.org/10.1007/978-3-030-58545-7_40

7. Chen, L.C., Papandreou, G., Kokkinos, I., Murphy, K., Yuille, A.L.: DeepLab: semantic image segmentation with deep convolutional nets, atrous convolution, and fully connected CRFs. IEEE Trans. Pattern Anal. Mach. Intell. **40**(4), 834–848 (2017)
8. Chen, L.C., Papandreou, G., Kokkinos, I., Murphy, K., Yuille, A.L.: DeepLab: semantic image segmentation with deep convolutional nets, atrous convolution, and fully connected CRFs. IEEE Trans. Pattern Anal. Mach. Intell. **40**(4), 834–848 (2018). https://doi.org/10.1109/tpami.2017.2699184, http://dx.doi.org/10.1109/TPAMI.2017.2699184
9. Chen, Y.H., Chen, W.Y., Chen, Y.T., Tsai, B.C., Wang, Y.C.F., Sun, M.: No more discrimination: cross city adaptation of road scene segmenters. In: 2017 IEEE International Conference on Computer Vision (ICCV), pp. 2011–2020. IEEE (2017). https://doi.org/10.1109/ICCV.2017.220, http://ieeexplore.ieee.org/document/8237482/
10. Cicek, S., Soatto, S.: Unsupervised domain adaptation via regularized conditional alignment. CoRR (2019). http://arxiv.org/abs/1905.10885
11. Cordts, M., et al.: The cityscapes dataset for semantic urban scene understanding (2016)
12. Dundar, A., Liu, M.Y., Yu, Z., Wang, T.C., Zedlewski, J., Kautz, J.: Domain stylization: a fast covariance matching framework towards domain adaptation. IEEE Trans. Pattern Anal. Mach. Intell. p. 1 (2020). https://doi.org/10.1109/TPAMI.2020.2969421
13. Furlanello, T., Lipton, Z., Tschannen, M., Itti, L., Anandkumar, A.: Born again neural networks. In: International Conference on Machine Learning, pp. 1607–1616. PMLR (2018)
14. Ganin, Y., et al.: Domain-adversarial training of neural networks. The J. Mach. Learn. Res. **17**(1), 2030–2096 (2016)
15. He, K., Zhang, X., Ren, S., Sun, J.: Deep residual learning for image recognition. CoRR abs/1512.03385 (2015). http://arxiv.org/abs/1512.03385
16. Hoffman, J., et al.: CyCADA: cycle-consistent adversarial domain adaptation. In: Dy, J., Krause, A. (eds.) Proceedings of the 35th International Conference on Machine Learning. Proceedings of Machine Learning Research, vol. 80, pp. 1989–1998. PMLR, Stockholmsmässan, Stockholm Sweden, 10–15 July 2018
17. Hoffman, J., Wang, D., Yu, F., Darrell, T.: FCNs in the wild: pixel-level adversarial and constraint-based adaptation. CoRR (2016). http://arxiv.org/abs/1612.02649
18. Hoyer, L., Dai, D., Van Gool, L.: Daformer: improving network architectures and training strategies for domain-adaptive semantic segmentation. arXiv preprint arXiv:2111.14887 (2021)
19. Huang, X., Belongie, S.: Arbitrary style transfer in real-time with adaptive instance normalization. In: Proceedings of the IEEE International Conference on Computer Vision, pp. 1501–1510 (2017)
20. Ioffe, S., Szegedy, C.: Batch normalization: accelerating deep network training by reducing internal covariate shift. In: International Conference on Machine Learning, pp. 448–456. PMLR (2015)
21. Iwasawa, Y., Matsuo, Y.: Test-time classifier adjustment module for model-agnostic domain generalization. In: Beygelzimer, A., Dauphin, Y., Liang, P., Vaughan, J.W. (eds.) Advances in Neural Information Processing Systems (2021)
22. Kim, M., Byun, H.: Learning texture invariant representation for domain adaptation of semantic segmentation. In: 2020 IEEE/CVF Conference on Computer Vision and Pattern Recognition (CVPR), June 2020. https://doi.org/10.1109/cvpr42600.2020.01299

23. Klingner, M., Termöhlen, J.A., Ritterbach, J., Fingscheidt, T.: Unsupervised batchnorm adaptation (UBNA): a domain adaptation method for semantic segmentation without using source domain representations. In: Proceedings of the IEEE/CVF Winter Conference on Applications of Computer Vision, pp. 210–220 (2022)
24. Kuznietsov, Y., Proesmans, M., Van Gool, L.: Towards unsupervised online domain adaptation for semantic segmentation. In: Proceedings of the IEEE/CVF Winter Conference on Applications of Computer Vision, pp. 261–271 (2022)
25. Lao, Q., Jiang, X., Havaei, M., Bengio, Y.: Continuous domain adaptation with variational domain-agnostic feature replay. arXiv preprint arXiv:2003.04382 (2020)
26. Lee, D.: Pseudo-label : the simple and efficient semi-supervised learning method for deep neural networks. In: Workshop on Challenges in Representation Learning, ICML (2013)
27. Li, Y., Yuan, L., Vasconcelos, N.: Bidirectional learning for domain adaptation of semantic segmentation. In: 2019 IEEE/CVF Conference on Computer Vision and Pattern Recognition (CVPR), Jun 2019. https://doi.org/10.1109/cvpr.2019.00710
28. Liang, J., Hu, D., Feng, J.: Do we really need to access the source data? source hypothesis transfer for unsupervised domain adaptation. CoRR (2020). http://arxiv.org/abs/2002.08546
29. Liu, Y., Zhang, W., Wang, J.: Source-free domain adaptation for semantic segmentation (2021). http://arxiv.org/abs/2103.16372
30. Liu, Y., Kothari, P., van Delft, B.G., Bellot-Gurlet, B., Mordan, T., Alahi, A.: TTT++: when does self-supervised test-time training fail or thrive? In: Beygelzimer, A., Dauphin, Y., Liang, P., Vaughan, J.W. (eds.) Advances in Neural Information Processing Systems (2021)
31. Liu, Z., et al.: Open compound domain adaptation. In: 2020 IEEE/CVF Conference on Computer Vision and Pattern Recognition (CVPR), pp. 12403–12412. IEEE (2020). https://doi.org/10.1109/CVPR42600.2020.01242, https://ieeexplore.ieee.org/document/9157145/
32. Mei, K., Zhu, C., Zou, J., Zhang, S.: Instance adaptive self-training for unsupervised domain adaptation. In: Vedaldi, A., Bischof, H., Brox, T., Frahm, J.-M. (eds.) ECCV 2020. LNCS, vol. 12371, pp. 415–430. Springer, Cham (2020). https://doi.org/10.1007/978-3-030-58574-7_25
33. Pan, F., Shin, I., Rameau, F., Lee, S., Kweon, I.S.: Unsupervised intra-domain adaptation for semantic segmentation through self-supervision. In: 2020 IEEE/CVF Conference on Computer Vision and Pattern Recognition (CVPR), June 2020. https://doi.org/10.1109/cvpr42600.2020.00382
34. Poularikas, A.D.: The Handbook of Formulas and Tables for Signal Processing. The electrical engineering handbook series, CRC Press; Springer: IEEE Press (1999)
35. Sakaridis, C., Dai, D., Hecker, S., Van Gool, L.: Model adaptation with synthetic and real data for semantic dense foggy scene understanding (2018). http://arxiv.org/abs/1808.01265
36. Sohn, K., et al.: Fixmatch: simplifying semi-supervised learning with consistency and confidence. CoRR abs/2001.07685 (2020). https://arxiv.org/abs/2001.07685
37. Stan, S., Rostami, M.: Unsupervised model adaptation for continual semantic segmentation. In: AAAI (2021)
38. Su, P., Tang, S., Gao, P., Qiu, D., Zhao, N., Wang, X.: Gradient regularized contrastive learning for continual domain adaptation (2020). http://arxiv.org/abs/2007.12942
39. Sun, T., et al.: SHIFT: a synthetic driving dataset for continuous multi-task domain adaptation. In: Computer Vision and Pattern Recognition (2022)

40. Tonioni, A., Tosi, F., Poggi, M., Mattoccia, S., Stefano, L.D.: Real-time self-adaptive deep stereo. In: Proceedings of the IEEE/CVF Conference on Computer Vision and Pattern Recognition, pp. 195–204 (2019)
41. Tremblay, M., Halder, S.S., de Charette, R., Lalonde, J.-F.: Rain rendering for evaluating and improving robustness to bad weather. Int. J. Comput. Vision 1–20 (2020). https://doi.org/10.1007/s11263-020-01366-3
42. Tsai, Y.H., Hung, W.C., Schulter, S., Sohn, K., Yang, M.H., Chandraker, M.: Learning to adapt structured output space for semantic segmentation. In: 2018 IEEE/CVF Conference on Computer Vision and Pattern Recognition, June 2018. https://doi.org/10.1109/cvpr.2018.00780
43. Vu, T.H., Jain, H., Bucher, M., Cord, M., Pérez, P.: Dada: depth-aware domain adaptation in semantic segmentation. In: ICCV (2019)
44. Vu, T.H., Jain, H., Bucher, M., Cord, M., Perez, P.: Advent: adversarial entropy minimization for domain adaptation in semantic segmentation. In: 2019 IEEE/CVF Conference on Computer Vision and Pattern Recognition (CVPR), June 2019. https://doi.org/10.1109/cvpr.2019.00262
45. Vu, T.H., Jain, H., Bucher, M., Cord, M., Pérez, P.: ADVENT: adversarial entropy minimization for domain adaptation in semantic segmentation (2019) http://arxiv.org/abs/1811.12833
46. Wang, D., Shelhamer, E., Liu, S., Olshausen, B., Darrell, T.: Tent: fully test-time adaptation by entropy minimization. In: International Conference on Learning Representations (2021)
47. Wang, H., Shen, T., Zhang, W., Duan, L., Mei, T.: Classes matter: a fine-grained adversarial approach to cross-domain semantic segmentation. In: The European Conference on Computer Vision (ECCV), August 2020
48. Wang, Y., Ma, X., Chen, Z., Luo, Y., Yi, J., Bailey, J.: Symmetric cross entropy for robust learning with noisy labels (2019). http://arxiv.org/abs/1908.06112
49. Wu, Z., et al.: DCAN: dual channel-wise alignment networks for unsupervised scene adaptation. In: Ferrari, V., Hebert, M., Sminchisescu, C., Weiss, Y. (eds.) ECCV 2018. LNCS, vol. 11209, pp. 535–552. Springer, Cham (2018). https://doi.org/10.1007/978-3-030-01228-1_32
50. Wu, Z., Wang, X., Gonzalez, J., Goldstein, T., Davis, L.: ACE: adapting to changing environments for semantic segmentation. In: 2019 IEEE/CVF International Conference on Computer Vision (ICCV), pp. 2121–2130. IEEE (2019). https://doi.org/10.1109/ICCV.2019.00221, https://ieeexplore.ieee.org/document/9009823/
51. Wulfmeier, M., Bewley, A., Posner, I.: Incremental adversarial domain adaptation for continually changing environments (2018). http://arxiv.org/abs/1712.07436
52. Yang, Y., Soatto, S.: FDA: fourier domain adaptation for semantic segmentation. In: 2020 IEEE/CVF Conference on Computer Vision and Pattern Recognition (CVPR), pp. 4084–4094. IEEE (2020). https://doi.org/10.1109/CVPR42600.2020.00414, https://ieeexplore.ieee.org/document/9157228/
53. Yu, C., Wang, J., Peng, C., Gao, C., Yu, G., Sang, N.: Bisenet: bilateral segmentation network for real-time semantic segmentation. In: Proceedings of the European conference on computer vision (ECCV), pp. 325–341 (2018)
54. Yuan, Y., Chen, X., Chen, X., Wang, J.: Segmentation transformer: object-contextual representations for semantic segmentation. In: European Conference on Computer Vision (ECCV), vol. 1 (2021)
55. Zhai, X., Oliver, A., Kolesnikov, A., Beyer, L.: S4L: self-supervised semi-Supervised Learning. arXiv e-prints arXiv:1905.03670, May 2019

56. Zhang, P., Zhang, B., Zhang, T., Chen, D., Wang, Y., Wen, F.: Prototypical pseudo label denoising and target structure learning for domain adaptive semantic segmentation (2021). http://arxiv.org/abs/2101.10979
57. Zhang, Q., Zhang, J., Liu, W., Tao, D.: Category anchor-guided unsupervised domain adaptation for semantic segmentation. Adv. Neural Inf. Process. Syst. (2019). http://arxiv.org/abs/1910.13049
58. Zheng, Z., Yang, Y.: Unsupervised scene adaptation with memory regularization in vivo. In: Proceedings of the Twenty-Ninth International Joint Conference on Artificial Intelligence, July 2020. https://doi.org/10.24963/ijcai.2020/150, http://dx.doi.org/10.24963/ijcai.2020/150
59. Zhu, J.Y., Park, T., Isola, P., Efros, A.A.: Unpaired image-to-image translation using cycle-consistent adversarial networks. In: 2017 IEEE International Conference on Computer Vision (ICCV), October 2017. https://doi.org/10.1109/iccv.2017.244
60. Zou, Y., Yu, Z., Kumar, B., Wang, J.: Unsupervised domain adaptation for semantic segmentation via class-balanced self-training. In: Proceedings of the European Conference on Computer Vision (ECCV), pp. 289–305 (2018)
61. Zou, Y., Yu, Z., Liu, X., Kumar, B.V.K.V., Wang, J.: Confidence regularized self-training. In: 2019 IEEE/CVF International Conference on Computer Vision (ICCV), October 2019. https://doi.org/10.1109/iccv.2019.00608
62. Zou, Y., Yu, Z., Liu, X., Kumar, B., Wang, J.: Confidence regularized self-training. In: Proceedings of the IEEE/CVF International Conference on Computer Vision, pp. 5982–5991 (2019)

Source-Free Video Domain Adaptation by Learning Temporal Consistency for Action Recognition

Yecong Xu[1], Jianfei Yang[2], Haozhi Cao[2], Keyu Wu[1], Min Wu[1], and Zhenghua Chen[1(✉)]

[1] Institute for Infocomm Research, A*STAR, Singapore, Singapore
{xuyu0014,chen0832}@e.ntu.edu.sg, {wu_keyu,wumin}@i2r.a-star.edu.sg
[2] School of Electrical and Electronic Engineering, Nanyang Technological University, Singapore, Singapore
{yang0478,haozhi001}@e.ntu.edu.sg

Abstract. Video-based Unsupervised Domain Adaptation (VUDA) methods improve the robustness of video models, enabling them to be applied to action recognition tasks across different environments. However, these methods require constant access to source data during the adaptation process. Yet in many real-world applications, subjects and scenes in the source video domain should be irrelevant to those in the target video domain. With the increasing emphasis on data privacy, such methods that require source data access would raise serious privacy issues. Therefore, to cope with such concern, a more practical domain adaptation scenario is formulated as the *Source-Free Video-based Domain Adaptation* (SFVDA). Though there are a few methods for Source-Free Domain Adaptation (SFDA) on image data, these methods yield degenerating performance in SFVDA due to the multi-modality nature of videos, with the existence of additional temporal features. In this paper, we propose a novel Attentive Temporal Consistent Network (ATCoN) to address SFVDA by learning temporal consistency, guaranteed by two novel consistency objectives, namely feature consistency and source prediction consistency, performed across local temporal features. ATCoN further constructs effective overall temporal features by attending to local temporal features based on prediction confidence. Empirical results demonstrate the state-of-the-art performance of ATCoN across various cross-domain action recognition benchmarks. Code is provided at https://github.com/xuyu0010/ATCoN.

This research is jointly supported by A*STAR Singapore under its AME Programmatic Funds (Grant No. A20H6b0151) and Career Development Award (Grant No. C210112046), and by Nanyang Technological University, Singapore, under its NTU Presidential Postdoctoral Fellowship, "Adaptive Multimodal Learning for Robust Sensing and Recognition in Smart Cities" project fund.
Y. Xu and J. Yang—Equal Contributions.

Supplementary Information The online version contains supplementary material available at https://doi.org/10.1007/978-3-031-19830-4_9.

S. Avidan et al. (Eds.): ECCV 2022, LNCS 13694, pp. 147–164, 2022.
https://doi.org/10.1007/978-3-031-19830-4_9

Keywords: Source-Free Domain Adaptation · Video domain adaptation · Action recognition · Temporal consistency

1 Introduction

Video-based tasks such as action recognition have long been investigated considering their wide applications. Deep neural networks have made remarkable advances with the introduction of large-scale labeled datasets [14,24]. However, due to the expense of laborious video data annotation, sufficient labeled training videos may not be readily available in real-world scenarios. To avoid costly data annotation, various *Video-based Unsupervised Domain Adaptation* (VUDA) methods have been introduced to transfer knowledge from a labeled source video domain to an unlabeled target video domain by reducing discrepancies between source and target video domains [2,4,43]. VUDA methods greatly improve the robustness of video models, enabling them to be applied to action recognition tasks across different environments [41].

Though current VUDA methods [2,4,40,41] enable the transfer of knowledge across video domains, they all require access to source video data during the adaptation process. Yet action information usually contains the private and sensitive information of the actors, including their actions and the relevant scenes. Meanwhile, in real-world applications, such information in the source domain is usually irrelevant to those in the target domain and should be protected from the target domain. Therefore, current VUDA methods would raise serious privacy issues, which is more severe than that raised by image-based domain adaptation. To cope with the video data privacy issue, a more practical domain adaptation scenario is formulated as the *Source-Free Video-based Domain Adaptation* (SFVDA), where only well-trained source video models and unlabeled target domain data would be provided for adaptation.

With the absence of source data, current VUDA methods that mainly align target and source domains statistically [22,34] cannot be applied to the SFVDA problem. Recently, there are a few research efforts [18,21,48] that start exploring Source-Free Domain Adaptation (SFDA) with image data, where SFDA is tackled by adjusting target features to adapt to the source classifier [20]. The key idea is to learn discriminative latent target features while aligning source data distribution embedded within the source classifier. However, aligning videos without source data is even more challenging thanks to the fact that videos are characterized by their multi-modality nature, where temporal features are key components that are excluded in images.

While direct minimization of statistical discrepancy between target and source domains cannot be achieved due to the lack of source data, domain adaptation can also be achieved by aligning the embedded semantic information [19,39] via entropy-based approaches [29,37] such as maximizing mutual information [36] or neighborhood clustering [30]. These methods improve the discriminability of the target features which satisfy the cluster assumption [8], while increasing the source model transferability [45]. However, these methods are insufficient for aligning semantic information in videos. The reason is that overall temporal feature of a video can be constructed with a series of local temporal features, obtained through clips sampled from videos. Each local temporal feature should be discriminative in the first place. However, if each local temporal feature is individually discriminative yet mutually inconsistent, the local temporal features may not hold similar semantic information. Subsequently, the overall temporal feature may contain indistinct semantic information, and would not be discriminative. Instead, we hypothesize that for source videos, the extracted local temporal features are not only discriminative, but also consistent across each other and possess similar feature distribution patterns, which implies similar semantic information. Such hypothesis is termed as the *cross-temporal hypothesis*. If the target data aligns with the source data distribution, we assume that source-like representations are learned for target data, therefore the *cross-temporal hypothesis* should be satisfied by the target data representation. To this end, our method is designed such that the local temporal features are consistent in their feature representations, which would result in the corresponding overall temporal feature being effective and discriminative.

Meanwhile, since only the source model with the source classifier is available for adaptation, the relevance of the target data to source data distribution is highly correlated to the prediction of target data on the source classifier. Therefore, to better adapt target temporal features to the source classifier, the relevance of the corresponding local temporal features towards source data distribution should also be consistent. Such consistency can be interpreted as the source prediction consistency of local temporal features with respect to the fixed source classifier. Further, to improve the discriminability of the video feature, the overall temporal feature should be built by an attentive combination of local temporal features. The attentive combination builds upon the confidence of each local temporal feature towards its relevance to source data distribution.

To this end, we propose an **Attentive Temporal Consistent Network (ATCoN)** to address SFVDA uniformly. ATCoN leverages temporal features effectively by learning **temporal consistency** via **feature consistency** and **source prediction consistency** for local temporal features in a self-supervised manner. ATCoN further adapts target data to the source data distribution by attending to local temporal features with higher confidence over its relevance towards source data distribution, indicated as higher source prediction confidence.

In summary, our contributions are threefold. First, we formulated a practical and challenging *Source-Free Video Domain Adaptation* (SFVDA) problem. To the best of our knowledge, this is the first research that studies source-free transfer for video-based tasks, which aims to address data-privacy issues in VUDA. Secondly, we analyze the challenges underlying SFVDA and propose ATCoN to address the challenges uniformly. ATCoN aims to obtain effective and discriminative overall temporal features that satisfies the *cross-temporal hypothesis* by learning temporal consistency which is composed of both feature and source prediction consistency. ATCoN further aligns target data to the source data distribution without source data access by attending to local temporal features with high source prediction confidence. Finally, empirical results demonstrate the efficacy of our proposed ATCoN, achieving state-of-the-art performance across the multiple cross-domain action recognition benchmarks.

2 Related Work

Unsupervised Domain Adaptation (UDA) and Video-Based Unsupervised Domain Adaptation (VUDA). Current UDA and VUDA methods aim to distill shared knowledge across labeled source domains and unlabeled target domains. These methods improve the transferability and robustness of models. Generally, they could be divided into three categories: a) reconstruction-based methods [7,46], where domain-invariant features are obtained by encoders trained with data-reconstruction objectives, whose methods are commonly formulated as encoder-decoder networks; b) adversarial-based methods [2,41], where domain-invariant features are extracted by feature generators while leveraging domain discriminators, which are trained jointly in an adversarial manner [11], minimizing adversarial losses [6]; and c) discrepancy-based methods [31,44,49], which mitigate domain shifts across domains by applying metric learning approaches, minimizing metrics such as MMD [22] and CORAL [34]. By comparison, VUDA research lags behind UDA research, mainly due to the challenges brought by aligning temporal features in videos. However, with the introduction of various cross-domain video datasets such as UCF-HMDB$_{full}$ [2] and Sports-DA [43], there has been a significant increase in research interests for VUDA [3,4,26]. Despite the improvements in video model robustness brought by VUDA methods, all such methods require access to source data during the adaptation process. Such requirements could raise serious privacy concerns given the amount of private information of the relevant subject and scene in videos.

Source-Free Domain Adaptation (SFDA). With the increased importance of data privacy, there have been a few recent research efforts that investigate SFDA with images, which enable image models to be adapted to the target domain without access to source data. Among them, 3C-GAN [18] and SDDA [17] seek to produce novel target-style data that are similar to the source domain. Domain invariant features are then obtained by aligning the novel target-style data with the original target data via adversarial-based domain adaptation methods. Similarly, CPGA [28] tackles SFDA by generating avatar feature prototypes for each class, which are trained with the target features in an adversarial manner. Meanwhile, SHOT [20,21] exploits knowledge of source feature distribution by freezing the source classifier and matches target features to the source classifier by leveraging information maximization and pseudo-labeling. More recently, BAIT [47] extends MCD [31] to SFDA. Despite the advances made in the research of SFDA for images, SFVDA has not been tackled. Due to the amount of private data in videos, SFVDA is even more critical, yet is also more challenging given that temporal features must also be aligned. We propose to engage in SFVDA by utilizing temporal features via learning temporal consistency while attending to local temporal features with high confidence.

3 Proposed Method

In the scenario of *Source-Free Video Domain Adaptation* (SFVDA), we are only given a source video model that consists of the spatial feature extractor $G_{S,sp}$, the temporal feature extractor $G_{S,t}$ and the classifier H_S, and an unlabeled target domain $\mathcal{D}_T = \{V_{iT}\}_{i=1}^{n_T}$ with n_T i.i.d. videos, characterized by a probability distribution of p_T. The source model is generated by training its parameters $\theta_{S,sp}$, $\theta_{S,t}$, and θ_H with the labeled source domain $\mathcal{D}_S = \{(V_{iS}, y_{iS})\}_{i=1}^{n_S}$ containing n_S videos. We assume that both the labeled source domain videos and the unlabeled target domain videos share the same C classes, yet $\mathcal{D}_S$ is inaccessible when adapting the source model to $\mathcal{D}_T$.

Owing to the absence of the source domain during adaptation, SFVDA is more challenging while current VUDA methods cannot be applied. SFVDA should be tackled by adapting target video features to the source classifier, which contains information regarding source data distribution. The core is to extract source-like representations that satisfy the *cross-temporal hypothesis*, characterized by the consistency across local temporal features. We propose ATCoN, a novel network to transfer source models to the target domain by leveraging temporal features constructed attentively through learning temporal consistency in a self-supervised manner. We start with an introduction to the generation of the source model, followed by a thorough illustration of ATCoN.

3.1 Source Model Generation

A key prior for the transferred model to obtain effective temporal features is that the generated source model could extract precise temporal features. While conventional 3D-CNN-based extractors (e.g., 3D-ResNet [9] or I3D [1]) have been adopted in action recognition due to their performances, they extract spatio-temporal features jointly while temporal features are obtained implicitly by temporal pooling. In contrast, the Temporal Relation Network (TRN) [50] is adopted for SFVDA, thanks to its ability in obtaining more precise temporal features through reasoning over correlations between spatial representations, which corresponds with how humans would recognize actions.

Formally, an input source video with k frames can be expressed as $V_{iS} = \{f_{iS}^{(1)}, f_{iS}^{(2)}, ..., f_{iS}^{(k)}\}$, where $f_{iS}^{(j)}$ is the spatial representation of the j−th frame in the i−th source video obtained from the source spatial feature extractor $G_{S,sp}$. $G_{S,sp}$ is formulated as a 2D-CNN (e.g., ResNet [10]). The temporal feature of V_{iS} is subsequently obtained from the source temporal feature extractor $G_{S,t}$, constructed by a combination of multiple local temporal features. Each local temporal feature is built upon clips with r temporal-ordered sampled frames where $r \in [2, k]$. Formally, a local temporal feature for V_{iS}, $lt_{iS}^{(r)}$, is defined by:

$$lt_{iS}^{(r)} = \sum\nolimits_m g_S^{(r)}((V_{iS}^{(r)})_m), \tag{1}$$

where $(V_{iS}^{(r)})_m = \{f_{iS}^{(a)}, f_{iS}^{(b)}, ...\}_m$ is the m−th clip with r temporal-ordered frames. a and b are the frame indices, which may not be consecutive as the clip with temporal-ordered frames could be extracted with nonconsecutive frames, but should be both in the range of $[1, k]$ with $b > a$. The local temporal feature $lt_{iS}^{(r)}$ is computed by fusing the time ordered frame-level spatial features through

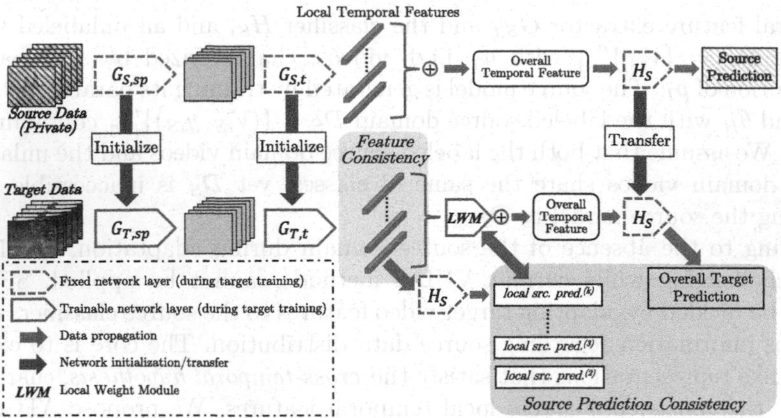

Fig. 1. Structure of the proposed ATCoN. ATCoN adopts the same network architecture for its spatial and temporal feature extractors as the source model, initialized by the source feature extractors. ATCoN extracts overall temporal features by learning *temporal consistency* over its local temporal features which includes both *feature consistency* and *source prediction consistency.* The *local weight module (LWM)* attends to more confident local temporal features. The overall target prediction is obtained by applying the *fixed* source classifier over the overall temporal feature. Dashed shapes indicates fixed network layers during adaptation.

the integration function $g_S^{(r)}$, implemented as a Multi-Layer Perceptron (MLP). $G_{S,t}$ is therefore a set of all integration functions $g_S^{(r)}$, namely $G_{S,t} = \{\forall_r g_S^{(r)}\}$. The final overall temporal feature $\mathbf{t}_{iS}$ is a simple mean aggregation applied across all local temporal features, defined as: $\mathbf{t}_{iS} = \frac{1}{k-1}\sum_r lt_{iS}^{(r)}$. The source prediction is further computed by applying a source classifier H_S over $\mathbf{t}_{iS}$. The source model is trained with the standard cross-entropy loss as the objective function, formulated as:

$$\mathcal{L}_{S,ce} = -\frac{1}{n_S}\sum\nolimits_{i=1}^{n_S} y_{iS} \log \sigma(H_S(\mathbf{t}_{iS})), \tag{2}$$

where σ is the softmax function whose c-th element is defined as $\sigma_c(x) = exp(x_c) / \sum_{c=1}^{C} exp(x_c)$. Inspired by [21], for the source model to be more discriminative and transferrable for better target data alignment, we further adopt the label smoothing technique [35] such that extracted features are encouraged to be distributed in tight clusters evenly separated [25]. By adopting the label smoothing technique, the objective function for training the source model can be further formulated as:

$$\mathcal{L}'_{S,ce} = -\frac{1}{n_S}\sum\nolimits_{i=1}^{n_S} y'_{iS} \log \sigma(H_S(\mathbf{t}_{iS})), \tag{3}$$

where y'_{iS} is the smoothed label computed as $y'_{iS} = (1-\epsilon)y_{iS} + \epsilon / C$ with ϵ being the smoothing parameter which is set to 0.1 empirically.

3.2 Attentive Temporal Consistent Network

With the absence of source data, conventional VUDA methods can no longer be applied. Instead, we tackle SFVDA from two perspectives: on the one hand, extracting effective overall temporal features that are discriminative and comply with the *cross-temporal hypothesis* in a self-supervised manner, without either target label or source data; on the other hand, aligning to the source data distribution via attending to local temporal features with higher confidence in its relevance towards the source data distribution. Following the above strategies, we develop an **Attentive Temporal Consistent Network (ATCoN)**, whose structure is presented in Fig. 1. With the same network architecture adopted for the target spatial and temporal feature extractors $G_{T,sp}$ $G_{T,t}$ as that of $G_{S,sp}$ $G_{S,t}$, $G_{T,sp}$ and $G_{T,t}$ are initialized by $G_{S,sp}$ and $G_{S,t}$ respectively. The overall temporal feature is obtained by learning temporal consistency over the local temporal features as well as the respective local source predictions, resulted by applying the source classifier H_S over the local temporal features directly. Note that the source classifier remains *fixed* throughout the adaptation process. Meanwhile, for attentive aggregation of target local temporal features, a *Local Weight Module (LWM)* is further designed.

Learning Temporal Consistency. As presented in Sect. 3.1, the different local temporal features are extracted via the multiple temporal-ordered frames, sampled from the input video. For a given input video, these local temporal features should represent the same action even if they may differ in spatial appearances. Therefore, the overall temporal feature is effective and discriminative when the corresponding local temporal features are consistent in feature representations. Given a target input video $V_T \in \mathcal{D}_T$ (with video index i omitted for simplicity), its local temporal features for the set of clips with $r1$ and $r2$ temporal frames ($r1, r2 \in [2, k]$), $lt_T^{(r1)}$ and $lt_T^{(r2)}$, are defined similarly to Eq. 1. If the local temporal features are consistent, then the cross-correlation matrix between $lt_T^{(r1)}$ and $lt_T^{(r2)}$ should be close to the identity matrix. The cross-correlation matrix is formulated by:

$$\mathcal{C}^{r1r2} = \left(\hat{lt}_T^{(r1)}\right)^T \hat{lt}_T^{(r2)}, \tag{4}$$

where $\hat{lt}$ is the normalized local temporal feature computed as:

$$\hat{lt} = \frac{lt - \mathbb{E}(lt)}{\sqrt{Var(lt) + \varepsilon}}, \tag{5}$$

with ε being a small bias value for numerical stability. The cross-correlation matrix $\mathcal{C}^{r1r2}$ is a square matrix with the size of $d \times d$, where d is the dimension of the local temporal feature. Since $\mathcal{C}^{r1r2}$ should ideally be close to an identity matrix, the feature consistency loss should maximize the similarity of the respective local temporal features while reducing redundancy between the components. Therefore, the feature consistency loss with respect to $\mathcal{C}^{r1r2}$ is expressed as:

$$\mathcal{L}_{fc}^{r1r2} = \textstyle\sum_i (1 - \mathcal{C}_{ii}^{r1r2})^2 + \lambda \sum_i \sum_{j \neq i} (\mathcal{C}_{ij}^{r1r2})^2, \tag{6}$$

where $i, j \in [0, d-1]$ are indexes of the local temporal feature dimension, while λ is a tradeoff constant. The final feature consistency loss is computed as the mean feature consistency loss over all cross-correlation matrices, with each matrix corresponding to a pair of local temporal features. The final feature consistency loss can be formulated as:

$$\mathcal{L}_{fc} = \frac{1}{N_{fc}} \left(\sum_{r1} \sum_{r2 \neq r1} \mathcal{L}_{fc}^{r1r2} \right), \tag{7}$$

where $N_{fc} = P_2^{k-1}$ is the total number of local temporal feature pairs.

Moreover, since the local temporal features of the same input video should be consistent by minimizing $\mathcal{L}_{fc}$, their relevance towards the source data distribution should also be consistent. With source data inaccessible, such relevance cannot be computed directly through measuring the divergence between source and target data distributions. Since the source classifier contains source data distribution, such relevance could instead be approximated by the prediction of the source classifier over the local temporal features. In other words, the consistency over the relevance of target local temporal features towards source data distribution is equivalent to the consistency over the source prediction of target local temporal features. Meanwhile, the target overall temporal feature is obtained by aggregating the respective local temporal features. It should contain similar motion information as the local temporal features. Therefore, the consistency over source prediction could be extended to the overall temporal feature.

Given local temporal features $lt_T^{(2)}, \ldots, lt_T^{(k)}$, the respective local source predictions $p_{lt,T}^{(2)}, \ldots, p_{lt,T}^{(k)}$ are obtained via the fixed source classifier H_S, following: $p_{lt,T}^{(r)} = H_S(lt_T^{(r)}), \forall r \in [2, k]$. An average local source prediction could be obtained by averaging over the local source predictions $\bar{p}_{lt,T} = \frac{1}{k-1} \sum_{r=2}^{k} p_{lt,T}^{(r)}$. To achieve source prediction consistency, we aim to minimize the divergence between each local source predictions and the average local source prediction:

$$\mathcal{L}_{pc}^{local} = \frac{1}{k-1} \left(\sum_{r=2}^{k} KL(\log \sigma(p_{lt,T}^{(r)}) \| \log \sigma(\bar{p}_{lt,T})) \right), \tag{8}$$

where $KL(p\|q)$ denotes the Kullback-Leibler (KL) divergence.

Further, the overall target prediction $p_{t,T}$ is computed by applying H_S to the target overall temporal feature $\mathbf{t}_T$, which is a simple mean aggregation applied across local temporal features $lt_T^{(2)}, \ldots, lt_T^{(k)}$. To incorporate $p_{t,T}$ into the source prediction consistency, we aim to minimize the absolute difference between $p_{t,T}$ and $\bar{p}_{lt,T}$, defined as:

$$\mathcal{L}_{pc}^{overall} = \sum_{c=1}^{C} |\log \sigma_c(p_{t,T}) - \log \sigma_c(\bar{p}_{lt,T})|. \tag{9}$$

The final source prediction consistency is achieved by joint minimization of the prediction divergence between each local source prediction and the average local source prediction, as well as between the overall target prediction and the average local source prediction, formulated as: $\mathcal{L}_{pc} = \alpha_{local} \mathcal{L}_{pc}^{local} + \alpha_{overall} \mathcal{L}_{pc}^{overall}$, where

α_{local} and $\alpha_{overall}$ are tradeoff constants. Learning temporal consistency is thus achieved by optimizing both the source prediction consistency loss and feature consistency loss jointly, expressed as: $\mathcal{L}_{tc} = \beta_{fc}\mathcal{L}_{fc} + \beta_{pc}\mathcal{L}_{pc}$, with β_{fc} and β_{pc} being the tradeoff hyperparameters.

Local Weight Module (LWM). While complying with the *cross-temporal hypothesis* via learning temporal consistency with feature and source prediction consistencies enables ATCoN to extract discriminative temporal features, we observe that the overall temporal feature $\mathbf{t}_T$ is constructed by simply averaging over all local temporal features. This would not be reasonable as the importance of each local temporal feature is commonly uneven. Therefore, we propose the *Local Weight Module (LWM)* to assign *local weights* to the local temporal features for subsequent attentive aggregation.

As mentioned in Sect. 3.2, ATCoN aims to tackle SFVDA by aligning target videos to the source data distribution. Therefore, LWM is designed such that local temporal features that are more confident towards its relevance to the source data distribution gains more attention, weighted by a *local relevance weight.* More specifically, following Sect. 3.2, the relevance towards source data distribution for $lt_T^{(r)}$ could be referred to its local source prediction $p_{lt,T}^{(r)} = H_S(lt_T^{(r)})$, from which the confidence score is computed. Subsequently, the confidence of $p_{lt,T}^{(r)}$ is defined as the additive inverse of its entropy computed over probabilities of all classes, formulated as:

$$\mathbb{C}(p_{lt,T}^{(r)}) = \sum\nolimits_{c=1}^{C} \sigma_c(p_{lt,T,c}^{(r)}) \log \sigma_c(p_{lt,T,c}^{(r)}). \tag{10}$$

The *local relevance weight* corresponding to the local temporal feature $lt_T^{(r)}$ is finally generated by adding a residual connection for more stable optimization, expressed as: $w_{lt_T^{(r)}} = 1 + \mathbb{C}(p_{lt,T}^{(r)})$. The *local relevance weight* is applied to obtain the weighted overall temporal feature $\mathbf{t}'_T$, which is the mean aggregation of the corresponding weighted local temporal features, computed as: $\mathbf{t}'_T = \frac{1}{k-1}\sum_r w_{lt_T^{(r)}}\, lt_T^{(r)}$. Meanwhile, *local relevance weight* is further applied to the local source predictions $p_{lt,T}^{(r)}$, where the source prediction consistency is learnt with relevance-weighted local source predictions $p_{lt,T}^{(r)\,\prime} = w_{lt_T^{(r)}} p_{lt,T}^{(r)}$.

ATCoN learns temporal consistency by learning feature consistency and source prediction consistency of local temporal features jointly. Inspired by prior works in SFDA [15,21,38], we further improve ATCoN from two aspects:

Information Maximization. The ideal overall temporal feature should be both individually certain and globally diverse. Therefore, we apply an Information Maximization (IM) loss over the weighted overall temporal feature as:

$$\mathcal{L}_{IM} = -\mathbb{E}_{V_T \in \mathbf{D}_T} \sum_{c=1}^{C} \sigma_c(H_S(\mathbf{t}'_T(V_T))) \log \sigma_c(H_S(\mathbf{t}'_T(V_T))) + \sum_{c=1}^{C} KL\left(\mathbb{E}_{V_T \in \mathbf{D}_T}[\sigma_c(H_S(\mathbf{t}'_T(V_T)))] \,\|\, \frac{1}{C}\right), \tag{11}$$

where $\mathbf{t}'_T(V_T)$ is the weighted overall temporal feature corresponding to target video V_T, while σ_c is the c-th element in the softmax.

Self-supervised Pseudo-label Generation. To further improve class-wise alignment of ATCoN with the lack of target label, we follow [20] and generate pseudo-labels for target videos in a self-supervised manner. Specifically, pseudo-labels are generated through a repeated k-means clustering process over the overall temporal feature, where the initial centroid for class c is attained by:

$$\mathbf{c}_c^{(0)} = \frac{\sum_{V_T \in \mathbf{D}_T} \sigma_c(H_S(\mathbf{t}'_T(V_T)))\, \mathbf{t}'_T(V_T)}{\sum_{V_T \in \mathbf{D}_T} \sigma_c(H_S(\mathbf{t}'_T(V_T)))}. \tag{12}$$

Subsequently, the initial pseudo-label of target data V_T is obtained by its nearest centroid, defined by: $\hat{y}_{V_T} = \arg\min_c \cos(\mathbf{t}'_T(V_T), \mathbf{c}_c^{(0)})$, where $\cos(\cdot,\cdot)$ denotes the cosine distance function. The initial centroids are further updated to characterize the category distribution of the target domain more reliably based on the initial pseudo-labels, formulated as:

$$\mathbf{c}_c^{(1)} = \frac{\sum_{V_T \in \mathbf{D}_T} \mathbb{I}(\hat{y}_{V_T} = c)\, \mathbf{t}'_T(V_T)}{\sum_{V_T \in \mathbf{D}_T} \mathbb{I}(\hat{y}_{V_T} = c)}, \tag{13}$$

with $\mathbb{I}(\cdot)$ being an indicator function. The pseudo-labels are finally renewed following the updated centroids with $\hat{y}_{V_T} = \arg\min_c \cos(\mathbf{t}'_T(V_T), \mathbf{c}_c^{(1)})$. ATCoN is further trained with the cross-entropy loss with respect to the pseudo-labels as:

$$\mathcal{L}_{T,ce} = -\frac{1}{n_T} \sum_{i=1}^{n_T} \hat{y}_{V_T} \log \sigma(H_S(\mathbf{t}'_T(V_T))), \tag{14}$$

where n_T is the total number of target videos.

Overall Objective. In summary, given a trained source model, the overall optimization objective of ATCoN is expressed as: $\mathcal{L} = \beta_{tc}\mathcal{L}_{tc} + \beta_{IM}\mathcal{L}_{IM} + \beta_{ce}\mathcal{L}_{T,ce}$, where β_{tc}, β_{IM}, and β_{ce} are tradeoff hyperparameters.

4 Experiments

In this section, we evaluate our proposed ATCoN across three cross-domain action recognition benchmarks including UCF-HMDB$_{full}$ [2], Daily-DA [43] and Sports-DA [43]. These benchmarks cover a wide range of cross-domain scenarios. We present superior results on all benchmarks. Further, ablation studies and empirical analysis of ATCoN are also presented to validate the architecture of ATCoN. *Code is provided at* https://github.com/xuyu0010/ATCoN.

4.1 Experimental Settings

Among the three benchmarks, **UCF-HMDB$_{full}$** is one of the most widely used cross-domain video dataset, which contains videos from two public datasets: UCF101 (U101) [33] and HMDB51 (H51) [16], a total of 3,209 videos in 12 action classes, with 2 cross-domain action recognition tasks. Meanwhile, **Daily-DA** is a more challenging dataset that incorporates both normal videos and low-illumination videos. It is constructed from four datasets : ARID (A11) [42], HMDB51 (H51), Moments-in-Time (MIT) [24], and Kinetics (K600) [14]. While HMDB51, Moments-in-Time, and Kinetics are widely used for action recognition benchmarking, ARID is a more recent dark dataset, comprised with videos shot under adverse illumination conditions. In total, **Daily-DA** includes 18,949 videos from 8 classes, with a total of 12 cross-domain action recognition tasks. **Sports-DA** is a large-scale cross-domain video dataset, built from UCF101 (U101), Sports-1M (S1M) [13], and Kinetics (K600), with 23 action classes and a total of 40,718 videos. With three different domains, **Sports-DA** contains 6 cross-domain action recognition tasks. For fair comparison, all methods adopt the TRN [50] as the backbone for video feature extraction, with the source model pre-trained on ImageNet [5]. Following [21], a Batch Normalization [12] and an additional fully connected layer are inserted while weight normalization [32] is applied to the last fully connected layer. All experiments are implemented with PyTorch [27] library. *More specifications on benchmark details and network implementation are provided in the Appendix.*

Table 1. Results for SFVDA on UCF-HMDB$_{full}$ and Sports-DA.

Methods	Source-free	UCF-HMDB$_{full}$			Sports-DA						
		U101→H51	H51→U101	Avg	K600→U101	K600→S1M	S1M→U101	S1M→K600	U101→K600	U101→S1M	Avg.
TRN	-	72.78	72.15	72.47	86.41	66.95	85.31	71.05	49.29	43.32	67.06
DANN	✗	74.44	75.13	74.79	86.60	66.79	89.32	70.53	61.77	48.73	70.62
MK-MMD	✗	74.72	79.69	77.21	86.49	66.18	87.37	71.43	64.17	**49.24**	70.81
TA^{3}N	✗	78.14	84.83	81.49	88.24	**70.56**	83.32	75.54	57.51	46.37	70.26
SFDA	✓	69.86	74.98	72.42	86.10	60.02	85.37	68.04	55.75	43.58	66.48
SHOT	✓	74.44	74.43	74.44	91.19	64.95	88.84	72.02	53.93	43.58	69.09
SHOT++	✓	71.11	68.13	69.62	90.01	63.11	88.01	70.34	44.75	40.95	66.20
MA	✓	74.45	67.36	70.91	91.04	65.95	87.84	71.88	60.75	39.41	69.48
BAIT	✓	75.33	76.36	75.85	92.27	66.61	88.33	72.85	57.25	44.67	70.33
CPGA	✓	75.82	68.16	71.99	89.42	66.26	86.49	72.55	55.22	44.53	69.08
ATCoN	✓	**79.72**	**85.29**	**82.51**	**93.62**	69.70	**90.64**	**75.99**	**65.24**	47.90	**73.85**

Table 2. Results for SFVDA on Daily-DA.

Methods	Source-free	Daily-DA												
		K600→A11	K600→H51	K600→MIT	MIT→A11	MIT→H51	MIT→K600	H51→A11	H51→MIT	H51→K600	A11→H51	A11→MIT	A11→K600	Avg.
TRN	–	20.87	36.66	29.00	22.11	43.75	53.10	13.81	22.00	37.10	17.20	14.75	24.38	27.89
DANN	✗	21.18	37.50	21.75	22.81	43.33	**58.76**	14.20	29.50	38.24	20.11	**19.75**	27.03	29.51
MK-MMD	✗	**21.66**	36.25	24.00	21.02	**50.42**	58.48	**20.35**	25.75	33.79	18.75	18.00	26.07	29.55
TA^{3}N	✗	19.87	37.67	31.53	21.57	43.01	55.47	14.38	25.71	38.39	14.92	15.56	23.42	28.49
SFDA	✓	12.57	44.95	27.50	15.96	35.19	49.23	13.08	24.25	24.86	16.29	13.25	25.22	25.19
SHOT	✓	12.03	44.58	29.50	15.28	36.67	51.04	13.58	24.25	21.24	17.08	14.00	24.35	25.30
SHOT++	✓	12.57	40.83	28.75	14.90	41.67	46.34	15.98	22.25	33.10	15.42	12.50	21.76	24.42
MA	✓	12.76	45.82	30.00	17.75	37.36	53.54	12.90	25.00	22.19	16.67	15.25	24.29	26.13
BAIT	✓	12.69	45.73	30.00	16.93	39.64	53.00	13.65	25.50	21.17	15.70	14.50	25.52	26.17
CPGA	✓	13.06	46.02	30.75	18.08	39.21	55.09	13.14	26.25	25.54	19.19	16.50	26.72	26.46
ATCoN	✓	17.21	**48.25**	**32.50**	**27.23**	47.35	57.66	17.92	**30.75**	**48.55**	**26.67**	17.25	**31.05**	**33.53**

4.2 Overall Results and Comparisons

We compare ATCoN with state-of-the-art SFDA approaches, as well as several competitive UDA/VUDA approaches. These include: SFDA [15], SHOT [20], SHOT++ [21], MA [18], BAIT [47] and CPGA [28] which are designed for source-free adaptation; as well as DANN [6], MK-MMD [22] and TA^{3}N that are designed for UDA/VUDA scenario. We also report the results of the source-only model (TRN), which is obtained by applying the model trained with source data directly to the target data. We report the top-1 accuracy on the target domains, averaged on 5 runs with identical settings for each approach. Table 1 and Table 2 show the performance of our proposed ATCoN compared with the above methods in the three cross-domain action recognition benchmarks.

The results in Table 1 and Table 2 show that the novel ATCoN achieves the best results among source-free methods on all 20 cross-domain tasks across the three cross-domain benchmarks, and outperforms previous source-free approaches considerably by noticeable margins. Notably, ATCoN exceeds all prior SFDA approaches designed for the image-based SFDA task (e.g., SHOT, MA, and CPGA) consistently by an average of more than 10% relative improvements on mean accuracy over the second-best performances across all 18 cross-domain tasks. The consistent improvements empirically justify the effectiveness of learning temporal consistency for obtaining discriminative overall temporal features while attending to local temporal features with high source prediction confidence. Our proposed ATCoN even exceeds the performance of VUDA methods which are trained with accessible source data under 13 cross-domain tasks, while the mean accuracies of our method are consistently higher than all VUDA methods evaluated across the three benchmarks. This further validates the capability of ATCoN in constructing effective temporal features.

Further, it could be observed that prior SFDA approaches could not tackle SFVDA well. Specifically, in 11 out of the 20 cross-domain tasks, more than half of the evaluated SFDA approaches result in performances inferior to that of the source-only model trained without any adaptation approaches. Prior SFDA approaches could only handle spatial features, while unable to obtain discriminative and transferrable temporal features, resulting in little or negative improvements compared to the source-only baseline. This further demonstrates the challenges faced when adapting video models under the source-free scenario. In particular, all tasks that involve ARID as the source or target domain in **Daily-DA** would lead to inferior results by prior SFDA approaches. This scenario could be further owed to the fact that videos in ARID are collected in adverse illumination with distinct statistical characteristics, leading to larger cross-domain gaps.

Table 3. Ablations studies of ATCoN on UCF-HMDB$_{full}$

Methods	U101→H51	H51→U101
Source-only (TRN)	72.78	72.15
ATCoN	**79.72**	**85.29**
ATCoN-*FC*	77.78	83.36
ATCoN-*PC*†	76.67	82.83
ATCoN-*PC*	77.50	83.01
ATCoN-*TC*	78.89	84.59

(a) Components of temporal consistency

Methods	U101→H51	H51→U101
Source-only (TRN)	72.78	72.15
ATCoN	**79.72**	**85.29**
ATCoN-*NA*	78.33	83.89
ATCoN-*A@F*	79.17	84.93
ATCoN-*A@P*	78.61	84.41

(b) Application of *local relevance weight*

4.3 Ablation Studies and Feature Visualization

To dive deeper into the effectiveness of ATCoN and validate its architecture, we perform detailed ablation studies and feature visualization. The ablation studies investigate ATCoN from two perspectives: firstly, the components of temporal consistency; and secondly the application of *local relevance weight* generated by *LWM*. All ablation studies are conducted utilizing the **UCF-HMDB$_{full}$** dataset with 2 cross-domain action recognition tasks, while TRN is adopted as the feature extractor backbone.

Temporal Consistency. We assess ATCoN against 4 variants to validate the design of the proposed temporal consistency loss $\mathcal{L}_{tc}$: **ATCoN-*FC***, where only the feature consistency is learnt; **ATCoN-*PC*†** and **ATCoN-*PC***, where only the source prediction consistency is learnt, with the overall target prediction not included for **ATCoN-*PC*†**; and finally **ATCoN-*TC***, where only the temporal consistency loss is learnt with both feature consistency and source prediction consistency. The above 4 variants would not apply both the IM loss and pseudo-label generation as proposed in Eq. 11 and 14 during training, while the *local relevance weight* in Sect. 3.2 is applied. Results in Table 3(a) demonstrate the efficacy of learning temporal consistency for constructing discriminative overall temporal features for tackling SFVDA. By learning either feature consistency or source prediction consistency, the network is able to outperform all prior SFDA approaches on both cross-domain tasks. Meanwhile, extending the source prediction consistency to the overall temporal feature further improves its efficacy. The superior performance of ATCoN-*TC* justifies that learning feature consistency and source prediction consistency complements each other.

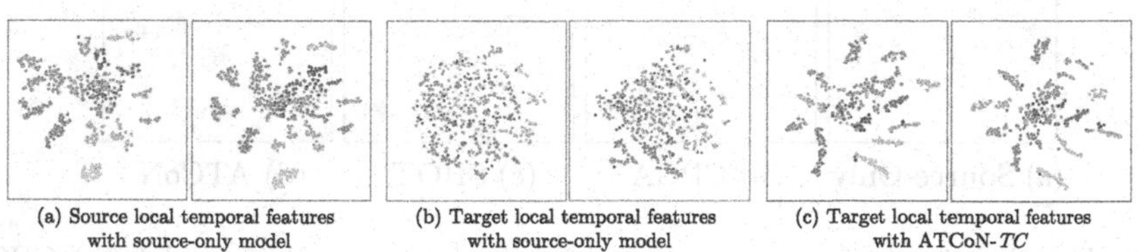

(a) Source local temporal features with source-only model (b) Target local temporal features with source-only model (c) Target local temporal features with ATCoN-*TC*

Fig. 2. t-SNE visualizations of local temporal features with class information. Different colors represent different classes.

Further, it could be observed that ATCoN performs slightly better than ATCoN-*TC*, thanks to the inclusion of both IM loss and pseudo-labeling in training the full ATCoN. However, compared to the improvements towards the baseline model performance brought by learning temporal consistency, the performance gain by applying both IM loss and pseudo-labeling is marginal. The comparison empirically proves that the key towards ATCoN's success lies more in the learning of temporal consistency.

Applying Local Relevance Weight. We propose the *local relevance weight* w_{lt} obtained from the *LWM* which attends to the local temporal features with high confidence over their relevance to the source data distribution. To justify the necessity of the w_{lt}, we compare ATCoN against 3 variants: **ATCoN-*NA***, where the *LWM* is not inserted thus w_{lt} is not obtained at all; **ATCoN-*A@F***, where w_{lt} is only applied for obtaining the overall temporal feature $\mathbf{t}'_T$; and **ATCoN-*A@P***, where w_{lt} is only applied to obtain the weighted local source prediction $p_{lt,T}^{(r)\,\prime}$. Both the IM loss and pseudo-label generation are adopted during the training of the three aforementioned variants. As illustrated in Table 3(b), applying *local relevance weight* brings consistent improvements wherever it has been applied, which justifies the necessity for such a weight. By employing the *local relevance weight* w_{lt}, ATCoN is able to obtain more discriminative temporal features. While w_{lt} bring further improvements on network performance, it should be noted that the improvement is relatively marginal compared to that brought by learning temporal consistency, which indicates that the proposed temporal consistency plays a more vital role in tackling SFVDA effectively.

Feature Visualization. To further understand the characteristics of ATCoN, we plot the t-SNE embeddings [23] of the features extracted. Specifically, we first prove our *cross-temporal hypothesis* by visualizing local temporal features learned by the source-only model on the source data and the target data, and local temporal features learned by ATCoN-*TC* for the H51→U101 task, as presented in Fig. 2. The local temporal features of the source data share similar distribution patterns, which confirms that they are both discriminative and consistent, with similar semantic information embedded. Meanwhile, the data distribution patterns of target data with the source model are inconsistent. In

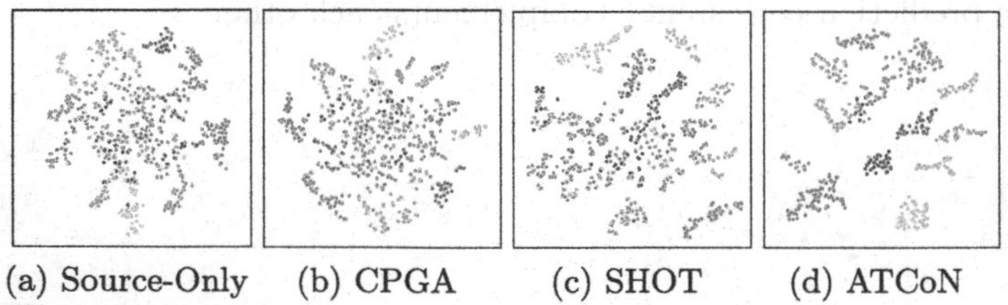

(a) Source-Only (b) CPGA (c) SHOT (d) ATCoN

Fig. 3. Visualization of features extracted by the (a) source-only model, (b) CPGA, (c) SHOT, and (d) ATCoN with class information. Different classes are marked by different colors.

comparison, by learning temporal consistency, ATCoN-*TC* is able to extract discriminative and relatively consistent local temporal features, satisfying the *cross-temporal hypothesis*. This implies that learning temporal consistency enables the learning of source-like representations for target data, and therefore is effective in aligning target data to source data distribution.

We further plot the t-SNE embeddings of the overall temporal features learnt by ATCoN, CPGA, and SHOT for the H51→U101 task with class information in the target domain. The results are presented in Fig. 3, where we can clearly observe that the features learned by ATCoN are much more clustered than those learned by other networks. This verifies that features learned by ATCoN are of higher discriminability, resulting in better SFVDA performance. In contrast, features learned by CPGA are even less clustered and discriminative than those learned by the source-only backbone, which corresponds to its inferior performance over the backbone in this task. The above observation implies the superiority of our ATCoN in tackling SFVDA while reflecting the challenges faced by prior SFDA approaches in tackling SFVDA.

5 Conclusion

In this work, we pioneer in formulating the challenging yet realistic Source-Free Video Domain Adaptation (SFVDA) problem, which addresses data-privacy issues in videos. We proposed a novel ATCoN to tackle SFVDA effectively. With source video data inaccessible, ATCoN tackles SFVDA via obtaining effective and discriminative overall temporal features satisfying the *cross-temporal hypothesis*, achieved by learning temporal consistency, guaranteed by both feature consistency and source prediction consistency. ATCoN further aims to align target data to the source distribution through attending to local temporal features with higher source prediction confidence. Extensive experiments and detailed ablation studies across multiple cross-domain action recognition benchmarks validate the superiority of our proposed ATCoN in tackling SFVDA.

References

1. Carreira, J., Zisserman, A.: Quo vadis, action recognition? a new model and the kinetics dataset. In: Proceedings of the IEEE Conference on Computer Vision and Pattern Recognition, pp. 6299–6308 (2017)
2. Chen, M.H., Kira, Z., AlRegib, G., Yoo, J., Chen, R., Zheng, J.: Temporal attentive alignment for large-scale video domain adaptation. In: Proceedings of the IEEE International Conference on Computer Vision, pp. 6321–6330 (2019)
3. Chen, M.H., Li, B., Bao, Y., AlRegib, G., Kira, Z.: Action segmentation with joint self-supervised temporal domain adaptation. In: Proceedings of the IEEE/CVF Conference on Computer Vision and Pattern Recognition, pp. 9454–9463 (2020)
4. Choi, J., Sharma, G., Schulter, S., Huang, J.-B.: Shuffle and attend: video domain adaptation. In: Vedaldi, A., Bischof, H., Brox, T., Frahm, J.-M. (eds.) ECCV 2020. LNCS, vol. 12357, pp. 678–695. Springer, Cham (2020). https://doi.org/10.1007/978-3-030-58610-2_40

5. Deng, J., Dong, W., Socher, R., Li, L.J., Li, K., Fei-Fei, L.: Imagenet: a large-scale hierarchical image database. In: 2009 IEEE Conference on Computer Vision and Pattern Recognition, pp. 248–255. IEEE (2009)
6. Ganin, Y., Lempitsky, V.: Unsupervised domain adaptation by backpropagation. In: International Conference on Machine Learning, pp. 1180–1189. PMLR (2015)
7. Ghifary, M., Kleijn, W.B., Zhang, M., Balduzzi, D., Li, W.: Deep reconstruction-classification networks for unsupervised domain adaptation. In: Leibe, B., Matas, J., Sebe, N., Welling, M. (eds.) ECCV 2016. LNCS, vol. 9908, pp. 597–613. Springer, Cham (2016). https://doi.org/10.1007/978-3-319-46493-0_36
8. Grandvalet, Y., Bengio, Y.: Semi-supervised learning by entropy minimization. Adv. Neural Inf. Process. Syst. **17** (2004)
9. Hara, K., Kataoka, H., Satoh, Y.: Learning spatio-temporal features with 3d residual networks for action recognition. In: Proceedings of the IEEE International Conference on Computer Vision Workshops, pp. 3154–3160 (2017). https://doi.org/10.1109/ICCVW.2017.373
10. He, K., Zhang, X., Ren, S., Sun, J.: Deep residual learning for image recognition. In: Proceedings of the IEEE Conference on Computer Vision and Pattern Recognition, pp. 770–778 (2016)
11. Huang, L., Joseph, A.D., Nelson, B., Rubinstein, B.I., Tygar, J.D.: Adversarial machine learning. In: Proceedings of the 4th ACM Workshop on Security and Artificial Intelligence, pp. 43–58 (2011)
12. Ioffe, S., Szegedy, C.: Batch normalization: accelerating deep network training by reducing internal covariate shift. In: International Conference on Machine Learning, pp. 448–456. PMLR (2015)
13. Karpathy, A., Toderici, G., Shetty, S., Leung, T., Sukthankar, R., Fei-Fei, L.: Large-scale video classification with convolutional neural networks. In: Proceedings of the IEEE Conference on Computer Vision and Pattern Recognition, pp. 1725–1732 (2014)
14. Kay, W., et al.: The kinetics human action video dataset (2017)
15. Kim, Y., Cho, D., Han, K., Panda, P., Hong, S.: Domain adaptation without source data. IEEE Trans. Artif. Intell. **2**(6), 508–518 (2021). https://doi.org/10.1109/TAI.2021.3110179
16. Kuehne, H., Jhuang, H., Garrote, E., Poggio, T., Serre, T.: Hmdb: a large video database for human motion recognition. In: 2011 International Conference on Computer Vision, pp. 2556–2563. IEEE (2011)
17. Kurmi, V.K., Subramanian, V.K., Namboodiri, V.P.: Domain impression: a source data free domain adaptation method. In: Proceedings of the IEEE/CVF Winter Conference on Applications of Computer Vision, pp. 615–625 (2021)
18. Li, R., Jiao, Q., Cao, W., Wong, H.S., Wu, S.: Model adaptation: unsupervised domain adaptation without source data. In: Proceedings of the IEEE/CVF Conference on Computer Vision and Pattern Recognition, pp. 9641–9650 (2020)
19. Li, S., et al.: Semantic concentration for domain adaptation. In: Proceedings of the IEEE/CVF International Conference on Computer Vision, pp. 9102–9111 (2021)
20. Liang, J., Hu, D., Feng, J.: Do we really need to access the source data? source hypothesis transfer for unsupervised domain adaptation. In: International Conference on Machine Learning, pp. 6028–6039. PMLR (2020)
21. Liang, J., Hu, D., Wang, Y., He, R., Feng, J.: Source data-absent unsupervised domain adaptation through hypothesis transfer and labeling transfer. IEEE Trans. Pattern Anal. Mach. Intell. **44**(11), 8602–8617 (2021)

22. Long, M., Cao, Y., Wang, J., Jordan, M.: Learning transferable features with deep adaptation networks. In: International Conference on Machine Learning, pp. 97–105. PMLR (2015)
23. Van der Maaten, L., Hinton, G.: Visualizing data using t-SNE. J. Mach. Learn. Res. **9**(11), 2579–2605 (2008)
24. Monfort, M., et al.: Moments in time dataset: one million videos for event understanding. IEEE Trans. Pattern Anal. Mach. Intell. **42**(2), 502–508 (2019)
25. Müller, R., Kornblith, S., Hinton, G.: When does label smoothing help? arXiv preprint arXiv:1906.02629 (2019)
26. Pan, B., Cao, Z., Adeli, E., Niebles, J.C.: Adversarial cross-domain action recognition with co-attention. In: AAAI, pp. 11815–11822 (2020)
27. Paszke, A., et al.: Pytorch: an imperative style, high-performance deep learning library. In: Advances in Neural Information Processing Systems, pp. 8026–8037 (2019)
28. Qiu, Z., et al.: Source-free domain adaptation via avatar prototype generation and adaptation. In: International Joint Conference on Artificial Intelligence (2021)
29. Saito, K., Kim, D., Sclaroff, S., Darrell, T., Saenko, K.: Semi-supervised domain adaptation via minimax entropy. In: Proceedings of the IEEE/CVF International Conference on Computer Vision, pp. 8050–8058 (2019)
30. Saito, K., Kim, D., Sclaroff, S., Saenko, K.: Universal domain adaptation through self supervision. Adv. Neural Inf. Process. Syst. **33**, 16282–16292 (2020)
31. Saito, K., Watanabe, K., Ushiku, Y., Harada, T.: Maximum classifier discrepancy for unsupervised domain adaptation. In: Proceedings of the IEEE Conference on Computer Vision and Pattern Recognition, pp. 3723–3732 (2018)
32. Salimans, T., Kingma, D.P.: Weight normalization: A simple reparameterization to accelerate training of deep neural networks. Adv. Neural Inf. Process. Syst. **29**, 901–909 (2016)
33. Soomro, K., Zamir, A.R., Shah, M.: Ucf101: a dataset of 101 human actions classes from videos in the wild. arXiv preprint arXiv:1212.0402 (2012)
34. Sun, B., Feng, J., Saenko, K.: Return of frustratingly easy domain adaptation. In: Proceedings of the AAAI Conference on Artificial Intelligence, vol. 30 (2016)
35. Szegedy, C., Vanhoucke, V., Ioffe, S., Shlens, J., Wojna, Z.: Rethinking the inception architecture for computer vision. In: Proceedings of the IEEE Conference on Computer Vision and Pattern Recognition, pp. 2818–2826 (2016)
36. Viola, P., Wells, W.M., III.: Alignment by maximization of mutual information. Int. J. Comput. Vision **24**(2), 137–154 (1997)
37. Vu, T.H., Jain, H., Bucher, M., Cord, M., Pérez, P.: Advent: adversarial entropy minimization for domain adaptation in semantic segmentation. In: Proceedings of the IEEE/CVF Conference on Computer Vision and Pattern Recognition, pp. 2517–2526 (2019)
38. Xia, H., Zhao, H., Ding, Z.: Adaptive adversarial network for source-free domain adaptation. In: Proceedings of the IEEE/CVF International Conference on Computer Vision, pp. 9010–9019 (2021)
39. Xie, S., Zheng, Z., Chen, L., Chen, C.: Learning semantic representations for unsupervised domain adaptation. In: International Conference on Machine Learning, pp. 5423–5432. PMLR (2018)
40. Xu, Y., Yang, J., Cao, H., Chen, Z., Li, Q., Mao, K.: Partial video domain adaptation with partial adversarial temporal attentive network. In: Proceedings of the IEEE/CVF International Conference on Computer Vision, pp. 9332–9341 (2021)
41. Xu, Y., Yang, J., Cao, H., Mao, K., Yin, J., See, S.: Aligning correlation information for domain adaptation in action recognition (2021)

42. Xu, Y., Yang, J., Cao, H., Mao, K., Yin, J., See, S.: ARID: a new dataset for recognizing action in the dark. In: Li, X., Wu, M., Chen, Z., Zhang, L. (eds.) DL-HAR 2021. CCIS, vol. 1370, pp. 70–84. Springer, Singapore (2021). https://doi.org/10.1007/978-981-16-0575-8_6
43. Xu, Y., et al.: Multi-source video domain adaptation with temporal attentive moment alignment. arXiv preprint arXiv:2109.09964 (2021)
44. Yang, J., Yang, J., Wang, S., Cao, S., Zou, H., Xie, L.: Advancing imbalanced domain adaptation: cluster-level discrepancy minimization with a comprehensive benchmark. IEEE Trans. Cybern., 1–12 (2021). https://doi.org/10.1109/TCYB.2021.3093888
45. Yang, J., Zou, H., Zhou, Y., Zeng, Z., Xie, L.: Mind the discriminability: asymmetric adversarial domain adaptation. In: Vedaldi, A., Bischof, H., Brox, T., Frahm, J.-M. (eds.) ECCV 2020. LNCS, vol. 12369, pp. 589–606. Springer, Cham (2020). https://doi.org/10.1007/978-3-030-58586-0_35
46. Yang, J., An, W., Wang, S., Zhu, X., Yan, C., Huang, J.: Label-driven reconstruction for domain adaptation in semantic segmentation. In: Vedaldi, A., Bischof, H., Brox, T., Frahm, J.-M. (eds.) ECCV 2020. LNCS, vol. 12372, pp. 480–498. Springer, Cham (2020). https://doi.org/10.1007/978-3-030-58583-9_29
47. Yang, S., Wang, Y., van de Weijer, J., Herranz, L., Jui, S.: Unsupervised domain adaptation without source data by casting a bait. arXiv preprint arXiv:2010.12427 (2020)
48. Yeh, H.W., Yang, B., Yuen, P.C., Harada, T.: Sofa: source-data-free feature alignment for unsupervised domain adaptation. In: Proceedings of the IEEE/CVF Winter Conference on Applications of Computer Vision, pp. 474–483 (2021)
49. Zhang, Y., Liu, T., Long, M., Jordan, M.: Bridging theory and algorithm for domain adaptation. In: International Conference on Machine Learning, pp. 7404–7413. PMLR (2019)
50. Zhou, B., Andonian, A., Oliva, A., Torralba, A.: Temporal relational reasoning in videos. In: Proceedings of the European Conference on Computer Vision (ECCV), pp. 803–818 (2018)

BMD: A General Class-Balanced Multicentric Dynamic Prototype Strategy for Source-Free Domain Adaptation

Sanqing Qu[1], Guang Chen[1(✉)], Jing Zhang[2], Zhijun Li[3], Wei He[4], and Dacheng Tao[2,5]

[1] Tongji University, Shanghai, China
{2011444,guangchen}@tongji.edu.cn
[2] The University of Sydney, Camperdown, Australia
jing.zhang1@sydney.edu.au
[3] University of Science and Technology of China, Hefei, China
[4] University of Science and Technology Beijing, Beijing, China
[5] JD Explore Academy, Beijing, China

Abstract. Source-free Domain Adaptation (SFDA) aims to adapt a pre-trained source model to the unlabeled target domain without accessing the well-labeled source data, which is a much more practical setting due to the data privacy, security, and transmission issues. To make up for the absence of source data, most existing methods introduced feature prototype based pseudo-labeling strategies to realize self-training model adaptation. However, feature prototypes are obtained by instance-level predictions based feature clustering, which is category-biased and tends to result in noisy labels since the visual domain gaps between source and target are usually different between categories. In addition, we found that a monocentric feature prototype may be ineffective to represent each category and introduce negative transfer, especially for those hard-transfer data. To address these issues, we propose a general class-**B**alanced **M**ulticentric **D**ynamic prototype (BMD) strategy for the SFDA task. Specifically, for each target category, we first introduce a global inter-class balanced sampling strategy to aggregate potential representative target samples. Then, we design an intra-class multicentric clustering strategy to achieve more robust and representative prototypes generation. In contrast to existing strategies that update the pseudo label at a fixed training period, we further introduce a dynamic pseudo labeling strategy to incorporate network update information during model adaptation. Extensive experiments show that the proposed model-agnostic BMD strategy significantly improves representative SFDA methods to yield new state-of-the-art results. The code is available at https://github.com/ispc-lab/BMD.

Supplementary Information The online version contains supplementary material available at https://doi.org/10.1007/978-3-031-19830-4_10.

S. Avidan et al. (Eds.): ECCV 2022, LNCS 13694, pp. 165–182, 2022.
https://doi.org/10.1007/978-3-031-19830-4_10

Keywords: Domain adaptation · Source-free · Class-balanced sampling · Multicentric prototype pseudo-labeling

1 Introduction

Deep neural networks have achieved remarkable success in various visual tasks at the expense of massive data collections and annotations [4,10,12,17,57] but still often generalized poorly to the unseen new domains due to the inter-domain discrepancy. To reduce the annotation burden when dealing with new domain data, unsupervised domain adaptation (UDA) methods have been developed by aligning the well-labeled source data and the unlabeled target data distribution, which have achieved promising results in object recognition [13,46,52,63], object detection [5,37,55], and semantic segmentation [14,60,61,64,65].

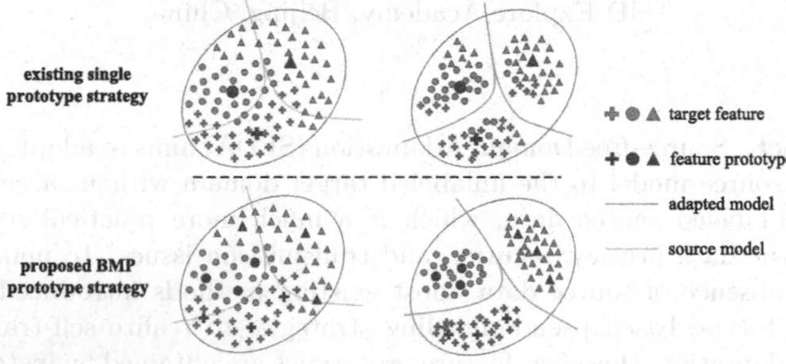

Fig. 1. Comparison between existing prototype strategy (left) and our BMD prototype strategy (right). During SFDA model adaptation, existing prototype strategies are monocentric and class-biased, which often lead to negative transfers for those hard-transfer instances, while our class-balanced multicentric dynamic prototype (BMD) strategy can effectively address the issue.

However, most existing UDA methods require to access the source and target data simultaneously during model adaptation, which is often impractical due to the concerns about data privacy, data security and data transmission efficiency. Therefore, current frontiers have emerged a few works [1,24,26,27,29,44,58,59] seeking to realize source-free domain adaptation (SFDA), where only a source pretrained model is available. To make up for the absence of source data, existing methods can be divided into two main categories: GAN based methods [24,29,44] and self-training based methods [1,26,27,58,59]. For those self-training methods, pseudo-labeling strategies based on feature prototypes are popular and offer promising results. [1,26,27] introduce a weighted k-means clustering based feature prototype generation strategy. However, existing strategies are implemented with instance-level prediction results, which are category-biased and tend to introducing noisy labels, since the visual (e.g. scale, appearance, etc.) domain gaps between source and target are usually different between categories [64,65]. In addition, we argue that due to the domain gap, a rough monocentric feature prototype for each category could not effectively represent the target data and would introduce negative transfer, especially for those hard-transfer data.

In light of the above issues, in this paper, we focus on existing self-training based SFDA methods and propose a general class-**B**alanced **M**ulticentric **D**ynamic (BMD) prototype strategy. Specifically, to avoid the gradual dominance of easy-transfer classes on prototype generation, for each target category we first introduce a novel inter-class balanced sampling strategy to aggregate the potential and representative data samples. Even though we can obtain category balanced feature prototype with above strategy, it is still inferior for those hard transfer data samples. Therefore, we then introduce an intra-class multicentric clustering strategy to generate multiple feature prototypes for each category to assign more robust and precise pseudo labels. In addition, we conjecture that existing strategies that update the pseudo label bank at a fixed training period, may not effectively exploit the dynamic information of network optimization. Thus, we further introduce a dynamic pseudo-labeling strategy to incorporate network update information during model adaptation. We compare our BMD strategy with existing methods in Fig. 1.

To evaluate the effectiveness and generality of our model agnostic strategy, we have applied our strategy to four existing representative methods (SHOT [26], SHOT++ [27], G-SFDA [59] and NRC [58]). Extensive experiments on four benchmark datasets (VisDA-C [40], Office-Home [53], Office-31 [45] and PointDA-10 [43]) show that our BMD strategy significantly improves these methods to yield new state-of-the-art performance.

Our contribution can be summarized as follows:

- We propose a general class-balanced multicentric dynamic prototype strategy BMD for SFDA tasks that is model-agnostic and can be applied to existing self-training based SFDA methods.
- To avoid the gradual dominance of easy-transfer classes on prototype generation, we propose a novel inter-class balanced sampling strategy to aggregate potential and representative data samples.
- To reduce the noisy labels for those hard-transfer data samples, we introduce an intra-class multicentric prototype strategy for each category to assign more robust and precise pseudo labels.
- We conducted extensive experiments to evaluate the effectiveness of our BMD strategy. The results show that the proposed strategy can significantly boost existing methods, e.g., improving SHOT [26] from 82.9% to 85.8% on VisDA-C and NRC [58] from 52.6% to 57.0% on PointDA-10.

2 Related Work

2.1 Unsupervised Domain Adaptation

In pursuit of transfering knowledge from a different but well-labeled source dataset to an unlabeled but relevant target dataset, unsupervised domain adaptation (UDA) has received considerable interests in recent years. Existing methods can be broadly classified into three categories: discrepancy based, reconstruction based, and adversarial based. Discrepancy based methods usually introduce a divergence criterion to measure the distance between the source and target data distributions, and then achieve model adaptation by minimizing the corresponding criterion, e.g. the maximum mean discrepancy (MMD) [31], the wasserstein metric [6], and the contrastive domain discrepancy [21]. Reconstruction based methods [2,15,35] typically introduce an auxiliary image reconstruction task that guides the network to extract domain-invariant features for model adaptation. Inspired by GAN, there are also approaches [13,30,47] that introduce domain discriminators to learn domain-invariant features in an adversarial manner. Despite of effectiveness, these methods require access to the source data, which is often impractical due to data privacy or security concerns.

2.2 Source-Free Domain Adaptation

Currently, there have been several works [1,24,26,27,29,44,58,59] attempting to realize source-free domain adaptation, where only a pre-trained source model and unlabeled target data are available. In these approaches, [24,29,44] introduce generative networks to generate pseudo-data similar to sources or targets, which are difficult and inefficient. Instead, self-training based on feature prototype could be a promising direction [1,26,27,49]. The most relevant papers to our BMD are SHOT [26] and SHOT++ [27], which introduce a weighted k-means clustering algorithm to generate feature prototype and then assign pseudo-labels based on prototype matching. However, their feature prototype generation process is category-biased and prone to introducing negative transfer for those hard-transfer data. In contrast, our BMD can obtain more robust and stable feature prototypes by introducing inter-class balanced sampling and intra-class multicentric prototypes generation. Our strategy may share some similarities in other fields approaches [16,41]. However, our methods are fundamentally different. Unlike these works which apply the labeled data to train a network to recognize the multimodal classes by introducing the multicentric prototypes, we explore the multicentric idea to assign preciser pseudo labels for those unlabeled data, especially those hard-transfer data, to achieve source-free model adaptation.

2.3 Imbalanced Learning

Massive studies [62] have been proposed for long-tail vision tasks to maintain diversity and balance predictions for minority categories. One straightforward idea is to perform category-balanced sampling [20,48,54] using prior knowledge about the category distributions. However, these strategies are not applicable to the UDA task because we do not have access to knowledge of the target distribution. For DA methods, [7,8] introduce a nuclear-norm regularization item to achieve balanced learning, and [64,65] design a self-training framework to realize class-balance segmentation adaptation. In the absence of labeled data, DeepCluster [3], one of the best self-supervised and class-balanced learning methods, generates pseudo-labels via k-means clustering and utilizes them to re-train the current model. Considering domain shift and absence of source data and leveraging advantages of existing methods, we design a novel and general class-balanced multicentric prototype strategy for SFDA.

3 Preliminary

In this paper, we consider the K-way object (2D images and 3D point cloud) recognition task. In the conventional UDA task, we are given two domain data, the labeled source domain with n_s samples as $\mathcal{D}_s = \{(x_s^i, y_s^i)\}_{i=1}^{n_s}$ where $x_s^i \in \mathcal{X}_s$, $y_s^i \in \mathcal{Y}_s$ and y_s^i is the corresponding label of data sample x_s^i, and the unlabeled target domain with n_t samples as $\mathcal{D}_t = \{(x_t^i)\}_{i=1}^{n_t}$ where $x_t^i \in \mathcal{X}_t$. The goal of UDA is to predict the labels $\{y_t^i\}_{i=1}^{n_t}$ of $\mathcal{D}_t$ where $y_t^i \in \mathcal{Y}_t$ with the well-labeled source domain $\mathcal{D}_s$. It is commonly assumed that the data space of $\mathcal{D}_s$ and $\mathcal{D}_t$ are distinct but label space are identical, i.e., $\mathcal{X}_s \neq \mathcal{X}_t$, $\mathcal{Y}_s = \mathcal{Y}_t$. But under the SFDA setting, the $\mathcal{D}_s$ is inaccessible and it is replaced by the source model. Assume that the source model f_s has been well-trained and it consists of two parts: a feature extractor g_s: $\mathcal{X}_s \to \mathbb{R}^d$ and a classifier h_s: $\mathbb{R}^d \to \mathbb{R}^K$, i.e., $f_s(x) = h_s(g_s(x))$. Here d is the dimension of the extracted feature. Therefore, the goal for SFDA is to learn the target model f_t: $\mathcal{X}_t \to \mathcal{Y}_t$ with only access to the source model f_s and the unlabeled target domain $\mathcal{D}_t$.

To transfer the knowledge from the pre-trained source model, feature prototype based pseudo-labeling strategy is a promising direction. Inspired by DeepCluster [3], existing feature prototype based pseudo-labeling strategies [1,26,27] first attain the prototype c_k for each class similar to weighted k-means clustering as follows:

$$c_k = \frac{\sum_{x_t \in \mathcal{X}_t} \delta_k(\hat{f}_t(x_t))\hat{g}_t(x_t)}{\sum_{x_t \in \mathcal{X}_t} \delta_k(\hat{f}_t(x_t))}, \tag{1}$$

where $\hat{f}_t = \hat{g}_t \circ \hat{h}_t$ denotes the previously learned target model and $\delta_k(\hat{f}_t(x_t))$ denotes the softmax probability of target instance x_t belonging to the k-th class. Then one can obtain the pseudo label $\hat{y}_t$ of target x_t via the nearest prototype classifier as:

$$\hat{y}_t = \arg\min_k D_f(\hat{g}_t(x_t), c_k), \tag{2}$$

where $D_f(a, b)$ measures the distance between a and b. One may iterate above process to obtain more stable prototype and pseudo labels like:

$$\begin{aligned} c_k &= \frac{\sum_{x_t \in \mathcal{X}_t} \mathbb{1}(\hat{y}_t = k)\ \hat{g}_t(x_t)}{\sum_{x_t \in \mathcal{X}_t} \mathbb{1}(\hat{y}_t = k)}, \\ \hat{y}_t &= \arg\min_k D_f(\hat{g}_t(x_t), c_k). \end{aligned} \tag{3}$$

where $\mathbb{1}(\cdot)$ is an indicator function.Thereafter, based on the obtained pseudo labels, one can realize self-training based model adaptation with the categorical cross-entropy (CE) loss as follows:

$$\mathcal{L}_{st} = -\frac{1}{n_t} \sum_{i=1}^{n_t} \sum_{k=1}^{K} \mathbb{1}_{[k=\hat{y}_t]} \log \delta_k(f_t(x_t^i))). \tag{4}$$

4 BMD Strategy

4.1 Inter-class Balanced Prototype

The visual domain gaps between source and target are typically different between categories, resulting in relatively higher prediction confidence scores for those easy-transfer classes in target domain [64,65]. Therefore, we conjecture that existing strategies are category-biased and tend to generating noisy labels for those hard data. To avoid the gradual dominance of easy-transfer classes on prototype generation, we propose a novel global inter-class balanced sampling strategy to aggregate those potential data samples. Different from existing methods that decide whether to sample instances based on the instance-level prediction results, we formulate this as a multiple instance learning (MIL) problem [11,25]. In MIL, individual samples are grouped in two bags, i.e., positive and negative bags. A positive bag contains at least one positive instance and a negative bag contains no positive instance. For a specific class k, we treat the target domain $\mathcal{D}_t$ as a combination of a positive bag and a negative bag, where each data instance x_t is represented by a feature vector $\hat{g}_t(x_t)$ and a classification result $p(x_t) = \delta(\hat{f}_t(x_t))$. Thus, the feature prototype for the k-th class is a representative of the positive bag. Since the *top* instances are most likely to be positive, we then aggregate the top-M $\delta_k(\hat{f}_t(x_t))$ scores represented instances along all target domain $\mathcal{D}_t$ for the k-th class as potential instances. After that we can average them to build the class-balanced feature prototype c_k and assign the pseudo label $\hat{y}_t$ as:

$$
\begin{aligned}
\mathcal{M}_k &= \mathop{\arg\max}_{\substack{x_t \in \mathcal{X}_t \\ |\mathcal{M}_k| = M}} \delta_k(\hat{f}_t(x_t)), \\
c_k &= \frac{1}{M} \sum_{i \in \mathcal{M}_k} \hat{g}_t(x_t^i), \\
\hat{y}_t &= \mathop{\arg\min}_{k} D_f(\hat{g}_t(x_t), c_k).
\end{aligned} \tag{5}
$$

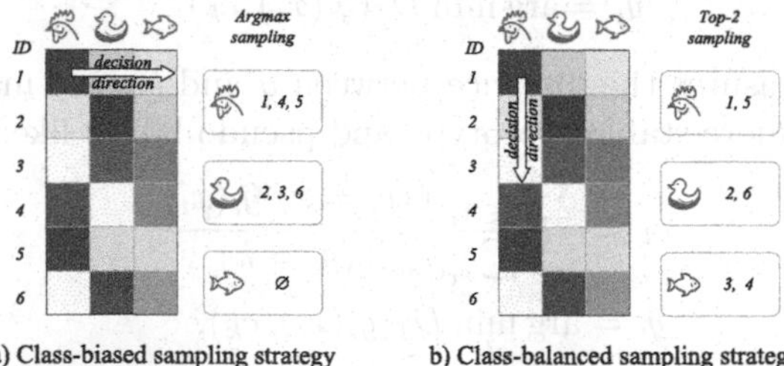

Fig. 2. A toy example compares the existing class-biased strategy (left) with BMD class-balanced strategy (right). To better understand the difference, we illustrate the decision direction of these two sampling strategies. In the presence of large domain gaps, existing strategy is prone to aggregating class-biased data instances.

where $M = \max\{1, \lfloor \frac{n_t}{r \times K} \rfloor\}$, r is a hyperparameter denoting the top-M selection ratio, and K is the number of object classes in the target domain. For simplicity, we refer to this class-balanced sampling based feature prototype pseudo-labeling strategy as BP. It is worth noting that our BP strategy is not based on local instance-level prediction results to decide whether to sample instances, but rather to select the top-M most likely instances to construct feature prototypes from a global perspective. Therefore, we argue that our strategy is inter-class balanced. We compare our class-balanced strategy with existing class-biased strategy in Fig. 2 with a toy example. We may iterate this process like existing methods to obtain more stable prototypes and pseudo labels as:

$$\begin{aligned}
\mathcal{M}_k &= \underset{\substack{x_t \in \mathcal{X}_t \\ |\mathcal{M}_k| = M}}{\arg\max} \frac{\exp\left(\hat{g}_t(x_t) \cdot c_k\right)}{\sum_{j=1}^{K} \exp\left(\hat{g}_t(x_t) \cdot c_j\right)}, \\
c_k &= \frac{1}{M} \sum_{i \in \mathcal{M}_k} \hat{g}_t(x_t^i), \\
\hat{y}_t &= \arg\min_k D_f(\hat{g}_t(x_t), c_k).
\end{aligned} \tag{6}$$

4.2 Intra-class Multicentric Prototype

Even though with the above strategy we can obtain class-balanced feature prototype and assign more robust pseudo labels, we found that a coarse monocentric feature prototype may be not effectively represent those ambiguous data and even introduce negative transfer. In contrast to [60] that introduces uncertainty for pseudo labels to mitigate the negative transfer caused by monocentric prototype, in this paper, we aim to assign more robust and precise label for each instance. Therefore, we propose an intra-class multicentric prototype strategy for each category to obtain more robust and precise pseudo label. We compare our multicentric strategy with existing monocentric strategy in Fig. 3.

Clustering is an essential data analysis technique for grouping unlabeled data in unsupervised learning [18]. In our implementations, assume the sampled data

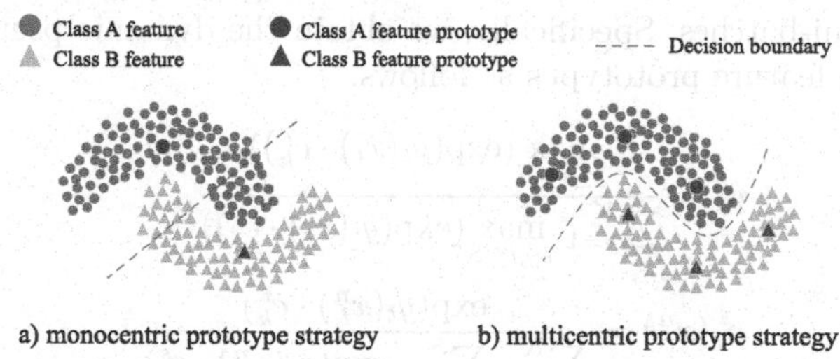

Fig. 3. Comparison between existing monocentric prototype strategy (left) and our proposed multicentric prototype strategy (right). We can conclude that with multicentric prototype strategy we would obtain more robust and precise decision boundaries during pseudo labels generation.

instances for k-th class as $\mathcal{X}_t^k$, the predefined multiple feature prototype number is S. We represent each data instance x_t as the extracted $\hat{g}_t(x_t)$, and apply the classical k-means [33] algorithm to realize intra-class clustering. Then for simplicity, we directly denote the S cluster centroids $\{c_k^i\}_{i=1}^S$ as intra-class multiple feature prototypes for the k-th class. After obtaining multiple feature prototypes for all categories, we can assign the pseudo-labels as follows:

$$\hat{y}_t = \arg\max_k \frac{\max\limits_{1\le i\le S}(\exp(\hat{g}_t(x_t)\cdot c_k^i))}{\sum_{j=1}^K \max\limits_{1\le i\le S}(\exp(\hat{g}_t(x_t)\cdot c_j^i))}, \tag{7}$$

where c_k^i is the i-th feature prototype of class k. For simplicity, we refer to this class-balanced sampling based multicentric pseudo-labeling strategy as BMP. We may also iterate this process like before to obtain more stable prototype and pseudo labels as:

$$\begin{aligned}
\mathcal{M}_k &= \arg\max_{\substack{x_t\in\mathcal{X}_t\\ |\mathcal{M}_k|=M}} \frac{\max\limits_{1\le i\le S}(\exp(\hat{g}_t(x_t)\cdot c_k^i))}{\sum_{j=1}^K \max\limits_{1\le i\le S}(\exp(\hat{g}_t(x_t)\cdot c_j^i))},\\
\{c_k^i\}_{i=1}^S &= \underset{n\in\mathcal{M}_k}{Kmeans}(\hat{g}_t(x_t^n)),\\
\hat{y}_t &= \arg\max_k \frac{\max\limits_{1\le i\le S}(\exp(\hat{g}_t(x_t)\cdot c_k^i))}{\sum_{j=1}^K \max\limits_{1\le i\le S}(\exp(\hat{g}_t(x_t)\cdot c_j^i))}.
\end{aligned} \tag{8}$$

4.3 Dynamic Pseudo Label

Existing strategies update the pseudo label bank at a fixed training period, which may not effectively exploit the updated network during optimization. Thus, we further explore a dynamic pseudo-labeling strategy to improve the target model performance. At the beginning of each epoch, we first update the multiple feature prototype for each class and the corresponding pseudo labels for each instance from a global perspective. And then, for each iteration step we update the feature prototypes as the exponentially moving average (EMA) [50] of the cluster centroids in mini-batches. Specifically, we obtain the dynamic pseudo labels $\hat{y}_t^d$ and update the feature prototypes as follows:

$$\begin{aligned}
\hat{y}_t^d &= \frac{\max\limits_{1\le i\le S}(\exp(\hat{g}_t(x_t)\cdot c_k^i))}{\sum_{j=1}^K \max\limits_{1\le i\le S}(\exp(\hat{g}_t(x_t)\cdot c_j^i))},\\
p_k^i(x_t^n) &= \frac{\exp(\hat{g}_t(x_t^n)\cdot c_k^i)}{\sum_{j=1}^K\sum_{s=1}^S \exp(\hat{g}_t(x_t^n)\cdot c_j^s)},\\
\hat{c}_k^i &= \frac{\sum_{n=1}^N \hat{g}_t(x_t^n)\cdot p_k^i(x_t^n)}{\sum_{n=1}^N p_k^i(x_t^n)},\\
c_k^i &\leftarrow \lambda c_k^i + (1-\lambda)\hat{c}_k^i.
\end{aligned} \tag{9}$$

where $p_k^i(x_t)$ denotes the similarity of instance x_t with existing feature prototypes, $\hat{c}_k^i$ represents the i-th feature prototype of class k calculated with current training minibatch, and λ is the momentum coefficient of EMA which we set to 0.9999. With the obtained dynamic pseudo labels $\hat{y}_t^d$, instead of using a standard cross-entropy loss, following [60], we adopt a more robust variant, symmetric cross-entropy loss (SCE) [56] to further enhance the noise-tolerance. Formally, the dynamic pseudo label loss is defined as follows:

$$\begin{aligned}\mathcal{L}_{dym} = -\frac{1}{N}\sum_{i=1}^{N}\sum_{k=1}^{K}\hat{y}_{t,k}^d \log \delta_k(f_t(x_t^i)) - \\ \frac{1}{N}\sum_{i=1}^{N}\sum_{k=1}^{K}\delta_k(f_t(x_t^i)) \log \hat{y}_{t,k}^d,\end{aligned} \tag{10}$$

However, the dynamic pseudo label did not take into account the potential for a large domain shift and may lead to less informative class prototypes, especially when many samples are misclassified, as it is updated based on the features of the local minibatch. Therefore, we combine the static pseudo label based self-training loss with the dynamic loss to achieve more stable results as :

$$\mathcal{L}_{bmd} = \alpha\mathcal{L}_{st} + \beta\mathcal{L}_{dym}. \tag{11}$$

where α and β are hyper-parameters to balance the two losses. Overall, we denote the combination of the class-balanced multicentric pseudo-labeling and dynamic pseudo labeling strategies as BMD.

5 Experiment

5.1 Experimental Setup

We conduct extensive experiments to evaluate the effectiveness of our BMD strategy covering several popular benchmarks and representative methods below.

Datasets. We evaluate our BMD strategy on three 2D image and one 3D point cloud recognition benchmarks. **Office-31** [45] is a standard benchmark that contains three domains (Amazon (**A**), DSLR (**D**), and Webcam (**W**)) and each domains contains 31 object classes under the office environment. **Office-Home** [53] is a challenging medium-sized benchmark that contains 4 domains (Real (**Rw**), Clipart (**Cl**), Art (**Ar**) and Product (**Pr**)) with 65 classes and a total of 15,500 images. **VisDA-C** [40] is a more challenging large-scale benchmark, which focus on 12-class synthetic-to-real object recognition tasks. Its source domain contains about 152k synthetic 3D object images while the target domain consists of 55k real object images sampled from Microsoft CoCo [28]. **PointDA-10** [43] is the first 3D dataset designed for domain adaptation on point cloud, which contains three domains (ModelNet-10, ShapeNet-10 and ScanNet-10). There are about 27.7k training and 5.1k testing frame point clouds.

Table 1. Classification accuracies (%) on small-sized office-31 dataset with ResNet-50 as backbone. SF denotes source-free.

Method	Venue	SF	A→D	A→W	D→A	D→W	W→A	W→D	**Avg.**
DANN [13]	JMLR 2016	✗	79.7	82.0	68.2	96.9	67.4	99.1	82.2
CDAN [30]	NeurIPS 2018	✗	92.9	94.1	71.0	98.6	69.3	100.0	87.7
MDD [63]	ICML 2019	✗	93.5	94.5	74.6	98.4	72.2	100.0	88.9
GVB-GD [9]	CVPR 2020	✗	95.0	94.8	73.4	98.7	73.7	100.0	89.3
SHOT [26]	ICML 2020	✓	94.0	90.1	74.7	98.4	74.3	99.9	88.6
SHOT w/ BMD	Ours		95.6	93.0	75.6	97.5	75.0	99.8	**89.4**
SHOT++ [27]	TPAMI 2021	✓	94.3	90.4	76.2	98.7	75.8	99.9	89.2
SHOT++ w/ BMD	Ours		96.2	94.2	76.0	98.0	76.0	100.0	**90.1**

Table 2. Accuracies (%) on medium-sized office-home dataset with ResNet-50 as backbone. [* using our reproduced performance]

Methods	Venue	SF	Ar→Cl	Ar→Pr	Ar→Re	Cl→Ar	Cl→Pr	Cl→Re	Pr→Ar	Pr→Cl	Pr→Re	Re→Ar	Re→Cl	Re→Pr	**Avg.**
CDAN [30]	NeurIPS 2018	✗	50.7	70.6	76.0	57.6	70.0	70.0	57.4	50.9	77.3	70.9	56.7	81.6	65.8
CDAN+BNM [7]	CVPR 2020	✗	56.2	73.7	79.0	63.1	73.6	74.0	62.4	54.8	80.7	72.4	58.9	83.5	69.4
GVB-GD [9]	CVPR 2020	✗	57.0	74.7	79.8	64.6	74.1	74.6	65.2	55.1	81.0	74.6	59.7	84.3	70.4
Fixbi [36]	CVPR 2021	✗	58.1	77.3	80.4	67.7	79.5	78.1	65.8	57.9	81.7	76.4	62.9	86.7	72.7
SHOT* [26]	ICML 2020	✓	54.3	78.1	80.3	68.3	79.1	80.1	68.7	54.1	82.0	73.1	57.0	83.0	71.5
SHOT w/ BMD	Ours		55.9	77.8	80.8	69.7	79.3	79.9	69.6	56.6	82.6	73.3	59.5	85.1	**72.5**
G-SFDA* [59]	ICCV 2021	✓	55.2	77.6	80.1	67.7	75.6	79.1	66.3	54.8	81.6	72.5	58.1	84.0	71.0
G-SFDA w/ BMD	Ours		56.0	78.2	80.4	69.1	79.0	79.4	67.5	55.8	82.4	73.7	58.7	83.8	**72.0**
SHOT++* [27]	TPAMI 2021	✓	55.9	79.1	81.8	69.9	81.3	81.0	70.3	56.2	83.6	72.9	59.0	84.3	72.9
SHOT++ w/ BMD	Ours		58.1	79.7	82.6	69.3	81.0	80.7	70.8	57.6	83.6	74.0	60.0	85.9	**73.6**

Baselines. We inject our BMD strategy to four existing SFDA methods to verify its versatility. **SHOT** [26] proposes to freeze the source classifier and fine-tunes the source features extraction module by maximizing the mutual information and feature prototype based pseudo labels. **SHOT++** [27] extends the SHOT [26] by introducing self-supervised learning for fine-tuning the feature extraction module and employing semi-supervised learning strategy to further improve the target domain performance. Different from SHOT and SHOT++ that introduce pseudo labeling strategy to realize model adaptation, **G-SFDA** [59] and **NRC** [58] explore the local neighborhood structure of the target data in feature space to realize model adaptation. Although these two approaches do not introduce pseudo labeling, we find that our BMD strategy still fits seamlessly with these methods and consistently improves their performance.

Implementation Details. For a fair comparison, we adopt the same network architecture and training recipe with baselines. Specifically, we adopt the ResNet-50 [17] pretrained on ImageNet [10] as backbone for Office-31 and Office-Home benchmarks, and the ResNet-101 for VisDA-C benchmark. As for PointDA-10, we utilize the PointNet [42] with local node aggregation network proposed in [43] as feature extraction backbone. To prepare the pretrained source model, following SHOT and NRC, we utilize the label smoothing [34] to increase the discriminability of the source model and facilitate the following target data alignment. During target model adaptation, to achieve source and target domain alignment, we fix the target classifier $h_t = h_s$ and update only the target feature extractor g_t initialized from g_s. Following previous methods, we apply the SGD optimizer with momentum 0.9 and the Adam optimizer for PointDA-10. The batch size is set to 64 for all benchmark datasets. We set the learning rate to 1e-2 for Office-31 and OfficeHome, 1e-3 for VisDA-C, and 1e-6 for PointDA-10. We train 30 epochs for all 2D image datasets and 50 epochs for PointDA. We set the hyperparamter r to 3 for all datasets, and $S = 4$ for Office-Home and VisDA-C, $S = 2$ for PointDA-10 and Office-31. We set $\alpha = 2$ and $\beta = 0.5$ for VisDA-C, $\alpha = 0.3$ and $\beta = 0.1$ for Office-31 and Office-Home, and $\alpha = 1.0$ and $\beta = 0.1$ PointDA-10. All experiments are conducted on a RTX-3090 GPU with PyTorch-1.7.

5.2 Results

2D Image Recognition. We first evaluate the effectiveness of our strategy with existing methods on three 2D image recognition datasets. The results are summarized in Table 1, 2, 3, the top part illustrates results for the traditional UDA methods with access to source data during model adaptation, and the bottom part presents results for the SFDA methods. As shown in Table 1, on **Office-31**, our BMD strategy can consistently improve SHOT and SHOT++ to yield new state-of-the-art performance, especially on the challenging A $\rightarrow$ D task, our BMD strategy can improve SHOT from 90.1% to 93.0% and SHOT++ from 90.4% to 94.2 %, respectively. As excepted in Table 2, on the medium-sized **Office-Home**, our BMD strategy can also consistently improve existing state-of-the-art methods. Specifically, by injecting BMD strategy, we can improve SHOT from 71.5% to 72.5%, G-SFDA from 71.0% to 72.0%, SHOT++ from 72.9% to 73.6%. For the large-scale synthetic-to-real **VisDA-C** dataset in Table 3, our BMD strategy can also significantly improve existing methods by a large margin, especially, we can improve SHOT from 82.9% to 85.7%, G-SFDA from 84.8% to 86.5%, NRC from 85.9% to 86.9% and SHOT++ from 87.3% to 88.7%. With our BMD strategy, SHOT++ can even achieve a performance comparable to the target supervised approach (88.7% vs 89.6%). In addition, on VisDA-C, we can find that with our strategy above methods can achieve more class-balanced performance. Especially for the challenging class 'truck', we can significantly improve SHOT from 58.2% to 70.8%, G-SFDA from 44.8% to 59.7%, and SHOT++ from 28.8% to 45.9%. We also report the standard deviation σ of the accuracy achieved by our method. The σ of SHOT w/BMD on Office-31 is 0.07, while the σ of SHOT w/BMD on VisDA-C is 0.11, showing that the improvement of using BMD in SHOT is significant. Beyond closet-set SFDA, we further evaluate BMD with SHOT on two other DA scenarios, multi-source [38] and multi-target [39]. Due to space limitations, we will present these experiments in the Appendix.

Table 3. Per-class accuracy (%) on large-scale VisDA-C validation set with ResNet-101 as backbone.

Methods	Venue	SF	plane	bcycl	bus	car	horse	knife	mcycl	person	plant	sktbrd	train	truck	**Avg.**
CDAN [30]	NeurIPS 2018	✗	85.2	66.9	83.0	50.8	84.2	74.9	88.1	74.5	83.4	76.0	81.9	38.0	73.9
SWD [22]	CVPR 2019	✗	90.8	82.5	81.7	70.5	91.7	69.5	86.3	77.5	87.4	63.6	85.6	29.2	76.4
MCC [19]	ECCV 2020	✗	88.7	80.3	80.5	71.5	90.1	93.2	85.0	71.6	89.4	73.8	85.0	36.9	78.8
STAR [32]	CVPR 2020	✗	95.0	84.0	84.6	73.0	91.6	91.8	85.9	78.4	94.4	84.7	87.0	42.2	82.7
FixBi [36]	CVPR 2021	✗	96.1	87.8	90.5	90.3	96.8	95.3	92.8	88.7	97.2	94.2	90.9	25.7	87.2
SHOT [26]	ICML 2020	✓	94.3	88.5	80.1	57.3	93.1	94.9	80.7	80.3	91.5	89.1	86.3	58.2	82.9
SHOT w/ BMD	Ours		96.2	87.8	81.4	61.7	95.0	97.5	87.9	82.9	92.6	88.8	87.4	70.8	**85.8**
G-SFDA [59]	ICCV 2021	✓	95.9	88.1	85.4	72.5	96.1	93.7	88.5	80.6	92.3	92.2	87.6	44.8	84.8
G-SFDA w/ BMD	Ours		95.9	87.5	83.9	75.7	96.5	96.6	91.4	81.8	95.9	88.4	85.1	59.7	**86.5**
NRC [58]	NeurIPS 2021	✓	96.8	91.3	82.4	62.4	96.2	95.9	86.1	80.6	94.8	94.1	90.4	59.7	85.9
NRC w/ BMD	Ours		96.7	87.2	85.0	75.6	96.8	97.0	91.6	84.9	94.7	89.0	88.6	55.6	**86.9**
SHOT++ [27]	TPAMI 2021	✓	97.7	88.4	90.2	86.3	97.9	98.6	92.9	84.1	97.1	92.2	93.6	28.8	87.3
SHOT++ w/ BMD	Ours		96.9	87.8	90.1	91.3	97.8	97.8	90.6	84.4	96.9	94.3	90.9	45.9	**88.7**
Target-Supervised	-	-	97.0	86.6	84.3	88.7	96.3	94.4	92.0	89.4	95.5	91.8	90.7	68.7	89.6

Table 4. Accuracies (%) on PointDA-10 dataset with PointNet [42] as backbone.

Method	Venue	SF	M→SC	M→SH	SC→M	SC→SH	SH→M	SH→SC	**Avg.**
ADDA [52]	CVPR 2017	✗	30.5	61.0	48.9	51.1	40.4	29.3	43.5
MCD [46]	CVPR 2018	✗	31.0	62.0	46.8	59.3	41.4	31.3	45.3
PointDAN [43]	NeurIPS 2019	✗	33.0	64.2	49.1	64.1	47.6	33.9	48.7
VDM [51]	Arxiv 2021	✓	30.9	58.4	45.3	61.8	61.0	40.8	49.7
SHOT [26]	ICML 2020	✓	31.8	62.1	67.6	56.9	75.8	24.3	53.1
SHOT w/ BMD	Ours		32.8	66.1	75.0	62.0	81.5	24.4	**57.0**
NRC [58]	NeurIPS 2021	✓	25.8	64.8	70.1	68.1	59.8	26.9	52.6
NRC w/ BMD	Ours		33.8	66.7	70.8	62.6	83.4	24.8	**57.0**

3D Point Cloud Recognition. In addition to 2D images, to verify the generality of our BMD strategy, we also conducted experiments on the 3D point cloud **PointDA-10** dataset. As shown in Table 4, our BMD strategy can also significantly improve existing methods by a large margin. Specifically, by injecting BMD strategy, we can improve SHOT from 53.1% to 57.0% and NRC from 52.6% to 57.0%. Especially on the challenging task, SH → M, we can improve SHOT from 75.8% to 81.5% and NRC from 59.8% to 83.4%.

5.3 Performance Analysis

Ablation Study. As we presented before, the core components of our BMD strategy are inter-class balanced sampling and intra-class multicentric prototype based pseudo label generation. In order to incorporate the network dynamic optimization information, we further introduce the EMA based dynamic pseudo label strategy. To study the advantage of each part of our BMD strategy, we conduct

Table 5. Ablation study on three UDA datasets.

Methods/Datasets	Office-Home	VisDA-C	PointDA-10
Source-model	59.6	46.6	39.4
SHOT w/ naive PL [23]	70.3	82.9	51.0
SHOT w/ mono PL [26]	71.5	82.9	53.1
SHOT w/ BP (ours)	72.0	83.8	55.0
SHOT w/ BMP (ours)	72.5	84.7	56.4
SHOT w/ BMD (ours)	72.5	85.7	57.0

Table 6. Statistics of class-wise performance on VisDA-C.

Methods	Acc avg μ ↑	Acc std σ ↓	Acc cv c_v ↓
SHOT [26]	82.9	12.857	0.155
SHOT w/ BMD	85.8	10.127	**0.118**
G-SFDA [59]	84.8	14.279	0.168
G-SFDA w/ BMD	86.5	10.766	**0.124**
SHOT++ [27]	87.3	19.027	0.218
SHOT++ w/ BMD	88.7	14.146	**0.159**

the ablation study on Office-Home, VisDA-C and PointDA-10 with SHOT, the results are summarized in Table 5. To verify the superiority of our BMD strategy, we also introduce two existing strategies, the naive argmax based pseudo label [23] strategy, and the monocentric prototype based pseudo label [26] strategy. As expected, the results show that the simple BP strategy can outperform existing strategies, which indicates the importance of the class-balanced sampling strategy for pseudo label generation. When we incorporate the intra-class multicentric prototype strategy with BP strategy, i.e. the BMP, the performance is further significantly boosted. We attribute this to the fact that the MP strategy introduce more fine-grained feature prototypes for each class, which allows the model to assign more accurate pseudo-labels for those hard-transfer data. As for the dynamic strategy, we find that it is not as effective as BP and BMP on the Office-Home and PointDA datasets. We suspect it may be due to the relatively small size of the datasets, thus the EMA-based dynamic feature prototypes cannot effectively utilize the information during training. Due to space limitations, we presented more ablation experiments in the Appendix.

Does Our Strategy Really Achieve More Class-Balanced Results? To verify whether our BMD strategy is really helpful in achieving the class-balanced results, in this part, we introduce the coefficient of variation (also known as the relative standard deviation) c_v as metric to evaluate the inter-class balance performance, which is a standardized measure of dispersion of a probability distribution or frequency distribution. Formally, the coefficient of variation is defined as $c_v = \frac{\sigma}{\mu}$, where σ and μ are the standard deviation and expected mean of the data distribution, respectively. We conduct experiments on VisDA-C dataset, the results are summarized in Table 6. As shown in this table, for all methods by injecting our BMD strategy we can arrive higher accuracy mean μ, lower standard deviation σ and lower coefficient of variation c_v, which demonstrates that our BMD strategy indeed facilitates existing methods to achieve more class-balanced performance. To verify the robustness, we also conducted the c_v experiments on PointDA, on task SC→M, SHOT gets 0.291, SHOT w/BMD is 0.186; NRC gets 0.464, NRC w/BMD is 0.301. These results further demonstrate that our BMD strategy can improve the existing methods to achieve class-balanced results.

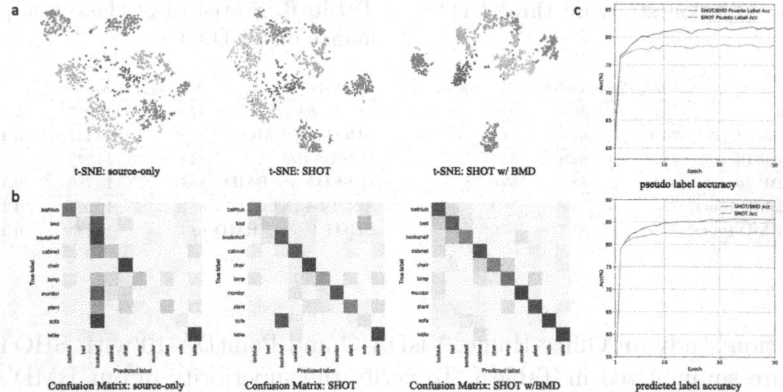

Fig. 4. **a**: The t-SNE visualization of target features for source model, SHOT, and SHOT w/ BMD on PointDA-10 (SC→M). **b**: The Confusion Matrix visualization for source model, SHOT, and SHOT w/BMD on PointDA-10 (SC→M). **c**: The pseudo and predicted label accuracy curves for SHOT, and SHOT w/BMD on VisDA-C.

Visualization. To demonstrate the superiority of our BMD strategy, we present the t-SNE feature and confusion matrix on PointDA-10 (SC→M), and the pseudo and predicted label accuracy curves on VisDA-C in Fig. 4. From Fig. 4a, we can see that after model adaptation by SHOT w/ BMD, the target features are more compactly clustered. The confusion matrix in Fig. 4b demonstrates that our BMD strategy can achieve more class-balanced accuracy compared to the vanilla SHOT. In particular, when there is severe class bias in the source model, e.g., for the hard-transfer *'sofa'* class, SHOT cannot achieve good model adaptation due to the severe domain gap, while BMD strategy can overcome this well by our inter-class balanced sampling. The accuracy curves in Fig. 4c further support that our BMD strategy can facilitate existing methods to achieve more superior pseudo labels and predicted labels during model adaptation.

6 Conclusion

In this paper, we present a general class-balanced multicentric dynamic (BMD) prototype strategy for source-free domain adaptation, which is model agnostic and can be applied to existing self-training based SFDA methods. Specifically, our BMD strategy consists of a novel inter-class balanced sampling strategy, an intra-class multicentric prototype strategy, and a dynamic feature prototype based pseudo-labeling strategy. We have injected our strategy into four existing representative methods and conducted experiments on both 2D images and 3D point cloud datasets. The results demonstrate that our BMD strategy can consistently and significantly boost existing methods to yield new state-of-the-art performance. For future work, we will extend our BMD strategy to those source-free dense prediction tasks.

Acknowledgments. This work was supported by Shanghai Municipal Science and Technology Major Project (No.2018SHZDZX01), ZJ Lab, Shanghai Center for Brain Science and Brain-Inspired Technology, and the National Natural Science Foundation of China under Grant 61906138, by Shanghai Rising Star Program (No. 21QC1400900).

References

1. Ahmed, S.M., Raychaudhuri, D.S., Paul, S., Oymak, S., Roy-Chowdhury, A.K.: Unsupervised multi-source domain adaptation without access to source data. In: CVPR (2021)
2. Bousmalis, K., Trigeorgis, G., Silberman, N., Krishnan, D., Erhan, D.: Domain separation networks. In: NeurIPS (2016)
3. Caron, M., Bojanowski, P., Joulin, A., Douze, M.: Deep clustering for unsupervised learning of visual features. In: ECCV (2018)
4. Chen, G., Chen, K., Zhang, L., Zhang, L., Knoll, A.: VCANet: vanishing-point-guided context-aware network for small road object detection. Automot. Innov. **4**(4), 400–412 (2021). https://doi.org/10.1007/s42154-021-00157-x
5. Chen, Y., Li, W., Sakaridis, C., Dai, D., Van Gool, L.: Domain adaptive faster r-cnn for object detection in the wild. In: CVPR (2018)
6. Courty, N., Flamary, R., Tuia, D., Rakotomamonjy, A.: Optimal transport for domain adaptation. IEEE TPAMI **39**(9), 1853–1865 (2016)
7. Cui, S., Wang, S., Zhuo, J., Li, L., Huang, Q., Tian, Q.: Towards discriminability and diversity: batch nuclear-norm maximization under label insufficient situations. In: CVPR (2020)
8. Cui, S., Wang, S., Zhuo, J., Li, L., Huang, Q., Tian, Q.: Fast batch nuclear-norm maximization and minimization for robust domain adaptation. arXiv preprint arXiv:2107.06154 (2021)
9. Cui, S., Wang, S., Zhuo, J., Su, C., Huang, Q., Tian, Q.: Gradually vanishing bridge for adversarial domain adaptation. In: CVPR (2020)
10. Deng, J., Dong, W., Socher, R., Li, L.J., Li, K., Fei-Fei, L.: Imagenet: a large-scale hierarchical image database. In: CVPR (2009)
11. Dietterich, T.G., Lathrop, R.H., Lozano-Pérez, T.: Solving the multiple instance problem with axis-parallel rectangles. Artif. Intell. **89**(1–2), 31–71 (1997)
12. Dosovitskiy, A., et al.: An image is worth 16 x 16 words: transformers for image recognition at scale. In: ICLR (2020)
13. Ganin, Y., et al.: Domain-adversarial training of neural networks. JMLR **17**(1), 2030–2096 (2016)
14. Gao, L., Zhang, J., Zhang, L., Tao, D.: Dsp: dual soft-paste for unsupervised domain adaptive semantic segmentation. In: ACM Multimedia (2021)
15. Ghifary, M., Kleijn, W.B., Zhang, M., Balduzzi, D., Li, W.: Deep reconstruction-classification networks for unsupervised domain adaptation. In: Leibe, B., Matas, J., Sebe, N., Welling, M. (eds.) ECCV 2016. LNCS, vol. 9908, pp. 597–613. Springer, Cham (2016). https://doi.org/10.1007/978-3-319-46493-0_36
16. Han, J., Luo, P., Wang, X.: Deep self-learning from noisy labels. In: Proceedings of the IEEE/CVF International Conference on Computer Vision, pp. 5138–5147 (2019)
17. He, K., Zhang, X., Ren, S., Sun, J.: Deep residual learning for image recognition. In: CVPR (2016)
18. Jain, A.K., Murty, M.N., Flynn, P.J.: Data clustering: a review. ACM comput. Surv. (CSUR) **31**(3), 264–323 (1999)

19. Jin, Y., Wang, X., Long, M., Wang, J.: Minimum class confusion for versatile domain adaptation. In: Vedaldi, A., Bischof, H., Brox, T., Frahm, J.-M. (eds.) ECCV 2020. LNCS, vol. 12366, pp. 464–480. Springer, Cham (2020). https://doi.org/10.1007/978-3-030-58589-1_28
20. Kang, B., et al.: Decoupling representation and classifier for long-tailed recognition. In: ICLR (2020)
21. Kang, G., Jiang, L., Yang, Y., Hauptmann, A.G.: Contrastive adaptation network for unsupervised domain adaptation. In: CVPR (2019)
22. Lee, C.Y., Batra, T., Baig, M.H., Ulbricht, D.: Sliced wasserstein discrepancy for unsupervised domain adaptation. In: CVPR (2019)
23. Lee, D.H., et al.: Pseudo-label: the simple and efficient semi-supervised learning method for deep neural networks. In: Workshop on Challenges in Representation Learning, ICML (2013)
24. Li, R., Jiao, Q., Cao, W., Wong, H.S., Wu, S.: Model adaptation: unsupervised domain adaptation without source data. In: CVPR (2020)
25. Li, W., Vasconcelos, N.: Multiple instance learning for soft bags via top instances. In: CVPR (2015)
26. Liang, J., Hu, D., Feng, J.: Do we really need to access the source data? source hypothesis transfer for unsupervised domain adaptation. In: ICML (2020)
27. Liang, J., Hu, D., Wang, Y., He, R., Feng, J.: Source data-absent unsupervised domain adaptation through hypothesis transfer and labeling transfer. IEEE TPAMI **44**(11), 8602–8617 (2021)
28. Lin, T.-Y., et al.: Microsoft coco: common objects in context. In: Fleet, D., Pajdla, T., Schiele, B., Tuytelaars, T. (eds.) ECCV 2014. LNCS, vol. 8693, pp. 740–755. Springer, Cham (2014). https://doi.org/10.1007/978-3-319-10602-1_48
29. Liu, Y., Zhang, W., Wang, J.: Source-free domain adaptation for semantic segmentation. In: CVPR (2021)
30. Long, M., Cao, Z., Wang, J., Jordan, M.I.: Conditional adversarial domain adaptation. In: NeurIPS (2018)
31. Long, M., Wang, J., Ding, G., Sun, J., Yu, P.S.: Transfer feature learning with joint distribution adaptation. In: ICCV (2013)
32. Lu, Z., Yang, Y., Zhu, X., Liu, C., Song, Y.Z., Xiang, T.: Stochastic classifiers for unsupervised domain adaptation. In: CVPR (2020)
33. MacQueen, J., et al.: Some methods for classification and analysis of multivariate observations. In: Proceedings of the fifth Berkeley Symposium on Mathematical Statistics and Probability. Oakland, CA, USA (1967)
34. Müller, R., Kornblith, S., Hinton, G.: When does label smoothing help? In: NeurIPS (2019)
35. Murez, Z., Kolouri, S., Kriegman, D., Ramamoorthi, R., Kim, K.: Image to image translation for domain adaptation. In: CVPR (2018)
36. Na, J., Jung, H., Chang, H.J., Hwang, W.: Fixbi: bridging domain spaces for unsupervised domain adaptation. In: CVPR (2021)
37. Oza, P., Sindagi, V.A., VS, V., Patel, V.M.: Unsupervised domain adaption of object detectors: a survey. arXiv preprint arXiv:2105.13502 (2021)
38. Peng, X., Bai, Q., Xia, X., Huang, Z., Saenko, K., Wang, B.: Moment matching for multi-source domain adaptation. In: ICCV (2019)
39. Peng, X., Huang, Z., Sun, X., Saenko, K.: Domain agnostic learning with disentangled representations. In: ICML. PMLR (2019)
40. Peng, X., Usman, B., Kaushik, N., Hoffman, J., Wang, D., Saenko, K.: Visda: the visual domain adaptation challenge. arXiv preprint arXiv:1710.06924 (2017)

41. Prabhu, V., Kannan, A., Ravuri, M., Chaplain, M., Sontag, D., Amatriain, X.: Few-shot learning for dermatological disease diagnosis. In: Machine Learning for Healthcare Conference, pp. 532–552. PMLR (2019)
42. Qi, C.R., Su, H., Mo, K., Guibas, L.J.: Pointnet: deep learning on point sets for 3d classification and segmentation. In: CVPR (2017)
43. Qin, C., You, H., Wang, L., Kuo, C.C.J., Fu, Y.: Pointdan: a multi-scale 3d domain adaption network for point cloud representation. In: NeurIPS (2019)
44. Qiu, Z., Zhang, Y., Lin, H., Niu, S., Liu, Y., Du, Q., Tan, M.: Source-free domain adaptation via avatar prototype generation and adaptation. In: IJCAI (2021)
45. Saenko, K., Kulis, B., Fritz, M., Darrell, T.: Adapting visual category models to new domains. In: Daniilidis, K., Maragos, P., Paragios, N. (eds.) ECCV 2010. LNCS, vol. 6314, pp. 213–226. Springer, Heidelberg (2010). https://doi.org/10.1007/978-3-642-15561-1_16
46. Saito, K., Watanabe, K., Ushiku, Y., Harada, T.: Maximum classifier discrepancy for unsupervised domain adaptation. In: CVPR (2018)
47. Shu, R., Bui, H.H., Narui, H., Ermon, S.: A dirt-t approach to unsupervised domain adaptation. In: ICLR (2018)
48. Song, J., Shen, C., Yang, Y., Liu, Y., Song, M.: Transductive unbiased embedding for zero-shot learning. In: CVPR (2018)
49. Tanwisuth, K., et al.: A prototype-oriented framework for unsupervised domain adaptation. In: NeurIPS (2021)
50. Tarvainen, A., Valpola, H.: Mean teachers are better role models: weight-averaged consistency targets improve semi-supervised deep learning results. In: NeurIPS (2017)
51. Tian, J., Zhang, J., Li, W., Xu, D.: Vdm-da: virtual domain modeling for source data-free domain adaptation. arXiv preprint arXiv:2103.14357 (2021)
52. Tzeng, E., Hoffman, J., Saenko, K., Darrell, T.: Adversarial discriminative domain adaptation. In: CVPR (2017)
53. Venkateswara, H., Eusebio, J., Chakraborty, S., Panchanathan, S.: Deep hashing network for unsupervised domain adaptation. In: CVPR (2017)
54. Wang, T., et al.: The devil is in classification: a simple framework for long-tail instance segmentation. In: Vedaldi, A., Bischof, H., Brox, T., Frahm, J.-M. (eds.) ECCV 2020. LNCS, vol. 12359, pp. 728–744. Springer, Cham (2020). https://doi.org/10.1007/978-3-030-58568-6_43
55. Wang, W., et al.: Exploring sequence feature alignment for domain adaptive detection transformers. In: ACM Multimedia (2021)
56. Wang, Y., Ma, X., Chen, Z., Luo, Y., Yi, J., Bailey, J.: Symmetric cross entropy for robust learning with noisy labels. In: ICCV (2019)
57. Xu, Y., Zhang, Q., Zhang, J., Tao, D.: Vitae: vision transformer advanced by exploring intrinsic inductive bias. In: NeurIPS (2021)
58. Yang, S., Wang, Y., van de Weijer, J., Herranz, L., Jui, S.: Exploiting the intrinsic neighborhood structure for source-free domain adaptation. In: NeurIPS (2021)
59. Yang, S., Wang, Y., van de Weijer, J., Herranz, L., Jui, S.: Generalized source-free domain adaptation. In: ICCV (2021)
60. Zhang, P., Zhang, B., Zhang, T., Chen, D., Wang, Y., Wen, F.: Prototypical pseudo label denoising and target structure learning for domain adaptive semantic segmentation. In: CVPR (2021)
61. Zhang, Q., Zhang, J., Liu, W., Tao, D.: Category anchor-guided unsupervised domain adaptation for semantic segmentation. In: NeurIPS (2019)
62. Zhang, Y., Kang, B., Hooi, B., Yan, S., Feng, J.: Deep long-tailed learning: a survey. arXiv preprint arXiv:2110.04596 (2021)

63. Zhang, Y., Liu, T., Long, M., Jordan, M.: Bridging theory and algorithm for domain adaptation. In: ICML (2019)
64. Zou, Y., Yu, Z., Kumar, B., Wang, J.: Unsupervised domain adaptation for semantic segmentation via class-balanced self-training. In: ECCV (2018)
65. Zou, Y., Yu, Z., Liu, X., Kumar, B., Wang, J.: Confidence regularized self-training. In: ICCV (2019)

Generalized Brain Image Synthesis with Transferable Convolutional Sparse Coding Networks

Yawen Huang[1], Feng Zheng[2(✉)], Xu Sun[1], Yuexiang Li[1], Ling Shao[3], and Yefeng Zheng[1(✉)]

[1] Tencent Jarvis Lab, Shenzhen, China
{yawenhuang,vicyxli,yefengzheng}@tencent.com
[2] Southern University of Science and Technology, Shenzhen, China
[3] Terminus Group, Beijing, China

Abstract. High inter-equipment variability and expensive examination costs of brain imaging remain key challenges in leveraging the heterogeneous scans effectively. Despite rapid growth in image-to-image translation with deep learning models, the target brain data may not always be achievable due to the specific attributes of brain imaging. In this paper, we present a novel generalized brain image synthesis method, powered by our transferable convolutional sparse coding networks, to address the lack of interpretable cross-modal medical image representation learning. The proposed approach masters the ability to imitate the machine-like anatomically meaningful imaging by translating features directly under a series of mathematical processings, leading to the reduced domain discrepancy while enhancing model transferability. Specifically, we first embed the globally normalized features into a domain discrepancy metric to learn the domain-invariant representations, then optimally preserve domain-specific geometrical property to reflect the intrinsic graph structures, and further penalize their subspace mismatching to reduce the generalization error. The overall framework is cast in a minimax setting, and the extensive experiments show that the proposed method yields state-of-the-art results on multiple datasets.

Keywords: Convolutional sparse coding networks · Image synthesis

1 Introduction

Neuroimaging techniques like magnetic resonance imaging (MRI) allow assessment of varying physical and chemical tissue properties of brain. Different pulse sequences, used in anatomical MRI, provide diverse and complementary information about the anatomical organization. However, a certain single imaging modality is relatively common in real clinical practice, due to the high inter-equipment variability, expensive examination costs and long acquisition time of

S. Avidan et al. (Eds.): ECCV 2022, LNCS 13694, pp. 183–199, 2022.
https://doi.org/10.1007/978-3-031-19830-4_11

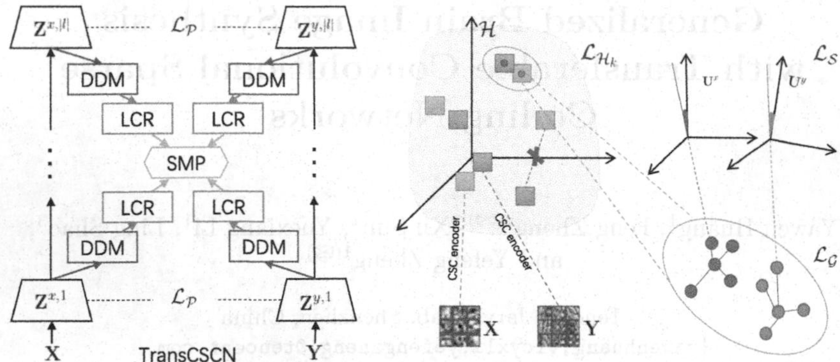

Fig. 1. Architecture of our TransCSCN. The first layer is the globally normalized CSC layer. DDM denotes a module calculating domain discrepancy metric $\mathcal{L}_{\mathcal{H}_k}$, the LCR module enforces Laplacian co-regularization $\mathcal{L}_{\mathcal{G}}$, and SMP enforces subspace mismatch penalization $\mathcal{L}_{\mathcal{S}}$. $\mathcal{L}_{\mathcal{P}}$ is the association loss. The right side shows the feature-leveled operation of each regularizer.

multi-modality imaging. The proliferation of multi-modal imaging is urgently needed for encouraging the comprehensive analysis and making accurate decisions.

Over the last decade, image synthesis technique has enabled transformational advances in various tasks, delivering superior performance on image-to-image translation ubiquitously [13,42]. These methods have also been widely used for medical image analysis [21], including cross-modal MRI synthesis [13], multi-modal image segmentation [26], registration [2], and tracking of anatomical structures [30]. Sparse-representation-based methods [34,35], as an early and trustworthy way, construct a linear function for mapping sparse codes and learning dictionaries jointly. The solution for such a celebrated model can be approximated using greedy algorithms but later known to be sub-optimal, because of highly redundant structure and damaged consistency. Convolutional sparse coding (CSC) [5,12] breaks this dilemma via modeling a shift invariant objective to obtain the coherent and compact representations via convolution. In addition to dictionary-based approaches, deep neural networks [38] have made rapid progress in image generation. The remarkable works are distributed in various applications such as style transfer [42] and sketch-to-photorealism generation [18].

Image synthesis algorithms indeed have achieved promising performance. However, for medical imaging, irrespective of the intrinsic anatomical meaning, requiring a large-scale standardized dataset, at the cost of a large number of parameters or computational complexity, is unacceptable for auxiliary clinical diagnosis and advanced research analysis. Specifically, early methods [7,31] seem to favor a shallow and redundant architecture with descriptors which cannot effectively capture image features, *e.g.*, by finding edges and pooling them. The architecture of recent networks makes feature extraction deeper by imposing a large amount of data and memory overhead in the implementation. However, collecting multi-modal medical images can be prohibitively hard or even implausible. The other issue is that most medical image synthesis works pursue the superficial consistency, omitting the underlying tissue information. Besides technical challenges, the complexity and heterogeneity of MRI remains a problem in leveraging the heterogeneous scans effectively, for example, imaging by different manufacturers (*e.g.*, Philips Achieva System vs. GE SIGNA system) and abundant sequences (*e.g.*, a turbo spin echo sequence vs. a single-shot EPI sequence). Taken together, a macro perspective expects that these weaknesses can be relieved by a compensatory solution, *i.e.*, constructing a new framework towards standardizing and expanding the synthesis reality for both visual and anatomical significance.

In view of the above challenges, we propose a novel Transferable Convolutional Sparse Coding Network (TransCSCN) that enables the learner to adapt to the target modal. This is done by mapping a latent space to generalize both intra-domain (*i.e.*, multiple imaging manufacturers for one modal) and cross-domains (*i.e.*, multiple modalities) while preserving the domain-specific geometries and their sub-manifolds. An overview of our TransCSCN is shown in Fig. 1. To summarize, this paper makes the following contributions:

- We propose a novel framework, *i.e.*, TransCSCN, for unsupervised brain image synthesis, where multiple objective-specific layers are adapted, resulting in mathematically interpretable formulations and anatomically meaningful results.
- A domain discrepancy metric is provided to embed the globally normalized features in the reproducing kernel Hilbert space to reduce the variant representations of similar tissues in different domains.
- The Laplacian co-regularization term is further devised to optimally preserve the geometric structures underlying the respective domains.
- Finally, a subspace mismatch regularizer is proposed to penalize the generalization error and variation.

2 Related Work

2.1 Domain Adaptation

Domain discrepancy severely degrades the model performance on cross-domain tasks. Luckily, significant effort has been devoted in the literature to provide adapted features or classifiers to new visual domains. Previous methods have tried to learn domain-invariant representations between source and target domains. Of these methods, Zhong *et al.* [40] proposed a transfer cross-validation method, which generalizes a learner across different domains by considering both marginal and conditional distributions. Qiu *et al.* [29] presented a function learning framework by adapting dictionaries learned from one visual domain to the other for smoothly varying domains utilizing regression. Recent work has focused on transferring deep neural network representations from a source dataset to a target domain where the labeled data may be sparse or non-existed. Deep adaptation network [23] explores feature transferability of deep CNNs in the task-specific layers embedded in a reproducing kernel Hilbert space to reduce the domain discrepancy. In [36], a curriculum manager was proposed as an independent network module to predict the transferability of source domain data and adversarially raise the error rate of a domain discriminator. Yu *et al.* [22] presented dynamic transfer by adapting model parameters to samples to address the domain conflict problem. While many domain adaptation or transformation algorithms for natural images are well explored by minimizing the distribution discrepancy, some disconnections still form non-negligible gaps between the natural and medical images.

2.2 Image-to-Image Translation

Image-to-image translation aims to transfer a source image into the style of a varying reference image. Conventional wisdom and early research [7] tackled this problem using nonparametric settings to resample the feature statistics of a given image texture. Roy *et al.* [31] provided a dictionary-learning-based brain image contrast synthesis approach by assuming that cross-modality patches have similar local geometry to linearly approximate the target image. Vemulapalli *et al.* [33] relaxed the supervision of fully paired data, by jointly maximizing both global mutual information and local spatial consistency to match the similarities across modalities. To circumvent the problem of lacking diversity and good quality, deep generative network was proposed after the introduction of neural style transfer algorithms. The popular works such as CycleGAN [42] are able to transfer rich local texture appearance cross domains, *e.g.*, translating between paintings and photographs. MSGAN [24] designed a mode seeking regularization term for conditional GANs to handle the mode collapse issue. Huang *et al.* [15] relaxed the supervision by matching similarities of both intra- and intre-modal data in feature-level, and then adopting the manifold penalization to handle the brain image synthesis problem. Mainstream image-to-image translation methods are tailored to adapting given modality and target modality; however, these methods have difficulties in modeling complex patterns of irregular distributions with heterogeneous variations.

3 Preliminaries

A natural way to cast the problem of learning a shallow architecture of shift-invariant representations into an optimization problem is a convolutional sparse coding (CSC) method [5]. CSC has gained popularity in computer vision and medical imaging, because of its ability to obtain a structured filter that facilitates a global handling of the image. CSC is remarkable when compared with traditional sparse coding, providing a more elegant way to represent data as the sum of filters convolved with sparsely distributed codes.

Given a set of observations $\{\mathbf{x}_1, \mathbf{x}_2, ..., \mathbf{x}_S\}$ in $\mathbb{R}^N$, CSC can be formulated as learning a set of sparse coefficient feature maps $\mathbf{z}_i \in \mathbb{R}^N$ convolved with filters $\mathbf{f}_i \in \mathbb{R}^M$, $\forall i = \{1, ..., K\}$. Its optimization problem boils down to:

$$\min_{\mathbf{f},\mathbf{z}} \frac{1}{2} \left\| \mathbf{x} - \sum_{i=1}^{K} \mathbf{f}_i * \mathbf{z}_i \right\|_2^2 + \lambda \sum_{i=1}^{K} \|\mathbf{z}_i\|_1 \ s.t. \ \|\mathbf{f}_i\|_2^2 \leq 1 \, \forall i = \{1, ..., K\}, \quad (1)$$

where $*$ denotes the 2D convolution operation, λ is the regularization parameter, $\mathbf{x}$ and $\mathbf{z}$ are the vectorized images, and $\mathbf{f}$ is the vectorized filter. The objective in Eq. (1) is difficult to optimize due to the convolutional decomposition mechanism. Motivated by Parseval's theorem and deconvolutional networks, Zeiler *et al.* [37] demonstrated that through an alternation strategy to solve a sequence of convex sub-problems until convergence is an efficient way. As a part of the proximal gradient methods, fast iterative shrinkage thresholding algorithm (FISTA) [3] provided an iterative approach for solving the l_1 penalized least squares problem with fast quadratic convergence. In parallel, the augmented Lagrange methods, such as the alternating direction method of multipliers (ADMM) [4], treated the optimization as sub-problems and computed the convolutions in the Fourier domain. The subsequent CSC based algorithms often rely on the ADMM formulation to circumvent the computational burdens of the inversion of a convolutional linear operation. For example, Heide *et al.* [12] exploited the mask matrices to deal with the incomplete samples, while Choudhury *et al.* [6] leveraged the matrix inverse lemma to achieve a global consensus in each of the estimates.

In this study, we consider a special case, where a source domain training set $\mathbf{X} \in \mathbb{R}^{N \times S}$ of S source modality samples and a target domain training set $\mathbf{Y} \in \mathbb{R}^{N \times T}$ of T target modality samples are given. The image synthesis task is then expected to learn both convolutional feature maps $\mathbf{Z}^x$ and $\mathbf{Z}^y$ over their corresponding filters $\mathbf{F}^x$ and $\mathbf{F}^y$, where the superscript is adopted to distinguish the variate from the source domain x or from the target domain y. The conventional solution following the independent scheme in Eq. (1), results in uncorrelated features. The joint representation learning groups two independent reconstruction errors in a single objective function, leading to a common set of feature maps (*i.e.*, $\mathbf{Z}^x \equiv \mathbf{Z}^y$) shared between source and target domains. The flexible joint learning strategy replaces the common feature assumption by constructing a linear projector $\mathbf{P}$ to calculate $\|\mathbf{Z}^x - \mathbf{P}\mathbf{Z}^y\|_2$, which is more reasonable.

4 Transferable Convolutional Sparse Coding Networks

The challenge of joint learning mainly arises when the target domain has no or only limited data pairing with the source domain. In other words, the assumption of the feature maps from one domain to be identical to those observed at the target domain is no longer valid, let alone the abundance of variations in single domain. In this paper, we address the dilemma of generalizability against multivariate nature of neuroimaging, by providing more flexibility in leveraging the large-scale heterogeneous medical data in an unsupervised manner, such that the learned transferable representations can close the source and target discrepancy.

Following the CSC approximation introduced in Sect. 3, a shallow convolutional structure on the learned matrices is constructed for the purpose of low-level feature extraction. Recent works [8,20] suggested to learn multiple levels of feature representations in a hierarchical architecture to deeply capture both low-level and mid-level features. As expected, CSCNets [15] were proposed to exploit the benefits of depth with convolutional filter learning to convey information with increasing austerity. Given $\mathbf{X}$ and $\mathbf{Y}$, the representations of the multilayered CSC can be formalized as $\mathbf{Z}^{x,|l|} = f(\mathbf{X}, \mathbf{F}^{x,|l-1|}, \lambda)$, $\mathbf{Z}^{y,|l|} = f(\mathbf{Y}, \mathbf{F}^{y,|l-1|}, \lambda)$, where $l \in \{1, 2, \ldots, L\}$ denotes the layer index, f is the feature extractor, $\mathbf{Z}^{x,|l|} \in \mathbb{R}^{N^{|l|} \times h^{|l|} w^{|l|}}$ and $\mathbf{Z}^{y,|l|} \in \mathbb{R}^{N^{|l|} \times h^{|l|} w^{|l|}}$ represent the l-th layered feature maps with tensor properties of height h and width w. Correspondingly, the layerwise projector $\mathbf{P}^{|l|}$ is updated as $\mathcal{L}_{\mathcal{P}}(\mathbf{Z}^{x,|l|}, \mathbf{Z}^{y,|l|}) = \|\mathbf{Z}^{x,|l|} - \mathbf{P}^{|l|}\mathbf{Z}^{y,|l|}\|_F^2 + \alpha\|\mathbf{P}^{|l|}\|_F^2$, where α is association mapping parameter. This can be solved as a set of the least squares problem.

4.1 Domain Discrepancy Metric

Despite the obvious cross-domain divergence, the variations such as different manufacturers and physical parameters in single domain are also harmful to model generalization. To approach this problem, we adopt the single domain unit normalization [15] and begin by a global normalization under $\mathbf{Z}^x$ and $\mathbf{Z}^y$. Then the features are scaled as $\frac{\mathbf{Z}^x}{\max(\|\mathbf{Z}^x\|_2)}$ and $\frac{\mathbf{Z}^y}{\max(\|\mathbf{Z}^y\|_2)}$, respectively. When the maximum of their norms is guaranteed to be unity, we project the features to a unit sphere to eliminate the scaling ambiguity globally as follows: $\hat{\mathbf{Z}}_i^x = \mathbf{Z}_i^x / (\max(\|\mathbf{Z}_i^x\|_2)\sqrt{1 - \left\|\frac{\mathbf{Z}_i^x}{\max(\|\mathbf{Z}_i^x\|_2)}\right\|^2}), \forall i \in \mathbb{R}^S$, $\hat{\mathbf{Z}}_j^y = \mathbf{Z}_j^y / (\max(\|\mathbf{Z}_j^y\|_2)\sqrt{1 - \left\|\frac{\mathbf{Z}_j^y}{\max(\|\mathbf{Z}_j^y\|_2)}\right\|^2}), \forall j \in \mathbb{R}^T$, where the general unit normalization criterion $\left\|\hat{\mathbf{Z}}_i^x\right\|_2^2 = 1, \forall i$ and $\left\|\hat{\mathbf{Z}}_j^y\right\|_2^2 = 1, \forall j$ can be satisfied. The globally normalized convolutional feature maps then become $\mathbf{Z}'^{x,|l|} = f(\hat{\mathbf{Z}}^{x,|l-1|}, \mathbf{F}^{x,|l-1|}, \lambda)$, $\mathbf{Z}'^{y,|l|} = f(\hat{\mathbf{Z}}^{y,|l-1|}, \mathbf{F}^{y,|l-1|}, \lambda)$, where the imposed upper layer of the representation $\hat{\mathbf{Z}}^{x,|l-1|}$ and $\hat{\mathbf{Z}}^{y,|l-1|}$ are treated as the intermediate representations.

The problem of adapting the source domain data to the target domain has been explored [14,23]. Of these methods, bounding the target error by superimposing a discrepancy metric between both domains is a direction to explore, which can be realized by the two-sample test statistics. Theoretically, given two samples coming from different domains following different probability distributions $p(\mathbf{x})$ and $p(\mathbf{y})$, the two-sample testing either accepts or rejects a null hypothesis $p(\mathbf{x}) = p(\mathbf{y})$, based on various metrics, such as the maximum mean discrepancy (MMD) [10]. This prior has motivated us to solve a natural domain variation in a generalized unsupervised way by learning the correlation-relaxed features of different domains more efficiently. On further consideration, the original MMD is restricted by the local generalization leading to the sub-optimal kernel problem, while the extended multi-kernel MMD (MK-MMD) criterion is more applicable to perform unbiased estimation. Suppose the reproducing kernel Hilbert space (RKHS) $\mathcal{H}_k$ induced with a characteristic kernel k on the vectorized element $\mathbf{Z}$ has a set of positive definite kernels $\{k_u\}_{u=1}^d, \forall u \in \{1, \cdots, d\}$. The MK-MMD then can be defined as the squared distance between kernel mean embeddings in $\mathcal{H}_k$ to minimize the domain gap and optimize the kernel selection,

$$\mathcal{L}_{\mathcal{H}_k}(X,Y) = \left\|\mathbb{E}_{p(\mathbf{x})}[f(\mathbf{X})] - \mathbb{E}_{p(\mathbf{y})}[f(\mathbf{Y})]\right\|^2_{\mathcal{H}_k}, \\ \forall\, k \in \mathcal{K} := \{\sum_{u=1}^{d} \beta_u k_u : \sum_{u=1}^{d} \beta_u = 1, \beta_u \geq 0\}, \tag{2}$$

where $\mathcal{K}$ is the convex combination of u positive definite kernels $\{k_u\}_{u=1}^d, \forall u$; β_u denotes the coefficient for constraining the characteristic of $\{k_u\}$; $f(\cdot)$ represents the feature mapping with $k(X,Y) = \langle f(\mathbf{X}), f(\mathbf{Y})\rangle_{\mathcal{H}_k}$; and $\mathcal{L}_{\mathcal{H}_k}$ can be interpreted as matching all orders of statistics with a property of $p(\mathbf{x}) = p(\mathbf{y})$ iff $\mathcal{L}_{\mathcal{H}_k}(X,Y) = 0$. As principally studied in MK-MMD, we are targeting to boost unpaired cross-modal data underlying the same distributions to be close to each other. Mathematically, the unsupervised method can be established by adding the MK-MMD-based layerwise regularizer $\mathcal{L}^l_{\mathcal{H}_k}$:

$$\min_f \max_k f(\hat{\mathbf{Z}}^{x,|l-1|}, \mathbf{F}^{x,|l-1|}, \lambda) + f(\hat{\mathbf{Z}}^{y,|l-1|}, \mathbf{F}^{y,|l-1|}, \lambda) \\ +\gamma \left\|\mathbb{E}_{p(\mathbf{x})}[\mathbf{Z}'^{x,|l|}] - \mathbb{E}_{p(\mathbf{y})}[\mathbf{Z}'^{y,|l|}]\right\|^2_{\mathcal{H}_k}, \tag{3}$$

where γ denotes the penalty parameter. Considering the kernel trick, $\mathcal{L}^l_{\mathcal{H}_k}$ can be expressed as the layered expectation of kernel function $\mathcal{L}^l_{\mathcal{H}_k} \triangleq \frac{1}{S^2}\sum_{i=1}^{S}\sum_{j=1}^{S} k(\mathbf{Z}_i'^{x,|l|}, \mathbf{Z}_j'^{x,|l|}) + \frac{1}{T^2}\sum_{i=1}^{T}\sum_{j=1}^{T} k(\mathbf{Z}_i'^{y,|l|}, \mathbf{Z}_j'^{y,|l|}) - \frac{2}{ST}\sum_{i=1}^{S}\sum_{j=1}^{T} k(\mathbf{Z}_i'^{x,|l|}, \mathbf{Z}_j'^{y,|l|})$, where $\mathbf{Z}_i'^{x,|l|}, \mathbf{Z}_j'^{x,|l|} \overset{iid}{\sim} p(\mathbf{x})$, and $\mathbf{Z}_i'^{y,|l|}, \mathbf{Z}_j'^{y,|l|} \overset{iid}{\sim} p(\mathbf{y})$, $k \in \mathcal{K}$, $\forall i, j$.

4.2 Laplacian Co-regularization

The representations learned in Eq. (3) encourage domain-invariant features against cross-modal distribution discrepancy; however, some important low-level details reflecting the domain-specific information are lost. With this limitation, the synthetic may be visually meaningful but lacking practical significance. Recent advances in exploring manifold assumption [41] reflect the geometric structure leading to a realistic and correct approximation. Based on the observation of graph Laplacian (*a.k.a.* manifold learning), we investigate how to preserve the complementary properties by introducing a Laplacian co-regularizer. To be specific, given $\mathbf{Z}'^{x,|l|}$ and $\mathbf{Z}_i'^{y,|l|}$ of $\mathbf{X}$ and $\mathbf{Y}$, respectively, two layerwise q-nearest neighbor graphs $\mathcal{G}^{x,|l|}$ and $\mathcal{G}^{y,|l|}$ can be constructed while each with g vertices [39]. Under the above definition, the Laplacian co-regularization $\mathcal{L}_{\mathcal{G}}(X,Y)$ is given as:

$$\sum_{i,j=1}^{g}\prod_{l\in L}(\mathbf{W}^{x,|l|}_{i,j}\left\|\mathbf{Z}_i'^{x,|l|} - \mathbf{Z}_j'^{x,|l|}\right\|^2 + \mathbf{W}^{y,|l|}_{i,j}\left\|\mathbf{Z}_i'^{y,|l|} - \mathbf{Z}_j'^{y,|l|}\right\|^2), \tag{4}$$

where $\mathbf{W}_{i,j}^{x,|l|}$ and $\mathbf{W}_{i,j}^{y,|l|}$ are the layered weight matrices of $\mathcal{G}^{x,|l|}$ and $\mathcal{G}^{y,|l|}$ having attributions of $\mathbf{W}_{i,j}^{x,|l|} = 1$, $\mathbf{W}_{i,j}^{y,|l|} = 1$ iff any two features $\mathbf{Z}_i^{\prime x,|l|}$ and $\mathbf{Z}_j^{\prime x,|l|}$ or $\mathbf{Z}_i^{\prime y,|l|}$ and $\mathbf{Z}_j^{\prime y,|l|}$ satisfying $\mathbf{Z}_i^{\prime x,|l|}$ or $\mathbf{Z}_i^{\prime y,|l|}$ is among the g-nearest neighbors of $\mathbf{Z}_j^{\prime x,|l|}$ or $\mathbf{Z}_j^{\prime y,|l|}$; otherwise, $\mathbf{W}_{i,j}^{x,|l|} = 0$, $\mathbf{W}_{i,j}^{y,|l|} = 0$.

The domain-specific graph structures are encoded into $\mathbf{W}_{i,j}^{x,|l|}$ and $\mathbf{W}_{i,j}^{y,|l|}$ with the corresponding layerwise diagonal matrices $\mathbf{D}^{x,|l|} = \mathrm{diag}(d_1^{x,|l|}, \cdots, d_g^{x,|l|})$ and $\mathbf{D}^{y,|l|} = \mathrm{diag}(d_1^{y,|l|}, \cdots, d_g^{y,|l|})$. The graph Laplacian provides $\mathcal{G} = \mathbf{D} - \mathbf{W}$, such that we can preserve the domain-specific geometrical structures by Eq. (4) updating as $\mathcal{L}_{\mathcal{G}}(X,Y) = \mathrm{Tr}(\mathbf{Z}^{\prime x,|l|}\mathcal{G}^{x,|l|}\mathbf{Z}^{\prime x,|l|^T} + \mathbf{Z}^{\prime y,|l|}\mathcal{G}^{y,|l|}\mathbf{Z}^{\prime y,|l|^T})$.

4.3 Subspace Mismatch Penalization

Considering the heterogeneity of medical images acquired on scanners from different manufacturers and with different physical parameters, all these properties induce conflicted and inconsistent features. The aforementioned formulations bridge the domain gap and enrich the domain-specific representation, but fail to cope with the variational tissue structures across domains. This means that performance may degrade when high-level features are insensitive to tissue boundaries, resulting in over-smoothness of the synthesis and potential scaling-based mismatching. To reduce the generalization error and better preserve the geometry in our synthesis task, we propose a subspace mismatch regularizer to constrain the veritable similar bases in their subspace. As suggested by [32], singular value decomposition (SVD) of the feature matrix can be exploited to enforce the constraint. In this work, we adopt the general SVD to get the layerwise orthogonal matrices $\mathbf{U}^{x,|l|}$ and $\mathbf{U}^{y,|l|}$: $\mathbf{Z}^{\prime x,|l|} = \mathbf{U}^{x,|l|}\mathbf{\Sigma}^{x,|l|}\mathbf{V}^{x,|l|^T}$, $\mathbf{Z}^{\prime y,|l|} = \mathbf{U}^{y,|l|}\mathbf{\Sigma}^{y,|l|}\mathbf{V}^{y,|l|^T}$. Here, $\mathbf{\Sigma}$ is the nonnegative real diagonal matrix, and $\mathbf{V}^T$ is the conjugate transpose of $\mathbf{V}$ denoting the right singular matrix. Following [32], we use principal angles to measure the subspace distance between two domains,

$$\mathbf{\Theta}^{|l|} = \min_{\mathbf{U}^{x,|l|},\mathbf{U}^{y,|l|}} \arccos\left(\frac{\mathbf{U}^{x,|l|^T}\mathbf{U}^{y,|l|}}{\left\|\mathbf{U}^{x,|l|}\right\|\left\|\mathbf{U}^{y,|l|}\right\|}\right),$$
$$\mathbf{U}^{x,|l|^T}\mathbf{U}^{y,|l|} = \mathbf{A}^{x,|l|}(\mathrm{diag}(\cos\Theta^{|l|}))\mathbf{A}^{y,|l|^T}, \tag{5}$$

where $\mathbf{\Theta}$ represents the principal angles and $\mathbf{A}$ is the weight matrix. The orthogonal bases are then matched by $\mathcal{L}_{\mathcal{S}}^{|l|} = \||\mathbf{A}|^{x,|l|} - |\mathbf{A}|^{y,|l|}\|_F^2$ in the feature-leveled subspaces.

4.4 Transfer Representation Learning

In our transfer representation learning, we construct the globally normalized features, the penalization of domain discrepancy, the regularization of domain-specific manifold, and the reduction of subspace mismatch. The overall objective function is then represented as follows:

Algorithm 1. Layerwise **F**-Step Optimization

Input: Training data $\mathbf{X}$, $\mathbf{Y}$, ρ^f
Initialize: $\mathbf{Z}_0^x$, $\mathbf{Z}_0^y$, $\mathbf{F}_0^x \in \mathbb{O}$, $\mathbf{F}_0^y \in \mathbb{O}$
$\mathbf{Z}_0^x \to \hat{\mathbf{Z}}_0^x$, $\mathbf{Z}_0^y \to \hat{\mathbf{Z}}_0^y$
while not converged **do**
  for $i = 1$ to B **do**
    $\arg\min_{\mathbf{F}^x,\mathbf{F}^y} \frac{1}{2}(\|\mathbf{X} - \mathbf{F}^x * \hat{\mathbf{Z}}^x\|_2^2 + \|\mathbf{X} - \mathbf{F}^y * \hat{\mathbf{Z}}^y\|_2^2 + \delta(\|\mathbf{F}^x - \tilde{\mathbf{F}}^x + \rho^{fx}\|_2^2 + \|\mathbf{F}^y - \tilde{\mathbf{F}}^y + \rho^{fy}\|_2^2)), s.t. \|\mathbf{f}_i^x\|_2^2 \leq 1, \|\mathbf{f}_i^y\|_2^2 \leq 1, \forall i$
  end for
  $\arg\min_{\tilde{\mathbf{F}}^x,\tilde{\mathbf{F}}^y} \text{ind}_C(\tilde{\mathbf{F}}^x) + \text{ind}_C(\tilde{\mathbf{F}}^y) + \frac{N\delta}{2}(\|\tilde{\mathbf{F}}^x - \bar{\mathbf{F}}^x - \bar{\rho}^{fx}\|_2^2 + \|\tilde{\mathbf{F}}^y - \bar{\mathbf{F}}^y - \bar{\rho}^{fy}\|_2^2)$
  for $i = 1$ to B **do**
    $\rho^{fx'} = \rho^{fx} + \mathbf{F}^x - \tilde{\mathbf{F}}^x, \rho^{fy'} = \rho^{fy} + \mathbf{F}^y - \tilde{\mathbf{F}}^y$
  end for
end while
Output: $\mathbf{F}^x$, $\mathbf{F}^y$

$$\min_{f,\mathcal{L}_\mathcal{P},\mathcal{L}_\mathcal{G},\mathcal{L}_\mathcal{S}} \max_k f(\mathbf{X},\lambda) + f(\mathbf{Y},\lambda) + \mathcal{L}_\mathcal{P} + \gamma\mathcal{L}_{\mathcal{H}_k} + \mathcal{L}_\mathcal{G} + \mathcal{L}_\mathcal{S}. \tag{6}$$

The resulting architecture is named as transferable convolutional sparse coding network (TransCSCN). Once the optimization is completed, we can obtain the trained filters $\mathbf{F}^x$, $\mathbf{F}^y$, convolutional feature maps $\mathbf{Z}^x$, $\mathbf{Z}^y$, and their projection matrices $\mathbf{P}$. The learned model is then applied to synthesize images across modalities. For the given test image $\mathbf{X}^t$, the correlated target modality version can be computed as $\mathbf{Y}^t = \mathbf{F}^y\hat{\mathbf{Z}}^{ty}$ with $\hat{\mathbf{Z}}^{ty} \approx \mathbf{P}\mathbf{Z}^{tx}$, where $\mathbf{Z}^{tx} = f(\mathbf{X}^t, \lambda)$.

4.5 Multilevel Optimization

The general CSCNet is convex in each variable of the i-th layer but not jointly convex. The solutions such as the coordinate descent allow to alternately minimize the objective over one block of the variables. Considering the large size of medical images which places great demands on computational efficiency, following [6,12], we reformulate the objective to an unconstrained optimization by introducing an indicator ind_C defined on the convex set of the constraints C,

$$\min_{f,\mathcal{L}_\mathcal{P},\mathcal{L}_\mathcal{G},\mathcal{L}_\mathcal{S}} \max_k f(\mathbf{X},\lambda)+f(\mathbf{Y},\lambda)+\text{ind}_C(\mathbf{F}^x)+\text{ind}_C(\mathbf{F}^y)+\mathcal{L}_\mathcal{P}+\gamma\mathcal{L}_{\mathcal{H}_k}+\mathcal{L}_\mathcal{G}+\mathcal{L}_\mathcal{S}. \tag{7}$$

Equation (7) then can be solved efficiently by splitting with respect to the filters $\mathbf{F}$, feature maps $\mathbf{Z}$, and the relationship operator $\mathbf{P}$.

F-Step Subproblem: We first exploit the l-th layer filter learning by solving,

$$\begin{aligned} &\arg\min_f f(\hat{\mathbf{Z}}^{x,|l|}, \mathbf{F}^{x,|l|}) + f(\hat{\mathbf{Z}}^{y,|l|}, \mathbf{F}^{y,|l|}) + \text{ind}_C(\tilde{\mathbf{F}}^{x,|l|}) \\ &+ \text{ind}_C(\tilde{\mathbf{F}}^{y,|l|}), s.t. \|\mathbf{f}_k^{x,|l|}\|_2^2 \leq 1, \mathbf{f}_k^{y,|l|}\|_2^2 \leq 1, \forall k, \end{aligned} \tag{8}$$

Algorithm 2. Layerwise **Z**-Step Optimization

Input: Training data $\mathbf{X}$, $\mathbf{Y}$, ρ^z, λ, γ

Initialize: $\mathbf{Z}_0^x$, $\mathbf{Z}_0^y$, $\mathbf{F}_0^x$, $\mathbf{F}_0^y$, $\mathbf{P}_0$

$\mathbf{Z}_0^x \to \hat{\mathbf{Z}}_0^x$, $\mathbf{Z}_0^y \to \hat{\mathbf{Z}}_0^y$

Let $\hat{\mathbf{Z}}_0^y \leftarrow \hat{\mathbf{Z}}_0^x \mathbf{P}_0$

while not converged **do**

  for $i = 1$ to B **do**

    $\arg\min_{f,\mathcal{L}_\mathcal{P},\mathcal{L}_\mathcal{G},\mathcal{L}_\mathcal{S}} \max_k f(\mathbf{X},\lambda) + f(\mathbf{Y},\lambda) + \mathcal{L}_\mathcal{P} + \gamma\mathcal{L}_{\mathcal{H}_k} + \mathcal{L}_\mathcal{G} + \mathcal{L}_\mathcal{S} + \frac{\delta}{2}(\|\hat{\mathbf{Z}}^x - \tilde{\mathbf{Z}}^x + \rho^{zx}\|_2^2 + \|\hat{\mathbf{Z}}^y - \tilde{\mathbf{Z}}^y + \rho^{zy}\|_2^2)$

  end for

  $\arg\min_{\tilde{\mathbf{Z}}^x,\tilde{\mathbf{Z}}^y} \|\tilde{\mathbf{Z}}^x\|_1 + \|\tilde{\mathbf{Z}}^Y\|_1 + \frac{N\delta}{2}(\|\hat{\mathbf{Z}}^x - \tilde{\mathbf{Z}}^x - \bar{\rho}^{zx}\|_2^2 + \|\hat{\mathbf{Z}}^y - \tilde{\mathbf{Z}}^y - \bar{\rho}^{zy}\|_2^2)$

  for $i = 1$ to B **do**

    $\rho^{zx\prime} = \rho^{zx} + \hat{\mathbf{Z}}^x - \tilde{\mathbf{Z}}^x, \rho^{zy\prime} = \rho^{zy} + \hat{\mathbf{Z}}^y - \tilde{\mathbf{Z}}^y$

  end for

end while

Output: $\mathbf{Z}^x$, $\mathbf{Z}^y$, $\mathbf{P}$

where $\tilde{\mathbf{F}}$ means the shared global variable introduced as the slack variable which is subjected to $\mathbf{F} - \tilde{\mathbf{F}} = 0$. Then the optimization with respect to Eq. (8) can be solved by the ADMM strategy derived from the augmented Lagrangian (Lagrange multiplier ρ) with respect to other variables, yielding Algorithm 1.

Z-Step Subproblem: Alternatively, we optimize the layered convolutional least squares with the corresponding filters and other regularization. The subproblem of learning convolutional sparse feature maps then can be written as:

$$\begin{aligned}\min_{f,\mathcal{L}_\mathcal{P},\mathcal{L}_\mathcal{G},\mathcal{L}_\mathcal{S}} \max_k & f(\hat{\mathbf{Z}}^{x,|l|}, \mathbf{F}^{x,|l|}, \lambda) + f(\hat{\mathbf{Z}}^{y,|l|}, \mathbf{F}^{y,|l|}, \lambda) + \||\mathbf{A}|^{x,|l|} - |\mathbf{A}|^{y,|l|}\|_F^2 \\ & + \gamma\left\|\mathbb{E}_{p(\mathbf{x})}[\mathbf{Z}'^{x,|l|}] - \mathbb{E}_{p(\mathbf{y})}[\mathbf{Z}'^{y,|l|}]\right\|_{\mathcal{H}_k}^2 + \|\mathbf{Z}^{x,|l|} - \mathbf{P}^{|l|}\mathbf{Z}^{y,|l|}\|_F^2 \\ & + \alpha\|\mathbf{P}^{|l|}\|_F^2 + \mathrm{Tr}(\mathbf{Z}'^{x,|l|}\mathcal{G}^{x,|l|}\mathbf{Z}'^{x,|l|^T} + \mathbf{Z}'^{y,|l|}\mathcal{G}^{y,|l|}\mathbf{Z}'^{y,|l|^T}).\end{aligned} \tag{9}$$

Like the subproblem of **F**-step, **Z** can be learned in a similar fashion by taking the form of Tikhonov-regularized least squares [19] and facilitating vector-wise manipulations. Through coordinate descent, we derive the **Z**-step subproblem in Algorithm 2.

P-Step Subproblem: Updating the projection matrix, which is only associated with **P**, can be incorporated into the optimization process as:

$$\arg\min_{\mathbf{P}} \|\mathbf{Z}^{x,|l|} - \mathbf{P}^{|l|}\mathbf{Z}^{y,|l|}\|_F^2 + \alpha\|\mathbf{P}^{|l|}\|_F^2. \tag{10}$$

5 Experiments

5.1 Network Architecture

We take the architecture proposed in [11] as the backbone, and construct a nine-layer TransCSCN constrained by different regularizers. All brain volumes

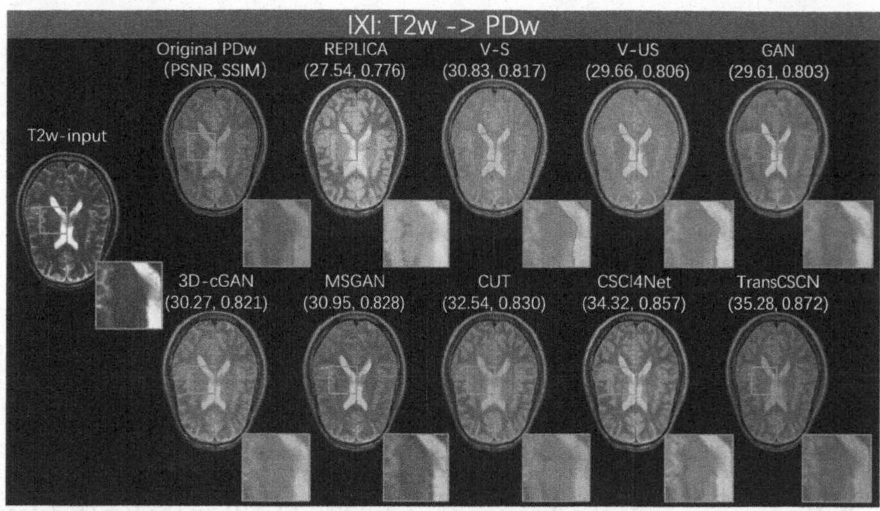

Fig. 2. Visual comparisons of different methods for T2w→PDw on the IXI dataset [1].

are split to 2D slices, and the spatial subsampling operation is fulfilled by our layerwise TransCSCN with a stride of 2 in the last two bottleneck layers, while batch normalization is incorporated after each layer to facilitate the convergence, and the last layer is followed by a global average pooling layer. We train the network for a total of 200 epochs using the Adam solver with a learning rate of 0.0002 and a batch size of 32. The other parameters are set as $\lambda = 0.2$, $\alpha = 0.15$, $\gamma = 1$, and the layered MK-MMD with Gaussian kernels have bandwidths equipped as median pairwise squared distances.

5.2 Experimental Setup

We validate our method on two public multi-modality brain datasets, *viz.* IXI[1] and BraTS[2] databsets, respectively. The IXI dataset involves 578 healthy subjects each imaged using a matrix of $256 \times 256 \times v$ ($v = 112 \sim 136$) scanned from three hospitals (Hammer Smith Hospital, Guy's Hospital, and Institute of Psychiatry) by different Magnetic Resonance Imaging (MRI) systems (Philips and GE). The BraTS dataset, instead, provides multi-modal brain tumor subjects, contributing 225 valid cases. It is worth noting that our experiments are relatively comprehensive since both healthy subjects and pathological data are covered. To be specific, we adopt Proton Density weighted (PDw) and T2w MRI scans (with significant difference) from the IXI dataset, and T1w and Fluid Attenuated Inversion Recovery (FLAIR) acquisitions (with significant difference) from the BraTS dataset. Physically, PDw data recognizes fluid and fat; T2w data reflects intermediate-bright fat and bright fluid; T1w data provides good contrast between Gray Matter (GM) and White Matter (WM); FLAIR data exhibits

[1] https://brain-development.org/ixi-dataset/.
[2] https://www.med.upenn.edu/sbia/brats2018/data.html.

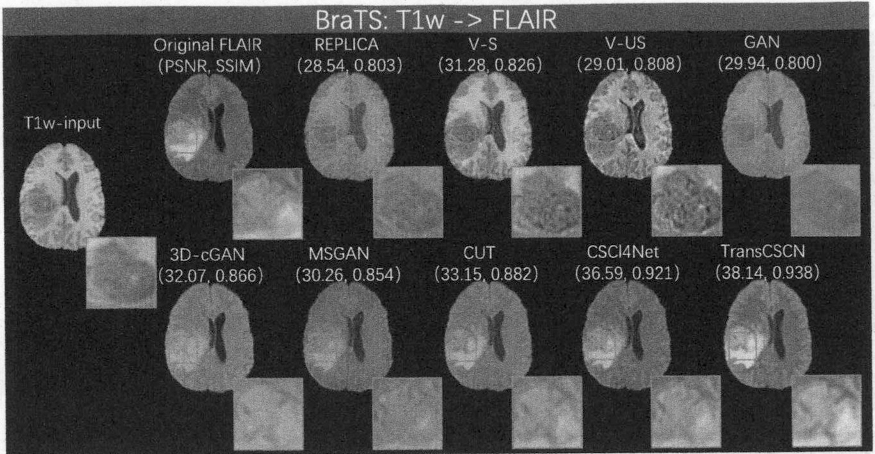

Fig. 3. Visual comparisons of different methods for T1→FLAIR on the BraTS dataset [25].

brighter GM than WM and Cerebrospinal Fluid (CSF) is dark, instead of bright. The conducted evaluations are divided into two parts, resulting in four tasks: (1) generating T2-w images from PD-w acquisitions and *vice versa* on the IXI dataset; (2) synthesizing FLAIR data from T1w images and *vice versa* on the BraTS dataset. We fix the number of test cases, *i.e.*, 80 for the IXI and 45 for the BraTS, respectively, and select 60 samples from the IXI and 20 samples from the BraTS for our validation. We construct the fully unsupervised training data with 219 unpaired PDw & T2w MRI for the IXI and 80 unpaired T2w & FLAIR MRI for the BraTS, respectively, after discarding half of the data pairs. The hyper-parameters of TransCSCN are tuned on our validation set. In addition to the visual effort, the anatomical accuracy needs equal attention. To this end, we calculate the segmentation results of the synthesized data and compare with their ground truths.[3] Both real scans and the synthesized results are fed into the segmentation tool, *i.e.*, FMRIB software library (FSL[4] [16]) to segment major tissue classes (GM, WM, and CSF) of brain, and the yielded results are averagely shown for each brain volume. The tissue prior probability templates are based on averaged multiple automatic segmentation in standard space from the IXI and BraTS datasets, respectively. The evaluation criteria include PSNR, SSIM and Dice score to quantitatively assess the quality of the synthesized results.

5.3 Comparison Methods

We compare our results against several state-of-the-art cross-modality synthesis algorithms including REPLICA [17], V-S and V-US [33], GAN [9], 3D-cGAN [27],

[3] Ground truths are calculated through a well-known segmentation tool on the real scans.

[4] https://fsl.fmrib.ox.ac.uk/fsl/fslwiki/.

Table 1. Quantitative evaluation of the quality of synthesized images using different methods on the IXI [1] and BraTS [25] datasets.

Metric (avg.)	REPLICA	V-S	V-US	GAN	3D-cGAN	MSGAN	CUT	CSCℓ_4Net	TransCSCN	Improvements ↑
IXI: T2w → PDw										
PSNR (dB)	*31.27*	33.87	32.99	32.25	32.76	32.98	34.06	36.64	**37.18**	0.54∼5.91
SSIM	*0.807*	0.851	0.836	0.831	0.851	0.856	0.876	0.900	**0.904**	0.004∼0.097
Dice (in %)	70.33	68.35	68.02	*66.52*	75.94	72.55	75.64	80.73	**82.03**	1.3∼15.51
IXI: PDw → T2w										
PSNR (dB)	*32.27*	34.28	32.87	33.46	35.08	35.63	36.97	38.08	**39.14**	1.06∼6.87
SSIM	*0.865*	0.919	0.902	0.901	0.899	0.899	0.910	0.959	**0.960**	0.002∼0.095
Dice (in %)	76.13	70.33	*69.66*	69.74	80.25	80.01	82.13	87.62	**88.59**	0.97∼18.93
BraTS: T1w → FLAIR										
PSNR (dB)	*31.60*	32.07	31.85	32.47	33.92	31.85	34.36	37.36	**39.12**	1.76∼7.52
SSIM	*0.811*	0.842	0.833	0.835	0.880	0.870	0.902	0.935	**0.943**	0.008∼0.131
Dice (in %)	70.92	69.89	69.44	*69.26*	73.94	74.02	78.92	84.07	**85.68**	1.61∼16.42
BraTS: FLAIR → T1w										
PSNR (dB)	*31.65*	33.00	31.80	31.93	32.89	33.72	34.96	36.51	**37.44**	0.93∼5.79
SSIM	*0.825*	0.857	0.842	0.847	0.881	0.860	0.887	0.911	**0.924**	0.013∼0.099
Dice (in %)	72.01	70.23	69.90	*69.62*	78.89	77.00	80.06	82.58	**84.02**	1.44∼12.01

MSGAN [24], CUT [28], and CSCℓ_4Net [15]. Note that REPLICA, V-S, GAN and MSGAN are the supervised methods, and we follow the defined rule and input paired data for their training. Others are all unsupervised approaches, thus we input our manually selected unpaired images for training. Moreover, following [17,27,33], the brain MRI scans are bias-field corrected. For fair comparison, we empirically set all methods following the recommended bias correction to obtain the best performance. Except for outer comparison, we also provide the ablation study for measuring the impact of each proposed penalization term.

5.4 Empirical Analysis

We evaluate both visual quality and segmentation performance of the synthesized data, and show the quantitative results along with others. The generality of our TransCSCN is explored by testing on many tasks distributed in two independent datasets with consistent property. Specifically, we demonstrate both visual and quantitative results in Figs. 2 and 3 and Table 1, respectively. The visual measurements are shown as the average value of the synthesis performance by PSNR and SSIM. The averaged segmentation results (referred as Dice score) potentially reflect the anatomical significance. In Figs. 2 and 3, we show two sets of synthesized results by different methods and the corresponding ground truths. We found that our method can generate more realistic results with well approximated appearance and better quantitative outcomes. Table 1 demonstrates the summarized performance between TransCSCN and other compared methods over different datasets on different tasks. The last row of Table 1 shows the performance boost over the worst compared results and the best compared results, respectively. In particular, TransCSCN consistently outperforms all advanced approaches and significantly boosts the performances especially

Table 2. Our comprehensive ablation study shows the effects of each proposed regularization on the IXI dataset [1] for T2w → PDw task, and on the BraTS dataset [25] for T1w → FLAIR task.

IXI: T2w → PDw							
CSCNet	GN	$\mathcal{L}_{\mathcal{H}_k}$	$\mathcal{L}_{\mathcal{G}}$	$\mathcal{L}_{\mathcal{S}}$	PSNR (dB)	SSIM	Dice (%)
✓					32.57	0.845	70.71
✓	✓				34.11	0.852	74.54
✓		✓			34.92	0.851	74.76
✓			✓		33.98	0.858	77.23
✓				✓	34.19	0.857	75.60
✓	✓	✓			36.09	0.881	78.03
✓	✓		✓		36.07	0.878	79.63
✓	✓			✓	36.05	0.861	79.62
✓		✓	✓		36.08	0.873	79.78
✓		✓		✓	36.05	0.879	79.82
✓			✓	✓	35.88	0.870	78.89
✓	✓	✓	✓		36.64	0.894	81.25
✓	✓	✓		✓	36.52	0.889	81.29
✓		✓	✓	✓	36.21	0.882	80.34
✓	✓	✓	✓	✓	**37.18**	**0.904**	**82.03**

BraTS: T1w → FLAIR							
CSCNet	GN	$\mathcal{L}_{\mathcal{H}_k}$	$\mathcal{L}_{\mathcal{G}}$	$\mathcal{L}_{\mathcal{S}}$	PSNR (dB)	SSIM	Dice (%)
✓					30.08	0.806	64.19
✓	✓				31.67	0.836	71.08
✓		✓			33.94	0.872	72.33
✓			✓		32.83	0.866	75.06
✓				✓	34.12	0.872	75.82
✓	✓	✓			36.30	0.895	78.23
✓	✓		✓		36.08	0.901	80.23
✓	✓			✓	37.35	0.922	81.66
✓		✓	✓		37.89	0.922	81.87
✓		✓		✓	37.87	0.921	81.58
✓			✓	✓	36.75	0.920	81.29
✓	✓	✓	✓		38.64	0.933	83.83
✓	✓	✓		✓	38.59	0.932	83.29
✓		✓	✓	✓	37.96	0.929	82.03
✓	✓	✓	✓	✓	**39.12**	**0.943**	**85.68**

in the experiments "T1-w → FLAIR" on the BraTS dataset. Our best case achieves 7.52dB (in PSNR) and 0.131 (in SSIM) improvements over the worst one (REPLICA), while the performance of segmentation is boosted by 16.42% compared to the worst baseline (GAN). We notice that REPLICA generates visually weaker results but plausible segmentation results. Instead, the appearance quality of GAN seems slightly better than REPLICA, but getting the worst Dice overlap. We also investigate the variants of our models to explore effectiveness of each module. For the T1w → FLAIR experiments on the BraTS, we separately adopt GN, $\mathcal{L}_{\mathcal{H}_k}$, $\mathcal{L}_{\mathcal{G}}$, $\mathcal{L}_{\mathcal{S}}$ and freely combine them upon the baseline CSCNet to investigate the effects in terms of image quality and their segmentation performance, where the detailed results are shown in Table 2 as our comprehensive ablation study (GN means global normalization). We observe that with the assistance of $\mathcal{L}_{\mathcal{H}_k}$, $\mathcal{L}_{\mathcal{G}}$, $\mathcal{L}_{\mathcal{H}_k}$ and $\mathcal{L}_{\mathcal{S}}$, both visual and segmentation results are improved greatly. The appearance score is sensitive to $\mathcal{L}_{\mathcal{G}}$, while the Dice overlap is sensitive to $\mathcal{L}_{\mathcal{G}}$ and $\mathcal{L}_{\mathcal{S}}$.

6 Conclusions

In this paper, we proposed a transferable convolutional sparse coding network for generalizing brain image synthesis task. The proposed method delves into the feature representations that jointly learns the cross-domain transferable features while taking the benefits of both deeper mining and optimal regularization. With the globally normalized convolutional sparse coding net, we exploited the domain discrepancy metric, Laplacian co-regularization, and subspace mismatch penalization for minimizing the domain divergence, preserving the local geometries, and reducing the generalization errors. TransCSCN was evaluated on different datasets, and showed promising results outperforming a number of recent approaches consistently. In future work, we plan to explore the performance of TransCSCN on other medical image processing tasks such as confronting artifacts.

References

1. IXI – Information eXtraction from Images. https://brain-development.org/ixi-dataset/
2. Arar, M., Ginger, Y., Danon, D., Bermano, A.H., Cohen-Or, D.: Unsupervised multi-modal image registration via geometry preserving image-to-image translation. In: IEEE CVPR, pp. 13410–13419 (2020)
3. Beck, A., Teboulle, M.: A fast iterative shrinkage-thresholding algorithm for linear inverse problems. SIAM J. Imaging Sci. **2**(1), 183–202 (2009)
4. Boyd, S., Parikh, N., Chu, E., Peleato, B., Eckstein, J., et al.: Distributed optimization and statistical learning via the alternating direction method of multipliers. Found. Trends® Mach. Learn. **3**(1), 1–122 (2011)
5. Bristow, H., Eriksson, A., Lucey, S.: Fast convolutional sparse coding. In: IEEE CVPR. pp. 391–398 (2013)
6. Choudhury, B., Swanson, R., Heide, F., Wetzstein, G., Heidrich, W.: Consensus convolutional sparse coding. In: IEEE ICCV, pp. 4280–4288 (2017)
7. Efros, A.A., Freeman, W.T.: Image quilting for texture synthesis and transfer. In: SIGGRAPH. pp. 341–346 (2001)
8. Goodfellow, I., Bengio, Y., Courville, A.: Deep Learning. MIT Press, Cambridge (2016)
9. Goodfellow, I., et al.: Generative adversarial networks. Commun. ACM **63**(11), 139–144 (2020)
10. Gretton, A., Borgwardt, K., Rasch, M.J., Scholkopf, B., Smola, A.J.: A kernel method for the two-sample problem. arXiv preprint arXiv:0805.2368 (2008)
11. He, K., Zhang, X., Ren, S., Sun, J.: Deep residual learning for image recognition. In: IEEE CVPR, pp. 770–778 (2016)
12. Heide, F., Heidrich, W., Wetzstein, G.: Fast and flexible convolutional sparse coding. In: IEEE CVPR, pp. 5135–5143 (2015)
13. Huang, Y., Shao, L., Frangi, A.F.: DOTE: dual cOnvolutional filTer lEarning for super-resolution and cross-modality synthesis in MRI. In: Descoteaux, M., Maier-Hein, L., Franz, A., Jannin, P., Collins, D.L., Duchesne, S. (eds.) MICCAI 2017. LNCS, vol. 10435, pp. 89–98. Springer, Cham (2017). https://doi.org/10.1007/978-3-319-66179-7_11
14. Huang, Y., Shao, L., Frangi, A.F.: Simultaneous super-resolution and cross-modality synthesis of 3D medical images using weakly-supervised joint convolutional sparse coding. In: IEEE CVPR, pp. 6070–6079 (2017)
15. Huang, Y., Zheng, F., Wang, D., Huang, W., Scott, M.R., Shao, L.: Brain image synthesis with unsupervised multivariate canonical CSCl4Net. In: IEEE CVPR, pp. 5881–5890 (2021)
16. Jenkinson, M., Beckmann, C.F., Behrens, T.E., Woolrich, M.W., Smith, S.M.: FSL. Neuroimage **62**(2), 782–790 (2012)
17. Jog, A., Carass, A., Roy, S., Pham, D.L., Prince, J.L.: Random forest regression for magnetic resonance image synthesis. MIA **35**, 475–488 (2017)
18. Johnson, J., Alahi, A., Fei-Fei, L.: Perceptual losses for real-time style transfer and super-resolution. In: Leibe, B., Matas, J., Sebe, N., Welling, M. (eds.) ECCV 2016. LNCS, vol. 9906, pp. 694–711. Springer, Cham (2016). https://doi.org/10.1007/978-3-319-46475-6_43

19. Kempen, V., Vliet, V.: The influence of the regularization parameter and the first estimate on the performance of Tikhonov regularized non-linear image restoration algorithms. J. Microsc. **198**(1), 63–75 (2000)
20. LeCun, Y., Bengio, Y., Hinton, G.: Deep learning. Nature **521**(7553), 436–444 (2015)
21. Li, Y., Shen, L.: Skin lesion analysis towards melanoma detection using deep learning network. Sensors **18**(2), 556 (2018)
22. Li, Y., Yuan, L., Chen, Y., Wang, P., Vasconcelos, N.: Dynamic transfer for multi-source domain adaptation. In: IEEE CVPR, pp. 10998–11007 (2021)
23. Long, M., Cao, Y., Wang, J., Jordan, M.: Learning transferable features with deep adaptation networks. In: ICML, pp. 97–105. PMLR (2015)
24. Mao, Q., Lee, H.Y., Tseng, H.Y., Ma, S., Yang, M.H.: Mode seeking generative adversarial networks for diverse image synthesis. In: IEEE CVPR, pp. 1429–1437 (2019)
25. Menze, B.H., Jakab, A., Bauer, S., et al.: The multimodal brain tumor image segmentation benchmark (BraTS). IEEE TMI **34**(10), 1993–2024 (2015)
26. Mondal, A.K., Dolz, J., Desrosiers, C.: Few-shot 3D multi-modal medical image segmentation using generative adversarial learning. arXiv preprint arXiv:1810.12241 (2018)
27. Pan, Y., Liu, M., Lian, C., Zhou, T., Xia, Y., Shen, D.: Synthesizing missing PET from MRI with cycle-consistent generative adversarial networks for Alzheimer's disease diagnosis. In: Frangi, A.F., Schnabel, J.A., Davatzikos, C., Alberola-López, C., Fichtinger, G. (eds.) MICCAI 2018. LNCS, vol. 11072, pp. 455–463. Springer, Cham (2018). https://doi.org/10.1007/978-3-030-00931-1_52
28. Park, T., Efros, A.A., Zhang, R., Zhu, J.-Y.: Contrastive learning for unpaired image-to-image translation. In: Vedaldi, A., Bischof, H., Brox, T., Frahm, J.-M. (eds.) ECCV 2020. LNCS, vol. 12354, pp. 319–345. Springer, Cham (2020). https://doi.org/10.1007/978-3-030-58545-7_19
29. Qiu, Q., Patel, V.M., Turaga, P., Chellappa, R.: Domain adaptive dictionary learning. In: Fitzgibbon, A., Lazebnik, S., Perona, P., Sato, Y., Schmid, C. (eds.) ECCV 2012. LNCS, vol. 7575, pp. 631–645. Springer, Heidelberg (2012). https://doi.org/10.1007/978-3-642-33765-9_45
30. Rosenthal, M., Weeks, S., Aylward, S., Bullitt, E., Fuchs, H.: Intraoperative tracking of anatomical structures using fluoroscopy and a vascular balloon catheter. In: Niessen, W.J., Viergever, M.A. (eds.) MICCAI 2001. LNCS, vol. 2208, pp. 1253–1254. Springer, Heidelberg (2001). https://doi.org/10.1007/3-540-45468-3_183
31. Roy, S., Carass, A., Prince, J.L.: Magnetic resonance image example-based contrast synthesis. IEEE TMI **32**(12), 2348–2363 (2013)
32. Van Loan, C.F., Golub, G.: Matrix computations (Johns Hopkins studies in mathematical sciences) (1996)
33. Vemulapalli, R., Van Nguyen, H., Zhou, S.K.: Unsupervised cross-modal synthesis of subject-specific scans. In: IEEE ICCV, pp. 630–638 (2015)
34. Wang, H., Li, Y., He, N., Ma, K., Meng, D., Zheng, Y.: DICDNet: deep interpretable convolutional dictionary network for metal artifact reduction in CT images. IEEE TMI **41**(4), 869–880 (2021)
35. Yang, J., Wright, J., Huang, T.S., Ma, Y.: Image super-resolution via sparse representation. IEEE TIP **19**(11), 2861–2873 (2010)
36. Yang, L., Balaji, Y., Lim, S.-N., Shrivastava, A.: Curriculum manager for source selection in multi-source domain adaptation. In: Vedaldi, A., Bischof, H., Brox, T., Frahm, J.-M. (eds.) ECCV 2020. LNCS, vol. 12359, pp. 608–624. Springer, Cham (2020). https://doi.org/10.1007/978-3-030-58568-6_36

37. Zeiler, M.D., Krishnan, D., Taylor, G.W., Fergus, R.: Deconvolutional networks. In: IEEE CVPR, pp. 2528–2535. IEEE (2010)
38. Zhang, H., Mao, H., Long, Y., Yang, W., Shao, L.: A probabilistic zero-shot learning method via latent nonnegative prototype synthesis of unseen classes. IEEE Trans. Neural Netw. Learn Syst. **31**(7), 2361–2375 (2019)
39. Zheng, M., et al.: Graph regularized sparse coding for image representation. IEEE TIP **20**(5), 1327–1336 (2010)
40. Zhong, E., Fan, W., Yang, Q., Verscheure, O., Ren, J.: Cross validation framework to choose amongst models and datasets for transfer learning. In: Balcázar, J.L., Bonchi, F., Gionis, A., Sebag, M. (eds.) ECML PKDD 2010. LNCS (LNAI), vol. 6323, pp. 547–562. Springer, Heidelberg (2010). https://doi.org/10.1007/978-3-642-15939-8_35
41. Zhu, J.-Y., Krähenbühl, P., Shechtman, E., Efros, A.A.: Generative visual manipulation on the natural image manifold. In: Leibe, B., Matas, J., Sebe, N., Welling, M. (eds.) ECCV 2016. LNCS, vol. 9909, pp. 597–613. Springer, Cham (2016). https://doi.org/10.1007/978-3-319-46454-1_36
42. Zhu, J.Y., Park, T., Isola, P., Efros, A.A.: Unpaired image-to-image translation using cycle-consistent adversarial networks. In: IEEE ICCV, pp. 2223–2232 (2017)

Incomplete Multi-view Domain Adaptation via Channel Enhancement and Knowledge Transfer

Haifeng Xia[1](✉), Pu Wang[2], and Zhengming Ding[1]

[1] Department of Computer Science, Tulane University, New Orleans, USA
{hxia,zding1}@tulane.edu

[2] Mitsubishi Electric Research Laboratories, Cambridge, USA
pwany@merl.com

Abstract. Unsupervised domain adaptation (UDA) borrows well-labeled source knowledge to solve the specific task on unlabeled target domain with the assumption that both domains are from a single sensor, e.g., RGB or depth images. To boost model performance, multiple sensors are deployemd on new-produced devices like autonomous vehicles to benefit from enriched information. However, the model trained with multi-view data difficultly becomes compatible with conventional devices only with a single sensor. This scenario is defined as incomplete multi-view domain adaptation (**IMVDA**), which considers that the source domain consists of multi-view data while the target domain only includes single-view instances. To overcome this practical demand, this paper proposes a novel Channel Enhancement and Knowledge Transfer (**CEKT**) framework with two modules. Concretely, the source channel enhancement module distinguishes view-common from view-specific channels and explores channel similarity to magnify the representation of important channels. Moreover, the adaptive knowledge transfer module attempts to enhance target representation towards multi-view semantic through implicit missing view recovery and adaptive cross-domain alignment. Extensive experimental results illustrate the effectiveness of our method in solving the IMVDA challenge.

Keywords: Multi-view fusion · Domain adaptation

1 Introduction

Deep neural network (DNN) recently becomes the dominate technique in computer vision community due to its success on the real-world applications such as image classification [20,49,49], object detection [38] and image segmentation [13,33]. As a data-driven learning strategy, DNN generally requires considerable training samples with high-quality annotations to capture the intrinsic semantic knowledge. However, the data collection and manual annotation tend to be expensive and time-consuming [4,19,46]. To benefit from external resources,

S. Avidan et al. (Eds.): ECCV 2022, LNCS 13694, pp. 200–217, 2022.
https://doi.org/10.1007/978-3-031-19830-4_12

recent solutions pay more attentions to transfer learning, especially for unsupervised domain adaptation (UDA) [2,6,21,36].

UDA aims to transfer well-supervised source knowledge to assist the specific tasks in target domain without any annotation information [29,44]. However, data collection typically occurring in varying environments easily triggers the significant distribution discrepancy across source and target samples [12,45]. The main challenge of UDA is how to learn domain-invariant feature representations. Along with this direction, the UDA algorithms mainly explore metric-based scheme and adversarial training fashion. Specifically, one of the classical and effective metric-based strategies transforms target samples into source latent space and explore their sample-wise association to eliminate domain mismatch [1]. However, the alignment method needs to observe all data to accurately estimate the relation of source and target instances, which difficultly adjusts to the mini-batch training manner in DNN. In addition, the basic UDA setting considers that the images of source and target domain are merely captured by one sensor. But the practical application always deploys multiple sensors such as the autonomous vehicle to obtain more sufficient information to boost the model performance.

A few efforts [5,16] have explored multi-view domain adaptation (MVDA), where source and target data are both collected from multiple sensors. The intuitive idea is to convert MVDA into a UDA problem by independently aligning source and target instances within each view and fusing multi-view semantic information within individual domain. They have achieved promising performance on solving MVDA and abundant empirical studies illustrate that the simple alignment-and-fusion promotes model performance on identifying target samples with more enriched data collected by multiple sensors. However, equipment rehabilitation to upgrade previous single-sensor devices with multiple sensors causes additional cost overhead, which makes MVDA to be invalid for several practical application scenarios. Instead, we post a question that *"Can we develop more effective domain adaptation algorithms to benefit single-sensor target data from enriched source data with multiple sensors?"*. This problem is defined as incomplete multi-view domain adaptation (**IMVDA**), where there are multi-view complete data in source domain, while single-view instances in target domain. This problem is under insufficient exploration in the literature.

To overcome IMVDA challenge, we propose a novel method named Channel Enhancement and Knowledge Transfer (**CEKT**) shown in Fig. 1, which not only conducts multi-view semantic fusion within source domain but also transfers the integrated knowledge for the use of target domain. Concretely, CEKT explores the sparse attribution of channel to distinguish view-common from view-specific feature maps and exchanges view-specific channels across multiple views to fuse their semantic information. Furthermore, we develop a metric of channel similarity to highlight the representation of significant channels, which assists model learning with more discriminative features. Moreover, we introduce a parallel target model taking source and target samples from the same view as input. The source model trained in the first step teaches the target model to produce

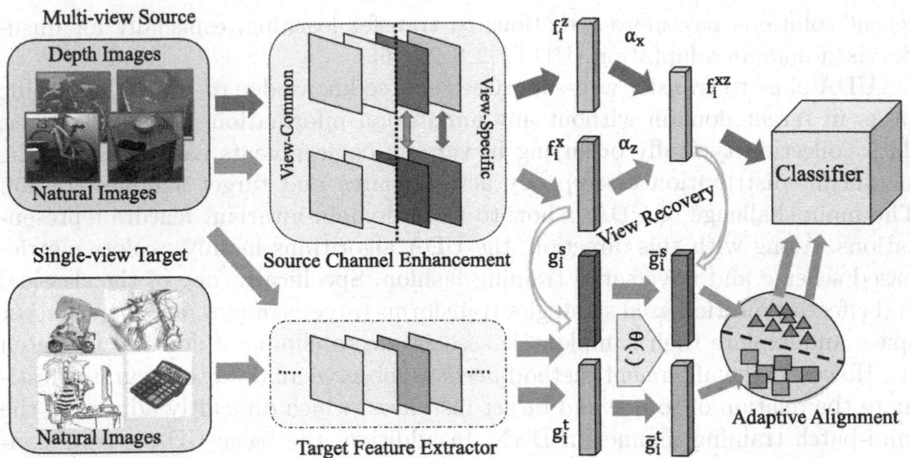

Fig. 1. Overview of our channel enhancement and knowledge transfer framework (CEKT) for incomplete multi-view domain adaptation (IMVDA). Specifically, the source channel enhancement module distinguishes view-common from view-specific channels and explores the channel similarity to emphasis essential representation. The source triggered missing view recovery teaches target model how to generate multi-view knowledge. And the adaptive alignment module aims to eliminate domain mismatch within the identical subspace.

multi-view semantic only with single view data. In addition, we propose a novel adaptive subspace alignment to gradually mitigate domain discrepancy in an end-to-end training manner. To sum up, the main contributions of this work are highlighted in three folds:

- First, our proposed CEKT introduces a novel channel enhancement mechanism to preserve considerable view-common semantic knowledge and exchange view-specific semantic to enrich the representation of each view. This module not only effectively achieves feature fusion but also emphasizes more discriminative features for the classification task.
- Second, the adaptive knowledge transfer module explores the supervision of source model to supervise the target model to approximate multi-view semantic information, which mitigates the negative influence of missing view on target domain. Simultaneously, we present a novel adaptive subspace alignment method to learn domain-invariant representations.
- Finally, we exploit many public-available real-world image datasets to imitate the IMVDA scenario and conduct abundant experiments to evaluate the performance of our CEKT. The corresponding experimental results and analysis fully demonstrate the effectiveness of our method.

2 Related Work

2.1 Domain Adaptation

Unsupervised domain adaptation (UDA) aims to borrow well-supervised source knowledge to assist the target learning without any label information [6,44,46]. And source and target instances belong to different distributions, yet share the identical label space [34]. The core task of UDA is to learn domain-invariant representations by gradually eliminating distribution mismatch. The mainstream learning mechanisms are considered as two types. One is metric-based alignment [32] which enforces source and target domains to share the identical statistics (e.g. mean and co-variance) and transform target samples into the source subspace via the estimation of cross-domain sample-wise association [1]. Another mature exploration adopts generative adversarial game between feature generator and discrimination to mitigate domain mismatch in latent feature space. In addition, [14] extends the conventional UDA by introducing more source domains to improve model generalization, which is named multi-source domain adaptation (MSDA). Similar with UDA based methods, [37] deploys multiple discriminators for arbitrary one source and target domains to independently achieve distribution alignment. However, the above problems generally assume that the instances per domain are captured with only one sensor, which prevents the development of technique. To improve model performance, abundant devices as autonomous vehicles are installed with multiple sensors to comprehensively perceive the open world. Thus, this work explores a practical and challenging IMVDA scenario, where source data are collected from multiple sensors while target samples are captured by the single sensor.

2.2 Multi-view Learning

Multi-view learning expects to access sufficient semantics via the joint utilization of multiple data sets [5,30,52]. Extensive empirical studies show significant performance improvement on object classification tasks [48,50] by using multiview data. The intuitive learning strategy is to discover the consistent hypothesis space across various views [22]. Specifically, [47] adopts a co-regularization manner to compress the search space of hypothesis function. Similarly, [28] presents an efficient dictionary learning and [24] utilizes a large-margin Gaussian process to find the intrinsic basis across multiple views. In addition, the clustering technique is introduced to discover complementary semantic knowledge from different views [43]. And the multi-view spectral embedding is developed to integrate feature representation. Although these multi-view methods produce positive effect given complete views, they assume the multi-view samples are from the identical distribution, which is not the case for the real-world applications. Instead, we not only consider multi-view knowledge fusion but also conduct simple yet effective knowledge transfer across multiple domains to address the IMVDA problem.

3 Proposed Method

3.1 Preliminary and Motivation

Formally for the IMVDA problem, we are given the well-annotated source domain with enriched views[1] as $\mathcal{D}_s = \{(\mathbf{x}_i^s, \mathbf{z}_i^s, y_i)\}_{i=1}^{n_s}$ and the unlabeled target domain with only single view as $\mathcal{D}_t = \{\mathbf{x}_i^t\}_{i=1}^{n_t}$, where $\mathbf{x}$ and $\mathbf{z}$ denote two view-paired samples, y represents the corresponding source label, and n_s and n_t are the number of source and target samples, respectively. The goal of IMVDA is to transfer the enriched view information and well-annotated label information in the source domain to improve the single-view target recognition.

Therefore, two-fold challenges should be considered: 1) How to effectively integrate multi-view semantics to boost performance of model, and 2) How to transfer knowledge from multi-view source domain to single view target one. To address these questions, we propose a novel solution named Channel Enhancement and Knowledge Transfer (CEKT) framework as Fig. 1. Concretely, CEKT involves two components, i.e., a source channel enhanced network and an adaptive knowledge transfer network. The former one aims to distinguish view-common channels from view-specific channels where semantic fusion occurs and exploit cross-view channel similarity to enhance the representation of necessary channels. The latter one attempts to adaptively learn a target-to-source projection to mitigate the domain mismatch.

3.2 Source Channel Enhanced Network

Cross-View Channel Enhancement. Batch normalization (BN) [17] is widely used in deep neural networks to scale the hidden features of the specific layer to accelerate convergence and avoid the model collapse as:

$$\hat{h}_c = \gamma_c \frac{(h_c - \mu_c)}{\sqrt{\sigma_c^2 + \epsilon}} + \beta_c, \tag{1}$$

where h_c, $\hat{h}_c$ mean the input and output of the BN module, μ_c, σ_c are the mean and variance of the c-th channel, and γ_c, β_c are trainable parameters. However, from the perspective of channel exchange [43], the model training gradually neglects the representation of task-irrelevant channels as $\gamma_c \to 0$, and multi-view data cause the channels $(h_{x,c}, h_{z,c})$ from $(\mathbf{x}^s, \mathbf{z}^s)$ to be activated differently. Then, Wang et. al. proposed channel exchange for two views to compensate each other as [43]:

$$\hat{h}_{x/z,c} = \gamma_{z/x,c} \frac{(h_{z/x,c} - \mu_{z/x,c})}{\sqrt{\sigma_{z/x,c}^2 + \epsilon}} + \beta_{z/x,c}, \quad \text{if} \quad \gamma_{x/z,c} < \delta, \tag{2}$$

[1] This paper considers the case that the source domain contains two views while target domain includes only single view.

where δ is an adjustable threshold, and a sparse regularization term $\sum_{c=1}^{C} |\gamma_{x/z,c}|$ is introduced to encourage more channel exchanges. Such channel exchange totally relies on the learned $\gamma_{x/z,c}$, which makes channel exchange in an unsupervised fashion without considering sharing channels across views.

Thus, we develop a Cross-view Channel Enhancement (C^{2}E) module. Specifically, for one concrete layer, all channels are divided into two groups: view-common channels and view-specific ones. Under this condition, we suppose view-common channels tend to involve considerable shared semantics, where the corresponding parameters $\gamma_{x/z,c}$ should be compact rather than sparse, and view-specific channels carry the unique information for each view and should be exchanged and enhanced. With this consideration, the ℓ_1-norm over the parameters is a promising manner to highlight the difference across view-specific channels. In implementation, we consider the first half of all feature maps as the view-common channels and the remaining ones as view-specific parts. Thus, we adopt the following constraint for parameters $\gamma_{x/z}$ as:

$$\min_{\gamma_{l,c}} \mathcal{L}_\gamma = \sum_{l=1}^{L} \left(\sum_{c=1}^{\lfloor C/2 \rfloor} \gamma_{l,c}^2 + \sum_{c=\lfloor C/2 \rfloor}^{C} |\gamma_{l,c}| \right), \tag{3}$$

where we omit the superscript (x, z) for convenience, C and $\lfloor C/2 \rfloor$ mean the number of channel and the rounding or flooring operation, and L is the number of network layers attached with the BN module. It is worth noting that only the view-specific channels participate in the channel exchange via Eq. (2). Through the above strategy, we not only achieve feature fusion but also preserve as much view-common semantics as possible. Hence, $\gamma_{x/z,c} \geq \delta$ illustrates that this channel can contribute to the classification task.

To further enhance the channels shared across views, we propose a strategy to identify those channels and amplify their presence during batch normalization. As two views data present the identical content in various forms, their representations to the necessary information such as the contour of object tend to be similar or even consistent. In other words, the c-th channel with a high similarity across two views should be considered as an important component with a high confidence. Thus, the similarity (s_c) of two views at channel c is defined as:

$$s_c = \frac{\exp(-\|\mu_{x,c} - \mu_{z,c}\|_2/\eta)}{\sum_{c=1}^{C} \exp(-\|\mu_{x,c} - \mu_{z,c}\|_2/\eta)}, \tag{4}$$

where $\sum_c s_c = 1$ and η controls the change of scale. Then, we first adjust the importance of channel with $\hat{h}_{x/z,c} = (1 + s_c)\hat{h}_{x/z,c}$ before the channel exchange in Eq. (2). For instance, when the two channels are very different, corresponding s_c plays a small fraction of the similarity vector and, hence, the importance of the c-th channel is not augmented with a relatively small s_c.

Data-Dependant Cross-View Fusion. For now, our module is easily applied into most deep neural network $\mathcal{F}(\cdot)$ mapping the original image into the high-level features $\mathbf{f}_x = \mathcal{F}(\mathbf{x})$ or $\mathbf{f}_z = \mathcal{F}(\mathbf{z})$. To further learn robust features, we adopt a data-dependant fusion manner to obtain these high-level representations as:

$$\mathbf{f}_{xz} = \alpha_x \mathcal{F}(\mathbf{x}) + \alpha_z \mathcal{F}(\mathbf{z}), \tag{5}$$

where $\alpha_{x/z}$ are the probability score for two views and we plug in the softmax layer $\mathbf{s}(\cdot)$ to $\mathcal{F}(\mathbf{x})$ and $\mathcal{F}(\mathbf{z})$ to learn the data-dependant fusion weights.

Finally, the multi-class source classifier $\mathcal{C}(\cdot)$ takes the fused features as input to generate the prediction. The objective function for training the source model is formulated as:

$$\min_{\mathcal{F},\mathcal{C},\mathbf{s},\gamma} \mathcal{L}_s = \sum_{i=1}^{n_s} \mathcal{L}_c\Big(\mathcal{C}(\mathbf{f}_{xz}^i), y_i\Big) + \lambda_\gamma \mathcal{L}_\gamma, \tag{6}$$

where λ_γ is a trade-off parameter and $\mathcal{L}_c(\cdot,\cdot)$ is the classical cross-entropy loss.

3.3 Adaptive Knowledge Transfer Network

The target domain lacks one view and exists considerable distribution difference with source domain, which makes it unreasonable to directly identify target samples with multi-view source model. Thus, the current challenge is how to effectively transfer source fused knowledge to the target domain. Along with this direction, we construct a novel adaptive knowledge transfer network (AKT), whose core is to associate two domains with source view data x_i^s as the bridge. Concretely, we introduce an additional target network $\mathcal{G}(\cdot)$ with the same network architecture to source and the conventional BN module.

Source Triggered Missing View Recovery. To guide the target network with the ability for missing view, we allow source sample $\mathbf{x}_i^s$ and target sample $\mathbf{x}_j^t$ to pass through the target network $\mathcal{G}(\cdot)$ so that we can obtain the high-level features, i.e., $\mathbf{g}_i^s = \mathcal{G}(\mathbf{x}_i^s)$ and $\mathbf{g}_j^t = \mathcal{G}(\mathbf{x}_j^t)$. Following that, we deploy one dimensionality-identical full-connection layer with trainable parameter θ to obtain $\bar{\mathbf{g}}_i^s$ and $\bar{\mathbf{g}}_j^t$, which aims to recover the missing view information for the target network by mapping one view to two-view fused representation.

Since the target model does not directly touch $\mathbf{z}_i^s$, we expect to learn the fused semantic only with one source view data. As DNN manifests strong approximation capability by using the convolution layers and non-linear mapping [8], it fits better to the given target. Inspired by this observation, when accessing the fused representations with fixed source model, we make $\mathbf{g}_i^s$ and $\bar{\mathbf{g}}_i^s$ approximate $\mathbf{f}_x^i$ and $\mathbf{f}_{xz}^i$, respectively, to mimic the fused semantic features. Hence, we propose a source triggered missing view recovery term as:

$$\min_{\mathcal{G},\theta} \mathcal{L}_g = \sum_{i=1}^{n_s} \Big(\|\mathbf{g}_i^s - \mathbf{f}_x^i\|_2^2 + \|\bar{\mathbf{g}}_i^s - \mathbf{f}_{xz}^i\|_2^2\Big). \tag{7}$$

In this way, the source model teaches the target one to offset the absence of the other view. Moreover, as $\mathbf{x}^s$ and $\mathbf{x}^t$ belong to the same view, the imitative manner brings semantics of the other view to feature learning of target samples. Certainly, the significant domain shift across $\mathbf{x}^s$ and $\mathbf{x}^t$ obstructs the delivery of additional semantic knowledge to the target domain. Thus, the target model needs to achieve distribution alignment by gradually eliminating the cross-domain discrepancy.

Adaptive Cross-Domain Alignment. The direct alignment approach is first to transform all source and target instances into the shared latent space and then to reduce the sample-wise distance with the manifold theory. The formulation of this classical strategy [1] is:

$$\min_{\mathbf{A}^{st}} \|\bar{\mathbf{G}}^s - \mathbf{A}^{st}\bar{\mathbf{G}}^t\|_{\mathrm{F}}^2 + \Omega(\mathbf{A}^{st}), \tag{8}$$

where $\|\cdot\|_{\mathrm{F}}$ denotes the Frobenius norm, $\bar{\mathbf{G}}^{s/t}$ is the feature matrix of all samples $\bar{\mathbf{g}}_i^{s/t}$, and $\mathbf{A}^{st}$ is defined as the transformation matrix mapping target features into the source feature subspace, and $\Omega(\mathbf{A}^{st})$ denotes a regularization term over $\mathbf{A}^{st}$ such as the ℓ_2-norm or ℓ_1-norm. This strategy achieves promising performance on domain adaptation with shallow feature extractors [9]. However, the feature transformation requires simultaneous access to all samples, which the mini-batch training mechanism used in DNN hardly satisfies. Meanwhile, a direct computation of $\mathbf{A}^{st}$ within each mini-batch is unreasonable since the insufficient samples fail to accurately capture the association of samples. To break the bottleneck, we present an adaptive alignment solution involving two fully connected layers without bias terms. The features $\bar{\mathbf{g}}_i^s$ and $\bar{\mathbf{g}}_j^t$ are fed into it to calculate the similarity $\mathbf{A}_{ij}^{st}$ via:

$$\mathbf{A}_{ij}^{st} = \delta\Big(\langle W_s\bar{\mathbf{g}}_i^s, W_t\bar{\mathbf{g}}_j^t\rangle\Big), \tag{9}$$

where $W_{s/t}$ is the projection matrix, $\delta(\cdot)$ denotes an activation function such as ReLU, and $\langle\cdot,\cdot\rangle$ denotes the inner product operation. During the update of $W_{s/t}$, the inputs are fixed. As the model training, $W_{s/t}$ gradually learns the intrinsic distribution information of overall dataset and can accurately estimate the sample-wise relationship.

On the other hand, we can access to the category probability of sample with $\mathbf{p}_i^{s/t} = \mathcal{C}(\bar{\mathbf{g}}_i^{s/t})$. As $\mathbf{p}_i^{s/t}$ with more discriminative information can reflect the structural relation of hidden features via $\bar{\mathbf{A}}_{ij}^{st} = \langle\mathbf{p}_i^s, \mathbf{p}_j^t\rangle$, we propose the adaptive cross-domain alignment as:

$$\min_{\mathcal{G},\theta,W_{s/t}} \mathcal{L}_a = \|\bar{\mathbf{G}}^s - \mathbf{A}^{st}\bar{\mathbf{G}}^t\|_{\mathrm{F}}^2 + \|\mathbf{A}^{st} - \bar{\mathbf{A}}^{st}\|_{\ell_1}, \tag{10}$$

where $\|\cdot\|_{\ell_1}$ denotes the ℓ_1-norm. $\mathbf{A}^{st}$ and $\bar{\mathbf{A}}^{st}$ are normalized along the row dimension. According to the guidance of adaptive similarity $\mathbf{A}^{st}$, the source features can be represented by the similar ones in target domain, and Eq. (10) effectively reduces their divergence to mitigate the domain mismatch.

3.4 Overall Objective

We first finalize the objective function for the target model. To preserve abundant source knowledge, we adopt source annotations to supervise the target model training. Similar to [27], the pseudo labels of target samples are explored to make target features more discriminative. Specifically, for each epoch, the predictions of target samples (y_j^t) with the fixed target model are used to calculate the class centers, $\mathcal{O}_k = \frac{1}{n_k}\sum_{j=1}^{n_t}\mathbb{I}(y_j^t = k)\bar{\mathbf{g}}_j^t$, where n_k is the number of target samples from the k-th class and $\mathbb{I}(\cdot)$ is the indicator function. With the class centers, the K-means clustering is adopted to reassign the optimized labels $\hat{y}_j^t$ to target samples. The loss function to the target model is defined as:

$$\min_{\mathcal{G},\theta,\mathcal{C},W_{s/t}} \mathcal{L}_t = \mathcal{L}_c^s + \lambda_g\mathcal{L}_g + \lambda_\tau(\mathcal{L}_a + \mathcal{L}_c^t), \tag{11}$$

where $\mathcal{L}_c^s$ denotes source supervision loss as $\sum_{i=1}^{n_s}\mathcal{L}_c(\mathcal{C}(\bar{\mathbf{g}}_i^s), y_i^s)$, $\mathcal{L}_c^t$ denotes the pseudo target supervision loss as $\sum_{j=1}^{n_t}\mathcal{L}_c(\mathcal{C}(\bar{\mathbf{g}}_i^t), \hat{y}_j^t)$, and λ_g, λ_τ are trade-off parameters. To avoid the negative effect in the beginning, we define λ_τ as $\frac{1-\exp(-10\tau)}{1+\exp(-10\tau)}$ with the changing of epoch number (τ).

Then, for the overall training strategy, we adopt an iterative training manner to optimize both source and target networks. Concretely, Eq. (6) is used to optimize the parameters of source model with the fixed target network $\mathcal{G}(\cdot)$ and then we update target model via Eq. (11) with the frozen source network $\mathcal{F}(\cdot)$.

3.5 Theoretical Analysis

In Eq. (3), we adopt two different constraints on the scaling factors $\gamma_{l,c}$, which enable the network to **actively** learn view-specific and view-common knowledge in various channels, respectively. Similar with [42], we deduce the following theorem to explain why the $\sum_{c=\lfloor C/2\rfloor}^{C}|\gamma_{l,c}|$ can assist the model to capture view-specific information and the function of $\sum_{c=1}^{\lfloor C/2\rfloor}\gamma_{l,c}^2$.

Theorem 1. *The proposed $\sum_{c=\lfloor C/2\rfloor}^{C}|\gamma_{l,c}|$ will definitely make the corresponding scaling factors towards zero with the probability $2\Phi(\lambda_\gamma(\frac{\partial\mathcal{L}_c}{\partial h_c})^{-1}) - 1$, where the $\Phi(\cdot)$ denotes the cumulative probability of standard Gaussian. To be simple, the subscript l of $\gamma_{l,c}$ is mitigated.*

Proof. According to Eq. (6), it is straightforward to deduce the derivative of $\mathcal{L}_s$ with respect to $\gamma_c, c \in [C/2, C]$ as the following:

$$\frac{\partial\mathcal{L}_s}{\partial\gamma_c} = \begin{cases} \dfrac{\partial\mathcal{L}_c}{\partial\hat{h}_c}\dfrac{(h_{z/x,c} - \mu_{z/x,c})}{\sqrt{\sigma_{z/x,c}^2 + \epsilon}} + \lambda_\gamma\dfrac{\partial\mathcal{L}_\gamma}{\partial\gamma_c}, & \gamma_c > 0 \\ \dfrac{\partial\mathcal{L}_c}{\partial\hat{h}_c}\dfrac{(h_{z/x,c} - \mu_{z/x,c})}{\sqrt{\sigma_{z/x,c}^2 + \epsilon}} - \lambda_\gamma\dfrac{\partial\mathcal{L}_\gamma}{\partial\gamma_c}, & \gamma_c < 0 \end{cases} \tag{12}$$

When the model training approaches convergence, the derivative of $\mathcal{L}_c$ w.r.t $\hat{h}_c$ approximates zero. Due to $\lambda\gamma > 0$, we easily achieve the following inequality:

$$\begin{cases} \frac{(h_{z/x,c} - \mu_{z/x,c})}{\sqrt{\sigma^2_{z/x,c} + \epsilon}} > -\lambda_\gamma(\frac{\partial \mathcal{L}_c}{\partial \hat{h}_c})^{-1}, & \gamma_c > 0 \\ \frac{(h_{z/x,c} - \mu_{z/x,c})}{\sqrt{\sigma^2_{z/x,c} + \epsilon}} < \lambda_\gamma(\frac{\partial \mathcal{L}_c}{\partial \hat{h}_c})^{-1}, & \gamma_c < 0 \end{cases} \tag{13}$$

With the central limit theorem, we can convert the above inequality into the probability formulation:

$$\mathbb{P}\Big(-\lambda_\gamma(\frac{\partial \mathcal{L}_c}{\partial \hat{h}_c})^{-1} < \frac{(h_{z/x,c} - \mu_{z/x,c})}{\sqrt{\sigma^2_{z/x,c} + \epsilon}} < \lambda_\gamma(\frac{\partial \mathcal{L}_c}{\partial \hat{h}_c})^{-1}\Big) = 2\Phi(\lambda_\gamma(\frac{\partial \mathcal{L}_c}{\partial \hat{h}_c})^{-1}) - 1. \tag{14}$$

The model convergence means $\frac{\partial \mathcal{L}_c}{\partial \hat{h}_c} \to 0$ so that the above probability approximates one. It suggests the scaling factors to these channels will become zero with high-probability. Multi-view images are likely to activate different channels in this part for the classification task. Thus, we consider these channel information as view-specific content. Inversely, benefit from the ℓ_2-norm analysis [51], the $\gamma_c, c \in [1, C/2)$ will be dense non-zero values with the constraint $\sum_{c=1}^{\lfloor C/2 \rfloor} \gamma^2_{l,c}$. These channels across various views are both activated to learn semantic from the identical location of images or feature maps and tend to include the similar even consistent patterns , which are defined as view-common channels.

4 Experiments

4.1 Experimental Details

♢ **Datasets:** i). **RGB-D** dataset [23] is a large-scale household objects dataset including 51 categories and each specific object is captured by Kinect style 3D camera (30 Hz) generating RGB and depth images at the same time. ii). **B3DO** [18] is a popular 3D benchmark database with RGB and depth image pairs from 83 object categories. And these images are collected from real domestic and office-environments by Microsoft Kinect sensor. iii). **Office-31** [39] is a standard multi-domain RGB image benchmark including Amazon (**A**), Webcam (**W**) and DSLR (**D**), which are gathered with different cameras. And all domains share the identical label space with 31 categories. iv). **Office-Home** [41] as a large-scale cross-domain dataset involves four domains as Art Painting (**Ar**), Clipart (**Cl**), Product (**Pr**) and Real World (**Rw**) with significant image style difference. And each domain includes the same 65 object classes. v). **Caltech-256** (**C**) [11] is a classical natural image database with 30,607 images from 257 objects.

In IMVDA experiments, we consider RGB-D and B3DO as two multi-view (RGB and Depth) well-annotated source domains, while the Caltech-256 or each domain of Office-31 and Office-Home as the unlabeled target domain to mimic the incomplete multi-view scenario. For each specific adaptation task, we select the shared categories across source and target domains. Concretely, the number of categories for tasks **RGB-D→Office31**, **RGB-D→Office-Home**, **RGB-D→Caltech-256** are 8, 13 and 10, respectively, while that for **B3DO→Office31**, **B3DO→Office-Home**, **B3DO→Caltech-256** are 27, 14 and 8, respectively.

◇ **Implementation Details:** The implementation of our model is based on pytorch platform. And we adopt the pre-trained ResNet-50 [15] without the last FC layer as the feature extractor for source and target models, and $W_{s/t} \in \mathbb{R}^{64\times256}$, $\{\mathbf{F}_i^{x/z}, \mathbf{F}_i^{xz}, \mathbf{G}_i^{s/t}, \bar{\mathbf{G}}_i^{s/t}\} \in \mathbb{R}^{256}$. Moreover, the stochastic gradient descent (SGD) optimizer with momentum 0.9 is used to optimize all parameters. The learning rate and batch size are 1e-3 and 96. The ϵ and δ are set as 1e-6 and 0.02 for all experiments. Our source code is available https://github.com/HaifengXia/IMVDA.

Table 1. Object classification accuracy (%) of target domain with **RGB-D** datasets as multi-view source domain. We adopt **bold** to highlight the best result and show the second best one with <u>underline</u>.

Method	A	D	W	Ar	Cl	Pr	Rw	C	Avg
ResNet [15]	61.75	79.37	81.73	35.90	28.86	48.01	52.68	74.82	57.89
DANN [10]	67.98	81.51	82.35	46.42	35.50	48.99	63.15	75.42	62.67
CDAN+E [31]	66.15	84.37	85.06	46.95	34.42	51.04	63.30	78.32	63.70
SRDC [40]	68.28	<u>87.70</u>	<u>87.77</u>	<u>51.57</u>	35.96	58.00	<u>66.44</u>	<u>81.45</u>	67.14
CGDM [7]	65.48	84.57	84.59	43.26	36.80	53.54	63.20	77.49	63.62
FixBi [35]	<u>69.07</u>	85.04	86.59	50.29	**38.33**	<u>61.53</u>	65.58	81.14	<u>67.19</u>
M3SDA [37]	66.11	85.70	85.86	45.10	<u>37.00</u>	56.53	64.96	80.71	65.25
DRT [26]	67.86	86.79	86.57	46.00	35.55	57.28	64.97	80.62	65.71
Ours	**70.79**	**89.68**	**90.87**	**56.17**	35.46	**66.86**	**70.33**	**84.21**	**70.55**

Table 2. Object classification accuracy (%) of target domain with **B3DO** datasets as multi-view source domain. We adopt **bold** to highlight the best result and show the second best one with <u>underline</u>.

Method	A	D	W	Ar	Cl	Pr	Rw	C	Avg
ResNet [15]	31.98	49.54	44.35	48.54	35.53	50.56	57.70	48.56	45.85
DANN [10]	44.05	63.53	62.35	59.61	40.05	67.09	74.98	68.18	59.98
CDAN+E [31]	47.70	66.75	64.69	62.00	43.93	70.29	77.93	71.35	63.08
SRDC [40]	49.47	<u>68.67</u>	<u>66.74</u>	<u>64.44</u>	<u>45.85</u>	<u>72.77</u>	79.73	<u>73.55</u>	<u>65.15</u>
CGDM [7]	47.19	66.07	64.09	61.23	43.15	69.70	76.97	70.42	62.35
FixBi [35]	<u>49.67</u>	68.59	66.69	63.97	45.41	71.72	<u>80.23</u>	72.82	64.89
M3SDA [37]	47.76	66.55	64.92	62.01	44.86	71.17	77.51	71.96	63.34
DRT [26]	47.75	67.59	66.01	63.00	44.22	70.84	78.62	72.82	63.86
Ours	**50.02**	**71.87**	**70.23**	**68.00**	**47.40**	**76.61**	**82.81**	**77.21**	**68.02**

◇ **Baselines:** In term of IMVDA, since source and target domains both involve one identical view data, the conventional unsupervised domain adaptation methods can exploit these samples to achieve alignment and identify target samples. Thus, we evaluate the DANN [10], CDAN+E [31], SRDC [40], CGDM [7], FixBi [35] under IMVDA scenario. Moreover, each view data of source domain can be considered as one independent domain. The multi-source domain adaptation methods M3SDA [37] and DRT [26] are used to solve IMVDA challenges. And we adopt their published source code and empirically search optimal parameters to conduct experiments.

4.2 Comparison of Results

The main experimental results in terms of target recognition accuracy are summarized in Table 1 and Table 2. According to the evaluation performance, we can easily achieve several significant conclusions. **First**, our method outperforms other baselines by a large margin on the average classification accuracy. Specifically, with RGB-D dataset as source domain, our CEKT surpasses the second best comparison (i.e., FixBi) by 3.36%. It illustrates the deployment of multi-view information effectively boosts the model performance on target domain even with considerable distribution shift. **Second**, we notice that our CEKT obtains much higher classification accuracy than others on the task RGB-D→Ar. As we all know, the images of Art Painting domain in Office-Home include lots of texture information to describe each object. On the other hand, depth sensor integrates more spatial information into depth images to clearly show the contour of object, which provides more discriminative semantic to the classification task. However, M3SDA and DRT, taking advantage of depth images to train the model, still fail to effectively assist the recognition of unlabeled target samples. These observations demonstrate our proposed solution not only emphasizes the specific semantic of depth images via source cross-view channel enhancement but also transfers such knowledge from source domain to target domain by reducing the negative influence of missing view with adaptive knowledge transfer network.

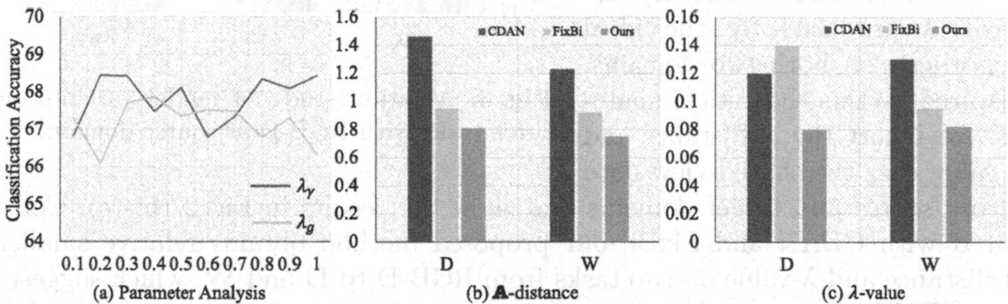

Fig. 2. Parameter analysis & Transfer ability. (a) Target classification accuracy with the varying parameters λ_γ and λ_g from 0.1 to 1.0 with B3DO as source domain. (b) $\mathcal{A}$-distance of source and target features from the same view data with RGB-D as source domain. (c) λ-value of three methods with tasks from RGB-D to D and W.

Third, comparison of Table 1 and Table 2 shows that B3DO has larger distribution difference than RGB-D to the other target domain in Office-31, Office-Home and Caltech-256, as we achieve worse results by directly recognizing the target based on ResNet features. However, our proposed CEKT model can still achieve very close results no matter which source is used. In details, we improve the average accuracy from 57.89% to 70.55% by using RGB-D as source, while promote the average accuracy from 45.85% to 68.02% by using B3DO as source.

4.3 Empirical Analysis

Parameter Sensitivity. During training model, there are two parameters (λ_γ, λ_g) in our designed CEKT framework which are manually adjusted. These two parameters are changed from 0.1 to 1.0 with step size 0.1. To analyse the model sensitivity to them, we record the classification accuracy of target domain with various parameter selection on task from B3DO to **Ar**, which is shown in Fig. 2 (a). On the whole, the model is not sensitive to the change of parameters. However, larger λ_γ can easily bring more benefits to the model, while the smaller λ_g results in better performance, which further illustrates the proposed channel enhancement module effectively assists model to learning discriminative features. Note that for the selection of parameters, we randomly select 10% source samples as validation set for each tentative and use it to evaluate the model performance.
Transfer Ability. In addition, Ben-David theoretically points out the learning bound of domain adaptation [3] is determined by three parts: 1) the expected error $\varepsilon_s(h)$ of hypothesis h on source domain; 2) the $\mathcal{A}$-distance defined as $d_{\mathcal{H}\Delta\mathcal{H}} = 2(1-2\xi)$ measuring the domain mismatch, where ξ is the error from a trained domain classifier distinguishing source from target ones; 3) the error λ produced by the ideal hypothesis on both two domains. Inspired by this theoretical analysis, we report the $\mathcal{A}$-distance and λ-value over the shared-view data across source and target domains and show the results in Fig. 2 (b)-(c). Compared with CDAN and FixBi, our proposed method obtains relative smaller $\mathcal{A}$-distance and λ-value on two tasks from RGB-D to **D** and **W**, which suggests that CEKT learns a model with a higher generalization ability.

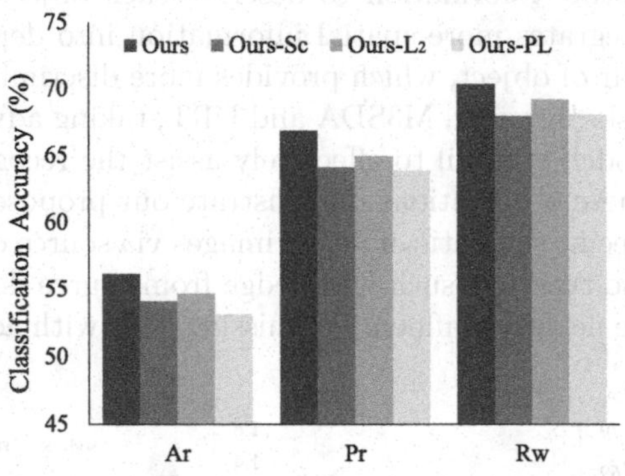

Fig. 3. Ablation study of model variants on three tasks with RGB-D as source domain.

Ablation Study. To clearly reflect the contribution of each component to the model performance, we carry out experiments on three knowledge transfer tasks with RGB-D as source domain by removing the corresponding operations. As previous mentioned, the source channel enhanced network actively discovers the view-common and view-specific parts via Eq. (3) and encourages the representation of important channels with Eq. (9). Thus, we replace Eq. (3) with $\sum_{c=1}^{C} |\gamma_{x/z,c}|$ (Ours-L$_2$) and attempt to remove Eq. (9) as Ours-Sc to study their effect. In addition, the model training adopts pseudo labels to facilitate feature with more discriminative power, and we further add a variant without the pseudo labeling as Ours-PL. Figure 3 reports the corresponding results with various methods on three tasks. According to it, we discover the enhancement with channel similarity and pseudo labels both produce significant and positive influence on improving model performance on target domain. Moreover, the sparse constraint for parameters $\gamma_{x/z,c}$ as [43] also results in the performance degradation, which further verifies the necessity of the preservation for the view-common channel split in multi-view data analysis.

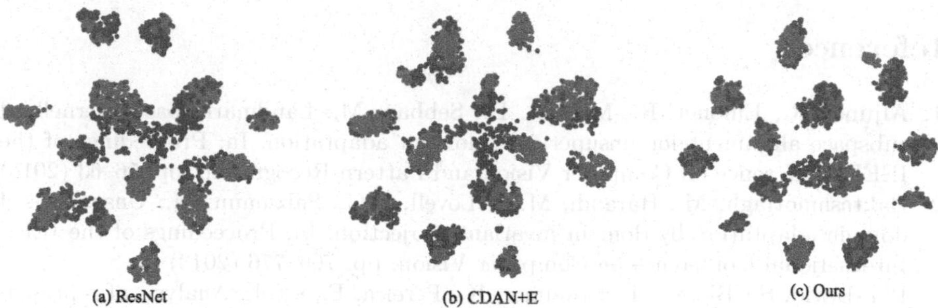

Fig. 4. Feature Visualization with t-SNE in 2D plane. The source and target features are represented by red and blue, respectively. And the experiment aims to transfer knowledge from RGB-D to **Ar** in Office-Home. (Color figure online)

Feature Visualization. To further understand the situation of distribution alignment, we follow [25] to visualize source and target features from the same view in 2D-plane, shown in Fig. 4. Concretely, we access to the high-level features $\bar{\mathbf{G}}_i^{s/t}$ from the well-trained target model and adopt t-SNE technique to draw them in the canvas. Moreover, the experiment is carried out on adaptation task from RGB-D to **Pr** and ResNet as well as CDAN+E are considered as the competitors. According to the visualization results, it is easy to observe that there exist more overlaps between source and target features, compared with other baselines, which shows our method successfully mitigates the domain shift and better align them. Moreover, we notice that the classification boundary is more explicit than that in ResNet and CDAN+E. It suggests CEKT effectively learns the discriminative features for classification task.

5 Conclusion

Unsupervised domain adaptation (UDA) aims to learn the domain-invariant knowledge across well-supervised source and unlabeled target samples to enhance the model generalization ability. However, UDA assumes the instances per domain are captured by single sensor, which difficultly matches the practical scenario with multi-view data. This paper considered a practical and challenging problem named incomplete multi-view domain adaptation (IMVDA) which access to multi-view source data and single-view target samples. To overcome the challenge, we proposed a novel learning framework channel enhancement and knowledge transfer (CEKT). Concretely, CEKT first explored channel attributions to conduct semantic fusion and enhance the representation of view-common channels to learn more discriminative features. Moreover, adaptive knowledge transfer module not only brought multi-view knowledge to single-view feature learning but also achieved simple yet effective alignment across source and target domains. Considerable experimental results and analysis fully demonstrated our CEKT effectively broke the bottleneck of IMVDA by improving the performance.

References

1. Aljundi, R., Emonet, R., Muselet, D., Sebban, M.: Landmarks-based kernelized subspace alignment for unsupervised domain adaptation. In: Proceedings of the IEEE Conference on Computer Vision and Pattern Recognition, pp. 56–63 (2015)
2. Baktashmotlagh, M., Harandi, M.T., Lovell, B.C., Salzmann, M.: Unsupervised domain adaptation by domain invariant projection. In: Proceedings of the IEEE International Conference on Computer Vision, pp. 769–776 (2013)
3. Ben-David, S., Blitzer, J., Crammer, K., Pereira, F., et al.: Analysis of representations for domain adaptation. Adv. Neural Inf. Process. Syst. **19**, 137 (2007)
4. Deng, J., Dong, W., Socher, R., Li, L.J., Li, K., Fei-Fei, L.: Imagenet: a large-scale hierarchical image database. In: 2009 IEEE Conference on Computer Vision and Pattern Recognition, pp. 248–255. IEEE (2009)
5. Ding, Z., Fu, Y.: Low-rank common subspace for multi-view learning. In: 2014 IEEE international conference on Data Mining, pp. 110–119. IEEE (2014)
6. Ding, Z., Li, S., Shao, M., Fu, Y.: Graph adaptive knowledge transfer for unsupervised domain adaptation. In: Proceedings of the European Conference on Computer Vision (ECCV), pp. 37–52 (2018)
7. Du, Z., Li, J., Su, H., Zhu, L., Lu, K.: Cross-domain gradient discrepancy minimization for unsupervised domain adaptation. In: Proceedings of the IEEE/CVF Conference on Computer Vision and Pattern Recognition, pp. 3937–3946 (2021)
8. Elbrächter, D., Perekrestenko, D., Grohs, P., Bölcskei, H.: Deep neural network approximation theory. IEEE Trans. Inf. Theory **67**(5), 2581–2623 (2021)
9. Fernando, B., Habrard, A., Sebban, M., Tuytelaars, T.: Unsupervised visual domain adaptation using subspace alignment. In: Proceedings of the IEEE International Conference on Computer Vision, pp. 2960–2967 (2013)
10. Ganin, Y., et al.: Domain-adversarial training of neural networks. J. Mach. Learn. Res. **17**(1), 2030–2096 (2016)
11. Griffin, G., Holub, A., Perona, P.: Caltech-256 object category dataset (2007)
12. Guan, D., Huang, J., Lu, S., Xiao, A.: Scale variance minimization for unsupervised domain adaptation in image segmentation. Pattern Recognit. **112**, 107764 (2021)
13. Guan, D., Huang, J., Xiao, A., Lu, S., Cao, Y.: Uncertainty-aware unsupervised domain adaptation in object detection. IEEE Trans. Multimedia **24**, 2502–2514 (2021)

14. He, J., Jia, X., Chen, S., Liu, J.: Multi-source domain adaptation with collaborative learning for semantic segmentation. In: Proceedings of the IEEE/CVF Conference on Computer Vision and Pattern Recognition, pp. 11008–11017 (2021)
15. He, K., Zhang, X., Ren, S., Sun, J.: Deep residual learning for image recognition. In: Proceedings of the IEEE Conference on Computer vision and Pattern Recognition, pp. 770–778 (2016)
16. He, Y., Tian, Y., Liu, D.: Multi-view transfer learning with privileged learning framework. Neurocomputing **335**, 131–142 (2019)
17. Ioffe, S., Szegedy, C.: Batch normalization: accelerating deep network training by reducing internal covariate shift. In: International Conference on Machine Learning, pp. 448–456. PMLR (2015)
18. Janoch, A., et al.: A Category-Level 3D Object dataset: putting the Kinect to Work. In: Fossati, A., Gall, J., Grabner, H., Ren, X., Konolige, K. (eds.) Consumer Depth Cameras for Computer Vision. Advances in Computer Vision and Pattern Recognition, pp 141–165. Springer, London (2013). https://doi.org/10.1007/978-1-4471-4640-7_8
19. Jing, T., Liu, H., Ding, Z.: Towards novel target discovery through open-set domain adaptation. In: Proceedings of the IEEE/CVF International Conference on Computer Vision, pp. 9322–9331 (2021)
20. Jing, T., Xia, H., Hamm, J., Ding, Z.: Augmented multi-modality fusion for generalized zero-shot sketch-based visual retrieval. IEEE Trans. Image Process. **31**, 3657–3668 (2022)
21. Kang, G., Jiang, L., Yang, Y., Hauptmann, A.G.: Contrastive adaptation network for unsupervised domain adaptation. In: Proceedings of the IEEE/CVF Conference on Computer Vision and Pattern Recognition, pp. 4893–4902 (2019)
22. Kumar, A., Rai, P., Daume, H.: Co-regularized multi-view spectral clustering. Adv. Neural Inf. Process. Syst. **24**, 1413–1421 (2011)
23. Lai, K., Bo, L., Ren, X., Fox, D.: A large-scale hierarchical multi-view rgb-d object dataset. In: 2011 IEEE International Conference on Robotics and Automation, pp. 1817–1824. IEEE (2011)
24. Li, J., Li, Z., Lu, G., Xu, Y., Zhang, B., Zhang, D.: Asymmetric gaussian process multi-view learning for visual classification. Inf. Fusion **65**, 108–118 (2021)
25. Li, R., Jiao, Q., Cao, W., Wong, H.S., Wu, S.: Model adaptation: unsupervised domain adaptation without source data. In: Proceedings of the IEEE/CVF Conference on Computer Vision and Pattern Recognition, pp. 9641–9650 (2020)
26. Li, Y., Yuan, L., Chen, Y., Wang, P., Vasconcelos, N.: Dynamic transfer for multi-source domain adaptation. In: Proceedings of the IEEE/CVF Conference on Computer Vision and Pattern Recognition, pp. 10998–11007 (2021)
27. Liang, J., Hu, D., Feng, J.: Do we really need to access the source data? source hypothesis transfer for unsupervised domain adaptation. In: International Conference on Machine Learning, pp. 6028–6039. PMLR (2020)
28. Liu, B., Chen, X., Xiao, Y., Li, W., Liu, L., Liu, C.: An efficient dictionary-based multi-view learning method. Inf. Sci. **576**, 157–172 (2021)
29. Liu, X., et al.: Adversarial unsupervised domain adaptation with conditional and label shift: infer, align and iterate. In: Proceedings of the IEEE/CVF International Conference on Computer Vision, pp. 10367–10376 (2021)
30. Liu, Y., Wang, L., Bai, Y., Qin, C., Ding, Z., Fu, Y.: Generative view-correlation adaptation for semi-supervised multi-view learning. In: Vedaldi, A., Bischof, H., Brox, T., Frahm, J.-M. (eds.) ECCV 2020. LNCS, vol. 12359, pp. 318–334. Springer, Cham (2020). https://doi.org/10.1007/978-3-030-58568-6_19

31. Long, M., Cao, Z., Wang, J., Jordan, M.I.: Conditional adversarial domain adaptation. arXiv preprint arXiv:1705.10667 (2017)
32. Long, M., Zhu, H., Wang, J., Jordan, M.I.: Deep transfer learning with joint adaptation networks. In: International Conference on Machine Learning, pp. 2208–2217. PMLR (2017)
33. Lu, X., Wang, W., Danelljan, M., Zhou, T., Shen, J., Van Gool, L.: Video object segmentation with episodic graph memory networks. In: Vedaldi, A., Bischof, H., Brox, T., Frahm, J.-M. (eds.) ECCV 2020. LNCS, vol. 12348, pp. 661–679. Springer, Cham (2020). https://doi.org/10.1007/978-3-030-58580-8_39
34. Lu, Z., Yang, Y., Zhu, X., Liu, C., Song, Y.Z., Xiang, T.: Stochastic classifiers for unsupervised domain adaptation. In: Proceedings of the IEEE/CVF Conference on Computer Vision and Pattern Recognition, pp. 9111–9120 (2020)
35. Na, J., Jung, H., Chang, H.J., Hwang, W.: Fixbi: bridging domain spaces for unsupervised domain adaptation. In: Proceedings of the IEEE/CVF Conference on Computer Vision and Pattern Recognition, pp. 1094–1103 (2021)
36. Pan, Y., Yao, T., Li, Y., Wang, Y., Ngo, C.W., Mei, T.: Transferrable prototypical networks for unsupervised domain adaptation. In: Proceedings of the IEEE/CVF Conference on Computer Vision and Pattern Recognition, pp. 2239–2247 (2019)
37. Peng, X., Bai, Q., Xia, X., Huang, Z., Saenko, K., Wang, B.: Moment matching for multi-source domain adaptation. In: Proceedings of the IEEE/CVF International Conference on Computer Vision, pp. 1406–1415 (2019)
38. Redmon, J., Divvala, S., Girshick, R., Farhadi, A.: You only look once: unified, real-time object detection. In: Proceedings of the IEEE Conference on Computer Vision and Pattern Recognition, pp. 779–788 (2016)
39. Saenko, K., Kulis, B., Fritz, M., Darrell, T.: Adapting visual category models to new domains. In: Daniilidis, K., Maragos, P., Paragios, N. (eds.) ECCV 2010. LNCS, vol. 6314, pp. 213–226. Springer, Heidelberg (2010). https://doi.org/10.1007/978-3-642-15561-1_16
40. Tang, H., Chen, K., Jia, K.: Unsupervised domain adaptation via structurally regularized deep clustering. In: Proceedings of the IEEE/CVF Conference on Computer Vision and Pattern Recognition, pp. 8725–8735 (2020)
41. Venkateswara, H., Eusebio, J., Chakraborty, S., Panchanathan, S.: Deep hashing network for unsupervised domain adaptation. In: Proceedings of the IEEE Conference on Computer Vision and Pattern Recognition, pp. 5018–5027 (2017)
42. Wang, M., et al.: Interbn: channel fusion for adversarial unsupervised domain adaptation. In: Proceedings of the 29th ACM International Conference on Multimedia, pp. 3691–3700 (2021)
43. Wang, Q., Cheng, J., Gao, Q., Zhao, G., Jiao, L.: Deep multi-view subspace clustering with unified and discriminative learning. IEEE Trans. Multimedia **23**, 3483–3493 (2020)
44. Xia, H., Ding, Z.: Structure preserving generative cross-domain learning. In: Proceedings of the IEEE/CVF Conference on Computer Vision and Pattern Recognition, pp. 4364–4373 (2020)
45. Xia, H., Ding, Z.: Cross-domain collaborative normalization via structural knowledge. In: AAAI 2022 (2022)
46. Xia, H., Jing, T., Ding, Z.: Maximum structural generation discrepancy for unsupervised domain adaptation. IEEE Trans. Pattern Anal. Mach. Intell. (2022)
47. Xu, H., Zhang, X., Xia, W., Gao, Q., Gao, X.: Low-rank tensor constrained co-regularized multi-view spectral clustering. Neural Networks **132**, 245–252 (2020)
48. Zhang, C., Cui, Y., Han, Z., Zhou, J.T., Fu, H., Hu, Q.: Deep partial multi-view learning. IEEE Trans. Pattern Anal. Mach. Intell. **44**, 2402–2415 (2020)

49. Zhang, C., Cai, Y., Lin, G., Shen, C.: Deepemd: few-shot image classification with differentiable earth mover's distance and structured classifiers. In: Proceedings of the IEEE/CVF Conference on Computer Vision and Pattern Recognition, pp. 12203–12213 (2020)
50. Zhang, D., et al.: Direct quantification of coronary artery stenosis through hierarchical attentive multi-view learning. IEEE Trans. Med. Imaging **39**(12), 4322–4334 (2020)
51. Zhang, L., Yang, M., Feng, X.: Sparse representation or collaborative representation: which helps face recognition? In: 2011 International Conference on Computer Vision, pp. 471–478. IEEE (2011)
52. Zhao, J., Xie, X., Xu, X., Sun, S.: Multi-view learning overview: recent progress and new challenges. Inf. Fusion **38**, 43–54 (2017)

DistPro: Searching a Fast Knowledge Distillation Process via Meta Optimization

Xueqing Deng[1,3](✉), Dawei Sun[2], Shawn Newsam[3], and Peng Wang[1]

[1] ByteDance Inc., Beijing, China
{xueqingdeng,peng.wang}@bytedance.com

[2] ECE, UIUC, Beijing, China
daweis2@illinois.edu

[3] EECS, UC Merced, Beijing, China
snewsam@ucmerced.edu

Abstract. Recent Knowledge distillation (KD) studies show that different manually designed schemes impact the learned results significantly. Yet, in KD, automatically searching an optimal distillation scheme has not yet been well explored. In this paper, we propose `DistPro`, a novel framework which searches for an optimal KD process via differentiable meta-learning. Specifically, given a pair of student and teacher networks, `DistPro` first sets up a rich set of KD connections from the transmitting layers of the teacher to the receiving layers of the student, and in the meanwhile, various transforms are also proposed for comparing feature maps along their pathways for distillation. Then, each combination of connection and transform (pathway) is associated with a stochastic weighting process which indicates its importance at every step during the distillation. At the searching stage, the process can be effectively learned through our proposed bi-level meta-optimization strategy. At the distillation stage, `DistPro` adopts the learned processes for knowledge distillation, which significantly improves the student accuracy especially when faster training is required. Lastly, we find the learned processes can be generalized between similar tasks and networks. In our experiments, `DistPro` produces state-of-the-art (SoTA) accuracy under varying number of learning epochs on popular datasets, *i.e.* CIFAR100 and ImageNet, which demonstrates the effectiveness of our framework. Codes are available at https://github.com/xdeng7/DistPro.

1 Introduction

Knowledge distillation (KD) is proposed to effectively transfer knowledge from a well performing larger/teacher deep neural network (DNN) to a given smaller/

X. Deng and D. Sun—These authors contributed equally to this work.

Supplementary Information The online version contains supplementary material available at https://doi.org/10.1007/978-3-031-19830-4_13.

S. Avidan et al. (Eds.): ECCV 2022, LNCS 13694, pp. 218–235, 2022.
https://doi.org/10.1007/978-3-031-19830-4_13

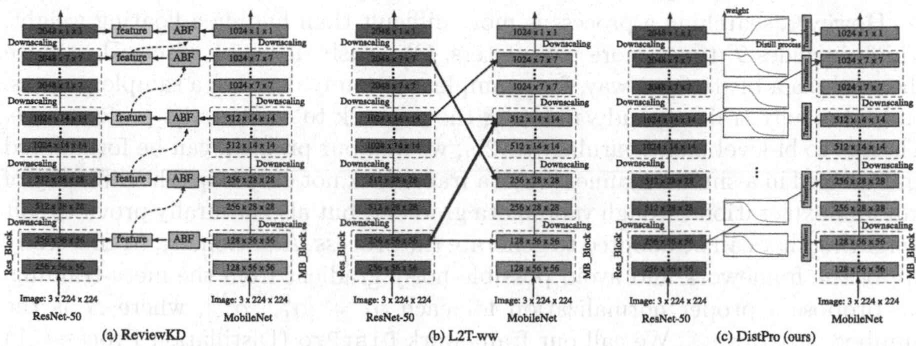

Fig. 1. Comparisons of distillation methods for learning process between teacher and student models. (a) Knowledge Review [4] proposes fixed sampled pathways by enumerating different configurations. (b) L2T-ww [18], adopts a meta-learning framework to learn a floating weight for each selected pathway. (c) Our framework learns distillation process for each pathway.

student network, where the learned student network often learns faster or performs better than that with a vanilla training strategy solely using ground truths.

Since its first appearance in DNN learning [14], KD has achieved remarkable success in training efficient models for image classification [50], image segmentation [26], object detection [3], *etc*, contributing to its wide application in various model deployment over mobile-phones or other low-power computing devices [28]. Nowadays, KD has become a popular technique in industry to develop distilled DNNs to deal with billions of data per day.

To improve the distillation efficiency and accuracy, numerous handcrafted KD design schemes have been proposed, *e.g.*, designing different distillation losses at outputs [26,44], manually assigning intermediate features maps for additional KD guidance [49,50]. However, recent studies [11,27,48] indicate that the effectiveness of those proposed KD techniques varies on the networks and tasks. Some recent works propose to search some configurations to conclude a better KD scheme. For instance, ReviewKD [4] (Fig. 1(a)) proposes to evaluate a subset from a total of 16 pathways by enabling and disabling partial of them for image classification task. It comes to the conclusion that partial pathways are always redundant. However, our experimental results show that it does not hold to a semantic segmentation task, and after conducting a research of the pathways, we may obtain better results. L2T-ww [18] (Fig. 1(b)) takes a further step, it can not only set up multiple distillation pathways between feature maps, but also learn a floating weight for each pathway, showing better performance than fixed weight. This inspires us to explore better KD schemes, and as motivated by the learning rate scheduler, shown in Fig. 1(c), we propose the concept of distillation process for each pathway i, *i.e.* $\mathcal{A}^i = \{\alpha_t^i\}_{t=1}^T$, where T is the number of distillation steps. Thus, it can result in dynamic changes of the importance for each pathway along the whole distillation procedure. Our work shows that such a process is beneficial to acceleration.

However, searching a process is more difficult than finding a floating weight, which includes T times more parameters. Obviously, it is not practical to solve the goal via a brute force way, for example, randomly drawing a sample process, and later fully training and validating the network to evaluate its performance. Thanks to bi-level meta-learning [10,25], we find our problem can be formulated and tackled in a similar manner. Such a framework not only skips the difficulty of random exploration through valid meta gradient, but also naturally provides soft weighting that can be adopted to generate the process. Additionally, to effectively apply the framework and avoid possible noisy gradient from the meta-training, we propose a proper normalization for each $\alpha_t = [\alpha_t^0, \cdot, \alpha_t^N]$, where N is the number of pathways. We call our framework `DistPro` (Distillation Process). In our experiments, we show that `DistPro` produces better results on various tasks, such as classification with CIFAR100 [22] and ImageNet1K [7], segmentation with CityScapes [6] and depth estimation with NYUv2 [32].

Finally, we find our learned process remains similar with minor variations across different network architectures and tasks as long as it uses the same proposed pathways and transforms. This indicates that the process can be generalized to new tasks. In practice, we transfer the process learned by CIFAR100 to ImageNet1K, and show that it improves over the baselines and accelerates the distillation (2x faster than ReviewKD [4] as shown in Table 3).

In summary, our contributions are three-folds 1) We propose a meta-learning framework for KD, *i.e.* DistPro, to efficiently learn an optimal process to perform KD. 2) We verify `DistPro` over various configurations, architecture and task settings, yielding significant improvement over other SoTA methods. 3) Through the experiments, we find the process that can generalize across tasks and networks, can potentially benefit KD in new tasks without additional searching.

2 Related Works

Knowledge Distillation. Starting under the name knowledge transfer [2,42], knowledge distillation (KD) is later popularized owing to Hinton et.al [14] for training efficient neural networks. Thereafter, it has been a popular field in the past few years, in terms of designing KD losses [43,44], combination with multiple tasks [8,33] or dealing with specific issues, eg few-shot learning [20], long-tail recognition [45]. Here, we majorly highlight the works that are closely related to ours, in order to locate our contributions.

According to a recent survey [11], current KD literature includes multiple knowledge types, eg response-based [31], feature-based [13,35] and relation-based [41] knowledge. For distillation algorithms, various distillation criteria are proposed such as adversarial-based [43], attention-based [17], graph-based [24] and lifelong distillation [5] etc. Finally, based on a certain task, KD can also extend with different task-aware metrics, eg speech [33], NLP [8] etc. In our principle, we hope all the surveyed KD schemes, ie knowledge types, methods under certain task settings, can be pooled with a universal way to a search space, in order to find the best distillation. While in this paper, we take the first step towards this goal by exploring a sub-field in this whole space, which is already a challenging problem to solve. Specifically, we adopt the setting of offline distillation with feature-based and response-based knowledge, where both network responses and intermediate feature maps are adopted for KD. For KD method, we use attention-based methods to compare feature responses, and apply the KD model to vision tasks including classification, segmentation and depth estimation.

Inside this field, knowledge review [4] and L2T-ww [18] are the most related to our work. The former investigates the importance of a few pathways and propose a knowledge review mechanism with a novel connection pattern, ie, residual learning framework. It provides SoTA results in several commonly comparison benchmarks. The latter learns a fixed weights for a few intermediate pathways for few-shot knowledge transfer. As shown in Fig. 1, `DistPro` finds a distillation process. Therefore, we extend the search space. In addition, for dense prediction tasks, one related work is IFVD [44], which proposes an intra-class feature variation comparison (IFVD). `DistPro` is free to extend to dense prediction tasks, and it also obtain extra benefits after combined with IFVD.

Meta-learning for KD/Hyperparameters. To automate the learning of a KD scheme, we investigated a wide range of efficient meta-learning methods in other fields that we might adopt. For examples, L2L [1] proposes to learn a hyperparameter scheduling scheme through a RNN-based meta-network. Franceschi et.al [10] propose an gradient-based approach without external meta-networks. Later, these meta-learning ideas have also been utilized in tasks of few-shot learning (eg learning to reweight [34]), learning cross-task knowledge transfer(eg learning to transfer [18]), and neural architecture search (NAS)(eg DARTS [25]). Although these methods share similar framework, it is critical to have essential embedded domain knowledge and task-aware adjustment to make it work. In our case, inspired by these methods, we majorly utilize the gradient-based strategy due to its efficiency for KD scheme learning, and also first to propose using the learnt process additional to the learnt importance factor.

Finally, knowledge distillation for NAS has also drawn significant attention recently. For example, Liu et.al [27] try to find student models that are best for distilling a given teacher, while Yao et.al [48] propose to search architectures of both the student and the teacher models based on a certain distillation loss. Though different from our scenario, *i.e.* fixed student-teacher architectures, it raises another important question of how to find the Pareto optimal inside the union space of architectures and KD schemes under certain resource constraint, which we hope could inspire future researches.

3 Approach

In this section, we elaborate `DistPro` by first setting up KD pathways with intermediate features in order to construct our search space, establishing the notations and definition of our KD scheme. Then, we derive the gradient for generating our process for the scheme. At last, the overall algorithm is presented.

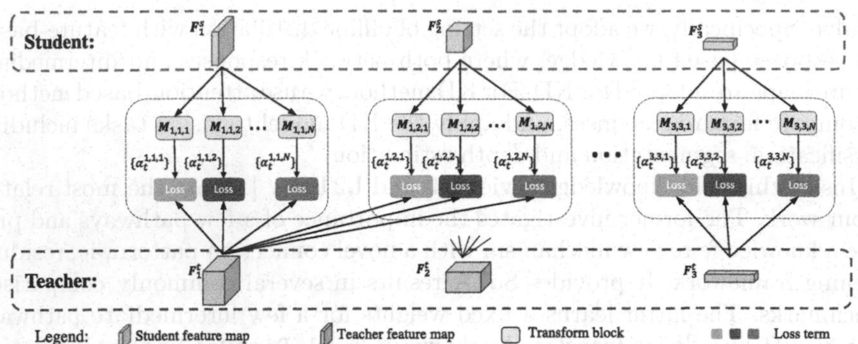

Fig. 2. Illustration of the search space. Two groups of feature maps are selected from the student and the teacher. For each pair of feature maps $\mathcal{F}_j^s$ and $\mathcal{F}_i^t$, we insert N candidate transform blocks $M_{i,j,1}, M_{i,j,2}, \cdots, M_{i,j,N}$ and get N loss terms. For each loss term, a distill process $\mathcal{A}^{i,j,k} = \{\alpha_t^{i,j,k}\}_{t=1}^T$ is assigned.

3.1 KD with Intermediate Features

Numerous prior works [4,19] have demonstrated that intermediate feature maps from neural network can benefit distillation. Motivated by this, we design our approach using feature maps. Let the student neural network be $\mathcal{S}$ and the teacher neural network be $\mathcal{T}$. Given an input example $\mathbf{X}$, the output of the student network is as follows

$$\mathcal{S}(\mathbf{X}) := \mathcal{S}_{L_s} \circ \cdots \circ \mathcal{S}_2 \circ \mathcal{S}_1(\mathbf{X}), \tag{1}$$

where $\mathcal{S}_i$ is the i-th layer of the neural network and L_s is the number of layers. The k-th intermediate feature map $\mathcal{F}_k^s$ of the student is defined as follows,

$$\mathcal{F}_k^s(\mathbf{X}) := \mathcal{S}_k \circ \cdots \circ \mathcal{S}_2 \circ \mathcal{S}_1(\mathbf{X}),\ 1 \leq k \leq L_s.$$

Similarly, the feature map of the teacher is denoted by $\mathcal{F}_k^t$, $1 \leq k \leq L_t$.

Knowledge can be distilled from a pathway between i-th feature map of the teacher and j-th feature map of the student by penalizing the difference between these two feature maps, ie, $\mathcal{F}_i^t$ and $\mathcal{F}_j^s$. Since the feature maps may come from any stage of the network, they may not be in the same shape and thus not directly comparable. Therefore, additional computation are required to align these two feature maps into the same shape. To this end, a transform block is added after $\mathcal{F}_j^s$, which could be in any forms of differentiable computation. In our experiments, the transform block consists of multiple convolution layers and an interpolation layer to align the spatial and channel resolution of the feature map. Denoting the transform block by $\mathcal{M}$, then the loss term measuring the difference between these two feature maps is as follows,

$$\ell(\mathcal{F}_j^s, \mathcal{F}_i^t) := \delta(\mathcal{M}(\mathcal{F}_j^s), \mathcal{F}_i^t),$$

where δ is the optional distance function, which could be L1 distance or L2 distance as used in [19], etc.

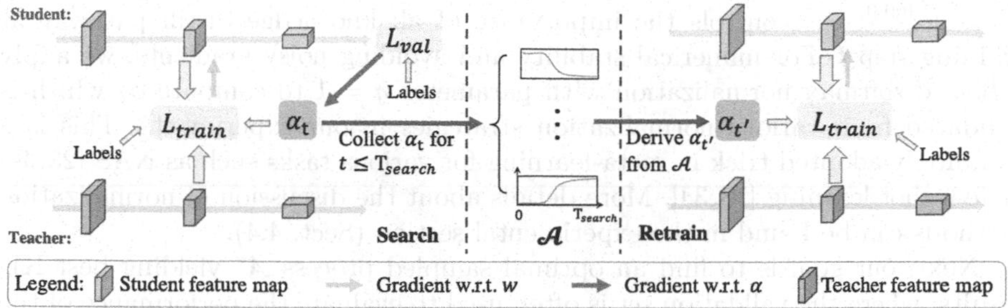

Fig. 3. Two phases of the proposed algorithm. In the search phase, student θ and α_t are computed. In the retrain phase, the learned process of $\mathcal{A} = \{\alpha_t, 0 \leq t \leq T_{search}\}$ is interpolated to be used for KD, and only θ is updated.

3.2 The Distillation Process

Now we will be able to build pathways to connect any feature layer of the teacher to any layer of the student with appropriate transforms. However, as discussed in Sect. 1, not all of these pathways are beneficial. This motivates us to design an approach to find out the importance of each possible pathway by assigning an importance factor for it. Different from the existing work [4,18], the importance factor here is a process. Formally, a stochastic weight process $\mathcal{A}^i = \{\alpha_t^i\}_{t=1}^T$ is associated with the pathway i, where T is the total learning steps. Here, α_t^i describes the importance factor at different learning step t (Fig. 3).

Let $D_{train} := \{(\mathbf{X}_i, y_i)\}_{i=1}^{|D_{train}|}$ and $D_{val} := \{(\mathbf{X}_i, y_i)\}_{i=1}^{|D_{val}|}$ be the training set and the validation set respectively, where y_i is the label of sample $\mathbf{X}_i$. We assume that for each pair of feature maps, $\mathcal{F}_i^t$ and $\mathcal{F}_j^s$, we have N candidate predefined transforms, $\mathbf{M}_{i,j,1}, \mathbf{M}_{i,j,2}, \cdots, \mathbf{M}_{i,j,N}$. The connections together with the transforms construct our search space as shown in Fig. 2.

We now define the search objective which consists of the optimizations of the student network and $\mathcal{A}$. The student network is trained on the training set with a loss encoding the supervision from both the ground truth label and the neural network. Specifically, denoting the parameters of the student and the transforms by θ, the loss on the training set at learning step t is defined as follows,

$$
\begin{aligned}
L_{train}(\theta_t, \alpha_t) = \frac{1}{|D_{train}|} \sum_{(\mathbf{X},y)\in D_{train}} \Big(& \delta_{label}(\mathcal{S}(\mathbf{X}), y) \\
& + \sum_{i=1}^{L_{te}} \sum_{j=1}^{L_s} \sum_{k=1}^{N} \alpha_t^{i,j,k} \delta\left(\mathbf{M}_{i,j,k}\left(\mathcal{F}_j^s(\mathbf{X})\right), \mathcal{F}_i^t(\mathbf{X})\right) \Big), \\
\alpha_t^{i,j,k} = \frac{\exp(\tilde{\alpha}_t^{i,j,k})}{\sum_{i,j,k} \exp(\tilde{\alpha}_t^{i,j,k}) + \exp(g)} &
\end{aligned} \tag{2}
$$

where $\alpha_t^{i,j,k} \in \mathbb{R}_{\geq 0}^{L_{te} \times L_s \times N}$ are the importance factors at training step t and δ_{label} is a distance function measuring difference between predictions and labels. Here,

$\alpha_t = [\alpha_t^{0,0,0}, \cdots]$ controls the importance of all knowledge distill pathway at training step t. For numerical stability and avoiding noisy gradients, we apply a biased softmax normalization with parameter $g = 1$ to compute α_t which is validated from various normalization strategies in our experiments. This is a commonly adopted trick in meta-learning for various tasks such as NAS [25,46] or few-shot learning [18,34]. More details about the discussion of normalization methods can be found in the experimental section (Sect. 4.4).

Next, our goal is to find an optimal sampled process $\mathcal{A}^*$ yielding best KD results, where the validation set is often used to evaluate the performance of the student trained on unseen inputs. To this end, following [25], the validation loss is adopted to evaluate the quality of $\mathcal{A}$, which is defined as follows,

$$L_{val}(\theta) := \frac{1}{|D_{val}|} \sum_{(\mathbf{X},y) \in D_{val}} \delta_{label}(\mathcal{S}(\mathbf{X}), y).$$

Finally, we formulate the bi-level optimization problem over $\mathcal{A}$ and network parameter θ as:

$$\begin{aligned} \min_{\mathcal{A}} \quad & L_{val}\left(\theta^*(\mathcal{A})\right) \\ \text{s.t.} \quad & \theta^*(\mathcal{A}) = \arg \mathrm{f}_\theta \quad L_{train}(\Theta, \mathcal{A}). \end{aligned} \tag{3}$$

where $\theta^*(\mathcal{A})$ is the parameters of the student neural network trained with the loss process defined with $\mathcal{A}$, *i.e.* $L_{train}(\Theta, \mathcal{A}) = \{L_{train}(\theta_t, \alpha_t)\}_{t=1}^{T}$. The ultimate goal of the optimization is to find an $\mathcal{A}$ such that the loss on the validation set is minimized. Note here, similar problem has been proposed in NAS [25,46] asking for a fixed architecture, but our problem is harder, and can be optimized if we enforce all the value in $\mathcal{A}$ to be the same. However, similarly, we are able to apply gradient-based method following the chain-rule to solve this problem.

3.3 Learning the Process $\mathcal{A}$

From the formulation in Eq. 3, directly solving the issue is intractable. Therefore, we propose two assumptions to simplify the problem. First, smooth assumption which means the next step of the process should be closed to previous one. This is commonly adopted in DNN training with stochastic gradient decent (SGD) with a learning rate scheduler [21]. Second, similar learning procedure assumption, which means among different distillation training given a teacher/student pair, at same step t, the student will have similar parameter θ_t. This assumption allows us to search for $\mathcal{A}$ with a single training procedure, which also holds from our experiments when batch size is relatively large (*e.g.* 512 for ImageNet).

Based on these assumptions, we let $\alpha_{t+1} = \alpha_t + \gamma \Delta(\alpha_t|\theta_t)$, where γ controls its changing ratio to be small. Then, we are able to adopt a greedy strategy to break the original problem of Eq. 3 down to a sequence of single steps of optimization, which can be defined as,

$$\begin{aligned} \alpha_{t+1} &= \alpha_t - \gamma \nabla_\alpha L_{val}\left(\theta_{t+1}(\alpha_t)\right) \\ \text{s.t} \quad \theta_{t+1}(\alpha_t) &= \theta_t - \xi \nabla_\theta L_{train}(\theta_t, \alpha_t) \end{aligned}$$

Algorithm 1 DistPro

Input: Full train data set D; Pre-trained teacher; Initialization of α_0, θ_0; Number of iterations T_{search} and T.
Output: Trained student.

Split D into D_{train} and D_{val}.
Let $t = 0$.
while $t < T_{search}$ **do**
  Compute α_t with descending the gradient approximation in Eq. 5 and do normalization.
  Update θ_t by descending $\nabla_\theta L_{train}(\theta_t; \alpha_t)$ in Eq. 2.
  Push the current α_t to $\mathcal{A}$.
end while
Interpolate $\mathcal{A}$ with length of T.
Set $D_{train} = D$ or use a new D_{train} in another task.
Reset $t = 0$.
while $t < T$ **do**
  Load the α_t corresponding to the current t.
  Update θ by descending $\nabla_\theta L_{train}(\theta, \alpha_t)$.
end while

where ξ is the learning rate of inner optimization for training student network. In practice, the inner optimization can be solved with more sophisticated gradient-based method, eg, gradient descent with momentum. In those cases, Eq. 4 has to be modified accordingly, but all the following analysis still applies.

Next, we apply the chain rule to Eq. 4 and get

$$\nabla_\alpha L_{val}\left(\theta_t - \xi \nabla_\theta L_{train}(\theta_t, \alpha_t)\right) = -\xi \nabla^2_{\alpha,\theta} L_{train}(\theta_t, \alpha_t) \nabla_\theta L_{val}(\theta_{t+1}), \quad (4)$$

However, the above expression contains second-order derivatives, which is still computational expensive. Next, we approximate this second-order derivative with finite difference as introduced in [25]. Let ϵ be a small positive scalar and define the notation $\theta^{\pm} = \theta \pm \epsilon \nabla_\theta L_{val}(\theta_{t+1})$. Then, we have

$$\nabla^2_{\alpha,\theta} L_{train}(\theta_t, \alpha_t) \nabla_\theta L_{val}(\theta_{t+1}) = \frac{\nabla_\alpha L_{train}(\theta^+, \alpha_t) - \nabla_\alpha L_{train}(\theta^-, \alpha_t)}{2\epsilon}. \quad (5)$$

Finally, we set an initial value $\alpha_0 = 1$ and launch the greedy learning procedure. Once learned, we push all computed α_t with T steps to a sequence, which is served as a sample of learned stochastic distillation process $\mathcal{A}$, and it can be used for retraining the student network with KD in the same or similar tasks.

3.4 Acceleration and Adopting $\mathcal{A}$ for KD

Now let us take a closer look at the approximation. To evaluate the expression in Eq. 5, the following items have to be computed. First, computing θ_{t+1} requires a forward and backward pass of the student, and a forward pass of the teacher. Then, computing $\theta^{\pm}$ requires another forward and backward pass of the student.

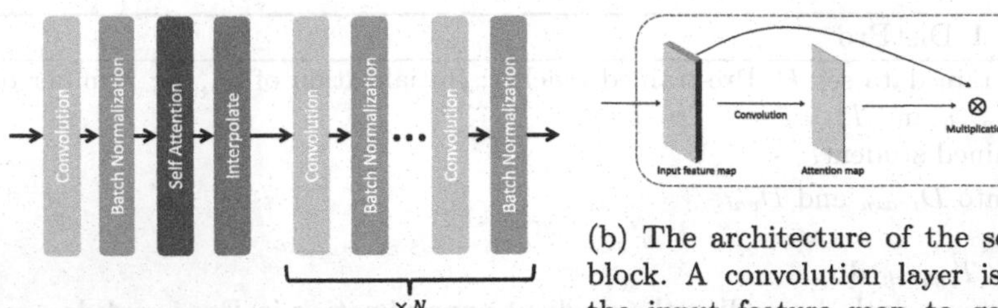

(a) The architecture of the transform block. The self-attention block is illustrated in Fig. 4b.

(b) The architecture of the self-attention block. A convolution layer is applied to the input feature map to generate a 1-channel attention map. Then the input feature map is multiplied with the attention map.

Fig. 4. Transform blocks

Finally, computing $\nabla_\alpha L_{train}(\theta^{\pm}, \alpha_t)$ requires two forward passes of the student. In conclusion, evaluating the approximated gradient in Eq. 5 entails one forward pass of the teacher, and four forward passes and two backward passes of the student in total. This is a time consuming process, especially when the required KD learning epoch is large, *e.g.* ≥ 100.

In meta-learning NAS literature, to avoid 2_{nd} order approximation, researchers commonly adopt 1_{st} order training [25,46] solely based on training loss. However, this is not practical in our case since the hyperparameters are defined over training loss. 1_{st} order gradient over α_t will simply drive all value to 0. Therefore, in our case, we choose to reduce the learning epochs of $\mathcal{A}$ to T_{search}, which is much smaller than T, and then expand it to a sequence with length T using linear interpolation. The choices of T_{search} can be dynamically adjusted based on the dataset size, which will be elaborated in Sect. 4.

Additionally, since we have more pathways than other KD strategy [4], therefore, the loss computation cost can not be ignored. To reduce the cost, at step t, we use a clip function to all $\tilde{\alpha}_t$ in Eq. 2 with a threshold $\tau = 0.5$, and drop corresponding computation when $\tilde{\alpha}_t \leq \tau$. This can save us 60% of loss computational cost in average, resulting in comparable KD time with our baselines.

In summary, the overall `DistPro` process is presented in Algorithm 1, where two phases of the algorithm are explained in order. The first phase is for searching the scheme $\mathcal{A}$. To this end, α_t and θ_t are computed alternately. The α_t obtained in each step is stored for future usage. The Second phase is for retraining the neural network with all the available training data and the searched $\mathcal{A}$.

4 Experiments

In this section, we evaluate the proposed approach on several benchmark tasks including image classification, semantic segmentation, and depth estimation. For image classification, we consider the popularly used dataset CIFAR100 and ImageNet1K. For semantic segmentation and depth estimation, we consider CityScapes [6] and NYUv2 [32] respectively. To make fair comparison, we

Table 1. Results on CIFAR100. Results are averaged over 5 runs. Variances are in the parentheses. "*" represents our reproduced results. In "Equally weighted", we do not use the searched α in the retrain phase. Instead, each element of α is uniformly set to $1/L$, where L is the length of α. In "Use α_T", the finally converged α is used at each iteration of the retrain phase.

Teacher Student	WRN-40-2 WRN-16-2	WRN-40-2 ShuffleNet-v1	ResNet32x4 ShuffleNet-v1	ResNet32x4 ShuffleNet-v2	ResNet56 ResNet20	ResNet110 ResNet32
Teacher Acc	76.51	76.51	79.45	79.45	73.28	74.13
Student Acc	73.26 (0.050)	70.50 (0.360)	70.50 (0.360)	71.82 (0.062)	69.06 (0.052)	71.14 (0.061)
L2T-ww* [18]	–	–	76.35	77.39	–	–
CRD [39]	75.64	76.27	75.12	76.05	71.63	
SSKD [47]	76.04	76.47*	77.21*	77.49*	71.49	–
ReviewKD* [4]	76.20 (0.030)	77.14 (0.015)	76.41 (0.063)	77.37 (0.069)	71.89 (0.056)	73.16 (0.029)
Equally weighted	75.50 (0.010)	74.28 (0.085)	73.54 (0.120)	74.39 (0.119)	70.89 (0.065)	73.19 (0.052)
Use α_T	76.25 (0.034)	77.19 (0.074)	77.15 (0.043)	76.64 (1.335)	71.24 (0.014)	73.58 (0.012)
DistPro	**76.36 (0.005)**	**77.24 (0.063)**	**77.18 (0.047)**	**77.54 (0.059)**	**72.03 (0.022)**	**73.74 (0.011)**

use exactly the same training setting and hyper-parameters for all the methods, including data pre-processing, learning rate scheduler, number of training epochs, batch size, etc. We first demonstrate the effectiveness of `DistPro` for classification on CIFAR100. Then, we provide more analysis with a larger-scale dataset, ImageNet1K. At last, we show the results of dense prection tasks and ablation study. All experiments are performed with Tesla-V100 GPUs.

4.1 Classification on CIFAR100

Implementation Details. We follow the same data pre-processing approach as in [4]. Similarly, we select a group of representative network architectures including ResNet [12], WideResNet [51], MobileNet [16,36], and ShuffleNet [30, 52]. We follow the same training setting in [4] for distillation. We train the models for 240 epochs and decay the learning rate by 0.1 for every 30 epochs after the first 150 epochs. Batch size is 128 for all the models. We train the models with the same setting five times and report the mean and variance of the accuracy on the testing set, to demonstrate the improvements are significant. As mentioned, before distillation training, we need to obtain the distillation process by searching described as below.

To search the process $\mathcal{A}$, we randomly split the original training set into two subdatasets, 80% of the images for training and 20% for validating. We run the search for 40 epochs and decay the learning rate for θ (parameters of the student) by 0.1 at epoch 10, 20, and 30. The learning rate for α is set to 0.05. Following the settings in [4], we did not use all feature maps for knowledge distillation but only the ones after each downsampling stage. Transform blocks are used to transform the student feature map. Figure 4a shows the block architecture. The size of the pathways is 27, as we use 3 transform blocks and 9 connections. To make fair comparison, we follow the same HCL distillation loss in [4]. Once the process is obtained, in order to align the searched distillation process, linear interpolation is used to expand the process of $\mathcal{A}$ from 40 epoch (search stage) to 240 epochs (retrain stage) during KD.

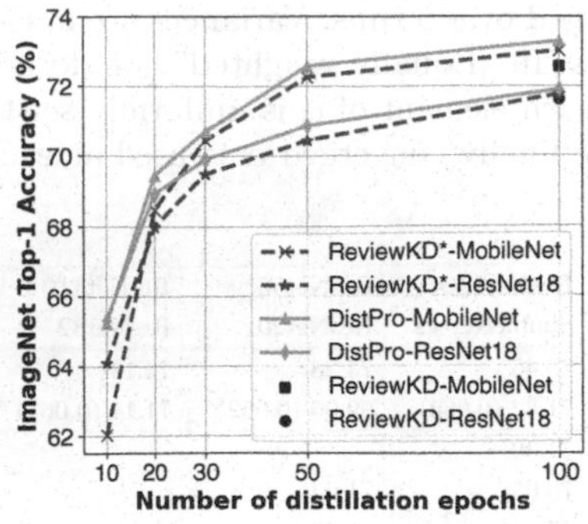

Fig. 5. Comparison study on fast distillation on ImageNet1K.

Table 2. Comparison study on numbers of distillation epochs to achieve same top-1 accuracy on ImageNet1K (lower the better).

	Network	ReviewKD [4]	DistPro(Ours)
Top-1	MobileNet	72.56	72.54
#Epochs		100	**50**
Top-1	ResNet18	71.61	71.59
#Epochs		100	**65**
Top-1	DeiT	73.44	73.41
#Epochs		150	**100**

Results. The quantitative results are summarized in Table 1. First two rows show the architecture of teacher and student network and their accuracy without distillation correspondingly. In the line of "ReviewKD*", we list the results reproduced using the code released by the author [4]. To demonstrate learning the α is essential, we first assign equally weighted α to all the pathways. As shown in line "Equally weighted", the results are worse than ReviewKD, indicating the selected pathways from ReviewKD are useful. For ablation, we first adopt the learned α_T at the end of the process. As shown in "Use α_T", it outperforms ReviewKD in multiple settings. The last row shows the results adopting the learned process $\mathcal{A}$, which outperforms ReviewKD significantly.

4.2 Classification on ImageNet1K

Implementation Details. We follow the search strategy used in CIFAR100 and training configurations in [4] with a batch size of 512 (4GPUs are used). The selected student/teacher networks are MobileNet/ResNet50, ResNet18/ResNet34 and DeiT-tiny [40]/ViT-B [9]. We adopt a different architecture of transform block for DeiT. At searching stage, we search $\mathcal{A}$ with Tiny-ImageNet [23] for 20 epochs. We adopt cosine lr scheduler for learning the student network. For search space, 1 transform block is used, while we consider 5 feature maps in the networks, and build 15 pathways by removing some pathways following [4] due to limited GPU memory. At KD stage, we train the network for various epochs with initial learning rate of 0.1, and cosine scheduler. It takes 4 GPU hours for searching and 80 GPU hours for distill with 100 epochs. More details (ViT transform block, selected pathways etc.) can be found in supplementary.

Fast Distillation. From prior works [38], KD is used to accelerate the network learning especially with large dataset. This is due to the fact that its accuracy can be increased using only Ground Truth labels if the network is trained with a large number of epochs [15]. Previous works [4] only check the results stopping at 100 epochs. Here, we argue that it is also important to evaluate the results with less training cost, which is another important index for evaluating KD methods. This will be useful for the applications requiring fast learning of the network.

Table 3. Results of transferring searched $\mathcal{A}$ cross search-retrain datasets and search-retrain networks performed on ImageNet1K with 100 epochs. Top-1 accuracy on validation set is reported.

Setting	Search dataset	Retrain dataset	Teacher	Student	Top-1 (%)
(a)	Tiny-ImageNet	ImageNet1K	ResNet50	MobileNet	73.26
	CIFAR100	ImageNet1K	ResNet50	MobileNet	73.20
Setting	Search teacher	Search student	Retrain teacher	Retrain student	Top-1 (%)
(b)	ResNet34	ResNet18	ResNet34	ResNet18	71.89
	ResNet50	MobileNet	ResNet34	ResNet18	71.87

Table 4. Comparison study on ImageNet1K. Settings are (a) teacher: ResNet-50, student: MobileNet; (b) teacher: ResNet-34, student: ResNet-18; (c) teacher: ViT-B, student: DeiT-tiny. ReviewKD* denotes our reproduced experimental results with cosine learning rate scheduler.

Setting	Acc. (%)	Teacher	Student	OFD [13]	LONDON [37]	SCKD [53]	ReviewKD [4]	ReviewKD*	DistPro
(a)	Top1	76.16	68.87	71.25	72.36	72.4	72.56	73.12	**73.26**
	Top5	93.86	88.76	90.34	91.03	–	91.00	91.22	**91.27**
(b)	Top1	73.31	69.75	70.81	–	71.3	71.61	71.76	**71.89**
	Top5	91.42	89.07	89.98	–	–	90.51	90.67	**90.76**
(c)	Top-1	85.1	73.41	–	–	–	–	73.44	**73.51**

Here, we show `DistPro` reaches much better trade-off between training cost and accuracy. In Fig. 5, `DistPro` with different network architectures (red curves) outperforms ReviewKD with the same setting (dashed blue curves) at all proposed training epochs. The performance gain is larger when less training cost is required, *e.g.* it is 3.22% on MobileNet with 10 epochs (65.25% vs 62.03%), while decreased to 0.14% with 100 epochs, which is still a decent improvement. Similar results are observed with ResNet18. Note here for all results with various epochs, we adopt the same learning process $\mathcal{A}$, where the time cost can be ignored comparing to that of KD. In Table 2, we show the number of epochs saved by `DistPro` when achieving the same accuracy using ReviewKD [4]. For instance, in training MobileNet, `DistPro` only use 50 epochs to achieve 72.54%, which is comparable to ReviewKD trained with 100 epochs (72.56%), yielding 2x acceleration. Similar acceleration is also observed with ResNet18 and DeiT.

Transfer $\mathcal{A}$. Here, we study whether learned $\mathcal{A}$ can be transferred across datasets and similar architectures. Table 3 shows the results. In setting (a), we resize the image in CIFAR100 to 224 × 224, and do the process search on CIFAR100, where the search cost is only 2 GPU hours. As shown at last column, it only downgrades accuracy by 0.06%, which is comparable with full results searched with ImageNet, demonstrating the process could be transferred across datasets. In setting (b), we adopt the searched process with student/teacher networks of MobileNet/ResNet50 to networks of ResNet18/ResNet34 since they have same feature pathways at similar corresponding layers. As shown, the results are closed, demonstrating the process could be transferred.

Table 5. mIoU (%) on CityScapes (higher the better). Results are averaged over 5 runs. Standard deviation in the parentheses.

Teacher	ResNet101
Student	MobileNet-v2
Baseline	66.92 (0.00721)
IFVD [44]	68.31 (0.00264)
SCKD [53]	68.25 (0.00307)
+ReviewKD [4]	69.03 (0.00373)
+Equally Weighted α	68.49 (0.00793)
+DistPro	**69.12 (0.00462)**

Table 6. Estimation error on NYUv2 (lower the better).

Teacher	ResNet50
Student	ResNet18
Baseline	0.2032
KD	0.2045
ReviewKD [4]	0.1983
Equally Weighted α	0.2030
DistPro	**0.1972**

Table 7. Performance of different normalization methods on CIFRA-100. concat($\tilde{\alpha}$, 1) concatenate $\tilde{\alpha}$ with a scalar 1. Results are averaged over 5 runs.

Normalization	Acc
softmax(concat($\tilde{\alpha}$, 1))	**79.78**
softmax($\tilde{\alpha}$)	79.41
$\frac{\tilde{\alpha}}{\|\tilde{\alpha}\|_1+1}$	79.47
$\frac{\tilde{\alpha}}{\|\tilde{\alpha}\|_1}$	79.20
sigmoid($\tilde{\alpha}$)	78.80

Best Results. Finally, Table 4 shows the quantitative results comparing with various SoTA baselines. As mentioned, we adopt cosine scheduler while ReviewKD [4] adopts step scheduler. To make it fair, we retrain ReviewKD with cosine scheduler, and list the results in the column of ReviewKD*. As shown in the table, for three distillation settings, DistPro outperform the existing methods achieving top-1 accuracy of 73.26% for MobileNet, 71.89% for ResNet18 and 73.51% for DeiT respectively, yielding new SoTA results for all these networks.

4.3 Dense Prediction Tasks

CityScapes is a popular semantic segmentation dataset with pixel class labels [6]. We compare to a SoTA segmentation KD method IFVD [44] and adopt their released code. IFVD is a response-based KD method, therefore can be combined with feature-based distillation method including ReviewKD and DistPro, which are shown as "+ReviewKD" and "+DistPro" respectively in Table 5. We adopt student of MobileNet-v2 to compare against another SoTA results from SCKD [53]. Please note here for simplicity and numerical stability, we disable adversarial loss of the original IFVD. From the table, "+DistPro" outperforms all competing methods.

NYUv2 is a dataset widely used for depth estimation [32]. The experiments are based on the code released in S2D [29]. We compare DistPro with the plain KD, where we treat teacher output as ground truth, and ReviewKD with intermediate feature maps. Root mean squared errors (RMSE) are summarized in Table 6, and it shows that DistPro is also beneficial.

4.4 Ablation Study

Is it Always Beneficial to Transfer Knowledge Only from Lower-Level Feature Maps to Higher-Level Feature Maps? In Table 6 of [4], the authors conducted a group of experiments on CIFAR100, which show that

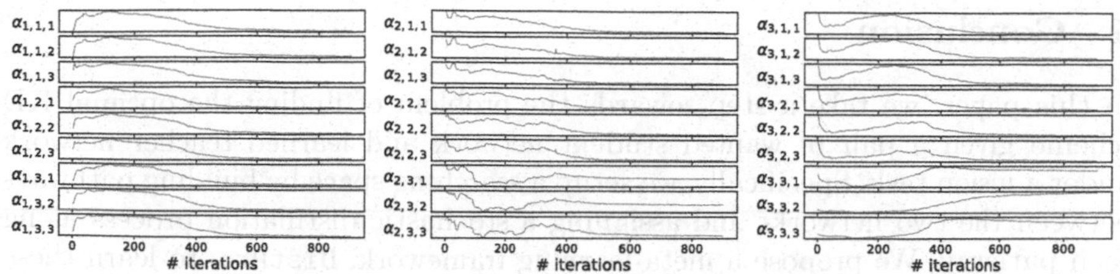

Fig. 6. Searched distillation process performed on CIFAR100 with WRN-40-2 as teacher and WRN-16-2 as student. x-axis is the number of iterations. The left image contains $\alpha[1,:,:]$, i.e., all the elements corresponding to the lowest-level feature map of the teacher. The middle one corresponds to $\alpha[2,:,:]$, and the right one corresponds to $\alpha[3,:,:]$.

only pathways from lower-level feature maps in teacher to higher-level feature maps in student are beneficial. However, we conducted similar experiments on CityScapes, the results did not support this claim. Specifically, using pathways from the last feature map to the first three feature maps results in mIoU 73.9% on ResNet18, while using pathways from all lower-level feature maps to higher level ones as in [4] results in 73.5%. This suggests that the optimal teaching scheme need to be searched w.r.t larger space. Also, the results in Table 5 also show that our searched process is better than the hand-crafted one.

Intuition of Process $\mathcal{A}$. In Fig. 6, we show how the learned sample of $\mathcal{A}$ changes with time in search stage of distilling WRN-40-2 to WRN-16-2. Similar observations are found in other settings. The figure indicates that at the early stage of the training, the optimized teaching scheme focuses on transferring knowledge from low-level feature maps of the teacher to the student. As training goes, the optimized teaching scheme gradually moves on to the higher-level feature maps of the teacher. Intuitively, high-level feature maps encode highly abstracted information of the input image and thus are harder to learn from compared to the low-level feature maps. `DistPro` is able to automatically find a teaching scheme to make use of this intuition.

Normalization of α_t. As mentioned before, we apply normalization to α_t ((2)) for numerical stability after 2_{nd} gradient approximation. In this study, we evaluate several normalization strategies. Let the unnormalized parameters be $\tilde{\alpha_t}$ and the normalized ones be α_t. In the following, we view α_t as a vector of length L. The experiments are conducted on CIFAR100 with WRN-28-4 as teacher and WRN-16-4 as student. The results are shown in Table 7, and the proposed biased softmax normalization outperforms others. Intuitively, due to the appended scalar 1, the value of $\tilde{\alpha_t}$ can be compared against 1, and a constant value yields a label smoothing [31] effect for the distribution.

5 Conclusion

In this paper, we take a step towards the problem of finding the optimal KD scheme given a pair of wanted student network and learned teacher network under a vision task. Specifically, we setup a searching space by building pathways between the two networks and assigning a stochastic distillation process along each pathway. We propose a meta-learning framework, `DistPro`, to learn these processes efficiently, and find effective ones to perform KD with intermediate features. We demonstrate its benefits over image classification, and dense predictions such as image segmentation and depth estimation. We hope our method could inspire the field of KD to further expand the scope, and its cooperation with other techniques such as NAS and hyper-parameter tuning.

References

1. Andrychowicz, M., et al.: Learning to learn by gradient descent by gradient descent. In: Advances in Neural Information Processing Systems, pp. 3981–3989 (2016)
2. Buciluǎ, C., Caruana, R., Niculescu-Mizil, A.: Model compression. In: Proceedings of the 12th ACM SIGKDD International Conference on Knowledge Discovery and Data Mining, pp. 535–541 (2006)
3. Chen, G., Choi, W., Yu, X., Han, T., Chandraker, M.: Learning efficient object detection models with knowledge distillation. Adv. Neural Inf. Process. Syst. **30** (2017)
4. Chen, P., Liu, S., Zhao, H., Jia, J.: Distilling knowledge via knowledge review. In: Proceedings of the IEEE/CVF Conference on Computer Vision and Pattern Recognition, pp. 5008–5017 (2021)
5. Chen, Z., Liu, B.: Lifelong machine learning. Synth. Lect. Artif. Intell. Mach. Learn. **12**(3), 1–207 (2018)
6. Cordts, M., et al.: The cityscapes dataset for semantic urban scene understanding. In: Proceedings of the IEEE Conference on Computer Vision and Pattern Recognition (CVPR) (2016)
7. Deng, J., Dong, W., Socher, R., Li, L.J., Li, K., Fei-Fei, L.: ImageNet: a large-scale Hierarchical Image Database. In: CVPR09 (2009)
8. Devlin, J., Chang, M.W., Lee, K., Toutanova, K.: Bert: pre-training of deep bidirectional transformers for language understanding. arXiv preprint arXiv:1810.04805 (2018)
9. Dosovitskiy, A., et al.: An image is worth 16 x 16 words: transformers for image recognition at scale. arXiv preprint arXiv:2010.11929 (2020)
10. Franceschi, L., Frasconi, P., Salzo, S., Grazzi, R., Pontil, M.: Bilevel programming for hyperparameter optimization and meta-learning. In: International Conference on Machine Learning, pp. 1568–1577. PMLR (2018)
11. Gou, J., Yu, B., Maybank, S.J., Tao, D.: Knowledge distillation: a survey. Int. J. Comput. Vision **129**(6), 1789–1819 (2021)
12. He, K., Zhang, X., Ren, S., Sun, J.: Deep residual learning for image recognition. In: Proceedings of the IEEE Conference on Computer Vision and Pattern Recognition, pp. 770–778 (2016)
13. Heo, B., Kim, J., Yun, S., Park, H., Kwak, N., Choi, J.Y.: A comprehensive overhaul of feature distillation. In: Proceedings of the IEEE/CVF International Conference on Computer Vision, pp. 1921–1930 (2019)

14. Hinton, G., Vinyals, O., Dean, J.: Distilling the knowledge in a neural network (2015)
15. Hoffer, E., Hubara, I., Soudry, D.: Train longer, generalize better: closing the generalization gap in large batch training of neural networks. Adv. Neural Inf. Process. Syst. **30** (2017)
16. Howard, A.G., et al.: Mobilenets: efficient convolutional neural networks for mobile vision applications. arXiv preprint arXiv:1704.04861 (2017)
17. Huang, Z., Wang, N.: Like what you like: knowledge distill via neuron selectivity transfer. arXiv preprint arXiv:1707.01219 (2017)
18. Jang, Y., Lee, H., Hwang, S.J., Shin, J.: Learning what and where to transfer. In: International Conference on Machine Learning, pp. 3030–3039. PMLR (2019)
19. Ji, M., Heo, B., Park, S.: Show, attend and distill: Knowledge distillation via attention-based feature matching. In: Proceedings of the AAAI Conference on Artificial Intelligence, vol. 35, pp. 7945–7952 (2021)
20. Kimura, A., Ghahramani, Z., Takeuchi, K., Iwata, T., Ueda, N.: Few-shot learning of neural networks from scratch by pseudo example optimization. arXiv preprint arXiv:1802.03039 (2018)
21. Kingma, D.P., Ba, J.: Adam: a method for stochastic optimization. arXiv preprint arXiv:1412.6980 (2014)
22. Krizhevsky, A., Hinton, G., et al.: Learning multiple layers of features from tiny images (2009)
23. Le, Y., Yang, X.: Tiny imagenet visual recognition challenge. CS 231N **7**(7), 3 (2015)
24. Lee, S., Song, B.C.: Graph-based knowledge distillation by multi-head attention network. arXiv preprint arXiv:1907.02226 (2019)
25. Liu, H., Simonyan, K., Yang, Y.: Darts: differentiable architecture search. In: International Conference on Learning Representations (2019)
26. Liu, Y., Chen, K., Liu, C., Qin, Z., Luo, Z., Wang, J.: Structured knowledge distillation for semantic segmentation. In: Proceedings of the IEEE/CVF Conference on Computer Vision and Pattern Recognition, pp. 2604–2613 (2019)
27. Liu, Y., et al.: Search to distill: Pearls are everywhere but not the eyes. In: Proceedings of the IEEE/CVF Conference on Computer Vision and Pattern Recognition, pp. 7539–7548 (2020)
28. Lyu, L., Chen, C.H.: Differentially private knowledge distillation for mobile analytics. In: Proceedings of the 43rd International ACM SIGIR Conference on Research and Development in Information Retrieval, pp. 1809–1812 (2020)
29. Ma, F., Karaman, S.: Sparse-to-dense: depth prediction from sparse depth samples and a single image. In: 2018 IEEE International Conference on Robotics and Automation (ICRA), pp. 4796–4803. IEEE (2018)
30. Ma, N., Zhang, X., Zheng, H.T., Sun, J.: Shufflenet v2: practical guidelines for efficient CNN architecture design. In: Proceedings of the European Conference on Computer Vision (ECCV), pp. 116–131 (2018)
31. Müller, R., Kornblith, S., Hinton, G.E.: When does label smoothing help? Adv. Neural Inf. Process. Syst. **32** (2019)
32. Silberman, N., Hoiem, D., Kohli, P., Fergus, R.: Indoor segmentation and support inference from RGBD images. In: Fitzgibbon, A., Lazebnik, S., Perona, P., Sato, Y., Schmid, C. (eds.) ECCV 2012. LNCS, vol. 7576, pp. 746–760. Springer, Heidelberg (2012). https://doi.org/10.1007/978-3-642-33715-4_54
33. Oord, A., et al.: Parallel wavenet: fast high-fidelity speech synthesis. In: International Conference on Machine Learning, pp. 3918–3926. PMLR (2018)

34. Ren, M., Zeng, W., Yang, B., Urtasun, R.: Learning to reweight examples for robust deep learning. In: International Conference on Machine Learning, pp. 4334–4343. PMLR (2018)
35. Romero, A., Ballas, N., Kahou, S., Chassang, A., Gatta, C., Bengio, Y.: Fitnets: hints for thin deep nets. CoRR abs/1412.6550 (2015)
36. Sandler, M., Howard, A., Zhu, M., Zhmoginov, A., Chen, L.C.: Mobilenetv 2: inverted residuals and linear bottlenecks. In: Proceedings of the IEEE Conference on Computer Vision and Pattern Recognition, pp. 4510–4520 (2018)
37. Shang, Y., Duan, B., Zong, Z., Nie, L., Yan, Y.: Lipschitz continuity guided knowledge distillation. In: Proceedings of the IEEE/CVF International Conference on Computer Vision, pp. 10675–10684 (2021)
38. Shen, Z., Xing, E.: A fast knowledge distillation framework for visual recognition. arXiv preprint arXiv:2112.01528 (2021)
39. Tian, Y., Krishnan, D., Isola, P.: Contrastive representation distillation. In: International Conference on Learning Representations (2020)
40. Touvron, H., Cord, M., Douze, M., Massa, F., Sablayrolles, A., Jégou, H.: Training data-efficient image transformers & distillation through attention. In: International Conference on Machine Learning, pp. 10347–10357. PMLR (2021)
41. Tung, F., Mori, G.: Similarity-preserving knowledge distillation. In: Proceedings of the IEEE/CVF International Conference on Computer Vision, pp. 1365–1374 (2019)
42. Urner, R., Shalev-Shwartz, S., Ben-David, S.: Access to unlabeled data can speed up prediction time. In: ICML (2011)
43. Wang, X., Zhang, R., Sun, Y., Qi, J.: Kdgan: knowledge distillation with generative adversarial networks. In: NeurIPS, pp. 783–794 (2018)
44. Wang, Y., Zhou, W., Jiang, T., Bai, X., Xu, Y.: Intra-class feature variation distillation for semantic segmentation. In: Vedaldi, A., Bischof, H., Brox, T., Frahm, J.-M. (eds.) ECCV 2020. LNCS, vol. 12352, pp. 346–362. Springer, Cham (2020). https://doi.org/10.1007/978-3-030-58571-6_21
45. Xiang, L., Ding, G., Han, J.: Learning from multiple experts: self-paced knowledge distillation for long-tailed classification. In: Vedaldi, A., Bischof, H., Brox, T., Frahm, J.-M. (eds.) ECCV 2020. LNCS, vol. 12350, pp. 247–263. Springer, Cham (2020). https://doi.org/10.1007/978-3-030-58558-7_15
46. Xie, S., Zheng, H., Liu, C., Lin, L.: SNAS: stochastic neural architecture search. In: International Conference on Learning Representations (2019). https://openreview.net/forum?id=rylqooRqK7
47. Xu, G., Liu, Z., Li, X., Loy, C.C.: Knowledge distillation meets self-supervision. In: European Conference on Computer Vision (ECCV) (2020)
48. Yao, L., Pi, R., Xu, H., Zhang, W., Li, Z., Zhang, T.: Joint-detnas: upgrade your detector with NAS, pruning and dynamic distillation. In: Proceedings of the IEEE/CVF Conference on Computer Vision and Pattern Recognition, pp. 10175–10184 (2021)
49. Yim, J., Joo, D., Bae, J., Kim, J.: A gift from knowledge distillation: fast optimization, network minimization and transfer learning. In: Proceedings of the IEEE Conference on Computer Vision and Pattern Recognition, pp. 4133–4141 (2017)
50. Zagoruyko, S., Komodakis, N.: Paying more attention to attention: improving the performance of convolutional neural networks via attention transfer. arXiv preprint arXiv:1612.03928 (2016)
51. Zagoruyko, S., Komodakis, N.: Wide residual networks. arXiv preprint arXiv:1605.07146 (2016)

52. Zhang, X., Zhou, X., Lin, M., Sun, J.: Shufflenet: an extremely efficient convolutional neural network for mobile devices. In: Proceedings of the IEEE Conference on Computer Vision and Pattern Recognition, pp. 6848–6856 (2018)
53. Zhu, Y., Wang, Y.: Student customized knowledge distillation: bridging the gap between student and teacher. In: Proceedings of the IEEE/CVF International Conference on Computer Vision, pp. 5057–5066 (2021)

ML-BPM: Multi-teacher Learning with Bidirectional Photometric Mixing for Open Compound Domain Adaptation in Semantic Segmentation

Fei Pan[1], Sungsu Hur[1], Seokju Lee[2], Junsik Kim[3], and In So Kweon[1](✉)

[1] KAIST, Daejeon, South Korea
{feipan,sshuh1215,iskweon77}@kaist.ac.kr
[2] KENTECH, Daejeon, South Korea
slee@kentech.ac.kr
[3] Harvard University, Cambridge, USA

Abstract. Open compound domain adaptation (OCDA) considers the target domain as the compound of multiple unknown homogeneous subdomains. The goal of OCDA is to minimize the domain gap between the labeled source domain and the unlabeled compound target domain, which benefits the model generalization to the unseen domains. Current OCDA for semantic segmentation methods adopt manual domain separation and employ a single model to simultaneously adapt to all the target subdomains. However, adapting to a target subdomain might hinder the model from adapting to other dissimilar target subdomains, which leads to limited performance. In this work, we introduce a multi-teacher framework with bidirectional photometric mixing to separately adapt to every target subdomain. First, we present an automatic domain separation to find the optimal number of subdomains. On this basis, we propose a multi-teacher framework in which each teacher model uses bidirectional photometric mixing to adapt to one target subdomain. Furthermore, we conduct an adaptive distillation to learn a student model and apply consistency regularization to improve the student generalization. Experimental results on benchmark datasets show the efficacy of the proposed approach for both the compound domain and the open domains against existing state-of-the-art approaches.

Keywords: Domain adaptation · Open compound domain adaptation · Semantic segmentation · Multi-teacher distillation

1 Introduction

Semantic segmentation is a fundamental task in finding applications to many problems, including robotics [34], autonomous driving [35], and medical diagnosis [16]. Recently, deep learning-based semantic segmentation approaches [12,35,

Supplementary Information The online version contains supplementary material available at https://doi.org/10.1007/978-3-031-19830-4_14.

S. Avidan et al. (Eds.): ECCV 2022, LNCS 13694, pp. 236–251, 2022.
https://doi.org/10.1007/978-3-031-19830-4_14

36] have achieved remarkable progress. However, their effectiveness and generalization ability require a large amount of pixel-wised annotated data which are expensive to collect. To reduce the cost of data collection and annotation, numerous synthetic datasets have been proposed [21,22]. However, the models trained on synthetic data tend to poorly generalize to real images. To cope with this issue, unsupervised domain adaptation (UDA) methods [17,25,26,28,33,37] have proposed to align the domain gap between the source and the target domain. Despite the efficacy of UDA techniques, most of these works rely on the strong assumption that the target data is composed of a single homogeneous domain. This assumption is often violated in real-world scenarios. As an illustration in autonomous driving, the target data will likely be composed of various subdomains such as night, snow, rain, etc. Therefore, directly applying the current UDA approaches to these target data might deliver limited performance. This paper focuses on the challenging problem of open compound domain adaptation (OCDA) in semantic segmentation where the target domain is unlabeled and contains multiple homogeneous subdomains. The goal of OCDA is to adapt a model to a compound target domain and to further enhance the model generalization to the unseen domains.

To perform OCDA, Liu *et al.* [13] propose an easy-to-hard curriculum learning strategy, where samples closer to the source domain will be chosen first for adaptation. However, it does not fully take advantage of the subdomain boundaries information in the compound target domain. To explicitly consider this information, current OCDA works [8,19] propose to separate the target compound domain into multiple subdomains based on image style information. Existing works use a manual domain separation method; they also employ a single model to simultaneously adapt to all the target subdomain. However, adapting to a target subdomain might hinder the model from adapting to other dissimilar target subdomains, which leads to limited performance. We propose a multi-teacher framework with bidirectional photometric mixing for open compound domain adaptation in semantic segmentation to tackle this issue. First, we propose automatic domain separation to find the optimal number of subdomains and split the target compound domain. Then, we present a multi-teacher framework in which each teacher model uses bidirectional photometric mixing to adapt to one target subdomain. On this basis, we conduct adaptive distillation to learn a student model and apply a fast and short online updating using consistency regularization to improve the student's generalization to the open domains. We evaluate our approach on the benchmark datasets. The proposed approach outperforms all the existing state-of-the-art OCDA techniques and the latest UDA techniques for domain adaptation and domain generalization task.

The Contribution of this Work. (1) we propose automatic domain separation to find the optimal number of target subdomains; (2) we present a multi-teacher framework with bidirectional photometric mixing to reduce the domain gaps between the source domain and every target subdomain separately; (3) we further conduct an adaptive distillation to learn a student model and apply consistency regularization to improve the student generalization to the open domains.

2 Related Work

Unsupervised Domain Adaptation. Unsupervised domain adaptation (UDA) techniques are used to reduce the expensive cost of pixel-wise labeling tasks like semantic segmentation. In UDA, adversarial learning is used actively to align input-level style using image translation, feature distribution, or structured output [10,17,27–29]. Alternatively, self-training approaches [2,25,33,37] have also recently demonstrated compelling performance in this context. While these works have shown significant improvement, adopting those works directly for practical usage shows limitations due to its restricted setting dealing with only single source and single target. Despite the improvement provided by UDA techniques, their applicability to real scenarios remains restricted by the implicit assumption that the target data contains images from a single distribution.

Domain Generalization. The purpose of domain generalization (DG) is to train a model – solely using source domain data – such that it can perform reliable predictions on unseen domain. While DG is an essential problem, a few works have attempted to address this problem in the task of semantic segmentation. DG for semantic segmentation shows two main streams: augmentation-based and network-based approaches. The augmentation-based approaches [11,30] propose to significantly augment the training data via an additional style dataset to learn domain-invariant representation. The network-based approaches [4,18] attempt to modify the structure of the network to minimize domain-specific information (such as colors or styles) such that the resulting model mainly focuses on the content-specific information. Even though DG for semantic segmentation has achieve obvious progress, their performance is inevitably lower than several UDA methods due to the absence of the target images, which is capable of providing abundant domain-specific information.

Open Compound Domain Adaptation. Liu *et al.* [13] firstly suggests Open Compound Domain Adaptation (OCDA) that handles unlabeled compound heterogeneous target domain and unseen open domain. While Liu *et al.* [13] propose a curriculum learning strategy, it fails to consider the specific information of each target subdomain. Current OCDA works [8,19] propose to separate the compound target domain into multiple subdomains to handle the intra-domain gaps. Gong *et al.* [8] adopt domain-specific batch normalization for adaptation. Park *et al.* [19] utilize GAN-based image translation and adversarial training to exploit domain invariant features from multiple subdomains (Fig. 1).

3 Generating Optimal Subdomains

3.1 Automatic Domain Separation

Our work assumes that the domain-specific property of images comes from their styles. Existing works adopt a predefined parameter to decide the number of subdomains, which might lead to a nonoptimal domain adaptation performance;

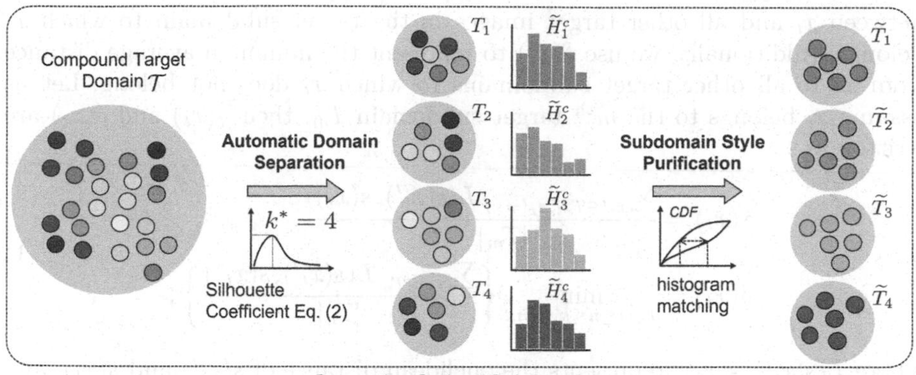

Fig. 1. The part of generating optimal subdomains consists of automatic domain separation (ADS) and subdomain style purification (SSP). In ADS, we adopt Silhouette Coefficient [23] to find the optimal number of subdomains k^*. In SSP, we calculate mean of histogram $\widetilde{H}_m^c$ for the mth target subdomain T_m according to Eq. 4, and the purified subdomain is denoted as $\widetilde{T}_m$.

furthermore, they rely on a pre-trained CNN-based encoder to extract the style information for the subdomain discovery. However, we propose an automatic domain separation (ADS) to effectively separate the target domain using the distribution of pixel values of the target images. The proposed ADS is capable of predicting the optimal number of subdomains without relying on any predefined parameters and extracting the image style information without relying on any pre-trained CNN models. We denote the source domain as $\mathcal{S}$, and the unlabeled compound target domain as $\mathcal{T}$. We also assume compound target domain contains k latent subdomains: $\{T_1, \ldots, T_k\}$, which lack of clear prior knowledge to distinguish themselves. The goal of ADS is to find the optimal number of subdomains k^* and separate $\mathcal{T}$ into several subdomains accordingly.

Current work [14] suggests a simple yet effective style translation method by matching the distribution of pixel values on LAB color space. Thus, we adopt LAB space into ADS to extract the style information of the target image. Given a target RGB image $x_t \in \mathcal{T}$ as input, we convert it into LAB color space $rgb2lab(x_t)$. The three channels in LAB color space are represented as l, a, and b. Then, we compute the histograms of the pixel values for all three channels in LAB color space: $H^l(x_t), H^a(x_t)$, and $H^b(x_t)$. The histograms are concatenated and represented as the style information of x_t. Let $s(x_t) = H^l(x_t)^\frown H^a(x_t)^\frown H^b(x_t)$ denote the concatenated histograms of x_t, and we take $s(x_t)$ as input to ADS for domain separation. However, most existing clustering algorithms require a hyperparameter to determine the number of clusters. Directly applying a naive clustering might lead to a nonoptimal adaptation performance. Thus, we propose to find the optimal number k^* of the subdomains using Silhouette Coefficient (SC) [23]. Suppose the target domain $\mathcal{T}$ is separated into k subdomains, $\{T_1, \ldots, T_k\}$. For each target image x_t, we denote $\gamma(x_t)$ as the average distance between x_t and all other target images in the target subdomain to which x_t belongs. Additionally, we use $\delta(x_t)$ to represent the minimum average distance from x_t to all other target subdomains to which x_t does not belong. Let us assume x_t belongs to the mth target subdomain T_m, then $\gamma(x_t)$ and $\delta(x_t)$ are written as

$$\gamma(x_t) = \frac{\sum_{x_t' \in T_m, x_t' \neq x_t} L(s(x_t'), s(x_t))}{|T_m| - 1},$$
$$\delta(x_t) = \min_{T_n : 1 \leq n \leq k, n \neq m} \left\{ \frac{\sum_{x_t' \in T_n} L(s(x_t'), s(x_t))}{|T_n|} \right\}, \tag{1}$$

where $L(s(x_t'), s(x_t))$ represents the euclidean distance of $s(x_t')$ and $s(x_t)$, and $|T_m|$ is the number of the target images in T_m. The SC score for k number of the target subdomains is given by

$$SC(k) = \sum_{x_t \in T} \frac{\delta(x_t) - \gamma(x_t)}{\max(\gamma(x_t), \delta(x_t))}. \tag{2}$$

Hence, the goal of the proposed ADS is to find k^* for

$$k^* = \arg\max_k SC(k). \tag{3}$$

3.2 Subdomain Style Purification

With the help fo automatic domain separation, the number of abnormal samples with different styles is small inside each target subdomain. Though these abnormal samples might be useful for the model's generalization, they could also lead to a negative transfer, which further hinders the model from learning domain invariant features in a specific subdomain. To cope with it, we propose to purify the style distribution of the target images inside each subdomain. We design a subdomain style purification (SSP) module to effectively make similar styles for the images within the same subdomain. Given the mth target subdomain T_m, we adopt the histograms of LAB color space $\{(H^l(x_t), H^a(x_t), H^b(x_t)); \forall x_t \in T_m\}$ (mentioned in 3.1), and then we compute the mean of the histograms for all the three channels, represented by $\widetilde{H}^l_m$, $\widetilde{H}^a_m$, and $\widetilde{H}^b_m$, and this process is achieved by

$$\widetilde{H}^c_m = \frac{\sum_{x_t \in T_m} H^c(x_t)}{|T_m|}; \forall c \in \{l, a, b\}, \tag{4}$$

where $|T_m|$ represents the number of the target images in T_m. We take $\{\widetilde{H}^l_m, \widetilde{H}^a_m, \widetilde{H}^b_m\}$ as the standard style for T_m. For each target RGB image $x_t \in T_m$, we change the style of x_t to generate the RGB new image $\tilde{x}_t$ by the histogram matching [20] on $\widetilde{H}^l_m$, $\widetilde{H}^a_m$, and $\widetilde{H}^b_m$ on the LAB color space. The process of SSP is done for all the subdomains $\{T_1, \ldots, T_{k^*}\}$. We denote the purified subdomains after SSP as $\{\widetilde{T}_1, \ldots, \widetilde{T}_{k^*}\}$.

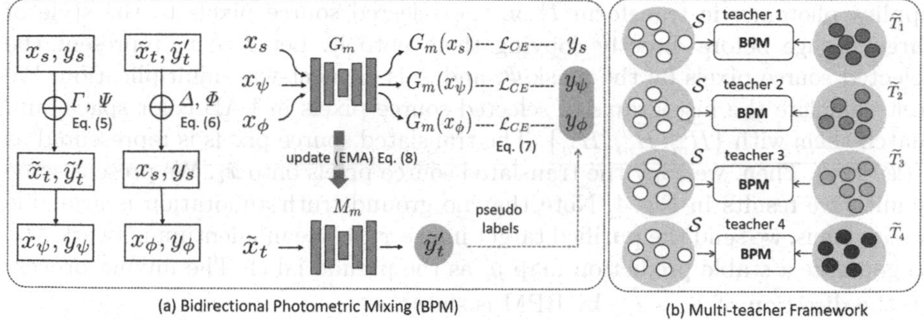

Fig. 2. (a) The architecture of the proposed bidirectional photometric mixing. (b) The diagram of the multi-teacher learning framework.

4 Multi-teacher Framework

4.1 Bidirectional Photometric Mixing

Through automatic domain separation and subdomain style purification (mentioned in 3.1 and 3.2), the compound domain $\mathcal{T}$ is automatically separated into multiple subdomains $\{\widetilde{T}_1, \ldots, \widetilde{T}_{k^*}\}$, where k^* represents the optimal number of the subdomains. Our next plan is to minimize the domain gap between the source domain and each target subdomain. A recent UDA work DACS [25] presents a mixing-based UDA technique for semantic segmentation. Inspired by DACS, we propose bidirectional photometric mixing (BPM) to minimize the domain gap between the source domain and each target subdomain separately. Compared with DACS, the proposed BPM adopts a photometric transform to decrease the style inconsistency of the mixed images to reduce the pixel-level domain gap. On this basis, BPM applies a bidirectional mixing scheme to provide a more robust regularization for training. The architecture of BPM is shown in Fig. 2(a). The proposed BPM contains a domain adaptive segmentation network G_m and a momentum network M_m that improves the stability of pseudo labels. Let $(x_s, y_s) \in \mathcal{S}$ denote the source RGB image and its pixel-wise annotation map, $x_s \in \mathbb{R}^{H\times W\times 3}$, $y_s \in \mathbb{R}^{H\times W}$. And $(\tilde{x}_t) \in \widetilde{T}_m$ represent a purified target RGB image from the mth purified subdomain $\widetilde{T}_m$, $\tilde{x}_t \in \mathbb{R}^{H\times W\times 3}$. Note that H and W represent the size of height and width. Our BPM applies the mixing in two directions: $\mathcal{S} \to \widetilde{T}_m$ and $\widetilde{T}_m \to \mathcal{S}$.

On the direction of mixing from $\mathcal{S} \to \widetilde{T}_m$, we choose ClassMix [15] because the source image x_s has the pixel-wise annotation map y_s. We first randomly select some classes from y_s. Then, we define $\Psi \in \{0,1\}^{H\times W}$ as a binary mask in which $\Psi(h,w) = 1$ when the pixel position (h,w) of x_s belongs to the selected classes, and $\Psi(h,w) = 0$ otherwise. While ClassMix suggests directly copying the corresponding pixels of selected classes of x_s onto $\tilde{x}_t$, the mixed image generated by ClassMix contains inconsistent style distribution which might hinder the adaptation performance. To cope with the limitation, the proposed BPM applies photometric transform Γ on the selected source pixels to the style of target image before directly copying them onto it. Let $\Psi \odot x_s$ represent the selected source pixels by the mask Ψ, and $\odot$ is element-wise multiplication. We first calculate the histograms of selected source pixels in LAB color space, and match them with $\{\widetilde{H}_m^l, \widetilde{H}_m^a, \widetilde{H}_m^b\}$. The translated source pixels is represented as $\Gamma(\Psi \odot x_s)$. Then, we copy the translated source pixels onto $\tilde{x}_t$. We present some qualitative results in Fig. 4. Note that no ground-truth annotation is available for $\tilde{x}_t$. Thus, we send the purified target image $\tilde{x}_t$ to the momentum network M_m to generate a stable prediction map $\tilde{y}_t'$ as the pseudo label. The mixing process on the direction of $\mathcal{S} \rightarrow \widetilde{T}_m$ by BPM is shown as

$$\begin{aligned} x_\psi &= \Gamma(\Psi \odot x_s) + (\mathbf{1} - \Psi) \odot \tilde{x}_t, \\ y_\psi &= \Psi \odot y_s + (\mathbf{1} - \Psi) \odot \tilde{y}_t', \end{aligned} \tag{5}$$

where x_ψ is the generated mixed image, y_ψ is the corresponding mixed pseudo label, and $\Gamma(\cdot)$ is the photometric transform of the source selected pixels by histogram matching on LAB color space.

On the direction of mixing from $\widetilde{T}_m \rightarrow \mathcal{S}$, however, it is impossible to choose ClassMix since no ground-truth annotation is available for $\tilde{x}_t$. Inspired by CutMix [31], we generate another binary mask $\Phi \in \{0,1\}^{H \times W}$ by sampling rectangular bounding box (d_x, d_y, d_w, d_h) according to the uniform distribution; $d_x \sim U(0, W), d_y \sim U(0, H), d_w = W\sqrt{1-\eta}, d_h = H\sqrt{1-\eta}$, where $\eta \sim U(0,1)$, (H, W) are the height and width of the image. The binary mask Φ is formed by filling with 1 the pixel positions inside the bounding box, and filling with 0 other positions. With the help of Φ, we select the target pixels $\Phi \odot \tilde{x}_t$ and transform them into the source style. The transformed target pixel is represented by $\Delta(\Phi \odot \tilde{x}_t)$. Then we paste them onto the source image x_s. We present the mixing of $\widetilde{T}_m \rightarrow \mathcal{S}$ at

$$\begin{aligned} x_\phi &= \Delta(\Phi \odot \tilde{x}_t) + (\mathbf{1} - \Phi) \odot x_s, \\ y_\phi &= \Phi \odot \tilde{y}_t' + (\mathbf{1} - \Phi) \odot y_s, \end{aligned} \tag{6}$$

where x_ϕ is the other generated mixed image, y_ϕ is the corresponding mixed pseudo label, and $\Delta(\cdot)$ is the photometric transform of the target selected pixels by histogram matching on LAB color space.

we (x_ψ, y_ψ) (x_ϕ, y_ϕ) and (x_s, y_s) to train the segmentation network G_m and the momentum network M_m. We first optimize the parameters of G_m through

$$\begin{aligned} \mathcal{L}_{BGM}(\theta_m) = \sum_{\forall x_s \in S} \sum_{\forall \tilde{x}_t \in \widetilde{T}_m} \Big[& \mathcal{L}_{CE}\Big(G_m(x_s), y_s\Big) + \alpha \mathcal{L}_{CE}\Big(G_m(x_\psi), y_\psi\Big) \\ & + \beta \mathcal{L}_{CE}\Big(G_m(x_\phi), y_\phi\Big)\Big] \end{aligned}, \tag{7}$$

where θ_m represent the parameters of G_m, $\mathcal{L}_{CE}$ is the cross-entropy loss for the predicted segmentation maps and the ground-truth or pseudo labels, α and β are the hyper-parameters to control the effect of the mixing of both the directions for the loss function. To help the momentum network M_m provide stable pseudo labels, we update the parameters of M_m, represented by θ_m', using an exponential moving average (EMA) with a momentum $\lambda \in [0,1]$. After finishing the training iteration t, θ'_m is updated by

$$\theta'^{\,t+1}_m = \lambda \theta'^{\,t}_m + (1-\lambda)\theta_m. \tag{8}$$

4.2 Multi-teacher Adaptive Knowledge Distillation

We propose a multi-teacher framework followed by an adaptive knowledge distillation to align the domain gaps between the source domain and all the target subdomains. Given a purified subdomain $\widetilde{T}_m$, we adopt a BPM as a specific teacher model to minimize the domain gap between $\mathcal{S}$ and $\widetilde{T}_m$. And we train the proposed multi-teacher framework by minimizing the loss function $\mathcal{L}_{MT}$ on all the teacher models, *i.e.*,

$$\mathcal{L}_{MT} = \sum_{m=1}^{k^*} \mathcal{L}_{BGM}(\theta_m), \tag{9}$$

where $\mathcal{L}_{BGM}(\theta_m)$ (defined in Eq. 7) is the loss function of the segmentation network G_m in the mth teacher model, and k^* is the optimal number of the subdomains. Moreover, We learn a segmentation network G_{sd} as the student network via an adaptive knowledge distillation from all the teacher networks $\{G_m : 1 \leq m \leq k^*\}$. Given a random target data from $x_t \in \mathcal{T}$, we send x_t to all the teachers model, and the student is to learn from a weighted average of the all teacher's predictions $O_w(x_t)$, based on the teacher's confidence score. We adopt the entropy of G_m's prediction map $G_m(x_t) \in \mathbb{R}^{H\times W\times C}$ as the confidence of the mth teacher model, where C is the total number of classes we consider. Thus, the weight w_m for the mth teacher and the average prediction $G_{out}(x_t)$ are formulated as

$$\begin{aligned} w_m &= \frac{\sum_{h,w,c} G_m(x_t)\log\left[G_m(x_t)\right]}{\sum_{m'}\sum_{h,w,c} G_{m'}(x_t)\log\left[G_{m'}(x_t)\right]}, \\ G_{out}(x_t) &= \sum_{m=1}^{k^*} w_m G_m(x_t). \end{aligned} \tag{10}$$

On this basis, we optimize the student segmentation network G_{sd} with a distillation loss $\mathcal{L}_D$ defined by

$$\mathcal{L}_D = \sum_{x_t \in \mathcal{T}} \mathcal{L}_{KL}\Big[G_{sd}(x_t)||G_{out}(x_t)\Big], \tag{11}$$

where $\mathcal{L}_{KL}$ is KL divergence loss function between the output of G_{sd} and G_{out}. The goal of the multi-teacher adaptive knowledge distillation is to achieve the optimal parameters $\theta_{sd}{}^*$ of the student segmentation network G_{sd} by

$$\theta_{sd}{}^* = \min_{\theta_{sd}} \mathcal{L}_{MT} + \mathcal{L}_D. \tag{12}$$

Online Updating with Consistency Regularization. To evaluate the generalization of our approach, we directly evaluate our student network on the open domains as shown in Table 2a and Table 2b. Additionally, after finishing the compound domain adaptation training, we also provide a fast and short online updating for the student network using consistency regularization. This would further boost the generalization of the student network. Given an RGB image x_o from an open domain, we first match the style of x_o to other standard styles from the existing target subdomains. The standard styles are defined as the mean histograms $\{\widetilde{H}^l_m, \widetilde{H}^a_m, \widetilde{H}^b_m\}$ (defined in 3.2). The newly transformed images are $\{x^m_o; 1 \leq m \leq k^*\}$, where x^m_o is generated by matching x_o to the style of the mth subdomain $\widetilde{T}_m$. Thus, we conduct an online updating for the student network G_{sd} by

$$\min_{\theta_{sd}} \sum_{m=1}^{k^*} \mathcal{L}_1\big(G_{sd}(x^m_o), G_{sd}(x_o)\big), \tag{13}$$

where $\mathcal{L}_1$ is the mean absolute loss. After the online updating, we test the student network with newly learnt parameters again on the open domains.

5 Experiments

5.1 Experimental Setup

Dataset. In this work, we adopt the synthetic datasets, including GTA5 [21] and SYNTHIA [22] as the source domains. GTA5 contains 24,966 annotated images of $1,914 \times 1,052$ resolution. SYNTHIA consists of 9,400 images with $1,280 \times 760$ resolution. Furthermore, we adopt C-Driving [13] as the compound target domains which contains real images of $1,280 \times 720$ resolution collected from different weather conditions. Following the settings of previous works [8,13,19], we use the 14,697 rainy, snowy, cloudy images as the compound target domain and adopt 627 overcast images as the open domain. We also use ACDC [24] as another compound target domain and the evaluation results are shown in supplementary material. We further adopt Cityscapes [5], KITTI [1], and WildDash [32] as the open domains to evaluate the generalization ability of the proposed approach.

Implementation Details. We adopt DeepLab-V2 [3] with ResNet101 backbone [9] pre-trained on ImageNet [6]. All the images from target domain are rescaled into $1,280 \times 720$ and then randomly cropped into 640×360. The batch size is set up with 2 and the total number of training iterations is 2.5×10^5. We adopt stochastic gradient descent to optimize all the segmentation networks, with a weight decay of 5×10^{-4} and momentum of 0.9. The learning rate is set up with an initial value of 2.5×10^{-4} and decreased by polynomial decay with an exponent of 0.9. The momentum network has the same network architecture as the segmentation network. Existing mixing techniques contain CutMix [31],

Table 1. The performance comparison of mean IoU on the compound domain. Our approach is compared with the state-of-the-art UDA and OCDA approaches on (a) GTA5→C-Driving and (b) SYNTHIA→C-Driving benchmark dataset with ResNet-101 as the backbone. Note that mIoU[11] represents the mean IoU of 11 classes, excluding the class with *.

(a) GTA5→C-Driving

Method	Type	road	sidewalk	building	wall	fence	pole	light	sign	veg	terrain	sky	person	rider	car	truck	bus	train	mbike	bike	mIoU
Source	-	73.4	12.5	62.8	6.0	15.8	19.4	10.9	21.1	54.6	13.9	76.7	34.5	12.4	68.1	31.0	12.8	0.0	10.1	1.9	28.3
CDAS [13]	OCDA	79.1	9.4	67.2	12.3	15.0	20.1	14.8	23.8	65.0	22.9	82.6	40.4	7.2	73.0	27.1	18.3	0.0	16.1	1.5	31.4
CSFU [8]	OCDA	80.1	12.2	70.8	9.4	24.5	22.8	19.1	30.3	68.5	28.9	82.7	47.0	16.4	79.9	36.6	18.8	0.0	13.5	1.4	34.9
SAC [2]	UDA	81.5	23.8	72.0	10.3	27.8	23.0	18.2	34.1	70.3	27.9	87.8	45.0	16.9	77.6	38.5	19.8	0.0	14.0	2.7	36.4
DACS [25]	UDA	81.9	24.0	72.2	11.9	28.6	24.2	18.3	35.4	**71.8**	28.0	87.7	44.9	15.6	78.4	39.1	**24.9**	0.1	6.9	1.9	36.6
DHA[19]	OCDA	79.9	14.5	71.4	**13.1**	32.0	**27.1**	20.7	35.3	70.5	27.5	86.4	47.3	23.3	77.6	44.0	18.0	0.1	13.7	2.5	37.1
Ours	OCDA	**85.3**	**26.2**	**72.8**	10.6	**33.1**	26.9	**24.6**	**39.4**	70.8	**32.5**	**87.9**	**47.6**	**29.2**	**84.8**	**46.0**	22.8	**0.2**	**16.7**	**5.8**	**40.2**

(b) SYNTHIA→C-Driving

Method	Type	road	sidewalk	building	wall	fence	pole	light	sign*	veg	sky	person	rider*	car	bus*	mbike*	bike*	mIoU[16]	mIoU[11]
Source	-	33.9	11.9	42.5	1.5	0.0	14.7	0.0	1.3	56.8	76.5	13.3	7.4	57.8	12.5	2.1	1.6	20.9	28.1
CDAS [13]	OCDA	54.5	13.0	53.9	0.8	0.0	18.2	13.0	13.2	**60.0**	78.9	17.6	3.1	64.2	12.2	2.1	1.5	25.3	34.0
CSFU [8]	OCDA	69.6	12.2	50.9	1.3	0.0	16.7	12.1	13.6	56.2	75.8	20.0	4.8	68.2	14.1	0.9	1.2	26.1	34.8
SAC [2]	UDA	69.8	13.4	56.2	1.7	0.0	20.0	9.6	13.7	52.5	78.1	29.1	15.5	68.9	10.9	**3.2**	1.2	27.7	36.3
DACS [25]	UDA	62.1	**15.2**	48.8	0.3	0.0	19.7	10.3	9.6	57.8	**84.4**	35.2	18.9	67.8	16.0	2.2	1.7	28.1	36.5
DHA [19]	OCDA	67.5	2.5	54.6	0.2	0.0	**25.8**	13.4	**27.1**	58.0	83.9	36.0	6.1	71.6	**28.9**	2.2	1.8	29.9	37.6
Ours	OCDA	**73.4**	**15.2**	**57.1**	**1.8**	0.0	23.2	**13.5**	23.9	59.9	83.3	**40.3**	**22.3**	**72.2**	23.3	2.3	**2.2**	**32.1**	**40.0**

CowMix [7] and ClassMix [15]. We adopt ClassMix on the mixing direction of the source domain to the target domain, and we apply CutMix on the mixing direction of the target domain to the source domain. Both α and β are set up with 1 in the experiments. To increase the robustness of the segmentation model, we adopt data augmentations, including flipping, color jittering, and Gaussian blurring on the mixed images.

5.2 Results

To demonstrate the efficacy of our approach, we conduct experiments on the benchmark datasets of GTA5→C-Driving and SYNTHIA→C-Driving. We first compare our approach with the existing state-of-the-art OCDA approaches: CDAS [13], DHA [19], and CSFU [8]. Furthermore, we compare the proposed approach with the current state-of-the-art UDA approaches SAC [2] and DACS [25].

Compound Domain Adaptation. We first compare the performance of our approach with existing state-of-the-art OCDA and UDA approaches on GTA5 →C-Driving, shown in Table 1a. All the results are generated on the validation set of C-Driving. Training only with the source data leads to 28.3% of mean IoU over the 19 classes. As the first work in OCDA, CDAS achieves 31.4% on the mean IoU of all the classes. CSFU generates 34.9% of mean IoU, and DHA

Table 2. The comparison of mean IoU on the open domains. The domain generalization (DG) model is trained only with the source domain. All the models are tested on the validation set of C-Driving Open (O), cityscapes (C), KITTI (K), and wildDash (W). We also present the scores of our approach without online updating (w/o Updating) and with online updating (w/ Updating).

(a) GTA5 as the source domain.

	GTA5					
Method	Type	O	C	K	W	Avg
CSFU [8]	OCDA	38.9	38.6	37.9	29.1	36.1
DACS [25]	UDA	39.7	37.0	40.2	30.7	36.9
RobustNet [4]	DG	38.1	38.3	40.5	30.8	37.0
DHC [19]	OCDA	39.4	38.8	40.1	30.9	37.5
Ours (w/o Updating)	OCDA	41.8	40.9	44.0	32.9	40.0
Ours (w/ Updating)	OCDA	42.5	41.7	44.3	34.6	40.8

(b) SYNTHIA as the source domain.

	SYNTHIA					
Method	Type	O	C	K	W	Avg
CSFU [8]	OCDA	36.2	34.9	32.4	27.6	32.8
DACS [25]	UDA	36.8	37.0	37.4	28.8	35.0
RobustNet [4]	DG	37.1	38.3	40.1	29.6	36.3
DHC [19]	OCDA	38.9	38.0	40.6	30.0	36.9
Ours (w/o Updating)	OCDA	41.5	40.3	42.7	30.1	38.7
Ours (w/ Updating)	OCDA	42.6	41.1	43.4	30.9	39.5

produces 37.1% of mean IoU. This is because both CSFU and DHA adopt the subdomain separation step and GAN framework, and DHA uses a more effective multi-discriminator to minimize the domain gaps. In comparison, the latest UDA approaches DACS and SAC show 36.6% and 36.4%, outperforming both CDAS and CSFU. The reason behind is that both DACS and SAC adopt various self-supervision techniques to minimize the domain gaps, which proves to be more effective than GAN-based approaches. In comparison, the proposed approach demonstrates effectiveness on this benchmark dataset with 40.2% of mean IoU over all classes.

We present experimental results on SYNTHIA→C-Driving shown in Table 1b. We consider the 11 classes for final evaluation. The proposed method achieves 40.0% of mean IoU over the 11 classes. For other OCDA approaches, DHA achieves 37.6%, CSFU produces 34.8%, and CDAS generates 34.0% of mean IoU. Moreover, the UDA approaches DACS and SAC generate 36.5% and 36.3% of mean IoU. Our approach outperforms all the existing OCDA approaches and the latest UDA approaches.

Generalization to the Open Domains. We also evaluate the domain generalization of the proposed approach against existing UDA and OCDA approaches. The results are presented in Table 2a and 2b. Our work is compared with the latest domain generalization (DG) approach RobustNet [4]. For all the UDA and OCDA approaches, we first train them with the labeled source and the unlabeled target images, and we evaluate their performance with the validation of the open domains. RobustNet generates 37.0% of mean IoU in Table 2a and 36.3% of mean IoU in Table 2b. Note that RobustNet only requires labeled source data during training. This shows that the DG approach is more effective in generalizing to the open domains than the existing UDA and OCDA approaches DACS and CSFU. Without any online updating, our approach achieves 40.0% of mean IoU in Table 2a and 38.7% of mean IoU in Table 2b. Our approach outperforms all the UDA approaches, OCDA approaches, and the DG approach listed in the table.

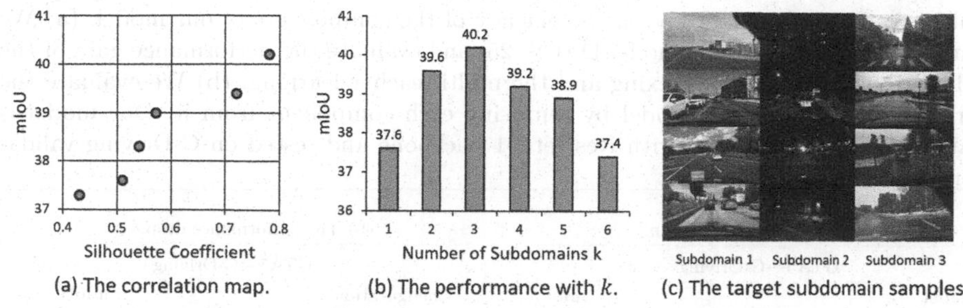

(a) The correlation map. (b) The performance with k. (c) The target subdomain samples.

Fig. 3. We conduct the ablation study on the proposed automatic domain separation using GTA5→C-Driving with ResNet101 backbone. (a) The scatterplot shows the correlation between our approach's mean IoU and the Silhouette Coefficient score. (b) The mean IoU of our approach with different number of subdomains k. (c) The sample images from the subdomains of the C-Driving dataset.

The reason might be that our approach is more powerful for learning the domain invariant features which improve the generalization of the model toward novel domains. The performance gain of our approach with updating further shows the efficacy of the proposed online updating with consistency regularization.

5.3 Ablation Study

Generating Optimal Subdomains. We first conduct the ablation study on the correlation between the mean IoU of the proposed approach with Silhouette Coefficient (SC) score on the subdomain separation in Fig. 3(a). It shows a positive correlation, which means that the SC score is effectively finds the optimal number of subdomains for the compound target domain. Moreover, we evaluate the mean IoU score with the different number of subdomains k in Fig. 3(b). Finally, we set up $k = 3$ and present the sample images from the subdomains of the C-Driving dataset in Fig. 3(c). We also evaluate the efficacy of the proposed subdomain style purification (SSP) in Table 3b. Without using SSP, the performance drops 0.5% of mean IoU.

Multi-teacher and Single Model. The ablation study on the multi-teacher learning of our proposed approach is presented in Table 3a and Table 3b. Applying a single model in our approach delivers 38.0% of mean IoU, leading to the the most significant drop 2.2%, shown in Table 3b. We further combine DACS with multi-teacher learning, and the mean IoU reaches from 36.6% to 39.1%. We argue that utilizing a single model is less effective than the multi-teacher models. Because adapting to one subdomain might hinder the single model from adapting to other dissimilar subdomains. Thus, we employ a multi-teacher framework in which each teacher adapts to one subdomain separately. And the multiple teachers together provide a comprehensive guide to the student model to adapt to all the target subdomains. We further present the qualitative results about

Table 3. The ablation study on the efficacy of the components of our model. (a) We compare with one baseline model DACS [25] and evaluate the performance gain of the bidirectional photometric mixing and the multi-teacher learning. (b) We evaluate the performance drop of our model by removing each component from it. Our model is trained GTA5→C-Driving with ResNet101 backbone and tested on C-Driving validation set.

(a) The performance gain.

GTA5→C-Driving	
Model	mIoU
DACS [25]	36.6
DACS + Multi-teacher Learning	39.1
DACS + Bidirectional Mixing	37.3
DACS + Photometric Mixing (Γ, Δ)	37.4
DACS + Bidirectional Photometric Mixing	37.8
Ours	40.2

(b) The performance drop.

GTA5→C-Driving		
Configuration	mIoU	Gap
w/o Multi-teacher Learning	38.0	-2.2
w/o Mixing on One Direction ($\alpha = 0$)	38.5	-1.7
w/o Mixing on One Direction ($\beta = 0$)	38.9	-1.3
w/o Subdomain Style Purification	39.7	-0.5
w/o Adaptive Distillation	39.6	-0.6
Full Framework	40.2	-

Fig. 4. We compare the mixed images from the source domain to the target domain. (a) the source image; (b) the target image; (c) the mixed images without using photometric transform, and the style inconsistency exists; (d) the mixed images using photometric transform, and the style inconsistency is mitigated; (e) the mask to crop the source image.

the target image prediction maps from each subdomain by the multi-teachers and the single-teacher model in Fig. 5.

Bidirectional Photometric Mixing. We further conduct the ablation study for the bidirectional photometric mixing (BPM), shown in Table 3a and Table 3b. Our model is trained on GTA5 → C-Driving with ResNet101 backbone and tested on C-Driving validation set. By making $\alpha = 0$ to remove the mixing on one direction (ClassMix), the mean IoU drops 1.7%, while making $\beta = 0$ to remove the other directional mixing (CutMix), it decreases by 1.3%. This suggests that ClassMix contributes slightly more to the final performance. We also use the baseline model DACS for an in-depth analysis. We add the bidirectional photometric mixing with the DACS, the performance increase from 36.6% to

Fig. 5. We present the predicted segmentation maps of the target images from every target subdomain. The maps in the second row are generated using a single model. The maps in the third row are generated using the multi-teacher models.

37.8% shown in Table 3a; we then combine DACS with only bidirectional mixing, the mean IoU rise up to 37.3%; we further add DACS with only photometric transform on mixing (use Γ and Δ), the mean IoU reaches to 37.4%. The reason behind is that DACS utilizes a simple mixing method that contains only one direction and generates the mixed image with the style inconsistency inside. However, we propose a bidirectional mixing scheme and apply the photometric transform to mitigate the style inconsistency on the generated images. We present the qualitative results to show this issue in Fig. 4. The style inconsistency is mitigated in Fig. 4(d) compared with Fig. 4(c) on the mixing direction from the source domain to the target domain.

6 Conclusion

Open compound domain adaptation (OCDA) considers the target domain as the compound of multiple unknown subdomains. In this work, we first propose automatic domain separation to find the optimal number of subdomains. Then we design a multi-teacher framework with bidirectional photometric mixing to align the domain gap between the source domain and the compound target domain, and we further evaluate its generalization to novel domains. Our current work is only focused on segmentation task and we leave the study on other visual tasks for future research.

Acknowledgment. This work was supported by the Korea Institute of Energy Technology Evaluation and Planning (KETEP) and the Ministry of Trade, Industry & Energy (MOTIE) of the Republic of Korea (No. 20224000000100).

References

1. Abu Alhaija, H., Mustikovela, S.K., Mescheder, L., Geiger, A., Rother, C.: Augmented reality meets computer vision: efficient data generation for urban driving scenes. IJCV **126**(9), 961–972 (2018)
2. Araslanov, N., Roth, S.: Self-supervised augmentation consistency for adapting semantic segmentation. In: CVPR, pp. 15384–15394 (2021)
3. Chen, L.C., Papandreou, G., Kokkinos, I., Murphy, K., Yuille, A.L.: Deeplab: semantic image segmentation with deep convolutional nets, atrous convolution, and fully connected CRFs. PAMI **40**(4), 834–848 (2017)
4. Choi, S., Jung, S., Yun, H., Kim, J.T., Kim, S., Choo, J.: Robustnet: improving domain generalization in urban-scene segmentation via instance selective whitening. In: CVPR, pp. 11580–11590 (2021)
5. Cordts, M., et al.: The cityscapes dataset for semantic urban scene understanding. In: CVPR, pp. 3213–3223 (2016)
6. Deng, J., Dong, W., Socher, R., Li, L.J., Li, K., Fei-Fei, L.: Imagenet: a large-scale hierarchical image database. In: CVPR, pp. 248–255. IEEE (2009)
7. French, G., Oliver, A., Salimans, T.: Milking cowmask for semi-supervised image classification. arXiv preprint arXiv:2003.12022 (2020)
8. Gong, R., et al.: Cluster, split, fuse, and update: meta-learning for open compound domain adaptive semantic segmentation. In: CVPR, pp. 8344–8354 (2021)
9. He, K., Zhang, X., Ren, S., Sun, J.: Deep residual learning for image recognition. In: CVPR, pp. 770–778 (2016)
10. Hoffman, J., et al.: Cycada: cycle-consistent adversarial domain adaptation. In: ICML, pp. 1989–1998. PMLR (2018)
11. Huang, J., Guan, D., Xiao, A., Lu, S.: Fsdr: frequency space domain randomization for domain generalization. In: CVPR, pp. 6891–6902 (2021)
12. Huang, Z., Wang, X., Huang, L., Huang, C., Wei, Y., Liu, W.: CCNet: criss-cross attention for semantic segmentation. In: CVPR, pp. 603–612 (2019)
13. Liu, Z., et al.: Open compound domain adaptation. In: CVPR, pp. 12406–12415 (2020)
14. Ma, H., Lin, X., Wu, Z., Yu, Y.: Coarse-to-fine domain adaptive semantic segmentation with photometric alignment and category-center regularization. In: CVPR, pp. 4051–4060 (2021)
15. Olsson, V., Tranheden, W., Pinto, J., Svensson, L.: Classmix: segmentation-based data augmentation for semi-supervised learning. In: WACV, pp. 1369–1378 (2021)
16. Ouyang, C., Biffi, C., Chen, C., Kart, T., Qiu, H., Rueckert, D.: Self-supervision with superpixels: training few-shot medical image segmentation without annotation. In: Vedaldi, A., Bischof, H., Brox, T., Frahm, J.-M. (eds.) ECCV 2020. LNCS, vol. 12374, pp. 762–780. Springer, Cham (2020). https://doi.org/10.1007/978-3-030-58526-6_45
17. Pan, F., Shin, I., Rameau, F., Lee, S., Kweon, I.S.: Unsupervised intra-domain adaptation for semantic segmentation through self-supervision. In: CVPR, pp. 3764–3773 (2020)
18. Pan, X., Luo, P., Shi, J., Tang, X.: Two at once: enhancing learning and generalization capacities via ibn-net. In: ECCV, pp. 464–479 (2018)
19. Park, K., Woo, S., Shin, I., Kweon, I.S.: Discover, hallucinate, and adapt: open compound domain adaptation for semantic segmentation. In: NeurIPS (2020)
20. Rafael, C.G., Richard, E.W., Steven, L.E., Woods, R., Eddins, S.: Digital Image Processing Using MATLAB. Tata McGraw-Hill, New York (2010)

21. Richter, S.R., Vineet, V., Roth, S., Koltun, V.: Playing for data: ground truth from computer games. In: Leibe, B., Matas, J., Sebe, N., Welling, M. (eds.) ECCV 2016. LNCS, vol. 9906, pp. 102–118. Springer, Cham (2016). https://doi.org/10.1007/978-3-319-46475-6_7
22. Ros, G., Sellart, L., Materzynska, J., Vazquez, D., Lopez, A.: The SYNTHIA dataset: a large collection of synthetic images for semantic segmentation of urban scenes. In: CVPR (2016)
23. Rousseeuw, P.J.: Silhouettes: a graphical aid to the interpretation and validation of cluster analysis. JCAM **20**, 53–65 (1987)
24. Sakaridis, C., Dai, D., Van Gool, L.: ACDC: the adverse conditions dataset with correspondences for semantic driving scene understanding. In: ICCV, pp. 10765–10775 (2021)
25. Tranheden, W., Olsson, V., Pinto, J., Svensson, L.: Dacs: domain adaptation via cross-domain mixed sampling. In: WACV, pp. 1379–1389 (2021)
26. Tsai, Y.H., Hung, W.C., Schulter, S., Sohn, K., Yang, M.H., Chandraker, M.: Learning to adapt structured output space for semantic segmentation. In: CVPR (2018)
27. Tsai, Y.H., Hung, W.C., Schulter, S., Sohn, K., Yang, M.H., Chandraker, M.: Learning to adapt structured output space for semantic segmentation. In: CVPR, pp. 7472–7481 (2018)
28. Vu, T.H., Jain, H., Bucher, M., Cord, M., Pérez, P.: Advent: adversarial entropy minimization for domain adaptation in semantic segmentation. In: CVPR (2019)
29. Wang, Z., et al.: Differential treatment for stuff and things: a simple unsupervised domain adaptation method for semantic segmentation. In: CVPR, pp. 12635–12644 (2020)
30. Yue, X., Zhang, Y., Zhao, S., Sangiovanni-Vincentelli, A., Keutzer, K., Gong, B.: Domain randomization and pyramid consistency: simulation-to-real generalization without accessing target domain data. In: ICCV, pp. 2100–2110 (2019)
31. Yun, S., Han, D., Oh, S.J., Chun, S., Choe, J., Yoo, Y.: Cutmix: regularization strategy to train strong classifiers with localizable features. In: CVPR, pp. 6023–6032 (2019)
32. Zendel, O., Honauer, K., Murschitz, M., Steininger, D., Dominguez, G.F.: Wilddash-creating hazard-aware benchmarks. In: ECCV, pp. 402–416 (2018)
33. Zhang, P., Zhang, B., Zhang, T., Chen, D., Wang, Y., Wen, F.: Prototypical pseudo label denoising and target structure learning for domain adaptive semantic segmentation. In: CVPR (2021)
34. Zhang, X., Zhou, X., Lin, M., Sun, J.: Shufflenet: an extremely efficient convolutional neural network for mobile devices. In: CVPR, pp. 6848–6856 (2018)
35. Zhao, H., Shi, J., Qi, X., Wang, X., Jia, J.: Pyramid scene parsing network. In: CVPR, pp. 2881–2890 (2017)
36. Zheng, S., et al.: Rethinking semantic segmentation from a sequence-to-sequence perspective with transformers. In: CVPR, pp. 6881–6890 (2021)
37. Zou, Y., Yu, Z., Kumar, B., Wang, J.: Unsupervised domain adaptation for semantic segmentation via class-balanced self-training. In: ECCV, pp. 289–305 (2018)

PACTran: PAC-Bayesian Metrics for Estimating the Transferability of Pretrained Models to Classification Tasks

Nan Ding(✉), Xi Chen, Tomer Levinboim, Soravit Changpinyo, and Radu Soricut

Google Research, Mountain View, USA
{dingnan,chillxichen,tomerl,schangpi,rsoricut}@google.com

Abstract. With the increasing abundance of pretrained models in recent years, the problem of selecting the best pretrained checkpoint for a particular downstream classification task has been gaining increased attention. Although several methods have recently been proposed to tackle the selection problem (e.g. LEEP, H-score), these methods resort to applying heuristics that are not well motivated by learning theory. In this paper we present PACTran, a theoretically grounded family of metrics for pretrained model selection and transferability measurement. We first show how to derive PACTran metrics from the optimal PAC-Bayesian bound under the transfer learning setting. We then empirically evaluate three metric instantiations of PACTran on a number of vision tasks (VTAB) as well as a language-and-vision (OKVQA) task. An analysis of the results shows PACTran is a more consistent and effective transferability measure compared to existing selection methods.

1 Introduction

Recent advances in machine learning and neural networks have resulted in effective but extremely over-parameterized models [9,37], sometimes referred to as foundation models [6]. Despite the fact that their training recipe and data are often available, training such models requires access to computational resources that are well beyond the reach of an average machine learning user or group. At the same time, many such model checkpoints (parameter snapshots at a particular training step) have been made publicly available in platforms such as Tensorflow-Hubs[1] [1] and Huggingface[2] [47], so that ML users who are interested in a certain model configuration need only write a few lines of code to initialize their own model from a public checkpoint, and continue fine-tuning on their

[1] https://www.tensorflow.org/hub.
[2] https://huggingface.co/.

Supplementary Information The online version contains supplementary material available at https://doi.org/10.1007/978-3-031-19830-4_15.

S. Avidan et al. (Eds.): ECCV 2022, LNCS 13694, pp. 252–268, 2022.
https://doi.org/10.1007/978-3-031-19830-4_15

downstream task of interest without incurring the cost of pretraining a model themselves. However, as the number of such models and checkpoints increases, a natural question of selection arises – is it possible to tell which initialization checkpoint is most suitable for a given downstream task without brute-force fine-tuning from all the available checkpoints?

To answer this question in the context of classification tasks, a number of existing approaches have been recently proposed. For example, the LEEP metric [33] assumes the pretrained model was trained on a source classification task, and then estimates the likelihood of an empirical predictor which maps source labels to target (downstream) labels for classifying the target data. On the other hand, the H-score metric [3] casts the classification problem as a linear regression task involving the representations of the penultimate layer and the target labels.

Unfortunately, both these methods resort to heuristics or approximations to arrive at their estimate. Specifically, the empirical predictor used by LEEP is not the optimal solution to its associated objective function. Furthermore, the predictor and the metric are estimated on the same dataset, which is prone to overfitting. On the other hand, the least squares solution of H-score is generally not a valid approximation to the commonly-used cross-entropy loss for classification, unless the dependence between the label and the input feature is weak [23], which rarely holds in practice.

In this paper we present PACTran, a theoretically grounded framework for deriving metrics that measure the transferability of pretrained models to downstream classification tasks. Our framework seeks an optimal yet efficient PAC-Bayesian bound [16,31] to the generalization error in a transfer learning setting, and the error is based on the cross-entropy loss between the prediction and the labels, as is commonly used in classification. That is, the PACTran framework enjoys at least one of two advantages compared to previous methods: (1) It is based on learning theory (as opposed to LEEP) through PAC-Bayesian bounds that measure the generalization gap, and (2) it is compatible with classification, since it relies on the cross-entropy loss (as opposed to H-score).

We instantiate the PACTran framework with three different priors, yielding three new transferability metrics: PACTran-Dirichlet, PACTran-Gamma and PACTran-Gaussian. Our experiments empirically evaluate and compare these new metrics against a number of baseline metrics over various image classification tasks in the Visual Task Adaptation Benchmark (VTAB) [51]. Furthermore, we also evaluate our metrics over the multimodal Open-Knowledge VQA [19,30] task, which contains both image and text.

2 Transferability Metrics: A Quick Review

In this section, we describe the transferability problem and review several transferability metrics which will be used as baselines in our experiments. We begin by describing the setup of Transfer Learning, where the goal is to leverage knowledge acquired on a source task in order to solve a new target task. Specifically, let M denote a model checkpoint already pretrained to solve a source task, and let S denote a dataset for the target (downstream) task, such that $S = \{(\mathbf{x}_1, y_1), \ldots, (\mathbf{x}_n, y_N)\}$ with inputs $\mathbf{x} \in \mathcal{X}$ and target labels $y \in \mathcal{Y}$. Transfer learning seeks to transfer the knowledge already encoded in M by finetuning from M using S.

At the same time, given multiple pretrained checkpoints M, another problem arises – is it possible to know which of the pretrained checkpoints is most suitable for the downstream task S, without incurring the cost of fine-tuning from each of them? To this end, several effective and computationally efficient transferability metrics have been proposed and are summarized below.

2.1 LEEP

Given a checkpoint M of a model pretrained on a source classification task, LEEP [33] estimates the transferability of M to the target dataset S by first computing two types of probabilities: (1) the predicted distribution $M(\mathbf{x}_i)$ over the source label set $\mathcal{Z}$ of the pretraining task, where we let $M(\mathbf{x}_i)_z$ denote the output probability of the z-th source label, and (2) the empirical conditional distribution $\hat{p}(y|z)$ of the target label y given the source label z,

$$\hat{p}(y|z) = \frac{\hat{p}(y,z)}{\sum_y \hat{p}(y,z)}, \text{where } \hat{p}(y,z) = \frac{1}{N} \sum_{(x_i,y_i)\in S} M(\mathbf{x}_i)_z \cdot \delta(y_i = y). \quad (1)$$

The LEEP measure is then defined as the logarithm of the marginal likelihood $\hat{p}(\mathbf{y}|\mathbf{x})$ (called EEP) given the empirical predictor $\hat{p}(y|z)$ and $M(\mathbf{x})$,

$$R_{LEEP} = \frac{1}{N} \sum_{(x_i,y_i)\in S} \log \hat{p}(y_i|\mathbf{x}_i) = \frac{1}{N} \sum_{(x_i,y_i)\in S} \log \left(\sum_{z\in\mathcal{Z}} \hat{p}(y_i|z) M(\mathbf{x}_i)_z \right). \quad (2)$$

LEEP was proposed as an improvement over the Conditional Entropy (CE) measure [42] which itself is an information theoretic approach that measures the transferability between two classification tasks by analyzing the correlation between their label sequences $Y = \{y_1, \ldots, y_N\}$ and $Z = \{z_1, \ldots, z_N\}$. In [33] the authors show that LEEP is an upper bound of negative CE and outperforms it empirically as a transferability metric. However, from a theoretic stand point the LEEP formulation suffers from a few deficiencies. For example, plugging in the empirical conditional distribution $\hat{p}(y|z)$ into Eq. (2) is not guaranteed to maximize the target log-likelihood $\log \hat{p}(\mathbf{y}|\mathbf{x})$. Furthermore, both $\hat{p}(y|z)$ and $\log \hat{p}(\mathbf{y}|\mathbf{x})$ are computed over S, which make the latter prone to overfitting and behave more similarly to training error as opposed to generalization error.

2.2 $\mathcal{N}$-LEEP

Another limitation of the LEEP measure (as well as CE) is that it can only be applied to measure the transferability of pretrained classification models. In addition, LEEP's performance degrades when the number of source classes is considerably smaller than the number of target classes. To overcome these issues, several methods that propose using the outputs $f(\mathbf{x})$ of the penultimate layer.

In $\mathcal{N}$-LEEP [29], the authors suggest to first apply Principal Component Analysis (PCA) on the penultimate layer outputs $f(\mathbf{x})$ to reduce their dimension and then fit a Gaussian Mixture Model (GMM) to the PCA-reduced representation $\mathbf{s}(\mathbf{x})$, so that $p(\mathbf{s}) = \sum_{v\in\mathcal{V}} \alpha_v \mathcal{N}(\mathbf{s}|\mathbf{u}_v, \mathbf{\Sigma}_v)$ and the posterior of the cluster assignment

$$p(v|\mathbf{x}) = p(v|\mathbf{s}) \propto \alpha_v \mathcal{N}(\mathbf{s}|\mathbf{u}_v, \mathbf{\Sigma}_v) \tag{3}$$

are used to replace $M(\mathbf{x})_z$ in Eq. (1). The rest of the procedure follows the same as in Eq. (2).

The $\mathcal{N}$-LEEP method [29] conjectures that the cluster assignment $p(v|\mathbf{s})$ is more reliable than the class assignment $M(\mathbf{x})_z$, because the GMM fitting is learned from the downstream target data, while the softmax classifier of LEEP is learned over the pretrained source data. Since $\mathcal{N}$-LEEP is a extension of LEEP, it also inherits its aforementioned problems such as the non-optimality of the log-likelihood, as well as the lack of generalization consideration.

2.3 H-Score

The H-score [3] transferability metric is also not restricted to pretrained classifiers. The idea for H-score comes from the matrix factorization of the divergence transition matrix (DTM) $\tilde{B} = \frac{p(x,y)}{\sqrt{p(x)p(y)}} - \sqrt{p(x)p(y)}$, for discrete random variables $\mathbf{x}$ and $\mathbf{y}$. It is shown in [23] that, under the assumption of sufficiently small $\tilde{B}$, the solution of the cross-entropy loss coincides with the following solution of the matrix decomposition:

$$\Psi^* = \underset{\Psi}{\operatorname{argmin}} \|\tilde{B} - \Phi(\mathbf{x})^\top \Psi\|_F^2, \text{ where } \Phi(\mathbf{x}) = \sqrt{p(\mathbf{x})} f(\mathbf{x}). \tag{4}$$

After plugging in the least squares solution $\Psi^* = \tilde{B}\Phi(\Phi^\top\Phi)^{-1}$, Eq. (4) becomes $\|\tilde{B}\|_F^2 - \|\tilde{B}\Phi(\Phi^\top\Phi)^{-\frac{1}{2}}\|_F^2$, in which the second term is defined as the H-score:

$$H = \|\tilde{B}\Phi(\Phi^\top\Phi)^{-\frac{1}{2}}\|_F^2 = \operatorname{tr}(\operatorname{cov}(f(\mathbf{x})))^{-1}\operatorname{cov}(\mathbb{E}_{p(x|y)}[f(\mathbf{x})|y]). \tag{5}$$

Compared to LEEP, H-score is more theoretically solid, in that it is optimal with respect to its loss. However, the key drawback of the H-score is that the optimality is based on the least squares objective, which is rarely used for classification. As proven in [23], the least squares solution is a valid approximation to the cross-entropy classification loss only when label $\mathbf{y}$ and input $\mathbf{x}$ are weakly dependent, which is clearly not the case in general.

2.4 LogME

Similarly to H-Score, the Log Marginal Evidence (LogME) [49] transferability metric also uses a least squares objective function. However, to avoid overfitting, instead of directly minimizing the Gaussian based log-likelihood (a.k.a the squared-loss) $\mathbf{w}^* = \text{argmin}_{\mathbf{w}} \|\mathbf{y} - \mathbf{f}^\top \mathbf{w}\|_F^2$, LogME uses Bayesian averaging to improve its generalization ability. That is, the LogME metric uses the marginal evidence of the target task $p(y|\mathbf{f}) = \int p(\mathbf{w})p(y|\mathbf{f}, \mathbf{w})d\mathbf{w}$. When $p(\mathbf{w})$ is defined as a Gaussian prior and $p(y|\mathbf{f}, \mathbf{w})$ is a Gaussian likelihood, then $p(y|\mathbf{f})$ can be analytically estimated.

LogME shares the same theoretical problems as H-score due to its dependence on the least squares objective, however, by relying on the marginal evidence it is less prone to overfitting [49] which potentially improves its generalization ability.

3 PACTran

In this section, we first briefly review the PAC-Bayesian bound [17,31] in the supervised learning setting. We then show how to leverage this bound for measuring transferability as the PACTran metric (Sect. 3.1). Specifically, we derive three instances of the PACTran metric based on the cross entropy loss using three different prior distributions: two based on conjugate priors with the Dirichlet and Gamma distributions (Sect. 3.2 and 3.3), and a third with a non-conjugate Gaussian prior (Sect. 3.4).

3.1 PAC-Bayesian Bounds for Supervised and Transfer Learning

Consider a learning task with data distribution D where examples are denoted as $u = (x, y)$. A hypothesis h from the hypothesis space H allows us to make predictions for each input x. The quality of the predictions is measured by a loss function $l(h, u)$, and the goal is to minimize the expected loss $L(h, D) = \mathbb{E}_{u \sim D} l(h, u)$. Typically, the data distribution D is unknown, and instead we are given a set of N (training) examples $S \sim D^N = \{u_i \sim D\}_{i=1}^N$, in which case the empirical error on S is simply $\hat{L}(h, S) = \frac{1}{N}\sum_{i=1}^N l(h, u_i)$. The gap between $L(h, D)$ and $\hat{L}(h, S)$ is known as the generalization gap of h. Based on this, various forms of PAC (Probably Approximately Correct) bounds have been studied in the ML community over the last few decades [7,43].

A key drawback of the PAC bounds is that the worst-case analysis (via the union bound over all $h \in H$) makes the bound vacuous for modern machine learning approaches [25,52]. To address this drawback, PAC-Bayesian learning [17,31] goes one step further by bounding the generalization gap of distributions over H, which can be optimized to obtain a non-vacuous bound [14,25]. In particular, let us assume that the learner has some prior knowledge of the hypothesis space H in the form of a prior distribution $P(h)$. Once the learner observes a training dataset S, it updates its prior P into a posterior distribution Q. The expected error of the posterior Q is called the Gibbs error $L(Q, D) = \mathbb{E}_{h \sim Q} L(h, D)$, and its empirical counterpart is $\hat{L}(Q, S) = \mathbb{E}_{h \sim Q} \hat{L}(h, S)$. The PAC-Bayesian framework provides the following upper bound [16,31] over $L(Q, D)$ based on its empirical estimate $\hat{L}(Q, S)$:

Theorem 1. *[16] Given a data distribution D, a hypothesis space H, a prior P, a confidence level $\delta \in (0,1]$, and $\lambda > 0$, with probability at least $1-\delta$ over samples $S \sim D^N$, for all posterior Q,*

$$L(Q,D) \leq \hat{L}(Q,S) + \frac{1}{\lambda} D_{KL}(Q\|P) + C(\delta,\lambda,N) \tag{6}$$

where $C(\delta,\lambda,N)$ is a constant independent of the posterior Q.

The hyperparameter λ can be adjusted to balance between the divergence and the constant C terms, where a common choice is $\lambda \propto N$ (see [11,16,38]).

In the transfer learning setting, starting from a pretrained checkpoint M that is encoded within the prior $P(h)$, $L(Q,D)$ measures the generalization error of a posterior Q after it was finetuned over the downstream data S. Furthermore, by minimizing the RHS of the bound (Eq. (6)) with respect to $Q \in \mathcal{Q}_M$, one can obtain a posterior Q that has low transfer error $L(Q,D)$. Therefore, to measure the transferability of a pretrained checkpoint M, we define a family of metrics *PACTran* by optimizing the PAC-Bayesian bound (ignoring the constant C since it is the same for all checkpoints):

$$\min_{Q \in \mathcal{Q}_M} \hat{L}(Q,S) + \frac{1}{\lambda} D_{KL}(Q\|P). \tag{7}$$

For computational efficiency, we restrict the domain of $\mathcal{Q}_M$ in which the feature network of the pretrained checkpoint M remains fixed. Since all $h \in dom(\mathcal{Q}_M)$ shares the same feature network, we can simplify P as the prior distribution of the top classification layer of the network only; and Q as the posterior distribution of the top layer after finetuning. Despite this restriction, PACTran appears promising in comparing the transferability of pretrained checkpoints even after full-model finetuning.

According to [16], the so-called Gibbs posterior Q^* that minimizes the objective of Eq. (7) takes the form of $Q^*(h) = P(h)\exp(-\lambda\hat{L}(h,S))/Z(S)$, where $Z(S)$ is equal to the marginal evidence $\int P(h)\exp(-\lambda\hat{L}(h,S))dh$. Plugging in $Q^*(h)$ back into Eq. (7), the resulting optimal PAC-Bayesian bound equals to $-\frac{1}{\lambda}\log Z(S)$. Note however, that computing $\log Z(S)$ is only analytically feasible, when the prior $P(h)$ and the likelihood function $\exp(-\lambda\hat{L}(h,S))$ are conjugate, for example, when both are Gaussians as in LogME [49].

In this paper, we focus on metrics for which $\hat{L}(h,S)$ is based on the cross-entropy loss, as it is more compatible with classification tasks (in which case $\exp(-L(Q,D))$ is an estimate of the expected test accuracy). From a theoretical perspective, this makes the PACTran metric preferable to LEEP (which is not optimal over the cross entropy loss) as well as LogME and H-score metrics (whose proposed solution is based on the squared loss instead of the classification loss of the downstream task).

In what follows, we derive three instantiations of the bound using the conjugate Dirichlet and Gamma priors whose solution can be found with a fast variational approach, and the non-conjugate Gaussian prior, which requires gradient optimization.

3.2 PACTran with a Dirichlet Prior

Given the target data $S = \{(\mathbf{x}_1, y_1), \ldots, (\mathbf{x}_N, y_N)\} \in (\mathcal{X}, \mathcal{Y})$, let us assume that the pretrained model M provides a probability vector $M(\mathbf{x})$ where $\sum_z M(\mathbf{x})_z = 1$. Here, $z \in \mathcal{Z}$ can either be defined over the set of source label as in LEEP or over the Gaussian clusters as in $\mathcal{N}$-LEEP. We restrict the top layer to a set of l_1-normalized vectors $\mathbf{W} = \{\mathbf{w}_1, \ldots, \mathbf{w}_{|\mathcal{Z}|}\}$ in the probability simplex, where for each vector $\mathbf{w}_z$ we have $\sum_{y \in \mathcal{Y}} w_{yz} = 1, w_{yz} \geq 0$, and then define the marginal likelihood as:

$$p(y_i|\mathbf{x}_i, \mathbf{W}) = \sum_z p(y_i, z|\mathbf{x}_i, \mathbf{W}) = \sum_z M(\mathbf{x}_i)_z w_{y_i z}. \tag{8}$$

We assign a Dirichlet prior $P(\mathbf{w}_z)$ on these vectors and let $\lambda = N$ for simplicity. Using the above definitions, we can rewrite $\log Z(S)$ as

$$\log \int \prod_z P(\mathbf{w}_z) \prod_i \left(\sum_z p(y_i, z_i = z|\mathbf{x}_i, \mathbf{W}) \right) d\mathbf{W}$$

$$= \log \sum_{z_1} \cdots \sum_{z_N} \int \left(\frac{\prod_z \Gamma(\sum_y \alpha_y)}{\prod_z \prod_y \Gamma(\alpha_y)} \right) \prod_z \prod_y w_{yz}^{n_{yz} + \alpha_y - 1} \prod_i M(\mathbf{x}_i)_{z_i} d\mathbf{W}, \tag{9}$$

where $\Gamma(\cdot)$ is the well-known Gamma function. The form of the resulting model is similar to Latent Dirichlet Allocation (LDA) [5]. Evaluating Eq. (9) exactly is considered intractable, as it involves a summation over $\mathbf{z}$ which has $|\mathcal{Z}|^N$ different configurations. Therefore, we turn to the variational inference approach as in [4,5] to optimize the evidence lower bound (ELBO). The PACTran-Dirichlet is the negation of the optimal ELBO, and equals to (see details in A.1):

$$\sum_z \left(\log C(\tilde{\alpha}_z) - \log C(\alpha_z) + \sum_i q^*(z_i = z) \left(\log q^*(z_i = z) - \log M(\mathbf{x}_i)_z \right) \right), \tag{10}$$

where,

$$q^*(z_i = z) = \operatorname{softmax}\left(\log M(\mathbf{x}_i)_z + \Psi(\tilde{\alpha}_{y_i z}) - \Psi(\sum_y \tilde{\alpha}_{yz}) \right),$$

$$\tilde{\alpha}_{yz} = \alpha_{yz} + \sum_i q^*(z_i = z)\delta(y_i = y), \text{ and } C(\boldsymbol{\alpha}_z) = \frac{\Gamma(\sum_y \alpha_{yz})}{\prod_y \Gamma(\alpha_{yz})},$$

where $\Psi(\cdot)$ denotes the digamma-function.

It is worth noting that the PACTran-Dirichlet metric Eq. (10) is a valid PAC-Bayesian upper bound to the generalization error (up to a constant). That is because Eq. (10) is the negation of ELBO which upper bounds the negative log evidence $-\log Z(S)$ which itself is an upper bound of $L(Q^*, D)$. Furthermore, both upper bounds are optimally tight with respect to their hypothesis spaces in consideration: the variational distribution q^* optimizes the ELBO over all the independent approximate distributions q, and the Gibbs posterior $Q^*(h)$ optimizes the PAC-Bayes bound (6) over all the base-learner Q.

3.3 PACTran with a Gamma Prior

Instead of using a set of l_1-normalized vectors $\mathbf{W}$, we can also relax the constraint by working on a matrix of non-negative variables $\mathbf{V} = \{v_{yz}\}$ whose prior is chosen to be the gamma distribution $P(v_{yz}) = Gamma(a_y, b)$. Unlike the normalized vectors $\mathbf{W}$, where $\sum_{y\in\mathcal{Y}}\sum_{z\in\mathcal{Z}} M(\mathbf{x})_z w_{yz} = 1$ is automatically satisfied, when using unnormalized $\mathbf{V}$, we need to normalize the output explicitly,

$$p(y_i, z|\mathbf{x}_i, \mathbf{V}) = \frac{M(\mathbf{x}_i)_z v_{y_i z}}{\sum_{y\in\mathcal{Y}}\sum_{z\in\mathcal{Z}} M(\mathbf{x}_i)_z v_{yz}}. \tag{11}$$

Note that $M(\mathbf{x}_i)$ is also not required to be normalized, which potentially makes the use case of Eq. (11) broader. Even with a normalized $M(\mathbf{x}_i)$, Eq. (11) strictly subsumes Eq. (8), because the former is only normalized once, while the latter is normalized $|\mathcal{Z}|$ times for each $\mathbf{w}_z$. In addition, since v_{yz} appears in both denominator and numerator, their scaling cancels out. Therefore, we fix a simple scaling coefficient $b = 1$ for all Gamma priors.

The rest of the Bayesian inference is similar to that of PACTran-Dirichlet. The PACTran-Gamma metric is the negative ELBO after applying the variational principles, and equals to (see details in A.2):

$$\begin{aligned}&\sum_y\sum_z (\log\Gamma(a_y) - \log\Gamma(\tilde{a}_{yz})) + \sum_i \log\tilde{\lambda}_i \\ &+\sum_i\sum_z q^*(z_i = z)\left(\log q^*(z_i = z) - \log M(x_i)_z\right),\end{aligned} \tag{12}$$

where,

$$q^*(z_i = z) = \text{softmax}\left(\log M(\mathbf{x}_i)_z + \Psi(\tilde{a}_{y_i z})\right),$$
$$\tilde{a}_{yz} = a_y + \sum_i q^*(z_i = z)\delta(y_i = y), \quad \tilde{\lambda}_i = \sum_y\sum_z M(\mathbf{x}_i)_z\tilde{a}_{yz}.$$

PACTran-Gamma metric is also a valid PAC-Bayesian upper bound to the generalization error, for the same reasons as the PACTran-Dirichlet metric.

3.4 PACTran with a Gaussian Prior

In the previous sections, we focus on the cases when the source model outputs normalized (in the Dirichlet prior case) or non-negative vectors (in the Gamma prior case). When the pretraining model is not based on classification tasks, one needs to add additional components (such as the Gaussian mixture models in $\mathcal{N}$-LEEP) to obtain those outputs. Here, we present another metric PACTran-Gaussian which relies only on penultimate layer representations $f(\mathbf{x})$. In PACTran-Gaussian, the prior P and posterior Q are both Gaussian distributions, where $P(\boldsymbol{\theta}) \sim \mathcal{N}(0, \sigma_0^2\mathbf{I})$ and $Q(\boldsymbol{\theta}) \sim \mathcal{N}(\boldsymbol{\theta}_q, \boldsymbol{\Sigma}_q)$. For computational efficiency, we consider $\boldsymbol{\Sigma}_q = \sigma_q^2\mathbf{I}$ only. Note that although both LogME and PACTran-Gaussian use Gaussian priors and posteriors on $\boldsymbol{\theta}$, a main difference is that the former applies the squared loss, while the latter applies the cross-entropy loss (see more discussions in A.3). However, since the Gaussian prior is not conjugate to the exponentiated cross-entropy loss, we derive the bound using 2nd order approximations and a reparameterization trick as in [44],

$$\begin{aligned}
&\hat{L}(Q,S)+\frac{1}{\lambda}D_{KL}(Q\|P)\\
\simeq&\hat{L}(\boldsymbol{\theta}_q,S)+\mathbb{E}_{\epsilon\sim\mathcal{N}(0,\mathbf{I})}[\sigma_q\epsilon^\top\nabla\hat{L}(\boldsymbol{\theta}_q,S)+\frac{\sigma_q^2}{2}\epsilon^\top\nabla^2\hat{L}(\boldsymbol{\theta}_q,S)\epsilon\\
&+\frac{1}{\lambda}\log\mathcal{N}(\boldsymbol{\theta}_q+\sigma_q\epsilon|\boldsymbol{\theta}_q,\sigma_q^2\mathbf{I})-\frac{1}{\lambda}\log\mathcal{N}(\boldsymbol{\theta}_q+\sigma_q\epsilon|0,\sigma_0^2\mathbf{I})]\\
=&\hat{L}(\boldsymbol{\theta}_q,S)+\frac{\sigma_q^2}{2}\mathrm{Tr}(\nabla^2\hat{L}(\boldsymbol{\theta}_q,S))+\frac{KD}{2\lambda}(\log\frac{\sigma_0^2}{\sigma_q^2}-1+\frac{\sigma_q^2}{\sigma_0^2}+\frac{\|\boldsymbol{\theta}_q\|_F^2}{KD\sigma_0^2}).
\end{aligned}\tag{13}$$

The results of minimizing Eq. (13) with respect to σ_q and $\boldsymbol{\theta}_q$ yield the following optimal σ_* and $\boldsymbol{\theta}_*$ (see details in A.3),

$$\frac{\sigma_0^2}{\sigma_*^2}=1+\frac{\beta}{KD}\mathrm{Tr}(\nabla^2\hat{L}(\boldsymbol{\theta}_*,S)),\quad \boldsymbol{\theta}_*=\operatorname*{argmin}_{\boldsymbol{\theta}_q}\left\{\hat{L}(\boldsymbol{\theta}_q,S)+\frac{\|\boldsymbol{\theta}_q\|_F^2}{2\beta}\right\},$$

where $\beta=\lambda\sigma_0^2$, So that we reach the following PACTran-Gaussian metric,

$$\underbrace{\hat{L}(\boldsymbol{\theta}_*,S)+\frac{\|\boldsymbol{\theta}_*\|_F^2}{2\beta}}_{RER}+\underbrace{\frac{KD\sigma_0^2}{2\beta}\log\frac{\sigma_0^2}{\sigma_*^2}}_{FR}.\tag{14}$$

In Eq. (14), the first two terms are simply the l_2-regularized empirical risk (RER). The third term is a "flatness regularizer" (FR) that involves the trace of the Hessian of the empirical risk $\mathrm{Tr}(\nabla^2\hat{L}(\boldsymbol{\theta}_*,S))$ and has a simple closed-form solution for the cross-entropy loss (provided in A.3). It is accepted wisdom that a model generalizes better when its optimum is relatively flat [14,32,44] (low trace of Hessian). Empirically, we observe that the FR term is extremely effective in preventing the metrics from overfitting even though metric evaluation is done only on the training set.

It is also worth noting that there are two subtle, yet critical, differences between the derivations of our bound Eq. (14) and the ones in [44]. First, our mean parameter $\boldsymbol{\theta}_*$ is a minimum of Eq. (13), while in [44] it is an arbitrary model parameter. Second, in [44], σ_0 and σ_* were tied together during the optimization of σ_*, which violates the assumption of the PAC-Bayes theorem where the prior must be data independent. Instead, our σ_* is not only optimal, but also leaves σ_0 data independent.

4 Empirical Studies

In this section, we evaluate the PACTran metrics: PACTran-Dirichlet, PACTran-Gamma and PACTran-Gaussian, over several transfer learning benchmarks, and compare them against other existing transferability metrics including LEEP, NCE, $\mathcal{N}$-LEEP, H-Score, LogME.

4.1 The Neural Checkpoint Ranking Benchmark (NeuCRaB)

Pretrained Checkpoints. Following NeuCRaB [29] (Group I), we collected a set of 16 ResNet-50 based checkpoints trained with various types of supervision. These checkpoints were pretrained on ImageNet with different training strategies, which include 5 models via self-supervised learning (Jigsaw [35], Relative Patch Location [12], Exemplar [13], Rotation [18], and Sup-Rotation [50]), 6 models via discriminators of generative models (WAE-UKL [39], WAE-GAN, WAE-MMD [41], Cond-BigGAN, Uncond-BigGAN [8], and VAE [26]), 2 via semi-supervised learning (Semi-Rotation-10% and Semi-Exemplar-10% [50]), one with a hybrid supervised loss (Sup-Exemplar-100% [50]), one by supervised learning of a standard Resnet50 (Sup-100% [21]), and lastly, one by supervised learning of a Resnet50 with identity mappings (Feature Vector [22]).

Downstream Tasks. Following NeuCRaB [29], we adopt the Visual Task Adaptation Benchmark (VTAB) [51] and study diverse downstream tasks. The original NeuCRaB only contains four tasks: Caltech101 [15], Flowers102 [34], Patch Camelyon [46] and Sun397 [48]. In order to compare the transferability metrics on a wider variety of downstream tasks, we added 5 more tasks: DMLAB [51], CBIS-DDSM [40], Cifar10 [27], Oxford IIIT Pet [36] and Smallnorb(azimuth) [28]. These new tasks not only enrich the task categories, but also span the full range of the number of classes per tasks (single-digit, double-digit, and 100+ classes), which allows us to analyze the performance of transferability metrics according to the number of classes. In particular, we group these tasks according to the number of output classes: tasks with 100+ classes include Caltech101 (102 classes), Flowers102 (102 classes), Sun397 (397 classes); tasks with 10–99 classes include Cifar10 (10 classes), Oxford IIIT Pet (37 classes) and Smallnorb(azimuth) (18 classes); tasks with 2–9 classes include Patch Camelyon (2 classes), DMLAB (6 classes), and CBIS-DDSM (5 classes).

Evaluating the Transferability Metrics. We use the Kendall-Tau rank correlation coefficient to correlate between the transferability metric scores and the testing error of the finetuned checkpoints. The "ground-truth" testing error that corresponds to each pretrained checkpoint M is obtained by finetuning M on the downstream training set multiple times and setting the ground-truth testing error e_M to the lowest test error among the runs (See details in B.3).

Experimental Settings. Since it is crucial for a transferability metric to be highly efficient compared to the finetuning, we focus our experiments on limited-data settings. Let K denote the number of classes, D the feature dimension and N the number of examples for computing the metric. We consider three data settings with increasing average number of samples per class $N/K \in \{2, 5, 10\}$ (to avoid having too few examples, we also set a lower bound for $N \geq 20$). For each N/K setting, we subsample N samples from the training set of each downstream task 5 times. The transferability metrics are then evaluated over the 5 splits and their average Kendall-Tau correlation is reported. Compared to evaluating the metrics on the full training set, the limited-data setting significantly reduces the cost of penultimate-layer feature extraction, which is usually orders of magnitude more expensive than computing the metrics themselves (see Table 2).

Besides the aforementioned baseline transferability metrics (LEEP, $\mathcal{N}$-LEEP, H-score, LogME), we also include two additional metrics based on linear classification. The LINEAR metric is based on the training loss of a regularized linear classifier (the sum of the first two terms of Eq. (14)). The second metric LINEAR-VALID splits the subsampled dataset into two equally sized folds, trains a linear classifer on one fold and computes the validation error on the other. The regularizing coefficients for both metrics are $\beta \in \{0.1, 1.0, 10\} \cdot N$. For LINEAR-VALID, the model with the lowest validation error is chosen. For LINEAR, since there is no validation set, we select the β that maximizes the Kendall correlation between the loss and LINEAR-VALID's validation error across checkpoints.

For $\mathcal{N}$-LEEP, we follow the recipe from [29] and set the PCA energy percentage to 80% and the number of Gaussian components to the number of classes in the downstream task. For PACTran-Dirichlet and PACTran-Gamma, we set $\alpha_y = \hat{p}(y)$. For PACTran-Gaussian, we report two sets of results: In PT-Gauss$_{fix}$, we fix the two hyperparameters to $\beta = 10N$ and $\sigma_0^2 = \frac{100}{D}$. In PT-Gauss$_{grid}$, we perform a hyperparameters grid-search over $\beta \in \{0.1, 1.0, 10\} \cdot N$ and $\sigma_0^2 \in \{1.0, 10, 100, 1000\} \cdot \frac{1}{D}$ and select the hyperparameters (β, σ_0^2) that maximize the Kendall correlation between the PT-Gauss$_{grid}$ metric scores and LINEAR-VALID's validation errors across checkpoints. More detailed discussions about the hyperparameters are available in B.5.

Results and Analysis. Table 1 reports the Kendall-Tau correlations of the various transferability metrics. Table 2 reports the GFLOPS per metric for each task as well as those of the feature extraction stage from the pretrained checkpoints. For LINEAR and PT-Gauss$_{grid}$, we include the GFLOPS for all hyperparameter runs as well as hyperparameter selection for LINEAR-VALID.

Although LEEP is the fastest algorithm, its averaged performance is worse than most other metrics. All other metrics employ more expensive components (PCA and GMM for $\mathcal{N}$-LEEP and $\mathcal{N}$-PT-Dir/Gam, SVD for Hscore and LogME, and L-BFGS for LINEAR and PT-Gauss) but are still 1–2 orders of magnitude faster to compute than feature extraction from the penultimate layer.

$\mathcal{N}$-LEEP, which obtains the source class assignments by applying GMM on the penultimate layer outputs, performs much better than LEEP on average. In addition, PACTran-Dirichlet and PACTran-Gamma with the GMM assignments (denoted as $\mathcal{N}$-PT-Dir and $\mathcal{N}$-PT-Gam) perform similarly to the $\mathcal{N}$-LEEP algorithm, which indicates that the EEP estimator is surprisingly close to Bayesian optimal based on the GMM assignments of the VTAB tasks.

Among the algorithms that use the L-BFGS optimizer, LINEAR-VALID performs better than LINEAR for large K. However, for small K LINEAR-VALID becomes worse, probably because the training and validation splits are too small. In contrast, the PT-Gauss metrics are consistently among the best metrics across all settings, which provides clear evidence that the 3rd "flatness" term (Eq. (14)) plays a crucial role in predicting generalization error. For example, they are the only metrics with correlation 0.4 or higher on 2–9 classes.

In comparing between PT-Gauss$_{grid}$ and PT-Gauss$_{fix}$, we find that PT-Gauss$_{grid}$ usually performs well whenever LINEAR-VALID's does (since it depends on it for hyperparameter selection). On the other hand, when LINEAR-VALID is worse (K is small), PT-Gauss$_{fix}$ outperforms PT-Gauss$_{grid}$.

Table 1. Kendall-Tau correlations on the NeuCRaB experiments with different N/K, where K is the number of classes, N the number of examples for computing the metric.

$N/K = 2$	100+ classes	10–99 classes	2–9 classes	Average
LEEP	0.202	0.005	0.041	0.083
$\mathcal{N}$-LEEP	0.723	0.401	0.077	0.401
H-score	0.413	0.106	0.185	0.235
LogME	0.308	0.067	0.071	0.149
LINEAR	0.231	0.072	0.114	0.139
LINEAR-VALID	0.750	0.309	0.063	0.374
$\mathcal{N}$-PT-Dir	0.760	0.327	0.099	0.395
$\mathcal{N}$-PT-Gam	0.763	0.333	0.108	0.401
PT-Gauss$_{grid}$	**0.868**	0.664	**0.509**	**0.680**
PT-Gauss$_{fix}$	0.770	**0.683**	**0.509**	0.654
$N/K = 5$	100+ classes	10–99 classes	2–9 classes	Average
LEEP	0.112	0.082	0.023	0.109
$\mathcal{N}$-LEEP	0.795	0.536	0.096	0.476
H-score	0.412	0.141	0.118	0.224
LogME	0.421	0.093	0.075	0.196
LINEAR	0.253	0.084	0.122	0.153
LINEAR-VALID	0.807	0.411	0.044	0.420
$\mathcal{N}$-PT-Dir	**0.826**	0.458	0.140	0.475
$\mathcal{N}$-PT-Gam	**0.825**	0.462	0.151	0.479
PT-Gauss$_{grid}$	0.793	**0.716**	0.412	0.641
PT-Gauss$_{fix}$	**0.832**	0.675	**0.512**	**0.673**
$N/K = 10$	100+ classes	10–99 classes	2–9 classes	Average
LEEP	0.276	0.079	0.049	0.134
$\mathcal{N}$-LEEP	0.822	0.520	0.148	0.497
Hscore	0.461	0.318	0.158	0.313
LogME	0.488	0.138	0.073	0.233
LINEAR	0.325	0.089	0.109	0.174
LINEAR-VALID	**0.835**	0.482	0.123	0.480
$\mathcal{N}$-PT-Dir	**0.839**	0.446	0.134	0.473
$\mathcal{N}$-PT-Gam	**0.839**	0.452	0.140	0.477
PT-Gauss$_{grid}$	0.769	**0.678**	0.429	0.625
PT-Gauss$_{fix}$	0.778	0.609	**0.534**	**0.641**

4.2 Visual Question Answering

We further conduct experiments over the multi-modal VQA task. Following common practice ([2,20]), we treat VQA as a classification task (vocab-based VQA). That is, we construct a vocabulary based on the top answers in the training sets and classify into one of those labels.

Table 2. GFLOPS of running each metrics and the penultimate-layer feature extraction stage on the subsampled datasets, when $N/K = 10$.

GFLOPS	100+ classes	10–99 classes	2–9 classes
LEEP	6.40E-1	2.00E-2	1.55E-3
$\mathcal{N}$-LEEP	2.09E2	1.40E0	7.25E-2
Hscore	1.33E2	1.30E2	1.29E2
LogME	1.34E2	1.30E2	1.29E2
LINEAR	2.89E2	9.03E0	7.07E-1
LINEAR-VALID	9.64E1	3.02E0	2.36E-1
$\mathcal{N}$-PT-Dir	2.09E2	1.40E0	7.25E-2
$\mathcal{N}$-PT-Gam	2.09E2	1.40E0	7.25E-2
PT-Gauss$_{grid}$	2.90E2	9.07E0	7.10E-1
PT-Gauss$_{fix}$	6.45E1	2.02E0	1.58E-1
Penultimate Feature	3.88E3	6.84E2	1.90E2

Pretrained Checkpoints. We apply the state-of-art VQA model architecture, which fuses image and question representations in a multimodal Transformer model [45] (see C.1). We pretrain the VQA models over 9 datasets, including: VQA-v2 [20], GQA [24], V7W [53], CNETVQA, TP-COLOR-COCO, TP-COLOR-CC3M, TP-COLOR-CC12M, VQ2A-COCO, and VQ2A-CC3M [10]. The detailed descriptions of the datasets are provided in C.2.

For each pretraining dataset, we consider 3 different model sizes and 4 different finetuning hyperparameter settings. For model sizes, the number of layers t of the text-encoder and m of the multimodal-encoder is varied from $(t, m) \in \{(6, 3), (9, 5), (12, 7)\}$. For hyperparameters, the dropout ratios are varied from $\{0, 0.1\}$. We use two learning schedules: a constant learning rate of 0.0005 and a decay learning rate starting at 0.2. For each of these 12 settings, we set batch size to 128, and save a checkpoint after 100,000 iterations.

Downstream Task. We chose the OKVQA dataset [30] because the task requires additional knowledge beyond its own training set, and it has been shown that proper pretraining brings significant benefits to performance [10, 30].

Experimental Settings. Finetuning details are available in C.3. The hyperparameter settings match the NeuCRaB experiments. Otherwise, we vary the number of data examples for metric computation from $N \in \{40, 100, 200\}$ and restrict the examples from the top 20 answers such that $N/K \in \{2, 5, 10\}$. For each N, we create 5 subsamples of the OKVQA train set. Each metric is then evaluated on the 5 splits and the average correlation score is reported.

Results and Analysis. In total, there are $108 = 9 \times 12$ checkpoints that span 9 different pretraining datasets, and 12 different model configurations. In Table 3, we report their results in 3 different ways: (1) "CD" (cross pretraining data sources), reports the averaged correlation of metrics across the 9 different

Table 3. Kendall-Tau correlations on the OKVQA experiments with different N.

N	40			100			200		
	CD	CM	Total	CD	CM	Total	CD	CM	Total
LEEP	0.420	0.337	0.471	0.430	0.373	0.492	0.435	0.402	0.508
$\mathcal{N}$-LEEP	0.309	0.077	0.295	0.452	0.232	0.427	0.503	0.329	0.480
Hscore	0.220	0.048	0.198	0.253	0.079	0.222	0.233	0.116	0.243
LogME	0.350	0.141	0.402	0.343	0.154	0.395	0.357	0.160	0.397
LINEAR	0.355	0.137	0.410	0.351	0.167	0.407	0.382	0.209	0.423
LINEAR-VALID	**0.488**	0.118	0.430	0.526	0.172	0.474	0.579	0.360	0.528
PT-Dir	0.253	0.329	0.301	0.449	**0.418**	0.480	0.460	**0.469**	0.503
PT-Gam	0.453	**0.348**	**0.490**	0.518	**0.411**	**0.544**	0.522	0.430	0.532
$\mathcal{N}$-PT-Dir	0.424	0.093	0.358	0.522	0.277	0.476	0.548	0.335	0.504
$\mathcal{N}$-PT-Gam	0.421	0.092	0.353	0.524	0.278	0.474	0.547	0.333	0.504
PT-Gauss$_{grid}$	**0.480**	0.272	0.451	**0.566**	0.349	**0.544**	**0.617**	0.391	**0.582**

pretraining datasets for each of the 12 model configurations; (2) "CM" (cross models), reports the averaged correlation of metrics cross the 12 model configurations for each of the 9 pretraining datasets; and (3) "Total", reports the correlation over all 108 checkpoints.

As can be seen, when the pretraining tasks are classification based, LEEP performs much better compared to the "mixed supervision" tasks in the previous section. On the other hand, PACTran-Gamma outperforms LEEP and PACTran-Dirichlet, which indicates that an unnormalized weight transfer matrix is more helpful in these setting. LINEAR-VALID is a strong baseline, especially as more data examples are provided. Finally, we see that PACTran-Gauss (with $\beta = 0.1N$ and $\sigma_0^2 = \frac{1}{D}$ from the grid search) provides competitive performance in all cases, and is consistently among the best in evaluating transferability from different pretraining datasets ("CD").

5 Conclusion

In this paper we presented PACTran, a PAC-Bayesian based framework for measuring the transferability of pretrained checkpoints to downstream tasks. Our method significantly improves upon previous methods in that it is both theoretically sound as well as compatible with downstream classification tasks. We instantiated three variant PACTran metrics using different hypothesis spaces and priors and conducted experiments over a set of vision tasks (VTAB) and a vision-and-language task (OKVQA). We showed that some PACTran variants can provide theoretical justification for existing methods. For example, ($\mathcal{N}$-)PT-Dir and ($\mathcal{N}$-)PT-Gam metrics subsume ($\mathcal{N}$-)LEEP, in which the finetuning head sits on top of the pretrained classification head (or a GMM). Our experiments also showed that several of the baseline metrics are unable to measure checkpoint transferability better than a simple linear classification and validation baseline

(LINEAR-VALID). On the other hand, the proposed PT-Gauss metric behaved well as a measure of transferability in a limited data setting and consistently exhibited high correlation with the test performance of models finetuned on the downstream tasks. Possibly, this is because it more closely matches the setup of the finetuned model, where the finetuning head is placed directly on the penultimate layer and trained with a cross-entropy loss.

References

1. Abadi, M., et al.: TensorFlow: large-scale machine learning on heterogeneous systems (2015). https://www.tensorflow.org/ software available from tensorflow.org
2. Antol, S., et al.: VQA: visual question answering. In: ICCV (2015)
3. Bao, Y., et al.: An information-theoretic approach to transferability in task transfer learning. In: 2019 IEEE International Conference on Image Processing (ICIP), pp. 2309–2313. IEEE (2019)
4. Blei, D.M., Kucukelbir, A., McAuliffe, J.D.: Variational inference: a review for statisticians. J. Am. Stat. Assoc. **112**(518), 859–877 (2017)
5. Blei, D.M., Ng, A.Y., Jordan, M.I.: Latent dirichlet allocation. J. Mach. Learn. Res. **3**, 993–1022 (2003)
6. Bommasani, R., et al.: On the opportunities and risks of foundation models (2021)
7. Bousquet, O., Boucheron, S., Lugosi, G.: Introduction to statistical learning theory. In: Bousquet, O., von Luxburg, U., Rätsch, G. (eds.) ML -2003. LNCS (LNAI), vol. 3176, pp. 169–207. Springer, Heidelberg (2004). https://doi.org/10.1007/978-3-540-28650-9_8
8. Brock, A., Donahue, J., Simonyan, K.: Large scale GAN training for high fidelity natural image synthesis (2019)
9. Brown, T., et al.: Language models are few-shot learners. Adv. Neural Inf. Process. Syst. **33**, 1877–1901 (2020)
10. Changpinyo, S., Kukliansky, D., Szpektor, I., Chen, X., Ding, N., Soricut, R.: All you may need for VQA are image captions. In: NAACL (2022)
11. Ding, N., Chen, X., Levinboim, T., Goodman, S., Soricut, R.: Bridging the gap between practice and PAC-bayes theory in few-shot meta-learning. Adv. Neural Inf. Process. Syst. **34**, 29506–29516 (2021)
12. Doersch, C., Gupta, A., Efros, A.A.: Unsupervised visual representation learning by context prediction (2016)
13. Dosovitskiy, A., Springenberg, J.T., Riedmiller, M., Brox, T.: Discriminative unsupervised feature learning with convolutional neural networks. In: Ghahramani, Z., Welling, M., Cortes, C., Lawrence, N., Weinberger, K.Q. (eds.) Advances in Neural Information Processing Systems. vol. 27. Curran Associates, Inc. (2014)
14. Dziugaite, G.K., Roy, D.M.: Computing nonvacuous generalization bounds for deep (stochastic) neural networks with many more parameters than training data. arXiv preprint arXiv:1703.11008 (2017)
15. Fei-Fei, L., Fergus, R., Perona, P.: Learning generative visual models from few training examples: an incremental bayesian approach tested on 101 object categories. In: Computer Vision and Pattern Recognition Workshop (2004)
16. Germain, P., Bach, F., Lacoste, A., Lacoste-Julien, S.: PAC-bayesian theory meets bayesian inference. Adv. Neural Inf. Process. Syst. **29**, 1884–1892 (2016)
17. Germain, P., Lacasse, A., Laviolette, F., Marchand, M.: PAC-bayesian learning of linear classifiers. In: Proceedings of the 26th Annual International Conference on Machine Learning, pp. 353–360 (2009)

18. Gidaris, S., Singh, P., Komodakis, N.: Unsupervised representation learning by predicting image rotations (2018)
19. Goyal, Y., Khot, T., Summers-Stay, D., Batra, D., Parikh, D.: Making the V in VQA matter: elevating the role of image understanding in visual question answering. In: Conference on Computer Vision and Pattern Recognition (CVPR) (2017)
20. Goyal, Y., Khot, T., Summers-Stay, D., Batra, D., Parikh, D.: Making the V in VQA matter: elevating the role of image understanding in visual question answering. In: CVPR (2017)
21. He, K., Zhang, X., Ren, S., Sun, J.: Deep residual learning for image recognition. In: 2016 IEEE Conference on Computer Vision and Pattern Recognition (CVPR), pp. 770–778 (2016). https://doi.org/10.1109/CVPR.2016.90
22. He, K., Zhang, X., Ren, S., Sun, J.: Identity mappings in deep residual networks (2016)
23. Huang, S.L., Makur, A., Wornell, G.W., Zheng, L.: On universal features for high-dimensional learning and inference. arXiv preprint arXiv:1911.09105 (2019)
24. Hudson, D.A., Manning, C.D.: GQA: A new dataset for real-world visual reasoning and compositional question answering. In: CVPR (2019)
25. Jiang, Y., Neyshabur, B., Mobahi, H., Krishnan, D., Bengio, S.: Fantastic generalization measures and where to find them. In: ICLR (2020)
26. Kingma, D.P., Welling, M.: Auto-encoding variational bayes (2014)
27. Krizhevsky, A.: Learning multiple layers of features from tiny images. University of Toronto, Technical Report (2009)
28. LeCun, Y., Huang, F.J., Bottou, L.: Learning methods for generic object recognition with invariance to pose and lighting. In: Proceedings of the 2004 IEEE Computer Society Conference on Computer Vision and Pattern Recognition, vol. 2, pp. II-104 (2004)
29. Li, Y., et al.: Ranking neural checkpoints. In: Proceedings of the IEEE/CVF Conference on Computer Vision and Pattern Recognition. pp. 2663–2673 (2021)
30. Marino, K., Rastegari, M., Farhadi, A., Mottaghi, R.: Ok-vqa: a visual question answering benchmark requiring external knowledge. In: Conference on Computer Vision and Pattern Recognition (CVPR) (2019)
31. McAllester, D.A.: Some PAC-bayesian theorems. Mach. Learn. **37**(3), 355–363 (1999)
32. Neyshabur, B., Bhojanapalli, S., McAllester, D., Srebro, N.: Exploring generalization in deep learning. Adv. Neural Inf. Process. Syst. **30** (2017)
33. Nguyen, C., Hassner, T., Seeger, M., Archambeau, C.: Leep: a new measure to evaluate transferability of learned representations. In: International Conference on Machine Learning, pp. 7294–7305. PMLR (2020)
34. Nilsback, M.E., Zisserman, A.: Automated flower classification over a large number of classes. In: Proceedings of the Indian Conference on Computer Vision, Graphics and Image Processing, December 2008
35. Noroozi, M., Favaro, P.: Unsupervised learning of visual representations by solving jigsaw puzzles (2017)
36. Parkhi, O.M., Vedaldi, A., Zisserman, A., Jawahar, C.V.: Cats and dogs. In: IEEE Conference on Computer Vision and Pattern Recognition (2012)
37. Raffel, C., et al.: Exploring the limits of transfer learning with a unified text-to-text transformer. JMLR (2020)
38. Rothfuss, J., Fortuin, V., Josifoski, M., Krause, A.: Pacoh: bayes-optimal meta-learning with pac-guarantees. In: International Conference on Machine Learning, pp. 9116–9126. PMLR (2021)

39. Rubenstein, P., Bousquet, O., Djolonga, J., Riquelme, C., Tolstikhin, I.O.: Practical and consistent estimation of f-divergences. In: Advances in Neural Information Processing Systems, vol. 32 (2019)
40. Sawyer-Lee, R., Gimenez, F., Hoogi, A., Rubin, D.: Curated breast imaging subset of DDSM (2016). https://doi.org/10.7937/k9/tcia.2016.7o02s9cy
41. Tolstikhin, I., Bousquet, O., Gelly, S., Schoelkopf, B.: Wasserstein auto-encoders (2019)
42. Tran, A.T., Nguyen, C.V., Hassner, T.: Transferability and hardness of supervised classification tasks. In: Proceedings of the IEEE/CVF International Conference on Computer Vision, pp. 1395–1405 (2019)
43. Tripuraneni, N., Jordan, M., Jin, C.: On the theory of transfer learning: the importance of task diversity. Adv. Neural Inf. Process. Syst **33**, 7852–7862 (2020)
44. Tsuzuku, Y., Sato, I., Sugiyama, M.: Normalized flat minima: exploring scale invariant definition of flat minima for neural networks using PAC-Bayesian analysis. In: Proceedings of the 37th International Conference on Machine Learning, pp. 9636–9647 (2020)
45. Vaswani, A., et al.: Attention is all you need. In: NeurIPS (2017)
46. Veeling, B.S., Linmans, J., Winkens, J., Cohen, T., Welling, M.: Rotation equivariant CNNs for digital pathology (2018). https://doi.org/10.1007/978-3-030-00934-2-24
47. Wolf, T., et al.: Huggingface's transformers: state-of-the-art natural language processing. arXiv preprint arXiv:1910.03771 (2019)
48. Xiao, J., Hays, J., Ehinger, K.A., Oliva, A., Torralba, A.: Sun database: large-scale scene recognition from abbey to zoo. In: 2010 IEEE Computer Society Conference on Computer Vision and Pattern Recognition, pp. 3485–3492, June 2010. https://doi.org/10.1109/CVPR.2010.5539970
49. You, K., Liu, Y., Wang, J., Long, M.: Logme: practical assessment of pre-trained models for transfer learning. In: International Conference on Machine Learning, pp. 12133–12143. PMLR (2021)
50. Zhai, X., Oliver, A., Kolesnikov, A., Beyer, L.: S4l: self-supervised semi-supervised learning. In: 2019 IEEE/CVF International Conference on Computer Vision (ICCV), pp. 1476–1485 (2019). https://doi.org/10.1109/ICCV.2019.00156
51. Zhai, X., et al.: A large-scale study of representation learning with the visual task adaptation benchmark. arXiv preprint arXiv:1910.04867 (2019)
52. Zhang, C., Bengio, S., Hardt, M., Recht, B., Vinyals, O.: Understanding deep learning (still) requires rethinking generalization. Commun. ACM **64**(3), 107–115 (2021)
53. Zhu, Y., Groth, O., Bernstein, M., Li, F.F.: Visual7W: grounded question answering in images. In: CVPR (2016)

Personalized Education: Blind Knowledge Distillation

Xiang Deng[1(✉)], Jian Zheng[2], and Zhongfei Zhang[1]

[1] State University of New York at Binghamton, Binghamton, USA
xdeng7@binghamton.edu, zhongfei@cs.binghamton.edu
[2] Amazon, Bellevue, USA
nzhengji@amazon.com

Abstract. Knowledge distillation compresses a large model (teacher) to a smaller one by letting the student imitate the outputs of the teacher. An interesting question is why the student still typically underperforms the teacher after the imitation. The existing literature usually attributes this to model capacity differences between them. However, capacity differences are unavoidable in model compression, and even large capacity differences are desired for achieving high compression rates. By designing exploratory experiments with theoretical analysis, we find that model capacity differences are not necessarily the root reason; instead the distillation data matter when the student capacity is greater than a threshold. In light of this, we propose personalized education (PE) to first help each student adaptively find its own blind knowledge region (BKR) where the student has not captured the knowledge from the teacher, and then teach the student on this region. Extensive experiments on several benchmark datasets demonstrate that PE substantially reduces the performance gap between students and teachers, even enables small students to outperform large teachers, and also beats the state-of-the-art approaches. Code link: https://github.com/Xiang-Deng-DL/PEBKD.

Keywords: Knowledge distillation · Model compression · Classification

1 Introduction

The successes of deep neural networks (DNNs) [10,23] are accompanied with the requirements of large amounts of computation and memory, which seriously restricts their deployment on resource-limited devices. One widely used solution is knowledge distillation (KD) [16] that compresses a large model (teacher) to a small one (student) by enforcing the student to mimic the outputs of the teacher. However, there is typically still a performance gap between them even if the student has imitated the outputs of the teacher. Figuring out the reason for this gap is essential for further improving the student performance.

Supplementary Information The online version contains supplementary material available at https://doi.org/10.1007/978-3-031-19830-4_16.

S. Avidan et al. (Eds.): ECCV 2022, LNCS 13694, pp. 269–285, 2022.
https://doi.org/10.1007/978-3-031-19830-4_16

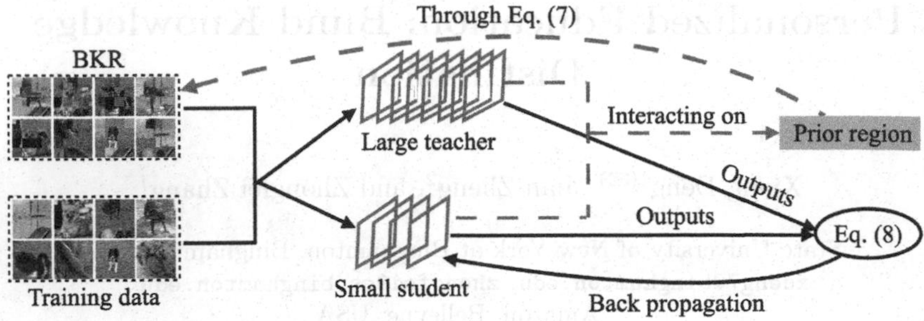

Fig. 1. Overview of PE

Mirzadeh et al. [27] argue that the model capacity difference causes the failure for transferring the knowledge from a large teacher to a small student, thus leading to a performance gap. Similarly, Cho and Hariharan [5] point out that as the teacher grows in capacity and accuracy, it is difficult for the student to emulate the teacher. However, the capacity reason is trivial for improving the student performance, since capacity differences are unavoidable in model compression. More essentially, large capacity differences are desired in model compression for achieving high compression rates. In light of this, we conduct simulation experiments (in Sect. 4) and find that in most experimental settings of the existing literature [34], the reason for the performance gap is not necessarily the capacity difference as the student is powerful enough to memorize the teacher's outputs. Instead, the reason lies in *distillation data* on which the knowledge is transferred.

In reality, it is not rare for human students to do better than their teachers. These excellent human students not only well capture the knowledge from their teachers but also learn more related knowledge on their own. This gives an insight for students in KD to match or outperform their teachers. We find that the students in KD have not well captured the knowledge from their teachers as they only mimic the behavior of the teachers on sparse training data points. We thus propose to go beyond the sparse, in-distribution distillation. However, simply going beyond distribution may not be optimal as different students master different levels of knowledge from the teacher. Similar to human students needing personalized education based on their own situations, we propose personalized education (PE) for KD to assist each student to spot and learn its own blind knowledge region (BKR) where the student fails to learn well from the teacher.

As image samples lie in a large, high-dimensional space, directly learning the BKRs in the full space is impossible and also not all samples in the large space are beneficial to the student. We thus learn BKR from a prior region where the samples share similar patterns with the training data (in-distribution) samples. We propose MixPatch as the prior region that linearly combines the patches in two images with different coefficients. MixPatch is inspired by but different from Mixup [43] that linearly combines two full images with a coefficient. Mixup is thus a special case of MixPatch when the patch size in MixPatch is set to the full image size. MixPatch theoretically can generate any image when the patch size is set to 1×1. MixPatch is also different from CutMix [40] that cuts a patch from one image and pastes it to another image. Unlike Mixup and CutMix, MixPatch is specially designed for KD instead of standard supervised learning, since it is almost impossible to directly generate the corresponding labels for MixPatch images in standard supervised learning while Mixup and CutMix can linearly combine the ground-truth labels to generate labels for new samples. Thanks to the pretrained teacher which can provide supervision signals, MixPatch can be specially used in KD. With MixPatch as the prior region, as shown in Fig. 1, PE first lets a student interact with the teacher to find its own BKR from the prior region and then lets it learn from the teacher on the BKR.

Our main contributions are summarized as follows:

- Different from the common belief that model capacity differences result in the performance gap between small students and large teachers, we find through designing exploratory experiments that capacity differences are not necessarily the root reason but the distillation data matter when student capacities are greater than a threshold.
- Different from the existing work focusing on designing different criteria to align representations or logits between teachers and students, we study knowledge distillation from a novel (data) perspective and accordingly propose personalized education (PE). PE goes beyond in-distribution distillation and adaptively learns the BKR for each student from a prior region.
- We propose a novel, simple yet effective data augmentation strategy (i.e., MixPatch) specially designed for KD, which addresses the limited image diversity issue of Mixup. It can be separately used or serve as a part of PE to enhance the student performance.
- Extensive experiments on several benchmark datasets demonstrate that PE reduces the student-teacher performance gap substantially, even enables small students to match or outperform large teachers, and also betas the existing SOTA approaches significantly. Furthermore, PE is also compatible with the existing SOTA approaches to further largely improve their performances.

2 Related Work

Knowledge Distillation. Hinton et al. [16] propose KD that trains a student network by using the softened logits of a teacher network as the targets. Different from one-hot labels, the soft targets contain instance-to-class similarity information (i.e., dark knowledge) learned by the teacher. However, KD only transfers the logits but fails to transfer the representations. Many approaches thus have been proposed to align the representations learned by a student and a teacher. Fitnets [31] lets a student imitate the intermediate features of a teacher through regressions. CRD [34] transfers representations by using contrastive learning. SSKD [38] uses extra self-supervised learning tasks to enhance the knowledge transfer. Other distillation approaches [1–5,7–9,12,14,15,17–19,21,24,28,29,33,37,39,42,44,45] utilize different criteria to align the feature representations or logits between a teacher and a student. Different from these efforts focusing on designing different fitting criteria, we address knowledge distillation from a data perspective by exploring the blind knowledge regions for students.

Teacher-Student Performance Gaps. Mirzadeh et al. [27] observe that the model capacity gap results in the failure for transferring knowledge from a large teacher to a small student, thus causing a performance gap. To reduce this gap, they propose a multi-step KD framework by using several intermediate-size networks (teacher assistants). However, the students still underperform the teachers substantially. Cho and Hariharan [5] argue that as the teacher grows in capacity and accuracy, it is difficult for the student to emulate the teacher. To reduce the influence of the large capacity gap, they regularize both the teacher and the distillation process by early stopping. We find that capacity differences are not necessarily the root reason when student capacities are greater than a threshold.

Mixup. MixPatch is proposed as a prior region in PE, which is inspired by Mixup [43] and aims to address the image diversity issue of Miuxp. Mixup [43] linearly interpolates a pair of training samples and their one-hot labels to generate new data. Linear combination of samples can preserve some patterns in the original samples, which can be beneficial to model learning. However, the simple linear interpolation can only generate limited samples, which is not enough for PE to learn the BKR. We thus propose MixPatch to address this issue by linearly combining the patches in two images with different coefficients. Mixup is thus a special case of MixPatch when the patch size in MixPatch is set to the image size. Furthermore, setting the patch size to 1 pixel can theoretically generate any image in the sample space. MixPatch is also substantially different from CutMix [40] where the patch is cut from one image and pasted into another image. Another related technique is ActiveMixup [36] which uses Mixup to generate a big image pool and then actively selects the images that the classifier has a low confidence on. However, the strategy ignores critical images that the classifier has a high confidence on but with a wrong prediction. The proposed PE addresses this issue by letting the student interact with the teacher to find its own BKR.

3 Reformulating KD

KD [16] aligns the outputs of a student and a teacher over training data $D_t = (X_t, Y_t) = \{(x_i, y_i)\}_{i=0}^n$ where X_t and Y_t are the training samples and the ground truth, respectively. The complete objective is written as:

$$\mathcal{L}_{KD} = \sum_{(x_t, y_t) \in D_t} [\alpha \mathcal{L}_{CE}(S_\theta(x_t), y_t) + \beta \mathcal{L}_{KL}(S_\theta, T, x_t)] \tag{1}$$

where α and β are the weights for balancing the contributions of the two terms; S_θ and T denote a student network with parameters θ and a pretrained teacher network, respectively; $\mathcal{L}_{CE}$ is the regular cross-entropy loss; $\mathcal{L}_{KL}$ is the distillation loss for transferring knowledge from the teacher to the student:

$$\mathcal{L}_{KL}(S_\theta, T, x_t) = \tau^2 \mathcal{K}\left(\sigma\left(\frac{T(x_t)}{\tau}\right), \sigma\left(\frac{S_\theta(x_t)}{\tau}\right)\right) \tag{2}$$

where σ is the softmax function; τ is a temperature to generate soft labels; $\mathcal{K}$ denotes KL-divergence. KD can be considered as using a function S_θ to fit another function T.

Note that in (1), $\mathcal{L}_{CE}$ requires both data samples X_t and the corresponding ground truth Y_t while $\mathcal{L}_{KL}$ only needs data samples X_t for distilling the teacher knowledge. In light of the difference, **we consider KD from a semi-supervised perspective** and reformulate (1) in a more general form:

$$\mathcal{L} = \sum_{(x_t,y_t)\in(X_t,Y_t)} \alpha\mathcal{L}_{CE}(S_\theta(x_t), y_t) + \sum_{x_d\in X_d} \beta\mathcal{L}_{KL}(S_\theta, T, x_d) \tag{3}$$

where we introduce a new concept: **distillation dataset** X_d is a set of samples on which the knowledge is transferred from a teacher to a student. The first term in the right hand side of (3) is supervised while the second term is unsupervised. It is obvious that the widely used objective (1) is a special case of (3) when X_d is set to X_t.

4 Why Small Students Underperform Large Teachers?

In this section, we systematically examine the reason for the performance gap between small students and large teachers. We first introduce several definitions.

Definition 1. *Memorization Error (ME): For a given task with data sample distribution $P(x)$, ME measures the degree of a student S_θ fitting the outputs of a teacher T over $P(x)$:*

$$E(S_\theta, T, P) = \mathop{\mathbb{E}}_{x\sim P(x)} M(T(x), S_\theta(x)) \tag{4}$$

where M denotes a distance metric such as KL-divergence or mean square error.

When ME is (or extremely close to) 0, it means that the student can completely memorize the outputs of the teacher over the data distribution. In this paper, we take KL-divergence as M.

Definition 2. *Capable Students (CSTs) and Incapable Students (ISTs): network S_θ is a CST of teacher T on a task with data sample distribution P if there exists θ such that $E(S_\theta, T, P)$=0; otherwise, it is an IST.*

Note that whether a student is a CST or IST is determined by its own capacity, the complexity of the teacher function T, and the task data distribution P. Obviously, a CST is able to fully fit the teacher outputs over data distribution $P(x)$. In contrast, an IST does not have the capacity to fit the teacher. For ISTs, the common belief holds that the student-teacher capacity gap causes the performance gap. For example, we cannot expect a two-layer neural network with 1000 parameters to fit the outputs of ResNet-101 with 1.7M parameters on CIFAR-100. However, in the current SOTA approaches and applications [34], the commonly used students are modern neural network architectures, such as ResNet-32, ResNet8×4, VGG-8, and WRN-16-2. We empirically show that

Table 1. ME of different networks on CIFAR-10, CIFAR-100, and Tiny ImageNet. All the values are accurate to 1 decimal place.

Teacher (#Params)	WRN-40-2 (2.26M)	VGG-13 (9.46M)	ResNet32×4 (7.43M)	ResNet-110 (1.74M)	ResNet32×4 (7.43M)	VGG-13 (9.46M)	VGG-13 (9.46M)
Student (#Params)	WRN-16-2 (0.70M)	VGG-8 (3.97M)	ResNet8×4 (1.23M)	ResNet-32 (0.47M)	ShuffleNetV2 (1.36M)	SN2 (0.0284M)	SN3 (0.0298M)
CIFAR-10	0.0	0.0	0.0	0.0	0.0	1.7	0.1
CIFAR-100	0.0	0.0	0.0	0.0	0.0	2.4	0.3
Tiny ImageNet	0.0	0.0	0.0	0.0	0.0	4.2	1.9

these models are CSTs on commonly used benchmark datasets, i.e., CIFAR-10, CIFAR-100, and Tiny ImageNet.

To check whether student S_θ is a CST of teacher T on a task, we minimize ME to check whether $E(S_\theta, T, P)$ can achieve 0. However, in practice, it is impossible to calculate $E(S_\theta, T, P)$ as the data distribution P is typically unknown. Fortunately, we have the access to a set of training data (X_t, Y_t). With the training data, we approximate ME $E(S_\theta, T, P)$ with the empirical error:

$$E_{em}(S_\theta, T, X_t) = \frac{1}{|X_t|} \sum_{x_t \in X_t} M(T(x_t), S_\theta(x_t)) \tag{5}$$

For comparison, we also evaluate two tiny neural networks which are expected to be ISTs, i.e., SN-2 and SN-3 with two and three layers, respectively. We report the ME in Table 1, where we adopt the students and the teachers that share the same architectures (e.g., WRN-40-2 and WRN-16-2) or use different architectures (e.g., ResNet32×4 and ShuffleNetV2). As expected, the widely used students achieve ME 0.0[1] on all the three benchmark datasets while the tiny networks (i.e., SN2 and SN3) have large ME (e.g., 2.4 and 4.2), which demonstrates that the widely used students are CSTs. However, as shown in Table 2, these students (i.e., KD) after distillation still underperform the teachers by a significant margin on the test data. This indicates that these students have well learned the knowledge on sparse training data points but have not well captured the local function shapes of the teachers within the data distribution so that they fail on the test data. This suggests the following proposition:

Proposition 1. *In KD, for CSTs, only fitting the teacher function on sparse training data points cannot enable them to well capture the in-distribution function shape of the teacher (i.e., in-distribution knowledge), thus leading to a performance gap. For ISTs, capacity differences cause the performance gap.*

We further conduct exploratory experiments to verify this proposition and the theoretical proof of the proposition is given in Appendix A. The exploratory experiments compare the student performances in the following two settings:

[1] Note that all the ME values in Table 1 are accurate to 1 decimal place. 0.0 is not exact 0 but is extremely close to 0.

Table 2. Simulation results on CIFAR-100 in terms of test accuracy (%). Underline denotes that small students outperform large teachers.

Teacher Student	ResNet32×4 ResNet8×4	WRN-40-2 WRN-16-2	VGG-13 VGG-8	ResNet32×4 ShuffleNetV2	VGG-13 SN2	VGG-13 SN3
Teacher	79.63	76.46	75.38	79.63	75.38	75.38
Vanilla student	72.51	73.64	70.68	73.12	26.29	55.31
Student type	CST	CST	CST	CST	IST	IST
KD	73.33	74.92	72.98	74.45	26.04	55.32
Simulation KD	**79.91**	**78.46**	**77.99**	**81.64**	25.58	57.50

(a) setting the distillation dataset to training data points; (b) setting the distillation dataset to real data distribution $P(x)$. As $P(x)$ is typically unknown in practice, we conduct a simulation experiment on CIFAR-100. We suppose that the union of the training dataset and the test dataset in CIFAR-100 can accurately represent the real data distribution for this task. Then we randomly draw data samples from the vicinity around the training data and the test data as the distillation dataset, i.e., X_d in Eq. (3). Consequently, the distillation dataset can sufficiently represent the real data sample distribution. Note that in this experiment, we **never spy the ground truth of the test samples**, since the distillation dataset X_d does not use ground truth as shown in Eq. (3). This means that the students are trained without any additional supervision compared with the teachers as training datset (X_t, Y_t) in Eq. (3) does not change. Since CSTs are able to fully memorize the outputs of the teachers, we expect them to achieve the same accuracies as or higher accuracies than those of the teachers. In contrast, we expect ISTs to achieve lower accuracies than those of the teachers. Table 2 shows the simulation results. As expected, all the CSTs outperform the teachers in the simulation experiments (i.e., Simulation KD). This is due to the following facts: first, by using the simulated distillation dataset, the distillation objective in Eq. (3) makes the CSTs fully capture the knowledge of the teachers within the data distribution; second, the cross-entropy objective in Eq. (3) enables the CSTs to learn their own knowledge. Consequently, CSTs contain both the teacher knowledge and the knowledge learned on their own, which results in better performances than those of the teachers. SN2 and SN3 still underperform the teachers in the simulation experiments due to their limited capacities. These results empirically validate the proposition.

The simulation experiments also suggest a way for CSTs to outperform large teachers. That is to sufficiently distill the knowledge from the teachers with a well representative distillation dataset. Unfortunately, it is impossible to have such a distillation dataset as the real data sample distribution $P(x)$ is typically unknown in reality. As directly modelling the high-dimensional data distribution from sparse data points is even more difficult than training the classifier itself, we propose to go beyond in-distribution distillation by using out-of-distribution (OOD) samples to assist distillation based on the following proposition:

Proposition 2. *Out-of-distribution (OOD) samples can be beneficial to knowledge distillation, but not all OOD samples are beneficial.*

The theoretical proof of this proposition is given in Appendix B.

5 Personalized Education

Although OOD samples can be useful for KD, simply going beyond the distribution may not be optimal, given the fact that different students master different levels of knowledge from the teacher. We thus further propose personalized education (PE) which automatically spots the blind knowledge region (BKR) for each student where the student has not well learned from the teacher. Due to the large, high-dimensional image space, finding the beneficial BKR from the full space is difficult or even impossible. We thus learn the BKR from a prior region where the OOD samples share similar local patterns to the original training data (i.e., in-distribution data). One can design the prior region based on the prior knowledge that they have about the target task. A prior region example is given below.

5.1 MixPatch

Mixup [43] linearly interpolates two training images to generate a new image which can preserver or share similar patterns to the original images. However, the diversities of the generated images are limited by the simple linear interpolation. CutMix [40] suffers a similar issue as it only cuts one patch from one image and pastes it to another image. To increase the image sample diversity and preserve similar local patterns to the original image, we propose MixPatch that linearly interpolates the patches in two images with different coefficients.

MixPatch has two hyper-parameters, i.e., patch size $s_h \times s_w$ where s_h and s_w are the height and width of the patch, and beta-distribution parameter a that is used to generate the coefficients. Suppose that the image size is $h \times w$ where h and w are the height and the width of the image, respectively (the channel size is omitted here); then the image is split into $m = \lceil \frac{h}{s_h} \rceil \times \lceil \frac{w}{s_w} \rceil$ patches, where $\lceil x \rceil$ is the ceiling function that returns the smallest integer that is greater than or equal to x.

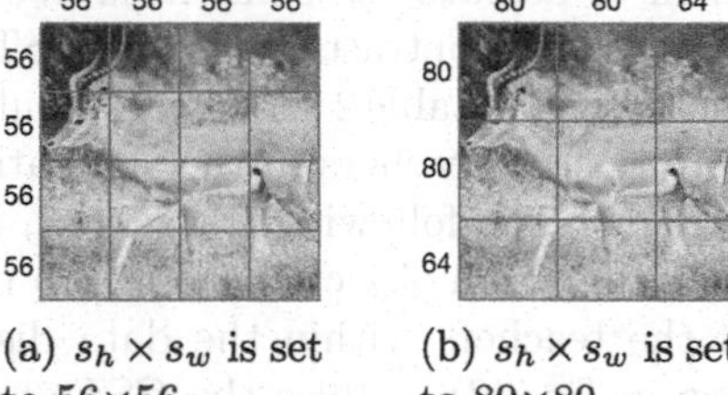

(a) $s_h \times s_w$ is set to 56×56. (b) $s_h \times s_w$ is set to 80×80.

Fig. 2. An image of size 224×224 are split into patches with different $s_h \times s_w$.

When h and w are divisible by s_h and s_w respectively, the sizes of the m patches are all equal to $s_h \times s_w$. One intuitive example is given in Fig. 2(a) where all the 16 patches are 56×56. On the contrary, when the image size is not divisible by the patch size, some of the patches have a size smaller than $s_h \times s_w$, with one example shown in Fig. 2(b) where 80 × 64 smaller than 80 × 80.

Each images x_i can thus be represented by m patches, i.e., $[h_{i0}, h_{i1}, ..., h_{im}]$, where h_{ij} is the jth patch in image x_i. MixPatch generates a new image $\hat{x}_z$ by linearly combining the patches of two random training images x_i and x_k with different coefficients:

$$\hat{h}_{zj} = \lambda_j h_{ij} + (1 - \lambda_j) h_{kj},\ j = 0, 1, 2, ..., m \tag{6}$$

where $\hat{h}_{zj}$ is the jth patch of new sample $\hat{x}_z$, i.e., $\hat{x}_z = [\hat{h}_{z0}, \hat{h}_{z1}, ..., \hat{h}_{zm}]$, and $\lambda_j \sim Beta(a, a)$ where a is the beta-distribution parameter.

We can see that when patch size $s_h \times s_w$ is set to image size $h \times w$, MixPath is reduced to Mixup, which indicates that Mixup is a special case of MixPatch. Furthermore, when patch size is set to 1×1 (i.e., 1 pixel), MixPatch is able to generate any images by tuning λ_j but loses the information of the local patterns in the original images. Therefore, the patch size controls the contributions of the new image diversity and the local pattern information. Another difference between MixPatch and Mixup is that MixPatch is specially designed for KD as it is difficult to directly generate labels for these new images in standard supervised learning. Thanks to the pretrained teacher in KD, the student can make use of these MixPatch samples by imitating the outputs of the teacher on them.

MixPatch samples can be used in two ways to assist distillation. One way is to directly use them to enhance the student knowledge by manually tuning and then freezing hyper-parameter patch size $s_h \times s_w$ and parameter a, but it may not be the optimal. The other way is to adaptively update the patch size and the distribution parameter by letting the student interact with the teacher during the training process.

5.2 Blind Knowledge Region Discovery

PE aims to help each small student spot its own BKR from a prior region by the interaction with the teacher. We propose a gradient-free search strategy to find the BKR for each student from the MixPatch prior region. Since the input images to modern DNNs are typically fix-sized with the height equal to the width (e.g., 224 × 224 for ImageNet image), for simplicity, we use one parameter s to represent the patch size by assuming $s = s_h = s_w$, and one parameter h to denote the image size by assuming $h = w$.

The MixPatch region is then determined by two hyper-parameter a and s that control coefficient (i.e., λ) distribution and the patch size, respectively. PE spots the BKR for a student from a set of candidate regions. The candidate values for a are typically set to $\mathbf{a} = \{0.1, 0.5, 1.0\}$ and those for s are set to $\mathbf{s} = \{h, \frac{h}{2}, ..., \frac{h}{n}\}$ where n is an integer. As a BKR is where the student has not well learned the knowledge from the teacher, we can search the BKR by maximizing the output differences of the student and the teacher on the prior region:

$$\text{argmax}_{a,s} \underset{\hat{x} \sim \text{MixPatch}(a,s)}{\mathbb{E}} \mathcal{L}_{KL}(S_\theta, T, \hat{x}), \text{ for } a \in \mathbf{a} \; s \in \mathbf{S} \tag{7}$$

PE adaptively searches the BKR with (7) every k epochs to update a and s. Note that this search process is very fast as it is gradient-free.

The BKR samples are then added to the distillation dataset X_d in Eq. (3). PE thus can be considered as a data-driven approach that enhances the student by enforcing it to mimic the behavior of the teacher on its own BKR:

$$\mathcal{L}_{\text{PE}} = \mathcal{L}_{\text{KD}} + \sum_{\hat{x} \in \text{BKR}} \mathcal{L}_{KL}(S_\theta, T, \hat{x}) \tag{8}$$

Table 3. Effects of different components in PE.

Teacher	Student	Teacher	Vanilla student	KD	KD+Mixup	KD+MixPatch	PE
WRN-40-2	WRN-16-2	76.46	73.64	74.92	75.56	75.94	**76.57**
VGG-13	VGG-8	75.38	70.68	72.98	74.58	74.93	**75.41**

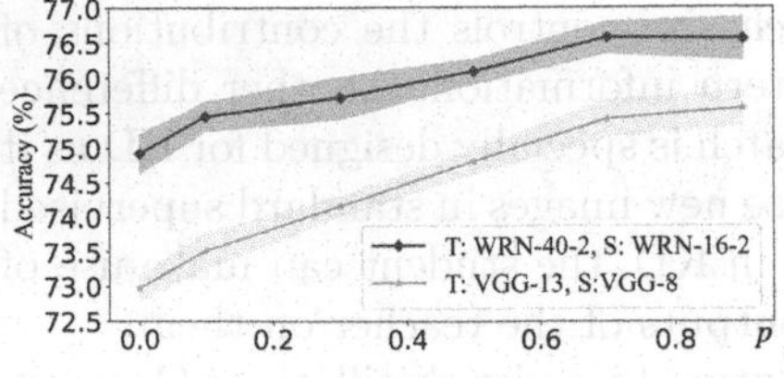

Fig. 3. Effects of p.

Fig. 4. Effects of update interval k.

where BKR = MixPatch($\overline{a}, \overline{s}$); $\overline{a}$ and $\overline{s}$ are the optimally identified values by (7) and updated every k epochs. By adaptively learning the BKR, PE is expected to enhance CSTs to match the performance of the teacher or largely reduce their performance gap.

6 Experiments

In this section, we aim to answer the following questions:
Q1: Ablation studies regarding MixPatch and the personalized education in PE.
Q2: Can PE enable small students to outperform large teachers or substantially reduce their performance gap?
Q3: Can PE outperform other similar data-driven approaches?
Q4: Is PE compatible with other SOTA distillation approaches?
Q5: Does PE indeed reduce teacher-student function shape differences?
Q6: What do the BKR images from the MixPatch prior region look like?

The experiments are conducted on the three widely used knowledge distillation benchmark datasets, i.e., CIFAR-100 [22], Tiny ImageNet[2], and ImageNet [6]. For a fair comparison, we adopt the architectures used in the existing literature (**we have shown that most of them are CSTs in Sect.** 4.) including ResNet [13], WRN [41], VGG [32], and ShuffleNet [26].

6.1 Answers to Q1

The ablation studies are conducted on CIFAR-100 with two teacher-student pairs of WRN-40-2 and WRN-16-2, and VGG-13 and VGG-8.

Effects of the Components in PE. PE uses the proposed MixPatch as the prior region, which is inspired by Mixup. We thus first show the superiority

[2] https://tiny-imagenet.herokuapp.com.

Table 4. Comparison results on CIFAR-100 in terms of test accuracy (%). Underline denotes students matching or outperforming teachers.

Teacher (#Params)	WRN-40-2 (2.26M)	resnet-110 (1.74M)	VGG-13 (9.46M)	ResNet32×4 (7.43M)	ResNet50 (23.71M)	ResNet32×4 (7.43M)	WRN-40-2 (2.26M)
Student (#Params)	WRN-16-2 (0.70M)	ResNet-32 (0.47M)	VGG-8 (3.97M)	ResNet8×4 (1.23M)	VGG-8 (3.97M)	ShuffleNetV2 (1.36M)	ShuffleNetV1 (0.95M)
Teacher	76.46	74.31	75.38	79.63	79.10	79.63	76.46
Vanilla student	73.64	71.14	70.68	72.51	70.68	73.12	70.77
KD	74.92 ± 0.28	73.08 ± 0.18	72.98 ± 0.19	73.33 ± 0.25	73.81 ± 0.13	74.45 ± 0.27	74.83 ± 0.17
GANKD	75.05 ± 0.30	72.87 ± 0.35	73.09 ± 0.28	73.46 ± 0.33	73.68 ± 0.27	74.61 ± 0.29	74.88 ± 0.22
Mixup	75.56 ± 0.15	73.67 ± 0.22	74.58 ± 0.27	75.86 ± 0.30	75.15 ± 0.23	77.63 ± 0.20	77.05 ± 0.29
ActiveMixKD	75.60 ± 0.35	73.21 ± 0.28	74.50 ± 0.29	75.98 ± 0.19	75.13 ± 0.25	77.22 ± 0.17	77.01 ± 0.20
PE(Ours)	**76.57 ± 0.23**	**74.35 ± 0.19**	**75.41 ± 0.25**	**76.27 ± 0.20**	**75.81 ± 0.23**	**79.83 ± 0.14**	**77.78 ± 0.22**

of MixPatch over Mixup and then show the effectiveness of (7) for spotting BKRs. As shown in Table 3, KD+MixPatch performs better than KD+Mixup on both pairs of teachers and students, which validates the superiority of MixPatch over Mixup for assisting KD. Furthermore, personalized education (PE) further enhances the performances of KD+MixPatch significantly on both pairs, even beating the teachers, which indicates the effectiveness of Eq. (7) for spotting BKRs.

Effects of the Number of BKR Samples. PE can theoretically find infinite BKR samples to assist distillation. However, the diversity of them is also limited by the original data. We randomly use the BKR samples with probability p and the training samples with $1-p$ as the distillation data in each optimization step so that we can control the number of BKR samples. Figure 3 presents the effects of p on CIFAR-100. As expected, with the number of BKR samples increasing, the performance first increases and then becomes stable.

Effects of the Update Frequency. PE updates the BKR every k epochs in the training process. The effects of k are presented in Fig. 4. It is observed that overall the performance of PE is not sensitive to k. However, when the BKR is updated too frequently (i.e., too small k), the student cannot have enough epochs to learn the current BKR, which leads to an inferior performance. Similarly, when the update frequency is too small, the performance of the student is also inferior, since not enough BKRs are found in the training process.

6.2 Answers to Q2 and Q3

We examine whether PE can indeed enable small students to outperform large teachers or substantially reduce their performance gap and compare it with the approaches along the same line. PE is a data-driven approach while the existing approaches focus on using different criteria to align the representations or logits of the teacher and the student. We thus design three data-driven baselines for reference (the comparison with non-data-driven SOTA approaches such as CRD [34] and SSKD [38] is reported in Appendix C):

Table 5. Comparison results on Tiny ImageNet.

Teacher Student	WRN-40-2 WRN-40-1		VGG-13 VGG-8		WRN-40-2 VGG-8	
	Top-1 (%)	Top-5 (%)	Top-1 (%)	Top-5 (%)	Top-1 (%)	Top-5 (%)
Teacher	61.84	84.11	61.62	81.71	61.84	84.11
Vanilla student	55.39	79.87	55.46	78.15	55.46	78.15
KD	56.25 ± 0.15	81.11 ± 0.19	60.19 ± 0.21	81.61 ± 0.30	58.25 ± 0.25	82.51 ± 0.18
GANKD	55.71 ± 0.26	80.13 ± 0.16	60.32 ± 0.11	81.90 ± 0.23	58.49 ± 0.35	82.73 ± 0.20
MixupKD	56.80 ± 0.28	81.29 ± 0.15	61.64 ± 0.15	82.81 ± 0.13	59.16 ± 0.19	82.10 ± 0.10
ActiveMixKD	56.66 ± 0.16	81.52 ± 0.30	61.23 ± 0.29	83.07 ± 0.12	59.09 ± 0.14	82.24 ± 0.19
PE (Ours)	**58.74 ± 0.17**	**82.59 ± 0.13**	**62.40 ± 0.29**	**83.57 ± 0.16**	**59.91 ± 0.18**	**82.98 ± 0.07**

(1) GANKD: As analysed in Sect. 4, only fitting the teacher outputs at sparse data points cannot enable students to well capture the in-distribution shape of the teacher function. One natural idea is to use generative adversarial networks (GANs) [11, 25] to learn the data distribution and then use the generator to generate fake data to assist distillation.
(2) MixupKD[3]: MixupKD uses Mixup[4] samples to assist distillation.
(3) ActiveMixKD: ActiveMixup [36] is originally proposed to train a classifier in data-few cases. It first uses Mixup to generate an image pool and then selects the images that the classifier has a low confidence on. ActiveMixKD adds these ActiveMixup samples to the distillation dataset.

CIFAR-100. The performances on CIFAR-100 are reported in Table 4. It is observed that there is an obvious performance gap between the students and the teachers in KD for different pairs. By enhancing each student on its own BKR, PE enables small students to **match or outperform** large teachers on five of the seven teacher-student pairs, and also substantially reduces the performance gap on the other two pairs. For example, the performance gap between teacher ResNet32×4 and student ResNet8×4 is reduced from 6.30 (KD) to 3.36 (PE). Note that there is no guarantee for PE to make small students match or outperform teachers as the BKR in PE cannot fully compensate for the unknown data sample distribution. Furthermore, PE also outperforms the data-driven competitors significantly. The reason for the superior performances of PE over GANKD is that modelling high-dimensional data distribution from sparse data points is even more challenging than training the classifier itself, which results in a nontrivial data discrepancy between the generated images and the real training images. This also causes that GANKD sometimes even underperforms KD. PE also beats ActiveMixKD significantly, since ActiveMixup ignores the critical samples that the student has a high confidence but with a wrong prediction and

[3] CutMix performs almost the same with Mixup for assisting KD but is slower so that we simply adopt Mixup as the baseline here.

[4] The core code for this baseline is borrowed from this publicly accessible implementation: https://github.com/facebookresearch/mixup-cifar10.

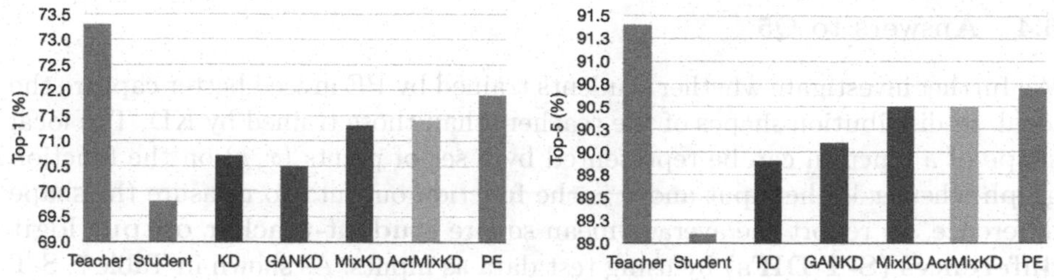

Fig. 5. Comparison on ImageNet

it also fails to interact with the teacher. In contrast, PE adaptively spots the BKRs for each student by interacting with the teacher. PE also outperforms Mixup due to the diverseness of MixPatch images in PE.

Tiny ImageNet. We further evaluate PE on Tiny ImageNet. As shown in Table 5, PE beats all the competitors in terms of both Top-1 and Top-5 accuracies on all the three pairs, and even enables the small student VGG-8 to significantly outperform the teacher VGG-13, which demonstrates the superiority of PE and the promise of addressing knowledge distillation from data perspectives.

ImageNet. To investigate whether PE is applicable to large scale datasets, we conduct experiments on ImageNet. We follow CRD [34] to use ResNet-34 and ResNet-18 as the teacher and the student, respectively. As shown in Fig. 5, by exploring the knowledge in the BKR, PE reduces the teacher-student performance gap significantly and also outperforms the competitors in terms of Top-1 and Top-5 accuracies, which demonstrates the applicability and usefulness of PE on large scale datasets. Nevertheless, the small student still underperforms the large teacher. Further examination reveals that ResNet-18 is an IST of ResNet-34 on the large and complex dataset ImageNet with ME 0.8, which indicates that the capacity difference can be the reason for the performance gap on ImageNet.

6.3 Answers to Q4

We further explore whether PE can be generalized to other SOTA distillation approaches inlcuding FitNet [31], AT [42], SP [35], CC [30], VID [2], RKD [28], PKT [29], AB [15], FT [20], NST [17], CRD [34], and SSKD [38]. The BKR searched by PE is used to enhance these SOTA approaches. We use WRN-40-2 and WRN-16-2 as the teacher and the student, respectively. Table 6 reports the results on CIFAR-100. It is observed that the enhanced counterparts (PE+Methods) consistently and substantially outperform the original methods even for the strong baselines like CRD and SSKD, which demonstrates the compatibility and usefulness of PE on different distillation approaches.

6.4 Answers to Q5

We further investigate whether students trained by PE indeed better capture the local, in-distribution shapes of the teachers than those trained by KD. The local shape of a function can be represented by a set of points (x, y) on the function graph where x is the input and y is the function output. To measure the shape difference, we report the average mean square **student-teacher output logit differences (S-T DIFs)** by using test data as inputs. As shown in Table 7, S-T DIFs of PE are consistently smaller than those of KD on all the seven pairs, which validates that the student shapes of PE are closer to the teacher shapes and indicates that the BKRs in PE are indeed beneficial to the students for capturing the local shapes of the teacher functions.

Table 6. Generalization (or Compatibility) of PE on SOTA distillation methods.

	FitNet	AT	SP	CC	VID	RKD	PKT	AB	FT	NST	CRD	SSKD
Methods	75.75	75.28	75.34	75.09	74.79	75.40	75.33	68.89	75.15	74.67	76.04	76.04
PE+Methods	**76.63**	**76.37**	**75.50**	**75.88**	**75.78**	**76.49**	**76.23**	**72.20**	**75.48**	**75.86**	**76.81**	**76.45**

Table 7. S-T DIFs (shape differences) on CIFAR-100

Teacher	WRN-40-2	resnet-110	VGG-13	ResNet32×4	ResNet-50	ResNet32×4	WRN-40-2
Student	WRN-16-2	resnet-32	VGG-8	ResNet8×4	VGG-8	ShuffleNetV2	ShuffleNetV1
KD	2.39	3.74	1.55	2.06	1.90	1.23	2.13
PE	1.74	2.92	1.15	1.53	1.37	0.77	1.52

Fig. 6. MixPatch images from the BKR on ImageNet.

6.5 Answers to Q6

PE adaptively learns the BKR from the MixPatch prior region for a student by interacting with the teacher. We show some BKR samples in Fig. 6. It is observed that these samples share similar local patterns with the original images.

7 Conclusion

In this paper, we study why small students typically underperform large teachers in KD and how they can outperform large teachers. Through designing exploratory experiments with theoretical analysis, we find that model capacity differences are not necessarily the root reason and the distillation data matter when the student capacity is greater than a threshold. Inspired by this, we propose to our best knowledge the first personalized distillation approach PE that goes beyond in-distribution distillation and adaptively learns the blind knowledge region for each student through interacting with the teacher. Extensive experiments demonstrate that PE substantially reduces the student-teacher performance gap and even enables small students to outperform large teachers.

References

1. Aguilar, G., Ling, Y., Zhang, Y., Yao, B., Fan, X., Guo, E.: Knowledge distillation from internal representations. arXiv preprint arXiv:1910.03723 (2019)
2. Ahn, S., Hu, S.X., Damianou, A., Lawrence, N.D., Dai, Z.: Variational information distillation for knowledge transfer. In: Proceedings of the IEEE Conference on Computer Vision and Pattern Recognition, pp. 9163–9171 (2019)
3. Chen, L., Wang, D., Gan, Z., Liu, J., Henao, R., Carin, L.: Wasserstein contrastive representation distillation. In: Proceedings of the IEEE/CVF Conference on Computer Vision and Pattern Recognition, pp. 16296–16305 (2021)
4. Chen, P., Liu, S., Zhao, H., Jia, J.: Distilling knowledge via knowledge review. In: Proceedings of the IEEE/CVF Conference on Computer Vision and Pattern Recognition, pp. 5008–5017 (2021)
5. Cho, J.H., Hariharan, B.: On the efficacy of knowledge distillation. In: Proceedings of the IEEE International Conference on Computer Vision, pp. 4794–4802 (2019)
6. Deng, J., Dong, W., Socher, R., Li, L.J., Li, K., Fei-Fei, L.: ImageNet: a large-scale hierarchical image database. In: CVPR09 (2009)
7. Deng, X., Zhang, Z.: Comprehensive knowledge distillation with causal intervention. Adv. Neural Inf. Process. Syst. **34**, 22158–22170 (2021)
8. Deng, X., Zhang, Z.: Graph-free knowledge distillation for graph neural networks. In: Proceedings of the 30th International Joint Conference on Artificial Intelligence (2021)
9. Deng, X., Zhang, Z.: Learning with retrospection. In: Proceedings of the AAAI Conference on Artificial Intelligence (2021)
10. Goodfellow, I., Bengio, Y., Courville, A., Bengio, Y.: Deep Learning, vol. 1. MIT Press, Cambridge (2016)
11. Goodfellow, I., et al.: Generative adversarial nets. In: Advances in Neural Information Processing Systems, pp. 2672–2680 (2014)
12. Han, X., Song, X., Yao, Y., Xu, X.S., Nie, L.: Neural compatibility modeling with probabilistic knowledge distillation. IEEE Trans. Image Process. **29**, 871–882 (2019)
13. He, K., Zhang, X., Ren, S., Sun, J.: Deep residual learning for image recognition. In: Proceedings of the IEEE Conference on Computer Vision and Pattern Recognition, pp. 770–778 (2016)

14. Heo, B., Kim, J., Yun, S., Park, H., Kwak, N., Choi, J.Y.: A comprehensive overhaul of feature distillation. In: Proceedings of the IEEE International Conference on Computer Vision, pp. 1921–1930 (2019)
15. Heo, B., Lee, M., Yun, S., Choi, J.Y.: Knowledge transfer via distillation of activation boundaries formed by hidden neurons. In: Proceedings of the AAAI Conference on Artificial Intelligence, vol. 33, pp. 3779–3787 (2019)
16. Hinton, G., Vinyals, O., Dean, J.: Distilling the knowledge in a neural network. arXiv preprint arXiv:1503.02531 (2015)
17. Huang, Z., Wang, N.: Like what you like: Knowledge distill via neuron selectivity transfer. arXiv preprint arXiv:1707.01219 (2017)
18. Huang, Z., et al.: Revisiting knowledge distillation: an inheritance and exploration framework. In: Proceedings of the IEEE/CVF Conference on Computer Vision and Pattern Recognition, pp. 3579–3588 (2021)
19. Yang, J., Martinez, B., Bulat, A., Tzimiropoulos, G.: Knowledge distillation vis softmax regression representation learning. In: International Conference on Learning Representations (2021)
20. Kim, J., Park, S., Kwak, N.: Paraphrasing complex network: Network compression via factor transfer. In: Advances in Neural Information Processing Systems, pp. 2760–2769 (2018)
21. Koratana, A., Kang, D., Bailis, P., Zaharia, M.: Lit: Learned intermediate representation training for model compression. In: International Conference on Machine Learning, pp. 3509–3518 (2019)
22. Krizhevsky, A., Hinton, G.: Learning multiple layers of features from tiny images. Technical Report, Citeseer (2009)
23. Krizhevsky, A., Sutskever, I., Hinton, G.E.: Imagenet classification with deep convolutional neural networks. In: Advances in Neural Information Processing Systems, pp. 1097–1105 (2012)
24. Li, X., Li, S., Omar, B., Wu, F., Li, X.: Reskd: residual-guided knowledge distillation. IEEE Trans. Image Process. **30**, 4735–4746 (2021)
25. Liu, R., Fusi, N., Mackey, L.: Teacher-student compression with generative adversarial networks. arXiv preprint arXiv:1812.02271 (2018)
26. Ma, N., Zhang, X., Zheng, H.T., Sun, J.: Shufflenet v2: practical guidelines for efficient CNN architecture design. In: Proceedings of the European Conference on Computer Vision (ECCV), pp. 116–131 (2018)
27. Mirzadeh, S.I., Farajtabar, M., Li, A., Levine, N., Matsukawa, A., Ghasemzadeh, H.: Improved knowledge distillation via teacher assistant. In: AAAI Conference on Artificial Intelligence (2020)
28. Park, W., Kim, D., Lu, Y., Cho, M.: Relational knowledge distillation. In: Proceedings of the IEEE Conference on Computer Vision and Pattern Recognition, pp. 3967–3976 (2019)
29. Passalis, N., Tefas, A.: Learning deep representations with probabilistic knowledge transfer. In: Proceedings of the European Conference on Computer Vision (ECCV), pp. 268–284 (2018)
30. Peng, B., et al.: Correlation congruence for knowledge distillation. In: Proceedings of the IEEE International Conference on Computer Vision, pp. 5007–5016 (2019)
31. Romero, A., Ballas, N., Kahou, S.E., Chassang, A., Gatta, C., Bengio, Y.: Fitnets: hints for thin deep nets. In: International Conference on Learning Representations (2015)
32. Simonyan, K., Zisserman, A.: Very deep convolutional networks for large-scale image recognition. In: International Conference on Learning Representations (2015)

33. Srinivas, S., Fleuret, F.: Knowledge transfer with Jacobian matching. In: Dy, J., Krause, A. (eds.) Proceedings of the 35th International Conference on Machine Learning. Proceedings of Machine Learning Research, vol. 80, pp. 4723–4731. PMLR, Stockholmsmässan, Stockholm Sweden, 10–15 July 2018
34. Tian, Y., Krishnan, D., Isola, P.: Contrastive representation distillation. In: International Conference on Learning Representations (2020)
35. Tung, F., Mori, G.: Similarity-preserving knowledge distillation. In: Proceedings of the IEEE International Conference on Computer Vision, pp. 1365–1374 (2019)
36. Wang, D., Li, Y., Wang, L., Gong, B.: Neural networks are more productive teachers than human raters: active mixup for data-efficient knowledge distillation from a blackbox model. In: Proceedings of the IEEE/CVF Conference on Computer Vision and Pattern Recognition, pp. 1498–1507 (2020)
37. Wang, X., Zhang, R., Sun, Y., Qi, J.: Kdgan: Knowledge distillation with generative adversarial networks. In: Advances in Neural Information Processing Systems, pp. 775–786 (2018)
38. Xu, G., Liu, Z., Li, X., Loy, C.C.: Knowledge distillation meets self-supervision. In: Vedaldi, A., Bischof, H., Brox, T., Frahm, J.-M. (eds.) ECCV 2020. LNCS, vol. 12354, pp. 588–604. Springer, Cham (2020). https://doi.org/10.1007/978-3-030-58545-7_34
39. Yim, J., Joo, D., Bae, J., Kim, J.: A gift from knowledge distillation: fast optimization, network minimization and transfer learning. In: Proceedings of the IEEE Conference on Computer Vision and Pattern Recognition, pp. 4133–4141 (2017)
40. Yun, S., Han, D., Oh, S.J., Chun, S., Choe, J., Yoo, Y.: Cutmix: regularization strategy to train strong classifiers with localizable features. In: Proceedings of the IEEE/CVF international conference on computer vision, pp. 6023–6032 (2019)
41. Zagoruyko, S., Komodakis, N.: Wide residual networks. In: BMVC (2016)
42. Zagoruyko, S., Komodakis, N.: Paying more attention to attention: improving the performance of convolutional neural networks via attention transfer. In: International Conference on Learning Representations (2017)
43. Zhang, H., Cisse, M., Dauphin, Y.N., Lopez-Paz, D.: mixup: beyond empirical risk minimization. International Conference on Learning Representations (2018). https://openreview.net/forum?id=r1Ddp1-Rb
44. Zhou, H., et al.: Rethinking soft labels for knowledge distillation: a bias-variance tradeoff perspective. In: International Conference on Learning Representations (2021)
45. Zhu, J., et al.: Complementary relation contrastive distillation. In: Proceedings of the IEEE/CVF Conference on Computer Vision and Pattern Recognition, pp. 9260–9269 (2021)

Not All Models Are Equal: Predicting Model Transferability in a Self-challenging Fisher Space

Wenqi Shao[1,2(✉)], Xun Zhao[2], Yixiao Ge[2(✉)], Zhaoyang Zhang[1], Lei Yang[3], Xiaogang Wang[1], Ying Shan[2], and Ping Luo[4]

[1] The Chinese University of Hong Kong, Ma Liu Shui, Hong Kong
weqish@link.cuhk.edu.hk

[2] ARC Lab, Tencent PCG, Shenzhen, China
{yixiaoge,yingsshan}@tencent.com

[3] Applied Model Center, Tencent PCG, Shenzhen, China

[4] The University of Hong Kong, Pok Fu Lam, Hong Kong

Abstract. This paper addresses an important problem of ranking the pre-trained deep neural networks and screening the most transferable ones for downstream tasks. It is challenging because the ground-truth model ranking for each task can only be generated by fine-tuning the pre-trained models on the target dataset, which is brute-force and computationally expensive. Recent advanced methods proposed several lightweight transferability metrics to predict the fine-tuning results. However, these approaches only capture static representations but neglect the fine-tuning dynamics. To this end, this paper proposes a new transferability metric, called **S**elf-challenging **F**isher **D**iscriminant **A**nalysis (**SFDA**), which has many appealing benefits that existing works do not have. First, SFDA can embed the static features into a Fisher space and refine them for better separability between classes. Second, SFDA uses a self-challenging mechanism to encourage different pre-trained models to differentiate on hard examples. Third, SFDA can easily select multiple pre-trained models for the model ensemble. Extensive experiments on 33 pre-trained models of 11 downstream tasks show that SFDA is efficient, effective, and robust when measuring the transferability of pre-trained models. For instance, compared with the state-of-the-art method NLEEP, SFDA demonstrates an average of 59.1% gain while bringing 22.5x speedup in wall-clock time. The code will be available at https://github.com/TencentARC/SFDA.

Keywords: Transfer learning · Model ranking · Image classification

1 Introduction

Due to the wide applications of DNNs [11,17,18], an increasing number of pre-trained models are produced by training on different source datasets (*e.g.*,

Supplementary Information The online version contains supplementary material available at https://doi.org/10.1007/978-3-031-19830-4_17.

S. Avidan et al. (Eds.): ECCV 2022, LNCS 13694, pp. 286–302, 2022.
https://doi.org/10.1007/978-3-031-19830-4_17

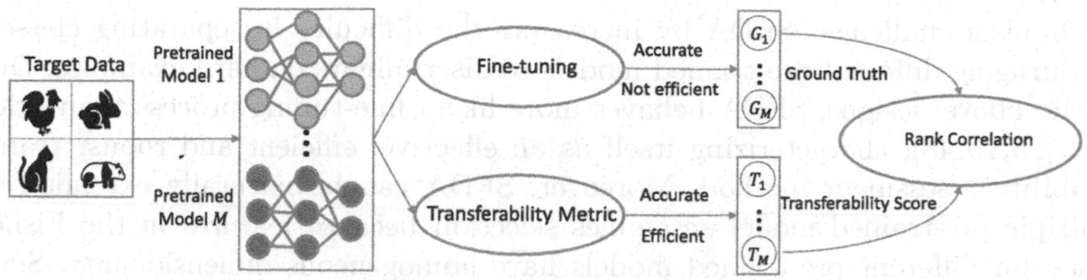

Fig. 1. The diagram of the task of ranking pre-trained models. The ground truth of the problem is to fine-tune pre-trained models and collect fine-tuning accuracy $\{G_m\}_{m=1}^M$. However, it is inefficient to enumerate all models in a fine-tuning procedure with a hyper-parameters sweep. An efficient approach is to adopt several lightweight transferability metrics to predict the fine-tuning results. Each metric produces transferability scores $\{T_m\}_{m=1}^M$ for all pre-trained models. An evaluation based on rank correlation such as Kendall's tau assesses the transferability metric.

ImageNet [23]), with different learning strategies (*e.g.*, self-supervised learning [15,16]). These pre-trained models are crucial in providing a good warm start for fine-tuning on target tasks in transfer learning. An interesting question naturally emerges: given the numerous pre-trained models, how can we properly and quickly rank the models thereby selecting the best ones for a certain target task.

Ranking pre-trained models is critical for transfer learning from a practical perspective. Due to the lack of sufficient labelled data in various domains (*e.g.*, object detection), a pre-trained model with expert knowledge is highly desired for initialization of downstream tasks in these domains. Ranking pre-trained models is also challenging, as the optimal pre-trained model is usually task-specific [25]. The pre-trained model ranking method should be efficient and generic enough so that the best model can be quickly selected for downstream tasks.

The ground-truth ranking of pre-trained models is obtained by fine-tuning pre-trained models on the target dataset and ranking them by the test accuracies, as shown in Fig. 1. Brute-force fine-tuning is obviously time-consuming and computationally expensive. For instance, fine-tuning one pre-trained model on one target dataset usually costs several GPU hours, selecting the optimal pre-trained model out of 10 models on 10 target tasks would cost many GPU days. Recent works propose several lightweight transferability metrics such as LEEP [29] and LogME [48] to substitute cumbersome fine-tuning procedure. Although these metrics are efficient to obtain, they simply measure the quality of pre-trained models by their static features, preventing themselves from characterizing the dynamics of the fine-tuning process, as shown in Fig. 2.

In this paper, we propose a new transferability metric for ranking pre-trained models, namely **S**elf-challenging **F**isher **D**iscriminant **A**nalysis (**SFDA**). To approximate the fine-tuning process, SFDA captures two significant features of fine-tuning, i.e. classes separability and discrimination on hard examples, as shown in Fig. 3. Towards this goal, we equip SFDA with a regularized FDA (Reg-FDA) module and a self-challenging mechanism. On the one hand, the Reg-FDA module projects the static features to a Fisher space where the updated features present better class separability. On the other hand, the self-challenging mechanism challenges SFDA by increasing the difficulty in separating classes, encouraging different pre-trained models to discriminate on hard examples. Due to the above designs, SFDA behaves more like a fine-tuning process than prior arts [25,29,48], characterizing itself as an effective, efficient and robust transferability assessment method. Moreover, SFDA can be naturally extended to multiple pre-trained model ensembles selection because features in the Fisher space for different pre-trained models have homogeneous dimensionality. Such homogeneity makes it possible to consider the complementarity between models.

The **contributions** of this work are three-fold. (1) We propose a new transferability metric named Self-challenging Fisher Discriminant Analysis (SFDA) which is effective, efficient and robust for ranking pre-trained models. (2) SFDA can be naturally extended to multiple pre-trained model ensembles selection. (3) Extensive experiments on 33 pre-trained models produced by different types of architectures and training strategies over 11 downstream classification tasks demonstrate the effectiveness of SFDA. For example, SFDA shows an average of 59.1% gain in the rank correlation with the ground truth fine-tuning accuracy while bringing 22.5× speedup in wall-clock time compared with previous state-of-the-art method NLEEP.

2 Related Work

Transfer Learning. Transfer learning [37,39] has been extensively investigated in the form of different learning tasks such as domain adaptation [26,41] and task transfer learning [49]. In deep learning, transfer learning mainly comes in the form of inductive transfer, which usually refers to the paradigm of adapting the pre-trained models to target tasks [20,46]. With the rapid development of deep learning in applications, numerous pre-trained models have been stored, such as HuggingFace Transformers [42]. This paper focuses on ranking pre-trained models and selecting the best performing model for the target task. Unlike task transfer learning, where the prior knowledge in the source domain is known, ranking pre-trained models only has access to the pre-trained model itself. Hence, the method for ranking pre-trained models should be generic and efficient enough to apply to various pre-trained models and target tasks.

Transferability of Pre-trained Models. Measuring the transferability of pre-trained models on a target task has recently attracted much attention due to the broad practicability. LEEP [29] is a well-known early work studying this problem. It estimates the empirical joint probability of source and target label space. Hence, LEEP only works when the pre-trained model has a classification head that outputs source label probability. To pursue a more generic transferability method, NLEEP [25] generate a pseudo classification head by a Gaussian Mixture Model and LogME [48] directly model the relationship between features extracted from the pre-trained models and their labels by marginalized likelihood. Although these metrics are easy to compute, they fail to characterize the dynamics of fine-tuning process, making the performance far from idealism. This paper proposes a new transferability metric that behaves more like fine-tuning by projecting features into a self-challenging Fisher space.

3 Preliminaries

In this section, we first present the setup, ground truth and evaluation protocol of the task of ranking pre-trained models and then introduce existing transferability metrics.

Problem Setup. A target dataset with N labeled data samples denoted as $\mathcal{T} = \{(x_n, y_n)\}_{n=1}^{N}$ and M pre-trained models $\{\phi_m = (\theta_m, h_m)\}_{m=1}^{M}$ are given. Each model ϕ_m consists of a feature extractor θ_m producing a D-dimension feature (i.e. $\hat{x} = \theta_m(x) \in \mathbb{R}^D$) and a classification head h_m outputting label prediction probability given input x [11,17]. The task of pre-trained model ranking is to generate a score for each pre-trained model thereby the best model can be identified according to the ranking list.

Fine-Tuning as Ground Truth. After fine-tuning all pre-trained models with hyper-parameters sweep on the target training dataset, the highest scores of evaluation metrics (e.g. test accuracy) are returned. The fine-tuning accuracies of different pre-trained models are denoted as $\{G_m\}_{m=1}^{M}$, which are recognized as the ground truth of pre-trained model ranking [25,48].

Transferability Metric. For each pre-trained model ϕ_m, a transferability metric outputs a scalar score T_m by

$$T_m = \sum_{i=1}^{N} \log p(y_i|x_i; \theta_m, h_m) \tag{1}$$

where (x_i, y_i) denotes the i-th data point in target dataset $\mathcal{T}$. A larger T_m indicates that model ϕ_i can perform better on target $\mathcal{T}$. As we can see from Fig. 2, transferability metrics differ in modelling label prediction probability $p(y_i|x_i; \theta_m, h_m)$. For instance, prior arts such as LEEP [29] obtain the probability based on static features $\hat{x}$, while ignoring that fine-tuning would update $\hat{x}$. Instead, our proposed SFDA is carefully designed to behave more like fine-tuning, as will be introduced in Sect. 4.

Evaluation Protocol. Basically, if ϕ_i has higher classification accuracy than ϕ_j (i.e. $G_i > G_j$), $T_i > T_j$ is also expected. Hence, a rank-based correlation between $\{T_m\}_{m=1}^{M}$ and $\{G_m\}_{m=1}^{M}$ is competent to evaluate the effectiveness of transferability metrics. We use *weighted Kendall's* τ_w (detailed in Appendix Sect. A.1) by following the common practice [25,48], where larger τ_w indicates better correlation and better transferability metric.

4 Self-challenging Fisher Discriminant Analysis

We propose a Self-challenging Fisher Discriminant Analysis (SFDA) for the problem of pre-trained model ranking. SFDA consists of two critical ingredients: a module of Regularized Fisher Discriminant Analysis (Reg-FDA) and a self-challenging mechanism motivated by two important observations in fine-tuning.

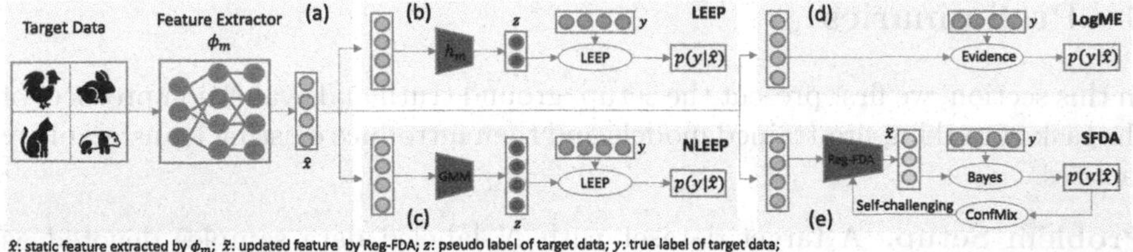

Fig. 2. Comparison of different transferability metrics including LEEP [29], NLEEP [25], LogME [48] and our proposed SFDA. (a) shows a transferability metric rely on the static representation $\hat{x}$. (b–d) show that these metrics differentiate in modeling label prediction $p(y|\hat{x})$. Specifically, LEEP, NLEEP, and LogME calculate transferability score by static features $\hat{x}$, making it difficult to approximate fine-tuning as fine-tuning would update $\hat{x}$. Our proposed SFDA behaves more like fine-tuning in terms of classes separability and discrimination on hard examples, which are achieved by the module of Reg-FDA and a self-mechanism with the proposed ConfMix noise in (e).

As shown in Fig. 3(a and b), fine-tuning pre-trained model would update static features $\{\hat{x}_i\}_{i=1}^N$ for better classes separability. Moreover, Fig. 3(d) show that different pre-trained models discriminate on hard examples during fine-tuning. Hence, the Reg-FDA and self-challenging mechanism are carefully designed to encourage classes separability and discrimination on hard examples. Algorithm 1 (see Appendix Sect. A.2) illustrates the whole pipeline of our proposed SFDA.

Notation. SFDA operates on static features $\hat{x} = \theta_m(x)$. Assume the target dataset $\mathcal{T} = \{(\hat{x}_n, y_n)\}_{n=1}^N$ has C classes, we split it into classes. Then we have $\mathcal{T} = \{\hat{x}_n^{(1)}\}_{n=1}^{N_1} \cup \cdots \cup \{\hat{x}_n^{(C)}\}_{n=1}^{N_C}$, where $\hat{x}_n^{(c)}$ denotes the n-th instance of the c-th class and N_c denote the sample size of the c-th class ($\sum_{c=1}^C N_c = N$).

4.1 Regularized FDA

To approximate fine-tuning procedure, the primary thing is to transform $\{\hat{x}_i\}_{i=1}^N$ to a space such that the classes on target $\mathcal{T}$ are separated as much as possible as shown in Fig. 3(b). Therefore, we propose Regularized Fisher Discriminant Analysis (Reg-FDA) for two reasons. First, Reg-FDA promotes classes separability by inheriting the merits from conventional FDA [28] that can maximize between scatter of classes and minimize within scatter of each class. Second, the optimization problem for Reg-FDA has a straightforward solution, which avoids gradient optimization and allows for efficient computation.

Formulation of Reg-FDA. Reg-FDA defines a transformation that projects $\hat{x} \in \mathbb{R}^D$ into $\tilde{x} \in \mathbb{R}^{D'}$ by a projection matrix $U \in \mathbb{R}^{D \times D'}$. We have $\tilde{x} := U^\top \hat{x}$, where

$$U = \arg\max_U \frac{d_B(U)}{d_W(U)} \overset{\text{def}}{=} \frac{|U^\top S_B U|}{|U^\top[(1-\lambda)S_W + \lambda I]U|} \tag{2}$$

In Eq. (2), $d_B(U) = |U^\top S_B U|$ and $d_W(U) = |U^\top \tilde{S}_W U|$ represent between scatter of classes and within scatter of every class, where $\tilde{S}_W = (1-\lambda)S_W + \lambda I$

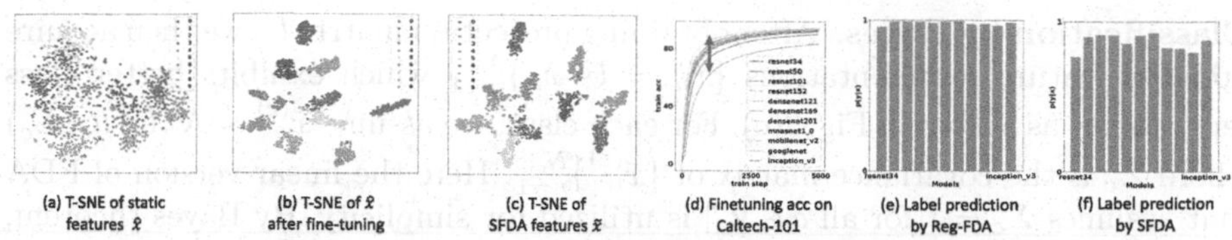

(a) T-SNE of static features $\hat{\mathcal{X}}$
(b) T-SNE of $\hat{\mathcal{X}}$ after fine-tuning
(c) T-SNE of SFDA features $\tilde{\mathcal{X}}$
(d) Finetuning acc on Caltech-101
(e) Label prediction by Reg-FDA
(f) Label prediction by SFDA

Fig. 3. (a–c) show that similar to fine-tuning our SFDA can update static features for better classes separability on the CIFAR-10 dataset. Deep models often fit easy examples in the early training stage while learning hard examples in the later training stage [2,50]. Hence, (d) presents that different pre-trained models discriminate on hard examples. (e) and (f) show that SFDA can produce more discriminative label prediction results than Reg-FDA because the self-mechanism in SFDA encourages the different pre-trained models to discriminate on hard examples.

and I is an identity matrix. Moreover, $S_B = \sum_{c=1}^{C} N_c(\mu_c - \mu)(\mu_c - \mu)^\top$ and $S_W = \sum_{c=1}^{C}\sum_{n=1}^{N_c}(\hat{x}_n^{(c)} - \mu_c)(\hat{x}_n^{(c)} - \mu_c)^\top$ are between and within scatter matrix respectively. Here $\mu = \sum_{n=1}^{N} \hat{x}_n$ and $\mu_c = \sum_{n=1}^{N_c} \hat{x}_n^{(c)}$ represent the mean of data and the mean of c-th class respectively. $\lambda \in [0, 1]$ in Eq. (2) is a regularization coefficient used to trade off the inter-class separation and intra-class compactness. Reg-FDA degrades into FDA [28] when $\lambda = 0$.

Adaptive Regularization Strength. We treat $\lambda \in [0, 1]$ as an regularization strength adaptive to different feature distribution. The motivation is that Reg-FDA can deal with diverse distribution of features $\{\hat{x}_i\}_{i=1}^{N}$ extracted from different pre-trained models when λ is adaptively varied. For example, self-supervised ResNet-50 with Infomin has a larger within scatter of classes than its supervised counterpart on CIFAR-10 dataset as shown in Fig. 5 of Appendix Sect. A.3, implying that ResNet-50 with Infomin needs stronger supervision on minimizing within scatter of every class for better classes separation. Motivated by this intuition we instantiate λ as follows,

$$\lambda = \exp^{-a\sigma(S_W)} \text{ where } \sigma(S_W) = \max_{u \in \mathbb{R}^D, \|u\|_2=1} u^\top S_W u. \tag{3}$$

In Eq. (3), a is a positive constant and $\sigma(S_W)$ is the largest eigenvalue of S_W by definition. A larger $\sigma(S_W)$ indicates the larger within scatter. Hence, a smaller λ should be used for the stronger supervision on minimizing within scatter.

Efficient Computation of Reg-FDA. The optimization problem in Eq. (2) can be solved efficiently as follows,

$$S_B u_k = v_k \tilde{S}_W u_k \tag{4}$$

Equation (4) is a generalized eigenvalues problem with v_k being the k-th eigenvalue and u_k being the corresponding eigenvector. Note that u_k constitutes the k-th column vector of the matrix U. The generalized eigenvalues problem can be efficiently solved by existing machine learning packages. Moreover, $\sigma(S_B)$ in Eq. (3) is also easily obtained by the Iteration method, which only involves a matrix-vector product as provided in Appendix Sect. A.2.

Classification by Bayes. After obtaining projection matrix U, we then acquire updated feature representations $\{\tilde{x}_n = U^\top \hat{x}_n\}_{n=1}^N$ which exhibits better class separability as shown in Fig. 3(c). For each class, we assume $\tilde{x}_n^{(c)} \sim \mathcal{N}(U^\top \mu_c, \Sigma_c)$ where Σ_c is the covariance matrix of $\{\tilde{x}_n^{(c)}\}_{n=1}^{N_c}$. Here the linear version of FDA that assumes $\Sigma_c = I$ for all $c \in [C]$ is utilized for simplicity. By Bayes theorem, given a sample $\tilde{x}_n$, the score function for label c is acquired by

$$\delta_c(\hat{x}_n) = \hat{x}_n{}^\top U U^\top \mu_c - \frac{1}{2}\mu_c{}^\top U U^\top \mu_c + \log q_c \tag{5}$$

which is a linear equation in terms of $\hat{x}_n$. In Eq. (5), q_c is the prior probability of the c-th class, which is estimated by $q_c = N_c/N$. We normalize $\delta_c(\hat{x}_n)$, $c = 1 \cdots C$ with softmax function to obtain the final class prediction probability

$$p(y_n|\hat{x}_n) = \frac{\exp^{\delta_{y_n}(\hat{x}_n)}}{\sum_{c=1}^C \exp^{\delta_c(\hat{x}_n)}} \tag{6}$$

Substituting Eq. (6) into Eq. (1) gives us the transferability metric score of Reg-FDA.

4.2 Self-challenging Mechanism by Noise Augmentation

Though Reg-FDA can project static features for better classes separability, pre-trained models perform differently on hard examples during fine-tuning (Fig. 3(d)). We propose a self-challenging mechanism augmented by the proposed Confidential Mix (ConfMix) noise to encourage pre-trained models to discriminate on hard examples. The self-challenging framework consists of a two-stage Reg-FDA. In the first stage, the Reg-FDA provides a confidential probability of correctly classifying each sample through Eq. (6). In the second stage, the Reg-FDA challenges the classification accuracy in the first stage by ConfMix.

Formulation of ConfMix. We denote $p(y_n|\hat{x}_n)$ in Eq. (6) as p_n. Since p_n represents the confidential probability of correctly classifying n-th sample in target dataset, a smaller p_n indicates larger difficulty in classifying $(\hat{x}_n, y_n)$. To increase the difficulty of classification, ConfMix builds Reg-FDA in the second stage on the convex combination of the underlying sample and the mean of its outer classes by p_n, as written by

$$\bar{x}_n = p_n \hat{x}_n + (1 - p_n)\mu_{c \neq y_n} \tag{7}$$

where $\mu_{c\neq y_n} = \frac{1}{N - N_{y_n}} \sum_{n=1, y_n \neq c}^N \hat{x}_n$ denotes the outer classes mean relative to the c-th class.

Analysis of ConfMix. We show that ConfMix increases classification difficulty and improves the discrimination on hard examples for pre-trained models. Through Eq. (7), $\hat{x}_n$ is moved to its outer classes by ConfMix. Hence, different classes would be closer to each other, increasing the difficulty in separating

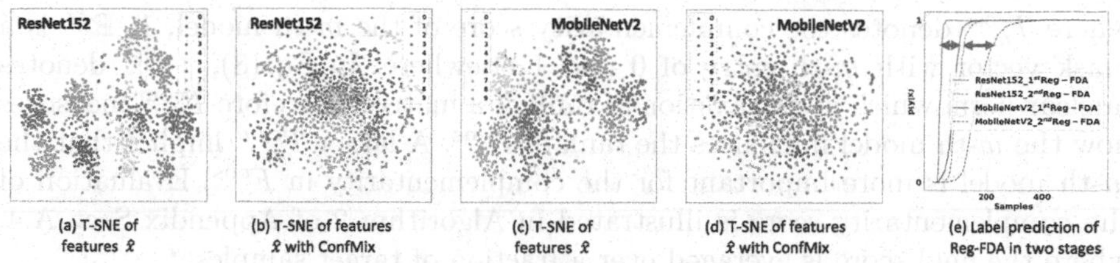

(a) T-SNE of features $\hat{x}$ (b) T-SNE of features $\hat{x}$ with ConfMix (c) T-SNE of features $\hat{x}$ (d) T-SNE of features $\hat{x}$ with ConfMix (e) Label prediction of Reg-FDA in two stages

Fig. 4. (a–d) show that our proposed ConfMix noise reduces separability between classes on both ResNet-152 and MobileNetV2. (e) shows that ConfMix increases the classification difficulty and encourages pre-trained models to differentiate on hard examples. The results are obtained on a fraction of the CIFAR-10 dataset.

classes by Reg-FDA. For example, Fig. 4 show that ConfMix encourages separate feature distribution between classes. Moreover, the final classification probability $p(y_n|\bar{x}_n)$ obtained by Reg-FDA in the second stage is lower than $p(y_n|\hat{x}_n)$ in the first stage, which means the classification by Reg-FDA becomes more difficult. In addition, we also observe from Fig. 3(e and f) and Fig. 4(e) that the difference between pre-trained models on hard examples are enlarged.

4.3 Extension to Top-k Model Ensembles Selection

Top-k model ensembles selection utilizes k pre-trained models to perform ensemble transfer learning. The k models are selected to obtain the best performance on target tasks. The main challenge of top-k model selection is the heterogeneous feature representations extracted from different pre-trained models. For example, ResNet-50 outputs a feature with the dimension of 2048 while the features extracted from ResNet-18 are 512-D. Such heterogeneity makes it difficult to compare different pre-trained models. To simplify the problem, recent works propose to select k models by top-k ranked transferability metrics. Despite the simplicity, it fails to consider the relationship between models. In other words, transferability metrics can only measure how well a single model performs on a target task. However, the complementarity between models should also be considered in ensemble transfer learning [6,30].

Homogeneous Features by SFDA. Fortunately, our proposed SFDA can deal with heterogeneous feature representations by the projection of U. By SFDA, we have $\tilde{x} = U^{\mathsf{T}}\hat{x} \in \mathbb{R}^{D'}$ where $D' = \min\{D, C-1\}$. Note that $\hat{x} \in \mathbb{R}^{D}$ where D varies for different models. Fortunately, the projected features of different models by SFDA have homogeneous dimension of $D' = C - 1$. Here we assume $D \geq C - 1$ which is a common case in practice.

Complementarity Score. By SFDA, we can collect an ensemble of homogeneous features on a model basis given a sample, as denoted by $F^{\text{ens}} = [\tilde{x}^1, \cdots, \tilde{x}^M] \in \mathbb{R}^{M \times D'}$. Hence, each model is now represented by each row of F^{ens}. An ablative approach [51] is employed to evaluate how a model is complementary to other models, as given by

$$T_m^{\text{com}} = \|F^{\text{ens}}\|_* - \|F^{\text{ens}} \odot 1_m\|_* \tag{8}$$

where T_m^{com} denotes the complementarity score of the m-th model, $1_m\mathbb{R}^M$ is a mask vector with m-th entry of 0 and 1 elsewhere. In Eq. (8), $\|\cdot\|_*$ denotes nuclear norm which is a relaxation of rank of a matrix Therefore T_m^{com} measures how the m-th model influences the rank of F^{ens}. A larger T_m^{com} implies that the m-th model is more important for the complementarity in F^{ens}. Evaluation of the complementarity score is illustrated in Algorithm 2 of Appendix Sect. A.4, where the final score is averaged over a fraction of target samples.

Ensemble Score. The total ensemble score for selecting top-k models is determined by combining SFDA and complementarity scores. The former evaluates the transferability of a single model, and the latter measures the complementarity between models. Putting them together yields

$$T_m^{\text{ens}} = rT_m^{\text{SFDA}} + (1-r)T_m^{\text{com}} \tag{9}$$

where T_m^{SFDA} and T_m^{com} denotes the transferability score and complementarity score. r is a weight ratio to balance two scores. Empirically, we set $r = 0.5$. We select top-k ranked models by T_m^{ens} to perform ensemble transfer learning.

5 Experiments

This section evaluates our method SFDA on different categories of pre-trained models, including both supervised and self-supervised Convolutional Neural Network (CNN) models and recently-popular vision transformer models [11,34] (see Appendix B.2). Moreover, we also show the effectiveness of SFDA in the top-k ensembles selection of pre-trained models. The evaluation is performed on 11 standard classification benchmark in transfer learning. Finally, we conduct an ablation study to analyze our SFDA (also see Appendix B.4).

5.1 Benchmarks

Target Datasets. We adopt 11 classification benchmarks widely used in the transfer learning study, including FGVC Aircraft [27], Caltech-101 [14], Stanford Cars [21], CIFAR-10 [22], CIFAR-100 [22], DTD [10], Oxford 102 Flowers [31], Food-101 [4], Oxford-IIIT Pets [32], SUN397 [44], and VOC2007 [13]. These datasets cover a broad range of classification tasks, which includes scene, texture, and coarse/fine-grained image classification.

Ground Truth. We can obtain the ground-truth ranking by fine-tuning all pre-trained models with hyper-parameters sweeping on target datasets. Here we consider the normal training setting which is more general in practice than other sparse training methods [53]. Details of target datasets and fine-tuning schemes are described in Appendix Sect. B.1

5.2 Evaluation on Supervised CNN Models

Models. We first evaluate the performance of transferability metrics on ranking pre-trained supervised CNN models. We select 11 widely-used models including

Table 1. Comparison of different transferability metrics on supervised CNN models in rank correlation τ_w with the ground truth and the wall-clock time. A larger τ_w indicates the better transferability assessment of pre-trained models. The best results are denoted in bold. A shorter wall-clock time suggests that the transferability metric is more efficient to obtain. Our proposed SFDA achieves the best transferability prediction over 11 target tasks while being much more efficient than NLEEP.

	Aircraft	Caltech	Cars	CF-10	CF-100	DTD	Flowers	Food	Pets	SUN	VOC
Weighted Kendall's tau τ_w											
LEEP	−0.234	0.605	0.367	0.824	0.677	0.486	−0.243	0.491	0.389	0.701	0.446
LogME	0.506	0.435	**0.576**	0.852	0.692	0.647	0.111	0.385	0.411	0.511	0.478
NLEEP	0.495	0.661	0.265	0.806	0.823	**0.777**	0.215	0.624	0.599	**0.807**	0.654
SFDA	**0.615**	**0.737**	0.487	**0.949**	**0.866**	0.597	**0.542**	**0.815**	**0.734**	0.703	**0.763**
Wall-Clock time (s)											
LEEP	5.1	4.9	8.3	22.3	23.8	3.5	3.8	37.1	3.9	21.1	4.8
LogME	11.5	11.0	18.3	23.5	36.9	8.7	10.9	54.0	9.4	51.8	9.7
NLEEP	253.8	488.7	973.8	1.1e4	1.7e4	146.0	294.0	2.0e4	580.8	8.6e3	678.8
SFDA	91.9	246.2	274.6	576.6	617.9	171.9	167.2	703.7	181.2	560.5	75.0

ResNet-34 [17], ResNet-50 [17], ResNet-101 [17], ResNet-152 [17], DenseNet-121 [19], DenseNet-169 [19], DenseNet-201 [19], MNet-A1 [38], MobileNetV2 [33], GoogleNet [35], and InceptionV3 [36]. All these models are trained on ImageNet dataset [23]. We fine-tune these models on the 11 target datasets to obtain the ground truth (original results are shown in Appendix Sect. B.1). In addition, the transferability scores of metrics including LEEP, NLEEP, LogME and our SFDA are also calculated by following the paradigm in Fig. 2. We re-implement these algorithms in our framework for a fair comparison.

Performance Comparison. We assess transferability metrics by weighted Ken-dall's tau τ_w that measures the rank correlation between ground truth and metrics scores. We compare SFDA with previous LEEP, LogME, and NLEEP. As shown in Table 1, SFDA achieves the best rank correlation τ_w with the ground truth on 8 target datasets. For example, SFDA outperforms NLEEP by 0.327, 0.191, and 0.160 rank correlation τ_w on Flowers, Food, and Pets, respectively. On these three datasets, the relative improvements are 152.1%, 30.6%, and 26.7%, respectively, showing the effectiveness of our SFDA in measuring the transferability of pre-trained models. On the other hand, for the remaining 3 target datasets (i.e. Cars, DTD, and SUN397), our SFDA still has a marginal gap compared to the best-performing transferability metric.

Wall-Clock Time Comparison. We also provide wall-clock time comparison in Table 1. The wall-clock time measures how long it takes for each metric to calculate the transferability scores of all models on a target dataset. We can see that both LEEP and LogME are fast to obtain on all target tasks. However, LEEP and LogME are not stable in measuring the transferability score of pre-trained models for all target tasks. For example, the rank correlation τ_w of

Table 2. Comparison of different transferability metrics on self-supervised CNN models regarding τ_w and the wall-clock time. Our proposed SFDA achieves the best transferability assessment over 11 target tasks and exhibits higher efficiency than NLEEP.

	Aircraft	Caltech	Cars	CF-10	CF-100	DTD	Flowers	Food	Pets	SUN	VOC
Weighted Kendall's tau τ_w											
LogME	0.223	0.051	0.375	0.295	−0.008	0.627	0.604	0.570	0.684	0.217	0.158
NLEEP	−0.029	**0.525**	0.486	−0.044	0.276	0.641	0.534	0.574	**0.792**	0.719	−0.101
SFDA	**0.254**	0.523	**0.515**	**0.619**	**0.548**	**0.749**	**0.773**	**0.685**	0.586	0.698	**0.568**
Wall-Clock time (s)											
LogME	33.5	33.0	72.7	89.3	116.0	15.0	41.0	140.1	40.9	112.5	16.7
NLEEP	581.7	787.7	1.6e3	8.0e3	2.1e4	332.7	322.3	1.1e4	186.5	3.9e4	678.8
SFDA	300.7	316.4	553.4	504.1	753.1	170.2	335.1	980.7	157.7	992.5	134.7

LogME and LEEP on multiple target datasets such as Flowers, Food, and Pets are lower than 0.5, implying that they are ineffective in measuring transferability on these downstream tasks. Moreover, NLEEP performs well on a large number of target tasks. But the computation of NLEEP on some target datasets costs even several hours, which is comparable with the fine-tuning procedure.

As we can see from Table 1, our SFDA can measure transferability of models well while only requiring several hundred seconds for computation on all target tasks, achieving a better trade-off between assessment of transferability and computation consumption than other methods.

5.3 Evaluation on Self-supervised CNN Models

Models. In transfer learning, self-supervised pre-trained models generally have better transferability than their supervised counterpart [12,16]. Moreover, the different self-supervised algorithms would provide diverse feature representation for a downstream task [12]. Hence, it is essential to investigate selecting the best self-supervised pre-trained model for a target task. To this end, we build a pool of self-supervised pre-trained models with ResNet-50 [17], including BYOL [15], Deepclusterv2 [5], Infomin [40], MoCov1 [16], MoCov2 [9], Instance Discrimination [43], PCLv1 [24], PCLv2 [24], Selav2 [3], SimCLRv1 [7], SimCLRv2 [8], and SWAV [10]. Our goal is to rank these self-supervised models on 11 downstream tasks in Sect. 5.1.

Performance Comparison. We compare our SFDA with LogME and NLEEP on transferability assessment in rank correlation τ_w with the ground truth. Because self-supervised models usually do not have a classifier, LEEP is not included for comparison as it relies on a classifier to calculate transferability score. As shown in Table 2, SFDA still performs consistently well in measuring the transferability of self-supervised models. On the contrary, LogME and NLEEP fail on some target tasks. For example, LogME and NLEEP have a negative of small positive rank correlation on Aircraft and CIFAR-100. Averaging

Table 3. Separate effects of components in SFDA. Three variants of SFDA are considered: (1) LogME + ConfMix; (2) SFDA w/o ConfMix; (3) SFDA with $\lambda = 0.5$ in Eq. (3). We see that both Reg-FDA and the self-challenging mechanism achieved by ConfMix are crucial to SFDA.

Variants	Aircraft	Caltech	Cars	CF-10	CF-100	DTD	Flowers	Food	Pets	SUN	VOC
(1)	0.408	0.324	0.365	0.924	0.571	0.328	0.023	0.466	0.390	0.419	0.695
(2)	0.481	0.676	0.403	0.887	0.773	0.471	**0.668**	0.812	0.652	0.606	0.721
(3)	0.424	0.627	0.178	0.931	0.828	0.458	0.228	0.802	0.409	0.651	0.650
SFDA	**0.615**	**0.737**	**0.487**	**0.949**	**0.866**	**0.597**	0.542	**0.815**	**0.734**	**0.703**	**0.763**

Table 4. Comparison between SFDA and re-training head in terms of τ_w. Our proposed SFDA generally performs better than re-training head over 11 target tasks.

	Aircraft	Caltech	Cars	CF-10	CF-100	DTD	Flowers	Food	Pets	SUN	VOC
Weighted Kendall's tau τ_w											
Re-Head	−0.008	**0.590**	**0.666**	0.583	0.501	0.721	0.661	**0.787**	**0.703**	0.637	0.490
SFDA	**0.254**	0.523	0.515	**0.619**	**0.548**	**0.749**	**0.773**	0.685	0.586	**0.698**	**0.568**
Wall-Clock time (s)											
Fine-tune	3.3e5	2.8e5	2.7e5	2.5e5	2.5e5	3.1e5	3.8e5	2.6e5	2.9e5	3.9e5	2.9e5
Re-Head	2211	2198	2246	2219	2215	2210	2173	2211	2232	2228	2375
SFDA	300.7	316.4	553.4	504.1	753.1	170.2	335.1	980.7	157.7	992.5	134.7

τ_w over 11 target tasks, the improvement of SFDA (0.593) over LogME (0.345) and NLEEP (0.397) are 71.9% and 49.4%, respectively. The results demonstrate the effectiveness of our SFDA in transferability assessment.

Wall-Clock Time Comparison. As shown in Table 2, LogME and SFDA usually take tens of seconds to calculate transferability score on all target tasks, while NLEEP may cost several hours on some target datasets. Though LogME is fast, it is not stable, as mentioned above. Instead, our SFDA adapts to different pre-trained models and requires several hundred seconds on all target tasks. Hence, SFDA is still effective and efficient in evaluating the transferability of self-supervised models.

5.4 Extension to Top-k Model Ensembles Selection

Our proposed SFDA is competent for the problem of top-k model ensembles selection as SFDA makes features extracted from different models homogeneous. Due to the homogeneity, the complementarity between models is considered by SFDA through Eq. (8), which we denoted as SFDA^{com} as shown in Table 10 of Appendix. To verify the effectiveness of SFDA^{com} in top-k model ensembles selection, we compare it with baselines [1,47] that select k models by top-k ranked LogME, NLEEP. We also experimented on selecting k models by top-k ranked SFDA. When k models are selected, we perform ensemble fine-tuning on 11 target tasks respectively by following the paradigm in [1]. The final ensemble

Table 5. Comparison on all CNN models in Sect. 5.2 and Sect. 5.3. The weighted Kendall's tau τ_w is used to assess transferability metrics. Our SFDA is still better at measuring the transferability of pre-trained models than LogME and NLEEP.

Method	Aircraft	Caltech	Cars	CF-10	CF-100	DTD	Flowers	Food	Pets	SUN	VOC
LogME	0.168	0.033	**0.506**	0.687	0.507	0.580	0.301	0.535	0.629	0.284	0.531
NLEEP	−0.026	0.714	0.099	0.491	0.653	**0.766**	0.373	0.233	0.768	**0.716**	0.637
SFDA	**0.350**	**0.791**	0.450	**0.748**	**0.803**	0.544	**0.741**	**0.743**	**0.788**	0.537	**0.798**

fine-tuning accuracy is used to compare different ensemble transferability metrics. Wee can see from Table 10 in Appendix B.3 that SFDA^{com} leads to higher fine-tuning accuracy on most target tasks than other metrics.

5.5 Ablation Analysis

The Effect of Reg-FDA and Self-challenging Mechanism. SFDA consists of a Reg-FDA module and a self-challenging mechanism achieved by ConfMix. Here we study their separate effects on transferability assessment. To this end, we evaluate the transferability of supervised CNN models in Sect. 5.2 with the following variants of SFDA, (1) SFDA with Reg-FDA replaced by LogME because LogME can also output a label prediction probability; (2) SFDA w/o ConfMix; and (3) SFDA with a fixed regularization coefficient $\lambda = 0.5$ in Eq. (2). The results are reported in Table 3. From (1), we see that 'LogME + ConfMix' performs worse than SFDA ('Reg-FDA + ConfMix'), indicating that the ConfMix cooperates better with Reg-FDA than LogME. The main reason is that our Reg-FDA projects features for better class separability, and ConfMix increases the difficulty in separating classes features. But LogME has nothing to do with classes separability. Moreover, comparing (2) and SFDA, we conclude that self-mechanism achieved by ConfMix can consistently improve the performance on 11 downstream tasks. Lastly, an adaptive regularization term in Eq. (3) helps SFDA deal with various feature distributions. Fixing the regularization strength leads to worse transferability assessment as shown in Table 3 (3).

Comparison with Re-training Head. Re-training head is a widely-adopted tool to measure how well the features extracted from the pre-trained model can predict their labels by a classification head. It freezes the extracted features and trains the classification head only. After training, the head produces the labels of features. Hence, we can obtain re-training head accuracy. Though re-training head simplifies the fine-tuning process, it is still built on static representations and requires a grid search for hyper-parameters such as learning rate and regularization strength. Hence, re-training head is less efficient and effective than our SFDA. Table 4 shows that SFDA is more effective in measuring the transferability of pre-trained models than the re-training head. In particular, our SFDA is more than 600x faster than brute-force fine-tuning in running time.

Performance on Total Pre-trained Model Hubs. In practice, we may have a large-scale pre-trained model hubs rather than categorized ones in Sect. 5.2–5.3. In this case, we need to rank a variety of pre-trained models. To this end, we consolidate the pre-trained models from supervised CNN models in Sect. 5.2 and self-supervised CNN models in Sect. 5.3 into one group (including 23 pre-trained models in total), then applying the ranking methods on it. The results are shown in Table 5. The results further reveal that our SFDA performs consistently well on a larger group of pre-trained models compared to LogME and NLEEP.

6 Conclusions and Discussions

The rapid development of deep learning produces many deep models pre-trained on different source datasets with various learning strategies. Given numerous pre-trained models, it is practical to consider how to rank them and screen the best ones for target tasks. In this work, we answer this question by proposing a new transferability metric named Self-challenging Fisher Discriminant Analysis (SFDA). SFDA build upon a regularized Fisher Discriminate Analysis and a self-challenging mechanism. Compared with prior arts, SFDA behaves more like fine-tuning in terms of classes separability and discrimination on hard examples, characterizing itself as an efficient, effective and robust transferability assessment method. Moreover, SFDA can be naturally extended to multiple pre-trained model ensemble selection where complementarity between models is essential for better ensemble performance on downstream tasks. SFDA measures transferability by mimicking the fine-tuning procedure for downstream classification tasks.

Discussions. Although SFDA is fast and effective in measuring transferability of pre-trained models, it can only used in downstream classification tasks. Several future works are worth investigating in pursuit of a more universal metric. Firstly, an interesting future work would be how to extend SFDA in other types of target tasks such as regression tasks by characterizing the features of fine-tuning on these tasks. Secondly, investigating SFDA in out-of-distribution setting [45,52] could also be a fruitful future direction.

Acknowledgement. We thank anonymous reviewers from the venue ECCV 2022 for their valuable comments. We also thank Xiuzhe Wu and Ruichen Luo for their helpful discussions. Ping Luo is supported by the General Research Fund of HK No. 27208720, No. 17212120, and No. 17200622.

References

1. Agostinelli, A., Uijlings, J., Mensink, T., Ferrari, V.: Transferability metrics for selecting source model ensembles. arXiv preprint arXiv:2111.13011 (2021)

2. Arazo, E., Ortego, D., Albert, P., O'Connor, N., McGuinness, K.: Unsupervised label noise modeling and loss correction. In: International Conference on Machine Learning, pp. 312–321. PMLR (2019)
3. Asano, Y.M., Rupprecht, C., Vedaldi, A.: Self-labelling via simultaneous clustering and representation learning. arXiv preprint arXiv:1911.05371 (2019)
4. Bossard, L., Guillaumin, M., Van Gool, L.: Food-101 – mining discriminative components with random forests. In: Fleet, D., Pajdla, T., Schiele, B., Tuytelaars, T. (eds.) ECCV 2014. LNCS, vol. 8694, pp. 446–461. Springer, Cham (2014). https://doi.org/10.1007/978-3-319-10599-4_29
5. Caron, M., Bojanowski, P., Joulin, A., Douze, M.: Deep clustering for unsupervised learning of visual features. In: Ferrari, V., Hebert, M., Sminchisescu, C., Weiss, Y. (eds.) Computer Vision – ECCV 2018. LNCS, vol. 11218, pp. 139–156. Springer, Cham (2018). https://doi.org/10.1007/978-3-030-01264-9_9
6. Chang, K.H.: Complementarity in Data Mining. University of California, Los Angeles (2015)
7. Chen, T., Kornblith, S., Norouzi, M., Hinton, G.: A simple framework for contrastive learning of visual representations. In: International Conference on Machine Learning, pp. 1597–1607. PMLR (2020)
8. Chen, T., Kornblith, S., Swersky, K., Norouzi, M., Hinton, G.E.: Big self-supervised models are strong semi-supervised learners. In: Advances in Neural Information Processing Systems, pp. 22243–22255 (2020)
9. Chen, X., Fan, H., Girshick, R., He, K.: Improved baselines with momentum contrastive learning. arXiv preprint arXiv:2003.04297 (2020)
10. Cimpoi, M., Maji, S., Kokkinos, I., Mohamed, S., Vedaldi, A.: Describing textures in the wild. In: Proceedings of the IEEE Conference on Computer Vision and Pattern Recognition, pp. 3606–3613 (2014)
11. Dosovitskiy, A., et al.: An image is worth 16x16 words: transformers for image recognition at scale. arXiv preprint arXiv:2010.11929 (2020)
12. Ericsson, L., Gouk, H., Hospedales, T.M.: How well do self-supervised models transfer? In: Proceedings of the IEEE/CVF Conference on Computer Vision and Pattern Recognition, pp. 5414–5423 (2021)
13. Everingham, M., Van Gool, L., Williams, C.K., Winn, J., Zisserman, A.: The pascal visual object classes (VOC) challenge. Int. J. Comput. Vision **2**, 303–338 (2010)
14. Fei-Fei, L., Fergus, R., Perona, P.: Learning generative visual models from few training examples: an incremental Bayesian approach tested on 101 object categories. In: 2004 Conference on Computer Vision and Pattern Recognition Workshop, p. 178. IEEE (2004)
15. Grill, J.B., et al.: Bootstrap your own latent-a new approach to self-supervised learning. In: Advances in Neural Information Processing Systems, pp. 21271–21284 (2020)
16. He, K., Fan, H., Wu, Y., Xie, S., Girshick, R.: Momentum contrast for unsupervised visual representation learning. In: Proceedings of the IEEE/CVF Conference on Computer Vision and Pattern Recognition, pp. 9729–9738 (2020)
17. He, K., Zhang, X., Ren, S., Sun, J.: Deep residual learning for image recognition. In: Proceedings of the IEEE Conference on Computer Vision and Pattern Recognition, pp. 770–778 (2016)
18. He, K., Zhang, X., Ren, S., Sun, J.: Identity mappings in deep residual networks. In: Leibe, B., Matas, J., Sebe, N., Welling, M. (eds.) ECCV 2016. LNCS, vol. 9908, pp. 630–645. Springer, Cham (2016). https://doi.org/10.1007/978-3-319-46493-0_38

19. Huang, G., Liu, Z., Van Der Maaten, L., Weinberger, K.Q.: Densely connected convolutional networks. In: Proceedings of the IEEE Conference on Computer Vision and Pattern Recognition, pp. 4700–4708 (2017)
20. Kornblith, S., Shlens, J., Le, Q.V.: Do better ImageNet models transfer better? In: Proceedings of the IEEE/CVF Conference on Computer Vision and Pattern Recognition, pp. 2661–2671 (2019)
21. Krause, J., Deng, J., Stark, M., Fei-Fei, L.: Collecting a large-scale dataset of fine-grained cars (2013)
22. Krizhevsky, A., Hinton, G., et al.: Learning multiple layers of features from tiny images (2009)
23. Krizhevsky, A., Sutskever, I., Hinton, G.E.: ImageNet classification with deep convolutional neural networks. In: Advances in Neural Information Processing Systems (2012)
24. Li, J., Zhou, P., Xiong, C., Hoi, S.C.: Prototypical contrastive learning of unsupervised representations. arXiv preprint arXiv:2005.04966 (2020)
25. Li, Y., et al.: Ranking neural checkpoints. In: Proceedings of the IEEE/CVF Conference on Computer Vision and Pattern Recognition, pp. 2663–2673 (2021)
26. Long, M., Cao, Y., Wang, J., Jordan, M.: Learning transferable features with deep adaptation networks. In: International Conference on Machine Learning, pp. 97–105. PMLR (2015)
27. Maji, S., Rahtu, E., Kannala, J., Blaschko, M., Vedaldi, A.: Fine-grained visual classification of aircraft. arXiv preprint arXiv:1306.5151 (2013)
28. Mika, S., Ratsch, G., Weston, J., Scholkopf, B., Mullers, K.R.: Fisher discriminant analysis with kernels. In: Neural Networks for Signal Processing IX: Proceedings of the 1999 IEEE Signal Processing Society Workshop (Cat. No. 98th8468), pp. 41–48. IEEE (1999)
29. Nguyen, C., Hassner, T., Seeger, M., Archambeau, C.: LEEP: a new measure to evaluate transferability of learned representations. In: International Conference on Machine Learning, pp. 7294–7305. PMLR (2020)
30. Nguyen, H., Chang, M.: Complementary ensemble learning. arXiv preprint arXiv:2111.08449 (2021)
31. Nilsback, M.E., Zisserman, A.: Automated flower classification over a large number of classes. In: 2008 Sixth Indian Conference on Computer Vision, Graphics & Image Processing, pp. 722–729. IEEE (2008)
32. Parkhi, O.M., Vedaldi, A., Zisserman, A., Jawahar, C.: Cats and dogs. In: 2012 IEEE Conference on Computer Vision and Pattern Recognition, pp. 3498–3505. IEEE (2012)
33. Sandler, M., Howard, A., Zhu, M., Zhmoginov, A., Chen, L.C.: MobileNetV 2: inverted residuals and linear bottlenecks. In: Proceedings of the IEEE Conference on Computer Vision and Pattern Recognition, pp. 4510–4520 (2018)
34. Shao, W., et al.: Dynamic token normalization improves vision transformer. arXiv preprint arXiv:2112.02624 (2021)
35. Szegedy, C., et al.: Going deeper with convolutions. In: Proceedings of the IEEE Conference on Computer Vision and Pattern Recognition, pp. 1–9 (2015)
36. Szegedy, C., Vanhoucke, V., Ioffe, S., Shlens, J., Wojna, Z.: Rethinking the inception architecture for computer vision. In: Proceedings of the IEEE Conference on Computer Vision and Pattern Recognition, pp. 2818–2826 (2016)
37. Tan, C., Sun, F., Kong, T., Zhang, W., Yang, C., Liu, C.: A survey on deep transfer learning. In: Kůrková, V., Manolopoulos, Y., Hammer, B., Iliadis, L., Maglogiannis, I. (eds.) ICANN 2018. LNCS, vol. 11141, pp. 270–279. Springer, Cham (2018). https://doi.org/10.1007/978-3-030-01424-7_27

38. Tan, M., et al.: MNASNet: platform-aware neural architecture search for mobile. In: Proceedings of the IEEE/CVF Conference on Computer Vision and Pattern Recognition, pp. 2820–2828 (2019)
39. Thrun, S., Pratt, L.: Learning to learn: introduction and overview. In: Thrun, S., Pratt, L. (eds.) Learning to Learn, pp. 3–17. Springer, Boston (1998). https://doi.org/10.1007/978-1-4615-5529-2_1
40. Tian, Y., Sun, C., Poole, B., Krishnan, D., Schmid, C., Isola, P.: What makes for good views for contrastive learning? Advances in Neural Information Processing Systems, pp. 6827–6839 (2020)
41. Wang, M., Deng, W.: Deep visual domain adaptation: a survey. In: Neurocomputing, pp. 135–153 (2018)
42. Wolf, T., et al.: Huggingface's transformers: state-of-the-art natural language processing. arXiv preprint arXiv:1910.03771 (2019)
43. Wu, Z., Xiong, Y., Yu, S.X., Lin, D.: Unsupervised feature learning via non-parametric instance discrimination. In: Proceedings of the IEEE Conference on Computer Vision and Pattern Recognition, pp. 3733–3742 (2018)
44. Xiao, J., Hays, J., Ehinger, K.A., Oliva, A., Torralba, A.: Sun database: large-scale scene recognition from abbey to zoo. In: 2010 IEEE Computer Society Conference on Computer Vision and Pattern Recognition, pp. 3485–3492. IEEE (2010)
45. Yang, J., Zhou, K., Li, Y., Liu, Z.: Generalized out-of-distribution detection: a survey. arXiv preprint arXiv:2110.11334 (2021)
46. Yosinski, J., Clune, J., Bengio, Y., Lipson, H.: How transferable are features in deep neural networks? (2014)
47. You, K., Liu, Y., Wang, J., Jordan, M.I., Long, M.: Ranking and tuning pre-trained models: a new paradigm of exploiting model hubs. arXiv preprint arXiv:2110.10545 (2021)
48. You, K., Liu, Y., Wang, J., Long, M.: LogME: practical assessment of pre-trained models for transfer learning. In: International Conference on Machine Learning, pp. 12133–12143. PMLR (2021)
49. Zamir, A.R., Sax, A., Shen, W., Guibas, L.J., Malik, J., Savarese, S.: Taskonomy: disentangling task transfer learning. In: Proceedings of the IEEE Conference on Computer Vision and Pattern Recognition, pp. 3712–3722 (2018)
50. Zhang, C., Bengio, S., Hardt, M., Recht, B., Vinyals, O.: Understanding deep learning (still) requires rethinking generalization. Commun. ACM **64**(3), 107–115 (2021)
51. Zhou, K., Yang, Y., Qiao, Y., Xiang, T.: Domain adaptive ensemble learning. IEEE Trans. Image Process. **30**, 8008–8018 (2021)
52. Zhou, X., et al.: Model agnostic sample reweighting for out-of-distribution learning. In: International Conference on Machine Learning, pp. 27203–27221. PMLR (2022)
53. Zhou, X., Zhang, W., Xu, H., Zhang, T.: Effective sparsification of neural networks with global sparsity constraint. In: Proceedings of the IEEE/CVF Conference on Computer Vision and Pattern Recognition, pp. 3599–3608 (2021)

How Stable Are Transferability Metrics Evaluations?

Andrea Agostinelli(✉), Michal Pándy, Jasper Uijlings, Thomas Mensink, and Vittorio Ferrari

Google Research, Zurich, Switzerland
{agostinelli,michalpandy,jrru,mensink,vittoferrari}@google.com

Abstract. Transferability metrics is a maturing field with increasing interest, which aims at providing heuristics for selecting the most suitable source models to transfer to a given target dataset, without fine-tuning them all. However, existing works rely on custom experimental setups which differ across papers, leading to inconsistent conclusions about which transferability metrics work best. In this paper we conduct a large-scale study by systematically constructing a broad range of 715k experimental setup variations. We discover that even small variations to an experimental setup lead to different conclusions about the superiority of a transferability metric over another. Then we propose better evaluations by aggregating across many experiments, enabling to reach more stable conclusions. As a result, we reveal the superiority of LogME at selecting good source datasets to transfer from in a semantic segmentation scenario, $\mathcal{N}$LEEP at selecting good source architectures in an image classification scenario, and GBC at determining which target task benefits most from a given source model. Yet, no single transferability metric works best in all scenarios.

1 Introduction

Transfer learning aims to re-use knowledge learned on a source task to help learning a target task, for which typically there is only little training data. The most prevalent method of transfer learning in computer vision is to pre-train a source model on a large source dataset (*e.g.*, ILSVRC'12 [66]), and then fine-tune it on the target dataset [5,17,29,31,40,69,94]. However, different target tasks benefit from using different source model architectures [13,32,55,64] or pre-training on different source datasets [51,56,88]. Hence, a key challenge is determining which source model is best suited for which target task, and doing so in a computationally efficient manner.

Transferability metrics [2,6,8,23,24,49,57,59,71,72,75,77,89] provide heuristics for selecting the most suitable source models for a given target dataset, without

M. Pándy—Currently at Waymo.

Supplementary Information The online version contains supplementary material available at https://doi.org/10.1007/978-3-031-19830-4_18.

S. Avidan et al. (Eds.): ECCV 2022, LNCS 13694, pp. 303–321, 2022.
https://doi.org/10.1007/978-3-031-19830-4_18

explicitly fine-tuning them all. These methods generally work by applying a source model to the target dataset to compute embeddings or predictions. Then they efficiently assess how compatible these embeddings/predictions are with the target labels. This provides a proxy for how well the source model transfers to the target task.

Transferability metrics is a maturing field with numerous contributions and increasing interest [2,6,49,57,59,75,77,89]. However, existing works rely on custom experimental settings without standardized benchmarks, which leads to inconsistent conclusions across different papers. In particular, contradicting conclusions often appear when comparing findings across papers. For example, while NCE [77] consistently outperforms LEEP [57] in [89], LEEP outperforms NCE in both [75] and [57]. Furthermore LogME outperforms LEEP [89], but LEEP outperforms LogME in [59]. This raises questions about how stable conclusions are across different experimental setups and if there truly is a single best transferability metric.

The primary goal of our work is to evaluate the stability of experimental setup for transferability estimation. We observe that a single experiment typically consists of three components: (1) a choice of the pool of source models; (2) a choice of the target dataset; (3) a choice of the measure used to evaluate how well transferability metrics perform. We vary each of these components in a large-scale systematic study of two scenarios: selecting good source datasets for semantic segmentation (Sect. 5), and selecting good source model architectures for image classification (Sect. 6). In total we construct a large set of **715k experiments**, several orders of magnitude larger than previous works [6,49,57,59,89] (and in a computationally efficient way). The source code for our experiments and analysis is publicly available[1]. Based on these experiments: (A) We demonstrate that even small variations to an experimental setup leads to very different conclusions about the superiority of a transferability metric over another. (B) We provide a systematic analysis to investigate which of the three setup components contributes the most to the instability of experimental outcomes. (C) We propose better evaluations by aggregating outcomes from a broad set of diverse experiments, reducing the experimental uncertainty and enabling to reach more stable conclusions. Concretely, we reveal that LogME is the best transferability metric in our first scenario (selecting source datasets for semantic segmentation); $\mathcal{N}$LEEP is the best in our second scenario (selecting source model architectures for image classification). Moreover, we also consider a third, somewhat separate scenario about determining which target task benefits most from a given source model, among a pool of target tasks constructed by subsampling out of a large target dataset (in the supplementary material). In this scenario GBC is the best metric. So, no single transferability metric works best in all scenarios.

[1] github.com/google-research/google-research/tree/master/stable_transfer.

2 Related Work

Transfer Learning. Training a deep neural network for a specific task often requires a large amount of data which can be difficult to obtain. The goal of transfer learning [9,62,76] is to leverage information from a source task with easily obtainable data, to improve performance on a target problem where data is scarce. Pre-training a neural network on large datasets and fine-tuning it on a target dataset is the most prevalent method of transfer learning in computer vision. For these reasons, there exists a wide array of large-scale source datasets, such as ILSVRC'12 [66], ImageNet21k [63], or Open Images [47]. In addition, recent works consider the use of unlabeled source datasets via self-supervised pre-training [14,15,30]. Other research studies settings in which transfer learning is effective. Taskonomy [91] develops connections between visual tasks (*e.g.* semantic segmentation, depth prediction, etc.), Mensink et al. [51] perform extensive experimental investigations in semantic segmentation settings, Mustafa et al. [53] focus on evaluating transfer learning for medical purposes, and Ding et al. [22] explore applications to human activity recognition. For a more general survey of transfer learning, we refer the reader to Weiss et al. [83].

Transferability Metrics. Transferability metrics provide efficient heuristics for determining which pre-trained models are most suitable for a specific target task. To generate transferability metrics, *label comparison-based methods* leverage the labels of the source and target domains. These methods generally assume equivalence between source and target domain labels or obtain pseudo-labels by executing the source model on the target domain. Methods in this category include NCE [77] and LEEP [57]. *Source embedding-based* methods use the feature extractor of a pre-trained neural network to embed target domain images. Transferability metrics are then computed using the embeddings and their corresponding labels. These methods include GBC [59], LogME [89], and $\mathcal{N}$LEEP [49]. To conclude, *optimal transport-based* methods [4,75] develop cost functions usable within the optimal transport framework to determine transferability between two datasets. See Sect. 3 for a more detailed description of state-of-the-art tranferability metrics.

Overview of Experimental Stability. Several works study experimental settings and analyse methods' performance with the aim of solidifying an area of research. In the field of graph neural networks (GNNs), Errica et al. [26] evaluate and compare GNNs across a large suite of experiments, while Dwivedi et al. [25] and Shchur et al. [68] point out issues with GNN evaluation and propose evaluation improvements. In reinforcement learning (RL), Whiteson et al. [84] discuss RL evaluation principles, Jordan et al. [42] discover flaws with RL evaluation metrics, and Colas et al. [19] study the necessary number of seeds for stable RL testing. In computer vision, Hoiem et al. [34] and Hosang et al. [35] analyse the stability of object detectors, Zendel et al. [92] discuss the quality of testing data, Xian et al. [86] evaluate state-of-the-art in zero-shot learning, and Abnar et al. [1] assess the trade-offs of upstream and downstream model performance. Our work provides clarity about good experimental settings for research in transferability metrics.

3 Background

We first discuss the basics of transferability metrics and how they are evaluated. At a high level, the overall pipeline in most papers is [2,6,49,57,59,75,77,89]: (1) a transferability metric considers a source model S and a target dataset T and predicts a transferability score M. M predicts how well S will transfer to T (Sect. 3.1). (2) compute the true accuracy of transferring from S on T by fine-tuning it on the target training set, then applying the fine-tuned model on the target test set, and finally evaluate accuracy A based on the ground-truth (Sect. 3.2). (3) evaluate the quality of the transferability metric by checking how well M predicted true accuracy A (Sect. 3.3).

3.1 Transferability Metrics

In our paper we compare the following transferability metrics M.

H-score. H-score [6] is based on the intuition that a model transfers well to a target dataset if the target embeddings have low inter-class variance and low feature redundancy. These quantities are computed by constructing the inter-class and data covariance matrices.

LEEP & $\mathcal{N}$LEEP. LEEP [57] first predicts pseudo-labels by applying the source model on the target images. These predictions are then used for computing a log-likelihood between the target labels and the source model predictions. The core idea is that if the predictions are 'clustered' around individual target labels, adaptation to the target dataset should be easier. $\mathcal{N}$LEEP [49] extends this idea by first embedding the target images using the source feature extractor and then fitting a Gaussian mixture model (GMM) on them. The GMM is said to provide a better density estimator for the pseudo-labels than the classification head in the original LEEP.

LogME. After embedding the target images using the source feature extractor, LogME [89] computes the probability of the target labels conditioned on these embeddings (i.e. the evidence of target labels). By setting up a graphical model and using independence assumptions between samples, the authors propose an efficient algorithm for computing such evidence.

GBC. GBC [59] measures the statistical overlap between classes of the target dataset, after representing the target images in the embedding space determined by the source feature extractor. The intuition is that the more classes overlap in that space, the more difficult it will be to achieve high accuracy after fine-tuning the source model. The overlap is estimated using the Bhattacharyya coefficient between multivariate Gaussians fitted to each class.

3.2 True Accuracy of Transfer Learning

We compute the true accuracy A of the source model S on the target test set after fine-tuning on the target training set. A represents how well S transfers to the target T. We note that we fine-tune the full source model on the target training dataset, rather than just the classification head.

3.3 Evaluating the Quality of a Transferability Metric

We introduce common measures for evaluating transferability metrics. Suppose we wish to evaluate a transferability metric M given a source pool S containing n source models, and a target dataset T. Hence, we have access to n transferability metric values M_i, each with its corresponding test accuracy A_i associated with source model S_i. An evaluation measure captures how well M_i relates to A_i (i.e. higher values of transferability M_i predict higher values of true accuracy A_i).

Pearson Correlation Coefficient [7] **(ρ).** It measures linear correlation between M_i and A_i across $i \in [1 .. n]$. For transferability metrics that tend to be linear with respect to test scores (e.g., LEEP [57]), it provides a straightforward way for measuring performance. The disadvantage is that low ρ correlation does not imply a bad a performing transferability metric. The transferability rankings could be correct even though M_i and A_i are non-linearly related.

Kendall Rank Correlation Coefficient [43] **(τ).** The core idea is that we should have $M_i > M_j$ if $A_i > A_j$. Based on this, τ is computed as:

$$\tau = \frac{1}{\binom{n}{2}} \sum_{i<j} \operatorname{sgn}(M_i - M_j) * \operatorname{sgn}(A_i - A_j) \tag{1}$$

Equation (1) can be interpreted as averaging over the agreements (+1) or disagreements (−1) in rankings between transferability metrics and test scores. Hence, $\tau \in [-1, 1]$ and high τ implies a strong correlation between the rankings of source models according to M_i and according to A_i. τ does not rely on linearity assumptions and gives a holistic idea for the overall ranking performance. The downside is that τ gives equal importance to all source models, regardless of their performance. However, practitioners ultimately care about a transferability metric's ability to correctly rank only the few best performing models.

Weighted Kendall Rank Correlation Coefficient (τ_w). To prioritize the top-performing models, we may assign higher weights to them. Models with higher A_i within the sum in Eq. (1) should be weighted more. Hence, two transferability metrics that would perform the same in terms of τ can now be discriminated based on which metric ranks top models better in τ_w. We still have $\tau_w \in [-1, 1]$ and now the evaluation measure reflects practitioners' priorities. We assume a hyperbolic drop-off in model importance with decreasing ranks in terms of A_i, which is implemented in the Sklearn library [61].

Relative Top-1 Accuracy [49] **(*Rel*@1).** It measures how close model k with the highest predicted transferability ($k = \operatorname{argmax}_i M_i$) performs, in terms of accuracy A_k, compared to the highest performing model ($\max_i A_i$). It is computed as $Rel@1 = \frac{A_k}{\max_i A_i}$. Since $A_k \leq \max_i A_i$, we have $1 \geq Rel@1 \geq 0$. The benefit of *Rel*@1 is that there could be multiple models that perform within a close margin of the top model, which in terms of $Rel@1$ would obtain similar performance scores. Since τ and τ_w are not sensitive to the actual value of the test scores of models, the evaluation of a particular transferability metric could vary drastically different even if similar-performing source models change order in the ranked lists (which can happen even for small fluctuations in the values of M_i or A_i).

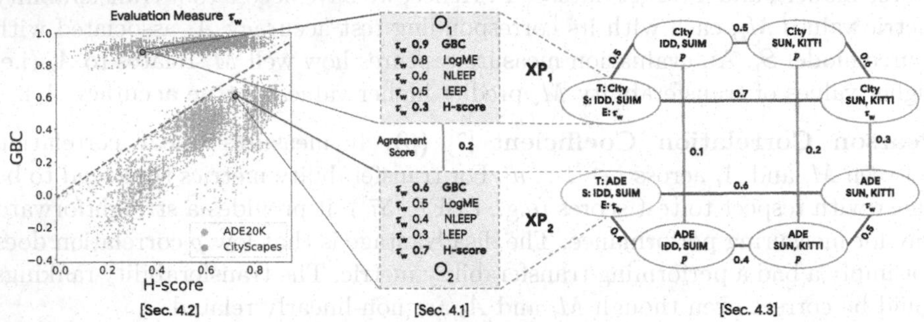

Fig. 1. An experiment XP is represented as a graph node, composed of source pool $\mathcal{S}$, target dataset T and evaluation measure E. We compare two experiments XP_1 and XP_2 by comparing their outcomes O_1 and O_2. We do it qualitatively with a scatter plot (left) and quantitatively with a graph (right). For the latter we connect experiments that differ by a single variation in either $\mathcal{S}$ (—), T (|) or E (/). We compute the agreement score between the outcomes of each two connected experiments $(\text{XP}_i, \text{XP}_j)$ (edge value).

4 Methodology

Our goal is to investigate the experimental stability of protocols to evaluate transferability metrics. We first rigorously define what constitutes a single experiment and identify its three main components (Sect. 4.1). We then investigate the effects of small variations on each of these components both qualitatively (Sect. 4.2, Fig. 1 left) and quantitatively (Sect. 4.3, Fig. 1 right). Finally, in Sect. 4.4 we define how we create a huge set of experiments that allows us to explore the influence of varying each component on the evaluation of transferability metrics. At the same time, the sheer size of our experiments helps to reduce experimental uncertainty and improve their stability.

4.1 A Single Experiment with Its Three Components

Given a set of transferability metrics, the outcome O of an experiment XP is a measure of quality for each transferability metric (Fig. 1, middle). A single experiment consists of three components whose choice influences its outcome: (1) A *pool of source models* $\mathcal{S}$. It can be created by training the same model architecture on different source datasets [2,59], or by training different model architectures on the same source dataset [57,89], or a combination of both [49]. (2) A *target dataset* T, which cannot be any dataset in the source pool. (3) An *evaluation measure* E to determine the quality of each transferability metric. Hence we can represent one experiment as $\mathrm{XP}(\mathcal{S}, T, E) \rightarrow O$ (Fig. 1).

We can compare two experiments XP_i and XP_j by looking at differences in their outcomes O_i and O_j. For example, the experiments XP_1 and XP_2 are composed of the same source pool $\mathcal{S}$ (i.e. IDD, SUIM), the same evaluation measure E (i.e. τ_w), but different target datasets T (i.e. ADE20k vs CityScapes). These experiments produce divergent outcomes, as GBC > H-score on XP_1, whereas H-score > GBC on XP_2.

We use these definitions to investigate how varying the components of an experimental setup ($\mathcal{S}$, T, E) affects the outcome O across experiments. We note that an experimental setup is stable if small variations of $\mathcal{S}$, T, or E produce similar outcomes (and unstable if small variations produces divergent outcomes).

4.2 Qualitative Analysis of Experimental Setup Stability

We qualitatively compare a large number of experiments by displaying their outcomes in a scatter plot (Fig. 1). Each point represents a single experiment and compares the quality of a transferability metric (*e.g.* H-score) to the quality of another (*e.g.* GBC) as assessed by a fixed evaluation measure E (τ_w in this example). Each experiment is colored according to its target dataset T. The dotted red line represents $x = y$; for points on this line both transferability metrics are equally good. If points are either all above or below the line, this means that one transferability metric consistently outperforms the other, suggesting the experiment is stable.

We can study how variations in the source pool $\mathcal{S}$ influence the outcome by looking at the distribution of points of the same color (i.e. on the same target dataset T). In Fig. 1, in all experiments where the target dataset is CityScapes (magenta), GBC consistently outperforms H-score. Hence this experiment is stable with respect to variations in the source pool. To study the influence of varying the target dataset T, we can compare whole point clouds (in different colors). In this case, for T = ADE20k H-score consistently outperforms GBC, which contradicts with what found for T = CityScapes. Hence this experiment setup is unstable when varying the target dataset. Finally, we can compare the influence of varying the evaluation measure E by comparing two scatter plots which differ only in the choice of E (*e.g.* Fig. 3b vs Fig. 5b).

4.3 Quantitative Measures of Experimental Setup Stability

Setup Stability (SS). We want to quantify the overall effect of varying exactly a single component $\mathcal{S}$, T or E of an experimental setup. To do so, we consider pairs of experiments which differ in only one component. Each edge in Fig. 1 (right) connects two experiments and is colored based on which component is different between them. Experiments which differ in two or more components are not connected.

We now detail how we measure the Setup Stability for a single component (*e.g.* T in green). First, for each pair of experiments which differ only in T, we calculate an agreement score between their outcomes: the rank correlation τ between the two lists of transferability metrics as ranked by their quality For example, the agreement score between XP_1 and XP_2 in our example is 0.2 (middle of Fig. 1). Then we average agreement scores over all experiment pairs which differ only in T (i.e. green edges in Fig. 1, right side). We call this aggregated measure the *Setup Stability* (SS). It is 1 when all experiments produce the same outcome, and indicates a stable setup. In contrast, a score of 0 implies there is no agreement at all across the experiment outcomes (very unstable). In our example in Fig. 1, the SS for T equals to $\frac{1}{4}(.2 + .1 + .2 + .3) = 0.20$.

Table 1. Volume of experiments for evaluating transferability metrics in various papers. We systematically construct 715k experiments by varying the source pool $\mathcal{S}$, target dataset T and evaluation measure E. In contrast, previous works have at most 500 experiments. All stats are about the scenario of selecting source models for a given target. Some papers [6,49,57,59,75] also report the converse case (determining which target task benefits most from a given source model). Even when including it, no previous work reports more than 508 experiments [75]. The OTCE paper [75] constructs 500 experiments by randomly sampling 100 target tasks within each of the 5 target datasets used. We note that the H-score paper [6] only reports in this converse scenario (and only 1 experiment).

		Ours	LEEP [57]	$\mathcal{N}$LEEP [49]	LogME [89]	GBC [59]	OTCE [75]
Selecting	#sources	17	0	16	0	17	4
Source datasets (Sect. 5)	#targets	17	0	4	0	17	5
Selecting	#sources	19	9	13	24	9	0
Cource architectures (Sect. 6)	#targets	9	1	4	17	8	0
Evaluation measures (Sect. 3.3)	#E	4	1	6	1	2	1
Constructing XPs (Sect. 4.4)	# experiments	715k	1	48	19	50	500

Win Rate. We introduce the *win rate* to assess whether a particular transferability metric is the best across many experiments. The win rate of a transferability metric is the percentage of experiments where it is the best metric (i.e. outperforms all other metrics in that experiment). We report the win rate for each of the four evaluation measures E individually, which provides another view of its influence. We also consider the win rate across all experiments, as the final, most aggregated assessment of a transferability metric.

4.4 Constructing 715k Experiments

We need to construct a set of experiments which vary along each of the three components $\mathcal{S}, T$, and E. This set needs to be extremely large to properly investigate the influence of each component and to be able to reduce experimental uncertainty when deciding which transferability metrics work best. In Sects. 5 and 6 we will study in-depth two scenarios about selecting good source models for the tasks of semantic segmentation and image classification. In total we construct *715k experiments*. This is several orders of magnitude more than other works on transferability metrics, which all have at most 500 experiments when selecting source models (Table 1).

5 Scenario 1: Selecting a Good Source Dataset in Semantic Segmentation

Experimental Setup. We consider the scenario of selecting good source datasets to transfer from on the task of semantic segmentation. We use a total of 17 datasets from a wide range of image domains: Pascal Context [52], Pascal VOC [27], ADE20K [93], COCO [12,45,50], KITTI [3], CamVid [10], CityScapes [20], IDD [78], BDD [90], MVD [54], ISPRS [65], iSAID [81,85], SUN RGB-D [73], ScanNet [21], SUIM [41], vKITTI2 [11,28] and vGallery [82]. We use a fixed model architecture composed of a HRNetV2-W48 backbone [80] with a linear classifier on top, as this model achieves state-of-the-art performances on dense prediction tasks [48,51,80]. We create a total of 17 source models by training HRNetV2-W48 on the full training set of each source dataset.

Now we create many setup variations. First, each dataset plays the role of target, in turn. For each target the other 16 datasets are sources, leading to 16 source models. To construct many different source pools $\mathcal{S}$, we consider all combinations of 11 out of 16 source models, resulting in $\binom{16}{11}$ source pools. Finally, we consider four evaluation measures E. Hence we have a total of $17 \times \binom{16}{11} \times 4 =$ 297k experiments, spanning variations across source pool $\mathcal{S}$, target dataset T and evaluation measure E. Importantly, while we consider a very large space of setup variations, this only requires training 17 source models and fine-tuning each 16 times, which is computationally efficient.

When fine-tuning on the target training set, we follow the low-shot setup of [51]: we limit it to 150 images for each dataset (except COCO and ADE20k, on which we use 1000 images as they contain a large number of classes). We follow [2] and apply the transferability metrics to semantic segmentation by subsampling 1000 pixels per image. As in [2], we sample pixels inversely proportionally to the frequency of their class labels in the target dataset.

Qualitative Analysis. We perform here the qualitative analysis described in Sect. 4.2. We fix the evaluation measure E to be τ_w and visualize experiments with variations of source pool $\mathcal{S}$ and target dataset T. Figure 2 shows comparisons for all possible pairs of transferability metrics. If we compare LogME to LEEP (Fig. 2-left), the experiments evaluated on the target dataset T = iSAID (red) form a group below the red line, indicating LEEP consistently outperforms LogME. Conversely, for both T = COCO (brown) and T = SUIM (pink), LogME consistently outperforms LEEP. This shows the experimental instability w.r.t. variations of T. If we look at T = ADE (light blue), the experiments are centered on the red line and stray quite far from it on *both sides.* This means that contradicting outcomes are found also when varying the source pool $\mathcal{S}$. The same observation holds for T = vGallery (purple).

In fact, we can find many cases where the outcome of an experiment is wildly different even when varying only a single setup component (Fig. 3). In Fig. 3a, we see that for T = ADE20K H-score outperforms LogME, whereas for T = CityScapes the opposite is true. Next, Fig. 3b show two examples where changing only the evaluation measure E leads to conflicting outcomes. On T = COCO, for $E = \tau_W$ $\mathcal{N}$LEEP is better than H-score (most points are above the line), whereas for $E = \rho$ the opposite is true (large dense cluster below the line). A similar contradicting result is observed on T = Pascal VOC for LEEP and GBC. Finally, we look at varying the source pool $\mathcal{S}$ in Fig. 3c. We see that in each of these example plots the points are scattered on both sides of the $x = y$ line, indicating contradicting outcomes within each plot.

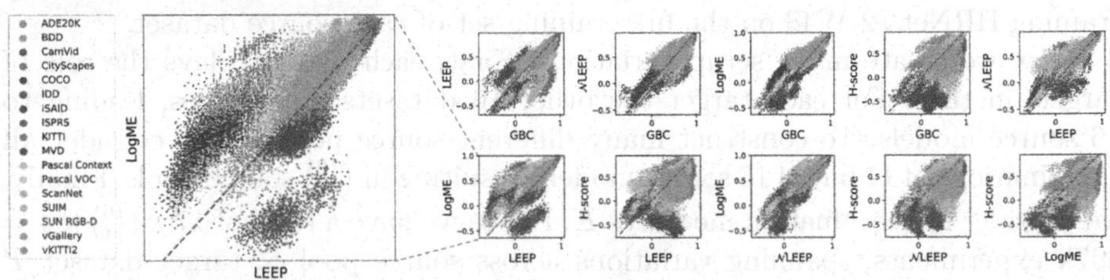

Fig. 2. Each point reports the quality of two transferability metrics in terms of τ_w (within a single experiment). In each plot we vary the source pool $\mathcal{S}$ and target dataset T. Points on the red line mean that the two transferability metrics have equal quality. For some comparisons the setup is not stable w.r.t T and $\mathcal{S}$, as different points fall above and below the line, hence they produce divergent outcomes. (Color figure online)

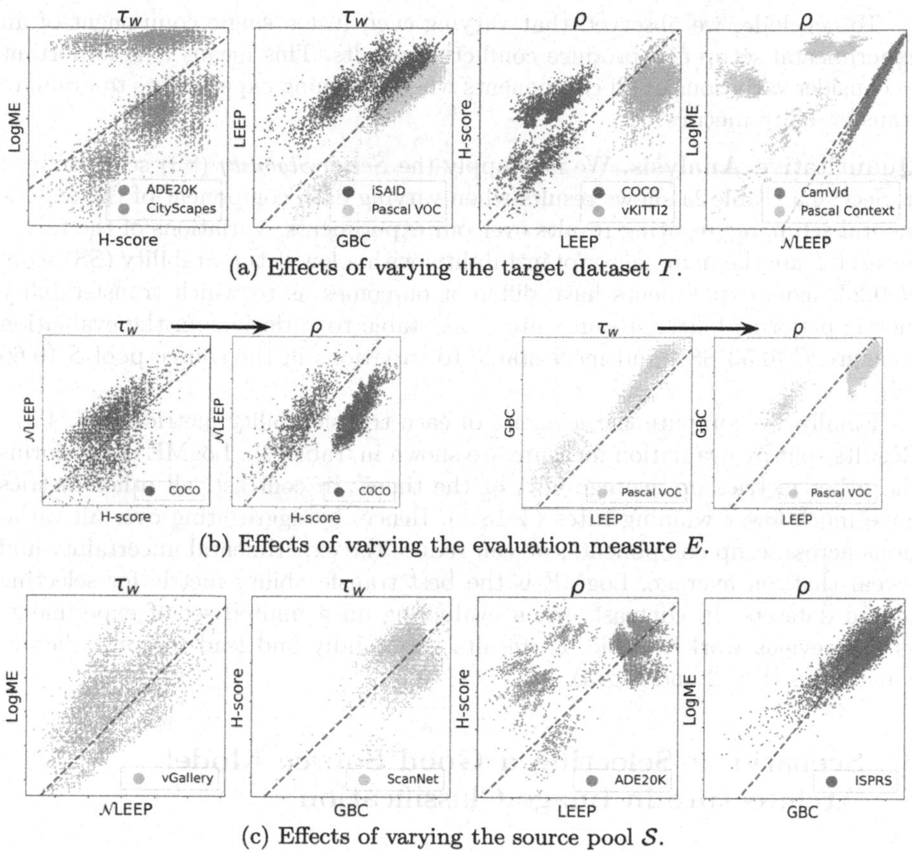

Fig. 3. Examples of how changing experimental setup components produces different winning metrics across experiments.

Table 2. Aggregate quantitative analysis for Sect. 5. (a) *Setup Stability* (SS) score for variations of source pool $\mathcal{S}$, target dataset T or evaluation measure E. (b) *Win rate* (**%W**) for each transferability metric and evaluation measure. LogME is on average the best metric.

	SS score
$\neq$ **T**	0.23
$\neq$ **E**	0.53
$\neq \mathcal{S}$	0.60

(a)

	%W τ_w	**%W** τ	**%W** ρ	**%W** *Rel*@1	**Avg**
GBC	20	16	10	5	13
LEEP	11	13	11	2	9
$\mathcal{N}$**LEEP**	7	3	5	2	4
LogME	**52**	**55**	**68**	**49**	**56**
H-score	10	13	6	42	18

(b)

To conclude, we observed that varying even just a single component of an experimental setup can produce conflicting results. This means it is important to consider variations of all components when designing experiments to evaluate transferability metrics.

Quantitative Analysis. We now apply the *Setup Stability* (SS) score defined in Sect. 4.3. Table 2a shows results when varying each component of the experimental setup, aggregating results over our experiments. Variations of the target dataset T are the main factor of instability: with a low Setup Stability (SS) score of 0.23, most experiments have different outcomes as to which transferability metric performs better. Results are more stable to variations in the evaluation measure E (0.53 SS), and most stable to variations in the source pool $\mathcal{S}$ (0.60 SS).

Finally, we compute the *win rate* of each transferability metric (Sect. 4.3) . Results split by evaluation measure are shown in Table 2b. LogME outperforms the other metrics on average 56% of the times. In contrast, all other metrics have much lower winning rates (4–18%). Hence, by aggregating over all variations across setup components, we can reduce the experimental uncertainty and reveal that, on average, LogME is the best transferability metric for selecting source datasets. In contrast, when evaluating on a limited set of experiments as in previous works (Table 1), results vary wildly and lead to contradictory conclusions (Fig. 2 and Fig. 3).

6 Scenario 2: Selecting a Good Source Model Architecture in Image Classification

Experimental Setup. We consider the scenario of selecting good source model architectures to transfer from on the task of image classification, as in [49,57,59,89]. We fix the source dataset to ImageNet. The goal is to select which architecture would lead to the best transfer learning results on a given target dataset. We use 9 target datasets: CIFAR10 & 100 [46], Imagenette [38], Oxford IIIT Pets [60], Caltech-USCD Birds 2011 [79], Stanford Dogs [44], Oxford Flowers 102 [58], SUN-397 [87], and DTD [18]. We consider a total of 19 source architectures: ResNet-50 & ResNet-101 [32], ResNetV2-50, ResNetV2-101 & ResNetV2-152 [33], DenseNet-121, DenseNet-169 & DenseNet-201 [39], MobileNet [37], MobileNetV2 [67], MobileNetV3 [36], EfficientNetB0, EfficientNetB1, EfficientNetB2 & EfficientNetB3 [74], NASNet Mobile [95], VGG16 & VGG19 [70], Xception [16]. We train 19 source models, each with a *different* model architecture but all trained on the *same* source dataset ImageNet [66].

Now we create many setup variations. To construct many different source pools, we consider all combinations of 14 out of 19 source models, resulting in $\binom{19}{14}$ source pools. Finally, we consider four evaluation measures E, and the 9 target datasets above. Hence we have a total of $9 \times \binom{19}{14} \times 4 = 418$k experiments.

Qualitative Analysis. We perform the qualitative analysis described in Sect. 4.2. We fix the evaluation measure E to be ρ and we visualize experiments with variations of source pool $\mathcal{S}$ and target dataset T. Figure 4 shows comparisons for all possible pairs of transferability metrics. Similar to Sect. 5 we observe that many experiments within the same plot fall on either sides of the red line with a large spread. Hence outcomes are not stable. In particular, on the left-side plot, for T = Oxford Pets (pink) GBC consistently outperforms LogME, whereas for T = Imagenette (purple) LogME consistently outperforms GBC.

As before, there exists multiple examples where changing a single experimental setup component is sufficient to produce divergent outcomes across experiments (Fig. 5). For example, in Fig. 5a for T = CIFAR10, LogME outperforms GBC, while for T = Caltech Birds the opposite is true. Moreover, in Fig. 5b we can clearly see the mass of the points move when changing E. For example, on the left LogME performs about equally to GBC when using $E = \tau_w$, whereas GBC is the best when using $E = \rho$. Finally, when varying only the source pool $\mathcal{S}$ in Fig. 5c we see points scattered on both sides of the line within each individual plot. Hence the choice of each experimental setup component can have a large effect on the outcome.

Quantitative Analysis. We now quantify the influence of varying experimental setup components by computing the *Setup Stability* (SS) score defined in Sect. 4.3. Results are shown in Table 3a. Varying the target dataset has the biggest impact (0.62 SS) on the instability of the experimental outcomes, followed by the evaluation measure (0.69 SS) and the source pool (0.80 SS). This is in line with the observations in Sect. 5, except that the overall scores are higher, indicating that the outcomes across experiments are broadly more consistent.

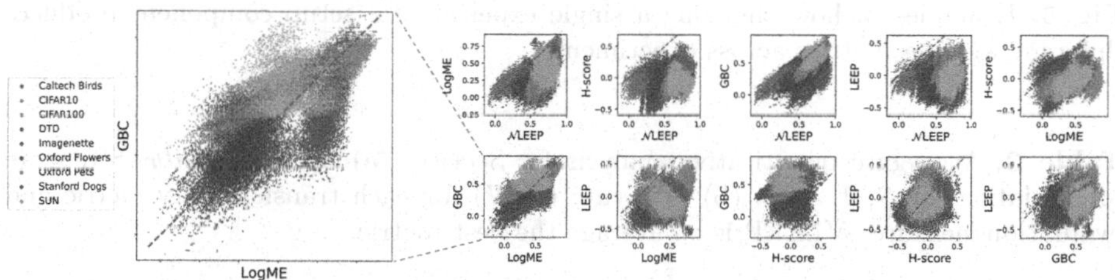

Fig. 4. Each point reports the quality of two transferability metrics in terms of ρ (within a single experiment). In each plot we vary the source pool $\mathcal{S}$ and target dataset T. Points on the red line mean that the two transferability metrics have equal quality. For some comparisons the setup is not stable w.r.t T and $\mathcal{S}$, as different points fall above and below the line, hence they produce divergent outcomes (i.e. LEEP vs H-score and GBC vs LogME).

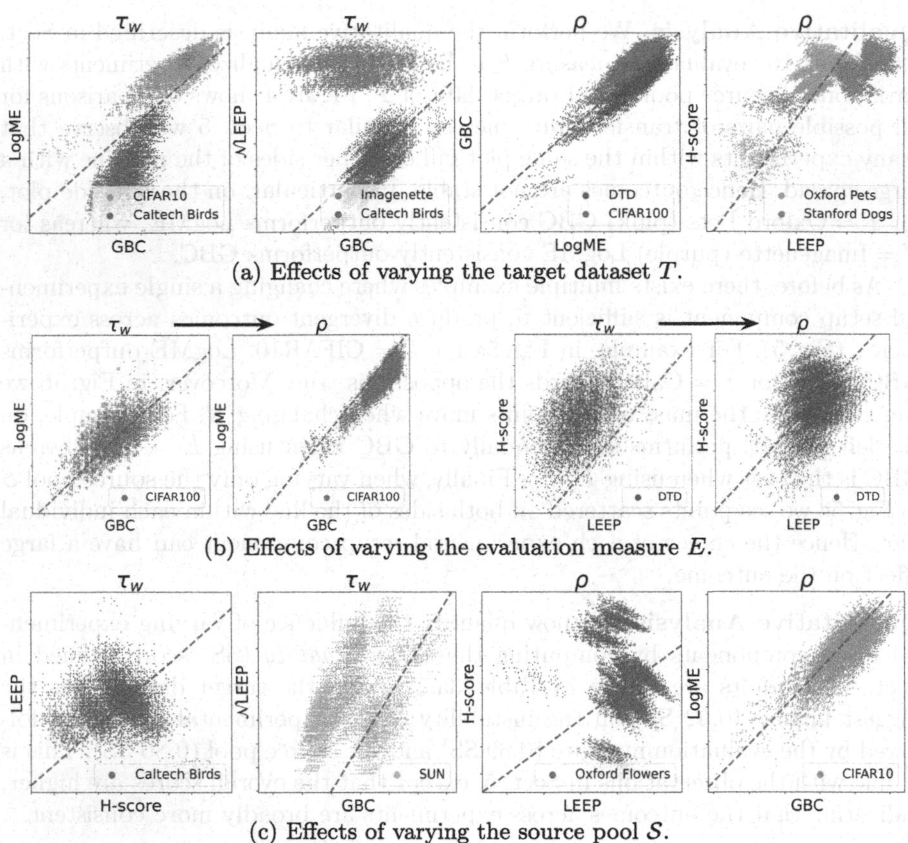

(a) Effects of varying the target dataset T.

(b) Effects of varying the evaluation measure E.

(c) Effects of varying the source pool $\mathcal{S}$.

Fig. 5. Examples of how changing a single experimental setup component produces different winning metrics across experiments.

Table 3. Aggregate quantitative analysis for Sect. 6. (a) *Setup stability* (SS) score for variations of $\mathcal{S}$, T & E. (b) *Win rate* (**%W**) for each transferability metric and evaluation measure. $\mathcal{N}$LEEP is on average the best metric.

	SS score
$\neq$ **T**	0.62
$\neq$ **E**	0.69
$\neq \mathcal{S}$	0.80

(a)

	%W τ_w	**%W** τ	**%W** p	**%W** *Rel*@1	**Avg**
GBC	12	4	5	4	6
LEEP	0	0	0	2	1
$\mathcal{N}$LEEP	**80**	**91**	**93**	30	**73**
LogME	8	5	2	**53**	17
H-score	0	0	0	11	3

(b)

Table 3b shows the *win rate* of each transferability metric against all others, for each evaluation measure. $\mathcal{N}$LEEP outperforms on average the other metrics in 73% of the experiments, while LEEP and H-score performs poorly (1 and 3% winning rates, respectively). Hence, by aggregating over many experiments we reveal a clear winner transferability metric in this scenario: $\mathcal{N}$LEEP. Moreover, LogME can be considered a good second place since it is the best for $E = Rel@1$.

Importantly, the conclusion in this scenario differs substantially from the previous scenario: In Sect. 5, LogME was the best while $\mathcal{N}$LEEP was the worst. Now, $\mathcal{N}$LEEP is the best while LogME is a good second. Hence even though we aggregate over many experiments, we still find different conclusions for even larger changes in our setup (*scenarios*): changing both the nature of the source pool (i.e. different source datasets vs different source model architectures) and the nature of the task (semantic segmentation vs image classification).

7 Conclusion

Our work investigates for the first time the stability of experiments to evaluate transferability metrics. We base our investigation on a systematic analysis of over 715k experiments. We show that even small variations across experiment setups leads to divergent conclusions about the superiority of a transferability metric over another. Then we improve stability by aggregating outcomes across many experiments. As a result, we reveal the superiority of LogME at selecting good source datasets to transfer from, and $\mathcal{N}$LEEP at selecting good source architectures. Finally, in the third scenario, we show that GBC is best for determining which target task benefits most from a given source model (see supp. mat.). Hence, no single transferability metric works best in all scenarios.

In this work all scenarios feature source and target tasks of identical types (*i.e.*, both segmentation, or both classification). However, the proposed experimental protocols and analysis methods are not restricted to this setting. Hence, we leave to future work investigations of the experimental stability of transferability metrics when source and target task types differ.

References

1. Abnar, S., Dehghani, M., Neyshabur, B., Sedghi, H.: Exploring the limits of large scale pre-training. In: ICLR (2022)
2. Agostinelli, A., Uijlings, J., Mensink, T., Ferrari, V.: Transferability metrics for selecting source model ensembles. In: CVPR (2021)
3. Alhaija, H., Mustikovela, S., Mescheder, L., Geiger, A., Rother, C.: Augmented reality meets computer vision : efficient data generation for urban driving scenes. Int. J. Comput. Vision. **126**, 961–972 (2018)
4. Alvarez-Melis, D., Fusi, N.: Geometric dataset distances via optimal transport. In: NeurIPS (2020)

5. Azizpour, H., Razavian, A.S., Sullivan, J., Maki, A., Carlsson, S.: Factors of transferability for a generic convnet representation. IEEE Trans. Pattern Anal. Mach. Intell. **38** (2015)
6. Bao, Y., et al.: An information-theoretic approach to transferability in task transfer learning. In: ICIP (2019)
7. Benesty, J., Chen, J., Huang, Y., Cohen, I.: Pearson Correlation Coefficient. In: Noise Reduction in Speech Processing. Springer, Dordrecht (2009). https://doi.org/10.1007/978-1-4020-5614-7_2569
8. Bolya, D., Mittapalli, R., Hoffman, J.: Scalable diverse model selection for accessible transfer learning. In: NeurIPS (2021)
9. Bozinovski, S., Fulgosi, A.: The influence of pattern similarity and transfer of learning upon training of a base perceptron b2 (original in Croatian). In: Proceedings of the Symposium Informatica, pp. 3–121 (1976)
10. Brostow, G.J., Fauqueur, J., Cipolla, R.: Semantic object classes in video: a high-definition ground truth database. Patt. Rec. Letters **30**(2), 88–97 (2009)
11. Cabon, Y., Murray, N., Humenberger, M.: Virtual kitti 2. arXiv (2020)
12. Caesar, H., Uijlings, J., Ferrari, V.: COCO-stuff: thing and stuff classes in context. In: CVPR (2018)
13. Chen, L.C., Papandreou, G., Kokkinos, I., Murphy, K., Yuille, A.: DeepLab: semantic image segmentation with deep convolutional nets, atrous convolution, and fully connected CRFs. IEEE Trans. Pattern Anal. Mach. Intell. **40**, 834 –848 (2018)
14. Chen, T., Kornblith, S., Norouzi, M., Hinton, G.: A simple framework for contrastive learning of visual representations. In: ICML (2020)
15. Chen, X., He, K.: Exploring simple siamese representation learning. In: CVPR (2021)
16. Chollet, F.: Xception: deep learning with depthwise separable convolutions. In: CVPR (2017)
17. Chu, B., Madhavan, V., Beijbom, O., Hoffman, J., Darrell, T.: Best practices for fine-tuning visual classifiers to new domains. In: ECCV (2016)
18. Cimpoi, M., Maji, S., Kokkinos, I., Mohamed, S., Vedaldi, A.: Describing textures in the wild. In: CVPR (2014)
19. Colas, C., Sigaud, O., Oudeyer, P.Y.: How many random seeds? statistical power analysis in deep reinforcement learning experiments. arXiv preprint arXiv:1806.08295 (2018)
20. Cordts, M., et al.: The cityscapes dataset for semantic urban scene understanding. In: CVPR (2016)
21. Dai, A., Chang, A.X., Savva, M., Halber, M., Funkhouser, T., Nießner, M.: ScanNet: richly-annotated 3d reconstructions of indoor scenes. In: CVPR (2017)
22. Ding, R., et al.: Empirical study and improvement on deep transfer learning for human activity recognition. Sensors **19**(1), 57 (2019)
23. Dwivedi, K., Huang, J., Cichy, R.M., Roig, G.: Duality diagram similarity: a generic framework for initialization selection in task transfer learning. In: ECCV (2020)
24. Dwivedi, K., Roig, G.: Representation similarity analysis for efficient task taxonomy and transfer learning. In: CVPR (2019)
25. Dwivedi, V.P., Joshi, C.K., Laurent, T., Bengio, Y., Bresson, X.: Benchmarking graph neural networks. arXiv preprint arXiv:2003.00982 (2020)
26. Errica, F., Podda, M., Bacciu, D., Micheli, A.: A fair comparison of graph neural networks for graph classification. arXiv preprint arXiv:1912.09893 (2019)
27. Everingham, M., Van Gool, L., Williams, C.K.I., Winn, J., Zisserman, A.: The PASCAL visual object classes challenge 2012 (VOC2012) Results. http://www.pascal-network.org/challenges/VOC/voc2012/workshop/index.html (2012)

28. Gaidon, A., Wang, Q., Cabon, Y., Vig, E.: Virtual worlds as proxy for multi-object tracking analysis. In: CVPR (2016)
29. Girshick, R.: Fast R-CNN. In: ICCV (2015)
30. He, K., Fan, H., Wu, Y., Xie, S., Girshick, R.: Momentum contrast for unsupervised visual representation learning. In: CVPR (2020)
31. He, K., Gkioxari, G., Dollár, P., Girshick, R.: Mask R-CNN. In: ICCV (2017)
32. He, K., Zhang, X., Ren, S., Sun, J.: Deep residual learning for image recognition. In: CVPR (2016)
33. He, K., Zhang, X., Ren, S., Sun, J.: Identity mappings in deep residual networks. In: ECCV (2016)
34. Hoiem, D., Chodpathumwan, Y., Dai, Q.: Diagnosing error in object detectors. In: ECCV (2012)
35. Hosang, J., Benenson, R., Dollár, P., Schiele, B.: What makes for effective detection proposals? IEEE Trans. on PAMI **38**(4), 814–830 (2015)
36. Howard, A., et al.: Searching for mobilenetv3. In: ICCV (2019)
37. Howard, A.G., et al.: MobileNets: efficient convolutional neural networks for mobile vision applications. Tech. rep., arXiv (2017)
38. Howard, J.: Imagenette..http://github.com/fastai/imagenette/
39. Huang, G., Liu, Z., Van Der Maaten, L., Weinberger, K.Q.: Densely connected convolutional networks. In: CVPR (2017)
40. Huh, M., Agrawal, P., Efros, A.: What makes imagenet good for transfer learning? In: NeurIPS LSCVS Workshop (2016)
41. Islam, M.J., et al.: Semantic segmentation of Underwater Imagery: Dataset and Benchmark. In: IROS (2020)
42. Jordan, S., Chandak, Y., Cohen, D., Zhang, M., Thomas, P.: Evaluating the performance of reinforcement learning algorithms. In: ICML (2020)
43. Kendall, M.G.: A new measure of rank correlation. Biometrika **30**(1/2), 81–93 (1938)
44. Khosla, A., Jayadevaprakash, N., Yao, B., Fei-Fei, L.: Novel dataset for fine-grained image categorization. In: CVPR Workshops (2011)
45. Kirillov, A., He, K., Girshick, R., Rother, C., Dollár, P.: Panoptic segmentation. In: CVPR (2019)
46. Krizhevsky, A.: Learning multiple layers of features from tiny images. University of Toronto, Tech. rep. (2009)
47. Kuznetsova, A., Rom, H., Alldrin, N., Uijlings, J., Krasin, I., Pont-Tuset, J., Kamali, S., Popov, S., Malloci, M., Kolesnikov, A., Duerig, T., Ferrari, V.: The open images dataset v4. IJCV **128**(7), 1956–1981 (2020)
48. Lambert, J., Liu, Z., Sener, O., Hays, J., Koltun, V.: MSeg: a composite dataset for multi-domain semantic segmentation. In: CVPR (2020)
49. Li, Y., et al.: Ranking neural checkpoints. In: CVPR (2021)
50. Lin, T.Y., et al.: Microsoft COCO: common objects in context. In: ECCV (2014)
51. Mensink, T., Uijlings, J., Kuznetsova, A., Gygli, M., Ferrari, V.: Factors of influence for transfer learning across diverse appearance domains and task types. IEEE Trans. Pattern, Anal. Mach. Intel. Early Access)(2021)
52. Mottaghi, R., et al.: The role of context for object detection and semantic segmentation in the wild. In: CVPR (2014)
53. Mustafa, B., et al.: Supervised transfer learning at scale for medical imaging. arXiv preprint arXiv:2101.05913 (2021)
54. Neuhold, G., Ollmann, T., Rota Bulò, S., Kontschieder, P.: The mapillary vistas dataset for semantic understanding of street scenes. In: ICCV (2017)

55. Newell, A., Yang, K., Deng, J.: Stacked hourglass networks for human pose estimation. In: Leibe, B., Matas, J., Sebe, N., Welling, M. (eds.) ECCV 2016. LNCS, vol. 9912, pp. 483–499. Springer, Cham (2016). https://doi.org/10.1007/978-3-319-46484-8_29
56. Ngiam, J., Peng, D., Vasudevan, V., Kornblith, S., Le, Q.V., Pang, R.: Domain adaptive transfer learning with specialist models. arXiv (2018)
57. Nguyen, C., Hassner, T., Seeger, M., Archambeau, C.: LEEP: a new measure to evaluate transferability of learned representations. In: ICML (2020)
58. Nilsback, M.E., Zisserman, A.: Automated flower classification over a large number of classes. In: Indian Conference on CVGIP (2008)
59. Pándy, M., Agostinelli, A., Uijlings, J., Ferrari, V., Mensink, T.: Transferability estimation using bhattacharyya class separability. In: CVPR (2022)
60. Parkhi, O.M., Vedaldi, A., Zisserman, A., Jawahar, C.: Cats and dogs. In: CVPR (2012)
61. Pedregosa, F., et al.: Scikit-learn: machine learning in Python. J. Mach. Learn. Res. **12**, 2825–2830 (2011)
62. Pratt, L.Y.: Discriminability-based transfer between neural networks. In: NeurIPS (1992)
63. Ridnik, T., Ben-Baruch, E., Noy, A., Zelnik-Manor, L.: Imagenet-21k pretraining for the masses. arXiv preprint arXiv:2104.10972 (2021)
64. Ronneberger, O., Fischer, P., Brox, T.: U-Net: convolutional networks for biomedical image segmentation. In: MICCAI (2015)
65. Rottensteiner, F., Sohn, G., Gerke, M., Wegner, J.D., Breitkopf, U., Jung, J.: Results of the isprs benchmark on urban object detection and 3D building reconstruction. ISPRS J. Photogramm. Remote Sens. **93**, 256–271 (2014)
66. Russakovsky, O., et al.: ImageNet large scale visual recognition challenge. Int. J. Comput. Vission **115**, 211–252 (2015)
67. Sandler, M., Howard, A.G., Zhu, M., Zhmoginov, A., Chen, L.: Mobilenetv 2: inverted residuals and linear bottleneck. In: CVPR (2018)
68. Shchur, O., Mumme, M., Bojchevski, A., Günnemann, S.: Pitfalls of graph neural network evaluation. arXiv preprint arXiv:1811.05868 (2018)
69. Shelhamer, E., Long, J., Darrell, T.: Fully convolutional networks for semantic segmentation. IEEE Trans. Pattern Aanal. Mach. Intel. **39**, 640–651 (2016)
70. Simonyan, K., Zisserman, A.: Very deep convolutional networks for large-scale image recognition. In: ICLR (2015)
71. Song, J., Chen, Y., Wang, X., Shen, C., Song, M.: Deep model transferability from attribution maps. In: NeurIPS (2019)
72. Song, J., et al.: DEPARA: deep attribution graph for deep knowledge transferability. In: CVPR (2020)
73. Song, S., Lichtenberg, S., Xiao, J.: SUN RGB-D: a RGB-D scene understanding benchmark suite. In: CVPR (2015)
74. Tan, M., Le, Q.: Efficientnet: rethinking model scaling for convolutional neural networks. In: ICML (2019)
75. Tan, Y., Li, Y., Huang, S.L.: OTCE: a transferability metric for cross-domain cross-task representations. In: CVPR (2021)
76. Thrun, S., Pratt, L.: Learning to Learn. Springer, New York (2012). https://doi.org/10.1007/978-1-4615-5529-2
77. Tran, A.T., Nguyen, C.V., Hassner, T.: Transferability and hardness of supervised classification tasks. In: CVPR (2019)

78. Varma, G., Subramanian, A., Namboodiri, A., Chandraker, M., Jawahar, C.: IDD: a dataset for exploring problems of autonomous navigation in unconstrained environments. In: Proceedings of WACV (2019)
79. Wah, C., Branson, S., Welinder, P., Perona, P., Belongie, S.: The Caltech-UCSD Birds-200-2011 Dataset. Tech. Rep. CNS-TR-2011-001, California Institute of Technology (2011)
80. Wang, J., et al.: Deep high-resolution representation learning for visual recognition. IEEE Trans. Pattern Anal. Mach Intell. (2020)
81. Waqas Zamir, S., et al.: iSAID: a large-scale dataset for instance segmentation in aerial images. In: CVPR Workshops (2019)
82. Weinzaepfel, P., Csurka, G., Cabon, Y., Humenberger, M.: Visual localization by learning objects-of-interest dense match regression. In: CVPR (2019)
83. Weiss, K., Khoshgoftaar, T.M., Wang, D.D.: A survey of transfer learning. J. Big Data **3**(1), 1–40 (2016). https://doi.org/10.1186/s40537-016-0043-6
84. Whiteson, S., Littman, M.L.: Introduction to the special issue on empirical evaluations in reinforcement learning. Mach. Learn. **84**(1-2), 1 (2011)
85. Xia, G.S., et al.: DOTA: a large-scale dataset for object detection in aerial images. In: CVPR (2018)
86. Xian, Y., Lampert, C.H., Schiele, B., Akata, Z.: Zero-shot learning-a comprehensive evaluation of the good, the bad and the ugly. IEEE Trans. Pattern Anal. Mach. Intell. **41**(9), 2251–2265 (2019)
87. Xiao, J., Hays, J., Ehinger, K., Oliva, A., Torralba, A.: SUN database: Large-scale scene recognition from Abbey to Zoo. In: CVPR (2010)
88. Yan, X., Acuna, D., Fidler, S.: Neural data server: a large-scale search engine for transfer learning data. In: CVPR (2020)
89. You, K., Liu, Y., Wang, J., Long, M.: LogME: practical assessment of pre-trained models for transfer learning. In: ICML (2021)
90. Yu, F., et al.: Bdd100k: a diverse driving dataset for heterogeneous multitask learning. In: CVPR (2020)
91. Zamir, A.R., Sax, A., Shen, W., Guibas, L.J., Malik, J., Savarese, S.: Taskonomy: Disentangling task transfer learning. In: CVPR (2018)
92. Zendel, O., Murschitz, M., Humenberger, M., Herzner, W.: How good is my test data? introducing safety analysis for computer vision. Int. J. Comput. Vision **125**(1), 95–109 (2017)
93. Zhou, B., Zhao, H., Puig, X., Fidler, S., Barriuso, A., Torralba, A.: Scene parsing through ADE20K dataset. In: CVPR (2017)
94. Zhou, X., Wang, D., Krähenbühl, P.: Objects as points. In: arXiv (2019)
95. Zoph, B., Vasudevan, V., Shlens, J., Le, Q.V.: Learning transferable architectures for scalable image recognition. In: CVPR (2018)

Attention Diversification for Domain Generalization

Rang Meng[1], Xianfeng Li[1], Weijie Chen[1,2(✉)], Shicai Yang[1(✉)], Jie Song[2], Xinchao Wang[3], Lei Zhang[4], Mingli Song[2], Di Xie[1], and Shiliang Pu[1]

[1] Hikvision Research Institute, Hangzhou, China
{mengrang,lixianfeng6,chenweijie5,yangshicai,xiedi, pushiliang.hri}@hikvision.com

[2] Zhejiang University, Hangzhou, China
{sjie,songml}@zju.edu.cn

[3] National University of Singapore, Singapore, Singapore
xinchao@nus.edu.sg

[4] Chongqing University, Chongqing, China
leizhang@cqu.edu.cn

Abstract. Convolutional neural networks (CNNs) have demonstrated gratifying results at learning discriminative features. However, when applied to unseen domains, state-of-the-art models are usually prone to errors due to domain shift. After investigating this issue from the perspective of shortcut learning, we find the devils lie in the fact that models trained on different domains merely bias to different domain-specific features yet overlook diverse task-related features. Under this guidance, a novel *Attention Diversification* framework is proposed, in which Intra-Model and Inter-Model Attention Diversification Regularization are collaborated to reassign appropriate attention to diverse task-related features. Briefly, Intra-Model Attention Diversification Regularization is equipped on the high-level feature maps to achieve in-channel discrimination and cross-channel diversification via forcing different channels to pay their most salient attention to different spatial locations. Besides, Inter-Model Attention Diversification Regularization is proposed to further provide task-related attention diversification and domain-related attention suppression, which is a paradigm of "*simulate, divide and assemble*": simulate domain shift via exploiting multiple domain-specific models, divide attention maps into task-related and domain-related groups, and assemble them within each group respectively to execute regularization. Extensive experiments and analyses are conducted on various benchmarks to demonstrate that our method achieves state-of-the-art performance over other competing methods. Code is available at https://github.com/hikvision-research/DomainGeneralization.

Keywords: Domain generalization · Attention diversification

R. Meng and X. Li—Equal contribution.

S. Avidan et al. (Eds.): ECCV 2022, LNCS 13694, pp. 322–340, 2022.
https://doi.org/10.1007/978-3-031-19830-4_19

1 Introduction

Domain is clarified as the feature space and marginal probability distribution for a specific dataset [2,3]. And domain shift reveals the discrepancy between source and target domains [2,3,57], which induces the models trained on source domains to perform defectively on an unseen target domain. Domain adaptation (DA) aims to remedy this issue of domain shift for various tasks in cases that target data is available [7, 8,29,32,36,39,49,62,72,73]. However, the domain shift is usually agnostic in real-world scenarios since the target data is not available for training. This issue inspires the research area of domain generalization (DG) [1,22,27,28,30,34,41,43,45,47,51,52, 54,74,75,78–80], which is aimed to make models trained on seen domains achieve accurate predictions on unseen domainss, i.e., the conditional distribution $P(Y|X)$ is robust with shifted marginal distribution $P(X)$.

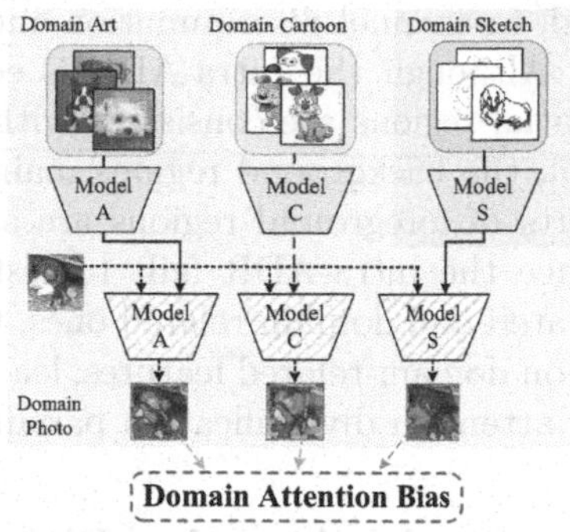

Fig. 1. The visualization of domain attention bias on PACS dataset. Domain-specific models trained on different domains (ACS) pay attention to different regions when they are tested on an unseen domain (P).

Canonical DG focuses on learning a domain-invariant feature distribution $P(F(X))$ across domains for the robustness of conditional distribution $P(Y|F(X))$. In fact, the domain issue can be revisited from the perspective of shortcut learning [15], which indicates that models attempt to find the simplest solution to solve a given task. Models trained on specific domains merely pay attention to salient domain-related features while overlooking other diverse task-related information. When the domain shifts, the discrimination of the biased features will not be held on the unseen domain, leading to the shift of the conditional distribution. This problematic phenomenon is dubbed as "domain attention bias" as shown in Fig. 1.

In this paper, we propose the *Attention Diversification* framework, in which the attention mechanism is served as the bridge to achieve the invariance of conditional distribution. In our framework, the proposed Intra-Model Attention Diversification Regularization (Intra-ADR) and Inter-Model Attention Diversification Regularization (Inter-ADR) are collaborated to rearrange appropriate spatial attention to diverse task-related features from coarse to fine. The reasons why the two components are designed in our framework are detailed as follows:

Intra-model Attention Diversification Regularization. According to *the principle of maximum entropy* [18], when estimating the probability distribution, we should select that distribution which leaves us the largest uncertainty under our constraints, so that we cannot bring any additional assumptions into our computation. That is, when testing the unseen domains, each task-related feature is equally-useful (i.e., the maximum entropy), driving us to propose Intra-ADR, which coarsely recalls overlooked features outside the domain attention bias as much as possible. This is done via forcing different channels to pay attention to different spatial locations, leading all spatial locations to be activated. To this end, in-channel discrimination and cross-channel diversification are facilitated.

Although the Intra-ADR is equipped upon the high-level features, not all spatial regions are consistent with the semantics of the categories. As stated in [15], the background regions mainly involve domain-related features, and some parts of foreground regions are also affected by domain-specific styles [21,23]. Since the Intra-ADR fails to distinguish features at the finer level into task-related and domain-related ones, the excessive attention is incidentally imposed upon domain-related features, leading to the conditional distribution shift. Thus, an attention diversification paradigm at a finer level is necessary.

Inter-model Attention Diversification Regularization. To handle the aforementioned issue, features that Intra-ADR coarsely recalls ought to be further refined by Inter-ADR. Thus, the diverse attention for task-related features is encouraged, yet the excessive attention for domain-related ones is suppressed. Inter-ADR is a paradigm of "*simulate, divide and assemble*". Specifically, 1) "*simulate*": we train multiple domain-specific models for each seen domain, and then infer these models on samples from other training domains to simulate domain shift. In addition, the attention maps and predictions for agnostic domains are generated; 2) "*divide*": we divide attention maps from domain-specific models and domain-aggregated model into the task-related and domain-related groups, according to whether the model predictions is consistent with the corresponding ground truth; 3) "*assemble*": attention maps from different models are assembled within each group as the task-related and domain-related inter-model attention maps, respectively. Finally, the attention maps of the domain-aggregated model can be regularized with the task-related and domain-related inter-model attention maps, to diversify task-related attention regions yet suppress domain-related attention regions.

Extensive experiments and analyses are conducted on multiple domain generalization datasets. Our optimization method achieves state-of-the-art results. It is worth emphasizing that our method can bring further performance improvement in conjunction with other DG methods.

2 Related Works

Domain Generalization. The analysis in [2] proves that the features tend to be general and can be transferred to unseen domains if they are invariant across different domains. Following this research, a sequence of domain alignment methods is proposed, which reduce the feature discrepancy among multiple source domains via aligning domain-invariant features. These methods enable models to generalize well to unseen target domains. Specifically, they use explicit feature alignment by minimizing the maximum mean discrepancy (MMD) [58] or using Instance Normalization (IN) layers [43]. Alternatively, [22,47] adopt domain adversarial learning for domain alignment, which trains a discriminator to distinguish the domains while training feature extractors to cheat the domain discriminator for learning domain-invariant features. Besides, the ability of generalizing to unseen domains will increase as training data covering more diverse domains. Several domain diversification attempts had been implemented in previous works: swapping the shape or style information of two images [25], mixing instance-level features of training samples across domains [78], altering the location and scene of objects [46], and simulating the actual environment for generating more training data [56]. In contrast, we investigate the issue of DG inspired by shortcut learning and maximum entropy principle. Besides, we introduce visual attention in our proposed method to boost DG, which is seldom studied in prior works.

Visual Attention. Visual attention has been widely used in deep learning and achieves remarkable advances [59,69]. It has been exploited in computer vision tasks such as image recognition [9,10,33,48,61,71] and object detection among others [6,16,35,66,67]. CAM [77] provides the attention visualization of feature maps for model interpretable analysis. In essence, visual attention can be interpreted as an allocation mechanism for the model learning resource: it assigns high weights to what the model considers valuable, and vice versa, assigns low weight to what the model considered negligible [70]. Motivated by this mechanism, many computer vision tasks achieve breakthrough. For example, many fine-grained image classification methods learn multi-attention to capture sufficient subtle inter-category differences [14,53,68,76]. Recently, self-attention [13,20,64] has emerged to model the long-range dependencies. In the field of transfer learning, Attentional Heterogeneous Transfer (AHT) [40] designed a new heterogeneous transfer learning approach to transfer knowledge from an optimized subset of source domain samples to a target domain. Transferable Attention for Domain Adaptation (TADA) [63] is proposed to use transferable global and local attention with multi-region-level domain discriminators to pick out the images and the transferable areas of the image.

Our work finds that CNN allocates sufficient attention to domain-related features, but insufficient attention to task-related features conversely. Under this consideration, we adopt spatial attention as a bridge to learn diverse transferable features to mitigate domain shifts.

3 Method

Our proposed *Attention Diversification* framework is composed of Intra-ADR and Inter-ADR as shown in Fig. 2. Our framework aims to deny shortcut learning, which ignores numerous task-related features. The Intra-ADR and Inter-ADR are collaborated to diversify attention regions for task-related features.

Notations. Given $\mathcal{S}$ training domains $\{\mathcal{D}_d\}_{d=1}^{\mathcal{S}}$, where $\mathcal{D}_d = \{(x_i^d, y_i^d)\}_{i=1}^{N_d}$ with N_d labeled samples covering Z categories. Let $\mathcal{M}$ denote the CNN model used for image classification. Suppose $\mathcal{X}_j^b \in R^{\mathcal{C}^b \times \mathcal{H}^b \times \mathcal{W}^b}$ denote the feature maps output from the b-th block of the model $\mathcal{M}_j$, where $\mathcal{C}^b$, $\mathcal{H}^b$ and $\mathcal{W}^b$ denote the channel number, height and width of $\mathcal{X}_j^b$, and $b \in \{1, ..., B\}$. We denote

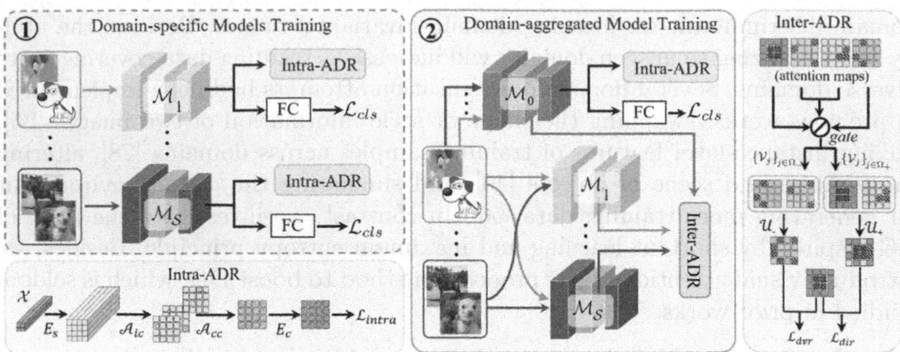

Fig. 2. The pipeline of our proposed *Attention Diversification* framework, which is composed of Intra-ADR and Inter-ADR.

the domain-specific models and domain-aggregated model as $\{\mathcal{M}_j\}_{j=0}^{\mathcal{S}}$, where $\mathcal{M}_1, ..., \mathcal{M}_\mathcal{S}$ represent the former which is trained on the corresponding single training domain, and $\mathcal{M}_0$ represents the later which is trained on multiple training domains. For the image classification task, the cross-entropy loss is employed as supervision:

$$\mathcal{L}_{cls} = \mathcal{L}_{CE}(\mathcal{M}_j(x_i^d), y_i^d) \quad (1)$$

3.1 Intra-model Attention Diversification Regularization

In this section, we introduce the design of Intra-ADR, which forces different channels to pay their most salient attention to different spatial locations, leading all spatial locations to be activated. To this end, potential features at all spatial regions are learned as much as possible. Intra-ADR is equipped upon the feature maps $\mathcal{X}^B$ for the last convolutional block.

In-Channel Attention Map. We perform normalization to each channel in $\mathcal{X}^B$ via spatial softmax, and obtain in-channel attention maps for different channels. In doing so, the maximum of the sum of all in-channel attention maps is permanently fixed as 1:

$$\mathcal{A}_{ic}(\mathcal{X}_{c,h,w}^B) = \frac{exp(\mathcal{X}_{c,h,w}^B)}{\sum_{h=1}^{\mathcal{H}^B} \sum_{w=1}^{\mathcal{W}^B} exp(\mathcal{X}_{c,h,w}^B)} \quad (2)$$

where $\mathcal{A}_{ic}(\cdot)$ is the operation of spatial softmax, and $\mathcal{X}_{c,h,w}^B$ denotes the pixel at the spatial location (h, w) of the c-th channel in $\mathcal{X}^B$. In this way, when the magnitudes of the selected pixels are enhanced, pixels in the remaining spatial location will be suppressed conversely. This means that attention is concentrated on the selected pixels and then we obtain "sparse" in-channel attention maps.

Cross-Channel Attention Map. Inspired by the maxout operation in [17], we enforce Pixel-wise Cross-Channel Maximization upon $\mathcal{A}_{ic}$ to obtain the cross-channel attention map:

$$\mathcal{A}_{cc}(\mathcal{X}^B_{c,h,w}) = \max_{c=1,2,\ldots,\mathcal{C}^B} \mathcal{A}_{ic}(\mathcal{X}^B_{c,h,w}) \tag{3}$$

where $\mathcal{A}_{cc}(\cdot)$ is the Pixel-wise Cross-Channel Maximization, and $\mathcal{A}_{cc}(\mathcal{X}^B_{c,h,w}) \in \mathbb{R}^{\mathcal{H}^B \times \mathcal{W}^B}$ contains the most representative pixels across different channels. Thus, when we maximize the sum of $\mathcal{A}_{cc}(\mathcal{X}^B_{c,h,w})$, all spatial locations are extremely activated to achieve "*dense*" features.

Spatial-Channel Joint Expanding Module. However, the involving channels in the cross-channel attention map are limited because of the following observation: take ResNet-50 with input size of 224 [19] as an example, the number of spatial location of $\mathcal{X}^B$ ($\mathcal{H}^B \times \mathcal{W}^B = 49$) is far less than that of channels ($\mathcal{C}^B = 2048$). The majority of channels are not involved in regularization, leading to that lots of features cannot get sufficient attention. To remedy this issue, we propose a Spatial-Channel joint Expanding module (SCE) to enlarge both the spatial scope and involved channel number in the cross-channel attention map. SCE consists of two strategies:

- *Spatial Expanding.* The spatial expanding block is composed of a deconvolutional layer, an instance normalization layer and a ReLU activation layer. This is done for two-folder reasons: i) deconvolution can enlarge the resolution of feature maps to offset the gap between channel number and spatial location number; ii) deconvolution can provide more detailed semantic clues. The output of spatial expanding block $\mathbb{X}^B$ can be expressed as:

$$\mathbb{X}^B = E_s(\mathcal{X}^B_{c,h,w}) \tag{4}$$

  where E_s is the spatial expanding block, $\mathbb{X}^B \in \mathbb{R}^{\mathcal{C}^B \times \mathtt{H}^B \times \mathtt{W}^B}$, $\mathtt{H}^B = s * \mathcal{H}^B$ and $\mathtt{W}^B = s * \mathcal{W}^B$. $s > 1$ is a scale factor.
- *Channel Expanding.* We involve more channels in the cross-channel attention map via the Pixel-wise Cross-Channel Top-k selection, which averages the most activated k pixels across channels:

$$\mathbb{A}_{cc}(\mathbb{X}^B_{c,h,w}) = E_c(\mathcal{A}_{ic}(\mathbb{X}^B_{c,h,w})) = \max_{c=1,2,\ldots,\mathcal{C}^B}(k) \ \mathcal{A}_{ic}(\mathbb{X}^B_{c,h,w}) \tag{5}$$

  where k is the number of selected channels, $\mathbb{A}_{cc}(\mathbb{X}_{c,h,w})$ is the output of SCE, and $\max(k)(\cdot)$ is the operation of averaging the most activated k pixels across channels. Note that SCE can make the cross-channel attention map involve $k \cdot s$ times channels compared with the original one.

Intra-model Regularization. We impose SCE upon the output feature maps from the last convolutional block, and formulate the Intra-ADR term via maximizing the average value of $\mathbb{A}_{cc}(\mathbb{X}^B_{c,h,w})$:

$$\mathcal{L}_{intra} = -\frac{1}{\mathtt{HW}} \sum_{h=1}^{\mathtt{H}} \sum_{w=1}^{\mathtt{W}} \max_{c=1,2,\ldots,\mathcal{C}^B}(k) \;\; \mathcal{A}_{ic}(\mathbb{X}^B_{c,h,w}) \tag{6}$$

3.2 Inter-model Attention Diversification Regularization

In this section, we introduce the other component of our proposed framework, i.e., Inter-ADR, which refines the attention assignment of Intra-ADR by a paradigm of "*simulate, divide and assemble*". This is done to diversify task-related features yet suppress the domain-related features. Details are as follows:

Simulate Domain Shift. We train the domain-specific models $\{\mathcal{M}_j\}_{j=1}^{\mathcal{S}}$ on each source domain with $\mathcal{L}_{intra}$ in Eq. 6 and $\mathcal{L}_{cls}$ in Eq. 1. We do not only infer each sample on its own domain-specific model but also on other domain-specific models to simulate domain shift. Then we obtain the cross-channel attention maps for the b-th block $\{\{\mathcal{V}_j^b\}_{b=1}^B\}_{j=0}^{\mathcal{S}}$ from each domain-specific model in the same manner of Intra-ADR (without spatial expanding block) :

$$\mathcal{V}_j^b = \max_{c=1,2,\ldots,\mathcal{C}^b}(\mathcal{C}^b) \; \mathcal{A}_{ic}(\mathcal{X}_j^b) \tag{7}$$

Divide Attention Maps Across Models. The models prediction $\hat{y}_j$ is utilized as the criterion to divide cross-channel attention maps $\{\{\mathcal{V}_j^b\}_{b=1}^B\}_{j=0}^{\mathcal{S}}$ from different models. $\{\{\mathcal{V}_j^b\}_{b=1}^B\}_{j=0}^{\mathcal{S}}$ are divided into two groups: if the prediction $\hat{y}_j$ agrees with the corresponding ground truth, $\{\mathcal{V}_j^b\}_{j=1}^B$ are viewed as task-related features, otherwise domain-related features. Let $\{\{\mathcal{V}_j^b\}_{b=1}^B\}_{j\in\Omega_+}$ and $\{\{\mathcal{V}_j^b\}_{b=1}^B\}_{j\in\Omega_-}$ denote the two groups respectively:

$$j \in \begin{cases} \Omega_+, \text{if} \;\; \hat{y}_i^j = y_i^d \\ \Omega_-, \text{otherwise} \end{cases} \quad s.t. \;\; j = 0, ..., \mathcal{S} \tag{8}$$

Assemble Attention Maps in Each Group. We assemble the cross-channel attention maps for each group via Pixel-wise Cross-Model Maximization, which is similar to Pixel-wise Cross-Channel Maximization in Eq. 3:

$$\mathcal{U}_+^b = \max_{j\in\Omega_+} \mathcal{V}_j^b, \quad \mathcal{U}_-^b = \max_{j\in\Omega_-} \mathcal{V}_j^b \tag{9}$$

where $\mathcal{U}_+^b$ and $\mathcal{U}_-^b$ are the task-related and domain-related inter-model attention map, respectively. Thanks to the Pixel-wise Cross-model Maximization, $\mathcal{U}_+^b$ contains appropriate attention regions attributed to correct predictions under domain shift. On the other hand, $\mathcal{U}_-^b$ includes the most salient attention locations, which involve the domain-related features leading to error predictions.

Inter-model Regularization. After dividing and assembling the attention maps across models, we exploit the inter-model attention map to force the cross-channel attention maps $\{\mathcal{V}_0^b\}_{b=1}^B$ of the domain-aggregated model to encourage task-related features yet suppress domain-related features.

Algorithm 1: Attention Diversification Training Schema

input : training data $\{\mathcal{D}\}_{d=1}^{\mathcal{S}}$, domain-specific models $\{\mathcal{M}_j\}_{j=1}^{\mathcal{S}}$, domain-aggregated model $\mathcal{M}_0$

output: trained domain-aggregated model $\mathcal{M}_0$;

for d *in* $\{1, ..., \mathcal{S}\}$ **do**

  Train domain-specific models $\mathcal{M}_{j=d}$ on the domain $\mathcal{D}_d$ with cross-entropy $\mathcal{L}_{cls}^d$ in Eqn. (1) and Intra-ADR losses $\mathcal{L}_{intra}^d$ in Eqn. (6) ;

end

for $\{x_i^d, y_i^d\}$ *in* $\{\mathcal{D}\}_{d=1}^{\mathcal{S}}$ **do**

  Generate predictions and cross-channel attention maps for domain-specific and domain-aggregated models: $\{\hat{y}_i^j = \mathcal{M}_j(x_i^d)\}_{j=0}^{\mathcal{S}}$;$\{\{\mathcal{V}_j^b\}_{b=1}^{B}\}_{j=0}^{\mathcal{S}}$;

  Divide cross-channel attention maps from multiple models into two group based on whether the prediction agrees with the ground truth using Eqn. (8): $\{\{\mathcal{V}_j^b\}_{b=1}^{B}\}_{j\in\Omega_+}, \{\{\mathcal{V}_j^b\}_{b=1}^{B}\}_{j\in\Omega_-} \leftarrow \{\{\mathcal{V}_j^b\}_{b=1}^{B}\}_{j=0}^{\mathcal{S}}$;

  Generate task-related and domain-related inter-model attention maps $\{\mathcal{U}_+^b\}_{b=1}^{B}$ and $\{\mathcal{U}_-^b\}_{b=1}^{B}$ using Eqn. (9);

  Calculate $\mathcal{L}_{dir}$ and $\mathcal{L}_{dvr}$ using Eqn. (10) and Eqn. (11);

  Train domain-aggregated model $\mathcal{M}_0$ with $\mathcal{L}_{total}$ in Eqn. (13)

end

On the one hand, we minimize the Euclidean distance between $\{\mathcal{V}_0\}_{b=1}^{B}$ and $\{\mathcal{U}_+^b\}_{b=1}^{B}$ to enhance attention regions involving task-related features:

$$\mathcal{L}_{dir} = \sum_{b=1}^{B} \|(\mathcal{V}_0^b - \mathcal{U}_+^b)\|_2 \tag{10}$$

On the other hand, we ought to suppress the attention regions involving domain-related features, which are accidentally included during Intra-ADR. This is done through maximizing the Euclidean distance between $\{\mathcal{V}_0\}_{b=1}^{B}$ and $\{\mathcal{U}_-^b\}_{b=1}^{B}$:

$$\mathcal{L}_{dvr} = -\sum_{b=1}^{B} \|(\mathcal{V}_0^b - \mathcal{U}_-^b)\|_2 \tag{11}$$

Therefore, the Inter-ADR term can be expressed as:

$$\mathcal{L}_{inter} = \lambda_{dir} \cdot \mathcal{L}_{dir} + \lambda_{dvr} \cdot \mathcal{L}_{dvr} \tag{12}$$

where λ_{dir} and λ_{dvr} are the hyperparameters to balance the two losses.

Training Scheme. Our framework is trained in a two-stage manner, which includes domain-specific models training and domain-aggregated-model training as shown in Algorithem 1. In the first stage, only Eq. 6 is used for attention diversification. In the second stage, both Eq. 6 and Eq. 12 are involved into attention diversification training. The total loss is:

$$\mathcal{L}_{total} = \mathcal{L}_{cls} + \lambda_{intra} \cdot \mathcal{L}_{intra} + \lambda_{dir} \cdot \mathcal{L}_{dir} + \lambda_{dvr} \cdot \mathcal{L}_{dvr} \tag{13}$$

Table 1. Leave-one-domain-out generalization results on PACS dataset.

Methods	References	Art	Cartoon	Photo	Sketch	Avg.	Art	Cartoon	Photo	Sketch	Avg.
		ResNet-18					*ResNet-50*				
Baseline	–	79.0	74.3	94.9	71.4	79.9	86.2	78.7	97.6	70.6	83.2
MetaReg [1]	NeurIPS'18	83.7	77.2	95.5	70.3	81.7	87.2	79.2	97.6	70.3	83.6
MASF [12]	NeurIPS'19	80.2	77.1	94.9	71.6	81.0	82.8	80.4	95.0	72.2	82.6
Epi-FCR [26]	ICCV'19	82.1	77.0	93.9	73.0	81.5	–	–	–	–	–
JiGen [4]	CVPR'19	79.4	75.2	96.0	71.3	80.5	–	–	–	–	–
DMG [5]	ECCV'20	76.9	80.4	93.4	75.2	81.5	82.6	78.1	94.5	78.3	83.4
RSC [21]	ECCV'20	84.4	80.3	95.9	80.8	85.1	87.8	82.1	97.9	83.3	87.9
MixStyle [78]	ICLR'21	84.1	78.8	96.1	75.9	83.7	–	–	–	–	–
SelfReg [24]	ICCV'21	82.3	78.4	**96.2**	77.5	83.6	87.9	79.4	96.8	78.3	85.6
DAML [50]	CVPR'21	83.0	74.1	95.6	78.1	82.7	–	–	–	–	–
SagNet [42]	CVPR'21	83.6	77.7	95.5	76.3	83.3	81.1	75.4	95.7	77.2	82.3
FACT [65]	CVPR'21	85.4	78.4	95.2	79.2	84.5	**89.6**	81.7	96.8	84.4	88.1
Intra-ADR	Ours	82.4	79.4	95.3	82.3	84.9	87.7	81.2	97.1	83.8	87.5
I^2-ADR	Ours	82.9	80.8	95.0	83.5	85.6	88.5	83.2	95.2	**85.8**	88.2
MixStyle + Intra-ADR	Ours	**86.0**	80.3	96.0	84.4	86.7	88.6	83.2	98.0	85.2	88.7
MixStyle + I^2-ADR	Ours	85.3	**81.2**	95.4	**86.1**	**87.0**	87.7	**84.5**	**98.2**	85.6	**89.2**

4 Experiments

In this section, we demonstrate the effectiveness of our *Attention Diversification* framework on three mainstream DG benchmarks. For convenience, we abbreviate our *Attention Diversification* framework to I^2-ADR.

4.1 Experimental Setup

Datasets. PACS [27] is a common DG benchmark that contains 9991 images of 7 categories from 4 different domains, i.e., Art (A), Cartoon (C), Photo (P), and Sketch (S). **Office-home** [60] contains images sharing 65 categories from 4 different domains around 15,579 images, i.e., Art (Ar), Clipart (Cl), Product (Pr), and Real-World (Rw). **DomainNet** [44] is a very large DG dataset, consisting of about 600K images with 345 categories from 6 different domains, i.e., Clipart (C), Infograph (I), Painting (P), Quickdraw (Q), Real (R), Sketch (S).

Implementation Details. Our framework is trained from ImageNet [11] pre-trained models. We utilize an SGD optimizer, batch size of 64 and weight-decay of 0.0004 with 150 epochs for optimization. The initial learning rate is set 0.008 and adjusted by a cosine annealing schedule. Following the standard augmentation protocol in [4], we train our framework with horizontal flipping, random cropping, color jittering, and grayscale conversion. We follow the standard data splits and leave-one-domain-out evaluation protocol as the prior work [4]. The best models are selected based on the validation split of training domains. The accuracy for test domains is reported and averaged over three runs. We mainly use ResNet-18/50 as the backbones. Note that the same backbone is adopted

Table 2. Office-Home under ResNet-18.

Methods	Ar	Cl	Pr	Rw	Avg.
ResNet-18					
Baseline	57.8	52.7	73.5	74.8	64.7
RSC [21]	58.4	47.9	71.6	74.5	63.1
MixStyle [78]	58.7	53.4	74.2	75.9	65.5
SagNet [42]	60.2	45.4	70.4	73.4	62.3
FACT [65]	60.3	54.9	74.5	**76.6**	66.6
Intra-ADR	64.5	54.0	73.9	74.7	66.8
I^2-ADR	66.4	53.3	74.9	75.3	67.5
MixStyle + Intra-ADR	65.9	55.3	74.3	75.1	67.7
MixStyle + I^2-ADR	**66.8**	**56.8**	**75.3**	75.7	**68.7**

Table 3. Office-Home under ResNet-50.

Methods	Ar	Cl	Pr	Rw	Avg.
ResNet-50					
Baseline	61.3	52.4	75.8	76.6	66.5
MLDG [28]	61.5	53.2	75.0	77.5	66.8
RSC [21]	50.7	51.4	74.8	75.1	65.5
SelfReg [24]	63.6	53.1	76.9	78.1	67.9
SagNet [42]	63.4	54.8	75.8	78.3	68.1
Intra-ADR	67.3	54.1	78.8	78.8	69.8
I^2-ADR	70.3	55.1	80.7	79.2	71.4
MixStyle + Intra-ADR	69.5	55.9	80.6	80.4	71.4
MixStyle + I^2-ADR	**71.1**	**56.9**	**81.8**	**80.5**	**72.5**

among the domain-aggregated and the domain-specific models. We set the hyper-parameters, λ_{intra}, λ_{dir}, and λ_{dvr} as 0.005, 2 and 1 for all datasets, respectively. Our framework is implemented with PyTorch on NVIDIA Tesla V100 GPUs.

4.2 Comparison with State-of-the-Arts

Results on PACS. Our framework achieves SOTA results on PACS dataset with both ResNet-18 and ResNet-50. In Table 1, the average performance of our framework achieves 85.6% and 88.2% with ResNet-18 and ResNet-50, respectively. Our framework provides impressive improvements of 5.7% and 5.0% compared with the corresponding baselines. Compared with other SOTA results, our framework surpasses other competing DG methods. Note that one component of our framework for recalling overlooked features in shortcut learning, Intra-ADR, can be surprisingly superior to most of DG methods. Moreover, Inter-ADR can further lift the DG performance of Intra-ADR and other competing DG methods.

Results on Office-Home. From Table 2 and Table 3, it can be observed that the baseline has a strong performance on Office-Home. Many previous DG methods cannot improve or perform worse than the baseline. Nevertheless, our framework achieves 67.5% and 71.4% with ResNet-18 and ResNet-50, respectively. Moreover, the proposed I^2-ADR surpasses the majority of other related methods, including the latest MixStyle [78], RSC [21], and FACT [65]. Notably, the Intra-ADR can achieve SOTA results of 66.8% and 69.8% on Office-Home with ResNet-18 and ResNet-50, respectively. Results on Office-Home justify the impact of each component of our framework.

Results on DomainNet. DomainNet is a very challenging large-scale dataset. The comparisons between our framework and other DG methods are reported in Table 4. The number of data in DomainNet is much larger than other DG benchmarks, leading to be very challenging to use ResNet-18 as the backbone. Fortunately, our framework using ResNet-18 achieves competing results on DomainNet. In addition, the performance of Intra-ADR and I^2-ADR using ResNet-50 are

Table 4. Leave-one-domain-out generalization results on DomainNet dataset.

Methods	References	Clipart	Infograph	Painting	Quickdraw	Real	Sketch	Avg.
ResNet-18								
Baseline	-	57.1	17.6	43.2	13.8	54.9	39.4	37.6
MetaReg [1]	NeurIPS'18	53.7	**21.1**	**45.3**	10.6	**58.5**	42.3	38.6
DMG [5]	ECCV'20	**60.1**	18.8	44.5	**14.2**	54.7	41.7	**39.0**
Intra-ADR	Ours	57.3 ± 0.1	14.9 ± 0.3	42.8 ± 0.2	12.2 ± 0.4	52.9 ± 0.5	46.0 ± 0.2	37.7
I^2-ADR	Ours	57.3 ± 0.3	15.2 ± 0.3	44.1 ± 0.1	12.1 ± 0.4	53.9 ± 0.6	46.7 ± 0.2	38.2
MixStyle + Intra-ADR	Ours	57.4 ± 0.2	15.3 ± 0.1	43.3 ± 0.2	12.3 ± 0.4	53.5 ± 0.3	46.5 ± 0.2	38.1
MixStyle + I^2-ADR	Ours	57.4 ± 0.4	15.7 ± 0.2	44.7 ± 0.1	12.3 ± 0.4	54.4 ± 0.2	$\mathbf{47.4 \pm 0.1}$	38.7
ResNet-50								
Baseline	-	62.2	19.9	45.5	13.8	57.5	44.4	40.5
MetaReg [1]	NeurIPS'18	59.8	**25.6**	**50.2**	11.5	**64.6**	50.1	43.6
MLDG [28]	AAAI'18	59.1 ± 0.2	19.1 ± 0.3	45.8 ± 0.7	13.4 ± 0.3	59.6 ± 0.2	50.2 ± 0.4	41.2
C-DANN [31]	ECCV'18	54.6 ± 0.4	17.3 ± 0.1	43.7 ± 0.9	12.1 ± 0.7	56.2 ± 0.4	45.9 ± 0.5	38.3
RSC [21]	ECCV'20	55.0 ± 1.2	18.3 ± 0.5	44.4 ± 0.6	12.2 ± 0.2	55.7 ± 0.7	47.8 ± 0.9	38.9
DMG [5]	ECCV'20	**65.2**	22.2	50.0	**15.7**	59.6	49.0	43.6
SagNet [42]	CVPR'21	57.7 ± 0.3	19.0 ± 0.2	45.3 ± 0.3	12.7 ± 0.5	58.1 ± 0.5	48.8 ± 0.2	40.3
SelfReg [24]	ICCV'21	60.7 ± 0.1	21.6 ± 0.1	49.4 ± 0.2	12.7 ± 0.1	60.7 ± 0.1	51.7 ± 0.1	42.8
Intra-ADR	Ours	63.6 ± 0.1	20.0 ± 0.1	49.4 ± 0.1	14.8 ± 0.3	60.0 ± 0.4	$\mathbf{54.4 \pm 0.1}$	43.7
I^2-ADR	Ours	64.4 ± 0.2	20.2 ± 0.6	49.2 ± 0.5	15.0 ± 0.2	61.6 ± 0.4	53.3 ± 0.1	44.0
MixStyle + Intra-ADR	Ours	63.9 ± 0.1	20.1 ± 0.5	49.4 ± 0.2	15.0 ± 0.4	60.4 ± 0.3	$\mathbf{54.4 \pm 0.1}$	43.9
MixStyle + I^2-ADR	Ours	64.1 ± 0.1	20.4 ± 0.2	49.2 ± 0.4	15.1 ± 0.2	61.3 ± 0.4	54.3 ± 0.4	**44.1**

Table 5. Ablation studies on the three components contained in I^2-ADR.

Method	$\mathcal{L}_{intra}$	$\mathcal{L}_{dir}$	$\mathcal{L}_{dvr}$	Art	Cartoon	Photo	Sketch	Avg.
I^2-ADR	✓	–	–	82.4	79.4	95.3	82.3	84.9
	-	✓	✓	82.3	80.0	95.1	82.6	85.0
	✓	✓	–	82.7	80.5	95.0	83.2	85.4
	✓	–	✓	82.5	80.2	95.1	82.9	85.2
	✓	✓	✓	**82.9**	**80.8**	95.0	**83.5**	**85.6**

Table 6. Ablation studies on two strategies in SCE module.

Method	E_s	E_c	Art	Cartoon	Photo	Sketch	Avg.
Intra-ADR	–	–	81.3	77.3	94.7	78.8	83.0
	–	✓	80.0	77.2	**96.0**	80.9	83.5
	✓	–	81.9	79.3	95.5	79.3	84.0
	✓	✓	**82.4**	**79.4**	95.3	**82.3**	**84.9**

among the top ones. We notice that the performance of our framework exceeds that of SelfReg [24] by 1.6% and DMG [5] by 0.4%, respectively. This again verifies the superiority of our framework.

4.3 Ablation Studies

In this section, we carry out various ablation studies to dissect the effectiveness of our proposed *Attention Diversification* framework. All ablation studies are conducted on PACS dataset with ResNet-18.

Analysis for SCE Module. We conduct ablation studies on SCE module to analyze the effectiveness of each component in SCE module. There are two critical strategies, Spatial Expanding (E_s) and Channel Expanding (E_c) designed to facilitate the effectiveness of the Intra-ADR on the high-level features. As

Table 7. Ablation studies on the equipped positions of Intra-ADR.

Methods	**Art**	**Cartoon**	**Photo**	**Sketch**	**Avg.**
Intra-ADR (res1)	80.8	78.4	94.7	80.1	83.5
Intra-ADR (res2)	81.0	78.6	94.9	80.7	83.8
Intra-ADR (res3)	<u>81.8</u>	<u>78.8</u>	<u>95.5</u>	<u>81.1</u>	<u>84.3</u>
Intra-ADR (res4)	**82.4**	**79.4**	**95.3**	**82.3**	**84.9**

Table 8. Ablation studies on the equipped positions of Inter-ADR.

Methods	Art	Cartoon	**Photo**	Sketch	Avg.
Intra-ADR	82.4	79.4	<u>95.3</u>	82.3	84.9
+ Inter-ADR (res1)	**83.0**	79.3	**95.5**	82.9	85.2
+ Inter-ADR (res12)	82.6	80.0	<u>95.3</u>	83.0	85.2
+ Inter-ADR (res123)	82.7	<u>80.5</u>	95.1	<u>83.2</u>	<u>85.4</u>
+ Inter-ADR (res1234)	<u>82.9</u>	**80.8**	95.0	**83.5**	**85.6**

Table 9. The seen domain performance of our proposed method.

Methods	Backbone	C&P&S	A&P&S	A&C&S	A&C&P
Baseline	ResNet-18	**96.4**	95.6	95.0	95.6
Intra-ADR		96.2	**96.5**	94.9	96.3
I^2-ADR		96.3	96.3	**95.1**	**96.6**
Baseline	ResNet-50	96.9	**96.8**	95.6	97.3
Intra-ADR		97.4	96.7	95.5	**97.4**
I^2-ADR		**97.6**	96.7	**97.2**	97.1

Table 10. Ablation studies on the scale factor s and selected channels number k.

(k, s)	Art	Cartoon	Photo	Sketch	Avg.
(2, 2)	82.0	78.1	95.1	81.0	84.1
(2, 4)	<u>82.2</u>	77.9	**96.0**	81.0	84.3
(4, 2)	82.1	78.2	95.0	81.2	84.2
(4, 4)	<u>82.4</u>	77.9	**96.0**	81.0	84.5
(10, 2)	**82.4**	**79.4**	95.3	**82.3**	**84.9**
(10, 4)	**82.4**	<u>79.2</u>	<u>95.6</u>	<u>82.2</u>	**84.9**

shown in Table 6, we can observe that both E_s and E_c can improve the ability of generalization across domains, and the gains of E_s are slightly better than E_c. Note that the performance w/ E_c on (A, C) is indeed worse than that w/o E_c (baseline Intra-ADR), but the performance w/ E_c is better than the baseline on average. On the other hand, we analyze the effect of the two crucial hyperparameters in SCE Module, the scale factor s in E_s and the selected channels number k in E_c. As shown in Table 10, the average performance increases as the channel number is expanded. Besides, The scale factor also has a significant impact on the effectiveness of Intra-ADR. We set $k = 10$, $s = 2$ as the default setting for all experiments.

Analysis for Different Losses in $\mathbf{I^2}$-ADR. We conduct ablation studies to investigate the effectiveness of the three losses in I^2-ADR. As shown in Table 5, the first row denotes the results of Intra-ADR, the second row denotes the results of Inter-ADR. We can observe that $\mathcal{L}_{dir} + \mathcal{L}_{dvr}$ contributes to the impressive improvement of 0.7% on the average performance compared with Intra-ADR. After removing $\mathcal{L}_{dir}$ which diversifies task-related attention regions, there is a drop of 0.4% compared with $\mathcal{L}_{dir} + \mathcal{L}_{dvr}$, but still an improvement of 0.3% compared with Intra-ADR. Besides, after removing $\mathcal{L}_{dvr}$ that suppresses the domain-related attention regions, $\mathcal{L}_{dir}$ solely surpasses the Intra-ADR by 0.5%, but losses 0.2% compared with $\mathcal{L}_{dir} + \mathcal{L}_{dvr}$.

Analysis for the Positions of Intra-ADR and Inter-ADR. Extensive works have been discussed that different layers of CNNs have different effects on the information flow [37,38,55]. Here we also analyze the equipped positions of the proposed two modules, Intra-ADR and Inter-ADR. Let's denote 4 bottleneck stages of a standard ResNet backbone as *res1-4*. For instance, *res1* means the outputted feature maps of the first bottleneck stage. As shown in Table 7, Intra-ADR is limited when equipped upon the low- and middle-level feature maps, but provides an impressive improvement when upon the high-level. Besides, the hierarchical Inter-ADR achieves a significant impact on the average performance. Thereby, Intra-ADR is ewuipped on the highest layer to diversify task-related features instead of introducing too many domain-related features. Inter-ADR is equipped upon multi-level layers to facilitate information flow with a mechanism of distinguishing the task- and domain-related features.

4.4 Discussions and Visualization

Performance on Seen Domains. In this section, we report the performance of our framework on the seen domains from PACS dataset. As shown in Table 9, "A","C","P","S" in the first row represent the classification accuracy on seen domains, including Art, Cartoon, Photo and Sketch, respectively. The performance of our framework, whether Intra-ADR or I^2-ADR, surpasses that of the baseline on almost all sub-tasks using ResNet-18 and ResNet-50, respectively. This verifies that our framework also improves the in-domain generalization.

Single-Source Domain Generalization. We further evaluate our framework on single-source DG tasks. Since the Inter-ADR is not suitable for single-source DG tasks, we only report the results of Intra-ADR. Results are reported as the average accuracy among single source-target pairs. As shown in Table 11, the performance of Intra-ADR is among the top ones. This indicates that the Intra-ADR can handle both the multiple-source and single-source DG tasks, and demonstrate that diverse features effectively can avoid shortcut learning.

Orthogonality to Other DG Methods. Our method can also boost the performance of other DG methods. As shown in Table 1-4, a new SOTA performance is achieved by combining our framework with MixStyle [78] and is superior to other competing DG works by a significant margin.

Table 11. Performance comparison on single-source DG. We train our methods with a single source domain and evaluate with other remaining target domains.

	Target domain																			
Source domain	**Baseline**					**RSC** [21] (ECCV'20)					**SelfReg** [24] (ICCV'21)					**Intra-ADR** (Ours)				
	A	C	P	S	Avg.	A	C	P	S	Avg.	A	C	P	S	Avg.	A	C	P	S	Avg.
A	-	61.3	96.1	52.3	69.9	-	62.5	96.3	53.2	70.7	-	65.2	96.6	55.9	<u>72.6</u>	-	64.8	94.4	64.3	**74.5**
C	64.1	-	81.8	75.8	73.9	69.0	-	85.9	70.4	<u>75.1</u>	72.1	-	87.5	70.1	**76.6**	66.7	-	83.8	74.9	<u>75.1</u>
P	66.1	29.5	-	32.3	41.6	66.3	26.5	-	32.1	41.6	67.7	29.0	-	33.7	<u>43.5</u>	67.8	40.3	-	39.5	**49.2**
S	38.6	60.5	48.0	-	<u>48.3</u>	38.0	56.4	47.4	-	47.3	37.2	54.0	46.1	-	45.8	42.7	61.5	46.6	-	**50.3**
Avg.	56.2	<u>50.4</u>	74.6	<u>53.4</u>	58.6	57.8	48.5	<u>76.5</u>	51.9	58.7	<u>59.0</u>	47.4	**76.7**	53.3	<u>59.6</u>	**59.1**	**55.5**	74.9	**59.6**	**62.3**

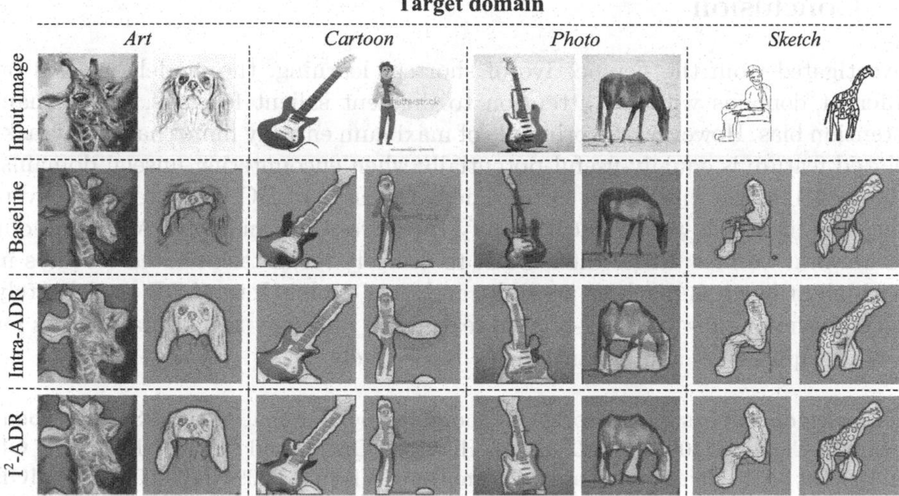

Fig. 3. Attention visualization on the testing domains of PACS with ResNet-18.

Attention Visualization. We visualize the attention maps to verify our motivation and the effectiveness of our framework. The attention maps on samples from testing split of the 4 domains in PACS are shown in Fig. 3. The hotter colors denote the more salient attention value, while the cooler colors represent the lower value. To compare the differences of attention regions between the baseline and our framework more clearly, we retain the top normalized attention values (>= 0.7). We can see that the proposed Intra-ADR *de-facto* pays sufficient attention to diverse spatial locations, including the task-related regions and some domain-related features. Fortunately, Inter-ADR can suppress the domain-related regions and enhance the task-related regions.

Limitations. As shown in the last row of Fig. 3, there still exist some risks to maintain/enhance domain-related features in some cases. Although Inter-ADR is utilized to suppress domain-related features brought by baseline and Intra-ADR, which exploits the prediction to determine task- and domain-related features, the domain-related features will be maintained/enhanced once the corresponding cross-domain prediction is consistent with the ground-truth. Nevertheless, the proposed Intra-ADR and Inter-ADR boost the DG performance on average. The existing limitations are left as the future works.

5 Conclusion

Investigated from the perspective of shortcut learning, the models trained on different domains will pay attention to different salient features, aka domain attention bias. However, the principle of maximum entropy hints that every task-related feature is equally-useful potentially when encountering unseen domains. This novel insight enlightens us to remedy the issue of DG via Attention Diversification, in which we organically unify the Intra-ADR and Inter-ADR into our framework: we first utilize Intra-ADR to coarsely recall task-related features in the highest layer as much as possible, and then exploit Inter-ADR to delicately distinguish domain- and task-related features in multiple intermediate layers for further suppression and enhancement, respectively.

Acknowledgements. This work was sponsored by National Natural Science Foundation of China (62106220, U20B2066), Hikvision Open Fund (CCF-HIKVISION OF 20210002), NUS Faculty Research Committee (WBS: A-0009440-00-00), and MOE Academic Research Fund (AcRF) Tier-1 FRC Research Grant of Singapore (WBS: A-0009456-00-00).

References

1. Balaji, Y., Sankaranarayanan, S., Chellappa, R.: MetaReg: towards domain generalization using meta-regularization. In: NeurIPS (2018)
2. Ben-David, S., Blitzer, J., Crammer, K., Pereira, F.: Analysis of representations for domain adaptation. In: NIPS (2007)
3. Ben-David, S., Blitzer, J., Crammer, K., Kulesza, A., Pereira, F., Vaughan, J.W.: A theory of learning from different domains. Mach. Learn. **79**(1), 151–175 (2010)
4. Carlucci, F.M., D'Innocente, A., Bucci, S., Caputo, B., Tommasi, T.: Domain generalization by solving jigsaw puzzles. In: CVPR (2019)
5. Chattopadhyay, P., Balaji, Y., Hoffman, J.: Learning to balance specificity and invariance for in and out of domain generalization. In: ECCV (2020)
6. Chen, B., et al.: Label matching semi-supervised object detection. In: Proceedings of the IEEE/CVF Conference on Computer Vision and Pattern Recognition, pp. 14381–14390 (2022)
7. Chen, M., Chen, W., Yang, S., Song, J., Wang, X., Zhang, L., Yan, Y., Qi, D., Zhuang, Y., Xie, D., et al.: Learning domain adaptive object detection with probabilistic teacher. In: ICML (2022)
8. Chen, W., et al.: Self-supervised noisy label learning for source-free unsupervised domain adaptation. arXiv preprint arXiv:2102.11614 (2021)
9. Chen, W., Xie, D., Zhang, Y., Pu, S.: All you need is a few shifts: designing efficient convolutional neural networks for image classification. In: Proceedings of the IEEE/CVF Conference on Computer Vision and Pattern Recognition, pp. 7241–7250 (2019)
10. Chen, W., Zhang, Y., Xie, D., Pu, S.: A layer decomposition-recomposition framework for neuron pruning towards accurate lightweight networks. In: Proceedings of the AAAI Conference on Artificial Intelligence, vol. 33, pp. 3355–3362 (2019)
11. Deng, J., Dong, W., Socher, R., Li, L.J., Li, K., Fei-Fei, L.: ImageNet: a large-scale hierarchical image database. In: CVPR (2009)

12. Dou, Q., Castro, D.C., Kamnitsas, K., Glocker, B.: Domain generalization via model-agnostic learning of semantic features. In: NeurIPS (2019)
13. Fu, J., et al.: Dual attention network for scene segmentation. In: 2019 IEEE/CVF Conference on Computer Vision and Pattern Recognition (CVPR) (2020)
14. Gao, Y., Han, X., Wang, X., Huang, W., Scott, M.: Channel interaction networks for fine-grained image categorization. In: Proceedings of the AAAI Conference on Artificial Intelligence, vol. 34, pp. 10818–10825 (2020)
15. Geirhos, R., et al.: Shortcut learning in deep neural networks. Nat. Mach. Intell. **2**, 665–673 (2020)
16. Gong, K., et al.: PoseTriplet: co-evolving 3D human pose estimation, imitation, and hallucination under self-supervision. In: Proceedings of the IEEE/CVF Conference on Computer Vision and Pattern Recognition (2022)
17. Goodfellow, I., Warde-Farley, D., Mirza, M., Courville, A., Bengio, Y.: Maxout networks. In: ICML (2013)
18. Guiasu, S., Shenitzer, A.: The principle of maximum entropy. Math. Intell. **7**(1), 42–48 (1985). https://doi.org/10.1007/BF03023004
19. He, K., Zhang, X., Ren, S., Sun, J.: Deep residual learning for image recognition. In: CVPR (2016)
20. Hu, H., Gu, J., Zhang, Z., Dai, J., Wei, Y.: Relation networks for object detection. In: Proceedings of the IEEE Conference on Computer Vision and Pattern Recognition, pp. 3588–3597 (2018)
21. Huang, Z., Wang, H., Xing, E.P., Huang, D.: Self-challenging improves cross-domain generalization. In: ECCV (2020)
22. Jia, Y., Zhang, J., Shan, S., Chen, X.: Single-side domain generalization for face anti-spoofing. In: CVPR (2020)
23. Jing, Y., et al.: Dynamic instance normalization for arbitrary style transfer. In: AAAI (2020)
24. Kim, D., Yoo, Y., Park, S., Kim, J., Lee, J.: SelfReg: self-supervised contrastive regularization for domain generalization. In: Proceedings of the IEEE/CVF International Conference on Computer Vision (ICCV), pp. 9619–9628, October 2021
25. Li, B., Wu, F., Lim, S., Belongie, S., Weinberger, K.Q.: On feature normalization and data augmentation. In: CVPR (2021)
26. Li, D., Zhang, J., Yang, Y., Liu, C., Song, Y., Hospedales, T.M.: Episodic training for domain generalization. In: ICCV (2019)
27. Li, D., Yang, Y., Song, Y.Z., Hospedales, T.M.: Deeper, broader and artier domain generalization. In: Proceedings of the IEEE International Conference on Computer Vision, pp. 5542–5550 (2017)
28. Li, D., Yang, Y., Song, Y.Z., Hospedales, T.M.: Learning to generalize: meta-learning for domain generalization. In: Thirty-Second AAAI Conference on Artificial Intelligence (2018)
29. Li, X., et al.: A free lunch for unsupervised domain adaptive object detection without source data. In: Proceedings of the AAAI Conference on Artificial Intelligence, vol. 35, pp. 8474–8481 (2021)
30. Li, X., Dai, Y., Ge, Y., Liu, J., Shan, Y., Duan, L.: uncertainty modeling for out-of-distribution generalization. In: International Conference on Learning Representations (2022)
31. Li, Y., et al.: Deep domain generalization via conditional invariant adversarial networks. In: ECCV (2018)
32. Li, Z., Zhao, L., Chen, W., Yang, S., Xie, D., Pu, S.: Target-aware auto-augmentation for unsupervised domain adaptive object detection. In: ICASSP

2022–2022 IEEE International Conference on Acoustics, Speech and Signal Processing (ICASSP), pp. 3848–3852. IEEE (2022)
33. Lin, L., Liang, L., Jin, L., Chen, W.: Attribute-aware convolutional neural networks for facial beauty prediction. In: IJCAI, pp. 847–853 (2019)
34. Lin, L., et al.: Semi-supervised domain generalization in real world: New benchmark and strong baseline. arXiv preprint arXiv:2111.10221 (2021)
35. Liu, H., Yang, Y., Wang, X.: Overcoming catastrophic forgetting in graph neural networks. In: AAAI Conference on Artificial Intelligence (2021)
36. Long, M., Cao, Y., Wang, J., Jordan, M.: Learning transferable features with deep adaptation networks. In: ICML, pp. 97–105 (2015)
37. Matthew Zeiler, D., Rob, F.: Visualizing and understanding convolutional neural networks. In: ECCV (2014)
38. Meng, R., Chen, W., Xie, D., Zhang, Y., Pu, S.: Neural inheritance relation guided one-shot layer assignment search. In: Proceedings of the AAAI Conference on Artificial Intelligence, vol. 34, pp. 5158–5165 (2020)
39. Meng, R., et al.: Slimmable domain adaptation. In: Proceedings of the IEEE/CVF Conference on Computer Vision and Pattern Recognition, pp. 7141–7150 (2022)
40. Moon, S., Carbonell, J.G.: Completely heterogeneous transfer learning with attention - what and wahr not to transfer. In: IJCAI (2017)
41. Muandet, K., Balduzzi, D., Schölkopf, B.: Domain generalization via invariant feature representation. In: International Conference on Machine Learning, pp. 10–18. PMLR (2013)
42. Nam, H., Lee, H., Park, J., Yoon, W., Yoo, D.: Reducing domain gap by reducing style bias. In: CVPR (2021)
43. Pan, X., Luo, P., Shi, J., Tang, X.: Two at once: enhancing learning and generalization capacities via ibn-net. In: ECCV (2018)
44. Peng, X., Bai, Q., Xia, X., Huang, Z., Saenko, K., Wang, B.: Moment matching for multi-source domain adaptation. In: ICCV (2019)
45. Peng, X., Saenko, K.: Synthetic to real adaptation with generaitve correlation alignment networks. In: WACV (2018)
46. Prakash, A., et al.: Structured domain randomization: bridging the reality gap by context-aware synthetic data. In: ICRA (2019)
47. Rahman, M.M., Fookes, C., Baktashmotlagh, M., Sridharan, S.: Correlation-aware adversarial domain adaptation and generalization. Pattern Recogn. **100** (2020)
48. Ren, S., Zhou, D., He, S., Feng, J., Wang, X.: Shunted self-attention via multi-scale token aggregation. In: Proceedings of the IEEE/CVF Conference on Computer Vision and Pattern Recognition (2022)
49. Saito, K., Watanabe, K., Ushiku, Y., Harada, T.: Maximum classifier discrepancy for unsupervised domain adaptation. In: CVPR, pp. 3723–3732 (2018)
50. Shu, Y., Cao, Z., Wang, C., Wang, J., Long, M.: Open domain generalization with domain-augmented meta-learning. In: Proceedings of the IEEE/CVF Conference on Computer Vision and Pattern Recognition, pp. 9624–9633 (2021)
51. Sicilia, A., Zhao, X., Hwang, S.J.: Domain adversarial neural networks for domain generalization: When it works and how to improve. arXiv:2102.03924 (2021)
52. Song, J., et al.: Selective zero-shot classification with augmented attributes. In: Proceedings of the European Conference on Computer Vision (ECCV), pp. 468–483 (2018)
53. Sun, M., Yuan, Y., Zhou, F., Ding, E.: Multi-attention multi-class constraint for fine-grained image recognition. In: Ferrari, V., Hebert, M., Sminchisescu, C., Weiss, Y. (eds.) ECCV 2018. LNCS, vol. 11220, pp. 834–850. Springer, Cham (2018). https://doi.org/10.1007/978-3-030-01270-0_49

54. Sun, Z., et al.: Dynamic domain generalization. In: IJCAI (2022)
55. Tishby, N., Zaslavsky, N.: Deep learning and the information bottleneck principle. In: 2015 IEEE Information Theory Workshop (ITW), pp. 1–5. IEEE (2015)
56. Tobin, J., Fong, R., Ray, A., Schneider, J., Zaremba, W., Abbeel, P.: Domain randomization for transferring deep neural networks from simulation to the real world. In: IROS (2017)
57. Torralba, A., Efros, A.A.: Unbiased look at dataset bias. In: CVPR 2011, pp. 1521–1528. IEEE (2011)
58. Tzeng, E., Hoffman, J., Zhang, N., Saenko, K., Darrell, T.: Deep domain confusion: maximizing for domain invariance. arXiv:1412.3474 (2014)
59. Vaswani, A., et al.: Attention is all you need. In: NIPS (2017)
60. Venkateswara, H., Eusebio, J., Chakraborty, S., Panchanathan, S.: Deep hashing network for unsupervised domain adaptation. In: CVPR (2017)
61. Wang, F., et al.: Residual attention network for image classification. In: CVPR (2017)
62. Wang, M., et al.: InterBN: channel fusion for adversarial unsupervised domain adaptation. In: Proceedings of the 29th ACM International Conference on Multimedia, pp. 3691–3700 (2021)
63. Wang, X., Li, L., Ye, W., Long, M., Wang, J.: Transferable attention for domain adaptation. In: AAAI (2019)
64. Wang, X., Girshick, R., Gupta, A., He, K.: Non-local neural networks. In: Proceedings of the IEEE Conference on Computer Vision and Pattern Recognition, pp. 7794–7803 (2018)
65. Xu, Q., Zhang, R., Zhang, Y., Wang, Y., Tian, Q.: A Fourier-based framework for domain generalization. In: Proceedings of the IEEE/CVF Conference on Computer Vision and Pattern Recognition, pp. 14383–14392 (2021)
66. Xue, Y., et al.: Point2seq: detecting 3D objects as sequences. In: Proceedings of the IEEE/CVF Conference on Computer Vision and Pattern Recognition (2022)
67. Yang, X., Ye, J., Wang, X.: Factorizing knowledge in neural networks. In: European Conference on Computer Vision (2022)
68. Yang, Y., Feng, Z., Song, M., Wang, X.: Factorizable graph convolutional networks. In: Conference on Neural Information Processing Systems (2020)
69. Yang, Y., Qiu, J., Song, M., Tao, D., Wang, X.: Distilling knowledge from graph convolutional networks. In: Proceedings of the IEEE/CVF Conference on Computer Vision and Pattern Recognition (2020)
70. Yang, Y., Qiu, J., Song, M., Tao, D., Wang, X.: Learning propagation rules for attribution map generation. In: European Conference on Computer Vision (2020)
71. Yu, W., et al..: Metaformer is actually what you need for vision. In: Proceedings of the IEEE/CVF Conference on Computer Vision and Pattern Recognition (2022)
72. Yuan, P., et al.: Simulation-and-mining: towards accurate source-free unsupervised domain adaptive object detection. In: ICASSP 2022–2022 IEEE International Conference on Acoustics, Speech and Signal Processing (ICASSP), pp. 3843–3847. IEEE (2022)
73. Zhao, Y., Zhong, Z., Luo, Z., Lee, G.H., Sebe, N.: Source-free open compound domain adaptation in semantic segmentation. IEEE Trans. Circ. Syst. Video Technol. **32**, 7019–7032 (2022)
74. Zhao, Y., et al.: Learning to generalize unseen domains via memory-based multi-source meta-learning for person re-identification. In: Proceedings of IEEE Conference on Computer Vision and Pattern Recognition (CVPR) (2021)

75. Zhao, Y., Zhong, Z., Zhao, N., Sebe, N., Lee, G.H.: Style-hallucinated dual consistency learning for domain generalized semantic segmentation. In: Proceedings of the European Conference on Computer Vision (ECCV) (2022)
76. Zheng, H., Fu, J., Zha, Z.J., Luo, J.: Looking for the devil in the details: Learning trilinear attention sampling network for fine-grained image recognition. In: 2019 IEEE/CVF Conference on Computer Vision and Pattern Recognition (CVPR) (2019)
77. Zhou, B., Khosla, A., Lapedriza, A., Oliva, A., Torralba, A.: Learning deep features for discriminative localization. In: CVPR (2016)
78. Zhou, K., Yang, Y., Qiao, Y., Xiang, T.: Domain generalization with mixstyle. In: ICLR (2021)
79. Zhou, Q., Zhang, K.Y., Yao, T., Yi, R., Ding, S., Ma, L.: Adaptive mixture of experts learning for generalizable face anti-spoofing. In: Proceedings of the 30th ACM International Conference on Multimedia (2022)
80. Liu, Y., Stehouwer, J., Liu, X.: On disentangling spoof trace for generic face anti-spoofing. In: Vedaldi, A., Bischof, H., Brox, T., Frahm, J.-M. (eds.) ECCV 2020. LNCS, vol. 12363, pp. 406–422. Springer, Cham (2020). https://doi.org/10.1007/978-3-030-58523-5_24

ESS: Learning Event-Based Semantic Segmentation from Still Images

Zhaoning Sun[1,2], Nico Messikommer[1,2(✉)], Daniel Gehrig[1,2], and Davide Scaramuzza[1,2]

[1] Department of Informatics, University of Zurich, Zurich, Switzerland
[2] Department of Neuroinformatics, University of Zurich and ETH Zurich, Zurich, Switzerland
zhasun@student.ethz.ch, {nmessi,dgehrig,sdavide}@ifi.uzh.ch

Abstract. Retrieving accurate semantic information in challenging high dynamic range (HDR) and high-speed conditions remains an open challenge for image-based algorithms due to severe image degradations. Event cameras promise to address these challenges since they feature a much higher dynamic range and are resilient to motion blur. Nonetheless, semantic segmentation with event cameras is still in its infancy which is chiefly due to the lack of high-quality, labeled datasets. In this work, we introduce ESS (Event-based Semantic Segmentation), which tackles this problem by directly transferring the semantic segmentation task from existing labeled image datasets to unlabeled events via unsupervised domain adaptation (UDA). Compared to existing UDA methods, our approach aligns recurrent, motion-invariant event embeddings with image embeddings. For this reason, our method neither requires video data nor per-pixel alignment between images and events and, crucially, does not need to hallucinate motion from still images. Additionally, we introduce DSEC-Semantic, the first large-scale event-based dataset with fine-grained labels. We show that using image labels alone, ESS outperforms existing UDA approaches, and when combined with event labels, it even outperforms state-of-the-art supervised approaches on both DDD17 and DSEC-Semantic. Finally, ESS is general-purpose, which unlocks the vast amount of existing labeled image datasets and paves the way for new and exciting research directions in new fields previously inaccessible for event cameras.

Keywords: Transfer learning · Low-level vision · Segmentation

Multimedia Material. The code is available at https://github.com/uzh-rpg/ess, dataset at https://dsec.ifi.uzh.ch/dsec-semantic/ and video at https://youtu.be/Tby5c9IDsDc.

Z. Sun and N. Messikommer—Equal contribution.

Supplementary Information The online version contains supplementary material available at https://doi.org/10.1007/978-3-031-19830-4_20.

S. Avidan et al. (Eds.): ECCV 2022, LNCS 13694, pp. 341–357, 2022.
https://doi.org/10.1007/978-3-031-19830-4_20

1 Introduction

In recent years, event cameras have become attractive sensors in a wide range of applications, spanning both computer vision and robotics. In particular, thanks to their high dynamic range, microsecond-level latency, and resilience to motion blur, algorithms leveraging event data have made various breakthroughs in fields such as Simultaneous Localization and Mapping (SLAM) [23,29], computational photography [21,25] and high-speed obstacle avoidance [8]. Recently, event cameras have been increasingly applied in automotive settings [17,19,20], where they promise to solve computer vision tasks in challenging edge-case scenarios, such as when exiting a tunnel into bright sunlight [13,21] or when children unexpectedly jump in front of a car.

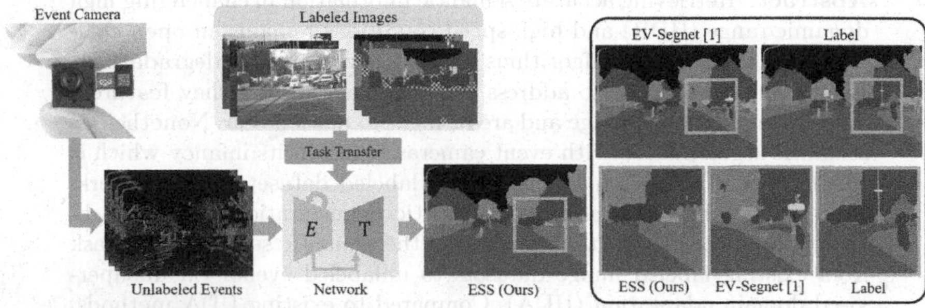

Fig. 1. In this work, we present ESS, a method for fine-grained event-based semantic segmentation. Due to the novelty of the sensor, only few datasets for event cameras are available. For this reason, we leverage existing image-based datasets for training neural networks for events using a novel UDA approach. Compared to existing methods, our approach does not require video or paired data and does not need to hallucinate motion to construct events. Our method can detect fine-grained objects, such as cars and pedestrians, outperforming state-of-the-art methods in UDA and supervised settings, on a common benchmark and our newly created benchmark with high-quality labels (right).

For the latter, extracting detailed and dense semantic information is essential for any automotive safety system. In particular, event-based semantic segmentation promises to significantly improve the reliability and safety of these systems by leveraging the robustness to lighting conditions and the low latency of event cameras. However, due to the novelty of the sensor, event-based semantic segmentation is still in its infancy, resulting in a lack of high-quality event-based semantic segmentation datasets. While some datasets exist [1,12], these are either synthetic or feature pseudo labels, which are produced by an image-based network running on low-quality grayscale images. As a result, methods trained on these datasets typically exhibit suboptimal performance [1,28].

In this work, we make significant strides toward high-quality event-based semantic segmentation by addressing the above limitation on two fronts: First, we generate a new event-based semantic segmentation dataset, named DSEC-Semantic, based on the stereo event camera dataset for driving scenarios (DSEC) [13]. The labels are generated via pseudo-labeling on high-quality RGB images and filtered by manual inspection. Second, we introduce ESS, a novel unsupervised domain adaptation (UDA) method specifically tailored to event data, which transfers a task from a labeled image dataset to an unlabeled event domain, see Fig. 1. Compared to other methods, it does not require video data [10] or per-pixel paired events and images [14,28] and does not need to hallucinate motion-imbued events from still images [18]. In fact, generating events from single images remains an ill-posed problem that so far has only been studied via adversarial learning, which is prone to mode collapse. Instead, our method produces a recurrent, motion-invariant event embedding, which is aligned with image embeddings during the training process, facilitating the transfer between domains.

We perform extensive evaluation both on the existing DDD17 [1,3] benchmark and our new DSEC-Semantic benchmark. On DDD17, we report a 6.98% higher mean intersection over union (mIoU) compared to other UDA methods, and when using additional event labels, ESS outperforms supervised methods by 2.57%. On DSEC-Semantic, we show a 4.17% higher mIoU when compared to other UDA approaches. Additionally, when combined with supervised learning, our method achieves 1.53% higher mIoU than other state-of-the-art supervised methods. Our contributions can be summarized as follows:

1. We present a UDA method that leverages image datasets to train neural networks for event data. It does this by directly aligning recurrent, motion-invariant event embeddings with image embedding without requiring paired data, video, or explicit event generation.
2. We show that our method outperforms existing state-of-the-art UDA and supervised methods both on an existing and our newly introduced benchmark.
3. We contribute a new high-quality dataset for event-based semantic segmentation, based on high-quality RGB frames from the large-scale DSEC dataset.

Finally, since ESS is general-purpose, it unlocks the virtually unlimited supply of existing image datasets, thereby democratizing them for event camera research. These datasets will pave the way for new and exciting research directions in new fields which were previously inaccessible for event cameras.

2 Related Work

2.1 Event-Based Semantic Segmentation

The first work to use events for the task of semantic segmentation was [1], which also introduced the first event-based semantic segmentation dataset based on the driving dataset DDD17 [3]. It used an Xception-type network [5] to show robust performance in edge-case scenarios, where standard images are overexposed. The semantic labels (also known as pseudo-labels) on DDD17 were generated by a pre-trained network running on the grayscale frames of the DAVIS346B [4]. This sensor features per-pixel aligned events and frames and has been useful for a variety of domain adaptation works. However, it has a low resolution and poor image quality, which results in significant artifacts in the resulting pseudo labels. Additionally, due to the low resolution of the DAVIS346B, multiple classes need to be merged, reducing the granularity of the labels. In parallel, the simulated EventScape dataset [13,15] includes high-quality semantic labels but was recorded in the CARLA simulator [7], and thus exhibits a sim-to-real gap.

Follow-up work by [10] improved on the results of [1] by leveraging additional labeled video datasets for events by augmenting training data with synthetic events converted from video. While this method allows networks to be trained on synthetic and real events resulting in a significant performance boost, it requires the availability of video datasets, which are not as common as datasets containing still images and are especially rare for semantic segmentation. For this reason, [28] combines labeled image datasets such as Cityscape [6] with unlabeled events and frames from a DAVIS to decrease the dependence on video data. In fact, they report an increase in the semantic segmentation performance but still rely on per-pixel paired data from a DAVIS for successful transfer. Another supervised semantic segmentation method [27] leverages the event-to-image transfer to help with the task of semantic segmentation. However, they rely on a labeled event dataset and do not consider recurrent event embeddings. Our method also leverages UDA for event-based semantic segmentation but differs from existing work in a few key points: *(i)* it only leverages datasets of still images, *(ii)* does not require per-pixel paired events and frames, and *(iii)* uses a recurrent network to generate motion-invariant event embeddings. Since UDA methods have become instrumental for event-based semantic segmentation, we review them next.

2.2 Unsupervised Domain Adaptation

A common challenge for novel sensors such as event cameras is the lack of labeled datasets. To tackle this challenge, multiple works try to leverage labeled images to train networks for event cameras. This transfer from a labeled source domain (images) to an unlabeled target domain (events) is generally defined as Unsupervised Domain Adaption (UDA).

Event-to-image reconstruction methods [2,21,22] were the first to address this setting. Most recently, E2VID [21] uses a recurrent network to convert events to video, which can then be processed with standard image-based networks. It, however, requires the overhead of converting events first to images and does not leverage unlabeled target events to help the task transfer from images to events. Instead of going from events to frames, VID2E converts labeled video sequences to event sequences. The synthetic events can then be used to train a network on the corresponding image labels, which transfers to real events. While this reduces the overhead of needing to convert events to video, it still cannot adapt to an unlabeled event domain. Moreover, it requires labeled video datasets, which excludes the majority of existing image datasets.

One of the first approaches to do explicit domain adaptation was network grafting [14], which replaces the encoder of a pre-trained image network with an event encoder, and finetuning it with paired events and images. However, it needs to be trained with a consistency loss, which requires paired event and image

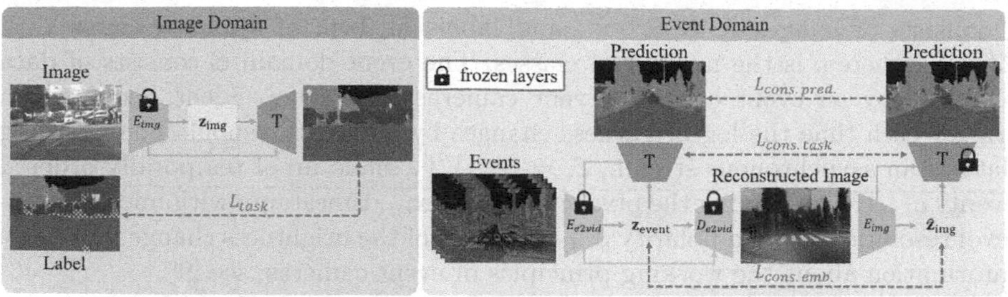

Fig. 2. Our method ESS, performs unsupervised domain adaptation by leveraging labeled image datasets (source domain, left) to train networks for event cameras in an unlabeled target domain (right). In the source domain, it performs supervised learning on the task network while not training the image encoder. In the event-domain, it uses the recurrent E2VID encoder to produce motion-invariant event embeddings, which are decoded and reencoded using the image encoder. Various consistency losses align these embeddings, forcing the image encoder to behave similarly to the event encoder. In this stage, both task and image encoder is trained. At test-time ESS simply uses the E2VID encoder and task decoder for prediction, and thus remains lightweight.

data, and is thus not be applicable in the UDA setting. Moreover, this constraint limits the kind of datasets that can be leveraged to those recorded with per-pixel aligned events and frames, which excludes most existing image datasets. EvDistill [28] lifted this limitation by instead leveraging unpaired events and images, with unlabeled events and labeled images. While this approach could transfer from unpaired Cityscapes labels to events from DDD17, they only report the segmentation performance based on paired images and events. Strictly speaking, this can thus not be considered as a UDA method. Instead, a pure UDA method for image-to-event transfer is [18], which splits the embedding space into motion-specific features and features shared by both image and events. They use adversarial learning to align image and event embedding spaces for the task of classification and object detection. However, this approach relies on generating fake events, which requires the hallucination of motion from still images. This hallucination is ill-posed and thus hinders the feature alignment, which is crucial for a successful task transfer from images to events. Our method, ESS, addresses these limitations by transferring from single images to events without the need for hallucinating motion. This task transfer is achieved by generating motion-invariant event embeddings, leveraging the pre-trained E2VID [21] encoder which are then aligned with the embedding space of single images via a dedicated image encoder. Since the resulting event embeddings do not contain motion information, they can be easily aligned in the embedding space, facilitating task transfer.

3 Approach

Our method transfers a task from a labeled source domain $\mathbb{I} = \{(I_i, \mathcal{L}_i)\}_{i=1}^{M}$ to an unlabeled target domain $\mathbb{E} = \{\mathcal{E}_i\}_{i=1}^{N}$. More specifically, the source domain

$\mathbb{I}$ consists of images $I_i \in \mathbb{R}^{H\times W}$ and labels in form of semantic maps $\mathcal{L} \in \mathbb{Z}_c^{H\times W}$, where c is the number of classes. The event domain $\mathbb{E}$ consists of data recorded by an event camera. Event cameras have independent pixels which trigger each time the log brightness changes by a fixed threshold. The resulting data is an asynchronous stream, $\mathcal{E}_i = \{e_{i,j}\}_{j=1}^{n_i}$ made up of temporally ordered events $e_{i,j}$, each encoding the pixel coordinate $\mathbf{x}_{i,j}$, timestamp with microsecond-level resolution $t_{i,j}$ and polarity $p_{i,j} \in \{-1, 1\}$ of the brightness change. For more information about the working principles of event cameras, see [9].

The goal of our approach is to train a neural network F which takes event sequences[1] $\mathcal{E}$ as input and outputs the task variable in form of pixel-wise semantic predictions $\mathcal{L}$. At training time, it only has access to image labels from the source domain $\mathbb{I}$, but can leverage unlabeled events from the target domain $\mathbb{E}$.

An overview of our method is shown in Fig. 2. Our method works by first encoding events into a motion-invariant embedding $\mathbf{z}_{\text{event}}$ using the E2VID [21] encoder E_{E2VID} and decoding these to an image reconstruction using the decoder D_{E2VID}. This event embedding preserves sufficient semantic information for the segmentation task but excludes motion information since it is used to reconstruct motion-invariant still images. The image reconstruction and events then formulate a pseudo pair in the source and target domain, which can be leveraged to align the embedding space. Consequently, we use an image encoder E_{img} to approximate the motion-invariant embedding. Finally, a shared task network T generates task predictions from image and event embeddings.

3.1 Network Overview

In a first step, we convert an event stream $\mathcal{E}$ to a sequence of grid-like representations [11], such as *voxel grids* [30] $\mathbf{V}_k$. Each voxel grid is constructed from non-overlapping windows with a fixed number of events, see supplementary for more details. Next, we produce a recurrent, multi-scale embedding $\mathbf{z}_{\text{event}}$, with

$$\mathbf{z}_{\text{event}}^k = E_{\text{E2VID}}(\mathbf{V}_k, \mathbf{z}_{\text{event}}^{k-1}), \quad k = 1, ..., N, \tag{1}$$

and $\mathbf{z}_{\text{event}} = \mathbf{z}_{\text{event}}^N$. Simultaneously, we train an image encoder E_{img} which produces image embeddings $\mathbf{z}_{\text{img}} = E_{\text{img}}(I)$. These embeddings are used in three branches of the training framework, see Fig. 2. First, we use the image and event embeddings to produce a task prediction via a task network T

$$\mathcal{L}_{\text{img}} = T(\mathbf{z}_{\text{img}}) \quad \text{and} \quad \mathcal{L}_{\text{event}} = T(\mathbf{z}_{\text{event}}), \tag{2}$$

with $\mathcal{L}_{\text{img/event}} \in \mathbb{R}^{H\times W\times c}$. Second, we also use the event embedding to generate an image reconstruction via the decoder D_{E2VID}, as $\hat{I} = D_{\text{E2VID}}(\mathbf{z}_{\text{event}})$, which results in a pseudo pair $(\hat{I}, \mathcal{E})$ in the source and target domain. Finally, E_{img} reencodes the resulting image and produces a task prediction

$$\hat{\mathbf{z}}_{\text{img}} = G\left(D_{\text{E2VID}}(\mathbf{z}_{\text{event}})\right) \quad \text{and} \quad \hat{\mathcal{L}}_{\text{img}} = T(\hat{\mathbf{z}}_{\text{img}}). \tag{3}$$

[1] For clarity, we omit the subscript i in the future.

Details of $D_{\text{E2VID}}, E_{\text{E2VID}}, E_{\text{img}}$ and T are given in the supplementary. In the following, we explain how the alignment of the motion-invariant embeddings is enforced by multiple consistency losses. This alignment is crucial since it ensures that the task decoder T can be applied in the event and image domain.

3.2 Aligning Motion-Invariant Embedding

With pseudo pairs $(\hat{I}, \mathcal{E})$ in the source and target domain, our method leverages several **consistency losses** to align the motion-invariant embeddings. Inspired by prior works [18,28], we enforce an alignment between event embeddings and reencoded event embeddings via an L_1 distance and between task predictions via the symmetric Jensen-Shannon divergence

$$L_{\text{cons. emb.}} = \|\mathbf{z}_{\text{event}} - \hat{\mathbf{z}}_{\text{img}}\|_1 \tag{4}$$

$$L_{\text{cons. pred.}} = \frac{1}{2} D_{\text{KL}}(T(\mathbf{z}_{\text{event}}) \| T(\hat{\mathbf{z}}_{\text{img}})) + \frac{1}{2} D_{\text{KL}}(T(\hat{\mathbf{z}}_{\text{img}}) \| T(\mathbf{z}_{\text{event}})). \tag{5}$$

Furthermore, we tighten the alignment by minimizing the L_1 distance between intermediate features $T^{(i)}(\mathbf{z}_{\text{event}})$ and $T^{(i)}(\hat{\mathbf{z}}_{\text{img}})$ produced while decoding the embeddings $\mathbf{z}_{\text{event}}$ and $\hat{\mathbf{z}}_{\text{img}}$ resulting in the following loss

$$L_{\text{cons. task}} = \sum_i \left\| T^{(i)}(\hat{\mathbf{z}}_{\text{img}}) - T^{(i)}(\mathbf{z}_{\text{event}}) \right\|_1. \tag{6}$$

3.3 Losses and Optimization

At each training step, we additionally compute the task loss in form of the cross-entropy and Dice loss in the image domain by leveraging the available labels $\mathcal{L}$,

$$L_{\text{task}} = \text{CrossEntropy}(T(\mathbf{z}_{\text{img}}), \mathcal{L}) + \text{Dice}(T(\mathbf{z}_{\text{img}}), \mathcal{L}). \tag{7}$$

Finally, we sum up the task loss and the consistency losses

$$L_{\text{total}} = \lambda_1 L_{\text{task}} + \lambda_2 L_{\text{cons. emb.}} + \lambda_3 L_{\text{cons. pred.}} + \lambda_4 L_{\text{cons. task}}, \tag{8}$$

where λ_1, λ_2, λ_3, and λ_4 are the hyper-parameters.

Optimization. We perform a two-stage network gradient accumulation for each optimization step, shown in Fig. 2. During the first stage (left), we use an image and label pair to compute the task loss, which we only use to update the network gradients of the task decoder T. During the second stage (right), we train on unlabeled events. Here, we freeze the E2VID encoder/decoder pair and the task network in the second branch (Fig. 2, top right). After computing the consistency losses, we accumulate the gradients for the image encoder E_{img} and the task decoder T in the first branch. We perform one parameter update step on the network after accumulating these gradients.

4 Experiments

We start off in Sect. 4.1, by validating our method on the commonly used DDD17 benchmark [1], where we compare against supervised [1,27], pixel-wise paired [28], and UDA methods [10,18,21]. We then introduce our newly generated DSEC-Semantic dataset in Sect. 4.2, which contains higher quality semantic labels, and report comparisons on this dataset. Finally, in Sect. 4.3 we perform ablation studies to verify the effectiveness of the proposed design choices. For more results, we refer to the supplementary.

Baseline Methods. We compare our task transfer method with the two state-of-the-art UDA approaches E2VID [21] and EV-Transfer [18]. For E2VID, we take the pre-trained network weights provided by the authors to convert events to grayscale images. We retrain a semantic segmentation network on labeled grayscale images from Cityscapes [6], which we then apply to the reconstructed images. E2VID is indeed a UDA method since it does not require a labeled event dataset nor paired image and event data. However, different from our method, it cannot be retrained for a specific target domain, performing zero-shot UDA.

In contrast, EV-Transfer [18] leverages unlabeled targets events for classification and object detection. To adapt the open-source implementation to semantic segmentation, we add the same task decoder as our method without skip connections. We report DDD17 results for EV-Distill [28] and DTL [27], but do not include them on DSEC-Semantic since open-source training code is not available, and they require paired images and events, which are not available on that dataset. Finally, we compare against the supervised methods VID2E [10] and EV-Segnet [1], which we retrain on DSEC-Semantic based on open-source code.

4.1 DDD17 for Semantic Segmentation

The DAVIS Driving Dataset (DDD17) for semantic segmentation targets automotive scenarios and contains 12 h of driving data recorded with a DAVIS [4], which provides per-pixel aligned and temporally synchronized events and grayscale frames. In [1], they used a pre-trained Xception network [5] to generate semantic pseudo-labels on the DAVIS frames. Since the DAVIS only features a low resolution, they fuse several classes and only provide labels for 6 merged classes: flat (road and pavement), background (construction and sky), object, vegetation, human, and vehicle. In this section, we will compare our method against related work in two settings: *(i)* in the UDA setting, where we only use unlabeled events, labeled frames and present them to the network in an unpaired fashion, and *(ii)* in a paired event and frame setting as well as in the supervised setting, where we introduce additional labels in the event-domain.

Implementation Details. We use Cityscapes [6] as the labeled source domain and DDD17 as the unlabeled target domain. The hyper-parameters λ_1, λ_2, λ_3, and λ_4 are set as 1, 0.01, 1, and 0.01, respectively. We set the learning rates as

Table 1. Performance of EV-Transfer, E2VID, VID2E, and our method on DDD17 in the UDA setting, in which the labels of Cityscapes and unlabeled events of DDD17 are available. Results report the mean and standard deviation of 3 runs with different random seeds except for the VID2E method which is taken from [10].

Method	Accuracy [%] ↑	mIoU [%] ↑
EV-Transfer [18]	47.37 ± 4.53	14.91 ± 0.61
E2VID [21]	83.24 ± 2.60	44.77 ± 3.70
VID2E [10]	85.93	45.48
ESS (ours)	$\mathbf{87.86 \pm 0.57}$	$\mathbf{52.46 \pm 0.63}$

Table 2. Results on DDD17 in the setting in which all of the available training data can be used. That includes real events with corresponding labels (events) and the possible combination with either synthetic events based on grayscale images of DDD17 (synthetic+events) or image labels (events+frames).

Method	Training data	Accuracy [%] ↑	mIoU [%] ↑
EVDistill [28]	Events	–	58.02
EV-SegNet [1]	Events	89.76	54.81
VID2E [10]	Synthetic+events	90.19	56.01
DTL [27]	Events	–	58.80
ESS (ours)	Events	**91.08**	**61.37**
ESS (ours)	Events+frames	90.37	60.43

1×10^{-5} for E_{img} and 1×10^{-4} for T. We empirically found that having a smaller learning rate on E_{img} and activating the accumulation of gradients for E_{img} in the first stage help improve the results. We train our model using the RAdam optimizer [16] with a batch-size of 16 for 50'000 iterations. Additionally, for the comparison with E2VID [21] in the UDA setting, we retrain the image encoder and task network (forming a U-Net) on grayscale images and labels from the Cityscapes dataset [6]. Similar to our method, we train [18] in our UDA setting with the same source and target domains. As commonly done, we report the accuracy as well as the mean intersection over union (mIoU) on the resulting segmentation maps, which better highlights the accuracy on smaller objects.

UDA Comparison. Table 1 shows that our method outperforms the runner-up VID2E by a large margin of 6.98% mIoU. VID2E converts DDD17 grayscale images to events and trains on the DDD17 labels. However, it suffers from a domain gap between synthetic and real events, which it cannot bridge using domain adaptation. Similarly, E2VID [21] cannot perform domain adaptation, which is why it achieves a lower performance. EV-Transfer [18] does domain adaptation but is still outperformed by our method. This is because we use a recurrent event encoder, which retains memory and can thus handle static scenes, which do not trigger events, leading to better predictions. Moreover, since our method aligns motion-invariant event embeddings, it does not rely on adversarial training and is therefore much simpler to train. Figure 3 shows qualitative results of the tested methods.

State-of-the-Art Comparison. Here, we show that, when combined with supervised learning, our method outperforms state-of-the-art methods. To do this, we add an additional task loss during training at the first task branch (Fig. 2, top right), which allows our method to simultaneously leverage image and event labels. We also compare against supervised methods DTL [27] and EV-Distill [26], which rely on the paired images and events provided by the DAVIS. We report results for two variations of our approach: The first is trained using only the recurrent encoder and task decoder, in a supervised setting using labeled events (Fig. 2, event domain, top left). The second combines supervised training on events with our full domain adaptation framework, including labeled

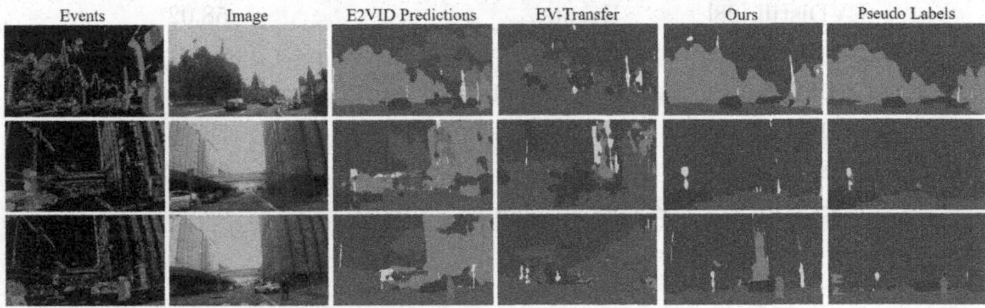

Fig. 3. Qualitative samples on DDD17 for the UDA setting, i.e., no event labels are available during training. Compared to EV-Transfer and E2VID, our method can more reliably predict smaller details such as people.

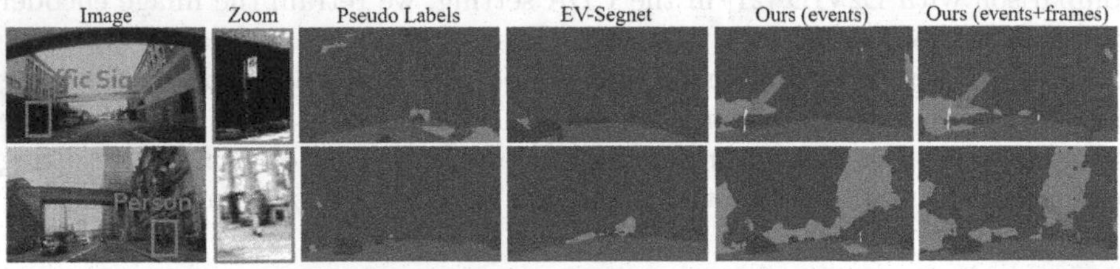

Fig. 4. Predictions of EV-Segnet and our method trained once purely with event labels (events) and once also with image labels (events+frames). Due to the low-quality of the DDD17 semantic labels, small objects are sometimes missed in the pseudo labels, (zoomed-in and brightened image patch in the red box). These objects are more reliable detected if our method is trained on the high-quality labels of Cityscapes. This can lead to a lower detection score on DDD17 even though the predictions of our method trained on events and frames provide more finegrained detections. (Color figure online)

images for improved performance. These methods are labeled with "events" and "events+frames" respectively in Table 2. As reported in Table 2, our method outperforms the runner-up DTL by 2.57% mIoU if trained in a supervised setting with events. DTL is a feed-forward network, which shows that our recurrent encoder boosts performance, especially in the near static scenes of DDD17. An additional advantage of our method compared to standard supervised methods is that it can leverage image labels in combination with event labels. From the Table 2, it can be observed that the additional image labels do not lead to a performance improvement. In fact, this can be explained by the fact that DDD17 semantic labels are not always accurate. In several examples (see Fig. 4), we found that our method predicted objects which were not present in the labels, but were clearly visible in the images and thus reduced the segmentation performance. Figure 4 shows that our method trained supervised on events and images sometimes provides more accurate predictions than the pseudo-labels from DDD17.

Fig. 5. We release a new semantic segmentation dataset for the DSEC [13] dataset. The pseudo labels are constructed based on the RGB images and a state-of-the-art frame-based segmentation network [24]. Compared to DDD17 [1,3] (left), our labels have a higher level of detail, seen in the zooms. Additionally, our dataset includes more classes (11 classes) compared to [1] (6 classes).

4.2 DSEC-Semantic

The semantic segmentation labels for DDD17 suffer from artifacts caused by the low-quality and low-resolution grayscale images, shown in Fig. 5. For this reason, we generate a new semantic segmentation dataset based on DSEC [13]. DSEC contains 53 driving sequences collected in a variety of urban and rural environments in Switzerland and was recorded with automotive-grade standard cameras and high-resolution event cameras. We use the pseudo labeling scheme adopted in [1] with the high-quality images provided by the left color FLIR Blackfly S USB3 with a resolution of 1440 × 1080. The semantic labels are generated by first warping the images from the left frame-based camera to the view of the left monochrome Prophesse Gen3.1 event camera with a resolution of 640 × 480. We then apply a state-of-the-art semantic segmentation method [24] to the warped images to generate the labels. By doing so, we obtain fine-grained labels for 19 classes, which we convert to 11 classes: background, building, fence, person, pole, road, sidewalk, vegetation, car, wall, and traffic sign. Since frame cameras suffer from image degradation in challenging illumination scenes, we only label the sequences recorded during the day, which results in 8082 labeled frames for the training and 2809 labeled frames for the test split. For more details, we refer to the supplementary. Compared to labels from DDD17, our labels feature much higher quality and more details, as can be observed in Fig. 5. We believe that our generated semantic labels can also spur future work in multi-modal semantic segmentation as the DSEC dataset includes measurements of a LiDAR, one frame-based, and one event-based stereo-camera pair.

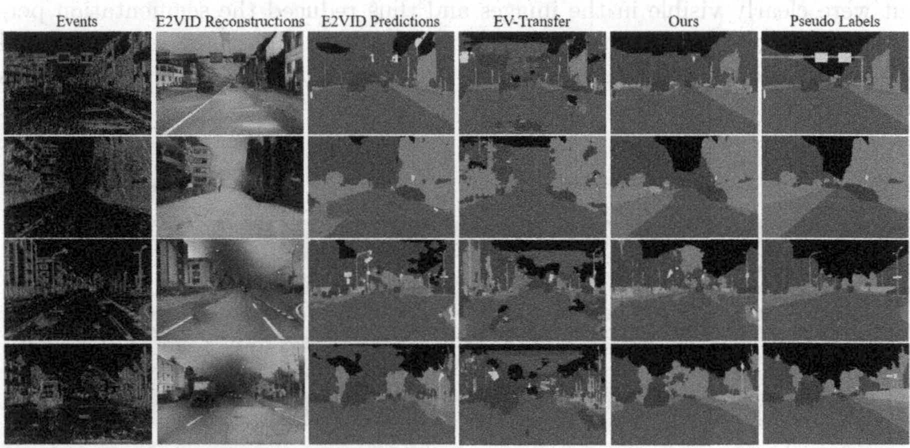

Fig. 6. Qualitative samples on DSEC-Semantic for the UDA setting, i.e., no event labels are available during training. Compared to EV-Transfer and E2VID, our method can more reliably predict smaller details such as persons.

Table 3. Performance of the UDA methods on DSEC-Semantic, which can leverage image labels and unpaired, unlabeled event data. Results report the mean and standard deviation of 3 runs with different random seeds.

Method	Labels	Accuracy [%] ↑	mIoU [%] ↑
EV-Transfer [18]	Frames	60.50 ± 2.50	23.20 ± 1.17
E2VID [21]	Frames	76.67 ± 3.39	40.70 ± 3.38
ESS (ours)	Frames	$\mathbf{84.04 \pm 0.12}$	$\mathbf{44.87 \pm 0.51}$

Implementation Details. Similar to the experiments on DDD17, we leverage the Cityscapes datasets as the labeled source dataset. The difference is that we use the DSEC-Semantic dataset as the target domain. The hyper-parameters λ_1, λ_2, λ_3, and λ_4 are now set as 1, 1, 1, and 1, respectively. We use the same RAdam optimizer to train our model with a larger learning rate of 5×10^{-4} (for both E_{img} and T), and a smaller batch-size of 8, for 25'000 iterations.

UDA Comparison. In this setting, we compare against the UDA methods [18,21], which can deal with unpaired, labeled image and unlabeled event data. As can be observed in Table 3, our method outperforms state-of-the-art UDA methods by a margin of 4.17% mIoU. Again, our method benefits from a recurrent architecture, and a simpler training regime that does not rely on adversarial training. Moreover, it can be adapted to the target domain, showing a large gap to methods that cannot do so, such as [21]. Figure 6 shows qualitative examples verifying the benefits of our method.

State-of-the-Art Comparison Here, we adopt the same setting as for the DDD17, where we train our method with a supervised task loss on training labels in the event domain. See Fig. 7 for qualitative samples. In this supervised setting, we compare against EV-Segnet [1]. Additionally, we also provide results for our method using both image and event labels during training. Without considering the image labels in the training, our method achieves a performance comparable with EV-Segnet with a higher accuracy score but a slightly lower mIoU, see Table 4. However, if we use the full potential of our method by using the image labels as well, we achieve state-of-the-art performance on DSEC-Semantic, outperforming EV-SegNet by 1.53% mIoU.

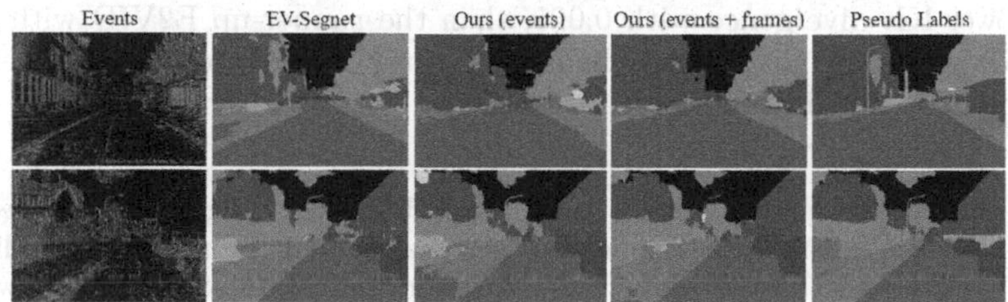

Fig. 7. Qualitative samples on DSEC-Semantic in the supervised setting, i.e., event labels are available during training. The combined training on image and event labels improves the semantic predictions. Importantly, at test-time all methods only use events.

Table 4. Results on DSEC-Semantic in the supervised setting, where event labels (events), image labels (labels), or both (events+frames) can be used.

Method	Labels	Accuracy [%] ↑	mIOU [%] ↑
EV-SegNet [1]	Events	88.61	51.76
ESS (ours)	Frames	84.17	45.38
ESS (ours)	Events	89.25	51.57
ESS (ours)	Events+frames	**89.37**	**53.29**

4.3 Ablation Studies

Loss importance. To verify the effectiveness of the proposed framework, we ablate the introduced loss functions by removing them during training. Table 5 reports the results of those experiments on DSEC-Semantic for the UDA setting. It can be observed that omitting the consistency loss in the embedding space, $L_{\text{cons. emb.}}$, leads to a 5.56% drop in mIoU, showing its importance to align the embedding spaces. Similarly, omitting $L_{\text{cons. pred.}}$ leads to a 1.28%, and omitting $L_{\text{cons. task.}}$ leads to a 2.09% drop, highlighting the importance of both.

Embedding Alignment. The studied UDA methods operate by aligning events and frame embeddings. For E2VID, these embeddings are image reconstructions and images, for EV-Transfer and our work, these are image and event embeddings. To study this alignment, we perform the following comparison: On DSEC-Semantic, we construct pairs of event and image embeddings, which we each decode to the logits of the semantic map, $T(\mathbf{z}_{\text{event}})$ and $T(\mathbf{z}_{\text{img}})$. While for EV-Transfer and our method, we use the dedicated task network to decode these embeddings, for the E2VID-baseline, we use the network trained on Cityscapes on both images and image reconstructions, to construct paired predictions. We then measure the consistency of these maps across pairs, via the symmetric KL divergence, which we report in Table 6. As can be seen, our approach has a three times lower KL divergence with 0.025, than the runner-up E2VID with 0.073. This indicates that our method aligns image and event embeddings better than other methods, facilitating domain transfer.

Table 5. Ablation experiments on DSEC-Semantic in the UDA setting.

Method	Accuracy [%] ↑	mIoU [%] ↑
w/o $L_{\text{cons. emb.}}$	80.86	39.31
w/o $L_{\text{cons. pred.}}$	83.62	43.59
w/o $L_{\text{cons. task}}$	82.50	42.78
w/o skip connect	78.79	38.08
ESS (ours)	**84.04**	**44.87**

Table 6. Alignment between image- and event-based predictions on DSEC-Semantic. Lower numbers mean better alignment.

Method	Dissimilarity↓
EV-Transfer [18]	0.120
E2VID [21]	0.073
ESS (ours)	**0.025**

5 Conclusion

Event cameras promise to enhance the reliability of autonomous systems by improving the robustness of semantic segmentation networks in edge case scenarios such as during the night or at high speeds. However, the lack of high-quality labeled datasets currently hinders the progress of event-based semantic segmentation. In this work, we tackled this problem, by introducing ESS, which leverages large-scale, labeled image datasets for event-based semantic segmentation, without requiring event labels or paired events and images. We thoroughly evaluated our method, both on the existing DDD17 benchmark, and the newly generated DSEC-Semantic benchmark, where we outperform existing state-of-the-art methods in UDA and supervised settings. DSEC-Semantic is a large-scale event-based dataset for semantic segmentation, with high-quality, fine-grained semantic labels, which will spur further research in event-based semantic scene understanding. While only evaluated for semantic segmentation, we believe that these performance gains can be transferred to other tasks. Our method unlocks the virtually unlimited supply of image-based datasets for event-based vision, enabling the exploration of previously inaccessible research fields for event cameras, such as panoptic segmentation, video captioning, action recognition etc.

Acknowledgment. This work was supported by the National Centre of Competence in Research (NCCR) Robotics through the Swiss National Science Foundation (SNSF) and the European Research Council (ERC) under grant agreement No. 864042 (AGILEFLIGHT).

References

1. Alonso, I., Murillo, A.C.: EV-SegNet: semantic segmentation for event-based cameras. In: IEEE Conference on Computer Vision and Pattern Recognition Workshops (CVPRW) (2019)
2. Bardow, P., Davison, A.J., Leutenegger, S.: Simultaneous optical flow and intensity estimation from an event camera. In: IEEE Conference on Computer Vision and Pattern Recognition (CVPR), pp. 884–892 (2016). https://doi.org/10.1109/CVPR.2016.102
3. Binas, J., Neil, D., Liu, S.C., Delbruck, T.: DDD17: end-to-end DAVIS driving dataset. In: ICML Workshop on Machine Learning for Autonomous Vehicles (2017)
4. Brandli, C., Berner, R., Yang, M., Liu, S.C., Delbruck, T.: A 240x180 130dB 3μs latency global shutter spatiotemporal vision sensor. IEEE J. Solid-State Circuits **49**(10), 2333–2341 (2014). https://doi.org/10.1109/JSSC.2014.2342715
5. Chollet, F.: Xception: Deep learning with depthwise separable convolutions. In: IEEE Conference on Computer Vision and Pattern Recognition (CVPR), pp. 1800–1807 (2017). https://doi.org/10.1109/CVPR.2017.195
6. Cordts, M., et al.: The cityscapes dataset for semantic urban scene understanding. In: IEEE Conference on Computer Vision and Pattern Recognition (CVPR) (2016)
7. Dosovitskiy, A., Ros, G., Codevilla, F., Lopez, A., Koltun, V.: CARLA: an open urban driving simulator. In: Conference on Robotics Learning (CoRL) (2017)
8. Falanga, D., Kleber, K., Scaramuzza, D.: Dynamic obstacle avoidance for quadrotors with event cameras. Sci. Robot. **5**(40), eaaz9712 (2020). https://doi.org/10.1126/scirobotics.aaz9712
9. Gallego, G., et al.: Event-based vision: a survey. IEEE Trans. Pattern Anal. Mach. Intell. (2020). https://doi.org/10.1109/TPAMI.2020.3008413
10. Gehrig, D., Gehrig, M., Hidalgo-Carrió, J., Scaramuzza, D.: Video to Events: recycling video datasets for event cameras. In: IEEE Conference on Computer Vision and Pattern Recognition (CVPR) (2020)
11. Gehrig, D., Loquercio, A., Derpanis, K.G., Scaramuzza, D.: End-to-end learning of representations for asynchronous event-based data. In: International Conference on Computer Vision (ICCV) (2019)

12. Gehrig, D., Rüegg, M., Gehrig, M., Hidalgo-Carrio, J., Scaramuzza, D.: Combining events and frames using recurrent asynchronous multimodal networks for monocular depth prediction. In: IEEE Robotic and Automation Letters (RA-L) (2021)
13. Gehrig, M., Aarents, W., Gehrig, D., Scaramuzza, D.: DSEC: a stereo event camera dataset for driving scenarios. In: IEEE Robotics and Automation Letters (2021). https://doi.org/10.1109/LRA.2021.3068942
14. Hu, Y., Delbruck, T., Liu, S.-C.: Learning to exploit multiple vision modalities by using grafted networks. In: Vedaldi, A., Bischof, H., Brox, T., Frahm, J.-M. (eds.) ECCV 2020. LNCS, vol. 12361, pp. 85–101. Springer, Cham (2020). https://doi.org/10.1007/978-3-030-58517-4_6
15. Hidalgo-Carrio, J., Gehrig, D., Scaramuzza, D.: Learning monocular dense depth from events. IEEE International Conference on 3D Vision (3DV) (2020)
16. Liu, L., et al.: On the variance of the adaptive learning rate and beyond. In: International Conference on Learning Representations (ICLR) (2020)
17. Maqueda, A.I., Loquercio, A., Gallego, G., García, N., Scaramuzza, D.: Event-based vision meets deep learning on steering prediction for self-driving cars. In: IEEE Conference on Computer Vision and Pattern Recognition (CVPR), pp. 5419–5427 (2018). https://doi.org/10.1109/CVPR.2018.00568
18. Messikommer, N., Gehrig, D., Gehrig, M., Scaramuzza, D.: Bridging the gap between events and frames through unsupervised domain adaptation. In: IEEE Robotics and Automation Letters (2022)
19. Muglikar, M., Moeys, D., Scaramuzza, D.: Event-guided depth sensing. In: IEEE International Conference on 3D Vision (3DV) (2021)
20. Perot, E., de Tournemire, P., Nitti, D., Masci, J., Sironi, A.: Learning to detect objects with a 1 megapixel event camera. In: Conference on Neural Information Processing Systems (NIPS) (2020)
21. Rebecq, H., Ranftl, R., Koltun, V., Scaramuzza, D.: High speed and high dynamic range video with an event camera. IEEE Trans. Pattern Anal. Mach. Intell. (2019). https://doi.org/10.1109/TPAMI.2019.2963386
22. Reinbacher, C., Graber, G., Pock, T.: Real-time intensity-image reconstruction for event cameras using manifold regularisation. In: British Machine Vision Conference (BMVC) (2016). https://doi.org/10.5244/C.30.9
23. Rosinol Vidal, A., Rebecq, H., Horstschaefer, T., Scaramuzza, D.: Ultimate SLAM? combining events, images, and IMU for robust visual SLAM in HDR and high speed scenarios. IEEE Robot. Autom. Lett. **3**(2), 994–1001 (2018). https://doi.org/10.1109/LRA.2018.2793357
24. Tao, A., Sapra, K., Catanzaro, B.: Hierarchical multi-scale attention for semantic segmentation. arXiv preprint arXiv:2005.10821 (2020)
25. Tulyakov, S., et al.: TimeLens: event-based video frame interpolation. IEEE Conference on Computer Vision and Pattern Recognition (CVPR) (2021)
26. Wang, L., Kim, T.K., Yoon, K.J.: EventSR: from asynchronous events to image reconstruction, restoration, and super-resolution via end-to-end adversarial learning. In: IEEE Conference on Computer Vision and Pattern Recognition (CVPR), pp. 8312–8322 (2020)
27. Wang, L., Chae, Y., Yoon, K.J.: Dual transfer learning for event-based end-task prediction via pluggable event to image translation. In: International Conference on Computer Vision (ICCV), pp. 2135–2145 (2021)
28. Wang, L., Chae, Y., Yoon, S.H., Kim, T.K., Yoon, K.J.: EvDistill: asynchronous events to end-task learning via bidirectional reconstruction-guided cross-modal knowledge distillation. In: IEEE Conference on Computer Vision and Pattern Recognition (CVPR) (2021)

29. Zhu, A.Z., Atanasov, N., Daniilidis, K.: Event-based visual inertial odometry. In: IEEE Conference on Computer Vision and Pattern Recognition (CVPR), pp. 5816–5824 (2017). https://doi.org/10.1109/CVPR.2017.616
30. Zhu, A.Z., Yuan, L., Chaney, K., Daniilidis, K.: Unsupervised event-based learning of optical flow, depth, and egomotion. In: IEEE Conference on Computer Vision and Pattern Recognition (CVPR) (2019)

An Efficient Spatio-Temporal Pyramid Transformer for Action Detection

Yuetian Weng[1], Zizheng Pan[1], Mingfei Han[1,2], Xiaojun Chang[2,3], and Bohan Zhuang[1(✉)]

[1] Department of Data Science & AI, Monash University, Melbourne, Australia
{yuetian.weng,zizheng.pan,mingfei.han,bohan.zhuang}@monash.edu
[2] ReLER Lab, AAII, University of Technology Sydney, Ultimo, Australia
xiaojun.chang@uts.edu.au
[3] School of Computing Technologies, RMIT University, Melbourne, Australia

Abstract. The task of action detection aims at deducing both the action category and localization of the start and end moment for each action instance in a long, untrimmed video. While vision Transformers have driven the recent advances in video understanding, it is non-trivial to design an efficient architecture for action detection due to the prohibitively expensive self-attentions over a long sequence of video clips. To this end, we present an efficient hierarchical Spatio-Temporal Pyramid Transformer (STPT) for action detection, building upon the fact that the early self-attention layers in Transformers still focus on local patterns. Specifically, we propose to use local window attention to encode rich local spatio-temporal representations in the early stages while applying global attention modules to capture long-term space-time dependencies in the later stages. In this way, our STPT can encode both locality and dependency with largely reduced redundancy, delivering a promising trade-off between accuracy and efficiency. For example, with only RGB input, the proposed STPT achieves 53.6% mAP on THUMOS14, surpassing I3D+AFSD RGB model by over 10% and performing favorably against state-of-the-art AFSD that uses additional flow features with 31% fewer GFLOPs, which serves as an effective and efficient end-to-end Transformer-based framework for action detection. Code is available at https://github.com/ziplab/STPT.

Keywords: Action detection · Efficient video transformers

1 Introduction

Action detection in lengthy, real-world videos is one of the crucial tasks in many video analysis applications, *e.g.*, sports analysis, autonomous driving. Action detection aims to localize and classify the action instances appearing in untrimmed videos, which essentially depends on learning strong spatio-temporal representations from videos.

Supplementary Information The online version contains supplementary material available at https://doi.org/10.1007/978-3-031-19830-4_21.

S. Avidan et al. (Eds.): ECCV 2022, LNCS 13694, pp. 358–375, 2022.
https://doi.org/10.1007/978-3-031-19830-4_21

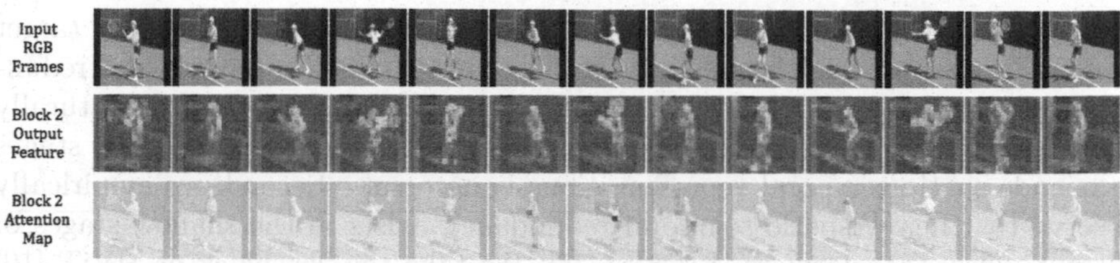

Fig. 1. Visualization of MViT [19]. We show the sampled input RGB frames, encoded feature maps and attention maps from the 2nd block of MViT. We find that such global attention in the early stages actually encodes local visual patterns in each RGB frame, but it is relatively redundant in successive frames. For illustration, a target query token in the middle frame (green anchor) only attends to its nearby tokens in adjacent frames while rarely interacting with tokens in distant frames (filled with red, the more darker the color, the higher the attention score). Therefore, attending to all spatio-temporal tokens leads to huge redundancy in encoding such local patterns. (Color figure online)

To date, the majority of action detection methods [12,32,38,54,66] are driven by 3D convolutional neural networks (CNNs), *e.g.*, C3D [56], I3D [10], to encode video segment features from video RGB frames and optical flows [71]. 3D convolution is compact and effective to aggregate contextual pixels within a small 3D region, *e.g.*, $3 \times 3 \times 3$, and thus reduce the spatio-temporal redundancy. However, the limited receptive field hinders the CNN-based models to capture long-term spatio-temporal dependencies. Alternatively, vision Transformers (ViTs) have shown the advantage [50] of capturing global dependencies via the self-attention mechanism in many computer vision tasks, such as image classification [18,47,55] and video action recognition [4,19,24,75]. Hierarchical ViTs [19] divide Transformer blocks into several stages and progressively reduce the spatial size of feature maps when the network goes deeper. However, the high-resolution feature maps of video clips in the early stages result in overlong token sequences. For instance, given an input video clip with $256 \times 96 \times 96$ RGB frames, the feature maps after the initial embedding layer requires more than 1000G Floating-point Operations (FLOPs) for a standard multi-head self-attention layer, which is impractical to train or evaluate. Therefore, how to efficiently handle spatio-temporal dependencies across overlong video frames is a fundamental challenge for action detection.

In this paper, we present an efficient Spatio-Temporal Pyramid Transformer (STPT) to tackle both spatio-temporal redundancy and long-range dependency, as illustrated in Fig. 2. Specifically, we propose a Local Spatio-Temporal Attention blocks (LSTA) to capture local patterns in the early stages while introducing Global Spatio-Temporal Attention blocks (GSTA) to handle long-range spatio-temporal relationships in the later stages. The motivation of this design comes from two aspects. First, considering the spatial dimension in videos, previous studies in CNNs and ViTs [27,50,65] have shown that shallow layers tend to capture local patterns in images (*e.g.*, texture, edges) while deep layers tend to learn high-level semantics or capture long-range dependencies. Besides, target motions across adjacent frames are subtle, which implies large temporal redundancy when encoding video representations [21,33,62]. Therefore, it naturally gives rise to the question of whether applying global attention at the early stages to encode spatio-temporal representations is necessary. Second, we empirically observe that heavy spatio-temporal redundancy exists in the shallow stages of current video Transformers [1,4,8,51,75]. We take the 2nd block of MViT [19] as an example and visualize its output features as well as the attention maps in Fig. 1. We observe that the self-attention in the shallow layers mainly focuses on neighboring tokens in a small spatial area and adjacent frames, rarely attending to other tokens in distant frames. Hence, aggregating all the visual tokens via self-attention in the early stages can bring noises to the informative local representations and incurs huge computational redundancy. By leveraging LSTA in the early stages, STPT significantly alleviates spatio-temporal redundancy and inherently benefits spatio-temporal representation learning, as target motions are highly correlated in a local spatial region and temporally subtle across adjacent frames.

To encourage locality inductive bias, recent studies propose to combine convolutions [63], MLPs [46] with Transformers or restrict self-attention within local windows [41], achieving favorable performance with reduced computational complexity. Moreover, from the theoretical perspective, locality inductive bias suppresses the negative Hessian eigenvalues, thus assisting in optimization by convexifying the loss landscape [48]. Different from these methods, we are the pioneering work to build a pure Transformer model that encodes both compact spatial and temporal locality while preserving the long-range dependency for the action detection task.

Finally, the proposed efficient Transformer is equipped with a temporal feature pyramid network (TFPN) to progressively reduce the spatial and temporal dimension and enlarge the receptive field into different scales. The multi-scale spatio-temporal feature representations are further utilized to predict the temporal boundaries and categories via an anchor-free prediction and refinement module.

In summary, our contributions are in three folds:

- We propose an efficient and effective Spatio-Temporal Pyramid Transformer (STPT) for action detection, which reduces the huge computational cost and redundancy while capturing long-range dependency in spatio-temporal representation learning.
- We devise local window attention to enhance local representations while reducing the spatio-temporal redundancy in shallow layers and retain the long-range dependency in deep layers with global self-attentions, achieving a favourable balance between efficiency and effectiveness.
- Finally, we conduct extensive experiments on standard benchmarks, *i.e.*, THUMOS14 and ActivityNet 1.3, by using pure RGB frame input. Compared with the methods that combining additional flow features, our STPT achieves

state-of-the-art results with reduced computational complexity, which makes a substantial stride for Transformer on the task of video action detection.

2 Related Work

2.1 Action Detection

Action detection aims at localizing the temporal boundaries of human activities in untrimmed videos and classifying the action categories [57]. Most existing works [22,32,38] utilize CNN-based models [10,49,56,60] pretrained on large-scale datasets (*e.g.*, Kinetics400 [10]) to extract spatio-temporal representations from a stack of RGB frames and/or optical flow frames. Anchor-based methods [13,22,66] retrieve fine-grained proposals by adjusting pre-defined multi-scale anchors while actionness-guided methods [36,38,77] instead learn the boundary confidence or actionness scores at all the temporal positions of the input video, which are matched and served as proposal candidates. Another line of research resorts to multi-scale towers [13,23] or temporal feature pyramids [37,40,74] to tackle the variation of action duration, utilizing high-resolution feature maps for short actions and feature maps with large receptive field for long actions, respectively. Recently, a new anchor-free detector [35] directly predicts the distance to the action boundaries and the action category for each frame. However, the local receptive field of 3D convolutions leads to the loss of temporal dependencies on untrimmed videos. To capture the action dependencies across frames, prior works introduce graph models [3,32,67,72,76], RNNs [6,7,70], and temporal Transformers [11,44,54] to capture these temporal relationships. However, the aforementioned methods rely on pre-extracted features from 3D convolution backbones and use head-only learning manner. In contrast, our STPT devises a pure Transformer model for efficiently and effectively learning spatio-temporal representations in an end-to-end manner, which encodes local patterns and global dependency via flexible token affinity learning in shallow and deep layers, respectively.

2.2 Video Transformers

ViTs are pushing the boundaries of recent video understanding research. In particular, VTN [45], LightVideoFormer [31] and STAM [51] introduce temporal Transformers to encode inter-frame relationships over the extracted image-level feature maps. ViViT [1], TimeSformer [4] and VidTr [75] propose to factorize along spatial and temporal dimensions on the granularity of encoder, attention block or dot-product computation. Similarly, SCT [73] proposes image chunk attention and shifted attention to model spatial and temporal relationships respectively. SMAVT [8] aggregates information from tokens located at the same spatial location within a local temporal window, while SIFAR [20] turns spatio-temporal patterns in video into purely spatial patterns in images, showing an image classifier can undertake the task of video understanding. However, these

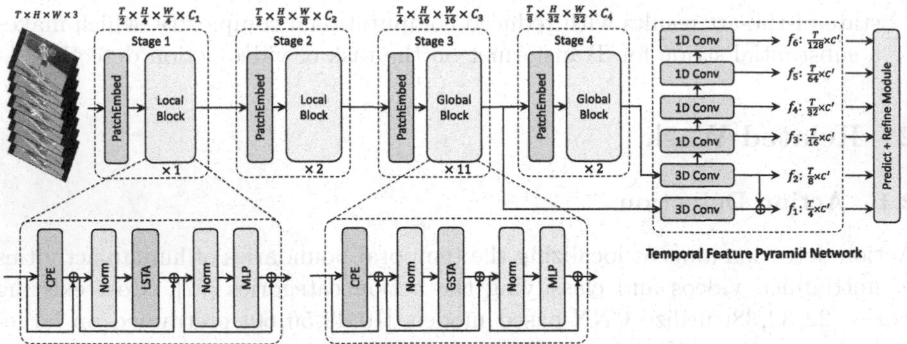

Fig. 2. Overall architecture of the proposed spatio-temporal pyramid Transformer. Given an input video X_{in}, our STPT is utilized to encode spatio-temporal representations and detect existing action instances. In the shallow layers, local blocks that constrain self-attention into local 3D windows tend to encode local patterns while reducing spatio-temporal redundancy. In deeper layers, global blocks retain long-range dependency over the token sequence. Features from the last stages are fed to the temporal feature pyramid network to predict the temporal boundaries and action categories via an anchor-free prediction and refinement module. Please refer to Sect. 3.1 for additional details.

studies lack hierarchical structure or model spatio-temporal dependencies separately, which may not be sufficient for the task of action detection. Targeting on these issues, MViT [19] presents a hierarchical Transformer to progressively shrink the spatio-temporal resolution of feature maps while expanding the channel as the network goes deeper. VideoSwin [42] proposes shifted window attention to limit the computation within a small local window, while Uniformer [33] unifies the spatio-temporal MobileNet block and self-attention and proposes an alternative multi-head relation aggregator. Different from the above methods, our model is purely Transformer based and jointly learns spatio-temporal representation. By flexibly involving locality constraint in early stages and data-specific global self-attentions in later stages, our model well addresses the challenges of spatio-temporal redundancy and dependency for action detection.

3 Method

3.1 Overall Architecture

The overall architecture of STPT is illustrated in Fig. 2. Let $X_{in} \in \mathbb{R}^{T \times H \times W \times 3}$ be an input video clip, where T, H and W represent the number, height and width of RGB frames, respectively. First, we divide the frame volume X_{in} into a series of overlapping 3D cubes, with the size of $3 \times 7 \times 7$. Then we exploit a 3D PatchEmbed module to aggregate contextual pixels from each cube and project each cube into dimension of 96, serving as the initial input for the subsequent pipeline. In practice, the 3D PatchEmbed module is a $3 \times 7 \times 7$ depth-wise convolution with stride $2 \times 4 \times 4$ and zero paddings. As a result, the input tensor X_{in} is downsampled to $\frac{T}{2} \times \frac{H}{4} \times \frac{W}{4}$.

Next, we divide the entire backbone into 4 stages. Letting $s \in [1, 2, 3, 4]$ be the index of each stage, we employ $L_s \in [1, 2, 11, 2]$ blocks at each stage, in which STPT Local Blocks are used to encode local spatio-temporal representations in the first two stages, and STPT Global Block are used to tackle long-term dependencies in the later stages. At the same time, from the 2nd stage, the spatial and temporal dimensions are gradually downsampled by the 3D PatchEmbed module. Following [19], by increasing the output dimension of the final MLP layer in the previous stage, the channel dimensions are gradually expanded before the transition to the next stage. The feature maps with different resolutions from the last two stages are then fed to the temporal feature pyramid network (TFPN) to obtain multiple resolution feature maps. Finally, the prediction and refinement modules are used to predict the start frame, end frame and the category of each anchor point on the multi-scale feature maps. The detailed architecture specifications are provided in Table 1.

3.2 Block Design in STPT

Formally, each STPT Block consists of three key modules: Conditional Positional Encoding (CPE), Multi-Head Spatio-Temporal Attention (MSTA), and multi-layer perceptron (MLP). Formally, letting X_{l-1} be the input of the l-th block, each block can be formulated as

$$X_{l-1} = \text{CPE}(X_{l-1}) + X_{l-1} \quad (1)$$

$$X'_{l-1} = \text{MSTA}(\text{LN}(X_{l-1})) + X_{l-1} \quad (2)$$

$$X_l = \text{MLP}(\text{LN}(X'_{l-1})) + X'_{l-1} \quad (3)$$

where $\text{LN}(\cdot)$ indicates the layer normalization [2] and MLP consists of two FC layers with GELU [26] non-linearity in between. Specifically, we first leverage CPE to integrate the spatio-temporal position information into each token. Then the MSTA module, which can be the Local spatio-temporal Attention (LSTA) or Global spatio-temporal Attention (GSTA), aggregates each token with its contextual tokens, followed by an MLP to perform channel mixing. As discussed above, we encode fine and local spatial-temporal representations in the early stages using LSTA and high-level semantics with long-term dependencies in the deep layers using GSTA, respectively. In the next, we elaborate the design for each module.

Conditional Positional Encoding. Since actions in videos are both spatial and temporal variant, we need to explicitly encode position information for all the visual tokens. Previous works [1,4,19] commonly adopt absolute positional encodings [18]. However, the length of token sequences is much longer for action detection compared to the one pretrained for action recognition tasks (*e.g.*, $128 \times 24 \times 24$ vs. $8 \times 56 \times 56$), which makes it difficult to utilize a fixed absolute positional

Table 1. Architecture specification of STPT. For the s-th stage, we denote P_s as the patch size, S_s as the kernel stride and R_s as the reduction ratio, where each dimension corresponding to the temporal size, height and width, respectively. L_s and C_s refer to the number of blocks and the channel dimension at the s-th stage, respectively. Furthermore, we denote W_{sl} as the window size at the l-th block in the s-th stage. We adopt an expanding ratio of 4 for all MLP layers in each block.

	Output size	Layer name	STPT
Stage1	$\frac{T}{2} \times \frac{H}{4} \times \frac{W}{4}$	PatchEmbed	$P_1 = 3 \times 7 \times 7$ $S_1 = 2 \times 4 \times 4$ $C_1 = 96$
		Local block	$L_1 = 1$ $W_{11} = 8 \times 8 \times 8$ $R_1 = 2 \times 8 \times 8$
Stage2	$\frac{T}{2} \times \frac{H}{8} \times \frac{W}{8}$	PatchEmbed	$P_2 = 3 \times 3 \times 3$ $S_2 = 1 \times 2 \times 2$ $C_2 = 192$
		Local block	$L_2 = 2$ $W_{21} = 8 \times 6 \times 6$ $W_{22} = 16 \times 4 \times 4$ $R_2 = 2 \times 2 \times 2$
Stage3	$\frac{T}{4} \times \frac{H}{16} \times \frac{W}{16}$	PatchEmbed	$P_3 = 3 \times 3 \times 3$ $S_3 = 2 \times 2 \times 2$ $C_3 = 384$
		Global block	$L_3 = 11$ $R_3 = 2 \times 2 \times 2$
Stage4	$\frac{T}{8} \times \frac{H}{32} \times \frac{W}{32}$	PatchEmbed	$P_4 = 3 \times 3 \times 3$ $S_4 = 2 \times 2 \times 2$ $C_4 = 768$
		Global block	$L_4 = 2$ $R_4 = 1 \times 1 \times 1$

encoding from a pretrained model. To tackle these problems, we make the spatio-temporal positional embedding conditioned on input features and extend the CPE proposed in [17] to the video domain, which can be formulated as

$$\text{CPE}(X) = \text{DWConv}(X), \tag{4}$$

where DWConv refers to a 3D depth-wise convolution with zero paddings. Previous works [17,28] have shown that tokens on the borders can be aware of their absolute positions when using convolutional layers with zero paddings. Therefore, the absolute position for each token can be encoded by progressively sliding convolutional kernels on the feature maps, justifying the design of our proposed CPE for introducing positional information into input features.

Local Spatio-Temporal Attention. As discussed in Sect. 1, global attention is redundant to encode local patterns in the shallow layers, thus leading to high computational cost owing to the high-resolution feature maps. Given an embedding $X \in \mathbb{R}^{T\times H\times W\times d}$ with channel dimension d, the complexity of self-attention is $\mathcal{O}(T^2H^2W^2d)$ [58]. Here, we propose to replace self-attention with LSTA to alleviate the redundancy.

Following the design of multi-head self-attention, LSTA first projects X into query $Q \in \mathbb{R}^{T\times H\times W\times d}$, key $K \in \mathbb{R}^{T\times H\times W\times d}$, and value $V \in \mathbb{R}^{T\times H\times W\times d}$ with linear transformations. For each tensor, we evenly divide it into $w_1 \times w_2 \times w_3$ partitions (sub-windows). Without loss of generality, we assume $T\%w_1 = 0$, $H\%w_2 = 0$ and $W\%w_3 = 0$, and thus each sub-window contains $\frac{THW}{w_1w_2w_3}$ tokens. We force each query token only attends to tokens within the same local 3D window, which helps encode local patterns via joint spatial-temporal relation aggregation and reduce the computational redundancy in the early stages.

To further improve the efficiency, we follow [19,61] to reduce both the spatial and temporal resolution of the keys and values within each local window, *i.e.*, $\bar{K} = R_K(K) \in \mathbb{R}^{T'\times H'\times W'\times d}$ and $\bar{V} = R_V(V) \in \mathbb{R}^{T'\times H'\times W'\times d}$, where $\bar{K}$, $\bar{V}$ are resolution-reduced keys and values, and R_K, R_V denote two independent reduction operations (*e.g.*, depth-wise convolution). T', H' and W' are the reduced temporal dimension, height and width. Thus, each sub-window of $\bar{K}$ and $\bar{V}$ contains $\frac{T'H'W'}{w_1w_2w_3}$ tokens after being divided into $w_1 \times w_2 \times w_3$ partitions. Specifically, the computational cost for each sub-window becomes $\mathcal{O}(\frac{THW}{w_1w_2w_3} \times \frac{T'H'W'}{w_1w_2w_3} \times d)$, and the total cost of LSTA is $\mathcal{O}(\frac{T'H'W'}{w_1w_2w_3} \times THWd)$, which is significantly efficient when $\frac{T'}{w_1} \ll T$, $\frac{H'}{w_2} \ll H$ and $\frac{W'}{w_3} \ll W$ and grows linearly with THW if $\frac{T'}{w_1}$, $\frac{H'}{w_2}$ and $\frac{W'}{w_3}$ are fixed.

By applying LSTA in the early stages, the model significantly alleviates spatio-temporal redundancy and efficiently encodes local spatio-temporal representations.

Global Spatio-Temporal Attention. To capture long-term dependencies, we employ GSTA in the deep layers. For more efficient aggregation, GSTA also uses the feature maps with reduced spatio-temporal resolution as the keys and values in the self-attention operations. Given a query token, GSTA compares it with all the tokens for aggregation. In this way, we ensure that the model captures global dependencies in the last stages. By combining LSTA in the shallow layers, the model forms an efficient and effective way of learning the spatio-temporal representations for action detection.

Relation to Existing Video Transformers. While [1,4] are based on space-time attention factorization, our method can encode the target motions by jointly aggregating spatio-temporal relations, without loss of spatio-temporal correspondence. Compared with MViT [19] which entirely utilizes global self-attentions, our model can resolve the long-range dependency while simultaneously reducing the local spatio-temporal redundancy. By removing the local redundancy in the early stages, our model outperforms MViT with a lower computational cost. Moreover, different from the spatio-temporal MobileNet block used in Uniformer [33], our LSTA is data-dependent [25,48] and flexible in terms of window size without introducing extra parameters, while the kernel parameters are fixed for the 3D convolutions in the spatio-temporal MobileNet block. Different from VideoSwin [42], we do not use shifted window mechanism to get a trade-off between locality and dependency. Compared with [14,16,34] which alternatively process local and global information within each block, we encode local and global spatio-temporal representations in the shallow and deep layers separately, tackling both redundancy and dependency in a concise manner.

3.3 Temporal Feature Pyramid

Given an untrimmed video, action detection aims to find the temporal boundaries and categories of action instances, with annotation denoted by $\{\psi_n = (t_n^s, t_n^e, c_n)\}_{n=1}^N$, where N is the number of action instances. For the n-th action instance ψ_n, t_n^s, t_n^e and c_n refer to the start time, end time and action label, respectively. As shown in Fig. 2, we first forward the video input X_{in} into the backbone to encode the spatio-temporal representations. The 3D feature maps extracted from the last two stages are then fed to TFPN to obtain multi-scale temporal feature maps. The motivation comes from the fact that multi-scale feature maps contribute to tackle the variation of action duration [13,23,64]. Specifically, we construct an M-level temporal feature pyramid $\{f_m\}_{m=1}^M$, where $f_m \in \mathbb{R}^{T_m \times C'}$ and T_m is the temporal dimension of the m-th level. The TFPN contains two 3D convolution layers followed by four 1D convolutional layers to progressively forms a featural hierarchy.

After obtaining the temporal feature pyramid, an anchor-free prediction and refinement module as in [35] is utilized to predict the boundary distances and class scores at each location i on f_m. Concretely, a two-branch tower including several temporal convolutional layers is employed to map f_m into two latent representations. The latent representations are then processed by a classification head and a localization head to get the class label $\hat{y}_i^C$ and boundary distances $(\hat{b}_i^s, \hat{b}_i^e)$ for each location i, respectively. To improve the confidence of the predictions, we further adjust the boundary distances with features extracted from a small region at the coarse boundary predicted above to obtain the modified offset as $(\Delta\hat{b}_i^s, \Delta\hat{b}_i^e)$, and the refinement action category label as $\hat{y}_i^R$. To obtain high quality proposals, we additionally predict the quality confidence η following [77]. Formally, for the i-th temporal location in the m-th TFPN layer, the final predicted start time $\hat{t}_{m,i}^s$, end time $\hat{t}_{m,i}^e$ and class label $\hat{y}_{m,i}$ can be formulated in the following form:

$$\hat{t}_{m,i}^s = \hat{b}_{m,i}^s + \frac{1}{2}(\hat{b}_{m,i}^e - \hat{b}_{m,i}^s)\Delta\hat{b}_i^s, \tag{5}$$

$$\hat{t}_{m,i}^e = \hat{b}_{m,i}^e + \frac{1}{2}(\hat{b}_{m,i}^e - \hat{b}_{m,i}^s)\Delta\hat{b}_i^e, \tag{6}$$

$$\hat{y}_{m,i} = \frac{1}{2}(\hat{y}_{m,i}^C + \hat{y}_{m,i}^R)\eta_{m,i}. \tag{7}$$

In the training process, we use a multi-task loss function based on the output of coarse and refined predictions, which can be formulated as

$$\mathcal{L} = \lambda_{cls}\mathcal{L}_{cls} + \lambda_{loc}\mathcal{L}_{loc} + \lambda_q\mathcal{L}_q, \tag{8}$$

where $\mathcal{L}_{cls}$, $\mathcal{L}_{loc}$ and $\mathcal{L}_q$ are losses corresponding to the classification, boundary regression and quality confidence prediction tasks, respectively, and λ_{cls}, λ_{loc}, λ_q are hyperparameters to balance the contribution of each task to the total loss. For the classification task, we use focal loss [39] between the predicted action scores from both prediction and refinement modules and the ground-truth categories, *i.e.*, $\mathcal{L}_{cls} = \mathcal{L}^C_{focal} + \mathcal{L}^R_{focal}$. The localization loss includes tIoU (temporal Interaction over Union) loss for the predicted coarse boundaries and L1 loss for refined offsets, respectively, *i.e.*, $\mathcal{L}_{loc} = \mathcal{L}^C_{tIoU} + \mathcal{L}^R_{L1}$. For the quality prediction task, $\mathcal{L}_q$ is computed in the same way as in [35].

4 Experiments

4.1 Datasets and Settings

Datasets. We present our experimental results on the commonly-used benchmarks THUMOS14 [29] and ActivityNet 1.3 [9]. THUMOS14 dataset is composed of 413 temporally annotated untrimmed videos with 20 action categories. We use the 200 videos in the validation set for training and evaluate our method on the 213 videos in the test set. ActivityNet 1.3 is a large-scale action understanding dataset for action recognition, action detection, proposal generation and dense captioning tasks, which contains 19,994 temporally labeled untrimmed videos with 200 action categories. We follow the former setting [38] to split this dataset into training, validation and testing sets based on the proportion of 2:1:1.

Metrics. We adopt mean Average Precision (mAP) at certain tIoU thresholds as the evaluation metric. On THUMOS14, we use tIoU thresholds {0.3, 0.4, 0.5, 0.6, 0.7}; on ActivityNet 1.3, we choose 10 values in the range of [0.5, 0.95] with a step size of 0.05 as tIoU thresholds following the official evaluation API.

Implementation Details. We build our STPT based on MViT [19]. The pipeline and architecture specifications have shown in Fig. 2 and Table 1, respectively. Follow common practice [35], we train and evaluate our model in an end-to-end manner, which takes as input pure RGB frames without using additional optical flow features. On THUMOS14, we sample RGB frames at 10 frames per second (fps) and split a video into clips, where each clip contains 256 frames. Adjacent clips have a temporal overlap of 30 and 128 frames at training and testing, respectively. For ActivityNet 1.3, we sample a clip of 768 frames at dynamic fps for each video. We set the spatial resolution as 96×96 and use data augmentation including random crop and horizontal flipping in training. For a fair comparison, we pretrain all the models on Kinetics400 [10] for 30 epochs under the same settings following [19]. Our model is trained for 16 epochs and 12 epochs on THUMOS14 and ActivityNet 1.3, respectively, using Adam [30] with a learning rate of 5×10^{-6} for backbone and 1×10^{-4} for other modules, and the weight decay is set to 1×10^{-3} and 1×10^{-4} for the two datasets. In post-processing, we apply soft-NMS [5] to suppress redundant predictions, where the tIoU threshold is set to 0.5 for THUMOS14 and 0.85 for ActivityNet 1.3. λ_{loc} is set to 10 for THUMOS14 and 1 for ActivityNet 1.3, and λ_{cls}, λ_q is set to 1.

Table 2. Performance comparison with state-of-the-art methods on THUMOS14, We measure the performance by mAP at different tIoU thresholds and average mAP in [0.3 : 0.1 : 0.7]. "*" indicates that the models are trained in an end-to-end manner. We measure the computational cost by GFLOPs based on a clip of 256 × 96 × 96 frames for them. "Flow" indicates using optical flow features.

Methods	GFLOPs	Backbone	Flow	0.3	0.4	0.5	0.6	0.7	Avg.
BSN [38]	455.4	TS	✓	53.5	45.0	36.9	28.4	20.0	36.8
BMN [36]	455.4	TS	✓	56.0	47.4	38.8	29.7	20.5	38.5
G-TAD [67]	444.2	TSN	✓	54.5	47.6	40.2	30.8	23.4	39.3
TAL [13]	157.0	I3D	✓	53.2	48.5	42.8	33.8	20.8	39.8
A2Net [69]	157.0	I3D	✓	58.6	54.1	45.5	32.5	17.2	41.6
G-TAD+PGCN [72]	157.0	I3D	✓	66.4	60.4	51.6	37.6	22.9	47.8
BMN-CSA [53]	455.4	TS	✓	64.4	58.0	49.2	38.2	27.8	47.5
AFSD* [35]	162.2	I3D	✓	67.3	62.4	55.5	43.7	31.1	52.0
DCAN [15]	444.2	TSN	✓	68.2	62.7	54.1	43.9	**32.6**	52.3
R-C3D* [66]	453.3	C3D		44.8	35.6	28.9	–	–	–
GTAN [43]	107.0	P3D		57.8	47.2	38.8	–	–	–
AFSD* [35]	84.4	I3D		–	–	45.9	35.0	23.4	43.5
BCNet+PGCN [68]	81.8	I3D		69.8	62.9	52.0	39.8	24.0	49.7
DaoTAD [59]	81.8	I3D		62.8	59.5	53.8	43.6	30.1	50.0
	167.6	MViT [19]		68.0	62.5	54.2	43.6	30.6	51.8
	120.9	VideoSwin [42]		69.5	64.1	54.7	42.6	27.7	51.7
	116.1	TimeSformer [4]		67.6	61.9	53.0	41.9	27.9	50.5
Ours*	111.2	STPT		**70.6**	**65.7**	**56.4**	**44.6**	30.5	**53.6**

4.2 Main Results

We compare our STPT with state-of-the-art approaches on the two datasets in Table 2 and Table 3. We also report the backbone used by each method, *e.g.*, I3D [10], TS [52], TSN [60], P3D [49], and whether the optical flows are used. For models that are end-to-end trainable, we directly report the computational cost for the whole model. For methods utilizing pre-extracted features or pre-generated action proposals, we also calculate the computational cost for the offline feature extraction stage under identical input settings for fair comparison.

On THUMOS14 dataset, our STPT, which only uses RGB frames, outperforms previous RGB models by a large margin and achieves comparable performance with methods using additional optical flows, reaching mAP 70.6%, 65.7%, 56.4% at tIoU thresholds 0.3, 0.4, 0.5, respectively. Specifically, our STPT provides 53.6%, a +10.1% average mAP boost over AFSD RGB model under identical settings. Besides, our model also outperforms the two-stream AFSD at most tIoU thresholds with less computational cost (111.2 vs. 162.2 GFLOPs).

On ActivityNet, with significant reduction of computational cost, our STPT also achieves comparable performance with the existing RGB models. Specifically, STPT still obtains slightly better mAPs than AFSD RGB model on all thresholds with less computational cost (134.1 vs. 248.7 GFLOPs). Notably, most previous models use optical flows to enhance motion modeling. However,

Table 3. Action localization results on ActivityNet 1.3 (validation set), measured by mAP(%) at different tIoU thresholds, and the average mAP in [0.5 : 0.05 : 0.95].

Models	GFLOPs	Backbone	Flow	0.5	0.75	0.95	Avg.
TAL [13]	471.3	I3D	✓	38.2	18.3	1.3	20.2
A2Net [69]	471.3	I3D	✓	43.6	28.7	3.7	27.8
BSN [38]	1367.0	TS	✓	46.5	30.0	8.0	30.0
BMN [36]	1367.0	TS	✓	50.1	34.8	8.3	33.9
G-TAD [67]	1367.0	TS	✓	50.4	34.6	9.0	34.1
BMN-CSA [53]	1367.0	TS	✓	52.4	36.7	5.2	35.4
AFSD* [35]	478.0	I3D	✓	52.4	35.3	6.5	34.4
DCAN [15]	1367.0	TS	✓	51.8	36.0	9.5	35.4
R-C3D* [66]	1360.0	C3D		26.8	–	–	12.7
GTAN [43]	320.0	P3D		52.6	34.1	8.9	34.3
AFSD* [35]	248.7	I3D		50.5	33.4	6.5	32.9
	172.4	MVIT [19]		50.1	32.7	5.9	32.2
	153.7	VideoSwin [42]		49.6	32.1	5.6	31.9
	140.6	TimeSformer [4]		51.1	33.3	6.0	33.1
Ours*	134.1	STPT		51.4	33.7	6.8	33.4

the adoption of an ensemble of flow features requires pre-extracting flow features using [71], which prevents these methods from end-to-end learning and also introduces huge computational cost. In contrast, our STPT can effectively encode the spatio-temporal representations from pure RGB frames, which is completely end-to-end trainable and computationally efficient.

It is worth to note that, compared with other representative video Transformers, our STPT achieves the best mAP on THUMOS14 and ActivityNet, which demonstrates the advantages of our architecture design that applying LSTA in shallow layers and GSTA in deeper layers in realizing the trade-off between locality and dependency. We also provide more comparison with other representative video Transformers in the supplementary.

4.3 Ablation Study

Effect of LSTA. As discussed in Sect. 1, MViT [19] suffers from heavy spatio-temporal redundancy in the shallow layers. We also investigate the computational cost of each layer and find that the heavy computation is caused by the global attention in the first two stages. To this end, we replace global attention with our efficient LSTA in the first two stages. As shown in Table 2, our STPT improves baseline MViT, which actually uses global self-attention in all the stages, by 1.4% on average mAP while reducing FLOPs by 55.4G on THUMOS14. Furthermore, we also compare our LSTA with factorized space-time

Table 4. Effect of our architecture design principle. We evaluate the performance of several combinations of blocks in terms of mAP. L/G refers to LSTA/GSTA blocks used in each stage. All models are equipped with CPE. The number of temporal tokens is set to 128, and the window size of temporal dimension for LSTA is set to 8.

Type	GFLOPs	0.3	0.4	0.5	0.6	0.7	Avg.
LLLL	101.8	64.7	59.4	50.8	40.0	26.5	48.3
LLLG	102.7	67.6	62.1	54.2	42.2	29.4	51.3
LGGG	151.4	69.4	63.5	55.0	42.9	29.2	52.0
GGGG	167.6	68.0	62.5	54.2	43.6	30.6	51.8
LLGG	111.4	69.1	63.7	55.2	44.2	29.3	52.3

Table 5. Effect of window size in terms of temporal dimension on THUMOS. We compare the performance (in mAP) and computational cost (in GFLOPs) for different scales of local window in each LSTA block. The number of temporal tokens is set to 128. Experiments are conducted on models without using CPE.

Window size	GFLOPs	0.3	0.4	0.5	0.6	0.7	Avg.
[1, 1, 1]	110.4	67.0	61.5	53.6	41.3	28.3	50.3
[4, 4, 4]	110.6	67.8	62.4	53.4	41.6	28.1	50.6
[8, 8, 8]	110.8	67.6	62.5	53.1	42.1	29.1	50.9
[8, 8, 16]	110.8	69.5	63.6	55.6	44.9	29.5	52.7
[16, 16, 16]	111.1	66.3	61.1	52.7	41.5	28.7	50.1

attention in [1,4]. As shown in Table 2 and Table 3, our LSTA leads to higher mAP scores than other attention designs with less computational cost, indicating the effectiveness and efficiency of the proposed module.

Effect of the Architecture Design. To explore the effect of our architecture design principle in STPT, we investigate all the possible combinations of LSTA (L) and GSTA (G). As shown in Table 4, when only using LSTA, the computational cost is light (LLLL). However, the mAP drops dramatically, since the network lacks the capacity of learning global dependency without GSTA. A significant improvement can be observed when replacing LSTA with GSTA in the 3rd stage, which indicates the importance of learning global dependency in the deeper layers for action detection. However, when applying GSTA in all stages (GGGG), the model leads to worse results and introduces heavy computational overhead (111.2G vs 166.6G). The main reason is that, without locality constraints, the model cannot extract detailed spatio-temporal patterns in the early stages. In our experiments, we choose LSTA and GSTA in the first two stages and the last two stages respectively to achieve a preferable balance between efficiency and effectiveness.

Effect of the Window Size. We compare the results of different window sizes in LSTA in terms of the temporal dimension. As shown in Table 5, LSTA is

Table 6. The effect of CPE when varying the number of temporal tokens on the performance (in mAP at different tIoU thresholds) and computational cost (in GFLOPs) on (a) THUMOS14 and (b) ActivityNet 1.3.

Length	GFLOPs	0.3	0.4	0.5	Avg.
64	83.2	68.2	62.2	53.0	50.7
64+CPE	84.7	68.2	62.5	54.3	51.1
128	110.8	69.5	63.6	55.6	52.7
128+CPE	111.2	70.6	65.7	56.4	53.6

(a) THUMOS14

Length	GFLOPs	0.5	0.75	0.95	Avg.
192	181.5	49.8	32.3	5.3	32.0
192+CPE	182.3	50.9	33.4	6.9	33.0
96	133.6	50.9	33.2	6.1	32.8
96+CPE	134.1	51.4	33.7	6.8	33.4

(b) ActivityNet 1.3

beneficial from the suitable window size. Moreover, it becomes equivalent to encode spatial patterns without temporal information when using only [1, 1, 1] in LSTA, where the model can not capture the motion variation of local patterns in the shallow layers, leading to performance drop for action detection. However, the setting of [16, 16, 16] leads to 0.5% average mAP drop compared to [8, 8, 8], showing that too large temporal window size brings noise to informative local representations, which also demonstrates the importance of involving locality inductive bias in early stages.

Effect of CPE. We verify the effectiveness of CPE in our STPT for the action detection task under the settings with different numbers of input tokens along temporal dimension. We carefully change the temporal stride in the first PatchEmbed layer, using dilated kernels to ensure more video frames are encoded into the token sequence while keeping the length of video clips identical to the setting in previous works [35]. Despite varying the number of input tokens, as shown in Table 6, CPE provides consistent performance gain on both datasets under all settings, with trivial computational cost introduced, *e.g.*, 0.9% average mAP improvement on THUMOS14 and 1.0% average mAP improvement on ActivityNet 1.3 under the setting of 128 and 192, respectively.

5 Conclusion and Future Work

In this paper, we have proposed a novel STPT, which tackles the challenges of both computational redundancy and long-range dependency in spatio-temporal representation learning for the task of action detection. Specifically, STPT applies LSTA in shallow layers to encode local patterns with reduced spatio-temporal redundancy and employs GSTA in the later stages to handle global dependencies. Extensive experiments on THUMOS14 and ActivityNet 1.3 have demonstrated that our STPT achieves a promising balance between accuracy and efficiency for the task of action detection. Future work may include extending our STPT to other dense prediction tasks in the video recognition field, *e.g.*, video segmentation and video captioning.

Acknowledgment. This work was partially supported by the NSFC under Grant (No. 61972315), Shaanxi Province International Science and Technology Cooperation Program Project-Key Projects No. 2022KWZ-14.

References

1. Arnab, A., Dehghani, M., Heigold, G., Sun, C., Lučić, M., Schmid, C.: ViViT: a video vision transformer. In: ICCV, pp. 6836–6846 (2021)
2. Ba, J.L., Kiros, J.R., Hinton, G.E.: Layer normalization. arXiv preprint arXiv:1607.06450 (2016)
3. Bai, Y., Wang, Y., Tong, Y., Yang, Y., Liu, Q., Liu, J.: Boundary content graph neural network for temporal action proposal generation. In: Vedaldi, A., Bischof, H., Brox, T., Frahm, J.-M. (eds.) ECCV 2020. LNCS, vol. 12373, pp. 121–137. Springer, Cham (2020). https://doi.org/10.1007/978-3-030-58604-1_8
4. Bertasius, G., Wang, H., Torresani, L.: Is space-time attention all you need for video understanding? In: ICML, pp. 813–824 (2021)
5. Bodla, N., Singh, B., Chellappa, R., Davis, L.S.: Soft-NMS-improving object detection with one line of code. In: ICCV, pp. 5561–5569 (2017)
6. Buch, S., Escorcia, V., Ghanem, B., Fei-Fei, L., Niebles, J.C.: End-to-end, single-stream temporal action detection in untrimmed videos. In: BMVC (2019)
7. Buch, S., Escorcia, V., Shen, C., Ghanem, B., Carlos Niebles, J.: SST: single-stream temporal action proposals. In: CVPR, pp. 2911–2920 (2017)
8. Bulat, A., Perez Rua, J.M., Sudhakaran, S., Martinez, B., Tzimiropoulos, G.: Space-time mixing attention for video transformer. In: NeurIPS, vol. 34 (2021)
9. Caba Heilbron, F., Escorcia, V., Ghanem, B., Carlos Niebles, J.: ActivityNet: a large-scale video benchmark for human activity understanding. In: CVPR, pp. 961–970 (2015)
10. Carreira, J., Zisserman, A.: Quo Vadis, action recognition? A new model and the kinetics dataset. In: CVPR, pp. 4724–4733 (2017)
11. Chang, S., Wang, P., Wang, F., Li, H., Feng, J.: Augmented transformer with adaptive graph for temporal action proposal generation. arXiv preprint arXiv:2103.16024 (2021)
12. Chang, X., et al.: MMVG-INF-ETROL@ TRECVID 2019: activities in extended video. In: TRECVID (2019)
13. Chao, Y.W., Vijayanarasimhan, S., Seybold, B., Ross, D.A., Deng, J., Sukthankar, R.: Rethinking the faster R-CNN architecture for temporal action localization. In: CVPR, pp. 1130–1139 (2018)
14. Chen, C.F., Panda, R., Fan, Q.: RegionViT: regional-to-local attention for vision transformers. In: ICLR (2022)
15. Chen, G., Zheng, Y., Wang, L., Lu, T.: DCAN: improving temporal action detection via dual context aggregation. In: AAAI (2022)
16. Chu, X., et al.: Twins: revisiting the design of spatial attention in vision transformers. In: NeurIPS (2021)
17. Chu, X., et al.: Conditional positional encodings for vision transformers. arXiv preprint arXiv:2102.10882 (2021)
18. Dosovitskiy, A., et al.: An image is worth 16x16 words: transformers for image recognition at scale. In: ICLR (2021)
19. Fan, H., et al.: Multiscale vision transformers. In: ICCV, pp. 6824–6835 (2021)
20. Fan, Q., Panda, R., et al.: An image classifier can suffice for video understanding. arXiv preprint arXiv:2106.14104 (2021)

21. Feichtenhofer, C., Fan, H., Malik, J., He, K.: SlowFast networks for video recognition. In: ICCV, pp. 6202–6211 (2019)
22. Gao, J., Yang, Z., Chen, K., Sun, C., Nevatia, R.: Turn tap: temporal unit regression network for temporal action proposals. In: ICCV, pp. 3628–3636 (2017)
23. Gong, G., Zheng, L., Mu, Y.: Scale matters: temporal scale aggregation network for precise action localization in untrimmed videos. In: ICME, pp. 1–6 (2020)
24. Han, M., et al.: Dual-AI: dual-path actor interaction learning for group activity recognition. In: CVPR (2022)
25. Han, Q., et al.: On the connection between local attention and dynamic depth-wise convolution. In: ICLR (2022)
26. Hendrycks, D., Gimpel, K.: Gaussian error linear units (GELUs). arXiv preprint arXiv:1606.08415 (2016)
27. Hou, Q., Cheng, M.M., Hu, X., Borji, A., Tu, Z., Torr, P.H.S.: Deeply supervised salient object detection with short connections. In: CVPR (2017)
28. Islam*, M.A., Jia*, S., Bruce, N.D.B.: How much position information do convolutional neural networks encode? In: ICLR (2020)
29. Jiang, Y.G., et al.: THUMOS challenge: action recognition with a large number of classes (2014)
30. Kingma, D.P., Ba, J.: Adam: a method for stochastic optimization. arXiv preprint arXiv:1412.6980 (2014)
31. Koot, R., Lu, H.: VideoLightFormer: lightweight action recognition using transformers. arXiv preprint arXiv:2107.00451 (2021)
32. Li, J., Liu, X., Zong, Z., Zhao, W., Zhang, M., Song, J.: Graph attention based proposal 3d convnets for action detection. In: AAAI, pp. 4626–4633, no. 04 (2020)
33. Li, K., et al.: UniFormer: unified transformer for efficient spatial-temporal representation learning. In: ICLR (2022)
34. Liang, Y., Zhou, P., Zimmermann, R., Yan, S.: DualFormer: local-global stratified transformer for efficient video recognition. arXiv preprint arXiv:2112.04674 (2021)
35. Lin, C., et al.: Learning salient boundary feature for anchor-free temporal action localization. In: CVPR, pp. 3320–3329 (2021)
36. Lin, T., Liu, X., Li, X., Ding, E., Wen, S.: BMN: boundary-matching network for temporal action proposal generation. In: ICCV, pp. 3889–3898 (2019)
37. Lin, T., Zhao, X., Shou, Z.: Single shot temporal action detection. In: ACM MM, pp. 988–996 (2017)
38. Lin, T., Zhao, X., Su, H., Wang, C., Yang, M.: BSN: boundary sensitive network for temporal action proposal generation. In: Ferrari, V., Hebert, M., Sminchisescu, C., Weiss, Y. (eds.) ECCV 2018. LNCS, vol. 11208, pp. 3–21. Springer, Cham (2018). https://doi.org/10.1007/978-3-030-01225-0_1
39. Lin, T.Y., Goyal, P., Girshick, R., He, K., Dollár, P.: Focal loss for dense object detection. In: ICCV, pp. 2980–2988 (2017)
40. Liu, Q., Wang, Z.: Progressive boundary refinement network for temporal action detection. In: AAAI, pp. 11612–11619 (2020)
41. Liu, Z., et al.: Swin transformer: hierarchical vision transformer using shifted windows. In: ICCV, pp. 10012–10022 (2021)
42. Liu, Z., et al.: Video swin transformer. arXiv preprint arXiv:2106.13230 (2021)
43. Long, F., Yao, T., Qiu, Z., Tian, X., Luo, J., Mei, T.: Gaussian temporal awareness networks for action localization. In: CVPR, pp. 344–353 (2019)
44. Nawhal, M., Mori, G.: Activity graph transformer for temporal action localization. arXiv preprint arXiv:2101.08540 (2021)
45. Neimark, D., Bar, O., Zohar, M., Asselmann, D.: Video transformer network. In: ICCV, pp. 3163–3172 (2021)

46. Pan, Z., Zhuang, B., He, H., Liu, J., Cai, J.: Less is more: pay less attention in vision transformers. In: AAAI (2022)
47. Pan, Z., Zhuang, B., Liu, J., He, H., Cai, J.: Scalable vision transformers with hierarchical pooling. In: ICCV, pp. 377–386 (2021)
48. Park, N., Kim, S.: How do vision transformers work? In: ICLR (2022)
49. Qiu, Z., Yao, T., Mei, T.: Learning spatio-temporal representation with pseudo-3d residual networks. In: ICCV, pp. 5533–5541 (2017)
50. Raghu, M., Unterthiner, T., Kornblith, S., Zhang, C., Dosovitskiy, A.: Do vision transformers see like convolutional neural networks? In: NeurIPS (2021)
51. Sharir, G., Noy, A., Zelnik-Manor, L.: An image is worth 16x16 words, what is a video worth? arXiv preprint arXiv:2103.13915 (2021)
52. Simonyan, K., Zisserman, A.: Two-stream convolutional networks for action recognition in videos. In: NeurIPS (2014)
53. Sridhar, D., Quader, N., Muralidharan, S., Li, Y., Dai, P., Lu, J.: Class semantics-based attention for action detection. In: ICCV, pp. 13739–13748 (2021)
54. Tan, J., Tang, J., Wang, L., Wu, G.: Relaxed transformer decoders for direct action proposal generation. In: ICCV, pp. 13526–13535 (2021)
55. Touvron, H., Cord, M., Douze, M., Massa, F., Sablayrolles, A., Jégou, H.: Training data-efficient image transformers & distillation through attention. In: ICML, pp. 10347–10357 (2021)
56. Tran, D., Bourdev, L., Fergus, R., Torresani, L., Paluri, M.: Learning spatiotemporal features with 3d convolutional networks. In: ICCV, pp. 4489–4497 (2015)
57. Vahdani, E., Tian, Y.: Deep learning-based action detection in untrimmed videos: a survey. arXiv preprint arXiv:2110.00111 (2021)
58. Vaswani, A., et al.: Attention is all you need. In: NeurIPS, vol. 30 (2017)
59. Wang, C., Cai, H., Zou, Y., Xiong, Y.: RGB stream is enough for temporal action detection. arXiv preprint arXiv:2107.04362 (2021)
60. Wang, L., et al.: Temporal segment networks for action recognition in videos. IEEE TPAMI **41**(11), 2740–2755 (2019)
61. Wang, W., et al.: Pyramid vision transformer: a versatile backbone for dense prediction without convolutions. In: ICCV, pp. 568–578 (2021)
62. Wang, Y., Chen, Z., Jiang, H., Song, S., Han, Y., Huang, G.: Adaptive focus for efficient video recognition. In: ICCV, pp. 16249–16258 (2021)
63. Wu, H., et al.: CVT: introducing convolutions to vision transformers. arXiv preprint arXiv:2103.15808 (2021)
64. Wu, J., et al.: Towards high-quality temporal action detection with sparse proposals. arXiv preprint arXiv:2109.08847 (2021)
65. Wu, Z., Su, L., Huang, Q.: Cascaded partial decoder for fast and accurate salient object detection. In: CVPR, pp. 3907–3916 (2019)
66. Xu, H., Das, A., Saenko, K.: R-C3D: region convolutional 3d network for temporal activity detection. In: ICCV, pp. 5783–5792 (2017)
67. Xu, M., Zhao, C., Rojas, D.S., Thabet, A., Ghanem, B.: G-TAD: sub-graph localization for temporal action detection. In: CVPR, pp. 10156–10165 (2020)
68. Yang, H., et al.: Temporal action proposal generation with background constraint. In: AAAI, vol. 36, pp. 3054–3062 (2022)
69. Yang, L., Peng, H., Zhang, D., Fu, J., Han, J.: Revisiting anchor mechanisms for temporal action localization. In: IEEE TIP, pp. 8535–8548 (2020)
70. Yeung, S., Russakovsky, O., Mori, G., Fei-Fei, L.: End-to-end learning of action detection from frame glimpses in videos. In: CVPR, pp. 2678–2687 (2016)

71. Zach, C., Pock, T., Bischof, H.: A duality based approach for realtime TV-L^1 optical flow. In: Hamprecht, F.A., Schnörr, C., Jähne, B. (eds.) DAGM 2007. LNCS, vol. 4713, pp. 214–223. Springer, Heidelberg (2007). https://doi.org/10.1007/978-3-540-74936-3_22
72. Zeng, R., et al.: Graph convolutional networks for temporal action localization. In: ICCV, pp. 7094–7103 (2019)
73. Zha, X., Zhu, W., Xun, L., Yang, S., Liu, J.: Shifted chunk transformer for spatio-temporal representational learning. In: NeurIPS, vol. 34 (2021)
74. Zhang, D., Dai, X., Wang, X., Wang, Y.: S3D: single shot multi-span detector via fully 3d convolutional networks. In: BMVC, p. 293 (2018)
75. Zhang, Y., et al.: VidTr: video transformer without convolutions. In: ICCV, pp. 13577–13587 (2021)
76. Zhao, C., Thabet, A.K., Ghanem, B.: Video self-stitching graph network for temporal action localization. In: ICCV, pp. 13658–13667 (2021)
77. Zhao, Y., Xiong, Y., Wang, L., Wu, Z., Tang, X., Lin, D.: Temporal action detection with structured segment networks. In: ICCV, pp. 2914–2923 (2017)

Human Trajectory Prediction via Neural Social Physics

Jiangbei Yue[1], Dinesh Manocha[2], and He Wang[1](✉)

[1] University of Leeds, Leeds, UK
H.E.Wang@leeds.ac.uk
[2] University of Maryland at College Park, College Park, USA

Abstract. Trajectory prediction has been widely pursued in many fields, and many *model-based* and *model-free* methods have been explored. The former include rule-based, geometric or optimization-based models, and the latter are mainly comprised of deep learning approaches. In this paper, we propose a new method combining both methodologies based on a new Neural Differential Equation model. Our new model (Neural Social Physics or NSP) is a deep neural network within which we use an explicit physics model with learnable parameters. The explicit physics model serves as a strong inductive bias in modeling pedestrian behaviors, while the rest of the network provides a strong data-fitting capability in terms of system parameter estimation and dynamics stochasticity modeling. We compare NSP with 15 recent deep learning methods on 6 datasets and improve the state-of-the-art performance by 5.56%–70%. Besides, we show that NSP has better generalizability in predicting plausible trajectories in drastically different scenarios where the density is 2–5 times as high as the testing data. Finally, we show that the physics model in NSP can provide plausible explanations for pedestrian behaviors, as opposed to black-box deep learning. Code is available: https://github.com/realcrane/Human-Trajectory-Prediction-via-Neural-Social-Physics.

Keywords: Human trajectory prediction · Neural differential equations

1 Introduction

Understanding human trajectories is key to many research areas such as physics, computer science and social sciences. Being able to learn behaviors with non-invasive sensors is important to analyzing the natural behaviors of humans. This problem has been widely studied in computer graphics, computer vision and machine learning [5]. Existing approaches generally fall into *model-based* and *model-free* methods. Early model-based methods tended to be empirical or

---

Supplementary Information The online version contains supplementary material available at https://doi.org/10.1007/978-3-031-19830-4_22.

S. Avidan et al. (Eds.): ECCV 2022, LNCS 13694, pp. 376–394, 2022.
https://doi.org/10.1007/978-3-031-19830-4_22

rule-based methods derived via the first-principles approach: summarizing observations into rules and deterministic systems based on fundamental assumptions on human motion. In such a perspective, social interactions can be modelled as forces in a particle system [20] or an optimization problem [8], and individuals can be influenced by affective states [36]. Later, data-driven model-based methods were introduced, in which the model behavior is still dominated by the assumptions on the dynamics, e.g. a linear dynamical system [19], but retains sufficient flexibility so that the model can be adjusted to fit observations. More recently, model-free methods based on deep learning have also been explored, and these demonstrate surprising trajectory prediction capability [1,9,14,16,18,29,31–33,37,38,48,49,55,70,76].

Empirical or rule-based methods possess good explainability because they are formed as explicit geometric optimization or ordinary/partial differentiable equations where specific terms correspond to certain behaviors. Therefore, they have been used for not only prediction but also analysis and simulation [58]. However, they are less effective in data fitting with respect to noise and are therefore unable to predict accurately, even when the model is calibrated on data [69]. Data-driven model-based methods (e.g., statistical machine learning) improve the ability of data fitting but are restricted by the specific statistical models employed which have limited capacities to learn from large amounts of data [19]. Finally, deep learning approaches excel at data fitting. They can learn from large datasets, but lack explainability and therefore have been mainly used for prediction rather than analysis and simulation [1,38,76].

We explore a model that can explain pedestrian behaviors and retain good data-fitting capabilities by combining model-based and model-free approaches. Inspired by recent research in neural differential equations [13,25,44,74,77], we propose a new crowd neural differentiable equation model consisting of two parts. The first is a deterministic model formulated using a differentiable equation. Although this equation can be arbitrary, we use a dynamical system inspired by the social force model [20]. In contrast to the social force model and its variants, the key parameters of our deterministic model are learnable through data instead of being hand-picked and fixed. The second part of our model captures complex uncertainty in the motion dynamics and observations via a Variational Autoencoder. Overall, the whole model is a deep neural network with an embedded explicit model; we call this model *Neural Social Physics* (NSP).

We demonstrate that our NSP model outperforms the state-of-the-art methods [9,14,16,18,29,31–33,37,38,48,49,55,70,76] in standard trajectory prediction tasks across various benchmark datasets [28,43,46] and metrics. In addition, we show that NSP can generalize to unseen scenarios with higher densities and still predict plausible motions with less collision between people, as opposed to pure black-box deep learning approaches. Finally, from the explicit model in NSP, we demonstrate that our method can provide plausible explanations for motions. Formally, (1) we propose a new neural differentiable equation model for trajectory prediction and analysis. (2) we propose a new mechanism to combine explicit and deterministic models with deep neural networks for crowd modeling. (3) We demonstrate the advantages of the NSP model in several aspects: prediction accuracy, generalization and explaining behaviors.

2 Related Work

2.1 Trajectory Analysis and Prediction

Statistical machine learning has been used for trajectory analysis in computer vision [11,15,26,42,64,66]. They aim to learn individual motion dynamics [75], structured latent patterns in data [63,64], anomalies [11,12], etc. These methods provide a certain level of explainability, but are limited in model capacity for learning from large amounts of data. Compared with these methods, our model leverages the ability of deep neural networks to handle high-dimensional and large data. More recently, deep learning has been exploited for trajectory prediction [53]. Recurrent neural networks (RNNs) [1,4,59] have been explored first due to their ability to learn from temporal data. Subsequently, other deep learning techniques and neural network architectures are introduced into trajectory prediction, such as Generative Adversarial Network (GAN) [18], conditional variational autoencoder (CVAE) [22,38,76] and Convolutional Neural Network (CNN) [39]. In order to capture the spatial features of trajectories and the interactions between pedestrians accurately, graph neural networks (GNNs) have also been used to reason and predict future trajectories [39,52]. Compared with existing deep learning methods, our method achieves better prediction accuracy. Further, our method has an explicit model which can explain pedestrian motions and lead to better generalizability. Very recently, attempts have been made in combining physics with deep learning for trajectory prediction [3,21,27]. But their methods are tied to specific physics models and are deterministic, while NSP is a general framework that aims to accommodate arbitrary physics models and is designed to be intrinsically stochastic to capture motion randomness.

2.2 Pedestrian and Crowd Simulation

Crowd simulation aims to generate trajectories given the initial position and destination of each agent [58], which essentially aims to predict individual motions. Empirical modelling and data-driven methods have been the two foundations in simulation [35,40]. Early research is dominated by empirical modelling or rule-based methods, where crowd motions are abstracted into mathematical equations and deterministic systems, such as flows [40], particle systems [20], and velocity and geometric optimization [8,51]. Meanwhile, data-driven methods using statistical machine learning have also been employed, e.g., using first-person vision to guide steering behaviors [35] or using trajectories to extract features to describe motions [23,67]. While the key parameters in these approaches are either fixed or learned from small datasets, our NSP model is more general. It can take existing deterministic systems as a component and provides better data-fitting capacity via deep neural networks. Compared with afore-mentioned model-based methods, our NSP can be regarded as using deep learning for model calibration. Our model possesses the ability to learn from large amount of data, which is difficult for traditional parameter estimation methods based on optimization or sampling [61]. Meanwhile, the formulation of our NSP is more general, flexible and data-driven than traditional model-based methods.

2.3 Deep Learning and Differential Equations

Solving differentiable equations (DE) with the assistance of deep learning has recently spiked strong interests [13,24,74,77]. Based on the involvement depth of deep learning, the research can be categorized into deep learning assisted DE, differentiable physics, neural differential equations and physics-informed neural networks (PINNs). Deep learning assisted DE involves accelerating various steps during the DE solve, such as Finite Element mesh generation [72,73]. The deeper involvement of neural networks is shown in differentiable physics and neural differential equations, where the former aims to make the whole simulation process differentiable [17,30,68], and the latter focuses on the part of the equations being parameterized by neural networks [50]. PINNs aim to bypass the DE solve and use NN for prediction [10,45]. Highly inspired by the research above, we propose a new neural differential equations model in a new application domain for human trajectory prediction.

3 Methodology

3.1 Neural Social Physics (NSP)

At any time t, the position p_i^t of the ith pedestrian can be observed in a crowd. Then a trajectory can be represented as a function of time $q(t)$, where we have discrete observations in time up to T, $\{q^0, q^1, \cdots, q^T\}$. An observation or *state* of a person at time t is represented by $q^t = [p^t, \dot{p}^t]^{\mathbf{T}}$ where p, $\dot{p} \in \mathbb{R}^2$ are the position and velocity. For most datasets, p is given and $\dot{p}$ can be estimated via finite difference. Given an observation q_n^t of the nth person, we consider her neighborhood set Ω_n^t containing other nearby pedestrians $\{q_j^t : j \in \Omega_n^t\}$. The neighborhood is also a function of time $\Omega(t)$. Then, in NSP the dynamics of a person (agent) in a crowd can be formulated as:

$$\frac{dq}{dt}(t) = f_{\theta,\phi}(t, q(t), \Omega(t), q^T, E) + \alpha_\phi(t, q^{t:t-M}) \tag{1}$$

where θ and ϕ are learnable parameters, E represents the environment. θ contains interpretable parameters explained later and ϕ contains uninterpretable parameters (e.g. neural network weights). The agent dynamics are governed by f which depends on time t, its current state $q(t)$, its time-varying neighborhood $\Omega(t)$ and the environment E. Similar to existing work, we assume there is dynamics stochasticity in NSP. But unlike them which assume simple forms (e.g. white noise) [19], we model time-varying stochasticity in a more general form: as a function of time, the current state and the brief history of the agent, $\alpha_\phi(t, q^{t:t-M})$. Then we have the following equation in NSP:

$$q^T = q^0 + \int_{t=0}^{T} f_{\theta,\phi}(t, q(t), \Omega(t), q^T, E) + \alpha_\phi(t, q^{t:t-M})dt \tag{2}$$

given the initial and final condition $q(0) = q^0$ and $q(T) = q^T$.

Physics models have been widely used to model crowd dynamics [20,40]. To leverage their interpretability, we model the dynamics as a physical system in NSP. Assuming the second-order differentiability of $p(t)$, NSP expands $q(t)$ via Taylor's series for a first-order approximation:

$$q(t+\triangle t) \approx q(t) + \dot{q}(t)\triangle t = \begin{pmatrix} p(t) \\ \dot{p}(t) \end{pmatrix} + \triangle t \begin{pmatrix} \dot{p}(t) + \alpha(t, q^{t:t-M}) \\ \ddot{p}(t) \end{pmatrix} \tag{3}$$

where $\triangle t$ is the time step. The stochasticity $\alpha(t, q^{t:t-M})$ is assumed to only influence $\dot{p}$. Equation 3 is general and any dynamical system with second-order differentiability can be employed here. Below, we realize NSP by combining a type of physics models-social force models (SFM) [20] and neural networks. We refer to our model NSP-SFM.

3.2 NSP-SFM

We design the NSP-SFM by assuming each person acts as a particle in a particle system and each particle is governed by Newton's second law of motion. $\ddot{p}(t)$ is designed to be dependent on three forces: goal attraction F_{goal}, inter-agent repulsion F_{col} and environment repulsion F_{env}.

$$\ddot{p}(t) = F_{goal}(t, q^T, q^t) + F_{col}(t, q^t, \Omega^t) + F_{env}(t, q^t, E) \tag{4}$$

where E is the environment and explained later. However, unlike [20], the three forces are partially realized by neural networks, turning Eq. 1 into a neural differential equation. The overall model is shown in Fig. 1. Note that, in Eq. 1, we assume p^T is given, although it is not available during prediction. Therefore, we employ a Goal Sampling Network (GSN) to sample p^T. During testing, we either first sample a p^T for prediction or require the user to input p^T. The GSN is similar to a part of Y-net [37] and pre-trained, and detailed in the supplementary materials.

Given the current state and the goal, we compute F_{goal} using the Goal-Network NN_{ϕ_1} in Eq. 5 (Fig. 2 Left), F_{col} using the Collision-Network NN_{ϕ_2} in

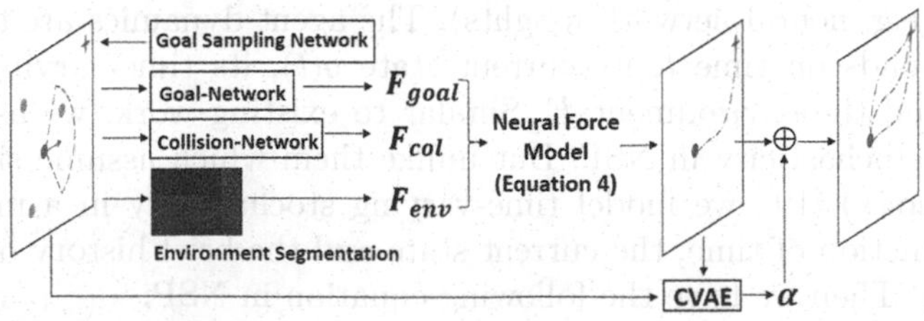

Fig. 1. Overview of NSP-SFM. F_{goal}, F_{col} and F_{env} are estimated in every time step by Goal-Network, Collision-Network and Eq. 7 before solving Eq. 4. The output is used to update the position and velocity which are then combined with the estimated noise from α for the final prediction

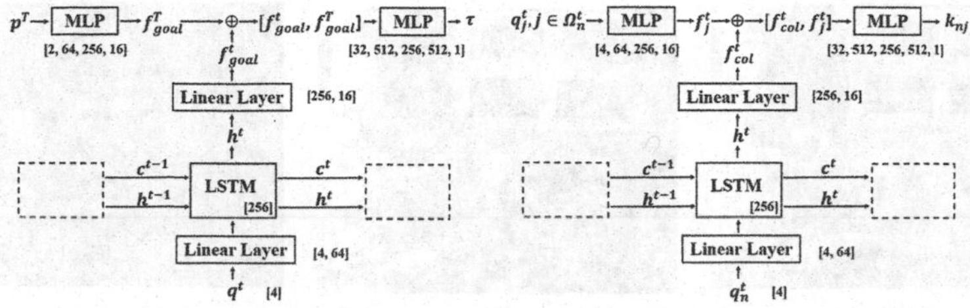

Fig. 2. Left: Goal-Network and Right: Collision-Network. The numbers in square brackets show both the number and dimension of the layers in each component.

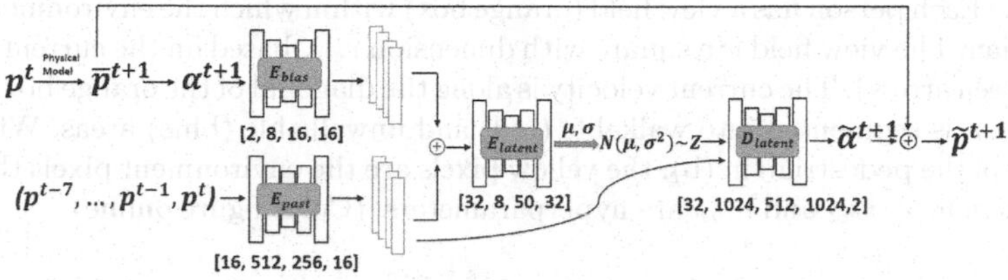

Fig. 3. The architecture of the CVAE, where $\bar{p}^{t+1}$ is the intermediate prediction out of our force model and $\alpha^{t+1} = p^{t+1} - \bar{p}^{t+1}$. Encoder E_{bias}, E_{past}, E_{latent} and decoder D_{latent} are all MLP networks with dimensions indicated in the square brackets. More Details of the network can be found in the supplementary material

Eq. 6 (Fig. 2 Right) and F_{env} using Eq. 7 directly. The Goal-Network encodes q^t then feeds it into a Long Short Term Memory (LSTM) network to capture dynamics. After a linear transformation, the LSTM output is concatenated with the embedded p^T. Finally, τ is computed by an MLP (multi-layer perceptron). In Collision-Network, the architecture is similar. Every agent q_j^t in the neighborhood Ω_n^t is encoded and concatenated with the encoded agent q_n^t. Then k_{nj} is computed. τ and k_{nj} are interpretable key parameters of F_{goal} and F_{col}. The corresponding parameter in F_{env} is k_{env}. Finally, we show our network for α for stochasticity modeling in Fig. 3.

Goal Attraction. Pedestrians are always drawn to destinations, which can be abstracted into a goal attraction force. At time t, a pedestrian has a desired walking direction e^t determined by the goal p^T and the current position p^t: $e^t = \frac{p^T - p^t}{\|p^T - p^t\|}$. If there are no other forces, she will change her current velocity to the desired velocity $v_{des}^t = v_0^t e^t$ where v_0^t and e^t are the magnitude and direction respectively. Instead of using a fixed v_0 as in [20], we update v_0^t at every t to mimic the change of the desired speed as the pedestrian approaches the destination: $v_0^t = \frac{\|p^T - p^t\|}{(T-t)\Delta t}$. Therefore, the desired velocity is defined as $v_{des}^t = v_0^t e^t = \frac{p^T - p^t}{(T-t)\Delta t}$. The goal attraction force F_{goal} represents the tendency of a pedestrian changing her current velocity $\dot{p}^t$ to the desired velocity v_{des}^t within time τ:

$$F_{goal} = \frac{1}{\tau}(v_{des}^t - \dot{p}^t) \text{ where } \tau = NN_{\phi_1}(q^t, p^T) \tag{5}$$

Fig. 4. (a) The neighborhood $\Omega(t)$ of a person is a sector within a circle (centered at this person with radius r_{col}) spanned by an angle ω from the current velocity vector (green arrow). (b) Each person has a view field (orange box) within which the environment repels a pedestrian. The view field is a square with dimension r_{env} based on the current velocity vector (green arrow). The current velocity is along the diagonal of the orange box. (c) The environment is segmented into walkable (red) and unwalkable (blue) areas. Within the view field of the pedestrian in (b), the yellow pixels are the environment pixels that repel the pedestrian. ω, r_{col} and r_{env} are hyperparameters. (Color figure online)

where τ is learned through a neural network (NN) parameterized by ϕ_1.

Inter-agent Repulsion. Pedestrians often steer to avoid potential collisions and maintain personal space when other people are in the immediate neighborhood (Fig. 4 a). Given an agent j in Ω_n^t of agent n and her state q_j^t, agent j repels agent n based on $r_{nj} = p_n^t - p_j^t$:

$$F_{col}^{nj} = -\nabla_{r_{nj}} \mathcal{U}_{nj}\left(\|r_{nj}\|\right), \text{ where } \mathcal{U}_{nj}\left(\|r_{nj}\|\right) = r_{col} k_{nj} e^{-\|r_{nj}\|/r_{col}} \tag{6}$$

where we employ a repulsive potential field $\mathcal{U}_{nj}\left(\|r_{nj}\|\right)$ modeled by a monotonic decreasing function of $\|r_{nj}\|$. Then the repulsive force caused by agent $j \in \Omega_n^t$ to agent n is the gradient of $\mathcal{U}_{nj}$. Previously, simple functions such as symmetric elliptic fields were employed for $\mathcal{U}_{nj}$ [20]. Here, we model $\mathcal{U}_{nj}$ as a time-varying field parameterized by k_{nj} which is learned via a neural network. Instead of directly learning k_{nj}, we set $k_{nj} = a * sigmoid(NN_{\phi_2}(q_n^t, q_{j,j\in\Omega_n^t}^t)) + b$. a and b are hyperparameters to ensure that the learned k_{nj} value is valid. If we have m agents at time t in Ω_n^t, the net repulsive force on agent n is: $F_{col}^n = \sum_{j=0}^m F_{col}^{nj}$.

Environment Repulsion. Besides collisions with others, people also avoid nearby obstacles. We model the repulsion from the environment as:

$$F_{env} = \frac{k_{env}}{\|p_n^t - p_{obs}\|}\left(\frac{p_n^t - p_{obs}}{\|p_n^t - p_{obs}\|}\right) \tag{7}$$

where p_{obs} is the position of the obstacle and k_{env} is a learnable parameter. NSP-SFM learns k_{env} directly via back-propagation and stochastic gradient descent. Since the environment is big, we assume the agent mainly focuses on her view field (Fig. 4b) within which the environment (Fig. 4c) repels the pedestrian. We calculate p_{obs} as the center of the pixels that are classified as obstacles in the view field of an agent. k_{env} is shared among all obstacles. So far, we have introduced all the interpretable parameters $\theta = \{\tau, k_{nj}, k_{env}\}$ in Eq. 1.

Dynamics Stochasticity $\alpha(t, q^{t:t-M})$. Trajectory prediction needs to explicitly model the motion randomness caused by intrinsic motion stochasticity and observational noises [62,63]. We employ a more general setting by assuming the noise distribution can have arbitrary shapes and is also time varying, unlike previous formulations such as white noise [19] which is too restrictive. Generally, learning such functions requires large amounts of data, as it is unconstrained. To constrain the learning, we further assume the noise is *Normally* distributed in a latent space, rather than in the data space.

Given a prediction $\bar{p}^{t+1}$ without dynamics stochasticity and its corresponding observation p^{t+1}, there is an error $\alpha^{t+1} = \bar{p}^{t+1} - p^{t+1}$. To model the arbitrary and time-varying shape of the distribution of α^{t+1}, we assume it depends on the brief history $p^{t:t-M}$ which implicitly considers the environment and other people. Then the conditional likelihood of α^{t+1} is: $P(\alpha^{t+1}|p^{t:t-M}) = \int P(\alpha^{t+1}|p^{t:t-M}, z)P(z)dz$, where z is a latent variable. Assuming a mapping $Q(z|\alpha^{t+1}, p^{t:t-M})$ and z being *Normally* distributed, minimizing the KL divergence between Q, i.e., the variational posterior, and $P(z|\alpha^{t+1}, p^{t:t-M})$ leads to a conditional Variational Autoencoder (CVAE) [54].

Our overall loss function is defined as $L = l_{traj} + l_{cvae}$ where:

$$
\begin{aligned}
l_{traj} =& \frac{1}{N(T-M)} \sum_{n=1}^{N} \sum_{t=M+1}^{T} \|p_n^t - \bar{p}_n^t\|_2^2 \\
l_{cvae} =& \frac{1}{N(T-M)} \sum_{n=1}^{N} \sum_{t=M+1}^{T} \{\|\alpha_n^t - \tilde{\alpha}_n^t\|_2^2 \\
& + \lambda D_{KL}(Q(z|\alpha_n^t, p^{t:t-M})||P(z|\alpha_n^t, p^{t:t-M}))\}
\end{aligned} \quad (8)
$$

N is the total number of samples, M is the length of the history, and T is the total length of the trajectory. l_{traj} minimizes the difference between the predicted position and the ground-truth, while l_{cvae} learns the distribution of randomness α. During training, in each iteration, we assume the first $M+1$ frames of the trajectory are given and run the forward pass iteratively to predict the rest of the trajectory, then back-propagate to compute the gradient to update all parameters. During the forward pass, we use a semi-implicit scheme for stability: $\dot{p}^{t+1} = \dot{p}^t + \Delta t \ddot{p}^t$ and $p^{t+1} = p^t + \Delta t \dot{p}^{t+1}$. We employ a progressive training scheme for the sub-nets. We first train Goal-Network with l_{traj} only, then fix Goal-Network and add Collision-Network and F_{env} for training using l_{traj}. Finally, we fix Goal-Network, Collision-Network and F_{env}, add α for training under l_{cvae}. We find this progressive training significantly improves the convergence speed. This is because we first train the deterministic part with the main forces added gradually, which converges quickly. Then the stochasticity part is trained separately to capture complex randomness. Please see the supplementary material for implementation details.

3.3 NSP Vs. Deep Neural Networks

One big difference between NSP and existing deep learning is the deterministic system embedded in NSP. Instead of learning any function mapping the input to the output (as black box deep learning does), the deterministic system acts as a strong inductive bias and constrains the functional space within which the target mapping should lie. This is because a PDE family can be seen as a flow connecting the input and the output space [2], and the learning is essentially a process of finding the most fitting PDE within this flow. In addition to better data-fitting capability, this strong inductive bias also comes with two other advantages. First, the learned model can help explain motions because the PDE we employ is a physics system where the learnable parameters have physical meanings. Second, after learning, the PDE can be used to predict motions in drastically different scenes (e.g., with higher densities) and generate more plausible trajectories (e.g., fewer collisions). This is difficult for existing deep learning as it requires to extrapolate significantly to unseen interactions between pedestrians.

4 Experiments

4.1 Datasets

We employ six widely used datasets in human trajectory prediction tasks: the Stanford Drone Dataset [46], ETH Hotel, ETH University [43], UCY University, Zara1, and Zara2 datasets [28]. **Stanford Drone Dataset (SDD):** SDD contains videos of a university campus with six classes of agents with rich interactions. SDD includes about 185,000 interactions between different agents and approximately 40,000 interactions between the agent and the environment. **ETH/UCY Datasets:** The datasets consist of human trajectories across five scenes recording the world coordinates of pedestrians. Following previous research [37,38], we adopt the standard leave-one-out evaluation protocol, where the model is trained on four sub-datasets and evaluated one. Since our goal sampling network and F_{env} need to work in the pixel space, we project the world coordinates in ETH/UCY into the pixel space using the homography matrices provided in Y-net [37]. When computing the prediction error, we project the predictions in the pixel space back into the world space. Finally, for SDD and ETH/UCY, we follow previous work [37,47] to segment trajectories into 20-frame samples and split the dataset for training/testing. Given the first 8 ($M = 7$) frames, we train NSP to predict the remaining 12 frames for each trajectory.

4.2 Trajectory Prediction

Average Displacement Error (ADE) and Final Displacement Error (FDE) are employed as previous research [1,18,37,38]. ADE is calculated as the l_2 error between a predicted trajectory and the ground truth, averaged over the entire trajectory. FDE is calculated as the l_2 error between the predicted final point and the ground truth. Following prior works, in the presence of multiple possible future predictions, the minimal error is reported. We compare our NSP-SFM

Table 1. Results on ETH/UCY and SDD based standard-sampling. NSP-SFM outperforms all baseline methods in both ADE and FDE. 20 samples are used in prediction and the minimal error is reported. $M = 7$ in all experiments. The unit is meters on ETH/UCY and pixels on SDD.

Methods	Metrics	ETH	Hotel	UNIV	ZARA1	ZARA2	AVG	SDD
S-GAN [18]	ADE	0.81	0.72	0.60	0.34	0.42	0.58	27.23
	FDE	1.52	1.61	1.26	0.69	0.84	1.18	41.44
Sophie [48]	ADE	0.70	0.76	0.54	0.30	0.38	0.54	16.27
	FDE	1.43	1.67	1.24	0.63	0.78	1.15	29.38
CF-VAE [9]	ADE	N/A	N/A	N/A	N/A	N/A	N/A	12.60
	FDE	N/A	N/A	N/A	N/A	N/A	N/A	22.30
CGNS [29]	ADE	0.62	0.70	0.48	0.32	0.35	0.49	15.6
	FDE	1.40	0.93	1.22	0.59	0.71	0.97	28.2
NEXT [33]	ADE	0.73	0.30	0.60	0.38	0.31	0.46	N/A
	FDE	1.65	0.59	1.27	0.81	0.68	1.00	N/A
P2TIRL [14]	ADE	N/A	N/A	N/A	N/A	N/A	N/A	12.58
	FDE	N/A	N/A	N/A	N/A	N/A	N/A	22.07
SimAug [31]	ADE	N/A	N/A	N/A	N/A	N/A	N/A	10.27
	FDE	N/A	N/A	N/A	N/A	N/A	N/A	19.71
PECNet [38]	ADE	0.54	0.18	0.35	0.22	0.17	0.29	9.96
	FDE	0.87	0.24	0.60	0.39	0.30	0.48	15.88
Traj++ [49]	ADE	0.39	0.12	**0.20**	**0.15**	**0.11**	0.19	N/A
	FDE	0.83	0.21	0.44	0.33	0.25	0.41	N/A
Multiverse [32]	ADE	N/A	N/A	N/A	N/A	N/A	N/A	14.78
	FDE	N/A	N/A	N/A	N/A	N/A	N/A	27.09
Y-net [37]	ADE	0.28	0.10	0.24	0.17	0.13	0.18	7.85
	FDE	0.33	0.14	0.41	**0.27**	0.22	0.27	11.85
SIT [55]	ADE	0.38	0.11	**0.20**	0.16	0.12	0.19	N/A
	FDE	0.88	0.21	0.46	0.37	0.27	0.44	N/A
Social DualCVAE [16]	ADE	0.66	0.34	0.39	0.27	0.24	0.38	N/A
	FDE	1.18	0.61	0.74	0.48	0.42	0.69	N/A
CSCNet [70]	ADE	0.51	0.22	0.36	0.31	0.47	0.37	14.63
	FDE	1.05	0.42	0.81	0.68	1.02	0.79	26.91
NSP-SFM (Ours)	ADE	**0.25**	**0.09**	0.21	0.16	0.12	**0.17**	**6.52**
	FDE	**0.24**	**0.13**	**0.38**	**0.27**	**0.20**	**0.24**	**10.61**

with an extensive list of baselines, including published papers and unpublished technical reports: Social GAN (S-GAN) [18], Sophie [48], Conditional Flow VAE (CF-VAE) [9], Conditional Generative Neural System (CGNS) [29], NEXT [33], P2TIRL [14], SimAug [31], PECNet [38], Traj++ [49], Multiverse [32], Y-Net [37], SIT [55], S-CSR [76], Social-DualCVAE [16] and CSCNet [70]. We divide the baselines into two groups due to their setting differences. All baseline methods except S-CSR report the minimal error out of 20 sampled trajectories. S-CSR achieved better results by predicting 20 possible states in each step, and it is the only method adopting such sampling to our best knowledge. We refer to the former as standard-sampling and the latter as ultra-sampling. We compare NSP-SFM with S-CSR and other baseline methods under their respective settings.

Standard-sampling results are shown in Table 1. On SDD, NSP-SFM outperforms the best baseline Y-Net by 16.94% and 10.46% in ADE and FDE, respectively. In ETH/UCY, the improvement on average is 5.56% and 11.11%

Table 2. Results on ETH/UCY (left) and SDD (right) based on ultra-sampling. 20 samples per step are used for prediction and the overall minimal error is reported. NSP-SFM outperforms S-CSR on both datasets in ADE and FDE.

Methods	Metrics	ETH	Hotel	UNIV	ZARA1	ZARA2	Avg	SDD
S-CSR [76]	ADE	0.19	0.06	0.13	0.06	0.06	0.10	2.77
	FDE	0.35	**0.07**	0.21	0.07	0.08	0.16	3.45
NSP-SFM	ADE	**0.07**	**0.03**	**0.03**	**0.02**	**0.02**	**0.03**	**1.78**
	FDE	**0.09**	**0.07**	**0.04**	**0.04**	**0.04**	**0.06**	**3.44**

Fig. 5. Red dots are observed, green dots are our prediction and black dots are the ground-truth. Blue dots are pedestrians. F_{goal}, F_{col} and F_{env} are shown as yellow, light blue and black arrows for a person. The orange areas are the view field for avoiding collisions with other people (left) and the environment (middle). They provide plausible explanations of individual behaviors such as steering. Left and middle show the major influence of different forces. Right shows motion randomness captured by our model. (Color figure online)

in ADE and FDE, with the maximal ADE improvement 12.5% in UNIV and the maximal FDE improvement 27.27% in ETH. We also compare NSP-SFM with S-CSR in Table 2. NSP-SFM outperforms S-CSR on ETH/UCY by 70% and 62.5% on average in ADE and FDE. In SDD, the improvement is 35.74% and 0.3% (Table 2). S-CSR is stochastic and learns per-step distributions, which enables it to draw 20 samples for every step during prediction. Therefore, the min error of S-CSR is much smaller than the other baselines. Similarly, NSP-SFM also learns a per-step distribution (the α function) despite its main behavior being dictated by a deterministic system. Under the same ultra-sampling setting, NSP-SFM outperforms S-CSR.

4.3 Generalization to Unseen Scenarios

We evaluate NSP-SFM on significantly different scenarios after training. We increase the scene density as it is a major factor in pedestrian dynamics [41]. This is through randomly sampling initial and goal positions and let NSP-SFM predict the trajectories. Since there is no ground truth, to evaluate the prediction plausibility, we employ collision rate because it is widely adopted [34] and parsimonious: regardless of the specific behaviors of agents, they do not penetrate each other in the real world. The collision rate is computed based on the percentage of trajectories colliding with one another. We treat each agent as a disc with radius $r = 0.2\,\mathrm{m}$ in ECY/UCY and $r = 15$ pixels in SDD. Once the distance between two agents falls below $2\,r$, we count the two trajectories as in collision. Due to the tracking error and the distorted images, the ground truth r is hard to obtain. We need to estimate r. If it is too large, the collision rate will be high in all cases; otherwise the collision rate will be too low, e.g., $r = 0$ will give 0% collision rate all the time. Therefore, we did a search and found that the above values are reasonable as they keep the collision rate of the ground-truth data approximately zero. We show two experiments. The first is the collision rate on the testing data, and the second is scenarios with higher densities. While the first is mainly to compare the plausibility of the prediction, the second is to test the model generalizability. For comparison, we choose two state-of-the-art baseline methods: Y-net and S-CSR. Y-net is published which achieves the best performance, while S-CSR is unpublished but claims to achieve better performance.

Table 3 shows the comparison of the collision rate. NSP-SFM outperforms the baseline methods in generating trajectories with fewer collisions. Y-net and S-CSR also perform well on the testing data because their predictions are close to the ground-truth. Nevertheless, they are still worse than NSP-SFM. Next, we test drastically different scenarios. We use ZARA2 and coupa0 (a sub-dataset from SDD) as the environment and randomly sample the initial positions and goals for 32 and 50 agents respectively. Because the highest number of people that simultaneously appear in the scene is 14 in ZARA2 and 11 in coupa0, we effectively increase the density by 2–5 times. For NSP-SFM, the initial and goal positions are sufficient. For Y-net and S-CSR which require 8 frames (3.2 s) as input, we use NSP-SFM to simulate the first 8 frames of each agent, then feed them into both baselines. Table 4 shows the results of three experiments. Since the density is significantly higher than the data, both Y-net and S-CSR cause much higher collision rate. While NSP-SFM's collision rate also occasionally increases (i.e. SDD) compared with Table 3, it is far more plausible.

4.4 Interpretability of Prediction

Unlike black-box deep learning methods, NSP-SFM has an embedded explainable model. While predicting a trajectory, NSP can also provide plausible explanations of the motion, by estimating the 'forces' exerted on a specific person. This potentially enables NSP-SFM to be used in applications beyond prediction, e.g. behavior analysis [71]. Figure 5 Left shows that a person, instead of directly walking towards the goal, steered upwards (the green trajectory in the orange area). This could be explained by the strong repulsive force (the light blue arrow) which is generated by the potential collisions with the agents in front of this person, in line with existing studies [41]. Similar explanations can be made in Fig. 5 Middle, where all three forces are present. F_{env} (the black arrow) is the most prominent, as expected, as the person is very close to the car. The repulsive force (light blue arrow) also plays a role due to the person in front of the agent (the blue dot in the orange area).

Table 3. Collision rate on testing data in ETH/UCY and SDD. NSP-SFM universally outperforms all baseline methods.

Methods	ETH	Hotel	UNIV	ZARA1	ZARA2	Avg	SDD
Y-net	0	0	1.51%	0.82%	1.31%	0.73%	0.47%
S-CSR	0	0	1.82%	0.41%	1.31%	0.71%	**0.42%**
NSP-SFM	**0**	**0**	**1.48%**	**0**	**0.66%**	**0.43%**	**0.42%**

Table 4. Collision rates of the generalization experiments on ZARA2 (Z) and coupa0 (C). NSP-SFM shows strong generalizability in unseen high density scenarios.

Methods	Z(1)	Z(2)	Z(3)	Z(avg)	C(1)	C(2)	C(3)	C(avg)
Y-net	1.8%	2.2%	2.0%	2.0%	2.8%	2.9%	3.8%	3.2%
S-CSR	3.2%	2.4%	1.8%	2.5%	2.5%	1.7%	1.9%	2.0%
NSP-SFM	**0.2%**	**0.2%**	**0**	**0.1%**	**0.6%**	**0.6%**	**0.6%**	**0.6%**

Table 5. Ablation study on SDD. (w/o) means without CVAE and (w) means with CVAE. F_{goal} is goal attraction only and NSP-SFM is all three forces.

SDD	F_{goal}(w/o)	NSP-SFM(w/o)	NSP-SFM(w)
ADE	6.57	6.52	1.78
FDE	10.68	10.61	3.44

Figure 5 Right shows an example where motion randomness is captured by NSP. In this example, there was no other pedestrian and the person was not close to any obstacle. However, the trajectory still significantly deviates from a straight line, which cannot be fully explained by e.g. the principle of minimal energy expenditure [60]. The deviation could be caused by unobserved factors, e.g. the agent changing her goal or being distracted by something on the side. These factors do not only affect the trajectory but also the dynamics, e.g. sudden changes of velocity. These unobserved random factors are implicitly captured by the CVAE in NSP-SFM. More results are in the supplementary material.

We emphasize that NSP-SFM merely provides plausible explanations and by no means the only possible explanations. Although explaining behaviors based on physics models has been widely used, there can be alternative explanations [65]. Visualizing the forces is merely one possible way. Theoretically, it is also possible to visualize deep neural networks, e.g. layer activation. However, it is unclear how or which layer to visualize to explain the motion. Overall, NSP-SFM is more explainable than black-box deep learning.

4.5 Ablation Study

To further investigate the roles of different components, we conduct an ablation study on SDD with three settings: F_{goal}(w/o) with goal attraction only, i.e. omitting other components such as F_{col}, F_{env} and dynamics stochasticity; NSP-SFM

Fig. 6. Red, green and cyan dots are observations, prediction and ground-truth respectively. From left to right: ground truth, F_{goal}(w/o), NSP-SFM(w/o) and NSP-SFM(w). (Color figure online)

(w/o) without dynamics stochasticity; and NSP-SFM (w) the full model. The results are shown in Table 5. Interestingly, F_{goal}(w/o) can already achieve good results. This is understandable as it is trained first in our progressive training scheme and catches most of the dynamics. NSP-SFM (w/o) further improves the performance. The improvement seems to be small but we find the other repulsive forces are crucial for trajectories with irregular geometries such as avoiding obstacles. Further NSP-SFM (w) significantly improves the results because it enables NSP to learn the dynamics stochasticity via a per-step distribution. We show one example in Fig. 6 in all settings. More ablation experiments can be found in the supplementary material.

5 Conclusions, Limitations, and Future Work

In this paper, we have proposed a new Neural Differential Equation model for trajectory prediction. Through exhaustive evaluation and comparison, our model, Neural Social Physics, has proven to be more accurate in trajectory prediction, generalize well in significantly different scenarios and can provide possible explanations for motions. The major limitation of NSP lies in the physics model, which overly simplifies people into 2D particles. In real-world scenarios, people are much more complex, and their motions can be influenced by other factors such as their affective states or interact with dense scenarios [6,7]. It would be useful to extend our NSP framework by incorporating these ideas and handle complex systems such as fluids/fields/agent-based modeling can be adopted to replace the components in Eq. 3. In the future, we would like to extend the current framework to model high-density crowds, where continuum models or reciprocal velocity obstacles need to be used. We would also like to incorporate learning-based collision detection techniques into this framework [56,57].

Acknowledgements. This project has received funding from the European Union's Horizon 2020 research and innovation programme under grant agreement No 899739 CrowdDNA.

References

1. Alahi, A., Goel, K., Ramanathan, V., Robicquet, A., Fei-Fei, L., Savarese, S.: Social LSTM: human trajectory prediction in crowded spaces. In: Proceedings of the IEEE Conference on Computer Vision and Pattern Recognition, pp. 961–971 (2016)
2. Álvarez León, L.M., Esclarín Monreal, J., Lefébure, M., Sánchez, J.: A PDE model for computing the optical flow. In: CEDYA XVI (1999)
3. Antonucci, A., Papini, G.P.R., Palopoli, L., Fontanelli, D.: Generating reliable and efficient predictions of human motion: a promising encounter between physics and neural networks. arXiv preprint arXiv:2006.08429 (2020)
4. Bartoli, F., Lisanti, G., Ballan, L., Del Bimbo, A.: Context-aware trajectory prediction. In: 2018 24th International Conference on Pattern Recognition (ICPR), pp. 1941–1946. IEEE (2018)
5. Bendali-Braham, M., Weber, J., Forestier, G., Idoumghar, L., Muller, P.A.: Recent trends in crowd analysis: a review. Mach. Learn. Appl. **4**, 100023 (2021)
6. Bera, A., Manocha, D.: Realtime multilevel crowd tracking using reciprocal velocity obstacles. In: 2014 22nd International Conference on Pattern Recognition, pp. 4164–4169. IEEE (2014)
7. Bera, A., Randhavane, T., Manocha, D.: Aggressive, tense or shy? identifying personality traits from crowd videos. In: IJCAI, pp. 112–118 (2017)
8. van den Berg, J., Lin, M., Manocha, D.: Reciprocal velocity obstacles for real-time multi-agent navigation. In: 2008 IEEE International Conference on Robotics and Automation (2008)
9. Bhattacharyya, A., Hanselmann, M., Fritz, M., Schiele, B., Straehle, C.N.: Conditional flow variational autoencoders for structured sequence prediction. In: 4th Workshop on Bayesian Deep Learning. bayesiandeeplearning. org (2019)
10. Cai, S., Mao, Z., Wang, Z., Yin, M., Karniadakis, G.E.: Physics-informed neural networks (pinns) for fluid mechanics: a review. Acta Mech. Sinica **37**, 1727–1738 (2022)
11. Chaker, R., Al Aghbari, Z., Junejo, I.N.: Social network model for crowd anomaly detection and localization. Pattern Recogn. **61**, 266–281 (2017)
12. Charalambous, P., Karamouzas, I., Guy, S.J., Chrysanthou, Y.: A data-driven framework for visual crowd analysis. Comput. Graphi. Forum **33**, 41–50. Wiley Online Library (2014)
13. Chen, R.T., Rubanova, Y., Bettencourt, J., Duvenaud, D.K.: Neural ordinary differential equations. In: 32nd Conference on Neural Information Processing Systems (NeurIPS 2018), vol. 33 (2018)
14. Deo, N., Trivedi, M.M.: Trajectory forecasts in unknown environments conditioned on grid-based plans. arXiv preprint arXiv:2001.00735 (2020)
15. Ellis, D., Sommerlade, E., Reid, I.: Modelling pedestrian trajectory patterns with gaussian processes. In: 2009 IEEE 12th International Conference on Computer Vision Workshops, ICCV Workshops, pp. 1229–1234. IEEE (2009)
16. Gao, J., Shi, X., Yu, J.J.: Social-dualcvae: multimodal trajectory forecasting based on social interactions pattern aware and dual conditional variational auto-encoder. arXiv preprint arXiv:2202.03954 (2022)
17. Gong, D., Zhu, Z., Andrew, B., Wang, H.: Fine-grained differentiable physics: a yarn-level model for fabrics. In: International Conference on Learning Representations (2022)

18. Gupta, A., Johnson, J., Fei-Fei, L., Savarese, S., Alahi, A.: Social GAN: socially acceptable trajectories with generative adversarial networks. In: Proceedings of the IEEE Conference on Computer Vision and Pattern Recognition, pp. 2255–2264 (2018)
19. He, F., Xia, Y., Zhao, X., Wang, H.: Informative scene decomposition for crowd analysis, comparison and simulation guidance. ACM Trans. Graph. **4**(39) (2020)
20. Helbing, D., Molnar, P.: Social force model for pedestrian dynamics. Phys. Rev. E **51**(5), 4282 (1995)
21. Hossain, S., Johora, F.T., Müller, J.P., Hartmann, S., Reinhardt, A.: SFMGNet: A physics-based neural network to predict pedestrian trajectories. arXiv (2022)
22. Ivanovic, B., Pavone, M.: The trajectron: probabilistic multi-agent trajectory modeling with dynamic spatiotemporal graphs. In: Proceedings of the IEEE/CVF International Conference on Computer Vision, pp. 2375–2384 (2019)
23. Karamouzas, I., Sohre, N., Hu, R., Guy, S.J.: Crowd space: a predictive crowd analysis technique. ACM Trans. Graph. **37**(6), 1–14 (2018)
24. Karniadakis, G.E., Kevrekidis, I.G., Lu, L., Perdikaris, P., Wang, S., Yang, L.: Physics-informed machine learning. Nat. Rev. Phys. **3**, 422–440 (2021)
25. Kidger, P.: On neural differential equations (2022)
26. Kim, S., Bera, A., Manocha, D.: Interactive crowd content generation and analysis using trajectory-level behavior learning. In: 2015 IEEE International Symposium on Multimedia (ISM), pp. 21–26. IEEE (2015)
27. Kreiss, S.: Deep social force. arXiv preprint arXiv:2109.12081 (2021)
28. Lerner, A., Chrysanthou, Y., Lischinski, D.: Crowds by example. Comput. Graph. Forum **26**, 655–664. Wiley Online Library (2007)
29. Li, J., Ma, H., Tomizuka, M.: Conditional generative neural system for probabilistic trajectory prediction. In: 2019 IEEE/RSJ International Conference on Intelligent Robots and Systems (IROS), pp. 6150–6156. IEEE (2019)
30. Liang, J., Lin, M., Koltun, V.: Differentiable cloth simulation for inverse problems. In: Advances in Neural Information Processing Systems, vol. 32 (2019)
31. Liang, J., Jiang, L., Hauptmann, A.: SimAug: learning robust representations from 3d simulation for pedestrian trajectory prediction in unseen cameras. arXiv preprint arXiv:2004.02022 2 (2020)
32. Liang, J., Jiang, L., Murphy, K., Yu, T., Hauptmann, A.: The garden of forking paths: Towards multi-future trajectory prediction. In: Proceedings of the IEEE/CVF Conference on Computer Vision and Pattern Recognition, pp. 10508–10518 (2020)
33. Liang, J., Jiang, L., Niebles, J.C., Hauptmann, A.G., Fei-Fei, L.: Peeking into the future: predicting future person activities and locations in videos. In: Proceedings of the IEEE/CVF Conference on Computer Vision and Pattern Recognition, pp. 5725–5734 (2019)
34. Liu, Y., Yan, Q., Alahi, A.: Social NCE: contrastive learning of socially-aware motion representations. In: Proceedings of the IEEE/CVF International Conference on Computer Vision, pp. 15118–15129 (2021)
35. López, A., Chaumette, F., Marchand, E., Pettré, J.: Character navigation in dynamic environments based on optical flow. Comput. Graphi. Forum **38**, 181–192. Wiley Online Library (2019)
36. Luo, L., et al.: Agent-based human behavior modeling for crowd simulation. Comput. Anim. Virtual Worlds **19** (2008)
37. Mangalam, K., An, Y., Girase, H., Malik, J.: From goals, waypoints & paths to long term human trajectory forecasting. In: Proceedings of the IEEE/CVF International Conference on Computer Vision, pp. 15233–15242 (2021)

38. Mangalam, K., Girase, H., Agarwal, S., Lee, K.-H., Adeli, E., Malik, J., Gaidon, A.: It is not the journey but the destination: endpoint conditioned trajectory prediction. In: Vedaldi, A., Bischof, H., Brox, T., Frahm, J.-M. (eds.) ECCV 2020. LNCS, vol. 12347, pp. 759–776. Springer, Cham (2020). https://doi.org/10.1007/978-3-030-58536-5_45
39. Mohamed, A., Qian, K., Elhoseiny, M., Claudel, C.: Social-STGCNN: a social spatio-temporal graph convolutional neural network for human trajectory prediction. In: Proceedings of the IEEE/CVF Conference on Computer Vision and Pattern Recognition, pp. 14424–14432 (2020)
40. Narain, R., Golas, A., Curtis, S., Lin, M.C.: Aggregate dynamics for dense crowd simulation. In: ACM SIGGRAPH Asia 2009 papers, pp. 1–8 (2009)
41. Narang, S., Best, A., Curtis, S., Manocha, D.: Generating pedestrian trajectories consistent with the fundamental diagram based on physiological and psychological factors. PLoS ONE **10**(4), e0117856 (2015)
42. Oliver, N.M., Rosario, B., Pentland, A.P.: A Bayesian computer vision system for modeling human interactions. IEEE Trans. Pattern Anal. Mach. Intell. **22**(8), 831–843 (2000)
43. Pellegrini, S., Ess, A., Van Gool, L.: Improving data association by joint modeling of pedestrian trajectories and groupings. In: Daniilidis, K., Maragos, P., Paragios, N. (eds.) ECCV 2010. LNCS, vol. 6311, pp. 452–465. Springer, Heidelberg (2010). https://doi.org/10.1007/978-3-642-15549-9_33
44. Rackauckas, C., et al.: Universal differential equations for scientific machine learning. arXiv preprint arXiv:2001.04385 (2020)
45. Raissi, M., Perdikaris, P., Karniadakis, G.E.: Physics-informed neural networks: a deep learning framework for solving forward and inverse problems involving nonlinear partial differential equations. J. Comput. Phys. **378**, 686–707 (2019)
46. Robicquet, A., Sadeghian, A., Alahi, A., Savarese, S.: Learning social etiquette: human trajectory understanding in crowded scenes. In: Leibe, B., Matas, J., Sebe, N., Welling, M. (eds.) ECCV 2016. LNCS, vol. 9912, pp. 549–565. Springer, Cham (2016). https://doi.org/10.1007/978-3-319-46484-8_33
47. Sadeghian, A., Kosaraju, V., Gupta, A., Savarese, S., Alahi, A.: TrajNet: towards a benchmark for human trajectory prediction. arXiv preprint (2018)
48. Sadeghian, A., Kosaraju, V., Sadeghian, A., Hirose, N., Rezatofighi, H., Savarese, S.: Sophie: an attentive GAN for predicting paths compliant to social and physical constraints. In: Proceedings of the IEEE/CVF Conference on Computer Vision and Pattern Recognition, pp. 1349–1358 (2019)
49. Salzmann, T., Ivanovic, B., Chakravarty, P., Pavone, M.: Trajectron++: Dynamically-feasible trajectory forecasting with heterogeneous data. In: Vedaldi, A., Bischof, H., Brox, T., Frahm, J.-M. (eds.) ECCV 2020. LNCS, vol. 12363, pp. 683–700. Springer, Cham (2020). https://doi.org/10.1007/978-3-030-58523-5_40
50. Shen, S., et al.: High-order differentiable autoencoder for nonlinear model reduction. ACM Trans. Graph. **40**(4) (2021)
51. Shen, Y., Henry, J., Wang, H., Ho, E.S.L., Komura, T., Shum, H.P.H.: Data-driven crowd motion control with multi-touch gestures. Comput. Graph. Forum (2018). https://doi.org/10.1111/cgf.13333
52. Shi, L., Wang, L., Long, C., Zhou, S., Zhou, M., Niu, Z., Hua, G.: SGCN: sparse graph convolution network for pedestrian trajectory prediction. In: Proceedings of the IEEE/CVF Conference on Computer Vision and Pattern Recognition, pp. 8994–9003 (2021)
53. Sighencea, B.I., Stanciu, R.I., Căleanu, C.D.: A review of deep learning-based methods for pedestrian trajectory prediction. Sensors **21**(22), 7543 (2021)

54. Sohn, K., Lee, H., Yan, X.: Learning structured output representation using deep conditional generative models. In: Proceedings of the 28th International Conference on Neural Information Processing Systems, vol. 2 (2015)
55. Su, T., Meng, Y., Xu, Y.: Pedestrian trajectory prediction via spatial interaction transformer network. In: 2021 IEEE Intelligent Vehicles Symposium Workshops (IV Workshops), pp. 154–159. IEEE (2021)
56. Tan, Q., Pan, Z., Manocha, D.: Lcollision: Fast generation of collision-free human poses using learned non-penetration constraints. In: Proceedings of the AAAI Conference on Artificial Intelligence, vol. 35, pp. 3913–3921 (2021)
57. Tan, Q., Pan, Z., Smith, B., Shiratori, T., Manocha, D.: N-penetrate: Active learning of neural collision handler for complex 3d mesh deformations. In: International Conference on Machine Learning, pp. 21037–21049. PMLR (2022)
58. Van Toll, W., Pettré, J.: Algorithms for microscopic crowd simulation: advancements in the 2010s. Comput. Graph. Forum **40**(2) (2021)
59. Vemula, A., Muelling, K., Oh, J.: Social attention: modeling attention in human crowds. In: 2018 IEEE International Conference on Robotics and Automation (ICRA), pp. 4601–4607. IEEE (2018)
60. Virtanen, A.: Energy-based pedestrian navigation. In: Proceedings of 20th ITS World Congress, pp. 1–9 (2013)
61. Wan, Z., Hu, X., He, H., Guo, Y.: A learning based approach for social force model parameter estimation. In: IJCNN, pp. 4058–4064. IEEE (2017)
62. Wang, H., Ondřej, J., O'Sullivan, C.: Path patterns: analyzing and comparing real and simulated crowds. In: ACM SIGGRAPH Symposium on Interactive 3D Graphics and Games 2016, pp. 49–57 (2016)
63. Wang, H., Ondřej, J., O'Sullivan, C.: Trending paths: a new semantic-level metric for comparing simulated and real crowd data. IEEE Trans. Visual. Comput. Graph. **99**, 1–1 (2016)
64. Wang, H., O'Sullivan, C.: Globally Continuous and non-Marconian crowd activity analysis from videos. In: Leibe, B., Matas, J., Sebe, N., Welling, M. (eds.) ECCV 2016. LNCS, vol. 9909, pp. 527–544. Springer, Cham (2016). https://doi.org/10.1007/978-3-319-46454-1_32
65. Wang, P.: Understanding social-force model in psychological principles of collective behavior. arXiv preprint arXiv:1605.05146 (2016)
66. Wang, X., Ma, K.T., Ng, G.W., Grimson, W.E.L.: Trajectory analysis and semantic region modeling using nonparametric hierarchical Bayesian models. Int. J. Comput. Vision **95**(3), 287–312 (2011)
67. Wei, J., Fan, W., Li, Z., Guo, Y., Fang, Y., Wang, J.: Simulating crowd evacuation in a social force model with iterative extended state observer. J. Adv. Transp. **2020** (2020)
68. Werling, K., Omens, D., Lee, J., Exarchos, I., Liu, C.K.: Fast and feature-complete differentiable physics for articulated rigid bodies with contact. CoRR abs/2103.16021 (2021)
69. Wolinski, D., J. Guy, S., Olivier, A.H., Lin, M., Manocha, D., Pettré, J.: Parameter estimation and comparative evaluation of crowd simulations. Comput. Graph. Forum **33**(2), 303–312 (2014)
70. Xia, B., Wong, C., Peng, Q., Yuan, W., You, X.: CscNet: contextual semantic consistency network for trajectory prediction in crowded spaces. Pattern Recog. **126**,, 108552 (2022)
71. Zeng, W., Chen, P., Nakamura, H., Iryo-Asano, M.: Application of social force model to pedestrian behavior analysis at signalized crosswalk. Transp. Res. Part C Emerg. Ttechnol. **40**, 143–159 (2014)

72. Zhang, Z., Jimack, P.K., Wang, H.: MeshingNet3D: efficient generation of adapted tetrahedral meshes for computational mechanics. Adv. Eng. Softw. **157**, 103021 (2021)
73. Zhang, Z., Wang, Y., Jimack, P.K., Wang, H.: MeshingNet: a new mesh generation method based on deep learning. In: Krzhizhanovskaya, W., et al. (eds.) ICCS 2020. LNCS, vol. 12139, pp. 186–198. Springer, Cham (2020). https://doi.org/10.1007/978-3-030-50420-5_14
74. Zhong, Y.D., Dey, B., Chakraborty, A.: Symplectic ode-net: Learning hamiltonian dynamics with control. arXiv preprint arXiv:1909.12077 (2019)
75. Zhou, B., Wang, X., Tang, X.: Random field topic model for semantic region analysis in crowded scenes from tracklets. In: CVPR 2011, pp. 3441–3448. IEEE (2011)
76. Zhou, H., Ren, D., Yang, X., Fan, M., Huang, H.: Sliding sequential CVAE with time variant socially-aware rethinking for trajectory prediction. arXiv preprint arXiv:2110.15016 (2021)
77. Zubov, K., et al.: Neuralpde: automating physics-informed neural networks (pinns) with error approximations. CoRR abs/2107.09443 (2021)

Towards Open Set Video Anomaly Detection

Yuansheng Zhu(✉), Wentao Bao, and Qi Yu

Rochester Institute of Technology, Rochester, USA
{yz7008,wb6219,qi.yu}@rit.edu

Abstract. Open Set Video Anomaly Detection (OpenVAD) aims to identify abnormal events from video data where both known anomalies and novel ones exist in testing. Unsupervised models learned solely from normal videos are applicable to any testing anomalies but suffer from a high false positive rate. In contrast, weakly supervised methods are effective in detecting known anomalies but could fail in an open world. We develop a novel weakly supervised method for the OpenVAD problem by integrating evidential deep learning (EDL) and normalizing flows (NFs) into a multiple instance learning (MIL) framework. Specifically, we propose to use graph neural networks and triplet loss to learn discriminative features for training the EDL classifier, where the EDL is capable of identifying the unknown anomalies by quantifying the uncertainty. Moreover, we develop an uncertainty-aware selection strategy to obtain clean anomaly instances and a NFs module to generate the pseudo anomalies. Our method is superior to existing approaches by inheriting the advantages of both the unsupervised NFs and the weakly-supervised MIL framework. Experimental results on multiple real-world video datasets show the effectiveness of our method.

Keywords: Video anomaly detection · Weakly supervised learning · Open set recognition · Normalizing flows

1 Introduction

Traditional video anomaly detection aims to detect abnormal events that significantly deviate from normal ones. Examples of such abnormal events include human crimes, natural disasters, and traffic accidents, to name a few. It has been successfully applied to many real-world applications [32]. However, unseen novel anomalies may occur after a well-trained supervised model has been deployed in an open world. Being aware of the unseen anomalies essentially leads to the Open-set Video Anomaly Detection (OpenVAD) problem (see Fig. 1), which is under-explored in literature despite being critical to real-world applications.

Supplementary Information The online version contains supplementary material available at https://doi.org/10.1007/978-3-031-19830-4_23.

S. Avidan et al. (Eds.): ECCV 2022, LNCS 13694, pp. 395–412, 2022.
https://doi.org/10.1007/978-3-031-19830-4_23

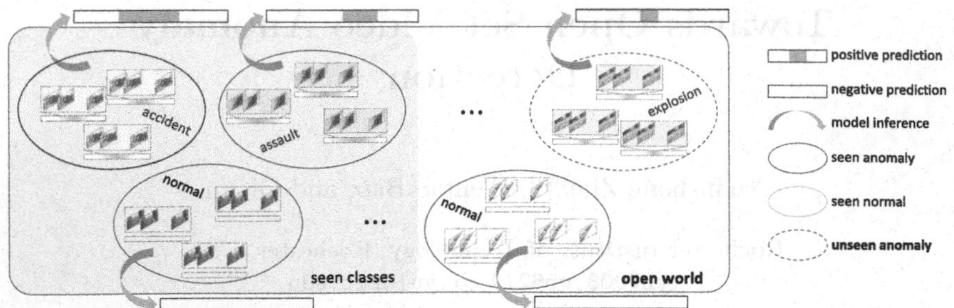

Fig. 1. OpenVAD Task. We propose to conduct OpenVAD through the weakly-supervised video anomaly detection in an open world. In training, only a closed-set of anomaly videos with video-level annotations are observed along with normal videos. In testing, the model is asked to identify and localize the anomaly events from videos in an open world where arbitrary unseen anomalies could exist.

Unsupervised learning is one of the typical ways to handle unseen anomalies in existing literature [16,28,29,47,55]. They aim to learn representative features of normal events only from normal videos. However, as unsupervised methods neglect the anomaly information, they are in general less effective to detect complicated anomalies that are similar to normal samples in the feature space [4]. Besides, (weakly-)supervised methods can use annotated anomaly videos so that their performances are generally better. However, the learned models are limited to detecting a closed set of anomaly categories and unable to handle the arbitrary unseen anomalies. Inspired by the recent advances in open set recognition [2,3, 13,36], we propose to perform video anomaly detection in an open world by extending the existing weakly-supervised video anomaly detection paradigm. The goal is to achieve accurate anomaly detection in an open set by learning a model only with video-level annotations from a closed subset of anomaly types.

Most existing works [42,46,51,62] formulate weakly supervised anomaly detection as a multiple instance learning (MIL) problem [10], where a video is modeled as a bag of instances (*e.g.,* video clips). Due to the lack of fine-grained instance labels, simply assigning all instances in an abnormal (*i.e.,* positive) bag with the same anomaly label inevitably incurs severe labeling noise. Such noise further results in a high false positive rate, *i.e.,* falsely treating normal events as abnormal ones, when using a trained model for detection. Therefore, it is essential to select the clean anomaly instances in MIL. Besides, to enable the MIL model to be aware of the unseen anomaly in testing, the open space risk of MIL should be bounded while it is under-explored in the existing literature.

To tackle these challenges, we first leverage graph neural networks (GCNs) and a triplet loss to learn representative instance features. Then, we instantiate the MIL with evidential deep learning (EDL) [2,37,39] and use the predicted evidence to help select anomaly instances with high *cleanness* for robust MIL training. To bound the open space risk, an unsupervised normalizing flows (NFs) is learned from normal instances, which allows us to sample pseudo anomaly samples from the low density area of the instance distribution.

We are among the first few attempts that address video anomaly detection in the open set setting, where arbitrary unseen anomaly events could appear in testing. This is fundamentally more challenging than a using fully-supervised training process as adopted by some existing efforts in [4,34] and some of these methods are not suitable to tackle high-dimensional video data. Though there are few works [12,23] with a similar open set assumption, our task definition is more realistic in real-world, where the model is weakly-supervised and aims to identify arbitrary unknown anomaly events in testing. By effectively leveraging any available anomaly videos through weakly supervised learning in novel ways, our approach also achieves better detection performance than few existing open set anomaly detection methods (*e.g.,* [27]) that solely rely on normal videos to initialize a detection model through unsupervised learning. In summary, the key contributions are threefold:

- We formulate a novel MIL framework for the OpenVAD problem to detect both seen and unseen video anomalies in a challenging open-world setting.
- We integrate MIL with a normalizing flow-based generative model and evidential learning for high-quality anomaly instance selection.
- We conduct extensive experiments and the results show significant superiority to existing unsupervised and weak supervised learning approaches.

2 Related Work

Video Anomaly Detection. Existing methods to detect anomalies from videos can be categorized into two groups: 1) unsupervised learning and 2) weakly supervised learning. Unsupervised approaches are motivated by the premise that anomaly events are fundamentally challenging to completely enumerate and characterize. Therefore, these approaches conduct either dictionary learning/sparse coding [29,61] or construct a deep auto-encoder [8,47,53]. Unlike unsupervised approaches, weakly supervised approaches [17,27,42,46,51,62] use both normal videos and anomaly videos for training. They take advantage of normal videos and leverage additional anomaly videos to train a binary classifier over the video clips. Among existing weakly supervised approaches, one representative approach leverages a deep auto-encoder to locate clips in anomaly videos with low reconstruction scores and then further reduces these scores through margin learning [27]. Some other approaches [17,42,62] formulate this problem as multiple instance learning (MIL) problem and build an instance-level classifier. To train the classifier properly, these MIL models select one or a set of instances from a positive bag to feed into the classifier and either a fixed number of instances are selected [17,42] or a predefined threshold is set as the selection criterion [62]. Previous MIL based approaches achieve superior performance compared to unsupervised counterparts. The core design of these approaches lies in the measurement of *cleanness* and the instance selection strategy. In this paper, we empirically show that the top-k strategy is robust, which inspires us to develop the *cleanness* measurement and an instance selection strategy by introducing the evidence based learning method.

Open Set Recognition. Open Set Recognition (OSR) aims to identify the unknowns while keeping reasonable closed set performance in the open set testing. Since the unknowns are never seen by the model and are out-of-distribution (OOD) with respect to the in-distributional (ID) training data, they are referred to as "unknown unknown class" in existing literature [14,54]. In contrast, the exact classes of ID data are known and are called "known known classes". The OSR approaches attempt to classify test samples from "known known classes" and detect test samples from "unknown unknown classes". The most recent work [31] encourages learning a multi-class classifier to give low activation values for external OOD data and large values for ID data. Some works do not depend on external OOD data in training by using either specialized loss functions [2,7] or unknown class generation [63]. Other works [3,59] address the OSR problem by integrating probabilistic density estimation in the latent feature space with a multi-class classifier. Our proposed OpenVAD and the traditional OSR problems can both be regarded as a generalized OOD detection problem [54], because of the semantic distribution shift between testing and training datasets. A key distinction of the proposed OpenVAD is that it does not care about if an anomaly video is from seen or unseen categories in testing. Instead, it focuses on distinguishing arbitrary anomaly activities from normal ones in an open world.

3 Methodology

Our work aims to handle the OpenVAD problem under a weakly supervised setting. Specifically, a model is trained using normal videos and a closed set of untrimmed anomaly videos with video (or bag)-level labels. Each anomaly video contains at least one anomaly event (*i.e.*, positive instance). The model is tested in an open world, where unseen anomaly events may occur, and the model is expected to robustly identify all anomaly clips (*i.e.*, segments of a video) during testing. Since we only have access to the video-level anomaly class labels, MIL provides an ideal learning framework to leverage the weakly supervised learning signals. Specifically, an untrimmed video is regarded as a bag X, which contains N temporal clips as instances in the bag: $X = \{\mathbf{x}_1, \ldots, \mathbf{x}_N\}$. The learning objective of MIL is to train an instance-level binary classifier $\Phi : \mathbf{x}_n \rightarrow y_n$ with only bag-level class label $Y \in \{0, 1\}$ in the training, while the instance-level labels $y_n \in \{0, 1\}$ with $y_n \in \{y_1, \ldots, y_N\}$ are not available. In MIL, a positive bag $(X, Y = 1)$ contains at least one positive instance (*e.g.*, anomaly event), *i.e.*, $\exists n \in [1, N], y_n = 1$, while a negative bag consists of only negative instances (*e.g.*, normal event), *i.e.*, $\forall n \in [1, N], y_n = 0$.

For the OpenVAD problem, the model is expected to handle the semantically shifted testing data that contains unseen anomaly events. In testing, given an untrimmed video, the model is expected to identify the anomaly clips, which could be either seen or unseen anomaly if the video contains any anomaly events.

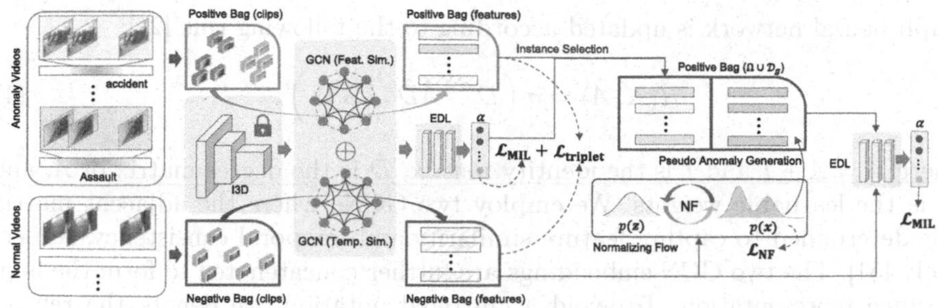

Fig. 2. Overview of the OpenVAD Framework. We first integrate two GCNs feature extractors and the evidential deep learning (EDL) into the multiple instance learning (MIL), which are learned by $\mathcal{L}_{\text{MIL}} + \mathcal{L}_{\text{triplet}}$. Then, the classification confidence and uncertainty from the trained EDL head are used to select instances with high *cleanness*. We further utilize the GCNs features of normal video clips to train a normalizing flow model, from which pseudo anomaly features are generated. Together with the normal videos, the selected clean anomaly and the generated pseudo anomaly are gathered to refine the EDL head by $\mathcal{L}_{\text{MIL}}$.

Overview of the Framework. Our method is developed as a MIL framework, as shown in Fig. 2. The instances are structured as graph data to address the temporal consistency and feature similarity of video clips. The MIL framework consists of two graph convolutional networks (GCN) followed by an evidential deep learning (EDL) head, which are trained by weakly-supervised MIL loss and triplet loss. The classification confidence and uncertainty are used to select clean anomaly instances for robust MIL training. To reduce the open space risk in OpenVAD tasks, we further utilize normal videos to train a normalizing flow (NF) model to generate pseudo anomalies. The selected and generated anomalies are used to fine-tune the EDL classification head. In testing, our model could correctly identify an unseen anomaly event from untrimmed video data. See Appendix Section A for the summary of notations.

3.1 Instance Feature Representation Learning

We take advantage of a pre-trained action recognition backbone (*e.g.*, I3D [5]) to extract features of raw video clips, denoted as $\mathbf{x}$. Given the temporal and visual similarity of close clips in a video, we propose to enhance the feature $\mathbf{x}$ by constructing temporal and feature similarity graphs, respectively. Furthermore, to enlarge the feature discrepancy between normal and anomaly instances, a triplet learning constraint is introduced in the feature embedding space.

More specifically, since each bag is formed from a video, there exist natural dependencies among instances in the bag. Thus, video clips that are located closely in temporal and feature space should have similar feature representation. We leverage a graph neural network to model such dependency. Given a graph defined by the adjacency matrix A and graph node features X (*i.e.*, a bag), the graph neural network is updated according to the following rule [21]:

$$\mathcal{H}(X, A) = \sigma\left(\hat{D}^{-\frac{1}{2}}\hat{A}\hat{D}^{-\frac{1}{2}}XW\right), \tag{1}$$

where $\hat{A} = A + I$ and I is the identity matrix, $\hat{D}$ is the degree matrix of $\hat{A}$, and W is the learnable weights. We employ two GCNs where the adjacent matrix A is determined to capture feature similarity and temporal consistency, respectively [51]. The two GCN embeddings are further concatenated to form the final instance representation. To avoid a cluttered notation, we denote the refined instance representation as $\mathcal{H}(\mathbf{x})$.

The GCNs help to compactly embed the neighbouring instances in the same bag. When multiple bags are involved, we further employ a triplet loss to achieve good separability of instances from different classes and compactness of instances in the same class. A triplet consists of an anchor instance, a paired instance from the same class as the anchor, and an unpaired instance from a different class from the anchor, which are sampled from the collection Ω (defined in Eq. (4)). The triplet loss is given by

$$\mathcal{L}_{triplet} = [d_{ap} - d_{an} + m]_{+} \tag{2}$$

where m is the margin that controls the desired difference between the paired distance d_{ap} and unpaired distance d_{an}.

In addition to GCNs, the consistency loss function [42,46] and other network architectures [46] (*e.g.,* LSTM and CNN) also have been investigated to model the relationship among instances. We choose GCNs because they have been proved to be effective in close set video anomaly detection tasks [51,62]. However, the representation learning in the open world is more complex than in a close set. The triplet loss will make the normal data stay close to each other while remaining dissimilar to the seen anomaly. This facilitating a normalizing flow (NF) to learn their distribution in the following stage.

3.2 Uncertainty-Aware Multiple Instance Learning

To train an instance-level classifier with only bag-level annotations, a naive solution is to assign a noisy version of label y_n for each instance $\mathbf{x}_n$ by directly using the bag-level label, *i.e.,* $y_n = Y$. As a result, most of instances in the positive bag may be incorrectly labelled (due to normal video clips in anomaly videos) during model training. These mislabeled instances may degrade the model performance as the learning targets are noisy. Furthermore, a MIL model instantiated by deep neural networks (DNNs) is usually sensitive to noisy labels because DNNs are of high capacity to fit random labels [58]. Therefore, instance selection from positive bags poses a critical issue that may significantly impact the performance of a MIL model [51,62].

To address this challenge, top-k methods (*e.g.,* [24]) select the "most positive" instances from the positive bag in training. Two recent works [46,51] adapt this technique and achieve decent performance in close set video anomaly detection tasks. Most top-k methods follow a "sort-then-rank" process, where a critical step is to determine the *cleanness* of each instance to evaluate how likely the instance is a clean positive one (*i.e.*, an anomaly event). In this work, we propose to quantify the classification uncertainty by evidential deep learning. We then introduce an instance selection approach based on uncertainty and confidence.

Given an instance $\mathbf{x}$, we introduce a binary random variable $p \in \{0, 1\}$ that represents the chance that it is an anomaly, which follows a Bernoulli distribution. Similar to EDL [37], we further introduce a Beta distribution $\text{Beta}(\boldsymbol{\alpha})$ as the conjugate prior of the Bernoulli likelihood. In our framework, the learning objective is to train a DNN to directly predict the Beta distribution parameter $\boldsymbol{\alpha}$ instead of p. According to Subjective Logic and evidence theory [18,38], the predicted parameters $\boldsymbol{\alpha} = (\alpha_+, \alpha_-)^\top$ can be regarded as the evidences over the positive (anomaly) and negative (normal) classes, which can be expressed as

$$\boldsymbol{\alpha} = \Phi(\mathcal{H}(\mathbf{x})) + \mathbf{a}W \tag{3}$$

where $\mathbf{a} = (a_+, a_-)^\top$ is the base rate with $a_+ = a_- = 1/2$ and $W = 2$ in our binary case; $\mathcal{H}$ and Φ denote GCNs based backbone as the feature extractor and a DNN as the EDL classification head, respectively. The GCNs encode the relationship among instances in a bag and output discriminative video clip features. In practice, the EDL classification head consists of two fully connected layers and ReLU activation to predict non-negative class-wise logits. The predictions α_+ and α_- correspond to the instance class $y = 1$ and $y = 0$ respectively, indicating the virtual quantity of evidence to support $\mathbf{x}$ to be classified as positive or negative.

The benefit of placing the Beta prior on the Bernoulli likelihood is that the prediction uncertainty can be efficiently and accurately quantified according to recent Dirichlet-based models [22], enabling the MIL model to *know what it does not know*. The predicted probabilities are the ratios of the evidence, *i.e.*, $\mathbb{E}[p_+] = \alpha_+/\alpha_0$ and $\mathbb{E}[p_-] = \alpha_-/\alpha_0$, where $\alpha_0 = \alpha_+ + \alpha_-$, and the evidential uncertainty (or vacuity) is quantified as $u = 2/\alpha_0$.

Based on the evidential uncertainty above, we propose to train the MIL by selecting the *clean* samples, which form a set:

$$\Omega = \left\{ \mathbf{x}_i | p_+^{(i)} \geq \tau_p, \alpha_+^{(i)} \geq \tau_u \right\}, \tag{4}$$

where $p_+^{(i)}$ and $\alpha_+^{(i)}$ are the confidence score and evidence that support the sample $\mathbf{x}_i$ being classified as an anomaly; τ_p and τ_u are thresholds to control the size of the set. The MIL model is trained by minimizing the Type II maximum likelihood loss (MLL) [37]:

$$\mathcal{L}_{\text{MIL}}(\mathbf{x}'_i) = \sum_{k=1}^{2} \left[\hat{y}_k^{(i)} \left(\log(\alpha_0^{(i)}) - \log(\alpha_k^{(i)}) \right) \right] \tag{5}$$

where the training sample $\mathbf{x}'_i$ is from either the selected set Ω or the negative bag $\mathcal{N} = \{\mathbf{x}_i | y_i = 0\}$, *i.e.*, $\mathbf{x}'_i \in \Omega \cup \mathcal{N}$, $\hat{y}$ is the one-hot version of the label

y. The benefit of Type II MLL lies in that it not only enforces the predicted probability to be as close to the ground-truth bag label, but also increases the evidence for observed data to support better instance selection.

MIL is intrinsically learning using the noisy labels, which is a long-standing challenge. Recent research approaches this problem generally from sample selection [30,52,56,57], sample re-weighting [6,50], and meta-learning [25,60] perspectives. We choose to explore sample selection because it is well-justified and empirically works well. The sample selection methods often leverage the memorization effect of DNNs to identify the clean samples, which stems from the observation that DNNs tend to fit clean samples faster than noisy ones [1]. Here, τ_p in Eq. (4) is derived from the memorization effect, which encourages Ω to retain those qualified samples, *i.e.*, samples whose predicted probability p_+ is most close to the learning target, $y = 1$. However, sample selection methods could severally suffer from the bias confirmation [45] caused by incorrect selection, which is challenging to solve. The proposed uncertainty aware MIL is distinguished from exiting efforts [42,48,51] for mitigating the bias confirmation by filtering out fluctuating samples (*i.e.*, those with a small α_+ less than τ_u), which may be incorrectly selected if only p_+ is considered.

3.3 Pseudo Anomaly Generation

For the OpenVAD problem, open space risk should be bounded in training so that the model could be aware of the semantically shifted unseen data. However, unseen anomaly videos are not available during training under the open set setting. Inspired by recent generative open set modeling [13,35] and normalizing flows (NFs), we propose to leverage NFs to generate pseudo anomaly instances in the latent feature space.

NFs are the flow-based deep generative models that could explicitly learn the probability density of data [43,44]. It has been shown effective for realistic data generation, exact posterior inference, and exact density estimation. NFs consist of composition of invertible learnable functions f_l to transform between a simple distribution $p(\mathbf{z})$ and the complex data distribution $p(\mathbf{x})$, *i.e.*, $\mathbf{z} = f(\mathbf{x})$ and $\mathbf{x} = f^{-1}(\mathbf{z})$ where $f = f_1 \circ \cdots \circ f_L$. To enable exact density estimation and data generation, the invertible transformation is constructed following the change-of-variable rule:

$$p(\mathbf{x}) = p(\mathbf{z}) \left| \det \left(\frac{\partial f(\mathbf{x})}{\partial \mathbf{x}^\top} \right) \right| \tag{6}$$

where $\mathbf{z}$ typically follows a non-informative Gaussian distribution. Equation (6) is associated with the determinant of Jacobian, which can be efficiently computed when a proper bijective function f_l is designed to make the Jacobian triangular. Recent NF models such as RealNVP [11], Glow [19], and IAF [20] use different coupling layers to address the functional invertibility and computational efficiency of the transformation f_l based on deep neural networks. In this paper, we adopt the IAF model because it is efficient for sampling purpose, which is critical for pseudo anomaly generation. The coupling layer f_l is designed as

$$x_i = z_i \times s(\mathbf{z}_{1:i-1}) + t(\mathbf{z}_{1:i-1}), \tag{7}$$

where x_i and z_i are the i-th entries of feature vector $\mathbf{x}$ and $\mathbf{z}$, respectively. The scaling and shifting functions s and t are instantiated by deep neural networks.

To train the flow model, the goal is to maximize the log-likelihood of the normal video data, which is equivalent to minimizing the following objective:

$$\mathcal{L}_{\text{NF}} = \mathbb{E}_{\mathcal{D}(X,Y=0)}\left[-\log p(\mathcal{H}(\mathbf{x}))\right] \tag{8}$$

Note that here we learn the flow model f in the latent feature space $\mathcal{H}(\mathbf{x})$. This alleviates the difficulty of directly learning in a high-dimensional space.

The generation is based on the assumption that pseudo anomalies are outliers with respect to the normal class. Therefore, a pseudo anomaly instance $\tilde{\mathbf{x}}$ should be sampled from the low density region of the probability distribution of the normal class $p(\mathbf{x}|y=0)$. In this paper, we first use the tractable $p(\mathbf{z})$ to repeatedly sample the latent feature $\tilde{\mathbf{z}}_i$. Then, the pseudo samples are generated by the flow model of the normal class, *i.e.*, $\tilde{\mathbf{x}} = g(\tilde{\mathbf{z}}; y=0)$ where $g(\cdot) = f^{-1}(\cdot)$. Finally, only the pseudo samples with low density (*i.e.*, with a small $p(\tilde{\mathbf{x}}|y=0)$) are preserved as pseudo anomaly instances. The following equations summarize this procedure:

$$\tilde{\mathbf{z}} \sim p(\mathbf{z}),\ \tilde{\mathbf{x}} = g(\tilde{\mathbf{z}}; y=0),\ \mathcal{D}_g = \{\tilde{\mathbf{x}} | p(\tilde{\mathbf{x}}|y=0) \leq \epsilon\} \tag{9}$$

where $p(\tilde{\mathbf{x}}|y=0) = p(\mathbf{z}) \left|\det\left(\frac{\partial f(\mathbf{x})}{\partial \mathbf{x}^T}\right)\right|$. The benefit of generating pseudo anomaly instances from normal class distribution is that the class boundary of the normal class is constrained by the pseudo anomalies so that the open space risk is well managed. Regarding the way of generating pseudo anomaly instances, unlike previous work [35] that generates in the pixel space, we perform generation in the feature space, similar to [13]. Spawning from the feature space has dual advantages over spawning from the pixel space: 1) the latent space has a much lower dimension, which allows fast sampling for the NFs, and 2) the latent features are more discriminative than the raw pixels [9]; thus the generated data are less likely to be negatively impacted by the background noise in the video data. In contrast, [13] uses the Gaussian mixtures to model the class-wise in-distribution data density. We argue that the Gaussian distribution is not flexible to model the complex in-distribution data. NFs can seamlessly solve this problem owing to its high capability via a deep composition of the bejiection function f.

NFs have a high capability of density estimation while free of supervision. A natural question that arises is whether we can directly ensemble the prediction results of a normalizing flow and a classifier. Ensemble is widely used yet seems to be simpler than pseudo anomaly generation. However, we remark that the ensembles can not inherit the benefit from unsupervised learning and (weakly-) supervised learning paradigms. This is because that NFs cannot detect the complicated anomaly (*e.g.*, anomaly samples that look similar to normal ones), which is consistent with the observations in [33]. Our motivation is to only leverage the strengths (*i.e.*, generating anomaly) and avoid weaknesses (*i.e.*, detecting anomaly) of NFs.

3.4 Multi-stage Model Training and Inference

Since NFs are used for generating pseudo anomaly instances for the target MIL model, we propose a multi-stage model training scheme. Specifically, we first train a feature encoder $\mathcal{H}(\cdot)$ and an EDL classifier $\Phi(\cdot)$ by minimizing the weighted sum of MIL loss and triplet loss. Then, the feature encoder $\mathcal{H}$ is frozen and the flow model $f(\cdot)$ is trained in an unsupervised way using only normal videos. Finally, the EDL classifier is fine-tuned by using the selected positive instances, the generated pseudo anomaly instances, and the normal videos. Algorithm 1 shows the details of the training process. It is worth to note that during inference, the flow model does not involve additional overhead we use the prediction of EDL classifiers to score samples and the anomaly score is defined as the mean probability of being an anomaly: $\mathbb{E}[p_+] = \frac{\alpha_+}{\alpha_0}$.

Algorithm 1 Multi-stage training

Input: $\mathcal{D}_{train} = \{X, Y\}$, number of epochs for training EDL model (Φ) and NFs model (f) T_{EDL}, T_{NFs}, thresholds τ_p, τ_p, ϵ, loss weight β
Output: feature encoder $\mathcal{H}$, EDL classifier Φ.
 ▷ *Stage 1*: Warmup training
  Train $\mathcal{H}$ and Φ by minimizing $\mathcal{L}_{\text{MIL}} + \beta\mathcal{L}_{triplet}$.
 ▷ *Stage 2*: Freeze $\mathcal{H}$ and train f
 for $t \in [1, T_{\text{NFs}}]$ **do**
  Fetch m normal videos, *i.e.*, $\{\mathbf{x}_i\}_{i=1}^m \sim \mathcal{D}_{train}(X, Y = 0)$.
  Update NFs model f by minimizing $\mathcal{L}_{\text{NF}}$.
 end for
 ▷ *Stage 3*: Freeze $\mathcal{H}$ and f, and fine-tune Φ
 for $t \in [1, T_{\text{EDL}}]$ **do**
  Fetch m normal and anomaly videos from $\mathcal{D}_{train}$.
  Construct the clean positive set Ω using Eq. (4).
  Augment Ω by sampling m pseudo anomalies using Eq (9), i.e., $\Omega \leftarrow \Omega \cup \mathcal{D}_g$.
  Update EDL model Φ by minimizing $\mathcal{L}_{\text{EDL}}$.
 end for

---

4 Experiments

Since OpenVAD is less explored, no standard evaluation setup is available for this type of task. To adequately assess the method and inform the practical choice, we develop a benchmark and test several state-of-the-art methods. Through comprehensive comparison on various datasets, we demonstrate the effectiveness of the proposed framework. More experiments details and results can be found in the Appendix, and the link to the source code is available in https://github.com/YUZ128pitt/Towards-OpenVAD.git.

4.1 Datasets and Evaluation Setup

We conduct experiments on three video anomaly detection datasets of different scales. Videos in these datasets are untrimmed, and only video-level labels are provided during training. The frame-level annotations are used for evaluation purpose. Detailed information for these three datasets is as follows:

- **XD Violence** [51]: This dataset contains totally 4,754 videos collected from movies, online videos, sport streaming, surveillance cameras and CCTVs. There are five types of anomaly events, and each anomaly video may contain one or more types of anomalies, including *Abuse, Riot, Shooting, Fighting, Car accident*, and *Explosion.*
- **UCF Crime** [42]: This dataset contains totally 1,900 videos collected from surveillance cameras from variant scenes. There 13 different types of violence-related anomaly videos: *Abuse, Burglary, Robbery, Stealing, Shooting, Shoplifting, Assault, Fighting, Arson, Explosion, Arrest, Road Accident*, and *Vandalism.* There are 1,610 training videos (of which 810 are anomaly) and 290 test videos (of which 140 are anomaly).
- **ShanghaiTech Campus** [26]: This dataset consists videos from 13 scenes with different light conditions and camera angles. Anomaly events are defined as actions that contain sudden motions, such as *chasing* and *brawling*, but there is no anomaly type labels. We follow the split in [62], in which there are totally 238 training videos (of which 63 are anomaly) and 199 testing (of which 44 are anomaly) videos.

Evaluation Setup. For the OpenVAD task, we consider a more realistic setting, where testing data contains unseen novel anomalies. To simulate unseen anomaly, we remove one or more types of anomaly from the training data on XD Violence and UCF Crime. We vary the size of anomaly training videos to get comprehensive results under different ratios of unseen anomaly scenarios. For example, in XD-Violence, there are six types of testing anomalies, and we train a model with 1, 2, 3, and 4 types of anomaly videos along with normal videos. We randomly remove a certain number of training anomaly classes and repeat them three times to reduce the evaluation bias of seen anomaly. These evaluation sets reflect our assumption about the most realistic video anomaly detection scenario in an open world. We further test our method with limited number of anomaly videos on the ShanghaiTech dataset. Since no anomaly labels are provided in this dataset, we randomly choose a small subset of anomaly videos for model training. We follow the previous work to use Area under Operating Characteristic curve (AUC-ROC) as the metric on UCF-Crime and ShanghaiTech, and use Area under Precision and Recall curve (AUC-PR) on the XD-Violence dataset. Both AUC-ROC and AUC-PR depict the overall performance using a sliding threshold, and a larger value indicates better performance.

4.2 Comparison with State-of-the-Arts

We use the pre-trained I3D classifier [5] to extract features for every non-overlapped video clip (each clip is a collection of 16 consecutive frames) in a video. During training, we uniformly sample 200/200/32 (XD-Violence/UCF-Crime/ShanghaiTech) video clips features to create a bag with the same size.

Our model shares the core design across three datasets and different tasks. We use two layers of GCNs and construct the EDL model with two fully connected layers stacked with a ReLU activation function. For the NFs, we use the 5 consecutive IAF [20]. See Appendix Section B for more implementation details.

Table 1. AUC-PR (%) results on XD-Violence for anomaly frame detection with various number of **seen anomaly classes**. Methods with (*) in the first column are unsupervised, while the rest are weakly-supervised.

NUM. SEEN ANOMALY	0	1	2	3	4
OCSVM [40] (*)	27.25	–	–	–	–
CONV-AE [16] (*)	30.77	–	–	–	–
WU *et al.* [51] (OFF-LINE)	–	40.67	50.34	60.53	67.77
WU *et al.* [51] (ON-LINE)	–	39.13	50.20	58.87	64.29
RTFM [46]	–	43.54	50.88	58.52	63.65
OURS	–	**45.65**	**54.65**	**64.40**	**69.61**

Results on XD-Violence. Table 1 shows the AUC-PR scores in detecting anomaly frames in settings where 6 types of anomaly activities appear in testing, while only 1, 2, 3, or 4 types of them are seen during training. Our method outperforms both unsupervised and weakly supervised ones in all cases. In particular, our method achieves a significant performance gain when very few anomalies are seen, which clearly justifies its capability in the open world setting. Hasan *et al.* [16] and OCSVM [40] do not rely on anomaly videos compared to other methods. Hasan *et al.* surpasses the OCSVM by around 3% on AUC-PR. However, weakly supervised methods perform much better when there are anomaly videos available for training. Even in the extreme case when only 1 out of 6 types of anomalies are seen, the weakly supervised methods can outperform the unsupervised ones by more than 10%. Moreover, more anomaly videos for training further boost the performance of weakly supervised methods. Our method also achieves better a AUC-ROC score than other weakly supervised methods, indicating that our method makes less false positive predictions (see additional experimental results in Appendix Section D).

Results on UCF-Crime. Table 2 shows that AUC-ROC scores in detecting anomaly frames when 13 types of the anomaly appear during testing, only 1, 3, 6, and 9 types of these anomaly are seen. Results in Table 2 show that our method consistently outperforms all baselines under all training settings. To our surprise, all weakly supervised methods can achieve relatively good performance even when a small subset of the anomaly is seen. It could be due to that most

Table 2. AUC-ROC (%) results on UCF-Crime for video anomaly detection with various number of **seen anomaly classes**. Methods with (*) in the first column are unsupervised, while the rest are weakly-supervised.

NUM. SEEN ANOMALY	0	1	3	6	9
SOHRAB*et al.* [41] (*)	58.50	–	–	–	–
LU *et al.* [29] (*)	65.51	–	–	–	–
BODS [49] (*)	68.26	–	–	–	–
GODS [49] (*)	70.46	–	–	–	–
CONV-AE [16] (*)	50.60	–	–	–	–
WU *et al.* [51] (OFF-LINE)	–	73.22	75.15	78.46	79.96
WU *et al.* [51] (ON-LINE)	–	73.78	74.64	77.84	79.11
RTFM [46]	–	75.91	76.98	77.68	79.55
OURS	–	**76.73**	**77.78**	**78.82**	**80.14**

Table 3. AUC-ROC (%) results on ShanghaiTech for video anomaly detection with various number of **seen anomaly videos**. Methods with (*) in the first column are unsupervised, while the rest are weakly-supervised.

NUM. SEEN ANOMALY	0	5	10	15	25
FRAME-PRED [28] (*)	73.40	–	–	–	–
MEM-AE [15] (*)	71.20	–	–	–	–
MNAD [15] (*)	70.50	–	–	–	–
VEC [55] (*)	74.80	–	–	–	–
CONV-AE [16] (*)	60.85	–	–	–	–
WU *et al.* [51] (OFF-LINE)	–	65.83	81.54	83.47	88.81
WU *et al.* [51] (ON-LINE)	–	66.27	81.03	82.42	88.61
RTFM [46]	–	70.59	83.42	81.50	86.33
OURS	–	**80.40**	**88.24**	**85.58**	**93.99**

anomalous behaviours are related to human activities, and there is somehow high correlation among various anomalies, *e.g., Abuse*, *Assault*, and *Vandalism*. RTFM [46] achieves better performance than Wu *et al.* [51] when fewer anomaly classes are seen, which may be owing to its feature magnitude component. Nevertheless, our method achieves the most stable performance under various training setups, implying that our proposed framework is robust by learning a compact decision boundary.

Results on ShanghaiTech. Table 3 shows the AUC-ROC under an imbalance scenario: only a few anomalies are available for training. Results indicate that our method performs better in this challenging setting when only 25 or fewer anomaly videos are available for training. In that case, our method outperforms both RTFM [46] and Wu *et al.* [51] by a large margin. In most cases, the performance advantage is more significant when fewer videos are available. This clearly indicates the effectiveness of the proposed method.

4.3 Ablation Study

We conduct ablation study to validate the proposed three components in our framework, *i.e.*, (i) triplet loss defined in Eq. (2), (ii) evidence criteria defined in Eq. (4), and (iii) pseudo anomaly generation. Specifically, we incrementally remove/replace them and compare the performance on XD-Violence, which is the largest dataset with most videos. When removing the evidence criteria, we set the Ω to include all samples. To evaluate the quality of pseudo anomalies, we replace it with a Gaussian noise.

Table 4. Ablation study results (%) on XD-Violence

Triplet loss	Evidence criteria	Pseudo anomaly	1 seen anomaly		4 seen anomaly	
			AUC-PR	AUC-ROC	AUC-PR	AUC-ROC
√	√	√	**45.65**	**72.50**	**69.61**	**88.25**
	√	√	45.26	61.30	69.14	83.57
		√	41.79	67.07	68.82	84.78
			40.94	66.83	66.61	84.09

Table 4 validates the contribution of each proposed technique. It shows that the combination of the three components achieves the best AUC-PR and AUC-ROC scores, indicating that all these three components positively contribute to the performance of our framework. Notably, the triplet loss contributes the most to the performance gain. This demonstrates the important role of instance representation learning for video anomaly detection. Besides, we note that the evidence criteria produce better AUC-PR scores while worse AUC-ROC scores. This can be explained that the evidence criteria drive the decision boundary toward the positive side in the feature space as it filters out the noisy labels. As a result, the false positive predictions are less while the false negative predictions might increase. Lastly, once the pseudo anomaly generation is applied, the performances of both AUC-PR and AUC-ROC are improved.

5 Conclusion

In this paper, we present a new approach for the OpenVAD problem under weak supervision, which is a highly challenging task by previous unsupervised and weakly supervised methods when being used alone. The OpenVAD scenario is the most realistic scenario in real-world applications, as the anomaly events are fundamentally difficult to be fully enumerated, characterized, and modeled. To address the unique challenges, the proposed framework integrates unsupervised learning (*i.e.*, NFs) and weakly supervised learning (*i.e.*, MIL) in novel ways to benefit from the advantages of both while not suffering from their individual limitations. Different from existing unsupervised methods, the proposed approach makes use of any available anomaly videos without expensive labelling costs. Unlike other weakly supervised methods, our method can detect any type of seen and unseen anomalies in an open world.

Acknowledgements. This research is supported by an Office of Naval Research (ONR) grant N00014-18-1-2875 and an Army Research Office (ARO) grant W911NF-21-1-0236. The views and conclusions in this document are those of the authors and should not be interpreted as representing the official policies, either expressed or implied, of the ONR, the ARO, or the U.S. Government.

References

1. Arpit, D., et al.: A closer look at memorization in deep networks. In: International Conference on Machine Learning, pp. 233–242. PMLR (2017)
2. Bao, W., Yu, Q., Kong, Y.: Evidential deep learning for open set action recognition. In: Proceedings of the IEEE/CVF International Conference on Computer Vision (ICCV), pp. 13349–13358, October 2021
3. Bendale, A., Boult, T.E.: Towards open set deep networks. In: Proceedings of the IEEE Conference on Computer Vision and Pattern Recognition, pp. 1563–1572 (2016)
4. Borisyak, M., Ryzhikov, A., Ustyuzhanin, A., Derkach, D., Ratnikov, F., Mineeva, O.: (1 + epsilon)- class classification: an anomaly detection method for highly imbalanced or incomplete data sets. arXiv preprint arXiv:1906.06096 (2019)
5. Carreira, J., Zisserman, A.: Quo Vadis, action recognition? A new model and the kinetics dataset. In: Proceedings of the IEEE Conference on Computer Vision and Pattern Recognition, pp. 6299–6308 (2017)
6. Chang, H.S., Learned-Miller, E., McCallum, A.: Active bias: training more accurate neural networks by emphasizing high variance samples. arXiv preprint arXiv:1704.07433 (2017)
7. Charpentier, B., Zügner, D., Günnemann, S.: Posterior network: uncertainty estimation without OOD samples via density-based pseudo-counts. arXiv preprint arXiv:2006.09239 (2020)
8. Chen, Z., Tian, Y., Zeng, W., Huang, T.: Detecting abnormal behaviors in surveillance videos based on fuzzy clustering and multiple auto-encoders. In: 2015 IEEE International Conference on Multimedia and Expo (ICME), pp. 1–6. IEEE (2015)
9. Cho, M., Kim, T., Kim, W.J., Cho, S., Lee, S.: Unsupervised video anomaly detection via normalizing flows with implicit latent features. Pattern Recogn. **129**, 108703 (2022)
10. Dietterich, T.G., Lathrop, R.H., Lozano-Pérez, T.: Solving the multiple instance problem with axis-parallel rectangles. Artif. Intell. **89**(1–2), 31–71 (1997)
11. Dinh, L., Sohl-Dickstein, J., Bengio, S.: Density estimation using real NVP. In: ICLR (2017)
12. Doshi, K., Yilmaz, Y.: Rethinking video anomaly detection-a continual learning approach. In: Proceedings of the IEEE/CVF Winter Conference on Applications of Computer Vision, pp. 3961–3970 (2022)
13. Du, X., Wang, Z., Cai, M., Li, Y.: VOS: learning what you don't know by virtual outlier synthesis. arXiv preprint arXiv:2202.01197 (2022)

14. Geng, C., Huang, S.J., Chen, S.: Recent advances in open set recognition: a survey. IEEE Trans. Pattern Anal. Mach. Intell. **43**, 3614–3631 (2020)
15. Gong, D., et al.: Memorizing normality to detect anomaly: memory-augmented deep autoencoder for unsupervised anomaly detection. In: Proceedings of the ICCV, pp. 1705–1714 (2019)
16. Hasan, M., Choi, J., Neumann, J., Roy-Chowdhury, A.K., Davis, L.S.: Learning temporal regularity in video sequences. In: Proceedings of the IEEE Conference on Computer Vision and Pattern Recognition, pp. 733–742 (2016)
17. He, C., Shao, J., Sun, J.: An anomaly-introduced learning method for abnormal event detection. Multimedia Tools Appl. **77**(22), 29573–29588 (2017). https://doi.org/10.1007/s11042-017-5255-z
18. Jøsang, A.: Subjective Logic. Springer, Cham (2016). https://doi.org/10.1007/978-3-319-42337-1
19. Kingma, D.P., Dhariwal, P.: Glow: generative flow with invertible 1x1 convolutions. In: Advances in Neural Information Processing Systems (NIPS) (2018)
20. Kingma, D.P., Salimans, T., Jozefowicz, R., Chen, X., Sutskever, I., Welling, M.: Improved variational inference with inverse autoregressive flow. Adv. Neural. Inf. Process. Syst. **29**, 4743–4751 (2016)
21. Kipf, T.N., Welling, M.: Semi-supervised classification with graph convolutional networks. arXiv preprint arXiv:1609.02907 (2016)
22. Kopetzki, A.K., Charpentier, B., Zügner, D., Giri, S., Günnemann, S.: Evaluating robustness of predictive uncertainty estimation: are dirichlet-based models reliable? In: International Conference on Machine Learning, pp. 5707–5718. PMLR (2021)
23. Kopuklu, O., Zheng, J., Xu, H., Rigoll, G.: Driver anomaly detection: a dataset and contrastive learning approach. In: Proceedings of the IEEE/CVF Winter Conference on Applications of Computer Vision, pp. 91–100 (2021)
24. Li, W., Vasconcelos, N.: Multiple instance learning for soft bags via top instances. In: CVPR, pp. 4277–4285 (2015). https://doi.org/10.1109/CVPR.2015.7299056
25. Li, Z., Hoiem, D.: Learning without forgetting. IEEE Trans. Pattern Anal. Mach. Intell. **40**(12), 2935–2947 (2017)
26. Liu, W., Luo, W., Lian, D., Gao, S.: Future frame prediction for anomaly detection - a new baseline. In: 2018 IEEE Conference on Computer Vision and Pattern Recognition (CVPR) (2018)
27. Liu, W., Luo, W., Li, Z., Zhao, P., Gao, S., et al.: Margin learning embedded prediction for video anomaly detection with a few anomalies. In: Proceedings of the 28th International Joint Conference on Artificial Intelligence, pp. 3023–3030. AAAI Press (2019)
28. Liu, W., Luo, W., Lian, D., Gao, S.: Future frame prediction for anomaly detection-a new baseline. In: Proceedings of the IEEE Conference on Computer Vision and Pattern Recognition, pp. 6536–6545 (2018)
29. Lu, C., Shi, J., Jia, J.: Abnormal event detection at 150 FPS in MATLAB. In: Proceedings of ICCV, pp. 2720–2727 (2013)
30. Malach, E., Shalev-Shwartz, S.: Decoupling "when to update" from "how to update". arXiv preprint arXiv:1706.02613 (2017)
31. Perera, P., Patel, V.M.: Deep transfer learning for multiple class novelty detection. In: Proceedings of the IEEE/CVF Conference on Computer Vision and Pattern Recognition, pp. 11544–11552 (2019)
32. Ramachandra, B., Jones, M., Vatsavai, R.R.: A survey of single-scene video anomaly detection. IEEE Trans. Pattern Anal. Mach. Intell. **44**, 2293–2312 (2020)
33. Ren, J., et al.: Likelihood ratios for out-of-distribution detection. Advances in Neural Information Processing Systems 32 (2019)

34. Ryzhikov, A., Borisyak, M., Ustyuzhanin, A., Derkach, D.: Normalizing flows for deep anomaly detection. arXiv preprint arXiv:1912.09323 (2019)
35. Ryzhikov, A., Borisyak, M., Ustyuzhanin, A., Derkach, D.: NFAD: fixing anomaly detection using normalizing flows. PeerJ Comput. Sci. **7**, e757 (2021). https://doi.org/10.7717/peerj-cs.757
36. Scheirer, W.J., de Rezende Rocha, A., Sapkota, A., Boult, T.E.: Toward open set recognition. IEEE Trans. Pattern Anal. Mach. Intell. **35**(7), 1757–1772 (2012)
37. Sensoy, M., Kaplan, L., Kandemir, M.: Evidential deep learning to quantify classification uncertainty. arXiv preprint arXiv:1806.01768 (2018)
38. Sentz, K., Ferson, S., et al.: Combination of evidence in Dempster-Shafer theory, vol. 4015. Sandia National Laboratories Albuquerque (2002)
39. Shi, W., Zhao, X., Chen, F., Yu, Q.: Multifaceted uncertainty estimation for label-efficient deep learning. Advances in Neural Information Processing Systems 33 (2020)
40. Smeureanu, S., Ionescu, R.T., Popescu, M., Alexe, B.: Deep appearance features for abnormal behavior detection in video. In: Battiato, S., Gallo, G., Schettini, R., Stanco, F. (eds.) ICIAP 2017. LNCS, vol. 10485, pp. 779–789. Springer, Cham (2017). https://doi.org/10.1007/978-3-319-68548-9_70
41. Sohrab, F., Raitoharju, J., Gabbouj, M., Iosifidis, A.: Subspace support vector data description. In: 2018 24th International Conference on Pattern Recognition (ICPR), pp. 722–727. IEEE (2018)
42. Sultani, W., Chen, C., Shah, M.: Real-world anomaly detection in surveillance videos. In: Proceedings of the IEEE Conference on Computer Vision and Pattern Recognition, pp. 6479–6488 (2018)
43. Tabak, E.G., Turner, C.V.: A family of nonparametric density estimation algorithms. Commun. Pure Appl. Math. **66**(2), 145–164 (2013)
44. Tabak, E.G., Vanden-Eijnden, E.: Density estimation by dual ascent of the log-likelihood. Commun. Math. Sci. **8**(1), 217–233 (2010)
45. Tarvainen, A., Valpola, H.: Mean teachers are better role models: weight-averaged consistency targets improve semi-supervised deep learning results. arXiv preprint arXiv:1703.01780 (2017)
46. Tian, Y., Pang, G., Chen, Y., Singh, R., Verjans, J.W., Carneiro, G.: Weakly-supervised video anomaly detection with robust temporal feature magnitude learning. In: Proceedings of the IEEE/CVF International Conference on Computer Vision (2021)
47. Tran, H.T., Hogg, D.: Anomaly detection using a convolutional winner-take-all autoencoder. In: Proceedings of the British Machine Vision Conference 2017. British Machine Vision Association (2017)
48. Wan, B., Fang, Y., Xia, X., Mei, J.: Weakly supervised video anomaly detection via center-guided discriminative learning. In: ICME, pp. 1–6. IEEE (2020)
49. Wang, J., Cherian, A.: GODS: generalized one-class discriminative subspaces for anomaly detection. In: Proceedings of ICCV, pp. 8201–8211 (2019)
50. Wang, R., Liu, T., Tao, D.: Multiclass learning with partially corrupted labels. IEEE Trans. Neural Netw. Learn. Syst. **29**(6), 2568–2580 (2017)
51. Wu, P., et al.: Not only look, but also listen: learning multimodal violence detection under weak supervision. In: Vedaldi, A., Bischof, H., Brox, T., Frahm, J.-M. (eds.) ECCV 2020. LNCS, vol. 12375, pp. 322–339. Springer, Cham (2020). https://doi.org/10.1007/978-3-030-58577-8_20
52. Xia, X., et al.: Sample selection with uncertainty of losses for learning with noisy labels. arXiv preprint arXiv:2106.00445 (2021)

53. Yang, H., Wang, B., Lin, S., Wipf, D., Guo, M., Guo, B.: Unsupervised extraction of video highlights via robust recurrent auto-encoders. In: Proceedings of ICCV, pp. 4633–4641 (2015)
54. Yang, J., Zhou, K., Li, Y., Liu, Z.: Generalized out-of-distribution detection: a survey. arXiv preprint arXiv:2110.11334 (2021)
55. Yu, G., et al.: Cloze test helps: effective video anomaly detection via learning to complete video events. arXiv preprint arXiv:2008.11988 (2020)
56. Yu, X., Han, B., Yao, J., Niu, G., Tsang, I., Sugiyama, M.: How does disagreement help generalization against label corruption? In: International Conference on Machine Learning, pp. 7164–7173. PMLR (2019)
57. Zaheer, M.Z., Mahmood, A., Shin, H., Lee, S.I.: A self-reasoning framework for anomaly detection using video-level labels. IEEE Signal Process. Lett. **27**, 1705–1709 (2020)
58. Zhang, C., Bengio, S., Hardt, M., Recht, B., Vinyals, O.: Understanding deep learning (still) requires rethinking generalization. Commun. ACM **64**(3), 107–115 (2021)
59. Zhang, H., Li, A., Guo, J., Guo, Y.: Hybrid models for open set recognition. In: Vedaldi, A., Bischof, H., Brox, T., Frahm, J.-M. (eds.) ECCV 2020. LNCS, vol. 12348, pp. 102–117. Springer, Cham (2020). https://doi.org/10.1007/978-3-030-58580-8_7
60. Zhang, Z., Zhang, H., Arik, S.O., Lee, H., Pfister, T.: Distilling effective supervision from severe label noise. In: Proceedings of the IEEE/CVF Conference on Computer Vision and Pattern Recognition, pp. 9294–9303 (2020)
61. Zhao, B., Fei-Fei, L., Xing, E.P.: Online detection of unusual events in videos via dynamic sparse coding. In: CVPR 2011, pp. 3313–3320. IEEE (2011)
62. Zhong, J.X., Li, N., Kong, W., Liu, S., Li, T.H., Li, G.: Graph convolutional label noise cleaner: train a plug-and-play action classifier for anomaly detection. In: Proceedings of the IEEE Conference on Computer Vision and Pattern Recognition, pp. 1237–1246 (2019)
63. Zhou, D.W., Ye, H.J., Zhan, D.C.: Learning placeholders for open-set recognition. In: Proceedings of the IEEE/CVF Conference on Computer Vision and Pattern Recognition, pp. 4401–4410 (2021)

EclipSE: Efficient Long-Range Video Retrieval Using Sight and Sound

Yan-Bo Lin(✉), Jie Lei, Mohit Bansal, and Gedas Bertasius

Department of Computer Science, University of North Carolina at Chapel Hill, Chapel Hill, USA
{yblin,jielei,mbansal,gedas}@cs.unc.edu

Abstract. We introduce an audiovisual method for long-range text-to-video retrieval. Unlike previous approaches designed for short video retrieval (e.g., 5–15 s in duration), our approach aims to retrieve minute-long videos that capture complex human actions. One challenge of standard video-only approaches is the large computational cost associated with processing hundreds of densely extracted frames from such long videos. To address this issue, we propose to replace parts of the video with compact audio cues that succinctly summarize dynamic audio events and are cheap to process. Our method, named EclipSE (Efficient CLIP with Sound Encoding), adapts the popular CLIP model to an audiovisual video setting, by adding a unified audiovisual transformer block that captures complementary cues from the video and audio streams. In addition to being 2.92× faster and 2.34× memory-efficient than long-range video-only approaches, our method also achieves better text-to-video retrieval accuracy on several diverse long-range video datasets such as ActivityNet, QVHighlights, YouCook2, DiDeMo, and Charades. Our code is available at https://github.com/GenjiB/ECLIPSE.

1 Introduction

Fueled by the growing availability of video data, the last few years have witnessed remarkable progress in text-to-video retrieval [1–8]. However, modern video retrieval systems are predominantly designed for very short videos (e.g., 5–15 s in length). In contrast, the majority of real-world videos often capture complex human actions, which may last several minutes or even hours. For example, consider yourself performing a complex activity of making Japanese Souffle Pancakes, which may take a couple of hours. In a scenario when you forget some of the steps in the recipe, it would be helpful to retrieve a relevant several-minute-long video segment demonstrating how to perform those steps. However, the traditional short-range video retrieval models would struggle with this task due to their inability to analyze longer videos. Combining the strengths of audio and video modalities, we aim to address this limitation by proposing an efficient audiovisual text-to-video retrieval system focused on long-range videos.

Supplementary Information The online version contains supplementary material available at https://doi.org/10.1007/978-3-031-19830-4_24.

S. Avidan et al. (Eds.): ECCV 2022, LNCS 13694, pp. 413–430, 2022.
https://doi.org/10.1007/978-3-031-19830-4_24

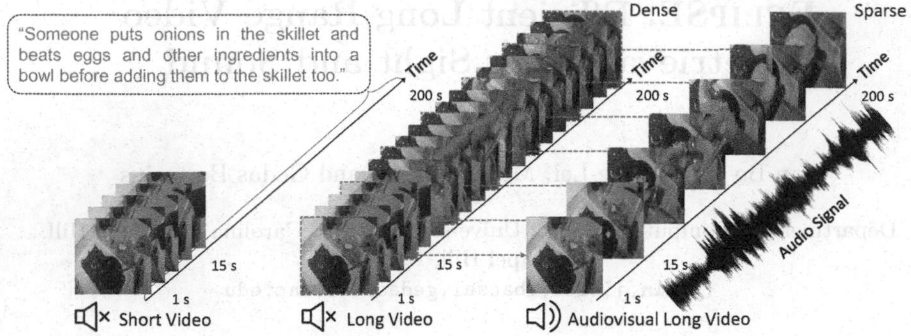

Fig. 1. Comparison of different high-level frameworks for long-range text-to-video retrieval. Most traditional text-to-video retrieval methods (**Leftmost Column**) are designed for short videos (e.g., 5–15 s in duration). Adapting these approaches to several-minute long videos by stacking more input frames (**Middle Column**) is impractical due to excessive computational cost. Instead, our proposed framework operates on sparsely sampled video frames and dense audio cues, which are cheaper to process (**Rightmost Column**). In addition to being more efficient, our framework also achieves higher text-to-video retrieval accuracy than standard video-only approaches.

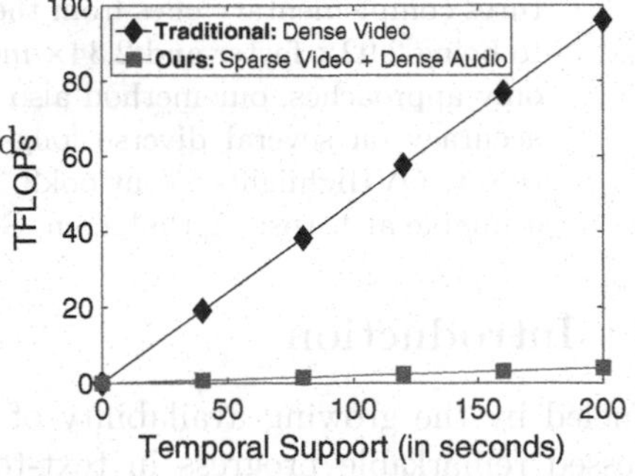

Fig. 2. Our audiovisual framework scales to long videos more efficiently than dense video-only approaches.

Among prior vision-and-language methods [1,2,9–14], CLIP [15] stands out as one of the most widely adopted models. Several recent approaches extended CLIP to video [16] by independently processing individual video frames and then averaging their predictions across time. However, these approaches are often impractical in the long-range video setting because of the large computational cost required to process hundreds of densely extracted video frames (see Fig. 2). Furthermore, while video modality is rich in the information it stores, it also has high informational redundancy (i.e., the video content often changes little in neighboring frames). In contrast, audio can compactly capture information related to human actions [17, 18], objects [19–21], scenes [22,23] and other complex events [24] while also being cheaper to process [25] than the raw video. For instance, consider a video of a person frying the eggs in a pan. In this example, most of the relevant visual information (e.g., kitchen stove, pan, eggs, etc.) can be captured in just a few video frames, while the temporal dynamics in the scene can be succinctly encoded in the audio stream (e.g., the sounds of the eggs sizzling in a pan, etc.).

Based on this motivation, we introduce ECLIPSE, an Efficient CLIP with Sound Encoding. Instead of processing many densely-extracted frames from a long video (the middle column in Fig. 1), our framework leverages complementary audio and video cues by operating on sparsely sampled video frames accompanied by dense audio (the rightmost column in Fig. 1). We demonstrate that compared to dense video-only approaches, our framework is not only more efficient but it is also more accurate.

Our approach adapts CLIP to long-range videos by incorporating a dual-pathway audiovisual attention block into every layer of the Transformer backbone. Such a cross-modal attention mechanism allows our model to (i) incorporate long-range temporal cues from the audio stream into the visual representation, and (ii) conversely inject rich visual features from the video modality into audio representation for improved audio feature expressivity. Such bi-directional exchange of information ensures that both modalities benefit from each other in order to maximize the performance of the downstream application (i.e., long-range text-to-video retrieval). Additionally, we demonstrate that our audiovisual attention block can be easily incorporated into pretrained transformer models such as CLIP [15] without re-training the new model from scratch.

We validate EcLipSE on several diverse long-range video retrieval benchmarks and show that it achieves state-of-the-art results on ActivityNet [26], QVHighlights [27], DiDeMo [28], YouCook2 [29], and Charades [30] while being 2.92× faster and 2.34× memory-efficient than long-range video-only methods.

In summary, our contributions are threefold. First, we propose EcLipSE, an audiovisual adaptation of CLIP that leverages complementary video and audio cues for long-range video retrieval. Second, we demonstrate that compared to long-range video-only approaches, our audiovisual framework leads to better video retrieval results at a reduced computational cost. Lastly, we provide comprehensive ablation studies investigating the success factors of EcLipSE .

2 Related Work

Text-to-Video Retrieval. The association of text descriptions and videos provides rich supervisory signals for developing robust text-to-video retrieval systems. Self-supervised learning approaches in this area achieve impressive results using contrastive loss [3,31–36], masked language modeling [37–41], or masked feature prediction [42]. Additionally, several prior methods propose to incorporate rich audio/speech information for video-and-text representations learning, either by fusing cross-modal signals [6,43,44] or masking inputs from different modalities during training [7,45]. Furthermore, with large-scale pre-training on millions of image and text pairs, CLIP [15] has achieved impressive results on a wide array of vision-and-language tasks. Recently, CLIP-based approaches [13,14,16,46–51] have also been used in video by aggregating image-level outputs across different time steps.

Unlike these prior methods, which are designed for short-range videos (e.g., 5–15 s), we aim to design an audivosual framework for retrieving long videos (e.g., several minutes in length). Compared to the existing CLIP-based approaches, which are difficult to adapt to long videos due to the large computational cost of processing many densely-extracted video frames, we propose to leverage compact audio cues in order to reduce the need for the costly video modality. This enables efficient adaptation of CLIP to long video retrieval.

Audiovisual Learning. Audio and video synchronization is commonly used for self-supervised audio-visual learning [19,22,23,52–59]. Aside from self-supervised learning, many recent methods were proposed for audio-visual event classification [17,24,25,60,61]. Furthermore, the recent popularity of Transformers [62–65] have enabled a wide array of architectures for jointly modeling audio and video data [66–72]. Compared to these prior approaches, our approach focuses on efficient long-range text-to-video retrieval. Specifically, we aim to leverage audio cues in order to reduce the computational cost of processing long videos.

Long Sequence Modeling. Recent work in the natural language processing (NLP) domain [73–75] proposed to approximate the self-attention operator for long sequence modeling. While these approaches are effective in NLP, they are still very costly in the video domain due to the high dimensionality of video inputs. Furthermore, as demonstrated by recent work in the video domain [75], such approximation techniques lead to a substantial accuracy drop while producing limited efficiency gains for video recognition tasks. Additionally, we note that these approximation mechanisms are often incompatible with pretrained vision-and-language models such as CLIP (due to different network architectures).

3 ECLIPSE: Efficient CLIP with Sound Encoding

Our goal is to design an efficient framework that leverages audiovisual cues for long-range text-to-video retrieval. Instead of processing many densely-extracted frames from a long video, which is costly, our framework operates on sparsely sampled video frames accompanied by dense audio. We adapt CLIP to long-range videos by adding a dual-pathway audiovisual attention block into every layer of the Transformer backbone. Our video retrieval framework consists of three high-level components: (i) multimodal input embeddings, (ii) an audiovisual backbone for processing video and audio modalities, and (iii) a contrastive video-to-text matching objective. Below we provide more details behind each of these components. We also illustrate our framework in Fig. 3.

3.1 Obtaining Multimodal Input Embeddings

Video, Audio and Text Inputs. Our framework takes audio, video, and text modalities as its inputs. For video modality, we consider video clips $X \in \mathbb{R}^{T \times H \times W \times 3}$ consisting of T RGB frames of size $H \times W$, sampled uniformly from the whole input video. For audio, we use T audio spectrograms $Z \in \mathbb{R}^{T \times M \times C}$, each spanning t seconds and centered around each of T video frames. Here, M and C depict spatial spectrogram dimensions. Lastly, the text is represented as a sequence $y = (y_1, \ldots, y_L)$ where y_i represents a distinct word in the textual video description and L is the length of the description (i.e., the number of words).

Video Patch Decomposition. Following the ViT [63], we decompose each frame into N non-overlapping patches, each of size $P \times P$, and flatten these patches into vectors $\mathbf{x}_{(p,t)} \in \mathbb{R}^{3P^2}$ where $p = 1, \dots, N$ denotes spatial locations and $t = 1, \dots, T$ indicates a frame index.

Video Patch Embeddings. Video patches from each frame $\mathbf{x}_{(p,t)}$ are linearly mapped into vectors $\mathbf{v}_{(p,t)}^{(0)} \in \mathbb{R}^d$, for $p = 1 \dots N$, and $t = 1 \dots T$. Afterward, we also augment each visual token with spatiotemporal position information as is done in [76]. A specialized CLS token $\mathbf{v}_{cls}^{(0)}$ is prepended to the visual sequence of each frame. Finally, the embeddings $\mathbf{V}^{(0)} \in \mathbb{R}^{T \times (N+1) \times d}$ are used as visual inputs to our ECLIPSE model.

Audio Embeddings. Given an audio spectrogram $Z_t \in \mathbb{R}^{M \times C}$, an audio encoder maps it into audio embeddings $\mathbf{A}_t^{(0)} \in \mathbb{R}^d$ for each timestep $t = 1 \dots T$ where as before, T denotes the number of video frames. We note that the audio encoder can be either a CNN [77–79] or a Transformer [80,81]. Afterward, the audio embeddings $\mathbf{A}^{(0)} \in \mathbb{R}^{T \times d}$ are fed into ECLIPSE together with the visual tokens $\mathbf{V}^{(0)} \in \mathbb{R}^{T \times (N+1) \times d}$.

Text Embeddings. We use a pretrained CLIP [15] text encoder to embed a textual video description $y = (y_1, \dots, y_L)$ into a textual embedding $\mathbf{g} \in \mathbb{R}^d$ where $\mathbf{g}$ corresponds to the CLS token of a given text sequence.

3.2 Audiovisual Attention Block

Although videos contain rich information, they are also redundant and costly to process. In contrast, audio is more compact and cheaper. Thus, we propose an audiovisual attention block that gradually incorporates relevant audio cues into the visual representation. Our audiovisual attention block consists of three distinct attention schemes: (i) spatial visual attention, (ii) audio-to-video attention, and (iii) video-to-audio attention. We next describe each of these attention schemes in more detail.

Multi-head Self-attention. All of our three attention schemes are implemented using a standard multi-head self-attention:

$$\text{MHA}(\mathbf{Q}, \mathbf{K}, \mathbf{V}) = \text{Softmax}\left(\frac{\mathbf{Q}\mathbf{K}^{\top}}{\sqrt{d}}\right)\mathbf{V}, \tag{1}$$

where $\mathbf{Q}, \mathbf{K}, \mathbf{V}$ are the query, key and value matrices obtained using learnable projection weights $\mathbf{W}^Q, \mathbf{W}^K, \mathbf{W}^V \in \mathbb{R}^{d \times d}$ respectively. With this formal description of the MHA function, we can now proceed to the definitions of the three attention schemes in our audiovisual attention block.

Spatial Attention. In order to preserve the pretrained network structure of CLIP, we use an identical spatial attention scheme as in CLIP. Intuitively, spatial attention enables our model to obtain discriminative frame-level representation

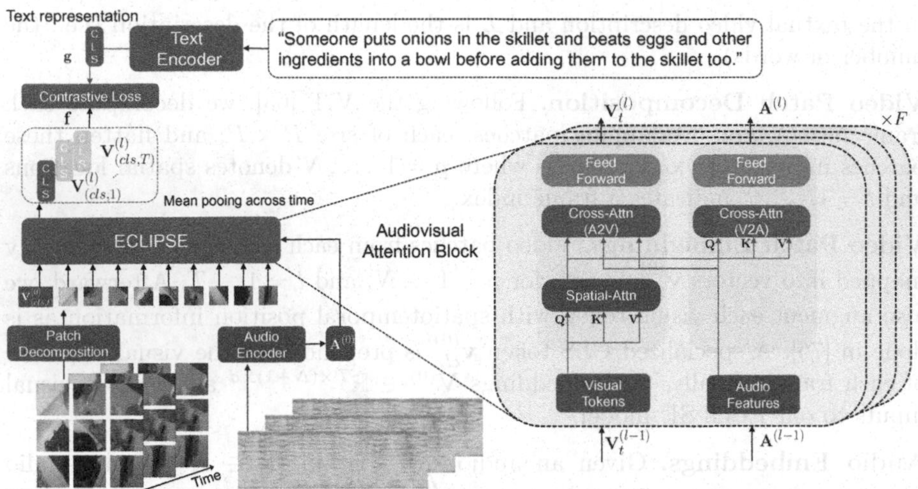

Fig. 3. We adapt CLIP [15] to long-range text-to-video retrieval by adding an efficient audiovisual attention block into the Transformer architecture. First, we obtain fixed dimensional text, audio, and visual feature embeddings. Afterward, the visual and audio embeddings are fed into our EcLIPSE audiovisual backbone, which injects relevant audio information to video and vice-versa. This is accomplished using a dual-pathway audiovisual attention block (illustrated on the right), which is stacked on top of each other F times. Afterward, the audiovisual video segments are aggregated using temporal pooling, and the model is optimized by maximizing the similarity between audiovisual and textual embeddings using a contrastive loss function.

by aggregating relevant information from the visual tokens in the individual video frames. We can implement this scheme using our previously defined MHA function as:

$$\mathbf{S}_t^{(\ell)} = \text{MHA}(\mathbf{V}_t^{(\ell-1)}, \mathbf{V}_t^{(\ell-1)}, \mathbf{V}_t^{(\ell-1)}) + \mathbf{V}_t^{(\ell-1)}. \tag{2}$$

Here, $\mathbf{S}_t^{(\ell)} \in \mathbb{R}^{(N+1)\times d}$ is our newly computed spatial self-attention representation for frame t, and $\mathbf{V}_t^{(\ell-1)}$ is a visual patch representation for frame t from the previous transformer layer $l-1$, which is used as input to the transformer layer l. Note that in the spatial self-attention, the multi-head self-attention is applied independently for each of T video frames. As discussed above, this enables us to preserve the network structure of the original CLIP model, which is essential for good text-to-video retrieval performance. For brevity, we omit the layer normalization operation, which is applied to $\mathbf{V}_t^{(\ell)}$ before feeding it to the spatial attention block. The right part of Fig. 3 provides a visual illustration of where spatial attention fits within our audiovisual attention block.

Audio-to-Video Attention (A2V). To efficiently incorporate temporal audio cues into static video frame representation, we use an audio-to-video (A2V) attention mechanism, which is also illustrated in the right part of Fig. 3 (labeled as Cross-Attn A2V module). This operation can be written as:

$$\mathbf{V}_t^{(\ell)} = \text{MHA}(\mathbf{S}_t^{(\ell-1)}, \mathbf{A}^{(\ell-1)}, \mathbf{A}^{(\ell-1)}) + \mathbf{S}_t^{(\ell-1)}. \tag{3}$$

Here, $\mathbf{A}^{(\ell-1)} \in \mathbb{R}^{T\times d}$ depicts our previously defined audio representation at layer $l-1$, and $\mathbf{S}_t^{(\ell-1)} \in \mathbb{R}^{(N+1)\times d}$ denotes a spatial video representation at timestep t computed using our previously defined spatial attention block. Intuitively, the new visual representation $\mathbf{V}_t^{(\ell)}$ is computed as a weighted summation of the audio features, which enables the model to incorporate long-range audio cues into the visual features. Furthermore, because the audio representation is compact, the operation above can be implemented efficiently.

Video-to-Audio Attention (V2A). Conversely, to inject rich visual information into compact audio features, we use a video-to-audio (V2A) attention mechanism (illustrated in Fig. 3 as Cross-Attn V2A module). We implement this attention scheme as:

$$\mathbf{A}_t^{(\ell)} = \text{MHA}(\mathbf{A}_t^{(\ell-1)}, \mathbf{S}_t^{(\ell-1)}, \mathbf{S}_t^{(\ell-1)}) + \mathbf{A}_t^{(\ell-1)}. \tag{4}$$

At a high level, the operation above computes a new audio feature representation for each timestep t as a weighted combination of all the visual token features at timestep t. This allows us to improve the richness of the audio representation.

Final Audiovisual Representation. Following CLIP4Clip [16], we stack our audiovisual attention block F times (F typically being set to 12). Afterward, we perform temporal pooling over the CLS tokens across all video frames, to obtain the final audiovisual representation $\mathbf{f} \in \mathbb{R}^d$.

3.3 Loss Function

We use the same contrastive video-to-text matching loss as in [16]. Specifically, we compute the similarity between text and video using a normalized dot product between the two embeddings $\mathbf{f}$ and $\mathbf{g}$. We consider the matching text-video pairs in a given batch as positive samples and all the other pairs in that same batch as negative samples. To train our model, we minimize the sum of the video-to-text and text-to-video matching losses [16].

3.4 Implementation Details

Our ECLIPSE follows CLIP4Clip [16] setting where text encoder and visual encoder are initialized with CLIP weights [15]. Specifically, we initialize the spatial attention weights with the weights from CLIP. We also use CLIP weights to initialize both of our cross-modal attention blocks. We attach zero-initialized linear projection layers to the outputs of both cross-modal attention blocks so that the initial outputs of these blocks would be set to zero. Unless otherwise noted, for all of our experiments, we use a ViT-B/32 with uniformly sampled 32-frame inputs spanning the whole input video. The visual frames are extracted at 3 fps. We implement EcLipSE using Pytorch [82] and conduct the training on four NVIDIA A6000 GPUs. For a fair comparison with the baselines, we set the batch size to 64. For audio encoder, we use ResNet-18 [83] pre-trained on VGGSound [79]. We sample 10-second audio clips in the neighborhood around the sampled video frame and process the raw audio into a spectrogram as is done in [79]. We train our model with Adam optimizer [84] and set the learning rate to $1e-7$ for text encoder and spatial attention in Eq. 2. The frame-level *CLS* tokens are averaged to obtain the final video embedding.

Furthermore, the maximum text input is set to 64 tokens for DiDeMo and QVHighlight, and 128 for ActivityNet Captions and YouCook2.

4 Experimental Setup

4.1 Downstream Datasets

We evaluate EcLipSE on five diverse long-range datasets: ActivityNet Captions [26], QVHighlights [27], DiDeMo [28], YouCook2 [29], and Charades [30].

ActivityNet Captions. [26] consists of 20,000 YouTube human activity videos, each annotated with temporally localized sentence descriptions, with a total of 100,000 sentences. The average video length is 180 s, which makes this dataset well suited for verifying our model's ability to retrieve long-range videos. We follow [2,6,16,85] to evaluate paragraph-to-video retrieval, where we concatenate all the sentence descriptions to form a paragraph. Since there is no test set provided, we evaluate the video retrieval results on the *val1* split.

QVHighlights. [27] contains 3,164 videos (10,148 clips) from YouTube, covering a wide range of topics, including everyday activities in lifestyle vlog videos to social and political activities in news videos. Each video is temporally annotated with multiple text queries describing distinct spans of the video. The average video length is around 8 min. The original dataset is created for moment localization and highlight detection. Here we re-purpose it for text-to-video retrieval by evaluating it in paragraph-to-video retrieval setup as ActivityNet Captions. We use the standard splits for training, validation, and testing.

DiDeMo. [28] contains 10,464 Flickr videos with 40,543 temporally localized sentences. The average video length is 30 s. Similar to ActivityNet Caption, we evaluate paragraph-to-video retrieval on DiDeMo. We use the standard splits for training, validation, and testing.

YouCook2. [29] consists of 2,000 videos capturing 89 complex recipes with total duration of 176 h. The average video length is 5.26 min. Each video is annotated with multiple temporally localized captions. Similar to ActivityNet Captions, we evaluate all methods in the paragraph-to-video retrieval setting. We use standard splits for training, validation, and testing.

Charades. [30] contains 9,848 videos with the corresponding textual descriptions. The average video length is about 28 s. We use standard train and test splits for training and testing.

Table 1. ActivityNet captions. We compare EclipSE with previous video retrieval methods. In the column Pretrain, C,G,H,W,CW,V denote COCO Captions [86], Visual Genome Captions [87], HowTo100M [88], WIT [15], CC3M [89]+WebVid2M [3] and VGGSound [79] datasets respectively. The performance is evaluated using text-to-video retrieval R@1, R@5, R@10 and MnR metrics. EclipSE achieves the best reported accuracy on this benchmark. We also note that using a stronger visual backbone (i.e., ViT-B/16 vs. ViT-B/32) also leads to better video retrieval performance.

Method	Pretrain	Frames	R@1 ↑	R@5 ↑	R@10 ↑	MnR ↓
CE [43]	–	–	18.2	47.7	–	23.1
ClipBERT [9]	C+G	40	21.3	49.0	–	–
TT-CE [1]	–	64	23.4	57.2	–	–
MMT [6]	H	–	28.7	61.4	–	16.0
FiT [3]	CW	32	28.9	57.8	71.2	–
SSB [31]	H	–	29.2	61.6	–	–
HiT [2]	H	–	29.6	60.7	–	–
CLIP4Clip [16] (ViT-B/32)	W	64	40.7	71.8	83.4	8.2
EclipSE (ViT-B/32)	W+V	32	**42.3**	**73.2**	**83.8**	**8.2**
EclipSE (ViT-B/16)	W+V	32	**45.3**	**75.7**	**86.2**	**6.2**

4.2 Evaluation Metrics

We use standard video retrieval evaluation metrics [9,16] such as text-to-video *R*@1, *R*@5, *R*@10, and mean rank (MnR) to validate the effectiveness of our EclipSE model. Since our model is built on CLIP, which is pretrained on a large-scale image-and-text dataset [15], the comparisons with some of the previous methods are not directly applicable. Therefore, in all of our evaluations, we use a publicly available state-of-the-art CLIP4Clip [16] video retrieval system as our primary baseline.

5 Results and Analysis

5.1 ActivityNet Captions

Comparison to the State-of-the-Art. In Table 1, we report the results of our method on ActivityNet Captions. These results indicate several interesting findings. First, we notice that the gap between CLIP-based methods (i.e., CLIP4Clip, EclipSE) and other previous approaches is significant (>10% in R@1 metric). This result justifies our motivation to build on the powerful CLIP model. Second, our results indicate that EclipSE outperforms CLIP4Clip by a substantial margin (1.6% in R@1), which suggests the usefulness of temporal audio cues. Third, we also note that unlike CLIP4Clip, which operates on 64 frame inputs, EclipSE achieves higher accuracy while processing fewer frames (i.e., 32). Lastly, we show that using a stronger visual backbone (i.e., ViT-B/16 vs. ViT-B/32) leads to improved video retrieval performance.

Accuracy vs. Number of Frames. We next investigate the trade-off between video retrieval accuracy and the number of input frames. In Fig. 4, we plot the long-range text-to-video retrieval accuracy (i.e., R@1) as a function of the number of input frames. Based on these results, we observe that ECLIPSE consistently outperforms CLIP4Clip in 8, 32 and 96-frame regimes. Furthermore, we notice that ECLIPSE achieves higher accuracy than CLIP4Clip even when operating on a much smaller number of video frames (e.g., 32 vs 96).

Computational Cost Analysis. We note that compared to the video-only approaches, our proposed ECLIPSE uses an additional audio modality. However, we would also like to emphasize that we use audio to improve the efficiency of the costly video-only approaches rather than merely improving the absolute video retrieval accuracy. In Table 2, we compare the computational cost of a 96-frame CLIP4Clip with our 32-frame ECLIPSE. Based on these results, we observe that ECLIPSE uses 2.3× less GPU memory, runs 2.92× faster, and achieves better accuracy (42.3 vs. 41.7) than CLIP4Clip. This suggests that replacing the costly video modality with the audio makes our retrieval framework more efficient and also improves its accuracy.

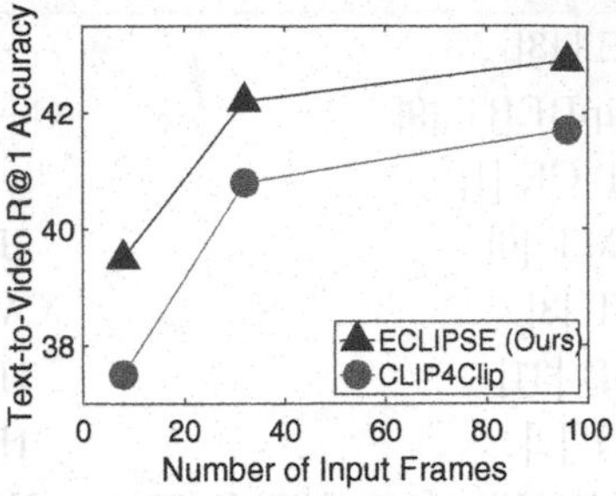

Fig. 4. We compare ECLIPSE with CLIP4Clip with a varying number of frames. Our method outperforms CLIP4Clip while using the same number or even fewer frames.

5.2 Results on Other Long-Range Datasets

Next, we validate our approach on four other long-range video datasets: QVHighlights [27] (QVH), DiDeMo [28], YouCook2 [29] (YC2), and Charades [30]. Since long-range video retrieval is a relatively unexplored subarea of research, we note that QVHighlights, YouCook2, and Charades are not formally used for the long-range video retrieval task. However, all three of these datasets contain (i) long videos and (ii) multiple annotated text descriptions of short-term segments within each long video. Thus, to re-purpose these datasets for long-range text-to-video retrieval, we follow the protocol of ActivityNet Captions [26]. Specifically, we concatenate the textual descriptions of all short-term segments in a given long video and treat it as a paragraph-to-video retrieval task similar to [26]. In our comparisons, we also include other recent video retrieval methods such as ClipBERT [9], Frozen in Time (FiT) [3], and CLIP4Clip [16].

In Table 3, we show that a 32-frame ECLIPSE with a ViT-B/32 backbone outperforms prior methods on all four datasets. Additionally, we point out that our method is more efficient than both FiT [3] and CLIP4Clip [16] (827 vs. 1251 vs. 1426 in GFLOPs).

Potential Overlap Between Audio and Video Datasets. Next, we want to verify that the videos used to pretrain our audio encoders were not present in the test sets of the video retrieval benchmarks. Upon our investigation, we found

Table 2. We compare the computational cost of a 32-frame EclipSE with a 96-frame CLIP4Clip [16] on ActivityNet Captions. Both methods are built using a ViT-B/32 architecture. Despite using fewer frames, EclipSE outperforms CLIP4Clip. Additionally, our method uses 2.3× less GPU memory, runs 2.92× faster and is generally more efficient as indicated by the number of GFLOPs (i.e., 827 vs 1251).

Method	Num. Frames	Inference GFLOPs ↓	GPU Mem. (in MB) ↓	Samples per Sec. ↑	T2V R@1 ↑
CLIP4Clip	96	1251	24,802	17.39	41.7
EclipSE	32	**827**	**10,637**	**50.93**	**42.3**

Table 3. Our results on QVHighlights [27] (QVH), YouCook2 [29] (YC2), Charades [30] and DiDeMo [28] using the *R*@1 T2V metric. A 32-frame EclipSE with a ViT-B/32 backbone outperforms prior approaches while also being more efficient.

Method	Pretrain	Frames	QVH	DiDeMo	YC2	Charades	GFLOPs
ClipBERT [9]	C+G	32	43.2	20.4	29.8	6.7	-
FiT [3]	CW	32	55.0	35.8	32.2	11.9	1426
CLIP4Clip [16]	W	96	70.2	42.5	37.6	13.9	1251
EclipSE	W+V	32	**70.8**	**44.2**	**38.5**	**15.7**	**827**

that the overlap between VGGSound, which was used to pretrain our best audio model, and ActivityNet Captions was small, i.e., 42 out of 4, 926 videos (0.8%). Furthermore, there were no overlaps between the VGGSound and all of the other datasets. To validate that our original conclusions on ActivityNet still hold, we conducted additional experiments on the deduplicated ActivityNet dataset where the overlapping test videos were removed. We used the same CLIP4Clip and EclipSE methods as in Table 1. We report that EclipSE achieved 42.3% T2V R@1 accuracy while CLIP4Clip obtained 40.8%. Both of these results are almost identical to the results in Table 1 (i.e., 42.3% and 40.7% respectively).

5.3 Ablation Studies

Next, we investigate how different design choices of our model affect the long-range video retrieval accuracy on the ActivityNet Captions dataset [26].

Audiovisual Block Design. First, we validate the effectiveness of our audiovisual attention block by comparing it to (i) a joint audiovisual attention that processes concatenated video and audio tokens, (ii) the variant of our model that only uses audio-to-video (A2V) attention (Eq. 3) and (iii) our final model that uses both audio-to-video (A2V) and video-to-audio (V2A) attentions (Eq. 3 and Eq. 4). For efficiency, all models are trained using 8-frame inputs.

From the results in Fig. 5a, we observe that using a bi-directional audiovisual attention (i.e., both audio-to-video (A2V) and video-to-audio (V2A)) leads to the best *R*@1 text-to-video retrieval accuracy on ActivityNet.

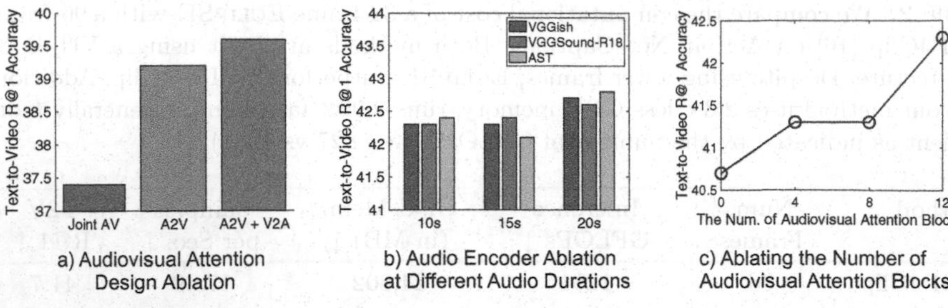

Fig. 5. **(a)** In the left subfigure, we study different audiovisual block design. Joint AV refers to standard self-attention applied to concatenated audio and video tokens. A2V refers to a single cross-modal audio-to-video attention block (Eq. 3). Lastly, A2V+V2A depicts our dual-pathway attention block design (Eq. 3 and Eq. 4). Based on these results, we observe that dual-pathway attention achieves the best performance. For efficiency, we use 8 frame inputs for these experiments. **(b)** In the middle subfigure, we also investigate different audio encoders applied to different duration audio segments. These results indicate that (i) longer audio typically improves the performance, (ii) ECLIPSE is robust to different audio encoders. **(c)** In the right subfigure, we study video retrieval accuracy as a function of the number of audiovisual attention blocks. Based on these results, we observe that injecting our proposed audiovisual attention block into every layer of our 12-layer ECLIPSE model leads to the best performance.

Different Audio Encoders. Next, we study how different audio encoders affect the video retrieval performance of our model. Specifically, we experiment with CNN-based audio encoders such as VGGish [78] and VGGSound [79], and also a transformer-based audio encoder AST [81]. Our results in Fig. 5b suggest that our framework is robust to the choice of an audio encoder, as all three audio encoders produce a similar performance.

Audio Duration. Additionally, we investigate how audio duration affects the accuracy of a long-range video retrieval task. In Fig. 5b, we experiment with audio spectrograms of 10, 20, and 30 s. Our results indicate that longer audio duration leads to better performance. However, the performance gain is relatively small (i.e., 0.5% in R@1), suggesting that 10s audio spectrograms are typically sufficient to capture relevant audio cues.

The Number of Audiovisual Attention Blocks. In Fig. 5c, we also study the video retrieval performance (using R@1) as a function of the number of audiovisual attention blocks in our 12-layer ECLIPSE model. Using k audiovisual attention blocks implies that these k audiovisual blocks are injected into the first k layers of the network while the remaining $12 - k$ layers only consider visual information. Our results indicate that video retrieval performance decreases when we use fewer audiovisual attention blocks. In other words, our method achieves the best video retrieval accuracy when the audiovisual attention block is inserted into every layer of our ECLIPSE architecture.

The Importance of CLIP Pretraining. To highlight the importance of CLIP pretraining, we compare CLIP pretraining with the ImageNet-21k pretraining.

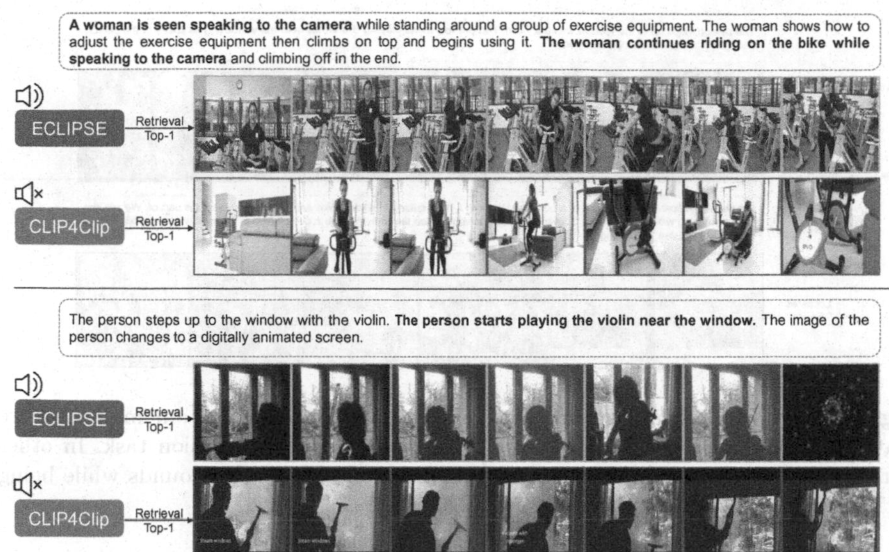

Fig. 6. Here, we illustrate our qualitative retrieval results on ActivityNet Captions [26]. We compare our audiovisual ECLIPSE model with a video-only CLIP4Clip [16]. For a given a textual query (depicted in a green block), we visualize each method's top-1 retrieved video. Our results indicate that the video-only CLIP4Clip struggles with retrieval when textual queries include audio event descriptions, e.g., "a woman speaking to the camera", "a person playing the violin," etc. (see bolded text). In these cases, CLIP4Clip fails to retrieve the correct video instances, whereas ECLIPSE effectively leverages audiovisual cues for a successful retrieval. (Color figure online)

We use the ViT-B/32 architecture for these experiments. We report that compared to the ImageNet-21k pretraining, CLIP pretraining leads to 27.1%, 34.6%, 24.2%, 42.5% better T2V R@1 retrieval accuracy on ActivityNet, DiDeMo, YouCook2, and QVHighlights respectively. These results suggest that CLIP pretraining is essential for good downstream video retrieval performance.

Single Modality Baselines. We also report the results of (i) 180-s audio-only, (ii) 64-frame video-only, and (iii) our 32-frame audiovisual methods. On ActivityNet Captions, the three approaches achieve 2.7%, 40.7%, and 42.3% R1 T2V retrieval accuracy respectively. These results indicate that jointly modeling audio and video achieves the best accuracy. We also note that while audio alone obtains poor accuracy, audio effectively complements video in our audiovisual approach. We observe similar trends on all other datasets too.

5.4 Qualitative Results

Video Retrieval Results. In Fig. 6, we also illustrate some of the qualitative video retrieval results on ActivityNet Captions [26]. Specifically, for a given textual query (illustrated in the green blocks in Fig. 6), we visualize the top-1 retrieved video by our audiovisual ECLIPSE and the video-only CLIP4Clip baseline. Based on these results, we observe that the video-only CLIP4Clip method

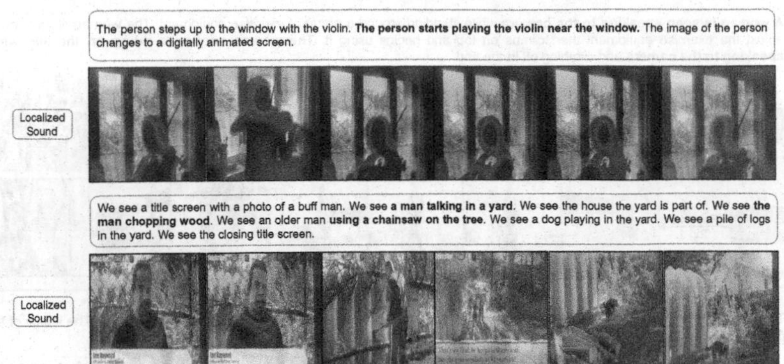

Fig. 7. Here, we illustrate qualitative sound localization results of our method. Note that our ECLIPSE is not explicitly trained for the sound localization task. In other words, ECLIPSE learns implicit associations between objects and sounds while being optimized with respect to the video retrieval task.

struggles to retrieve videos for textual queries that include audio-based event descriptions. For instance, in the first example of Fig. 6, the textual query mentions an audio-based event of "a woman speaking to the camera" (see bolded text). Furthermore, the textual query in the second example also involves a sound event of "a person playing the violin."

Since CLIP4Clip, does not have any audiovisual modeling capabilities, it fails to retrieve the correct video in these cases. In contrast, ECLIPSE retrieves the correct videos in all three illustrated cases, thus, highlighting the importance of incorporating video and audio cues for effective long-range video retrieval.

Sound Localization Results. In Fig. 7, we also demonstrate qualitative sound localization results of our method. By computing the similarity between audio features and visual patches, we can obtain saliency maps that are indicative of sound sources in the video. Note that our method does not require any additional sound localization training objective. In other words, ECLIPSE successfully learns associations between sound sources and objects (e.g., a woman talking, a man playing the violin, a man using a chainsaw) as a byproduct of being trained for the video retrieval task.

6 Conclusions

In this paper, we present a novel audiovisual framework, ECLIPSE, for long-range video retrieval. By replacing costly and redundant parts of the video, with compact audio cues, ECLIPSE efficiently processes long-range videos while also obtaining better performance than standard video-only methods. Our audiovisual framework is (i) flexible, (ii) fast, (iii) memory-efficient, and (iv) it achieves state-of-the-art results on five diverse long-range video benchmarks. In the future, we plan to extend our method to other multimodal video understanding tasks such as video question answering and video captioning.

References

1. Croitoru, I., et al.: Crossmodal generalized distillation for text-video retrieval. In ICCV, Teachtext (2021)
2. Liu, S., Fan, H., Qian, S., Chen, Y., Ding, W., Wang, Z.: Hierarchical transformer with momentum contrast for video-text retrieval. In: ICCV (2021)
3. Bain, M., Nagrani, A., Varol, G., Zisserman, A.: Frozen in time: a joint video and image encoder for end-to-end retrieval. In: ICCV (2021)
4. Wang, X., Zhu, L., Yang, Y.: T2VLAD: global-local sequence alignment for text-video retrieval. In: CVPR (2021)
5. Wray, M., Doughty, H., Damen, D.: On semantic similarity in video retrieval. In: CVPR (2021)
6. Gabeur, V., Sun, C., Alahari, K., Schmid, C.: Multi-modal transformer for video retrieval. In: ECCV (2020)
7. Gabeur, V., Nagrani, A., Sun, C., Alahari, K., Schmid, C.: Masking modalities for cross-modal video retrieval. In: WACV (2022)
8. Hu, X., et al.: Contrastive pre-training for zero-shot video-text understanding. In: EMNLP, VideoCLIP (2021)
9. Lei, J., et al.: ClipBERT for video-and-language learning via sparse sampling. In: CVPR (2021)
10. Dong, J., Li, X., Snoek, C.G.M.: Word2VisualVec: image and video to sentence matching by visual feature prediction. arXiv Preprint (2016)
11. Xu, R., Xiong, C., Chen, W., Corso, J.: Jointly modeling deep video and compositional text to bridge vision and language in a unified framework. In: AAAI (2015)
12. Kiros, R., Salakhutdinov, R., Zemel, R.S.: Unifying visual-semantic embeddings with multimodal neural language models. arXiv Preprint (2014)
13. Fang, H., Xiong, P., Xu, L., Chen, Y.: Clip2Video: Mastering video-text retrieval via image clip. arXiv Preprint (2021)
14. Gao, Z., et al.: CLIP2TV: an empirical study on transformer-based methods for video-text retrieval. arXiv Preprint (2021)
15. Radford, A., et al.: Learning transferable visual models from natural language supervision. In: ICML (2021)
16. Luo, H., et al.: CLIP4Clip: an empirical study of clip for end to end video clip retrieval. arXiv Preprint (2021)
17. Nagrani, A., Yang, S., Arnab, A., Jansen, A., Schmid, C., Sun, C.: Attention bottlenecks for multimodal fusion. In: NeurIPS (2021)
18. Kazakos, E., Huh, J., Nagrani, A., Zisserman, A., Damen, D.: Multimodal egocentric action recognition. In: BMVC (2021)
19. Arandjelović, R., Zisserman, A.: Objects that sound. In: ECCV (2018)
20. Vasudevan, A.B., Dai, D., Van Gool, L.: Sound and visual representation learning with multiple pretraining tasks, In: CVPR (2022)
21. Afouras, T., Asano, Y.M., Fagan, F., Vedaldi, A., Metze, F.: Self-supervised object detection from audio-visual correspondence. In: CVPR (2022)
22. Aytar, Y., Vondrick, C., Torralba, A.: Learning sound representations from unlabeled video. In: NeurIPS, SoundNet (2016)
23. lwassel, H., Mahajan, D., Torresani, L., Ghanem, B., Tran, D.: Self-supervised learning by cross-modal audio-video clustering. In: NeurIPS (2020)
24. Lin, Y.-B., Tseng, H.-Y., Lee, H.-Y., Lin, Y.-Y., Yang, M.-H.: Exploring cross-video and cross-modality signals for weakly-supervised audio-visual video parsing. In: NeurIPS (2021)

25. Gao, R., Tae-Hyun, O., Grauman, K., Torresani, L.: Action recognition by previewing audio. In: CVPR (2020)
26. Krishna, R., Hata, K., Ren, F., Fei-Fei, L., Carlos Niebles, J.: Dense-captioning events in videos. In: ICCV (2017)
27. Lei, J., Berg, T.L., Bansal, M.: QVHighlights: detecting moments and highlights in videos via natural language queries. In: NeurIPS (2021)
28. Hendricks, L.A., Wang, O., Shechtman, E., Sivic, J., Darrell, T., Russell, B.: Localizing moments in video with natural language. In: ICCV (2017)
29. Zhou, L., Xu, C., Corso, J.J.: Towards automatic learning of procedures from web instructional videos. In: AAAI (2018)
30. Sigurdsson, G.A., Varol, G., Wang, X., Farhadi, A., Laptev, A., Gupta, A.: Hollywood in homes: crowdsourcing data collection for activity understanding. In: ECCV (2016)
31. Patrick, M., et al.: Support-set bottlenecks for video-text representation learning. In: ICLR (2021)
32. Amrani, E., Ben-Ari, R., Rotman, D., Bronstein, A.: Noise estimation using density estimation for self-supervised multimodal learning. In: AAAI (2020)
33. Miech, A., Alayrac, J.-P., Smaira, L., Laptev, I., Sivic, J., Zisserman, A.: End-to-end learning of visual representations from uncurated instructional videos. In: CVPR (2020)
34. Wray, M., Larlus, D., Csurka, G., Damen, D.: Fine-grained action retrieval through multiple parts-of-speech embeddings. In: ICCV (2019)
35. Ge, Y., et al.: Bridging video-text retrieval with maultiple choice questions. In: CVPR (2022)
36. Haoyu, L., Fei, N., Huo, Y., Gao, Y., Zhiwu, L., Rong Wen, J.: Collaborative two-stream vision-language pre-training model for cross-modal retrieval. In: CVPR (2022)
37. Wang, J., et al.: Object-aware video-language pre-training for retrieval. In: CVPR (2022)
38. Zhu, L., Yang, Y.: ActBERT: learning global-local video-text representations. In: CVPR (2020)
39. Li, L., et al.: Hierarchical encoder for Video+Language omni-representation pre-training. In: EMNLP (2020)
40. Yu, Y., Kim, J., Kim, G.: A joint sequence fusion model for video question answering and retrieval. In: ECCV (2018)
41. Yu, Y., Ko, H., Choi, J., Kim, G.: End-to-end concept word detection for video captioning, retrieval, and question answering. In: CVPR (2017)
42. Luo, H., et al.: UniVL: a unified video and language pre-training model for multimodal understanding and generation. arXiv Preprint (2020)
43. Liu, Y., Albanie, S., Nagrani, A., Zisserman, A.: Video retrieval using representations from collaborative experts. In: BMVC (2019)
44. Mithun, N.C., Li, J., Metze, F., Roy-Chowdhury, A.M.: Learning joint embedding with multimodal cues for cross-modal video-text retrieval. In: ICMR (2018)
45. Miech, A., Laptev, I., Sivic, J.: Learning a text-video embedding from incomplete and heterogeneous data. arXiv Preprint (2018)
46. Cheng, X., Lin, H., Wu, X., Yang, F., Shen, D.: Improving video-text retrieval by multi-stream corpus alignment and dual SoftMax loss. arXiv Preprint (2021)
47. Wang, Z., Wu, Y., Narasimhan, K., Russakovsky, O.: Multi-query video retrieval. arXiv Preprint (2022)
48. Dzabraev, M., Kalashnikov, M., Komkov, S., Petiushko. A.: Multidomain multimodal transformer for video retrieval. In: CVPRW (2021)

49. Portillo-Quintero, J.A., Ortiz-Bayliss, J.C., Terashima-Marín, H.: A straightforward framework for video retrieval using clip. In: MCPR (2021)
50. Gorti, S.K., et al.: Cross-modal language-video attention for text-video retrieval. In CVPR (2022)
51. Bain, M., Nagrani, A., Varol, G., Zisserman, A.: A clip-hitchhiker's guide to long video retrieval. arXiv Preprint (2022)
52. Owens, A., Efros, A.A.: Audio-visual scene analysis with self-supervised multisensory features. In: ECCV (2018)
53. Korbar, B., Tran, D., Torresani, L.: Cooperative learning of audio and video models from self-supervised synchronization. In: NeurIPS (2018)
54. Arandjelovic, R., Zisserman, A.: Look, listen and learn. In: ICCV (2017)
55. Owens, A., Jiajun, W., McDermott, J.H., Freeman, W.T., Torralba, A.: Ambient sound provides supervision for visual learning. In: ECCV (2016)
56. Asano, Y.M., Patrick, M., Rupprecht, C., Vedaldi, A.: Labelling unlabelled videos from scratch with multi-modal self-supervision. In: NeurIPS (2020)
57. Ma, S., Zeng, Z., McDuff, D., Song, Y.: Active contrastive learning of audio-visual video representations. In: ICLR (2021)
58. Morgado, P., Vasconcelos, N., Misra, I.: Audio-visual instance discrimination with cross-modal agreement. In: CVPR (2021)
59. Morgado, P., Misra, I., Vasconcelos, N.: Robust audio-visual instance discrimination. In: CVPR (2021)
60. Lin, Y.-B., Li, Y.-J., Wang, Y.-G.F.: Dual-modality seq2seq network for audio-visual event localization. In: ICASSP (2019)
61. Ma, S., Zeng, Z., McDuff, D., Song, Y.: Contrastive learning of global and local video representations. In: NeurIPS (2021)
62. Zhang, Y., Doughty, H., Shao, L., Snoek, C.G.M.: Audio-adaptive activity recognition across video domains. In: CVPR (2022)
63. Dosovitskiy, D., et al.: An image is worth 16x16 words: transformers for image recognition at scale. In: ICLR (2021)
64. Lin, Y.-B., Wang, Y.-C.F.: Audiovisual transformer with instance attention for audio-visual event localization. In: ACCV (2020)
65. Vaswani, A., et al.: Attention is all you need. In: NeurIPS (2017)
66. Shvetsova, N., et al.: Everything at once-multi-modal fusion transformer for video retrieval. In: CVPR (2022)
67. Zellers, R., et al.: Neural script knowledge through vision and language and sound. In CVPR (2022)
68. Akbari, H., et al.: VATT: transformers for multimodal self-supervised learning from raw video, audio and text. In: NeurIPS (2021)
69. Zhao, Y., Hessel, J., Yu, Y., Lu, X., Zellers, R., Choi, Y.: Connecting the dots between audio and text without parallel data through visual knowledge transfer. arXiv Preprint (2021)
70. Alayrac, J.-B., et al.: Self-supervised multimodal versatile networks. In: NeurIPS (2020)
71. Chen, B., et al.: Multimodal clustering networks for self-supervised learning from unlabeled videos. In: ICCV (2021)
72. Lin, Y.-B., Frank Wang, Y-C.: Exploiting audio-visual consistency with partial supervision for spatial audio generation. In: AAAI (2021)
73. Wang, S., et al.: Self-attention with linear complexity. arXiv Preprint, Linformer (2020)
74. Choromanski, K.M.: Rethinking attention with performers. In: ICLR (2021)

75. Patrick, M., et al.: Trajectory attention in video transformers. In: NeurIPS (2021)
76. Bertasius, G., Wang, H., Torresani, L.: Is space-time attention all you need for video understanding? In: ICML (2021)
77. Gemmeke, J.F., et al.: Audio set: an ontology and human-labeled dataset for audio events. In: ICASSP (2017)
78. Hershey, S., et al.: CNN architectures for large-scale audio classification. In: ICASSP (2017)
79. Chen, H., Xie, W., Vedaldi, A., Zisserman, A.: A large-scale audio-visual dataset. In: ICASSP (2020)
80. Gong, Y., Chung, Y.-A., Glass, J.: Audio spectrogram transformer. In INTEER-SPEECH,AST (2021)
81. Gong, Y., Chung, Y.-A., Glass, J.: Improving audio tagging with pretraining, sampling, labeling, and aggregation. In: TASLP (2021)
82. Paszke, A., et al.: Pytorch: an imperative style, high-performance deep learning library. In: NeurIPS (2019)
83. He, K., Zhang, X., Ren, S., Sun, J.: Deep residual learning for image recognition. In: CVPR (2016)
84. Kingma, D.P., Ba, J.: Adam: a method for stochastic optimization. In: ICLR (2015)
85. Zhang, B., Hu, H., Sha, F.: Cross-modal and hierarchical modeling of video and text. In: Ferrari, V., Hebert, M., Sminchisescu, C., Weiss, Y. (eds.) ECCV 2018. LNCS, vol. 11217, pp. 385–401. Springer, Cham (2018). https://doi.org/10.1007/978-3-030-01261-8_23
86. Chen, X., et al.: Data collection and evaluation server. arXiv Preprint, Microsoft coco captions (2015)
87. Krishna, R., et al.: Visual genome: connecting language and vision using crowdsourced dense image annotations. In: IJCV (2017)
88. Miech, A., et al.: Howto100m: Learning a text-video embedding by watching hundred million narrated video clips. In: ICCV (2019)
89. Sharma, P., Ding, N., Goodman, S., Soricut, R.: Conceptual captions: A cleaned, hypernymed, image alt-text dataset for automatic image captioning. In: ACL (2018)

Joint-Modal Label Denoising for Weakly-Supervised Audio-Visual Video Parsing

Haoyue Cheng[1,2], Zhaoyang Liu[2], Hang Zhou[3], Chen Qian[2], Wayne Wu[2], and Limin Wang[1,4(✉)]

[1] State Key Laboratory for Novel Software Technology, Nanjing University, Nanjing, China
lmwang@nju.edu.cn

[2] SenseTime Research, Shanghai, China
qianchen@sensetime.com

[3] CUHK - Sensetime Joint Lab, Hong Kong, China
zhouhang@link.cuhk.edu.hk

[4] Shanghai AI Laboratory, Shanghai, China

Abstract. This paper focuses on the weakly-supervised audio-visual video parsing task, which aims to recognize all events belonging to each modality and localize their temporal boundaries. This task is challenging because only overall labels indicating the video events are provided for training. However, an event might be labeled but not appear in one of the modalities, which results in a modality-specific noisy label problem. In this work, we propose a training strategy to identify and remove modality-specific noisy labels dynamically. It is motivated by two key observations: 1) networks tend to learn clean samples first; and 2) a labeled event would appear in at least one modality. Specifically, we sort the losses of all instances within a mini-batch individually in each modality, and then select noisy samples according to the relationships between intra-modal and inter-modal losses. Besides, we also propose a simple but valid noise ratio estimation method by calculating the proportion of instances whose confidence is below a preset threshold. Our method makes large improvements over the previous state of the arts (*e.g.*, from 60.0% to 63.8% in segment-level visual metric), which demonstrates the effectiveness of our approach. Code and trained models are publicly available at https://github.com/MCG-NJU/JoMoLD.

Keywords: Audio-visual video parsing · Multi-modal learning · Weakly-supervised learning · Label denoising

Supplementary Information The online version contains supplementary material available at https://doi.org/10.1007/978-3-031-19830-4_25.

S. Avidan et al. (Eds.): ECCV 2022, LNCS 13694, pp. 431–448, 2022.
https://doi.org/10.1007/978-3-031-19830-4_25

1 Introduction

Many works show that the audio-visual clues play a crucial role in comprehensive video understanding [3,30,45]. However, most studies on audio-visual joint learning [17,31,38] assume that the two modalities are correlated or even temporally synchronized, which is not always the case. For example, the sound of a car might be out of sight, but such information is still crucial for real-world perception. To this end, Tian *et al.* [37] proposed the **audio-visual video parsing** (AVVP) task without consistency restriction, which aims to recognize all events belonging to each modality and localize their temporal boundaries.

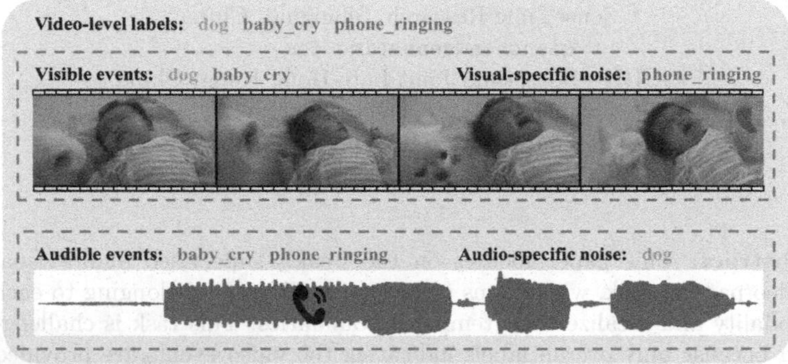

Fig. 1. An example to illustrate modality-specific noise in weakly-supervised AVVP task. An infant accompanied by a dog is sleeping. Then, the phone bell rings and it frightens the baby to cry. In this example, the visible events in the whole video are " dog" and " baby_cry_infant_cry". The audible events are " telephone_bell_ringing" and " baby_cry_infant_cry". Thus, the " dog" can be treated as audio-specific noise, and " telephone_bell_ringing" is regarded as visual-specific noise.

AVVP task is formulated in a weakly-supervised manner since precisely annotating labels would be expensive and time-consuming. Event labels are provided for each video in the training set, but the events' detailed modality and temporal location are unavailable. This manner is termed Multimodal Multiple Instance Learning (MMIL). The weakly-supervised setting and audio-visual inconsistency lead to a serious issue: **modality-specific noise**. Modality-specific noise is related to *the event clues that do not appear in one of the two modalities*. Taking Fig. 1 as an example, the event "telephone_bell_ringing" only appears in the audio track and can not be perceived from the visual track, which thus is an improper supervised signal for visual modality and can be regarded as a visual-specific noisy label. We argue that lowering the interference of modality-specific noise can significantly advance the quality of audio-visual video parsing.

The pioneers in audio-visual video parsing have made sustained efforts to learn the spatio-temporal clues under such a weakly-supervised setting. HAN [37] adopts a hybrid attention network optimized with a label smoothing mechanism, but it still suffers from the modality-specific noise. MA [43] exchanges audio or visual tracks between two unrelated videos to yield reliable event labels for each modality. However, since the cross-modal aggregation in [43] is trained by paired audio-visual features, this might interfere with the uncertainty-assessing procedure on their re-assembled videos. As the previous label denoising methods [21,29,42,47] focus on unimodal patterns, leveraging the cross-modal correlation to alleviate modality-specific noise still remains to be studied further. Consequently, we design a novel training strategy to mitigate the impacts of modality-specific noise for weakly-supervised audio-visual video parsing.

In this paper, we propose the **Joint-Modal Label Denoising (JoMoLD)** training strategy to dynamically alleviate **modality-specific noise** through careful loss analysis for both modalities. We take the inspiration from two observations. 1) Neural networks tend to learn cleanly labeled samples first, and gradually memorize noisy ones [6,22,48]. As a result, most noisily labeled data would be more challenging to learn than correctly labeled ones. From the view of loss patterns, the loss of cleanly labeled samples would be lower than noisily labeled ones. 2) Under the weakly supervised training setting, an event label ought not to serve as noise for both modalities, *i.e.*, this event appears in at least one modality. According to these observations, the loss of a noisily labeled modality tends to be higher than the loss of the other modality where the event appears. We call this phenomenon *loss inconsistency among different modalities.*

Based on the above analysis, we leverage audio and visual loss patterns to remove modality-specific noisy labels for each modality. First, we design a noise estimator to approximately pre-estimate the noise ratio per category individually for each modality, which guides our proposed training strategy in determining the modality-specific noise. Then, when training the parsing model, we rank the losses within a mini-batch separately for two modalities. Based on the pre-estimated noise ratios, we treat the labels with inconsistent losses between two modalities as modality-specific noise. For each iteration in the training phase, we remove modality-specific noisy labels from their corresponding modality before back-propagation. This training strategy makes the parsing network robust to modality-specific noise under the weakly-supervised setting of AVVP. Our experiment results significantly outperform the previous state of the arts, which validates the effectiveness of our proposed method.

In summary, we make the following contributions:

- *First*, we develop a noise ratio estimator to calculate the modality-specific noise ratios, which play a crucial role in determining the noise selection.
- *Second*, we propose a general and dynamic training paradigm, namely Joint-Modal Label Denoising (JoMoLD), to alleviate the issue of modality-specific noise from the perspective of joint-modal label denoising on weakly-supervised AVVP task.
- *Finally*, the experiments on the LLP dataset validate the effectiveness of our method. Especially, the segment-level visual metric is improved from 60.0% to 63.8% over the state of the art.

2 Related Work

2.1 Audio-Visual Learning

Audio-visual joint learning has derived a variety of tasks, such as audio-visual representation learning [1,3,7,12,20], audio-visual sound separation [9,10,50,51], sound source localization [4,33], audio-visual video captioning [16,32,36], audio-visual event localization [23,44,52], and audio-visual action recognition [11,30,45]. Most of these works are based on the assumption that audio and visual signals are always semantically corresponding and temporally synchronized.

For audio-visual representation learning, [7] and [12] transfer discriminative visual knowledge from pre-trained visual models into the audio modality. Alwassel *et al.* [1] leverage unsupervised clustering results within one modality as a supervised signal to the other modality. Other works explore learning instance-level audio-visual correspondence. Arandjelovic *et al.* [3] design a pretext task to learn correspondent representations between images and audio. Korbar *et al.* [20] further utilize the temporal synchronization between audio and visual streams.

2.2 Weakly-Supervised AVVP

Audio-visual video parsing (AVVP) task [37] breaks the restriction that audio and visual signals are definitely aligned. Due to the difficulty of exhaustive manual annotations, the audio-visual video parsing task is under the weakly-supervised setting, where only the video-level labels are provided for training.

To tackle the weakly-supervised AVVP task, previous work [37] proposes a hybrid attention network and attentive Multimodal Multiple Instance Learning (MMIL) Pooling mechanism to aggregate all features. Wu *et al.* [43] refine individual modality labels by swapping audio or visual tracks between two unrelated videos. Nevertheless, they independently refine modality labels without considering the relationship between the two modality labels. Our work obtains more precise modality-specific labels in a joint-modal label denoising manner.

2.3 Learning with Label Noise

Deep neural networks have been demonstrated to learn clean samples first, and gradually memorize samples with noisy labels [6,13,22,48]. Recent works [25] show that such early-learning and memorization phenomena can even be observed in linear models. Many works are trying to handle this problem from different perspectives. One kind of methods [19,40,49] designs reasonable loss functions or regularization mechanisms to reduce overfitting noise. Semi-supervised learning is also adopted in some works [21,27].

Two types of methods related to our approach are learning on selected clean samples [13,26,29,47] and correcting noisy labels [5,34,35,46]. Han *et al.* [13] propose "Co-teaching", which optimizes two models on clean samples selected by the paired network. To prevent the two networks converging to a consensus,

"Co-teaching+" [47] is proposed to combine "Co-teaching" with "Update by Disagreement" [26] strategy. These collaborative learning with label noise methods are motivated by "Co-training" [8] in semi-supervised training. Tanaka *et al.* [35] utilize model output to reassign labels for noisy samples. However, most of these works focus on single-modal label denoising, and cannot be directly utilized for multi-modal label denoising.

Some multi-modal learning works [2,18] also try to mitigate the effects of noisy labels. Amrani *et al.* [2] propose to reduce multi-modal noise estimation to a multi-modal density estimation problem. Hu *et al.* [18] propose a "Robust Clustering loss" to make the model focus on clean samples instead of noisy ones. However, these methods do not explore the correlation between multi-modalities and have not addressed the multi-modal noisy labels problem.

Our work deals with the issue of modality-specific noisy labels in weakly-supervised AVVP task. We aim to generate more reliable modality-specific labels considering cross-modal connections.

3 Method

Our main idea is to utilize the cross-modal loss patterns to perceive modality-specific noise, which is compatible with off-the-shelf networks (*e.g.*, [37]) on weakly-supervised AVVP task. In this section, we elaborately introduce our proposed method, *i.e.*, **Joint-Modal Label Denoising** (JoMoLD). Firstly, we formulate the problem statement along with the baseline framework in Sect. 3.1. Secondly, the noise estimator is proposed to calculate modality-specific noise ratios in Sect. 3.2. Thirdly, we design an effective algorithm to remove modality-specific noisy labels by pre-estimated noise ratios in Sect. 3.3. Lastly, we give an insightful discussion of our method in Sect. 3.4.

3.1 Preliminaries

Problem Statement. This task aims to detect audible events or visible events that appear in each segment of a video, which is formulated as a Multimodal Multiple Instance Learning (MMIL) problem with C event categories by Tian *et al.* [37]. Specifically, given a T-second video sequence $\{A_t, V_t\}_{t=1}^{T}$, A_t denotes $t\text{-}th$ segment in audio track and V_t denotes $t\text{-}th$ segment in visual track. During evaluation, let (y_t^a, y_t^v, y_t^{av}) denote audio, visual and audio-visual event labels at $t\text{-}th$ segment, respectively. Note that y_t^a, y_t^v and y_t^{av} are $\{0,1\}^C$ vectors, indicating the presence or absence of each event category. The audio-visual event represents this event occurs in both visual track and audio track at time t. However, as a weakly-supervised task, we can only access video-level event label $y \in \{0,1\}^C$ instead of accurate segment-level labels during training. In other words, we only know which events occurred in a video, but can not acquire when events occur and in which modality the events appear. Following the practice in [37], we use pre-trained off-the-shelf networks to extract local audio and visual features $\{f_t^a, f_t^v\}_{t=1}^{T}$ for each segment.

Baseline Framework. We here use previous work [37] (denoted as $\mathcal{F}$) as our important baseline. To capture temporal context and leverage the clues in different modalities, Tian *et al.* [37] adopt self-attention and cross-attention mechanisms to aggregate inner-modal and intra-modal information on segment features. Furthermore, an attentive MMIL Pooling mechanism is proposed to yield modality-level and video-level predictions. As a multi-label multi-class learning task, it naturally uses binary cross-entropy (BCE) loss to optimize the model. In the baseline, the video-level label y is used to supervise both modality-level and video-level predictions. Due to the modality-specific noise, we argue that such a fashion is misleading for model training. Therefore, we develop a dynamic training strategy, termed **Joint-Modal Label Denoising** (JoMoLD), to alleviate the effect of modality-specific noise during training.

3.2 Estimating Noise Ratios

Our algorithm requires pre-estimating the modality-specific noise ratio per category, which assists our model in determining which labels should be removed during training. Since the real modality-specific noise ratios are unavailable in the training phase, we design a simple yet effective manner to approximately estimate noise ratios. The key insight is that the baseline model trained on this task already has a certain capacity for discriminating noisy labels.

Specifically, we train a noise estimator $\mathcal{H}$ following baseline [37] with one notable modification: removing the cross-modal attention in the overall pipeline. As cross-modal attention exchanges the information between audio and visual features, it practically interferes with the noise estimation for each modality. Experiment in Table 2c has proved this point. Let $\hat{\mathbf{P}}^a, \hat{\mathbf{P}}^v \in \mathbb{R}^{N\times C}$ denote the audio and visual predictions of $\mathcal{H}$, and $\bar{P}^a, \bar{P}^v \in \mathbb{R}^C$ are the mean of predictions for each category. $\mathbf{Y} \in \{0,1\}^{N\times C}$ are video-level labels. Note that N is the number of videos in training set. Then, we need to define which labels are probably noise. For example, we argue the annotated *c-th* category label for *i-th* video, *i.e.* $\mathbf{Y}[i,c] = 1$, is not reliable for audio modality if $\hat{\mathbf{P}}^a[i,c]/\bar{P}^a[c]$ is lower than a pre-set threshold θ^a. Here, $\hat{\mathbf{P}}^a[i,c]$ is normalized by $\bar{P}^a[c]$ so as to alleviate the impact of imbalanced distribution of predictions in each event category. The procedure of estimating noise ratio for *c-th* category is summarized as follows:

$$\begin{aligned}
\mathbf{r}^a[c] &= \frac{\sum_{i=1}^{N} \mathbb{I}(\hat{\mathbf{P}}^a[i,c]/\bar{P}^a[c] < \theta^a) \times \mathbf{Y}[i,c]}{\sum_{i=1}^{N} \mathbf{Y}[i,c]}, \\
\mathbf{r}^v[c] &= \frac{\sum_{i=1}^{N} \mathbb{I}(\hat{\mathbf{P}}^v[i,c]/\bar{P}^v[c] < \theta^v) \times \mathbf{Y}[i,c]}{\sum_{i=1}^{N} \mathbf{Y}[i,c]},
\end{aligned} \tag{1}$$

where $\mathbf{r}^a$ ($\mathbf{r}^v$) $\in \mathbb{R}^C$ denotes noise ratios of positive labels in audio (visual) track for C categories, $\mathbb{I}$ is the indicator function, and "$\times$" denotes multiplication. Note that θ^a (θ^v) can be seen as the confidence to determine noisy labels for audio (visual) modality. Table 2b shows that final performance of our proposed method is not sensitive to θ^a and θ^v. The estimated noise ratios will be used as a priori knowledge for the label denoising procedure.

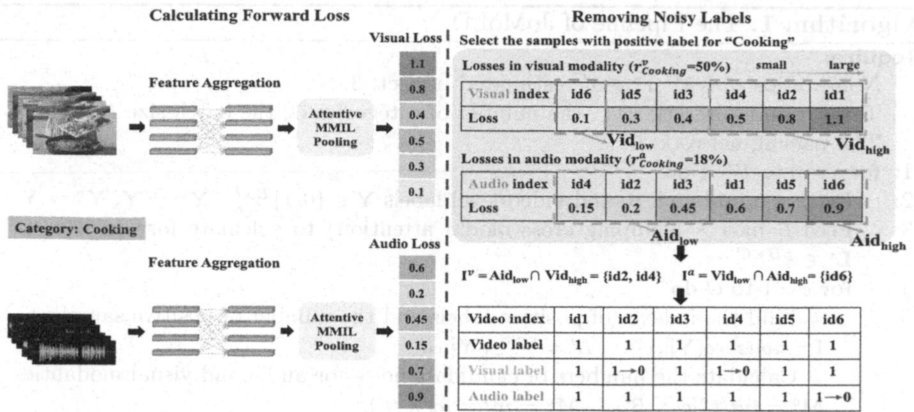

Fig. 2. The proposed modality-specific label denoising procedure. The label denoising procedure consists of **Calculating Foward Loss** and **Removing Noisy Labels**. In this case, we represent the label denoising process for the "Cooking" event in a batch of videos. In calculating forward loss, we aggregate the intra-modal features, obtain the modality-level predictions, and further calculate the modality losses. Based on the estimated noise ratios $\mathbf{r}^v_{Cooking}$ and the sorted visual losses, we obtain the indices of noisy samples for visual modality, *i.e.* $\mathbf{I}^v$. Then we remove the video labels for videos by $\mathbf{I}^v$ to generate refined visual labels. In the figure, "$\rightarrow 0$" denotes the label of "Cooking" is removed. The same procedure is applied to audio modality label denoising.

Generally, our noise estimator is essentially different from Wu *et al.* [43]. They exchange the audio tracks between two unrelated videos to filter out the noisy labels and re-train the model from scratch based on refined labels. On the one hand, as cross-modal attention aggregates multi-modal clues, the modality-level predictions would affect each other. Thus it is improper to assess the uncertainty of event labels for each modality when using cross-modal attention. On the other hand, the refined labels will be fixed after the label refinement procedure in [43]. It causes that even the wrongly refined labels would also be used to re-train the parsing model in the whole re-training phase. In contrast, our method alleviates the potential negative impacts of cross-modal attention in the phase of noise estimation. Furthermore, modality-specific noisy labels are removed dynamically, which is expected to tolerate some improper refinements in the previous training. Even though the intrinsic biases might exist in the noise estimator, the estimated noise ratios are still effective for our modality-specific label denoising algorithm, which is also validated in experiments.

3.3 Modality-Specific Label Denoising

In this section, our goal is to remove modality-specific noisy labels and optimize the parsing model $\mathcal{F}$ with the refined labels. Therefore, we need to solve a tricky issue: how to identify the modality-specific noisy labels. As illustrated in Fig. 2,

Algorithm 1. The Pipeline of JoMoLD

Require:

Noise ratios $\mathbf{r}^a \in \mathbb{R}^C, \mathbf{r}^v \in \mathbb{R}^C$ estimated in Sect. 3.2

Total training iterations Γ, the number of categories C, the batch size B

The parsing network $\mathcal{F}$

for $i = 0$ to Γ - 1 **do**

  Fetch a mini-batch $\mathcal{B}$, and video-level labels $\mathbf{Y} \in \{0,1\}^{B \times C}$, $\mathbf{Y}^a = \mathbf{Y}$, $\mathbf{Y}^v = \mathbf{Y}$

  Feed $\mathcal{B}$ into $\mathcal{F}$ (skipping cross-modal attention) to calculate forward loss $\mathbf{L}^a$, $\mathbf{L}^v \in \mathbb{R}^{B \times C}$

  for $c = 1$ to C **do**

    # Find the indexes of positive labels and the number of positive samples

    $\mathbf{I} = nonzero(\mathbf{Y}[:, c]), \quad B' = \sum_{i=1}^{B} \mathbf{Y}[:, c]$

    # Calculate the numbers of candidate noise for audio and visual modalities

    $\mathbf{M}^a = int(\mathbf{r}^a[c] \times B'), \quad \mathbf{M}^v = int(\mathbf{r}^v[c] \times B')$

    # Determine the indexes of audio noise in batch $\mathcal{B}$

    $\mathbf{I}^a = \mathbf{I}[\mathcal{G}(-\mathbf{L}^a[\mathbf{I}, c], \mathbf{M}^a)] \cap \mathbf{I}[\mathcal{G}(\mathbf{L}^v[\mathbf{I}, c], \mathbf{M}^a)]$

    # Determine the indexes of visual noise in batch $\mathcal{B}$

    $\mathbf{I}^v = \mathbf{I}[\mathcal{G}(-\mathbf{L}^v[\mathbf{I}, c], \mathbf{M}^v)] \cap \mathbf{I}[\mathcal{G}(\mathbf{L}^a[\mathbf{I}, c], \mathbf{M}^v)]$

    # Remove noisy labels

    $\mathbf{Y}^a[\mathbf{I}^a, c] = 0, \quad \mathbf{Y}^v[\mathbf{I}^v, c] = 0$

  end for

  Feed $\mathcal{B}$ into $\mathcal{F}$, and utilize $\mathbf{Y}$, $\mathbf{Y}^a$ and $\mathbf{Y}^v$ to optimize network $\mathcal{F}$

end for

our modality-specific label denoising procedure can be summarized as two steps: a) **Calculating Forward Loss** and b) **Removing Noisy Labels**. As a general training strategy, we adopt the model in [37] as our backbone network $\mathcal{F}$ to verify our method.

First, in the step of **Calculating Forward Loss**, losses are calculated in each modality for removing the noisy labels. Specifically, we feed the extracted local features of a batch of videos into the network, and calculate the BCE losses for each modality. Here, cross-modal attention is skipped in this step to avoid interference of cross-modal feature aggregation. Note that the losses calculated in this step are only utilized to remove noisy labels but not optimize the network. Let B represent the batch size, $\mathbf{L}^a, \mathbf{L}^v \in \mathbb{R}^{B \times C}$ denote the BCE losses in audio and visual modalities.

Second, in the step of **Removing Noisy Labels**, modality-specific noisy labels are determined according to the loss patterns based on estimated noise ratios $\mathbf{r}^a$ and $\mathbf{r}^v$. We here define a function for better introducing the procedure of removing labels:

$$\mathcal{G}(\mathcal{L}, n) = argsort(\mathcal{L})[0 : n], \tag{2}$$

where $\mathcal{L}$ denotes the losses of a batch of samples, and n is the parameter to control the number of selected indexes. $argsort(\mathcal{L})$ is a function that sorts $\mathcal{L}$ in ascending order and returns the indexes of sorted losses. We use $argsort(-\mathcal{L})$ to obtain the indexes of losses $\mathcal{L}$ sorted in descending order. The $nonzero(\cdot)$ is a function that returns the indexes of samples whose value is not 0. The procedure to determine which labels are modality-specific noise corresponds to Step 5 in Algorithm 1. Intuitively, taking audio-specific label denoising as an example, we argue that a positive label with a high loss in the audio modality and a low loss in visual modality would be an audio-specific noisy label. We have discussed the interpretability and reasonability of the way to determine noisy labels in Sect. 3.4. The identified modality-specific noisy labels are removed from $\mathbf{Y}$, to generate refined modality labels $\mathbf{Y}^a$ and $\mathbf{Y}^v$.

Lastly, in each training iteration, we feed the batch $\mathcal{B}$ to network $\mathcal{F}$ to obtain predictions. The refined labels $\mathbf{Y}^a$, $\mathbf{Y}^v$ and $\mathbf{Y}$ serve as supervised signals for audio predictions, visual predictions, and video predictions, respectively. Experimental results in Sect. 4 have validated the effectiveness of our method.

3.4 Discussion

As we have mentioned above, we first train the noise estimator $\mathcal{H}$ to estimate the modality-specific noise ratios for each category. $\mathcal{H}$ is modified from the baseline $\mathcal{F}$ [37] by removing cross-modal attention. After that, we adopt the noise ratios to guide the training process. We use the network $\mathcal{F}$ as our parsing model, but skip the cross-modal attention during **calculating forward loss**. Finally, there is still confronted with two critical questions about the motivation of our method:

1) Why do we regard the event labels with higher losses as the candidate noise set by using intra-modal loss patterns? As analyzed previously, deep neural networks are prone to learn clean labels first, but over-fit the noisy labels with more training epochs [6,22,48]. In other words, the losses of clean labels would drop faster than noisy labels. Built upon this observation, we argue that noisy labels are more likely to exist in the samples with higher losses.

2) Why do cross-modal cues make more evident improvement for determining the modality-specific noise? If we directly treat the event labels with higher losses as noise, some hard labels would not be seen by the model during training in extreme circumstances. We observe that a video-level event label typically appears in at least one modality. In this sense, if one label has a higher loss in audio modality but a lower loss in the visual modality, it means evident clues have appeared in visual rather than audio modality. Therefore, we speculate that this label may be noisy for audio modality with high confidence. It is effective to utilize the complementary knowledge to recheck label noise, which is also verified in Table 2d.

4 Experiments

This section elaborates on our experiments' details and compares our proposed JoMoLD with state-of-the-art methods. In the ablation studies, we present the effect of each module. We conduct a qualitative analysis and show the advantages of our JoMoLD over state-of-the-art methods.

4.1 Experiment Settings

Dataset. We evaluate our method for weakly-supervised AVVP task on the *Look, Listen, and Parse* (LLP) dataset. It consists of 11849 10-s videos with 25 event categories. The categories cover a wide range of domains such as human activities, animal activities, music performance, *etc.* We utilize the official data split for training and evaluation. There are 10000 videos for training and 1849 validation-test videos for evaluation.

Evaluation Metrics. We evaluate the parsing performance of all events (audio, visual, and audio-visual events) under segment-level and event-level metrics. We use both segment-level and event-level F-scores as metrics. The former metrics evaluate the segment-wise prediction performance. The latter metrics are designed to extract events with consecutive positive snippets in the same event categories, and 0.5 is used as the mIoU threshold to compute event-level F-scores. Moreover, we also assess the comprehensive performance for all events by "Type@AV" and "Event@AV" metrics. Type@AV is calculated by averaging audio, visual, and audio-visual metrics. Event@AV computes the results considering all audio and visual events instead of averaging metrics. Abbreviations of metric names are represented in all experiment tables, where "A" denotes audio events, "V" represents visual events, "AV" denotes audio-visual events, "Type" indicates Type@AV, and "Event" denotes "Event@AV".

Implementation Details. Following the data preprocessing in [37,43], we decode a 10-s video into 10 segments, and each segment contains 8 frames. We use pre-trained ResNet152 [14] and R(2+1)D [39] to capture the appearance and motion features and concatenate them as low-level visual features. For audio, we adopt pre-trained VGGish [15] to yield audio features. Adam optimizer is used to train the model, and the learning rate 5e-4 drops by a factor of 0.25 for every 6 epochs. We train the model for 25 epochs with batch size 128.

4.2 Comparison with State-of-the-Art Methods

We compare our method with different types of methods: weakly-supervised sound event detection methods TALNet [41], weakly-supervised action localization methods STPN [28] and CMCS [24], modified audio-visual event localization methods AVE [38] and AVSD [23], the state-of-the-art AVVP methods HAN [37] and MA [43]. In addition, Co-teaching+ [47] and JoCoR [42] are famous for learning with label noise methods that focus on single-modal tasks but not multi-modal tasks. On this weakly-supervised AVVP task, we reproduce the variants of these two methods [42,47] utilizing the backbone in HAN to compare with our method. The variants of these two methods are denoted as "HAN *w/*Co-teaching+" (*abbr.* HC) and "HAN *w/* JoCoR" (*abbr.* HJ).

Table 1 shows the results of JoMoLD and other state-of-the-art methods on the LLP test dataset. Our JoMoLD here adopts the optimal settings studied

Table 1. Comparisons with the state-of-the-art methods on the test set of LLP. JoMoLD achieves the best performance among them. "CL" denotes the contrastive learning proposed in MA [43]. We simply add "CL" loss into the existing loss functions when optimizing the network, but do not utilize it in label denoising. Results of our method combined with "CL" proves the flexibility and effectiveness of JoMoLD. "-" denotes this result is not available.

Methods		Segment-level					Event-Level				
		A	V	AV	Type	Event	A	V	AV	Type	Event
TALNet [41]		50.0	–	–	–	–	41.7	–	–	–	–
STPN [28]		–	46.5	–	–	–	–	41.5	–	–	–
CMCS [24]		–	48.1	–	–	–	–	45.1	–	–	–
AVE [38]		49.9	37.3	37.0	41.4	43.6	43.6	32.4	32.6	36.2	37.4
AVSDN [23]		47.8	52.0	37.1	45.7	50.8	34.1	46.3	26.5	35.6	37.7
HAN [37]		60.1	52.9	48.9	54.0	55.4	51.3	48.9	43.0	47.7	48.0
HAN *w/* Co-teaching+ (HC) [47]		59.4	56.7	52.0	56.0	56.3	50.7	53.9	46.6	50.4	48.7
HAN *w/* JoCoR (HJ) [42]		61.0	58.2	53.1	57.4	57.7	52.8	54.7	46.7	51.4	50.3
MA [43]	*w/o* CL	59.8	57.5	52.6	56.6	56.6	52.1	54.4	45.8	50.8	49.4
	w/ CL	60.3	60.0	55.1	58.9	57.9	53.6	56.4	49.0	53.0	50.6
JoMoLD (Ours)	*w/o* CL	60.6	62.2	56.0	59.6	58.6	53.1	58.9	49.4	53.8	51.4
	***w/* CL**	**61.3**	**63.8**	**57.2**	**60.8**	**59.9**	**53.9**	**59.9**	**49.6**	**54.5**	**52.5**

by Sect. 4.3. As a label denoising strategy, JoMoLD can combine with other feature learning methods to achieve higher performance, such as contrastive learning proposed in MA [43]. Notably, our method outperforms the state-of-the-art methods (*e.g.*, HC, HJ, and MA) by a non-negligible margin. For example, JoMoLD is higher than MA by 3.8 points in the segment-level visual event parsing metric. These results demonstrate the effectiveness of our strategy of joint-modal label denoising.

4.3 Ablation Studies

This section performs ablation studies on estimating noise ratios and modality-specific label denoising, respectively. Segment-level metrics are reported if not stated. The optimal settings are explored by the following ablations.

Ablation Studies on Estimating Noise Ratios: *Study the Effectiveness of Noise Estimator.* To verify the importance of the noise estimator, we compare the performance of using a series of hand-crafted noise ratios to guide the label denoising procedure. These manually set noise ratios contain no prior information. As shown in Table 2a, our noise estimator provides sound guidance in determining noisy labels.

Study Thresholds for Noise Estimation. We study the impact of thresholds, *i.e.*, θ^a and θ^v, in noise ratio estimation. A lower threshold leads to smaller noise ratios and vice versa. Since the predictions of the noise estimator are normalized by the mean value per category, θ^a (θ^v) may be more than 1. We find in Table 2b that our method is robust when θ^a and θ^v are within a reasonable range.

Table 2. Ablation studies. Tables 2a, 2b, and 2c are studies on estimating noise ratios. Tables 2d, 2e and 2f are ablations on modality-specific label denoising.

(a) **Study the effectiveness of noise ratio estimator**. The constant noise ratios are hand-crafted.

Noise Ratio	A	V	AV	Type	Event
0.1	60.9	53.9	51.4	55.4	55.4
0.2	61.3	54.4	52.0	55.9	55.9
0.3	60.8	55.2	51.6	55.9	56.1
0.4	60.2	56.6	53.0	56.6	56.2
0.5	58.4	58.3	53.2	56.6	55.9
Estimated ratios	**61.3**	**63.8**	**57.2**	**60.8**	**59.9**

(b) **Study thresholds for noise estimation.** Segment-level Type@AV results are reported.

audio θ^a \ visual θ^v	1.6	1.7	1.8	1.9	2.0
0.5	58.3	58.9	60.6	60.5	60.0
0.6	58.9	58.8	**60.8**	60.5	60.5
0.7	58.5	59.0	60.8	60.7	60.4
0.8	58.3	59.3	60.7	60.6	60.4

(c) **Study the impact of cross-modal attention on noise estimator**. "cm attn." represents cross-modal attention.

Estimator	A	V	AV	Type	Event
w/ cm attn.	60.9	55.9	52.9	56.6	56.3
***w/o* cm attn.**	**61.3**	**63.8**	**57.2**	**60.8**	**59.9**

(d) **Intra-modal label denoising *vs.* Joint-modal label denoising**. "InMoLD" indicates Intra-modal label denoising.

Methods	A	V	AV	Type	Event
InMoLD	59.6	58.5	51.8	56.6	57.8
JoMoLD	**61.3**	**63.8**	**57.2**	**60.8**	**59.9**

(e) **Single-modal label denoising *vs.* joint-modal label denoising.** "Audio only" or "Visual only" denotes that label denoising is performed only for audio or visual track.

Modality	A	V	AV	Type	Event
Audio only	61.3	53.2	50.3	54.9	56.2
Visual only	61.0	62.7	56.2	60.0	59.2
both (JoMoLD)	**61.3**	**63.8**	**57.2**	**60.8**	**59.9**

(f) **Study the warm-up of noise ratios.** The noise ratios will be increased from 0 to its real values during the period of warm-up.

Warm-up epochs	A	V	AV	Type	Event
no warm-up	60.6	63.3	56.3	60.1	59.0
0.7	61.1	63.6	56.8	60.5	59.7
0.8	60.9	63.8	56.6	60.4	59.5
0.9	**61.3**	**63.8**	**57.2**	**60.8**	**59.9**
1.0	61.3	63.7	56.8	60.6	59.7

Study the Impact of Cross-modal Attention on Noise Estimator. As shown in Table 2c, it leads to a noticeable performance drop when training the noise estimator with cross-modal attention. Since cross-attention mixes the clues between modalities, it causes improper noise estimation for each modality. Experiments also verify the rationality of removing cross-attention in the noise estimator.

Ablation Studies on Modality-Specific Label Denoising: *Intra-modal Label Denoising vs. Joint-modal Label Denoising.* Experiments in Table 2d demonstrates the superiority of JoMoLD over intra-modal label denoising (InMoLD). The latter does not consider cross-modal clues for label denoising. Specifically, for audio modality, InMoLD only considers the labels of samples with high losses in audio modality as audio noise, and does not check whether the losses in the visual modality of these samples are low. The procedure is the same for visual modality label denoising. JoMoLD makes good use of the intuition that a label would not serve as noise for both modalities, so a confident noisy label should enjoy the different loss patterns between two modalities.

Single-modal Label Denoising vs. Joint-modal Label Denoising. Single-modal label denoising adopts the same method as joint-modal label denoising, but

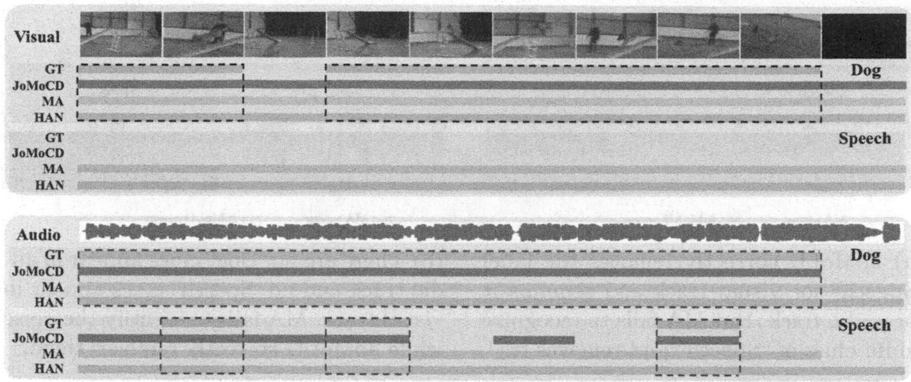

Fig. 3. Qualitative comparisons with the state-of-the-art mothods. We detail the parsing visualization results of "Dog" and "Speech" categories for visual and audio modalities. "GT" denotes the ground truth annotations. We compare JoMoLD, MA [43] and HAN [37] with GT. Generally, JoMoLD achieves better parsing results.

conducts label denoising only for a single modality. Table 2e shows that denoising labels for the visual track brings more improvement than the audio track. This might be because LLP is an audio-dominant dataset with more visual noise. Moreover, removing noisy labels for both modalities brings further improvement.

Study Warm-up Strategy. At the beginning of the training, the model treats clean and noisy labels alike, so we cannot distinguish them from the losses. In order to avoid selection bias in the early training, we adopt a warm-up strategy. It gradually increases the noise ratios from zero to the pre-computed values during warm-up epochs. The results are shown in Table 2f. Because warm-up strategy is not a critical step in JoMoLD, we omit it in Algorithm 1 for clarity.

4.4 Qualitative Analysis

Video Parsing Visualization. Figure 3 visualizes the parsing results of JoMoLD, MA [43] and HAN [37] as well as the ground truth annotation "GT". This video contains audio events "Dog" and "Speech", and visual event "Dog". Our method achieves the best performance in event recognition and localization among three methods. In detail, MA and HAN wrongly predict the "Speech" event in the visual track while JoMoLD correctly predicts no "Speech" event in the visual track. This can be credited to our more accurate label denoising procedure during training. For the audio track, JoMoLD makes more precise detection results than the other two for the event "Dog" and "Speech". Nevertheless, our method still makes mistakes for some segments. Due to the lack of segment-level supervised signals, there is still room for our method to improve performance.

Label Denoising Visualization. We visualize two cases of label denoising results of JoMoLD and MA [43] in Fig. 4. The first case displays a motorcy-

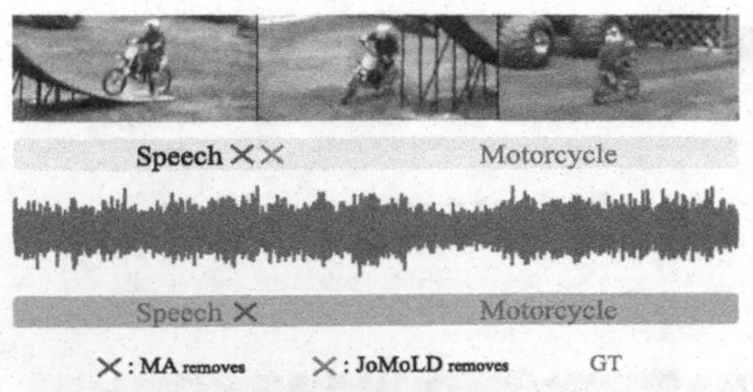

(a) JoMoLD correctly removes the label "Speech" for visual track and remains it for audio track. But MA fails to recognize audio clues of "Speech" and removes it.

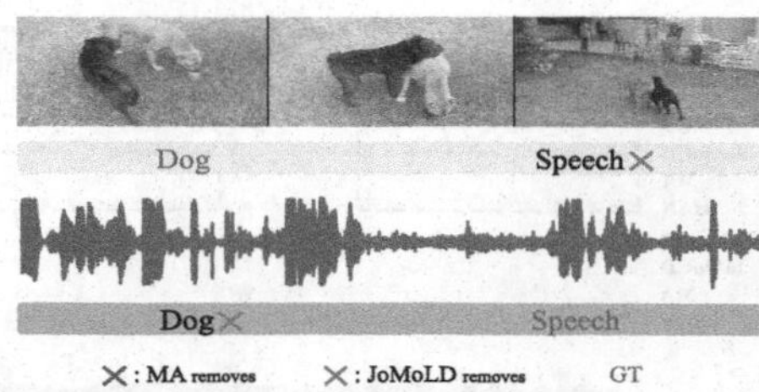

(b) There are no "Dog" clues appear in audio track and no "Speech" clues appear in visual track. MA fails to identify the noise while JoMoLD correctly removes them.

Fig. 4. Comparisons of label denoising results between JoMoLD and MA.

cle race. The event "Motorcycle" can be perceived from both modalities, but "Speech" is from the off-screen audience. In the second case, the event "Dog" only appears in the visual track and "Speech" in the audio track. MA makes mistakes in both two cases. When identifying noisy labels, MA exchanges the audio tracks of one video with another video whose label sets do not intersect. So the modality predictions of the newly assembled video are lowered when cross-attended to the unrelated modality. While our method does not confuse the video content, and successfully removes noisy labels while retaining correct labels.

More visualizations are presented in the supplementary material.

5 Conclusions

In our work, we focus on weakly-supervised audio-visual video parsing task. We are committed to solving the modality-specific label noise issue, which degenerates parsing performance according to our analysis. We notice that the clean and noisy labels present different loss patterns, and an annotated event label would not be noise for both modalities. Thus we take the different loss levels of the two modalities as the noise and remove the noisy labels. Extensive experiments show that our Joint-Modal Label Denoising method selects modality-specific noise more accurately and improves performance over the state of the arts. As for the limitations, more large-scale datasets of the weakly-supervised AVVP task are expected to further validate our method in future work.

Acknowledgements. This work is supported by National Natural Science Foundation of China (No.62076119, No.61921006), Program for Innovative Talents and Entrepreneur in Jiangsu Province, and Collaborative Innovation Center of Novel Software Technology and Industrialization.

References

1. Alwassel, H., Mahajan, D., Korbar, B., Torresani, L., Ghanem, B., Tran, D.: Self-supervised learning by cross-modal audio-video clustering. In: 34th Conference on Neural Information Processing Systems (NeurIPS 2020). NeurIPS (2020)
2. Amrani, E., Ben-Ari, R., Rotman, D., Bronstein, A.: Noise estimation using density estimation for self-supervised multimodal learning. In: Proceedings of the AAAI Conference on Artificial Intelligence. vol. 35, pp. 6644–6652 (2021)
3. Arandjelovic, R., Zisserman, A.: Look, listen and learn. In: Proceedings of the IEEE International Conference on Computer Vision, pp. 609–617 (2017)
4. Arandjelovic, R., Zisserman, A.: Objects that sound. In: Proceedings of the European conference on computer vision (ECCV), pp. 435–451 (2018)
5. Arazo, E., Ortego, D., Albert, P., O'Connor, N., McGuinness, K.: Unsupervised label noise modeling and loss correction. In: International Conference on Machine Learning, pp. 312–321. PMLR (2019)
6. Arpit, D., et al.: A closer look at memorization in deep networks. In: International Conference on Machine Learning, pp. 233–242. PMLR (2017)
7. Aytar, Y., Vondrick, C., Torralba, A.: Soundnet: learning sound representations from unlabeled video. Adv. Neural Inf. Process. Syst. **29**, 892–900 (2016)
8. Blum, A., Mitchell, T.: Combining labeled and unlabeled data with co-training. In: Proceedings of the eleventh annual conference on Computational learning theory, pp. 92–100 (1998)
9. Ephrat, A., et al.: Looking to listen at the cocktail party: a speaker-independent audio-visual model for speech separation. ACM Trans. Grap. (TOG) **37**(4), 1–11 (2018)
10. Gao, R., Grauman, K.: Visualvoice: Audio-visual speech separation with cross-modal consistency. In: Proceedings of the IEEE/CVF Conference on Computer Vision and Pattern Recognition, pp. 15495–15505 (2021)
11. Gao, R., Oh, T.H., Grauman, K., Torresani, L.: Listen to look: Action recognition by previewing audio. In: Proceedings of the IEEE/CVF Conference on Computer Vision and Pattern Recognition, pp. 10457–10467 (2020)
12. Gupta, S., Hoffman, J., Malik, J.: Cross modal distillation for supervision transfer. In: Proceedings of the IEEE Conference on Computer Vision and Pattern Recognition, pp. 2827–2836 (2016)
13. Han, B., et.al.: Co-teaching: robust training of deep neural networks with extremely noisy labels. In: Proceedings of the 32nd International Conference on Neural Information Processing Systems, pp. 8536–8546 (2018)
14. He, K., Zhang, X., Ren, S., Sun, J.: Deep residual learning for image recognition. In: Proceedings of the IEEE Conference on Computer Vision and Pattern Recognition, pp. 770–778 (2016)
15. Hershey, S., et al.: Cnn architectures for large-scale audio classification. In: 2017 IEEE International Conference on Acoustics, Speech and Signal Processing (icassp), pp. 131–135. IEEE (2017)
16. Hori, C., et.al.: Attention-based multimodal fusion for video description. In: Proceedings of the IEEE international conference on computer vision, pp. 4193–4202 (2017)
17. Hu, D., Nie, F., Li, X.: Deep multimodal clustering for unsupervised audiovisual learning. In: Proceedings of the IEEE/CVF Conference on Computer Vision and Pattern Recognition, pp. 9248–9257 (2019)

18. Hu, P., Peng, X., Zhu, H., Zhen, L., Lin, J.: Learning cross-modal retrieval with noisy labels. In: Proceedings of the IEEE/CVF Conference on Computer Vision and Pattern Recognition, pp. 5403–5413 (2021)
19. Kim, Y., Yun, J., Shon, H., Kim, J.: Joint negative and positive learning for noisy labels. In: Proceedings of the IEEE/CVF Conference on Computer Vision and Pattern Recognition, pp. 9442–9451 (2021)
20. Korbar, B., Tran, D., Torresani, L.: Cooperative learning of audio and video models from self-supervised synchronization. In: Proceedings of the 32nd International Conference on Neural Information Processing Systems, pp. 7774–7785 (2018)
21. Li, J., Socher, R., Hoi, S.C.H.: Dividemix: Learning with noisy labels as semi-supervised learning. ArXiv abs/2002.07394 (2020)
22. Li, M., Soltanolkotabi, M., Oymak, S.: Gradient descent with early stopping is provably robust to label noise for overparameterized neural networks. In: The 23rd International Conference on Artificial Intelligence and Statistics (2020)
23. Lin, Y.B., Li, Y.J., Wang, Y.C.F.: Dual-modality seq2seq network for audio-visual event localization. In: ICASSP 2019–2019 IEEE International Conference on Acoustics, Speech and Signal Processing (ICASSP), pp. 2002–2006. IEEE (2019)
24. Liu, D., Jiang, T., Wang, Y.: Completeness modeling and context separation for weakly supervised temporal action localization. In: Proceedings of the IEEE/CVF Conference on Computer Vision and Pattern Recognition, pp. 1298–1307 (2019)
25. Liu, S., Niles-Weed, J., Razavian, N., Fernandez-Granda, C.: Early-learning regularization prevents memorization of noisy labels. Adv. Neural Inf. Process. Sys. 33 (2020)
26. Malach, E., Shalev-Shwartz, S.: Decoupling" when to update" from" how to update". In: Proceedings of the 31st International Conference on Neural Information Processing Systems, pp. 961–971 (2017)
27. Mandal, D., Bharadwaj, S., Biswas, S.: A novel self-supervised re-labeling approach for training with noisy labels. In: Proceedings of the IEEE/CVF Winter Conference on Applications of Computer Vision, pp. 1381–1390 (2020)
28. Nguyen, P., Liu, T., Prasad, G., Han, B.: Weakly supervised action localization by sparse temporal pooling network. In: Proceedings of the IEEE Conference on Computer Vision and Pattern Recognition, pp. 6752–6761 (2018)
29. Nguyen, T., Mummadi, C., Ngo, T., Beggel, L., Brox, T.: Self: learning to filter noisy labels with self-ensembling. In: International Conference on Learning Representations (ICLR) (2020)
30. Panda, R., et al.: Adamml: Adaptive multi-modal learning for efficient video recognition. arXiv preprint arXiv:2105.05165 (2021)
31. Pedro Morgado, Nuno Vasconcelos, I.M.: Audio-visual instance discrimination with cross-modal agreement. In: Computer Vision and Pattern Recognition (CVPR), IEEE/CVF Conf. on (2021)
32. Rahman, T., Xu, B., Sigal, L.: Watch, listen and tell: Multi-modal weakly supervised dense event captioning. In: Proceedings of the IEEE/CVF International Conference on Computer Vision, pp. 8908–8917 (2019)
33. Senocak, A., Oh, T.H., Kim, J., Yang, M.H., Kweon, I.S.: Learning to localize sound source in visual scenes. In: Proceedings of the IEEE Conference on Computer Vision and Pattern Recognition, pp. 4358–4366 (2018)
34. Song, H., Kim, M., Lee, J.G.: Selfie: Refurbishing unclean samples for robust deep learning. In: International Conference on Machine Learning, pp. 5907–5915. PMLR (2019)

35. Tanaka, D., Ikami, D., Yamasaki, T., Aizawa, K.: Joint optimization framework for learning with noisy labels. In: Proceedings of the IEEE Conference on Computer Vision and Pattern Recognition, pp. 5552–5560 (2018)
36. Tian, Y., Guan, C., Goodman, J., Moore, M., Xu, C.: An attempt towards interpretable audio-visual video captioning. arXiv preprint arXiv:1812.02872 (2018)
37. Tian, Y., Li, D., Xu, C.: Unified multisensory perception: weakly-supervised audio-visual video parsing. In: Vedaldi, A., Bischof, H., Brox, T., Frahm, J.-M. (eds.) ECCV 2020. LNCS, vol. 12348, pp. 436–454. Springer, Cham (2020). https://doi.org/10.1007/978-3-030-58580-8_26
38. Tian, Y., Shi, J., Li, B., Duan, Z., Xu, C.: Audio-visual event localization in unconstrained videos. In: Proceedings of the European Conference on Computer Vision (ECCV), pp. 247–263 (2018)
39. Tran, D., Wang, H., Torresani, L., Ray, J., LeCun, Y., Paluri, M.: A closer look at spatiotemporal convolutions for action recognition. In: Proceedings of the IEEE conference on Computer Vision and Pattern Recognition, pp. 6450–6459 (2018)
40. Wang, Y., Ma, X., Chen, Z., Luo, Y., Yi, J., Bailey, J.: Symmetric cross entropy for robust learning with noisy labels. In: Proceedings of the IEEE/CVF International Conference on Computer Vision, pp. 322–330 (2019)
41. Wang, Y., Li, J., Metze, F.: A comparison of five multiple instance learning pooling functions for sound event detection with weak labeling. In: ICASSP 2019–2019 IEEE International Conference on Acoustics, Speech and Signal Processing (ICASSP), pp. 31–35. IEEE (2019)
42. Wei, H., Feng, L., Chen, X., An, B.: Combating noisy labels by agreement: A joint training method with co-regularization. In: Proceedings of the IEEE/CVF Conference on Computer Vision and Pattern Recognition, pp. 13726–13735 (2020)
43. Wu, Y., Yang, Y.: Exploring heterogeneous clues for weakly-supervised audio-visual video parsing. In: Proceedings of the IEEE/CVF Conference on Computer Vision and Pattern Recognition, pp. 1326–1335 (2021)
44. Wu, Y., Zhu, L., Yan, Y., Yang, Y.: Dual attention matching for audio-visual event localization. In: Proceedings of the IEEE/CVF international conference on computer vision, pp. 6292–6300 (2019)
45. Xiao, F., Lee, Y.J., Grauman, K., Malik, J., Feichtenhofer, C.: Audiovisual slowfast networks for video recognition. arXiv preprint arXiv:2001.08740 (2020)
46. Yi, K., Wu, J.: Probabilistic end-to-end noise correction for learning with noisy labels. In: Proceedings of the IEEE/CVF Conference on Computer Vision and Pattern Recognition, pp. 7017–7025 (2019)
47. Yu, X., Han, B., Yao, J., Niu, G., Tsang, I., Sugiyama, M.: How does disagreement help generalization against label corruption? In: International Conference on Machine Learning, pp. 7164–7173. PMLR (2019)
48. Zhang, C., Bengio, S., Hardt, M., Recht, B., Vinyals, O.: Understanding deep learning requires rethinking generalization (2016). arXiv preprint arXiv:1611.03530 (2017)
49. Zhang, Z., Sabuncu, M.R.: Generalized cross entropy loss for training deep neural networks with noisy labels. In: 32nd Conference on Neural Information Processing Systems (NeurIPS) (2018)
50. Zhao, H., Gan, C., Rouditchenko, A., Vondrick, C., McDermott, J., Torralba, A.: The sound of pixels. In: Proceedings of the European Conference on Computer Vision (ECCV), pp. 570–586 (2018)

51. Zhou, H., Xu, X., Lin, D., Wang, X., Liu, Z.: Sep-stereo: visually guided stereophonic audio generation by associating source separation. In: Vedaldi, A., Bischof, H., Brox, T., Frahm, J.-M. (eds.) ECCV 2020. LNCS, vol. 12357, pp. 52–69. Springer, Cham (2020). https://doi.org/10.1007/978-3-030-58610-2_4
52. Zhou, J., Zheng, L., Zhong, Y., Hao, S., Wang, M.: Positive sample propagation along the audio-visual event line. In: Proceedings of the IEEE/CVF Conference on Computer Vision and Pattern Recognition, pp. 8436–8444 (2021)

Less Than Few: Self-shot Video Instance Segmentation

Pengwan Yang[1,2](✉), Yuki M. Asano[1,2], Pascal Mettes[2], and Cees G. M. Snoek[1,2]

[1] QUVA Lab, University of Amsterdam, Amsterdam, The Netherlands
[2] Institute of Informatics, University of Amsterdam, Amsterdam, The Netherlands
yangpengwan2016@gmail.com

Abstract. The goal of this paper is to bypass the need for labelled examples in few-shot video understanding at run time. While proven effective, in many practical video settings even labelling a few examples appears unrealistic. This is especially true as the level of details in spatio-temporal video understanding and with it, the complexity of annotations continues to increase. Rather than performing few-shot learning with a human oracle to provide a few densely labelled support videos, we propose to automatically learn to find appropriate support videos given a query. We call this self-shot learning and we outline a simple self-supervised learning method to generate an embedding space well-suited for unsupervised retrieval of relevant samples. To showcase this novel setting, we tackle, for the first time, video instance segmentation in a self-shot (and few-shot) setting, where the goal is to segment instances at the pixel-level across the spatial and temporal domains. We provide strong baseline performances that utilize a novel transformer-based model and show that self-shot learning can even surpass few-shot and can be positively combined for further performance gains. Experiments on new benchmarks show that our approach achieves strong performance, is competitive to oracle support in some settings, scales to large unlabelled video collections, and can be combined in a semi-supervised setting. Code: https://github.com/PengWan-Yang/self-shot

1 Introduction

The goal of this paper is to decrease the reliance on humans to provide labelled examples in few-shot video understanding. While impressive few-shot video classification [11,38,56], localization [26,69,71] and detection [25,70] results have been reported, in many practical video settings even labelling a few examples may appear unrealistic. This is especially true as the level of spatio-temporal video understanding and with it, the complexity of annotations continues to increase. Consider for example the problem of video instance segmentation

Supplementary Information The online version contains supplementary material available at https://doi.org/10.1007/978-3-031-19830-4_26.

S. Avidan et al. (Eds.): ECCV 2022, LNCS 13694, pp. 449–466, 2022.
https://doi.org/10.1007/978-3-031-19830-4_26

[9,64,68], where datasets for example contain around 1.6 K annotated frames for just a single object class. We deem it unlikely that an interacting user, that is looking to segment a "query" video with unknown instances, is willing to provide pixel-precise annotations masks for all objects in a frame for each video in the support set, despite this being a setting which is typical for more classical, image-based few-shot learning scenarios. Thus, rather than relying on a human oracle to provide a few densely labeled support videos, we propose to automatically learn to find appropriate support videos given a query.

For this, we introduce the notion of *self-shot* learning, in which the need for labelled video clips at test-time is abolished. Instead, one is provided with a large unlabelled pool of videos from which samples potentially relevant to the query video can be retrieved and utilized in a strictly unsupervised fashion. We address this by adapting a simple self-supervised learning method [60] to generate an embedding space well-suited for unsupervised retrieval of relevant samples. To showcase this novel setting, we go beyond just bounding box detection and temporal localization and instead tackle, for the first time, *video instance segmentation* in a self-shot (and few-shot) setting, where the goal is to segment instances at the pixel-level across the spatial and temporal domains.

Overall, we make three contributions in this paper:

1. We propose the setting of self-shot learning. While annotations are used during training (similar to few-shot), at test-time, new classes are evaluated *without* any annotations, but with access to an unlabelled dataset.
2. We investigate this new setting for a particularly annotation-heavy scenario, that of video instance segmentation, for which we propose new splits to establish a self-shot (and few-shot) benchmark.
3. Finally, we provide strong baseline performances that utilize a novel transformer-based model and show that self-shot learning can even surpass few-shot and can be positively combined for further performance gains.

2 Related Work

Video few-shot learning. There is limited related work on the few-shot learning setup for videos. Initial works have explored few-shot learning for the task of video classification [38,73]. For example, OSS-Metric Learning [38] measures similarity of pairs of video to enable few-shot video classification. Yang *et al.* [67] introduce few-shot action localization in time, where a few positive labelled and several negative labelled support videos steer the localization via an end-to-end meta-learning strategy. Xu *et al.* [66] and Zhang *et al.* [71] also perform few-shot temporal action localization with the assistance of video-level class annotations. To further free the need for labels, a new research line is emerging, called few-shot common action localization, where the common action in a long untrimmed query video is localized in time [26,69] or both in time and in space [25,70] based on a few support videos containing the same action. Wang *et al.* [62] segment objects that simultaneously exist in multiple individual videos. However, all of the input videos need to contain exactly the same object instances, which is not necessary in our self-shot setting where relevant support videos can be self-retrieved. Closest to our work is few-shot spatio-temporal action localization by Yang *et al.* [70], who adopt a transformer-based action detection architecture and extend to localizing actions at pixel level. They propose a mask head upon the action detection boxes to perform the binary classification for the pixels inside each detected box. In this paper, we propose the new task of self-shot video instance segmentation that operates on objects instead of actions, predicts the segmentation directly, removes the need for having predefined (labelled) support videos, and encapsulates the few-shot setting as a special case.

Video zero-shot learning. Various video tasks have been investigated from a zero-shot perspective. Zhang *et al.* [72] can localize the unseen activities in time in a long untrimmed video based on the label embeddings. Spatio-temporal action localization is also explored in zero-shot setting by linking actions to relevant objects [34,45,46], or by leveraging trimmed videos used for action classification [35]. Wang *et al.* [63] achieve zero-shot video object segmentation by proposing a novel attentive graph neural network which can iteratively fuse information over video graphs. Lu *et al.* [44] can distinguish foreground/background in a zero-shot manner, but it relies on supervised prior knowledge, *e.g.*class activation maps obtained from a pre-trained image classifier. Dave *et al.* [22] can segment the moving objects in videos, even ones unseen in training. Just like the zero-shot setting, we also aim to segment unseen object instances in videos, without any labelled support videos. But we try to leverage self-retrieved (free) support videos to boost the performance.

Self-supervised learning. Self-supervision has been proposed as a method to obtain feature representations without labels. This has been accomplished by geometric pretext tasks [28,50,52], clustering [5,13,14,27] or more recently contrastive [17,19,36,49,65] and teacher-student approaches [15,29]. These have also been extended to the video domain [2,4,8,24,30,37,39,53,54,58]. In this work we use self-supervised learning to construct an embedding space well-suited for retrieving semantically relevant videos to support video instance segmentation. Note that this use of support samples is fundamentally different to how it has been used in other self-supervised works such as [23] or [55], where they are only used as random subsets to aid contrastive learning. Instead, support samples are the goal of our self-shot method. To this end, we compare the use of noise contrastive methods [65] and the differentiable ranking loss [60] extended to the video domain.

Video instance segmentation (VIS). VIS [9,68] requires classifying, segmenting, and tracking instances over all frames in a given video. With the introduction of the YouTube-VIS dataset, which contains dense pixel-level annotations across consecutive frames [68], considerable progress has been made in tackling this challenging task. State-of-the-art methods typically develop sophisticated pipelines and rely on heavy supervision and complex heuristic rules to associate the instances across frames. As two representative methods, MaskTrack R-

CNN [68] extends the Mask R-CNN model [32] with a pair-wise identity branch to solve the instance association problem in VIS, while MaskProp [9] introduces a multi-stage framework [16] for propagating instance masks in time. In contrast, VisTR [64] builds a DETR-based pipeline [12] for the VIS task in a query-based end-to-end fashion, which can supervise and segment the instances across frames as sequences. In this paper we adopt the spirit of VisTR to treat instance segmentation in a query video as a sequence prediction problem. Different from the usual VIS task, our self-support video instance segmentation task focuses on recognizing, segmenting, and tracking the instances in a query video containing novel classes – from just a few retrieved support videos and without knowing any annotations.

3 Problem Definition and Benchmarking

3.1 Task Definition

Our goal is video instance segmentation in a query video without having access to any labelled training examples with the same instances as in the query. Instead, we consider a self-shot scenario where we have an unlabelled pool of videos that we can use to help guide the instance segmentation. To that end, we denote a set of seen classes as $\mathcal{S}$ and a disjoint set of unseen classes as $\mathcal{U}$, where $\mathcal{S} \cap \mathcal{U} = \emptyset$. Let $\mathcal{D}_\mathcal{S} = \{(x, y) | x \in \mathcal{X}, y \in \mathcal{Y}^\mathcal{S}\}$ represent the set of labelled training data on seen classes, where x is the pixel-wise feature embeddings from the visual space $\mathcal{X}$, y is the corresponding pixel-wise label in the label space $\mathcal{Y}^\mathcal{S}$ of seen classes. $\mathcal{D}_\mathcal{U}$ denotes the set of unlabelled videos on unseen classes. Our self-shot learning shares with few-shot and zero-shot learning the same goal to learn a model from $\mathcal{D}_\mathcal{S}$ and predict the label of each pixel for videos in $\mathcal{D}_\mathcal{U}$. However, they differ in their objective and expected data availability:

Few-shot learning. For each unseen class $c \in \mathcal{U}$, a handful of predefined support videos $\mathcal{V}_c^k$ are provided, where k is small. Then for each query video $Q_c \in \mathcal{D}_\mathcal{U}$, the small set of support videos containing exactly the same class $\mathcal{V}_c^k$ function as guidance videos to predict a segmentation for the unseen object class c.

Zero-shot learning. In the most conventional zero-shot strategy [34,40,46,72], all class labels $\mathcal{C}{=}\mathcal{S} \cup \mathcal{U}$ are provided and mapped through semantic embeddings to vector representations $\{v_c | c \in \mathcal{C}\}$. Then a joint visual-text perspective helps the model learned on the seen classes generalize to the unseen classes.

Self-shot learning. Instead of predefined supports or semantic class labels, self-shot learning relies on an unsupervised manner to retrieve support videos $\{\mathcal{V}_{Q_c} | \mathcal{V}_{Q_c} \in \mathbb{S}\}$ for each query video $Q_c, c \in \mathcal{U}$ from a collection of unlabelled videos $\mathbb{S}$. It leverages the discovered support videos as guidance for predicting an instance segmentation. Self-shot learning can be viewed as a framework to obtain noisy few-shot examples without the need for human annotations.

3.2 Datasets

Since self-shot video instance segmentation is a new task, we set up two benchmarks through the reorganization of two existing (many-shot) video instance segmentation datasets, namely YouTube-VIS [68] (2021 version) and OVIS [57].

Self-VIS. YouTube-VIS contains 2,985 videos in the training set where the instance mask annotations are publicly available. The annotated instances cover 40 instance categories and a minority of the videos have instances of more than one classes. To build a setting with videos containing one singe instance class, we discard videos with multiple instance classes and obtain a total of 2,123 videos. We randomly select 30 classes for training and 10 classes for validation and testing.

Self-OVIS. Occluded VIS (OVIS) provides 607 videos with annotated instance masks. Among the 25 instance categories in OVIS, 17 are for training and 8 for validation and testing. With more instances of multiple classes per video, and more frequent occlusions, the setting of OVIS is much harder than the one of YouTue-VIS. More details are provided in Table A in the Appendix. During training, the query video and support videos are randomly paired according to the common instances present, while the pairs are fixed for validation and testing for reproducibility.

YouTube-8M Segments. The YouTube-8M Segments dataset is a subset of the YouTube-8M dataset proposed in the same paper [1]. It contains about 237 K 5-second videos extracted from around 50 K source videos and while it contains annotations, we do not use any of the labels. Instead, we adopt YouTube-8M Segments as our unlabelled video database $\mathbb{S}$ for self-shot retrieval and call the self-shot benchmarks

4 Finding Support Videos Through Self-shot Learning

The purpose of self-shot learning is to retrieve videos from a large, unlabelled video dataset that will aid in performing inference on the query video, specifically for the task of instance segmentation in this paper. To this end, we train an encoder that will yield an embedding space well suited for video retrieval by adopting components of self-supervised representation learning methods MoCo v1 to v3 [18,20,31], multiple-instance NCE [47] and self-supervised ranking [60].

For self-shot learning, we are given an unlabelled video collection $\mathbb{S}$. Each clip is encoded by two visual encoders, Φ and $\tilde{\Phi}$, where $\tilde{\Phi}$ is updated as the exponential moving-average of Φ as in [20,31]. With this setup we evaluate self-shot retrieval with two different losses: noise-contrastive instance discrimination and ranking.

The contrastive loss $\mathcal{L}_{\text{NCE}}$ in our case is given by setting positive pairs to be different temporal crops of a single video, while negative pairs are constructed from other instances of the dataset. Let $V_i \in \mathbb{S}$ denote a single unlabelled video and let $v \in V_i$ denote one of its temporal crops. Then we naturally arrive at the following multiple-instance NCE [47] formulation:

$$\mathcal{L}_{\text{NCE}}(v) = -\log \frac{\sum_{v^+} \exp\langle \Phi(v) \cdot \tilde{\Phi}(v^+)\rangle_\tau}{\sum_{(v^+ \cup v^-)} \exp\langle \Phi(v) \cdot \tilde{\Phi}(v^+)\rangle_\tau)}, \tag{1}$$

where $\langle \cdot, \cdot \rangle_\tau$, is a temperature-scaled dot-product, and v^+ is the positive set defined as $V_i \setminus v$ and v^- is the negative set, corresponding to crops from other videos in $\mathbb{S}$.

We further experiment with transplanting a differentiable ranking loss from [60], to the setting of using two encoders. The ranking loss is a less aggressive form of enforcing self-invariance than the NCE loss, and is given by learning an embedding space in which a set of positive videos is ranked *above* a set of negative videos, when comparing distances in feature space. More precisely,

$$\mathcal{L}_{\text{Rank}}(v) = -\log \sum_{v^+} \frac{R_{\Phi(v)}(\tilde{\Phi}(v), \tilde{\Phi}(v^+))}{R_{\Phi(v)}(\tilde{\Phi}(v), \tilde{\Phi}(v^+) \cup \tilde{\Phi}(v^-))}, \tag{2}$$

where $R_a(b, c)$ is a differentiable function to rank video b among all videos in the set $\{c\}$ with respect to the query video a [10,60].

Once the feature spaces are learned, the final step is **retrieving relevant support videos using only the query itself**. For query video q, we use the self-supervised trained encoder Φ and a simple k-nearest neighbor (kNN) approach. The self-shot support videos for query q is obtained as:

$$\text{self-shot}(q) = k\text{NN}(\Phi(q), \Phi(\mathbb{S})). \tag{3}$$

Note that this simple kNN approach allows us to use self-shot learning as a *plug-and-play* component, which can be used to replace supervised support videos or to extend these in a semi-supervised manner. This setup is generally applicable, we focus on video instance segmentation as testbed in this paper, due to the hefty annotation demand for supervised settings.

Implementation Details. We follow the uniform frame sampling method in [3] for mapping a video to a sequence of tokens of a Vision Transformer of size B (ViT-B). In each mini-batch, we use 160 $5 \times 224 \times 224$ video segments from 32 videos. The patch-size of ViT-B is 16×16. We keep the memory queue [31] and the length is 1280. We train for 40 epochs with the AdamW optimizer [43], with an initial learning rating of 10^{-4}, which we decay by 10 at epoch 25. Further details are provided in the Appendix.

5 A Self-shot and Few-Shot VIS Transformer

Equipped with self-shot learning, we examine a research problem with a high annotation cost: video instance segmentation. Hence our goal is to segment and track the object instances of interest in a query video. We do however not assume access to training videos labelled with the same instance classes, temporal boundaries, or mask annotations as support for the query video at test-time. In essence, the query video is on its own and we are instead given a collection of unlabelled videos. We seek to find a few unlabelled support videos from this collection through self-shot learning. While we aim for self-shot learning, few-shot video instance segmentation using a few support videos has not yet been investigated either. Hence, we first introduce a baseline sequence-to-sequence transformer approach to solve video instance segmentation given semantically similar (support) videos. At the core of our approach is a common instance segmentation transformer, which contains three stages with three functions: (*i*) encoding and extracting of features for query and support videos, (*ii*) learning of pixel-level similarities for the query features by leveraging cross-attention, and (*iii*) prediction of instance mask sequences across space and time through decoding. Each step is detailed below.

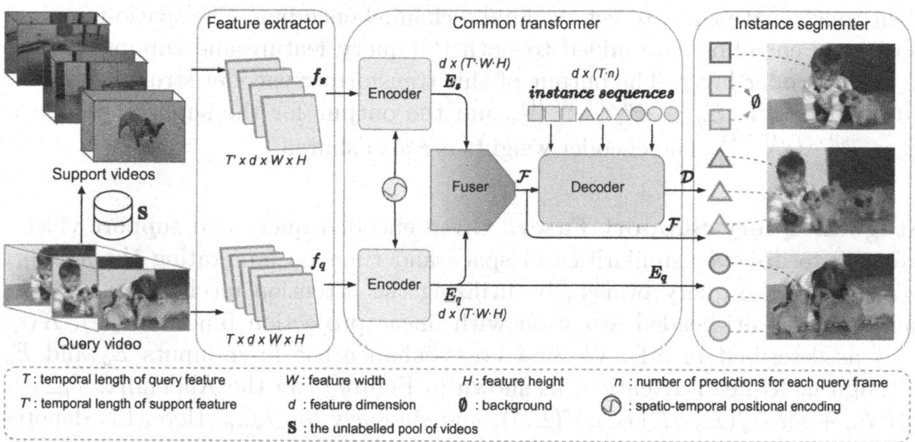

Fig. 1. Overview of the self-shot and few-shot VIS transformer. In the feature extraction stage, given a query video and a handful of (self-shot) support videos, the backbone extracts features of individual image frames, then the image features are concatenated in the frame order to form clip-level features for the query and support videos. In the common transformer, the encoder models the pixel-level similarity for the query and support features respectively, the fuser leverages the similarity between the query feature and the support feature, and the decoder learns the similarity between instances along the time dimension. In the prediction stage, the instance sequences are inferred in the query video

Feature Extraction. We adopt a modified ResNet-50 [33] with a bigger receptive field for feature extraction, with the complete architecture given in the Appendix. We let a single query video and a few support videos go through the backbone to extract the pixel-level image frame feature sequences. Assume that the query video contains T frames and the support videos contain T' frames in total. The backbone generates a lower-resolution activation map for each frame in the query video and support videos, then the frame features are concatenated to form video clip level features for the query and support videos. The query video feature is denoted as $f_q \in \mathbb{R}^{T \times d \times W \times H}$ and the support feature is $f_s \in \mathbb{R}^{T' \times d \times W \times H}$. The weights of the backbone are shared between the query and support videos.

Stage 1: Spatio-Temporal Transformer Encoder. We first feed the extracted video features into the transformer encoder structure and flatten the spatial and temporal dimensions of f_q and f_s in 2D feature maps of size $d\times(T{\cdot}W{\cdot}H)$ and $d\times(T'{\cdot}W{\cdot}H)$. Since the image-encoder based backbone is permutation-invariant, we append spatio-temporal positional encodings [7,51] to the inputs as the instance segmentation task requires precise spatial and temporal information. Specially, for all spatio-temporal coordinates of each dimension, we independently use $d/3$ sine and cosine functions with different frequencies. We then concatenate them to get the final d channel encoding. The spatio-temporal positional encodings are added to both the query feature and support feature in each encoder layer. The output of this transformer encoder structure for the query branch is $E_q \in \mathbb{R}^{d\times(T\cdot W\cdot H)}$, and the output for the support branch is $E_s \in \mathbb{R}^{d\times(T'\cdot W\cdot H)}$. The encoder weights are also shared.

Stage 2: Query-Support Fuser. Given encoded query and support videos, we seek to discover similarities in space and time by integrating the support branch into the query branch, by utilizing the attention mechanism. Let $\mathbb{MA}$ denote the multi-headed attention with linear projection function $Q(\cdot)$, $K(\cdot)$, $V(\cdot)$ as described in [61]. We first cross-enhance the fuser inputs E_q and E_s through multi-head attention, as shown in Figure A in the Appendix: $f_{q\leftarrow s} = \mathrm{LN}(E_q + \mathbb{MA}(Q(E_q), K(E_s), V(E_s)))$, and similarly for $f_{s\leftarrow q}$. Here, LN denotes the layer normalization operation [6]. Next, the support branch is fused into the query branch to get the fused feature $\widetilde{F}$:

$$\widetilde{F} = \mathrm{LN}(f_{q\leftarrow s} + \mathbb{MA}(Q(f_{q\leftarrow s}), K(f_{s\leftarrow q}), V(f_{s\leftarrow q}))). \tag{4}$$

In addition, a feed-forward network (2-layer MLP) is applied to $\widetilde{F}$ in a residual fashion for increased modelling ability, yielding output of the fuser: $\mathcal{F} = \mathrm{LN}(\widetilde{F} + \mathrm{FFN}(\widetilde{F}))$.

Stage 3: Decoding and Predicting. The spatio-temporal decoder aims to decode the most discriminative pixel features that can represent the instances of each frame. We introduce a fixed number of input embeddings to represent the instance features across time and space, which we call *instance sequences.* Assuming that the model decodes n instances per frame, the number of instances for the T frames in the query video is $N{=}n{\cdot}T$. The *instance sequences* are learned by the spatio-temporal decoder and take the output of the query-support fuser $\mathcal{F}$ and *instance sequences* as input, to outputs N instance features, denoted as $\mathcal{D}$, as shown in Fig. 1. Finally, the instance segmenter predicts the mask sequence for each instance. For each frame in the query video, we feed the instance features $\mathcal{D}$ and the fused feature $\mathcal{F}$ into an attention module to obtain the attention maps. The attention maps are then concatenated with the encoded query feature E_q and the fused feature $\mathcal{F}$, followed by a deformable convolution layer [21]. In this way, we obtain the mask features for each instance of the different frames in the query video. We denote the mask feature for instance i of frame t is $g_{i,t} \in \mathbb{R}^{1\times a\times W_0\times H_0}$, where a is the channel number, W_0 and H_0 are the feature width and height. Finally, the instance segmenter uses the accumulated features to output the mask sequence for each instance (see Appendix for details). and outputs the mask sequence $m_i \in \mathbb{R}^{1\times 1\times T\times W_0\times H_0}$ for the instance i directly.

Training loss. To score predicted instances with respect to the ground truth, we introduce an optimal bipartite matching between predicted and ground truth instances, in the spirit of [12,64] (see Appendix for details). Given the optimal assignment, the next step is to compute the training loss $\mathcal{L}_{\text{train}}$, which is a linear combination of a negative log-likelihood for *foreground/background* prediction, a box loss and mask loss for the instance sequences:

$$\begin{aligned}\mathcal{L}_{\text{train}}(y,\hat{y}) = \sum_{i=1}^{n}[(-\log \hat{p}_{\hat{\sigma}(i)}(c_i))+ \\ \mathcal{L}_{\text{box}}(b_i,\hat{b}_{\hat{\sigma}(i)}) + \lambda_{\text{mask}}\cdot\mathcal{L}_{\text{mask}}(m_i,\hat{m}_{\hat{\sigma}(i)})],\end{aligned} \tag{5}$$

here $c_i{=}$*foreground*, and $\hat{\sigma}$ is the optimal assignment, $\hat{p}_{\sigma(i)}(c_i)$ denotes the probability of c_i with index $\sigma(i)$, b_i denotes the ground truth box sequences. This training loss is used to train the whole video instance segmentation framework end-to-end. For the bounding box loss we employ the generalize IoU loss as prescribed in [59], while we use a linear combination of the dice loss [48] and focal loss [41] for the mask loss. The full loss equations are provided in the Appendix. As a result we obtain an end-to-end framework that is guided by support videos and able to segment instances in a query video.

Implementation Details. As the largest video length in Self-VIS is 32, we take 32 as the query video clip length T. The support video clip length is set to 24. If the original video is too short or too long, we pad it with the last frame or cut it at a random position. All videos are resized to a 320×280 resolution before they are fed into the backbone. The model predicts 10 instances for each query frame, thus the total instance number is 320. In the common transformer structure, we use 6 encoder, 3 fuser, 6 decoder layers of width 288 with 8 attention heads.

The model is trained with AdamW [43], setting the initial common transformer's learning rate to 10^{-4}, the backbone's learning rate to 10^{-5}. The model is trained for 20 epochs, with the learning rate decay by 10 at 14 epochs. We initialize our backbone with the weights pretrained on the COCO dataset [42]. Further details are provided in the Appendix.

The main evaluation metric is average precision, with the video Intersection over Union (IoU) of the mask sequences as threshold. The IoU threshold is set to 0.5 unless specified otherwise.

6 Results

Self-shot Evaluation. We first evaluate the potential of self-shot learning on the introduced video instance segmentation benchmarks. We use the introduced transformer and compare to both oracle upper bounds and self-supervised baselines for obtaining support videos as input to the transformer.

In Table 1, we compare a broad range of feature spaces for providing relevant support videos given a query video. We first find that utilizing random videos from the unlabelled dataset as support already provides a non-trivial instance segmentation performance (row *a*), but still with a considerable gap to the oracle baseline where each support video is manually curated to have matching instance classes with the query video. Self-shot learning brings large benefits over randomly picking support videos (rows *(c)-(f)*). We first establish a baseline of using ImageNet-pretrained features for obtaining relevant support samples in row *(c)*, as well as finetuning these features using a non-parametric

Table 1. Self-shot evaluation. The unsupervised support videos come from the Youtube-8M Segments dataset and video instance segmentation performance is evaluated on the test set of Self-VIS. For comparability, we include baselines using random videos or fully supervised oracle videos as support. Inference-time support-increase is evaluated in the $5 + (n)$ columns where extra n support videos are used at inference. The strongest self-support is competitive with a 1-shot oracle-support

		Support				
		1	5	5+(1)	5+(3)	5+(5)
Retrieval based on						
(a)	Random videos	44.3	44.9	44.8	45.1	45.1
(b)	Oracle/labels	53.2	56.6	56.1	57.6	57.8
Self-shot variants						
(c)	Inception fixed	46.9	48.3	48.5	48.2	48.4
(d)	Inception MoCo	49.4	51.6	51.9	51.7	51.9
(e)	Video MIL-NCE	50.1	52.5	52.6	52.9	53.3
(f)	Video Rank	51.4	54.3	54.6	55.2	55.4

instance retrieval loss [65] using MoCo [31] in row *(d)*, which adds around 2.5–3.5% in performance. Next, we utilize a more sophisticated MIL-NCE loss [47] and a rank-based retrieval loss [60] to learn *video-clip* embeddings (see Appendix for details). With this we find that row *(f)* in Tab. 1 achieves strong gains of 6–10% in absolute performance compared to the random baseline and more than 3–7% compared to frozen ImageNet features and use this for subsequent experiments. Besides the finding that all features obtained in a self-supervised fashion improve over the supervised frame-based features ones we also establish that the self-supervised task does matter too, as we find the ranking loss well-suited for retrieving relevant support videos. We conclude that the strongest self-support can almost close the gap with the oracle-support baseline, even though self-shot support videos are not guaranteed to have matching classes.

Self-shot versus Zero-Shot Learning. To further quantify the effectiveness of self-shot learning for finding support videos, we compare to zero-shot learning on two different tasks: video instance segmentation and temporal action localization. For video instance segmentation, all experiments run on the Self-VIS dataset and as zero-shot baselines we utilize the methods from Dave *et al.* [22] and Lu *et al.* [44]. Dave *et al.*can segment moving objects in videos, even the ones unseen in training. Lu *et al.*can distinguish foreground/background in a zero-shot manner. For temporal action localization, we follow the setup of Yang *et al.* [69], which also provides the temporal action localization pipeline and the reorganized dataset derived from Thumos14. Zhang *et al.* [72] provide the zero-shot method for temporal action localization. They can localize the unseen activities in a long untrimmed video based on the label embeddings, which means class labels are needed during inference. In Table 2, we report the video instance segmentation and temporal action localization results. We find that on both settings our self-shot approach improves over the zero-shot alternatives, indicating that automatically obtaining support videos in an unsupervised manner and using them for their respective video task obtains favorable results over a semantic

Table 2. Self-shot versus zero-shot learning for video instance segmentation and temporal action localization. For Temporal action localization, we follow the setup of Yang *et al.* [69] on the Thumos14 dataset. The metric is video-mAP with an overlap threshold of 0.5. We find that our self-shot perspective is better suited for segmentation and localization in videos than zero-shot baselines

	Self-VIS			Thumos14		
	0	1	5	0	1	5
Zero-shot learning [22]	47.4	–	–	–	–	–
Zero-shot learning [44]	48.1	–	–	–	-	–
Zero-shot learning [72]	–	–	–	43.4	–	–
Self-shot learning	–	51.4	54.3	–	45.8	47.3
Self-shot learning k+(5)	-	54.6	55.4	-	47.7	48.0

Table 3. VIS transformer ablation under self-shot setting. The decoder achieves competitive performance by itself. It improves when the encoder processes the videos. A considerable performance gain happens when the fuser passes messages from the support branch to the query branch. Performance is best with all three modules

Encoder	Fuser	Decoder	Self-VIS		Self-OVIS	
			1 self-shot	5 self-shots	1 self-shot	5 self-shots
		✓	40.7	40.8	13.7	14.4
✓		✓	42.4	42.2	14.3	15.7
	✓	✓	49.1	51.5	19.6	21.0
✓	✓	✓	**51.4**	**54.3**	**20.6**	**23.7**

transfer of information from seen to unseen visual classes. In the Appendix, we also provide results where we use zero-shot learning to help find support videos, which is also not as effective as self-shot learning.

Transformer Ablation. In Table 3, we show the effect of the three components in our video instance segmentation transformer when using both one and five self-shot support videos. We find that all three components matter for maximizing segmentation performance. Especially the introduced fuser module is important and adds 8.4% 1-shot performance compared to the baseline, while the encoder adds 1.7%. When combined, the encoder yields an additional 2.3% gain on top of the fuser-only baseline, showing that having sufficient encoding capacity before fusing leads to better performance. In the appendix we also establish that the proposed baseline is competitive both against previous works adapted for the novel video instance segmentation setting, as well as against established methods for an image segmentation setting. Overall, we conclude that the proposed transformer is effective for video instance segmentation using a few support videos.

Table 4. Video difficulty ablation. (a): Performance when varying the number of instances on Self-VIS. High scores can be obtained when the common instances are not too many (no more than 3), segmentation of more than 4 instances in a query video remains challenging. **(b)**: Performance when varying the number of classes on Self-OVIS. When the common instances come from multiple classes, segmentation becomes harder

(a) Instance number in query video

	Instance number				
	1	2	3	4	≥5
1 self-shot	52.1	51.7	49.5	44.7	41.6
5 self-shots	54.8	54.6	52.9	50.2	45.5

(b) Class number in query video

	Class number			
	1	2	3	≥4
1 self-shot	23.4	20.7	17.1	8.6
5 self-shots	26.2	23.3	19.4	9.4

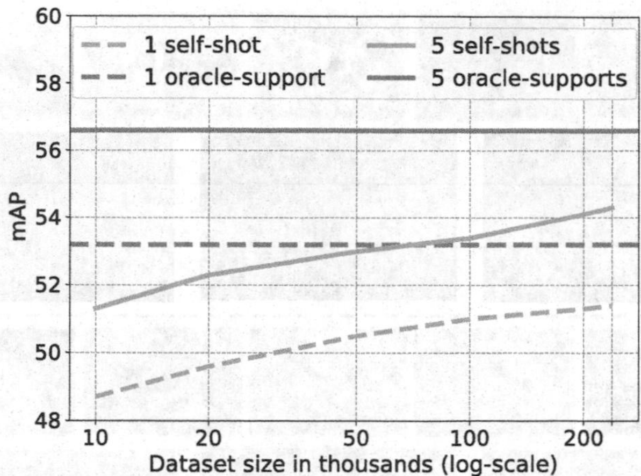

Fig. 2. Scalability of self-shot learning. Performance scales positively with the increase in unlabelled videos available and 5 self-supports outperforms using 1 oracle-support for >75K videos

Video Difficulty Ablation. Next, we ablate the effect of the number of instances and number of classes in the query video on the segmentation performance in Table 4. As each video in the Self-VIS dataset contains instances from just a single class, we use this to analyze the stability of our model with regard to the number of instances. The result is shown in Table 4a, and we find performance only mildly declines for a moderate increase, up to 3, in number of instances in the query video. Next, we use the more difficult Self-OVIS dataset to study the robustness against more diverse videos that contain more instances from multiple classes. As shown in Table 4b, the method still works well with more than one instance per video, though performance naturally declines with this added difficulty for the task.

Scaling Unsupervised Support. The quality of the self-shot learning is bounded by the quality of the videos in the unlabelled video collection. In Fig. 2 we show how self-shot video instance segmentation scales with unlabelled dataset size. We find that at around 75 K videos, our self-shot approach with 5 videos already *outperforms the 1-shot oracle-support* baseline. While we cannot perform experiments using even larger dataset sizes, we can see that even at 237 K videos, the performance is still rising steeply on a typical log-datasize scale. Based on this result, oracle-support from a labelled dataset of limited size might not even present a top-line for the same number of support videos and as we have shown in Table 1 can be further boosted with inference-time increase in number of supports. Thus, this shows that using larger unlabelled video datasets and conducting retrieval presents an effective method for scalable video instance segmentation. In Fig. 3 we provide qualitative examples of self-shot learning.

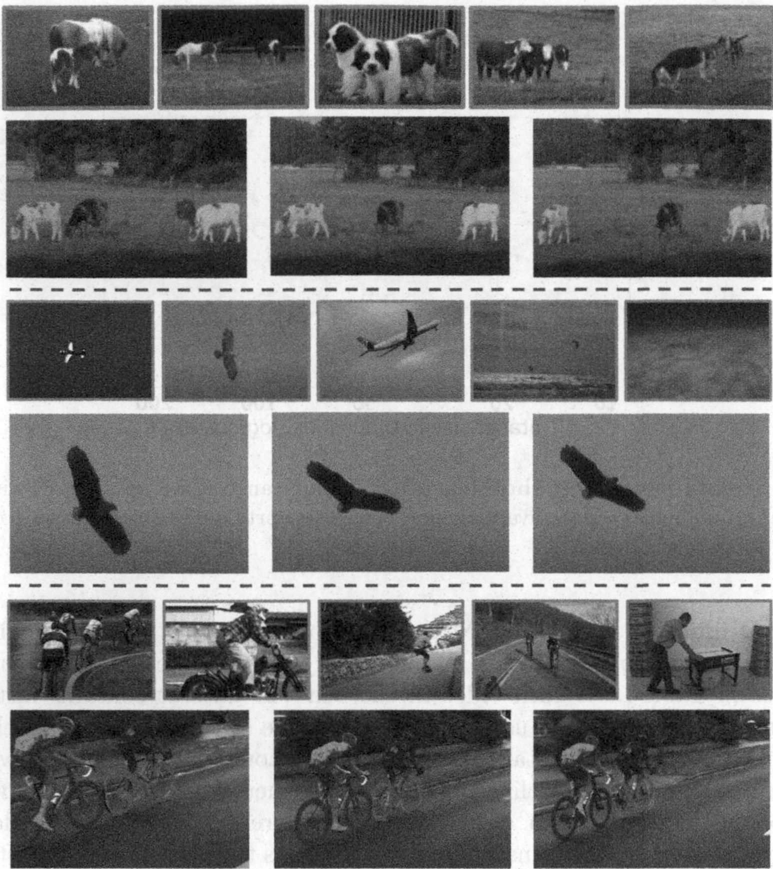

Fig. 3. Qualitative examples. Three examples of self-shot videos (top) and the resulting instance segmented query video (bottom)

Semi-shot Learning. In the final experiment, we show results for combining self-shot and oracle support videos. In this setting, we are given a few oracle support videos and use these to help find more support videos in a self-shot manner, arriving at a semi-shot alternative. In Table 5, we show using a single oracle video and 4 self-shot videos boosts performance by 1.9% and achieves 55.1% mAP, thus almost reaching the performance when using 5 oracle-support videos, all without any further annotation requirements.

Table 5. Semi-shot learning. We show that the performance increases when adding additional self-shot videos to the oracle-support videos, arriving at a semi-shot alternative. We find that such a hybrid setting can quickly close the gap to few-shot learning with ground truth support videos, further highlighting the potential of self-shot learning for video instance segmentation

	# Oracle-support					
	0	1	2	3	4	5
# Self-shot 0		53.2	53.9	55.0	55.7	56.6
1	51.4	53.6	54.5	55.1	56.0	
2	52.3	54.2	54.8	55.9		
3	52.8	54.7	55.2			
4	53.6	55.1				
5	54.3					

7 Discussion

Limitations. While we have proposed and explored the task of self-shot video instance segmentation, we have done so in a sequential fashion: The support set generation is detached from the segmentation pipeline. While this allows for better analysis of the method, performance can likely be further improved by training in an end-to-end fashion. We are also limited by the unlabelled video dataset size because of our computational resources. As shown in Fig. 2, larger dataset sizes will likely further highlight the benefit of utilizing self-shot learning.

Conclusions. This paper proposed the task of self-shot learning. We have analysed and proposed this in the most annotation intense setting, that of video instance segmentation where existence of oracle support can be considered unrealistic. For this we develop a novel transformer based instance segmentation baseline and outline how to obtain support videos automatically from an unlabelled pool through self-supervision. Experiments show that our approach achieves strong performance, can already outperform oracle support in some settings, is scalable, and can be combined in a semi-supervised setting.

Acknowledgments. This work is financially supported by Qualcomm Technologies Inc., the University of Amsterdam and the allowance Top consortia for Knowledge and Innovation (TKIs) from the Netherlands Ministry of Economic Affairs and Climate Policy.

References

1. Abu-El-Haija, S., et al.: Youtube-8m: a large-scale video classification benchmark. arXiv (2016)

2. Alwassel, H., Mahajan, D., Korbar, B., Torresani, L., Ghanem, B., Tran, D.: Self-supervised learning by cross-modal audio-video clustering. In: NeurIPS (2020)
3. Arnab, A., Dehghani, M., Heigold, G., Sun, C., Lučić, M., Schmid, C.: Vivit: a video vision transformer. arXiv (2021)
4. Asano, Y.M., Patrick, M., Rupprecht, C., Vedaldi, A.: Labelling unlabelled videos from scratch with multi-modal self-supervision. In: NeurIPS (2020)
5. Asano, Y.M., Rupprecht, C., Vedaldi, A.: Self-labelling via simultaneous clustering and representation learning. In: ICLR (2020)
6. Ba, J.L., Kiros, J.R., Hinton, G.E.: Layer normalization. In: STAT (2016)
7. Bello, I., Zoph, B., Vaswani, A., Shlens, J., Le, Q.V.: Attention augmented convolutional networks. In: ICCV (2019)
8. Benaim, S., et al.: SpeedNet: learning the speediness in videos. In: CVPR, pp. 9922–9931 (2020)
9. Bertasius, G., Torresani, L.: Classifying, segmenting, and tracking object instances in video with mask propagation. In: CVPR (2020)
10. Brown, A., Xie, W., Kalogeiton, V., Zisserman, A.: Smooth-AP: smoothing the path towards large-scale image retrieval. In: Vedaldi, A., Bischof, H., Brox, T., Frahm, J.-M. (eds.) ECCV 2020. LNCS, vol. 12354, pp. 677–694. Springer, Cham (2020). https://doi.org/10.1007/978-3-030-58545-7_39
11. Cao, K., Ji, J., Cao, Z., Chang, C.Y., Niebles, J.C.: Few-shot video classification via temporal alignment. In: CVPR (2020)
12. Carion, N., Massa, F., Synnaeve, G., Usunier, N., Kirillov, A., Zagoruyko, S.: End-to-end object detection with transformers. In: Vedaldi, A., Bischof, H., Brox, T., Frahm, J.-M. (eds.) ECCV 2020. LNCS, vol. 12346, pp. 213–229. Springer, Cham (2020). https://doi.org/10.1007/978-3-030-58452-8_13
13. Caron, M., Bojanowski, P., Joulin, A., Douze, M.: Deep clustering for unsupervised learning of visual features. In: ECCV (2018)
14. Caron, M., Misra, I., Mairal, J., Goyal, P., Bojanowski, P., Joulin, A.: Unsupervised learning of visual features by contrasting cluster assignments. In: NeurIPS (2020)
15. Caron, M., Touvron, H., Misra, I., Jégou, H., Mairal, J., Bojanowski, P., Joulin, A.: Emerging properties in self-supervised vision transformers. arXiv (2021)
16. Chen, K., et al.: Hybrid task cascade for instance segmentation. In: CVPR (2019)
17. Chen, T., Kornblith, S., Norouzi, M., Hinton, G.E.: A simple framework for contrastive learning of visual representations. In: ICML (2020)
18. Chen, X., Fan, H., Girshick, R., He, K.: Improved baselines with momentum contrastive learning. arXiv (2020)
19. Chen, X., He, K.: Exploring simple siamese representation learning. In: CVPR (2021)
20. Chen, X., Xie, S., He, K.: An empirical study of training self-supervised vision transformers. arXiv (2021)
21. Dai, J., Qi, H., Xiong, Y., Li, Y., Zhang, G., Hu, H., Wei, Y.: Deformable convolutional networks. In: ICCV (2017)
22. Dave, A., Tokmakov, P., Ramanan, D.: Towards segmenting anything that moves. In: ICCV Workshops (2019)
23. Dwibedi, D., Aytar, Y., Tompson, J., Sermanet, P., Zisserman, A.: With a little help from my friends: nearest-neighbor contrastive learning of visual representations. In: ICCV (2021)
24. Feichtenhofer, C., Fan, H., Xiong, B., Girshick, R., He, K.: A large-scale study on unsupervised spatiotemporal representation learning. In: CVPR, pp. 3299–3309 (2021)

25. Feng, Y., Ma, L., Liu, W., Luo, J.: Spatio-temporal video re-localization by warp lstm. In: CVPR (2019)
26. Feng, Y., Ma, L., Liu, W., Zhang, T., Luo, J.: Video re-localization. In: ECCV (2018)
27. Gidaris, S., Bursuc, A., Komodakis, N., Pérez, P., Cord, M.: Learning representations by predicting bags of visual words. In: CVPR, pp. 6928–6938 (2020)
28. Gidaris, S., Singh, P., Komodakis, N.: Unsupervised representation learning by predicting image rotations. In: ICLR (2018)
29. Grill, J.B., et al.: Bootstrap your own latent: A new approach to self-supervised learning. In: NeurIPS (2020)
30. Han, T., Xie, W., Zisserman, A.: Self-supervised co-training for video representation learning. In: NeurIPS (2020)
31. He, K., Fan, H., Wu, Y., Xie, S., Girshick, R.: Momentum contrast for unsupervised visual representation learning. In: CVPR (2020)
32. He, K., Gkioxari, G., Dollár, P., Girshick, R.: Mask r-cnn. In: ICCV (2017)
33. He, K., Zhang, X., Ren, S., Sun, J.: Deep residual learning for image recognition. In: CVPR (2016)
34. Jain, M., van Gemert, J.C., Mensink, T., Snoek, C.G.M.: Objects2action: Classifying and localizing actions without any video example. In: ICCV (2015)
35. Jain, M., Ghodrati, A., Snoek, C.G.M.: ActionBytes: Learning from trimmed videos to localize actions. In: CVPR (2020)
36. Kalantidis, Y., Sariyildiz, M.B., Pion, N., Weinzaepfel, P., Larlus, D.: Hard negative mixing for contrastive learning. In: NeurIPS (2020)
37. Kim, D., Cho, D., Kweon, I.S.: Self-supervised video representation learning with space-time cubic puzzles. In: AAAI, pp. 8545–8552 (2019)
38. Kliper-Gross, O., Hassner, T., Wolf, L.: One shot similarity metric learning for action recognition. In: International Workshop on Similarity-Based Pattern Recognition (2011)
39. Korbar, B., Tran, D., Torresani, L.: Cooperative learning of audio and video models from self-supervised synchronization. In: NeurIPS (2018)
40. Li, P., Wei, Y., Yang, Y.: Consistent structural relation learning for zero-shot segmentation. In: NeurIPS (2020)
41. Lin, T.Y., Goyal, P., Girshick, R., He, K., Dollár, P.: Focal loss for dense object detection. In: ICCV (2017)
42. Lin, T.Y., et al.: Microsoft COCO: common objects in context. In: Fleet, D., Pajdla, T., Schiele, B., Tuytelaars, T. (eds.) ECCV 2014. LNCS, vol. 8693, pp. 740–755. Springer, Cham (2014). https://doi.org/10.1007/978-3-319-10602-1_48
43. Loshchilov, I., Hutter, F.: Decoupled weight decay regularization. In: ICLR (2017)
44. Lu, X., Wang, W., Shen, J., Tai, Y.W., Crandall, D.J., Hoi, S.C.: Learning video object segmentation from unlabeled videos. In: CVPR (2020)
45. Mettes, P., Snoek, C.G.M.: Spatial-aware object embeddings for zero-shot localization and classification of actions. In: ICCV (2017)
46. Mettes, P., Thong, W., Snoek, C.G.M.: Object priors for classifying and localizing unseen actions. In: IJCV (2021)
47. Miech, A., Alayrac, J.B., Smaira, L., Laptev, I., Sivic, J., Zisserman, A.: End-to-end learning of visual representations from uncurated instructional videos. In: CVPR (2020)
48. Milletari, F., Navab, N., Ahmadi, S.A.: V-net: Fully convolutional neural networks for volumetric medical image segmentation. In: 3DV (2016)
49. Misra, I., van der Maaten, L.: Self-supervised learning of pretext-invariant representations. In: CVPR (2020)

50. Noroozi, M., Favaro, P.: Unsupervised learning of visual representations by solving jigsaw puzzles. In: Leibe, B., Matas, J., Sebe, N., Welling, M. (eds.) ECCV 2016. LNCS, vol. 9910, pp. 69–84. Springer, Cham (2016). https://doi.org/10.1007/978-3-319-46466-4_5
51. Parmar, N., Vaswani, A., Uszkoreit, J., Kaiser, Ł., Shazeer, N., Ku, A., Tran, D.: Image transformer. In: ICML (2018)
52. Pathak, D., Krähenbühl, P., Donahue, J., Darrell, T., Efros, A.: Context encoders: Feature learning by inpainting. In: CVPR (2016)
53. Patrick, M., Asano, Y.M., Huang, B., Misra, I., Metze, F., Henriques, J., Vedaldi, A.: Space-time crop & attend: improving cross-modal video representation learning. In: ICCV (2021)
54. Patrick, M., et al.: On compositions of transformations in contrastive self-supervised learning. In: ICCV, pp. 9577–9587 (2021)
55. Patrick, M., et al.: Support-set bottlenecks for video-text representation learning. In: ICLR (2021)
56. Perrett, T., Masullo, A., Burghardt, T., Mirmehdi, M., Damen, D.: Temporal-relational crosstransformers for few-shot action recognition. In: CVPR (2021)
57. Qi, J., et al.: Occluded video instance segmentation. arXiv (2021)
58. Qian, R., et al.: Spatiotemporal contrastive video representation learning. In: CVPR, pp. 6964–6974 (2021)
59. Rezatofighi, H., Tsoi, N., Gwak, J., Sadeghian, A., Reid, I., Savarese, S.: Generalized intersection over union: a metric and a loss for bounding box regression. In: CVPR (2019)
60. Varamesh, A., Diba, A., Tuytelaars, T., Van Gool, L.: Self-supervised ranking for representation learning. In: NeurIPS (2020)
61. Vaswani, A., et al.: Attention is all you need. In: NIPS (2017)
62. Wang, L., Hua, G., Sukthankar, R., Xue, J., Niu, Z., Zheng, N.: Video object discovery and co-segmentation with extremely weak supervision. In: TPAMI (2016)
63. Wang, W., Lu, X., Shen, J., Crandall, D.J., Shao, L.: Zero-shot video object segmentation via attentive graph neural networks. In: ICCV (2019)
64. Wang, Y., Xu, Z., Wang, X., Shen, C., Cheng, B., Shen, H., Xia, H.: End-to-end video instance segmentation with transformers. In: CVPR (2021)
65. Wu, Z., Xiong, Y., Stella, X.Y., Lin, D.: Unsupervised feature learning via non-parametric instance discrimination. In: CVPR (2018)
66. Xu, H., Sun, X., Tzeng, E., Das, A., Saenko, K., Darrell, T.: Revisiting few-shot activity detection with class similarity control. arXiv (2020)
67. Yang, H., He, X., Porikli, F.: One-shot action localization by learning sequence matching network. In: CVPR (2018)
68. Yang, L., Fan, Y., Xu, N.: Video instance segmentation. In: CVPR (2019)
69. Yang, P., Hu, V.T., Mettes, P., Snoek, C.G.M.: Localizing the common action among a few videos. In: Vedaldi, A., Bischof, H., Brox, T., Frahm, J.-M. (eds.) ECCV 2020. LNCS, vol. 12352, pp. 505–521. Springer, Cham (2020). https://doi.org/10.1007/978-3-030-58571-6_30
70. Yang, P., Mettes, P., Snoek, C.G.M.: Few-shot transformation of common actions into time and space. In: CVPR (2021)
71. Zhang, D., Dai, X., Wang, Y.F.: Metal: Minimum effort temporal activity localization in untrimmed videos. In: CVPR (2020)
72. Zhang, L., et al.: Zstad: zero-shot temporal activity detection. In: CVPR (2020)
73. Zhu, L., Yang, Y.: Compound memory networks for few-shot video classification. In: ECCV (2018)

Adaptive Face Forgery Detection in Cross Domain

Luchuan Song[1], Zheng Fang[2(✉)], Xiaodan Li[3], Xiaoyi Dong[1], Zhenchao Jin[1], Yuefeng Chen[3], and Siwei Lyu[4]

[1] University of Science and Technology of China, Hefei, China
{slc0826,dlight,blwx96}@mail.ustc.edu.cn
[2] Shopee Inc., Singapore, Singapore
fangzheng0827@gmail.com
[3] Alibaba Group, Hangzhou, China
{fiona.lxd,yuefeng.chenyf}@alibaba-inc.com
[4] University at Buffalo, Buffalo, USA
siweilyu@buffalo.edu

Abstract. It is necessary to develop effective face forgery detection methods with constantly evolving technologies in synthesizing realistic faces which raises serious risks on malicious face tampering. A large and growing body of literature has investigated deep learning-based approaches, especially those taking frequency clues into consideration, have achieved remarkable progress on detecting fake faces. The method based on frequency clues result in the inconsistency across frames and make the final detection result unstable even in the same deepfake video. So, these patterns are still inadequate and unstable. In addition to this, the inconsistency problem in the previous methods is significantly exacerbated due to the diversities among various forgery methods. To address this problem, we propose a novel deep learning framework for face forgery detection in cross domain. The proposed framework explores on mining the potential consistency through the correlated representations across multiple frames as well as the complementary clues from both RGB and frequency domains. We also introduce an instance discrimination module to determine the discriminative results center for each frame across the video, which is a strategy that adaptive adjust with during inference.

Keywords: Face forgery detection · Adaptive discriminative centers

1 Introduction

With the rapid developments of face forgery techniques [1,2,25,31,42,45], manipulated media (the images and videos) with highly realistic forged faces can be easily generated by off-the-shelf softwares. These advanced face forgery technologies may be abused for malicious purposes, such as generating fake statement

Supplementary Information The online version contains supplementary material available at https://doi.org/10.1007/978-3-031-19830-4_27.

S. Avidan et al. (Eds.): ECCV 2022, LNCS 13694, pp. 467–484, 2022.
https://doi.org/10.1007/978-3-031-19830-4_27

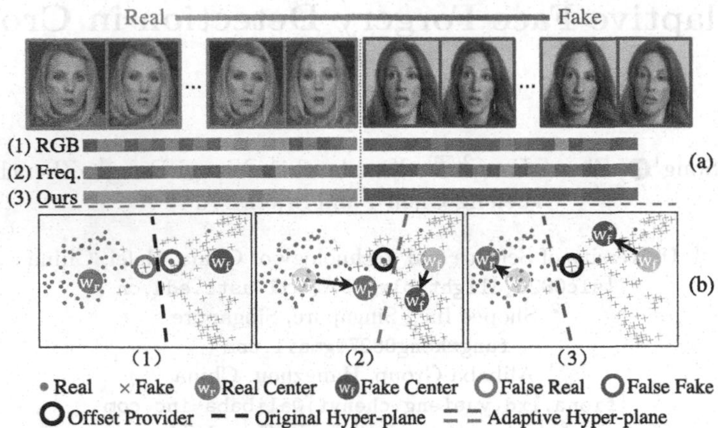

Fig. 1. (a) Probability of the face being fake (red) or real (green). (1)–(3) correspond to the prediction results from Xception, frequency based Xception and our proposed CD-Net, respectively. (b) T-SNE embedding visualization. Instances close to the hyper-plane are easy to be erroneously predicted, since the single classification hyper-plane may be not appropriate for all instances (in (b-1)). Predictions can be corrected by adjusting the hyper-plane adaptively for each instance (in (b-2,3)). (Color figure online)

videos, causing trust issues and security concerns of the general public. Alternatively, recent studies begin to focus on various clues, *e.g.* RGB pattern [11,15], temporal feature [4,34], optical flow [5], frequency [18,20,35,40,50], local facial region [10,47,55], forgery boundary [27] and biometric signals [12,13,37], to capture more robust features for forgery detection. These approaches achieve remarkable performance improvements on several public benchmark datasets.

Albeit the promising performance achieved by previous detection models, they are far from the ultimate solution to the problem. In particular, most existing deep convolutional neural network (CNN) based solutions suffer from several distinct limitations.

As shown in Fig. 1(a-1), though Xception-based detection [11] can make a correct prediction on a given video with voting strategies, it still makes some wrong predictions on several frames, resulting in low frame-level prediction. Moreover, the frame-level detection results are highly inconsistent across faces within multiple frames, even though they share the same identity, accessories, background and *etc.*. This means that for DeepFake videos detection, the Xception [11] cannot give a robust classification performance due to the unstable discriminative center. Apart from the RGB domain feature, several approaches [35,40] use information in the frequency domain to boost the performance on face forgery detection. Existing methods using features based on frequency patterns are effective in general image classification [27,49,55] show that such models are able to find statistical features. There are some artifacts in the existing GAN-based and graphics-based face synthesis methods [24,44], it is exposed with frequency-aware clues and the performance of frequency augmented Xception can be improved to some extent [40], as shown in Fig. 1(a-2). Nonetheless, the frequency features may be inadequate and there remains significant cross-frame inconsistency in the predictions. Therefore, we need to improve the cross-frame detection consistency, especially for faces from the same subject, to further improve the performance of detection algorithms.

Another limitation of existing works originates from the large intra-class distance caused by various artifacts on fake faces. We treat the forgery detection problem as a binary classification problem. It optimizes a one-fold discriminative plane $\mathcal{P}$ decided by the class centers, *i.e.*positive center $\mathbf{w}_\mathrm{f}$ and the corresponding negative center $\mathbf{w}_\mathrm{r}$. During training, these centers will be optimized to achieve an optimal discriminative performance. The final optimized classification hyper-plane based on SoftMax in previous methods is determined by the discriminative centers. This fixed hyper-plane cannot divide the real and fake faces in all frames accurately. In particular, those instances near the discriminative plane tend to be ambiguous for classification, as shown in Fig. 1(b-1). However, to the best of our knowledge, this discrimination inconsistency has not been addressed in previous face forgery detection works.

To solve the inter-frame and inter-instance instability of current forgery detection methods, we propose a novel deep architecture focusing on both *consistent* feature extraction and *discriminative* center adjusting, named as CD-Net. The proposed CD-Net consists of two novel components: *Dual-domain Intra-Consistency Module (DICM)* and *Instance-Discrimination Module (IDM)*. The DICM is designed to enhance intra-consistency by promoting the correlation of features from multiple frames in a video. In contrast with existing methods where either only the temporal consistency is considered in the final embedding (Two-branch RNN [35], STIL [22]), nor temporal information is utilized in frequency-based methods (F^3-Net [40]), the proposed DICM utilizes both temporal and frequency information at the feature level. In this way, it can boost the intra-consistent representations in both the RGB and frequency domains by extracting communal patterns existed in different frames, as shown in Fig. 1(a-3). To give a robust classification performance, we further propose a novel component *Instance-Discrimination Module (IDM)* in CD-Net, which aims to make the predictions adaptive to the features of individual instance and adjust the discriminative centers based on the features of each individual instance. As far as we know, there is no similar approach to explore the intra-class distance of various artifacts and the primary discriminative center of the whole training set is not suitable for those hard fake instances. As shown in Fig. 1(b-2,3), IDM extracts the offsets from the instance feature and adjust centers for real&fake instances to get the instance-adaptive discriminative centers $\mathbf{w}_\mathrm{r}^*$ and $\mathbf{w}_\mathrm{f}^*$. Helped with the instance-level offsets, the false predictions can be corrected with the adjusted discriminative hyper-plane determined by $\mathbf{w}_\mathrm{r}^*$ and $\mathbf{w}_\mathrm{f}^*$.

To validate the effectiveness of the proposed CD-Net for face forgery detection, we experiment on two different backbones under both the in-domain and out-domain settings. Experimental results show that the proposed method can achieve state-of-the-art performance on various datasets, showing a promising result for face forgery detection. Our contributions are summarized as follows:

1) We introduce a *Dual-domain Intra-Consistency Module (DICM)* to improve consistency and stability of instance representation, which is extracted based on multiple frames in various domains, *i.e.*RGB and frequency patterns.
2) We introduce an *Instance-Discrimination Module (IDM)* to adjust the discriminative centers. It can dynamically adjust the position of the hyper-plane according to the input instance, which can help to improve the detection performance further.
3) We verify that our approach can achieve state-of-the-art performance on several widely-used datasets under both in-domain and out-domain settings.

2 Related Works

Spatial-Based Forgery Detection. Early approaches mainly focus on examining the appearance features in the spatial domain such as RGB or HSV color spaces. A few studies [27,33,55] extract color-space features for classification. GramNet [33] extracts global textures to tackle the distortion perturbations. Face X-ray [27] explores the detection task on locating the boundary of face forgery. PCL [55] employs 1×1 convolution module and extracts the relationship between each pixel in spatial. However, these approaches only utilize the RGB/spatial information, and some important features are difficult to be discovered with CNN models, especially on fake media with fewer artifacts. These clues are generally better revealed in the frequency domain, this is often the case with heavily compressed frames.

Frequency-Based Forgery Detection. Recently there is a growing number of studies [10,35,40,49,50] focus on frequency features. F^3-Net [40] uses frequency-aware image decomposition and local frequency statistics to mine forgery patterns while Two-branch RNN [35] uses the Laplacian of Gaussian operator and merges information extracted from both the RGB domain and the frequency domain. Nevertheless, the frequency information extractors used in these approaches are limited to each face itself, without considering faces of the same person in other frames of the video, and the correlation of features extracted from multiple frames in network backbone is absent.

3 CD-NET

In this section, we describe the proposed CD-Net in detail. As shown in Fig. 2, given a sequence of extracted faces from the input video and its corresponding frequency maps extracted via DCT and IDCT transforms, the proposed DICM performs element-wise summation over frequency and RGB features for robust classification. Last, the dual-domain features are merged and fed into the IDM module to dynamically adjust the hyper-plane by the bias and output the final fake score of the input sequence.

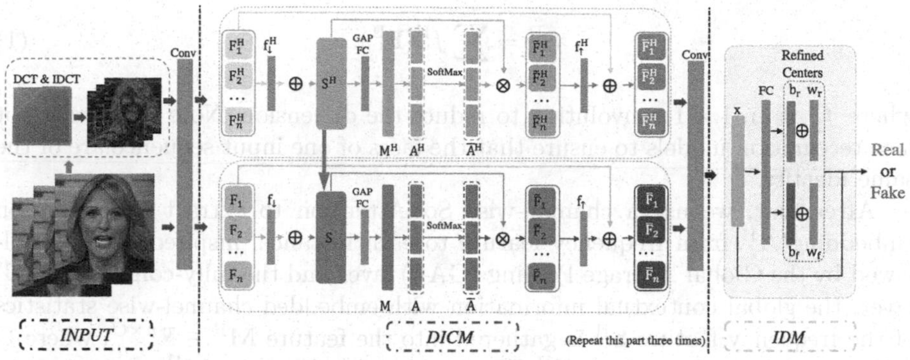

Fig. 2. The overview of the CD-Net. From left to right are the input modules, *Dual-domain Intra-Consistency Module (DICM)* and *Instance-Discrimination Module (IDM)*. The DICM takes RGB features and frequency features as input to obtain stable dual-domain feature for IDM classification. The IDM adaptively adjusting discriminative centers based on the individual instance. The "Repeat this part three times" represents the concatenation of three identical modules. ⊗ and ⊕ are element-wise multiplication and summation respectively.

3.1 Dual-Domain Intra-consistency Module

Forgery face videos are usually generated in a frame-by-frame manner. In other words, each fake frame is generated individually, which may result in artifacts in temporal dimension. However, most previous studies [33,35,40,55] only adopt features from the current face frame in the backbone, without considering other frames in the video, which leads to inadequate forgery-patterns and introduces inconsistency in predictions. Though some methods [28] propose to model the sequence smoothness along the temporal dimension, their applications are limited in frame-level detection. We argue that for a robust model, the fake faces' features of the same identity in multiple frames should be consistent with each other. For this, instead of focusing on the modeling in temporal dimension, we propose a Dual-domain Intra-Consistency Module (DICM) to extract consistent representations in both the RGB and the frequency domain from the input multiple n frames to inter-act with each other. The architecture of DICM is shown in the Fig. 2. Three DICM modules are cascaded in our CD-Net.

In order to improve the robustness of classification through frequency and RGB information, we extract features in a dual-domain way. For the frequency domain, given the features $\{\mathbf{F}^{\mathrm{H}}_1, \mathbf{F}^{\mathrm{H}}_2, \cdots, \mathbf{F}^{\mathrm{H}}_n\}$ of the input multiple faces where n is the number of frames ($n = 3$ in our experiments), it will be fed into the *Intra-Consistency Module (ICM)* to extract generalized communal frequency maps $\mathbf{S}^{\mathrm{H}}$. Specifically, we first perform element-wise summation over the frequency features from the sequence to acquire the common feature $\mathbf{S}^{\mathrm{H}}$, to enhance the features activated by most frames and weaken the noise features. Formally, we have:

$$\mathbf{S}^{\mathrm{H}} = \sum_{i}^{n} f_{\downarrow}^{\mathrm{H}}(\mathbf{F}_i^{\mathrm{H}}), \tag{1}$$

where $f_{\downarrow}^{\mathrm{H}}$ is an 1×1 convolution to reduce the dimension. Note that we adopt face recognition models to ensure that the faces of one input sequence are of the same identity.

After that, we use a channel-wise SoftAttention to extract the attention embedding $\bar{\mathbf{A}}_i^{\mathrm{H}}$ from frequency feature to each instance, inspired by [53]. Followed by the Global Average Pooling (GAP) layer and the fully-connected (FC) layer, the global contextual information with embedded channel-wise statistics of the frequency feature $\mathbf{S}^{\mathrm{H}}$ is gathered into the feature $\mathbf{M}^{\mathrm{H}} \in \mathbb{R}^{n \times C}$, where C is the number of channels in $\mathbf{F}_i^{\mathrm{H}}$. We further transform the $\mathbf{M}^{\mathrm{H}}$ to the feature $\mathbf{A}^{\mathrm{H}} \in \mathbb{R}^{n \times C}$ with each row represents the global contextual information for a single frame. The $\mathbf{M}^{\mathrm{H}}$ is reshaped to feature $\mathbf{A}^{\mathrm{H}} \in \mathbb{R}^{n \times C}$ with each row represents the global contextual information for a single frame. Since the communal feature required by each instance is different, a SoftMax function is performed on $\mathbf{A}_i^{\mathrm{H}}$ to get the channel-wise SoftAttention embedding $\bar{\mathbf{A}}_i^{\mathrm{H}}$. The architecture for extracting the RGB feature is the same as the frequency branch. Formally, the c-th channel of $\bar{\mathbf{A}}_i^{\mathrm{H}}$ is calculated as:

$$\bar{\mathbf{A}}_i^{\mathrm{H}}(c) = \frac{\exp(\mathbf{A}_i^{\mathrm{H}}(c))}{\sum_j^n \exp(\mathbf{A}_j^{\mathrm{H}}(c))}, \tag{2}$$

This channel-wise attention is performed on the dual-domain feature $\mathbf{S}^{\mathrm{H}}$ and $\mathbf{S}$ to extract robust supplementary feature for each instance to enhance the prediction stability. The original feature and the robust supplementary feature are summed together as the refined output $\bar{\mathbf{F}}_i^{\mathrm{H}}$:

$$\bar{\mathbf{F}}_i^{\mathrm{H}} = f_{\uparrow}^{\mathrm{H}}(\mathbf{S}^{\mathrm{H}} \otimes \bar{\mathbf{A}}_i^{\mathrm{H}}) \oplus \mathbf{F}_i^{\mathrm{H}}, \tag{3}$$

where $\otimes$ and $\oplus$ are element-wise multiplication and element-wise summation respectively. $f_{\uparrow}^{\mathrm{H}}$ is the 1×1 convolution for restoring the dimension to the size of the original input.

To make full use of the frequency information together with the RGB information, the frequency communal feature $\mathbf{S}^{\mathrm{H}}$ is merged to the RGB communal feature $\mathbf{S}$. Other parts of the architecture for extracting the RGB feature is the same as the frequency branch. The merge operation concatenates $\mathbf{S}^{\mathrm{H}}$ and $\mathbf{S}$ on channel, and then pass the concatenated features through the fully-connected layer to downsample to origin channel. The merged feature utilizes both RGB maps and frequency maps, which is then used to enhance the stability of the RGB features learned from different instances as mentioned above. Finally, the output of DICM is the concatenate of the refined frequency squence $\{\mathbf{F}_1^{\mathrm{H}}, \mathbf{F}_2^{\mathrm{H}}, \cdots, \mathbf{F}_n^{\mathrm{H}}\}$ and refined RGB squence $\{\mathbf{F}_1, \mathbf{F}_2, \cdots, \mathbf{F}_n\}$.

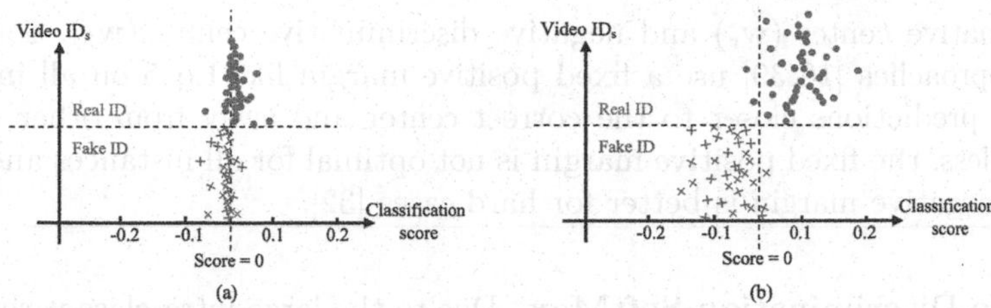

Fig. 3. Toy examples under the normalized SoftMax in (a) and Instance-Discrimination SoftMax in (b). We perform this on 30 real videos and 30 fake videos. The "Video IDs" represents different video markers, and the "Classification score" represents the prediction score get from the classification centers. From (a), the clusters are all around score 0. But from (b), the clusters will be sparser and the classification is more robust.

3.2 Instance-Discrimination Module

Apart from the prediction inconsistency of features, discriminative centers based on the whole training set is another problem for face forgery detection. The discriminative centers need to cover all data, so as to be adaptable to on unseen data. However, the original center based on the whole training set is not suitable for the requirement, especially when there are ambiguous cases near the classification hyper-plane.

We propose a novel Instance-Discrimination Module to adaptively adjust the discriminative center based on the instance itself to make robust and efficient predictions.

The input to IDM $\mathbf{x}$ is the Max-Pooling output of DICM, which is an embedding feature vector. And the corresponding label as y (real or fake), then the conditional probability output (fake score) $P(Y = y|\mathbf{x})$ by a deep neural network can be estimated via the SoftMax operator after FC layer:

$$P(Y = y|\mathbf{x}) = \frac{\exp(\mathbf{w}_y^\top \mathbf{x})}{\sum_j^N \exp(\mathbf{w}_j^\top \mathbf{x})}, \tag{4}$$

where $[\mathbf{w}_1, \cdots, \mathbf{w}_N] \in \mathbb{R}^{d \times N}$ is the weight tensor of the last fully-connected layer. N denotes the number of classes (N is 2 in our task). d is the dimension of embeddings.

The normalized SoftMax is:

$$P(Y = y|\mathbf{x}) = \frac{\exp(\tau \frac{\mathbf{w}_y^\top}{\|\mathbf{w}_y^\top\|_2} \frac{\mathbf{x}}{\|\mathbf{x}\|_2})}{\sum_j^N \exp(\tau \frac{\mathbf{w}_j^\top}{\|\mathbf{w}_j^\top\|_2} \frac{\mathbf{x}}{\|\mathbf{x}\|_2})}, \tag{5}$$

where τ is a scaling factor. Different from Eq. 4, $[\mathbf{w}_1, \cdots, \mathbf{w}_N]$ can be viewed as the discriminative centers, this is because the embedding $\mathbf{x}$ will calculate its cosine distance with $\mathbf{w}_0$ and $\mathbf{w}_1$. The $\mathbf{w}_0$ and $\mathbf{w}_1$ can be considered as positive discriminative center ($\mathbf{w}_\text{r}$) and negative discriminative center ($\mathbf{w}_\text{f}$). Some previous approaches [16,39] use a fixed positive margin like Eq. 5 on all instances to make predictions closer to the correct center and away from other centers. Nonetheless, the fixed positive margin is not optimal for all instances and sometimes a negative margin is better for hard cases [32].

Instance-Discrimination SoftMax. Due to the large intra-class variances in large-scale face datasets, the learned discriminative centers can not appropriately represent some instances distributed differently from the most instances (*i.e.*, instances with few visible artifacts). In this paper, we propose the IDM to adaptively adjust the discriminative centers based on the instance itself. The architecture of IDM is illustrated in Fig. 2(a). Two fully-connected layers gathered with Batch Normalization and ReLU are utilized to extract bias embeddings $\mathbf{b}_\text{r}$ and $\mathbf{b}_\text{f}$ for classification centers $\mathbf{w}_\text{r}$ and $\mathbf{w}_\text{f}$, respectively. Our Instance-Discrimination SoftMax is formalized as:

$$P(Y=y|\mathbf{x}) = \frac{\exp(\tau \frac{\mathbf{w}_y^\top + \mathbf{b}_y^\top(\mathbf{x})}{\|\mathbf{w}_y^\top + \mathbf{b}_y^\top(\mathbf{x})\|_2} \frac{\mathbf{x}}{\|\mathbf{x}\|_2})}{\sum_j^N \exp(\tau \frac{\mathbf{w}_j^\top + \mathbf{b}_j^\top(\mathbf{x})}{\|\mathbf{w}_j^\top + \mathbf{b}_j^\top(\mathbf{x})\|_2} \frac{\mathbf{x}}{\|\mathbf{x}\|_2})}, \tag{6}$$

and the corresponding loss $L(\mathbf{x}, y) = -logP(Y = y|\mathbf{x})$. The IDM adjust discriminative centers based on each individual instance. To give insight into it, we compare the difference of Cosine Similarity between normalized SoftMax (T_Norm) and Instance-Discrimination SoftMax (T_IDM), specifically,

$$\begin{aligned}
T_\text{Norm} &= \frac{\mathbf{w}^\top}{\|\mathbf{w}^\top\|_2} \frac{\mathbf{x}}{\|\mathbf{x}\|_2}, T_\text{Bias} = \frac{\mathbf{b}^\top(\mathbf{x})}{\|\mathbf{b}^\top(\mathbf{x})\|_2};\\
T_\text{IDM} &= \frac{\mathbf{w}^\top + \mathbf{b}^\top(\mathbf{x})}{\|\mathbf{w}^\top + \mathbf{b}^\top(\mathbf{x})\|_2} \frac{\mathbf{x}}{\|\mathbf{x}\|_2}\\
&= \frac{\mathbf{w}^\top}{\|\mathbf{w}^\top + \mathbf{b}^\top(\mathbf{x})\|_2} \frac{\mathbf{x}}{\|\mathbf{x}\|_2} + \frac{\mathbf{b}^\top}{\|\mathbf{w}^\top + \mathbf{b}^\top(\mathbf{x})\|_2} \frac{\mathbf{x}}{\|\mathbf{x}\|_2}\\
&= \frac{\left\|\mathbf{w}^\top\right\|_2}{\|\mathbf{w}^\top + \mathbf{b}^\top(\mathbf{x})\|_2} \left(\frac{\mathbf{w}^\top}{\|\mathbf{w}^\top\|_2} \frac{\mathbf{x}}{\|\mathbf{x}\|_2}\right) + \frac{\left\|\mathbf{b}^\top(\mathbf{x})\right\|_2}{\|\mathbf{w}^\top + \mathbf{b}^\top(\mathbf{x})\|_2} \left(\frac{\mathbf{b}^\top(\mathbf{x})}{\|\mathbf{b}^\top(\mathbf{x})\|_2} \frac{\mathbf{x}}{\|\mathbf{x}\|_2}\right)\\
&= \frac{\left\|\mathbf{w}^\top\right\|_2}{\|\mathbf{w}^\top + \mathbf{b}^\top(\mathbf{x})\|_2} T_\text{Norm} + \frac{\left\|\mathbf{b}^\top(\mathbf{x})\right\|_2}{\|\mathbf{w}^\top + \mathbf{b}^\top(\mathbf{x})\|_2} T_\text{Bias}\\
&= \alpha T_\text{Norm} - \epsilon,
\end{aligned} \tag{7}$$

where $\alpha = \frac{\|\mathbf{w}^\top\|_2}{\|\mathbf{w}^\top + \mathbf{b}^\top(\mathbf{x})\|_2}$ serves as temperature on T_Norm. T_Bias is the Cosine Similarity between bias embedding and discriminative center. $\epsilon = -\frac{\|\mathbf{b}^\top(\mathbf{x})\|_2}{\|\mathbf{w}^\top + \mathbf{b}^\top(\mathbf{x})\|_2} T_\text{Bias}$ can be viewed as the adaptive margin performed on each instance.

From Eq. 7, we can find that the proposed T_IDM consists of both original similarity T_Norm and the adaptive margin ϵ. Different from the fixed positive margin in previous work [16], ϵ can be either positive or negative, and is derived from the instance feature. Note that previous studies [16,26,39] only apply the margin on the the discriminative center corresponding to ground-truth, however, single-side margin is unreasonable for adaptive margin learning. In our Instance-Discrimination SoftMax, the adaptive margin ϵ is used in both real center and fake center to achieve the balance in the training period and force the network to learn effective bias on each center. Besides, the adaptive margin ϵ is used in both training and testing as a learned offset on discriminative centers in IDM rather than only applied in training to simply improve the intra-class compactness like previous work [16,26]. ϵ can be viewed as the adaptive margin performed on each instance.

The final discriminative center is the summation of primary center and the predicted center bias. In contrast, when directly extracting discriminative centers from the instance feature, that is essentially the same with baseline which regresses the logits with FC. In IDM, center bias is utilized to adjust primary discriminative centers, which forces the center bias to learn the relationship between instance feature and primary discriminative centers. We give a comparison of toy examples of Instance-Discrimination SoftMax and normalized SoftMax in Fig. 3, in which we use the same instance feature. The proposed Instance-Discrimination SoftMax can be treated as adaptive margins (either positive or negative) for instances, promoting the optimal performance on all cases.

4 Experiments

4.1 Setting

Datasets. We conduct experiments on several widely-used datasets, including FaceForensics++ (FF++) [42], DeeperForensics [25], Celeb-DF v2 [31] and Deepfake Detection Challenge (DFDC) dataset [17]. Both GAN-based (such as DeeperForensics [25]) and graphics-based (such as FF++ NeuralTextures [46]) forgery datasets are considered. We follow previous settings used in their corresponding datasets and compare with other methods respectively.

Metrics. We use the Area Under the Receiver Operating Characteristic Curve (AUC) and Accuracy score (Acc) as our evaluation metrics following previous methods [27,35,40]. In our experiments, AUC is used as the main metric since it is not affected by class imbalance and threshold. Although Acc is widely-used in face forgery detection, we assume that Acc is improper for this task, mainly caused by the sensitivity on class imbalance and the choice of threshold as mentioned in [35]. For fair comparison, Acc is calculated with the threshold of 0.5 without any threshold adjusting tricks. The video-level results are calculated by averaging all frame-level results by default.

To quantify the stability of the proposed method, two metrics are utilized in experiments, namely *Proportion of Unstable Predictions (PUP)* and *Correction Rate (CR)*. PUP_θ represents the proportion of unstable videos with the max score gap among frames higher than θ. Smaller PUP_θ indicates better stability. CR represents the proportion of same-video frame pairs which are originally get

Table 1. In-domain quantitative results on FF++ dataset with all quality settings. LQ indicates low quality (heavy compression), HQ indicates high quality (light compression) and RAW indicates videos with raw resolution. The bold results are the best. The reported approaches are spited based on whether utilizing 3D Convolution in backbone. The Acc of F^3-Net [40] with threshold of 0.5. The † implies re-implementation.

Methods	AUC (LQ)	Acc. (LQ)	AUC (HQ)	Acc. (HQ)	AUC (RAW)	Acc. (RAW)
Steg. features [21]	–	55.98%	–	70.97%	–	97.63%
LD-CNN [14]	–	58.69%	–	78.45%	–	98.57%
Constrained conv. [6]	–	66.84%	–	82.97%	–	98.74%
CustomPooling CNN [41]	–	61.18%	–	79.08%	–	97.03%
MesoNet [3]	–	70.47%	–	83.10%	–	95.23%
Face X-ray [27]	0.616	–	0.874	–	0.987	–
Two-branch RNN [35]	0.911	86.34%	0.991	96.43%	–	–
Xception [11]	0.925	84.11%	0.963	95.04%	0.992	98.77%
STIL† [22]	0.948	86.31%	0.986	98.57%	0.993	99.04%
PCL&I2G† [55]	0.939	87.02%	0.990	98.85%	0.997	99.78%
F^3-Net (Xception) [40]	0.933	86.89%	0.981	97.31%	0.998	99.84%
CD-Net (Xception)	**0.952**	**88.12%**	**0.999**	**98.75%**	**0.999**	**99.91%**
I3D [8]	–	87.43%	–	–	–	–
3D ResNet [23]	–	83.86%	–	–	–	–
3D ResNeXt [51]	–	85.14%	–	–	–	–
3D R50-FTCN [56]	0.966	92.35%	0.995	98.59%	0.997	99.84%
Slowfast [19]	0.936	88.25%	0.982	96.92%	0.994	99.34%
F^3-Net (Slowfast) [40]	0.958	92.37%	0.993	98.64%	0.999	99.91%
CD-Net (Slowfast)	**0.985**	**93.21%**	**0.999**	**98.93%**	**0.999**	**99.91%**

different predictions in baseline and are corrected after applying other methods. Higher CR indicates better ability on improving stability.

Implementation Details. In our experiments, Xception [11] pre-trained on the ImageNet dataset is used as the backbone. When training with IDM, we firstly fix the IDM to train the rest parameters with cross-entropy loss [54] until converged. Then we unfreeze the IDM and fine-tune the whole network. To demonstrate the generalization of the proposed methods, we also conduct experiments to validate the effectiveness of DICM and IDM on an exsiting video-based backbone, *i.e.*SlowFast R-101 [19] pre-trained on Kinetics-700 [7]. The DICM directly uses the frames in the slow pathway of SlowFast to extract the communal feature. IDM is attached at the end of SlowFast similar to Xception.

4.2 Comparison with Previous Methods

Face Forgery Detection. The results on FF++ are listed in Table 1. Our CD-Net outperforms all the previous methods on all quality settings, *i.e.*, LQ

Table 2. Out-domain Video-level evaluation on DFDC [17] and Celeb-DF v2 [30]. The CD-Net[1,2,3] represents the backbone of CD-Net are Xception-raw, Xception-c23 and Xception-40 respectively. The best results are bolded. † implies re-implementation.

Methods	DFDC	Celeb-DF v2	Methods	DFDC	Celeb-DF v2
Two-Branch [35]	–	0.767	PCL&I2G [55]	0.675	0.900
CNN-aug [50]	0.721	0.756	3DR50-FTCN [56]	0.740	0.869
CNN-GRU [43]	0.689	0.698	Multi-task [38]	0.681	0.757
FWA [29]	0.695	0.673	PatchForensics [9]	0.656	0.696
Face X-ray [27]	0.655	0.795	STIL† [22]	0.661	0.715
VA-LogReg [36]	0.680	0.651	DSP-FWA [29]	0.630	0.693
Xception-raw [11]	0.709	0.655	**CD-Net[1]**	**0.783**	0.877
Xception-c23 [11]	0.717	0.635	**CD-Net[2]**	0.770	0.885
Xception-c40 [11]	0.709	0.655	**CD-Net[3]**	0.753	**0.921**

(c40, compressed with the quantization of 40), HQ (c23, quantization of 23) and RAW respectively. Benefited from the consistent representations on forgery patterns and instance-adaptive discriminative centers, our Xception-based model performs much better than other image-based approaches, with 0.952 in AUC and 88.12% in Acc respectively, which is even better than most video-based approaches. When utilizing the same backbone (*i.e.*, Slowfast [19]), our CD-Net gains significant improvement compare with F^3-Net (Slowfast), with 0.984 and 93.13% of AUC and Acc in comparison to 0.958 and 92.37%, in LQ task. We further calculate the confidence intervals of the AUC and Acc in Table 1 over three repeating runs (the last three checkpoints) to verify that our model is a reliable model rather than randomly obtained. The confidence intervals are pretty small and our CD-Net is stably better than previous approaches on all quality settings even in the case of the lower bound of the score.

The comparison between our method and frequency information based methods [35,40] is shown in Table 1. Although the frequency-based methods are greatly improved compared to the other, our method still has outstanding performance than them, which achieves the best Acc and AUC at any resolution on FF++ dataset than frequency-based methods (*e.g.*, LQ (AUC): 88.12% *v.s.* 86.89%). Meanwhile, our method also has advantages over temporal-based methods [56] (*e.g.*, LQ (AUC): 88.12% *v.s.* 86.31%). Our DICM is more robust as it depends on the RGB and frequency feature existed in multiple frames other than the temporal cues, which boosts the consistency of predictions from different frames.

Generalization Out Domain. To validate the effectiveness of the proposed method, we perform the out-domain experiments on DFDC [17] and Celeb-DF v2 [31] with the models trained on FF++ (c23) datasets. The results are listed in Table 2. Following the previous studies [22,55,56], the video-level AUC scores

Table 3. Ablation study of our method on FF++ c40 (low quality) with AUC metric to evaluate the effects of components. PUP_θ represents the proportion of videos with the frame-level score gap higher than θ, the smaller the better. CR represents the proportion of corrected unstable frame pairs in baseline, the bigger the better.

ID	DICM	IDM	AUC	$PUP_{0.7}$	$PUP_{0.5}$	$PUP_{0.3}$	CR
1	–	–	0.925	66.1%	66.1%	67.4%	–
2	√	–	0.944	29.0%	41.7%	48.9%	78.82%
3	–	√	0.938	35.7%	60.9%	66.6%	55.35%
4	√	√	**0.952**	**26.1%**	**39.4%**	**48.7%**	**80.67%**

on DFDC and Celeb-DF v2 are presented in experiments. We copy the result from the papers [25,48,55,56], and we also re-implementate the results without open release code († in the Table 2) to complete the missing values. For our CD-Net, we conduct experiments on FF++ with different resolutions and the results are listed in the Table 2. Even when compared with strong state-of-the-art methods, *i.e.*PCL&I2G [55] and 3D R50-FTCN [56], our method still has advantages on Acc score (0.783*v.s.*0.740) and AUC score(0.921*v.s.*0.900) in terms of different resolutions. The CD-Net[1] (Xception-c40) based CD-Net achieves the best performance on DFDC since the heavily compressed data boost the model to acquire more generalized patterns. Our CD-Net outperforms the Xception baseline on all quality settings with much higher AUC score on Celeb-DF v2 and better Acc score on DFDC, demonstrating the robustness of our CD-Net on the unseen data.

4.3 Ablation Study

Effectiveness of DICM & IDM. To evaluate the effectiveness of the proposed DICM and IDM, we quantitatively evaluate our model and its variants: 1) the naked Xception as the baseline (ID 1), 2) Xception with DICM, 3) Xception with IDM, 4) Xception with both DICM and IDM (CD-Net). Both the AUC score and the prediction stability are reported in Table 3. Smaller PUP_θ represents better stability with a small prediction score gap among frames. Higher CR corresponds to better ability on improving stability.

As shown in Table 3, even if only utilizing DICM (ID 2) or IDM (ID 3), significant improvement on detection performance is achieved with AUC score 0.944 and 0.938 respectively. When using both DICM and IDM (ID 4), our method achieves the best performance with 0.952 AUC, much better than the 0.925 of baseline. Furthermore, as shown in the ROC curves in Fig. 4(a), CD-Net achieves the best performance with higher true positive rate, demonstrates the effectiveness in mining consistent representations on forgery patterns. The results of stability are positively related with detection performance where higher AUC corresponds to lower PUP and higher CR. The $PUP_{0.7}$ of CD-Net is smaller than half of the baseline with 26.1% in comparison to 66.1%, and 80.67% inconsistent frame pairs in baseline are corrected by CD-Net.

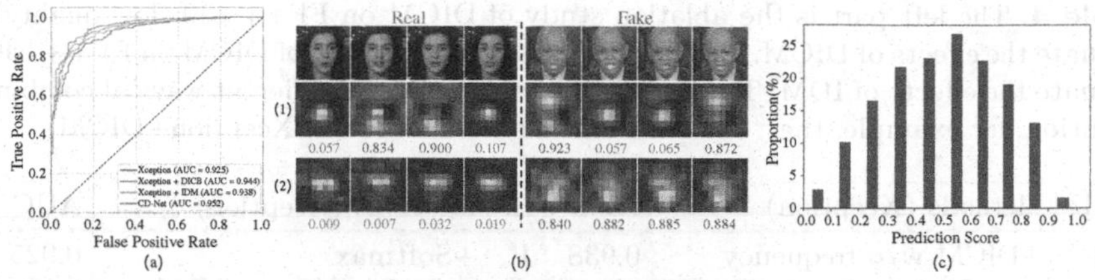

Fig. 4. (a) ROC Curve of the models in ablation studies. (b) The visualization of feature map extracted by Xception (1) and the proposed "Xception + DICM" (2). (c) The proportion of corrected instances after applying IDM relative to the total instances.

DICM. To demonstrate the benefits of utilizing correlation among frames on both frequency and RGB in DICM, we evaluate the proposed DICM and its variants by removing or replacing some components, *i.e.*, 1) the proposed DICM without frequency component, denoted as DICM w/o frequency (ID 1), 2) the proposed DICM without using correlation among frames, denoted as DICM w/o correlation (ID 2). All the experiments are under the same hyper-parameters for fair comparisons. The performance of each variants is listed in left part of Table 4. To demonstrate the improvement in DICM is not introduced by simply using multiple frames, we conduct experiments on multiple frames with other components, *i.e.*, 1) Xception using 3D convolution (Conv) to correlate features among different frames, denoted as "+ 3D Conv" (ID 3). The 3D Conv based model (ID 3) utilizes the similar architecture with singe Intra-consistency Module (ICM) by replacing the summation and SoftAttention with 3D Conv, and the number of parameters in 3D Conv is 27 times of ICM when the count of frames is 3. It shows the efficiency and effectiveness of our DICM. And we further demonstrate the importance of frequency feature as supplementary for RGB domain by quantitatively evaluating the DICM with different kinds of information, *i.e.*, low-frequency, frequency and original image. The model with frequency components (ID 6) achieves the best scores, which indicates that frequency is more complementary with others.

To better understand the effectiveness of DICM, the visualization of feature maps extracted by Xception and the "+ DICM" are shown in Fig. 4(b). Benefited from the communal patterns existed in various frames, these mispredictions in Fig. 4(b-1) have been corrected. Besides, in Fig. 4(b-2), predictions achieve a consistent representation for explicitly utilizing the correlation among frames.

IDM. For better conditioning on the discriminative centers based on instance itself, our IDM is performed gathered with normalized Softmax. To demonstrate the effectiveness of the proposed IDM, we conduct experiments to compare with other classification module, *i.e.*, 1) Xception with Softmax (ID 1*), 2) Xception with normalized Softmax (ID 2*), 3) Xception with ArcFace [16] (ID 3*), 4) Xception with SoftTriple [39] (ID 4*). The result is listed in the right part of Table 4. There is nearly no performance difference between the Softmax and the

Table 4. The left part is the ablation study of DICM on FF++ c40 (low quality) to evaluate the effects of DICM. The right part is ablation study of DICM on FF++ c40 to evaluate the effects of IDM. The "+" in the table indicates different ways of combining Xception, for example, the "+ DICM" means the method of Xception+DICM.

ID	Methods (Xception)	AUC	ID	Methods (Xception)	AUC
1	+DICM w/o frequency	0.938	1*	+Softmax	0.925
2	+DICM w/o correlation	0.932	2*	+Norm Softmax [52]	0.924
3	+3D Conv	0.931	3*	+ArcFace [16]	0.923
4	+DICM w/ Original Image	0.941	4*	+SoftTriple [39]	0.926
5	+DICM w/ Low-frequency	0.939	5*	+IDM w/ Bias on Embed.	0.929
6	+DICM	**0.944**	6*	+IDM	**0.938**

normalized Softmax, while our IDM gains a significant improvement with 0.938 in AUC. There are also some previous studies using the metric learning during the training period, such as ArcFace [16] uses a fixed positive margin and SoftTriple [39] uses multiple centers for classification. The proposed IDM achieves excellent performances comparing with these previous metric-based models. The fixed positive margin is not suitable for all instances in ArcFace while the multiple centers used in SoftTriple need the prior knowledge to pre-set the center number and an additional regulation is used to merge centers. The IDM is more versatile than the above-mentioned empirical methods and achieves excellent performances on the FF++. The average ratio between the center bias and the primary discriminative center 1:2.51, which demonstrates the importance of center bias on adjusting centers.

To adjust the distance of the instance relative to the discriminative centers, the bias can be either trained to modify the discriminative centers or the instance itself. However, when adjusting the discriminative centers, the model can modify both the distance between the instance relative to the discriminative centers and the distance on the internal of discriminative centers. The latter one could be served as the temperature to pull or push discriminative centers close or away from each other. We perform experiments to utilize the bias on the instance embedding, as shown in right of Table 4(ID 5*), the result of "+IDM w/ Bias on Embedding" is 0.929 AUC score, slightly better than baseline while worse than using bias on the discriminative centers, demonstrating the advantage of adjusting on discriminative centers.

We further analyze the specific influence of IDM on different predicted score ranges in the test set. As shown in Fig. 4(c), horizontal axis represents the predicted (by baseline without IDM) score range, and vertical axis shows the proportion of corrected instances relative to the total instances after applying IDM. The major corrected instances score range from 0.4 to 0.7 and are close to the original discriminative hyper-plane. Benefited from the instance-adaptive adjusting on discriminative centers in IDM, the ambiguous predictions can be corrected to maintain consistent performance on various instances.

5 Conclusions

In this paper, we propose an innovative face forgery detection framework CD-Net that repair defects of the inconsistency of forgery patterns and the suboptimal discriminative centers existed in current approaches. The proposed framework is composed of two components: DICM and IDM. The DICM utilizes the communal feature existed in multiple frames in both frequency domain and RGB domain to promote the stability and consistency. The IDM is capable of adaptively adjusting discriminative centers based on the individual instance feature. Extensive experiments demonstrate the effectiveness and significance of our approaches in-domain detection, robustness on distortions and the unseen data.

References

1. Deepfakes. https://github.com/deepfakes/faceswap/
2. Faceswap. https://github.com/MarekKowalski/FaceSwap/
3. Afchar, D., Nozick, V., Yamagishi, J., Echizen, I.: Mesonet: a compact facial video forgery detection network. In: 2018 IEEE International Workshop on Information Forensics and Security (WIFS), pp. 1–7. IEEE (2018)
4. Agarwal, S., El-Gaaly, T., Farid, H., Lim, S.N.: Detecting deep-fake videos from appearance and behavior. arXiv preprint arXiv:2004.14491 (2020)
5. Amerini, I., Galteri, L., Caldelli, R., Del Bimbo, A.: Deepfake video detection through optical flow based cnn. In: Proceedings of the IEEE International Conference on Computer Vision Workshops (2019)
6. Bayar, B., Stamm, M.C.: A deep learning approach to universal image manipulation detection using a new convolutional layer. In: Proceedings of the 4th ACM Workshop on Information Hiding and Multimedia Security, pp. 5–10 (2016)
7. Carreira, J., Noland, E., Hillier, C., Zisserman, A.: A short note on the kinetics-700 human action dataset. arXiv preprint arXiv:1907.06987 (2019)
8. Carreira, J., Zisserman, A.: Quo vadis, action recognition? a new model and the kinetics dataset. In: proceedings of the IEEE Conference on Computer Vision and Pattern Recognition, pp. 6299–6308 (2017)
9. Chai, L., Bau, D., Lim, S.N., Isola, P.: What makes fake images detectable? understanding properties that generalize. arXiv preprint arXiv:2008.10588 (2020)
10. Chen, Z., Yang, H.: Manipulated face detector: joint spatial and frequency domain attention network. arXiv preprint arXiv:2005.02958 (2020)
11. Chollet, F.: Xception: deep learning with depthwise separable convolutions. In: Proceedings of the IEEE Conference on Computer Vision and Pattern Recognition, pp. 1251–1258 (2017)
12. Ciftci, U.A., Demir, I., Yin, L.: Fakecatcher: detection of synthetic portrait videos using biological signals. IEEE Trans. Pattern Anal. Mach. Intell. (2020)
13. Ciftci, U.A., Demir, I., Yin, L.: How do the hearts of deep fakes beat? deep fake source detection via interpreting residuals with biological signals. arXiv preprint arXiv:2008.11363 (2020)
14. Cozzolino, D., Poggi, G., Verdoliva, L.: Recasting residual-based local descriptors as convolutional neural networks: an application to image forgery detection. In: Proceedings of the 5th ACM Workshop on Information Hiding and Multimedia Security, pp. 159–164 (2017)

15. Dang, H., Liu, F., Stehouwer, J., Liu, X., Jain, A.K.: On the detection of digital face manipulation. In: Proceedings of the IEEE/CVF Conference on Computer Vision and Pattern Recognition, pp. 5781–5790 (2020)
16. Deng, J., Guo, J., Xue, N., Zafeiriou, S.: Arcface: additive angular margin loss for deep face recognition. In: Proceedings of the IEEE Conference on Computer Vision and Pattern Recognition, pp. 4690–4699 (2019)
17. Dolhansky, B., Howes, R., Pflaum, B., Baram, N., Ferrer, C.C.: The deepfake detection challenge (dfdc) preview dataset. arXiv preprint arXiv:1910.08854 (2019)
18. Durall, R., Keuper, M., Pfreundt, F.J., Keuper, J.: Unmasking deepfakes with simple features. arXiv preprint arXiv:1911.00686 (2019)
19. Feichtenhofer, C., Fan, H., Malik, J., He, K.: Slowfast networks for video recognition. In: Proceedings of the IEEE International Conference on Computer Vision, pp. 6202–6211 (2019)
20. Frank, J., Eisenhofer, T., Schönherr, L., Fischer, A., Kolossa, D., Holz, T.: Leveraging frequency analysis for deep fake image recognition. arXiv preprint arXiv:2003.08685 (2020)
21. Fridrich, J., Kodovsky, J.: Rich models for steganalysis of digital images. IEEE Trans. Inf. Forensics Secur. **7**(3), 868–882 (2012)
22. Gu, Z., et al.: Spatiotemporal inconsistency learning for deepfake video detection. In: Proceedings of the 29th ACM International Conference on Multimedia, pp. 3473–3481 (2021)
23. Hara, K., Kataoka, H., Satoh, Y.: Can spatiotemporal 3D CNNs retrace the history of 2D cnns and imagenet? In: Proceedings of the IEEE conference on Computer Vision and Pattern Recognition, pp. 6546–6555 (2018)
24. He, Y., et al.: Forgerynet: a versatile benchmark for comprehensive forgery analysis. In: Proceedings of the IEEE/CVF Conference on Computer Vision and Pattern Recognition, pp. 4360–4369 (2021)
25. Jiang, L., Li, R., Wu, W., Qian, C., Loy, C.C.: Deeperforensics-1.0: a large-scale dataset for real-world face forgery detection. In: 2020 IEEE/CVF Conference on Computer Vision and Pattern Recognition (CVPR), pp. 2886–2895. IEEE (2020)
26. Kumar, A., Bhavsar, A., Verma, R.: Detecting deepfakes with metric learning. In: 2020 8th International Workshop on Biometrics and Forensics (IWBF), pp. 1–6 (2020). https://doi.org/10.1109/IWBF49977.2020.9107962
27. Li, L., et al.: Face x-ray for more general face forgery detection. In: Proceedings of the IEEE/CVF Conference on Computer Vision and Pattern Recognition, pp. 5001–5010 (2020)
28. Li, X., et al.: Sharp multiple instance learning for deepfake video detection. In: Proceedings of the 28th ACM International Conference on Multimedia, pp. 1864–1872 (2020)
29. Li, Y., Lyu, S.: Exposing deepfake videos by detecting face warping artifacts. arXiv preprint arXiv:1811.00656 (2018)
30. Li, Y., Yang, X., Sun, P., Qi, H., Lyu, S.: Celeb-df (v2): a new dataset for deepfake forensics. arXiv preprint arXiv:1909.12962 (2019)
31. Li, Y., Yang, X., Sun, P., Qi, H., Lyu, S.: Celeb-df: a large-scale challenging dataset for deepfake forensics. In: Proceedings of the IEEE/CVF Conference on Computer Vision and Pattern Recognition, pp. 3207–3216 (2020)
32. Liu, B., et al.: Negative margin matters: understanding margin in few-shot classification. arXiv preprint arXiv:2003.12060 (2020)
33. Liu, Z., Qi, X., Torr, P.H.: Global texture enhancement for fake face detection in the wild. In: Proceedings of the IEEE/CVF Conference on Computer Vision and Pattern Recognition, pp. 8060–8069 (2020)

34. Mas Montserrat, D., et al.: Deepfakes detection with automatic face weighting. In: Proceedings of the IEEE/CVF Conference on Computer Vision and Pattern Recognition Workshops, pp. 668–669 (2020)
35. Masi, I., Killekar, A., Mascarenhas, R.M., Gurudatt, S.P., AbdAlmageed, W.: Two-branch recurrent network for isolating deepfakes in videos. arXiv preprint arXiv:2008.03412 (2020)
36. Matern, F., Riess, C., Stamminger, M.: Exploiting visual artifacts to expose deepfakes and face manipulations. In: 2019 IEEE Winter Applications of Computer Vision Workshops (WACVW), pp. 83–92. IEEE (2019)
37. Mittal, T., Bhattacharya, U., Chandra, R., Bera, A., Manocha, D.: Emotions don't lie: a deepfake detection method using audio-visual affective cues. arXiv preprint arXiv:2003.06711 (2020)
38. Nguyen, H.H., Fang, F., Yamagishi, J., Echizen, I.: Multi-task learning for detecting and segmenting manipulated facial images and videos. arXiv preprint arXiv:1906.06876 (2019)
39. Qian, Q., Shang, L., Sun, B., Hu, J., Li, H., Jin, R.: Softtriple loss: deep metric learning without triplet sampling. In: Proceedings of the IEEE International Conference on Computer Vision, pp. 6450–6458 (2019)
40. Qian, Y., Yin, G., Sheng, L., Chen, Z., Shao, J.: Thinking in frequency: face forgery detection by mining frequency-aware clues. arXiv preprint arXiv:2007.09355 (2020)
41. Rahmouni, N., Nozick, V., Yamagishi, J., Echizen, I.: Distinguishing computer graphics from natural images using convolution neural networks. In: 2017 IEEE Workshop on Information Forensics and Security (WIFS), pp. 1–6. IEEE (2017)
42. Rossler, A., Cozzolino, D., Verdoliva, L., Riess, C., Thies, J., Nießner, M.: Faceforensics++: learning to detect manipulated facial images. In: Proceedings of the IEEE International Conference on Computer Vision, pp. 1–11 (2019)
43. Sabir, E., Cheng, J., Jaiswal, A., AbdAlmageed, W., Masi, I., Natarajan, P.: Recurrent convolutional strategies for face manipulation detection in videos. Interfaces (GUI) **3**(1), 80–87 (2019)
44. Song, L., Liu, B., Yin, G., Dong, X., Zhang, Y., Bai, J.X.: Tacr-net: editing on deep video and voice portraits. In: Proceedings of the 29th ACM International Conference on Multimedia, pp. 478–486 (2021)
45. Song, L., Yin, G., Liu, B., Zhang, Y., Yu, N.: Fsft-net: face transfer video generation with few-shot views. In: 2021 IEEE International Conference on Image Processing (ICIP), pp. 3582–3586. IEEE (2021)
46. Thies, J., Zollhöfer, M., Nießner, M.: Deferred neural rendering: image synthesis using neural textures. ACM Trans. Graph. (TOG) **38**(4), 1–12 (2019)
47. Tolosana, R., Romero-Tapiador, S., Fierrez, J., Vera-Rodriguez, R.: Deepfakes evolution: analysis of facial regions and fake detection performance. arXiv preprint arXiv:2004.07532 (2020)
48. Tran, D., Bourdev, L., Fergus, R., Torresani, L., Paluri, M.: Learning spatiotemporal features with 3D convolutional networks. In: Proceedings of the IEEE International Conference on Computer Vision, pp. 4489–4497 (2015)
49. Wang, H., Wu, X., Huang, Z., Xing, E.P.: High-frequency component helps explain the generalization of convolutional neural networks. In: Proceedings of the IEEE/CVF Conference on Computer Vision and Pattern Recognition, pp. 8684–8694 (2020)
50. Wang, S.Y., Wang, O., Zhang, R., Owens, A., Efros, A.A.: Cnn-generated images are surprisingly easy to spot... for now. In: Proceedings of the IEEE Conference on Computer Vision and Pattern Recognition, vol. 7 (2020)

51. Wang, Y., Dantcheva, A.: A video is worth more than 1000 lies: comparing 3dcnn approaches for detecting deepfakes. In: FG 2020, 15th IEEE International Conference on Automatic Face and Gesture Recognition, Buenos Aires, Argentina, 18–22 May 2020 (2020)
52. Zhai, A., Wu, H.Y.: Classification is a strong baseline for deep metric learning (2019)
53. Zhang, H., et al.: Resnest: split-attention networks. arXiv preprint arXiv:2004.08955 (2020)
54. Zhang, Z., Sabuncu, M.: Generalized cross entropy loss for training deep neural networks with noisy labels. Adv. Neural Inf. Process. Syst. **31**, 1–11 (2018)
55. Zhao, T., Xu, X., Xu, M., Ding, H., Xiong, Y., Xia, W.: Learning self-consistency for deepfake detection. In: Proceedings of the IEEE/CVF International Conference on Computer Vision, pp. 15023–15033 (2021)
56. Zheng, Y., Bao, J., Chen, D., Zeng, M., Wen, F.: Exploring temporal coherence for more general video face forgery detection. In: Proceedings of the IEEE/CVF International Conference on Computer Vision, pp. 15044–15054 (2021)

Real-Time Online Video Detection with Temporal Smoothing Transformers

Yue Zhao(✉) and Philipp Krähenbühl

University of Texas at Austin, Austin, TX 78712, USA
{yzhao,philkr}@cs.utexas.edu

Abstract. Streaming video recognition reasons about objects and their actions in every frame of a video. A good streaming recognition model captures both long-term dynamics and short-term changes of video. Unfortunately, in most existing methods, the computational complexity grows linearly or quadratically with the length of the considered dynamics. This issue is particularly pronounced in transformer-based architectures. To address this issue, we reformulate the cross-attention in a video transformer through the lens of kernel and apply two kinds of temporal smoothing kernel: A box kernel or a Laplace kernel. The resulting streaming attention reuses much of the computation from frame to frame, and only requires a constant time update each frame. Based on this idea, we build TeSTra, a Temporal Smoothing Transformer, that takes in arbitrarily long inputs with constant caching and computing overhead. Specifically, it runs 6× faster than equivalent sliding-window based transformers with 2,048 frames in a streaming setting. Furthermore, thanks to the increased temporal span, TeSTra achieves state-of-the-art results on THUMOS'14 and EPIC-Kitchen-100, two standard online action detection and action anticipation datasets. A real-time version of TeSTra outperforms all but one prior approaches on the THUMOS'14 dataset.

Keywords: Online action detection · Action anticipation · Transformer · Temporal smoothing kernel

1 Introduction

The problem of online action detection [10] and anticipation [29] aims to determine what action is happening or will happen shortly at each time step without seeing the future. The challenge for online action detection is (1) how to effectively retain both the long-term trends and short-term cues when encoding the history and (2) how to efficiently compute at each time step in the streaming setting when the history gets longer. Recurrent models such as LSTM [22] and GRU [7] excel at updating the output recurrently but do not benefit from increasing sequence length due to the training difficulty [49]. Attention-based models [43], like Long Short-Term Transformer (LSTR) [53], are capable of handling sequences up to 8 min long with impressive prediction results. However, in the streaming setting, the attention computation of the long-term memory

S. Avidan et al. (Eds.): ECCV 2022, LNCS 13694, pp. 485–502, 2022.
https://doi.org/10.1007/978-3-031-19830-4_28

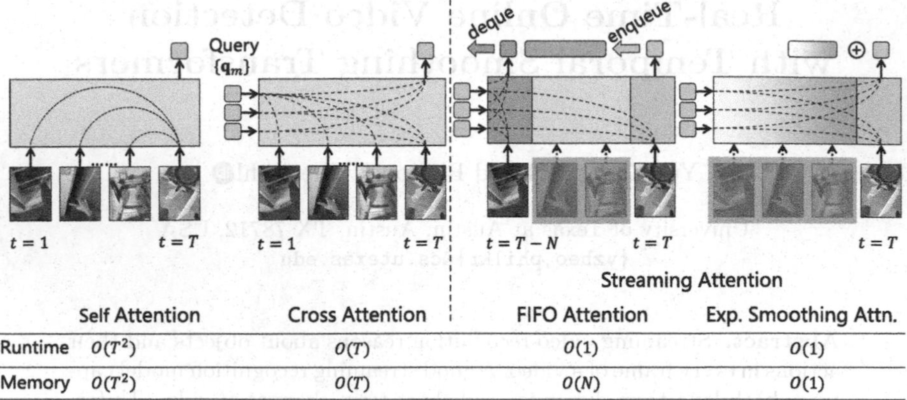

Fig. 1. A comparison of traditional attention computation (left) in streaming videos and our streaming attention (right). Unlike traditional approaches, our approach has a constant runtime per frame. Exponential smoothing attention has a constant memory footprint as well

has to be recomputed for each streaming window considered. Therefore, the computational cost per frame is proportional to the sequence length.

In this paper, we propose an effective and efficient approach, *Temporal Smoothing Transformers* (TeSTra), to encode sufficiently long history with constant inference cost at each time step. TeSTra relies on an efficient attention that reuses much of the attention computation between consecutive frames. We reformulate attention through a kernel perspective [38,42] and explore two temporal kernels: a Box kernel and a Laplace kernel. Both kernels lead to an efficient streaming attention computation. A box kernel results in a First In First Out (FIFO) attention computation with a constant runtime update, but linear memory costs. A Laplace kernel results in an exponential smoothing attention with constant runtime and memory costs. Figure 1 shows a comparison of traditional attention for streaming videos and our streaming attention. Both formulations exploit the fact that in streaming recognition queries used in cross attention are learned parameters and fixed during inference. During training, we use windowed attention in its original matrix multiplication form (with explicitly computed kernels). This allows us to enjoy all the GPU parallelism of modern transformer training. At test time, we switch to efficient streaming implementations.

To show the effectiveness of TeSTra, we conduct extensive experiments on standard benchmarks for online action detection and anticipation, namely THUMOS'14 [24] and EPIC-Kitchen-100 [9]. TeSTra achieves state-of-the-art performance on both benchmarks. Running at 142.8 FPS alone, TeSTra can serve as a building block for streaming video recognition with low latency. When we include an accelerated optical flow computing method and an image-based feature extractor, the overall system can run as fast as 41.1 FPS and achieves 67.3% mAP on THUMOS'14, outperforming all but one prior approaches. Code is publicly available at https://github.com/zhaoyue-zephyrus/TeSTra/.

2 Related Work

Online Action Detection and Anticipation. Online action detection [10], also known as early action detection [21], aims to detect the start of an action in a video stream as soon as it happens. Much of prior work builds ever longer-term temporal reasoning using various recurrent units or networks [11,13,52]. Xu *et al.* [52] perform online detection (classification) on current frame and prediction the near-future actions simultaneously. StartNet [18] decomposes the online detection into two stages: action classification and start localization. The recently proposed LSTR [53] enlarges the effective temporal context to as long as 512 s by adopting the highly flexible cross-attention mechanism in Transformer [43]. However, the induced computation cost is proportional to the temporal span. In contrast, our streaming attention incurs the same constant runtime cost independent of temporal span.

Action anticipation [19], or forecasting [29], aims to predict the action *before* it occurs. Vondrick *et al.* [44] propose to anticipate by regressing the representations of future frames from past ones. Zeng *et al.* [57] and Rhinehart *et al.* [37] use inverse reinforcement learning to perform forecasting at multiple levels. For egocentric videos anticipation may additionally incorporate the camera wearer's trajectory [35], eye gaze [32], hand-object interaction [30], and environment affordance [34]. In this paper, we handle the problem by taking longer history into account, which is a general approach to both third-person and egocentric videos.

Transformers and its Efficient Variants. Since the Transformer architecture was introduced in [43], much work has gone into improving the efficiency of dot-product attention. Low-rank approximation on attention matrix [6,47] factorizes the attention matrix into two lower-rank matrices. Different efficient learnable sparsity patterns, such as locality-sensitive hashing [28], differentiable sorting [40] or fixed patterns [5,56], reduce the total number of attention operations. Query-based cross attention mechanisms compress longer-term input into a fixed-size representation via memory [31,36] or recurrence [8]. Based on a kernel-reformation [42], Katharopoulos *et al.* [27] propose linear attention by decomposing the kernel function $\kappa(\mathbf{q}_m, \mathbf{k}_n)$ between a query-key pair into a product between the feature mapping of query and key, *i.e.* $\phi(\mathbf{q}_m)^\top \cdot \phi(\mathbf{k}_n)$. In computer vision, Transformers are made more efficient by (1) leveraging hierarchy using shifted local window [33] and pooling attention [14], (2) applying axial attention on separate dimensions [45], and (3) using asymmetric attention (cross attention) to squeeze high-dimensional inputs into tighter latent variables [26]. In speech recognition, transformers are tailored to streaming decoding by integrating recurrence [60] or memory [51]. In this paper, we follow the kernel interpretation of Tsai *et al.* [42], and show how to efficiently update streaming attention kernels.

Efficient Video Processing. Videos are notoriously expensive to process. TSN [46] suggests sampling frames sparsely and running 2D CNNs on the selected frames. MVCNN [58] and CoViAR [50] directly learn video representation from compressed videos. X3D [15] and CSN [41] reduce computation FLOPs by leveraging channel-wise separable convolution. However, 3D CNN takes video clips as input whose span can be 2–3 s, therefore may not be the best solution in a low-latency application. Par-Inception [3] tackles the latency issue by introducing depth-parallelism to the vanilla I3D [4] at increased implementation difficulty. Most of the previous methods focus on trimmed videos whose duration is often in several seconds while our method focuses on streaming videos whose length can be as long as hours. However, many of these 3D CNNs may form a good backbone to our system.

3 Preliminaries

Attention. The attention mechanism [43] is a weighted addition of the input features. The weights are guided by the similarities between the key and query elements on an input sequence:

$$\text{Attention}(\mathbf{Q}, \mathbf{X}) = \text{Softmax}\left(\frac{\mathbf{Q}\mathbf{K}^\top}{\sqrt{C}}\right) \cdot \mathbf{V} = \text{Softmax}\left(\frac{\mathbf{Q} \cdot (\mathbf{X}\mathbf{W}_k)^\top}{\sqrt{C}}\right) \cdot \mathbf{X}\mathbf{W}_v, \tag{1}$$

where $\mathbf{Q} \in \mathcal{R}^{M \times C}$ is a set of M queries, $\mathbf{X} = \left[\cdots \mathbf{x}_n \cdots\right]^\top \in \mathcal{R}^{N \times d}$ is the sequence of N input tokens, $\mathbf{W}_{k/v} \in \mathcal{R}^{d \times C}$ is the weight to map the input to key/value vector and C is the feature dimension of $\mathbf{x}_n^\top \mathbf{W}_k$. For self-attention computes queries from the inputs sequence $\mathbf{Q} = \mathbf{X}\mathbf{W}_q$ ($M = N$ in this case). Cross-attention uses a queries $\mathbf{Q}$ that do not relate to the input sequence $\mathbf{X}$ (generally $M \neq N$ in this case). Cross-attention is commonly used in the encoder-decoder architecture [43]. Cross-attention with $M \ll N$ is also used to efficiently encode large amounts of data into a fixed-size representation [26,53].

Attention as Kernels. The distance computation in attention is similar to the mechanism of kernel learning [38]. Tsai *et al.* [42] reformulated Eq. (1) from the perspective of kernels:

$$\text{Attention}(\mathbf{q}_m, \{\mathbf{x}_n\}) = \frac{\sum_{n=1}^{N} \kappa(\mathbf{q}_m, \mathbf{k}_n)\mathbf{v}_n}{\sum_{n=1}^{N} \kappa(\mathbf{q}_m, \mathbf{k}_n)}, \tag{2}$$

where $\kappa(\cdot, \cdot) : \mathcal{R}^C \times \mathcal{R}^C \to \mathcal{R}^+$ is a generalized kernel function, which depicts the similarity between the pair of input vectors. Equation (1) is equivalent to Eq. (2) for a kernel $\kappa(\mathbf{q}_m, \mathbf{k}_n) = \exp(\frac{\mathbf{q}_m^\top \mathbf{k}_n}{\sqrt{C}})$. In the next section, we show that this kernel perspective leads to an efficient streaming formulation of attention in the context of streaming video recognition.

4 Efficient Attention on Streaming Input

We use cross-attention to summarize a large stream of past frames into a fixed size context representation. We use a fixed number learned queries and variable number of keys and values from past frames as input. See Fig. 1 for an example.

In streaming tasks, we are constantly receiving input and want to generate the corresponding output on the fly. Examples include simultaneous interpretation or online detection in broadcast videos. Let $\mathbf{x}_{[1:t]} = \{\mathbf{x}_1, \mathbf{x}_2, \cdots, \mathbf{x}_t\}$ denote a sequence of encoded past video frames for the current time-step t. The encoder may use an image-based [20,25] or short-clip-based [4,15] CNN. Top-performing video models [53] summarize large parts of the video through cross-attention on either the entire sequence, *i.e.* Attention$(\mathbf{q}_1 \ldots \mathbf{q}_M, \mathbf{x}_{[1:t]})$ or a chunk of input by sliding a N-sized temporal window, *i.e.* Attention$(\mathbf{q}_1 \ldots \mathbf{q}_M, \mathbf{x}_{[t-N+1:t]})$. Mathematically, this attention operation is captured in Eq. (2). Here, a small number of queries $\{\mathbf{q}_1 \ldots \mathbf{q}_M\}$ summarize a large temporal context. Queries combine learned parameters $\{\boldsymbol{\lambda}_1 \ldots \boldsymbol{\lambda}_M\}$ with a temporal embedding ω_t of the current frame: $\mathbf{q}_m = \boldsymbol{\lambda}_m + \omega_t$. Keys $\{\mathbf{k}_1 \ldots \mathbf{k}_t\}$ combine a frame-level embeddings $\mathbf{f}_n = \mathbf{W}_k^\top \mathbf{x}_n$ with a temporal embedding ω_t: $\mathbf{k}_n = \mathbf{f}_n + \omega_n$. Values $\{\mathbf{v}_1 \ldots \mathbf{v}_t\}$ use the same frame-level features $\mathbf{v}_n = \mathbf{W}_v^\top \mathbf{x}_n$. In this setup, keys and values of past frames remain unchanged, learned queries are constant during inference, only the temporal query embedding changes frame to frame. This changing temporal embedding does change the attention kernel κ for each new frame. This means in a streaming setting, we have no choice but to recompute the entire attention operation frame after frame. This recomputation grows linearly with the size N of the temporal context considered. Next, we show how a reformulation of the attention mechanism leads to a much more efficient streaming evaluation.

Streaming Attention. Note, that both queries and keys combine a temporal and feature-level embedding in their distance kernel $\kappa(\mathbf{q}_m, \mathbf{k}_n) = \kappa(\boldsymbol{\lambda}_m + \omega_t, \mathbf{f}_n + \omega_n)$. In *Streaming Attention*, we simple split this kernel into temporal and feature component: $K(\omega_t, \omega_n)\kappa(\boldsymbol{\lambda}_m, \mathbf{f}_n)$. The *Streaming Attention* operation reduces to

$$\text{Stream-Attention}(\mathbf{q}_m, \mathbf{x}_{[1:t]}) = \frac{\sum_{n=1}^{t} K(\omega_t, \omega_n)\kappa(\boldsymbol{\lambda}_m, \mathbf{f}_n)\mathbf{v}_n}{\sum_{n=1}^{t} K(\omega_t, \omega_n)\kappa(\boldsymbol{\lambda}_m, \mathbf{f}_n)}. \tag{3}$$

Most of the features and kernels used in this attention block remain constant throughout the streaming setting. Moving from timestep t to $t+1$ only changes the temporal kernel $K(\omega_t, \omega_n)$ to $K(\omega_{t+1}, \omega_n)$ and adds one more element $(\mathbf{f}_{t+1}, \mathbf{v}_{t+1})$. Because of the change in the temporal kernel, a naive evaluation of streaming attention (3) still requires a linear runtime in the size of the temporal context. However, the right choice of a temporal kernel can alleviate this. Here, we explore two kernels: A box (or uniform) kernel $K_B(\omega_t, \omega_n) = 1_{[t-n<N]}$ and a Laplace kernel $K_L(\omega_t, \omega_n) = \exp(-\lambda(t-n))$ for $\lambda > 0$. Each of these kernels leads to an efficient streaming attention mechanism. A box kernel results in first-in-first-out (FIFO) attentionw while a Laplace kernel leads to exponential smoothing attention. Figure 2 provides an overview of both kernels.

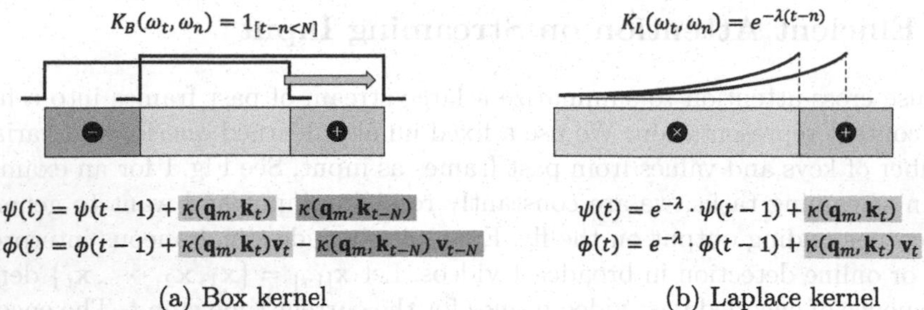

$K_B(\omega_t, \omega_n) = 1_{[t-n<N]}$
$K_L(\omega_t, \omega_n) = e^{-\lambda(t-n)}$
$\psi(t) = \psi(t-1) + \kappa(\mathbf{q}_m, \mathbf{k}_t) - \kappa(\mathbf{q}_m, \mathbf{k}_{t-N})$
$\phi(t) = \phi(t-1) + \kappa(\mathbf{q}_m, \mathbf{k}_t)\mathbf{v}_t - \kappa(\mathbf{q}_m, \mathbf{k}_{t-N})\mathbf{v}_{t-N}$
$\psi(t) = e^{-\lambda} \cdot \psi(t-1) + \kappa(\mathbf{q}_m, \mathbf{k}_t)$
$\phi(t) = e^{-\lambda} \cdot \phi(t-1) + \kappa(\mathbf{q}_m, \mathbf{k}_t)\mathbf{v}_t$
(a) Box kernel
(b) Laplace kernel

Fig. 2. A visualization of a box kernel (a) and Laplace kernel (b) and their streaming computation

FIFO Attention. Let us define the numerator and denominator of Eq. (3) to be two intermediate variables

$$\text{Stream-Attention}(\mathbf{q}_m, \mathbf{x}_{[1:t]}) = \frac{\phi(t)}{\psi(t)}. \tag{4}$$

Both $\phi(t) = \sum_{n=1}^{t} K_B(\omega_t, \omega_n)\kappa(\boldsymbol{\lambda}_m, \mathbf{f}_n)\mathbf{v}_n$ and $\psi(t) = \sum_{n=1}^{t} K_B(\omega_t, \omega_n)\kappa(\boldsymbol{\lambda}_m, \mathbf{f}_n)$ are updated by the following recursion as the streaming attention progresses:

$$\begin{aligned}\phi(t+1) &= \phi(t) + \kappa(\boldsymbol{\lambda}_m, \mathbf{f}_t)\mathbf{v}_t - \kappa(\boldsymbol{\lambda}_m, \mathbf{f}_{t-N})\mathbf{v}_{t-N} \\ \psi(t+1) &= \psi(t) + \kappa(\boldsymbol{\lambda}_m, \mathbf{f}_t)\mathbf{v}_t - \kappa(\boldsymbol{\lambda}_m, \mathbf{f}_{t-N}),\end{aligned} \tag{5}$$

where $\kappa(\boldsymbol{\lambda}_m, \mathbf{f}_{t-N}) = 0$ and $\mathbf{v}_{t-N} = 0$ for $t \leq N$, $\phi(0) = 0$ and $\psi(0) = 0$.

Like a FIFO queue, we keep track of $\phi(t)$ and $\psi(t)$ and update them by subtracting the quantity contributed by the input at time $(t-N)$ and adding up the one at time t in the long run. Therefore, we call this formulation *FIFO-Attention*. The advantage of FIFO-Attention is that the computational cost becomes $O(MC)$ for M queries and values of C channels. Neither the effective window size N nor the actual time-step t influences the runtime. However, the subtraction operation in Eq. (5) requires us to keep a window of features and kernel values in memory. Hence, the memory complexity is still $O(N)$. The Laplace kernel addresses this issue.

Exponential Smoothing Attention. The Laplace kernel K_L allows for an even more efficient recursive update:

$$\begin{aligned}\tilde{\phi}(t) &= e^{-\lambda}\tilde{\phi}(t-1) + \kappa(\boldsymbol{\lambda}_m, \mathbf{f}_t)\mathbf{v}_t \\ \tilde{\psi}(t) &= e^{-\lambda}\tilde{\psi}(t-1) + \kappa(\boldsymbol{\lambda}_m, \mathbf{f}_t),\end{aligned} \tag{6}$$

where $\tilde{\phi}(0) = 0$ and $\tilde{\psi}(0) = 0$. The parameters λ controls the temporal extent of the attention. The above operation (6) is known as exponential smoothing [23]. Therefore we name this attention *Exponential Smoothing Attention*, or *ES-Attention* for short. Both ES- and FIFO-Attention reduce to the same operation if $\lambda = 0$ and the windows size $N \to \infty$. The time complexity of ES-Attention is

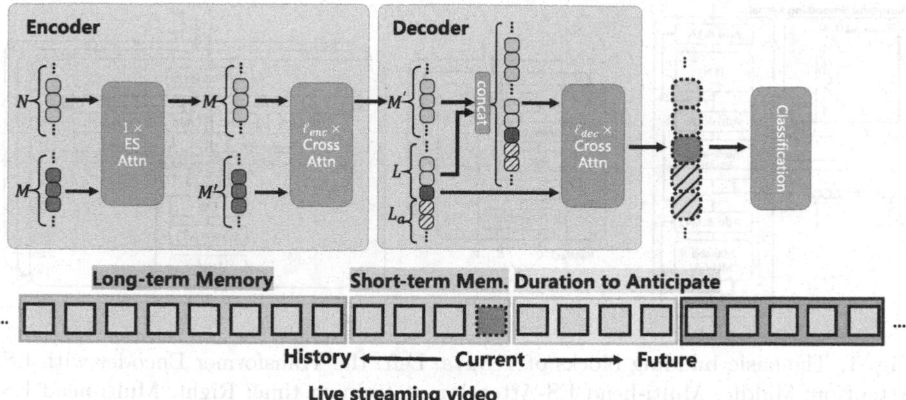

Fig. 3. Overview of our streaming attention architecture TeSTra. The basic setup follows LSTR [53]: A long-term memory compresses a long temporal history into M representative queries. A short-term attention mechanism uses the compressed memory and a short history of frames to compute current and future actions. The main advantage of TeSTra is that the long-memory incurs only constant cost, and thus allows for much more efficient long-term reasoning

also constant in the temporal window considered $O(MC)$. More importantly, the space complexity reduces from $O(N)$ to $O(1)$ since we only maintain $\tilde{\psi}$, $\tilde{\phi}$ and no longer keep values in our window around. Exponential smoothing instead slowly reduces the influence of older keys and values in the attention.

Video Recognition with Streaming Attention. The streaming attention can replace the vanilla cross-attention in current Transformer architectures with minimal modification. Specifically, we follow LSTR architecture [53] for all our experiments, due to its state-of-the-art performance on online action detection. The overall architecture of TeSTra is sketched in Fig. 3. Given a sequence of encoded vectors $\mathbf{x}_{[1:t]} = \{\mathbf{x}_1, \mathbf{x}_2, \cdots, \mathbf{x}_t\}$, where t refers to the current time stamp, we divide the historic frames into two parts: short-term memory $\mathbf{x}_{[t-L+1:t]}$ if size $L \leq 32$ and long-term memory which contains the rest of distant inputs, namely $\mathbf{x}_{[1:t-L]}$. The architecture follows an encoder-decoder [43,53] design. The encoder module encodes the long-term memory into $M = 16$ query features. The decoder uses the query features and short-term memory to predict current and anticipated actions.

The encoder has two stages of memory compression. First, it uses an ES-Attention-based Transformer decoder unit [43] to compress the long-term memory into M latent vectors $\mathbf{Z}$ using learnable queries $\mathbf{Q}$.

$$\begin{aligned}\mathbf{Q}' &= \text{Attention}(\mathbf{Q}, \mathbf{Q}),\\ \mathbf{Z}' &= \text{ES-Attention}(\sigma(\mathbf{Q}'), \mathbf{X}_{[1:t-L]}),\\ \mathbf{Z} &= \text{FFN}(\sigma(\mathbf{Z}')),\end{aligned} \tag{7}$$

where σ denotes the nonlinear mapping which is composed of a skip connection with $\mathbf{Q}$ followed by a LayerNorm [1]. Next, the compressed vectors are further

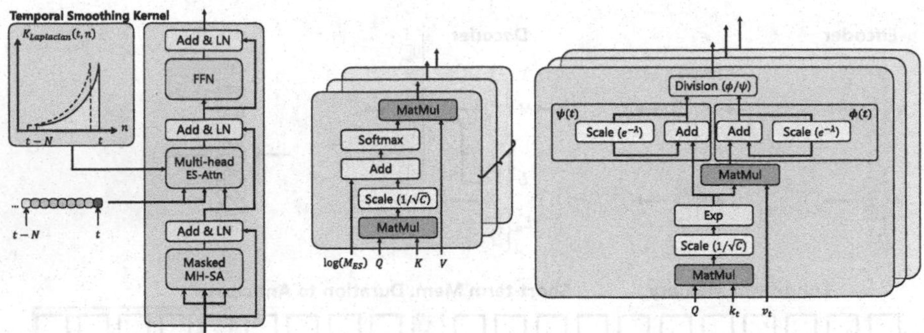

Fig. 4. The basic building blocks of TeSTra. Left: the Transformer Encoder with ES-Attention; Middle: Multi-head ES-Attention at training time; Right: Multi-head ES-Attention at inference time

cross-attended by M' learnable queries through ℓ_{enc} decoder units into $\mathbf{Z}_{\ell_{enc}}$. Strictly speaking, it should be possible to learn $\mathbf{Q}'$ directly. However, the training dynamics of transformer work out better using a self-attention block first. Figure 4 shows an overview of the encoder.

The decoder uses the short-term memory as queries to attend the compressed memory and retrieve relevant information through a stack of ℓ_{dec} decoder units.

$$\begin{aligned} \mathbf{X}'_{[t-L+1:t]} &= \text{Attention}(\mathbf{X}_{[t-L+1:t]}, \mathbf{X}_{[t-L+1:t]}), \\ \mathbf{O}' &= \text{Attention}(\mathbf{X}'_{[t-L+1:t]}, \left[\mathbf{Z}_{\ell_{enc}} \parallel \mathbf{X}_{[t-L+1:t]}\right]), \\ \mathbf{O} &= \text{FFN}(\sigma(\mathbf{O}')), \end{aligned} \tag{8}$$

In Eq. (8), we construct the key/value tokens by concatenating $[\cdot \parallel \cdot]$ both the compressed long-term memory and short-term memory to incorporate all the known historic information. This proves to be effective for action anticipation, where the closer memory is more important to indicate the upcoming action. The L output vectors are then passed through a linear layer to produces the scores $\mathbf{s}_{[t-L+1:t]} \in \mathcal{R}^{L\times(K+1)}$ over K action classes plus one non-action (background) class[1]. At inference time, we take the score $\mathbf{s}_t$ to be online detection result. In action anticipation, the frames in the anticipating duration are not observable. We thus attach L_a learnable tokens after short-term memory predict L_a anticipated actions $\mathbf{s}_{[t+1:t+L_a]}$.

Training TeSTra. At inference time, we naturally apply the recursion in Eq. (6) in the streaming setting. During training, however, it is computationally inefficient to feed all historic inputs and update them recursively on a modern GPU architecture. To handle this, we cut the video into a clip $\mathbf{x}_{t-L-N+1:t}$. Multiple clips share the same length N and thus can be packed into a batch. Furthermore, instead of recursion, we compute the attention in matrix form:

[1] $\mathbf{s}_t \in \mathcal{R}^K$ if the background class is absent.

$$\text{ES-Attention}_{train}(\mathbf{Q}'', \mathbf{X}) = \text{Softmax}\left(\log(\mathbf{M}_{ES}) + \frac{\mathbf{Q}''\mathbf{K}^\top}{\sqrt{C}}\right) \cdot \mathbf{V}, \tag{9}$$

$$\mathbf{M}_{ES} = \begin{bmatrix} e^{-\lambda(N-1)} & e^{-\lambda(N-2)} & \dots & 1 \\ e^{-\lambda(N-1)} & e^{-\lambda(N-2)} & \dots & 1 \\ \vdots & \vdots & & \vdots \\ e^{-\lambda(N-1)} & e^{-\lambda(N-2)} & \dots & 1 \end{bmatrix}, \tag{10}$$

where $\log(\cdot)$ takes the element-wise logarithm of a matrix and the exponential smoothing matrix $\mathbf{M}_{ES} \in \mathcal{R}^{M \times N}$ is a Vandermonde matrix. Since we train on the windowed input and test on un-windowed streaming input, we select a decay factor λ and window size N such that $e^{-\lambda(N-1)}$ is sufficiently small. This minimizes the effect of a potential train-test gap. Figure 4 shows the difference between training and inference for streaming attention.

We use the cross-entropy loss to predict both current and anticipated actions. Following [19,53], we predict actions for all frames in short-term memory for a stronger supervisory signal. We use a causal attention mask [43] on the short-term memory to avoid future actions from influencing our predictions.

5 Experiments

5.1 Experimental Setup

Datasets. We conduct experiments on THUMOS'14 [24] and Epic-Kitchen-100 (EK100) [9]. THUMOS'14 contains 413 untrimmed videos annotated with 20 actions. We train our model on the validation set (200 videos) and evaluate on the test set (213 videos). Epic-Kitchen-100 contains 100 h of egocentric videos with 90K action segments. The narrations are mapped into 97 verb classes and 300 noun classes. We follow the train/val split given by Furnari *et al.* [16].

Evaluation Metrics. For THUMOS'14, we measure the performance of both online action detection and anticipation with per-frame mean average precision (mAP). Anticipation mAP uses an anticipation period τ_o which varies from 0.25 s to 2.0 s with a stride of 0.25 s. Online detection mAP is as a special case of anticipation mAP at $\tau_o = 0$. EK-100 uses mean Top-5 Verb/Noun/Action Recall to measure anticipation performance per instance with a predefined $\tau_o = 1$ s [9].

Implementation Details. On THUMOS14, we pre-process the videos into 24 FPS, extract the two-stream deep features pretrained on ActivityNet or Kinetics following Xu *et al.* [53]. The visual stream is a ResNet-50 [20] while the motion stream uses BN-Inception [25]. On EK100, we pre-process the videos into 30 FPS and fine-tune the two-stream TSN [46] on EK100 action classification task with ImageNet-pretrained parameters, following Furnari *et al.* [16]. Our model is not restricted to using 2D CNNs as backbone. Efficient 3D CNN such as X3D [15] is also applicable but the longer input span might cause higher latency.

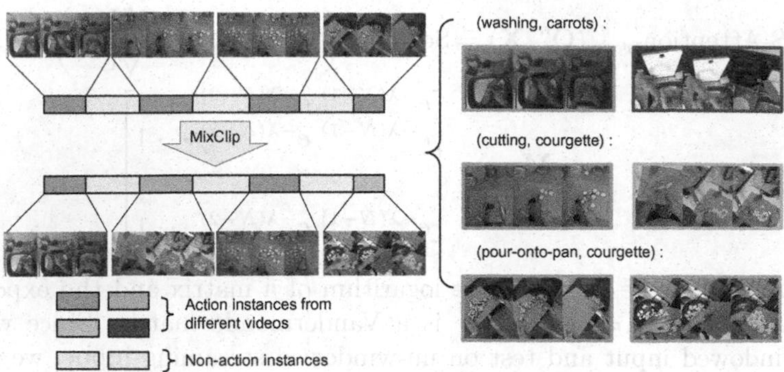

Fig. 5. Illustration of MixClip. In the example sequence, we have 4 action instances and 2 of them are replaced by another clip that comes from another video but is annotated with the same action category

The training procedure of TeSTra on THUMOS'14 follows Xu *et al.* [53] for fair comparison. Specifically, we train TeSTra with batch size of 16 for 25 epochs using Adam optimizer with a weight decay of 5e–5 and a base learning rate of 7e–5. We apply a cosine annealing schedule with linear warm-up, *i.e.* the learning rate linearly increases from 0 to 7e–5 in the first 10 epochs and then decays following a cosine function.

MixClip. The model takes as input both short clips as working memory and frames in the longer history as long-term memory. The duration of long history is significantly larger (often 10×) than the short clip. This means that two neighboring clips of interest share a large portion of historical frames. This causes the model to overfit to those scene-related cues and fail to generalize to unseen scenarios. To resolve this, we propose a simple augmentation technique called *MixClip* which increases the diversity of long history by composing short clips from different recordings into each other.

Assume that the long memory is composed of a sequence of action instances $\{(t_i^{(s)}, t_i^{(e)}, a_i)\}$, where $t_i^{(s)}, t_i^{(e)}$ denotes the start and end time while a_i denotes the action label. With probability p_{mc}, each of the action instances may be replaced with another instance with the same label from a different video. This input feature sequence is randomly cropped if the new instance's duration longer. Otherwise, the input feature sequence is padded to ensure that the length of history is unchanged for ease of implementation. Figure 5 gives an illustration.

MixClip is inspired by some popular augmentation techniques widely used in image classifications, such as CutOut [12], Mixup [59], and CutMix [54].

5.2 Main Results

THUMOS'14. We conduct both online action detection and anticipation experiments on THUMOS'14. In both tasks, the backbone network from which

Table 1. Result of online action detection on THUMOS'14. $^{\natural}$ denotes optical flow computed by NVIDIA Optical Flow SDK, a faster alternative to TV-L1 [55]. More detailed runtime analysis will be provided in Sect. 5.4

(a) Using ANet-pretrained feature

Method	mAP
RED [17]	45.3
IDN [13]	50.0
TRN [52]	47.2
OadTR [48]	58.3
LSTR [53]	65.3
Ours	**68.2**

(b) Using Kinetics-pretrained feature

Method	mAP
IDN [13]	60.3
TRN [52]	62.1
OadTR [48]	65.2
LSTR [53]	69.5
Ours$^{\natural}$	<u>67.3</u>
Ours	**71.2**

Table 2. Result of online action anticipation on THUMOS'14. † was reproduced by us because LSTR [53] only reported ActivityNet-pretrained results

Method	Pre-train	mAP@τ_o								Average
		0.25	0.50	0.75	1.0	1.25	1.50	1.75	2.0	
RED [17]	ANet1.3	45.3	42.1	39.6	37.5	35.8	34.4	33.2	32.1	37.5
TRN [52]		45.1	42.4	40.7	39.1	37.7	36.4	35.3	34.3	38.9
TTM [48]		45.9	43.7	42.4	41.0	39.9	39.4	37.9	37.3	40.9
LSTR [53]		–	–	–	–	–	–	–	–	50.1
Ours		64.7	61.8	58.7	55.7	53.2	51.1	49.2	47.8	**55.3**
TTM [48]	K400	46.8	45.5	44.6	43.6	41.9	41.1	40.4	38.7	42.8
LSTR† [53]		60.4	58.6	56.0	53.3	50.9	48.9	47.1	45.7	52.6
Ours		66.2	63.5	60.5	57.4	54.8	52.6	50.5	48.9	**56.8**

the feature is extracted is pretrained on either ActivityNet v1.3 [2] or Kinetics [4]. Table 1 shows the results of online action detection. TeSTra surpasses the previous states-of-the-art by a large margin. We also adopt NVIDIA Optical Flow SDK (NVOFA)[2] for faster optical flow computation. NVOFA can run as fast as 1K FPS on a 240×180 image sequence on a modern GPU. We denote the model that takes NVOFA optical flow as input to be TeSTra$^{\natural}$. We observe some performance drop, but an mAP of 67.3% is still competitive. Most importantly, the runtime of the entire pipeline is significantly sped up. More detailed discussion on runtime analysis will be provided in Sect. 5.4. All results use ES-Attention.

Table 2 shows the results of online action anticipation. TeSTra with Kinetics-pretrained feature achieves an average mAP of 56.8%, outperforming all previous methods. For fair comparison, we also rerun LSTR [53] using the same Kinetics-pretrained feature. This improved LSTR is still 4% below TeSTra.

[2] https://developer.nvidia.com/opticalflow-sdk.

Table 3. Result of action anticipation on EK100. The upper half lists RGB-only methods; in lower half all types of inputs are allowed

Method	Input	Pre-train	Overall			Unseen			Tail		
			Verb	Noun	Action	Verb	Noun	Action	Verb	Noun	Action
RULSTM [16]	RGB	IN-1k	27.5	29.0	13.3	29.8	23.8	13.1	19.9	21.4	10.6
AVT [19]		IN-1k	27.2	30.7	13.6	–	–	–	–	–	–
AVT [19]		IN-21k	30.2	31.7	14.9	–	–	–	–	–	–
Ours		IN-1k	26.8	36.2	17.0	27.1	30.1	13.3	19.3	28.6	13.7
RULSTM [16]	RGB +OF +Obj	IN-1k	27.8	30.8	14.0	28.8	27.2	14.2	19.8	22.0	11.1
TempAgg [39]		IN-1k	23.2	31.4	14.7	28.0	26.2	14.5	14.5	22.5	11.8
AVT+ [19]		IN-1k	25.5	31.8	14.8	25.5	23.6	11.5	18.5	25.8	12.6
AVT+ [19]		IN-21k	28.2	32.0	15.9	29.5	23.9	11.9	21.1	25.8	14.1
Ours	RGB+OF	IN-1k	30.8	35.8	17.6	29.6	26.0	12.8	23.2	29.2	14.2

EK100. We compare TeSTra with prior works on the EPIC-Kitchen-100 action anticipation track [9] in Table 3. We split the results into two halves: the upper half contains methods with only RGB inputs and the lower half uses additional information, such as optical flow and object feature. Using the same ImageNet-1k-pretrained feature, TeSTra significantly outperforms RULSTM [16] and AVT [19] on the action-level recall. The improvement is most pronounced in the increase noun-level recall. This demonstrates the effectiveness of incorporating longer input for anticipation. The long-memory recalls many objects that appeared previously. TeSTra with RGB+OF achieves 4.4% higher verb-level recall than TeSTra with only RGB. One reason for this our early-fusion. Unlike late-fusion approaches, RULSTM and AVT+, we concatenate RGB and optical-flow feature at the beginning so that motion-related feature can be more effectively leveraged. Again, all results use ES-Attention.

5.3 Ablation Studies

We conduct ablation experiments on EK100 to study the role of each module in the architecture. Our full ablations uses the RGB-only model, but conclusions generally hold for two-stream input as well.

Temporal Smoothing Kernels. We first verify the correctness of the temporal smoothing kernels at inference time in Table 4. If we apply the box kernel and apply the FIFO recursion defined in Eq. (5), the result is 16.14%. However, if we use the exponential smoothing recursion defined in Eq. (6) with decay factor $\lambda = 0$, action recall drops by $0.2 \sim 0.4\%$ on unseen and tail classes. This indicates the necessity to cache historic elements and pop them when the queue becomes full. When using the Laplace kernel, we compare batch mode where windowed attention is computed using Eq. (9) and stream mode where exponential smoothing recursion is computed using Eq. (6). The results are consistent (less than 0.05% difference).

Table 4. Temporal smoothing kernels. Using explicit windowed-attention and stream-attention under the Laplace kernel yield consistent results

Kernel type	Test mode	Overall	Unseen	Tail
		Act. rec.	Act. rec.	Act. rec.
Box	FIFO (Eq. (5))	16.14	12.64	12.89
Box	ES (Eq. (6); $\lambda = 0$)	16.08	12.22	12.70
Laplace	ES (Eq. (9))	16.95	13.33	13.73
Laplace	ES (Eq. (6))	16.94	13.28	13.72

Table 5. Ablation studies on position embeddings. Temporal position embeddings are unnecessary for long-term memory, justifying our design of separate the temporal smoothing kernel and feature vector

PE @ long memory	PE @ short memory	Overall act. rec.
✗	✓	17.0
✓	✓	16.8
✗	✗	15.7

Effectiveness of Positional Embedding. The rationale behind streaming attention is that we can separate the attention kernel into temporal and feature components. To justify this, we add a temporal positional embedding in the long-term memory and observe no performance improvement from Table 5. We also try to remove the temporal embedding in the short-term memory but this changes the result significantly (–1.3%).

Effectiveness of MixClip. Table 6a shows the effect of MixClip rate on the anticipation result. When no MixClip is applied, the baseline drops to 15.5% action recall. The performance consistently improves with MixClip and achieves the best (17.0%) at $p_{mc} = 0.5$.

Fusing Long- and Short-Term Memory. Table 6b compares different ways of fusing long- and short-term memory. The naive way is to treat long- and short-term memory separately, *i.e.* (1) use the TeSTra encoder to compress distant inputs and (2) use closer inputs as queries in the TeSTra decoder to attend to this compressed set of vectors. We observe that this no-fuse approach achieves 15.9% which is even 0.2% lower than short-memory-only baseline, where $N = 0$ and the TeSTra decoder is instantiated by self-attention. This indicates that we might need to incorporate the relationship within the short-term memory too. To achieve this, we try to augment long-term memory by attaching short-term memory, denoted by "@ long mem.", but see no significant improvement. It might be because long-term memory is much longer than the short-term one so

Table 6. Ablation studies on MixClip and long-/short-term memory fusing

(a) The effect of MixClip

MixClip rate	0	0.2	0.5	0.8
Overall v. rec.	25.8	26.0	26.8	26.2
Overall n. rec.	34.6	35.3	36.2	35.2
Overall act. rec.	15.5	16.0	17.0	16.2

(b) Long- and short-term memory fusion

How to fuse	Overall act. rec.
w/o. long mem.	16.1
no fuse	15.9
@ long mem.	16.0
@ comp. mem.	17.0

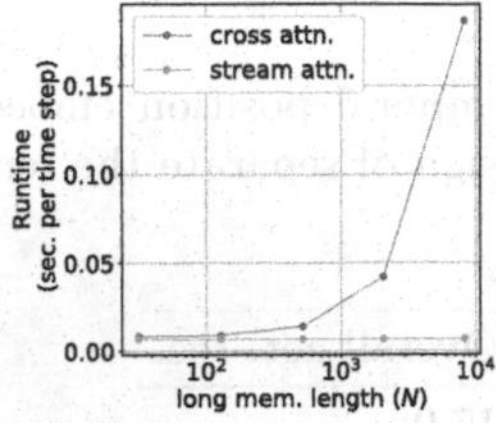

Fig. 6. Runtime comparison between vanilla cross attention and our exponential smoothing attention

Table 7. Runtime profile (in FPS) for the entire detection system. Real-time TeSTra uses NVOFA optical-flow while the default one uses TV-L1 [55]

	OF comp.	RGB feat.	OF feat.	TeSTra	Total
Ours$^{\lightning}$	1,000	150.0	104.7	142.8	41.1
Ours	19.3				12.6

that the short-term information is overwhelmed at the first stage of compression. Since the memory length after compressed is in the same order as the short-term memory, we concatenate both ("@ comp. mem.") and get 17.0% action recall, improving the naive way by 1.1%.

5.4 Runtime Analysis

Finally, we study the runtime speed of TeSTra using an NVIDIA Quadro RTX 6000 GPU. Figure 6 shows the comparison of inference speed between LSTR with cross attention and TeSTra with ES-Attention. We choose the length of the long memory N to be $\{32, 128, 512, 2048, 8196\}$. We can clearly see that the runtime per time step scales linearly for cross-attention-based LSTR but keeps constant for TeSTra. Specifically, TeSTra runs at a speed of 142.8 FPS. If we integrate TeSTra into the online detection system, we need to take into account of the computation overhead by the optical flow computation and feature extraction. The runtime profile is summarized in Table 7. The full TeSTra runs at 12.6 FPS. The bottleneck is computing optical flow using TV-L1 algorithm [55]. Using the NVOFA, the real-time TeSTra can run at 41.1 FPS.

6 Conclusion

We propose stream attention based on the kernel-based reformulation of cross-attention and apply two kinds of temporal smoothing kernels that reduce the inference computation to constant cost per frame. The resultant temporal smoothing transformer achieves excellent performance while running at a low latency. We hope that our design can shed some light on developing more efficient models for long-term videos understanding.

Acknowledgement. This material is in part based upon work supported by the National Science Foundation under Grant No. IIS-1845485, IIS-2006820, and the NSF Institute for Foundations of Machine Learning.

References

1. Ba, J.L., Kiros, J.R., Hinton, G.E.: Layer normalization. arXiv preprint arXiv:1607.06450 (2016)
2. Caba Heilbron, F., Escorcia, V., Ghanem, B., Carlos Niebles, J.: Activitynet: a large-scale video benchmark for human activity understanding. In: CVPR (2015)
3. Carreira, J., Pătrăucean, V., Mazare, L., Zisserman, A., Osindero, S.: Massively parallel video networks. In: Ferrari, V., Hebert, M., Sminchisescu, C., Weiss, Y. (eds.) ECCV 2018. LNCS, vol. 11208, pp. 680–697. Springer, Cham (2018). https://doi.org/10.1007/978-3-030-01225-0_40
4. Carreira, J., Zisserman, A.: Quo vadis, action recognition? a new model and the kinetics dataset. In: CVPR (2017)
5. Child, R., Gray, S., Radford, A., Sutskever, I.: Generating long sequences with sparse transformers. arXiv preprint arXiv:1904.10509 (2019)
6. Choromanski, K.M., et al.: Rethinking attention with performers. In: ICLR (2021)
7. Chung, J., Gulcehre, C., Cho, K., Bengio, Y.: Empirical evaluation of gated recurrent neural networks on sequence modeling. In: Deep Learning and Representation Learning Workshop (2014)
8. Dai, Z., Yang, Z., Yang, Y., Carbonell, J.G., Le, Q., Salakhutdinov, R.: Transformer-xl: attentive language models beyond a fixed-length context. In: ACL (2019)
9. Damen, D., et al.: Rescaling egocentric vision: collection, pipeline and challenges for EPIC-KITCHENS-100. Int. J. Comput. Vision **130**(1), 33–55 (2021). https://doi.org/10.1007/s11263-021-01531-2
10. De Geest, R., Gavves, E., Ghodrati, A., Li, Z., Snoek, C., Tuytelaars, T.: Online action detection. In: Leibe, B., Matas, J., Sebe, N., Welling, M. (eds.) ECCV 2016. LNCS, vol. 9909, pp. 269–284. Springer, Cham (2016). https://doi.org/10.1007/978-3-319-46454-1_17
11. De Geest, R., Tuytelaars, T.: Modeling temporal structure with LSTM for online action detection. In: WACV (2018)
12. DeVries, T., Taylor, G.W.: Improved regularization of convolutional neural networks with cutout. arXiv preprint arXiv:1708.04552 (2017)
13. Eun, H., Moon, J., Park, J., Jung, C., Kim, C.: Learning to discriminate information for online action detection. In: CVPR (2020)
14. Fan, H., et al.: Multiscale vision transformers. In: ICCV (2021)

15. Feichtenhofer, C.: X3D: expanding architectures for efficient video recognition. In: CVPR (2020)
16. Furnari, A., Farinella, G.M.: Rolling-unrolling LSTMs for action anticipation from first-person video. TPAMI **43**, 4021–4036 (2020)
17. Gao, J., Yang, Z., Nevatia, R.: Red: reinforced encoder-decoder networks for action anticipation. In: BMVC (2017)
18. Gao, M., Xu, M., Davis, L.S., Socher, R., Xiong, C.: Startnet: online detection of action start in untrimmed videos. In: ICCV (2019)
19. Girdhar, R., Grauman, K.: Anticipative video transformer. In: ICCV (2021)
20. He, K., Zhang, X., Ren, S., Sun, J.: Deep residual learning for image recognition. In: CVPR (2016)
21. Hoai, M., De la Torre, F.: Max-margin early event detectors. IJCV **107**(2), 191–202 (2014)
22. Hochreiter, S., Schmidhuber, J.: Long short-term memory. Neural Comput. **9**(8), 1735–1780 (1997)
23. Holt, C.C.: Forecasting seasonals and trends by exponentially weighted moving averages. Int. J. Forecast. **20**(1), 5–10 (2004)
24. Idrees, H., et al.: The THUMOS challenge on action recognition for videos "in the wild". In: CVIU (2016). http://arxiv.org/abs/1604.06182
25. Ioffe, S., Szegedy, C.: Batch normalization: accelerating deep network training by reducing internal covariate shift. In: ICML (2015)
26. Jaegle, A., Gimeno, F., Brock, A., Vinyals, O., Zisserman, A., Carreira, J.: Perceiver: general perception with iterative attention. In: ICML (2021)
27. Katharopoulos, A., Vyas, A., Pappas, N., Fleuret, F.: Transformers are rnns: fast autoregressive transformers with linear attention. In: ICML (2020)
28. Kitaev, N., Kaiser, L., Levskaya, A.: Reformer: the efficient transformer. In: ICLR (2020)
29. Kitani, K.M., Ziebart, B.D., Bagnell, J.A., Hebert, M.: Activity forecasting. In: Fitzgibbon, A., Lazebnik, S., Perona, P., Sato, Y., Schmid, C. (eds.) ECCV 2012. LNCS, vol. 7575, pp. 201–214. Springer, Heidelberg (2012). https://doi.org/10.1007/978-3-642-33765-9_15
30. Koppula, H., Saxena, A.: Learning spatio-temporal structure from rgb-d videos for human activity detection and anticipation. In: ICML (2013)
31. Lei, J., Wang, L., Shen, Y., Yu, D., Berg, T., Bansal, M.: Mart: memory-augmented recurrent transformer for coherent video paragraph captioning. In: ACL (2020)
32. Li, Y., Liu, M., Rehg, J.M.: In the eye of beholder: joint learning of gaze and actions in first person video. In: Ferrari, V., Hebert, M., Sminchisescu, C., Weiss, Y. (eds.) ECCV 2018. LNCS, vol. 11209, pp. 639–655. Springer, Cham (2018). https://doi.org/10.1007/978-3-030-01228-1_38
33. Liu, Z., et al.: Swin transformer: hierarchical vision transformer using shifted windows. In: ICCV (2021)
34. Nagarajan, T., Li, Y., Feichtenhofer, C., Grauman, K.: Ego-topo: environment affordances from egocentric video. In: CVPR (2020)
35. Park, H.S., Hwang, J.J., Niu, Y., Shi, J.: Egocentric future localization. In: CVPR (2016)
36. Rae, J.W., Potapenko, A., Jayakumar, S.M., Hillier, C., Lillicrap, T.P.: Compressive transformers for long-range sequence modelling. In: ICLR (2020)
37. Rhinehart, N., Kitani, K.M.: First-person activity forecasting with online inverse reinforcement learning. In: ICCV (2017)

38. Schölkopf, B., Smola, A.J., Bach, F., et al.: Learning with Kernels: Support Vector Machines, Regularization, Optimization, and Beyond. MIT press, Cambridge (2002)
39. Sener, F., Singhania, D., Yao, A.: Temporal aggregate representations for long-range video understanding. In: Vedaldi, A., Bischof, H., Brox, T., Frahm, J.-M. (eds.) ECCV 2020. LNCS, vol. 12361, pp. 154–171. Springer, Cham (2020). https://doi.org/10.1007/978-3-030-58517-4_10
40. Tay, Y., Bahri, D., Yang, L., Metzler, D., Juan, D.C.: Sparse sinkhorn attention. In: ICML (2020)
41. Tran, D., Wang, H., Torresani, L., Feiszli, M.: Video classification with channel-separated convolutional networks. In: ICCV (2019)
42. Tsai, Y.H.H., Bai, S., Yamada, M., Morency, L.P., Salakhutdinov, R.: Transformer dissection: an unified understanding for transformer's attention via the lens of kernel. In: EMNLP (2019)
43. Vaswani, A., et al.: Attention is all you need. In: NeurIPS (2017)
44. Vondrick, C., Pirsiavash, H., Torralba, A.: Anticipating visual representations from unlabeled video. In: CVPR (2016)
45. Wang, H., Zhu, Y., Green, B., Adam, H., Yuille, A., Chen, L.-C.: Axial-DeepLab: stand-alone axial-attention for panoptic segmentation. In: Vedaldi, A., Bischof, H., Brox, T., Frahm, J.-M. (eds.) ECCV 2020. LNCS, vol. 12349, pp. 108–126. Springer, Cham (2020). https://doi.org/10.1007/978-3-030-58548-8_7
46. Wang, L., et al.: Temporal segment networks for action recognition in videos. T-PAMI **41**, 2740–2755 (2018)
47. Wang, S., Li, B.Z., Khabsa, M., Fang, H., Ma, H.: Linformer: self-attention with linear complexity. arXiv preprint arXiv:2006.04768 (2020)
48. Wang, X., et al.: OadTR: online action detection with transformers. In: ICCV (2021)
49. Werbos, P.J.: Backpropagation through time: what it does and how to do it. Proc. IEEE **78**(10), 1550–1560 (1990)
50. Wu, C.Y., Zaheer, M., Hu, H., Manmatha, R., Smola, A.J., Krähenbühl, P.: Compressed video action recognition. In: CVPR (2018)
51. Wu, C., Wang, Y., Shi, Y., Yeh, C.F., Zhang, F.: Streaming transformer-based acoustic models using self-attention with augmented memory. In: Interspeech (2020)
52. Xu, M., Gao, M., Chen, Y.T., Davis, L.S., Crandall, D.J.: Temporal recurrent networks for online action detection. In: ICCV (2019)
53. Xu, M., et al.: Long short-term transformer for online action detection. In: NeurIPS (2021)
54. Yun, S., Han, D., Oh, S.J., Chun, S., Choe, J., Yoo, Y.: Cutmix: regularization strategy to train strong classifiers with localizable features. In: ICCV (2019)
55. Zach, C., Pock, T., Bischof, H.: A duality based approach for realtime TV-L^1 optical flow. In: Hamprecht, F.A., Schnörr, C., Jähne, B. (eds.) DAGM 2007. LNCS, vol. 4713, pp. 214–223. Springer, Heidelberg (2007). https://doi.org/10.1007/978-3-540-74936-3_22
56. Zaheer, M., et al.: Big bird: transformers for longer sequences. In: NeurIPS, vol. 33 (2020)
57. Zeng, K.H., Shen, W.B., Huang, D.A., Sun, M., Carlos Niebles, J.: Visual forecasting by imitating dynamics in natural sequences. In: ICCV (2017)
58. Zhang, B., Wang, L., Wang, Z., Qiao, Y., Wang, H.: Real-time action recognition with enhanced motion vector cnns. In: CVPR (2016)

59. Zhang, H., Cisse, M., Dauphin, Y.N., Lopez-Paz, D.: mixup: beyond empirical risk minimization. In: ICLR (2018)
60. Zhang, Q., et al.: Transformer transducer: a streamable speech recognition model with transformer encoders and rnn-t loss. In: ICASSP (2020)

TALLFormer: Temporal Action Localization with a Long-Memory Transformer

Feng Cheng and Gedas Bertasius(✉)

Department of Computer Science, University of North Carolina at Chapel Hill, Chapel Hill, USA
{fengchan,gedas}@cs.unc.edu

Abstract. Most modern approaches in temporal action localization divide this problem into two parts: (i) short-term feature extraction and (ii) long-range temporal boundary localization. Due to the high GPU memory cost caused by processing long untrimmed videos, many methods sacrifice the representational power of the short-term feature extractor by either freezing the backbone or using a small spatial video resolution. This issue becomes even worse with the recent video transformer models, many of which have quadratic memory complexity. To address these issues, we propose TALLFormer, a memory-efficient and end-to-end trainable **T**emporal **A**ction **L**ocalization transformer with **L**ong-term memory. Our long-term memory mechanism eliminates the need for processing hundreds of redundant video frames during each training iteration, thus, significantly reducing the GPU memory consumption and training time. These efficiency savings allow us (i) to use a powerful video transformer feature extractor without freezing the backbone or reducing the spatial video resolution, while (ii) also maintaining long-range temporal boundary localization capability. With only RGB frames as input and no external action recognition classifier, TALLFormer outperforms previous state-of-the-arts by a large margin, achieving an average mAP of 59.1% on THUMOS14 and 35.6% on ActivityNet-1.3. The code is public available (https://github.com/klauscc/TALLFormer.)

1 Introduction

With the rapid growth of video media, video understanding has become an important area of computer vision. As a fundamental task in video understanding, Temporal Action Localization (TAL) aims to localize temporal boundaries and classify the actions for each action instance in a long untrimmed video.

Because many actions span long temporal extent (e.g., 50–100 s), most prior approaches in TAL [2,6,23,25,27,33,45,53,62], divide this problem into two

Supplementary Information The online version contains supplementary material available at https://doi.org/10.1007/978-3-031-19830-4_29.

S. Avidan et al. (Eds.): ECCV 2022, LNCS 13694, pp. 503–521, 2022.
https://doi.org/10.1007/978-3-031-19830-4_29

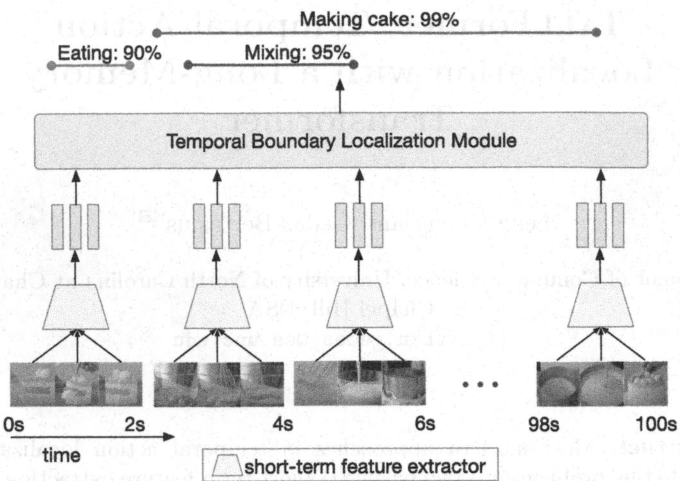

Fig. 1. A general framework for temporal action localization (TAL). The short-term feature extractor extracts the features for each short-term clip. Then, the long-term temporal boundary localization module uses the features of all short-term clips in the video to predict the action boundaries and categories. Due to excessive training time and GPU memory cost, many prior TAL methods restrict the representational power of the short-term feature extractor by either freezing the backbone or operating on small spatial video resolution. While effective at reducing the computational burden, these techniques also significantly degrade TAL performance.

parts: (i) short-term feature extraction and (ii) long-range temporal boundary localization. As shown in Fig. 1, the first part involves sampling many consecutive short clips (e.g., each spanning 1–2 s) from a long untrimmed video and extracting short-term features from them. In the second part, the model uses the extracted features of all short-term clips (i.e., spanning the entire duration of an untrimmed video) for predicting action boundaries and categories. Thus, based on these observations, it is natural to conclude that an ideal TAL model should consist of (i) a powerful short-term feature extractor and (ii) a precise temporal boundary localization module.

However, due to the high GPU memory cost needed to process long untrimmed videos, the majority of existing methods sacrifice the representational power of short-term feature extractor, by either freezing the backbone [25,27,53] or using a very small spatial video resolution (e.g., 96×96) [23,45]. While both of these techniques are highly effective at reducing GPU memory consumption, they also degrade the quality of extracted short-term features, which leads to a significantly lower TAL accuracy. For example, as shown in Table 1, in order to save memory, reducing spatial resolution from 168×168 to 112×112 leads to 2.3% mAP drop; using a smaller backbone also reduces the mAP by 2.1%; freezing the backbone leads to a severe drop in mAP (∼8–9%).

In parallel, we note that the recent introduction of powerful video transformer models [3,32] have achieved impressive results on various video understanding problems such as action recognition. However, these models have made the above-described GPU memory issues even worse. Due to the quadratic complexity of self-attention, video transformers require even more GPU memory than traditional CNNs. As a result, it is challenging to adapt these models to the TAL task, which generally requires a lot of GPU memory even when using CNN-based models. The commonly used GPU memory saving techniques such as Checkpointing [7], Mixed Precision [34], can alleviate these computational issues. However, as shown in Table 1, even when using these techniques, the GPU memory cost of applying video transformers (e.g., VideoSwin [32]) to TAL is very large.

Table 1. We study several important factors for short-term feature extraction on THUMOS14: (i) spatial video resolution, (ii) transformer backbone complexity, and (iii) the number of frozen backbone stages. For these experiments, we use Swin [32], which consists of 4 stages where i frozen stages means that the first i stages in the backbone are frozen. We use DaoTAD [45] codebase to conduct these experiments. Additionally, we note that in all of these experiments, we incorporate Checkpointing [7] to reduce GPU memory usage. GPU Memory (Mem) is measured in Gigabytes. Based on these results, we note that **(a)** increasing the spatial resolution leads to large mAP improvement(∼2.3%) but also quadratic memory consumption, **(b)** using larger backbones also improves the mAP, and lastly, **(c)** freezing the backbone leads to a severe drop in performance (∼8–9%).

(a) Spatial video resolution (SVR) analysis. The backbone is Swin-T with the first 2 stages frozen.

SVR	mAP(%)	Mem
112 × 112	52.8	**15**
168 × 168	**55.1**	34
224 × 224	-	OOM

(b) Studying the backbone complexity. Spatial resolution is 112 × 112. The first 2 stages of backbone are frozen.

Backbone	mAP(%)	Mem
Swin-T	52.8	**15**
Swin-S	53.3	17
Swin-B	**54.7**	20

(c) The number of frozen backbone stages (FBS). Spatial resolution is 112 × 112. The backbone is Swin-T.

FBS	mAP(%)	Mem
4	44.3	**3**
2	52.8	14
0	**53.8**	26

Thus, with these computational issues in mind, we propose TALLFormer, a memory-efficient and end-to-end trainable **T**emporal **A**ction **L**ocalization Transformer with a **L**ong-memory mechanism. Our key observation is that most videos are highly redundant, i.e., their content changes little in most neighboring frames. This raises the question of whether every single frame from a long untrimmed video needs to be processed during each training iteration. Motivated by this observation, we design TALLFormer to process only a fraction of randomly selected frames at each training iteration, which significantly reduces the training time and GPU memory requirements. For the remaining (i.e., not selected) video frames, the video features are sampled from long-term memory, which stores the features of all previously processed frames for that particular video. Note that the features from long-term memory do not have to be re-computed online, and they also do not require backpropagating the gradients, which makes long video processing much more efficient.

As the short-term feature extractor evolves throughout training, the video features in long-term memory are also evolving, i.e., the newly computed features for a given video are used to replace the old features in long-term memory. Compared to previous TAL approaches, TALLFormer has several main advantages. First, our model can be trained end-to-end on long, high spatial resolution videos beyond the constraints of finite GPU memory. Second, our framework is flexible as we can incorporate any state-of-the-art short-term video transformer model into TALLFormer, thus, benefiting from future improvements in the video transformer design. Lastly, unlike many previous TAL methods [2,25,27,33,53,62] that rely on external action recognition classifiers, TALLFormer is a unified framework that predicts action boundaries and categories with a single model. Despite being simpler, and only operating on RGB inputs, TALLFormer achieves an average mAP of 59.1% on THUMOS14 and 35.6% on ActivityNet-1.3, thus, outperforming the current state-of-the-arts by 7.1% and 1.2% respectively.

2 Related Work

Action Recognition. Action recognition is a fundamental short-term modeling task in video understanding. With the success of deep learning, a vast array of methods [5,11,12,21,22,24,42,43,46–48,55] utilize 2D and 3D CNNs to achieve impressive performance on standard action recognition benchmarks [5]. Recently, Vision Transformer-based methods [3,10,32,56] have been shown to outperform previous CNN-based methods by a large margin. Due to the large scale pretraining on action recognition datasets, the pretrained models from this domain are widely used in temporal action localization as a short-term feature extractor. One limitation of modern video transformer models is that due to the quadratic memory complexity of self-attention [44], these models are slow to train and they require a lot of GPU memory. As a result, it is difficult to apply them to long-term modeling tasks such as temporal action localization.

Temporal Action Localization (TAL). Due to finite GPU memory constraints, most existing methods [1,2,6,25,27,33,41,53,60,62] use pre-extracted action recognition features as inputs to the TAL model. However, since those features are extracted using models [5,17] that are pretrained on different datasets, using these features for TAL often leads to suboptimal performance. To address these issues, recent methods AFSD [23] and DaoTAD [45] proposed end-to-end trainable frameworks. However, to fit into finite GPU memory, these models operate on very low spatial video resolutions (e.g., 96×96 and 112×112 respectively), which leads to a significant drop in TAL accuracy. To the best of our knowledge, none of the existing methods are capable of end-to-end training with both high spatial resolution and long temporal extent. We aim to address this issue by proposing a simple, end-to-end trainable, transformer-based TAL method that can operate on long high-resolution video inputs.

Besides end-to-end training ability, we also note that most TAL methods can be categorized into two groups: (i) single-stage detectors, and (ii) two-stage detectors that require external action recognition classifiers. One-stage detectors [26,29,50,59] perform action localization and classification at the same time. In comparison, the two-stage methods [2,13,14,23,25,27,30,36,38,40,53,57,63] only predict action boundaries and then use the predictions of an external action recognition classifier to assign an action class to a given video segment. Despite the elegance and simplicity of one-stage methods, the two-stage methods typically have a much higher detection accuracy. In this work, we will show that even without relying on the external action recognition classifier, our TALLFormer still achieves state-of-the-art results on several major TAL benchmarks.

Memory-Saving Techniques. Applying transformer-based methods to TAL poses many GPU memory challenges due to the quadratic memory complexity of self-attention. There are several general memory-saving techniques, including Gradient Checkpointing [7] and Mixed Precision [34], which reduce the GPU memory usage by about 50%. We note that our proposed approach is complementary to these techniques. In fact, we use Gradient Checkpointing [7] in many of our experiments, thus, demonstrating that our proposed method works well in conjunction with these prior memory-saving techniques.

Furthermore, we note that several methods from Natural Language Processing (NLP) such as LinFormer [49] and Performer [9] propose to reduce the memory complexity of standard self-attention by approximating the attention using low-rank matrix decomposition. While being effective in NLP, those approximation methods work poorly when applied to video recognition [35].

3 TALLFormer

Given an untrimmed video $V = \{x_t\}_{t=1}^{T} \in \mathbb{R}^{C \times T \times H \times W}$ with T RGB frames, our TALLFormer model aims to predict a set of action instances $\Phi_V = \{\phi_m\}_{m=1}^{M}$ where M is the number of action instances in V. Each action instance $\phi_m = (s_m, e_m, c_m, p_m)$ is a four-element tuple that represents the start timestamp of action, end timestamp of action, action class and probability of this instance respectively.

As shown in Fig. 2, TALLFormer consists of four components: (i) a short-term Transformer encoder, (ii) a long memory module, (iii) a temporal consistency module and (iv) a temporal boundary localization module. First, we randomly sample a subset of short video clips, and process them using the short-term Transformer encoder. The remaining features are directly sampled from long-term memory, which stores previously computed features of all frames for that particular video input. Afterward, all of these features (i.e., from the short-term

Transformer encoder and long-term memory) are fed into a temporal consistency module that effectively fuses them in order to map them to a similar feature space, i.e., to alleviate potential issues caused by differing feature distributions from the feature extractor and long-term memory. Lastly, the temporal boundary localization module processes these features and produces temporal boundaries and action categories for each detected action instance. We now describe each of these components in more detail.

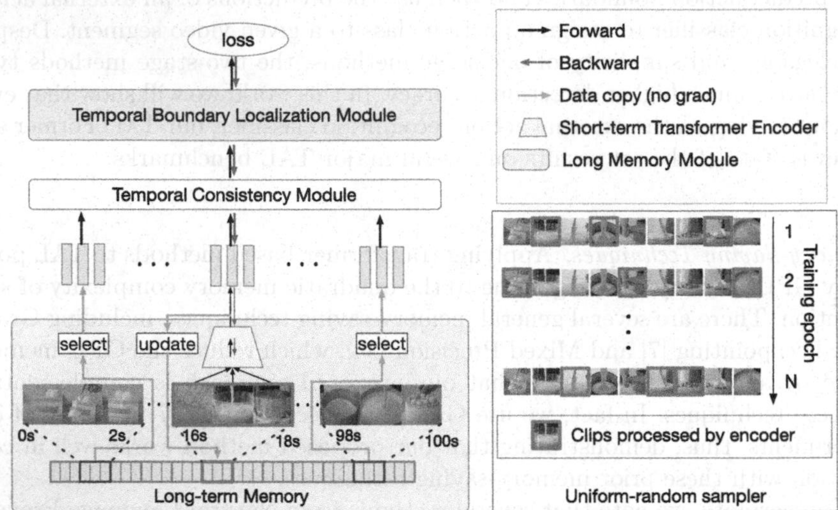

Fig. 2. An illustration of our proposed TALLFormer model. Our method consists of four high-level components: (i) a short-term Transformer encoder, (ii) a long memory module, (iii) a temporal consistency module and (iv) a temporal boundary localization module. The short-term Transformer encoder only extracts features from a few randomly sampled video clips. The rest of the features are sampled from long-term memory. All features are then fed into a temporal consistency module to ensure smooth feature fusion. Lastly, the temporal boundary localization module outputs temporal boundaries and action categories for each action instance. Afterward, the features extracted by the short-term encoder are used to update the corresponding features in long-term memory.

3.1 Short-Term Transformer Encoder

Our Shor-term Transformer Encoder considers many consecutive short clips (i.e., spanning 1–2 s) from a long untrimmed video. In order to avoid computing dense features for every single clip, we randomly sample a fixed number of such clips and feed them into our encoder.

Formally, for each input video V we divide it into N_c non-overlapping clips $c = \{c_m\}_{m=1}^{N_c}$ where $c_m \in \mathbb{R}^{L_c \times H \times W \times 3}$. The input video is shifted at most L_c

frames to ensure the clip-division changes at each epoch. A uniform sampler first samples the indices $I \in \mathbb{R}^{N_s}$ of clips that will be processed by the encoder. The indices of the remaining (i.e., not sampled) clips are denoted as $I' \in \mathbb{R}^{N_c - N_s}$. The encoder then processes each sampled clip c_i to extract low-dimensional features $f_{c_i} \in \mathbb{R}^{L_f \times C_f}$ to produce features $f_I^{(s)} = \{f_{c_{I_1}}, f_{c_{I_2}}, ..., f_{c_{I_{N_s}}}\} \in \mathbb{R}^{N_s \times L_f \times C_f}$.

Note that during each training iteration, the Transformer encoder only processes a small fraction of clips from the whole input video. The remaining clips are sampled from the long memory module (described in Sect. 3.2). This enables TALLFormer to be trained end-to-end on long high spatial resolution videos without (i) reducing the spatial video resolution, (ii) freezing the backbone, or (iii) resorting to a weak short-term feature extraction backbone. We use the recent VideoSwin [32] as our short-term Transformer encoder, which achieved impressive results on several popular action recognition benchmarks [5,15].

3.2 Long Memory Module

Our proposed Long Memory Module (LMM) enables TALLFormer to be trained on long and high-resolution videos. Inspired by [8,58], we propose LMM to cache the features computed by our short-term Transformer encoder for all short-term video clips. For the remaining clips (denoted by the indices I') that are not processed by the short-term Transformer encoder, LMM samples the features $f_{I'}^{(l)} \in \mathbb{R}^{(N_c - N_s) \times L_f \times C_f}$ from long-term memory. Following this step, we then update long-term memory with the features $f_I^{(s)}$ extracted by the short-term Transformer encoder. Note that before training, we initialize the LMM with the features extracted by our short-term Transformer encoder.

Such a scheme works well in the TAL setting because the short-term Transformer encoder is already pretrained on a large-scale external action recognition dataset (e.g., Kinetics) and thus, it evolves more slowly than the other modules in the network (i.e., it uses a smaller learning rate than the other parts of the network). Thus, "approximating" short-term features with the features from LMM provides large efficiency gains (both in terms of training time and GPU memory), while still achieving excellent TAL accuracy, which we demonstrate in our experimental section. Compared to prior methods [16,51,54,58] that use memory bank as auxiliary information, our LMM serves as an approximation to the short-term encoder. Both the features from LMM and short-term encoder are directly used to produce the final predictions of our method.

Overall, compared to standard end-to-end training, TALLFormer only needs to process a fraction of input clips, which saves the memory and computational cost by a rate of $r = \frac{N_s}{N_c}$. This then allows us to (i) use a powerful transformer-based feature extractor without freezing its backbone or reducing the spatial video resolution and (ii) still maintain the ability to precisely localize long-range temporal boundaries of actions. Note that during inference, we extract all features using a short-term Transformer encoder (i.e., without using LMM).

3.3 Temporal Consistency Module

Due to different feature distributions between (i) the online extracted Transformer features $f_I^{(s)}$ and (ii) LMM-cached offline features $f_{I'}^{(l)}$, we need to reduce temporal inconsistency among clip-level features across the whole input video. To be more precise, the features that are processed online (i.e., using our short-term Transformer encoder) are extracted using the latest short-term encoder. In contrast, most clip-level features stored in the LMM are extracted using the same short-term Transformer encoder but from the previous iterations. Thus, the short-term features associated with different clips might have different feature distributions, which can potentially degrade TAL performance. To address this issue, we propose a simple, yet effective Temporal Consistency Module (TCM).

The idea is to make the features from both sources more consistent by allowing them to interact with each other. Due to the effectiveness of standard self-attention to capture global long-range dependencies, we design TCM as an L attention layer subnetwork. Formally, given the video features $g = [f_I^{(l)}; f_{I'}^{(s)}]$, the TCM refines the features using three Transformer layers:

$$h^{(i)} = \text{TransformerLayer}(h^{(i-1)}) \tag{1}$$

where $i \in [1, L]$ is the layer index, $h^{(0)} = g$ and $h^{(L)}$ is the refined features of TCM. The TransformerLayer uses relative positional encoding as in Swin [31], GELU [18] activation, and Droppath [19].

Conceptually, our self-attention-based TCM subnetwork allows our model to refine potentially inconsistent features by incorporating temporal information from the entire untrimmed input video into feature vectors associated with individual video clips. In our experimental section, we demonstrate the effectiveness of such long-range TCM module.

3.4 Temporal Boundary Localization Module

The Temporal Boundary Localization Module (TBLM) utilizes the features of all clips produced by the TCM to predict the action boundaries and categories.The TBLMs in most existing methods [2,23,25,27,33,41,53,60,62] especially for difficult datasets (e.g., ActivityNet [4]) are two-stage detectors that require external action classification classifiers, which is costly and cumbersome. Our analysis into this problem reveals that the reason that many prior methods rely on external classifiers is because of a weak short-term encoder. Specifically, as discussed above, many prior methods have to either freeze the backbone or use small spatial video resolution in order to save GPU memory. This then leads to poor action classification performance, which requires these methods to adapt an external action recognition classifier. In contrast, we note that TALLFormer utilizes a strong short-term encoder while achieving strong performance on both action classification and localization using a one-stage TBLM.

We build upon the existing methods [23,45] by simply adding a shared linear action recognition classifier to each action proposal. For datasets where each video only contains one action category such as ActivityNet [4], we add the linear classifier on the temporally averaged features of the TCM with a 50% dropout. Due to the strong representational power of TALLFormer, this simple modification achieves a high action classification accuracy and thus, eliminates the necessity for an external action recognition classifier. We use the same loss functions as the previous methods [23,45] and Focal Loss [28] for the added linear action recognition layer. See more details in Supplementary 1.2.

4 Experiments

4.1 Datasets and Evaluation Metrics

Datasets. We conduct our evaluations on the two commonly-used benchmark datasets THUMOS14 [20], and ActivityNet-1.3 [4]. THUMOS14 contains 200 untrimmed validation videos and 213 untrimmed testing videos with temporal annotations from 20 categories. ActivityNet-1.3 contains 15,000 videos for training and 5,000 videos for validation. Additionally, we also evaluate on the large-scale HACS-Segment [61] dataset, which contains 38K untrimmed videos for training and 6K for validation. Following previous works [23,25,45], on THUMOS14, we train on the validation set and evaluate on the test set. On ActivityNet-1.3 and HACS-Segment we train on the training set and evaluate on the validation set.

Evaluation Metrics. As is standard, we use mean Average Precision (mAP) to report our results. The Intersection over Union (IoU) thresholds are set to [0.3 : 0.1 : 0.7] for THUMOS14 and [0.5 : 0.05 : 0.95] for ActivityNet-1.3 and HACS-Segment.

4.2 Implementation Details

The flexibility of our framework allows us to consider any transformer-based model as our short-term feature extractor. Due to its superior accuracy, we adopt Video Swin Transformer [32] pretrained on Kinetics-400 [5]. The number of layers L in TCM is set to 3 and Droppath rate is 0.1. Our temporal boundary localization module (TBLM) is designed using the techniques from DaoTAD [45] and AFSD [23] for THUMOS14 and ActivityNet-1.3 respectively. Unlike previous methods that operate on (i) RGB and (ii) optical flow frames inputs, our TALLFormer only uses RGB frames. The frames are resized to 256×256 and cropped to 224×224 unless stated otherwise.

During training, we apply common data augmentations on both datasets, including random crop, random horizontal flipping, random rotate and other photometric distortions such as random brightness and contrast. For the other training and inference details, we follow DaoTAD for THUMOS14 and AFSD for ActivityNet-1.3 with minor modifications as below. The inference and all the other settings are kept the same. Gradient Checkpointing [7] is applied to all our models. Our models are trained on 4× RTX A6000 GPUs.

THUMOS14. We extract RGB frames with 15fps. Because 99.5% of action instances in the validation set span less than 32 s, we consider 480 frames as inputs. The batch size is set to 4 on each GPU. Since in DaoTAD, clip features are temporally downsampled by 8, but in Swin Transformer the temporal downsampling rate is only 2, we add two Convolutional layers with stride 2 before the TCM to keep the same temporal downsampling rate as in DaoTAD.

ActivityNet-1.3. As is done in prior work [23], we resize all videos to 768 RGB frames. The batch size is set to 1 on each GPU. For simplicity, we remove the boundary consistency learning module in AFSD. Our model is trained for 10 epochs instead of 16 as used in the original AFSD.

4.3 Comparison with Short-Term and Long-Term Baselines

We next conduct a thorough empirical study investigating the importance of short-term vs. long-term modeling for the TAL task. We focus our comparisons on three of our baselines, which are compared under the same finite GPU memory constraints, i.e., either 12GB (RTX 3080) or 32GB (Tesla V100).

Table 2. Comparing TALLFormer with several of our own short-term and long-term baselines on THUMOS14. We use a powerful video Swin-B as the Feature Extractor (**FE**) for all models. All models operate on videos with a Spatial Resolution (**SR**) of 224 × 224. LT-Frozen is a long-term baseline that uses a frozen feature extractor but long Temporal Support (**TS**). ST-E2E is a short-term end-to-end trainable baseline with an unfrozen backbone but short temporal support. TALLFormer provides the best trade-off between short-term and long-term modeling among these baselines.

Mem cap (GB/GPU)	Model type	Short-term			Long-term		mAP(%)			
		FE	E2E	SR	TS(s)	Fps	0.3	0.5	0.7	Avg
12	LT-Frozen	Swin-B	✗	224	32	15	70.2	55.4	29.4	52.7
	ST-E2E	Swin-B	✓	224	8	8	63.1	46.6	16.0	42.9
		Swin-B	✓	224	32	2	55.4	32.2	8.4	31.9
		Swin-B	✓	224	4	15	50.5	33.9	13.4	32.8
	TALLFormer	Swin-B	✓	224	32	15	**76.1**	**63.1**	**34.2**	**59.0**
32	LT-Frozen	Swin-B	✗	224	32	15	70.2	55.4	29.4	52.7
	ST-E2E	Swin-B	✓	224	32	8	72.7	59.8	33.3	56.3
		Swin-B	✓	224	12	15	72.8	58.6	30.0	55.1
	TALLFormer	Swin-B	✓	224	32	15	**76.0**	**63.2**	**34.5**	**59.2**

LT-Frozen: For this Long-Term modeling baseline, we use a powerful yet frozen Video Swin-B as the feature extractor. A similar strategy of freezing the feature extractor is commonly used in many prior methods [25,27,53] as the GPU memory savings from freezing the backbone enable long-range temporal modeling needed by TAL. All models are trained under a finite GPU memory constraint.

ST-E2E: Unlike LT-Frozen baseline, the Short-Term End-to-End trainable baseline uses a Swin-B feature extractor (*not frozen*) that operates on 224×224 video frame inputs. While benefiting from end-to-end trainability, due to the GPU memory limitation, this baseline can only span either (i) short temporal extent with dense video frame sampling or (ii) long temporal extent with sparse video frame sampling. We study both of these ST-E2E variants.

TALLFormer: Compared to the previous two baselines, we believe that our approach achieves the best trade-off between short-term and long-term modeling. In other words, the short-term feature extractor in our framework can be trained end-to-end on high spatial resolution videos. Furthermore, our long-term memory module enables the model to maintain strong long-term modeling capability for precise temporal boundary localization.

Analysis. From Table 2, we observe that long-term modeling is important, i.e., reducing the temporal support in ST-E2E leads to sub-optimal performance. With a 32 GB GPU memory limit, ST-E2E with a maximum temporal support of 12 s achieves 4.1% lower average mAP than TALLFormer with 32 s temporal support. We also point out that the ST-E2E variant that spans 32 s using sparsely sampled frames (i.e., 8 vs. 15 fps) also produces 2.9% worse performance than TALLFormer. We observe similar trends for the models trained under the 12 GB GPU memory constraint. Additionally, our results indicate that the end-to-end training of a short-term feature extractor is also important as LT-Frozen baseline achieves 6.5% lower accuracy than TALLFormer. We observe this trend in both 12 GB and 32 GB GPU memory settings.

Overall, we can conclude that TALLFormer achieves the best accuracy-memory trade-offs under both 12 GB and 32 GB GPU memory constraints. Specifically, TALLFormer outperforms the LT-Frozen and ST-E2E baselines by a large margin especially with tighter GPU memory constraints (i.e. 12 GB).

4.4 Comparison to the State-of-the-Art

Next, we compare TALLFormer to the state-of-the-art methods as shown in Table 3. The upper part of Table 3 includes methods that operate on pre-extracted action recognition features. The middle section of Table 3 includes recently proposed end-to-end trainable methods, AFSD and DaoTAD, that operate on small spatial video resolutions (i.e., 96×96 and 112×112 respectively) to fit into GPU memory. Lastly, in the bottom part of the table, we include our TALLFormer, which can be trained end-to-end on long 224×224 videos.

We experiment with three variants of our method. First, we introduce a variant, named TALLFormer-12, which is cheap enough to fit in a 12GB memory GPU, with two backbones I3D and Swin-B for fair comparison with prior methods. Additionally, for the first variant (using I3D backbone), we use the clip sampling rate $r = 0.4$ on THUMOS14 and $r = 1/3$ on AcitivityNet-1.3, whereas for the latter variant (using Swin-B backbone) the clip sampling rate is set to

$r = 0.15$ for THUMOS14 and $r = 1/8$ for ActivityNet-1.3. Lastly, our best performing variant is TALLFormer-32 with Swin-B as its backbone, which uses a clip sampling-rate of $r = 0.4$ for THUMOS and $r = 0.375$ for ActivityNet. We set these sampling rates so that our model would fit in the available GPU memory.

THUMOS14. The results in Table 3 (the left part of the table), indicate several interesting trends. First, we notice that despite using a small spatial resolution, the end-to-end trainable methods such as AFSD and DaoTAD, outperform methods that operate on pre-extracted action recognition features by a large margin. Second, our results indicate that the memory-constrained TALLFormer-12 with an I3D backbone outperforms a strong AFSD baseline by a substantial margin according to all evaluation metrics. Moreover, when increasing the GPU memory constraints, TALLFormer-12 achieves 7.2% higher accuracy on average than AFSD. We note that the GPU consumption for TALLFormer is 29 GB, which is still within the capacity of the mainstream Tesla V100 GPUs. We also point out that even when using the same amount of GPU memory as prior methods, our method still largely outperforms previous SOTAs, i.e., TALLFormer-12 with I3D backbone and VSwin-B backbone outperforms AFSD by 1.9% and 7.0%.

ActivityNet. First, we point out that all the previous methods achieve strong TAL results on ActivityNet while relying on an external action recognition classifier [52], which ensembles the predictions from ResNet-200 and Inception-V2 models operating on RGB and optical flow inputs. Instead, we simplify this pipeline by predicting action boundaries and categories using a single model. Not only is our proposed framework simpler and more efficient, but it also outperforms all previous approaches by 1.2% using RGB inputs alone. One interesting observation is that TALLFormer with I3D backbone is 6.5% lower than TALLFormer with a Swin-B backbone. Our analysis of this result reveals that TALLFormer-12 variant with an I3D backbone achieves a low video-level action recognition accuracy (78.2%) while the accuracy of TALLFormer-12 with Swin-B backbone is 90.1%. We also note that the accuracy of an external action recognition classifier [52] used by AFSD is 88.9%. This empirical finding also explains why all previous methods require an external action recognition classifier.

HACS. We train TALLFormer with Swin-B as backbone using the same network structure and hyperparameters as in AcitivityNet-1.3. We report these results in Table 4. These results suggest that similar to our previously considered datasets, TALLFormer also achieves state-of-the-art results on the HACS-Segment dataset. Specifically, it outperforms the GTAD [53] and BMN [25,36] baselines by 9.1% and 0.7% average mAP respectively without an external classifier.

Inference Speed Discussion. Compared with previous methods, we use a larger backbone and higher spatial resolution. On the other hand, our proposed framework is much simpler than the frameworks of many prior TAL methods.

Table 3. Comparison to the state-of-the-art on THUMOS14 and ActivityNet-v1.3. **FE** and **E2E** denote the feature extractor backbone and whether a method is end-to-end trainable respectively. The feature extractor backbones include TS [39], I3D [5], P3D [37] and Swin-B [32] (denoted as SW). **Flow** and **Ext. Cls.** denote whether each method uses optical flow as input and whether an external action recognition classifier is needed respectively. Note that AFSD relies on an external classifier on ActivityNet-1.3.

Method	FE	E2E	Flow	Ext. Cls.	mAP								Mem (GB)
					THUMOS14				ActivityNet-1.3				
					0.3	0.5	0.7	Avg.	0.5	0.75	0.95	Avg.	
BSN [27]	TS	✗	✓	✓	53.5	36.9	20.0	36.8	46.5	30.0	8.0	30.0	–
BMN [25]	TS	✗	✓	✓	56.0	38.8	20.5	38.5	50.1	34.8	8.3	33.9	–
BC-GNN [2]	TS	✗	✓	✓	57.1	40.4	23.1	40.2	50.6	34.8	**9.4**	34.3	–
BU-TAL [62]	I3D	✗	✓	✓	53.9	45.4	28.5	43.3	43.5	33.9	9.2	30.1	–
GTAN [33]	P3D	✗	✓	✓	57.8	38.8	–	–	52.6	34.1	8.9	34.3	–
G-TAD [53]	TS	✗	✓	✓	54.5	40.2	23.4	39.3	50.4	34.6	9.0	34.1	–
TAL [6]	I3D	✗	✓	✗	53.2	42.8	20.8	39.8	38.2	18.3	1.3	20.2	–
RTD-Action [41]	TS	✗	✓	✓	68.3	51.9	23.7	49.0	47.2	30.7	8.6	30.8	–
VSGN [60]	TS	✗	✓	✓	66.7	52.4	30.4	50.2	52.4	36.0	8.4	35.1	–
AFSD [23]	I3D	✓	✓	–	67.3	55.5	31.1	52.0	52.4	35.3	6.5	34.4	12
DaoTAD [45]	I3D	✓	✗	✗	62.8	53.8	30.1	50.0	–	–	–	–	11
DaoTAD [45]	SW	✓	✗	✗	72.7	59.8	33.3	56.3	–	–	–	–	30
TALLFormer-12	I3D	✓	✗	✗	68.4	57.6	30.8	53.9	41.3	27.3	6.3	27.2	12
TALLFormer-12	SW	✓	✗	✗	**76.1**	63.1	34.2	59.0	51.4	34.0	7.6	33.7	12
TALLFormer-32	SW	✓	✗	✗	76.0	**63.2**	**34.5**	**59.2**	**54.1**	**36.2**	7.9	**35.6**	29

Table 4. Our results (in mAP) on the HACS-Segment dataset.

Backbone	mAP(%)			
	0.5	0.75	0.95	Avg.
GTAD [53]	–	–	–	27.5
BMN [25,36]	52.5	**36.4**	10.4	35.8
TALLFormer	**55.0**	36.1	**11.8**	**36.5**

In particular, we use a single model with only RGB frames as input while most previous methods adopt a two-stream approach that requires an external action classifier. This is costly, because (i) optical flow extraction is slow and because (ii) training and inference of an external action classifier is also time-consuming.

Due to the complexity of the existing systems, and the lack of publicly available implementations, it is difficult to quantitatively measure the inference speed of many prior methods. However, we note that in general, TALLFormer provides a much simpler, elegant and more efficient framework to the TAL problem. For example, consider performing inference on AcitivyNet-1.3 using a RTX A6000 GPU. The overall inference speed of a recent state-of-the-art AFSD [23]

Table 5. Ablation studies on THUMOS14: **(a)** TALLFormer works well even for a small sampling rate r; **(b)** The temporal consistency module leads to 1.5% boost in the average mAP; **(c)** TALLFormer performs better with longer temporal support. For **(a)** the backbone is Swin-B with spatial resolution 224 × 224. For **(b)** and **(c)**, the backbone is Swin-T with spatial resolution 112 × 112.

(a) Analysis of the clip sampling rate r.

r	mAP(%)	Mem
0.15	59.0	12
0.3	59.4	22
0.4	59.2	29
0.6	**60.0**	45
1.0	–	OOM

(b) Importance of Temporal Consistency Module (TCM).

TCM	mAP(%)
✗	51.1
✓	**52.6**

(c) Temporal Support (TS) analysis.

TS (s)	mAP(%)
8	41.5
16	49.7
24	51.5
32	52.8
40	**53.3**

is 11.74 s/video, which includes (i) optical flow extraction, (ii) processing two modalities and (iii) performing video-level action classification using [52]. On the other hand, TALLFormer only costs 1.58 s/video while outperforming AFSD by 1.2% mAP.

4.5 Ablation Study

Lastly, we study various design choices of our TALLFormer model. Specifically, we investigate (i) TAL performance as a function of our clip sampling rate r, (ii) the importance of the temporal consistency module (TCM) and (iii) TAL performance as a function of temporal support. We present these results below.

Accuracy vs. Clip Sampling Rate. During training, our model samples a fraction of r total short-term clips from an untrimmed video input. We study the performance as a function of clip sampling rate r. From Table 1(a), we can observe that i) GPU memory usage is proportional to the sampling rate r; ii) standard end-to-end training ($r = 1$) causes out-of-memory (OOM) error; iii) TALLFormer performs quite well even with a very small sampling rate 0.15, i.e., the TAL accuracy in mAP drops by only 1.0% while reducing the GPU memory usage to only 12 GB (compared to > 45GB using $r = 1.0$)

Importance of Temporal Consistency Module (TCM). As shown in Table 5(b), our proposed TCM increases the average mAP by 1.5%, which indicates its importance to our overall framework. More conceptually, these results suggest that encouraging long-range interactions between the memory features, and the online-processed features can alleviate the feature distribution inconsistency issue, which is also suggested by the visualized features before and after TCM in Supplementary 2.1.

Analysis of Temporal Support. We evaluate TALLFormer when using different temporal support (measured in seconds). Based on the results in Table 5(c), we observe that longer temporal supports leads to consistently higher mAP.

5 Discussion

We present TALLFormer, a long-memory Transformer for temporal action localization. Our method is simple, flexible, and it can be efficiently trained on long high-resolution videos for TAL. Furthermore, we demonstrate that TALLFormer significantly outperforms previous TAL approaches on the THUMOS14 and ActivityNet-1.3 benchmarks.

Some readers might wonder whether optimizing the GPU memory usage for long-video processing is a valuable contribution since modern GPUs can accommodate larger and larger GPU memory requirements. Furthermore, there exist many prior memory saving techniques such as Gradient Checkpoint [7] and Mixed Precision [34]. Despite the advances in GPU hardware, and new developments in memory saving techniques, we believe that TALLFormer is still a valuable contribution to the research community. With the new developments in GPU hardware, the demands for higher resolution video analysis and larger models also grow. Thus, such demands pose new GPU memory-related challenges, especially for long-term video understanding tasks such as temporal action localization. We also note that TALLFormer can be easily combined with the existing memory-saving techniques, which we demonstrated in our experiments. Our future work involves extending our framework to various multimodal settings that involve processing both visual inputs and language.

References

1. Bagchi, A., Mahmood, J., Fernandes, D., Sarvadevabhatla, R.K.: Hear me out: fusional approaches for audio augmented temporal action localization. arXiv preprint arXiv:2106.14118 (2021)
2. Bai, Y., Wang, Y., Tong, Y., Yang, Y., Liu, Q., Liu, J.: Boundary content graph neural network for temporal action proposal generation. In: Vedaldi, A., Bischof, H., Brox, T., Frahm, J.-M. (eds.) ECCV 2020. LNCS, vol. 12373, pp. 121–137. Springer, Cham (2020). https://doi.org/10.1007/978-3-030-58604-1_8
3. Bertasius, G., Wang, H., Torresani, L.: Is space-time attention all you need for video understanding, vol. 2, no. p. 4. arXiv preprint arXiv:2102.05095 (2021)
4. Caba Heilbron, F., Escorcia, V., Ghanem, B., Carlos Niebles, J.: Activitynet: a large-scale video benchmark for human activity understanding. In: Proceedings of the IEEE Conference on Computer Vision and Pattern Recognition, pp. 961–970 (2015)
5. Carreira, J., Zisserman, A.: Quo vadis, action recognition? a new model and the kinetics dataset. In: proceedings of the IEEE Conference on Computer Vision and Pattern Recognition, pp. 6299–6308 (2017)

6. Chao, Y.W., Vijayanarasimhan, S., Seybold, B., Ross, D.A., Deng, J., Sukthankar, R.: Rethinking the faster r-cnn architecture for temporal action localization. In: Proceedings of the IEEE Conference on Computer Vision and Pattern Recognition, pp. 1130–1139 (2018)
7. Chen, T., Xu, B., Zhang, C., Guestrin, C.: Training deep nets with sublinear memory cost. arXiv:1604.06174 (2016)
8. Cheng, F., et al.: Stochastic backpropagation: a memory efficient strategy for training video models. In: Proceedings of the IEEE/CVF Conference on Computer Vision and Pattern Recognition, pp. 8301–8310 (2022)
9. Choromanski, K., et al.: Rethinking attention with performers. arXiv preprint arXiv:2009.14794 (2020)
10. Fan, H., et al.: Multiscale vision transformers. In: Proceedings of the IEEE/CVF International Conference on Computer Vision, pp. 6824–6835 (2021)
11. Feichtenhofer, C.: X3d: expanding architectures for efficient video recognition. In: Proceedings of the IEEE/CVF Conference on Computer Vision and Pattern Recognition, pp. 203–213 (2020)
12. Feichtenhofer, C., Fan, H., Malik, J., He, K.: Slowfast networks for video recognition. In: Proceedings of the IEEE/CVF International Conference on Computer Vision, pp. 6202–6211 (2019)
13. Gao, J., et al.: Accurate temporal action proposal generation with relation-aware pyramid network. In: Proceedings of the AAAI Conference on Artificial Intelligence, vol. 34, pp. 10810–10817 (2020)
14. Gao, J., Chen, K., Nevatia, R.: Ctap: complementary temporal action proposal generation. In: Proceedings of the European conference on computer vision (ECCV), pp. 68–83 (2018)
15. Goyal, R., et al.: The "something something" video database for learning and evaluating visual common sense. In: Proceedings of the IEEE International Conference on Computer Vision, pp. 5842–5850 (2017)
16. He, K., Fan, H., Wu, Y., Xie, S., Girshick, R.: Momentum contrast for unsupervised visual representation learning. In: Proceedings of the IEEE/CVF Conference on Computer Vision and Pattern Recognition, pp. 9729–9738 (2020)
17. He, K., Zhang, X., Ren, S., Sun, J.: Deep residual learning for image recognition. In: Proceedings of the IEEE Conference on Computer Vision and Pattern Recognition, pp. 770–778 (2016)
18. Hendrycks, D., Gimpel, K.: Gaussian error linear units (gelus). arXiv preprint arXiv:1606.08415 (2016)
19. Huang, G., Sun, Yu., Liu, Z., Sedra, D., Weinberger, K.Q.: Deep networks with stochastic depth. In: Leibe, B., Matas, J., Sebe, N., Welling, M. (eds.) ECCV 2016. LNCS, vol. 9908, pp. 646–661. Springer, Cham (2016). https://doi.org/10.1007/978-3-319-46493-0_39
20. Idrees, H., et al.: The thumos challenge on action recognition for videos "in the wild". Comput. Vision Image Underst. **155**, 1–23 (2017)
21. Jiang, B., Wang, M., Gan, W., Wu, W., Yan, J.: Stm: spatiotemporal and motion encoding for action recognition. In: Proceedings of the IEEE/CVF International Conference on Computer Vision, pp. 2000–2009 (2019)
22. Kwon, H., Kim, M., Kwak, S., Cho, M.: MotionSqueeze: neural motion feature learning for video understanding. In: Vedaldi, A., Bischof, H., Brox, T., Frahm, J.-M. (eds.) ECCV 2020. LNCS, vol. 12361, pp. 345–362. Springer, Cham (2020). https://doi.org/10.1007/978-3-030-58517-4_21

23. Lin, C., et al.: Learning salient boundary feature for anchor-free temporal action localization. In: Proceedings of the IEEE/CVF Conference on Computer Vision and Pattern Recognition, pp. 3320–3329 (2021)
24. Lin, J., Gan, C., Han, S.: Tsm: temporal shift module for efficient video understanding. In: Proceedings of the IEEE/CVF International Conference on Computer Vision, pp. 7083–7093 (2019)
25. Lin, T., Liu, X., Li, X., Ding, E., Wen, S.: Bmn: boundary-matching network for temporal action proposal generation. In: Proceedings of the IEEE/CVF International Conference on Computer Vision, pp. 3889–3898 (2019)
26. Lin, T., Zhao, X., Shou, Z.: Single shot temporal action detection. In: Proceedings of the 25th ACM international conference on Multimedia, pp. 988–996 (2017)
27. Lin, T., Zhao, X., Su, H., Wang, C., Yang, M.: Bsn: boundary sensitive network for temporal action proposal generation. In: Proceedings of the European Conference on Computer Vision (ECCV), pp. 3–19 (2018)
28. Lin, T.Y., Goyal, P., Girshick, R., He, K., Dollár, P.: Focal loss for dense object detection. In: Proceedings of the IEEE International Conference on Computer Vision, pp. 2980–2988 (2017)
29. Liu, Q., Wang, Z.: Progressive boundary refinement network for temporal action detection. In: Proceedings of the AAAI Conference on Artificial Intelligence, vol. 34, pp. 11612–11619 (2020)
30. Liu, Y., Ma, L., Zhang, Y., Liu, W., Chang, S.F.: Multi-granularity generator for temporal action proposal. In: Proceedings of the IEEE/CVF Conference on Computer Vision and Pattern Recognition, pp. 3604–3613 (2019)
31. Liu, Z., et al.: Swin transformer: hierarchical vision transformer using shifted windows. In: Proceedings of the IEEE/CVF International Conference on Computer Vision, pp. 10012–10022 (2021)
32. Liu, Z., et al.: Video swin transformer. arXiv preprint arXiv:2106.13230 (2021)
33. Long, F., Yao, T., Qiu, Z., Tian, X., Luo, J., Mei, T.: Gaussian temporal awareness networks for action localization. In: Proceedings of the IEEE/CVF Conference on Computer Vision and Pattern Recognition, pp. 344–353 (2019)
34. Micikevicius, P., et al.: Mixed precision training. arXiv preprint arXiv:1710.03740 (2017)
35. Patrick, M., et al.: Keeping your eye on the ball: trajectory attention in video transformers. Adv. Neural Inf. Process. Syst. **34**, 12493–12506 (2021)
36. Qing, Z., et al.: Temporal context aggregation network for temporal action proposal refinement. In: Proceedings of the IEEE/CVF Conference on Computer Vision and Pattern Recognition, pp. 485–494 (2021)
37. Qiu, Z., Yao, T., Mei, T.: Learning spatio-temporal representation with pseudo-3D residual networks. In: proceedings of the IEEE International Conference on Computer Vision, pp. 5533–5541 (2017)
38. Shou, Z., Chan, J., Zareian, A., Miyazawa, K., Chang, S.F.: Cdc: convolutional-de-convolutional networks for precise temporal action localization in untrimmed videos. In: Proceedings of the IEEE Conference on Computer Vision and Pattern Recognition, pp. 5734–5743 (2017)
39. Simonyan, K., Zisserman, A.: Two-stream convolutional networks for action recognition in videos. Adv. Neural Inf. Process. Syst. **27**, 1–9 (2014)
40. Su, H., Gan, W., Wu, W., Qiao, Y., Yan, J.: Bsn++: complementary boundary regressor with scale-balanced relation modeling for temporal action proposal generation. arXiv preprint arXiv:2009.07641 (2020)

41. Tan, J., Tang, J., Wang, L., Wu, G.: Relaxed transformer decoders for direct action proposal generation. In: Proceedings of the IEEE/CVF International Conference on Computer Vision, pp. 13526–13535 (2021)
42. Tran, D., Bourdev, L., Fergus, R., Torresani, L., Paluri, M.: Learning spatiotemporal features with 3D convolutional networks. In: Proceedings of the IEEE International Conference on Computer Vision, pp. 4489–4497 (2015)
43. Tran, D., Wang, H., Torresani, L., Ray, J., LeCun, Y., Paluri, M.: A closer look at spatiotemporal convolutions for action recognition. In: Proceedings of the IEEE Conference on Computer Vision and Pattern Recognition, pp. 6450–6459 (2018)
44. Vaswani, A., et al.: Attention is all you need. Adv. Neural Inf. Process. Syst. **30**, 1–11 (2017)
45. Wang, C., Cai, H., Zou, Y., Xiong, Y.: Rgb stream is enough for temporal action detection. arXiv preprint arXiv:2107.04362 (2021)
46. Wang, L., Li, W., Li, W., Van Gool, L.: Appearance-and-relation networks for video classification. In: Proceedings of the IEEE Conference on Computer Vision and Pattern Recognition, pp. 1430–1439 (2018)
47. Wang, L., et al.: Temporal segment networks: towards good practices for deep action recognition. In: Leibe, B., Matas, J., Sebe, N., Welling, M. (eds.) ECCV 2016. LNCS, vol. 9912, pp. 20–36. Springer, Cham (2016). https://doi.org/10.1007/978-3-319-46484-8_2
48. Wang, L., et al.: Temporal segment networks for action recognition in videos. IEEE Trans. Pattern Anal. Mach. Intell. **41**(11), 2740–2755 (2018)
49. Wang, S., Li, B.Z., Khabsa, M., Fang, H., Ma, H.: Linformer: self-attention with linear complexity. arXiv preprint arXiv:2006.04768 (2020)
50. Wang, X., Gao, C., Zhang, S., Sang, N.: Multi-level temporal pyramid network for action detection. In: Peng, Y., et al. (eds.) PRCV 2020. LNCS, vol. 12306, pp. 41–54. Springer, Cham (2020). https://doi.org/10.1007/978-3-030-60639-8_4
51. Wu, C.Y., Feichtenhofer, C., Fan, H., He, K., Krahenbuhl, P., Girshick, R.: Long-term feature banks for detailed video understanding. In: Proceedings of the IEEE/CVF Conference on Computer Vision and Pattern Recognition, pp. 284–293 (2019)
52. Xiong, Y., et al.: Cuhk & ethz & siat submission to activitynet challenge 2016. arXiv preprint arXiv:1608.00797 (2016)
53. Xu, M., Zhao, C., Rojas, D.S., Thabet, A., Ghanem, B.: G-tad: sub-graph localization for temporal action detection. In: Proceedings of the IEEE/CVF Conference on Computer Vision and Pattern Recognition, pp. 10156–10165 (2020)
54. Xu, M., et al.: Long short-term transformer for online action detection. Adv. Neural Inf. Process. Syst. **34**, 1086–1099 (2021)
55. You, C., Han, L., Feng, A., Zhao, R., Tang, H., Fan, W.: Megan: memory enhanced graph attention network for space-time video super-resolution. In: Proceedings of the IEEE/CVF Winter Conference on Applications of Computer Vision, pp. 1401–1411 (2022)
56. You, C., et al.: Class-aware generative adversarial transformers for medical image segmentation. arXiv preprint arXiv:2201.10737 (2022)
57. Zeng, R., et al.: Graph convolutional networks for temporal action localization. In: Proceedings of the IEEE/CVF International Conference on Computer Vision, pp. 7094–7103 (2019)
58. Zhang, C., Gupta, A., Zisserman, A.: Temporal query networks for fine-grained video understanding. In: Proceedings of the IEEE/CVF Conference on Computer Vision and Pattern Recognition, pp. 4486–4496 (2021)

59. Zhang, D., Dai, X., Wang, X., Wang, Y.F.: S3d: single shot multi-span detector via fully 3d convolutional networks. arXiv preprint arXiv:1807.08069 (2018)
60. Zhao, C., Thabet, A.K., Ghanem, B.: Video self-stitching graph network for temporal action localization. In: Proceedings of the IEEE/CVF International Conference on Computer Vision, pp. 13658–13667 (2021)
61. Zhao, H., Torralba, A., Torresani, L., Yan, Z.: Hacs: human action clips and segments dataset for recognition and temporal localization. In: Proceedings of the IEEE/CVF International Conference on Computer Vision, pp. 8668–8678 (2019)
62. Zhao, P., Xie, L., Ju, C., Zhang, Y., Wang, Y., Tian, Q.: Bottom-up temporal action localization with mutual regularization. In: Vedaldi, A., Bischof, H., Brox, T., Frahm, J.-M. (eds.) ECCV 2020. LNCS, vol. 12353, pp. 539–555. Springer, Cham (2020). https://doi.org/10.1007/978-3-030-58598-3_32
63. Zhao, Y., Xiong, Y., Wang, L., Wu, Z., Tang, X., Lin, D.: Temporal action detection with structured segment networks. In: Proceedings of the IEEE International Conference on Computer Vision, pp. 2914–2923 (2017)

Mining Relations Among Cross-Frame Affinities for Video Semantic Segmentation

Guolei Sun[1], Yun Liu[1(✉)], Hao Tang[1], Ajad Chhatkuli[1], Le Zhang[2], and Luc Van Gool[1,3]

[1] Computer Vision Lab, ETH Zurich, Zürich, Switzerland
yun.liu@vision.ee.ethz.ch

[2] School of Information and Communication Engineering, UESTC, Chengdu, China

[3] VISICS, KU Leuven, Leuven, Belgium

Abstract. The essence of video semantic segmentation (VSS) is how to leverage temporal information for prediction. Previous efforts are mainly devoted to developing new techniques to calculate the cross-frame affinities such as optical flow and attention. Instead, this paper contributes from a different angle by mining relations among cross-frame affinities, upon which better temporal information aggregation could be achieved. We explore relations among affinities in two aspects: single-scale intrinsic correlations and multi-scale relations. Inspired by traditional feature processing, we propose Single-scale Affinity Refinement (SAR) and Multi-scale Affinity Aggregation (MAA). To make it feasible to execute MAA, we propose a Selective Token Masking (STM) strategy to select a subset of consistent reference tokens for different scales when calculating affinities, which also improves the efficiency of our method. At last, the cross-frame affinities strengthened by SAR and MAA are adopted for adaptively aggregating temporal information. Our experiments demonstrate that the proposed method performs favorably against state-of-the-art VSS methods. The code is publicly available at https://github.com/GuoleiSun/VSS-MRCFA.

Keywords: Video semantic segmentation · Cross-frame affinities · Single-scale Affinity Refinement · Multi-scale Affinity Aggregation

1 Introduction

Image semantic segmentation aims at classifying each pixel of the input image to one of the predefined class labels, which is one of the most fundamental tasks in visual intelligence. Deep neural networks have made tremendous progresses in this field [5,10,11,17,18,21,24,25,30,41,50,52,55,58], benefiting from the availability of large-scale image datasets [3,9,35,54] for semantic segmentation. However, in real life, we usually confront more complex scenarios in which a series of successive video frames need to be segmented. Thus, it is desirable to explore video semantic segmentation (VSS) by exploiting the temporal information.

S. Avidan et al. (Eds.): ECCV 2022, LNCS 13694, pp. 522–539, 2022.
https://doi.org/10.1007/978-3-031-19830-4_30

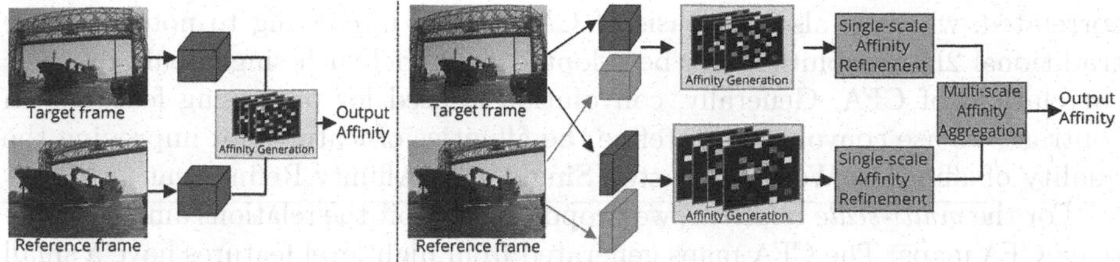

Fig. 1. *Left*: recent VSS methods [29,37] for which the affinity is directly forwarded to the next step (feature retrieval). The affinity is shown in a series of 2D maps. *Right*: We propose to mine the relations within the affinities before outputting the affinity, by Single-scale Affinity Refinement (SAR) and Multi-scale Affinity Aggregation (MAA).

The core of VSS is how to leverage temporal information. Most of the existing VSS works rely on the optical flow to model the temporal information. Specifically, they first compute the optical flow [14] that is further used to warp the features from neighboring video frames for feature alignment [16,22,28,33,36,48,56]. Then, the warped features can be simply aggregated. Although workable in certain scenarios, those methods are still unsatisfactory because i) the optical flow is error-prone and thus the error could be accumulated; ii) directly warping features may yield inevitable loss on the spatial correlations [20,31]. Hence, other approaches [29,37] directly aggregate the temporal information in the feature level using attention techniques, as shown in Fig. 1. Since they are conceptually simple and avoid the problems incurred by optical flow, we follow this way to exploit temporal information. In general, those methods first calculate the attentions/affinities between the target and the references, which are then used to generate the refined features. Though promising, they only consider the single-scale attention. What's more, they do not mine the relations within the affinities.

In this paper, we propose a novel approach MRCFA by Mining Relations among Cross-Frame Affinities for VSS. Specifically, we compute the **Cross-Frame Affinities (CFA)** between the features of the *target* frame and the *reference* frame. Hence, CFA is expected to have large activation for informative features and small activation for useless features. When aggregating the CFA-based temporal features, the informative features are highlighted and useless features are suppressed. As a result, the segmentation of the target frame would be improved by embedding temporal contexts. With the above analysis, the main focus of this paper is mining relations among CFA to improve the representation capability of CFA. Since deep neural networks usually generate multi-scale features and CFA can be calculated at different scales, we can obtain multi-scale CFA accordingly. Intuitively, the relations among CFA are twofold: single-scale intrinsic correlations and multi-scale relations.

For the *single-scale intrinsic correlations*, each feature token in a reference frame (*i.e.*, reference token) corresponds to a CFA map for the target frame. Intuitively, we have the observation that the CFA map of each reference token should be locally correlated as the feature map of the target frame is locally correlated, which is also the basis of CNNs. It is interesting to note that the traditional 2D convolution can be adopted to model such single-scale intrinsic correlations of CFA. Generally, convolution is used for processing features. In contrast, we use convolution to refine the affinities of features for improving the quality of affinities. We call this step Single-scale Affinity Refinement (SAR).

For the *multi-scale relations*, we propose to exploit the relations among multi-scale CFA maps. The CFA maps generated from high-level features have a small scale and a coarse representation, while the CFA maps generated from low-level features have a large scale and a fine representation. It is natural to aggregate multi-scale CFA maps using a high-to-low decoder structure so that the resulting CFA would contain both coarse and fine affinities. Generally, the decoder structure is usually used for fusing multi-scale features. In contrast, we build a decoder to aggregate the multi-scale affinities of features. We call this step Multi-scale Affinity Aggregation (MAA).

When we revisit the above MAA, one requirement arises: the reference tokens at different scales should have the same number and corresponding semantics; otherwise, it is impossible to connect a decoder. As discussed above, each reference token corresponds to a CFA map for the target frame. Only when two reference tokens have the same semantics, their CFA maps can be merged. For this goal, a simple solution is to downsample reference tokens at different scales into the same size. This also saves the computation due to the reduction of reference tokens. It inspires us to further reduce the computation by sampling reference tokens. To this end, we propose a **Selective Token Masking** strategy to select S most important reference tokens and abandon less important ones. Then, the relation mining among CFA is executed based on the selected tokens.

In summary, there are three aspects for mining relations among CFA: i) We propose Single-scale Affinity Refinement for refining the affinities among features, based on single-scale intrinsic correlations; 2) We further introduce Multi-scale Affinity Aggregation by using an affinity decoder for aggregating the multi-scale affinities among features; 3) To make it feasible to execute MAA and improve efficiency, we propose Selective Token Masking (STM) to generate a subset of consistent reference tokens for each scale. After strengthened with single-scale and multi-scale relations, the final CFA can be directly used for embedding reference features into the target frame. Extensive experiments show the superiority of our method over previous VSS methods. Besides, our exploration of affinities among features would provide a new perspective on VSS.

2 Related Works

2.1 Image Semantic Segmentation

Image semantic segmentation has always been a hot topic in image understanding since it plays an important role in many real applications such as autonomous driving, robotic perception, augmented reality, aerial image analysis, and medical image analysis. In the era of deep learning, various algorithms have been proposed to improve semantic segmentation. Those related works can be divided into two groups: CNN-based methods [1,5,8,12,19,40,41,44,49,51] and transformer-based methods [47,53]. Among CNN-based methods, FCN [41] is a pioneer work, which adopts fully convolutional networks and pixel-to-pixel classification. Since then, other methods [4,5,15,21,52,58] have been proposed to increase the receptive fields or representation ability of the network. Another group of works [47,53] is based on the transformer which is first proposed in natural language processing [45] and has the ability to capture global context [13]. Though tremendous progress has been achieved in image segmentation, researchers have paid more and more attention to VSS since video streams are a more realistic data modality.

2.2 Video Semantic Segmentation

Video semantic segmentation (VSS), aiming at classifying each pixel in each frame of a video into a predefined category, can be tackled by applying single image semantic segmentation algorithms [5–7,47,52] on each video frame. Though simple, this approach serves as an important baseline in VSS. One obvious drawback of this method is that the temporal information between consecutive frames is discarded and unexploited. Hence, dedicated VSS approaches [16, 20,22,23,27,28,31–34,36–38,42,46,48,57] are proposed to make use of the temporal dimension to segment videos.

Most of the current VSS approaches can be divided into two groups. The first group of approaches focuses on using temporal information to reduce computation. Specifically, LLVS [31], Accel [22], GSVNET [28] and EVS [38] conserve computation by propagating the features from the key frames to non-key frames. Similarly, DVSNet [17] divides the current frame into different regions and the regions which do not differ much from previous frames do not traverse the slow segmentation network, but a fast flow network. However, due to the fact that they save computation on some frames or regions, their performance is usually inferior to the single frame baseline. The second group of methods focuses on exploring temporal information to improve segmentation performance and prediction consistency across frames. Specifically, NetWarp [46] wraps the features of the reference frames for temporal aggregation. TDNet [20] aggregates the features of sequential frames with an attention propagation module. ETC [33] uses motion information to impose temporal consistency among predictions between sequential frames. STT [29], LMANet [37] and CFFM [43] exploit the features from reference frames to help segment the target frame by the attention mechanism. Despite the promising results, those methods do not consider correlation mining among cross-frame affinities. This paper provides a new perspective on VSS by mining the relations among affinities.

3 Methodology

In this section, we target VSS and present a novel approach MRCFA through Mining Relations among Cross-Frame Affinities. The main idea of MRCFA is to mine the relations among multi-scale affinities computed from multi-scale

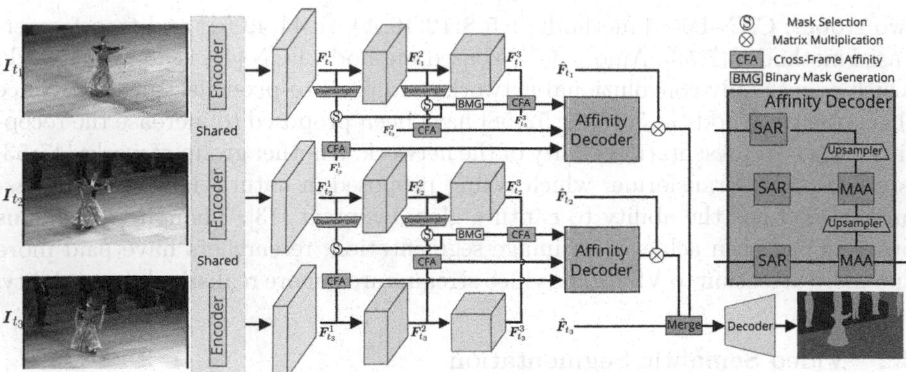

Fig. 2. Network overview of MRCFA. Our method is illustrated when the clip contains three frames ($T = 3$). The first two frames are reference frames while the last one is the target frame. All frames first go through the encoder to extract the multi-scale features ($L = 3$) from the intermediate layers. For each reference frame, we compute the Cross-Frame Affinities (CFA) across different scales of features. To save computation, Selective Token Masking is proposed. Then, the multi-scale affinities are input to an affinity decoder to learn a unified and informative affinity, through the Single-scale Affinity Refinement (SAR) module and Multi-scale Affinity Aggregation (MAA). The new representation of the target frame using the reference is obtained by exploiting the refined affinity to retrieve the corresponding reference features. Finally, all the new representations of the target are merged to segment the target. *Best viewed in color.*

intermediate features between the target frame and the reference frames, as illustrated in Fig. 2. We first provide the preliminaries in Sect. 3.1. Next, we introduce Single-scale Affinity Refinement (SAR) which independently refines each single-scale affinity in Sect. 3.2. After that, Multi-scare Affinities Aggregation (MAA) which merges affinities across various scales is presented in Sect. 3.3. Finally, we explain the Selective Token Masking mechanism (Sect. 3.4) to reduce the computation.

3.1 Preliminaries

Given a video clip $\{\boldsymbol{I}_{t_i} \in \mathbb{R}^{H\times W\times 3}\}_{i=1}^{T}$ containing T video frames and corresponding ground-truth masks $\{\boldsymbol{M}_{t_i} \in \mathbb{R}^{H\times W}\}_{i=1}^{T}$, our objective is to learn a VSS model. Without loss of generalizability, we focus on segmenting the last frame $\boldsymbol{I}_{t_T}$, which is referred as the target frame. All the previous frames $\{\boldsymbol{I}_{t_i}\}_{i=1}^{T-1}$ are referred as the reference frames. Each frame $\boldsymbol{I}_{t_i}$ is first input into an encoder to extract intermediate features $\{\boldsymbol{F}_{t_i}^{l} \in \mathbb{R}^{H_l W_l \times C_l}\}_{l=1}^{L}$ in various scales from L intermediate layers of the deep encoder, where H_l, W_l, C_l correspond to the height, width, number of channels of the feature map, respectively. For simplicity, multi-scale features $\{\boldsymbol{F}_{t_i}^{l}\}_{l=1}^{L}$ are in the order that shallow features are followed by deep features. We have $H_{l_1} \geq H_{l_2}$ and $W_{l_1} \geq W_{l_2}$, if $l_1 < l_2$. In this paper, we aim to exploit the contextual information in the reference frames to refine the features of the target frame and thus improve the target's segmentation.

Instead of simply modeling the affinities among frames for feature aggregation, we devote our efforts to mine relations among cross-frame affinities.

3.2 Single-scale Affinity Refinement

We start with introducing the process of generating multi-scale affinities between the target frame and each reference frame. We first map the features $\{\boldsymbol{F}_{t_T}^l\}_{l=1}^L$ of the target frames into the queries $\{\boldsymbol{Q}^l\}_{l=1}^L$ by a linear layer, as:

$$\boldsymbol{Q}^l = f(\boldsymbol{F}_{t_T}^l; \boldsymbol{W}_{query}^l), \tag{1}$$

where $\boldsymbol{W}_{query}^l \in \mathbb{R}^{C_l \times C_l}$ is the weight matrix of the linear layer f and $\boldsymbol{Q}^l \in \mathbb{R}^{H_l W_l \times C_l}$. Similarly, the multi-scale features $\{\boldsymbol{F}_{t_i}^l\}_{l=1}^L$ of the reference frame ($i \in [1, T-1]$) are also processed to generate the keys $\{\boldsymbol{K}_{t_i}^l\}_{l=1}^L$, as follows:

$$\boldsymbol{K}_{t_i}^l = f(\boldsymbol{F}_{t_i}^l; \boldsymbol{W}_{key}^l), \tag{2}$$

where $\boldsymbol{W}_{key}^l \in \mathbb{R}^{C_l \times C_l}$ is the corresponding weight matrix and $\boldsymbol{K}_{t_i}^l \in \mathbb{R}^{H_l W_l \times C_l}$. After obtaining the queries and the keys, we are ready to generate the affinities between the target frame $\boldsymbol{I}_{t_T}$ and each reference frame $\boldsymbol{I}_{t_i}$ ($i \in [1, T-1]$) across all scales. Then, **Cross-Frame Affinities (CFA)** are computed as:

$$\boldsymbol{A}_{t_i}^l = \boldsymbol{Q}^l \times \boldsymbol{K}_{t_i}^{l\top}, \tag{3}$$

where we have $\boldsymbol{A}_{t_i}^l \in \mathbb{R}^{H_l W_l \times H_l W_l}$, $l \in [1, L]$ and $i \in [1, T-1]$. It means that, at each scale, the target frame has an affinity map with each reference frame.

Based on the affinities $\{\boldsymbol{A}_{t_i}^l\}_{l=1}^L$, our affinity decoder is designed to mine the correlations between them to learn a better affinity between the target and the reference frame. As shown in Fig. 2, it is comprised of two modules: Single-scale Affinity Refinement (SAR) and Multi-scale Affinity Aggregation (MAA). Please refer to Sect. 1 for our motivations. In order to reduce computation and prepare the affinities for MAA module which requires the same number and corresponding semantics (see Sect. 1), our affinity decoder operates on $\{\tilde{\boldsymbol{A}}_{t_i}^l \in \mathbb{R}^{H_l W_l \times S}\}_{l=1}^L$, rather than $\{\boldsymbol{A}_{t_i}^l \in \mathbb{R}^{H_l W_l \times H_l W_l}\}_{l=1}^L$. The affinities $\tilde{\boldsymbol{A}}_{t_i}^l$ is a downsampled version of $\boldsymbol{A}_{t_i}^l$ along the second dimension, which will be explained in Sect. 3.4.

Single-scale Affinity Refinement (SAR). For the affinity matrix $\tilde{\boldsymbol{A}}_{t_i}^l$, each of its elements corresponds to a similarity between a token in the query and a token in the key. We reshape $\tilde{\boldsymbol{A}}_{t_i}^l$ from $\mathbb{R}^{H_l W_l \times S}$ to $\mathbb{R}^{H_l \times W_l \times S}$. In order to learn the correlation within the single-scale affinity $\tilde{\boldsymbol{A}}_{t_i}^l \in \mathbb{R}^{H_l \times W_l \times S}$, a straightforward way is to exploit 3D convolution. However, this approach suffers from two weaknesses. First, it requires a large amount of computational cost. Second, not all the activations within the 3D window are meaningful. Considering a 3D convolution with a kernel $\mathcal{K} \in \mathbb{R}^{k \times k \times k}$, the normal 3D convolution at the location $x = (x_1, x_2, x_3)$ is formulated as:

$$(\tilde{\boldsymbol{A}}_{t_i}^l * \mathcal{K})_x = \sum_{(o_1, o_2, o_3) \in \mathcal{N}(x)} \tilde{\boldsymbol{A}}_{t_i}^l(o_1, o_2, o_3) \mathcal{K}(o_1 - x_1, o_2 - x_2, o_3 - x_3), \tag{4}$$

where $\mathcal{N}(x)$ is the set of locations in the 3D window $(k \times k \times k)$ centered at x, and $|\mathcal{N}(x)| = k^3$. As seen in Eq. (4), all the neighbors along three dimensions are used to conduct the 3D convolution. However, the last dimension of $\tilde{\boldsymbol{A}}^l_{t_i}$ is the sparse selection in the key (Sect. 3.4) and thus does not contain spatial information. Including the neighbors along the last dimension could introduce noise and bring more complexity. Thus, we propose to refine the affinities across the first two dimension. For affinity $\tilde{\boldsymbol{A}}^l_{t_i}$ of each scale, we first permute it to $\mathbb{R}^{S \times H_l \times W_l}$ and then use 2D convolutions to learn the relations within the affinity. The refined affinity is denoted as $\bar{\boldsymbol{A}}^l_{t_i} \in \mathbb{R}^{S \times H_l \times W_l}$. This process can be formulated as:

$$\begin{aligned} \tilde{\boldsymbol{A}}^l_{t_i} &\in \mathbb{R}^{H_l \times W_l \times S} \rightarrow \tilde{\boldsymbol{A}}^l_{t_i} \in \mathbb{R}^{S \times H_l \times W_l}, \\ \bar{\boldsymbol{A}}^l_{t_i} &= G(\tilde{\boldsymbol{A}}^l_{t_i}), \end{aligned} \tag{5}$$

where G represents a few connvolutional layers. Due to the use of 2D convolution and the token reduction mentioned in Sect. 3.4, the refinement of affinities is fast. After refining affinity for each scale, we collect the refined affinities $\{\bar{\boldsymbol{A}}^l_{t_i}\}_{l=1}^L$ for all scales. Next, we present Multi-scale Affinity Aggregation (MAA) module.

3.3 Multi-scale Affinity Aggregation

Multi-scale Affinity Aggregation (MAA). The affinity from the deep features contains more semantic but more coarse information, while the affinity from the shallow features contains more fine-grained but less semantic information. Thus, we propose a **Multi-scale Affinity Aggregation** module to aggregate the information from small-scale affinities to large-scale affinities, as:

$$\begin{aligned} \boldsymbol{B}^L_{t_i} &= \bar{\boldsymbol{A}}^L_{t_i}, \\ \boldsymbol{B}^l_{t_i} &= G(\Gamma(\boldsymbol{B}^{l+1}_{t_i}) + \bar{\boldsymbol{A}}^l_{t_i}), \quad l = L-1, ..., 1, \end{aligned} \tag{6}$$

where Γ denotes upsampling operation to match the spatial size when necessary. By Eq. (6), we generate the final refined affinity $\boldsymbol{B}^1_{t_i}$ between the target frame $\boldsymbol{I}_{t_T}$ and each reference frame $\boldsymbol{I}_{t_i}$ $(i \in [1, L-1])$.

Feature Retrieval. For single-frame semantic segmentation, SegFormer [47] generates the final feature $\hat{\boldsymbol{F}}_{t_i} \in \mathbb{R}^{\hat{H}\hat{W} \times \hat{C}}$ by merging multiple intermediate features. The final features are informative and directly used to predict the segmentation mask [47]. Using the refined affinity $\boldsymbol{B}^1_{t_i}$ and the informative features $\hat{\boldsymbol{F}}_{t_i}$, we compute the new refined feature representations for the target frame. Specifically, the feature $\hat{\boldsymbol{F}}_{t_i}$ is first downsampled to the size of $\mathbb{R}^{H_L W_L \times \hat{C}}$. To correspond the refined affinity and the informative feature, we sample feature $\hat{\boldsymbol{F}}_{t_i}$ using the token selection mask $\boldsymbol{M}_{t_i}$ (Sect. 3.4) and obtain $\tilde{\boldsymbol{F}}_{t_i} \in \mathbb{R}^{S \times \hat{C}}$. The new feature representation for the target frame using the reference is obtained as:

$$\boldsymbol{B}^1_{t_i} \in \mathbb{R}^{S \times H_1 \times W_1} \rightarrow \boldsymbol{B}^1_{t_i} \in \mathbb{R}^{H_1 W_1 \times S}, \qquad \boldsymbol{O}_{t_i} = \boldsymbol{B}^1_{t_i} \times \tilde{\boldsymbol{F}}_{t_i}. \tag{7}$$

Intuitively, this step is to retrieve the informative features from the reference frame to the target frame using affinity. Computing Eq. (7) for all reference frames, we obtain the new representations of the target frame as $\{\boldsymbol{O}_{t_i}\}_{i=0}^{T-1}$.

The final feature used to segment the target frame is merged from $\{\boldsymbol{O}_{t_i}\}_{i=0}^{T-1}$ and $\hat{\boldsymbol{F}}_{t_L}$ as follows:

$$\boldsymbol{O}_{t_L} = \frac{1}{T-1}\Gamma(\sum_{i=1}^{T-1}\boldsymbol{O}_{t_i}) + \hat{\boldsymbol{F}}_{t_L}. \tag{8}$$

Finally, a simple MLP decoder projects $\boldsymbol{O}_{t_L}$ to the segmentation logits, and typical cross-entropy loss is used for training. In the test period, when segmenting the target frame I_{t_T}, the encoder only needs to generate the features for the current target while the reference frames are already processed in previous steps and the corresponding features can be directly used.

3.4 Selective Token Masking

As discussed in Sect. 1, there should be the same number of reference tokens with corresponding semantics across scales.Besides, computing cross-frame affinities requires a lot of computation. Thus, our affinity decoder does not process $\{\boldsymbol{A}_{t_i}^l \in \mathbb{R}^{H_l W_l \times H_l W_l}\}_{l=1}^L$, but rather its downsampled version $\{\tilde{\boldsymbol{A}}_{t_i}^l \in \mathbb{R}^{H_l W_l \times S}\}_{l=1}^L$. Here, we explain how to generate $\{\tilde{\boldsymbol{A}}_{t_i}^l\}_{l=1}^L$, by reducing the number of tokens in the multi-scale keys $\{\boldsymbol{K}_{t_i}^l\}_{l=1}^L$ before computing Eq. (3).

We exploit convolutional layers to downsample the multi-scale keys to the spatial size of $H_L \times W_L$. Specifically, for the key $\boldsymbol{K}_{t_i}^l$ ($l \in [1, L-1]$), we process it by a convolutional layer with both kernel and stride size of $(\frac{H_l}{H_L}, \frac{W_l}{W_L})$. As a result, we obtain new keys $\hat{\boldsymbol{K}}_{t_i}^l$ with smaller spatial size, which is given by

$$\begin{aligned}
\boldsymbol{K}_{t_i}^l &\in \mathbb{R}^{H_l W_l \times C_l} \rightarrow \boldsymbol{K}_{t_i}^l \in \mathbb{R}^{C_l \times H_l \times W_l}, \\
\hat{\boldsymbol{K}}_{t_i}^l &= g(\boldsymbol{K}_{t_i}^l; (\frac{H_l}{H_L}, \frac{W_l}{W_L}); (\frac{H_l}{H_L}, \frac{W_l}{W_L})), \\
\hat{\boldsymbol{K}}_{t_i}^l &\in \mathbb{R}^{C_l \times H_L \times W_L} \rightarrow \hat{\boldsymbol{K}}_{t_i}^l \in \mathbb{R}^{H_L W_L \times C_l}.
\end{aligned} \tag{9}$$

where $g(\cdot; (k_h, k_w); (s_h, s_w))$ represents a convolutional layer with the kernel size (k_h, k_w) and the stride (s_h, s_w). After this step, we obtain the downsampled keys $\{\hat{\boldsymbol{K}}_{t_i}^l\}_{l=1}^{L-1}$, where $\hat{\boldsymbol{K}}_{t_i}^l \in \mathbb{R}^{H_L W_L \times C_l}$, $l \in [1, L-1]$ and $i \in [1, T-1]$.

To further reduce the number of tokens in $\{\hat{\boldsymbol{K}}_{t_i}^l\}_{l=1}^{L-1}$, we propose to select important tokens and discard less important ones. The idea is to first compute the affinity for the deepest query/key pair ($\boldsymbol{Q}^L$ and $\boldsymbol{K}_{t_i}^L$), then generate a binary mask of important token locations, and finally select tokens in keys using the mask. The process of **Binary Mask Generation (BMG)** is in the following. The affinity between the deepest query and key is given by $\boldsymbol{A}_{t_i}^L \in \mathbb{R}^{H_L W_L \times H_L W_L}$, following Eq. (3). Next, we choose the top-n maximum elements across each column of $\boldsymbol{A}_{t_i}^L$, given by

$$\hat{\boldsymbol{A}}_{t_i}^L[:, j] = \arg\max_n(\boldsymbol{A}_{t_i}^L[:, j]), \qquad j \in [1, H_L W_L], \tag{10}$$

where $\arg\max_n$ means to take the top-n elements, and $\hat{\boldsymbol{A}}_{t_i}^L \in \mathbb{R}^{n \times H_L W_L}$. Then, we sum over the top-n elements and generate a token importance map $\boldsymbol{M}_{t_i}$ as

$$\boldsymbol{M}_{t_i} = \sum_{j=1}^{n} (\hat{\boldsymbol{A}}_{t_i}^L[j,:]), \tag{11}$$

in which we have $\boldsymbol{M}_{t_i} \in \mathbb{R}^{H_L W_L}$. We recover the spatial size of $\boldsymbol{M}_{t_i}$ by reshaping it to $\mathbb{R}^{H_L \times W_L}$. The token importance map $\boldsymbol{M}_{t_i}$ shows the importance level of every location in the key feature map. Since $\boldsymbol{M}_{t_i}$ is derived from the deepest/highest level of features, the token importance information it contains is semantic-oriented and can be shared in other shallow levels. We use it to sample the tokens in $\{\hat{\boldsymbol{K}}_{t_i}^l\}_{l=1}^{L-1}$. Specifically, we sample p percent of the locations with the top-p highest importance scores in $\boldsymbol{M}_{t_i}$, where p is referred as the token selection ratio. The binary token selection mask with p percent of the locations highlighted is denoted as $\tilde{\boldsymbol{M}}_{t_i}$. The location with the value 1 in $\tilde{\boldsymbol{M}}_{t_i}$ means the token importance is within the top-p percent and the corresponding token will be selected. The location with the value 0 in $\tilde{\boldsymbol{M}}_{t_i}$ means the token in that location is less important and will thus be discarded. The total number of locations with the value 1 in $\tilde{\boldsymbol{M}}_{t_i}$ is denoted by $S = pH_L W_L$.

Using mask $\tilde{\boldsymbol{M}}_{t_i}$, we select p percent of tokens in $\{\hat{\boldsymbol{K}}_{t_i}^l\}_{l=1}^{L-1}$. The keys after selection are denoted as $\{\tilde{\boldsymbol{K}}_{t_i}^l \in \mathbb{R}^{S \times C_l}\}_{l=1}^{L-1}$. With $\boldsymbol{Q}^l$ and $\tilde{\boldsymbol{K}}_{t_i}^l$, we compute the affinities $\{\tilde{\boldsymbol{A}}_{t_i}^l \in \mathbb{R}^{H_l W_l \times S}\}_{l=1}^{L-1}$ using Eq. (3). For $\boldsymbol{A}_{t_i}^L$, we also conduct sampling using $\tilde{\boldsymbol{M}}_{t_i}$ and obtain $\tilde{\boldsymbol{A}}_{t_i}^L \in \mathbb{R}^{H_L W_L \times S}$. Merging the affinities from all L scales gives final affinities of $\{\tilde{\boldsymbol{A}}_{t_i}^l \in \mathbb{R}^{H_l W_l \times S}\}_{l=1}^{L}$. After computing the affinities for all reference frames, we have the downsampled affinities $\{\{\tilde{\boldsymbol{A}}_{t_i}^l\}_{l=1}^{L}\}_{i=1}^{T-1}$.

4 Experiments

4.1 Experimental Setup

Datasets. Densely annotating video frames requires intensive manual labeling efforts. The widely used datasets for VSS are Cityscapes [9] and CamVid [2] datasets. However, these datasets only contain sparse annotations, which limits the exploration of temporal information. Fortunately, the Video Scene Parsing in the Wild (VSPW) dataset [34] is proposed to facilitate the progress of this field. It is currently the largest-scale VSS dataset with 198,244 training frames, 24,502 validation frames and 28,887 test frames. For each video, 15 frames per second are densely annotated for 124 categories. These aspects make VSPW the best benchmark for VSS up till now. Hence, most of our experiments are conducted on VSPW. To further demonstrate the effectiveness of MRCFA, we also show results on Cityscapes, for which only one out of 30 frames is annotated.

Implementation Details. For the encoder, we use the MiT backbones as in Segformer [47], which have been pretrained on ImageNet-1K [39]. For VSPW

Table 1. The impact of the selection of reference frames.

Methods	T	t_1	t_2	t_3	mIoU ↑	mVC$_8$ ↑	mVC$_{16}$ ↑
SegFormer [47]	–	–	–	–	36.5	84.7	79.9
MRCFA (Ours)	2	−1	–	–	38.0	85.9	81.2
	2	−3	–	–	38.1	85.5	80.7
	2	−6	–	–	38.2	85.1	80.3
	2	−9	–	–	37.4	85.5	81.2
	3	−6	−3	–	38.4	87.0	82.1
	3	−9	−6	–	38.4	86.9	82.0
	4	−9	−6	−3	**38.9**	**88.8**	**84.4**

Table 2. The impact of token selection ratio p. The row which best deals with the trade-off between performance and computation resources is shown in **black bold**.

p	mIoU ↑	mVC$_8$ ↑	mVC$_{16}$ ↑	Memory (M) ↓	FPS (f/s) ↑
100%	39.4	89.2	84.9	1068	32.9
90%	39.1	89.1	84.8	1035	34.2
70%	39.1	88.2	83.9	969	36.8
50%	**38.9**	**88.8**	**84.4**	**903 (15.4%)**	**40.1 (21.9%)**
30%	38.5	86.7	81.9	838	43.5
10%	35.9	86.2	81.7	773	47.2

dataset, three reference frames are used, which are 9, 6 and 3 frames ahead of the target, following [34]. Three-scale features from the last three transformer blocks are used to compute the cross-frame affinities and mine their correlations. For the Mask-based Token Selection (MTS), we set $p = 80\%$ for MiT-B0 and $p = 50\%$ for other backbones unless otherwise specified. For training augmentations, we use random resizing, horizontal flipping, and photometric distortion to process the original images. Then, the images are randomly cropped to the size of 480×480 to train the network. We set the batch size as 8 during training. The models are all trained with AdamW optimizer for a maximum of 160k iterations and "poly" learning rate schedule. The initial learning rate is 6e-5. For simplicity, we perform the single-scale test on the whole image, rather than the sliding window test or multi-scale test. The input images are resized to 480×853 for VSPW. We also do not perform any post-processing such as CRF [26]. For Cityscape, the input image is cropped to 512×1024 during training and resized to the same resolution during inference. And we use two reference frames and four-scale features. The number of frames being processed per second (FPS) is computed in a single Quadro RTX 6000 GPU (24G memory).

Evaluation Metrics. To evaluate the segmentation results, we adopt the commonly used metrics of Mean IoU (mIoU) and Weighted IoU (WIoU), following [41]. We also use Video Consistency (VC) [34] to evaluate the category consistency among the adjacent frames in the video, following [34]. Formally, video consistency VC_n for n consecutive frames for a video clips $\{\boldsymbol{I}_c\}_{c=1}^{C}$, is computed by: $\mathrm{VC}_n = \frac{1}{C-n+1}\sum_{i=1}^{C-n+1} \frac{(\cap_i^{i+n-1}\boldsymbol{S}_i)\cap(\cap_i^{i+n-1}\boldsymbol{S}_i^{'})}{\cap_i^{i+n-1}\boldsymbol{S}_i}$, where $C \geq n$. $\boldsymbol{S}_i$ and $\boldsymbol{S}_i^{'}$ are the ground-truth mask and predicted mask for i^{th} frame, respectively. We compute the mean of video consistency VC_n for all videos in the dataset as mVC_n. Following [34], we compute mVC_8 and mVC_{16} to evaluate the visual consistency of the predicted masks. Please refer to [34] for more details about VC.

4.2 Ablation Studies

We conduct ablation studies on the large-scale VSPW dataset [34] to validate the key designs of MRCFA. For fairness, we adopt the same settings as in Sect. 4.1 unless otherwise specified. The ablation studies are conducted on MiT-B1 backbone.

Influence of the Reference Frames. We study the performance of our method with respect to different choices of reference frames in Table 1. We have the following observations. First, using a single reference frame largely improves the segmentation performance (mIoU). For example, when using a single reference frame which is 3 frames ahead of the target one, the mIoU improvement over the baseline (SegFormer) is 1.6%, *i.e.*, 38.1 over 36.5. Further adding more reference frames, better segmentation performance is observed. The best mIoU of 38.9 is obtained when using reference frames of 9, 6, and 3 frames ahead of the target. Second, for the prediction consistency metrics (mVC_8 and mVC_{16}), the advantage of exploiting more reference frames is more obvious. For example, using one reference frame ($t_1 = -6$) gives mVC_8 and mVC_{16} of 85.1 and 80.3, improving the baseline by 0.4% and 0.4%, respectively. However, when using three reference frames ($t_1 = -9$, $t_2 = -6$, $t_3 = -3$), the achieved mVC_8 and mVC_{16} are much more superior to the baseline, improving by 4.1% and 4.5%. The results are reasonable because using more reference frames gives the model a bigger view of the previously predicted features and thus generates more consistent predictions.

Influence of Token Selection Ratio p. We study the influence of the token selection ratio p in terms of performance and computational resources in Table 2. Smaller p represents that less number of tokens in the key features are selected and thus less computation resource is required. Hence, there is a trade-off between the segmentation performance and the required resources (GPU memory and additional latency). In the experiments, when reducing $p = 100\%$ to 50%, the performance reduces slightly (0.5 in mIoU) while the GPU memory reduces by 15.4% and FPS increases by 21.9%. When further reducing p to 10%, the performance largely decreases in terms of mIoU, mVC_8 and mVC_{16}. The reason is that too many tokens are discarded in the reference frames and the remained tokens are not informative enough to provide the required contexts for segmenting the target frame. To sum up, the best trade-off is achieved when $p = 50\%$.

Influence of the Feature Scales. For VSPW dataset, we use three-scale features output from the last three transformer blocks. Here, we conduct an ablation study on the impact of the used feature scales. The results are shown in Table 3. It can be observed that using the features from the last stage ($L = 1$) or the last two stages ($L = 2$) gives inferior performance while consuming less computational resources and achieving faster running speed. When using three-scale features, the best results are achieved in terms of mIoU, mVC_8, and mVC_{16}. This is due to the fact that the features in different scales contain complementary information, and the proposed affinity decoder successfully mines this information through learning correlations between multi-scale affinities.

Table 3. Ablation study on the number of feature scales (L). Using more scales of features for our method progressively increases the performance.

L	mIoU ↑	mVC_8 ↑	mVC_{16} ↑	Params (M) ↓	FPS (f/s) ↑
1	37.5	87.7	83.1	14.8	44.3
2	38.1	87.5	82.5	15.3	43.8
3	**38.9**	**88.8**	**84.4**	16.2	40.1

Table 4. Ablation study on the affinity decoder. Within our design, SAR and MAA are essential parts which contribute to the refinement of the affinity.

Methods	SAR	MAA	mIoU ↑	mVC_8 ↑	mVC_{16} ↑	Params (M) ↓
SegFormer	–	–	36.5	84.7	79.9	13.8
Feature pyramid	–	–	37.8	87.0	82.0	16.2
Affinity decoder	✓	✗	37.8	87.1	82.6	16.2
	✗	✓	37.4	88.3	83.6	16.2
	✓	✓	**38.9**	**88.8**	**84.4**	16.2

Ablation Study on Affinity Decoder. We conduct ablation studies on the proposed affinity decoder. The results are shown in Table 4. Our affinity decoder processes the multi-scale affinities and generates a refined affinity matrix for each pair of the target and reference frames. It is reasonable to ask whether this design is better than the feature pyramid baseline. For this baseline (Feature Pyramid), we first compute the features for the target frame using the reference frame features at each scale and then merge those multi-scale features. For fair comparisons, we use a similar number of parameters for this baseline and other settings are also the same as ours. The result shows that while Feature Pyramid performs favorably over the single-frame baseline, our approach clearly surpasses it. It validates the effectiveness of the proposed affinity decoder.

As presented in Sect. 3.2, our affinity decoder has two modules: Single-scale Affinity Refinement (SAR) and Multi-scale Affinity Aggregation (MAA). The ablation study of two modules is provided in Table 4. Only using SAR, our method obtains the mIoU of 37.8, while only using MAA gives the mIoU of 37.4. Both variants are clearly better than the baseline, validating their effectiveness. Combining both modules, the proposed approach achieves the best mIoU, mVC_8, and mVC_{16}. It shows that both SAR and MAA are essential parts of the affinity decoder to learn better affinities to help segment the target frame.

4.3 Segmentation Results

The state-of-the-art comparisons on VSPW [34] dataset are shown in Table 5. Besides segmentation performance and visual consistency of the predicted masks, we also report the model complexity and FPS. According to the model size, the methods are divided into two groups: small models and large models.

Table 5. State-of-the-art comparison on the VSPW [34] validation set. MRCFA outperforms the compared methods on both accuracy (mIoU) and prediction consistency.

Methods	Backbone	mIoU ↑	Weighted IoU ↑	mVC_8 ↑	mVC_{16} ↑	Params (M) ↓	FPS (f/s) ↑
SegFormer [47]	MiT-B0	32.9	56.8	82.7	77.3	3.8	73.4
SegFormer [47]	MiT-B1	36.5	58.8	84.7	79.9	13.8	58.7
MRCFA (Ours)	MiT-B0	35.2	57.9	88.0	83.2	5.2	50.0
MRCFA (Ours)	MiT-B1	**38.9**	**60.0**	**88.8**	**84.4**	16.2	40.1
DeepLabv3+ [6]	ResNet-101	34.7	58.8	83.2	78.2	62.7	–
UperNet [46]	ResNet-101	36.5	58.6	82.6	76.1	83.2	–
PSPNet [52]	ResNet-101	36.5	58.1	84.2	79.6	70.5	13.9
OCRNet [50]	ResNet-101	36.7	59.2	84.0	79.0	58.1	14.3
ETC [33]	PSPNet	36.6	58.3	84.1	79.2	89.4	–
NetWarp [46]	PSPNet	37.0	57.9	84.4	79.4	89.4	–
ETC [33]	OCRNet	37.5	59.1	84.1	79.1	58.1	–
NetWarp [46]	OCRNet	37.5	58.9	84.0	79.0	58.1	–
$TCB_{st\text{-}ppm}$ [34]	ResNet-101	37.5	58.6	87.0	82.1	70.5	10.0
$TCB_{st\text{-}ocr}$ [34]	ResNet-101	37.4	59.3	86.9	82.0	58.1	5.5
$TCB_{st\text{-}ocr\text{-}mem}$ [34]	ResNet-101	37.8	59.5	87.9	84.0	58.1	5.5
SegFormer [47]	MiT-B2	43.9	63.7	86.0	81.2	24.8	39.2
SegFormer [47]	MiT-B5	48.2	65.1	87.8	83.7	82.1	17.2
MRCFA (Ours)	MiT-B2	45.3	64.7	90.3	86.2	27.3	32.1
MRCFA (Ours)	MiT-B5	**49.9**	**66.0**	**90.9**	**87.4**	84.5	15.7

Table 6. State-of-the-art comparison on the Cityscapes [9] val set.

Methods	Backbone	mIoU ↑	Params (M) ↓	FPS (f/s) ↑
FCN [41]	MobileNetV2	61.5	9.8	14.2
CC [42]	VGG-16	67.7	–	16.5
DFF [56]	ResNet-101	68.7	–	9.7
GRFP [36]	ResNet-101	69.4	–	3.2
PSPNet [52]	MobileNetV2	70.2	13.7	11.2
DVSN [48]	ResNet-101	70.3	–	19.8
Accel [22]	ResNet-101	72.1	–	3.6
ETC [33]	ResNet-18	71.1	13.2	9.5
SegFormer [47]	MiT-B0	71.9	3.7	58.5
MRCFA (Ours)	MiT-B0	72.8	4.2	33.3
SegFormer [47]	MiT-B1	74.1	13.8	46.8
MRCFA (Ours)	MiT-B1	**75.1**	14.9	21.5

Among all methods, our MRCFA achieves state-of-the-art performance and produces the most consistent segmentation masks across video frames. For small models, our method on MiT-B1 clearly outperforms the strong baseline SegFormer [47] by 2.4% in mIoU and 1.2% in weighted IoU. In terms of the visual consistency in the predicted masks, our approach is superior to other methods, surpassing the second best method with 4.1% and 4.5% in mVC_8 and mVC_{16}, respectively. For large models, MRCFA shows similar behavior. The results indicate that our method is effective in mining the relations between the target and reference frames through the designed modules: SAR and MAA.

Despite that our approach achieves impressive performance, it adds limited model complexity and latency. Specifically, compared to SegFormer (MiT-B2), MRCFA slightly increases the number of parameters from 24.8 M to 27.3 M and reduces the FPS from 39.2 to 32.1. The efficiency of our method benefits from the proposed STM mechanism for which we abandon unimportant tokens.

Fig. 3. Qualitative results. From *top* to *bottom*: the input frames, the predicted masks of SegFormer [47], the predictions of ours ($T = 3, t_1 = -3,\ t_2 = -6$), the predictions of ours ($T = 4, t_1 = -3,\ t_2 = -6,\ t_3 = -9$) and the ground-truth masks. Our model generates better results than the baseline in terms of accuracy and VC.

We conduct additional experiments on the semi-supervised Cityscapes [9] dataset, for which only one frame in each video clip is pixel-wise annotated.

Table 6 shows the results. Similar to VSPW, MRCFA also achieves state-of-the-art results among the compared approaches under the semi-supervised setting and has a fast running speed. Besides the quantitative comparisons analyzed above, we also qualitatively compare the proposed method with the baseline on the sampled video clips in Fig. 3. For the two samples, our method generates more accurate segmentation masks, which are also more visually consistent.

5 Conclusions

This paper presents a novel framework MRCFA for VSS. Different from previous methods, we aim at mining the relations among multi-scale Cross-Frame Affinities (CFA) in two aspects: single-scale intrinsic correlations and multi-scale relations. Accordingly, Single-scale Affinity Refinement (SAR) is proposed to independently refine the affinity of each scale, while Multi-scale Affinity Aggregation (MAA) is designed to merge the refined affinities across various scales. To reduce computation and facilitate MAA, Selective Token Masking (STM) is adopted to sample important tokens in keys for the reference frames. Combining all the novelties, MRCFA generates better affinity relations between the target and the reference frames without largely adding computational resources. Extensive experiments demonstrate the effectiveness and efficiency of MRCFA, by setting new state-of-the-arts. The key components are validated to be essential for our method by ablation studies. Overall, our exploration of mining the relations among affinities could provide a new perspective on VSS.

References

1. Ahn, J., Cho, S., Kwak, S.: Weakly supervised learning of instance segmentation with inter-pixel relations. In: IEEE CVPR, pp. 2209–2218 (2019)
2. Brostow, G.J., Fauqueur, J., Cipolla, R.: Semantic object classes in video: a high-definition ground truth database. Pattern Recogn. Lett. **30**(2), 88–97 (2009)
3. Caesar, H., Uijlings, J., Ferrari, V.: COCO-Stuff: thing and stuff classes in context. In: IEEE CVPR, pp. 1209–1218 (2018)
4. Chen, L.C., Papandreou, G., Kokkinos, I., Murphy, K., Yuille, A.L.: Semantic image segmentation with deep convolutional nets and fully connected CRFs. In: ICLR (2015)
5. Chen, L.C., Papandreou, G., Kokkinos, I., Murphy, K., Yuille, A.L.: DeepLab: semantic image segmentation with deep convolutional nets, atrous convolution, and fully connected CRFs. IEEE TPAMI **40**(4), 834–848 (2018)
6. Chen, L.C., Papandreou, G., Schroff, F., Adam, H.: Rethinking atrous convolution for semantic image segmentation. arXiv preprint arXiv:1706.05587 (2017)
7. Chen, L.-C., Zhu, Y., Papandreou, G., Schroff, F., Adam, H.: Encoder-decoder with atrous separable convolution for semantic image segmentation. In: Ferrari, V., Hebert, M., Sminchisescu, C., Weiss, Y. (eds.) ECCV 2018. LNCS, vol. 11211, pp. 833–851. Springer, Cham (2018). https://doi.org/10.1007/978-3-030-01234-2_49
8. Chen, W., et al.: Tensor low-rank reconstruction for semantic segmentation. In: Vedaldi, A., Bischof, H., Brox, T., Frahm, J.-M. (eds.) ECCV 2020. LNCS, vol. 12362, pp. 52–69. Springer, Cham (2020). https://doi.org/10.1007/978-3-030-58520-4_4

9. Cordts, M., et al.: The Cityscapes dataset for semantic urban scene understanding. In: IEEE CVPR, pp. 3213–3223 (2016)
10. Ding, H., Jiang, X., Liu, A.Q., Thalmann, N.M., Wang, G.: Boundary-aware feature propagation for scene segmentation. In: IEEE ICCV, pp. 6819–6829 (2019)
11. Ding, H., Jiang, X., Shuai, B., Liu, A.Q., Wang, G.: Context contrasted feature and gated multi-scale aggregation for scene segmentation. In: IEEE CVPR, pp. 2393–2402 (2018)
12. Ding, H., Jiang, X., Shuai, B., Liu, A.Q., Wang, G.: Semantic correlation promoted shape-variant context for segmentation. In: IEEE CVPR, pp. 8885–8894 (2019)
13. Dosovitskiy, A., et al.: An image is worth 16×16 words: transformers for image recognition at scale. In: ICLR (2021)
14. Dosovitskiy, A., et al.: FlowNet: learning optical flow with convolutional networks. In: IEEE ICCV, pp. 2758–2766 (2015)
15. Fu, J., et al.: Dual attention network for scene segmentation. In: IEEE CVPR, pp. 3146–3154 (2019)
16. Gadde, R., Jampani, V., Gehler, P.V.: Semantic video CNNs through representation warping. In: IEEE ICCV, pp. 4453–4462 (2017)
17. He, J., Deng, Z., Qiao, Y.: Dynamic multi-scale filters for semantic segmentation. In: IEEE ICCV, pp. 3562–3572 (2019)
18. He, J., Deng, Z., Zhou, L., Wang, Y., Qiao, Y.: Adaptive pyramid context network for semantic segmentation. In: IEEE CVPR, pp. 7519–7528 (2019)
19. Hsiao, C.W., Sun, C., Chen, H.T., Sun, M.: Specialize and fuse: pyramidal output representation for semantic segmentation. In: IEEE ICCV, pp. 7137–7146 (2021)
20. Hu, P., Caba, F., Wang, O., Lin, Z., Sclaroff, S., Perazzi, F.: Temporally distributed networks for fast video semantic segmentation. In: IEEE CVPR, pp. 8818–8827 (2020)
21. Huang, Z., Wang, X., Huang, L., Huang, C., Wei, Y., Liu, W.: CCNet: criss-cross attention for semantic segmentation. In: IEEE ICCV, pp. 603–612 (2019)
22. Jain, S., Wang, X., Gonzalez, J.E.: Accel: a corrective fusion network for efficient semantic segmentation on video. In: IEEE CVPR, pp. 8866–8875 (2019)
23. Jin, X., et al.: Video scene parsing with predictive feature learning. In: IEEE ICCV, pp. 5580–5588 (2017)
24. Jin, Z., et al.: Mining contextual information beyond image for semantic segmentation. In: IEEE ICCV, pp. 7231–7241 (2021)
25. Jin, Z., Liu, B., Chu, Q., Yu, N.: ISNet: integrate image-level and semantic-level context for semantic segmentation. In: IEEE ICCV, pp. 7189–7198 (2021)
26. Krähenbühl, P., Koltun, V.: Efficient inference in fully connected CRFs with Gaussian edge potentials. In: NeurIPS, pp. 109–117 (2011)
27. Kundu, A., Vineet, V., Koltun, V.: Feature space optimization for semantic video segmentation. In: IEEE CVPR, pp. 3168–3175 (2016)
28. Lee, S.P., Chen, S.C., Peng, W.H.: GSVNet: guided spatially-varying convolution for fast semantic segmentation on video. In: IEEE ICME, pp. 1–6 (2021)
29. Li, J., et al.: Video semantic segmentation via sparse temporal transformer. In: ACM MM, pp. 59–68 (2021)
30. Li, X., Yang, Y., Zhao, Q., Shen, T., Lin, Z., Liu, H.: Spatial pyramid based graph reasoning for semantic segmentation. In: IEEE CVPR, pp. 8950–8959 (2020)
31. Li, Y., Shi, J., Lin, D.: Low-latency video semantic segmentation. In: IEEE CVPR, pp. 5997–6005 (2018)
32. Liu, S., Wang, C., Qian, R., Yu, H., Bao, R., Sun, Y.: Surveillance video parsing with single frame supervision. In: IEEE CVPR, pp. 413–421 (2017)

33. Liu, Y., Shen, C., Yu, C., Wang, J.: Efficient semantic video segmentation with per-frame inference. In: Vedaldi, A., Bischof, H., Brox, T., Frahm, J.-M. (eds.) ECCV 2020. LNCS, vol. 12355, pp. 352–368. Springer, Cham (2020). https://doi.org/10.1007/978-3-030-58607-2_21
34. Miao, J., Wei, Y., Wu, Y., Liang, C., Li, G., Yang, Y.: VSPW: a large-scale dataset for video scene parsing in the wild. In: IEEE CVPR, pp. 4133–4143 (2021)
35. Neuhold, G., Ollmann, T., Rota Bulo, S., Kontschieder, P.: The Mapillary Vistas dataset for semantic understanding of street scenes. In: IEEE ICCV, pp. 4990–4999 (2017)
36. Nilsson, D., Sminchisescu, C.: Semantic video segmentation by gated recurrent flow propagation. In: IEEE CVPR, pp. 6819–6828 (2018)
37. Paul, M., Danelljan, M., Van Gool, L., Timofte, R.: Local memory attention for fast video semantic segmentation. In: IROS, pp. 1102–1109. IEEE (2021)
38. Paul, M., Mayer, C., Gool, L.V., Timofte, R.: Efficient video semantic segmentation with labels propagation and refinement. In: Winter Conference Application Computer Vision (WACV), pp. 2873–2882 (2020)
39. Russakovsky, O., et al.: ImageNet large scale visual recognition challenge. IJCV **115**(3), 211–252 (2015)
40. Seifi, S., Tuytelaars, T.: Attend and segment: attention guided active Semantic Segmentation. In: Vedaldi, A., Bischof, H., Brox, T., Frahm, J.-M. (eds.) ECCV 2020. LNCS, vol. 12370, pp. 305–321. Springer, Cham (2020). https://doi.org/10.1007/978-3-030-58595-2_19
41. Shelhamer, E., Long, J., Darrell, T.: Fully convolutional networks for semantic segmentation. IEEE TPAMI **39**(4), 640–651 (2017)
42. Shelhamer, E., Rakelly, K., Hoffman, J., Darrell, T.: Clockwork convnets for video semantic segmentation. In: Hua, G., Jégou, H. (eds.) ECCV 2016. LNCS, vol. 9915, pp. 852–868. Springer, Cham (2016). https://doi.org/10.1007/978-3-319-49409-8_69
43. Sun, G., Liu, Y., Ding, H., Probst, T., Van Gool, L.: Coarse-to-fine feature mining for video semantic segmentation. In: IEEE CVPR, pp. 3126–3137 (2022)
44. Sun, G., Wang, W., Dai, J., Van Gool, L.: Mining cross-image semantics for weakly supervised semantic segmentation. In: Vedaldi, A., Bischof, H., Brox, T., Frahm, J.-M. (eds.) ECCV 2020. LNCS, vol. 12347, pp. 347–365. Springer, Cham (2020). https://doi.org/10.1007/978-3-030-58536-5_21
45. Vaswani, A., et al.: Attention is all you need. In: NeurIPS, pp. 6000–6010 (2017)
46. Xiao, T., Liu, Y., Zhou, B., Jiang, Y., Sun, J.: Unified perceptual parsing for scene understanding. In: ECCV, pp. 418–434 (2018)
47. Xie, E., Wang, W., Yu, Z., Anandkumar, A., Alvarez, J.M., Luo, P.: SegFormer: simple and efficient design for semantic segmentation with transformers. In: NeurIPS (2021)
48. Xu, Y.S., Fu, T.J., Yang, H.K., Lee, C.Y.: Dynamic video segmentation network. In: IEEE CVPR, pp. 6556–6565 (2018)
49. Yang, M., Yu, K., Zhang, C., Li, Z., Yang, K.: DenseASPP for semantic segmentation in street scenes. In: IEEE CVPR, pp. 3684–3692 (2018)
50. Yuan, Y., Chen, X., Wang, J.: Object-contextual representations for semantic segmentation. In: Vedaldi, A., Bischof, H., Brox, T., Frahm, J.-M. (eds.) ECCV 2020. LNCS, vol. 12351, pp. 173–190. Springer, Cham (2020). https://doi.org/10.1007/978-3-030-58539-6_11
51. Zhang, F., et al.: ACFNet: attentional class feature network for semantic segmentation. In: IEEE ICCV, pp. 6798–6807 (2019)

52. Zhao, H., Shi, J., Qi, X., Wang, X., Jia, J.: Pyramid scene parsing network. In: IEEE CVPR, pp. 2881–2890 (2017)
53. Zheng, S., et al.: Rethinking semantic segmentation from a sequence-to-sequence perspective with transformers. In: IEEE CVPR, pp. 6881–6890 (2021)
54. Zhou, B., et al.: Semantic understanding of scenes through the ADE20K dataset. IJCV **127**(3), 302–321 (2019)
55. Zhou, Y., Sun, X., Zha, Z.J., Zeng, W.: Context-reinforced semantic segmentation. In: IEEE CVPR, pp. 4046–4055 (2019)
56. Zhu, X., Xiong, Y., Dai, J., Yuan, L., Wei, Y.: Deep feature flow for video recognition. In: IEEE CVPR, pp. 2349–2358 (2017)
57. Zhu, Y., et al.: Improving semantic segmentation via video propagation and label relaxation. In: IEEE CVPR, pp. 8856–8865 (2019)
58. Zhu, Z., Xu, M., Bai, S., Huang, T., Bai, X.: Asymmetric non-local neural networks for semantic segmentation. In: IEEE ICCV, pp. 593–602 (2019)

TL;DW? Summarizing Instructional Videos with Task Relevance and Cross-Modal Saliency

Medhini Narasimhan[1,2(✉)], Arsha Nagrani[2], Chen Sun[2,3], Michael Rubinstein[2], Trevor Darrell[1], Anna Rohrbach[1], and Cordelia Schmid[2]

[1] UC Berkeley, Berkeley, USA
medhini@berkeley.edu
[2] Google Research, Berkeley, USA
[3] Brown University, Berkeley, USA

https://medhini.github.io/ivsum

Abstract. YouTube users looking for instructions for a specific task may spend a long time browsing content trying to find the right video that matches their needs. Creating a visual summary (abridged version of a video) provides viewers with a quick overview and massively reduces search time. In this work, we focus on summarizing *instructional* videos, an under-explored area of video summarization. In comparison to generic videos, instructional videos can be parsed into semantically meaningful segments that correspond to important steps of the demonstrated task. Existing video summarization datasets rely on manual frame-level annotations, making them subjective and limited in size. To overcome this, we first automatically generate *pseudo summaries* for a corpus of instructional videos by exploiting two key assumptions: (i) relevant steps are likely to appear in multiple videos of the same task (*Task Relevance*), and (ii) they are more likely to be described by the demonstrator verbally (*Cross-Modal Saliency*). We propose an instructional video summarization network that combines a context-aware temporal video encoder and a segment scoring transformer. Using pseudo summaries as weak supervision, our network constructs a visual summary for an instructional video given only video and transcribed speech. To evaluate our model, we collect a high-quality test set, *WikiHow Summaries*, by scraping WikiHow articles that contain video demonstrations and visual depictions of steps allowing us to obtain the ground-truth summaries. We outperform several baselines and a state-of-the-art video summarization model on this new benchmark.

T. Darrell and A. Rohrbach—TL;DW? - Too Long; Didn't Watch?
M. Narasimhan—Work done while an intern at Google Research.
T. Darrell, A. Rohrbach, and C. Schmid—Equal contribution.

Supplementary Information The online version contains supplementary material available at https://doi.org/10.1007/978-3-031-19830-4_31.

S. Avidan et al. (Eds.): ECCV 2022, LNCS 13694, pp. 540–557, 2022.
https://doi.org/10.1007/978-3-031-19830-4_31

"To make a veggie black bean burger, start by ..."
Summary comprising of task relevant and salient steps in input video

Fig. 1. Summarizing Instructional Videos We introduce an approach for creating short visual summaries comprising steps that are most relevant to the task, as well as salient in the video, i.e. referenced in the speech. For example, given a long video on *"How to make a veggie burger"* shown above, the summary comprises key steps such as *fry ingredients, blend beans,* and *fry patty.*

1 Introduction

The search query *"How to make a veggie burger?"* on YouTube yields thousands of videos, each showing a slightly different technique for the same task. It is often time-consuming for a first-time burger maker to sift through this plethora of video content. Imagine instead, if they could watch a compact visual summary of each video which encapsulates all semantically meaningful steps relevant to the task. Such a summary could provide a quick overview of what the longer video has to offer, and may even answer some questions about the task without the viewer having to watch the whole video. In this work, we propose a method to create such succinct visual summaries from long instructional videos.

Since our goal is to summarize videos, we consider prior work on generic [9,34] and query-focused [33] video summarization. Generic video summarization datasets [9,34] tend to contain videos from *unrestricted domains* such as sports, news and day-to-day events. Given that annotations are obtained manually, the notion of what constitutes a good summary is subjective, and might differ from one annotator to the next. Query-focused video summarization partially overcomes this subjectivity by allowing users to customize a summary by specifying a natural language query [21,33]. However, both generic and query-focused approaches require datasets to be annotated manually at a per-frame level. This is very expensive, resulting in very small-scale datasets (25–50 videos) with limited utility and generalization.

Here, we focus on a specific domain - that of instructional videos [20,35,44]. We argue that a unique characteristic of these videos is that a summary can be clearly defined as a minimally sufficient *procedural* one, i.e., it must include the steps necessary to complete the task (see Fig. 1). To circumvent having to manually annotate our training data, we use an unsupervised algorithm to obtain weak supervision in the form of pseudo ground-truth summaries for a large corpus of instructional videos. We design our unsupervised objectives based on two hypotheses: (i) steps that are relevant to the task will appear across multiple videos of the same task, and (ii) salient steps are more likely to be described by the demonstrator verbally. In practice, we segment the video and group individual segments into steps based on their visual similarity. Then we compare the steps across videos of the same task to obtain *task relevance scores*. We also transcribe the videos using Automatic Speech Recognition (ASR) and compare the video segments to the transcript. We aggregate these *task relevance* and *cross-modal scores* to obtain the *importance scores* for all segments, i.e., our pseudo ground-truth summary.

Next, given an input video and transcribed speech, we train an instructional video summarization network (*IV-Sum*). IV-Sum learns to assign scores to short *video segments* using 3D video features which capture temporal context. Our network consists of a video encoder that learns context-aware temporal representations for each segment and a segment scoring transformer (SST) that then assigns importance scores to each segment. Our model is trained end-to-end using the importance scores from the pseudo summaries. Finally, we concatenate the highest scoring segments to form the final video summary.

While we can rely on pseudo ground-truth for training, we collect a clean, manually verified test set to evaluate our method. Since manually creating a labeled test set from scratch would be extremely expensive, we find a solution in the form of the WikiHow resource[1]. WikiHow articles often contain a link to an instructional video and a set of human-annotated steps present in the task along with corresponding images or short clips. To construct our test set (referred to as *WikiHow Summaries*), we automatically localize these images/clips in the video. We obtain localized segments for the images (using a window around the localized frame) and clips, and stitch the segments together to create a summary. This provides us with binary labels for each frame which serve as ground-truth annotations. We evaluate our model on *WikiHow Summaries* and compare it to several baselines and the state-of-the-art video summarization model CLIP-It [21]. Our model surpasses prior work and several baselines on three standard metrics (F-Score, Kendall [14], and Spearman [45] coefficients).

To summarize (pun intended), we introduce an approach for summarizing instructional videos that involves training our *IV-Sum* model on pseudo summaries created from a large corpus of instructional videos. *IV-Sum* learns to rank different segments in the video by learning context-aware temporal representations for each segment and a segment scoring transformer that assigns scores to segments based on their task relevance and cross-modal saliency. Our method is weakly-supervised (it only requires the task labels for videos), multimodal – uses both video and speech transcripts, and is scalable to large online corpora of instructional videos. We collect a high-quality test set, *WikiHow Summaries* for benchmarking instructional video summarization, which will be publicly released. Our model outperforms state-of-the-art video summarization methods on all met-

[1] https://www.wikihow.com/.

rics. Compared to the baselines, our method is especially good at capturing task relevant steps and assigning higher scores to salient frames, as seen through qualitative analysis.

2 Related Work

We review several lines of work related to summarization of instructional videos.
Generic Video Summarization. This task involves creating abridged versions of generic videos by stitching together short important clips from the original video [10,18,21,24,28,39,41–43]. Some of the more recent methods attempt to learn contextual representations to perform video summarization, via attention mechanism [7], graph based [24] or transformer-based [21] methods. Representative datasets include SumMe [9] and TVSum [34], where the ground-truth summaries were created by annotators assigning scores to each frame in the video, which is highly time consuming and expensive. As a consequence, the generic video summarization datasets are small and the quality of the summaries is often very subjective. Here, we focus on instructional videos which contain structure in the form of task steps, thus we have a clear definition of what a good summary should contain - a set of necessary steps for performing that specific task.

Query Focused Video Summarization. To address the subjectivity issues with Generic Summarization, Query Focused Video Summarization allowed for having user defined natural language queries to customize the summaries [13,33, 37]. A representative dataset is Query Focused Video Summarization [32]; it is very small and the queries correspond to a very narrow set of objects. In contrast, our task is large and we do not rely on any additional user input.

Step Localization. Step localization (also known as temporal action segmentation) is a related albeit distinct task. It typically implies predicting temporal boundaries of steps when the step labels [27,35,44] and even their ordering [2,4,6,11,16,26] are given. Representative datasets, COIN [35] and CrossTask [44] consist of instructional videos and a fixed set of steps for each task (from the WikiHow resource), and the task is to localize these steps in the video. Our task is different in that we are only given a video without corresponding input steps. Our model learns to pick out segments that correspond to relevant and salient steps in order to construct a video summary. We discuss and illustrate the shortcomings of the step localization annotations in Sect. 5 and Fig. 6.

Unsupervised Parsing of Instructional Videos. Closest to ours is the line of work on unsupervised video parsing and segmentation that discovers steps in instructional videos in an unsupervised manner [1,8,17,30,31]. However, these works - (1) do not focus on video summarization, thus they might miss some salient steps in video (2) often use very small datasets for training and evaluation that do not capture the broad range of instructional videos found in, e.g., COIN [35] and CrossTask [44].

3 Summarizing Instructional Videos

Overview. We propose a novel approach for constructing visual summaries of instructional videos. An instructional video typically consists of a visual demonstration of a specific task, e.g. *"How to make a pancake?"*. Our goal is to construct a visual summary of the input video containing only the steps that are crucial to the task and salient in the video, i.e. referenced in the speech. Figure 2 illustrates an outline of our approach. Our instructional video summarization pipeline consists of two stages - (i) first, we use a weakly supervised algorithm to generate pseudo summaries and frame-wise importance scores for a large corpus of instructional videos, relying only on the task label for each video (ii) next, using the pseudo summaries as supervision, we train an instructional video summarization network which takes as input the video and the corresponding transcribed speech and learns to assign scores to different segments in the input video. The network consists of a video encoder and a segment scoring transformer (SST) and is trained using the importance scores of the pseudo summaries. The final summary is constructed by selecting and concatenating the segments with high importance scores. We first describe our pseudo summary generation algorithm, followed by details on our instructional video summarizer (*IV-Sum*), and the inference procedure.

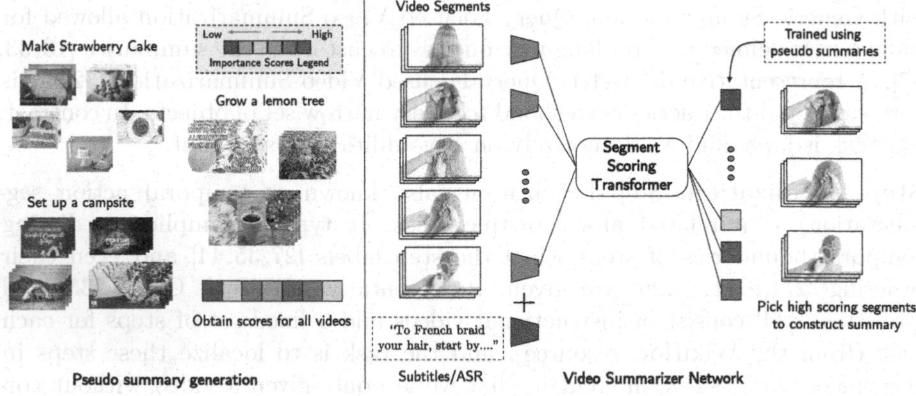

Fig. 2. Summarizing Instructional Videos. We first obtain pseudo summaries for a large collection of videos using our weakly supervised algorithm (more details in Fig. 3). Next, using the pseudo summaries as weak-supervision, we train our Instructional Video Summarizer (*IV-Sum*). It takes an input video along with the corresponding ASR transcript and learns to assign importance scores to each segment in the video. The final summary is a compilation of the high scoring video segments.

3.1 Generating Pseudo Summaries

Since manually collecting annotations for summarization is expensive and time consuming, we propose an automatic weakly supervised approach for generating summaries that may contain noise but have enough valuable signal for training a summarization network. The main intuition behind our pseudo summary generation pipeline is that given many videos of a task, steps that are crucial to the task are likely to appear across multiple videos (task relevance). Additionally, if a step is important, it is typical for the demonstrator to speak about this step either before, during, or after performing it. Therefore, the subtitles for the video obtained using Automatic Speech Recognition (ASR) will likely reference these key steps (cross-modal saliency). These two hypotheses shape our objectives for generating pseudo summaries.

Task Relevance. We first group videos based on the task. Say videos $V_i, i \in [1, \dots \mathcal{K}]$ are $\mathcal{K}$ videos from the same task, as shown in Fig. 3. For a given video, we divide it into $\mathcal{N}$ equally sized non-overlapping segments $s_i, i \in [1, \dots \mathcal{N}]$ and embed each segment using a pre-trained 3D CNN video encoder g_{vid} [19]. We merge segments along the time axis based on their dot-product similarity, i.e. if similarity of a segment to the one prior to it is greater than a threshold, the two are grouped together and the joint feature representation is an average of the feature representation of the two segments. The threshold for similarity is heuristically set to be 90% of the maximum similarity between any two segments in the video. We call these merged segments *steps*, as they typically correspond to semantic steps as we show through qualitative results in supplemental. We do this for all $\mathcal{K}$ videos in the task, and then compare each step to all the $\mathcal{S}$ steps across all $\mathcal{K}$ videos of the task. We assign *task relevance scores* trs_{S_i}, to each step $S_i, i \in \mathcal{S}$ based on its visual similarity to all the $\mathcal{S}$ steps from all K videos of this task, as shown below:

$$\text{trs}_{S_i} = \frac{1}{|\mathcal{S}|} \sum_{j \in \mathcal{S}} g_{vid}(S_i) \cdot g_{vid}(S_j)$$

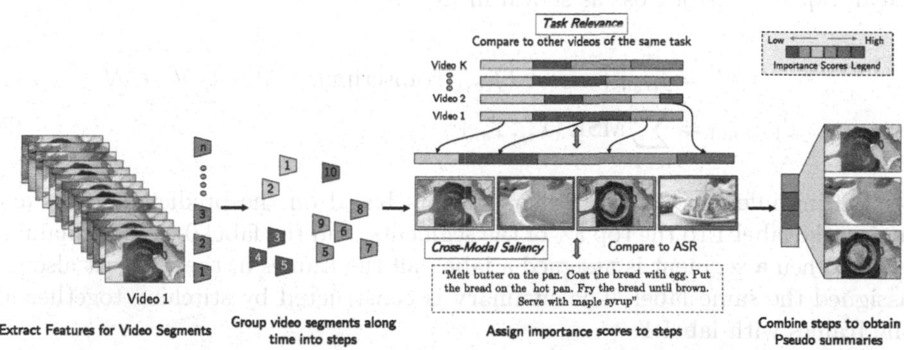

Fig. 3. Pseudo summary generation. To generate the pseudo summary, we first uniformly partition the video into segments, then group the segments based on visual similarity into steps (shown in different colors), assign *importance scores* to steps based on *Task Relevance* and *Cross-Modal Saliency*, and then pick high scoring steps to obtain pseudo summaries.

Cross-Modal Saliency. We also compare each video step to each sentence in the transcript of the same video. This enforces our idea that if a step is important, it will likely be referenced in the speech. To do this, we encode both, the input segments and the transcript sentences, using a pre-trained video-text model where the video and text streams are trained jointly using MIL-NCE loss [19]. Each visual step is assigned a *cross-modal score* by averaging its similarity over all the sentences.

Each step (and all the segments in it) is then assigned an importance score that is an average of the *task relevance* and the *cross-modal scores.* This constitutes our pseudo summary scores. For any given video, the top $t\%$ highest scoring steps are retained to be a part of the summary.

3.2 Instructional Video Summarizer (*IV-Sum*)

Recall that our goal is to construct a visual summary of any instructional video by picking out the important steps in it, without having to rely on other videos of the same task or the task label. To do this, we use the pseudo summaries generated above as weak supervision to train *IV-Sum*, which learns to assign importance scores to individual segments in the video using only the information in the video and the corresponding transcripts as seen in Fig. 2. While some prior summarization methods operate on independent frames [21,24], *IV-Sum* operates on non-overlapping segments $s_i, i \in [1, \ldots \mathcal{N}]$, and learns *context-aware temporal representations* using a 3D CNN video encoder f_{vid}. The transcript is projected onto the same embedding space using a text encoder f_{text}, and the text representations are concatenated individually to each of the segments. To contextualize information across several segments, we use a segment scoring encoder-only transformer [36] f_{trans} with positional embeddings, that assigns importance scores Y'_{s_i} to each segment as shown in Eq. 1. The network is trained using supervision from the importance scores of the pseudo summaries Y_{s_i}, using Mean-Squared Error Loss as shown in Eq. 2.

$$Y'_{s_i} = f_{\text{trans}}(\text{concat}\ (f_{\text{text}}(\text{transcript}), f_{\text{vid}}(s_i)))\ \forall\, i \in \mathcal{N} \tag{1}$$

$$\mathcal{L}_{\text{IV-Sum}} = \sum_{i \in \mathcal{N}} \text{MSE}\ (Y'_{s_i}, Y_{s_i}) \tag{2}$$

During inference, we sort the segments based on the predicted scores and assign the label 1 to the top $t\%$ of the segments, and the label 0 to the remaining ones. When a segment is assigned a label, all the frames in the segment also get assigned the same label. The summary is constructed by stitching together all the frames with label 1.

4 Instructional Video Summarization Datasets

We describe the details of the data collection process for the annotations used in our work—*Pseudo Summaries* annotations for training and the *WikiHow Summaries* annotations for evaluation.

Pseudo Summaries Training Dataset. As described in Sect. 3.1, we use the pseudo summary generation process for creating our training set. We use the videos and task annotations from COIN [35] and CrossTask [44] datasets for creating our training datasets.
COIN: COIN consists of 11K videos related to 180 tasks. As this is a dynamic YouTube dataset, we were able to obtain 8,521 videos at the time of this work.
Cross-Task: CrossTask consists of 4,700 instructional videos (of which we were able to access 3,675 videos) across 83 different tasks.
Pseudo Summaries: We combined the two datasets to create pseudo summaries comprising of 12,160 videos, whilst using the videos that were common to both datasets only once. They span 263 different tasks, have an average length of 3.09 min, and in total comprise of 628.53 h of content. The summary videos that were constructed using our pseudo ground-truth generation pipeline are 1.71 min long on an average, with each summary being 60% of the original video. While it is possible to construct pseudo summaries using the step-localization annotations, we show in Sec. 5 that such summaries may miss important steps or do not pick up on steps that are salient in the video. Moreover, our pseudo summary generation mechanism is weakly-supervised, requiring only task annotations and no step-localization annotations.

Table 1. Instructional Video Summarization Datasets Statistics. † Our *WikiHow Summaries* dataset was created automatically using a scalable pipeline, but manually verified for correctness.

	TVSum	SumMe	Pseudo Summaries	WikiHow Summaries
Number of videos	50	25	12160	2106
Annotation	Manual	Manual	Automatic	Manually verified†
Number of tasks/categories	10	25	185	20
Total Input Duration (h)	3.5	1.0	628.53	42.94

WikiHow Summaries Dataset. To provide a test bed for instructional video summarization, we automatically create and manually verify *WikiHow Summaries*, a video summarization dataset consisting of 2,106 input videos and summaries, where each video describes a unique task. Each article on the WikiHow Videos website consists of a main instructional video demonstrating a task that often includes promotional content, clips of the instructor speaking to the camera with no visual information of the task, and steps that are not crucial for performing the task. Viewers who want an overview of the task would prefer a shorter video without all of the aforementioned irrelevant information. The WikiHow articles (e.g., see How to Make Sushi Rice) contain exactly this: corresponding text that contains all the important steps in the video listed with accompanying images/clips illustrating the various steps in the task. These manually annotated articles are a good source for automatically creating ground-truth summaries for the main videos. We obtain the summaries and the corresponding labels and importance scores using the following process (see supp. for an overview figure):

1. Scraping WikiHow Videos. We scrape the WikiHow Videos website for all the long instructional videos along with each step and the images/video clips (GIFs) associated with the step.

2. Localizing Images/Clips. We automatically localize these images/clips in the main video by finding the closest match in the video. To localize an image, we compare ResNet50 [10] features of the image and to that of all the frames in the video. The most similar frame is selected and this step is localized in the input video to a 5 s window centered around the frame. If the step contains a video clip/GIF, we localize the first frame of the video clip/GIF in the input video by similarly comparing ResNet features, as above, and the localization is set to be the length of the step video clip.

3. Ground-Truth Summary from Localized Clips. We stitch the shorter localized clips together to create the ground truth summary video. Consequently, we assign labels to each frame in the input video, depending on whether it belongs to the input summary (label 1) or not (label 0). To obtain importance scores, we partition each input video into equally sized segments (same as in Sec. 3.2) and compute the importance score for each segment to be the average of the labels assigned to the individual frames in the segment.

4. Manual Verification. We verified that the summaries are at least 30% of the original video and manually fixed summaries that were extremely short/long.

Online Longevity and Scalability. We note that a common problem plaguing YouTube datasets today is shrinkage of datasets as user uploaded videos are taken down by users (e.g. Kinetics [3]). WikiHow articles are less likely to be taken down, and this is an actively growing resource as new How-To videos are released and added (25% growth since we collected the data). Hence there is a potential to continually increase the size of the dataset.

For each video, we provide the following: (i) frame-level binary labels (ii) the summary formed by combining the frames with label 1 (iii) segment-level importance scores between 0 and 1, which are computed as an average of the importance scores for all the frames in the segment (iv) the localization of the visual steps in the video (i.e. the frames associated with each step). We also scrape natural language descriptions of each step as a bonus that could be useful for future work. We divide our WikiHow dataset into 768 validation and 1,339 test videos. Table 1 shows the statistics of both our datasets. Both datasets are much larger in size compared to existing generic video summarization datasets, contain a broader range of tasks, and are scalable.

5 Experiments

Next, we describe the experimental setup and evaluation for instructional video summarization. We compare our method to several baselines, including CLIP-It [21], the state-of-the-art on generic and query-focused video summarization.

Implementation Details. For the video and text encoders, we use an S3D [38] network, initialized with weights from pre-training on HowTo100M [20] using the MIL-NCE loss [19]. We fine-tune the *mixed_5** layers and freeze the rest. The segment scoring transformer is an encoder consisting of 24 layers and 8 heads and is initialized randomly. The network is trained using the Adam optimizer [15], with learning rate of 0.01, and a batch size of 24. We use Distributed Data Parallel to train for 300 epochs across 8 NVIDIA RTX 2080 GPUs. Additional implementation details are mentioned in supplemental.

Metrics. To evaluate instructional video summaries, we follow the evaluation protocol used in past video summarization works [21,24,40] and report Precision, Recall and F-Score values. As described in Sect. 4, each video in the *WikiHow Summaries* dataset contains the ground-truth labels Y_l (binary labels for each frame in the video) and the ground-truth scores Y_s (importance scores in the range [0–1] for each segment in the video). We compare the binary labels predicted for the frames in the video Y_l', to the ground truth labels Y_l, and measure F-Score, Precision and Recall, as defined in prior summarization works [28,29].

Table 2. Instructional Video Summarization results on *WikiHow Summaries*. We compare F-Score, Kendall and Spearman correlation metrics of our method IV-Sum, to all the baselines. Our method achieves state-of-the-art on all three metrics.

Method				F-Score		τ [14]	ρ [45]
				Val	Test	Test	Test
	ASR	RGB	Pseudo				
Frame Cross-Modal Similarity	✓	✓	–	52.8	53.1	0.022	0.051
Segment Cross-Modal Similarity	✓	✓	–	55.1	55.5	0.034	0.060
Step Cross-Modal Similarity	✓	✓	–	57.9	58.3	0.037	0.061
CLIP-It with captions [21]	–	✓	–	22.5	22.1	0.036	0.064
CLIP-It with ASR [21]	✓	✓	–	27.9	27.2	0.055	0.088
CLIP-It with ASR	✓	✓	✓	62.5	61.8	0.093	0.191
IV-Sum without ASR	–	✓	✓	65.8	65.2	0.095	0.202
IV-Sum	✓	✓	✓	**67.9**	**67.3**	**0.101**	**0.212**

While these scores assess the quality of the predicted frame-wise binary labels, to assess the quality of the predicted segment-wise importance scores Y_s', we follow Otani *et al.* [23], and report results on the rank-based metrics Kendall's τ [14] and Spearman's ρ [45] correlation coefficients. We first rank the video frames according to the generated importance scores Y_s' and the ground-truth importance scores Y_s. We then compare the generated ranking to each ground-truth ranking of video segments for each video obtained from the frame-wise binary labels as described in Sec. 4. The final correlation score is computed by averaging over the individual scores for each video.

Baselines. We compare our method to the state-of-the-art video summarization model CLIP-It [21]. To validate the need for pseudo summaries, we construct three unsupervised baselines as alternatives to our pseudo summary generation algorithm. We first describe the three unsupervised baselines.

Frame Cross-Modal Similarity. We sample frames (at the same FPS used by our method) from an input video and compute the similarity between CLIP (ViT-B/32) [25] frame embeddings and CLIP text embeddings of each sentence in the transcript. The embeddings do not encode temporal information but leverage the priors learned by the CLIP model. Based on the scores assigned to each frame, we threshold $t\%$ of the higher scoring frames to be part of the summary. Frame scores are propagated to the segments they belong to, and the summary is a compilation of the chosen segments.

Segment Cross-Modal Similarity. We uniformly divide the video into segments and compute MIL-NCE [19] video features for each segment. We embed each sentence in the transcript to the same feature space using the MIL-NCE text encoder. We compute the pairwise similarity between all video segments and the sentences, and average over sentences to obtain a score for each segment.

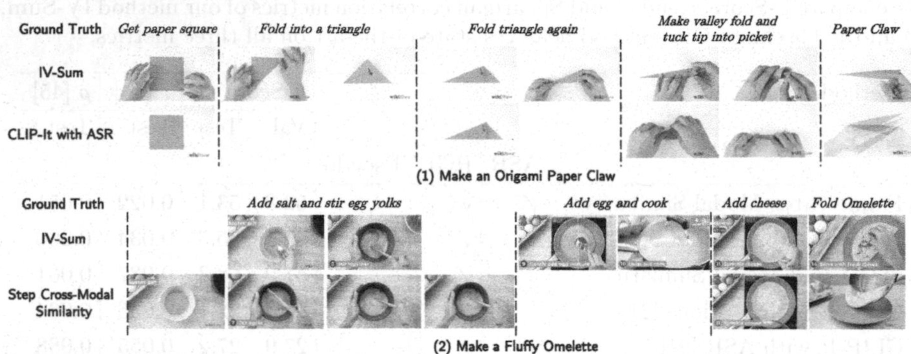

Fig. 4. Qualitative comparisons to baselines. We show the steps in the ground-truth as text (note we never train with step descriptions, these are shown here simply for illustrative purposes) and compare frames selected in summaries generated by our method IV-Sum, CLIP-It with ASR, and Step Cross-Modal Similarity. In (1), CLIP-It misses steps which are deemed important by our method (*"Fold into a triangle"*) and assigns higher scores to less salient frames for the step (*"Make valley fold and tuck tip into picket"*) where neither the valley fold nor the picket are clearly visible. In (2), Step Cross-Modal Similarity misses (*"Add egg and cook"*) and selects too many redundant frames for the step (*"Add salt and stir egg yolks"*).

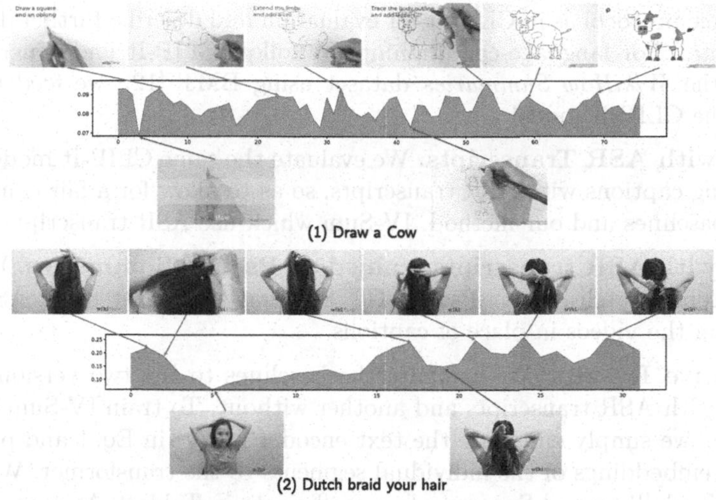

Fig. 5. Qualitative results. We show summaries from our method IV-Sum along with the predicted importance scores. The green and red arrows point to frames that were assigned a high and low scores, respectively. Our model correctly assigns higher scores to frames from all the steps that are relevant and lower scores to frames which aren't crucial to the task (as in (1)) and frames which don't belong to a step (as in (2)).

Our intuition is that since demonstrators typically describe the important steps shortly before, after or while performing them, a high similarity between the visuals and transcripts would directly correlate with the significance of the step. We filter $t\%$ of the highest scoring segments, where t is determined heuristically using the *WikiHow Summaries* validation set and is consistent across all baselines and our model. The filtered segments are stitched together to form the summary.

Step Cross-Modal Similarity. We first group segments into steps and then compare them to the ASR transcripts. For this we employ the technique described in Sect. 3.1, i.e. we extract MIL-NCE features for the video segments and group them together based on their similarity to form steps.[2] The embedding for a step is set to be the average of all the segment embeddings in it. If a step is similar to the transcript, all the segments in that step are chosen to be part of the summary. This baseline is the closest to our pseudo summary generation algorithm.

Next, we describe the CLIP-It baseline and ablations, trained with supervision.

CLIP-It with Captions. We evaluate CLIP-It [21] trained on TVSum [34], SumMe [9], OVP [22], and YouTube [5] against our *WikiHow Summaries*. We

[2] Since we process a single input video (not multiple videos per task), we can not use the Task Relevance component.

use the same protocol as in CLIP-It for evaluation and describe further details in supplemental. For language-conditioning, we follow CLIP-It and generate captions for the *WikiHow Summaries* dataset using BMT [12]; we feed these as input to the CLIP-It model.

CLIP-It with ASR Transcripts. We evaluate the same CLIP-It model above by replacing captions with ASR transcripts, so as to allow for a fair comparison with the baselines and our method, IV-Sum which use ASR transcripts.

CLIP-It with ASR transcripts trained on Pseudo Summaries. We train CLIP-It from scratch on our Pseudo-GT Summaries dataset using ASR transcripts from the videos in place of captions.

Quantitative Results. We compare the baselines to the two versions of IV-Sum, one with ASR transcripts and another without. To train IV-Sum without transcripts, we simply eliminate the text encoder (f_{text}) in Eq. 1 and pass only the visual embeddings of the individual segments to the transformer. We report F-Score, Kendall's τ and Spearman's ρ coefficients in Table 2. As seen, IV-Sum (both with and without ASR transcripts), outperforms all the baselines on all metrics. Particularly, we achieve notable improvements on the correlation metrics that compare the saliency scores, attesting to our model's capabilities to assign higher scores to segments that are more relevant. We also observe that CLIP-It trained using the pseudo summaries generated by our method has a strong boost in performance compared to CLIP-It trained on generic video summarization datasets, reinforcing the effectiveness of our pseudo summaries for training. The best method among the unsupervised ones is Step Cross-Modal Similarity, a "reduced" version of our pseudo summary generation method.

Qualitative Results. We present qualitative results in Fig. 4. We show frames in the summaries generated by our method IV-Sum, CLIP-It with ASR transcripts (trained on generic video summarization datasets), and Step Cross-Modal Similarity. We also list the steps in the ground-truth as text (for illustrative purposes). In Fig. 4 (1), CLIP-It misses the step *"Fold into a triangle"*, as it optimizes for diversity among the frames and was trained on a small dataset that does not generalize well to our domain. It also picks the less salient frames for the step *"Make valley fold and tuck tip into picket"*, whereas our model correctly identifies all the steps and assigns higher scores to the more salient frames. The summary from the Step Cross-Modal Similarity baseline, shown in Fig. 4 (2), assigns high scores to several redundant frames (*"Add salt and stir egg yolks"*), but misses "Add egg and cook".

Figure 5 shows results from our method along with the predicted frame-wise importance scores. The green and red arrows point to frames that are assigned the highest and lowest scores by our method, respectively. As seen, our method assigns high scores to frames in task relevant and salient steps and low scores to frames which aren't crucial to the step, like in Fig. 5 (1), or do not belong to a step, like in Fig. 5 (2) where the person is talking to the camera.

Ablations. We compare different approaches to generate pseudo summaries for training our instructional video summarizer network – (i) First, we ablate the

Fig. 6. Pseudo summaries vs step-localization annotations. We compare frames in our automated pseudo summary to the step localization manual annotations, aligned temporally. Frames corresponding to steps that are identified by our method but missed by step localization are highlighted in yellow. (Color figure online)

two objectives, Task Relevance and Cross-Modal Saliency, used to generate the pseudo summaries. (ii) Next, we replace the annotations from our pseudo summary generation pipeline with step localization annotations. We include model and loss ablations in the supplemental.

(i) Ablating Objectives. We ablate the two objectives, Task Relevance and Cross-Modal Saliency, used for generating pseudo summaries, in Table 3a. We train IV-Sum on different versions of pseudo summaries and report F-Scores on the *WikiHow Summaries* validation set. Combining both objectives is more effective than using each objective individually.

(ii) Using Step Localization Annotations. COIN and CrossTask datasets contain temporal localization annotations of a generic set of steps pertaining to the task in the videos. We use these annotations to extract the visual segments corresponding to the steps and concatenate them to form a summary. We assign binary labels to each frame, depending on whether they belong in the summary or not. We then use these step-localization summaries as supervision to train our model, IV-Sum with a weighted-CE loss [21] as this works best for binary labels.

Table 3. Pseudo summary variations. We report results on two variations of generating the pseudo summaries: (i) ablating the objectives (ii) using step localization annotations to generate pseudo summaries.

(a) **Ablating objectives.** We ablate the two objectives in our pseudo summary generation pipeline.

Method	F-Score
Task-Consistency only	64.1
Cross-Modal Similarity only	61.0
Both	67.9

(b) **Using Step-Localization Annotations.** We compare pseudo summaries from step-localization annotations with our approach.

Method	F-Score
IV-Sum (Step Localization)	57.6
IV-Sum (Ours)	66.8

In Tab. 3b, we compare this to IV-Sum trained on pseudo summaries generated using our pipeline and report F-Scores on our *WikiHow Summaries* validation set. As seen, IV-Sum trained on our generated summaries outperforms IV-Sum trained using step-localization summaries. We qualitatively compare our automatic pseudo summaries to the manually labeled step localization annotations in Fig. 6. Often the step annotations only cover a few steps and miss other crucial steps as shown in yellow in (1). In (2), we observe that our pseudo summary retrieves steps that are unique to the task which the step localization annotation doesn't include.

6 Conclusion

We introduce a novel approach for generating visual summaries of instructional videos—a practical task with broad applications. Specifically, we overcome the need to manually label data in two important ways. For training, we propose a weakly-supervised method to create pseudo summaries for a large number of instructional videos. For evaluation, we leverage WikiHow (its videos and step illustrations) to automatically build a *WikiHow Summaries* dataset. We manually verify that the obtained summaries are of high quality. We also propose an effective model to tackle instructional video summarization, IV-Sum, that uses temporal 3D CNN representations, unlike most prior work that relies on frame-level representations. We demonstrate that all components of the proposed approach are effective in a comprehensive ablation study.

Acknowledgements. We thank Daniel Fried and Bryan Seybold for valuable discussions and feedback on the draft. This work was supported in part by DoD including DARPA's LwLL, PTG and/or SemaFor programs, as well as BAIR's industrial alliance programs.

References

1. Alayrac, J.B., Bojanowski, P., Agrawal, N., Sivic, J., Laptev, I., Lacoste-Julien, S.: Unsupervised learning from narrated instruction videos. In: IEEE Conference on Computer Vision and Pattern Recognition (CVPR) (2016)
2. Bojanowski, P., et al.: Weakly supervised action labeling in videos under ordering constraints. In: Fleet, D., Pajdla, T., Schiele, B., Tuytelaars, T. (eds.) ECCV 2014. LNCS, vol. 8693, pp. 628–643. Springer, Cham (2014). https://doi.org/10.1007/978-3-319-10602-1_41
3. Carreira, J., Zisserman, A.: Quo vadis, action recognition? a new model and the kinetics dataset. IEEE Conference on Computer Vision and Pattern Recognition (CVPR) (2017)
4. Chang, C.Y., Huang, D.A., Sui, Y., Fei-Fei, L., Niebles, J.C.: D3TW: Discriminative differentiable dynamic time warping for weakly supervised action alignment and segmentation. In: IEEE Conference on Computer Vision and Pattern Recognition (CVPR) (2019)

5. De Avila, S.E.F., Lopes, A.P.B., da Luz Jr, A., de Albuquerque Araújo, A.: Vsumm: A mechanism designed to produce static video summaries and a novel evaluation method. Patt. Rec. Lett. **32**, 56–68 (2011)
6. Ding, L., Xu, C.: Weakly-supervised action segmentation with iterative soft boundary assignment. In: IEEE Conference on Computer Vision and Pattern Recognition (CVPR) (2018)
7. Fajtl, J., Sokeh, H.S., Argyriou, V., Monekosso, D., Remagnino, P.: Summarizing videos with attention. In: Asian Conference on Computer Vision (ACCV) (2018)
8. Fried, D., Alayrac, J.B., Blunsom, P., Dyer, C., Clark, S., Nematzadeh, A.: Learning to segment actions from observation and narration. In: Association for Computational Linguistics (2020)
9. Gygli, M., Grabner, H., Riemenschneider, H., Van Gool, L.: Creating summaries from user videos. In: Fleet, D., Pajdla, T., Schiele, B., Tuytelaars, T. (eds.) ECCV 2014. LNCS, vol. 8695, pp. 505–520. Springer, Cham (2014). https://doi.org/10.1007/978-3-319-10584-0_33
10. He, K., Zhang, X., Ren, S., Sun, J.: Deep residual learning for image recognition. In: IEEE Conference on Computer Vision and Pattern Recognition (CVPR) (2016)
11. Huang, D.-A., Fei-Fei, L., Niebles, J.C.: Connectionist temporal modeling for weakly supervised action labeling. In: Leibe, B., Matas, J., Sebe, N., Welling, M. (eds.) ECCV 2016. LNCS, vol. 9908, pp. 137–153. Springer, Cham (2016). https://doi.org/10.1007/978-3-319-46493-0_9
12. Iashin, V., Rahtu, E.: A better use of audio-visual cues: Dense video captioning with bi-modal transformer. In: British Machine Vision Conference (BMVC) (2020)
13. Kanehira, A., Gool, L.V., Ushiku, Y., Harada, T.: Viewpoint-aware video summarization. In: IEEE Conference on Computer Vision and Pattern Recognition (CVPR) (2018)
14. Kendall, M.G.: The treatment of ties in ranking problems. Biometrika **33**(3), 239–251 (1945)
15. Kingma, D.P., Ba, J.: Adam: A method for stochastic optimization. In: International Conference on Learning Representations (ICLR) (2015)
16. Kuehne, H., Richard, A., Gall, J.: Weakly supervised learning of actions from transcripts. In: CVIU (2017)
17. Kukleva, A., Kuehne, H., Sener, F., Gall, J.: Unsupervised learning of action classes with continuous temporal embedding. In: IEEE Conference on Computer Vision and Pattern Recognition (CVPR) (2019)
18. Mahasseni, B., Lam, M., Todorovic, S.: Unsupervised video summarization with adversarial lstm networks. In: IEEE Conference on Computer Vision and Pattern Recognition (CVPR) (2017)
19. Miech, A., Alayrac, J.B., Smaira, L., Laptev, I., Sivic, J., Zisserman, A.: End-to-end learning of visual representations from uncurated instructional videos. In: IEEE Conference on Computer Vision and Pattern Recognition (CVPR) (2020)
20. Miech, A., Zhukov, D., Alayrac, J.B., Tapaswi, M., Laptev, I., Sivic, J.: Howto100m: Learning a text-video embedding by watching hundred million narrated video clips. In: IEEE International Conference on Computer Vision (ICCV) (2019)
21. Narasimhan, M., Rohrbach, A., Darrell, T.: Clip-it! language-guided video summarization. In: Advances in Neural Information Processing Systems (NeurIPS) (2021)
22. Open video project. https://open-video.org/
23. Otani, M., Nakashima, Y., Rahtu, E., Heikkilä, J.: Rethinking the evaluation of video summaries. In: IEEE Conference on Computer Vision and Pattern Recognition (CVPR) (2019)

24. Park, J., Lee, J., Kim, I.-J., Sohn, K.: Sumgraph: Video summarization via recursive graph modeling. In: Vedaldi, A., Bischof, H., Brox, T., Frahm, J.-M. (eds.) ECCV 2020. LNCS, vol. 12370, pp. 647–663. Springer, Cham (2020). https://doi.org/10.1007/978-3-030-58595-2_39
25. Radford, A., et al.: Learning transferable visual models from natural language supervision. arXiv preprint arXiv:2103.00020 (2021)
26. Richard, A., Kuehne, H., Gall, J.: Weakly supervised action learning with RNN based fine-to-coarse modeling. In: IEEE Conference on Computer Vision and Pattern Recognition (CVPR) (2017)
27. Richard, A., Kuehne, H., Gall, J.: Action sets: Weakly supervised action segmentation without ordering constraints. In: IEEE Conference on Computer Vision and Pattern Recognition (CVPR) (2018)
28. Rochan, M., Wang, Y.: Video summarization by learning from unpaired data. In: IEEE Conference on Computer Vision and Pattern Recognition (CVPR) (2019)
29. Rochan, M., Ye, L., Wang, Y.: Video summarization using fully convolutional sequence networks. In: Ferrari, V., Hebert, M., Sminchisescu, C., Weiss, Y. (eds.) ECCV 2018. LNCS, vol. 11216, pp. 358–374. Springer, Cham (2018). https://doi.org/10.1007/978-3-030-01258-8_22
30. Sener, F., Yao, A.: Unsupervised learning and segmentation of complex activities from video. In: IEEE Conference on Computer Vision and Pattern Recognition (CVPR) (2018)
31. Sener, O., Zamir, A.R., Savarese, S., Saxena, A.: Unsupervised semantic parsing of video collections. In: IEEE International Conference on Computer Vision (ICCV) (2015)
32. Sharghi, A., Gong, B., Shah, M.: Query-focused extractive video summarization. In: Leibe, B., Matas, J., Sebe, N., Welling, M. (eds.) ECCV 2016. LNCS, vol. 9912, pp. 3–19. Springer, Cham (2016). https://doi.org/10.1007/978-3-319-46484-8_1
33. Sharghi, A., Laurel, J.S., Gong, B.: Query-focused video summarization: Dataset, evaluation, and a memory network based approach. In: IEEE Conference on Computer Vision and Pattern Recognition (CVPR) (2017)
34. Song, Y., Vallmitjana, J., Stent, A., Jaimes, A.: Tvsum: Summarizing web videos using titles. In: IEEE Conference on Computer Vision and Pattern Recognition (CVPR) (2015)
35. Tang, Y., et al.: Coin: A large-scale dataset for comprehensive instructional video analysis. In: IEEE Conference on Computer Vision and Pattern Recognition (CVPR) (2019)
36. Vaswani, A., et al.: Attention is all you need. In: Proceedings of the 31st International Conference on Neural Information Processing Systems, pp. 6000–6010 (2017)
37. Wei, H., Ni, B., Yan, Y., Yu, H., Yang, X., Yao, C.: Video summarization via semantic attended networks. In: The Association for the Advancement of Artificial Intelligence Conference (AAAI) (2018)
38. Xie, S., Sun, C., Huang, J., Tu, Z., Murphy, K.: Rethinking spatiotemporal feature learning: Speed-accuracy trade-offs in video classification. In: Ferrari, V., Hebert, M., Sminchisescu, C., Weiss, Y. (eds.) ECCV 2018. LNCS, vol. 11219, pp. 318–335. Springer, Cham (2018). https://doi.org/10.1007/978-3-030-01267-0_19
39. Yuan, L., Tay, F.E., Li, P., Zhou, L., Feng, J.: Cycle-sum: Cycle-consistent adversarial lstm networks for unsupervised video summarization. In: The Association for the Advancement of Artificial Intelligence Conference (AAAI) (2019)

40. Zhang, K., Chao, W.L., Sha, F., Grauman, K.: Summary transfer: Examplar-based subset selection for video summarization. In: IEEE Conference on Computer Vision and Pattern Recognition (CVPR) (2016)
41. Zhang, K., Chao, W.-L., Sha, F., Grauman, K.: Video summarization with long short-term memory. In: Leibe, B., Matas, J., Sebe, N., Welling, M. (eds.) ECCV 2016. LNCS, vol. 9911, pp. 766–782. Springer, Cham (2016). https://doi.org/10.1007/978-3-319-46478-7_47
42. Zhang, K., Grauman, K., Sha, F.: Retrospective encoders for video summarization. In: Ferrari, V., Hebert, M., Sminchisescu, C., Weiss, Y. (eds.) ECCV 2018. LNCS, vol. 11212, pp. 391–408. Springer, Cham (2018). https://doi.org/10.1007/978-3-030-01237-3_24
43. Zhao, B., Li, X., Lu, X.: Hsa-rnn: Hierarchical structure-adaptive rnn for video summarization. In: IEEE Conference on Computer Vision and Pattern Recognition (CVPR) (2018)
44. Zhukov, D., Alayrac, J.B., Cinbis, R.G., Fouhey, D., Laptev, I., Sivic, J.: Cross-task weakly supervised learning from instructional videos. In: IEEE Conference on Computer Vision and Pattern Recognition (CVPR) (2019)
45. Zwillinger, D., Kokoska, S.: Crc standard probability and statistics tables and formulae. CRC Press (1999)

Rethinking Learning Approaches for Long-Term Action Anticipation

Megha Nawhal[1(✉)], Akash Abdu Jyothi[1], and Greg Mori[1,2]

[1] Simon Fraser University, Burnaby, Canada
mnawhal@sfu.ca
[2] Borealis AI, Vancouver, Canada

Abstract. Action anticipation involves predicting future actions having observed the initial portion of a video. Typically, the observed video is processed as a whole to obtain a video-level representation of the ongoing activity in the video, which is then used for future prediction. We introduce ANTICIPATR which performs long-term action anticipation leveraging segment-level representations learned using individual segments from different activities, in addition to a video-level representation. We propose a two-stage learning approach to train a novel transformer-based model that uses these two types of representations to directly predict a set of future action instances over any given anticipation duration. Results on Breakfast, 50Salads, Epic-Kitchens-55, and EGTEA Gaze+ datasets demonstrate the effectiveness of our approach.

Keywords: Action anticipation · Transformer · Long-form videos

1 Introduction

The ability to envision future events is a crucial component of human intelligence which helps in decision making during our interactions with the environment. We are naturally capable of anticipating future events when interacting with the environment in a wide variety of scenarios. Similarly, anticipation capabilities are essential to practical AI systems that operate in complex environments and interact with other agents or humans (*e.g.*, wearable devices [55], human-robot interaction systems [28], autonomous vehicles [36,62]).

Existing anticipation methods have made considerable progress on the task of near-term action anticipation [9,10,13,14,16,18,37,59] that involves predicting the immediate next action that would occur over the course of a few seconds. While near-term anticipation is a valuable step towards the goal of future prediction in AI systems, going beyond short time-horizon prediction has applicability in a broader range of tasks that involve long-term interactions with the environment. The ability to anticipate actions over long time-horizons is imperative for applications such as efficient planning in robotic systems [8,15] and intelligent augmented reality systems.

Supplementary Information The online version contains supplementary material available at https://doi.org/10.1007/978-3-031-19830-4_32.

S. Avidan et al. (Eds.): ECCV 2022, LNCS 13694, pp. 558–576, 2022.
https://doi.org/10.1007/978-3-031-19830-4_32

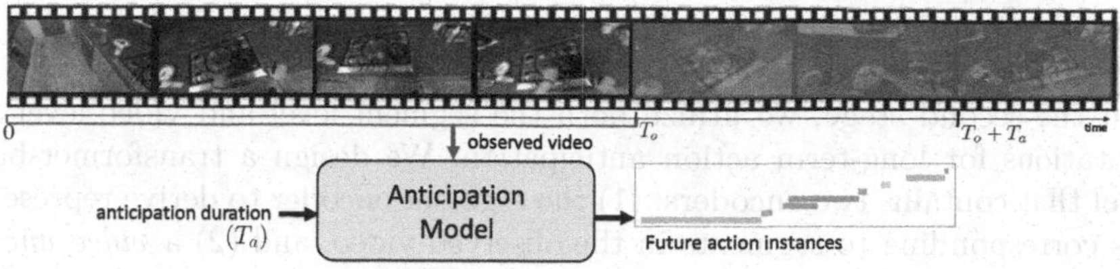

Fig. 1. Long-term action anticipation. Given the initial portion of an activity video $(0, \ldots, T_o)$ and anticipation duration T_a, the task is to predict the actions that would occur from time $T_o + 1$ to $T_o + T_a$. Our proposed anticipation model receives the observed video and the anticipation duration as inputs and directly predicts a set of future action instances. Here, the action anticipation is *long-term* – both the observed duration T_o and the anticipation duration T_a are in the order of minutes.

In this paper, we focus on long-term action anticipation. Figure 1 illustrates the problem – having observed an initial portion of an untrimmed activity video, we predict *what* actions would occur *when* in the future.

Long-term anticipation methods [2,12,15,25,51] predict future actions based on the information in the observed video (*i.e.*, an initial portion of an untrimmed activity video) that partially depicts the activity in the video. Current approaches rely on encoding the observed video (input) as a whole to obtain *video-level representations* to perform action anticipation.

We propose a novel approach that leverages segment-level and video-level representations for the task of long-term action anticipation. Consider the example in Fig. 1. The video depicts the activity *person making pasta* spanning several minutes. This activity has segments with actions such as *slice onion, put pesto, put courgette, add cheese.* One of these segments such as *put pesto* tends to co-occur with actions involving objects such as *courgette, onion,* or *cheese* in a specific order. However, other videos with a different activity, say, *person making pizza,* could potentially have a similar set and/or sequence of actions in a different kitchen scenario. As such, while a specific sequence of actions (*i.e.*, segments of a video) help denote an activity, an individual video segment (containing a single action) alone contains valuable information for predicting the future. Based on this intuition, we introduce an approach that leverages segment-level representations in conjunction with video-level representations for the task of long-term action anticipation. In so doing, our approach enables reasoning beyond the limited context of the input video sequence.

In this work, we propose ANTICIPATR that consists of a two-stage learning approach employed to train a transformer-based model for long-term anticipation (see Fig. 2 for an overview). In the first stage, we train a *segment encoder* to learn segment-level representations. As we focus on action anticipation, we design this training task based on co-occurrences of actions. Specifically, we train the segment encoder to learn *which future actions are likely to occur after a given segment*? Intuitively, consider a video segment showing a pizza pan being moved towards a microwave. Irrespective of the ongoing activity in the video that contains this segment, it is easy to anticipate that certain actions such as *open microwave*, *put pizza* and *close microwave* are more likely to follow than the actions *wash spoon* or *close tap*.

In the second stage, we utilize both the segment-level and video-level representations for long-term action anticipation. We design a transformer-based model that contains two encoders: (1) the segment encoder to derive representations corresponding to segments in the observed video, and (2) a *video encoder* to derive the video-level representations of the observed video. These encoded representations are then fed into an *anticipation decoder* that predicts actions that would occur in the future. Our model is designed to directly predict a set of future action instances, wherein, each element of the set (*i.e.*, an action instance) contains the start and end timestamps of the instance along with the action label. Using direct set prediction, our approach predicts the actions at all the timestamps over a given anticipation duration in a single forward pass.

To summarize, this paper makes the following contributions: (1) a novel learning approach for long-term action anticipation that leverages segment-level representations and video-level representations of the observed video, (2) a novel transformer-based model that receives a video and anticipation duration as inputs to predict future actions over the specified anticipation duration, (3) a direct set prediction formulation that enables single-pass prediction of actions, and (4) state-of-the-art performance on a diverse set of anticipation benchmarks: Breakfast [29], 50Salads [56], Epic-Kitchens-55 [9], and EGTEA Gaze+ [31]. Code is available at https://github.com/Nmegha2601/anticipatr

Overall, our work highlights the benefits of learning representations that capture different aspects of a video, and particularly demonstrates the value of such representations for action anticipation.

2 Related Work

Action Anticipation. Action anticipation is generally described as the prediction of actions before they occur. Prior research efforts have used various formulations of this problem depending on three variables: (1) anticipation format, *i.e.*, representation format of predicted actions, (2) anticipation duration, *i.e.*, duration over which actions are anticipated, and (3) model architectures.

Current approaches span a wide variety of anticipation formats involving different representations of prediction outcomes. They range from pixel-level representations such as frames or segmentations [5,33,34,39] and human trajectories [3,10,20,24,27,38] to label-level representations such as action labels [12–14,16,25,30,46,48,49,51,53,59,64,65] or temporal occurrences of actions [2,15,32,37,40,57] through to semantic representations such as affordances [28] and language descriptions of sub-activities [52]. We focus on label-level anticipation format and use ‘action anticipation’ to refer to this task.

Existing anticipation tasks can be grouped into two categories based on the anticipation duration: (1) near-term action anticipation, and (2) long-term action anticipation. In this paper, we focus on long-term action anticipation.

Near-Term anticipation involves predicting label for the immediate next action that would occur in the range of a few seconds having observed a short video segment of duration of a few seconds. Prior work propose a variety of temporal modeling techniques to encode the observed segment such as regression networks [59], reinforced encoder-decoder network [16], TCNs [63], temporal segment network [9], LSTMs [13,14,45], VAEs [40,61] and transformers [18].

Long-Term anticipation involves predicting action labels over long time-horizons in the range of several minutes having observed an initial portion of a video (observed duration of a few minutes). A popular formulation of this task involves prediction of a sequence of action labels having observed an initial portion of the video. Prior approaches encode the observed video as a whole to obtain a video-level representation. Using these representations, these approaches either predict actions recursively over individual future time instants or use time as a conditional parameter to predict action label for the given single time instant. The recursive methods [2,12,15,46,51] accumulate prediction error over time resulting in inaccurate anticipation outcomes for scenarios with long anticipation duration. The time-conditioned method [25] employs skip-connections based temporal models and aims to avoid error accumulation by directly predicting an action label for a specified future time instant in a single forward pass. However, this approach still requires multiple forward passes during inference as the task involves predicting actions at all future time instants over a given anticipation duration. Additionally, sparse skip connections used in [25] do not fully utilize the relations among the actions at intermediate future time instants while predicting action at a given future time instant. In contrast to these approaches based on video-level representations, our approach leverages segment-level representations (learned using individual segments across different activities) in conjunction with video-level representations. Both these representations are utilized to directly predict action instances corresponding to actions at all the time instants over a given anticipation duration in a single forward pass.

An alternate formulation of long-term anticipation proposed in [42] focuses on predicting a set of future action labels without inferring when they would occur. [42] extracts a graph representation of the video based on frame-level visual affordances and uses graph convolutional network to encode the graph representation to predict a set of action labels. In contrast, our approach leverages both the segment-level and video-level representations of the input video and a transformer-based model to predict action instances - both action labels and their corresponding timestamps.

Other methods design approaches to model uncertainty in predicting actions over long time horizons [1,44,46] and self-supervised learning [47].

Early Action Detection. The task of early action detection [21,35,50,54] involves recognizing an ongoing action in a video as early as possible given an initial portion of the video. Though the early action detection task is different from action anticipation (anticipation involves prediction of actions *before* they begin), the two tasks share the inspiration of future prediction.

Transformers in Computer Vision. The transformer architecture [58], originally proposed for machine translation task, has achieved state-of-the-art performance for many NLP tasks. In recent years, there has been a flurry of work on transformer architectures designed for high-level reasoning tasks on images and videos. Examples include object detection [6], image classification [11], spatio-temporal localization in videos [17], video instance segmentation [60], action recognition [4,66], action detection [43], multi-object tracking [41], next action anticipation [18], human-object interaction detection [26,67]. DETR [6] is a transformer model for object detection, wherein, the task is formulated as a set prediction problem. This work has since inspired transformer designs for similar vision tasks – video instance segmentation [60] and human-object interaction detection [67]. Inspired by these works, we propose a novel transformer architecture that uses two encoder to encode different representations derived from the input video and a decoder to predict the set of future action instances in a single pass. Our proposed decoder also receives anticipation duration as an input parameter to control the duration over which actions are predicted.

3 Action Anticipation with ANTICIPATR

In this section, we first describe our formulation of long-term action anticipation and then describe our approach.

Problem Formulation. Let $\mathbf{v}_o$ be an observed video containing T_o frames. Our goal is to predict the actions that occur from time $T_o + 1$ to $T_o + T_a$ where T_a is the anticipation duration, *i.e.*, the duration over which actions are predicted. Specifically, we predict a set $\mathcal{A} = \{a^i = (c^i, t_s^i, t_e^i)\}$ containing future action instances. The i-th element denotes an action instance a^i depicting action category c^i occurring from time t_s^i to t_e^i where $T_o < t_s^i < t_e^i \leq T_o + T_a$. Here, $c^i \in \mathcal{C}$ where $\mathcal{C}$ is the set of action classes in the dataset.

Intuitively, for action anticipation, the observed video as a whole helps provide a broad, video-level representation of the ongoing activity depicted in the video. However, the observed video is composed of several segments that individually also contain valuable information about future actions and provide an opportunity to capture the video with segment-level representations. Using this intuition, in this paper, we propose ANTICIPATR that leverages these two types of representations of the observed video for the task of long-term anticipation.

ANTICIPATR employs a two-stage learning approach to train a transformer-based model that takes an observed video as input and produces a set of future action instances as output. See Fig. 2 for an overview. In the first stage, we train a *segment encoder* that receives a segment (sequence of frames from a video) as input and predicts the set of action labels that would occur at any time in the future after the occurrence of the segment in the video. We refer to this stage as segment-level training (described in Sect. 3.1). As the segment encoder only operates over individual segments, it is unaware of the broader context of the activity induced by a specific sequence of segments in the observed video.

In the second stage, we train a *video encoder* and an *anticipation decoder* to be used along with the segment encoder for long-term action anticipation. The video encoder encodes the observed video to a video-level representation. The segment encoder (trained in the first stage) is fed with a sequence of segments from the observed video as input to obtain a segment-level representation of

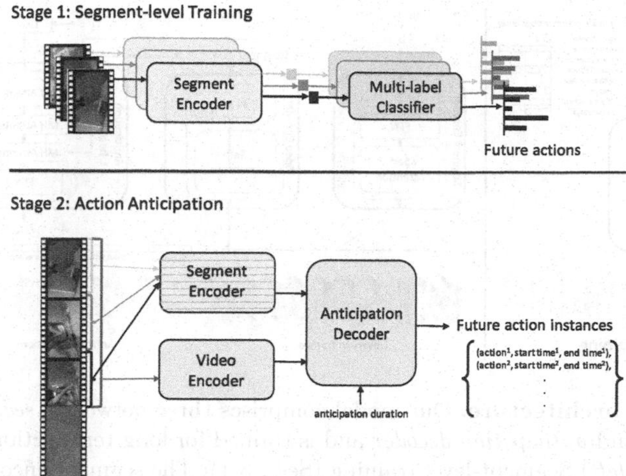

Fig. 2. Learning Approach. ANTICIPATR uses a two-stage learning approach. In the first stage, we perform segment-level training (refer to Sect. 3.1). Given a segment as input, we train a segment encoder to predict the set of action labels that would occur at any time after the occurrence of the segment in the activity video. In the second stage, we perform long-term action anticipation (refer to Sect. 3.2). We use video encoder to obtain video-level representation and segment encoder (trained in the first stage) is used to obtain segment-level representation. The anticipation decoder receives these two representations of the observed video to directly predict a set of action instances that would occur in the future over a given anticipation duration.

the video. The anticipation decoder receives the two representations along with the anticipation duration to predict a set of future action instances over the given anticipation duration in a single pass. The video encoder and anticipation decoder are trained using classification losses on the action labels and two temporal losses (L_1 loss and temporal IoU loss) on the timestamps while the segment encoder is kept unchanged. We refer to this second stage of training as action anticipation (see Sect. 3.2).

3.1 Stage 1: Segment-Level Training

In this stage, the segment encoder is trained on a segment-level prediction task to learn representations for individual segments. See Fig. 3 (*left*) for an overview.

Segment Encoder. We design the segment encoder network E_s as a sequence of ℓ_s transformer blocks containing a multi-head self-attention module followed by layernorm and a feed forward network [58]. This network is trained on the task of segment-level action anticipation.

Training. During training, the segment encoder receives a segment (sequence of frames from a video) as input and predicts the set of action labels that would occur at any time in the future (starting from the temporal boundary, *i.e.*, end of the segment until the end of that video) without inferring when they would occur. Depending on the segment, there could be multiple actions occurring

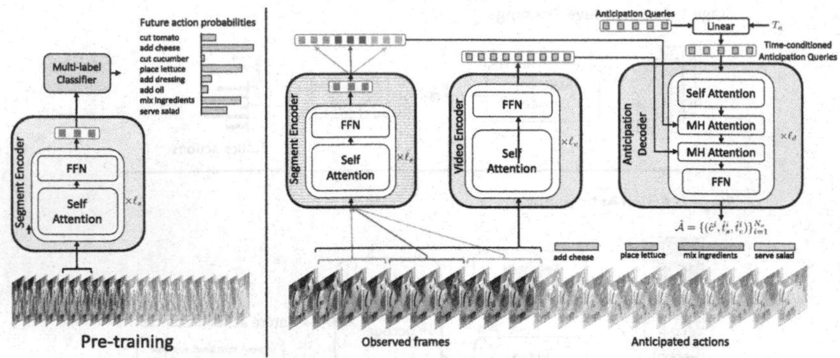

Fig. 3. Model architecture. Our model comprises three networks: *segment encoder*, *video encoder* and *anticipation decoder* and is trained for long-term action anticipation in two stages. (*left*) Segment-level training (Sect. 3.1): The segment encoder receives a segment as input and predicts a set of action labels that would occur at any time in the future (after the occurrence of segment in the video). (*right*) Action Anticipation (Sect. 3.2): The video encoder encodes the observed video to a video-level representation. Concurrently, the video is divided into a sequence of segments and each segment is fed into the segment encoder (trained in first stage) The anticipation decoder receives the two representations along with an anticipation duration as inputs to directly predict a set of future action instances over the given anticipation duration. [MH Attention: Multi-head Attention, FFN: Feed Forward Network.]

between the end of segment and end of video. Thus, we formulate this training task as a multi-class multi-label classification.

The training data for the segment encoder is derived from the training set in the original video dataset containing videos with action annotations. These input segments are obtained using the action boundaries provided in the training set. We do not require any additional annotations. Formally, given a video $\mathbf{v}$ containing T frames, a segment $\mathbf{v}_s^{(t',t'')}$, spanning time indices t' to t'' where $0 \leq t' < t'' < T$, is taken as input. For this segment, the target is a binary vector $\mathbf{c}_s$ (dimension $|\mathcal{C}|$) corresponding to the action labels that occur after the temporal boundary of the segment until the end of the video ($[\mathbf{v}^{t''+1}, \ldots, \mathbf{v}^T]$).

The segment encoder E_s receives the segment $\mathbf{v}_s^{(t',t'')}$ along with positional encodings $\mathbf{p}_s^{(t',t'')}$ (details in supplementary). The output of the encoder is an embedding $\mathbf{h} = [\mathbf{h}^1, \ldots, \mathbf{h}^{t''-t'+1}]$ of dimension $(t'' - t' + 1) \times d_s$ where d_s is the channel dimension. The output embeddings are then averaged along time dimension and fed into a linear layer F followed by a sigmoid activation σ to obtain future action probabilities $\hat{\mathbf{c}}_s$ of dimension $|\mathcal{C}|$, expressed as:

$$\begin{aligned} \mathbf{h} &= E_s\big(\mathbf{v}_s^{(t',t'')}, \mathbf{p}_s^{(t',t'')}\big) \\ \hat{\mathbf{c}}_s &= \sigma\left(F\bigg(\frac{1}{t''-t'+1}\sum_{i=1}^{t''-t'+1}\mathbf{h}^i\bigg)\right). \end{aligned} \tag{1}$$

Here, $\hat{\mathbf{c}}_s$ is the output of a multi-label classifier where each element c_s^j of $\hat{\mathbf{c}}_s$ denotes probability of corresponding action category $j \in \mathcal{C}$. This network is trained using binary cross entropy loss between the prediction vector $\hat{\mathbf{c}}_s$ and target vector $\mathbf{c}_s$. Once trained, the linear layer F is discarded and the segment encoder E_s is used to obtain segment-level representations for the action anticipation stage.

3.2 Stage 2: Action Anticipation

In the second stage of our approach, we use an encoder-decoder model that contains two encoders: (i) the segment encoder from the first stage, and (ii) a video encoder that encodes the observed video as a whole. The outputs of these two encoders along with an anticipation duration are fed into an anticipation decoder which uses the representations from the two encoders to predict a set of future action instances over the given anticipation duration. See Fig. 3 (*right*).

Video Encoder. The video encoder receives an observed video containing T_o frames. We denote the input as $\mathbf{v}_o = [\mathbf{v}^1, \ldots, \mathbf{v}^{T_o}]$. We design the encoder network E_v as a sequence of ℓ_v transformer blocks [58] containing a multi-head self-attention module followed by layernorm and feed forward network. The encoder receives the features corresponding to the observed video $\mathbf{v}_o$ as input. As the self-attention module is permutation-invariant, we provide additional information about the sequence in the form of sinusoidal positional encodings [58] $\mathbf{p}_o = [\mathbf{p}^1, \ldots, \mathbf{p}^{T_o}]$ (see supplementary for additional explanation). Here, each element in the positional encoding sequence is added to the corresponding element in the video features and then fed into the encoder block. The encoder models temporal relationships in the observed video and transforms the input sequence to a contextual representation $\mathbf{h}_v = [\mathbf{h}_v^1, \ldots, \mathbf{h}_v^{T_o}]$, expressed as:

$$\mathbf{h}_v = E_v(\mathbf{v}_o, \mathbf{p}_o). \tag{2}$$

Encoding Video Segments. Concurrent to the video encoder, the input video is divided into a sequence of segments using temporal sliding windows. Specifically, a temporal window of size k starting from frame index i obtains a segment $[\mathbf{v}^i, \ldots, \mathbf{v}^{i+k-1}]$, which is fed to the segment encoder to obtain the outputs $\mathbf{h}_s^i, \ldots, \mathbf{h}_s^{i+k-1}$. The starting index i slides across time with $i \in \{1, k+1, 2k+1, \ldots, (T_o - k + 1)\}$ generating the temporal windows, where the window size k is a hyperparameter. The outputs of the segment encoder for all temporal windows are concatenated to obtain $\mathbf{h}_s = [\mathbf{h}_s^1, \ldots, \mathbf{h}_s^{T_o}]$. During implementation, the representations can still be obtained in one forward pass of the segment encoder by stacking segments along the batch dimension of the input. This segment-level representation of the video is complementary to the video-level representation that encodes the ongoing activity in the video.

Anticipation Decoder. Given the video-level and the segment-level representations, the decoder aims to predict a set of future action instances over a given anticipation duration. The predicted set contains action instances of the form (label, start time, end time). The anticipation decoder receives the following inputs: (i) *anticipation queries* $\mathbf{q}_0$, (ii) anticipation duration T_a over which actions are to be predicted, (iii) encoded representation $\mathbf{h}_v$ from video encoder E_v, and (iv) encoded representation $\mathbf{h}_s$ from segment encoder E_s.

The anticipation queries contain N_a elements, *i.e.*, $\mathbf{q}_0 = [\mathbf{q}_0^1, \ldots, \mathbf{q}_0^{N_a}]$, wherein each query is a learnable positional encoding (more details in supplementary). We consider N_a as a hyperparameter that is constant for a dataset and is sufficiently larger than the maximum number of action instances to be anticipated per video in the overall dataset. Each query $\mathbf{q}_0^i$ is then fed into a linear layer (weights shared for all values of i) along with the anticipation duration T_a to obtain time-conditioned anticipation queries $\mathbf{q}_a^i$ for $i = 1, \ldots, N_a$. This time conditioning enables the anticipation decoder to predict actions over any specified anticipation duration.

The decoder network D consists of ℓ_d blocks, wherein, each block contains a cascade of attention layers. The first attention layer is the multi-head self-attention block which models relations among the anticipation queries. The second attention layer is a multi-head encoder-decoder attention layer that maps the queries and the segment-level representations from the segment encoder. And, the third attention layer is another multi-head encoder-decoder attention layer that maps the output of previous layer to the video-level representation corresponding to the input. This third attention layer is followed by a feedforward network. The output of the decoder $\mathbf{y} = [\mathbf{y}^1, \ldots, \mathbf{y}^{N_a}]$ serves as a latent representation of the action instances in the videos, expressed as:

$$\mathbf{y} = D(\mathbf{q}_a, \mathbf{h}_v, \mathbf{h}_s) \tag{3}$$

The decoder output is used to predict the set of action instances $\hat{\mathcal{A}} = \{\hat{a}^i = (\hat{c}^i, \hat{t}_s^i, \hat{t}_e^i)\}_{i=1}^{N_a}$. Each element in decoder output $\mathbf{y}^i$ is fed into a linear layer followed by softmax to obtain prediction probabilities $\hat{p}^i(c)$ where $c = 1, \ldots, |\mathcal{C}| + 1$ and $\hat{c}^i$ is the class corresponding to maximum probability. The number of queries N_a is larger than the maximum number of action instances per video in the dataset. Thus, we introduce an additional class label $\varnothing$ indicating no action. $\mathbf{y}^i$ is also fed into another feedforward network with ReLU to obtain corresponding start timestamps $\hat{t}_s^i$ and end timestamps $\hat{t}_e^i$.

Training. To compute the loss, we first align the predictions with the groundtruth set of action instances. This alignment is necessary as there is no fixed prior correspondence between the predicted and the groundtruth set of action instances. Here, the predicted set for any video contains N_a action instances, but the size of groundtruth set $\mathcal{A}$ varies based on the video and is smaller than the predicted set. Thus, we first pad the groundtruth set to make it the same size as the predicted set by adding $N_a - |\mathcal{A}|$ elements with label $\varnothing$ indicating no action. Then, we use a pair-wise greedy correspondence algorithm to align the groundtruth and predicted sets. Starting with the groundtruth instance having the longest duration, we match each groundtruth instance with the unmatched predicted instance that has the maximum temporal overlap with the groundtruth instance. This results in a one-to-one mapping for loss computation (more details in supplementary).

Consider the output of the set correspondence module as γ denoting the permutation of the predicted set of instances, *i.e.*, the groundtruth action instance a^i is matched to predicted instance $\hat{a}^{\gamma(i)}$ for $i = 1, \ldots, N_a$. Given this alignment, we compute loss $\mathcal{L}$ over all the matched pairs as a weighted combination of cross-entropy loss for classification, and two temporal losses: $L1$ loss and IoU loss ($\mathcal{L}_{iou}$) for prediction of segment timestamps, defined as:

$$\mathcal{L} = \sum_{i=1}^{N_a} \Big[- \log(\hat{p}^{\gamma(i)}(c^i)) + \mathbb{1}_{\{c^i \neq \varnothing\}} \lambda_{L1} ||s^i - \hat{s}^{\gamma(i)}||_1 + \mathbb{1}_{\{c^i \neq \varnothing\}} \lambda_{iou} \mathcal{L}_{iou}(s^i, \hat{s}^{\gamma(i)}) \Big], \tag{4}$$

where $\lambda_{iou}, \lambda_{L1} \in \mathbb{R}^+$ are hyperparameters, $s^i = [t_s^i, t_e^i]$, $\hat{s}^{\gamma(i)} = [\hat{t}_s^{\gamma(i)}, \hat{t}_e^{\gamma(i)}]$ and $\hat{p}^{\gamma(i)}(c^i)$ is the probability of the groundtruth class c^i for prediction $\gamma(i)$. The video encoder and anticipation decoder are jointly trained to minimize this loss. We do not fine-tune the segment encoder in this stage.

Inference. During inference, the video encoder takes the observed video as input and the segment encoder takes the chunked video (*i.e.*, non-overlapping segments of fixed length) as input. The inputs to the decoder are: (i) anticipation queries $\mathbf{q}_0 = 1, \ldots, N_a$ (a constant, regardless of input), (ii) anticipation duration T_a (varies based on the input video and the anticipation requirement), (iii) output representation from the video encoder, and (iv) output representation from the segment encoder. The decoder predicts a set of action instances. Thus, our approach allows us to build a model that can anticipate actions over any future duration in a single pass by simply controlling the input T_a to the decoder as shown by results in Table 1.

In summary, AnticipaTR uses a two-stage learning approach to train a transformer-based model (consisting of two encoders and one decoder) to predict a set of future action instances over any given anticipation duration. Our approach aims to perform action anticipation with segment-level representations learned using individual video segments in conjunction with video-level representations learned by encoding input video as a whole. Our model anticipates actions at all time instants over a given anticipation duration in a single forward pass by directly predicting a set of future action instances.

4 Experiments

We conducted extensive experiments and analysis to demonstrate the effectiveness of our proposed approach.

Datasets. We evaluate on four established benchmarks for this task. These datasets of untrimmed videos vary in scale, diversity of labels and video duration.

Breakfast [29] contains 1,712 videos each depicting one of 10 breakfast activities and annotated with action instances spanning 48 different action classes. On average, a video contains 6 action instances and has a duration of 2.3 min. For evaluation, we report the average across 4 splits from the original dataset.

Table 1. Results (Breakfast and 50Salads). We report the mean over classes accuracy for different observation/anticipation durations. Higher values indicate better performance. Note that "Sener *et al.* [51] (features+labels)" use action labels from a segmentation algorithm as additional input. Baseline results are from respective papers.

	Observation (β_o) →	20%				30%			
	Anticipation (β_a) →	10%	20%	30%	50%	10%	20%	30%	50%
Breakfast	RNN [2]	18.1	17.2	15.9	15.8	21.6	20.0	19.7	19.2
	CNN [2]	17.9	16.3	15.3	14.5	22.4	20.12	19.7	18.7
	RNN [2] + TCN	5.9	5.6	5.5	5.1	8.9	8.9	7.6	7.7
	CNN [2] + TCN	9.8	9.2	9.1	8.9	17.6	17.1	16.1	14.4
	Ke *et al.* [25]	18.4	17.2	16.4	15.8	22.7	20.4	19.6	19.7
	Farha *et al.* [12]	25.9	23.4	22.4	21.5	29.7	27.4	25.6	25.2
	Qi *et al.* [47]	25.6	21.0	18.5	16.0	27.3	23.6	20.8	17.3
	Sener *et al.* [51] (features)	24.2	21.1	20.0	18.1	30.4	26.3	23.8	21.2
	Sener *et al.* [51] (features+labels)	**37.4**	31.8	30.1	27.1	39.8	34.2	31.9	27.9
	ANTICIPATR **(Ours)**	**37.4**	**32.0**	**30.3**	**28.6**	**39.9**	**35.7**	**32.1**	**29.4**
50Salads	RNN [2]	30.1	25.4	18.7	13.5	30.8	17.2	14.8	9.8
	CNN [2]	21.2	19.0	15.9	9.8	29.1	20.1	17.5	10.9
	RNN [2] + TCN	32.3	25.5	19.1	14.1	26.1	17.7	16.3	12.9
	CNN [2] + TCN	16.0	14.7	12.1	9.9	19.2	14.7	13.2	11.2
	Ke *et al.* [25]	32.5	27.6	21.3	15.9	35.1	27.1	22.1	15.6
	Farha *et al.* [12]	34.8	28.4	21.8	15.2	34.4	23.7	18.9	15.9
	Sener *et al.* [51](features)	25.5	19.9	18.2	15.1	30.6	22.5	19.1	11.2
	Sener *et al.* [51](features+labels)	34.7	26.3	23.7	15.7	34.5	26.1	22.7	17.1
	Qi *et al.* [47]	37.9	28.8	21.3	11.1	37.5	24.1	17.1	09.1
	Piergiovanni *et al.* [46]	40.4	33.7	25.4	20.9	40.7	40.1	26.4	19.2
	ANTICIPATR **(Ours)**	**41.1**	**35.0**	**27.6**	**27.3**	**42.8**	**42.3**	**28.5**	**23.6**

50Salads [56] contains 50 videos, each showing a person preparing a salad. On average, there are 20 action instances per video spanning 17 action classes and duration is 6.4 min. Following the original dataset, we report the average across 5-fold cross-validation in our evaluation.

EGTEA Gaze+ (EGTEA+) [31] contains egocentric videos of 32 subjects following 7 recipes in a single kitchen. Each video depicts the preparation of a single dish. Each video is annotated with instances depicting interactions (*e.g.*, open drawer), spanning 53 objects and 19 actions.

EPIC-Kitchens-55 (EK-55). [9] contains videos of daily kitchen activities. It is annotated for interactions spanning 352 objects and 125 actions. It is larger than the aforementioned datasets, and contains unscripted activities.

We represent the input videos by feature representations used in the benchmarks (see supplementary for details).

Evaluation. To measure the performance of our model, we adopt the evaluation protocol followed by state-of-the-art methods for these benchmark datasets.

Table 2. Results (EK-55 and EGTEA+). We report mAP values for ALL classes, FREQUENT classes (>100 action instances) and RARE class (<10 action instances). Following [42], we report the mAP values averaged over different observation durations. Higher values implies better performance. Baseline results are from respective papers.

Method	EK-55			EGTEA+		
	ALL	FREQ	RARE	ALL	FREQ	RARE
RNN	32.6	52.3	23.3	70.4	76.6	54.3
I3D [7]	32.7	53.3	23.0	72.1	79.3	53.3
ActionVLAD [19]	29.8	53.5	18.6	73.3	79.0	58.6
Timeception [22]	35.6	55.9	26.1	74.1	79.7	59.7
VideoGraph [23]	22.5	49.4	14.0	67.7	77.1	47.2
EGO-TOPO [42]	38.0	56.9	**29.2**	73.5	80.7	54.7
ANTICIPATR**(Ours)**	**39.1**	**58.1**	29.1	**76.8**	**83.3**	**55.1**

For Breakfast and 50Salads, we report the mean over classes accuracy averaged over all future timestamps in the specified anticipation duration, *i.e.*, dense prediction evaluation as defined in [2,12,25]. We use $\beta_o\%$ of a full video as observation duration and predict the actions corresponding to following $\beta_a\%$ of the remaining video. As per the benchmarks, we sweep the values of $\beta_o \in \{20, 30\}$ and $\beta_a \in \{10, 20, 30, 50\}$ denoting different observation and anticipation durations respectively. Note that a single trained model is used for predicting at all these values of β_o and β_a by just varying the anticipation duration input to the decoder. Since the metric is computed over a dense anticipation timeline, we first convert our model predictions (set of action instances) into a timeline and then compute mean over classes accuracy (details in supplementary).

For EK-55 and EGTEA+, we compute a multi-label classification metric (mAP) over the target action classes as defined in [42]. $\alpha_o\%$ of each untrimmed video is given as input to predict all action classes in the future $(100 - \alpha_o)\%$ of the video, *i.e.*, until the end of the video. We sweep values of $\alpha_o \in \{25, 50, 75\}$ representing different observation durations. Since the metric is computed only over the future action classes, we take the union of the class labels of predicted action instances to compute mAP.

Comparison with State-of-the-Art. Table 1 shows the results for Breakfast and 50Salads datasets in the *'no groundtruth labels'* setting [25,51]. The results show that our approach outperforms existing methods by a considerable margin for different observation/anticipation durations. For these benchmarks, the most similar approach to ours is Sener *et al.* [51] where they propose self-attention methods for temporal aggregation for long-term video modeling. In the setting similar to ours where they use only visual features as input, our approach outperforms [51] with up to 13% improvement. Moreover, when they also use action labels from a segmentation algorithm as input, our approach is still competitive despite not using such additional inputs. In addition, the benefit of our approach is more apparent when the anticipation duration is longer.

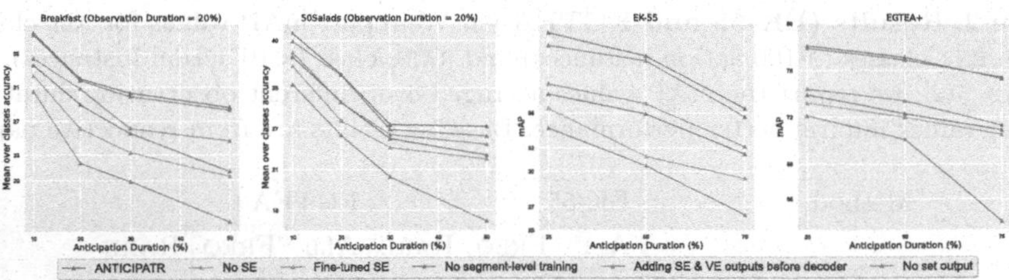

Fig. 4. Analysis. Quantitative evaluation of the anticipation performance of ablated versions of ANTICIPATR. [SE: segment encoder; VE: video encoder].

Table 2 shows results on the long-term action anticipation benchmarks for EK-55 and EGTEA+ datasets, as defined by [42]. The results show that our model achieves competitive results with the state-of-the-art method [42]. While this benchmark only considers prediction of future action labels, our results demonstrate that the segment prediction in our model acts as a beneficial auxiliary task for label prediction.

Impact of Segment-Level Training. Our two-stage learning approach separately learns video-level representations and segment-level representations. To analyze the impact of such two-stage training, we design following experiments.

(i) **Fine-tuned Segment Encoder.** In this experiment, we also fine-tune the segment encoder while training video encoder and decoder during the anticipation stage (Sect. 3.2). The results in Fig. 4 ('Fine-tuned SE') indicate that fine-tuning the segment encoder hurts the anticipation performance. We believe fine-tuning the segment encoder with anticipation loss (Eq. 4) perturbs the segment-level representation learned during first stage of training.

(ii) **No Segment-level Training.** In this experiment, we do not train the segment encoder network in a separate stage. Instead, we train all three networks (*i.e.*, segment encoder, video encoder and anticipation decoder) jointly for the task of long-term action anticipation using the anticipation loss function (Eq. 4). Here, the segment encoder receives videos chunked into short segments (same as the proposed two-stage training). However, it is directly tasked with solving a more difficult problem of simultaneously encoding segment-level representation and inferring its usage for long-term anticipation. The results for all datasets presented in Fig. 4 ('No Segment-level Training') illustrate that eliminating training of the segment encoder worsens the anticipation performance. This shows the value of learning the segment-level representations independently without being influenced by the overall activity in the input video.

In summary, these experiments demonstrate the importance of the two-stage learning approach and suggest that the two representations should be learned separately to serve their individual purposes during anticipation.

Impact of Segment Encoder. To evaluate the impact of learning segment-level representation, we conducted experiments without the segment encoder network. This ablated version only contains the video encoder and the anticipa-

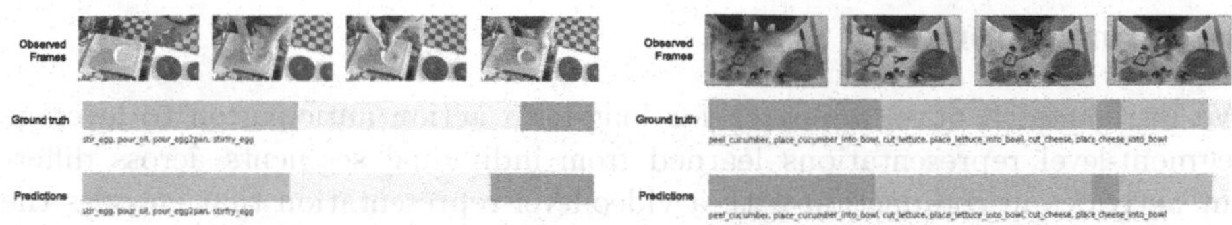

Fig. 5. Visualizations from Breakfast (left) and 50salads (right) where 20% of the video is observed and actions are anticipated over 50% of the remaining video.

tion decoder and is trained in a single-stage using the anticipation loss (Eq. 4). The results in Fig. 4 ('No SE') show that removing the segment-level representations considerably hurts the anticipation performance. This performance degradation is worse than just removing the segment-level training stage ('No segment-level training' in Fig. 4). Thus, this experiment validates the benefit of the segment-level stream of information for action anticipation.

Impact of Set-Based Output Representation. In our approach, we model the anticipation output as a set of action instances. We empirically validate this design by comparing with an alternative approach where the output is a sequence of action labels corresponding to the individual future time instants. We implement this by changing the anticipation queries (decoder input) during the anticipation stage – we provide positional encodings corresponding to each time instant over anticipation duration and directly predict the labels corresponding to these time instants. While the prediction for all time instants still happens in a single pass, the decoder is required to transform a large number of anticipation queries. The results in Fig. 4 ('No Set Output') show poor performance that worsen further as anticipation duration increases. This is largely because the number of queries is too high for the decoder for effective modeling.

Fusion of Encoder Outputs. To combine the representation from segment encoder and video encoder, our model uses two encoder-decoder attention layers in the decoder blocks. We tested an alternative approach wherein we fused the representations using a simple addition along temporal dimension before feeding into the decoder. Here, we modify the decoder blocks to contain a single encoder-decoder attention layer. The results in Fig. 4 ('Adding SE & VE before decoder') indicate that this fusion approach leads to a slight decrease in anticipation performance. We believe adding the representations before decoder forces the computation of encoder-decoder attention weights by considering both information streams at once. In contrast, our ANTICIPATR approach of computing attention one-by-one enables it to first filter out the relevant information from segment-level representations learned across different activities and then contextualize them into the specific context of the input video.

Visualizations. The examples in Fig. 5 shows that our model effectively anticipates future actions. Please refer to supplementary material for additional visualizations and analysis of failure cases.

5 Conclusion

We introduced a novel approach for long-term action anticipation to leverage segment-level representations learned from individual segments across different activities in conjunction with a video-level representation that encodes the observed video as a whole. We proposed a novel two-stage learning approach to train a transformer-based model that receives a video and an anticipation duration as inputs and predicts a set of future action instances over the given anticipation duration. Results showed that our approach achieves state-of-the-art performance on long-term action anticipation benchmarks for Breakfast, 50Salads, Epic-Kitchens-55, and EGTEA Gaze+ datasets. Overall, our work highlights the benefits of learning representations that capture information across different activities for action anticipation.

References

1. Abu Farha, Y., Gall, J.: Uncertainty-aware anticipation of activities. In: Proceedings of the IEEE/CVF International Conference on Computer Vision Workshops (2019)
2. Abu Farha, Y., Richard, A., Gall, J.: When will you do what?-Unticipating temporal occurrences of activities. In: Proceedings of the IEEE International Conference on Computer Vision (CVPR) (2018)
3. Alahi, A., Goel, K., Ramanathan, V., Robicquet, A., Fei-Fei, L., Savarese, S.: Social LSTM: human trajectory prediction in crowded spaces. In: Proceedings of the IEEE/CVF Conference on Computer Vision and Pattern Recognition (CVPR) (2016)
4. Arnab, A., Dehghani, M., Heigold, G., Sun, C., Lučić, M., Schmid, C.: Vivit: A video vision transformer. In: Proceedings of the IEEE/CVF International Conference on Computer Vision (ICCV) (2021)
5. Bhattacharyya, A., Fritz, M., Schiele, B.: Bayesian prediction of future street scenes using synthetic likelihoods. In: Proceedings of the International Conference on Learning Representations (ICLR) (2019)
6. Carion, N., Massa, F., Synnaeve, G., Usunier, N., Kirillov, A., Zagoruyko, S.: End-to-end object detection with transformers. In: Proceedings of the European Conference on Computer Vision (ECCV) (2020)
7. Carreira, J., Zisserman, A.: Quo Vadis, action recognition? a new model and the kinetics dataset. In: Proceedings of the IEEE/CVF Conference on Computer Vision and Pattern Recognition (CVPR) (2017)
8. Chang, C.Y., Huang, D.A., Xu, D., Adeli, E., Fei-Fei, L., Niebles, J.C.: Procedure planning in instructional videos. In: Proceedings of the European Conference on Computer Vision (ECCV) (2020)
9. Damen, D., et al.: scaling egocentric vision: The epic-kitchens dataset. In: Proceedings of the European Conference on Computer Vision (ECCV) (2018)
10. Dang, L., Nie, Y., Long, C., Zhang, Q., Li, G.: MSR-GCN: multi-scale residual graph convolution networks for human motion prediction. In: Proceedings of the IEEE/CVF International Conference on Computer Vision (ICCV) (2021)
11. Dosovitskiy, A., et al.: An image is worth 16x16 words: transformers for image recognition at scale. In: Proceedings of the International Conference on Learning Representations (ICLR) (2021)

12. Farha, Y.A., Ke, Q., Schiele, B., Gall, J.: Long-term anticipation of activities with cycle consistency. In: Proceedings of the German Conference on Pattern Recognition (GCPR) (2020)
13. Furnari, A., Farinella, G.: Rolling-unrolling LSTMs for action anticipation from first-person video. IEEE Trans. Pattern Anal. Mach. Intell. (99), 1–1 (TPAMI) (2020)
14. Furnari, A., Farinella, G.M.: What would you expect? Unticipating egocentric actions with rolling-unrolling LSTMs and modality attention. In: Proceedings of the IEEE International Conference on Computer Vision (CVPR) (2019)
15. Gammulle, H., Denman, S., Sridharan, S., Fookes, C.: Forecasting future action sequences with neural memory networks. In: Proceedings of the British Machine Vision Conference (BMVC) (2019)
16. Gao, J., Yang, Z., Nevatia, R.: RED: Reinforced encoder-decoder networks for action anticipation. In: Proceedings of the British Machine Vision Conference (BMVC) (2017)
17. Girdhar, R., Carreira, J., Doersch, C., Zisserman, A.: video action transformer network. In: Proceedings of the IEEE Conference on Computer Vision and Pattern Recognition (2019)
18. Girdhar, R., Grauman, K.: Anticipative video transformer. In: Proceedings of the IEEE/CVF International Conference on Computer Vision (ICCV) (2021)
19. Girdhar, R., Ramanan, D., Gupta, A., Sivic, J., Russell, B.: ActionVLAD: Learning spatio-temporal aggregation for action classification. In: Proceedings of the IEEE/CVF Conference on Computer Vision and Pattern Recognition (CVPR) (2017)
20. Hernandez, A., Gall, J., Moreno-Noguer, F.: Human motion prediction via spatio-temporal inpainting. In: Proceedings of the IEEE/CVF International Conference on Computer Vision (ICCV) (2019)
21. Hoai, M., De la Torre, F.: Max-margin early event detectors. In: 2012 IEEE Conference on Computer Vision and Pattern Recognition (2014)
22. Hussein, N., Gavves, E., Smeulders, A.W.: Timeception for complex action recognition. In: Proceedings of the IEEE/CVF Conference on Computer Vision and Pattern Recognition (CVPR) (2019)
23. Hussein, N., Gavves, E., Smeulders, A.W.: Videograph: Recognizing minutes-long human activities in videos. Proceedings of the IEEE/CVF International Conference on Computer Vision (ICCV) Workshop (2019)
24. Jain, A., Zamir, A.R., Savarese, S., Saxena, A.: Structural-RNN: deep learning on spatio-temporal graphs. In: Proceedings of the IEEE/CVF Conference on Computer Vision and Pattern Recognition (CVPR) (2016)
25. Ke, Q., Fritz, M., Schiele, B.: Time-conditioned action anticipation in one shot. In: Proceedings of the IEEE/CVF Conference on Computer Vision and Pattern Recognition (CVPR) (2019)
26. Kim, B., Lee, J., Kang, J., Kim, E.S., Kim, H.J.: Hotr: end-to-end human-object interaction detection with transformers. In: Proceedings of the IEEE/CVF Conference on Computer Vision and Pattern Recognition (CVPR) (2021)
27. Kitani, K.M., Ziebart, B.D., Bagnell, J.A., Hebert, M.: Activity forecasting. In: Proceedings of the European Conference on Computer Vision (ECCV) (2012)
28. Koppula, H.S., Saxena, A.: Anticipating human activities using object affordances for reactive robotic response. IEEE Trans. Pattern Anal. Mach. Intell. **38**, 14–29 (2015)

29. Kuehne, H., Arslan, A., Serre, T.: The language of actions: recovering the syntax and semantics of goal-directed human activities. In: Proceedings of the IEEE/CVF Conference on Computer Vision and Pattern Recognition (CVPR) (2014)
30. Lan, T., Chen, T.C., Savarese, S.: A hierarchical representation for future action prediction. In: Proceedings of the European Conference on Computer Vision (ECCV) (2014)
31. Li, Y., Liu, M., Rehg, J.M.: In the eye of beholder: Joint learning of gaze and actions in first person video. In: Proceedings of the European Conference on Computer Vision (ECCV) (2018)
32. Liang, J., Jiang, L., Niebles, J.C., Hauptmann, A.G., Fei-Fei, L.: Peeking into the future: predicting future person activities and locations in videos. In: Proceedings of the IEEE/CVF Conference on Computer Vision and Pattern Recognition (CVPR) (2019)
33. Liang, X., Lee, L., Dai, W., Xing, E.P.: Dual motion GAN for future-flow embedded video prediction. In: Proceedings of the IEEE/CVF International Conference on Computer Vision (ICCV) (2017)
34. Luc, P., Neverova, N., Couprie, C., Verbeek, J., LeCun, Y.: Predicting deeper into the future of semantic segmentation. In: Proceedings of the IEEE/CVF International Conference on Computer Vision (ICCV) (2017)
35. Ma, S., Sigal, L., Sclaroff, S.: Learning activity progression in lstms for activity detection and early detection. In: Proceedings of the IEEE/CVF Conference on Computer Vision and Pattern Recognition (CVPR) (2016)
36. Ma, Y., Zhu, X., Zhang, S., Yang, R., Wang, W., Manocha, D.: TrafficpRedict: Trajectory prediction for heterogeneous traffic-agents. In: Proceedings of the AAAI Conference on Artificial Intelligence (AAAI) (2019)
37. Mahmud, T., Hasan, M., Roy-Chowdhury, A.K.: Joint prediction of activity labels and starting times in untrimmed videos. In: Proceedings of the IEEE/CVF International Conference on Computer Vision (ICCV) (2017)
38. Martinez, J., Black, M.J., Romero, J.: On human motion prediction using recurrent neural networks. In: Proceedings of the IEEE/CVF Conference on Computer Vision and Pattern Recognition (CVPR) (2017)
39. Mathieu, M., Couprie, C., LeCun, Y.: Deep multi-scale video prediction beyond mean square error. In: Proceedings of the International Conference on Learning Representations (ICLR) (2016)
40. Mehrasa, N., Jyothi, A.A., Durand, T., He, J., Sigal, L., Mori, G.: A variational auto-encoder model for stochastic point processes. In: Proceedings of the IEEE/CVF Conference on Computer Vision and Pattern Recognition (CVPR) (2019)
41. Meinhardt, T., Kirillov, A., Leal-Taixe, L., Feichtenhofer, C.: Trackformer: Multi-object tracking with transformers. arXiv preprint arXiv:2101.02702 (2021)
42. Nagarajan, T., Li, Y., Feichtenhofer, C., Grauman, K.: Ego-topo: Environment affordances from egocentric video. In: Proceedings of the IEEE/CVF Conference on Computer Vision and Pattern Recognition (CVPR) (2020)
43. Nawhal, M., Mori, G.: Activity graph transformer for temporal action localization. arXiv preprint arXiv:2101.08540 (2021)
44. Ng, Y.B., Fernando, B.: Forecasting future action sequences with attention: a new approach to weakly supervised action forecasting. IEEE Trans. Image Process. (2020)
45. Osman, N., Camporese, G., Coscia, P., Ballan, L.: Slowfast rolling-unrolling lstms for action anticipation in egocentric videos. In: Proceedings of the IEEE/CVF International Conference on Computer Vision (ICCV) (2021)

46. Piergiovanni, A., Angelova, A., Toshev, A., Ryoo, M.S.: Adversarial generative grammars for human activity prediction. In: Proceedings of the European Conference on Computer Vision (ECCV) (2020)
47. Qi, Z., Wang, S., Su, C., Su, L., Huang, Q., Tian, Q.: Self-regulated learning for egocentric video activity anticipation. IEEE Trans. Pattern Analy. Mach. Intell. (Early Access 2021)
48. Rodin, I., Furnari, A., Mavroeidis, D., Farinella, G.M.: Untrimmed action anticipation. arXiv preprint arXiv:2202.04132 (2022)
49. Rodriguez, C., Fernando, B., Li, H.: Action anticipation by predicting future dynamic images. In: Proceedings of the European Conference on Computer Vision (ECCV) Workshops (2018)
50. Ryoo, M.S.: Human activity prediction: early recognition of ongoing activities from streaming videos. In: Proceedings of the IEEE/CVF International Conference on Computer Vision (ICCV) (2011)
51. Sener, F., Singhania, D., Yao, A.: Temporal aggregate representations for long-range video understanding. In: Proceedings of the European Conference on Computer Vision (ECCV) (2020)
52. Sener, F., Yao, A.: Zero-shot anticipation for instructional activities. In: Proceedings of the IEEE International Conference on Computer Vision (CVPR) (2019)
53. Shi, Y., Fernando, B., Hartley, R.: Action anticipation with RBF kernelized feature mapping RNN. In: Proceedings of the European Conference on Computer Vision (ECCV) (2018)
54. Shou, Z., et al.: Online detection of action start in untrimmed, streaming videos. In: Proceedings of the European Conference on Computer Vision (ECCV) (2018)
55. Soran, B., Farhadi, A., Shapiro, L.: Generating notifications for missing actions: Don't forget to turn the lights off! In: Proceedings of the IEEE/CVF International Conference on Computer Vision (ICCV) (2015)
56. Stein, S., McKenna, S.J.: Combining embedded accelerometers with computer vision for recognizing food preparation activities. In: Proceedings of the ACM International Joint Conference on Pervasive and Ubiquitous Computing (2013)
57. Sun, C., Shrivastava, A., Vondrick, C., Sukthankar, R., Murphy, K., Schmid, C.: Relational action forecasting. In: Proceedings of the IEEE/CVF Conference on Computer Vision and Pattern Recognition (CVPR) (2019)
58. Vaswani, A., et al.: Attention is all you need. In: 31st Conference on Neural Information Processing Systems (NIPS 2017), Long Beach, CA, USA (NIPS) (2017)
59. Vondrick, C., Pirsiavash, H., Torralba, A.: Anticipating visual representations from unlabeled video. In: Proceedings of the IEEE/CVF Conference on Computer Vision and Pattern Recognition (CVPR) (2016)
60. Wang, Y., et al: End-to-end video instance segmentation with transformers. Proceedings of the IEEE/CVF Conference on Computer Vision and Pattern Recognition (CVPR) (2021)
61. Wu, B., Nair, S., Martin-Martin, R., Fei-Fei, L., Finn, C.: Greedy hierarchical variational autoencoders for large-scale video prediction. In: Proceedings of the IEEE/CVF Conference on Computer Vision and Pattern Recognition (CVPR) (2021)
62. Yu, C., Ma, X., Ren, J., Zhao, H., Yi, S.: Spatio-temporal graph transformer networks for pedestrian trajectory prediction. In: Proceedings of the European Conference on Computer Vision (ECCV) (2020)
63. Zatsarynna, O., Abu Farha, Y., Gall, J.: Multi-modal temporal convolutional network for anticipating actions in egocentric videos. In: Proceedings of the

IEEE/CVF Conference on Computer Vision and Pattern Recognition (CVPR) (2021)
64. Zeng, K.H., Shen, W.B., Huang, D.A., Sun, M., Carlos Niebles, J.: Visual forecasting by imitating dynamics in natural sequences. In: Proceedings of the IEEE/CVF International Conference on Computer Vision (ICCV) (2017)
65. Zhang, H., Chen, F., Yao, A.: Weakly-supervised dense action anticipation. In: Proceedings of the British Machine Vision Conference (BMVC) (2021)
66. Zhang, Y., e al.: Vidtr: Video transformer without convolutions. In: Proceedings of the IEEE/CVF International Conference on Computer Vision (ICCV) (2021)
67. Zou, C., et al.: End-to-end human object interaction detection with hoi transformer. In: Proceedings of the IEEE/CVF Conference on Computer Vision and Pattern Recognition (CVPR) (2021)

DualFormer: Local-Global Stratified Transformer for Efficient Video Recognition

Yuxuan Liang[1,2(✉)], Pan Zhou[1], Roger Zimmermann[2], and Shuicheng Yan[1]

[1] Sea AI Lab, Beijing, Singapore
{zhoupan,ysc}@sea.com
[2] National University of Singapore, Singapore, Singapore
{yuxliang,rogerz}@comp.nus.edu.sg

Abstract. While transformers have shown great potential on video recognition with their strong capability of capturing long-range dependencies, they often suffer high computational costs induced by the self-attention to the huge number of 3D tokens. In this paper, we present a new transformer architecture termed DualFormer, which can efficiently perform space-time attention for video recognition. Concretely, DualFormer stratifies the full space-time attention into dual cascaded levels, i.e., to first learn fine-grained local interactions among nearby 3D tokens, and then to capture coarse-grained global dependencies between the query token and global pyramid contexts. Different from existing methods that apply space-time factorization or restrict attention computations within local windows for improving efficiency, our local-global stratification strategy can well capture both short- and long-range spatiotemporal dependencies, and meanwhile greatly reduces the number of keys and values in attention computation to boost efficiency. Experimental results verify the superiority of DualFormer on five video benchmarks against existing methods. In particular, DualFormer achieves 82.9%/85.2% top-1 accuracy on Kinetics-400/600 with ∼1000G inference FLOPs which is at least 3.2× fewer than existing methods with similar performance. We have released the source code at https://github.com/sail-sg/dualformer.

Keywords: Efficient video transformer · Local and global attention

1 Introduction

Video recognition is a fundamental task in computer vision, such as action recognition [5] and event detection [18]. Like in image-based tasks [17,27,44], Convolutional Neural Networks (CNNs) are often taken as backbones for video recognition models [5,12,13,32,48,50]. Though successful, it is challenging for convolutional architectures to capture *long-range spatiotemporal dependencies* across video frames due to their limited receptive field.

Supplementary Information The online version contains supplementary material available at https://doi.org/10.1007/978-3-031-19830-4_33.

S. Avidan et al. (Eds.): ECCV 2022, LNCS 13694, pp. 577–595, 2022.
https://doi.org/10.1007/978-3-031-19830-4_33

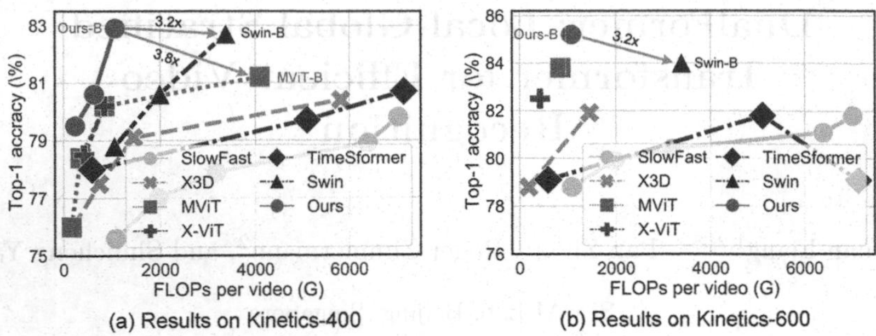

Fig. 1. Accuracy vs. FLOPs on Kinetics [25]. Ours-B is the base version of DualFormer.

Recently, transformers [51] have become an alternative paradigm for visual modeling beyond CNNs, demonstrating great potential in a series of image processing tasks [34,42,52,54,55,62]. A pioneering work is the Vision Transformer (ViT) [10] which replaces the inherent inductive bias of locality in convolutions by global relation modeling with multi-head self-attention (MSA) [51]. Soon the vision community extends the application of MSA from static images to videos considering its remarkable power for capturing long-range spatiotemporal dependencies [1,3,11,38]. Concretely, a video is first partitioned into non-overlapping 3D patches, similar as in NLP tasks [51], which then serve as input tokens for transformers to jointly learn short- and long-range relations within a video.

One of the major challenges for applying transformers to video data is their *low efficiency*. Due to the MSA operation, the computational cost of video transformers grows quadratically with the increasing number of tokens, and may even become totally unaffordable for some high spatial resolution or long videos. To alleviate this issue, TimeSformer [3] and ViViT [1] factorize the full space-time self-attention along temporal and spatial dimensions separately to achieve a balance between accuracy and efficiency in video recognition. Inspired by the observation that near tokens are usually more related than distant ones [46], Video Swin Transformer [35] applies the inductive bias of locality at each transformer layer via performing self-attention in the non-overlapping local windows. Though effective, both the space-time factorization and the local-window based attention scheme contradict the aim of applying full space-time attention, i.e., to *jointly* capture local and global spatiotemporal dependencies within one layer, and thus impair the performance of video transformers.

In this work, we present a new video transformer architecture entitled **DualFormer** for *efficient* video recognition. DualFormer stratifies the full space-time attention into dual cascaded levels: 1) *Local-Window based Multi-head Self-Attention* (LW-MSA) to extract short-range interactions among nearby tokens; and 2) *Global-Pyramid based MSA* (GP-MSA) to capture long-range dependencies between the query token and the coarse-grained global pyramid contexts. In this manner, DualFormer significantly reduces the number of keys and values in attention computation, and achieves much higher efficiency over existing video transformers [1,3,35] with comparable performance, as shown in Fig. 1.

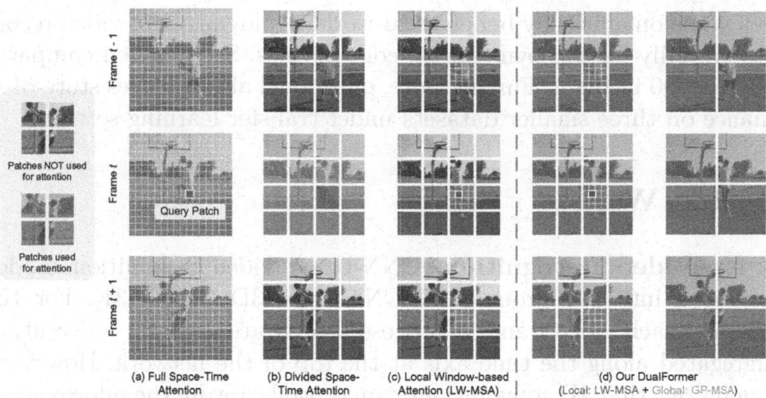

Fig. 2. Visualization of four space-time MSA schemes. For better illustration, we use 2D patch partitions. We denote in red the query patch and in non-red colors its attention targets for each scheme. Multiple highlighted colors in a scheme indicate the MSA separately applied along different dimensions. (a) Full space-time attention [3] has quadratic complexity w.r.t. the number of patches. (b) Divided space-time attention [3], where MSA is separately applied in temporal and spatial domains. (c) Local window-based attention [35] improves efficiency by restricting MSA computation within local windows, lacking interactions between distant patches. (d) Our dual-level MSA scheme stratifies the modeling of local and global relations. Given a query patch, we first use LW-MSA to compute attention weights within the local window. Then, the query patch attends to the multi-scale global priors (two scales here) via GP-MSA. (Color figure online)

Figure 2 shows how a query patch (in red) attends to its surroundings in a DualFormer block. Following the intuition that tokens closer to each other are more likely to be correlated [34,59], we first perform LW-MSA at a fine-grained level to allow each patch to interact with its neighbors within a local window. This strategy has also been verified to be efficient and memory-friendly by recent studies [6,8,34,35,59]. Next, at the global level, a query patch attends to the full region of interest at a coarse granularity via GP-MSA. To be specific, we first extract global contextual priors with different pyramid scales for multi-scale scene interpretation (see the two scales, i.e. small windows and large windows, in Fig. 2(d)). These global priors then pass global contextual information to the query tokens via MSA. Since such priors are extracted at a coarse-grained level, their number is much smaller than the original token number, leading to far less computation cost in capturing global information than the full space-time attention. In contrast to the space-time factorization in TimeSformer [3] and ViViT [1] and the locality-based scheme in Swin [35], this dual-level attention design not only enables our model to have the global receptive field at each block, but is also efficient in attention computations.

Extensive experimental results on five video benchmarks validate the superiority of our DualFormer in terms of accuracy and FLOPs. In particular, our DualFormer achieves 82.9%/85.2% top-1 accuracy on Kinetics-400/600 [25] with only ~1000 GFLOPs which is 3.2× and 16.2× fewer than the previous state-of-the-art methods, i.e., Swin [34] and ViViT [1], respectively. We strongly believe that such gains on efficiency benefit real-world deployments of video recognition models, especially for deployments on edge devices. See detailed comparison on Kinetics-400/600 in Fig. 1. Furthermore, our model also achieves state-of-the-art performance on three smaller datasets under transfer learning settings.

2 Related Work

CNNs for Video Recognition. CNN-based video recognition models can be categorized into two groups: 2D CNNs and 3D CNNs [31]. For the first group [24,53], each video frame is processed separately by 2D convolutions and then aggregated along the time axis at the top of the network. However, some studies point out that 2D convolutions cannot well capture the information along the temporal dimension [22,32,36,37]. The second group learns spatiotemporal video representation via 3D convolutions by aggregating space-time features and are difficult to optimize [15,16,21,48,58]. Thus, the current trend for 3D CNN-based video recognition is to boost efficiency. For example, I3D [5] expands pre-trained 2D CNNs [17,27,44]into 3D CNNs; some recent works[12,13,41,49,50,57] factorize 3D convolutions into spatial and temporal filters, demonstrating even higher accuracy than vanilla 3D CNNs. Unfortunately, most of the 2D and 3D CNNs cannot capture long-range spatiotemporal dependencies due to their limited receptive fields, which leads to sub-optimal recognition performance.

Transformers for Video Recognition. Recently, transformers are applied to model spatiotemporal dependencies for video recognition [1,3,4,11,35,38,39,61] by virtue of their great power in capturing long-range dependencies [8,10,34,47]. With pretraining on a large-scale image dataset, video transformers achieve promising performance on video benchmarks [1,3,35], such as Kinetics-400/600. However, the potential of video transformers is significantly limited by the considerable computational complexity of performing full space-time attention. Various approaches have been proposed to reduce such computation cost [1,3,4,35,61]. For instance, TimeSformer [3] factorizes the full space-time attention into spatial and temporal dimensions. Similarly, ViViT [1] examines three variants of space-time factorization for computation reduction. X-ViT [4] approximates the space-time attention by restricting the temporal attention to a local temporal window and using a mixing strategy. Video Swin Transformer [35] introduces an inductive bias of locality to transformers for video understanding. However, these attempts focus on either space-time factorization or restricting attention computation locally, crippling the capability of MSA in capturing long-range dependencies. To solve this, we present a new transformer called DualFormer to improve the efficiency of video transformers, by alternatively capturing fine-grained local interactions and coarse-grained global information within each block. Besides, there are some concurrent works enhancing transformers [29,60] or exploring self-supervised pretraining schemes [40,56] for video recognition.

3 Methodology

We start by summarizing the overall architecture of DualFormer in Sect. 3.1, and then elaborate on its basic block in Sect. 3.2 by well introducing the two types of attention, including Local-Window based Multi-head Self-Attention (LW-MSA) and Global-Pyramid based MSA (GP-MSA). Afterward, we explain the network configuration for constructing our DualFormer in Sect. 3.3. Finally, we discuss the differences between our DualFormer and related works in Sect. 3.4.

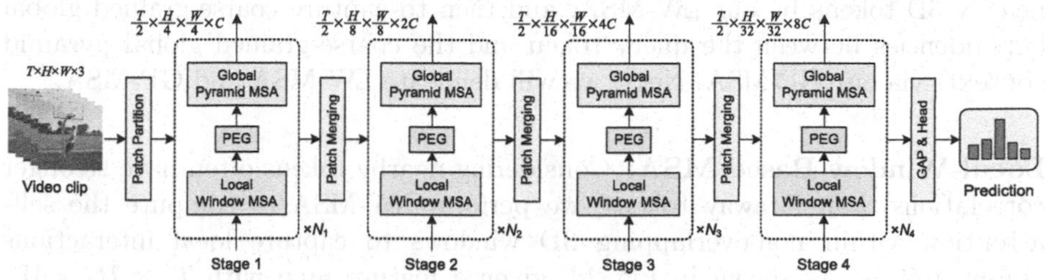

Fig. 3. Overall architecture of DualFormer. GAP: global average pooling.

3.1 Overall Architecture

Figure 3 shows the overall architecture of the proposed DualFormer. It takes a video clip $\mathcal{X} \in \mathbb{R}^{T\times H\times W\times 3}$ as input, where T stands for the number of frames and each frame consists of $H \times W \times 3$ pixels. To accommodate high-resolution video-based tasks, our model leverages a hierarchical design [11,34,35,59] to produce decreasing-resolution feature maps from early to late stages. First, we partition a video clip into non-overlapping 3D patches of size $2 \times 4 \times 4 \times 3$ and employ a linear layer for projection, resulting in $\frac{T}{2} \times \frac{H}{4} \times \frac{W}{4}$ visual tokens with feature channel dimension C. Then, as shown in Fig. 3, these tokens go through the four stages of DualFormer for learning visual representations. At each stage $s \in \{1, 2, 3, 4\}$, we sequentially stack N_s DualFormer blocks for spatiotemporal learning, where N_s controls the capacity of each model stage. Each DualFormer block consists of dual cascaded levels of self-attention mechanisms: LW-MSA for learning short-range interactions within local windows, and GP-MSA for capturing long-range context information within the whole video. Additionally, a convolution-based Position Encoding Generator (PEG) [9] is integrated into the first block of each stage (between the two types of MSA) to empower position-aware self-attention. After each stage, DualFormer follows the prior art [35] to utilize a patch merging layer to downsample the spatial size of the feature map by 2×, while the feature channel dimension is increased by 2×. Once the output of the last stage is obtained, DualFormer performs video recognition by applying a global average pooling (GAP) layer followed by a linear classifier.

3.2 DualFormer Block

As all blocks share the same architecture, we introduce each block by taking a block at the s-th stage as an example. Assume that the input feature map at the s-th stage is of resolution $T_s \times H_s \times W_s$ with channel dimension C_s, the complexity of the full space-time attention is $\mathcal{O}(T_s^2 H_s^2 W_s^2 C_s)$ which is too high to handle high-resolution videos in practice. To alleviate this efficiency issue, in each DualFormer block, we stratify the full space-time attention into dual cascaded levels, i.e., to first learn fine-grained local space-time interactions among nearby 3D tokens by our LW-MSA, and then to capture coarse-grained global dependencies between the query token and the coarse-grained global pyramid contexts via our GP-MSA. Next, we will delineate LW-MSA and GP-MSA.

Local-Window Based MSA. Considering nearby tokens often have stronger correlations than faraway tokens, we perform LW-MSA to compute the self-attention within non-overlapping 3D windows to capture local interactions among tokens. As shown in Fig. 2d, given a feature map with $T_s \times H_s \times W_s$ patch tokens with dimension C_s, we first evenly split it into non-overlapping small local windows, each of which is of size $t_s \times h_s \times w_s$, yielding $\frac{T_s}{t_s} \times \frac{H_s}{h_s} \times \frac{W_s}{w_s}$ windows. Next, we flatten all tokens within the (i, j, k)-th local window into $\mathbf{X}_{i,j,k} \in \mathbb{R}^{t_s h_s w_s \times C_s}$. Now we are ready to formulate our LW-MSA:

$$\mathbf{X}'_{ijk} = \mathrm{MSA}(\mathrm{LN}(\mathbf{X}_{ijk})) + \mathbf{X}_{ijk}, \quad \mathbf{Y}_{ijk} = \mathrm{MLP}\left(\mathrm{LN}\left(\mathbf{X}'_{ijk}\right)\right) + \mathbf{X}'_{ijk}, \tag{1}$$

where MSA, LN, and MLP denote a standard multi-head self-attention, a layer normalization [2], and a multi-layer perceptron, respectively. The computational complexity[1] of MSA within a local window is computed as $\mathcal{O}((t_s h_s w_s)^2 C_s)$. We further summarize the cost of all $\frac{T_s}{t_s} \times \frac{H_s}{h_s} \times \frac{W_s}{w_s}$ windows as follows:

$$\mathcal{O}(\text{LW-MSA}) = (t_s h_s w_s)^2 C_s \times \left(\frac{T_s H_s W_s}{t_s h_s w_s}\right) = t_s h_s w_s M_s C_s, \tag{2}$$

where $M_s = T_s H_s W_s$ is the token number. In this way, the complexity of our LW-MSA is $\frac{M_s}{t_s h_s w_s} \times$ less than that of full space-time attention $\mathcal{O}(M_s^2 C_s)$. Since videos often have a huge number of tokens (M_s is large) and the local window is of small size ($t_s h_s w_s$ is small), our LW-MSA enjoys much higher efficiency for video recognition. See the effects of t_s, h_s, w_s on the performance in Sect. 4.3.

Global-Pyramid Based MSA. While being efficient in computation, LW-MSA cripples the ability of MSA to capture global information. For example, a query patch cannot attend to a patch outside the local window. To tackle this issue, a shifted window strategy is proposed to enable a patch to communicate with the patches inside adjacent windows in [35]. Nevertheless, it is still difficult for patches to interact with distant windows. In this work, we propose GP-MSA as a complement for learning long-range dependencies within the whole video.

[1] For simplicity, we omit the complexity of MLP in this paper.

As a variant of MSA, our GP-MSA receives queries $\mathbf{Q}$, keys $\mathbf{K}$, and values $\mathbf{V}$ as input to capture the global information. For simplicity, we assume $\mathbf{Q}$, $\mathbf{K}$ and $\mathbf{V}$ are all in shape $M_s \times C_s$, where M_s is the number of tokens at the s-th stage. Different from the vanilla MSA, our GP-MSA proposes a simple yet effective method, termed **pyramid downsampling**, to reduce the spatiotemporal scale of $\mathbf{K}$ and $\mathbf{V}$ before performing MSA, so as to lessen the computational overheads and memory usage. Specifically, as illustrated by Fig. 4, our pyramid downsampling adopts three levels of depth-wise convolutions [7] to generate a set of global priors, where each prior is a spatiotemporal abstract of the original feature map under different pyramid scales. This operation allows the model to separate the feature map into non-overlapping regions and to build pooled representations for various locations. For example, the 1×1×1 prior (the orange cube in Fig. 4) denotes the coarsest scale with only a single value at each channel, which is similar to global average pooling [33] that covers the whole video, while the 2×2×2 prior (the yellow cube) indicates a summary of finer granularity. Then, as shown in Fig. 4, we flatten and concatenate these priors to be the new key-value of size $G \times C_s$, where G denotes the number of space-time locations, e.g., $G{=}\sum_{k=\{1,2,4\}} k^3{=}73$. After downsampling, we pass the global contextual information in these priors to each query patch via standard MSA.

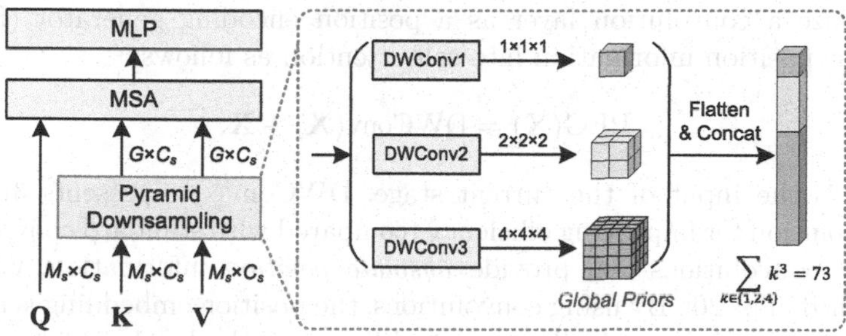

Fig. 4. The pipeline of GP-MSA. DWConv denotes depth-wise convolution [7] for generating global priors with multiple scales. For simplicity, we use a three-level pyramid (1×1×1, 2×2×2, and 4×4×4) for illustration. With pyramid downsampling, the computational cost and memory usage of GP-MSA are much lower than those of standard MSA due to reduction of the key/value number.

Complexity Analysis of GP-MSA. Without loss of generality, assume we have N_g pyramid scales for all stages and denote the size of global prior at the i-th scale as (k_1^i, k_2^i, k_3^i), where $k_1^i < T_s$, $k_2^i < H_s$ and $k_3^i < W_s$. The complexity of GP-MSA at the s-th stage is computed as:

$$\mathcal{O}(\text{GP-MSA}) = \underbrace{M_s C_s \sum_{i=1}^{N_g} k_1^i k_2^i k_3^i}_{\text{MSA}} + \underbrace{\sum_{i=1}^{N_g} \left(\frac{T_s H_s W_s}{k_1^i k_2^i k_3^i} k_1^i k_2^i k_3^i C_s \right)}_{\text{DWConv}}$$

$$= \left(\sum_{i=1}^{N_g} k_1^i k_2^i k_3^i + N_g \right) M_s C_s = (G + N_g) M_s C_s,$$

where $G = \sum_{i=1}^{N_g} k_1^i k_2^i k_3^i$ is the number of global priors, i.e., new keys or values after reduction. To further improve efficiency, we draw inspiration from R(2+1)D [50] to factorize the depth-wise convolution at each scale along temporal and spatial dimensions, which gives an even less complexity:

$$\mathcal{O}(\text{GP-MSA}) = \Big(G + \sum_{i=1}^{N_g}\Big(\frac{k_1^i}{T_s} + \frac{k_2^i k_3^i}{H_s W_s}\Big)\Big) M_s C_s \approx G M_s C_s < \underbrace{(G + N_g) M_s C_s}_{\text{Previous}} \ll \underbrace{M_s^2 C_s}_{\text{MSA}}. \quad (3)$$

Since G is generally much smaller than the number of tokens (M_s) in the original feature map, our GP-MSA significantly reduces the computational complexity and memory usage during learning global representations. For instance, at the first stage of DualFormer where G is 456 while M_s is 50176, the complexity has been reduced by ~110 times. In a nutshell, the overall complexity of MSA in a DualFormer block is the summation of LW-MSA in Eq. (2) and GP-LSA in Eq. (3), and is much smaller than the complexity of vanilla full-time self-attention, demonstrating the efficiency of our DualFormer.

Position Encoding Generator (PEG). As the self-attention operation is permutation-invariant, we draw inspiration from conditional positional encoding [9] to utilize a convolution layer as a position encoding generator (PEG) to encode the position information into self-attention as follows:

$$\text{PEG}(\mathbf{X}) = \text{DWConv}(\mathbf{X}) + \mathbf{X}, \quad (4)$$

where $\mathbf{X}$ is the input of the current stage. DWConv(·) represents 3D depth-wise convolution for improving efficiency (compared with standard convolutions). Primarily, convolutions can provide *absolute position* information, which has been verified in [9,20]. By using convolutions, the position embedding is no longer input-agnostic and dynamically generated based on the local neighbors of each token. Moreover, our PEG is permutation-variant since the permutation over inputs affects the order in local windows. In addition, the convolution kernels are applied to local windows everywhere in an input video, thus having similar responses to the objects with similar features, i.e., translation-invariant.

3.3 Model Configuration

Following Swin [35], we consider three network configurations (i.e., base, small and tiny) for our DualFormer. For the LW-MSA of all versions, its local window size is always (8, 7, 7), and its MLP expansion factor is always 4. In GP-MSA, we utilize two pyramid scales (8, 7, 7) and (4, 4, 4) at the first three stages for learning global contextual information. At the last stage, since the feature map size has become (16, 7, 7), we only extract one scale of global prior with (8, 7, 7) using a depth-wise convolution. More details can be found in Table 1.

Table 1. Model configurations of DualFormer, including three versions. p_i and C_i denote patch size and feature dimension at the i-th stage, respectively.

Stage	Layer	Tiny	Small	Base
Stage 1	Patch Merging	$p_1 = (2,4,4)$ $C_1 = 64$	$p_1 = (2,4,4)$ $C_1 = 96$	$p_1 = (2,4,4)$ $C_1 = 128$
Output: $\frac{T}{2}, \frac{H}{4}, \frac{W}{4}$	LW-MSA GP-MSA	$\begin{bmatrix} (8,7,7) \\ (4,4,4) \\ (8,7,7) \end{bmatrix} \times 1$	$\begin{bmatrix} (8,7,7) \\ (4,4,4) \\ (8,7,7) \end{bmatrix} \times 1$	$\begin{bmatrix} (8,7,7) \\ (4,4,4) \\ (8,7,7) \end{bmatrix} \times 1$
Stage 2	Patch Merging	$p_2 = (1,2,2)$ $C_2 = 128$	$p_2 = (1,2,2)$ $C_2 = 192$	$p_2 = (1,2,2)$ $C_2 = 256$
Output: $\frac{T}{2}, \frac{H}{8}, \frac{W}{8}$	LW-MSA GP-MSA	$\begin{bmatrix} (8,7,7) \\ (4,4,4) \\ (8,7,7) \end{bmatrix} \times 1$	$\begin{bmatrix} (8,7,7) \\ (4,4,4) \\ (8,7,7) \end{bmatrix} \times 1$	$\begin{bmatrix} (8,7,7) \\ (4,4,4) \\ (8,7,7) \end{bmatrix} \times 1$
Stage 3	Patch Merging	$p_3 = (1,2,2)$ $C_3 = 256$	$p_3 = (1,2,2)$ $C_3 = 384$	$p_3 = (1,2,2)$ $C_3 = 512$
Output: $\frac{T}{2}, \frac{H}{16}, \frac{W}{16}$	LW-MSA GP-MSA	$\begin{bmatrix} (8,7,7) \\ (4,4,4) \\ (8,7,7) \end{bmatrix} \times 5$	$\begin{bmatrix} (8,7,7) \\ (4,4,4) \\ (8,7,7) \end{bmatrix} \times 9$	$\begin{bmatrix} (8,7,7) \\ (4,4,4) \\ (8,7,7) \end{bmatrix} \times 9$
Stage 4	Patch Merging	$p_4 = (1,2,2)$ $C_4 = 512$	$p_4 = (1,2,2)$ $C_4 = 768$	$p_4 = (1,2,2)$ $C_4 = 1024$
Output: $\frac{T}{2}, \frac{H}{32}, \frac{W}{32}$	LW-MSA GP-MSA	$\begin{bmatrix} (8,7,7) \\ (8,7,7) \end{bmatrix} \times 2$	$\begin{bmatrix} (8,7,7) \\ (8,7,7) \end{bmatrix} \times 1$	$\begin{bmatrix} (8,7,7) \\ (8,7,7) \end{bmatrix} \times 1$

3.4 Discussion

Here, we compare our model with some related works mentioned in Sect. 2.

Comparison with Space-Time Factorization. The space-time attention factorization in TimeSformer [3] and ViViT [1] separately perform standard MSA in temporal and spatial domains, while DualFormer has two major differences. Firstly, our DualFormer factorizes the full space-time attention along another two dimensions, namely, local and global dependencies via LW-MSA and GP-MSA respectively in which both model temporal and spatial domains as a whole and thus better capture their complementary information. Secondly, for each domain, TimeSformer and ViViT still perform conventional MSA attention among all tokens. Differently, our LW-MSA and GP-MSA first considers the attention among nearby 3D tokens and then integrate the global information at the local-window level, which greatly reduces the number of keys and values for attention computation and boosts efficiency.

Comparison with Video Swin. Our DualFormer also distinguishes Swin [35] from their different ways for long-range relation modeling. In Swin, a shifting window strategy is proposed to empower cross-local-window interaction, and thus increases the receptive fields of MSA. Nevertheless, it is still non-trivial for this shifting scheme to learn the dependencies between distant patch tokens. In contrast, our DualFormer employs GP-MSA to *directly* capture the interaction between the query token and the coarse-grained global pyramid contexts, which is more explicit and efficient to learn the global spatiotemporal dependencies. Experimental results in Fig. 1 verify that DualFormer can achieve slightly higher accuracy while having at least 3× fewer FLOPs than Swin.

Comparison with Image-Based ViTs. Several image-based transformers with a local-to-global design, e.g., Twins [8] and RegionViT [6], are also relevant to our model. Compared to Twins, the major difference is the construction of global contexts. Since the objects across different frames in a video may vary in sizes, our DualFormer extracts multi-scale global contextual information via a pyramid downsampling module, while Twins only captures global information at a specific scale. Besides, Twins is originally designed for image processing and hence needs elaborate ways to generalize to spatiotemporal domains.

RegionViT differs from our model in how local tokens interact with global contexts. It generates coarse-grained regional tokens and fine-grained local tokens from an image with different patch sizes, where each regional token is associated with a set of local tokens based on their locations. All regional tokens are first passed through a standard MSA to exchange the information among regions, and then a local self-attention performs MSA where each takes one regional token and corresponding local tokens. In other words, the local token will only interact with the regional token that it belongs to, while each local token in DualFormer *directly* interacts with all multi-scale global contexts.

4 Experiments

We evaluate our approach on five popular video datasets. For action recognition, we use two versions of Kinetics [25], i.e., **Kinetics-400/Kinetics-600** which contain about 240K/370K training videos and 20k/28k validation videos, and has 400/600 action classes. For temporal modeling, since the Something-Something [14] dataset has expired, we test DualFormer on another fine-grained action benchmark, namely **Diving-48** [30] which consists of ∼18k videos with 48 diving classes. Finally, we examine transfer learning performance of our method on two smaller datasets, including **HMDB-51** [28] and **UCF-101** [45].

4.1 Implementation Details

Unless otherwise stated, our model receives a clip of 32 frames sampled from the original video using a temporal stride of 2 and spatial resolution of 224×224, yielding 16×56×56 tokens at the first stage. During inference, 4 temporal clips with a center crop (totally 4 space-time views) are exploited to compute accuracy.

Kinetics-400/600. For both Kinetics datasets, we use AdamW [26] optimizer with a batch size 64 and a cosine learning rate scheduler to train DualFormer for 30 epochs. Following Swin [35], we utilize different initial learning rates for the ImageNet-pretrained backbone (1e-4) and head (1e-3). We also use a linear warm-up for the first 2.5 epochs. To avoid overfitting, we set weight decay to 0.02, 0.02, 0.05 and stochastic depth drop rates [19] to 0.1, 0.2 and 0.3 for the tiny, small and base versions, respectively. Token labeling [23] is employed as augmentation to improve DualFormer-T/S. See more details in the Appendix.

Diving/HMDB/UCF. On these three datasets, we adopt AdamW [26] optimizer to train 16 epochs with one epoch of linear warm-up. The learning rate, batch size, weight decay and stochastic depth drop rate are the same as those for Kinetics. We use the pretrained weights on ImageNet-1K or Kinetics-400 for the model initialization for different settings.

4.2 Comparison to State-of-the-Art

Kinetics-400. We present the top-1 and top-5 accuracy of CNNs (upper part) and transformer-based methods (lower part) in Table 2. Compared to the best CNN-based method X3D-XXL [57], DualFormer-S achieves slightly higher accuracy while using **9.2**× fewer FLOPs. Compared to transformers (MViT-B,32×3

Table 2. Comparisons with state-of-the-art methods for action recognition on Kinetics-400/600. All models are trained and evaluated on 224×224 spatial resolution. $n \times s$ input indicates we feed n frames to the network sampled every s frames. FLOPs indicates the total floating point operations per second during inference. The magnitudes are Giga (10^9) and Mega (10^6) for FLOPs and Param, respectively. IN: ImageNet.

Method	Pretrain	Input	Views	Overall FLOPs	Param	Kinetics-400		Kinetics-600	
						Top-1	Top-5	Top-1	Top-5
R(2+1)D [50]	–	32 × 2	10 × 1	750	61.8	72.0	90.0	–	–
I3D [5]	IN-1K	32 × 2	–	108	25.0	72.1	90.3	–	–
SlowFast+NL [13]	–	–	10 × 3	7020	59.9	79.8	93.9	81.8	95.1
X3D-XL [12]	–	16 × 5	10 × 3	1452	11.0	79.1	93.9	81.9	95.5
X3D-XXL [12]	–	16 × 5	10 × 3	5823	20.3	80.4	94.6	–	–
ip-CSN-152 [49]	IG-65M	8	10 × 3	3270	32.8	82.5	95.3	–	–
ViT-B-VTN [38]	IN-21K	250 × 1	1 × 1	4218	11.0	78.6	93.7	–	–
TimeSformer-L [3]	IN-21K	96 × 4	1 × 3	7140	121.4	80.7	94.7	82.2	95.5
MViT-B, 32×3 [11]	–	32 × 3	1 × 5	850	36.6	80.2	94.4	83.8	96.3
MViT-B, 64×3 [11]	–	64 × 3	3 × 3	4095	36.6	81.2	95.1	–	–
VidTr-L [61]	IN-21K	32 × 2	10 × 3	10530	–	78.6	93.5	–	–
X-ViT (16×) [4]	IN-21K	16 × 4	1 × 3	850	–	80.2	94.7	84.5	96.3
ViViT-L/16×2 [1]	IN-21K	32 × 2	4 × 3	17352	310.8	80.6	94.7	82.5	95.6
ViViT-L/16×2 [1]	JFT-300M	32 × 2	4 × 3	17352	310.8	82.8	95.5	84.3	96.2
Swin-T [35]	IN-1K	32 × 2	4 × 3	1056	28.2	78.8	93.6	–	–
Swin-S [35]	IN-1K	32 × 2	4 × 3	1992	49.8	80.6	94.5	–	–
Swin-B [35]	IN-1K	32 × 2	4 × 3	3384	88.1	80.6	94.6	–	–
Swin-B [35]	IN-21K	32 × 2	4 × 3	3384	88.1	82.7	**95.5**	84.0	96.5
DualFormer-T (ours)	IN-1K	32 × 2	4 × 1	240	21.8	79.5	94.1	–	–
DualFormer-S (ours)	IN-1K	32 × 2	4 × 1	636	48.9	80.6	94.9	–	–
DualFormer-B (ours)	IN-1K	32 × 2	4 × 1	1072	86.8	81.1	95.0	–	–
DualFormer-B (ours)	IN-21K	32 × 2	4 × 1	1072	86.8	**82.9**	**95.5**	**85.2**	**96.6**

Table 3. Results on HMDB-51, UCF-101 and Diving-48 (DIVE). Baseline results are from protect [3,61]. We pretrain our models on Kinetics-400 and finetune them on these datasets, only except for DualFormer-T* which is pretrained on ImageNet-1K.

Method	Input	Views	FLOPs	DIVE	HMDB	UCF
I3D [5]	64×1	–	–	–	74.3	95.1
TSM [32]	8	–	–	–	70.7	94.5
TeiNet [36]	16	–	–	–	73.3	96.7
SlowFast [13]	16×8	–	–	77.6	–	–
VidTr-M [61]	16×4	10×3	5370	–	74.4	96.6
VidTr-L [61]	32×4	10×3	10530	–	74.4	96.7
TimeSformer [3]	8×4	1×3	590	75.0	–	–
TimeSformer-L [3]	96×4	1×3	7140	81.0	–	–
DualFormer-T*	16×4	4×1	28	75.4	74.6	96.3
DualFormer-T	16×4	4×1	28	75.9	75.0	96.6
DualFormer-S	32×4	4×1	636	81.2	76.2	97.4
DualFormer-S	32×4	4×3	1908	**81.8**	**76.4**	**97.5**

[11] and X-ViT [4]), DualFormer-S with similar computations brings ~0.4% gain on the top-1 accuracy. In contrast to Swin-T [35], DualFormer-T outperforms it by 0.7% on top-1 and 0.5% on top-5 score with **4.4**× fewer computational costs. We also witness 1.8% improvement on the top-1 accuracy when using ImageNet-21K to pretrain DualFormer-B compared to ImageNet-1K. With ImageNet-21K pretraining, DualFormer-B achieves the state-of-the-art results on both metrics while being dramatically faster than two recent transformer backbones: **16.2**× faster than ViViT-L [1] and **3.2**× faster than Swin-B [35]. See more details on accuracy vs. speed in Fig. 1.

Kinetics-600. As shown in Table 2, the results on Kinetics-600 are similar to those on Kinetics-400. DualFormer-B achieves the highest accuracy among these models. In particular, DualFormer-B brings **1.2%** gains on top-1 score and runs 3.2× faster than Swin-B. Compared to ViViT-L which is pretrained on a large-scale and private dataset JFM-300M, although our DualFormer-B is pretrained on a much smaller dataset (ImageNet-21K), it yields **0.9%** higher top-1 accuracy and requires **16.2**× fewer FLOPs.

Diving-48. Here we test our model on a temporally-heavy dataset. Due to a recently reported label issue of Diving-48, we only compare our model with SlowFast [13] and TimeSformer [3]. From Table 3, we observe that our DualFormer obtains a maximum **81.8%** top-1 score on Diving-48, significantly surpassing SlowFast. For TimeSformer-L which has **3.7**× FLOPs and receives 96 frames as input, our method still yields **0.8%** higher accuracy while using only 32 frames as input. These results verify the strong power of our model in temporal modeling.

Table 4. Experimental results of different combinations of LW-MSA (L) and GP-MSA (G) with DualFormer-T on Kinetics-400. G_1 and G_2 denote GP-MSA with only one pyramid scale (4,4,4) and (8,7,7), respectively. The gray row indicates our default setting.

Variants	FLOPs	Param	Top-1	Top-5
(LL, LL, LL, LL)	244	21.7	78.4	93.3
(GG, GG, GG, GG)	228	21.8	77.6	93.2
(LL, LL, LG, LG)	236	21.7	78.8	93.5
(LG, LG, LL, LL)	244	21.8	79.3	94.0
(LG_1, LG_1, LG_1, LG_1)	224	21.8	78.4	93.4
(LG_2, LG_2, LG_2, LG_2)	232	21.8	79.3	93.9
(LG, LG, LG, LG)	240	21.8	79.5	94.1

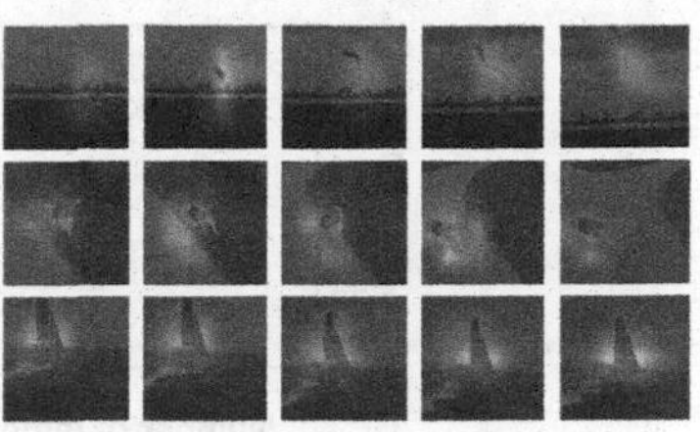

Fig. 5. Visualization of attention maps at the last layer generated by Grad-CAM protect [43] on Kinetics-400. Our model successfully learns to focus on the relevant parts in the video clip. Upper: flying kites. Middle: walking dogs. Below: sailing.

HMDB-51 and UCF-101. Lastly, we examine the transfer learning ability of our DualFormer over the split 1 of HMDB-51 and UCF-101. Table 3 reports the top-1 accuracy. With ImageNet-1K pretrained weights as initialization, our tiny version achieves comparable performance to VidTr-M [61] while using **192**$\times$ fewer FLOPs (see DualFormer-T* in Table 3). When pretrained on Kinetics-400, DualFormer-S with 12 testing views can outperform VidTr-L by a large accuracy margin **2%**/0.8% on HMDB and UCF while using only **18%** FLOPs of VidTr-L. This reveals the generalization potential of our model on small datasets.

4.3 Ablation Study

Effect of LW-MSA and GP-MSA. To study the effect of the dual-level MSA, we test different combinations of LW/GP-MSA to implement DualFormer-T. (LG, LG, LG, LG) denotes our default configuration, namely the one in Fig. 4, where each block sequentially performs LW-MSA and GP-MSA. For the four variants at the upper part of Table 4, LL and GG mean that the blocks at that stage only contain two LW-MSAs and two GP-MSAs, respectively. For example (LL, LL, LG, LG) means using blocks with two LW-MSAs at the first two stages and using a combination of LW-MSA and GP-MSA at the last two stages.

For a fair comparison, we slightly tune the hyperparameter to ensure their FLOPs and parameters to be similar. We report the accuracy of these variants on Kinetics-400 in the upper part of Table 4. Among these variants (GG, GG, GG, GG) performs the worst since the local context information is very important to a patch. The model with only LW-MSA degrades by 1.1% top-1 score (79.5%$\rightarrow$78.4%) due to a limited receptive field at every stage. By integrating GP-MSA to increase the receptive field, both (LL, LL, LG, LG) and (LG, LG, LL, LL) achieve better performance than the variants with only local or global modules. In particular, adding GP-MSA to the early stages benefits more

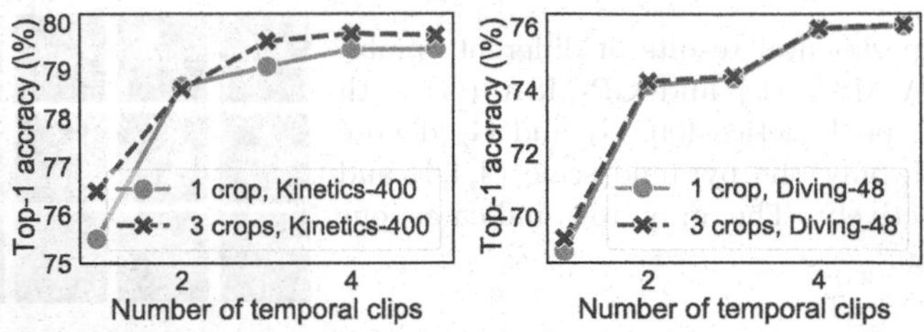

Fig. 6. Effect of space-time views on Kinetics-400 (left) and on Diving-48 (right).

than late stages, revealing the importance of GP-MSA to complement the early stages. Moreover, we evaluate the two pyramid scales in GP-MSA and report their results in the lower part of Table 4. Compared to our default setting, we can find a clear accuracy drop by removing either the (4, 4, 4) or (8, 7, 7) scale. In addition, some examples of attention visualization are shown in Fig. 5.

Effect of Testing Views. Previous methods employ multiple space-time views to boost performance during inference, e.g., 10×3 views in VidTr-L and 4×3 views in Swin. We investigate how the number of testing views affects the accuracy of DualFormer-T on Kinetics-400 and Diving-48. From Fig. 6, one can find that increasing the number of temporal clips can bring significant improvement on both datasets, while using more spatial crops does not always help. For example, using three spatial crops slightly outperforms the 1-crop counterpart on Diving-48. As the inference FLOPs is proportional to the space-time views, to trade off the computational cost and accuracy, our method uses a testing strategy of four temporal clips with a spatial crop (totally four) during the inference phase.

Effect of Window Size in LW-MSA. Window size is a crucial hyperparameter in LW-MSA. Hence, we test different window sizes to investigate their effect on model performance. As shown in Table 5, a larger window size in both temporal and spatial dimensions brings consistent gains in accuracy due to the increase of local receptive field, but also induces heavier computation. For an accuracy-speed balance, we choose (8, 7, 7) as our default setting. From this table, we also observe that reducing the number of input frames (e.g., 32→16) can dramatically improve efficiency but inevitably degrades the top-1 accuracy by ~1%.

Table 5. Effect of window size of LW-MSA with DualFormer-T on Kinetic-400. The gray row indicates the default configuration.

Input	Window Size	FLOPs	Top-1	Top-5
16×4	4×7×7	104	78.0	93.2
16×4	8×7×7	112	78.4	93.3
32×2	4×7×7	224	79.1	93.9
32×2	8×7×7	240	79.5	94.1
32×2	16×7×7	272	**79.7**	94.4
32×2	8×14×14	324	**79.7**	**94.5**

Table 6. Results of pyramid downsampling functions based on DualFormer-T on Kinetics-400.

Method	FLOPs	Param	Top-1
AvgPool	59	21.8	78.7
Conv	61	27.6	**79.5**
DWConv	60	21.8	**79.5**

Effect of Pyramid Downsampling Function. There are several alternative functions to generate global priors in GP-MSA, such as average pooling (AvgPool) and standard convolution (Conv). Here, we replace the depth-wise convolution (DWConv) with them on Kinetics-400 to investigate their effect. As reported in Table 6, our DWConv achieves comparable performance to Conv while using much fewer parameters. Our implementation also outperforms AvgPool by 0.8% on the top-1 score with similar computation costs.

Table 7. Effect of PEGs to DualFormer-T on the Kinetics-400 dataset.

Method	Top-1
w.o PEG	78.9
Absolute [3]	79.2
Relative [35]	79.3
DWConv	**79.5**

Table 8. Effect of temporal pooling in DualFormer-T on Kinetic-400. (i, j, k) means reducing the temporal resolution i, j, k times at the last 3 stages, respectively.

Rate	Patch Size	FLOPs	Param	Top-1	Top-5
1, 1, 1	(4, 4, 4)	112	21.8	78.5	93.3
2, 1, 1	(2, 4, 4)	136	21.8	78.7	93.5
1, 2, 1	(2, 4, 4)	152	21.9	78.8	93.5
1, 1, 2	(2, 4, 4)	216	22.3	79.2	93.9
1, 1, 1	(2, 4, 4)	240	21.8	**79.5**	**94.1**

Do We Need PEG? As depicted in Table 7, DualFormer without PEG suffers from a clear drop on the top-1 accuracy (79.5%→78.9%), which indicates the necessity of integrating position information in MSA. We further compare our DWConv-based PEG with an absolute position encoding (i.e., TimeSformer) and a relative bias-based method in Swin. As a result, our solution achieves 0.3% and 0.2% higher top-1 score than the absolute and relative method, respectively.

Effect of Temporal Pooling Rate. Our method follows [11,35] to utilize a multi-scale hierarchy. Such hierarchy is achieved by the patch merging layer at the beginning of the last three stages, where we downsample the spatial size of feature map by 2× and keep the original temporal resolution. Here, we discuss the effect of temporal pooling at the last three stages. According to the results in Table 8, even though such temporal pooling can further reduce the computational cost, it also leads to a decrease in the overall accuracy.

5 Conclusion

In this paper, we develop a transformer-based architecture with local-global attention stratification for efficient video recognition. Empirical study demonstrates that the proposed method achieves a better accuracy-speed trade-off on five popular video recognition datasets. In the future, we plan to remove the strong dependency on pretrained models and design a useful strategy to train our model from scratch. Another direction is to explore the use of our model in other applications, such as video segmentation and prediction.

Acknowledgement. We thank Quanhong Fu at Sea AI Lab for the help to improve the paper writing. This research is supported by Singapore Ministry of Education Academic Research Fund Tier 1 under MOE's official grant number T1 251RES2029.

References

1. Arnab, A., Dehghani, M., Heigold, G., Sun, C., Lučić, M., Schmid, C.: Vivit: A video vision transformer. arXiv preprint arXiv:2103.15691 (2021)
2. Ba, J.L., Kiros, J.R., Hinton, G.E.: Layer normalization. arXiv preprint arXiv:1607.06450 (2016)
3. Bertasius, G., Wang, H., Torresani, L.: Is space-time attention all you need for video understanding? arXiv preprint arXiv:2102.05095 (2021)
4. Bulat, A., Perez-Rua, J.M., Sudhakaran, S., Martinez, B., Tzimiropoulos, G.: Space-time mixing attention for video transformer. arXiv preprint arXiv:2106.05968 (2021)
5. Carreira, J., Zisserman, A.: Quo vadis, action recognition? a new model and the kinetics dataset. In: Proceedings of the IEEE Conference on Computer Vision and Pattern Recognition, pp. 6299–6308 (2017)
6. Chen, C.F., Panda, R., Fan, Q.: Regionvit: Regional-to-local attention for vision transformers. arXiv preprint arXiv:2106.02689 (2021)
7. Chollet, F.: Xception: Deep learning with depthwise separable convolutions. In: Proceedings of the IEEE Conference on Computer Vision and Pattern Recognition, pp. 1251–1258 (2017)
8. Chu, X., et al.: Twins: Revisiting the design of spatial attention in vision transformers. In: NeurIPS 2021 (2021)
9. Chu, X., et al.: Conditional positional encodings for vision transformers. arXiv preprint arXiv:2102.10882 (2021)
10. Dosovitskiy, A., et al.: An image is worth 16x16 words: Transformers for image recognition at scale. In: International Conference on Learning Representations (2020)
11. Fan, H., et al.: Multiscale vision transformers. arXiv preprint arXiv:2104.11227 (2021)

12. Feichtenhofer, C.: X3d: Expanding architectures for efficient video recognition. In: Proceedings of the IEEE/CVF Conference on Computer Vision and Pattern Recognition, pp. 203–213 (2020)
13. Feichtenhofer, C., Fan, H., Malik, J., He, K.: Slowfast networks for video recognition. In: Proceedings of the IEEE/CVF International Conference on Computer Vision, pp. 6202–6211 (2019)
14. Goyal, R., et al.: The" something something" video database for learning and evaluating visual common sense. In: Proceedings of the IEEE International Conference on Computer Vision, pp. 5842–5850 (2017)
15. Hara, K., Kataoka, H., Satoh, Y.: Learning spatio-temporal features with 3d residual networks for action recognition. In: Proceedings of the IEEE International Conference on Computer Vision Workshops, pp. 3154–3160 (2017)
16. Hara, K., Kataoka, H., Satoh, Y.: Can spatiotemporal 3d cnns retrace the history of 2d cnns and imagenet? In: Proceedings of the IEEE Conference on Computer Vision and Pattern Recognition, pp. 6546–6555 (2018)
17. He, K., Zhang, X., Ren, S., Sun, J.: Deep residual learning for image recognition. In: Proceedings of the IEEE Conference on Computer Vision and Pattern Recognition, pp. 770–778 (2016)
18. Hongeng, S., Nevatia, R., Bremond, F.: Video-based event recognition: activity representation and probabilistic recognition methods. Comput. Vis. Image Underst. **96**(2), 129–162 (2004)
19. Huang, G., Sun, Yu., Liu, Z., Sedra, D., Weinberger, K.Q.: Deep networks with stochastic depth. In: Leibe, B., Matas, J., Sebe, N., Welling, M. (eds.) ECCV 2016. LNCS, vol. 9908, pp. 646–661. Springer, Cham (2016). https://doi.org/10.1007/978-3-319-46493-0_39
20. Islam, M.A., Jia, S., Bruce, N.D.: How much position information do convolutional neural networks encode? arXiv preprint arXiv:2001.08248 (2020)
21. Ji, S., Xu, W., Yang, M., Yu, K.: 3d convolutional neural networks for human action recognition. IEEE Trans. Pattern Anal. Mach. Intell. **35**(1), 221–231 (2012)
22. Jiang, B., Wang, M., Gan, W., Wu, W., Yan, J.: Stm: Spatiotemporal and motion encoding for action recognition. In: Proceedings of the IEEE/CVF International Conference on Computer Vision, pp. 2000–2009 (2019)
23. Jiang, Z., et al.: Token labeling: Training a 85.5% top-1 accuracy vision transformer with 56m parameters on imagenet. arXiv preprint arXiv:2104.10858 (2021)
24. Karpathy, A., Toderici, G., Shetty, S., Leung, T., Sukthankar, R., Fei-Fei, L.: Large-scale video classification with convolutional neural networks. In: Proceedings of the IEEE conference on Computer Vision and Pattern Recognition, pp. 1725–1732 (2014)
25. Kay, W., et al.: The kinetics human action video dataset. arXiv preprint arXiv:1705.06950 (2017)
26. Kingma, D.P., Ba, J.: Adam: A method for stochastic optimization. arXiv preprint arXiv:1412.6980 (2014)
27. Krizhevsky, A., Sutskever, I., Hinton, G.E.: Imagenet classification with deep convolutional neural networks. Adv. Neural. Inf. Process. Syst. **25**, 1097–1105 (2012)
28. Kuehne, H., Jhuang, H., Garrote, E., Poggio, T., Serre, T.: Hmdb: a large video database for human motion recognition. In: 2011 International Conference on Computer Vision, pp. 2556–2563. IEEE (2011)
29. Li, K., et al.: Uniformer: Unified transformer for efficient spatial-temporal representation learning. In: International Conference on Learning Representations (2021)

30. Li, Y., Li, Y., Vasconcelos, N.: Resound: Towards action recognition without representation bias. In: Ferrari, V., Hebert, M., Sminchisescu, C., Weiss, Y. (eds.) ECCV 2018. LNCS, vol. 11210, pp. 520–535. Springer, Cham (2018). https://doi.org/10.1007/978-3-030-01231-1_32
31. Li, Z., Liu, F., Yang, W., Peng, S., Zhou, J.: A survey of convolutional neural networks: analysis, applications, and prospects. IEEE Trans. Neural Netw. Learn. Syst. (2021)
32. Lin, J., Gan, C., Han, S.: Tsm: Temporal shift module for efficient video understanding. In: Proceedings of the IEEE/CVF International Conference on Computer Vision, pp. 7083–7093 (2019)
33. Lin, M., Chen, Q., Yan, S.: Network in network. In: Bengio, Y., LeCun, Y. (eds.) 2nd International Conference on Learning Representations, ICLR 2014, Banff, AB, Canada, 14–16 April 2014. Conference Track Proceedings (2014)
34. Liu, Z., et al.: Swin transformer: Hierarchical vision transformer using shifted windows. In: International Conference on Computer Vision (ICCV) (2021)
35. Liu, Z., et al.: Video swin transformer. arXiv preprint arXiv:2106.13230 (2021)
36. Liu, Z., et al.: Teinet: Towards an efficient architecture for video recognition. In: Proceedings of the AAAI Conference on Artificial Intelligence, vol. 34, pp. 11669–11676 (2020)
37. Liu, Z., Wang, L., Wu, W., Qian, C., Lu, T.: Tam: Temporal adaptive module for video recognition. In: Proceedings of the IEEE/CVF International Conference on Computer Vision, pp. 13708–13718 (2021)
38. Neimark, D., Bar, O., Zohar, M., Asselmann, D.: Video transformer network. arXiv preprint arXiv:2102.00719 (2021)
39. Patrick, M., et al.: Keeping your eye on the ball: Trajectory attention in video transformers. arXiv preprint arXiv:2106.05392 (2021)
40. Qian, R., et al.: Spatiotemporal contrastive video representation learning. In: Proceedings of the IEEE/CVF Conference on Computer Vision and Pattern Recognition, pp. 6964–6974 (2021)
41. Qiu, Z., Yao, T., Mei, T.: Learning spatio-temporal representation with pseudo-3d residual networks. In: Proceedings of the IEEE International Conference on Computer Vision, pp. 5533–5541 (2017)
42. Ranftl, R., Bochkovskiy, A., Koltun, V.: Vision transformers for dense prediction. In: Proceedings of the IEEE/CVF International Conference on Computer Vision, pp. 12179–12188 (2021)
43. Selvaraju, R.R., Cogswell, M., Das, A., Vedantam, R., Parikh, D., Batra, D.: Grad-cam: Visual explanations from deep networks via gradient-based localization. In: Proceedings of the IEEE International Conference on Computer Vision, pp. 618–626 (2017)
44. Simonyan, K., Zisserman, A.: Very deep convolutional networks for large-scale image recognition. arXiv preprint arXiv:1409.1556 (2014)
45. Soomro, K., Zamir, A.R., Shah, M.: Ucf101: A dataset of 101 human actions classes from videos in the wild. arXiv preprint arXiv:1212.0402 (2012)
46. Tobler, W.R.: A computer movie simulating urban growth in the detroit region. Econ. Geogr. **46**(sup1), 234–240 (1970)
47. Touvron, H., Cord, M., Douze, M., Massa, F., Sablayrolles, A., Jégou, H.: Training data-efficient image transformers & distillation through attention. In: International Conference on Machine Learning, pp. 10347–10357. PMLR (2021)
48. Tran, D., Bourdev, L., Fergus, R., Torresani, L., Paluri, M.: Learning spatiotemporal features with 3d convolutional networks. In: Proceedings of the IEEE International Conference on Computer Vision, pp. 4489–4497 (2015)

49. Tran, D., Wang, H., Torresani, L., Feiszli, M.: Video classification with channel-separated convolutional networks. In: Proceedings of the IEEE/CVF International Conference on Computer Vision, pp. 5552–5561 (2019)
50. Tran, D., Wang, H., Torresani, L., Ray, J., LeCun, Y., Paluri, M.: A closer look at spatiotemporal convolutions for action recognition. In: Proceedings of the IEEE Conference on Computer Vision and Pattern Recognition, pp. 6450–6459 (2018)
51. Vaswani, A., et al.: Attention is all you need. In: Advances in Neural Information Processing Systems, pp. 5998–6008 (2017)
52. Wang, H., Zhu, Y., Adam, H., Yuille, A., Chen, L.C.: Max-deeplab: End-to-end panoptic segmentation with mask transformers. In: Proceedings of the IEEE/CVF Conference on Computer Vision and Pattern Recognition, pp. 5463–5474 (2021)
53. Wang, L., et al.: Temporal segment networks for action recognition in videos. IEEE Trans. Pattern Anal. Mach. Intell. **41**(11), 2740–2755 (2018)
54. Wang, W., et al.: Pyramid vision transformer: A versatile backbone for dense prediction without convolutions. arXiv preprint arXiv:2102.12122 (2021)
55. Wang, Y., et al.: End-to-end video instance segmentation with transformers. In: Proceedings of the IEEE/CVF Conference on Computer Vision and Pattern Recognition, pp. 8741–8750 (2021)
56. Wei, C., Fan, H., Xie, S., Wu, C.Y., Yuille, A., Feichtenhofer, C.: Masked feature prediction for self-supervised visual pre-training. arXiv preprint arXiv:2112.09133 (2021)
57. Xie, S., Sun, C., Huang, J., Tu, Z., Murphy, K.: Rethinking spatiotemporal feature learning: speed-accuracy Trade-offs in Video Classification. In: Ferrari, V., Hebert, M., Sminchisescu, C., Weiss, Y. (eds.) ECCV 2018. LNCS, vol. 11219, pp. 318–335. Springer, Cham (2018). https://doi.org/10.1007/978-3-030-01267-0_19
58. Xu, H., Das, A., Saenko, K.: R-c3d: Region convolutional 3d network for temporal activity detection. In: Proceedings of the IEEE International Conference on Computer Vision, pp. 5783–5792 (2017)
59. Yang, J., et al.: Focal self-attention for local-global interactions in vision transformers. arXiv preprint arXiv:2107.00641 (2021)
60. Zha, X., Zhu, W., Lv, T., Yang, S., Liu, J.: Shifted chunk transformer for spatio-temporal representational learning. arXiv preprint arXiv:2108.11575 (2021)
61. Zhang, Y., et al.: Vidtr: Video transformer without convolutions. In: Proceedings of the IEEE/CVF International Conference on Computer Vision, pp. 13577–13587 (2021)
62. Zhu, X., Su, W., Lu, L., Li, B., Wang, X., Dai, J.: Deformable detr: Deformable transformers for end-to-end object detection. arXiv preprint arXiv:2010.04159 (2020)

Hierarchical Feature Alignment Network for Unsupervised Video Object Segmentation

Gensheng Pei[1], Fumin Shen[2(✉)], Yazhou Yao[1], Guo-Sen Xie[1(✉)], Zhenmin Tang[1], and Jinhui Tang[1]

[1] Nanjing University of Science and Technology, Nanjing, China
yazhou.yao@njust.edu.cn, gsxiehm@gmail.com

[2] University of Electronic Science and Technology of China, Chengdu, China
fumin.shen@gmail.com

https://github.com/NUST-Machine-Intelligence-Laboratory/HFAN

Abstract. Optical flow is an easily conceived and precious cue for advancing unsupervised video object segmentation (UVOS). Most of the previous methods directly extract and fuse the motion and appearance features for segmenting target objects in the UVOS setting. However, optical flow is intrinsically an instantaneous velocity of all pixels among consecutive frames, thus making the motion features not aligned well with the primary objects among the corresponding frames. To solve the above challenge, we propose a concise, practical, and efficient architecture for appearance and motion feature alignment, dubbed hierarchical feature alignment network (HFAN). Specifically, the key merits in HFAN are the sequential **F**eature **A**lign**M**ent (FAM) module and the **F**eature **A**dapta**T**ion (FAT) module, which are leveraged for processing the appearance and motion features hierarchically. FAM is capable of aligning both appearance and motion features with the primary object semantic representations, respectively. Further, FAT is explicitly designed for the adaptive fusion of appearance and motion features to achieve a desirable trade-off between cross-modal features. Extensive experiments demonstrate the effectiveness of the proposed HFAN, which reaches a new state-of-the-art performance on DAVIS-16, achieving 88.7 $\mathcal{J}\&\mathcal{F}$ Mean, *i.e.*, a relative improvement of 3.5% over the best published result.

Keywords: Video object segmentation · Feature alignment

1 Introduction

Video object segmentation (VOS) aims to segment objects for each frame in a video sequence. Compared to semi-supervised VOS (SVOS), in which annotations are provided for the first frame at test time, unsupervised VOS (UVOS) is particularly challenging as it involves no prior knowledge and human interposing. This work focuses on the UVOS task, which has motivated numerous downstream segmentation topics [3,5,26,71,78].

S. Avidan et al. (Eds.): ECCV 2022, LNCS 13694, pp. 596–613, 2022.
https://doi.org/10.1007/978-3-031-19830-4_34

UVOS approaches can be grouped into three main subcategories: motion-based, appearance-based, and motion-appearance-based, depending on the utilizations of different feature types. By merely using motion information [45,59], the UVOS is transformed into a moving object segmentation (MOS) task. The main drawback of MOS is the risk of losing targets when the object is moving slowly or is stationary. Further, appearance-based methods [34,38,63,77] usually describe the target in detail using mature image segmentation techniques. However, the lack of prior knowledge on the primary objects in the unsupervised solution, almost always, can lead to mis-segmentation cases. By contrast, motion-appearance schemes [1,50,69,75,79] can mitigate the deficiencies of the above two types of methods. Appearance features compensate for the shortage of motion descriptions on semantic representations, and motion cues enable the high-quality candidate regions to be selected for appearance features.

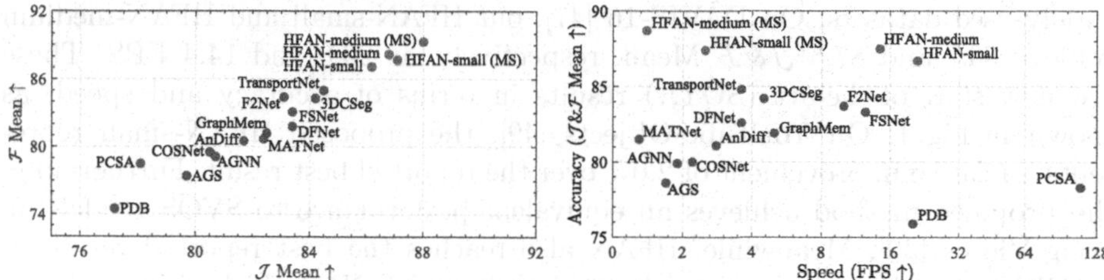

Fig. 1. Performance $\mathcal{J}$&$\mathcal{F}$ Mean versus inference speed FPS (frames per second) on DAVIS-16 [47]. Existing and proposed methods are marked with • and •, respectively.

As the leading motion-appearance scenario, optical flow guided UVOS methods have significantly advanced the performances of segmentation. Abandoning appearance modeling by converting VOS into a foreground motion prediction based purely on optical flow information does not handle static foreground objects well. However, two intrinsic drawbacks exist in these approaches. **First**, optical flow describes the velocity vector of per-pixel motion in a video, capturing the motion information between consecutive frames. As such, the positions of the primary objects in a frame and/or its corresponding optical flow are usually not well preserved. Most of the existing methods solely fuse the features of a frame and its corresponding optical flow without considering the respective alignments between the primary objects and the appearance/motion features. This inevitably leads to the loss of boundary information of the primary objects. **Second**, when facing occlusions, motion blur, fast-moving objects, and even stationary objects in UVOS, the inferior optical flow estimation directly affects the segmentation results of the final models. Especially, if optical flow estimation fails, the motion features of the primary objects in the video are invalidated accordingly. In this case, the unselective fusion of appearance and motion features is probably harmful to segmentation accuracy.

To tackle the above challenges, inspired by the current trend of optical flow guided UVOS [1,22,50,59,69,75,79], we propose a hierarchical feature alignment network (HFAN). It aligns the object positions with the motion/appearance features and adapts the aligned features for mitigating the cross-modal mismatch. Specifically, we construct a **F**eature **A**lign**M**ent (FAM) module to implement object-level alignment with appearance/motion features in the multi-level feature encoding stage. Considering that the spatial locations of appearance and ground-truth target regions are seamlessly matched, we generate the coarse segmentation probability mask by appearance features. Next, FAM leverages the same object regions (*i.e.*, coarse masks) to represent object-level alignment features for appearance and motion. Moreover, we build the **F**eature **A**dapta**T**ion (FAT) module to combine appearance and motion features after the alignment step. FAT aims to ensure the robustness of fused features by constructing an adaptive weight between appearance and motion features. Notably, the adaptive fusion of appearance and motion features could effectively relieve the harms of optical flow estimation failure and motion blur on segmentation results.

We assess the effectiveness and reliability of the proposed model on three widely-used datasets. On DAVIS-16 [47], our HFAN-small and HFAN-medium achieve 86.7 and 87.5 $\mathcal{J}\&\mathcal{F}$ Mean, respectively, at 20.8 and 14.4 FPS. These are new state-of-the-art (SOTA) results in terms of accuracy and speed, as shown in Fig. 1. On YouTube-Objects [49], the proposed HFAN-small represents a relative improvement of 2.0% over the reported best result. Furthermore, the proposed method achieves an equivalent performance to SVOS models on Long-Videos [32]. Meanwhile, HFAN also reaches the best reported result on DAVIS-16 for the video salient object detection (VSOD), which aims to detect salient regions in videos. In summary, HFAN provides an efficient solution and a new perspective on optical flow guided UVOS.

2 Related Work

2.1 Video Object Segmentation

Current video object segmentation is broadly classified as unsupervised VOS [58,63,65,70] and semi-supervised VOS [8,39,44,52] tasks. The main difference is whether they provide accurate pixel-level annotations for the first frame of the segmented video at inference. As research on VOS has progressed, interactive VOS methods [5,15,43] that utilize user interaction (*e.g.*, scribbles or clicks) as input to iteratively optimize segmentation results have yielded good performance. Referring VOS setting [18,24,51] arises from considering a different type of interaction, language-guided video expressions, *i.e.*, target objects referred by a given language descriptions. However, the expensive nature of high-quality annotated video data motivates the need for an elegant and unrestricted VOS setting. This paper focuses on UVOS, which does not use any human intervention during testing. Depending on whether the current methods use deep features or not, we further divide UVOS into two subcategories: *traditional* and *deep*.

The computer vision community has extensively studied the task of automatic binary video segmentation over nearly three decades. Early *traditional* models were typically based on specific heuristics related to the foreground (*i.e.*, target proposals [48], motion boundaries [45], salient objects [64]). They required hand-crafted low-level features (*e.g.*, SIFT, edges). Later, several methods (*e.g.*, point trajectories [42], background subtraction [12] and over-segmentation [10]) were proposed to segment and track all targets with different motions and appearances in the video. More recently, with the renaissance of artificial neural networks, *deep* models (*e.g.*, CNN [70,77], RNN [1,55,65], GNN [36,63]) have enabled UVOS to evolve rapidly. A quintessential example of an attempt to apply deep learning techniques in this field is LSMO [59], which learns a multilayer perceptron to detect moving objects. The computational burden is reduced by many subsequent approaches based on fully convolutional networks, such as two-stream structures [21,28,54,58], CNN-based encoder-decoder architectures [6,78,79], and Siamese network [34,37]. As the field of optical flow estimation [19,56,57] has flourished, more and more optical flow based UVOS methods [22,50,69,75] have gained tremendous performance improvements. The major difference from the optical flow-based approaches described above is that we reconsider the mismatch between frames and optical flow. Our HFAN performs hierarchical feature alignment and adaptation of motion-appearance features to achieve accurate feature representation of the primary objects in a video.

2.2 Feature Alignment

Feature alignment is widely used in various fields, *e.g.*, object detection [4,13,33], image segmentation [16,17,31,74], and person re-identification [40,62,72,73]. For object detection, feature alignment mainly involves the misalignment between anchor boxes and convolutional features, in addition to multiple anchors for the same point in the feature map. Existing image segmentation models generally adopt the feature pyramid networks (FPN) [33] to obtain different resolution feature maps to improve performance. However, this increases the loss of boundary information during downsampling and unaligned feature maps with different resolutions for upsampling. An effective way [16,31] is to align the features from the coarsest resolution to the finest resolution to match positions between feature maps. Aligning and adapting motion and appearance features of multi-level representations from the same encoder is implemented by our HFAN. Thus, it is guaranteed that hierarchical feature maps between the two modalities align their respective features based on the same primary objects.

3 The Proposed Method

Our HFAN consists of two modules: *feature alignment* (FAM, Sect. 3.2) and *feature adaptation* (FAT, Sect. 3.3). FAM aligns the hierarchical features of appearance and motion feature maps with the primary objects. FAT fuses these two aligned feature maps at the pixel-level with a learnable adaptive weight.

3.1 Task Definitions

Given an input video $\mathcal{I}$ with N frames, we can select each frame $\mathbf{I} \in \mathbb{R}^{H\times W\times 3}$, and calculate the relative optical flow $\mathbf{O} \in \mathbb{R}^{H\times W\times 3}$ (visualized as an RGB

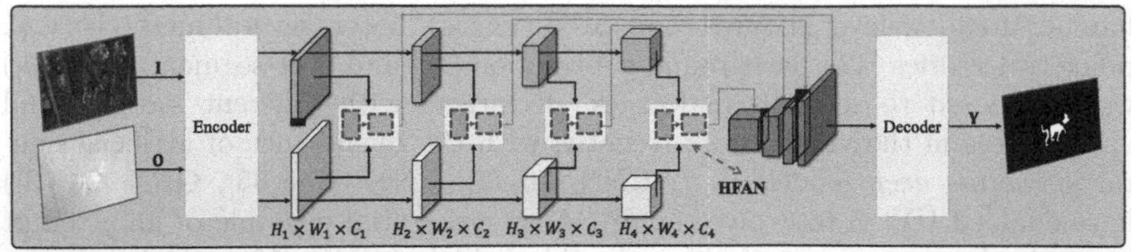

Fig. 2. The pipeline of HFAN. Frame **I** and optical flow **O** are used as inputs to extract hierarchical appearance and motion features, respectively, through an encoder with HFAN. And the excellent segmentation mask **Y** is obtained by the decoder.

image) by [57]. In the i-th stage of the multi-level feature representation ($i \in \{1, 2, 3, 4\}$), the appearance and motion features are denoted as $\mathbf{I}_i \in \mathbb{R}^{H_i \times W_i \times C_i}$ and $\mathbf{O}_i \in \mathbb{R}^{H_i \times W_i \times C_i}$, respectively. $H_i \times W_i$ indicates the feature resolution, where the value is set to $\frac{H}{2^{i+1}} \times \frac{W}{2^{i+1}}$. The proposed HFAN aims to generate object-level aligned, high-quality adapted features,

$$\mathbf{U}_i = \mathcal{F}_{\mathrm{HFAN}}(\mathbf{I}_i, \mathbf{O}_i) \in \mathbb{R}^{H_i \times W_i \times C_i}. \tag{1}$$

Here, $\mathcal{F}_{\mathrm{HFAN}}(\cdot, \cdot)$ contains two main modules, which are:

$$\hat{\mathbf{I}}_i, \hat{\mathbf{O}}_i = \mathcal{F}_{\mathrm{FAM}}(\mathbf{I}_i, \mathbf{O}_i), \mathbf{U}_i = \mathcal{F}_{\mathrm{FAT}}(\hat{\mathbf{I}}_i, \hat{\mathbf{O}}_i), \tag{2}$$

where $\mathcal{F}_{\mathrm{FAM}}$ conducts feature alignment for $\mathbf{I}_i$ and $\mathbf{O}_i$, and $\mathcal{F}_{\mathrm{FAT}}$ fuses aligned feature maps from $\mathcal{F}_{\mathrm{FAM}}$ by performing a multi-modal adaptive feature fusion. The overall architecture of the proposed method is shown in Fig. 2.

We adopt a lightweight MiT [66] backbone (ResNet [14] is also studied, see Sect. 4.2 for details.) and employ a decoder to yield the primary object binary mask $\mathbf{Y} \in \{0, 1\}^{H \times W}$ of the frame $\mathbf{I}$. Next, we illustrate in detail the two main modules of our proposed HFAN model, along with the training and inference phases.

3.2 Feature Alignment Module

Optical flow methods produce a dense motion vector field by generating a vector for each pixel, which is important auxiliary information for studying video analysis and representation. Former works [50, 69, 75, 79] using optical flow guidance have defaulted one video frame and its optical flow to aligned images. However, this hypothesis then holds approximately only if the motion between two consecutive frames is small. In addition, this solidification tends to result in poor accuracy along moving object boundaries. An intuitive concept is that although appearance features and motion features are unaligned, the bond between them is that they share the primary objects. Motivated by this, we design a feature alignment module specifically for the frame and optical flow to alleviate these issues. Firstly, FAM predicts the coarse segmentation probability of $\mathbf{I}_i$ to obtain

$$\mathbf{P}_i = \mathcal{F}_{\mathrm{CS}}(\mathbf{I}_i) \in \mathbb{R}^{H_i \times W_i \times N_{cls}}, \tag{3}$$

where $\mathcal{F}_{\text{CS}}(\cdot)$ represents the coarse segmentation probability mask implemented by a convolution block $\texttt{Conv}_{1\times1}(C_i, N_{cls}) \rightarrow \texttt{BN} \rightarrow \texttt{ReLU}$ on the appearance feature map $\mathbf{I}_i$, and N_{cls} denotes the number of categories. Here, BN indicates the batch normalization [20] and ReLU is the rectified linear unit [41]. This paper focuses on single foreground and background, so N_{cls} is set to 2.

The regions contained in the coarse probability mask $\mathbf{P}_i$ obtained by the original frame $\mathbf{I}_i$ are consistent with the primary object's areas to be segmented. Therefore, we design the feature alignment module, which only aligns the appearance and motion features separately for the mask regions. This way has the merit of reducing the computational cost while weakening the negative impact of the optical flow background noise on the segmentation. Subsequently, $\mathbf{P}_i$ obtained by Eq. (3) is a contextual representation of primary object regions co-built with the original appearance feature map. We design the category-specific semantic (CSS) module to represent the category semantic, formulated as

$$\begin{aligned} \mathbf{I}_i^{'} &= \texttt{permute}(\texttt{view}(\mathbf{I}_i)), \mathbf{P}_i^{'} = \texttt{softmax}(\texttt{view}(\mathbf{P}_i)), \\ \mathbf{M}_i &= \mathcal{F}_{\text{CSS}}(\mathbf{I}_i, \mathbf{P}_i) = \texttt{matmul}(\mathbf{I}_i^{'}, \mathbf{P}_i^{'}) \in \mathbb{R}^{C_i \times N_{cls} \times 1}, \end{aligned} \tag{4}$$

where view, permute and matmul indicate the reshaping, permuting tensor dimension and tensor product. softmax is also known as normalized exponential function. The prominent role of $\mathbf{M}_i$ is summarized in two points: **1)** the spatial compression of appearance features within a specific region $\mathbf{P}_i$; **2)** the construction of category-specific information shared by appearance and motion features. The interchange on feature and semantic levels performed by $\mathcal{F}_{\text{CSS}}$ makes it possible to seek common contexts for appearance-motion features.

Immediately afterward, the primary object context (POC) module is devised to perform object-level contextual alignment of appearance and motion features with the same $\mathbf{M}_i$. Inspired by self-attention [60], $\mathcal{F}_{\text{SA}}$ is achieved by

$$\begin{aligned} \mathcal{F}_{\text{SA}} &= \texttt{softmax}(\alpha \mathbf{Q}\mathbf{K}^{\text{T}})\mathbf{V}, \mathbf{Q} \in \{\mathbf{I}_i, \mathbf{O}_i\} \\ \mathbf{Q}, \mathbf{K}, \mathbf{V} &= \mathcal{F}_{\text{Query}}(\mathbf{Q}), \mathcal{F}_{\text{Key}}(\mathbf{M}_i), \mathcal{F}_{\text{Value}}(\mathbf{M}_i), \end{aligned} \tag{5}$$

where $\mathbf{Q}$, $\mathbf{K}$ and $\mathbf{V}$ denote the query, key and value obtained by three transformation operations of $\mathcal{F}_{\text{Query}}$, $\mathcal{F}_{\text{Key}}$ and $\mathcal{F}_{\text{Value}}$, respectively. They are formed by $\texttt{Conv}_{1\times1}(C_i, C_i/r) \rightarrow \texttt{BN} \rightarrow \texttt{ReLU}$. $\alpha = \frac{1}{\sqrt{C_i}}$ is a scaling factor. r is set to $C_i/16$ for channel reduction ratio and concat indicates the concatenation operation.

Our proposed POC module helps refine the target boundaries and alleviate the primary object shifts between the frame and optical flow. The POC module can be represented as follows:

$$\begin{aligned} \hat{\mathbf{I}}_i &= \mathcal{F}_{\text{POC}}(\mathbf{I}_i, \mathbf{M}_i) \in \mathbb{R}^{H_i \times W_i \times C_i}, \\ \hat{\mathbf{O}}_i &= \mathcal{F}_{\text{POC}}(\mathbf{O}_i, \mathbf{M}_i) \in \mathbb{R}^{H_i \times W_i \times C_i}, \end{aligned} \tag{6}$$

where $\hat{\mathbf{I}}_i$ and $\hat{\mathbf{O}}_i$ are appearance-aligned and motion-aligned feature maps, respectively.

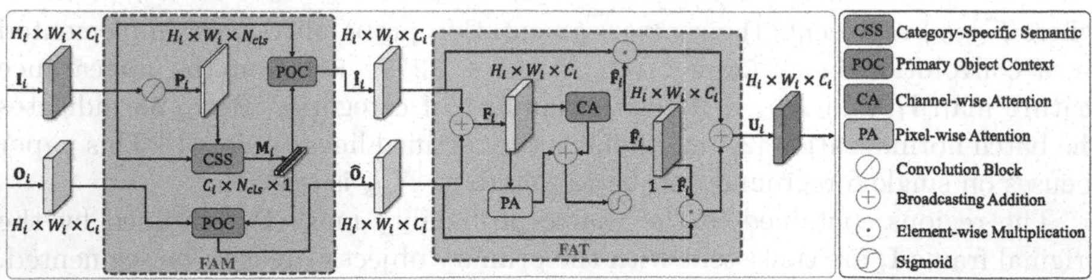

Fig. 3. Illustration of the proposed FAM and FAT modules. *Feature Alignment* and *Feature Adaptation* are applied on each hierarchical feature map to resolve the position and modal mismatches between optical flow and video frames. $\mathbf{U}_i$ denotes the alignment and adaptation features of stage $i \in \{1, 2, 3, 4\}$.

Compared to previous methods, FAM does not interact directly with appearance and motion features but employs CSS and POC modules to achieve contextual alignment of different modal features. As shown in Fig. 3-FAM, when $\mathbf{I}_i$ and $\mathbf{O}_i$ go through FAM, their respective features represent the shared primary object region $\mathbf{P}_i$, guided by $\mathbf{M}_i$. It ensures the feature independence of appearance $\hat{\mathbf{I}}_i$ and motion $\hat{\mathbf{O}}_i$ before the feature adaptation fusion phase.

3.3 Feature Adaptation Module

After the appearance and motion features are expressed based on the same object-contextual region, the aligned feature maps $\hat{\mathbf{I}}_i$ and $\hat{\mathbf{O}}_i$ have more boundary information and less background noise. However, when the optical flow estimation fails due to slow motion or stationary target objects, retaining all the optical flow features would cause a tremendous loss in segmentation performance. To this end, we require adaptive operations between cross-modal features for them. In this work, we propose the feature adaptation (FAT) module.

Specifically, we aggregate appearance-aligned and motion-aligned features and accordingly get the fused feature map $\mathbf{F}_i$, which embraces all the information of $\hat{\mathbf{I}}_i$ and $\hat{\mathbf{O}}_i$. The formula is directly expressed as $\mathbf{F}_i = \hat{\mathbf{I}}_i + \hat{\mathbf{O}}_i$. Here, $\mathbf{F}_i \in \mathbb{R}^{H_i \times W_i \times C_i}$ is treated as a semantic feature map after the superposition of appearance and motion contexts, equivalent to performing a skip connection operation [14,33] on different modal features of the same resolutions. Inspired by [30], channel-level and pixel-level semantic representations are obtained by

$$\begin{aligned} \mathbf{F}_i^{\mathrm{CA}} &= \mathcal{F}_{\mathrm{CA}}(\mathbf{F}_i) \in \mathbb{R}^{H_i \times W_i \times C_i}, \\ \mathbf{F}_i^{\mathrm{PA}} &= \mathcal{F}_{\mathrm{PA}}(\mathbf{F}_i) \in \mathbb{R}^{1 \times 1 \times C_i}, \end{aligned} \tag{7}$$

where $\mathcal{F}_{\mathrm{CA}}(\cdot)$ and $\mathcal{F}_{\mathrm{PA}}(\cdot)$ indicate channel-wise and pixel-wise attention operations are performed on $\mathbf{F}_i$.

Instead of using $\mathbf{F}_i$ directly as the fused appearance and motion features as in existing approaches [21,50,79], we propose to adapt these features. Specifically, we transform $\mathbf{F}_i$ into basis weight with feature adaptation to ensure stable feature representation capability even under low-quality motion information conditions (*e.g.*, occlusion and slow motion). The formula is expressed as

$$\begin{aligned}\hat{\mathbf{F}}_i &= \mathtt{sigmoid}(\mathbf{F}_i^{\mathrm{CA}} + \mathbf{F}_i^{\mathrm{PA}}) \in \mathbb{R}^{H_i \times W_i \times C_i},\\ \mathbf{U}_i &= \hat{\mathbf{I}}_i \odot \hat{\mathbf{F}}_i + \hat{\mathbf{O}}_i \odot (1 - \hat{\mathbf{F}}_i) \in \mathbb{R}^{H_i \times W_i \times C_i},\end{aligned} \tag{8}$$

where $\odot$ denotes the element-wise multiplication. At this point, details of FAT are introduced, and the workflow is illustrated in Fig. 3-FAT. Further observation of Eq. (8) shows that when $(1 - \hat{\mathbf{F}}_i)$ approaches 0, all information of $\mathbf{U}_i$ is provided by appearance features, while when $\hat{\mathbf{F}}_i$ reaches 0, all information of $\mathbf{U}_i$ is supplied by motion features. Meanwhile, $\hat{\mathbf{F}}_i$ is learnable, so it realizes the feature self-adaptation of the frame and optical flow.

3.4 Training and Inference

The multi-level features $\mathbf{U}_i$ $(i \in \{1, 2, 3, 4\})$ obtained through HFAN are fed to the decoder $\mathcal{F}_{\mathrm{DEC}}$, and the predicted segmentation mask $\mathbf{Q}$ is acquired

$$\mathbf{Q} = \mathcal{F}_{\mathrm{DEC}}(\mathbf{U}_{i|i=1,2,3,4}) \in \mathbb{R}^{H \times W \times N_{cls}}, \tag{9}$$

where $\mathcal{F}_{\mathrm{DEC}}(\cdot)$ utilizes a lightweight All-MLP decoder provided by [66] to ensure consistency with the encoder network MiT.

Our model is trained to minimize the loss function $\mathcal{L}$ as follows

$$\mathcal{L} = \frac{1}{H \times W} \sum_{p,q} \mathcal{L}_{\mathrm{CE}}(\mathbf{Q}_{[\cdot,p,q]}, \mathbf{G}_{[p,q]}), \tag{10}$$

where $\mathcal{L}_{\mathrm{CE}}$ is the Cross Entropy Loss. $\mathbf{G}$ stands for the ground-truth mask. $\sum_{p,q}$ denotes the sum over all positions on the frame $\mathbf{I}$. In the inference stage, $\mathbf{Q}$ from the decoder is passed directly through the $\mathtt{argmax}$ function to infer the final binary mask $\mathbf{Y}$. Prediction segmentation of video $\mathcal{I}$ without applying any post-processing techniques can be phrased as

$$\mathbf{Y} = \mathtt{argmax}(\mathbf{Q}) \in \{0, 1\}^{H \times W}. \tag{11}$$

4 Experiments

4.1 Experimental Setup

Datasets. We evaluate HFAN on three publicly available datasets with UVOS: DAVIS-16 [47], YouTube-Objects [49] and Long-Videos [32]. DAVIS-16 [47] contains a total of 50 videos, including 30 videos for training and 20 videos for validation. YouTube-Objects [49] includes 126 web videos divided into 10 categories with a total of more than 20,000 frames. Long-Videos [32] consists of three videos, each of which contains about **2500** frames per video sequence.

Implementation Details. We utilize PyTorch [46] and MMSegmentation codebase [7] to implement our model and train on two NVIDIA V100 with a mini-batch size of 8 per GPU. To achieve a better trade-off between accuracy and speed, we choose lightweight MiT-b1 and middleweight MiT-b2 as the backbones rather than the better but larger MiT-b3 to MiT-b5 [66]. Following [38,61,79], we pre-train our network on YouTube-VOS [67] and fine-tune on the training set of DAVIS-16 [47]. During training, we augment data online by random horizontal flipping, random resize with ratio 0.5–2.0, and random cropping to 512×512. We use AdamW optimizer to pre-train for 160K iterations and fine-tune for 4K iterations. The learning rates of pre-training and fine-tuning are set to $6e-5$ with a *poly* schedule and $1e-5$ with a *fixed* schedule, respectively. For obtaining an elegant end-to-end model, we do not employ training tricks like auxiliary head loss and online hard example mining [53]. Moreover, no post-processing techniques (*e.g.*, the widely used CRF [25]) are used in the inference phase. All inference processes for the experiments are performed using a single V100. We report UVOS performance using two standard evaluation metrics recommended by [47], *i.e.*, region similarity $\mathcal{J}$ and boundary accuracy $\mathcal{F}$.

4.2 Ablation Studies

To quantify the effect of each fundamental component in HFAN, we perform an exhaustive ablation study on the DAVIS-16 val-set [47]. For the fairness of the ablation results, we do not perform any post-processing techniques.

Impact of Data Input. To analyze the effect of appearance and motion features on performance, we first conduct an ablation study on the data input in Table 1. We adopt the video frame and corresponding optical flow as data inputs. A simple additive feature fusion approach is employed as the baseline. Compared to using a single input type, the baseline improves performance by providing richer appearance and motion cues. The ablation results illustrate that optical flow, which is deemed as the temporal consistency between video frames, requires the coaction of appearance features to achieve the desired effect.

Efficacy of Crucial Modules. When comparing our baseline with FAM, FAT, and HFAN, the results in Table 2 reveal that HFAN is a superior aggregate of FAM and FAT. Specifically, FAM improves 2.2% and 2.3% in terms of $\mathcal{J}$

Table 1. Ablation study for data input. All ablated versions utilize hierarchical architecture MiT-b1 as the backbone.

Input	$\mathcal{J}$ Mean ↑	$\Delta\mathcal{J}$	$\mathcal{F}$ Mean ↑	$\Delta\mathcal{F}$
Image frame only	79.1	-3.9	79.8	-3.5
Optical flow only	77.9	-5.1	76.5	-6.8
Baseline	83.0	–	83.3	–

Table 2. Ablation study for module. HFAN indicates a full model with integrated FAM and FAT modules.

Variant	$\mathcal{J}$ Mean ↑	$\Delta\mathcal{J}$	$\mathcal{F}$ Mean ↑	$\Delta\mathcal{F}$	FPS ↑
Baseline	83.0	–	83.3	–	22.0
Baseline + FAM	85.2	+2.2	85.6	+2.3	21.0
Baseline + FAT	85.0	+2.0	86.1	+2.8	21.4
Baseline + HFAN	86.2	+3.2	87.1	+3.8	20.8

Table 3. Ablation study on different backbones. Transformer-like and CNN-like versions are considered in the experimental ablation. For the test setup, SS/MS denotes single/multi-scale test.

Backbone	Test Setup	$\mathcal{J}$ Mean ↑	$\mathcal{F}$ Mean ↑	FPS ↑
MiT-b0	SS	81.5	80.8	24.0
	MS	83.4	82.3	3.4
MiT-b1	SS	86.2	87.1	20.8
	MS	87.1	87.7	2.5
MiT-b2	SS	86.8	88.2	14.4
	MS	88.0	89.3	1.4
MiT-b3	SS	86.8	88.8	10.6
	MS	88.2	90.0	1.0
Swin-Tiny	SS	86.0	87.3	12.8
	MS	87.2	87.9	1.1
ResNet-101	SS	86.6	87.3	12.4
	MS	87.3	87.9	1.3

Table 4. Ablation study on different input sizes and optical flow with MS test.

Size \ Method	RAFT $\mathcal{J}$ Mean ↑	RAFT $\mathcal{F}$ Mean ↑	PWCNet $\mathcal{J}$ Mean ↑	PWCNet $\mathcal{F}$ Mean ↑
384 × 384	86.2	86.6	84.5	84.7
448 × 448	86.9	87.5	85.3	85.7
480 × 480	86.9	87.6	85.5	85.9
512 × 512	87.1	87.7	85.7	86.0

Table 5. Ablation study on Transformer-like and CNN-like network architectures. Ablated results are obtained in same setups (RAFT, 512 × 512, and MS test).

Backbone \ Method	MATNet + CRF $\mathcal{J}$ Mean ↑	MATNet + CRF $\mathcal{F}$ Mean ↑	Ours $\mathcal{J}$ Mean ↑	Ours $\mathcal{F}$ Mean ↑
MiT-b1	83.8	82.6	87.1	87.7
MiT-b2	84.7	83.8	88.0	89.3
ResNet-101	84.0	82.9	87.3	87.9

Mean and $\mathcal{F}$ Mean, respectively. FAT increases by 2.0% on $\mathcal{J}$ Mean and 2.8% $\mathcal{F}$ Mean. The best performance gains achieved by HFAN, which is implemented by combining FAM and FAT modules, further demonstrates the effectiveness of proposed approach. For aligning features of co-foreground objects in different modal images, HFAN achieves a simple way to correct shift differences between video frames and their corresponding optical flow features. In addition, HFAN achieves adaptive selection in the feature fusion phase by learning feature adaptation weights. Figure 4 visualizes the ablated versions for Table 2. It can be found that FAM aligns the image and optical flow features to yield smoother and more refined object boundaries. Meanwhile, FAT enhances the image and optical flow features by adaptive transformation. Our HFAN inherits advantages of FAM and FAT, obtaining more finesse in the target region and removing a larger amount of noise in the non-target region.

Efficacy of Backbone. We investigate the effect of different backbone networks on accuracy and speed. The results of MiT-b0 to MiT-b3 [66] are shown in Table 3 (Note that we do not run experiments using MiT-b4 and MiT-b5 due to GPU memory limitations.). We find that the performance increases when enlarging the size of backbone networks. However, a larger network leads to a lower model efficiency and real-time speed. In addition, other types of backbone networks (*e.g.*, Swin Transformer [35] and ResNet [14]) also achieve competitive results.

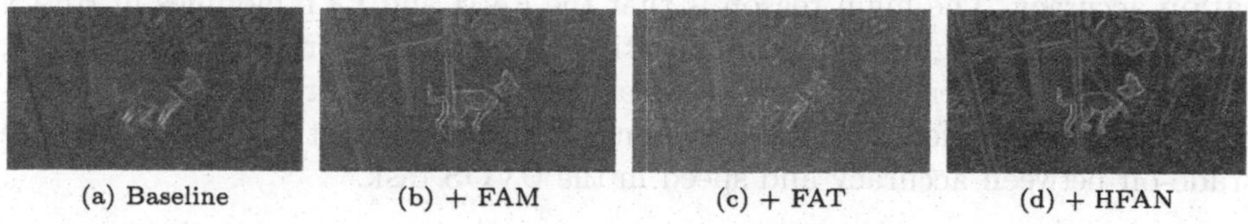
(a) Baseline (b) + FAM (c) + FAT (d) + HFAN

Fig. 4. Illustration of the first stage feature maps $\mathbf{U}_1$ from four ablated models.

This adequately demonstrates the generality of the proposed method. Given the trade-off between the model size and performance, we choose MiT-b1 and MiT-b2 as the small and medium backbone networks for HFAN, respectively.

Effect of Image Size and Optical Flow. Low-resolution image inputs generally degrade the performance of the segmentation model, while the use of different optical flow estimation methods also affects the final segmentation results. To study the effects of image size and optical flow estimation methods on the proposed method, we explore four different image size inputs and two well-known optical flow estimation methods. The ablation results are shown in Table 4, and we can find that **1)** the proposed method still has good performance under the low-resolution condition; **2)** RAFT [57] has better results than PWCNet [56] at the same resolution. The comprehensive analysis suggests that our method is not sensitive to the image resolution, while the optical flow estimation of different quality has a more obvious impact on the segmentation results.

Impact of Network Architecture. We further explore the impact of different network architectures on video segmentation methods. Table 5 shows the ablation results of Transformer-like (MiT [66]) and CNN-like (ResNet [14]) networks, and the analysis reveals that **1)** the performance ranking order of both methods (MATNet [79] and ours) is MiT-b2 > ResNet-101 > MiT-b1, and **2)** the proposed method outperforms MATNet (Note that results of MATNet are obtained by the CRF post-processing technique, while our results are not.) above 4.1% in terms of $\mathcal{J}\&\mathcal{F}$ Mean for the same network architecture. The above ablation results show that the large Transformer-like MiT-b2 [66] benefits from better visual perception and achieves better segmentation performance compared to CNN-like ResNet-101 [14].

4.3 Quantitative Results for UVOS

DAVIS-16. We compare the proposed model HFAN with SOTA methods on the public benchmark DAVIS-16 [47]. Table 6 shows the quantitative results. Our method outperforms all existing SOTA models by a significant margin on DAVIS-16. Specifically, our HFAN-small scores 86.7% $\mathcal{J}\&\mathcal{F}$ Mean and reaches 20.8 FPS in real-time speed. In contrast to RTNet [50], which employs both forward and backward optical flow and uses post-processing, HFAN-medium achieves 88.7% $\mathcal{J}\&\mathcal{F}$ Mean using only forward optical flow without any post-processing techniques. Compared with previous methods [22,50,69,75,79] using optical flow, our method exhibits significant superiority in terms of inference speed and segmentation accuracy. The main reason is that the FAM and FAT modules in HFAN perform feature alignment and adaptation for unaligned cross-modal features, allowing the decoder to utilize a more accurate feature representation. Quantitative results of different metrics demonstrate that our method achieves a nice trade-off between accuracy and speed in the UVOS task.

YouTube-Objects. To explore the universality of our proposed method to other video datasets, we perform validation experiments on the YouTube-Objects [49]

Table 6. Evaluation on DAVIS-16 [47]. 'small' and 'medium' indicate that the backbone networks of HFAN are MiT-b1 and MiT-b2, respectively. '†' means that the optical flow is used. 'PP' denotes post-processing. The three best scores are marked in red, blue and green for each metric, respectively. The inference speed (FPS) of each model contains all the necessary aspects for its generation of final results.

Method	Publication	PP	$\mathcal{J}$			$\mathcal{F}$			$\mathcal{J}\&\mathcal{F}$	FPS ↑
			Mean ↑	Recall ↑	Decay ↓	Mean ↑	Recall ↑	Decay ↓	Mean ↑	
PDB [55]	ECCV 2018	✓	77.2	90.1	0.9	74.5	84.4	-0.2	75.9	20.0
UOVOS† [80]	TIP 2019	✓	73.9	88.5	0.6	68.0	80.6	0.7	71.0	–
LSMO† [59]	IJCV 2019	✓	78.2	89.1	4.1	75.9	84.7	3.5	77.1	–
MotAdapt† [54]	ICRA 2019	✓	77.2	87.8	5.0	77.4	84.4	3.3	77.3	–
AGS [65]	CVPR 2019	✓	79.7	91.1	1.9	77.4	85.8	1.6	78.6	1.7
AGNN [63]	ICCV 2019	✓	80.7	94.0	0.0	79.1	90.5	0.0	79.9	1.9
COSNet [37]	CVPR 2019	✓	80.5	93.1	4.4	79.5	89.5	5.0	80.0	2.2
AnDiff [70]	ICCV 2019		81.7	90.9	2.2	80.5	85.1	0.6	81.1	2.8
PCSA [11]	AAAI 2020		78.1	90.0	4.4	78.5	88.1	4.1	78.3	110
EPO+† [1]	WACV 2020	✓	80.6	95.2	2.2	75.5	87.9	2.4	78.1	–
MATNet† [79]	AAAI 2020	✓	82.4	94.5	3.8	80.7	90.2	4.5	81.5	1.3
GraphMem [36]	ECCV 2020	✓	82.5	94.3	4.2	81.2	90.3	5.6	81.9	5.0
DFNet [77]	ECCV 2020	✓	83.4	94.4	4.2	81.8	89.0	3.7	82.6	3.6
3DCSeg [38]	BMVC 2020		84.2	95.8	7.4	84.3	92.4	5.5	84.2	4.5
F2Net [34]	AAAI 2021		83.1	95.7	0.0	84.4	92.3	0.8	83.7	10.0
FSNet† [22]	ICCV 2021	✓	83.4	94.5	3.2	83.1	90.2	2.6	83.3	12.5
AMC-Net† [69]	ICCV 2021	✓	84.5	96.4	2.8	84.6	93.8	2.5	84.6	–
TransportNet† [75]	ICCV 2021		84.5	–	–	85.0	–	–	84.8	3.6
RTNet† [50]	CVPR 2021	✓	85.6	96.1	–	84.7	93.8	–	85.2	–
Ours-small†(SS/MS)	–		86.2/87.1	96.7/96.8	4.6/4.8	87.1/87.7	95.5/95.3	2.3/2.5	86.7/87.4	20.8/2.5
Ours-medium†(SS/MS)			86.6/88.0	96.1/96.2	4.3/4.5	88.2/89.3	95.3/95.4	1.1/2.0	87.5/88.7	14.4/1.4

Table 7. Evaluation on YouTube-Objects [49]. The three best scores are marked in red, blue, and green for each object category over $\mathcal{J}$ Mean ↑.

Method	MOTAdapt [54]	LSMO [59]	LVO [58]	FSEG [21]	PDB [55]	SFL [6]	AGS [65]	COSNet [37]	AGNN [63]	MATNet [79]	AMCNet [69]	GraphMem [50]	RTNet [36]	**Ours-small**
Airplane	77.2	60.5	86.2	81.7	78.0	65.6	87.7	81.1	81.1	72.9	78.9	86.1	84.1	84.7
Bird	42.2	59.3	81.0	63.8	80.0	65.4	76.7	75.7	75.9	77.5	80.9	75.7	80.2	80.0
Boat	49.3	62.1	68.5	72.3	58.9	59.9	72.2	71.3	70.7	66.9	67.4	68.6	70.1	72.0
Car	68.6	72.3	69.3	74.9	76.5	64.0	78.6	77.6	78.1	79.0	82.0	82.4	79.5	76.1
Cat	46.3	66.3	58.8	68.4	63.0	58.9	69.2	66.5	67.9	73.7	69.0	65.9	71.8	76.0
Cow	64.2	67.9	68.5	68.0	64.1	51.2	64.6	69.8	69.7	67.4	69.6	70.5	70.1	71.2
Dog	66.1	70.0	61.7	69.4	70.1	54.1	73.3	76.8	77.4	75.9	75.8	77.1	71.3	76.9
Horse	64.8	65.4	53.9	60.4	67.6	64.8	64.4	67.4	67.3	63.2	63.0	72.2	65.1	71.0
Motorbike	44.6	55.5	60.8	62.7	58.4	52.6	62.1	67.7	68.3	62.6	63.4	63.8	64.6	64.3
Train	42.3	38.0	66.3	62.2	35.3	34.0	48.2	46.8	47.8	51.0	57.8	47.8	53.3	61.4
Average	58.1	64.3	67.5	68.4	65.5	57.1	69.7	70.5	70.8	69.0	71.1	71.4	71.0	73.4

test set without further fine-tuning its training set. The quantitative results of 10 categories in this dataset are shown in Table 7. Our method HFAN-small dose not reach SOTA across all categories but has better stability than other comparative methods. The proposed method is 2.0% higher than the second-best GraphMem [36] in terms of *average* $\mathcal{J}$ Mean. For 10 different object categories, the proposed method achieves its balanced performance over various challenging (*e.g.*, motion blur, occlusion, scale variation) video sequences. This is made possible by the sensible interaction of the proposed modules (FAM and FAT) for appearance and motion information.

Long-Videos. DAVIS [47] (**60+** frames per video sequence in average) only contains short-term video clips, while real-world videos tend to have more frames. To verify the performance of our HFAN in long-term video object segmentation, we evaluate it on the Long-Videos [32] val-set (approximate **2500** frames per video sequence). Table 8 shows the results under two types of supervision, SVOS and UVOS. By further observation, we can find that the proposed HFAN-medium has obtained the best result, achieving 81.7% over $\mathcal{J}\&\mathcal{F}$ Mean under the UVOS setting. Compared with the second-best method AGNN [63], our small model obtains an improvement of 7.0% on $\mathcal{J}\&\mathcal{F}$ Mean. Meanwhile, HFAN-medium achieves appealing results compared to SVOS methods. The results show that the temporal consistency provided by optical flow is also effective for long-term video object segmentation.

Table 8. Evaluation on Long-Videos [32]. The best results of SVOS and UVOS methods are marked in <u>underline</u> and **bold**, respectively.

Method	Supervision	$\mathcal{J}$			$\mathcal{F}$			$\mathcal{J}\&\mathcal{F}$Mean ↑
		Mean ↑	Recall ↑	Decay ↓	Mean ↑	Recall ↑	Decay ↓	
RVOS [61]	SVOS	10.2	6.7	13.0	14.3	11.7	<u>10.1</u>	12.2
A-GAME [23]		50.0	58.3	39.6	50.7	58.3	45.2	50.3
STM [44]		79.1	88.3	11.6	79.5	90.0	15.4	79.3
AFB-URR [32]		<u>82.7</u>	<u>91.7</u>	<u>11.5</u>	<u>83.8</u>	<u>91.7</u>	13.9	<u>83.3</u>
3DCSeg [38]	UVOS	34.2	38.6	11.6	33.1	28.1	15.6	33.7
MATNet [79]		66.4	73.7	10.9	69.3	77.2	10.6	67.9
AGNN [63]		68.3	77.2	13.0	68.6	77.2	16.6	68.5
Ours-small		74.9	82.5	14.8	76.1	86.0	16.0	75.5
Ours-medium		**80.2**	**91.2**	**9.4**	**83.2**	**96.5**	**7.1**	**81.7**

Table 9. Evaluation on DAVIS [47] for VSOD. The best scores are marked in **bold**.

Method	FGRN [27]	LTSI [2]	RCR [68]	MBN [29]	SSAV [9]	PCSA [11]	DCFNet [76]	FSNet [22]	Ours-small	Ours-medium
S_α ↑	0.838	0.876	0.886	0.887	0.893	0.902	0.914	0.920	0.934	**0.938**
E_ξ^{max} ↑	0.917	0.957	0.947	0.966	0.948	0.961	–	0.970	**0.983**	**0.983**
F_β^{max} ↑	0.783	0.850	0.848	0.862	0.861	0.880	0.900	0.907	0.929	**0.935**
MAE ↓	0.043	0.034	0.027	0.031	0.028	0.022	0.016	0.020	0.009	**0.008**

4.4 Quantitative Results for VSOD

The additional task VSOD, like UVOS, does not require first-frame annotation. To verify the performance of the proposed method on the VSOD setting, we perform a quantitative comparison with eight SOTA models on DAVIS [47].

Metrics. We employ four widely-used evaluation metrics including structure-measure S_α ($\alpha = 0.5$), max enhanced-alignment measure E_ξ^{max}, max F-measure F_β^{max} ($\beta^2 = 0.3$), and mean absolute error (MAE).

Results. As shown in Table 9, our HFAN outperforms all SOTA models. In particular, compared with DCFNet [76], S_α and F_β^{max} are improved by ∼2% and ∼3%, respectively. Compared to FSNet [22], HFAN achieves >1.3% performance gains on S_α, E_ξ^{max} and F_β^{max}, and reduces MAE by a factor of two. This significantly proves the adaptability of our method to similar tasks.

4.5 Qualitative Results

Figure 5 shows qualitative results of our HFAN model. We select five videos from DAVIS-16 [47], YouTube-Objects [49] and Long-Videos [32] test sets. These videos consist of several challenging frame sequences (*e.g.*, fast motion, scale variation, interacting objects and occlusion). As shown in the top two rows, our method yields desirable results for dynamic, similar, and complex backgrounds. Moreover, our proposed model has an accurate prediction for the occlusion boundary. In the third and fourth rows, satisfactory segmentation results are acquired in the presence of large-scale variation and object interaction cases.

Fig. 5. Qualitative results on three challenging video clips over time. From top to bottom: *bmx-trees*, *libby* and *soapbox* from DAVIS-16 [47], *dog-0028* from YouTube-Objects [49], and *rat* from Long-Videos [32].

5 Conclusion

We present a hierarchical feature alignment network, termed as HFAN, for addressing the contextual mismatch between appearance and motion features in the UVOS task. Firstly, to address the mismatch of primary object positions between video frames and their corresponding optical flows, our proposed FAM module relies on sharing primary objects in images across modalities to align appearance and motion features. Subsequently, for tackling the modal mismatch problem between aligned feature maps, the FAT module is designed to construct a feature adaptation weight to automatically enhance cross-modal features. With the alignment and adaptation of appearance and motion features achieved by FAM and FAT, HFAN could achieve a more accurate object segmentation. Experimental results show that the proposed method achieves SOTA performance in the unsupervised video object segmentation task.

Acknowledgment. This work was supported by the National Natural Science Foundation of China (No. 62102182 and 61976116), Natural Science Foundation of Jiangsu Province (No. BK20210327), and Fundamental Research Funds for the Central Universities (No. 30920021135).

References

1. Akhter, I., Ali, M., Faisal, M., Hartley, R.: Epo-net: Exploiting geometric constraints on dense trajectories for motion saliency. In: WACV (2020)
2. Chen, C., Wang, G., Peng, C., Zhang, X., Qin, H.: Improved robust video saliency detection based on long-term spatial-temporal information. In: TIP (2019)
3. Chen, T., Yao, Y., Zhang, L., Wang, Q., Xie, G., Shen, F.: Saliency guided inter- and intra-class relation constraints for weakly supervised semantic segmentation. In: TMM (2022)
4. Chen, Y., Han, C., Wang, N., Zhang, Z.: Revisiting feature alignment for one-stage object detection. arXiv preprint arXiv:1908.01570 (2019)
5. Cheng, H.K., Tai, Y.W., Tang, C.K.: Modular interactive video object segmentation: Interaction-to-mask, propagation and difference-aware fusion. In: CVPR (2021)
6. Cheng, J., Tsai, Y.H., Wang, S., Yang, M.H.: Segflow: Joint learning for video object segmentation and optical flow. In: ICCV (2017)
7. Contributors, M.: MMSegmentation: Openmmlab semantic segmentation toolbox and benchmark (2020). https://github.com/open-mmlab/mmsegmentation
8. Duke, B., Ahmed, A., Wolf, C., Aarabi, P., Taylor, G.W.: Sstvos: Sparse spatiotemporal transformers for video object segmentation. In: CVPR (2021)
9. Fan, D.P., Wang, W., Cheng, M.M., Shen, J.: Shifting more attention to video salient object detection. In: CVPR (2019)
10. Giordano, D., Murabito, F., Palazzo, S., Spampinato, C.: Superpixel-based video object segmentation using perceptual organization and location prior. In: CVPR (2015)
11. Gu, Y., Wang, L., Wang, Z., Liu, Y., Cheng, M.M., Lu, S.P.: Pyramid constrained self-attention network for fast video salient object detection. In: AAAI (2020)
12. Han, B., Davis, L.S.: Density-based multifeature background subtraction with support vector machine. In: TPAMI (2011)
13. Han, J., Ding, J., Li, J., Xia, G.S.: Align deep features for oriented object detection. In: TGRS (2021)
14. He, K., Zhang, X., Ren, S., Sun, J.: Deep residual learning for image recognition. In: CVPR (2016)
15. Heo, Y., Koh, Y.J., Kim, C.S.: Guided interactive video object segmentation using reliability-based attention maps. In: CVPR (2021)

16. Huang, S., Lu, Z., Cheng, R., He, C.: Fapn: Feature-aligned pyramid network for dense image prediction. In: ICCV (2021)
17. Huang, Z., Wei, Y., Wang, X., Shi, H., Liu, W., Huang, T.S.: Alignseg: Feature-aligned segmentation networks. In: TPAMI (2021)
18. Hui, T., et al.: Collaborative spatial-temporal modeling for language-queried video actor segmentation. In: CVPR (2021)
19. Ilg, E., Mayer, N., Saikia, T., Keuper, M., Dosovitskiy, A., Brox, T.: Flownet 2.0: Evolution of optical flow estimation with deep networks. In: CVPR (2017)
20. Ioffe, S., Szegedy, C.: Batch normalization: Accelerating deep network training by reducing internal covariate shift. In: ICML (2015)
21. Jain, S.D., Xiong, B., Grauman, K.: Fusionseg: Learning to combine motion and appearance for fully automatic segmentation of generic objects in videos. In: CVPR (2017)
22. Ji, G.P., Fu, K., Wu, Z., Fan, D.P., Shen, J., Shao, L.: Full-duplex strategy for video object segmentation. In: ICCV (2021)
23. Johnander, J., Danelljan, M., Brissman, E., Khan, F.S., Felsberg, M.: A generative appearance model for end-to-end video object segmentation. In: CVPR (2019)
24. Khoreva, A., Rohrbach, A., Schiele, B.: Video object segmentation with language referring expressions. In: ACCV (2018)
25. Krähenbühl, P., Koltun, V.: Efficient inference in fully connected crfs with gaussian edge potentials. In: NeurIPS (2011)
26. Lao, D., Zhu, P., Wonka, P., Sundaramoorthi, G.: Flow-guided video inpainting with scene templates. In: ICCV (2021)
27. Li, G., Xie, Y., Wei, T., Wang, K., Lin, L.: Flow guided recurrent neural encoder for video salient object detection. In: CVPR (2018)
28. Li, H., Chen, G., Li, G., Yu, Y.: Motion guided attention for video salient object detection. In: ICCV (2019)
29. Li, S., Seybold, B., Vorobyov, A., Lei, X., Kuo, C.-C.J.: Unsupervised video object segmentation with motion-based bilateral networks. In: Ferrari, V., Hebert, M., Sminchisescu, C., Weiss, Y. (eds.) ECCV 2018. LNCS, vol. 11207, pp. 215–231. Springer, Cham (2018). https://doi.org/10.1007/978-3-030-01219-9_13
30. Li, X., Wang, W., Hu, X., Yang, J.: Selective kernel networks. In: CVPR (2019)
31. Li, X., et al.: Semantic flow for fast and accurate scene parsing. In: Vedaldi, A., Bischof, H., Brox, T., Frahm, J.-M. (eds.) ECCV 2020. LNCS, vol. 12346, pp. 775–793. Springer, Cham (2020). https://doi.org/10.1007/978-3-030-58452-8_45
32. Liang, Y., Li, X., Jafari, N., Chen, Q.: Video object segmentation with adaptive feature bank and uncertain-region refinement. In: NeurIPS (2020)
33. Lin, T.Y., Dollár, P., Girshick, R., He, K., Hariharan, B., Belongie, S.: Feature pyramid networks for object detection. In: CVPR (2017)
34. Liu, D., Yu, D., Wang, C., Zhou, P.: F2net: Learning to focus on the foreground for unsupervised video object segmentation. In: AAAI (2021)
35. Liu, Z., et al.: Swin transformer: Hierarchical vision transformer using shifted windows. In: ICCV (2021)
36. Lu, X., Wang, W., Danelljan, M., Zhou, T., Shen, J., Van Gool, L.: Video object segmentation with episodic graph memory networks. In: Vedaldi, A., Bischof, H., Brox, T., Frahm, J.-M. (eds.) ECCV 2020. LNCS, vol. 12348, pp. 661–679. Springer, Cham (2020). https://doi.org/10.1007/978-3-030-58580-8_39
37. Lu, X., Wang, W., Ma, C., Shen, J., Shao, L., Porikli, F.: See more, know more: Unsupervised video object segmentation with co-attention siamese networks. In: CVPR (2019)

38. Mahadevan, S., Athar, A., Ošep, A., Hennen, S., Leal-Taixé, L., Leibe, B.: Making a case for 3d convolutions for object segmentation in videos. In: BMVC (2020)
39. Mao, Y., Wang, N., Zhou, W., Li, H.: Joint inductive and transductive learning for video object segmentation. In: ICCV (2021)
40. Miao, J., Wu, Y., Liu, P., Ding, Y., Yang, Y.: Pose-guided feature alignment for occluded person re-identification. In: ICCV (2019)
41. Nair, V., Hinton, G.E.: Rectified linear units improve restricted boltzmann machines. In: ICML (2010)
42. Ochs, P., Malik, J., Brox, T.: Segmentation of moving objects by long term video analysis. In: TPAMI (2013)
43. Oh, S.W., Lee, J.Y., Xu, N., Kim, S.J.: Fast user-guided video object segmentation by interaction-and-propagation networks. In: CVPR (2019)
44. Oh, S.W., Lee, J.Y., Xu, N., Kim, S.J.: Video object segmentation using space-time memory networks. In: ICCV (2019)
45. Papazoglou, A., Ferrari, V.: Fast object segmentation in unconstrained video. In: ICCV (2013)
46. Paszke, A., et al.: Pytorch: An imperative style, high-performance deep learning library. In: NeurIPS (2019)
47. Perazzi, F., Pont-Tuset, J., McWilliams, B., Van Gool, L., Gross, M., Sorkine-Hornung, A.: A benchmark dataset and evaluation methodology for video object segmentation. In: CVPR (2016)
48. Perazzi, F., Wang, O., Gross, M., Sorkine-Hornung, A.: Fully connected object proposals for video segmentation. In: ICCV (2015)
49. Prest, A., Leistner, C., Civera, J., Schmid, C., Ferrari, V.: Learning object class detectors from weakly annotated video. In: CVPR (2012)
50. Ren, S., Liu, W., Liu, Y., Chen, H., Han, G., He, S.: Reciprocal transformations for unsupervised video object segmentation. In: CVPR (2021)
51. Seo, S., Lee, J.-Y., Han, B.: Urvos: Unified referring video object segmentation network with a large-scale benchmark. In: Vedaldi, A., Bischof, H., Brox, T., Frahm, J.-M. (eds.) ECCV 2020. LNCS, vol. 12360, pp. 208–223. Springer, Cham (2020). https://doi.org/10.1007/978-3-030-58555-6_13
52. Seong, H., Oh, S.W., Lee, J.Y., Lee, S., Lee, S., Kim, E.: Hierarchical memory matching network for video object segmentation. In: ICCV (2021)
53. Shrivastava, A., Gupta, A., Girshick, R.: Training region-based object detectors with online hard example mining. In: CVPR (2016)
54. Siam, M., et al.: Video object segmentation using teacher-student adaptation in a human robot interaction (hri) setting. In: ICRA (2019)
55. Song, H., Wang, W., Zhao, S., Shen, J., Lam, K.-M.: Pyramid dilated deeper convlstm for video salient object detection. In: Ferrari, V., Hebert, M., Sminchisescu, C., Weiss, Y. (eds.) ECCV 2018. LNCS, vol. 11215, pp. 744–760. Springer, Cham (2018). https://doi.org/10.1007/978-3-030-01252-6_44
56. Sun, D., Yang, X., Liu, M.Y., Kautz, J.: Pwc-net: Cnns for optical flow using pyramid, warping, and cost volume. In: CVPR (2018)
57. Teed, Z., Deng, J.: Raft: Recurrent all-pairs field transforms for optical flow. In: Vedaldi, A., Bischof, H., Brox, T., Frahm, J.-M. (eds.) ECCV 2020. LNCS, vol. 12347, pp. 402–419. Springer, Cham (2020). https://doi.org/10.1007/978-3-030-58536-5_24
58. Tokmakov, P., Alahari, K., Schmid, C.: Learning video object segmentation with visual memory. In: ICCV (2017)
59. Tokmakov, P., Schmid, C., Alahari, K.: Learning to segment moving objects. In: IJCV (2019)

60. Vaswani, A., et al.: Attention is all you need. In: NeurIPS (2017)
61. Ventura, C., Bellver, M., Girbau, A., Salvador, A., Marques, F., Giro-i Nieto, X.: Rvos: End-to-end recurrent network for video object segmentation. In: CVPR (2019)
62. Wang, G., Zhang, T., Cheng, J., Liu, S., Yang, Y., Hou, Z.: Rgb-infrared cross-modality person re-identification via joint pixel and feature alignment. In: ICCV (2019)
63. Wang, W., Lu, X., Shen, J., Crandall, D.J., Shao, L.: Zero-shot video object segmentation via attentive graph neural networks. In: ICCV (2019)
64. Wang, W., Shen, J., Porikli, F.: Saliency-aware geodesic video object segmentation. In: CVPR (2015)
65. Wang, W., et al.: Learning unsupervised video object segmentation through visual attention. In: CVPR (2019)
66. Xie, E., Wang, W., Yu, Z., Anandkumar, A., Alvarez, J.M., Luo, P.: Segformer: Simple and efficient design for semantic segmentation with transformers. In: NeurIPS (2021)
67. Xu, N., et al.: YouTube-VOS: Sequence-to-sequence video object segmentation. In: Ferrari, V., Hebert, M., Sminchisescu, C., Weiss, Y. (eds.) ECCV 2018. LNCS, vol. 11209, pp. 603–619. Springer, Cham (2018). https://doi.org/10.1007/978-3-030-01228-1_36
68. Yan, P., et al.: Semi-supervised video salient object detection using pseudo-labels. In: ICCV (2019)
69. Yang, S., Zhang, L., Qi, J., Lu, H., Wang, S., Zhang, X.: Learning motion-appearance co-attention for zero-shot video object segmentation. In: ICCV (2021)
70. Yang, Z., Wang, Q., Bertinetto, L., Hu, W., Bai, S., Torr, P.H.: Anchor diffusion for unsupervised video object segmentation. In: ICCV (2019)
71. Yao, Y., et al.: Non-salient region object mining for weakly supervised semantic segmentation. In: CVPR (2021)
72. Yao, Y., et al.: Jo-src: A contrastive approach for combating noisy labels. In: CVPR (2021)
73. Yao, Y., Zhang, J., Shen, F., Hua, X., Xu, J., Tang, Z.: Exploiting web images for dataset construction: A domain robust approach. In: TMM (2017)
74. Yuan, Y., Chen, X., Wang, J.: Object-contextual representations for semantic segmentation. In: ECCV (2020)
75. Zhang, K., Zhao, Z., Liu, D., Liu, Q., Liu, B.: Deep transport network for unsupervised video object segmentation. In: ICCV (2021)
76. Zhang, M., et al.: Dynamic context-sensitive filtering network for video salient object detection. In: ICCV (2021)
77. Zhen, M., et al.: Learning discriminative feature with crf for unsupervised video object segmentation. In: Vedaldi, A., Bischof, H., Brox, T., Frahm, J.-M. (eds.) ECCV 2020. LNCS, vol. 12372, pp. 445–462. Springer, Cham (2020). https://doi.org/10.1007/978-3-030-58583-9_27
78. Zhou, T., Li, J., Li, X., Shao, L.: Target-aware object discovery and association for unsupervised video multi-object segmentation. In: CVPR (2021)
79. Zhou, T., Wang, S., Zhou, Y., Yao, Y., Li, J., Shao, L.: Motion-attentive transition for zero-shot video object segmentation. In: AAAI (2020)
80. Zhuo, T., Cheng, Z., Zhang, P., Wong, Y., Kankanhalli, M.: Unsupervised online video object segmentation with motion property understanding. In: TIP (2019)

PAC-Net: Highlight Your Video via History Preference Modeling

Hang Wang[1], Penghao Zhou[2], Chong Zhou[3], Zhao Zhang[4], and Xing Sun[5](✉)

[1] Huawei, Shenzhen, China
francis970625@gmail.com
[2] ByteDance, Beijing, China
patrick.phzhou@gmail.com
[3] Nanyang Technological University, Singapore, Singapore
chong033@ntu.edu.sg
[4] NanKai University, Tianjin, China
zzhang@mail.nankai.edu.cn
[5] Shopee, Singapore, Singapore
winfred.sun@gmail.com

Abstract. Autonomous highlight detection is crucial for video editing and video browsing on social media platforms. General video highlight detection aims at extracting the most interesting segments from the entire video. However, interest is subjective among different users. A naive solution is to train a model for each user but it is not practical due to the huge training expense. In this work, we propose a ***P**reference-**A**daptive **C**lassification* (PAC-Net) framework, which can model users' personalized preferences from their user history. Specifically, we design a *Decision Boundary Customizer* (DBC) module to dynamically generate the user-adaptive highlight classifier from the preference-related user history. In addition, we introduce *Mini-History* (Mi-Hi) mechanism to capture more fine-grained user-specific preferences. The final highlight prediction is jointly decided by the user's multiple preferences. Extensive experiments demonstrate that PAC-Net achieves state-of-the-art performance on the public benchmark dataset, whilst using substantially smaller networks.

Keywords: Personalized video highlight detection · User-adaptive learning · Decision boundary · User preference modeling

1 Introduction

Nowadays, people show growing interest in short videos to record and share their daily life. However, it is a laborious task to manually pick out the more attractive highlight parts from the long video to get a well-edited one. Therefore, autonomous video highlight detection arouses great attention in the vision community, and many efforts have been devoted into the study of general video highlight detection (VHD) [4,9,13,46,49].

S. Avidan et al. (Eds.): ECCV 2022, LNCS 13694, pp. 614–631, 2022.
https://doi.org/10.1007/978-3-031-19830-4_35

In real-world applications, a more practical task is personalized video highlight detection (P-VHD), which aims at extracting user-adaptive highlight predictions guided by annotated user history. Since user preferences vary a lot, it is very subjective when it comes to determining how interesting a video segment, *e.g.*, for a sports competition video, some prefer the scoring moments while some enjoy more teamwork plays. General VHD algorithms may not perform well due to the neglect of user's personal information. Such an issue calls for efficient and specialized techniques for P-VHD problem.

Fig. 1. Motivation of PAC-Net. A user has diverse preferences, and these preferences can be collected from user history and used as guidance for personalized prediction. In this example, the user is interested in singing, forest walks, food close-up, and Big Ben. In PAC-Net, we first summarize each preference with a classifier that can classify highlight parts and non-highlight parts for the corresponding preference. Then, multiple preference-specific classifiers jointly result in the final prediction for the input video.

PHD-GIFs [24] is the first attempt and it proposes a large-scale dataset as well as a baseline model. PHD-GIFs concatenates the historical highlight video segments with the input video so that the input contains the personalized information. Recently, Adaptive-H-FCSN [29] proposes to use adaptive instance normalization [11] that conditions on the user history along the temporal dimension, which utilizes the user history more effectively than direct concatenation.

In this paper, we propose a new perspective to better address the P-VHD problem. Imagine you are required to pick out several interesting segments from a new video for a customer, and you are also given several videos that have annotations indicating which frames the customer prefers, one intuitive solution is to first summarize the labeled history videos into assessment standards then apply these standards to the unlabeled video to filter out the desired contents. See Fig. 1 for an example. To mimic what a person would do, we propose a novel framework called *Preference-Adaptive Classification* (PAC-Net), which consists of two key components, *Decision Boundary Customizer* (DBC) module and *Mini-History* (Mi-Hi) mechanism.

Specifically, DBC is responsible for extracting the aforementioned assessment standards from the user history. In a nutshell, we represent each standard with a highlight classifier that draws a decision boundary between the highlighted frames and non-highlighted frames. DBC module is designed to dynamically generate such preference-specific classifier based on labeled user history. In fact, such process is a feature transformation from user history to the weights of the preference-related highlight classifier, and the generated classifier is responsible for the highlight prediction. During inference, by plugging in the history of a specific user, DBC could generate personalized classifier without any retraining. In order to encourage DBC to generate diverse highlight classifiers, we equip DBC with a regularization module to prevent the personalized highlight classifier from degenerating into a generic highlight classifier. In addition, we also find that previous methods discard the non-highlighted frames of the user history and only utilize the highlighted ones. However, the non-highlights could also be beneficial for the P-VHD task, *e.g.*, helping to eliminate the false positives. Therefore, we further enable DBC to take the non-highlighted user history as part of its inputs to generate a more precise highlight classifier.

The Mini-History (Mi-Hi) mechanism is proposed to make the assessment standards more fine-grained. Previous P-VHD methods view the user preferences at a user level, that is, concatenating features of all the highlighted frames into one feature vector thus each user only has one preference representation. However, as a matter of fact, one user could have diverse preferences, let alone one video could contain multiple topics. Therefore, we argue that user history could be utilized at a more fine-grained level. Mi-Hi mechanism makes it possible by extracting all highlight segments from user history and converting each preference-related highlight segment into a preference-specific highlight classifier by DBC. The final highlight prediction is jointly decided by all the classifiers.

To prove the effectiveness of PAC-Net, we conduct extensive experiments on PHD-GIFs dataset [24], the only related large-scale dataset for this task. The results show that PAC-Net outperforms state-of-the-art methods, with a relative improvement of 9% over Adaptive-H-FCSN. Comprehensive ablation experiments validate the effectiveness of our method, and we also provide visualizations for better understanding.

Our contributions are summarized as follows:

1. We propose PAC-Net, a novel framework for personalized video highlight detection, which achieves state-of-the-art performance on a large-scale benchmark dataset whilst using substantially smaller networks.
2. We design the Decision Boundary Customizer (DBC) module to dynamically generate the preference-related highlight classifier conditioned on labeled user history, which makes the highlight classifier user-adaptive.
3. To capture more fine-grained user preferences, we introduce the Mini-History (Mi-Hi) mechanism, where each historical highlight segment is first extracted and then converted into a highlight classifier by DBC, and the final prediction is jointly decided by user's multiple highlight classifiers.

2 Related Work

Personalized Video Highlight Detection. Video highlight detection aims at detecting the attractive clips from the whole video, which capture the important information in the video. Early works mainly focus on sports videos [32,38,44], and in recent years, the research area has been extended to general videos like social media videos [24,36] or first-person videos [48]. Most video highlight detectors do not consider user preference [3,9,10,13,42,46,48,49] and these general detectors are mostly ranking models, whose key idea is to rank the highlighted segments higher than the non-highlighted ones. For example, Video2GIF [9] proposes a deep model to generate a ranked list of segments according to their suitability as GIF. Recently, several works are proposed for P-VHD task. PHD-GIFs [24] is the first works for personalized video highlight detection and it also creates a large-scale dataset. PHD-GIFs is a ranking model as well but it concatenates the historical highlight segments into the input to capture the user's interests. Adaptive-H-FCSN [29] proposes T-AIN, which extends the adaptive instance normalization [11] to the time dimension. The T-AIN layer is conditioned on user history and is more effective than concatenating the input feature with the history feature. In this work, we tackle the P-VHD problem from a new perspective for better personalization.

Personalized Video Summarization. Video highlight detection is evolved from the video summarization task. The major difference is that video summarization targets on providing a concise overview of the entire video, while video highlight detection requires extracting the most interesting segments and does not enforce integrity. Early video summarization systems are based on heuristic rules and are fully unsupervised [15,16,20,22,25,26,35,40,52,55]. Later, as deep learning develops rapidly, several data-driven supervised approaches outperform the hand-crafted rules [5–8,18,21,28,45,50,51,54]. However, all the aforementioned video summarization methods are for general video summarization. To adapt a general model to be user-specific, one naive solution is to retrain the whole model or part of the model for each user, which, however, is usually infeasible in practice due to that retraining takes much more time than feed-forward computation and there might not be sufficient training data for just one user. Another line of work performs personalization with extra annotations, such as metadata (*e.g.*, user profiles) [1,2,12,37] and user interaction (*e.g.*, text queries) [19,23,33,34,41,47,53]. Note that, our method does not rely on either metadata or user interaction.

3 Methodology

The proposed PAC-Net consists of three components namely encoder, Decision Boundary Customizer (DBC), and Mini-History (Mi-Hi) mechanism. In this section, we first formally describe the personalized video highlight detection problem. Then we briefly go over the overview of the proposed PAC-Net framework and describe the details of the feature encoder. Finally, we elaborate on how the DBC enables personalization and how to utilize user history more precisely and flexibly with the Mi-Hi mechanism.

3.1 Problem Definition

Personalized video highlight detection (P-VHD) is a sub-problem of video highlight detection (VHD), but it is more practical and challenging than VHD. Thus, we first introduce the VHD then P-VHD for better understanding. The goal of VHD is to, for each frame in the input video, correctly predict the likelihood of its being highlight. We denote the input as $V_{in} \in \mathbb{R}^N$, where N denotes the number of frames. Each frame is annotated with 1 if is highlight, otherwise 0. The VHD problem is essentially a binary classification problem, that is, given a entire video, classifying each frame into either highlight or non-highlight category:

$$\mathrm{VHD}(v_i \mid V_{in}) = \begin{cases} 1, & \text{if } v_i \in \text{highlight} \\ 0, & \text{otherwise} \end{cases}, \tag{1}$$

where v_i denotes the feature of the i-th frame.

Compared to the general VHD, P-VHD task further requires the highlight detector to be adaptive to the different users' preferences, and such preferences are given by a set of history videos $\{H_1, H_2, ...H_M\}$ with highlight annotations of each user:

$$\text{P-VHD}(v_i \mid V_{in}, \{H_1...H_M\}) = \begin{cases} 1, & \text{if } v_i \in \text{highlight} \\ 0, & \text{otherwise} \end{cases}, \tag{2}$$

where M denotes the number of history videos.

3.2 Overview of PAC-Net

General VHD approaches do not consider the user history so they tend to highlight the common flavors of all the users. To achieve the goal of personalization, we propose the PAC-Net, which consists of encoder $\mathcal{F}$, Decision Boundary Customizer (DBC) module, and Mini-History (Mi-Hi) mechanism. The key idea of PAC-Net is that the standards for determining the highlights can be extracted from the user history and the extracted standards can be used to pick out the highlighted frames in the input query video. We represent each preference standard with a classifier that draws a decision boundary between the highlighted frames and non-highlighted frames. Such process is conducted by the DBC module, which is designed to convert user history into the parameters of the preference-specific highlight classifier.

In addition, prior P-VHD works view the history as holistic information by summarizing all user history into one preference vector, which is oversimplified and sub-optimal since one user could have diverse preferences let alone the segments in the same video could have multiple topics. To make the preferences more fine-grained, we propose the Mini-History (Mi-Hi) mechanism, where each highlight segment in history is picked out and converted to a preference-dependent highlight classifier by DBC, and the final highlight prediction for the input video is jointly decided by multiple preference-specific classifiers.

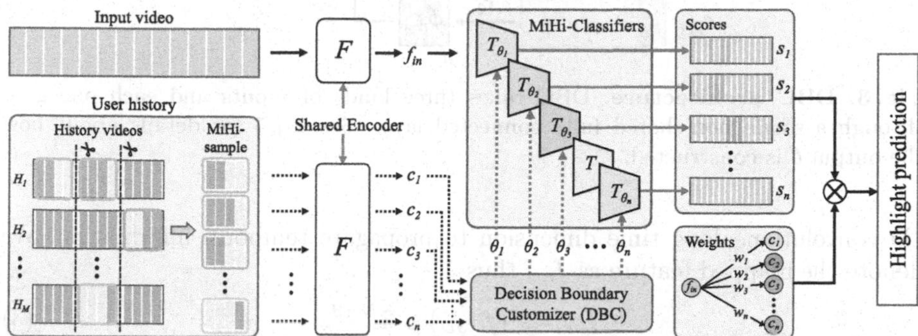

Fig. 2. PAC-Net architecture. PAC-Net consists of the encoder $\mathcal{F}$, DBC module, and Mi-Hi mechanism (highlighted with the gray background). In particular, DBC converts the preference-related history features c into the parameters θ of the highlight classifiers T_θ. And Mi-Hi mechanism corresponds to (1) splitting user history into multiple Mi-Hi samples (2) multiple Mi-Hi highlight classifiers generated by DBC, and (3) results fusion to get final prediction.

The whole pipeline of the PAC-Net framework is shown in Fig. 2. First, we split the history videos into equal-length segments and select the ones contained both highlighted frames and non-highlighted frames as Mi-Hi samples. Then, the input video and these Mi-Hi samples are fed into the shared encoder $\mathcal{F}$ and become input feature f_{in} and Mi-Hi features c_i. Next, DBC converts each Mi-Hi feature c_i into the parameters θ_i of a Mi-Hi highlight classifier T_{θ_i}. We apply all the Mi-Hi classifiers to input feature f_{in} and each one will predict a set of frame-level highlight scores. Finally, the final highlight result is produced by the weighted sum of predictions from all Mi-Hi classifiers.

3.3 Encoder

Following previous work [29], we use the fixed C3D [39] features for both training and testing to reduce the computational burden. The features are extracted by a C3D model pre-trained on the Sports-1M [14] dataset. Since the C3D [39] features are fixed, we further introduce an encode $\mathcal{F}$ to map the fixed input feature into a new feature space to facilitate later learning. Specifically, a standard U-Net [31] without the last fully connected layer serves as the encoder. The U-Net consists of 4 downsampling blocks and 4 upsampling blocks, and each block is composed of 2 temporal convolution layers.

For an input video $V_{in} \in \mathbb{R}^N$ with N frames, we first extract its C3D features $f_{C3D} \in \mathbb{R}^{N\times d}$, where d is the feature dimension. The encode performs temporal

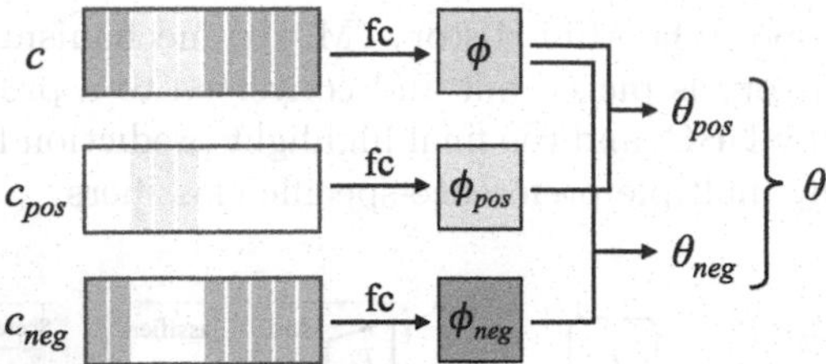

Fig. 3. DBC architecture. DBC takes three kinds of inputs and each one goes through a single non-shared fully connected layer. See Eq. 5 for details about how the output θ is constructed.

1D convolution along time dimension to propagate temporal information. We denote the mapped feature as f_{in}, thus

$$f_{in} = \mathcal{F}(f_{C3D}) \in \mathbb{R}^{N \times d}. \tag{3}$$

Note that C3D features only encode local motion information, and the encoder $\mathcal{F}$ equips features with contextual semantics.

3.4 Decision Boundary Customizer

Given a video with labels on the highlights, a person can easily summarize a standard to distinguish these highlights. And in PAC-Net, Decision Boundary Customizer (DBC) is designed for the same purpose, that is, building a customized classifier given a history clip. Briefly speaking, DBC learns to convert the feature c of a history clip into the parameters θ of the classifier T_θ,

$$\text{DBC: } c \rightarrow \theta. \tag{4}$$

The feature c of the historical segment contains a specific user preference, and the generated classifier T_θ represents the corresponding personal preference.

Figure 3 gives a graphical illustration of the proposed DBC. Given a historical highlight segment $c \in \mathbb{R}^{L \times d}$ with L frames, we first pick out the highlighted-frames-only segment c_{pos} and the non-highlighted-frames-only segment c_{neg} based on the user's label in order to explicitly input the highlight and non-highlight information to DBC. Then we pool all three features along the time dimension and each of them is fed into a non-shared fully connected layer. We denote these intermediate results as ϕ, ϕ_{pos}, and $\phi_{neg} \in \mathbb{R}^d$ respectively. Finally, the parameters $\theta \in \mathbb{R}^{d \times 2}$ of the classifier T_θ is generated by

$$\begin{aligned} \theta &= [\theta_{pos}; \theta_{neg}], \\ \theta_{pos} &= \phi + \phi_{pos}, \\ \theta_{neg} &= \phi + \phi_{neg}. \end{aligned} \tag{5}$$

The generated classifier T_θ is actually a single fully connected layer, which takes $f_{in} \in \mathbb{R}^{N \times d}$ as input and yields the prediction $T_\theta(f_{in}) \in \mathbb{R}^{N \times 2}$ with the second dimension denotes the likelihood of being highlight and non-highlight.

During training, it is not guaranteed that DBC will learn to generate diverse classifiers. In fact, it is easier for the DBC to generate only the classifiers that capture the general preferences. For instance, assume the input video is about baseball and there are three history videos about baseball, tennis, and golf respectively, the DBC will not receive any punishment by generating three similar classifiers that focus on swinging. This might potentially cause the model to degenerate to a general highlight detector. Thus, to enforce the DBC to focus on more detailed preferences and generate diverse classifiers, we propose a regularization module during training. Specifically, in addition to the input feature, we also apply the generated classifier to the corresponding historical feature that generates this highlight classifier and use cross-entropy loss to provide supervision. And the formula of the regularization loss is

$$\mathcal{L}_{reg} = \mathrm{CE}(T_\theta(c), Y_c), \tag{6}$$

where Y_c denotes the set of frame-level labels of c.

3.5 Mini-History

It's common sense that in real world a user could have diverse interests, which can be summarized from user history. Previous methods simply average the history so that one user would only have a holistic user-level history feature. We argue that user-level history feature might not be able to sufficiently represent the user preference since the user history could have diverse topics. Therefore, we introduce the Mini-History (Mi-Hi) mechanism that utilizes the history in a more fine-grained level. There are three steps in the Mi-Hi mechanism: (1) splitting the history videos into Mi-Hi samples (2) converting each Mi-Hi sample into corresponding preference-specific Mi-Hi classifier, and (3) fusing the predictions of all the Mi-Hi classifiers.

In specific, we split each history video into equal-length segments and keep only the ones that contain both highlighted and non-highlighted frames. We regard each kept segment as a Mi-Hi sample, and other segments are not used for training. Every Mi-Hi sample will get through the encoder $\mathcal{F}$ and get its feature c_i, which is then fed into the DBC to generate the parameters θ_i of a preference-specific highlight classifier T_{θ_i}, called Mi-Hi classifier,

$$\theta_i = \mathrm{DBC}(c_i). \tag{7}$$

Thus, if a user provides multiple Mi-Hi samples, there will be more than one highlight classifiers $\{T_{\theta_1} \dots T_{\theta_n}\}$. n denotes the number of Mi-Hi samples, and the number of Mi-Hi samples is greater or equal to the number of history videos ($n \geq M$) since a history video could contain more than one highlight segment. Each Mi-Hi sample corresponds to one specific Mi-Hi classifier. Applying each Mi-Hi classifier to the input video yields a prediction s_i. We calculate the weighted-sum of all the s_i to get the final highlight prediction,

$$s = \sum_{i}^{n} w_i \cdot s_i, \quad s_i = T_{\theta_i}(f_{in}). \tag{8}$$

And the weight w_i is computed by applying the radial basis function (RBF) kernel on the pooled input feature and pooled Mi-Hi feature followed by a SoftMax function:

$$\mathcal{K}(x, x') = \exp(-\frac{\|x - x'\|^2}{2\tau^2}), \tag{9}$$

$$w_i = \sigma\bigg(\mathcal{K}(\text{Pool}(c_i),\ \text{Pool}(f_{in}))\bigg), \tag{10}$$

where $\mathcal{K}(\cdot, \cdot)$ represents the RBF kernel, and τ is the temperature hyper-parameter. Pool$(\cdot)$ is a global pooling function along the time dimension, which converts a highlight $c \in \mathbb{R}^{L \times d}$ with L frames into Pool$(c) \in \mathbb{R}^d$, where d is feature dimension. σ denotes the SoftMax function.

Finally, the cross entropy between the prediction s and labels Y serves as the classification loss

$$\mathcal{L}_{cls} = \text{CE}(s, Y). \tag{11}$$

Besides, since there are multiple Mi-Hi features that input into the DBC, the regularization loss in Eq. 6 now becomes

$$\mathcal{L}_{reg} = \frac{1}{N} \sum_{i}^{N} \text{CE}(T_\theta(c_i), Y_{c_i}). \tag{12}$$

The overall training loss is the sum of $\mathcal{L}_{cls}$ and $\mathcal{L}_{reg}$,

$$\min\ \mathcal{L}_{cls} + \mathcal{L}_{reg}. \tag{13}$$

4 Experiments

In this section, we conduct extensive experiments on the largest benchmark dataset to verify the effectiveness of the proposed PAC-Net.

4.1 Experimental Setup

Dataset. All the experiments are conducted on the PHD-GIFs [24] dataset, which is by far the largest public highlight detection dataset with personalized highlight annotation, *i.e.*, user history. The original dataset contains 119,938 YouTube videos with 222,015 annotations from a total of 13,822 users, among which, 850 users are selected for testing. There are at least five history videos for each user, where the last video is reserved for the test set. Testing videos are clamped to a proper length to avoid extreme scenarios.

PHD-GIFs dataset only provides a list of YouTube URLs. Since some videos are no longer available on YouTube, we can not obtain the whole dataset. This problem has also been reported in Adaptive-H-FCSN [29]. This causes that the previous two works and ours conduct experiments on three different versions of the PHD-GIFs dataset. Thus, we collect several statistics of the dataset of each

Table 1. Statistics of three versions of the PHD-GIFs dataset. The dataset used in PHD-GIFs [24], Adaptive-H-FCSN [29], and ours is denoted as D_{v1}, D_{v2}, and D_{v3} respectively. The difference is caused by that the invalid YouTube URLs increase gradually.

Dataset	$\text{Users}_{(train+val)}$	Users_{test}	Total videos	Videos per user
D_{v1} [24]	12972	850	119938	9.25
D_{v2} [29]	7818	727	104828	12.27
D_{v3} (ours)	10146	675	95250	8.80

Table 2. Comparisons with state-of-the-art methods. We report the performance on three versions of PHD-GIFs dataset separately. On D_{v1} and D_{v2}, we report the results in their papers. On D_{v3}, we train the models marked with * with their official open-source code.

Methods	Params (M)	Dataset	mAP (%)
Video2GIF [9]	2.23	D_{v1}	15.69
PHD-GIFs [24]	–		16.68
Video2GIF [9]	2.23	D_{v2}	14.75
FCSN [30]	23.90		15.22
Adaptive-H-FCSN [29]	197.36		16.73
Video2GIF	2.23	D_{v3}	13.82
FCSN*	23.90		15.09
Adaptive-H-FCSN*	197.36		16.04
PAC-Net	5.89		**17.51**

paper for clear comparison as shown in Table 1. We denote the dataset in PHD-GIFs [24], Adaptive-H-FCSN [29], and ours as D_{v1}, D_{v2}, and D_{v3} respectively. Note that our version has the smallest video-user ratio.

Evaluation Metric. Following the former works [9,24,29] in video highlight detection, we also use the mean Average Precision (mAP) as the evaluation metric. The mAP summarizes the precision-recall curve of the detection results and has been extensively used in object detection and retrieval tasks to measure the accuracy of the model. We report the mAP on the test set. And the mAP is first calculated separately for each testing video and finally averaged.

Implementation Details. In all experiments, temperature parameter τ in RBF kernel and length of the Mi-Hi sample are set to 0.05 and 256 respectively. We train the model for 20 epochs with the Adam [17] optimizer (learning rate: 0.001, weight decay: 1×10^{-4}). The learning rate and weight decay are set to 0.001 and 0.0001 separately. And the training usually takes 8 to 9 h on 8 Nvidia Tesla V100 GPUs. Our method is implemented with the PyTorch [27] deep learning framework, and the source code will be released for reproducibility.

Table 3. Detailed improvement of the PAC-Net over baseline.

Gains (mAP)	≤0	0.0–2.0	2.0–5.0	≥5.0
Proportion (%)	2.3	48.9	35.2	13.6

Table 4. Ablation study experiments. PAC-Net(*) denotes the different modification based on our method. PR-Net$_{full}$ is our full method.

Methods	mAP(%)
PAC-Net$_{\mathrm{G}}$	15.28
PAC-Net$_{\mathrm{Agg}}$	15.67
PAC-Net$_{\mathrm{DBC}}$	15.89
PAC-Net$_{\mathrm{MiHi}}$	16.23
PAC-Net$_{\mathrm{H}}$	15.66
PAC-Net$_{full}$	**17.51**

4.2 Results

We compare our method with several previous state-of-the-art approaches including Video2GIF [9], FCSN [30], PHD-GIFs [24], and Adaptive-H-FCSN [29]. The first two are general video highlight detectors while the rest are personalized detectors. As we mentioned before, the datasets used in different papers are not exactly the same due to some YouTube URLs gradually becoming invalid. Therefore, for fair comparisons, we re-train previous methods with their official open-source code on our dataset.

As shown in Table 2, our method achieves state-of-the-art results and surpasses the second-best by 1.47 mAP, with a relative improvement of 9% over Adaptive-H-FCSN. Besides, Adaptive-H-FCSN performs worse on our dataset, and only obtains +0.95 mAP gain over FCSN. Such undesirable performance degradation implies that our dataset is more difficult and more challenging. Note that, despite our dataset having the smallest video-user ratio, we still get the highest mAP. We also report the number of parameters of each method. Our model has around thirty times fewer parameters than Adaptive-H-FCSN, but achieves the best performance, which illustrates the superiority of PAC-Net. Finally, In Table 3, We analyze the detailed performance improvement ratios of different users. From the table, we can see the vast majority of users have an obvious gain over baseline, which proves the effectiveness of our method.

4.3 Analysis

To evaluate the effectiveness of the different components in our proposed model and justify several design choices, comprehensive ablation study experiments are conducted on the PHD-GIFs dataset.

We first explore the usage of user history, and get two variants of PAC-Net named **PAC-Net**$_{\mathrm{G}}$ and **PAC-Net**$_{\mathrm{Agg}}$, where the former works as a baseline generic model

Table 5. Impact of number of user history. The number denotes the maximum number of historical videos that each user can use and M means no restriction is imposed.

# of hist.	0	1	2	3	5	M
mAP	15.28	15.53	15.84	16.38	17.02	**17.51**

Table 6. F-Score (%) performance comparison on SumMe [7] dataset. Note that unlike other SOTA methods, H-FCSN and our PAC-Net$_G$ are trained on the PHD-GIFs without fine-tuning on SumMe.

Methods	GAN$_{sup}$ [22]	DR-DSN$_{sup}$ [55]	S^{2}N [43]	H-FCSN [29]	PAC-Net$_G$
F-score	41.7	42.1	43.3	44.4	**44.6**

without the use of user history and the latter directly concatenate input feature with the user-level average history feature. Both PAC-Net$_G$ and PAC-Net$_{Agg}$ are composed of a feature encoder and a generic classifier for highlight prediction; To evaluate the effect of the major components in our method, two variants are studied: using DBC module only (**PAC-Net$_{DBC}$**) and using Mi-Hi mechanism only (**PAC-Net$_{MiHi}$**); To evaluate the effect of non-highlighted history, we remove the use of non-highlights of DBC and get the **PAC-Net$_H$** variant.

Improvement of Individual Module. Our main contributions can be summarized in two folds: DBC module for personalization and Mini-History for fine-grained utilization of user history. Therefore, we show how much each contribution improves the performance in Table 4. PAC-Net$_G$ does not utilize user history and serves as the baseline.

PAC-Net$_{MiHi}$ improves the baseline by 0.95 mAP, where Mi-Hi features and input features are trained with a shared classifier, whose parameters are not adaptive to users. Besides, to prove the performance gain does not all come from incorporating the user history into the model, we conduct another experiment (PAC-Net$_{Agg}$) where the input feature is concatenated with averaged history feature. PAC-Net$_{MiHi}$ still surpasses PAC-Net$_{Agg}$ by 0.56 mAP, which shows the fine-grained utilization of user history is more effective. In the PAC-Net$_{DBC}$, all the history videos of a user are concatenated into one giant history video, and the DBC is required to construct only one user-level classifier. Compared with the learned-and-fixed classifier in the baseline, DBC brings 0.61 mAP improvement. Finally, we show the Mini-History and DBC are complementary to each other. Based on Mini-History, DBC could generate various fine-grained Mi-Hi classifiers, which are more flexible and precise, and the full model could provide personalized highlight detection via the integration of multiple preference-specific decision boundaries. As a result, combining DBC with Mini-History significantly improves the baseline by 2.23 mAP, which is even greater than the sum of the improvements of each individual component.

Fig. 4. Qualitative comparisons between PAC-Net$_G$ and PAC-Net. We provide a few representative frames from input video and each historical highlight, respectively. We also show the highlighted frames detected by PAC-Net$_G$ and PAC-Net$_{full}$. These visualizations show that the user-adaptive model well extracts user's preference from user history, while general model PAC-Net$_G$ fails.

Importance of Non-highlighted History. Another difference from the previous work is that we are the first to utilize the non-highlighted history. To prove that non-highlighted history is beneficial to P-VHD, we perform an ablation study on whether to utilize the history non-highlights. As shown in Table 4, without non-highlighted history, the performance of PAC-Net$_H$ drops by 1.95 mAP. We think the usage of historical non-highlights plays an important role in defining a more precise decision boundary, which helps to eliminate the false positives and therefore makes the full PAC-Net model achieve better performance.

Discussion of the Number of User History Videos. In PHD-GIFs dataset, users do not have the same number of history videos and this is usually the case in practice. Hence, to test how much the number of user history affects the performance, we set several fixed upper-bounds of the max allowed history videos per user. Table 5 shows that as the number of allowed history videos increases, the performance gradually increases as expected, which demonstrates the good potential of our method. The trend indicates that as we acquire more history videos, more accurate user preferences can be built, which results in better performance.

Application to Video Summarization. Since highlight detection is highly related to video summarization, we also test our generic variant PAC-Net$_G$ on

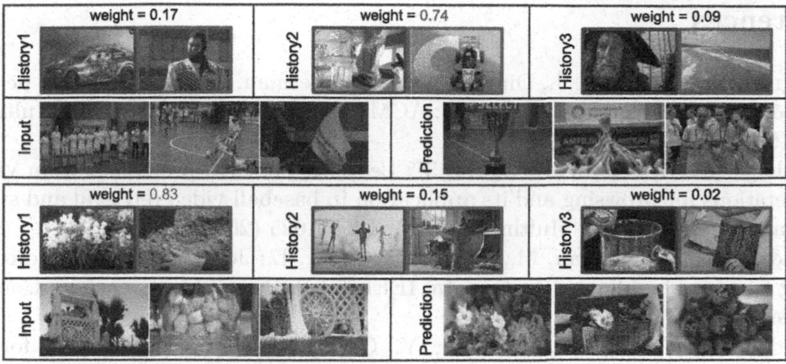

Fig. 5. Visualizations of the classifier weights during fusion. On the upper side, we choose one representative sample from each historical highlight. On the lower side, representative frames are selected from the input video and prediction respectively. As expected, the ***trophy*** and ***flower*** classifiers play the most importance part in two examples separately.

video summarization task. Following Adaptive-H-FCSN [29], we evaluate PAC-Net$_\mathrm{G}$ (trained on the PHD-GIFs [24] dataset) on *SumMe* [7] dataset without fine-tuning. Table 6 compares the F-Score of our PAC-Net$_\mathrm{G}$ and several state-of-the-art video summarization methods. It can be observed that the proposed PAC-Net$_\mathrm{G}$ achieves the best performance, verifying its effectiveness.

4.4 Visualizations

In Fig. 4, we provide several qualitative results as examples to compare the baseline PAC-Net$_\mathrm{G}$ and the full PAC-Net model. In these examples, PAC-Net$_\mathrm{full}$ obviously outperforms the baseline PAC-Net$_\mathrm{G}$. For example, the user in the second case likes the firefly and PAC-Net$_\mathrm{full}$ successfully highlights several close-ups of the firefly while the baseline fails. The visualization results illustrate that the fine-grained user preferences contained in user history play an important role for better personalized video highlight predictions.

Moreover, our fusion strategy assigns different weights to different Mi-Hi highlight classifiers. In Fig. 5, we visualize the focus of each classifier as well as its associated weight. It clearly shows that the highlight predictions are highly related to the Mi-Hi highlight classifier with the highest score.

5 Conclusion

We propose PAC-Net, a novel personalized video highlight detection framework, which extracts users' preferences from their history videos and makes highlight predictions based on the extracted preferences. As two core components of PAC-Net, DBC converts the user history into the parameters of the classifier, while Mi-Hi mechanism enables to utilize the user history at a fine-grained level. Extensive experiments and analytical studies verify the superiority of our approach.

References

1. Agnihotri, L., Kender, J., Dimitrova, N., Zimmerman, J.: Framework for personalized multimedia summarization. In: ACM International Conference on Multimedia (MM) (2005)
2. Babaguchi, N., Ohara, K., Ogura, T.: Learning personal preference from viewer's operations for browsing and its application to baseball video retrieval and summarization. IEEE Trans. Multimedia **9**(5), 1016–1025 (2007)
3. Badamdorj, T., Rochan, M., Wang, Y., Cheng, L.: Joint visual and audio learning for video highlight detection. In: IEEE International Conference on Computer Vision (ICCV) (2021)
4. Badamdorj, T., Rochan, M., Wang, Y., Cheng, L.: Contrastive learning for unsupervised video highlight detection. In: IEEE Conference on Computer Vision and Pattern Recognition (CVPR) (2022)
5. Chu, W.S., Song, Y., Jaimes, A.: Video co-summarization: Video summarization by visual co-occurrence. In: IEEE Conference on Computer Vision and Pattern Recognition (CVPR) (2015)
6. Gong, B., Chao, W.L., Grauman, K., Sha, F.: Diverse sequential subset selection for supervised video summarization. In: Advances in Neural Information Processing Systems (NeurIPS) (2014)
7. Gygli, M., Grabner, H., Riemenschneider, H., Van Gool, L.: Creating summaries from user videos. In: Fleet, D., Pajdla, T., Schiele, B., Tuytelaars, T. (eds.) ECCV 2014. LNCS, vol. 8695, pp. 505–520. Springer, Cham (2014). https://doi.org/10.1007/978-3-319-10584-0_33
8. Gygli, M., Grabner, H., Van Gool, L.: Video summarization by learning submodular mixtures of objectives. In: IEEE Conference on Computer Vision and Pattern Recognition (CVPR) (2015)
9. Gygli, M., Song, Y., Cao, L.: Video2gif: Automatic generation of animated gifs from video. In: IEEE Conference on Computer Vision and Pattern Recognition (CVPR) (2016)
10. Hong, F.-T., Huang, X., Li, W.-H., Zheng, W.-S.: MINI-Net: Multiple instance ranking network for video highlight detection. In: Vedaldi, A., Bischof, H., Brox, T., Frahm, J.-M. (eds.) ECCV 2020. LNCS, vol. 12358, pp. 345–360. Springer, Cham (2020). https://doi.org/10.1007/978-3-030-58601-0_21
11. Huang, X., Belongie, S.: Arbitrary style transfer in real-time with adaptive instance normalization. In: IEEE Conference on Computer Vision and Pattern Recognition (CVPR) (2017)
12. Jaimes, A., Echigo, T., Teraguchi, M., Satoh, F.: Learning personalized video highlights from detailed mpeg-7 metadata. In: IEEE Conference on Image Processing (ICIP) (2002)
13. Jiao, Y., Yang, X., Zhang, T., Huang, S., Xu, C.: Video highlight detection via deep ranking modeling. In: Pacific-Rim Symposium on Image and Video Technology (PSIVT) (2017)
14. Karpathy, A., Toderici, G., Shetty, S., Leung, T., Sukthankar, R., Fei-Fei, L.: Large-scale video classification with convolutional neural networks. In: IEEE Conference on Computer Vision and Pattern Recognition (CVPR) (2014)

15. Khosla, A., Hamid, R., Lin, C.J., Sundaresan, N.: Large-scale video summarization using web-image priors. In: IEEE Conference on Computer Vision and Pattern Recognition (CVPR) (2013)
16. Kim, G., Xing, E.P.: Reconstructing storyline graphs for image recommendation from web community photos. In: IEEE Conference on Computer Vision and Pattern Recognition (CVPR) (2014)
17. Kingma, D.P., Ba, J.: Adam: A method for stochastic optimization. In: International Conference on Learning Representations (ICLR) (2015)
18. Lee, Y.J., Ghosh, J., Grauman, K.: Discovering important people and objects for egocentric video summarization. In: IEEE Conference on Computer Vision and Pattern Recognition (CVPR) (2012)
19. Liu, W., Mei, T., Zhang, Y., Che, C., Luo, J.: Multi-task deep visual-semantic embedding for video thumbnail selection. In: IEEE Conference on Computer Vision and Pattern Recognition (CVPR) (2015)
20. Lu, Z., Grauman, K.: Story-driven summarization for egocentric video. In: IEEE Conference on Computer Vision and Pattern Recognition (CVPR) (2013)
21. Ma, Y.F., Hua, X.S., Lu, L., Zhang, H.J.: A generic framework of user attention model and its application in video summarization. IEEE Trans. Multimedia **7**(5), 907–919 (2005)
22. Mahasseni, B., Lam, M., Todorovic, S.: Unsupervised video summarization with adversarial lstm networks. In: IEEE Conference on Computer Vision and Pattern Recognition (CVPR) (2017)
23. Garcia del Molino, A., Boix, X., Lim, J.H., Tan, A.H.: Active video summarization: Customized summaries via on-line interaction with the user. In: Association for the Advancement of Artificial Intelligence (AAAI) (2017)
24. Garcia del Molino, A., Gygli, M.: Phd-gifs: personalized highlight detection for automatic gif creation. In: ACM International Conference on Multimedia (MM) (2018)
25. Ngo, C.W., Ma, Y.F., Zhang, H.J.: Automatic video summarization by graph modeling. In: IEEE International Conference on Computer Vision (ICCV) (2003)
26. Panda, R., Roy-Chowdhury, A.K.: Collaborative summarization of topic-related videos. In: IEEE Conference on Computer Vision and Pattern Recognition (CVPR) (2017)
27. Paszke, A., et al.: Automatic differentiation in pytorch. In: NeurIPS Workshop (2017)
28. Plummer, B.A., Brown, M., Lazebnik, S.: Enhancing video summarization via vision-language embedding. In: IEEE Conference on Computer Vision and Pattern Recognition (CVPR) (2017)
29. Rochan, M., Krishna Reddy, M.K., Ye, L., Wang, Y.: Adaptive video highlight detection by learning from user history. In: Vedaldi, A., Bischof, H., Brox, T., Frahm, J.-M. (eds.) ECCV 2020. LNCS, vol. 12366, pp. 261–278. Springer, Cham (2020). https://doi.org/10.1007/978-3-030-58589-1_16
30. Rochan, M., Ye, L., Wang, Y.: Video summarization using fully convolutional sequence networks. In: European Conference on Computer Vision (ECCV) (2018)
31. Ronneberger, O., Fischer, P., Brox, T.: U-net: Convolutional networks for biomedical image segmentation. In: International Conference on Medical Image Computing and Computer Assisted Intervention (MICCAI) (2015)
32. Rui, Y., Gupta, A., Acero, A.: Automatically extracting highlights for tv baseball programs. In: ACM International Conference on Multimedia (MM) (2000)
33. Sharghi, A., Gong, B., Shah, M.: Query-focused extractive video summarization. In: European Conference on Computer Vision (ECCV) (2016)

34. Singla, A., Tschiatschek, S., Krause, A.: Noisy submodular maximization via adaptive sampling with applications to crowdsourced image collection summarization. In: Association for the Advancement of Artificial Intelligence (AAAI) (2016)
35. Song, Y., Vallmitjana, J., Stent, A., Jaimes, A.: Tvsum: Summarizing web videos using titles. In: IEEE Conference on Computer Vision and Pattern Recognition (CVPR) (2015)
36. Sun, M., Farhadi, A., Seitz, S.M.: Ranking domain-specific highlights by analyzing edited videos. In: European Conference on Computer Vision (ECCV) (2014)
37. Takahashi, Y., Nitta, N., Babaguchi, N.: User and device adaptation for sports video content. In: IEEE International Conference on Multimedia and Expo (ICME) (2007)
38. Tang, H., Kwatra, V., Sargin, M.E., Gargi, U.: Detecting highlights in sports videos: Cricket as a test case. In: IEEE International Conference on Multimedia and Expo (ICME) (2011)
39. Tran, D., Bourdev, L., Fergus, R., Torresani, L., Paluri, M.: Learning spatiotemporal features with 3d convolutional networks. In: IEEE International Conference on Computer Vision (ICCV) (2015)
40. Truong, B.T., Venkatesh, S.: Video abstraction: A systematic review and classification. ACM Trans. Multimedia Comput. Commun. Appli. **3**(1), 3-es (2007)
41. Vasudevan, A.B., Gygli, M., Volokitin, A., Van Gool, L.: Query-adaptive video summarization via quality-aware relevance estimation. In: ACM International Conference on Multimedia (MM) (2017)
42. Wei, F., Wang, B., Ge, T., Jiang, Y., Li, W., Duan, L.: Learning pixel-level distinctions for video highlight detection. In: IEEE Conference on Computer Vision and Pattern Recognition (CVPR) (2022)
43. Wei, Z., et al.: Sequence-to-segment networks for segment detection. In: Advances in Neural Information Processing Systems (NeurIPS) (2018)
44. Xiong, Z., Radhakrishnan, R., Divakaran, A., Huang, T.S.: Highlights extraction from sports video based on an audio-visual marker detection framework. In: IEEE International Conference on Multimedia and Expo (ICME) (2005)
45. Xu, J., Mukherjee, L., Li, Y., Warner, J., Rehg, J.M., Singh, V.: Gaze-enabled egocentric video summarization via constrained submodular maximization. In: IEEE Conference on Computer Vision and Pattern Recognition (CVPR) (2015)
46. Xu, M., Wang, H., Ni, B., Zhu, R., Sun, Z., Wang, C.: Cross-category video highlight detection via set-based learning. In: IEEE International Conference on Computer Vision (ICCV) (2021)
47. Yang, H., Chaisorn, L., Zhao, Y., Neo, S.Y., Chua, T.S.: Videoqa: question answering on news video. In: ACM International Conference on Multimedia (MM) (2003)
48. Yao, T., Mei, T., Rui, Y.: Highlight detection with pairwise deep ranking for first-person video summarization. In: IEEE Conference on Computer Vision and Pattern Recognition (CVPR) (2016)
49. Yu, Y., Lee, S., Na, J., Kang, J., Kim, G.: A deep ranking model for spatio-temporal highlight detection from a 360○ video. In: Association for the Advancement of Artificial Intelligence (AAAI) (2018)
50. Zhang, K., Chao, W.L., Sha, F., Grauman, K.: Summary transfer: Exemplar-based subset selection for video summarization. In: IEEE Conference on Computer Vision and Pattern Recognition (CVPR) (2016)
51. Zhang, K., Chao, W.-L., Sha, F., Grauman, K.: Video summarization with long short-term memory. In: Leibe, B., Matas, J., Sebe, N., Welling, M. (eds.) ECCV 2016. LNCS, vol. 9911, pp. 766–782. Springer, Cham (2016). https://doi.org/10.1007/978-3-319-46478-7_47

52. Zhang, K., Grauman, K., Sha, F.: Retrospective encoders for video summarization. In: Ferrari, V., Hebert, M., Sminchisescu, C., Weiss, Y. (eds.) ECCV 2018. LNCS, vol. 11212, pp. 391–408. Springer, Cham (2018). https://doi.org/10.1007/978-3-030-01237-3_24
53. Zhang, Y., Kampffmeyer, M., Liang, X., Tan, M., Xing, E.P.: Query-conditioned three-player adversarial network for video summarization. In: British Machine Vision Conference (BMVC) (2018)
54. Zhao, B., Li, X., Lu, X.: Hierarchical recurrent neural network for video summarization. In: ACM International Conference on Multimedia (MM) (2017)
55. Zhou, K., Qiao, Y., Xiang, T.: Deep reinforcement learning for unsupervised video summarization with diversity-representativeness reward. In: Association for the Advancement of Artificial Intelligence (AAAI) (2018)

How Severe Is Benchmark-Sensitivity in Video Self-supervised Learning?

Fida Mohammad Thoker(✉), Hazel Doughty, Piyush Bagad, and Cees G. M. Snoek

University of Amsterdam, Amsterdam, Netherlands
f.m.thoker@uva.nl

Abstract. Despite the recent success of video self-supervised learning models, there is much still to be understood about their generalization capability. In this paper, we investigate how sensitive video self-supervised learning is to the current conventional benchmark and whether methods generalize beyond the canonical evaluation setting. We do this across four different factors of sensitivity: domain, samples, actions and task. Our study which encompasses over 500 experiments on 7 video datasets, 9 self-supervised methods and 6 video understanding tasks, reveals that current benchmarks in video self-supervised learning are not good indicators of generalization along these sensitivity factors. Further, we find that self-supervised methods considerably lag behind vanilla supervised pre-training, especially when domain shift is large and the amount of available downstream samples are low. From our analysis we distill the *SEVERE-benchmark*, a subset of our experiments, and discuss its implication for evaluating the generalizability of representations obtained by existing and future self-supervised video learning methods. Code is available at https://github.com/fmthoker/SEVERE-BENCHMARK.

Keywords: Self-supervised learning · Video representation learning · Video understanding

1 Introduction

Video self-supervised learning has progressed at a tremendous pace in recent years, e.g. [1,54,56–58,75], as it offers a crucial starting point from which to learn. This is especially important for video understanding applications, where annotating large amounts of data is extremely expensive, error-prone and sensitive to annotator bias. Hence, learning video representations through self-supervision is crucial, especially for use cases where the downstream video data is limited because of the domain, task or actions the video contains. However, the majority of current works in video self-supervised learning, e.g. [4,48,49,53,81], do

Supplementary Information The online version contains supplementary material available at https://doi.org/10.1007/978-3-031-19830-4_36.

S. Avidan et al. (Eds.): ECCV 2022, LNCS 13694, pp. 632–652, 2022.
https://doi.org/10.1007/978-3-031-19830-4_36

not test beyond standard benchmarks. The standard protocol is to use unlabeled Kinetics-400 [36] for pre-training and then measure performance by finetuning on two action recognition datasets: UCF-101 [65] and HMDB-51 [42]. While these benchmarks have facilitated the impressive progress of video self-supervised learning in recent years, they cannot indicate the generalizability of such methods as these pre-training and downstream datasets are all similar in appearance and the type of actions they contain. Some methods have started to report finetuning performance on additional datasets like Something-Something-v2 [25] in [20,56,75], Diving-48 [43] in [14,78], AVA [27] in [20,80,82] and EPIC-Kitchens-100 [13] in [82]. However, such evaluations are insufficient to understand the generalization of video self-supervised methods alone since they only add a single additional dataset, often without comparison to prior methods.

In this work, we address the essential need to gauge the sensitivity of existing video self-supervised methods to the current benchmark by thoroughly evaluating their performance for generalization across diverse downstream settings. Similar benchmarking studies have been performed for self-supervised pre-training in images [5,12,16,17,24,33,38,41,50,60,73,83,86], which investigate model transferability [16,33,50,74] or the importance of factors like pre-training dataset [12,24,41] and backbone architecture [38]. Unfortunately, lessons from these works do not directly transfer to video self-supervised learning. First, video self-supervised tasks are distinct from those of images as they are designed to understand the temporal dimension of video [14,56,75,82] in addition to the spatial understanding needed in images [9]. Second, video is multi-modal and several methods [4,49,54] are designed to exploit cross or multi-modal understanding, which is again absent in image-based methods. For videos, [20] extends four image-based self-supervised methods to videos and investigate their performance focusing on different pre-training setups. We take inspiration from this and benchmarking works in image self-supervised learning and perform a much-needed study for understanding the generalizability of self-supervised methods for video in relation to different downstream factors.

As our first contribution, we identify the problem of benchmark-sensitivity in video self-supervised learning and examine this sensitivity along the factors of domain, samples, actions and task. As our second contribution, we perform an extensive evaluation which spans a total of over 500 experiments with 9 video self-supervised learning methods across 7 video datasets and 6 video understanding tasks. We find that standard benchmarks in video self-supervised learning do not indicate generalization along the said sensitivity factors and vanilla supervised pre-training outperforms self-supervised pre-training, particularly when domain change is large and there are only a few downstream finetuning samples available. Third, we propose a subset of our experiments as the SEVERE-benchmark for future self-supervised learning methods to benchmark generalization capability. We also discuss the implication of this benchmark for evaluating the generalizability of representations obtained by existing methods as well as the nature of video self-supervised objectives that currently generalize well.

2 Identifying Benchmark Sensitivity

The vast majority of current works in video self-supervised learning evaluate their approach by pre-training on Kinetics-400 [36] and finetuning the learned representation for action recognition on UCF-101[65] and HMDB-51[42]. Some works [4,14,22,31,44,54,56,70,75] also report performance on video retrieval for UCF-101 and HMDB-51 and several recent works [58,59,82] compare linear evaluation performance on Kinetics-400. However, these downstream datasets are very similar to each other and also share many similarities with the pre-training dataset of Kinetics-400. Videos in all three datasets are collected from YouTube and are mostly recorded with a single camera containing a single well-positioned human actor. In terms of class labels, all datasets focus on similar, coarse-grained and mutually exclusive actions with many actions common between pre-training and downstream datasets. Besides all these data similarities, the existing evaluations also ignore a major benefit of self-supervised representation learning for videos, *i.e.* finetuning the representation with only a small amount of data samples and transferring to other video understanding tasks beyond action recognition. Hence, we believe the current benchmark standard is insufficiently equipped to gain a true understanding of where video self-supervised models are successful, as it cannot show the generalizability or the sensitivity of methods to factors such as domain shift, amount of finetuning data samples, action similarity or task shift. In this study, we identify the sensitivity of existing evaluations and thoroughly benchmark self-supervised video learning methods along four sensitivity factors as depicted in Fig. 1.

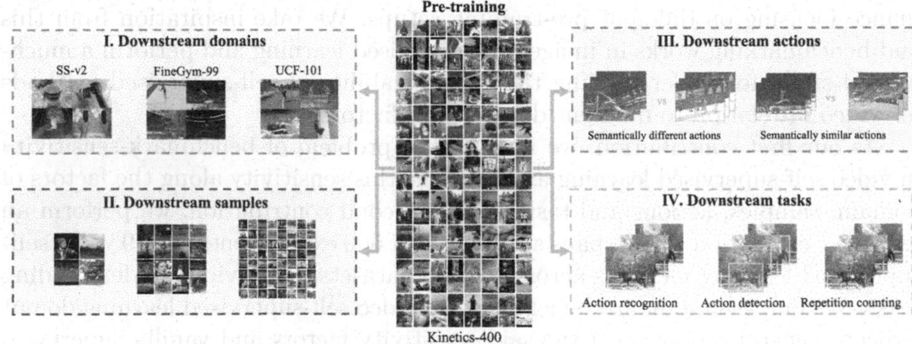

Fig. 1. Benchmark-sensitivity. We evaluate the sensitivity of 9 video self-supervised learning methods along 4 downstream factors which vary from the pre-training source: the domain, the samples, the actions and the task.

I. **Downstream domain.** First, we analyse whether features learned by self-supervised models transfer to datasets that vary in domain with respect to the pre-training dataset.

II. **Downstream samples.** Second, we evaluate the sensitivity of self-supervised methods to the number of downstream samples available for fine-tuning.
III. **Downstream actions.** Third, we investigate if self-supervised methods learn fine-grained features required to recognize semantically similar actions.
IV. **Downstream task.** Finally, we study the sensitivity of video self-supervised methods to the downstream task and question whether self-supervised features can be used beyond action recognition.

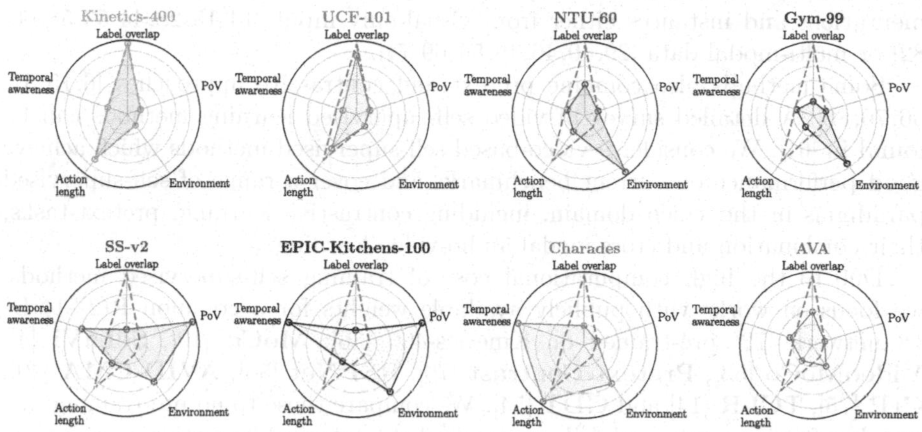

Fig. 2. Video dataset characteristics. Characterizing domain shift in datasets via difference in label overlap, point-of-view (PoV), environment, action length and temporal awareness with Kinetics-400 (shown by dotted line). Kinetics-400 and UCF-101 are highly similar to each other, while datasets like Something-Something-v2, EPIC-Kitchens-100 and Charades have different attributes compared to Kinetics-400.

2.1 Downstream Video Datasets

We evaluate various self-supervised models along our four sensitivity factors on 7 video datasets: **UCF-101** [65], **NTU-60** [62], **FineGym** (Gym-99) [63], **SomethingSomething-v2** (SS-v2) [25], **EPIC-Kitchens-100** (EK-100) [13], **Charades** [64] and **AVA** [27]. They include a considerable variety in video domain, the actions they contain and cover a range of video understanding tasks. To get a sense of the differences between these downstream datasets and the Kinetics-400 source dataset, we summarize their similarity to Kinetics-400 by radar plots in Fig. 2 based on several attributes. *Environment* refers to the variety of settings contained in the dataset. *Point-of-view* is whether a video is recorded from a first-person or third-person viewpoint. *Temporal awareness* defines the extent to which temporal context is required to recognize or detect actions. We quantify this as the point at which performance saturates with increasing temporal context in the input. *Label overlap* is the fraction of actions in a target dataset that are also present in Kinetics-400. *Action length* is the temporal length of the actions in seconds. Details are provided in the appendix.

2.2 Evaluated Self-supervised Video Learning Methods

Self-supervised learning methods in video can be grouped into two categories based on the objective they use: pretext task methods and contrastive learning methods. Pretext task methods use predictive tasks such as solving spatio-temporal jigsaw puzzles [2,32,37], rotation prediction [35], frame and clip order [21,48,68,81,84], video speed [7,11,34,77,85], video completion [45], predicting motion statistics [76], tracking random patches in video frames [75] or audio-visual clustering [3,4,8,30]. Contrastive learning methods discriminate between 'positive' and 'negative' pairs to learn invariances to certain data augmentations and instances either from visual-only input [14,15,28,44,53,58,66, 82] or multi-modal data [29,40,46,49,54,69,71].

Some methods also combine pretext and contrastive approaches [6,15,31, 56,70,88]. A detailed survey of video self-supervised learning methods can be found in [61]. We consider 9 video-based self-supervised methods which achieve good performance on current benchmarks and cover a range of self-supervised paradigms in the video domain, including contrastive learning, pretext-tasks, their combination and cross-modal audio-video learning.

Due to the high computational cost of training self-supervised methods, we focus on works with publicly available weights for a common R(2+1) D-18 network [72] pre-trained on Kinetics-400 [36]: **MoCo** [10], **SeLaVi** [4], **VideoMoCo** [53], **Pretext-Contrast** [70], **RSPNet** [56], **AVID-CMA** [49], **CtP** [75], **TCLR** [14] and **GDT** [54]. We compare these to no pre-training, *i.e.* training from scratch, and fully supervised pre-training for action recognition. It is worth noting that since we use publicly available models we cannot control the exact pre-training setup. There are subtle differences in the training regime for each method, such as the number of epochs, the data augmentations used and the batch size. Details of these differences are provided in the appendix. However, all models use the same backbone and pre-training dataset thus we can evaluate their downstream abilities in exactly the same way. To finetune for downstream tasks we simply attach a task-dependent head at the last layer of the pre-trained R(2+1) D-18 backbone to produce label predictions for the corresponding task. For a fair comparison, we use the same set of hyper-parameters, optimization and pre-processing during the downstream training of each model.

3 Sensitivity Factor I: Downstream Domain

We first investigate to what extent self-supervised methods learn features that are applicable to action recognition in any domain. We evaluate the suite of pre-trained models on UCF-101, NTU-60, Gym-99, SS-v2 and EK-100 for the task of action recognition. It is worth noting that as well as variety in domain, these datasets include variety in the amount of training data (9.5 k–168 k examples) and cardinality of classification (60–300 classes). We attach a single classification layer to the pre-trained backbone and evaluate the models' performance on the downstream task in two settings. First, **full finetuning** where we train the whole network from the initialization of the pre-trained weights. Second, **linear**

evaluation where we train the classification layer only using the frozen features of pre-trained backbones. We follow the standard splits proposed in the original datasets and report video-level top-1 accuracy on the test sets. The details about splits, pre-processing, training for each dataset are provided in the appendix.

Full Finetuning. The left part of Table 1 shows the results of full finetuning. From the results, it is clear that all self-supervised methods are very effective on UCF-101 as there is a significant gap between training from scratch and using self-supervised pre-training. This gap is reduced as the difference between Kinetics-400 and the downstream domain increases. SeLaVi, MoCo and AVID-CMA in particular are evidence of this as these methods suffer when datasets have higher temporal awareness and less label overlap with Kinetics-400. When moving from UCF-101 to NTU-60 and Gym-99 there is a change in the ordering of self-supervised methods. This demonstrates a high performance on UCF-101 does not guarantee a self-supervised model is generalizable to other domains. The change in ranking is even more prominent for SS-v2 and EK-100, which require the most temporal awareness and also shift to a first-person viewpoint. This is particularly noticeable for AVID-CMA. On these datasets, MoCo has similar results to no pre-training, which is evidence that video-specific self-supervised learning methods are needed and that image-based methods are insufficient. Overall, supervised pre-training achieves good performance across the board, outperforming self-supervised methods on the most similar domain (UCF-101) as well as the most dissimilar domains (SS-v2 and EK-100). Amidst the models tested, CtP, RSPNet, VideoMoCo and TCLR stand out as the self-supervised pre-training methods most generalizable to different domains.

Table 1. Sensitivity Factor I: Downstream Domain. Video self-supervised methods evaluated across datasets with increasing domain shift with respect to the source dataset (see Fig. 2). Colors denote relative rankings across methods for each dataset, ranging from low high. The ranking of methods is domain-sensitive for both finetuning and linear classification and becomes less and less correlated with the current UCF-101 benchmark as the domain shift increases.

Pre-training	Finetuning					Linear Evaluation					
	UCF101	NTU60	Gym99	SSv2	EK 100	K 400	UCF101	NTU60	Gym99	SSv2	EK 100
None	77.3	92.9	89.8	57.1	25.7	-	-	-	-	-	-
MoCo	83.3	93.4	90.7	57.1	26.4	34.5	65.4	16.0	21.2	7.4	21.4
VideoMoCo	84.9	94.1	90.3	59.0	43.6	31.0	66.3	51.6	41.6	19.5	25.7
SeLaVi	85.2	92.8	88.9	56.2	33.8	24.1	51.2	15.7	20.2	4.5	22.4
Pretext-Contrast	87.7	93.9	90.5	56.9	34.3	22.4	57.2	17.6	30.0	10.9	20.0
RSPNet	88.7	93.9	91.1	59.0	42.7	46.0	76.6	33.5	32.2	12.5	24.9
AVID-CMA	88.8	94.0	90.4	52.0	29.9	43.5	78.1	53.9	45.1	16.1	22.5
CtP	90.1	94.3	92.0	59.6	42.8	7.6	37.9	22.6	30.6	12.2	20.0
TCLR	90.8	94.1	91.6	59.8	36.2	19.9	63.3	33.5	33.0	10.8	21.8
GDT	91.3	93.9	90.5	58.0	37.3	38.6	75.7	38.2	34.2	11.9	25.3
Supervised	93.9	93.9	92.1	60.8	47.7	65.9	91.7	45.5	42.7	16.6	26.6

Linear Classification. The right part of Table 1 shows the results for linear classification. As with finetuning, the ranking among the self-supervised methods changes as the domain difference between the pre-training and the downstream dataset increases. For example, VideoMoCo ranks lower than GDT and RSPNet for UCF-101 and Kinetics-400 but ranks higher than both for all other datasets. This again demonstrates that performance on UCF-101 does not give a complete picture of a self-supervised model's success. We also observe that linear evaluation on Kinetics-400, as some papers report [58,59,82], has the same issue since it is highly correlated to UCF-101 performance. For UCF-101 and Kinetics-400, self-supervised models with contrastive objectives learn highly discriminative features compared to the non-contrastive models. This can be seen by comparing contrastive models AVID-CMA, GDT and RSPNet to non-contrastive SeLaVi and CtP. From the NTU-60 and Gym-99 results we observe that as the label overlap between the pre-training and the downstream dataset decreases, the performance gap between finetuning and linear evaluation increases considerably. This is true for both supervised and self-supervised pre-training. The most generalizable methods in the linear classification setting are contrastive methods VideoMoCo and AVID-CMA as well as supervised pre-training. Interestingly, there are cases where VideoMoCo and AVID-CMA even outperform supervised pre-training, namely for NTU-60, Gym-99 and SS-v2.

Conclusion. We observe from Table 1 that performance for both UCF-101 finetuning and Kinetics-400 linear evaluation is not indicative of how well a self-supervised video model generalizes to different downstream domains, with the ranking of methods changing substantially across datasets and whether full finetuning or linear classification is used.

4 Sensitivity Factor II: Downstream Samples

The previous section analyzed sensitivity to the downstream domain by evaluating performance on several different datasets. However, finetuning on each of these datasets uses a large number of labeled examples, which means training from scratch already obtains good performance. Not all domains and use cases have ample labeled video examples available, thus we investigate what the impact of the number of finetuning samples is and whether self-supervised methods can be beneficial in scenarios where we have little data to finetune with. We vary the amount of finetuning data, beginning from 1000 videos, sampled uniformly from the classes, and double the amount until we reach the full training set size. We report on four of the downstream datasets from the previous section: UCF-101, NTU-60, Gym-99 and SS-v2. The results are summarized in Fig. 3.

We first observe that the trends in the low data regime are different from those with the full data. The gap between supervised and self-supervised pre-training is much larger in low data settings, particularly for UCF-101 and Gym-99. NTU is an exception, where, with 1000–4000 samples CtP, GDT, AVID-CMA and

TCLR outperform supervised pre-training. As with changes in the downstream domain, change in the amount of downstream examples also causes a change in the ranking of self-supervised models. For example, on UCF-101, RSPNet is much more successful than CtP and TCLR when using only 1000 samples. This is because some self-supervised models benefit more than others from an increased amount of downstream samples. For example, CtP is one of the most generalizable pre-training strategies when finetuning with the full data on UCF-101, Gym-99 and SS-v2, but this is not the case with fewer training samples. Interestingly, GDT is consistently high in the ranking with low amounts of fine-tuning samples. This is likely due to the large number of temporal augmentations it uses, which help the generalization ability when the training data is limited.

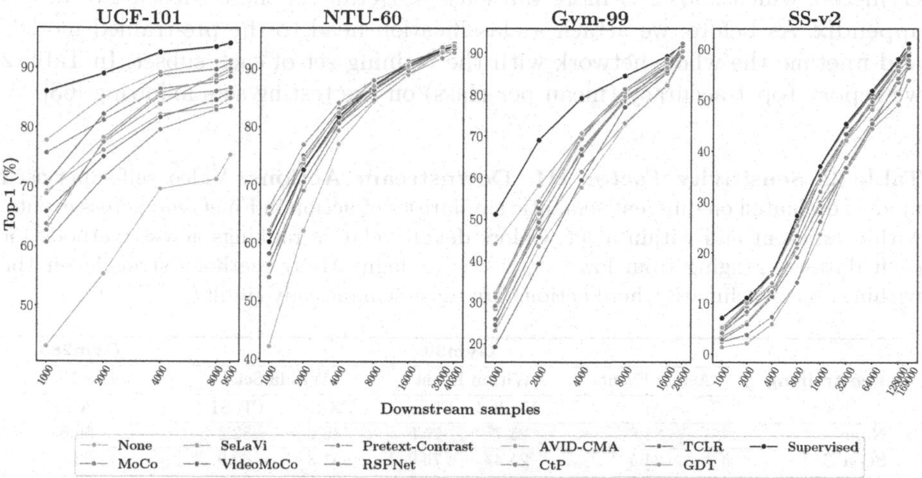

Fig. 3. Sensitivity Factor II: Downstream Samples. Comparison of video self-supervised learning methods using varying number of finetuning samples for four downstream datasets. Both the gap and rank among pre-training methods are sensitive to the number of samples available for finetuning.

> *Conclusion.* We observe from Fig. 3 that video self-supervised models are highly sensitive to the amount of samples available for finetuning, with both the gap and rank between methods changing considerably across sample sizes on each dataset.

5 Sensitivity Factor III: Downstream Actions

As indicated earlier, existing evaluations of self-supervised video learning methods have been limited to coarse-grained action recognition. In this section, we investigate whether current self-supervised tasks are only effective for these types of benchmarks or whether they are able to learn features that are useful for differentiating more challenging and semantically similar actions.

FineGym [63] provides us with an experimental setup to study sensitivity to this factor. The dataset contains different evaluations with varying levels of semantic similarity, namely action recognition *across all events*, *within an event* or *within a set*. Recognition *across all events* uses the whole of Gym-99 containing actions from four gymnastic events. For recognition *within an event* there are two subsets: Vault and Floor containing only actions from these two events. Recognition *within a set* has two subsets namely FX-S1, containing different *leaps-jumps-hops* in Floor, and UB-S1, which consists of types of *circles* in Uneven Bars. We also experiment with the long-tailed version of FineGym, Gym-288, which adds 189 more tail classes. Details of these subsets are in the appendix. As before, we attach a classification head to the pre-trained models and finetune the whole network with the training set of each subset. In Table 2 we report Top-1 accuracy (mean per-class) on the testing sets following [63].

Table 2. Sensitivity Factor III: Downstream Actions. Video self-supervised models evaluated on different semantic similarities of action in FineGym: across events, within an event and within a set. Colors denote relative rankings across methods for each dataset, ranging from low ▭ high. Many methods struggle on the within a set benchmark where actions are most semantically similar.

Pre-training	Gym99					Gym288
	Across Events	Within Event		Within Set		Across Events
	All	Vault	Floor	FX-S1	UB-S1	All
None	84.8	24.7	75.9	46.6	82.3	50.0
SeLaVi	84.5	25.4	76.0	51.3	80.9	52.8
AVID-CMA	85.7	30.4	82.7	68.0	87.3	52.5
VideoMoCo	85.9	28.4	79.5	57.3	83.9	54.1
Pretext-contrast	86.0	28.5	81.4	66.1	86.1	52.7
MoCo	86.5	33.2	83.3	65.0	84.5	55.1
GDT	86.6	36.9	83.6	66.0	83.4	55.4
RSPNet	86.9	33.4	82.7	65.4	83.6	55.2
TCLR	87.7	29.8	84.3	60.7	84.7	55.4
CtP	88.1	26.8	86.2	79.1	88.8	56.5
Supervised	88.6	37.7	86.1	79.0	87.1	58.4

Performance of self-supervised methods varies considerably across downstream actions. The methods that perform best on Gym-99 often do not generalize well to the subsets with higher semantic similarity among actions. This is particularly noticeable for RSPNet and TCLR which drop in the ranking for the within-set subsets. All self-supervised methods, except GDT, struggle on Vault, likely due to the intense motions. Surprisingly, MoCo performs reasonably well when actions are more semantically similar, and is comparable to GDT and RSPNet. The best self-supervised method for subsets with high semantic similarity is CtP. This is especially evident from FX-S1 where it outperforms the second-best self-supervised method, AVID-CMA, by 12%. As with downstream domain and samples, supervised pre-training generalizes better than self-supervised methods across downstream actions with only CtP achieving comparable performance.

Table 2 also compares balanced Gym-99 with long-tailed Gym-288. We observe that self-supervised methods are not robust to this change in distribution, with the gap in performance with respect to supervised pre-training increasing. However, the ranking remains consistent, meaning the performance on the balanced set is generally indicative of the performance on the long-tailed set.

Conclusion. Most self-supervised methods in Table 2 are sensitive to the actions present in the downstream dataset and do not generalize well to more semantically similar actions. This further emphasizes the need for proper evaluation of self-supervised methods beyond current coarse-grained action classification.

Table 3. Sensitivity Factor IV: Downstream Tasks. Transferability of self-supervised video learning methods across video understanding tasks. Colors denote relative rankings across methods for each task, ranging from low to high. Note that for repetition counting lower (error) is better. Self-supervised features are transferable to different downstream tasks when the domain shift is low, but struggle when there is also a domain shift. Action recognition on UCF-101 is not a good proxy for self-supervised video learning use cases where a downstream domain- and task-shift can be expected.

Pre-training	Task-shift within domain				Task-shift out of domain	
	Action Recognition	Action Detection	Repetition Counting	Arrow of Time	Multi-label Recognition	Action Detection
None	77.3	0.327	0.217	56.1	7.9	7.4
MoCo	83.3	0.416	0.208	80.3	8.3	11.7
VideoMoCo	84.9	0.440	0.185	72.9	10.5	13.1
SeLaVi	85.2	0.419	0.162	77.4	8.4	10.2
Pretext-contrast	87.7	0.462	0.164	77.2	8.9	12.7
RSPNet	88.7	0.467	0.145	87.0	9.0	14.1
AVID-CMA	88.8	0.435	0.148	83.3	8.2	10.0
CtP	90.1	0.465	0.178	77.1	9.6	10.0
TCLR	90.8	0.476	0.142	85.6	12.2	10.8
GDT	91.3	0.463	0.123	76.4	8.5	12.6
Supervised	93.9	0.482	0.132	77.0	23.5	17.9

6 Sensitivity Factor IV: Downstream Tasks

The fourth factor we investigate is whether self-supervised video models are sensitive to the downstream task or whether features learned by self-supervised models are useful to video understanding tasks beyond actionrecognition.

We evaluate this in two ways. First, we keep the domain fixed and evaluate different tasks in a domain similar to the pre-training dataset. We also explore further tasks by changing the domain and seeing how these two factors interplay.

Task-Shift Within Domain. We consider three different tasks which are all defined for UCF-101: spatio-temporal action detection [39], repetition counting [87] and arrow-of-time prediction [23]. Using UCF-101 allows us to keep the domain fixed across tasks and eliminates the impact of domain shift. Note that each task uses a different subset of the full UCF-101 dataset, however, the domain remains consistent. For each task, we use the R(2+1)D-18 networks as the pre-trained backbones as before and attach task-dependent heads. We report mean Average Precision for spatio-temporal localization [47], mean absolute counting error for repetition counting [87] and classification accuracy for arrow-of-time prediction [23, 79]. Further details are in the appendix.

From the results in Table 3, we observe that self-supervised learning is beneficial to tasks beyond action recognition, with almost all methods outperforming training from scratch on spatio-temporal action detection, repetition counting and arrow-of-time prediction. Action detection results are well correlated with action recognition. Repetition counting and arrow-of-time have less correlation with action recognition, suggesting that the current benchmark on UCF-101 action recognition by itself is not a good indication of how well self-supervised methods generalize to other tasks. For repetition counting and arrow-of-time prediction, some methods perform comparably to or outperform supervised pre-training. Notably, RSPNet and TCLR generalize the best across these tasks, with GDT also performing well on repetition counting. CtP ranks high on action recognition and detection but performs modestly for repetition counting. This shows that different methods have different task sensitivity, so a thorough evaluation along downstream tasks is needed.

Task-Shift Out of Domain. We also evaluate how well the self-supervised models generalize when both the domain and the task change. We do so with two popular video understanding benchmarks: long-term multi-label classification on Charades [64] and short-term spatio-temporal action detection on AVA [27]. For both, we follow the setup and training procedure from [19] with R(2+1)D-18 models as the pre-trained backbone and we measure performance in mean Average Precision. Details are in the appendix.

From the results in Table 3, we observe that supervised pre-training is far more generalizable than all self supervised methods, which all struggle considerably when both the domain and task change. For long-term action classification on Charades, TCLR is slightly better than other methods. On AVA, RSPNet is the best performing self-supervised method with VideoMoCo second. In Sect. 3, we earlier observed that these were two of the methods more robust to domain shift suggesting that this factor is key to success on AVA.

Conclusion. The results in Table 3 reveal that action classification performance on UCF-101 is mildly indicative for transferability of self-supervised features to other tasks on UCF-101. However, when methods pre-trained on Kinetics-400 are confronted with a domain change in addition to the task change, UCF-101 results are no longer a good proxy and the gap between supervised and self-supervised pre-training is large.

7 SEVERE-Benchmark

As evident from the results in previous sections, current video self-supervised methods are benchmark-sensitive to the four factors we have studied. Based on our findings, we propose the SEVERE-benchmark (SEnsitivity of VidEo REpresentations) for use in future works to more thoroughly evaluate new video self-supervised methods for generalization along the four sensitivity factors we have examined. Since we do not expect future works to run all the experiments from our study, we create a subset of experiments that are indicative benchmarks for each sensitivity factor and realistic to run. We summarize the benchmark composition in Table 4 and detail its motivation per factor. Standard deviations for the results we obtain on this benchmark can be found in the appendix.

Table 4. Proposed SEVERE-benchmark for evaluating video self-supervised methods for generalization along downstream domains, samples, actions and tasks.

Pre-training	Existing	SEVERE-benchmark							
		Domains		Samples		Actions		Tasks	
	UCF101	SS-v2	Gym-99	UCF (10^3)	Gym-99 (10^3)	FX-S1	UB-S1	UCF-RC	Charades-MLC
None	77.3	57.1	89.8	38.3	22.7	46.6	82.3	0.217	7.9
MoCo	83.3	57.1	90.7	60.4	30.9	65.0	84.5	0.208	8.3
VideoMoCo	84.9	59.0	90.3	65.4	20.6	57.3	83.9	0.185	10.5
SeLaVi	85.2	56.2	88.9	69.0	30.2	51.3	80.9	0.162	8.4
Pretext-Contrast	87.7	56.9	90.5	64.6	27.5	66.1	86.1	0.164	8.9
RSPNet	88.7	59.0	91.1	74.7	32.2	65.4	83.6	0.145	9.0
AVID-CMA	88.8	52.0	90.4	68.2	33.4	68.0	87.3	0.148	8.2
CtP	90.1	59.6	92.0	61.0	32.9	79.1	88.8	0.178	9.6
TCLR	90.8	59.8	91.6	72.6	26.3	60.7	84.7	0.142	12.2
GDT	91.3	58.0	90.5	78.4	45.6	66.0	83.4	0.123	8.5
Supervised	93.9	60.8	92.1	86.6	51.3	79.0	87.1	0.132	23.5

Downstream Domain. To measure a self-supervised model's domain sensitivity we recommend using Something-Something-v2 and FineGym-99. These two datasets come from domains distinct to Kinetics-400 and UCF-101 and also each other. FineGym-99 evaluates a model's ability to generalize to datasets with less distinctive backgrounds where there are few actions in common with Kinetics-400. SS-v2 evaluates the generalizability to actions that require high temporal awareness as well as the shift to a first-person viewpoint. It is evident from Table 4 that there are significant rank changes between UCF-101, Gym-99 and SS-v2 thus these three datasets provide a challenging subset for future methods.

Downstream Samples. For the sample sensitivity, we recommend using 1000 samples on UCF-101 and Gym-99. Using 1000 samples showed the most dramatic difference from the full dataset size particularly for these datasets where there is a considerable gap between self-supervised and supervised pre-training as well as considerable rank change among the methods.

Downstream Actions. To test generalizability to recognizing semantically similar actions, we recommend evaluating the two within-set granularities of Gym-99 *i.e.* FX-S1 and UB-S1. Both of these subsets have high semantic similarity between actions with methods currently struggling to generalize to both of these subsets as can be seen in Table 4. There is also a significant gap between supervised and most self-supervised pre-training methods for FX-S1, highlighting the potential for future works in this area.

Downstream Task. To evaluate the task sensitivity, we recommend using repetition counting on UCF-101 and multi-label classification on Charades. Repetition counting on UCF-101 highlights different strengths to action recognition as it allows investigation of a model's ability to generalize to a task that requires more temporal understanding without measuring the impact of the domain. We recommend multi-label classification on Charades as it is currently a very challenging task for self-supervised models and allows the combination of domain and task shift to be investigated. Code to compare on the SEVERE-benchmark is available at https://github.com/fmthoker/SEVERE-BENCHMARK.

8 Observations, Limitations and Recommendations

Observations. We hope that our study and resulting benchmark provides a helpful insight for future research to design novel self-supervised methods for generalizable video representation learning. From the benchmark results in Table 4, we observe that:

(i) There is no clear winner as different methods stand out in different downstream settings.
(ii) Supervised pre-training is dominant across all sensitivity factors, especially when the number of available downstream samples are limited and when there is a change in both the downstream domain and the downstream task.
(iii) Self-supervised contrastive methods that explicitly encourage features to be distinct across the temporal dimension transfer well. This is visible from the consistent performance of GDT, TCLR and RSPNet across different sensitivity factors.
(iv) Learning certain temporal invariances may prevent generalizability to temporal or fine-grained benchmarks. This is evident from GDT's performance on SS-v2 and UB-S1. These benchmarks require distinction between actions such as *moving something left* vs. *moving something right* in SS-v2 and *giant circle forwards* vs. *giant circle backwards* in UB-S1. The invariance to temporal reversal learned by GDT impacts its ability to recognize such

actions. Similarly, MoCo outperforming VideoMoCo on the FX-S1 and UB-S1 Gym-99 subsets suggests that invariance to frame dropout in VideMoCo can harm the performance on highly similar actions.

(v) Pretext-tasks specific to videos can be effective to learn more fine-grained features. CtP generalizes well both to different domains where the background is less indicative of the action and to more semantically similar actions. The pretext task is to track and estimate the position and size of image patches moving in a sequence of video frames. Such a formulation requires the network to learn to follow moving targets and ignore the static background information. CtP's generalization success demonstrates that contrastive learning is not the only way forward for self-supervised video representation learning.

(vi) Figure 4 shows the feature similarity on Kinetics using centered kernel alignment [52] between supervised pre-training and the best self-supervised methods *i.e.* GDT, RSPNet, TCLR, CtP. This figure illustrates that contrastive methods seem to imitate supervised pre-training as the correlation between supervised pre-training and the three contrastive methods (RSPNet, GDT and TCLR) is high. This explains the good performance of these methods on UCF-101 with 1000 examples. By contrast, CtP's features are far away from supervised pre-training. This is interesting because CtP generalizes well to new domains and actions, it shows that good generalization capability can be obtained without imitating supervised pre-training.

Limitations. While our study has highlighted the benchmark sensitivity of video self-supervised learning across four factors, there are many more factors that we do not consider in this work. Due to computational limits, we keep the source dataset fixed as Kinetics-400 and use publicly available pre-trained models. This means there is variability in the exact pre-training setup such as the spatial data augmentations that are used by each model. We hope that future works will explore impact of such pretraining factors as well as the impact of pre-training on other large-scale datasets such as Ego4D [26] for the generalization of video self-supervised models. Another limitation of our study is that we

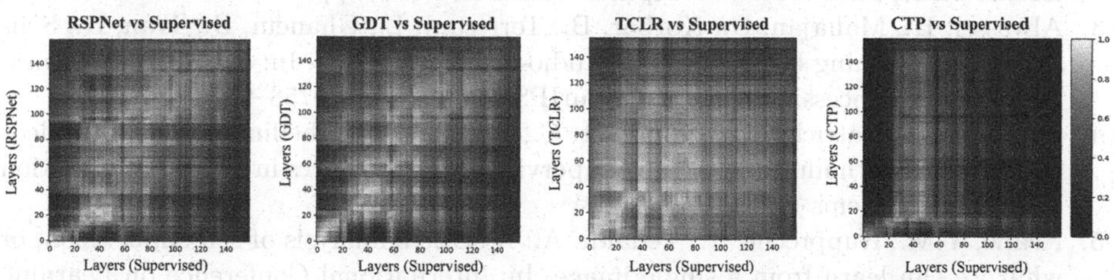

Fig. 4. Representation similarity between features of top self-supervised methods and supervised pre-training on Kinetics-400 validation set (using centered kernel alignment [52]). Contrastive methods have a high correlation with supervised pretraining, while CtP's features are far away. Thus, showing potential for both imitating supervised learning as well as learning features distinct to it.

only consider a fixed R(2+1)D-18 backbone, which is currently one of the most commonly used in video self-supervised learning. This allows our comparison between methods to be fair, however, it does limit the ability of methods to perform well on datasets such as EPIC-Kitchens-100. Another factor that could be explored further is the task. We have considered a selection of various video understanding tasks centered around human actions. However, there are many more video understanding tasks that could be explored such as human centric tasks like action anticipation [13] and temporal action detection[13], as well as non-human centric tasks like animal behavior analysis [18,51,67], multi-object tracking [55] and visual grounding [67].

Recommendations. Based on the results and our observations, we have several recommendations for future works in video self-supervised learning. (i) Our study has highlighted the need for more focus on generalizability of self-supervised learning methods, particularly along the domain and dataset size factors. (ii) Distinguishing across the temporal dimension is effective and is a useful direction to pursue further for generalizability. (iii) Pretext-tasks like the one used in CtP are good for the generalizability to domain and action, thus designing new video specific pretext tasks is a promising direction. This could also be combined with contrastive learning tasks to gain the benefits of both types of learning.

Acknowledgements. This work is part of the research programme Perspectief EDL with project number P16-25 project 3, which is financed by the Dutch Research Council (NWO) domain Applied and Engineering/ Sciences (TTW).

References

1. Afouras, T., Owens, A., Chung, J.S., Zisserman, A.: Self-supervised learning of audio-visual objects from video. In: Vedaldi, A., Bischof, H., Brox, T., Frahm, J.-M. (eds.) ECCV 2020. LNCS, vol. 12363, pp. 208–224. Springer, Cham (2020). https://doi.org/10.1007/978-3-030-58523-5_13
2. Ahsan, U., Madhok, R., Essa, I.: Video jigsaw: Unsupervised learning of spatiotemporal context for video action recognition. In: Proceedings of the IEEE Winter Conference on Applications of Computer Vision (WACV), pp. 179–189. IEEE (2019)
3. Alwassel, H., Mahajan, D., Korbar, B., Torresani, L., Ghanem, B., Tran, D.: Self-supervised learning by cross-modal audio-video clustering. In: Advances in Neural Information Processing Systems (NeurIPS), vol. 33, pp. 9758–9770 (2020)
4. Asano, Y.M., Patrick, M., Rupprecht, C., Vedaldi, A.: Labelling unlabelled videos from scratch with multi-modal self-supervision. In: Advances in Neural Information Processing Systems (NeurIPS) (2020)
5. Asano, Y.M., Rupprecht, C., Vedaldi, A.: A critical analysis of self-supervision, or what we can learn from a single image. In: International Conference on Learning Representations (ICLR) (2020)
6. Bai, Y., et al.: Can temporal information help with contrastive self-supervised learning? arXiv preprint arXiv:2011.13046 (2020)

7. Benaim, S., et al.: Speednet: Learning the speediness in videos. In: Proceedings of the IEEE/CVF Conference on Computer Vision and Pattern Recognition (CVPR), pp. 9922–9931 (2020)
8. Chen, B., et al.: Multimodal clustering networks for self-supervised learning from unlabeled videos. In: Proceedings of the IEEE/CVF International Conference on Computer Vision (CVPR), pp. 8012–8021 (2021)
9. Chen, T., Kornblith, S., Norouzi, M., Hinton, G.: A simple framework for contrastive learning of visual representations. In: Proceedings of the International Conference on Machine Learning (PMLR) (2020)
10. Chen, X., Fan, H., Girshick, R., He, K.: Improved baselines with momentum contrastive learning. arXiv preprint arXiv:2003.04297 (2020)
11. Cho, H., Kim, T., Chang, H.J., Hwang, W.: Self-supervised spatio-temporal representation learning using variable playback speed prediction. IEEE Access **9**, 79562–79571 (2021)
12. Cole, E., Yang, X., Wilber, K., Mac Aodha, O., Belongie, S.: When does contrastive visual representation learning work? In: Proceedings of the IEEE/CVF Conference on Computer Vision and Pattern Recognition (CVPR) (2022)
13. Damen, D., et al.: Rescaling egocentric vision: Collection, pipeline and challenges for EPIC-KITCHENS-100. Int. J. Comput. Vis. (IJCV) **130**, 33–55 (2021)
14. Dave, I., Gupta, R., Rizve, M.N., Shah, M.: Tclr: Temporal contrastive learning for video representation. In: Computer Vision and Image Understanding (CVIU), p. 103406 (2022)
15. Diba, A., et al.: Vi2clr: Video and image for visual contrastive learning of representation. In: Proceedings of the IEEE/CVF International Conference on Computer Vision (ICCV), pp. 1502–1512 (2021)
16. Ericsson, L., Gouk, H., Hospedales, T.M.: How well do self-supervised models transfer? In: Proceedings of the IEEE/CVF Conference on Computer Vision and Pattern Recognition (CVPR), pp. 5414–5423 (2021)
17. Ericsson, L., Gouk, H., Hospedales, T.M.: Why do self-supervised models transfer? investigating the impact of invariance on downstream tasks. arXiv preprint arXiv:2111.11398 (2021)
18. Eyjolfsdottir, E., et al.: Detecting social actions of fruit flies. In: Fleet, D., Pajdla, T., Schiele, B., Tuytelaars, T. (eds.) ECCV 2014. LNCS, vol. 8690, pp. 772–787. Springer, Cham (2014). https://doi.org/10.1007/978-3-319-10605-2_50
19. Feichtenhofer, C., Fan, H., Malik, J., He, K.: Slowfast networks for video recognition. In: Proceedings of the IEEE/CVF International Conference on Computer Vision (ICCV), pp. 6201–6210 (2019)
20. Feichtenhofer, C., Fan, H., Xiong, B., Girshick, R., He, K.: A large-scale study on unsupervised spatiotemporal representation learning. In: Proceedings of the IEEE/CVF Conference on Computer Vision and Pattern Recognition (CVPR), pp. 3299–3309 (2021)
21. Fernando, B., Bilen, H., Gavves, E., Gould, S.: Self-supervised video representation learning with odd-one-out networks. In: Proceedings of the IEEE Conference on Computer Vision and Pattern Recognition (CVPR), pp. 3636–3645 (2017)
22. Gavrilyuk, K., Jain, M., Karmanov, I., Snoek, C.G.M.: Motion-augmented self-training for video recognition at smaller scale. In: Proceedings of the IEEE/CVF International Conference on Computer Vision (ICCV), pp. 10429–10438 (2021)
23. Ghodrati, A., Gavves, E., Snoek, C.G.M.: Video time: Properties, encoders and evaluation. In: British Machine Vision Conference (BMVC) (2018)

24. Goyal, P., Mahajan, D., Gupta, A., Misra, I.: Scaling and benchmarking self-supervised visual representation learning. In: Proceedings of the IEEE/CVF International Conference on Computer Vision (ICCV), pp. 6391–6400 (2019)
25. Goyal, R., et al.: The "something something" video database for learning and evaluating visual common sense. In: Proceedings of the IEEE International Conference on Computer Vision (ICCV), pp. 5842–5850 (2017)
26. Grauman, K., et al.: Ego4d: Around the World in 3,000 Hours of Egocentric Video. In: Proceedings of the IEEE/CVF Conference on Computer Vision and Pattern Recognition (CVPR) (2022)
27. Gu, C., et al.: Ava: A video dataset of spatio-temporally localized atomic visual actions. In: Proceedings of the IEEE Conference on Computer Vision and Pattern Recognition (CVPR) (2018)
28. Han, T., Xie, W., Zisserman, A.: Video representation learning by dense predictive coding. In: Proceedings of the IEEE/CVF International Conference on Computer Vision Workshops (2019)
29. Han, T., Xie, W., Zisserman, A.: Self-supervised co-training for video representation learning. In: Advances in Neural Information Processing Systems (NeurIPS) (2020)
30. Hu, D., Nie, F., Li, X.: Deep multimodal clustering for unsupervised audiovisual learning. In: Proceedings of the IEEE/CVF Conference on Computer Vision and Pattern Recognition (CVPR), pp. 9248–9257 (2019)
31. Huang, D., et al.: Ascnet: Self-supervised video representation learning with appearance-speed consistency. In: Proceedings of the IEEE/CVF International Conference on Computer Vision (ICCV), pp. 8096–8105 (2021)
32. Huo, Y., et al.: Self-supervised video representation learning with constrained spatiotemporal jigsaw. In: Proceedings of the Thirtieth International Joint Conference on Artificial Intelligence (IJCAI) (2021)
33. Islam, A., Chen, C.F.R., Panda, R., Karlinsky, L., Radke, R., Feris, R.: A broad study on the transferability of visual representations with contrastive learning. In: Proceedings of the IEEE/CVF International Conference on Computer Vision (ICCV), pp. 8845–8855 (2021)
34. Jenni, S., Meishvili, G., Favaro, P.: Video representation learning by recognizing temporal transformations. In: Vedaldi, A., Bischof, H., Brox, T., Frahm, J.-M. (eds.) ECCV 2020. LNCS, vol. 12373, pp. 425–442. Springer, Cham (2020). https://doi.org/10.1007/978-3-030-58604-1_26
35. Jing, L., Yang, X., Liu, J., Tian, Y.: Self-supervised spatiotemporal feature learning via video rotation prediction. arXiv preprint arXiv:1811.11387 (2018)
36. Kay, W., et al.: The kinetics human action video dataset. arXiv preprint arXiv:1705.06950 (2017)
37. Kim, D., Cho, D., Kweon, I.S.: Self-supervised video representation learning with space-time cubic puzzles. In: Proceedings of the AAAI Conference on Artificial Intelligence, pp. 8545–8552 (2019)
38. Kolesnikov, A., Zhai, X., Beyer, L.: Revisiting self-supervised visual representation learning. In: Proceedings of the IEEE/CVF Conference on Computer Vision and Pattern Recognition (CVPR), pp. 1920–1929 (2019)
39. Köpüklü, O., Wei, X., Rigoll, G.: You only watch once: A unified CNN architecture for real-time spatiotemporal action localization. arXiv preprint arXiv:1911.06644 (2019)
40. Korbar, B., Tran, D., Torresani, L.: Cooperative learning of audio and video models from self-supervised synchronization. In: Advances in Neural Information Processing Systems (NeurIPS), vol. 31 (2018)

41. Kotar, K., Ilharco, G., Schmidt, L., Ehsani, K., Mottaghi, R.: Contrasting contrastive self-supervised representation learning pipelines. In: Proceedings of the IEEE/CVF International Conference on Computer Vision (ICCV), pp. 9949–9959 (2021)
42. Kuehne, H., Jhuang, H., Garrote, E., Poggio, T., Serre, T.: HMDB: a large video database for human motion recognition. In: Proceedings of the International Conference on Computer Vision (ICCV) (2011)
43. Li, Y., Li, Y., Vasconcelos, N.: RESOUND: Towards action recognition without representation bias. In: Ferrari, V., Hebert, M., Sminchisescu, C., Weiss, Y. (eds.) ECCV 2018. LNCS, vol. 11210, pp. 520–535. Springer, Cham (2018). https://doi.org/10.1007/978-3-030-01231-1_32
44. Lin, Y., Guo, X., Lu, Y.: Self-supervised video representation learning with meta-contrastive network. In: Proceedings of the IEEE/CVF International Conference on Computer Vision (ICCV), pp. 8239–8249 (2021)
45. Luo, D., et al.: Video cloze procedure for self-supervised spatio-temporal learning. In: Proceedings of the AAAI Conference on Artificial Intelligence, pp. 11701–11708 (2020)
46. Ma, S., Zeng, Z., McDuff, D., Song, Y.: Active contrastive learning of audio-visual video representations. In: International Conference on Learning Representations (ICLR) (2021)
47. Mettes, P., van Gemert, J.C., Snoek, C.G.M.: Spot On: Action localization from pointly-supervised proposals. In: Leibe, B., Matas, J., Sebe, N., Welling, M. (eds.) ECCV 2016. LNCS, vol. 9909, pp. 437–453. Springer, Cham (2016). https://doi.org/10.1007/978-3-319-46454-1_27
48. Misra, I., Zitnick, C.L., Hebert, M.: Shuffle and learn: unsupervised learning using temporal order verification. In: Leibe, B., Matas, J., Sebe, N., Welling, M. (eds.) ECCV 2016. LNCS, vol. 9905, pp. 527–544. Springer, Cham (2016). https://doi.org/10.1007/978-3-319-46448-0_32
49. Morgado, P., Vasconcelos, N., Misra, I.: Audio-visual instance discrimination with cross-modal agreement. In: Proceedings of the IEEE/CVF Conference on Computer Vision and Pattern Recognition (CVPR) (2021)
50. Newell, A., Deng, J.: How useful is self-supervised pretraining for visual tasks? In: Proceedings of the IEEE/CVF Conference on Computer Vision and Pattern Recognition (CVPR) (2020)
51. Ng, X.L., Ong, K.E., Zheng, Q., Ni, Y., Yeo, S.Y., Liu, J.: Animal kingdom: A large and diverse dataset for animal behavior understanding. In: Proceedings of the IEEE/CVF Conference on Computer Vision and Pattern Recognition (CVPR), pp. 19023–19034 (2022)
52. Nguyen, T., Raghu, M., Kornblith, S.: Do wide and deep networks learn the same things? uncovering how neural network representations vary with width and depth. In: International Conference on Learning Representations (ICLR) (2021)
53. Pan, T., Song, Y., Yang, T., Jiang, W., Liu, W.: Videomoco: Contrastive video representation learning with temporally adversarial examples. In: Proceedings of the IEEE/CVF Conference on Computer Vision and Pattern Recognition (CVPR), pp. 11205–11214 (2021)
54. Patrick, M., et al.: Multi-modal self-supervision from generalized data transformations. In: International Conference on Computer Vision (ICCV) (2021)
55. Pedersen, M., Haurum, J.B., Bengtson, S.H., Moeslund, T.B.: 3d-zef: A 3d zebrafish tracking benchmark dataset. In: Proceedings of the IEEE/CVF Conference on Computer Vision and Pattern Recognition, pp. 2426–2436 (2020)

56. Peihao, C., et al.: Rspnet: Relative speed perception for unsupervised video representation learning. In: The AAAI Conference on Artificial Intelligence (AAAI) (2021)
57. Piergiovanni, A., Angelova, A., Ryoo, M.S.: Evolving losses for unsupervised video representation learning. In: Proceedings of the IEEE/CVF Conference on Computer Vision and Pattern Recognition (CVPR), pp. 133–142 (2020)
58. Qian, R., et al.: Spatiotemporal contrastive video representation learning. In: Proceedings of the IEEE/CVF Conference on Computer Vision and Pattern Recognition (CVPR), pp. 6964–6974 (2021)
59. Recasens, A., et al.: Broaden your views for self-supervised video learning. In: Proceedings of the IEEE/CVF International Conference on Computer Vision (ICCV), pp. 1255–1265 (2021)
60. Sariyildiz, M.B., Kalantidis, Y., Larlus, D., Alahari, K.: Concept generalization in visual representation learning. In: Proceedings of the IEEE/CVF International Conference on Computer Vision (ICCV), pp. 9629–9639 (2021)
61. Schiappa, M.C., Rawat, Y.S., Shah, M.: Self-supervised learning for videos: A survey. arXiv preprint arXiv:2207.00419 (2022)
62. Shahroudy, A., Liu, J., Ng, T.T., Wang, G.: Ntu rgb+ d: A large scale dataset for 3d human activity analysis. In: Proceedings of the IEEE Conference on Computer Vision and Pattern Recognition (CVPR), pp. 1010–1019 (2016)
63. Shao, D., Zhao, Y., Dai, B., Lin, D.: Finegym: A hierarchical video dataset for fine-grained action understanding. In: Proceedings of the IEEE Conference on Computer Vision and Pattern Recognition (CVPR) (2020)
64. Sigurdsson, G.A., Varol, G., Wang, X., Farhadi, A., Laptev, I., Gupta, A.: Hollywood in homes: crowdsourcing data collection for activity understanding. In: Leibe, B., Matas, J., Sebe, N., Welling, M. (eds.) ECCV 2016. LNCS, vol. 9905, pp. 510–526. Springer, Cham (2016). https://doi.org/10.1007/978-3-319-46448-0_31
65. Soomro, K., Zamir, A.R., Shah, M.: Ucf101: A dataset of 101 human actions classes from videos in the wild. arXiv preprint arXiv:1212.0402 (2012)
66. Sun, C., Nagrani, A., Tian, Y., Schmid, C.: Composable augmentation encoding for video representation learning. In: Proceedings of the IEEE/CVF International Conference on Computer Vision (ICCV), pp. 8834–8844 (2021)
67. Sun, J.J., et al.: The multi-agent behavior dataset: Mouse dyadic social interactions. In: Vanschoren, J., Yeung, S. (eds.) Proceedings of the Neural Information Processing Systems Track on Datasets and Benchmarks (2021)
68. Suzuki, T., Itazuri, T., Hara, K., Kataoka, H.: Learning spatiotemporal 3d convolution with video order self-supervision. In: Leal-Taixé, L., Roth, S. (eds.) ECCV 2018. LNCS, vol. 11130, pp. 590–598. Springer, Cham (2019). https://doi.org/10.1007/978-3-030-11012-3_45
69. Tao, L., Wang, X., Yamasaki, T.: Self-supervised video representation learning using inter-intra contrastive framework. In: Proceedings of the 28th ACM International Conference on Multimedia (ACM MM), pp. 2193–2201 (2020)
70. Tao, L., Wang, X., Yamasaki, T.: Pretext-contrastive learning: Toward good practices in self-supervised video representation leaning. arXiv preprint arXiv:2010.15464 (2021)
71. Thoker, F.M., Doughty, H., Snoek, C.: Skeleton-contrastive 3d action representation learning. In: Proceedings of the 29th ACM International Conference on Multimedia, (ACM MM) (2021)

72. Tran, D., Wang, H., Torresani, L., Ray, J., LeCun, Y., Paluri, M.: A closer look at spatiotemporal convolutions for action recognition. In: Proceedings of the IEEE Conference on Computer Vision and Pattern Recognition (CVPR), pp. 6450–6459 (2018)
73. Van Horn, G., Cole, E., Beery, S., Wilber, K., Belongie, S., Mac Aodha, O.: Benchmarking representation learning for natural world image collections. In: Proceedings of the IEEE/CVF Conference on Computer Vision and Pattern Recognition (CVPR), pp. 12884–12893 (2021)
74. Wallace, B., Hariharan, B.: Extending and analyzing self-supervised learning across domains. In: Vedaldi, A., Bischof, H., Brox, T., Frahm, J.-M. (eds.) ECCV 2020. LNCS, vol. 12371, pp. 717–734. Springer, Cham (2020). https://doi.org/10.1007/978-3-030-58574-7_43
75. Wang, G., Zhou, Y., Luo, C., Xie, W., Zeng, W., Xiong, Z.: Unsupervised visual representation learning by tracking patches in video. In: Proceedings of the IEEE Conference on Computer Vision and Pattern Recognition (CVPR) (2021)
76. Wang, J., Jiao, J., Bao, L., He, S., Liu, Y., Liu, W.: Self-supervised spatio-temporal representation learning for videos by predicting motion and appearance statistics. In: Proceedings of the IEEE/CVF Conference on Computer Vision and Pattern Recognition (CVPR), pp. 4006–4015 (2019)
77. Wang, J., Jiao, J., Liu, Y.-H.: Self-supervised video representation learning by pace prediction. In: Vedaldi, A., Bischof, H., Brox, T., Frahm, J.-M. (eds.) ECCV 2020. LNCS, vol. 12362, pp. 504–521. Springer, Cham (2020). https://doi.org/10.1007/978-3-030-58520-4_30
78. Wang, J., et al.: Removing the background by adding the background: Towards background robust self-supervised video representation learning. In: Proceedings of the IEEE/CVF Conference on Computer Vision and Pattern Recognition (CVPR) (2021)
79. Wei, D., Lim, J.J., Zisserman, A., Freeman, W.T.: Learning and using the arrow of time. In: Proceedings of the IEEE Conference on Computer Vision and Pattern Recognition (CVPR), pp. 8052–8060 (2018)
80. Xiao, F., Tighe, J., Modolo, D.: Modist: Motion distillation for self-supervised video representation learning. arXiv preprint arXiv:2106.09703 (2021)
81. Xu, D., Xiao, J., Zhao, Z., Shao, J., Xie, D., Zhuang, Y.: Self-supervised spatiotemporal learning via video clip order prediction. In: Proceedings of the IEEE/CVF Conference on Computer Vision and Pattern Recognition (CVPR), pp. 10334–10343 (2019)
82. Yang, C., Xu, Y., Dai, B., Zhou, B.: Video representation learning with visual tempo consistency. arXiv preprint arXiv:2006.15489 (2020)
83. Yang, X., He, X., Liang, Y., Yang, Y., Zhang, S., Xie, P.: Transfer learning or self-supervised learning? a tale of two pretraining paradigms. arXiv preprint arXiv:2007.04234 (2020)
84. Yao, T., Zhang, Y., Qiu, Z., Pan, Y., Mei, T.: Seco: Exploring sequence supervision for unsupervised representation learning. In: AAAI, vol. 2, p. 7 (2021)
85. Yao, Y., Liu, C., Luo, D., Zhou, Y., Ye, Q.: Video playback rate perception for self-supervised spatio-temporal representation learning. In: Proceedings of the IEEE/CVF Conference on Computer Vision and Pattern Recognition (CVPR), pp. 6548–6557 (2020)
86. Zhai, X., et al.: A large-scale study of representation learning with the visual task adaptation benchmark. arXiv preprint arXiv:1910.04867 (2019)

87. Zhang, H., Xu, X., Han, G., He, S.: Context-aware and scale-insensitive temporal repetition counting. In: Proceedings of the IEEE/CVF Conference on Computer Vision and Pattern Recognition (CVPR) (2020)
88. Zhang, Y., et al.: Contrastive spatio-temporal pretext learning for self-supervised video representation. In: Proceedings of the AAAI Conference on Artificial Intelligenc (2022)

A Sliding Window Scheme for Online Temporal Action Localization

Young Hwi Kim, Hyolim Kang, and Seon Joo Kim(✉)

Yonsei University, 50 Yonsei-ro, Seodaemun-gu, Seoul, Republic of Korea
{younghwikim,hyolimkang,seonjookim}@yonsei.ac.kr

Abstract. Most online video understanding tasks aim to immediately process each streaming frame and output predictions frame-by-frame. For extension to instance-level predictions of existing online video tasks, Online Temporal Action Localization (On-TAL) has been recently proposed. However, simple On-TAL approaches of grouping per-frame predictions have limitations due to the lack of instance-level context. To this end, we propose Online Anchor Transformer (OAT) to extend the anchor-based action localization model to the online setting. We also introduce an online-applicable post-processing method that suppresses repetitive action proposals. Evaluations of On-TAL on THUMOS'14, MUSES, and BBDB show significant improvements in terms of mAP, and our model shows comparable performance to the state-of-the-art offline TAL methods with a minor change of the post-processing method. In addition to mAP evaluation, we additionally present a new online-oriented metric of early detection for On-TAL, and measure the responsiveness of each On-TAL approach.

Keywords: Online video understanding · Temporal Action Localization

1 Introduction

The rising amount of video production has increased the need for processing untrimmed videos. To automate the processing of untrimmed video, many researchers have attempted to solve the problems with deep neural networks (DNN). Temporal Action Localization (TAL) is one of the major untrimmed video understanding tasks, which detects the action instances with the class and the boundary information. Significant progress has been made in TAL recently by employing DNN [18,28,30,31,33,34].

As a challenging format of untrimmed videos, streaming video processing is receiving more attention in the surveillance system, live streaming services, and autonomous driving systems. Online Action Detection (OAD) is a task that takes one frame from the stream and immediately predicts the action class including

Supplementary Information The online version contains supplementary material available at https://doi.org/10.1007/978-3-031-19830-4_37.

S. Avidan et al. (Eds.): ECCV 2022, LNCS 13694, pp. 653–669, 2022.
https://doi.org/10.1007/978-3-031-19830-4_37

the non-action class. In addition, Online Detection of Action Start (ODAS) finds the action starting point as early as possible even before the start of an action. These tasks mainly target the high responsiveness of action detection. However, highly responsive systems are limited to specific applications, especially alarm systems, due to their frame-level output format. Although most video understanding tasks start from an action instance, aforementioned tasks do not consider instance-level contexts and are hard to apply to other applications.

To address these limitations on existing online video understanding tasks, an instance-level online video understanding task named Online Temporal Action Localization (On-TAL) [12] was recently introduced. On-TAL has two main differences with offline TAL: 1) by the online constraint, future frames cannot be accessed, and 2) modification of generated proposals in the past is not allowed, so the post-processing methods can only be applied on the currently generated proposals.

From these constraints, one of the obvious approaches to On-TAL is to get per-frame action predictions from the OAD backbone framework and to group them into action instances. However, grouping per-frame predictions fundamentally causes three issues of tick, fragmentation, and merging. The predicted action probabilities from OAD may fluctuate at non-action frames or in the middle of an action, and make ticks of an action instance or fragmented actions. In the case of consecutive actions, the OAD based methods cannot separate the action instances, making one merged action instance by the same action class.

To tackle these issues, we start with a TAL approach with the intuition that instance-level supervision would solve the limitations of the OAD based approaches. As we cannot access the future context by the first constraint of On-TAL, revisiting the sliding window scheme becomes a valid approach for On-TAL. The TAL methods with the sliding window approach [7,23] are not being actively utilized in recent works due to its restricted use of video contexts. Building rich video context has been receiving more attention lately [18,28,30,31,34] for TAL. However, we revisit the sliding window approach for online TAL and show its potential by reorganizing the framework and exploiting the state-of-the-art context encoders.

In this paper, we spotlight the sliding window scheme again, and propose an anchor-based model named Online Anchor Transformer (OAT) for On-TAL task. OAT employs the transformer encoder/decoder to encode a sliding window from each timeline and decode several anchor features from the encoded window features and the anchor query. The decoded anchor features are used to classify the action class and to regress the action end offset and the action length for the refinement of action boundaries.

Aside from accurate detection, another advantage of adopting the anchor-based approach for On-TAL is the ability to detect an action before the action ends. The anchor-based approach can make the action proposals earlier than the action ends, and those proposals are refined by the offset regression. On the contrary, OAD-based approaches must wait until the action ends as depicted in Fig. 1. Since the responsiveness is critical in online video understanding, we introduce a new online-oriented metric for On-TAL named Average Early Detected Time (AEDT), and compare it with other baseline On-TAL methods.

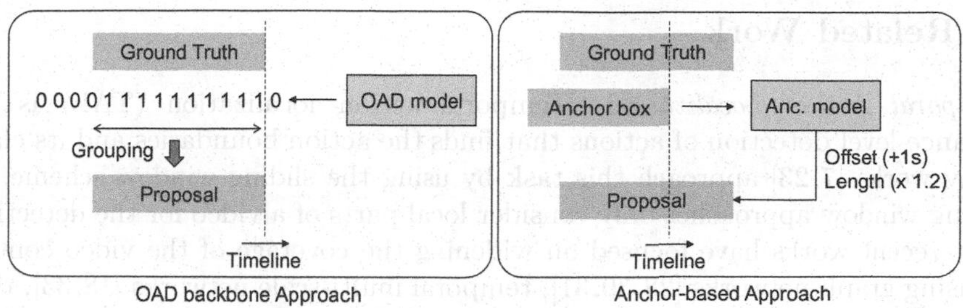

Fig. 1. Comparison of the OAD backbone approach and the anchor-based approach for Online Temporal Action Localization. When making an action instance proposal, the OAD backbone approach have to wait until the model predicts the end of an action. In contrast, Anchor-based approach can make proposals earlier than action ends, and refine them by the offset regression.

The anchor-based approach is not a master key, of course, since it produces a large amount of action proposals. Most TAL methods employ the post-processing of non-maximum suppression (NMS) to control excessive number of proposals, but this is not applicable to On-TAL by its second constraint. To deal with this, we propose Online Suppression Network (OSN) that approximates NMS without the use of the future context.

We evaluated our model on three online-applicable datasets, THUMOS'14 [11], MUSES [19], and BBDB [20]. Our method shows the state-of-the-art On-TAL performance by a significant margin. In addition, by simply changing the post-processing method to NMS, our model shows comparable performance compared to the state-of-the-art offline TAL methods, showing the potential of the sliding window scheme.

In summary, our contributions are described as follows:

- To avoid the fundamental limitations of OAD-based On-TAL approaches, we build the online-applicable anchor-based TAL framework using the sliding window scheme, which can significantly boost the performance and detect actions earlier than the action ends.
- We propose an online-oriented post-processing method named Online Suppression Network (OSN), which can approximate non-maximum suppression (NMS) without violating the online constraints.
- We introduce a new online-oriented metric for On-TAL named Average Early Detected Time (AEDT), which can indicate the responsiveness of the online video understanding task.
- Extensive experiments on THUMOS'14, MUSES, and BBDB show the effectiveness of our model for On-TAL, and comparison with offline TAL methods supports the potential of the sliding window scheme.

2 Related Work

Temporal Action Localization. Temporal action localization (TAL) is the instance-level detection of actions that finds the action boundaries and its class. Early works [7,23] approach this task by using the sliding window scheme. As sliding window approaches only consider local parts of a video for the detection, most recent works have focused on widening the coverage of the video context by using graph networks [28,30,31], temporal multi-scale networks [18,33], relations among the action proposals [3] or concatenating the global context [34]. For another branch of TAL approach, end-to-end training methods [15,27] are recently getting attention. Forced by the constraint of the input format (On-TAL), we draw attention to the sliding window approach again and narrow the performance gap to the approaches that use coarse to fine video contexts.

Online Video Understanding. As the start of the online video understanding, De Geest *et al.* [4] proposed the Online Action Detection (OAD) task which classifies per-frame action classes under the streaming video setting. Various approaches are studied for the OAD task, such as applying reinforcement learning [8], anticipating intermediate future [13,29], and building a new GRU-based neural network layer [5]. Recently, Wang *et al.* [26] designed a transformer-based model named OadTR which encodes past frames and decodes future frames to boost the performance of the OAD.

Aside from classifying action classes, Shou *et al.* [22] suggested Online Detection of Action Start (ODAS) that focuses on the action start. The goal of ODAS is detecting the action start frame as early as possible in streaming videos. The following work [9] improves the performance of ODAS by combining the conventional per-frame action classification and the class-agnostic start detection that is trained by reinforcement learning.

As another type of online video understanding, Online Temporal Action Localization (On-TAL) focuses on instance-level detection of actions. Kang *et al.* [12] firstly defined the On-TAL task, which takes a streaming video as an input and generates instance-level action proposals similar to TAL outputs. They grouped the predictions from a backbone OAD model with a method of context-aware actionness grouping (CAG). CAG is formalized into a Markov Decision Process (MDP), and trained by the imitation learning.

However, using OAD backbone causes inevitable limitations such as tick, fragmentation and merging. Our work excludes OAD backbones from the framework, and relieves such limitations by introducing the anchor-based framework. Although the anchor-based framework cannot be evaluated on frame-level detection (*e.g.* ODAS or OAD) as done in [12], our framework significantly boosts the On-TAL performance that are comparable to offline methods.

Post-Processing of Generated Proposals. The localization tasks, such as object detection and temporal action localization, use a proposal generation framework and typically employ the non-maximum suppression (NMS) method as its post-processing to reduce repetitive proposals. As a deep learning approach of NMS,

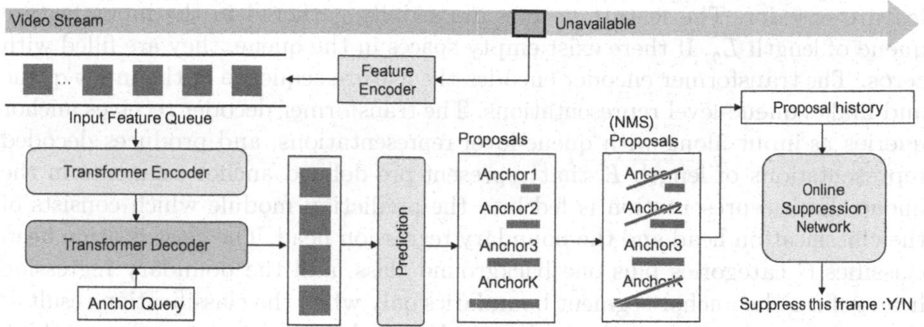

Fig. 2. Illustration of how OAT makes action proposals from a new input frame. The streaming video frames are encoded by the pre-trained feature encoder and the extracted features are gathered in the input feature queue. The transformer encoder generates queue-level features from the contents of the queue. With the anchor queries and the encoded features, the transformer decoder makes the anchor segment features of various anchor sizes. Each feature is fed into the prediction module that classifies the action and regresses the offset and the length for the action boundaries. To suppress repetitive proposals, we use the online post-processing method that consists of per-frame NMS and online suppression network.

Hosang *et al.* [10] suggested context-aware NMS methods for the purpose of removing threshold hyperparameters. In this paper, we propose Online Suppression Network (OSN) to enable online post-processing that does not use future context of videos.

3 Proposed Method

3.1 Problem Definition

Let $V = \{v_i\}_{i=1}^{T}$ and $\Psi = \{\psi_m\}_{m=1}^{M} = \{(s_m, e_m, c_m)\}_{m=1}^{M}$ denote an untrimmed video with T frames and its corresponding M label sets that have start time s_m, end time e_m and action category c_m. By the online constraint of On-TAL, we can observe the partial video $V_{1:t} = \{v_i\}_{i=1}^{t}$ at timestamp $t (1 \leq t \leq T)$. Given $V_{1:t}$, our goal is to generate action proposals as soon as action ends are detected, and recover Ψ in consecutive order. Once action proposals are generated, they are not allowed to be repaired or removed under the online constraint, so NMS-like post-processing cannot be applied to this task.

3.2 Architecture Overview

As depicted in Fig. 2, OAT consists of 4 main components: (1) transformer encoder, (2) transformer decoder, (3) prediction module, and (4) online post-processing. To have compact processing of incoming video frames, we convert k consecutive raw video frames to a video feature vector by the pre-trained feature encoder. The feature vectors are serially gathered in the input feature queue of length L_q. If there exist empty spaces in the queue, they are filled with zeros. The transformer encoder encodes the feature sequence of the input queue and makes queue-level representations. The transformer decoder receives anchor queries as input along with queue-level representations, and produces decoded representations of length K that represent pre-defined anchor segments in the queue. Each representation is fed into the prediction module which consists of the classification head and the boundary regression head. The classification head classifies C categories plus one background class, and the boundary regression head refines the anchor segment boundaries only when the classification result of the anchor segment is not the background class. As the post-processing method, NMS is applied to K action proposals from OAT and its results are enqueued to the proposal history. By looking at the proposal history, the online suppression network (OSN) decides to use the current frame as the final output or suppress the frame.

3.3 Transformer Encoder

Each video feature in the input feature queue is a locally encoded representation that is extracted by the pre-trained feature encoder. We convert the local features into the temporally contextual features by using a standard transformer encoder as described in [24].

Given feature vectors from the input feature queue at timestamp t, the feature sequence is fed into a linear projection layer and projected into D-dimensional feature space. We denote this as $\mathbf{X} = \{\mathbf{x}_i\}_{i=t-L_q+1}^{t} \in \mathbb{R}^{L_q \times D}$. To provide positional information, we apply the sinusoidal positional encoding PE,

$$\mathbf{p}_i = \mathbf{x}_i + PE_i. \tag{1}$$

Then, $\mathbf{P} = \{\mathbf{p}_i\}_{i=1}^{L_q}$ is encoded by transformer encoder.

The transformer encoder is a sequence of N_e blocks that are consist of multi-head self-attention and feed forward network. One block of transformer encoder f operates as:

$$f(\mathbf{X}) = \mathrm{FFN}(\mathbf{X}') + \mathbf{X}', \tag{2}$$

$$\mathbf{X}' = \mathrm{MultiAtt}(\mathbf{X}) + \mathbf{X}, \tag{3}$$

where FFN is a feed forward network, and MultiAtt is a multi-head self-attention layer. As our model have N_e blocks of encoder, it outputs $\mathbf{E} = f_{N_e} \circ \cdots \circ f_1(\mathbf{P}) \in \mathbb{R}^{L_q \times D}$.

3.4 Transformer Decoder

For every new input video frame, our model generates K action proposals that are learned by pre-defined anchors of the ground truth. Previously, the anchor segments of different length are physically cropped and reshaped into the same feature shape by various pooling methods. Our model integrates those complex steps, and generates anchor representations directly. The visualization of how the decoder is trained is reported in the supplementary material.

From the representation sequence $\mathbf{E}$ of length L_q from the encoder, we transform it to K-length representation sequence by using a standard transformer decoder. The transformer decoder has two types of inputs. One is a learnable anchor query $\mathbf{A} \in \mathbb{R}^{K\times D}$, and the other is the encoded queue-level context $\mathbf{E}$. Passing through the N_d blocks of multi-head self-attention (Eq. 3) and FFN (Eq. 2), the decoder outputs $\mathbf{D} \in \mathbb{R}^{K\times D}$.

3.5 Prediction Module and Loss Function

The decoded anchor representation $\mathbf{D}$ is fed into the prediction module that includes an action classification head and a boundary regression head. The classification head classifies the action category of the anchor segment including the background class. The boundary regression head predicts the distance between the target action end and the anchor segment's end (offset), and the ratio between the target action length and the anchor segment's length (length). Each head is a two-layered feed forward network and outputs $logit_c \in \mathbb{R}^{K\times(C+1)}$ and $\{logit_o, logit_l\} \in \mathbb{R}^{K\times 2}$, respectively.

During the training, we give the supervision of pre-defined anchors to the output of our model. We fix the end point of the anchors at the latest input frame, and define K anchors of various length (*e.g.* $\{L_q/8, L_q/4, L_q/2, L_q\}$). Then, we check the ground truth instances overlapping with each anchor and calculate Intersection-over-Union (IoU) between the ground truths and corresponding anchors. If IoU is higher than matching threshold θ_m, the anchor is matched to the ground truth and the loss $\mathcal{L}$ is calculated as follows:

$$\mathcal{L}_c = \sum_{i=1}^{K} \mathrm{CE}(\mathrm{softmax}(logit_{c,i}), g_{c,i}), \tag{4}$$

$$\mathcal{L}_o = \sum_{i=1}^{K} \mathrm{L1}(logit_{o,i} - \frac{g_{o,i} - a_{o,i}}{a_{l,i}}), \tag{5}$$

$$\mathcal{L}_l = \sum_{i=1}^{K} \mathrm{L1}(logit_{l,i} - \log\frac{g_{l,i}}{a_{l,i}}), \tag{6}$$

$$\mathcal{L} = \mathcal{L}_c + \mathcal{L}_o + \mathcal{L}_l, \tag{7}$$

where CE is the cross entropy loss, L1 is the L1 loss, g_c, g_o, g_l, a_o, a_l are the ground truth class, the ground truth action end, the ground truth action length, the anchor segment end, and the anchor segment length, respectively. Otherwise, the anchor is set to the background class and the boundary regression is omitted.

By fixing the end point of the anchors at the latest input frame, the proposals with the background class are generated at the early part of actions, and the anchors are matched to their ground truth in the middle and the end of the actions, which have enough context to predict precise action boundaries.

During the inference, our model makes K action proposals $\{(s_i, e_i, c_i)\}_{i=1}^{K}$ for every timestamp as follows:

$$c_i = \text{softmax}(logit_{c,i}), \tag{8}$$

$$e_i = a_{o,i} + a_{l,i} logit_{o,i}, \tag{9}$$

$$s_i = e_i - a_{l,i} \exp(logit_{l,i}). \tag{10}$$

3.6 Online Post-processing

As OAT generates action proposals for every new input, suppressing the repetitive proposals is critical to the detection performance. Conventional NMS that are used in offline TAL methods cannot be applied to our framework due to the online constraint. Without the access to the future information, the On-TAL model has to pick the best proposal from the repetitive proposals in the video time axis. Therefore, we apply a neural network that determines the best time to register to the final instance set Ψ, which is approximately similar frames as the frames selected by NMS.

The proposed OAT model generates K action proposals for every new input frames. Then, we remove the proposals with the background class and apply NMS among the outputs of the single frame. The confidence scores of the action proposals are enqueued to the proposal history queue $q_h \in [0,1]^{L_q \times C}$, which has the same length as the window size L_q and can store the confidence scores by C classes separately. q_h is fed into the neural network (FC-ReLU-FC-Sigmoid), and the network outputs the NMS selection probability $s \in [0,1]^C$. If s is a value larger than the suppression threshold θ_s, the generated proposal of the current frame is registered to the final action instance set Ψ. Once registered to the final set, all following proposal candidates with high IoU are ignored. The step-by-step details are described in the supplementary material.

For the training, we made input tables ($[0,1]^{L_v \times L_q \times C}$ where L_v is video length) from the confidence scores of OAT outputs, and made ground truth labels ($\{0,1\}^{L_v \times C}$) from the NMS-applied results of OAT. If the proposal that generated on timestamp t is selected by NMS, the frames of timestamp $t-1, t, t+1$ are set to 1, otherwise the frames are set to 0. OSN is trained by the binary cross entropy loss.

By this method, our framework can approximate NMS only with the past context that does not violate the online constraint. Note that our model can also operate in the offline setting by switching to the post-processing method that stacks all output proposals of all timestamp, and adopting NMS.

4 Experiments

4.1 Datasets

Following Kang *et al.* [12], we use THUMOS'14 [11] to evaluate our model. They also cited ActivityNet v1.3 [6], but mentioned that it is not suitable for On-TAL since the main objective of On-TAL is to detect multiple action instances in the streaming setting. Therefore, we find two more datasets with three conditions. The dataset should have boundary labels, multiple instances per video, and multiple classes per video. We use MUSES [19] and BBDB [20], which satisfy all conditions for evaluating our model.

THUMOS'14 [11] contains 200 training videos and 213 test videos with 20 action classes. The videos are sport-related untrimmed videos and have an average of 15 action instances per video.

MUSES [19] contains 3,697 videos, a total of 716 h with 25 action classes. The videos are from TV and movie dramas, and have an average of 8.5 action instances and 3.3 action classes per video. The action instances are multi-shot event, which makes the dataset challenging.

BBDB [20] contains 1,172 full baseball games, adding up to 4,254 h of videos with 30 classes. Since a single video is a full game, it has almost all classes in one video. Also, it has an average of 405 action instances per video. The lengths of videos are extremely long (over 2 h), so the methods of processing whole video at once are difficult to adopt to this dataset.

4.2 Evaluation Metric

For an easy comparison to existing On-TAL and offline TAL methods, we aggregate all generated action proposals after processing all frames in videos and use mean Average Precision (mAP) with different IoU thresholds. We chose IoU threshold values in $\{0.3, 0.4, 0.5, 0.6, 0.7\}$ to report.

Since mAP metric is calculated once after all frames are processed, it cannot evaluate how reactive the model is. As the secondary evaluation metric, we propose a new online-oriented metric, named Average Early Detected Time (AEDT).

Assume that we have the true positive action proposal set $\{(p_{s,i}, p_{e,i}, p_{g,i}, c_i)\}_{i=1}^{N_{tp}}$, where p_s, p_e, p_g, c, N_{tp} are the action start time, the action end time, the proposal generation time, the action class, and the number of true positives. Also, we have its corresponding ground truth set $\{(g_{s,i}, g_{e,i}, c_i)\}_{i=1}^{N_{tp}}$, where g_s, g_e are the start time and the end time of ground truth actions. To calculate how early the action proposal is generated, we subtract the ground truth action end time from the generated time of the action proposal. Formally, AEDT is defined as follows:

$$AEDT = \frac{1}{N_{tp}} \sum_{i=1}^{N_{tp}} (p_{g,i} - g_{e,i}). \tag{11}$$

4.3 Implementation Detail

As the video feature encoder for THUMOS'14, we use the two-stream TSN [25] trained on Kinetics [1]. On MUSES, we use the I3D [1] feature extractor following the conventions of previous MUSES work [19]. On BBDB, we use the RGB-stream of TSN (ResNet-50) after setting the videos into 6 fps.

For our network, we use $D = 1024$ feature dimensions for the transformer, 3 encoder blocks with 8 heads, and 5 decoder blocks with 4 heads. The threshold for matching the ground truth with the proposal (θ_m) is set to 0.5, the suppression network threshold (θ_s) is set to 0.1, and overlapping threshold (θ_o) is set to 0.3. For dataset specific parameters, we use the input queue size $L_q = 64$ and $K = 6$ anchors of size $\{4, 8, 16, 32, 48, 64\}$ for THUMOS'14, $L_q = 150$ and $K = 7$ anchors of $\{4, 9, 18, 37, 75, 112, 150\}$ on MUSES, and $L_q = 32$ and $K = 4$ anchors of $\{4, 8, 16, 32\}$ on BBDB. For training of the main network, we use Adam [14] optimizer with the learning rate of 0.0001, the weight decay of 0.0001, and the batch size of 128. The suppression network is separately trained with Adam optimizer with the learning rate of 0.0005, the weight decay of 0.0001, and the batch size of 128.

For the online execution, the per-frame process must be finished until the next frame comes. If a model executes faster than the frame sampling rate (*e.g.* 5 fps on THUMOS'14, 0.75 fps on MUSES, 1 fps on BBDB), it is applicable to online execution. The execution speed of our model is 70.5 fps on Nvidia RTX 2080 Ti GPU, which can be executed online.

4.4 Online Performance Comparison

To evaluate on the On-TAL task, we compare our model with the previous work (CAG-QIL) and the post-processing baseline (OAT-Naive). We set the post-processing method of OAT-Naive as registering the first proposal of the higher confidence score than the threshold to the final output set and ignore all following overlapping proposals.

As shown in Table 1, OAT performs significantly better than CAG-QIL, due to the advantages of the anchor-based approach. In Table 2, OAT can detect the action instance before the action ends which can be observed as minus values of AEDT. CAG-QIL, which is based on OAD grouping, shows near-zero values of AEDT, meaning that it detect action instances near the end of actions.

Comparing the post-processing methods, the naive approach shows the fastest detection of actions. However, the first detected proposal may not be accurate, so the mAP of the naive approach have inferior performance compared to OSN. On the other hand, OSN waits for the better proposal by approximating NMS, so it shows higher mAP and slower AEDT than the naive approach.

4.5 Offline Performance Comparison

As On-TAL is a newly proposed task, only a limited amount of works are available for the comparison. Therefore, we also compare our work with offline TAL methods in Tables 3 and 4. Although our work succeeded to narrow the performance gap between online and offline methods, there is still a performance gap to the state-of-the-art offline TAL methods. However, applying the video-level post-processing (OAT-NMS) boosts the performance and shows comparable performance to the state-of-the-art offline methods. For the post-processing method, we stack all generated action proposals in a video and apply NMS

Table 1. Comparison of mAP (%) at different tIoU thresholds with On-TAL baseline (CAG-QIL) on 3 datasets.

Dataset	Method	0.3	0.4	0.5	0.6	0.7
THUMOS'14	CAG-QIL [12]	48.4	40.8	33.0	24.2	16.2
	OAT-Naive	57.6	50.6	43.0	30.0	15.7
	OAT-OSN	**63.0**	**56.7**	**47.1**	**36.3**	**20.0**
MUSES	CAG-QIL [12]	8.5	6.5	4.2	2.8	1.9
	OAT-Naive	20.3	16.6	12.9	7.7	3.6
	OAT-OSN	**22.1**	**18.5**	**14.2**	**8.9**	**4.7**
BBDB	CAG-QIL [12]	36.2	35.3	32.9	28.5	21.8
	OAT-Naive	52.4	52.1	49.5	44.2	37.8
	OAT-OSN	**64.4**	**64.2**	**63.4**	**60.4**	**53.4**

Table 2. Comparison of AEDT (second) at different tIoU thresholds with On-TAL baseline (CAG-QIL) on 3 datasets.

Dataset	Method	0.3	0.4	0.5	0.6	0.7
THUMOS'14	CAG-QIL [12]	−0.11	−0.07	−0.08	−0.07	−0.04
	OAT-Naive	**−1.65**	**−1.66**	**−1.68**	**−1.73**	**−1.75**
	OAT-OSN	−1.28	−1.25	−1.25	−1.23	−1.21
MUSES	CAG-QIL [12]	−1.03	−0.69	−0.77	−0.79	−0.54
	OAT-Naive	**−18.57**	**−16.73**	−13.31	−11.05	**−9.80**
	OAT-OSN	−17.29	−16.08	**−13.99**	**−11.12**	−9.53
BBDB	CAG-QIL [12]	−0.02	0.03	0.10	0.17	0.21
	OAT-Naive	**−2.78**	**−2.78**	**−2.77**	**−2.75**	**−2.77**
	OAT-OSN	−0.15	−0.16	−0.16	−0.19	−0.25

to make final action proposals. Note that other factors, including the network design and hyperparameters, are the same except for the post-processing. Our model is not applicable to global or multi-scale contexts due to the processing constraints of online inputs, but the comparable performance to offline methods with the minor post-processing change shows that our model produces high quality action proposals as offline methods. This indicates that the performance gap between the online and the offline method may be minimized depending on the improvement of the controlling algorithm for repetitive proposals.

4.6 Qualitative Evaluation

As the qualitative result, we compare the output proposal sets of CAG-QIL and OAT-OSN in Fig. 3. For the OAD-based models like CAG-QIL, the per-frame predictions of OAD raise fundamental difficulties to group them into accurate action instances. In the case of the high confidence score on the non-action frames, CAG-QIL makes short action proposals that is not related to the ground

Table 3. Comparison of mAP (%) at different tIoU thresholds with *offline* TAL methods on THUMOS'14.

Method	0.3	0.4	0.5	0.6	0.7
CDC [21]	40.1	29.4	23.3	13.1	7.9
BSN [17]	53.5	45.0	36.9	28.4	20.0
TAL-Net [2]	53.2	48.5	42.8	33.8	20.8
BMN [16]	56.0	47.4	38.8	29.7	20.5
G-TAD [28]	54.5	47.6	40.2	30.8	23.4
PBRNet [18]	58.5	54.6	51.3	41.8	29.5
VSGN [31]	66.7	60.4	52.4	41.0	30.4
ContextLoc [34]	68.3	63.8	54.3	41.8	26.2
MUSES [19]	68.9	**64.0**	**56.9**	**46.3**	**31.0**
OAT-OSN	63.0	56.7	47.1	36.3	20.0
OAT-NMS	**69.7**	**64.0**	53.9	42.9	27.0

Table 4. Comparison of mAP (%) at different tIoU thresholds with *offline* TAL methods on MUSES and BBDB.

Dataset	Method	0.3	0.4	0.5	0.6	0.7
MUSES	MR [32]	12.9	11.3	9.2	7.6	5.9
	G-TAD [28]	19.1	14.8	11.1	7.4	4.7
	P-GCN [30]	19.9	17.1	13.1	9.7	5.4
	MUSES [19]	25.9	22.6	18.9	**15.0**	**10.6**
	OAT-OSN	22.1	18.5	14.2	8.9	4.7
	OAT-NMS	**27.7**	**24.3**	**19.9**	14.9	9.2
BBDB	Single frame [20]	10.0	7.9	3.4	2.5	1.6
	CDC [21]	26.1	22.2	11.3	9.5	6.1
	OAT-OSN	64.4	64.2	63.4	60.4	53.4
	OAT-NMS	**66.6**	**66.5**	**65.8**	**63.5**	**56.7**

truth actions (Fig. 3 (a)). In the opposite case of the low confidence score on the action frames, it makes one ground truth action into several fragmented action proposals (Fig. 3 (b)). OAD-base models also shows limitations when the actions are overlapping or repeat with short intervals (Fig 3 (c)), as CAG-QIL shows the merged proposals on consecutive actions. On the other hand, OAT uses instance-level context from anchors and it shows the advantages of overcoming the problems of tick, fragmentation, and merge.

5 Model Analysis

Rethinking Steps of Sliding Window Scheme. To share our observations of rethinking sliding window scheme, we show step-by-step results by changing the

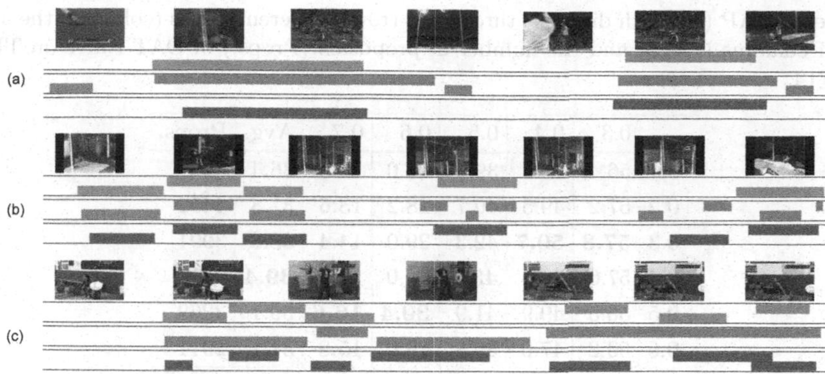

Fig. 3. Comparison on qualitative results of OAT-ONS with CAG-QIL [12]. Green is the ground truth, red is the result of CAG-QIL, and blue is the result of OAT-ONS. The rows are the examples of tick (a), fragmentation (b), and merge (c), respectively. (Color figure online)

Table 5. Comparison of mAP (%) with step-by-step changes of the anchor encoding components on THUMOS'14.

Method	0.3	0.4	0.5	0.6	0.7
Pooling-NMS	61.0	53.4	42.7	30.3	16.6
ConvNet-NMS	63.1	56.6	47.4	32.2	18.9
OAT-NMS	**69.7**	**64.0**	**53.9**	**42.9**	**27.0**

component from the baseline method in Table 5. All methods in this experiment shares the sliding window framework and the same post-processing for the fair comparison.

Firstly, we set the baseline by changing the transformers into the pooling layers for the anchor encoding (Pooling-NMS). As a straightforward extension of TURN [7], Pooling-NMS divides each anchor segment into three parts, and the features of each part are average-pooled, and the three features are concatenated for the anchor encodings. It shows the performance of 42.7% @tIoU = 0.5

For the next step, we try to use the convolutional networks for the anchor encoding (ConvNet-NMS). ConvNet-NMS has 2-layer convnets separately for each anchors, and the output shape of each convnets are the same. The performance gain of exploiting convnets is +4.7% @tIoU = 0.5, mainly achieved by the richer context than the average pooling.

Our method, OAT, shows +6.5% @tIoU = 0.5 gain from ConvNet-NMS. The sliding window includes background frames, so the transformer encoder makes rich representations including non-action contexts and its anchor decodings can make accurate action proposals. As the byproduct of finding the effective On-TAL framework, we found the sliding window, which is considered to be outdated for the offline TAL, shows the comparable performance to state-of-the-art offline TAL methods.

Table 6. mAP (%) with different thresholds (row), different tIoUs (column), the average of columns (Avg.), and the number of proposals (Props.) of OAT-Naive on THUMOS'14.

	0.3	0.4	0.5	0.6	0.7	Avg.	Props.
0.1	56.4	48.6	39.6	26.0	11.5	36.4	5247
0.2	57.2	49.5	40.7	28.2	13.6	37.8	4452
0.3	**57.8**	**50.7**	42.3	29.0	14.4	38.8	3991
0.4	57.6	50.6	**43.0**	30.0	15.7	**39.4**	3610
0.5	56.5	49.9	41.9	**30.4**	**16.6**	39.1	3269
0.6	53.2	47.0	39.8	29.6	15.8	37.1	2911

Naive Thresholding. To strengthen the effectiveness of ONS, we show the detailed results of OAT-Naive by changing threshold values. Our final selection of the threshold is 0.4, since it shows the best performance on average, as seen in Table 6.

The smaller thresholds can catch the actions with the low confidence scores, but increase the number of false positives causing the performance decrease at high tIoU. As the thresholds get larger, the number of proposals decreases, and the proposals with high confidence remain. However, it overlooks the detected actions with low confidence, causing the performance drop at low tIoU.

The simple change of thresholds cannot reach to the performance of NMS and its approximation, ONS. Those methods select the maximum confidence, which is a relative operation, and are able to suppress repetitive proposals of both low and high confidence.

6 Conclusion

In this paper, we proposed the anchor-based action localization model, named Online Anchor Transformer (OAT), to deal with Online Temporal Action Localization. In addition to OAT, we also proposed the Online Suppression Network which is an online-applicable post-processing method. Our model shows significantly better performance than the baseline in terms of both mAP and online responsiveness. By changing the post-processing method, our model performs comparably to state-of-the-art offline TAL methods, making inspirations for rethinking the sliding window scheme.

Acknowledgements. This work has partly supported by the National Research Foundation of Korea(NRF) grant funded by the Korea government(MSIT)(NRF-2022R1A2C2004509) and by Institute of Information communications Technology Planning Evaluation (IITP) grant funded by the Korea government(MSIT), Artificial Intelligence Innovation Hub under Grant 2021–0-02068, Artificial Intelligence Graduate School Program under Grant 2020–0-01361.

References

1. Carreira, J., Zisserman, A.: Quo vadis, action recognition? a new model and the kinetics dataset. In: Proceedings of the IEEE Conference on Computer Vision and Pattern Recognition (CVPR), pp. 6299–6308 (2017)
2. Chao, Y.W., Vijayanarasimhan, S., Seybold, B., Ross, D.A., Deng, J., Sukthankar, R.: Rethinking the faster R-CNN architecture for temporal action localization. In: Proceedings of the IEEE Conference on Computer Vision and Pattern Recognition (CVPR), pp. 1130–1139 (2018)
3. Chen, P., Gan, C., Shen, G., Huang, W., Zeng, R., Tan, M.: Relation attention for temporal action localization. IEEE Trans. Multimedia **22**(10), 2723–2733 (2019)
4. De Geest, R., Gavves, E., Ghodrati, A., Li, Z., Snoek, C., Tuytelaars, T.: Online action detection. In: Leibe, B., Matas, J., Sebe, N., Welling, M. (eds.) ECCV 2016. LNCS, vol. 9909, pp. 269–284. Springer, Cham (2016). https://doi.org/10.1007/978-3-319-46454-1_17
5. Eun, H., Moon, J., Park, J., Jung, C., Kim, C.: Learning to discriminate information for online action detection. In: Proceedings of the IEEE Conference on Computer Vision and Pattern Recognition (CVPR), pp. 809–818 (2020)
6. Heilbron, F.C., Escorcia, V., Ghanem, B., Niebles, J.C.: Activitynet: a large-scale video benchmark for human activity understanding. In: Proceedings of the IEEE Conference on Computer Vision and Pattern Recognition (CVPR), pp. 961–970 (2015)
7. Gao, J., Yang, Z., Chen, K., Sun, C., Nevatia, R.: Turn tap: temporal unit regression network for temporal action proposals. In: Proceedings of the IEEE International Conference on Computer Vision (ICCV), pp. 3628–3636 (2017)
8. Gao, J., Yang, Z., Nevatia, R.: RED: reinforced encoder-decoder networks for action anticipation. In: Proceedings of the British Machine Vision Conference (BMVC), pp. 1-11 (2017)
9. Gao, M., Xu, M., Davis, L.S., Socher, R., Xiong, C.: Startnet: online detection of action start in untrimmed videos. In: Proceedings of the IEEE International Conference on Computer Vision (ICCV), pp. 5542–5551 (2019)
10. Hosang, J., Benenson, R., Schiele, B.: Learning non-maximum suppression. In: Proceedings of the IEEE Conference on Computer Vision and Pattern Recognition (CVPR), pp. 4507–4515 (2017)
11. Jiang, Y.G., et al.: THUMOS challenge: action recognition with a large number of classes. https://crcv.ucf.edu/THUMOS14/ (2014)
12. Kang, H., Kim, K., Ko, Y., Kim, S.J.: CAG-QIL: context-aware actionness grouping via Q imitation learning for online temporal action localization. In: Proceedings of the IEEE International Conference on Computer Vision (ICCV), pp. 13729–13738 (2021)
13. Kim, Y.H., Nam, S., Kim, S.J.: Temporally smooth online action detection using cycle-consistent future anticipation. Pattern Recogn. **116**, 107954 (2021)
14. Kingma, D.P., Ba, J.: Adam: a method for stochastic optimization. arXiv preprint arXiv:1412.6980 (2014)
15. Lin, C., et al.: Learning salient boundary feature for anchor-free temporal action localization. In: Proceedings of the IEEE Conference on Computer Vision and Pattern Recognition (CVPR), pp. 3320–3329 (2021)
16. Lin, T., Liu, X., Li, X., Ding, E., Wen, S.: BMN: boundary-matching network for temporal action proposal generation. In: Proceedings of the IEEE International Conference on Computer Vision (ICCV), pp. 3889–3898 (2019)

17. Lin, T., Zhao, X., Su, H., Wang, C., Yang, M.: BSN: boundary sensitive network for temporal action proposal generation. In: Ferrari, V., Hebert, M., Sminchisescu, C., Weiss, Y. (eds.) ECCV 2018. LNCS, vol. 11208, pp. 3–21. Springer, Cham (2018). https://doi.org/10.1007/978-3-030-01225-0_1
18. Liu, Q., Wang, Z.: Progressive boundary refinement network for temporal action detection. In: Proceedings of the AAAI Conference on Artificial Intelligence, vol. 34, pp. 11612–11619 (2020)
19. Liu, X., Hu, Y., Bai, S., Ding, F., Bai, X., Torr, P.H.: Multi-shot temporal event localization: a benchmark. In: Proceedings of the IEEE Conference on Computer Vision and Pattern Recognition (CVPR), pp. 12596–12606 (2021)
20. Shim, M., Kim, Y.H., Kim, K., Kim, S.J.: Teaching machines to understand baseball games: large-scale baseball video database for multiple video understanding tasks. In: Ferrari, V., Hebert, M., Sminchisescu, C., Weiss, Y. (eds.) ECCV 2018. LNCS, vol. 11219, pp. 420–437. Springer, Cham (2018). https://doi.org/10.1007/978-3-030-01267-0_25
21. Shou, Z., Chan, J., Zareian, A., Miyazawa, K., Chang, S.F.: CDC: convolutional-de-convolutional networks for precise temporal action localization in untrimmed videos. In: Proceedings of the IEEE Conference on Computer Vision and Pattern Recognition (CVPR), pp. 5734–5743 (2017)
22. Shou, Z., et al.: Online detection of action start in untrimmed, streaming videos. In: Ferrari, V., Hebert, M., Sminchisescu, C., Weiss, Y. (eds.) ECCV 2018. LNCS, vol. 11207, pp. 551–568. Springer, Cham (2018). https://doi.org/10.1007/978-3-030-01219-9_33
23. Shou, Z., Wang, D., Chang, S.F.: Temporal action localization in untrimmed videos via multi-stage CNNs. In: Proceedings of the IEEE Conference on Computer Vision and Pattern Recognition (CVPR), pp. 1049–1058 (2016)
24. Vaswani, A., et al.: Attention is all you need. In: Proceedings of the Advances in Neural Information Processing Systems (NeurIPS) 30 (2017)
25. Wang, L., et al.: Temporal segment networks: towards good practices for deep action recognition. In: Leibe, B., Matas, J., Sebe, N., Welling, M. (eds.) ECCV 2016. LNCS, vol. 9912, pp. 20–36. Springer, Cham (2016). https://doi.org/10.1007/978-3-319-46484-8_2
26. Wang, X., et al.: OadTR: online action detection with transformers. In: Proceedings of the IEEE International Conference on Computer Vision (ICCV), pp. 7565–7575 (2021)
27. Xu, M., Perez Rua, J.M., Zhu, X., Ghanem, B., Martinez, B.: Low-fidelity video encoder optimization for temporal action localization. In: Proceedings of the Advances in Neural Information Processing Systems (NeurIPS) 34 (2021)
28. Xu, M., Zhao, C., Rojas, D.S., Thabet, A., Ghanem, B.: G-TAD: sub-graph localization for temporal action detection. In: Proceedings of the IEEE Conference on Computer Vision and Pattern Recognition (CVPR), pp. 10156–10165 (2020)
29. Xu, M., Gao, M., Chen, Y.T., Davis, L.S., Crandall, D.J.: Temporal recurrent networks for online action detection. In: Proceedings of the IEEE International Conference on Computer Vision (ICCV), pp. 5532–5541 (2019)
30. Zeng, R., et al.: Graph convolutional networks for temporal action localization. In: Proceedings of the IEEE International Conference on Computer Vision (ICCV), pp. 7094–7103 (2019)
31. Zhao, C., Thabet, A.K., Ghanem, B.: Video self-stitching graph network for temporal action localization. In: Proceedings of the IEEE International Conference on Computer Vision (ICCV), pp. 13658–13667 (2021)

32. Zhao, P., Xie, L., Ju, C., Zhang, Y., Wang, Y., Tian, Q.: Bottom-up temporal action localization with mutual regularization. In: Vedaldi, A., Bischof, H., Brox, T., Frahm, J.-M. (eds.) ECCV 2020. LNCS, vol. 12353, pp. 539–555. Springer, Cham (2020). https://doi.org/10.1007/978-3-030-58598-3_32
33. Zhao, Y., Xiong, Y., Wang, L., Wu, Z., Tang, X., Lin, D.: Temporal action detection with structured segment networks. In: Proceedings of the IEEE International Conference on Computer Vision (ICCV), pp. 2914–2923 (2017)
34. Zhu, Z., Tang, W., Wang, L., Zheng, N., Hua, G.: Enriching local and global contexts for temporal action localization. In: Proceedings of the IEEE International Conference on Computer Vision (ICCV), pp. 13516–13525 (2021)

ERA: Expert Retrieval and Assembly for Early Action Prediction

Lin Geng Foo[1], Tianjiao Li[1], Hossein Rahmani[2], Qiuhong Ke[3], and Jun Liu[1(✉)]

[1] ISTD Pillar, Singapore University of Technology and Design, Singapore, Singapore
{lingeng_foo,tianjiao_li}@mymail.sutd.edu.sg, jun_liu@sutd.edu.sg

[2] School of Computing and Communications, Lancaster University, Lancaster, UK
h.rahmani@lancaster.ac.uk

[3] Department of Data Science and AI, Monash University, Clayton, Australia
qiuhong.ke@monash.edvu

Abstract. Early action prediction aims to successfully predict the class label of an action before it is completely performed. This is a challenging task because the beginning stages of different actions can be very similar, with only minor subtle differences for discrimination. In this paper, we propose a novel Expert Retrieval and Assembly (ERA) module that retrieves and assembles a set of experts most specialized at using discriminative subtle differences, to distinguish an input sample from other highly similar samples. To encourage our model to effectively use subtle differences for early action prediction, we push experts to discriminate exclusively between samples that are highly similar, forcing these experts to learn to use subtle differences that exist between those samples. Additionally, we design an effective Expert Learning Rate Optimization method that balances the experts' optimization and leads to better performance. We evaluate our ERA module on four public action datasets and achieve state-of-the-art performance.

Keywords: Early action prediction · Dynamic networks · Expert retrieval

1 Introduction

The goal of early action prediction is to infer an action category at the early temporal stage, i.e., before the action is fully observed. This task is relevant to many practical applications, such as human-robot interaction [17,28,40], security surveillance [6,7,23] and self-driving vehicles [1,11,36] since a timely response is crucial in these scenarios. For example, for enhanced safety of self-driving

L. G. Foo and T. Li—Equal contribution.

Supplementary Information The online version contains supplementary material available at https://doi.org/10.1007/978-3-031-19830-4_38.

S. Avidan et al. (Eds.): ECCV 2022, LNCS 13694, pp. 670–688, 2022.
https://doi.org/10.1007/978-3-031-19830-4_38

vehicles, it is crucial that the actions of pedestrians can be predicted before they are fully completed, so that the vehicle can react promptly. Such utility of early action prediction has not gone unnoticed, and it has received a lot of research attention recently [15,30,50,54,55].

Previous works [30,55] show that one of the major challenges in early action prediction lies in the subtlety of the differences between some "hard" samples at the very beginning temporal stages, since only limited initial observations of the action sequences are seen and some important discriminative information in the middle or later parts of the sequences is not observed, greatly increasing the difficulty of making correct predictions. For instance, as shown in Fig. 1, though the human postures and motions in the full sequences of the actions "slapping" and "shaking hands" are quite different, their early parts are quite similar, with only subtle differences between them.

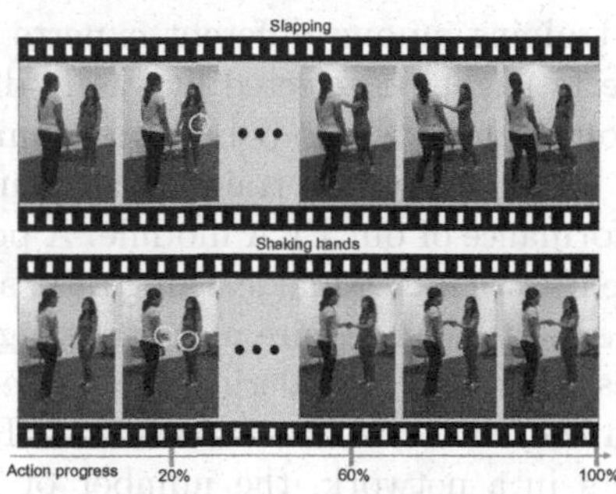

Fig. 1. Illustration of two actions at the early stage, taken from NTU RGB+D 120 [32]. Only subtle differences (highlighted in circles) exist for discrimination between the actions "Slapping" and "Shaking hands" at the early temporal stages (e.g., 20%). Best viewed in colour.

To tackle early action prediction, various types of deep networks have been proposed [30,54,55], but they still do not possess very good discrimination capabilities using subtle cues. In particular, deep networks prefer to learn to discriminate between the easier samples with major discriminative cues instead of the harder ones [20]. This can happen when we train the entire neural network by updating all its parameters using all samples – the gradients update all the parameters to contribute towards correctly classifying all these samples, which thus can lead to the network learning more *general patterns* that apply to more samples, as opposed to learning *specific subtle cues* to discriminate subtle differences that may only apply to a small subset of the data [12]. The performance drop from such sub-optimal training behaviour can be further exacerbated on the very challenging action prediction task, where there can be a lack of major discriminative cues at the early stages among different actions, and the importance of utilizing subtle differences is increased. Although recent work [30] on early action prediction has attempted to improve the discriminative ability on subtle cues through mining hard training samples, they train the parameters of the entire network using all samples, still leaving the network prone to sub-optimal performance with respect to subtle differences.

In this work, to improve the performance of deep networks on early action prediction, we propose an Expert Retrieval and Assembly (ERA) module that contains *non-experts* and *experts*. Unlike *non-experts* that contain parameters which are shared across all samples and capture general patterns that exist in many samples, *experts* are only trained on a subset of the data (according to their *keys*) and contain parameters that focus on encoding subtle differences to distinguish between highly similar samples. During the forward pass, a retrieval mechanism retrieves the most suitable experts, which are then assembled together with the non-experts to form a combination that is able to discriminate samples using an effective mix of general patterns and subtle differences. This retrieval mechanism is designed such that experts are retrieved by samples that are very similar, and thus, during training, the losses push the experts to learn *specialized discriminative subtle cues to distinguish exclusively between these similar samples*, encouraging the acquiring of expertise in exploiting relevant subtle cues. The proposed ERA module is *flexible*, and can be a plug-and-play replacement for traditional convolutional layers.

We design the ERA module with a set of experts to learn different subtle cues that exist across different actions. However, it is non-trivial to balance the training among different experts in the ERA module, especially when the experts might be selected by vastly different numbers of samples. For instance, as some subtle cues may be more common, a few experts are selected more often and might be better trained. Such unbalanced training may limit the overall performance of our ERA module. A possible solution could be for each expert to have its own individual learning rate, and we adjust these learning rates such that the experts that require more training will have correspondingly higher learning rates. However, considering the numerous experts in the ERA module, coupled with the envisioned scenario where ERA modules replace multiple convolutional layers in a network, the number of hyperparameters is too large for manual tuning to be practical. Thus, we design an Expert Learning Rate Optimization (ELRO) method that balances the training of experts within the ERA module, improving the overall performance.

In summary, our main contributions include: **(1)** We propose a novel ERA module that effectively utilizes subtle discriminative differences between similar actions through retrieval and assembly of the most suitable experts for action prediction. Our ERA module is a flexible plug-and-play module that can replace the traditional convolutional layer. **(2)** To balance the training among experts and further improve performance of the ERA module on early action prediction, we design an effective ELRO method. **(3)** We obtain state-of-the-art-performance on early action prediction on four widely used datasets by replacing convolutional layers of the baseline architectures with our ERA modules.

2 Related Work

Early Action Prediction refers to the task where only the front parts of each sequence are observed by the model. The loss of important discriminative information leads to a challenging scenario where subtle cues need to be properly utilized for successful discrimination. Different approaches [2,10,15,21,22,24–27,30,33,39,41,50,52,54,55,62] have been proposed to address the early action prediction problem. Li *et al.* [30] focused on the 3D early activity prediction task by mining hard instances and training the model to discriminate between them.

Ke *et al.* [22] proposed a Latent Global Network to learn how to transfer knowledge from full-length sequences to partially-observed sequences in an adversarial manner. Weng *et al.* [55] introduced a policy-based reinforcement learning mechanism to generate binary masks to preclude the negative category information leading to improved recognition accuracy. Wang *et al.* [54] proposed a teacher-student network architecture to distill the global information contained within the full action video from the teacher network to the student network.

In this work, unlike the above-mentioned methods, we explore the usage of a *dynamic model* that pushes expert parameters to effectively encode subtle differences. We propose a novel ERA module, which learns to discriminate among similar samples using subtle cues by retrieving and assembling relevant experts for each sample.

Action Recognition is the task where a model predicts the classes of actions based on their full action sequences. Input data can come from different modalities, such as RGB data [8,31,60,63–65] and skeletal data [4,5,34,38,44–46,48,67]. Here, we focus on early action prediction, which is important yet more challenging since the early segments of different actions can be highly similar [30,54,55].

Dynamic Networks refer to neural networks that adapt their parameters or structures according to the input. A variety of different methods have been explored, including dynamic depth [51,53,59], dynamic widths [37,43], weight generation [3,66], dynamic routing [29,58] and spatially dynamic [61] methods. In general, dynamic networks can be employed for their improved computational efficiency and representation power.

As our ERA module retrieves a different set of experts for each input sample, it can be considered a type of dynamic module. To the best of our knowledge, our ERA module is the first work that dynamically assigns experts to handle *subsets of similar samples during training*, pushing them to *gain expertise in exploiting subtle differences.* This relies on our novel retrieval mechanism involving key-query matching that retrieves experts to handle similar samples, which is different from existing mechanisms [3,37,43,66]. Moreover, we explore a novel ELRO method to further improve performance of our dynamic ERA module.

3 Method

Subtle differences among highly similar samples are difficult to be well-learned by deep neural networks that share all network parameters across all samples. When tackling the challenging early action prediction task, the importance of exploiting subtle cues is increased, as there can be a lack of major discriminative cues at the early stages of actions, which exacerbates the performance drop from the sub-optimal performance of deep networks using subtle cues.

Motivated by this, we design a novel ERA module with an expert-retrieval mechanism to better exploit subtle cues. The expert-retrieval mechanism retrieves experts (from the Expert Banks) with relevant expertise for each input sample, and assembles them with non-experts. By matching experts with input samples that are highly similar to each other during training, this mechanism allows experts to ignore distant samples, while pushing them to focus on distinguishing between highly similar samples by specializing in subtle differences.

Due to the uneven distribution of samples across different experts, there might be uneven training among experts, which limits performance of our ERA module. To mitigate this issue, an effective ELRO method is implemented during the training of the experts, which tunes their individual learning rates, resulting in a more effective training of experts and improved performance.

Below, we first describe the early action prediction task. Then, we introduce the ERA module and explain in detail how the expert-retrieval mechanism can encourage experts to specialize during training. Lastly, we describe our ELRO method.

3.1 Problem Formulation

A full-length action sequence can be represented as a set $S = \{s_t\}_{t=1}^{T}$ containing T frames, where s_t denotes the frame at the t-th time step. Following previous works [15,22,30], S is divided into N independent segments, with each segment containing $\frac{T}{N}$ frames. A partial sequence consists of a set of frames $P = \{s_t\}_{t=1}^{\tau}$, with τ being the last frame in any one of the N segments, i.e., $\tau = i\frac{T}{N}, i = \{1, 2, ..., N\}$. The task of early action prediction is to predict the class $c \in \{1, 2, ..., C\}$ of the activity that the partial sequence P belongs to, and different observation ratios $\frac{\tau}{T}$ of P are tested.

3.2 ERA Module

As shown in Fig. 2, our ERA module consists of *candidate experts* contained within multiple Expert Banks and a *non-expert block*. Considering that convolutional architectures have been shown to be effective for the early action prediction task [30,54], the experts are implemented as convolutional kernels. For ease of notation, we describe our method in a 2D convolutional kernel setting, even though it can be generalized to 1D, 3D or graph convolutions as well. This ability to generalize to other types of convolutions is important, as existing early action prediction architectures often use various types of convolutions, such as 3D convolutions [45] or graph + 2D convolutions [13].

Let an input be $X \in \mathbb{R}^{N_{in} \times N_h \times N_w}$, where N_{in}, N_h and N_w represent the channel, height and width dimensions of the input feature map. Note that here we omit the batch dimension for simplicity. Assume that, in the backbone model, input X is processed by a convolutional filter $W_{conv} \in \mathbb{R}^{N_{out} \times N_{in} \times b_h \times b_w}$, where N_{out} represents the number of output channels, and b_h and b_w represent the height and width of the convolutional kernel. We aim to replace W_{conv} with our ERA module, for better performance on early action prediction.

Specifically, we design our ERA module to also ultimately produce weights W_{ERA} of the same shape ($N_{out} \times N_{in} \times b_h \times b_w$) as W_{conv}, which can be seen as N_{out} kernels (each of shape $N_{in} \times b_h \times b_w$) that respectively produce each of the N_{out} output channels. More specifically, in our ERA Module, we split the N_{out} channels (and therefore also kernels) into two parts: d expert channels and $N_{out} - d$ non-expert channels, where d is a hyperparameter. To allow our d expert channels to specialize in subtle cues, we would like *each expert to be trained on only a subset of the data*, thus we introduce d Expert Banks containing

M candidate experts each, and retrieve only one expert from each Expert Bank per sample, such that the other $M-1$ candidate experts in the bank are unused for this sample. The $N_{out} - d$ non-expert kernels (collectively defined in a non-expert block $W_{nonexpert} \in \mathbb{R}^{(N_{out}-d)\times N_{in}\times b_h\times b_w}$) are shared over all samples, and thus tend to learn general patterns. We utilize a combination of both non-expert and expert kernels, because the usage of non-expert kernels to capture general patterns, is complementary with our experts that specialize at capturing subtle cues for discriminating between similar samples, and their combination leads to improvements on early action prediction.

1) Expert Banks. To facilitate our intention to let each expert be trained on only a subset of samples, we define d Expert Banks, each containing M candidate experts, as shown in Fig. 2. The M candidate experts in the p-th Expert Bank are all potential candidates that can be retrieved for the corresponding p-th expert channel.

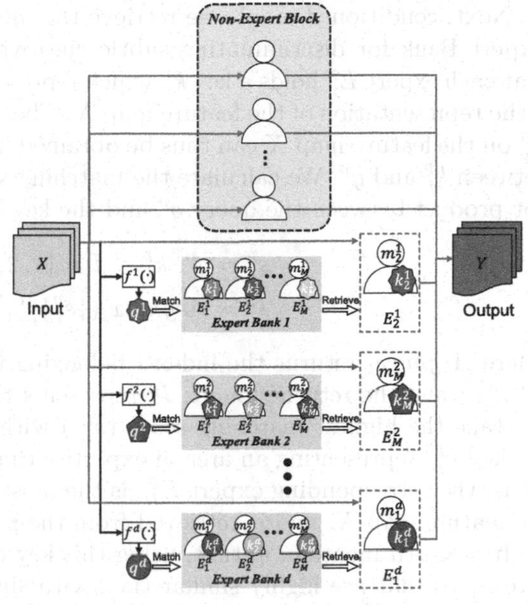

Fig. 2. Schema of our ERA module. Our ERA module contains N_{out} channels in total: $N_{out} - d$ non-expert channels (Top) and d expert channels (Bottom). Each expert channel retrieves its expert from a corresponding Expert Bank that contains M candidate experts, where each expert E_i^p consists of parameters m_i^p and a key k_i^p. The two important steps (i.e., retrieval and assembly) are indicated with red arrows. In the *retrieval* step, an expert will be retrieved from each Expert Bank through a key-query matching mechanism, such that d experts are retrieved across d expert channels. In the *assembly* step, the d retrieved experts are assembled and combined with the $N_{out}-d$ non-expert kernels to produce the output Y (with N_{out} channels).

We define the i-th expert in the p-th Expert Bank as E_i^p, where E_i^p contains convolutional kernel weights m_i^p and a key k_i^p. The key k_i^p is used for matching with the most suitable samples, and represents the *area of expertise* of this expert, as it determines the samples that the expert will be retrieved for. Meanwhile, the expert kernel m_i^p acts as a *specialized mechanism* to process the discriminative subtle cues on the input features that match the key k_i^p. The expert key k_i^p and kernel m_i^p are model parameters that are trained in an end-to-end manner. For each expert E_i^p, $m_i^p \in \mathbb{R}^{N_{in}\times b_h\times b_w}$ and $k_i^p \in \mathbb{R}^K$, where K represents the dimensionality of the key, and $K << N_{in} \times N_h \times N_w$ for efficiency.

2) Expert Retrieval. We now show how we can retrieve the most suitable expert from each Expert Bank for input X, taking the p-th Expert Bank as an example. As shown in Fig. 2, we first extract a compact and meaningful representation from the input feature map X. The query mapping function f^p maps the input feature map X to a lower-dimensional query $q^p \in \mathbb{R}^K$ as follows:

$$q^p = f^p(X). \tag{1}$$

This step transforms the feature map X into a query (vector) q^p of the dimensionality K.

Next, conditioned on q^p, we retrieve the most suitable expert from the p-th Expert Bank for discriminating subtle cues within the feature map X. Recall that each expert E_i^p holds a key k_i^p which represents its area of expertise, while q^p is the representation of the feature map X. The degree of suitability of the expert E_i^p on the feature map X can thus be obtained by calculating the matching score between k_i^p and q^p. We calculate the matching score s_i^p for each expert E_i^p using dot product between the query q^p and the key k_i^p as:

$$s_i^p = q^{p\top} k_i^p, \quad i = \{1, 2, ..., M\}. \tag{2}$$

$$I^p = Argmax_i(\{s_i^p\}_{i=1}^M), \tag{3}$$

where $Argmax_i$ returns the index i belonging to the largest element in the set $\{s_i^p\}_{i=1}^M$, and the returned index I^p represents the index of the retrieved expert. We take the highest matching score ($s_{I^p}^p$) within the set, as it will come from the key $k_{I^p}^p$ representing an area of expertise that matches the query q^p the best. Thus, the corresponding expert $E_{I^p}^p$ is the most suitable expert to be applied to the feature map X, and is retrieved from the p-th Expert Bank in this step.

It is worth mentioning that, using this key-query mechanism, the input feature maps that are highly similar (i.e., with similar q values) will tend to have high matching scores with the same key and retrieve the same expert. Crucially, this leads to the experts having to discriminate between highly similar input samples, pushing each expert to specialize in exploiting subtle cues for distinguishing between those similar samples to tackle early action prediction.

Above, we only show the operations on the p-th Expert Bank, but the same process is conducted for all d banks to retrieve d experts, which is shown in Fig. 2. Notably, this process (Eqs. 1, 2, 3) across d Expert Banks can be done in *parallel*, so it is *efficient*.

3) Expert Assembly. We assemble the retrieved expert kernels from all d Expert Banks (i.e., $\{m_{I^p}^p\}_{p=1}^d$) to form an expert block W_{expert} as follows:

$$W_{expert} = Concat(\{m_{I^p}^p\}_{p=1}^d), \tag{4}$$

where $W_{expert} \in \mathbb{R}^{d \times N_{in} \times b_h \times b_w}$ is composed of the parameters of the d experts that have the highest matching scores in the d banks, and *Concat* denotes concatenation along the channel dimension. These retrieved experts will be specialized in capturing multiple subtle cues in X, that distinguish between the true class of X and other similar classes for tackling early action prediction.

Finally, to form the full convolutional block W_{ERA}, we further assemble the non-expert block $W_{nonexpert}$ and the expert block W_{expert} (shown in Fig. 2) as:

$$W_{ERA} = Concat(W_{nonexpert}, W_{expert}). \tag{5}$$

The final assembled block W_{ERA} will be applied to the feature map in a similar manner to a traditional convolutional kernel W_{conv}. Notably, as W_{ERA} can directly replace W_{conv}, our ERA module is a plug-and-play module that can replace the basic convolutional layer.

To apply the ERA module to other types of convolutions that are used in early action prediction architectures, only minor changes need to be made. For 1D and 3D convolutions, we change the shape of m_i^p and $W_{nonexpert}$ according to the corresponding 1D or 3D kernel. As for graph convolutions, since many graph convolutions (as used in [45]) are implemented based on traditional convolutions with additional parameters and steps to account for adjacency information, thus we can also implement our method by replacing the contained convolutional kernel with our ERA module in these scenarios.

4) Analysis of specialization of experts. Next, we analyze how our ERA module allows experts to specialize in subtle cues through the expert-retrieval mechanism during training. This justification is rather important, as it explains why the retrieval of the most suitable d experts leads to better discrimination of subtle differences and tackles the sub-optimal training behaviour of the deep neural networks. We approach this by analyzing the differences between the gradients that update experts and non-experts *during backpropagation*.

Usually, the aggregated gradients $\bar{g}$ of a loss $\mathcal{L}$ w.r.t a model parameter w is computed by averaging over the entire batch with batch size B:

$$\bar{g} = \frac{1}{B}\sum_{j=1}^{B}\frac{\partial \mathcal{L}_j}{\partial w}. \tag{6}$$

The non-expert parameters are updated using $\bar{g}$ in Eq. 6, which trains the non-expert parameters to contribute towards classifying all samples, resulting in the learning of general patterns that apply to more samples, as opposed to subtle differences that occur only in a small subset of the data. If all parameters in a network are non-experts, this results in the network having sub-optimal performance with respect to subtle cues [20] and leads to worse performance on early action prediction.

In contrast, in our ERA module, not all experts are selected by each sample, as each expert is only retrieved for its most suitable samples. When backpropagating using the loss $\mathcal{L}$ on experts, the aggregated gradient $\bar{g}_i^p$ for the expert kernel weights m_i^p thus becomes:

$$\bar{g}_i^p = \frac{1}{|\mathcal{N}(k_i^p)|}\sum_{j\in\mathcal{N}(k_i^p)}\frac{\partial \mathcal{L}_j}{\partial m_i^p}, \tag{7}$$

where $\mathcal{N}(k_i^p)$ denotes the set of samples in the batch that select expert E_i^p (with key k_i^p and kernel m_i^p), i.e., $\mathcal{N}(k_i^p) = \{j \text{ s.t } I_j^p = i\}_{j=1}^B$, where I_j^p refers to the index of the selected expert in the p-th Expert Bank (I^p) for the j-th sample in the batch. The samples in $\mathcal{N}(k_i^p)$ are likely to be very similar, with only some subtle differences, due to their close proximity to k_i^p in the feature space.

If we train the expert E_i^p using the gradient $\bar{g}_i^p$ as in Eq. 7, the expert is only updated using samples that are closer to this expert's area of expertise, i.e., samples which are in $\mathcal{N}(k_i^p)$. Thus, as compared to $\bar{g}$, much more emphasis is placed on learning to distinguish between these similar samples in $\mathcal{N}(k_i^p)$ only, which *pushes the expert to learn to exploit subtle differences in these samples*, as opposed to general patterns that generally hold across all data.

3.3 Expert Learning Rate Optimization

Experts in our ERA modules, together with all other network parameters, are end-to-end trainable using backpropagation. However, due to the uneven distribution of samples across experts, some experts might be selected by more samples and be better trained than others, possibly causing imbalanced training that limits the performance of our ERA module. To mitigate this effect, we design an Expert Learning Rate Optimization (ELRO) method that optimizes the training among experts, leading to improved early action prediction accuracy. For ease of notation, in this section, we only use one ERA module, although this method can also work for multiple ERA modules. We introduce a set of expert learning rates $\beta = \{\beta_i^p\}_{i\in\{1..M\},p\in\{1..d\}}$ as additional parameters, where each element β_i^p is a scalar that balances the training of a corresponding expert E_i^p during backpropagation. Instead of using manual tuning to adjust the large set of β, we update β using a *meta-learning approach* in an end-to-end manner.

The core idea of meta-learning [9,47] is about "learning-to-learn", which in our case is *learning to optimize the learning rates* β for *improved training of experts.* This meta-optimization of β is conducted over two steps. Firstly, we simulate training on a training set while using the current β_i^p values to balance updates for each expert E_i^p respectively, to obtain a virtually updated *interim model.* Next, we evaluate the performance of this interim model on a validation set, and the gradients of these validation losses will *provide feedback on how we can adjust* β *to a more optimized* β' (which improves training of experts, and results in better performance on unseen validation samples). Finally, we then use the meta-optimized β' values for balancing expert updates during actual model training, which yields improvements in performance.

An illustration of our proposed ELRO method is shown in Fig. 3. Specifically, in each iteration, we draw two batches of training data that are non-overlapping, which we call training samples $\mathcal{D}_{train}$ and validation samples $\mathcal{D}_{val}$. Then, the following three steps are employed to update the model parameters.

(1) Virtual Training. We simulate the training on $\mathcal{D}_{train}$ by virtually updating all the model parameters other than β as follows:

$$\hat{w} = w - \alpha \nabla_w \mathcal{L}(w, \mathcal{E}; \mathcal{D}_{train}), \tag{8}$$

$$\hat{E}_i^p = E_i^p - \beta_i^p \nabla_{E_i^p} \mathcal{L}(w, \mathcal{E}; \mathcal{D}_{train}), i = \{1, .., M\}, p = \{1, .., d\}, \tag{9}$$

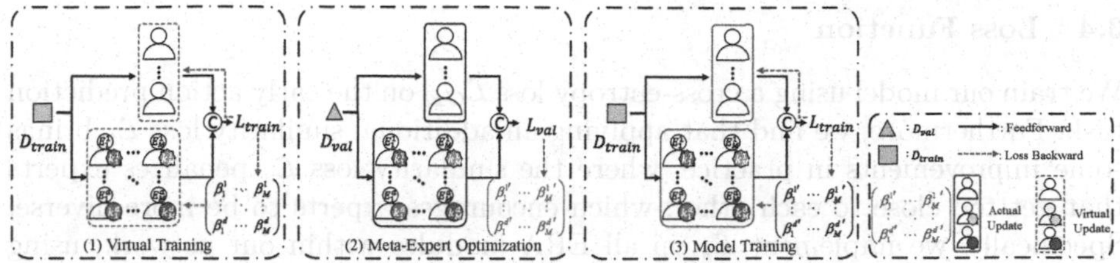

Fig. 3. Illustration of the Expert Learning Rate Optimization method. Two independent batches are sampled: training samples $\mathcal{D}_{train}$ and validation samples $\mathcal{D}_{val}$. Forward propagation paths are in black, while backpropagation paths are in red. The entire method consists of three phases: (1) Virtual Training, (2) Meta-Expert Optimization and (3) Model Training. At the Virtual Training step, all non-β model parameters are virtually updated using $\mathcal{D}_{train}$. At the Meta-Expert Optimization step, expert learning rate parameters β are dynamically updated using the gradients from validation loss $\mathcal{L}_{val}$. At the Model Training step, all non-β parameters are updated using $\mathcal{D}_{train}$ with updated β'. Best viewed in color. (Color figure online)

where w represents the non-expert parameters, $\mathcal{E}$ represents the set of experts $\{E_i^p\}_{i\in\{1..M\},p\in\{1..d\}}$, α is the learning rate (which is a fixed hyperparameter), and $\mathcal{L}$ refers to the supervised loss for the early action prediction task. Note that here the update of each expert E_i^p (which includes key k_i^p and kernel weights m_i^p) is scaled by β_i^p.

(2) Meta-expert Optimization. In this step, we evaluate the performance of the virtually updated model (consisting of $\hat{w}$ and $\hat{\mathcal{E}}$) on $\mathcal{D}_{val}$. The gradients w.r.t each expert learning rate β_i^p provide feedback on how β_i^p should be tuned for the virtually updated model to generalize better to unseen samples, as follows:

$$\beta_i^{p\prime} = \beta_i^p - \alpha \nabla_{\beta_i^p} \mathcal{L}(\hat{w}, \hat{\mathcal{E}}; \mathcal{D}_{val}), i = \{1, .., M\}, p = \{1, .., d\}. \tag{10}$$

Only β is updated in this step, and other parameters ($\hat{w}$ and $\hat{\mathcal{E}}$) remain fixed. Note that $\nabla_{\beta_i^p}$ takes gradients with respect to β_i^p as used in Eq. 9. This means that, by tuning β_i^p in Eq. 10, the newly updated expert learning rate $\beta_i^{p\prime}$ can provide better training for expert E_i^p if Eq. 9 is performed again.

(3) Model Training. After we obtain the set of meta-optimized expert learning rates $\beta' = \{\beta_i^{p\prime}\}_{i\in\{1..M\},p\in\{1..d\}}$, we can perform actual model training by updating model parameters $\mathcal{E}$ and w on $\mathcal{D}_{train}$ as:

$$w' = w - \alpha \nabla_w \mathcal{L}(w, \mathcal{E}; \mathcal{D}_{train}), \tag{11}$$

$$E_i^{p\prime} = E_i^p - \beta_i^{p\prime} \nabla_{E_i^p} \mathcal{L}(w, \mathcal{E}; \mathcal{D}_{train}), i = \{1, .., M\}, p = \{1, .., d\}, \tag{12}$$

In this step, the meta-optimized β' *balances the training of experts such that performance on unseen samples is improved.* This concludes one iteration of ELRO, where we have obtained updated parameters w', $\mathcal{E}'$ and β'. An outline of this algorithm is shown in the Supplementary Material.

3.4 Loss Function

We train our model using a cross-entropy loss $\mathcal{L}_{CE}$ on the early action prediction task. Furthermore, we find that applying an additional similarity loss $\mathcal{L}_s$ brings some improvements in practice, where the similarity loss $\mathcal{L}_s$ penalizes experts that get too close to each other, which encourages experts to be more diverse. Specifically, we implement $\mathcal{L}_s$ on all ERA modules within our network, using a negative pairwise mean-squared loss among expert kernels in each Expert Bank, i.e., using one ERA module as an example, $\mathcal{L}_s = \sum_{p=1}^{d} \sum_{i=1}^{M} \sum_{j \neq i} ||m_i^p - m_j^p||^2$. Overall, our loss $\mathcal{L}$ is then given by $\mathcal{L} = \mathcal{L}_{CE} - \gamma_s \mathcal{L}_s$, where γ_s is a hyperparameter that weights the relative significance of losses.

4 Experiments

To validate effectiveness of our ERA module for early action prediction, we conduct extensive experiments on both skeletal and RGB datasets. We experiment on the NTU RGB+D 60 (NTU60) [42], NTU RGB+D 120 (NTU120) [42] and SYSU [14] datasets for skeletal data, and the UCF-101 (UCF101) dataset [49] for RGB data.

4.1 Implementation Details

Network Architecture. Following the previous works [30,54], we use 2s-AGCN [45] and 3D ResNeXt-101 [13] as the backbone networks for skeletal and RGB datasets, respectively. As mentioned above, since the ERA module serves as a plug-and-play replacement for the conventional convolutional module, we uniformly replace 25% of convolutional layers with our ERA module in the backbone networks. Network hyperparameters $N_{in}, N_{out}, b_h, b_w$ at each layer follow the original settings in the backbone networks. Also, in each ERA module, $d = 0.2N_{out}$, i.e. 80% of the convolutional kernels are non-expert kernels and the other 20% are expert kernels, and $M = 5$.

For the mapping function f^p in Eq. 1, we first conduct average pooling across the spatial and temporal dimensions of the feature map before a linear layer is used to downsample to the dimensionality K, where K is set to 64.

Training. We perform experiments on Nvidia RTX 3090 GPU. For skeletal datasets, NTU60, NTU120 and SYSU, we follow [45] and set the initial learning rate α as 0.1, which then gradually decays to 0.001. The batch size B is 64. For RGB dataset UCF101, we follow the same experimental settings as [54]. Network parameters θ and expert learning rates β are updated using $\mathcal{L}$ defined in Sect. 3.4. γ_s is set to 0.1. Each β_i^p is initialized to α, and constrained to non-negative values. To allow end-to-end training of the retrieved experts in Eq. 3, Gumbel-Softmax [19] gradients are computed during backpropagation for the Argmax operation, with temperature τ set to 1.

Table 1. Performance comparison (%) of Early Action Prediction on NTU60 and SYSU. We follow the evaluation setting of [30,39,55] and [54] respectively. Even without ELRO, we can attain state-of-the-art performance. With ELRO, our method obtains further improvements.

Methods	Observation Ratios on NTU60						Observation Ratios on SYSU					
	20%	40%	60%	80%	100%	AUC	20%	40%	60%	80%	100%	AUC
Jain *et al.* [18]	7.07	18.98	44.55	63.84	71.09	37.38	31.61	53.37	68.71	73.96	75.53	57.23
Ke *et al.* [21]	8.34	26.97	56.78	75.13	80.43	45.63	26.76	52.86	72.32	79.40	80.71	58.89
Kong *et al.* [26]	-	-	-	-	-	-	51.75	58.83	67.17	73.83	74.67	61.33
Ma *et al.* [35]	-	-	-	-	-	-	57.08	71.25	75.42	77.50	76.67	67.85
Weng *et al.* [55]	35.56	54.63	67.08	72.91	75.53	57.51	-	-	-	-	-	-
Aliakbarian *et al.* [41]	27.41	59.26	72.43	78.10	79.09	59.98	56.11	71.01	78.39	80.31	78.50	69.12
Hu *et al.* [16]	-	-	-	-	-	-	56.67	75.42	80.42	82.50	79.58	71.25
Wang *et al.* [54]	35.85	58.45	73.86	80.06	82.01	60.97	63.33	75.00	81.67	86.25	87.92	74.31
Pang *et al.* [39]	33.30	56.94	74.50	80.51	81.54	61.07	-	-	-	-	-	-
Tran *et al.* [50]	24.60	57.70	76.90	85.70	88.10	62.80	-	-	-	-	-	-
Ke *et al.* [22]	32.12	63.82	77.02	82.45	83.19	64.22	58.81	74.21	82.18	84.42	83.14	72.55
HARD-Net [30]	42.39	72.24	82.99	86.75	87.54	70.56	-	-	-	-	-	-
Baseline	38.09	66.36	78.67	83.29	84.10	66.43	60.71	73.04	77.81	83.88	84.32	72.20
ERA-Net w/o ELRO	43.94	73.23	84.53	87.61	87.97	71.62	63.50	80.82	82.70	86.33	87.10	75.78
ERA-Net	**53.98**	**74.34**	**85.03**	**88.35**	**88.45**	**73.87**	**65.30**	**81.27**	**85.67**	**89.17**	**89.38**	**77.73**

4.2 Experiments on Early Action Prediction

NTU60 Dataset. [42] has been widely used for 3D action recognition and early action prediction. It is a large dataset that contains more than 56 thousand skeletal sequences from 60 activity classes. All human skeletons in the dataset contain 3D coordinates of 25 body joints. As noted in [30], this dataset is challenging for the 3D early action prediction task due to the presence of many classes with very similar starting sequences. We follow the evaluation protocol of [30].

We first compare the proposed ERA-Net with the state-of-the-art approaches on NTU60. The results over different observation ratios are shown in Table 1. Our full method is employed in the **ERA-Net** setting. In **ERA-Net w/o ELRO**, we use ERA modules but do not implement β to train experts using the proposed ELRO algorithm, instead we train using a single backpropagation step that updates all model parameters at each iteration. We also provide the **Baseline** setting for comparison, where the backbone is used without ERA modules.

We report the prediction accuracy at each observation ratio. Furthermore, we use the Area Under Curve (AUC) metric in our experiments, following previous works [30,39,55]. The AUC measures the average precision over all observation ratios and broadly summarizes each model's performance into a single metric. On NTU60, we achieve more than a 3 point improvement against existing state-of-the art method [30], suggesting that the ERA module effectively increases the discriminative capabilities on the early action prediction task.

One crucial observation is that ERA-Net outperforms existing methods more significantly when the observation ratio is low. For example, when the observation ratio is 20%, ERA-Net improves over state-of-the-art [30] by more than 11%, which further demonstrates that the ERA module is especially effective in

Table 2. Performance comparison (%) of Early Action Prediction on NTU120 and UCF101. As no prior works report NTU120 early action prediction results, we compare our method to the baseline. For UCF101, we follow the evaluation setting of [54].

Methods	Observation ratios on NTU120						Observation ratios on UCF101					
	20%	40%	60%	80%	100%	AUC	10%	30%	50%	70%	90%	AUC
MSRNN [16]	-	-	-	-	-	-	68.01	88.71	89.25	89.92	90.23	80.89
Wu *et al.* [56]	-	-	-	-	-	-	80.24	84.55	86.28	87.53	88.24	80.57
Wu *et al.* [57]	-	-	-	-	-	-	82.36	88.97	91.32	92.41	93.02	84.66
Wang *et al.* [54]	-	-	-	-	-	-	83.32	88.92	90.85	91.28	91.31	89.64
Baseline	23.14	32.49	59.07	75.61	81.18	50.03	82.88	89.02	89.64	91.12	91.96	89.30
ERA-Net w/o ELRO	29.60	43.45	65.14	78.03	82.01	55.52	86.99	91.49	93.63	94.24	94.40	92.51
ERA-Net	**31.73**	**45.67**	**67.08**	**78.84**	**82.43**	**57.02**	**89.14**	**92.39**	**94.29**	**95.45**	**95.72**	**93.64**

picking up subtle cues to tackle hard samples (where samples are more similar at the earlier stages).

SYSU Dataset. [14] is also commonly used for 3D action recognition and early action prediction. The dataset contains 480 skeletal sequences belonging to 12 action classes performed by 40 subjects. The human skeletons in this dataset contain 3D coordinates of 20 joints. We follow evaluation protocol of [54]. Comparisons against state-of-the-art methods are displayed in Table 1, where ERA-Net outperforms the current state-of-the-art [54] by about 3 points.

NTU120 Dataset. [32] is an extension of NTU60. It is currently the largest RGB+D dataset for 3D action analysis with more than 114k skeletal sequences and contains 120 activity classes. This dataset is challenging for the early action prediction task, containing many classes that are hard to classify without observing the full sequences. Comparisons are displayed in Table 2, where ERA-Net outperforms the baseline by about 7 points on the AUC metric. We also observe very large improvements at lower observation ratios, demonstrating the efficacy of our method for early action prediction.

UCF101 Dataset. [49] is a popular dataset containing 13,320 video clips of 101 classes of human activities. It is a commonly used dataset for action prediction from RGB videos. Comparisons against state-of-the-art action prediction methods are shown in Table 2, where ERA-Net outperforms current state-of-the-art methods [54,56,57] by 4 or more AUC points, showing that ERA provides gains for early action prediction on RGB video datasets as well.

4.3 Ablation Study

Impact of Number of Experts. We evaluate the ratio of experts and non-experts in Table 3(a). As performance peaks at 20 : 80, we set $d = 0.2N_{out}$, which allows for encoding of the most effective mix of general patterns and subtle cues within the layer.

Impact of Size of Expert Banks (M). We evaluate the size of Expert Banks in Table 3(b). We find that the performance increases moderately when M is

Table 3. Ablation studies conducted on NTU60. (a) Evaluation of ratios between number of experts and non-experts; (b) evaluation of size of Expert Banks M; (c) evaluation of the percentage (%) of convolutional layers replaced by ERA modules; (d) evaluation of the value of similarity loss weight γ_s; (e) evaluation of our dynamic retrieval mechanism against alternative static designs.

(a)		(b)		(c)		(d)		(e)	
Expert:Non-expert	AUC	M	AUC	% of ERA modules	AUC	γ_s	AUC	Method	AUC
0:100	66.43	1	66.43	0	66.43	0.05	72.92	Extra-Channel	67.55
20:80	73.87	2	71.55	25	73.87	0.1	73.87	Expert-Avg	68.02
60:40	71.22	5	73.87	50	73.79	0.2	73.85	ERA-Net	73.87
100:0	70.12	10	73.86	100	73.81	0.3	73.76		

increased from 2 to 5, and remains stable when we further increase it. We argue that this is because the representation capacity by setting $M = 5$ is sufficient to capture the subtle cues present in the dataset.

Impact of Number of ERA Modules. We ablate the decision of replacing 25% of convolutional layers with ERA modules in Table 3(c). We find that, above 25%, the performance does not increase further. This suggests that, at 25%, there is already sufficient representation capacity to handle the encoding of subtle cues.

Impact of Similarity Loss Weight (γ_s). We conduct ablation studies on the impact of γ_s in Table 3(d). $\gamma_s = 0.1$ performs the best. This because, when γ_s is set too low, the experts are not as diverse, and when it is set too high, the experts may lose focus on the main objective.

Impact of Dynamic Retrieval Mechanism. We evaluate our dynamic design by comparing our ERA module against other alternative static designs in Table 3(e). **Expert-Avg** averages the outputs of all experts within the Expert Bank (i.e. all experts are used for each input sample, without dynamic expert selection), while **Extra-Channel** adds extra channels to the traditional convolutional layer. *Notably, these alternative static designs use the same number of parameters as our ERA-Net.* We find that our dynamic retrieval mechanism provides significant improvement over these alternatives.

5 Conclusion

In this paper, we have proposed a novel plug-and-play ERA module for early action prediction. To encourage the experts to effectively use subtle differences for early action prediction, we push them to discriminate exclusively among similar samples. An Expert Learning Rate Optimization algorithm is further proposed to balance the training among numerous experts, which improves performance. Our method obtains state-of-the-art performance on four popular datasets.

Acknowledgement. This work is supported by National Research Foundation, Singapore under its AI Singapore Programme (AISG Award No: AISG-100E-2020-065), Ministry of Education Tier 1 Grant and SUTD Startup Research Grant.

References

1. Chaabane, M., Trabelsi, A., Blanchard, N., Beveridge, R.: Looking ahead: Anticipating pedestrians crossing with future frames prediction. In: Proceedings of the IEEE/CVF Winter Conference on Applications of Computer Vision, pp. 2297–2306 (2020)
2. Chen, L., Lu, J., Song, Z., Zhou, J.: Recurrent semantic preserving generation for action prediction. IEEE Trans. Circuits Syst. Video Technol. **31**(1), 231–245 (2020)
3. Chen, Y., Dai, X., Liu, M., Chen, D., Yuan, L., Liu, Z.: Dynamic convolution: Attention over convolution kernels. In: Proceedings of the IEEE/CVF Conference on Computer Vision and Pattern Recognition, pp. 11030–11039 (2020)
4. Chen, Y., Zhang, Z., Yuan, C., Li, B., Deng, Y., Hu, W.: Channel-wise topology refinement graph convolution for skeleton-based action recognition. In: Proceedings of the IEEE/CVF International Conference on Computer Vision, pp. 13359–13368 (2021)
5. Cheng, K., Zhang, Y., He, X., Chen, W., Cheng, J., Lu, H.: Skeleton-based action recognition with shift graph convolutional network. In: Proceedings of the IEEE/CVF Conference on Computer Vision and Pattern Recognition, pp. 183–192 (2020)
6. Emad, M., Ishack, M., Ahmed, M., Osama, M., Salah, M., Khoriba, G.: Early-anomaly prediction in surveillance cameras for security applications. In: 2021 International Mobile, Intelligent, and Ubiquitous Computing Conference (MIUCC), pp. 124–128. IEEE (2021)
7. Fatima, I., Fahim, M., Lee, Y.K., Lee, S.: A unified framework for activity recognition-based behavior analysis and action prediction in smart homes. Sensors **13**(2), 2682–2699 (2013)
8. Feichtenhofer, C., Fan, H., Malik, J., He, K.: SlowFast networks for video recognition. In: Proceedings of the IEEE/CVF International Conference on Computer Vision, pp. 6202–6211 (2019)
9. Finn, C., Abbeel, P., Levine, S.: Model-agnostic meta-learning for fast adaptation of deep networks. In: International Conference on Machine Learning, pp. 1126–1135. PMLR (2017)
10. Gammulle, H., Denman, S., Sridharan, S., Fookes, C.: Predicting the future: a jointly learnt model for action anticipation. In: Proceedings of the IEEE/CVF International Conference on Computer Vision, pp. 5562–5571 (2019)
11. Gujjar, P., Vaughan, R.: Classifying pedestrian actions in advance using predicted video of urban driving scenes. In: 2019 International Conference on Robotics and Automation (ICRA), pp. 2097–2103. IEEE (2019)
12. Han, Y., Huang, G., Song, S., Yang, L., Wang, H., Wang, Y.: Dynamic neural networks: A survey. arXiv preprint arXiv:2102.04906 (2021)
13. Hara, K., Kataoka, H., Satoh, Y.: Can spatiotemporal 3d CNNs retrace the history of 2d cnns and imagenet? In: Proceedings of the IEEE Conference on Computer Vision and Pattern Recognition, pp. 6546–6555 (2018)
14. Hu, J.F., Zheng, W.S., Lai, J., Zhang, J.: Jointly learning heterogeneous features for RGB-d activity recognition. In: Proceedings of the IEEE Conference on Computer Vision and Pattern Recognition, pp. 5344–5352 (2015)

15. Hu, J.-F., Zheng, W.-S., Ma, L., Wang, G., Lai, J.: Real-time RGB-D activity prediction by soft regression. In: Leibe, B., Matas, J., Sebe, N., Welling, M. (eds.) ECCV 2016. LNCS, vol. 9905, pp. 280–296. Springer, Cham (2016). https://doi.org/10.1007/978-3-319-46448-0_17
16. Hu, J.F., Zheng, W.S., Ma, L., Wang, G., Lai, J., Zhang, J.: Early action prediction by soft regression. IEEE Trans. Pattern Anal. Mach. Intell. **41**(11), 2568–2583 (2018)
17. Huang, C.M., Mutlu, B.: Anticipatory robot control for efficient human-robot collaboration. In: 2016 11th ACM/IEEE International Conference on Human-Robot Interaction (HRI), pp. 83–90. IEEE (2016)
18. Jain, A., Singh, A., Koppula, H.S., Soh, S., Saxena, A.: Recurrent neural networks for driver activity anticipation via sensory-fusion architecture. In: 2016 IEEE International Conference on Robotics and Automation (ICRA), pp. 3118–3125. IEEE (2016)
19. Jang, E., Gu, S., Poole, B.: Categorical reparameterization with Gumbel-Softmax. arXiv preprint arXiv:1611.01144 (2016)
20. Johnson, J.M., Khoshgoftaar, T.M.: Survey on deep learning with class imbalance. J. Big Data **6**(1), 1–54 (2019)
21. Ke, Q., Bennamoun, M., An, S., Sohel, F., Boussaid, F.: A new representation of skeleton sequences for 3D action recognition. In: Proceedings of the IEEE Conference on Computer Vision and Pattern Recognition, pp. 3288–3297 (2017)
22. Ke, Q., Bennamoun, M., Rahmani, H., An, S., Sohel, F., Boussaid, F.: Learning latent global network for skeleton-based action prediction. IEEE Trans. Image Process. **29**, 959–970 (2019)
23. Kong, Y., Fu, Y.: Human action recognition and prediction: a survey. arXiv preprint arXiv:1806.11230 (2018)
24. Kong, Y., Gao, S., Sun, B., Fu, Y.: Action prediction from videos via memorizing hard-to-predict samples. In: Proceedings of the AAAI Conference on Artificial Intelligence, vol. 32 (2018)
25. Kong, Y., Kit, D., Fu, Y.: A discriminative model with multiple temporal scales for action prediction. In: European conference on computer vision. pp. 596–611. Springer (2014)
26. Kong, Y., Tao, Z., Fu, Y.: Deep sequential context networks for action prediction. In: Proceedings of the IEEE Conference on Computer Vision and Pattern Recognition, pp. 1473–1481 (2017)
27. Kong, Y., Tao, Z., Fu, Y.: Adversarial action prediction networks. IEEE Trans. Pattern Anal. Mach. Intell. **42**(3), 539–553 (2018)
28. Koppula, H.S., Saxena, A.: Anticipating human activities using object affordances for reactive robotic response. IEEE Trans. Pattern Anal. Mach. Intell. **38**(1), 14–29 (2015)
29. Li, H., Wu, Z., Shrivastava, A., Davis, L.S.: 2D or not 2d? adaptive 3d convolution selection for efficient video recognition. In: CVPR, pp. 6155–6164 (2021)
30. Li, T., Liu, J., Zhang, W., Duan, L.: HARD-Net: hardness-AwaRe discrimination network for 3D early activity prediction. In: Vedaldi, A., Bischof, H., Brox, T., Frahm, J.-M. (eds.) ECCV 2020. LNCS, vol. 12356, pp. 420–436. Springer, Cham (2020). https://doi.org/10.1007/978-3-030-58621-8_25
31. Lin, J., Gan, C., Han, S.: TSM: temporal shift module for efficient video understanding. In: Proceedings of the IEEE/CVF International Conference on Computer Vision, pp. 7083–7093 (2019)

32. Liu, J., Shahroudy, A., Perez, M., Wang, G., Duan, L.Y., Kot, A.C.: NTU RGB+ D 120: a large-scale benchmark for 3d human activity understanding. IEEE Trans. Pattern Anal. Mach. Intell. **42**(10), 2684–2701 (2019)
33. Liu, J., Shahroudy, A., Wang, G., Duan, L.Y., Kot, A.C.: Skeleton-based online action prediction using scale selection network. IEEE Trans. Pattern Anal. Mach. Intell. **42**(6), 1453–1467 (2019)
34. Liu, Z., Zhang, H., Chen, Z., Wang, Z., Ouyang, W.: Disentangling and unifying graph convolutions for skeleton-based action recognition. In: Proceedings of the IEEE/CVF Conference on Computer Vision and Pattern Recognition, pp. 143–152 (2020)
35. Ma, S., Sigal, L., Sclaroff, S.: Learning activity progression in LSTMs for activity detection and early detection. In: Proceedings of the IEEE Conference on Computer Vision and Pattern Recognition, pp. 1942–1950 (2016)
36. Mavrogiannis, A., Chandra, R., Manocha, D.: B-gap: Behavior-guided action prediction for autonomous navigation. arXiv preprint arXiv:2011.03748 (2020)
37. Mullapudi, R.T., Mark, W.R., Shazeer, N., Fatahalian, K.: Hydranets: Specialized dynamic architectures for efficient inference. In: Proceedings of the IEEE Conference on Computer Vision and Pattern Recognition, pp. 8080–8089 (2018)
38. Nguyen, X.S.: GeomNet: a neural network based on Riemannian geometries of SPD matrix space and Cholesky space for 3d skeleton-based interaction recognition. In: Proceedings of the IEEE/CVF International Conference on Computer Vision, pp. 13379–13389 (2021)
39. Pang, G., Wang, X., Hu, J., Zhang, Q., Zheng, W.S.: DbdNet: learning bi-directional dynamics for early action prediction. In: IJCAI, pp. 897–903 (2019)
40. Reily, B., Han, F., Parker, L.E., Zhang, H.: Skeleton-based bio-inspired human activity prediction for real-time human-robot interaction. Auton. Robot. **42**(6), 1281–1298 (2018)
41. Sadegh Aliakbarian, M., Sadat Saleh, F., Salzmann, M., Fernando, B., Petersson, L., Andersson, L.: Encouraging lSTMs to anticipate actions very early. In: Proceedings of the IEEE International Conference on Computer Vision, pp. 280–289 (2017)
42. Shahroudy, A., Liu, J., Ng, T.T., Wang, G.: NTU RGB+ D: a large scale dataset for 3d human activity analysis. In: Proceedings of the IEEE Conference on Computer Vision and Pattern Recognition, pp. 1010–1019 (2016)
43. Shazeer, N., Mirhoseini, A., Maziarz, K., Davis, A., Le, Q., Hinton, G., Dean, J.: Outrageously large neural networks: the sparsely-gated mixture-of-experts layer (2017)
44. Shi, L., Zhang, Y., Cheng, J., Lu, H.: Skeleton-based action recognition with directed graph neural networks. In: Proceedings of the IEEE/CVF Conference on Computer Vision and Pattern Recognition, pp. 7912–7921 (2019)
45. Shi, L., Zhang, Y., Cheng, J., Lu, H.: Two-stream adaptive graph convolutional networks for skeleton-based action recognition. In: Proceedings of the IEEE/CVF Conference on Computer Vision and Pattern Recognition, pp. 12026–12035 (2019)
46. Shi, L., Zhang, Y., Cheng, J., Lu, H.: AdaSGN: adapting joint number and model size for efficient skeleton-based action recognition. In: Proceedings of the IEEE/CVF International Conference on Computer Vision, pp. 13413–13422 (2021)
47. Shu, J., et al.: Meta-Weight-Net: Learning an explicit mapping for sample weighting. In: : Proceedings of the 33rd International Conference on Neural Information Processing System (2019)

48. Song, Y.F., Zhang, Z., Shan, C., Wang, L.: Stronger, faster and more explainable: a graph convolutional baseline for skeleton-based action recognition. In: Proceedings of the 28th ACM International Conference on Multimedia, pp. 1625–1633 (2020)
49. Soomro, K., Zamir, A.R., Shah, M.: Ucf101: a dataset of 101 human actions classes from videos in the wild. arXiv preprint arXiv:1212.0402 (2012)
50. Tran, V., Balasubramanian, N., Hoai, M.: Progressive knowledge distillation for early action recognition. In: 2021 IEEE International Conference on Image Processing (ICIP), pp. 2583–2587. IEEE (2021)
51. Veit, A., Belongie, S.: Convolutional networks with adaptive inference graphs. In: Proceedings of the European Conference on Computer Vision (ECCV), pp. 3–18 (2018)
52. Wang, W., Chang, F., Liu, C., Li, G., Wang, B.: GA-Net: a guidance aware network for skeleton-based early activity recognition. IEEE Trans. Multim. Early Access (2021)
53. Wang, X., Yu, F., Dou, Z.Y., Darrell, T., Gonzalez, J.E.: SkipNet: learning dynamic routing in convolutional networks. In: Proceedings of the European Conference on Computer Vision (ECCV), pp. 409–424 (2018)
54. Wang, X., Hu, J.F., Lai, J.H., Zhang, J., Zheng, W.S.: Progressive teacher-student learning for early action prediction. In: Proceedings of the IEEE/CVF Conference on Computer Vision and Pattern Recognition, pp. 3556–3565 (2019)
55. Weng, J., Jiang, X., Zheng, W.L., Yuan, J.: Early action recognition with category exclusion using policy-based reinforcement learning. IEEE Trans. Circuits Syst. Video Technol. **30**(12), 4626–4638 (2020)
56. Wu, X., Wang, R., Hou, J., Lin, H., Luo, J.: Spatial-temporal relation reasoning for action prediction in videos. Int. J. Comput. Vision **129**(5), 1484–1505 (2021)
57. Wu, X., Zhao, J., Wang, R.: Anticipating future relations via graph growing for action prediction. In: Proceedings of the AAAI Conference on Artificial Intelligence, vol. 35, pp. 2952–2960 (2021)
58. Wu, Z., Li, H., Zheng, Y., Xiong, C., Jiang, Y., Davis, L.S.: A coarse-to-fine framework for resource efficient video recognition. Int. J. Comput. Vision **129**(11), 2965–2977 (2021)
59. Wu, Z., et al.: Blockdrop: Dynamic inference paths in residual networks. In: CVPR, pp. 8817–8826 (2018)
60. Xie, S., Sun, C., Huang, J., Tu, Z., Murphy, K.: Rethinking spatiotemporal feature learning: speed-accuracy trade-offs in video classification. In: Proceedings of the European Conference on Computer Vision (ECCV), pp. 305–321 (2018)
61. Xie, Z., Zhang, Z., Zhu, X., Huang, G., Lin, S.: Spatially adaptive inference with stochastic feature sampling and interpolation. In: Vedaldi, A., Bischof, H., Brox, T., Frahm, J.-M. (eds.) ECCV 2020. LNCS, vol. 12346, pp. 531–548. Springer, Cham (2020). https://doi.org/10.1007/978-3-030-58452-8_31
62. Xu, W., Yu, J., Miao, Z., Wan, L., Ji, Q.: Prediction-CGAN: human action prediction with conditional generative adversarial networks. In: Proceedings of the 27th ACM International Conference on Multimedia, pp. 611–619 (2019)
63. Yan, R., Tang, J., Shu, X., Li, Z., Tian, Q.: Participation-contributed temporal dynamic model for group activity recognition. In: Proceedings of the 26th ACM International Conference on Multimedia, pp. 1292–1300 (2018)
64. Yan, R., Xie, L., Tang, J., Shu, X., Tian, Q.: HiGCIN: hierarchical graph-based cross inference network for group activity recognition. IEEE Trans. Pattern Aanal. Mach. Intell. Early Access (2020)

65. Yan, R., Xie, L., Tang, J., Shu, X., Tian, Q.: Social adaptive module for weakly-supervised group activity recognition. In: Vedaldi, A., Bischof, H., Brox, T., Frahm, J.-M. (eds.) ECCV 2020. LNCS, vol. 12353, pp. 208–224. Springer, Cham (2020). https://doi.org/10.1007/978-3-030-58598-3_13
66. Yang, B., Bender, G., Le, Q.V., Ngiam, J.: CondConv: conditionally parameterized convolutions for efficient inference. In: Advances in Neural Information Processing Systems 32 (NeurIPS 2019) (2019)
67. Ye, F., Pu, S., Zhong, Q., Li, C., Xie, D., Tang, H.: Dynamic GCN: context-enriched topology learning for skeleton-based action recognition. In: Proceedings of the 28th ACM International Conference on Multimedia, pp. 55–63 (2020)

Dual Perspective Network for Audio-Visual Event Localization

Varshanth Rao[1(✉)], Md Ibrahim Khalil[1], Haoda Li[1,2], Peng Dai[1], and Juwei Lu[1]

[1] Huawei Noah's Ark Lab, Montreal, Canada
{varshanth.rao1,md.ibrahim.khalil,haoda.li, peng.dai,juwei.lu}@huawei.com
[2] University of Toronto, Toronto, Canada

Abstract. The Audio-Visual Event Localization (AVEL) problem involves tackling three core sub-tasks: the creation of efficient audio-visual representations using cross-modal guidance, the formation of short-term temporal feature aggregations, and its accumulation to achieve long-term dependency resolution. These sub-tasks are often performed by tailored modules, where the limited inter-module interaction restricts feature learning to a serialized manner. Past works have traditionally viewed videos as temporally sequenced multi-modal streams. We improve and extend on this view by proposing a novel architecture, the Dual Perspective Network (DPNet), that - (1) additionally operates on an intuitive *graph perspective* of a video to *simultaneously* facilitate cross-modal guidance and short-term temporal aggregation using a Graph Neural Network (GNN), (2) deploys a Temporal Convolutional Network (TCN) to achieve long-term dependency resolution, and (3) encourages interactive feature learning using a *cyclic feature refinement* process that alternates between the GNN and TCN. Further, we introduce the Relational Graph Convolutional Transformer, a novel GNN integrated into the DPNet, to express and attend each segment node's relational representation with its different relational neighborhoods. Lastly, we diversify the input to the DPNet through a new video augmentation technique called Replicate and Link, which outputs semantically identical video blends whose graph representations can be linked to that of the source videos. Experiments reveal that our DPNet framework outperforms prior state-of-the-art methods by large margins for the AVEL task on the public AVE dataset, while extensive ablation studies corroborate the efficacy of each proposed method.

1 Introduction

The rise of various multimedia platforms has resulted in the burgeon of videos across various sectors. The presence of various modalities within a video renders it a rich source of information. Videos stemming from real-life scenes often

Supplementary Information The online version contains supplementary material available at https://doi.org/10.1007/978-3-031-19830-4_39.

S. Avidan et al. (Eds.): ECCV 2022, LNCS 13694, pp. 689–704, 2022.
https://doi.org/10.1007/978-3-031-19830-4_39

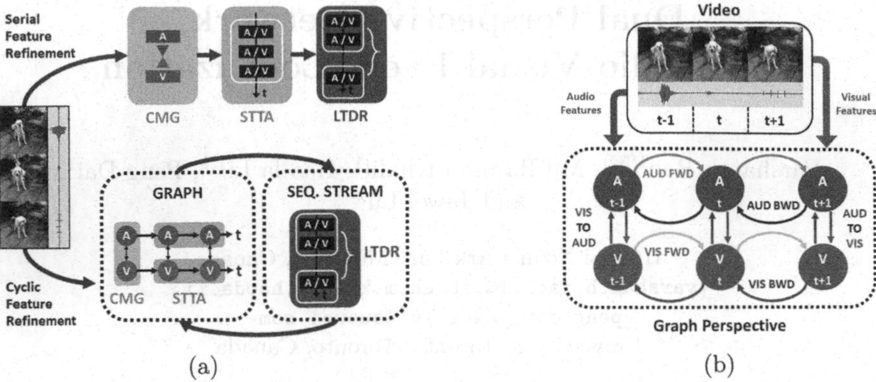

(a) (b)

Fig. 1. (a) Serial vs cyclic feature refinement involved in the execution of the three core AVEL sub-tasks: Cross-Modal Guidance (CMG), Short-Term Temporal Association (STTA), and Long-Term Dependency Resolution (LTDR). Serial feature refinement limits interaction between sub-task modules to a single pass. Valuable information acquired by the later modules are not conveyed to the earlier modules. Cyclic feature refinement alternates between graph and sequential stream perspectives, enriching the modal features by increasing information exchange between the modules. (b) Visualization of the graph perspective of a sample video. Segment-wise audio and visual features are represented by separate nodes, while edges constitute temporally directed and cross-modal relationships.

contain the audio and visual modalities in harmony. In order to understand, recognize and reaffirm events in one modality, processing the other modality can become a necessity. This is particularly true in the case of static sound sources such as an idling car, where it is difficult to recognize an audio-visual event (AVE) of a static car running without the disambiguation provided by the audio modality. The integrated processing of audio and visual modalities has bolstered methods in various tasks such as sound source localization and separation [1,11,17], synthesis of audio from visual data/visual data from audio [4,5], etc.

AVE Localization (AVEL) engulfs the core sub-tasks of (1) establishment of efficient audio-visual representations of segments through cross-modal guidance, (2) formation of short-term temporal associations to discern patches of event sequences and (3) their accumulation to store event contexts and resolve long-term temporal dependencies. Prior works view videos as sequential modal streams and devise separate modules to tackle these sub-tasks. The sub-network of [20] performs (1), that of [10] perform (1) and (2), while that of [26] perform all three. As illustrated in Fig. 1a, these modules seldom interact with each other apart from the order in which the pipeline is constructed, resulting in the limited serial feature refinement of a segment. Differently, we propose to view videos from an additional graph perspective with modal segment representations as nodes and their interconnections through temporally directed and cross-modal relationships as edges, as shown in Fig. 1b. By using GNNs on the video's graph, a node update encourages a modal segment's features to learn from its temporal neighbors as well as its modal counterparts, hence *simultaneously* addressing sub-tasks (1) and (2). Although deeper GNNs operating on these video graphs have larger temporal receptive fields, their innate nature induces the oversmoothing effect [8], making them undesirable to perform sub-task (3). Instead, we process the sequential stream perspective of a video using Temporal Convolutional Networks (TCNs) to implement long-term dependency resolution. Further, as shown in Fig. 1a, we alternately process the graph and sequential perspectives, allowing the three sub-tasks to co-refine the features to achieve cyclic feature refinement. We term this procedure as dual perspective processing and the corresponding network as the Dual Perspective Network (DPNet).

Since edges represent different relation types, we can leverage relational GNNs to compose relation-specific node updates. Prior relational GNNs such as Relational Graph Convolutional Network [15] and Relational Graph Attention Networks [3] assume that inter-node relationships are independent. Subsequently, the node updates are derived separately from each relational neighborhood because they are treated as isolated groups. However, in a video, the temporally directed and cross-modal connections between audio and visual segments are semantically related, hence breaking the assumption of relational independence. To induce cross-relational learning, we create a novel GNN called Relational Graph Convolutional Transformer (RGCT) which updates a segment node's relational representation by attending on and learning from its temporal and cross-modal neighborhoods.

An issue with the graph perspective is that segment nodes have limited neighbors of temporally directed and cross-modal nature. Given the segment labels, an effective way to enrich the graph representations is through graph expansion by interconnecting similar videos of the same event type. However, the expansion would be restricted to identical segment sequences, possibly with limited semantic context. Inspired by the CutMix technique [23], we devise a novel video augmentation strategy called Replicate and Link, which preserves the event composition and the semantic context of the original segment sequence. The graphs of the replicas and the originals can then be interlinked to achieve neighborhood expansion for each segment, hence allowing for diversified node updates.

We deploy the DPNet framework to tackle the AVEL problem under the supervised and weakly supervised setting on the public AVE dataset [18]. The contributions of our work are summarized below:

- We propose the Dual Perspective Network (DPNet) to alternately process videos as sequential modal streams, and as graphs. Different from prior works, the DPNet design addresses all the sub-tasks of the AVEL problem while achieving cyclic feature refinement.
- We introduce the Relational Graph Convolutional Transformer (RGCT) to update a node's relational representation by attending across the different relational neighborhoods. RGCTs are used in the DPNet to perform cross-modal guidance and short-term temporal aggregation.
- We design the Replicate and Link video augmentation technique to expand the training set by generating semantically identical replica videos, and enrich a video's graph representation through graph linkage with the replica.

– Experiments show that the DPNet outperforms prior works under the considered settings on the AVE dataset.

2 Related Works

Graphs in Temporal Action Localization (TAL): In TAL, prior works exploit a GNN's ability to perform neighborhood aggregation for refining segment or action proposal features. In [24], the action proposal features are treated as nodes and edges imply a significant temporal overlap or small inter-proposal distance. GNNs perform classification and boundary regression on the node features to achieve TAL. In [13], visual segments form the nodes and the edge weights between all segments are learned with a similarity metric. The learnt inter-segment relation assists in co-localization of similar actions. [22] construct a novel GCNeXt block which splits and operates on snippet nodes using two separate graphs to reflect temporal and semantic connectivity. The graphs are then merged and the updated features are used for performing action localization. Differently, to tackle the AVEL task, our graph constitutes segment nodes and temporal and cross-modal edges. Our GNN, the RGCT, refines segment features by attending across entire relational neighborhoods, rather than across constituent nodes.

Audio-Visual Event Localization (AVEL): The AVEL task entails the identification of temporal regions in a video corresponding to events which are both audible and visible. In [10], a unique Audio-Visual Transformer (AVT) produces short-term spatially attended feature maps corresponding to the sound source into an instance attention module to determine the extent of correlation between the audio and visual components. In [21], an audio-guided spatial-channel attention mechanism is used to refine visual features corresponding to the sound source. The audio features and the attended visual features are processed by blocks of cross-modal scaled dot product attention modules to co-refine modal features before performing segment-wise classification. Recently, [26] introduced a Positive Sample Propagation (PSP) module which calculates and thresholds a similarity matrix between all audio and visual segments. The PSP module then limits the refinement of segment features based on only the positively related connections. Different from prior works, we leverage the graph representation of videos to attend on short-term relationships defined according to temporal and cross-modal directions using GNNs and learn long-term relationships on the stream representation using temporal convolutions.

3 Methodology

3.1 Problem Statement

For the AVEL [18] task, each video sequence is split into N non-overlapping segments. The segment level event label is denoted by $y_t = \{y_t^c | y_t^c \in \{0,1\},$

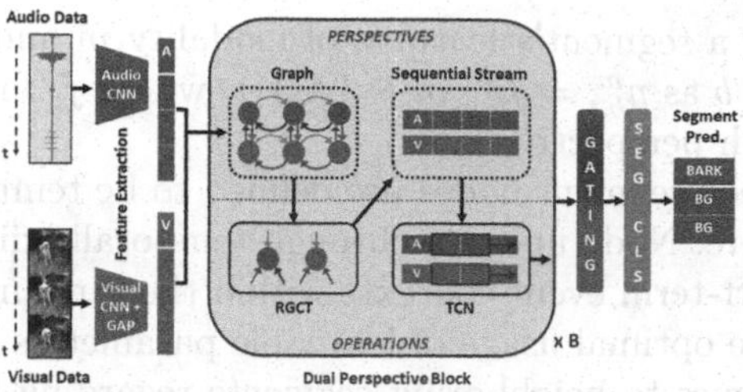

Fig. 2. Illustration of the DPNet used for the AVEL task. Audio and visual features are extracted from a video and fed to a series of Dual Perspective Blocks (DPBlocks). Each DPBlock first processes the graph perspective of the video using an RGCT layer and then processes the sequential stream perspective using a TCN layer. The output audio-visual features are gated and then subject to segment classification.

$\sum_{c=0}^{C-1} y_t^c = 1\}$ while the video level event label is denoted by $y = \{y^c | y^c \in \{0,1\}, \sum_{c=0}^{C-1} y^c = 1\}$. Here C denotes the number of event classes inclusive of a BG event indicating independently audible (or visible) events or the absence of an event. For each video segment, the audio and visual features are extracted and denoted as $\{f_t^A, f_t^V\}_{t=1}^N$ respectively. Here $f_t^A \in \mathcal{R}^{d_a}$ and $f_t^V \in \mathcal{R}^{d_v \times S}$ where d_a is the dimension of the audio features, d_v and S are the dimension and the spatial size of the visual feature maps respectively. Following [18], we fix the feature extractors and build our architecture on top of these local features. Supervised Event Localization (SEL) and Weakly Supervised Event Localization (WSEL) tasks entail the prediction of the segment level event label $\hat{y_t}$, wherein y_t is available to use for training in SEL and only the video level label y is available for WSEL.

3.2 Dual Perspective Network for AVE Localization

We address the three core sub-tasks of AVEL, namely, the establishment of efficient audio-visual representations through cross-modal guidance, the formation of short-term temporal associations, and their accumulation to store event contexts. The first two sub-tasks involve feature interaction within a small temporal neighborhood while the last involves learning to resolve long-term dependencies through the formation of a global understanding. To address the former, we employ GNNs on a video's graph perspective and we tackle the latter using modality-wise temporal convolutions on its sequential stream perspective. A block that sequentially processes both perspectives once is termed as a Dual Perspective Block (DPBlock) and the network with one or more DPBlocks as the Dual Perspective Network (DPNet). We visualize the DPNet architecture for the AVEL task in Fig. 2 and detail its mechanism below.

Graph Perspective: In the graph perspective of a video, a node represents an audio or visual segment's features local to the DPBlock. Concretely, we define a node representing a segment's features of modality m and time step t within a DPBlock of index b as $n_{b,t}^m = f_{b,t}^m, m \in \{A, V\}$, where $f_{b,t}^m$ represents the input features to the graph perspective layer.

The edges between segment nodes are defined to be temporally directed and cross-modal in nature. Node updates through temporally directed edges enable the encoding of short-term event contexts within the same modality. These contexts can lead to the optimal usage of learnable parameters. E.g., event borders can provide useful cues to neighboring segments regarding how to characterize the start or end of an event. Node updates through cross-modal edges perform cross-modal feature refinement which can assist to achieve a local consensus on an ambiguous AVE. E.g., for static sound sources like idling cars or church bells whose bell movements are occluded, the model can utilize the visual cue of the presence of the static candidate sound source while leveraging the audio signal to confirm the presence of the characteristic sound. All node updates execute simultaneously when the graph is processed using a GNN.

We denote the edge set representing the temporally forward relationships between segments of the same modality m as $\mathcal{E}_{b,r_f}^m$ and temporally backward relationships as $\mathcal{E}_{b,r_b}^m$. Further, we denote the edge set representing the audio to visual and visual to audio relationships between audio and visual segments as $\mathcal{E}_{b,r_{AV}}$ and $\mathcal{E}_{b,r_{VA}}$ respectively. We define $\mathcal{E}_{b,r_f}^m, \mathcal{E}_{b,r_b}^m, \mathcal{E}_{b,r_{AV}}$ and $\mathcal{E}_{b,r_{VA}}$ as:

$$\mathcal{E}_{b,r_f}^m = \{(n_{b,t}^m, n_{b,t+1}^m) | t \in \{1, 2, .., N-1\}\} \tag{1}$$

$$\mathcal{E}_{b,r_b}^m = \{(n_{b,t}^m, n_{b,t-1}^m) | t \in \{2, .., N-1, N\}\} \tag{2}$$

$$\mathcal{E}_{b,r_{AV}} = \{(n_{b,t}^A, n_{b,t}^V) | t \in \{1, 2, .., N\}\} \tag{3}$$

$$\mathcal{E}_{b,r_{VA}} = \{(n_{b,t}^V, n_{b,t}^A) | t \in \{1, 2, .., N\}\} \tag{4}$$

Summarizing the video's graph local to a DPBlock of index b as $\mathcal{G}_b = \{\mathcal{N}_b, \mathcal{E}_b\}$, where $\mathcal{N}_b = \{n_{b,t}^m | m \in \{A, V\}, t \in \{1, 2, .., N\}\}$ represents the modal segment node set and $\mathcal{E}_b = \mathcal{E}_{b,r_f}^m \cup \mathcal{E}_{b,r_b}^m \cup \mathcal{E}_{b,r_{AV}} \cup \mathcal{E}_{b,r_{VA}}$ represents the temporally directed and cross-modal edge set. We process $\mathcal{G}_b$ using a suitable GNN, $\mathcal{F}_b^{GNN}$.

Sequential Stream Perspective: Here, a video is described exclusively by modality-wise temporal sequences. By processing the video within a reference modality, the network learns to assist in forming short-term modality-specific contexts and gradually accumulates these to learn long-term dependencies. This procedure is critical since AVEs can be temporally well spaced. An exemplar case would be the animal sound AVEs which occur discontinuously and in short bursts. The model needs to characterize the entire event and remember the event context to recognize it if it occurs again within the video. We choose Temporal Convolutional Networks (TCNs) over RNNs to process each modal stream, as the former can potentially learn longer sequences than the latter [2].

Formally, we denote the input features of a segment of modality $m \in \{A, V\}$ and time step t to the sequential stream layer of DPBlock index b as $\tilde{f}_{b,t}^m$. The audio and visual streams are denoted respectively as $F_b^A = \{\tilde{f}_{b,t}^A, t \in \{1, 2, .., N\}\}$ and $F_b^V = \{\tilde{f}_{b,t}^V, t \in \{1, 2, .., N\}\}$. We employ TCN layers $\mathcal{F}_{b,A}^{TCN}$ and $\mathcal{F}_{b,V}^{TCN}$ with parameters W_b^A and W_b^V, kernel size k, and the Swish activation [12]:

$$\mathcal{F}_{b,A}^{TCN} = \text{Swish}(\text{TCN}(F_b^A, k; W_b^A)) \tag{5}$$

$$\mathcal{F}_{b,V}^{TCN} = \text{Swish}(\text{TCN}(F_b^V, k; W_b^V)) \tag{6}$$

Since $\mathcal{F}_{b,A}^{TCN}$ and $\mathcal{F}_{b,V}^{TCN}$ operate separately on audio and visual streams, we denote their parallel execution as $\mathcal{F}_b^{TCN}$.

Dual Perspective Network: We first denote the DPBlock of index b as $\mathcal{F}_b^{DPBlock}$ and define it as the sequential execution of $\mathcal{F}_b^{GNN}$ to $\mathcal{F}_b^{TCN}$. The DPNet backbone $\mathcal{F}^{DPNet}$ can be expressed as the sequence of B DPBlocks. Formally,

$$\mathcal{F}_b^{DPBlock} = \mathcal{F}_b^{GNN} \rightarrow \mathcal{F}_b^{TCN} \tag{7}$$

$$\mathcal{F}^{DPNet} = \mathcal{F}_1^{DPBlock} \rightarrow \mathcal{F}_2^{DPBlock} .. \rightarrow \mathcal{F}_B^{DPBlock} \tag{8}$$

For AVEL, we first subject f_t^V to a Global Average Pooling layer, yielding a condensed feature vector $\hat{f}_t^V \in \mathcal{R}^{d_v}$. An FC layer with parameters $W_a \in \mathcal{R}^{d_a \times d_v}$ is applied to f_t^A to yield $\hat{f}_t^A \in \mathcal{R}^{d_v}$. Next, we input $\{\hat{f}_t^A, \hat{f}_t^V\}_{t=1}^N$ to the DPNet backbone. The output audio and visual features of the DPNet backbone are denoted as $\{\hat{\hat{f}}_t^A, \hat{\hat{f}}_t^V\}_{t=1}^N$. We then learn a gating function $\mathcal{F}^G$ through an FC layer parameterized by W_G with a sigmoid activation that operates on a fusion of the features of both modalities. Finally, we apply $\mathcal{F}^G$ to yield the final localization features as a weighted consensus through the convex combination of both the modalities.

$$\mathcal{F}_t^G = \sigma(\text{FC}([\hat{\hat{f}}_t^A, \hat{\hat{f}}_t^V]; W_G)) \tag{9}$$

$$G_t^{AV} = \mathcal{F}_t^G \odot \hat{\hat{f}}_t^A + (1 - \mathcal{F}_t^G) \odot \hat{\hat{f}}_t^V \tag{10}$$

where [.] denotes concatenation and $\odot$ the element-wise product. We transform G_t^{AV} into localization predictions over C classes using an FC layer with a softmax activation.

$$\hat{y}_t = \text{Softmax}(\text{FC}(G_t^{AV}; W_{seg})) \tag{11}$$

The WSEL is formulated as a Multi-Instance Learning (MIL) problem, so we use MIL pooling to aggregate the segment predictions into a video level prediction $\hat{y}$. We use the cross-entropy loss to supervise the SEL and WSEL tasks using the segment-level (y_t) and video-level (y) labels respectively.

3.3 Relational Graph Convolutional Transformer

Earlier, we deduced that the temporally directed and cross-modal edges between audio and visual segment nodes are semantically related, which breaks the

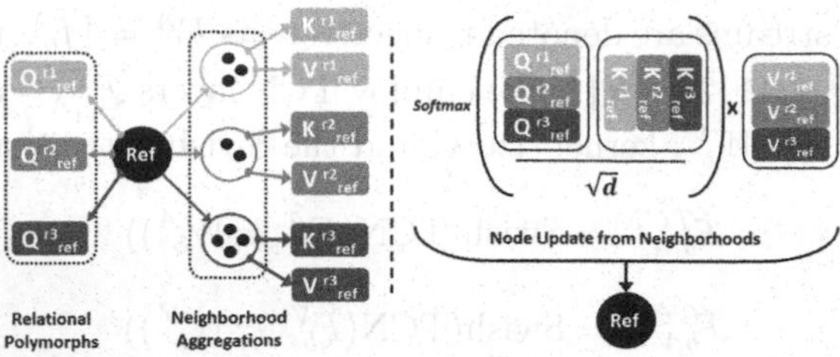

Fig. 3. Visualization of the mechanism of the RGCT. Here, different colors indicate the different relation types. A reference node "Ref" (audio/visual node) is projected into its relational polymorphs as query vectors, while its neigbhorhood aggregations are projected into key and value vectors. The cross-relational scaled dot product attention is used to compose the node update from the relational neighborhoods.

assumption of relational independence that fuels the prior GNNs like Relational Graph Convolutional Networks (RGCN) [15] and Relational Graph Attention Networks (RGAT) [3]. To leverage and extract the semantic relationships between the different edge types, we execute a *cross-relational attention mechanism* via a novel GNN called the Relational Graph Convolutional Transformer (RGCT), as shown in Fig. 3. The RGCT is deployed to the DPNet as the $\mathcal{F}_b^{GNN}$ in a DPBlock.

We simplify the graph notation by omitting reference to DPBlock b as $\mathcal{G} = \{\mathcal{N}, \mathcal{E}\}$. We denote the set of indices of the neighbor nodes to a reference node n_i under relation r as η_i^r, where $r \in R$, $R = \{r_{Af}, r_{Ab}, r_{Vf}, r_{Vb}, r_{AV}, r_{VA}\}$ represents the audio and visual temporally directed and cross-modal relationships defined earlier. Next, the neighborhood aggregation of η_i^r is defined as:

$$NA(\eta_i^r) = \frac{1}{|\eta_i^r|} \sum_{j \in \eta_i^r} n_j \tag{12}$$

Nodes can be expressed according to the different relationships it exhibits. These expressions are called *relational polymorphs* and they act as reservoirs of relation-specific details that can be captured from a node's general representation. E.g., a visual node of a person speaking can have the visual temporal forward polymorph encode the presence of the person in the next segment, while the visual to audio polymorph can associate the person's open mouth with the audible speech.

We transform a node n_i into a relational polymorph of type r using an FC layer parameterized by W_Q^r as a query vector $Q_i^r = \text{FC}(n_i; W_Q^r)$. Following the purpose of deriving cross-relational attention, we transform the neighborhood aggregations into key and value vectors parameterized by W_K^r and W_V^r respectively as $K_i^r = \text{FC}(\eta_i^r; W_K^r)$ and $V_i^r = \text{FC}(\eta_i^r; W_V^r)$. We collect the relational polymorphs and neighborhood aggregations of n_i, into single matrix representations as $Q_i = \overset{r}{\|} Q_i^r$, $K_i = \overset{r}{\|} K_i^r$ and $V_i = \overset{r}{\|} V_i^r$, where $\overset{r}{\|}$ is the stack operation over all $r \in R$, $(Q_i^r, K_i^r, V_i^r) \in \mathcal{R}^d$ and $(Q_i, K_i, V_i) \in \mathcal{R}^{|R| \times d}$. We build the cross-relational attention map $Att_i \in \mathcal{R}^{|R| \times |R|}$ and the relation-weighted neighborhood aggregation NA_{att} using scaled dot product attention [19] as follows:

$$Att_i = \text{Softmax}(\frac{Q_i K_i^T}{\sqrt{d}}) \tag{13}$$

$$NA_{att}(\eta_i) = Att_i V_i \tag{14}$$

To summarize $NA_{att}(\eta_i)$, we average along the relation axis r as $\overline{NA}_{att}(\eta_i) = avg_r(NA_{att}(\eta_i))$. Then, we project n_i to the feature space of $\overline{NA}_{att}$ using an FC layer parameterized by W_1, followed by the Swish activation function. Finally, we update the node n_i to n'_i using an FC parameterized by W_2:

$$\hat{n}_i = \text{Swish}(\text{FC}(n_i; W_1)) \tag{15}$$

$$n'_i = \text{Swish}(\text{FC}(\hat{n}_i + \text{DropOut}(\overline{NA}_{att}(\eta_i)); W_2)) \tag{16}$$

3.4 Replicate and Link Video Augmentation

Equations 1-4 reveal that a node in the video's graph possesses a small neighborhood. Small neighborhoods limit node updates and encourage nodes to overfit by creating rigid relation templates. We can alleviate overfitting by increasing the GNN layers to expose nodes to larger neighborhoods. However, on small graphs, this leads to the over-smoothing phenomenon [8]. We tackle this issue by expanding the neighborhood at run-time through the linkage of the graph representations of the original video with that of the semantically identical replicas. We term this video augmentation technique as Replicate and Link and visualize the process through an example in Fig. 4.

Replica Creation: Analogous to action instances in [9], we observe that AVEs can be decomposed into start, continuation, and end sub-events based on temporal progression. Sub-events of the same class type exhibit semantic similarities. E.g., the start sub-event of the helicopter event involves its lift-off from the helipad while its end sub-event often involves its landing and the termination

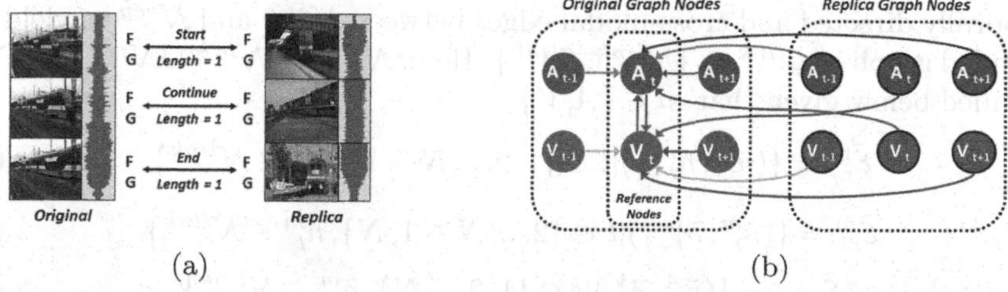

Fig. 4. (a) Illustration of the Replicate operation. A clip of a "Train" AVE is broken down into start, continue and end sub-events. Then, a replica clip of the *same sub-event sequence* is generated. Here, FG indicates the foreground train event. (b) Visualization of the Link operation wherein reference audio and visual nodes receive relevant edge connections from both the original and replica graphs

Algorithm 1: Replica Creation

Input: Original video O of event type e, start, continue and end sub-event databases

Output: Replica video R_O of event type e

```
Identify a sub-event sequence for O as SEQ_O = se_1, se_2, ..se_{N_se}, such that there
  exists sub-event samples of matching segment length for each se_i ∈ SEQ_O, in
  the se_i database
Initialize R_O to None
for i ← 1 to N_se do
  | Choose a random sample v from se_i database matching the segment length
  |   of se_i
  | Append v to R_O
end
```

of blade rotation. We propose that sub-event segments from different videos of the same event type can be swapped to synthesize semantically identical videos called replicas.

For each training set video of event type e, we first identify and extract the start and end sub-event segments using a one-segment context window around the event border. Next, we identify the continue sub-event segments as those which are wedged between a start and end sub-event. We copy and decompose a continue sub-event of length L into smaller continue sub-events of length $1, 2, .., L-1$. We store the respective sub-events into separate sub-event databases. Then, given an original video and the sub-event databases of event type e, we generate the replica using Algorithm 1. The discontinuity in context introduced by stitching sub-events from different videos allows the network to hone in on the discriminative features specific to the sound source.

Graph Linkage: Given replica videos of identical event sequences, we mutually expand the graph representations of the original and replica videos through graph linkage. Formally, given the graphs of the original and replica as $\mathcal{G}^{orig} = \{\mathcal{N}^{orig}, \mathcal{E}^{orig}\}$ and $\mathcal{G}^{rep} = \{\mathcal{N}^{rep}, \mathcal{E}^{rep}\}$, we merge $\mathcal{G}^{orig}$ and $\mathcal{G}^{rep}$ and then add temporally directed and cross-modal edges between $\mathcal{N}^{orig}$ and $\mathcal{N}^{rep}$ to yield the expanded graph as $\mathcal{G}^{link} = \{\mathcal{N}^{link}, \mathcal{E}^{link}\}$. Here, $\mathcal{N}^{link} = \mathcal{N}^{orig} \cup \mathcal{N}^{rep}$ and $\mathcal{E}^{link}$ is defined below given that $m \in \{A, V\}$:

$$\tilde{\mathcal{E}}^m_{r_f} = \{(\tilde{n}^m_t, \tilde{n}^m_{t+1}) | t \in \{1, 2, .., N-1\}, \tilde{n}^m_t \in \mathcal{N}^{link}\} \tag{17}$$

$$\tilde{\mathcal{E}}^m_{r_b} = \{(\tilde{n}^m_t, \tilde{n}^m_{t-1}) | t \in \{2, .., N-1, N\}, \tilde{n}^m_t \in \mathcal{N}^{link}\} \tag{18}$$

$$\tilde{\mathcal{E}}_{r_{AV}} = \{(\tilde{n}^A_t, \tilde{n}^V_t) | t \in \{1, 2, .., N\}, \tilde{n}^m_t \in \mathcal{N}^{link}\} \tag{19}$$

$$\tilde{\mathcal{E}}_{r_{VA}} = \{(\tilde{n}^V_t, \tilde{n}^A_t) | t \in \{1, 2, .., N\}, \tilde{n}^m_t \in \mathcal{N}^{link}\} \tag{20}$$

$$\mathcal{E}^{link} = \tilde{\mathcal{E}}^m_{r_f} \cup \tilde{\mathcal{E}}^m_{r_b} \cup \tilde{\mathcal{E}}_{r_{AV}} \cup \tilde{\mathcal{E}}_{r_{VA}} \tag{21}$$

Through graph linkage, we diversify the feature space of the aggregated neighborhoods (refer Eq. 12) and correspondingly influence the node update in Eq. 16.

4 Experiments

Dataset and Evaluation Metrics: The AVE dataset [18] is a subset of the AudioSet [6] containing 4143 videos covering 28 real-life event classes such as human speech, vehicle sounds, musical performances etc. Each video is evenly partitioned into 10 segments and each segment is 1 s long. Event labels are available at the segment and video level. AVEs are both audible and visible and spans for at least two seconds. We adopt the same train/validation/test split as [18]. Recently, [26] corrected the annotations for some test videos and report their performance on this corrected test set. We refer to the AVE dataset with the *original* test set as **O-AVE** and the one with the *corrected* version as **C-AVE**. Following all prior works, we evaluate the localization performance using the global classification accuracy of segment predictions.

Implementation Details: For a fair comparison with prior works, we utilize the same extracted audio and visual features (provided with the AVE dataset) using VGGish [7] and VGG19 [16] networks pretrained on AudioSet [6] and ImageNet [14] respectively. We implement the DPNet using PyTorch Geometric library. The DPNet is built with 4 DPBlocks, each with an RGCT operating first and configured with a dropout probability of 0.2, followed by a TCN layer of kernel size 3. The feature size is set to 768 for all transformations. We train the DPNet using a mini-batch of 48 videos, and use cosine annealing with warm restarts to cycle the learning rates every 20 epochs from 1 to 0.1 till epoch 300, and then to 0.01 till epoch 400. *Only for the SEL setting*, we dynamically generate and link one replica for each video in the mini-batch. For all our experiments, we fix the random seed values for all libraries to ensure reproducible results.

4.1 Quantitative Analysis

Comparisons with SoTA: We compare the AVEL performance of our DPNet on the AVE dataset under the SEL and WSEL settings with Audio-Visual Transformer (AVT) [10], Cross Modal Relation Aware Network (CMRAN) [21] and Positive Sample Propagation (PSP) Network [26]. Unlike prior works, DPNet uses GNNs and TCNs and performs cyclic feature refinement via dual perspective processing. As demonstrated in Table 1, the DPNet with our proposed RGCT outperforms prior works, validating the superiority of cyclic feature refinement. Specifically, DPNet outperforms the previous SoTA, CMRAN, on the O-AVE dataset by **1.53%** on the SEL task and by **1.56%** on the WSEL task. Also, on the C-AVE dataset, it surpasses the previous SoTA, PSP, by **1.88%** on the SEL task and by **1.65%** on the WSEL task.

Effectiveness of the Replicate and Link Augmentation: We investigate the role of the Replicate and Link augmentation technique for the AVEL task under the SEL setting and summarize the ablation in Table 2. We note that the base DPNet performs competitively against prior SoTA methods for the SEL

Table 1. Performance comparison with SoTAs for the SEL and WSEL tasks on the O-AVE and C-AVE datasets.

AVEL Method	Dataset	WSEL Acc (%)	SEL Acc (%)
AVT [10]	O-AVE	70.20	76.80
PSP [26]	O-AVE	72.93	76.84
CMRAN [21]	O-AVE	72.94	77.40
PSP [26]	C-AVE	73.50	77.80
DPNet (Ours w/ RGCT)	**O-AVE**	**74.50**	**78.93**
DPNet (Ours w/ RGCT)	**C-AVE**	**75.15**	**79.68**

Table 2. Ablation study for the Replicate and Link augmentation technique for the SEL task on the O-AVE and C-AVE datasets. Replicate indicates inclusion of the generated replicas during training. Link indicates the interconnection of the graph representations of the original and replica videos.

DPNet	Replicate	Link	O-AVE SEL Acc. (%)	C-AVE SEL Acc. (%)
✓			77.50	78.08
✓	✓		78.08	78.78
✓	✓	✓	78.93	79.68

task. We observe that the replication procedure brings a **∼0.6–0.7%** boost. On inspection, we observe large improvements (> 10%) on events that have high scope to focus on common event contexts rather than the sound source. Example contexts include the green fields where *horses* ride, uniformly colored walls where *clocks* sit, and surrounding traffic with *buses* in between. Further, by applying the link operation, we derive an additional **∼0.9%** increase in overall performance with major improvements visible on AVEs of rodents (+17%), female speech (+8%), and motorcycle (+7%). We observe that these categories benefit from a richer sound source localization due to the feature interpolation achieved during the neighborhood aggregation on the expanded graph representation.

Perspective Combinations: Here, we investigate the influence of each perspective by analyzing the performance of similarly sized networks which cover various perspective combinations. Results are presented in Table 3. Rows 1 and 2 respectively denote the RGAT [3] and RGCT only networks which process only the video's graph perspective. Row 3 denotes a TCN only network operating separately on the audio and visual streams. Rows 4 and 5 present the networks which respectively process the sequential stream (TCN) to graph perspectives (RGCT) and vice versa. The DPNet with Parallel Perspective Block (PPBlock) in row 6 performs parallel processing of both perspectives within a block using the split-transform-merge strategy, instead of the serial style we follow in the DPBlock. Finally, rows 7 and 8 indicate the DPNet with different RGCT-TCN

Table 3. Ablation study on the various networks tailored for different perspective combinations. Performance is reported for the SEL and WSEL tasks on the O-AVE dataset. For the SEL task, Base denotes performance of the network alone, Rep. denotes addition of replica videos during training, and Link denotes the inclusion of the link operation.

	Network	Perspective Setting	WSEL Acc. (%)	SEL Acc (%) Base	+ Rep	+ Link
1	RGAT Only	One	51.83	56.11	58.91	60.47
2	RGCT Only	Perspective	59.22	63.73	64.72	67.13
3	TCN Only	Only	70.20	74.60	76.10	N/A
4	TCN → RGCT	Two	59.40	64.17	66.80	70.08
5	RGCT → TCN	Perspectives	65.52	65.37	70.50	71.07
6	DPNet w/ PPBlock	Block-wise	71.42	74.82	76.32	77.36
7	DPNet w/ Graph Second	Two	73.70	76.55	78.01	78.60
8	**DPNet w/ Graph First**	Perspectives	**74.50**	**77.50**	**78.08**	**78.93**

order within a DPBlock as defined in Eq. 7. For all networks, the gating mechanism described in Eqs. 9 and 10 performs the feature fusion for localization. We perform hyperparameter tuning separately on each network to extract the best individual performances.

Within the graph-only perspective setting (rows 1 and 2), we observe that the proposed RGCT only network significantly outperforms the RGAT only network, highlighting the importance of executing the RGCT's cross-relational attention mechanism for the semantically related relationships. Additionally, we discover that the low results obtained using graph-based (sub)networks (rows 1, 2, 4, and 5) are caused by the oversmoothing effect by the GNN on the localization features which results in similar event predictions for many continuous segments within a video. Similarly, we observe that although the TCN layer in the last DPBlock of the DPNet in row 7 produces discriminative features, the subsequent RGCT layer smooths them across the temporal vicinity before localization, reducing the segment-wise localization performance. Within the DPNet designs (rows 6-8), although the DPNet w/ PPBlock is competitive, it falls short to that of DPNet w/ DPBlock (row 7 and 8). We attribute this to the reduced interaction between the parallel TCN and RGCT layers within a PPBlock as opposed to the richer interaction achieved during their sequential execution within a DPBlock of the DPNet. Finally, we observe that the inclusion of the Replicate and Link augmentation boosts the performance of all methods wherever applicable, with larger increments visible when the base network performance is relatively low.

4.2 Qualitative Analysis

For each relation r of a relevant audio/visual node n_i, we utilize the Class Activation Map [25] algorithm to visualize the Feature Activation Map (FAM) for

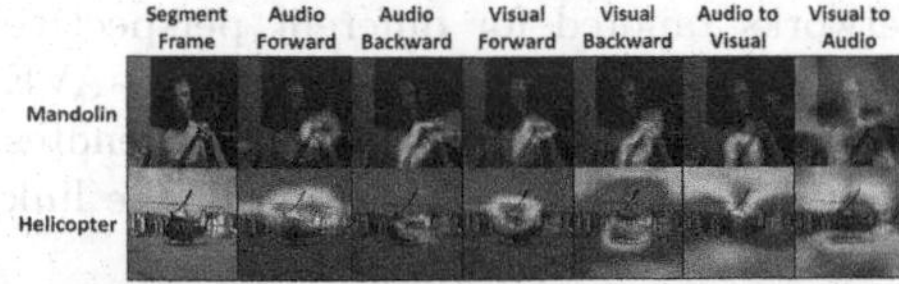

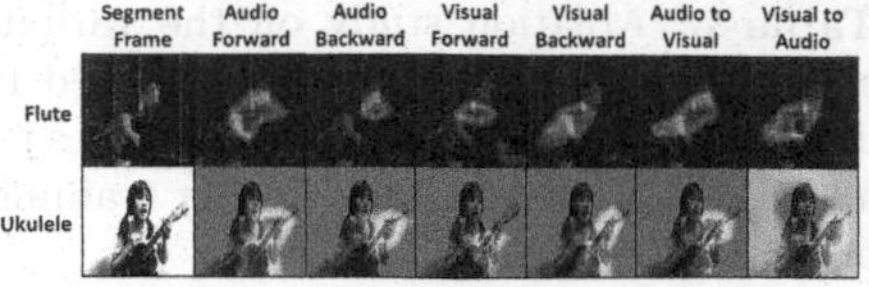

Fig. 5. Visualizations of the Feature Activation Maps from query projections of the audio and visual nodes into relational polymorphs. Each relational polymorph hones its focus onto spatial regions relevant to its semantic functionality, contributing to a rich node update

each relational polymorph, by taking the overall maximum activation (to avoid region inversions) of the query vector Q_i^r of the RGCT in the first DPBlock. Although FAMs here cannot be compared directly to attention maps of prior work, they offer insights into the model's decision-making process. In Fig. 5, we plot the FAMs of the relational polymorphs for segments from videos of different AVE types. We observe that temporally forward polymorphs focus on locating the spatial region(s) corresponding to the actual parts of the sound source, while the temporally backward polymorphs often concentrate on ensuring the presence of the sound source itself. E.g., the audio forward polymorph for the mandolin AVE captures the contact of the player's fingers with the mandolin, and that of the helicopter AVE focuses on the rotating blades. In contrast, the audio backward polymorph of the mandolin AVE targets the entire mandolin, and that of the helicopter focuses on the helicopter's body. Similar patterns can be discerned from the visual temporal polymorphs, although less consistently. Additionally, we perceive that the cross-modal polymorphs disseminate information about the sound source from the source modality's perspective. E.g., the audio to visual polymorph for the ukulele AVE focuses on both the player's mouth and ukulele since the person is singing and playing simultaneously. Similarly, for the flute AVE, both the player's mouth and the flute are targeted. In contrast, the visual to audio polymorphs rather focuses on the player's hand contact with the flute and ukulele. It is lucid that the model can focus on different visual regions via the relational polymorphs and this focus is calibrated according to the semantic functionality of the relation type.

5 Conclusion

In this paper, we proposed the DPNet to perform the AVEL task on a video by alternating between its sequential stream and the graph perspectives. By doing so, we achieve cyclic feature refinement between the modules performing cross-modal guidance, short-term temporal aggregation, and long-term dependency resolution. The RGCT was introduced to operate on the graph perspective and achieve cross-relational attention between the relational polymorphs of each node and its relational neighborhoods. The visualizations plotted in the qualitative analysis corroborate that the relational polymorphs implement focus on different spatial regions to propagate relation-specific information during the node update. For the SEL task, the Replicate and Link video augmentation technique enlarged the AVE dataset through the production of semantically identical video replicas and expanded the source video's graph through the interconnection with that of the replica's. Ablation studies demonstrate that both the Replicate and Link operations are effective in assisting the model for the SEL task. Additionally, we validate the superiority of the DPNet structure over other network designs which can operate on both video perspectives. Lastly, comparison results show that the DPNet framework outperforms prior methods in both the SEL and WSEL tasks by large margins.

References

1. Arandjelović, R., Zisserman, A.: Objects that sound. In: Ferrari, V., Hebert, M., Sminchisescu, C., Weiss, Y. (eds.) ECCV 2018. LNCS, vol. 11205, pp. 451–466. Springer, Cham (2018). https://doi.org/10.1007/978-3-030-01246-5_27
2. Bai, S., Kolter, J.Z., Koltun, V.: An empirical evaluation of generic convolutional and recurrent networks for sequence modeling. arXiv preprint arXiv:1803.01271 (2018)
3. Busbridge, D., Sherburn, D., Cavallo, P., Hammerla, N.Y.: Relational graph attention networks (2019)
4. Chatterjee, M., Cherian, A.: Sound2sight: generating visual dynamics from sound and context. In: Vedaldi, A., Bischof, H., Brox, T., Frahm, J.-M. (eds.) ECCV 2020. LNCS, vol. 12372, pp. 701–719. Springer, Cham (2020). https://doi.org/10.1007/978-3-030-58583-9_42
5. Gan, C., Huang, D., Chen, P., Tenenbaum, J.B., Torralba, A.: Foley music: learning to generate music from videos. In: Vedaldi, A., Bischof, H., Brox, T., Frahm, J.-M. (eds.) ECCV 2020. LNCS, vol. 12356, pp. 758–775. Springer, Cham (2020). https://doi.org/10.1007/978-3-030-58621-8_44
6. Gemmeke, J.F., et al.: Audio set: an ontology and human-labeled dataset for audio events. In: 2017 IEEE International Conference on Acoustics, Speech and Signal Processing (ICASSP), pp. 776–780 (2017)
7. Hershey, S., et al.: CNN architectures for large-scale audio classification. In: International Conference on Acoustics, Speech and Signal Processing (ICASSP) (2017). arXiv preprint arXiv:1609.09430
8. Li, Q., Han, Z., Wu, X.: Deeper insights into graph convolutional networks for semi-supervised learning. In: McIlraith, S.A., Weinberger, K.Q. (eds.) Proceedings of the Thirty-Second AAAI Conference on Artificial Intelligence, (AAAI-18), the 30th innovative Applications of Artificial Intelligence (IAAI-18), and the 8th AAAI Symposium on Educational Advances in Artificial Intelligence (EAAI-18), New Orleans, Louisiana, USA, 2–7 February 2018, pp. 3538–3545. AAAI Press (2018). http://www.aaai.org/ocs/index.php/AAAI/AAAI18/paper/view/16098
9. Lin, T., Zhao, X., Su, H., Wang, C., Yang, M.: BSN: boundary sensitive network for temporal action proposal generation. In: Ferrari, V., Hebert, M., Sminchisescu, C., Weiss, Y. (eds.) ECCV 2018. LNCS, vol. 11208, pp. 3–21. Springer, Cham (2018). https://doi.org/10.1007/978-3-030-01225-0_1
10. Lin, Y., Wang, Y.: Audiovisual transformer with instance attention for audio-visual event localization. In: ACCV (2020)

11. Owens, A., Efros, A.A.: Audio-visual scene analysis with self-supervised multisensory features. In: Ferrari, V., Hebert, M., Sminchisescu, C., Weiss, Y. (eds.) ECCV 2018. LNCS, vol. 11210, pp. 639–658. Springer, Cham (2018). https://doi.org/10.1007/978-3-030-01231-1_39
12. Ramachandran, P., Zoph, B., Le, Q.V.: Searching for activation functions (2017)
13. Rashid, M., Kjellström, H., Lee, Y.J.: Action graphs: weakly-supervised action localization with graph convolution networks. In: Winter Conference on Applications of Computer Vision (2020)
14. Russakovsky, O., et al.: ImageNet large scale visual recognition challenge. Int. J. Comput. Vision **115**(3), 211–252 (2015). https://doi.org/10.1007/s11263-015-0816-y
15. Schlichtkrull, M., Kipf, T.N., Bloem, P., van den Berg, R., Titov, I., Welling, M.: Modeling relational data with graph convolutional networks. In: Gangemi, A., et al. (eds.) The Semantic Web, pp. 593–607. Springer International Publishing, Cham (2018)
16. Simonyan, K., Zisserman, A.: Very deep convolutional networks for large-scale image recognition. arXiv preprint arXiv:1409.1556 (2014)
17. Tian, Y., Hu, D., Xu, C.: Cyclic co-learning of sounding object visual grounding and sound separation. In: CVPR (2021)
18. Tian, Y., Shi, J., Li, B., Duan, Z., Xu, C.: Audio-visual event localization in unconstrained videos. In: Ferrari, V., Hebert, M., Sminchisescu, C., Weiss, Y. (eds.) ECCV 2018. LNCS, vol. 11206, pp. 252–268. Springer, Cham (2018). https://doi.org/10.1007/978-3-030-01216-8_16
19. Vaswani, A., et al.: Attention is all you need. In: Guyon, I., et al. (eds.) Advances in Neural Information Processing Systems 30, pp. 5998–6008. Curran Associates, Inc. (2017). https://papers.nips.cc/paper/7181-attention-is-all-you-need.pdf
20. Wu, Y., Zhu, L., Yan, Y., Yang, Y.: Dual attention matching for audio-visual event localization. In: 2019 IEEE/CVF International Conference on Computer Vision (ICCV). IEEE (2019)
21. Xu, H., Zeng, R., Wu, Q., Tan, M., Gan, C.: Cross-modal relation-aware networks for audio-visual event localization. In: Proceedings of the 28th ACM International Conference on Multimedia (2020)
22. Xu, M., Zhao, C., Rojas, D.S., Thabet, A., Ghanem, B.: G-TAD: sub-graph localization for temporal action detection. In: Proceedings of the IEEE/CVF Conference on Computer Vision and Pattern Recognition (CVPR) (2020)
23. Yun, S., Han, D., Oh, S.J., Chun, S., Choe, J., Yoo, Y.: CutMix: regularization strategy to train strong classifiers with localizable features. In: 2019 IEEE/CVF International Conference on Computer Vision (ICCV), pp. 6022–6031 (2019)
24. Zeng, R., et al.: Graph convolutional networks for temporal action localization. In: ICCV (2019)
25. Zhou, B., Khosla, A., Lapedriza, A., Oliva, A., Torralba, A.: Learning deep features for discriminative localization. In: CVPR (2016)
26. Zhou, J., Zheng, L., Zhong, Y., Hao, S., Wang, M.: Positive sample propagation along the audio-visual event line. In: Proceedings of the IEEE Conference on Computer Vision and Pattern Recognition (CVPR) (2021)

NSNet: Non-saliency Suppression Sampler for Efficient Video Recognition

Boyang Xia[1,2], Wenhao Wu[3,4](✉), Haoran Wang[4], Rui Su[5], Dongliang He[4], Haosen Yang[6], Xiaoran Fan[2], and Wanli Ouyang[3,5]

[1] Key Lab of Intelligent Information Processing of Chinese Academy of Sciences (CAS), Institute of Computing Technology, CAS, Beijing, China
[2] University of Chinese Academy of Sciences, Beijing, China
[3] SenseTime Computer Vision Group, The University of Sydney, Sydney, Australia
whwu.ucas@gmail.com
[4] Baidu Inc., Beijing, China
[5] Shanghai AI Laboratory, Shanghai, China
[6] Harbin Institute of Technology, Harbin, China

Abstract. It is challenging for artificial intelligence systems to achieve accurate video recognition under the scenario of low computation costs. Adaptive inference based efficient video recognition methods typically preview videos and focus on salient parts to reduce computation costs. Most existing works focus on complex networks learning with video classification based objectives. Taking all frames as positive samples, few of them pay attention to the discrimination between positive samples (salient frames) and negative samples (non-salient frames) in supervisions. To fill this gap, in this paper, we propose a novel **Non-saliency Suppression Network (NSNet)**, which effectively suppresses the responses of non-salient frames. Specifically, on the frame level, effective pseudo labels that can distinguish between salient and non-salient frames are generated to guide the frame saliency learning. On the video level, a temporal attention module is learned under dual video-level supervisions on both the salient and the non-salient representations. Saliency measurements from both two levels are combined for exploitation of multi-granularity complementary information. Extensive experiments conducted on four well-known benchmarks verify our NSNet not only achieves the state-of-the-art accuracy-efficiency trade-off but also present a significantly faster (2.4∼4.3×) practical inference speed than state-of-the-art methods. Our project page is at https://lawrencexia2008.github.io/projects/nsnet.

Keywords: Video recognition · Adaptive inference · Temporal sampling

B. Xia and W. Wu— Co-first authorship. This work was done when Boyang was an intern at Baidu.

Supplementary Information The online version contains supplementary material available at https://doi.org/10.1007/978-3-031-19830-4_40.

S. Avidan et al. (Eds.): ECCV 2022, LNCS 13694, pp. 705–723, 2022.
https://doi.org/10.1007/978-3-031-19830-4_40

1 Introduction

The prevalence of digital devices exponentially increases the data amount of video content. Meanwhile, the proliferation of videos poses great challenges for existing video analysis systems, and consequently draws more and more attention from the research community. Thanks to the renaissance of deep neural networks [12,16,45], a surge of progress has been made to promote the development of advanced video understanding techniques [4,15,25,35,36,43,49,59]. Although achieving promising performance on some benchmarks [2,18] with supervised learning or unsupervised learning [6,14], many of them apply computationally heavy networks, which hinders their deployment to the practical applications, such as autonomous driving and personalized recommendations. Accordingly, building an efficient video understanding system is a crucial step towards widespread deployment in the real world.

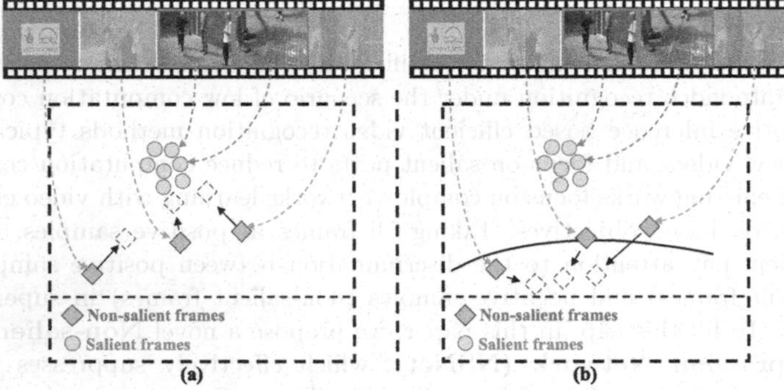

Fig. 1. A conceptual comparison between our proposed non-saliency suppression based sampler and existing approaches. (a) Feature space learned by sampler networks optimized by vanilla classification objectives with video labels. (b) Feature space learned by proposed NSNet. A video of *Hopscotch* is used for illustration. The arrows indicate the moving directions of frame features during training process. In (a), the features of non-salient frames, the 1st, 2nd, 5th frames are forced to cluster near the centroid of the category. In contrast, our approach introduce a *non-salient* category and those low saliency frames are labeled as *non-salient* and function as negative samples against the video category during training. In this way, features of the 1st, 2nd, 5th frames in (b) are pushed away to form another cluster of *non-salient* category.

To achieve efficient video recognition, a rich line of studies have been proposed, which roughly fall into two paradigms: i) **lightweight architecture based methods** and ii) **adaptive inference based methods**. The first category of approaches [23,50] devote to reducing the computational cost via designing lightweight networks. By contrast, another series of works propose to achieve efficient recognition by leveraging adaptive inference strategy to flexibly allocate resources according to the the saliency of frames. Specifically, the adaptive inference mechanism has been applied on multiple dimensions of video, including temporal sampling [20], spatial sampling [27,44], *etc.* Compared to the former, the adaptive inference based methods is easier to be incorporated into the existing advanced recognition backbones. For example, in the pipeline of a adaptive temporal sampling method, a sampler network is first trained based on lightweight feature to sample key frames, and then an off-the-shell computation-consuming recognizer is evoked on sampled frames for final recognition.

Semantic saliency of each frame is the fundamental basis for the adaptive inference based methods [20,30]. Nonetheless, it is difficult to obtain explicit supervision of frame-level saliency in the general setting of video recognition. Therefore, existing methods are mainly based on either reinforce learning (RL) or attention mechanism [10,27,51,56], where the agent (*resp.*, attention module) is optimized to take actions (*resp.*, attend) to those salient frames by classification objective based rewards (*resp.*, loss). In this way, the sampler is trained to determine the salient frames by using all frames as the positive samples of the corresponding video category, as shown in Fig. 1. Due to the lack of negative samples in training, it is hard for the sampler to accurately determine the non-salient frames from the salient ones within one video, which may easily overestimate the saliency of the non-salient frames. As a result, it is reasonable to introduce the negative samples for the frame-level video category classification objective based learning, which helps suppress the response of the non-salient frames to the video category during the sampling process.

To this end, we propose a novel **Non-saliency Suppression (NS) mechanism**, to provide negative-sample-aware supervision for saliency measurement, which can effectivly suppress the response of non-salient frames in the adaptive inference based framework. Specifically, the key principle is that the salient frames should belong to the corresponding video category while the non-salient frames should fall into a special category, which is distinguishable from all video categories. We term this special category as *non-salient* category, as shown in Fig. 1. As the video categories are the only annotation we can use during training, in order to guarantee high-quality negative samples (*i.e.*, the non-salient frames) in the frame-level saliency learning, we propose a Frame Scrutinize Module (FSM) to generate frame-level pseudo labels for supervision. By doing so, the salient frames can be effectively distinguished from the non-salient frames. In addition to the frame-level supervision, we then propose a temporal attention module named Video Glimpse Module (VGM) to compensate for high-level information of video events by using video-level supervision. In order to introduce NS mechanism on video level, we first formulate a video representation as a linear combination of two components: the representation of the salient parts and the representation of the non-salient parts of a video. Following the aforementioned principle, we then assign the label of that salient representation as current video label, and the label of non-salient representation as the special *non-salient* category.

Overall, our contributions are three-folds:

- We introduce the **Non-saliency Suppression mechanism** for suppressing the responses of non-salient frames, which considerably improve the discrimination power of the temporally sampled video representations without increment of computation overhead.

- We propose an discriminative and flexible multi-granularity frame sampling framework **N**on-saliency **S**uppression **Net**work (**NSNet**), which leverages supervisions from both video level and frame level to measure frame saliency. We design two specific schemes for realizing Non-saliency Suppression mechanism on the two granularities.
- Extensive experiments are conducted with multiple backbone architectures on four well-known benchmarks, *i.e.*, ActivityNet, FCVID, Mini-Kinetics and UCF101, which show that our NSNet achieves superior performance over existing state-of-the-art methods with limited computational costs.

2 Related Work

Video Recognition. Video Recognition has made significant progress in past decade for successful application of neural networks including 2D CNNs [42], 3D CNNs [3] and Transformers [1,53]. Although decent results are achieved by powerful spatiotemporal networks, it is still challenging for applying video recognition in resource-constraint scenarios for its superfluous computational complexity. TSM [23], TEA [22], MVFNet [50], *etc.*, try to realize temporal modelling with pure 2D CNNs to improve efficiency by shifting operations, motion based channel selection and multi views fusion. While P3D [31], S3D [58], R(2+1)D [40], SlowFast [7], Ada3D [21], DSANet [54] are proposed to improve the efficiency by decomposing 3D convolution or designing hybrid 2D-3D frameworks. Different from these approaches, we seek to achieve efficient video recognition by adaptively sampling salient frames and recognize selectively on a per-sample basis.

Adaptive Inference. The core idea of adaptive inference is to dynamically allocate computational resources (network layers, parameters, *etc.*) conditioned on the input to improve the trade-off between performance and cost [11,52]. For video analysis, adaptive inference are realized in several perspectives including temporal sampling, resolution, sub-networks and modality. FastForward [5], FrameGlimpse [60], AdaFrame [56], MARL [51] and OCSampler [24] model temporal sampling as a decision-making process, which is optimized by policy gradients or differentiable alternatives. ListenToLook [8], SMART [10], TSQNet [57] design temporal frame samplers based on attention mechanism. Besides temporal sampling, AdaFocus series [44,46] samples salient patches for each frame to reduce spatial redundancy. AR-Net [27], LiteEval [55], AdaMML [30] strategically allocate higher resolution, more powerful sub-networks, or more expensive modality to more informative frames, respectively.

The most closely related work to ours is an adaptive temporal sampling method, SCSampler [20], which proposes a frame-level classification task with video label and measure saliency based on classification confidence. However, there exist substantial differences between SCSampler and the proposed NSNet. SCSampler assigns each frame with the video label, while we argue that only the salient ones belong to video category, other ones should be labeled as a special category distinguishable from all semantic categories. Besides, we also consider to measure frame saliency with video level supervisions to enable context-aware saliency measurements, which is overlooked by SCSampler. Compared

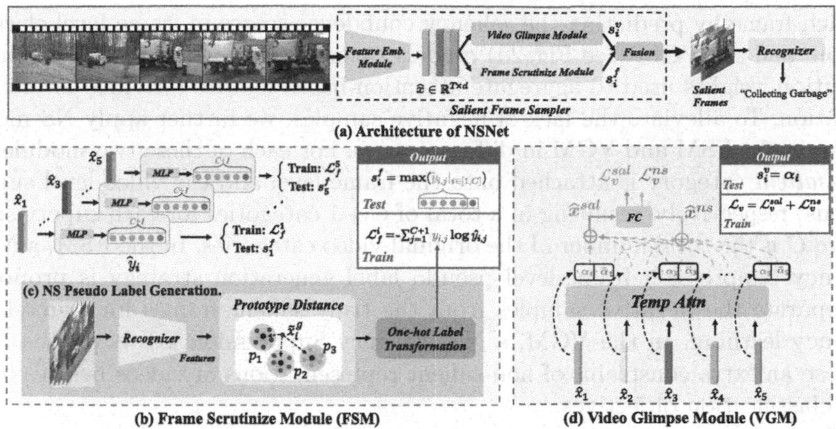

Fig. 2. An overview of architecture of NSNet. (a) shows the whole architecture. (b) shows the Frame Scrutinize Module (FSM), which estimates the saliency of each frame by the prediction confidence in frame-level classification. (c) shows the proposed Non-saliency Suppression (NS) frame-level pseudo label generation strategy based on the distance between each frame and video category prototypes. (d) shows the Video Glimpse module (VGM), which measures the saliency of each frame using temporal attentions in video-level classification.

with SCSampler, our NSNet achieves significantly superior performance with much less computational overhead.

3 Approach

3.1 Problem Definition

Let $V = \{x_i\}_{i=1}^{T}$ denote a video of T frames. Firstly, our NSNet is designed to select K most salient frames from all T frames. Then, the K salient frames are fed into a recognizer model, the predictions of which are aggregated to yield the final video-level prediction. The workflow of our system is illustrated in Fig. 2a. Note that we use an off-the-shell model as our recognizer, and therefore, the problem can be formulated as how to effectively sample the most salient frames from the input frames. In the following sections, we introduce the process of salient frames selection for our NSNet.

3.2 The Overview of NSNet

In this section, we elaborate on the proposed **N**on-saliency **S**uppression **Net**work (NSNet), which mainly consists of three components: a **Feature Embedding module (FEM)**, a **Frame Scrutinize module (FSM)**, and a **Video Glimpse module (VGM)**. The feature embedding module generates feature embedding from the input video frames. The FSM (see Fig. 2b) measures saliency of each frame by predicting the saliency confidence scores in frame-level classification, and the VGM (see Fig. 2d) models saliency of frames from the temporal attention weights used to aggregate attention-based feature for video-level classification. To alleviate the lack of negative samples, we further apply NS mechanism in the FSM and VGM in different ways. For each of these two modules, a *non-salient* category is attached onto the frame-level and the video-level supervisions, respectively, resulting in a total of $C+1$ categories for each supervision, where C is the total number of the original video categories. In the FSM, a Non-saliency Suppression frame-level pseudo label generation strategy is proposed to separate the negative samples from the truly salient frames for frame-level saliency learning. In the VGM, a Non-saliency Suppression loss is proposed to impose an extra constraint of non-salient representations of videos besides original classification objectives.

3.3 Feature Embedding Module (FEM)

Here we encode the input video frames $\{x_i\}_{i=1}^T$ into the robust feature sequence $\{\hat{x}_i\}_{i=1}^T$, which is then used by our FSM and VGM. Specifically, we first use the off-the-shelf lightweight feature extractor, *e.g.*, MobileNet, EfficientNet, *etc.*, to take the video frames as input and extract features for all frames. In order to allow message passing among features for all frames, we then apply a transformer encoder [41] on top of these features and output the feature sequence $\{\hat{x}_i\}_{i=1}^T$.

3.4 Frame Scrutinize Module (FSM)

In our FSM, we first generate frame-level Non-saliency Supression (NS) pseudo labels, and then use them as supervision to train our FSM to perform frame-level saliency classification and produce saliency scores. Details of our FSM are provided as follows.

Non-saliency Suppression Pseudo Label Generation. Here we denote the label of a video of the c-th category as a C-dimension one-hot vector $y_v \in \mathbb{R}^C$, where $y_{v,c} = 1$ and $y_{v,m} = 0|_{m\in[1,C],m\neq c}$. To distinguish between the salient frames and non-salient frames in frame labels, we then introduce a **guiding saliency score** g_i, which is obtained from the recognizer, *i.e.*, the one we used for final recognition as described in Sect. 3.1 (Fig. 2a). Although the classification response produced by the pre-trained model (*i.e.*, recognizer) is widely used for pseudo labeling in weakly-supervised learning [29,39,47], we propose a prototype-based strategy for more robust frame level pseudo label generation. According to [33,61], a sample could be more representative when it is closer to the centroid in feature space. As a result, we use distances of the feature for the i-th frame from the prototype features of all categories to obtain g_i. Specifically, we first use the recognizer to extract features and confidence scores on ground-truth category for all frames for each video in training set. Then the prototype feature of each category is then calculated by averaging all video features in that category. Here each video feature is obtained by applying average pooling on the features of the top-K frames based on the predicted confidence scores (see our Appendix for more details). The guiding saliency score g_i for the i-th frame is as follows:

$$g_i = \frac{e^{\phi(\tilde{x}_i^g, p_c)}}{\sum_{j=1}^{C} e^{\phi(\tilde{x}_i^g, p_j)}}, \tag{1}$$

where ϕ is a distance function measuring the similarity of two feature vectors, *e.g.*, Euclidean Distance, $\tilde{x}_i^g$ is the feature for the i-th frame extracted by the recognizer, p_j and p_c are the prototype features of the j-th category and the ground truth category, respectively. Finally, we use g_i to generate the NS pseudo label $y_i^{ns} = [\ g_i y_{v,1},\ g_i y_{v,2},\ \cdots\ g_i y_{v,C}, 1 - g_i] \in \mathbb{R}^{C+1}$.

Frame-Level Saliency Classification. After generating the NS pseudo labels, we then use them to train our FSM to perform frame-level saliency classification over the feature sequence $\{\hat{x}_i\}_{i=1}^{T}$. Mathematically, the frame-level classification objective is defined as follows:

$$\mathcal{L}_f = -\sum_{i=1}^{T}\sum_{j=1}^{C+1} y_{i,j}^{ns} \log(\hat{y}_{i,j}^{ns}), \tag{2}$$

where $y_{i,j}^{ns}$ is the element of the j-th category in y_i^{ns}, and $\hat{y}_{i,j}^{ns}$ is the classification prediction. It is noteworthy that y_i^{ns} is a soft one-hot target, the cross entropy loss of which is similar to label smooth [38]. During inference, the frames with very high response to any one of C categories are identified as salient frames. To this end, the maximum confidence across C semantic categories (except the $C+1$-th category) of classification score after softmax normalization is used for saliency measurement. We then apply additional softmax normalization along the time axis to obtain final saliency score s_i^f.

3.5 Video Glimpse Module (VGM)

In our VGM, we first generate attention weights $\alpha_i = \text{TempAttn}(\hat{x}_i)$ for the features of all observed frames, where $\text{TempAttn}(\cdot)$ is implemented by a fully-connected layer followed by a L1 normalization layer, which is used to rescale attention weights to $[0, 1]$ range. The features of all observed frames are then aggregated with the attention weights to generate the video salient representation $\hat{x}_v^{sal} = \sum_{i=1}^{T} \alpha_i \hat{x}_i$. To perform video-level classification, the salient representation of the video $\hat{x}_v^{sal}$ is fed to a fully-connected layer to compute the cross-entropy loss with video label. In order to guide our VGM to separate negative samples (non-salient frames) from positive samples (salient frames) of current video category, we propose a Non-saliency Suppression (NS) loss to impose a constraint other than the regular classification objective. During inference, the attention weights are used as saliency scores $\{s_i^v\}_{i=1}^{T}$. The details of the NS loss are described next.

Non-saliency Suppression Loss. It is obvious that all videos contains both salient and non-salient frames for a specific video category. Therefore, it is natural that a holistic video representation $\hat{x}_v$ can be formulated as a linear combination of the salient representation $\hat{x}_v^{sal}$ and the non-salient representation $\hat{x}_v^{ns}$ [29], *i.e.*, $\hat{x}_v = \hat{x}_v^{sal} + \gamma\hat{x}_v^{ns}$. The non-salient representation $\hat{x}_v^{ns}$ can be obtained as follows. We first compute the complementary part of attention weights $\overline{\alpha}_i = \frac{1}{T}(1-\alpha_i)$, and then aggregate the feature sequence with $\overline{\alpha}_i$ and produce the non-salient representation $\hat{x}_v^{ns} = \sum_{i=1}^{T} \overline{\alpha}_i\hat{x}_i$. In this way, a video can be regarded as a positive sample of both its ground truth category and *non-salient* category to different proportions, at the same time. Both $\hat{x}_v^{sal}$ and $\hat{x}_v^{ns}$ will be fed into the classification fully-connected layer to get different predictions $\hat{y}_v^{sal}$ and $\hat{y}_v^{ns}$. Then we defines labels for both $\hat{y}_v^{sal}$ and $\hat{y}_v^{ns}$: $y_v^{ns} = [0, 0, ..., 0, 1] \in \mathbb{R}^{C+1}$, $y_v^{sal} = [y_{v,1}, y_{v,2}, ...y_{v,C}, 0] \in \mathbb{R}^{C+1}$, where y_v is the original video label. The cross-entropy loss between $\hat{y}_v^{sal}$ and y_v^{sal} is the original classification loss $\mathcal{L}_{cls}$, and the one between $\hat{y}_v^{ns}$ and y_v^{ns} is the NS loss $\mathcal{L}_{ns}$. Consequently, the objective function of this module is defined as follows, where γ is the weight of $\mathcal{L}_{ns}$.

$$\mathcal{L}_v = \mathcal{L}_{cls} + \gamma\mathcal{L}_{ns}, \tag{3}$$

3.6 Learning Objectives

The overall objective function of our NSNet is formulated as follows:

$$\mathcal{L} = \mathcal{L}_v + \mathcal{L}_f, \tag{4}$$

where $\mathcal{L}_v$ and $\mathcal{L}_f$ denote the loss function of the VGM and the FSM, respectively. This objective not only drives model to conduct discriminative saliency measuring according to video semantics and frame discrepancy, but also facilitates information exchange between the video context and parts in shared feature encoding.

4 Experiments

4.1 Datasets and Evaluation Metrics

We evaluate our method on four large-scale video recognition benchmarks, *i.e.*, ActivityNet, FCVID, Mini-Kinetics and UCF101. ActivityNet [2] contains 19994 videos of 200 categories of most popular actions in daily life. FCVID [17] contains 91,223 videos collected from YouTube and divided into 239 classes covering most common events, objects, and scenes in our daily lives. Mini-Kinetics [27] is a subset of Kinetics [18] presented by [27], including 200 categories of videos of Kinetics, with 121k videos for training and 10k videos for validation. UCF101 [34] has 101 classes of actions and 13K videos with short duration (7.2 s). Mean Average Precision (mAP) is used as the main evaluation metric for ActivityNet and FCVID, while Top-1 accuracy is used for Mini-Kinetics and UCf-101 following previous works. We also report the computational cost (in FLOPs) to evaluate the efficiency of the proposed method. FLOPs of our method are composed of following parts: $P_{total} = P_{rec} \times K + P_{fem} + P_{vgm} + P_{fsm}$, where

$P_{rec}, P_{fem}, P_{vgm}, P_{fsm}$ represent the FLOPs of the recognizer, FEM, VGM and FSM, respectively. An example of FLOPs computation of our model with the setting in Table 2 is: 4.109×5 (ResNet-50 with 5 frames) + $(0.320 \times 16 + 0.315)$ (MobileNetv2 with 16 frames+transformer) + 0.004 + 0.002 = 25.99(G).

4.2 Implementation Details

Training. Following previous works [10,56], we mainly use MobileNetv2 [32] as the lightweight feature extractor in our FEM. Different high-capacity networks trained on target datasets are used as recognizers at the same time: ResNet family [12] and Swin-Transformer family [26], *etc.* For the transformer encoder in our FEM, 2 encoder layers with 8 heads and learnable positional embedding are used. The distance function ϕ in our FSM used for guiding saliency score is Euclidean Distance. The non-saliency suppression loss weight γ is set to 0.2. See Appendix for more details of training.

Inference. We fuse the results of FSM and VGM to obtain the final saliency measurements. Score *sum, max, mul* and index *union, intersect, join* are considered for fusion. See Appendix for details.

4.3 Main Results

Comparison with Simple Baselines. As shown in Table 1, we compare our approach with multiple hand-crafted sampling methods on ActivityNet and UCF101 with ResNet-101 and ResNet-50 as recognizers (without TSN training strategy [42]), respectively. The simple baselines include UNIFORM, RANDOM, DENSE, and TOP-K sampling. For UNIFORM and RANDOM, we uniformly and randomly sample 10 frames from all frames, respectively, while for TOP-K, we sample top 10 frames with highest predicted confidence scores (*i.e.*, the maximum confidence among all categories), from all frames. For our method, we first uniformly sample an observation number (100 for ActivityNet and 50 for UCF-101) of frames as the observation frames from the input videos, and then use our method to sample 5 frames from the observation frames. DENSE sampling makes use of all frames for recognition. We observe that our NSNet outperforms all simple baselines by a large margin on both two datasets. In ActivityNet, our method relatively outperforms the competitive but heavy TOP-K baseline by 2.4% in terms of mAP with 11.7× less GFLOPs, which verifies the effectiveness of our sampler. In UCF-101, the videos are much shorter than those in ActivityNet (7 s *v.s.*119 s on average), which constructs a much more difficult setting for sampler. However, the top-1 accuracy of our NSNet still relatively exceeds that of the most competitive DENSE baseline by 2.1% with much less GFLOPs, which demonstrates NSNet can improve the video classification performance on trimmed videos.

Comparison with SOTA on ActivityNet. We make a comprehensive comparison with recent state-of-the-art efficient video recognition methods on the

Table 1. Comparison with several hand-crafted sampling strategies. ResNet-101 and ResNet-50 are adopted as the recognizers for ActivityNet and UCF-101, respectively.

	ActivityNet		UCF101	
	mAP(%)	FLOPs	Top-1(%)	FLOPs
UNIFORM	68.6	195.8G	75.9	61.7G
RANDOM	68.1	195.8G	75.7	61.7G
DENSE	69.0	930.8G	76.1	753.4G
TOP-K	72.5	930.8G	74.5	753.4G
Ours	**74.9**	**73.2G**	**77.6**	**37.6G**

Table 2. Comparisons with SOTA efficient video recognition methods with ResNet50 as the main recognizer on the ActivityNet dataset. The backbones used for sampler and recognizer are reported. MBv2 denotes MobileNetv2.

Method	Backbone	mAP(%)	FLOPs
SCSampler [20]	MBv2+Res50	72.9	42.0G
AR-Net [27]	MBv2+ResNets	73.8	33.5G
AdaMML [30]	MBv2+Res50	73.9	94.0G
VideoIQ [37]	MBv2+Res50	74.8	28.1G
AdaFocus [44]	MBv2+Res50	75.0	26.6G
Dynamic-STE [19]	Res18+Res50	75.9	30.5G
FrameExit [9]	ResNet-50	76.1	26.1G
Ours	MBv2+Res50	**76.8**	**26.0G**

ActivityNet dataset in Table 2–3, and Fig. 3. As shown in Table 2, we compare our NSNet with other state-of-the-art efficient approaches using ResNet-50 as the recognizer. NSNet consistently outperforms all existing methods including sampler-based and sampler-free approaches. When compared with AR-Net [27], an adaptive resolution method, the mAP of our method improve by 3% with much less computational cost (**26.0G** *v.s.*33.5G). Our NSNet also outperforms AdaMML [30], an adaptive modality approach, by 2.9% in terms of mAP while having 3.6× less FLOPs. In addition, sampler-free approaches often have relatively low FLOPs, because they do not need sampling process. However, although our NSNet has extra computational on the sampling process, it can achieve higher accuracy than FrameExit [9](**76.8%** *v.s.*76.1%), a competing sampler-free framework, with comparable FLOPs, which demonstrates our sampler greatly improve the discrimination power of the video representation. In Table 3, we show the results of the SOTAs using ResNet-152 and more advanced backbones on the ActivityNet dataset. We can see that our NSNet outperforms the sampler-free methods P3D [31], RRA [63] by at least 1.7% in terms of mAP. When compared with competing sampler-based methods (MARL [51], ListenToLook [8], SMART [10]), our method still shows superiority over them. Besides, when using a more advanced transformer-based network Swin-Transformer [26] as the recognizer in our NSNet, the mAP can be further promoted to 94.3%, which is the highest performance on ActivityNet to our best knowledge.

Table 3. Comparisons with SOTA video recognition methods with ResNet152 and more advanced networks as the recognizers on the ActivityNet dataset.

Method	Recognizer	Pretrain	Top-1(%)	mAP(%)
ResNet-152 w/ ImageNet				
P3D [31]	ResNet-152	ImageNet	75.1	78.9
RRA [63]	ResNet-152	ImageNet	78.8	83.4
MARL [51]	ResNet-152	ImageNet	79.8	83.8
ListenToLook [8]	ResNet-152	ImageNet	80.3	84.2
Ours	ResNet-152	ImageNet	**80.7**	**85.1**
ResNet-152 w/ Kinetics				
SMART [10]	ResNet-152	Kinetics	–	84.4
Ours	ResNet-152	Kinetics	**84.5**	**88.7**
More Advanced Networks w/ Kinetics				
DSN [62]	R(2+1)D-34	Kinetics	82.6	87.8
Ada3D [21]	SlowOnly-50	Kinetics	–	84.0
ListenToLook [8]	R(2+1)D-152	Kinetics	–	89.9
MARL [51]	SEResNeXt-152	Kinetics	85.7	90.1
Ours	Swin-B	Kinetics	86.7	91.6
Ours	Swin-L	Kinetics	**90.2**	**94.3**

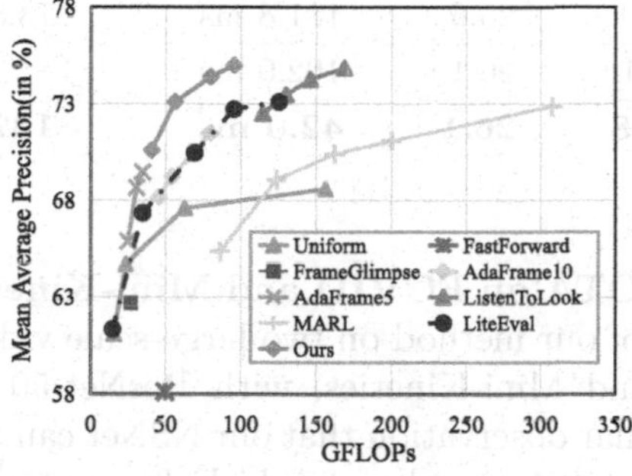

Fig. 3. Comparison with state-of-the-art sampling methods on ActivityNet dataset. Our proposed NSNet achieves better mAP with much fewer GLOPs (per video) than other methods. It is worth noting that we compare these methods with the same recognizer ResNet-101, under different computation budgets. The results are quoted from the published works [8,27].

Figure 3 illustrates the GFLOPs-mAP curve on the ActivityNet dataset. On this curve, the observation number T is set to 50, while the number of sampled frames K is tuned up as FLOPs budget increases. Following previous works [8, 51,55,56], we use ResNet-101 without TSN-style training as the recognizer. Our NSNet presents significant accuracy improvement with much lower GFLOPs than other methods.

Table 4. Comparison with previous methods on FCVID and Mini-Kinetics. Our NSNet consistently outperforms state-of-the-art in terms of accuracy and efficiency using ResNet-50 as the recognizer.

Methods	FCVID		Mini-Kinetics	
	mAP(%)	FLOPs	Top-1(%)	FLOPs
LiteEval [55]	80.0	94.3G	61.0	99.0G
AdaFrame [56]	80.2	75.1G	–	–
SCSampler [20]	81.0	42.0G	70.8	42.0G
AR-Net [27]	81.3	35.1G	71.7	32.0G
AdaFuse [28]	81.6	45.0G	72.3	23.0G
SMART [10]	82.1	–	–	–
VideoIQ [37]	82.7	27.0G	72.3	20.4G
Dynamic-STE [19]	–	–	72.7	18.3G
FrameExit [9]	–	–	72.8	19.7G
AdaFocus [44]	83.4	26.6G	72.9	38.6G
Ours	**83.9**	**26.0G**	**73.6**	**18.1G**

Table 5. Comparison of practical efficiency between SotA methods.

Method	mAP(%)	GFLOPs	Latency (bs = 1)	Throughput (bs = 32)
AdaFocus [44]	75.0	26.6	181.8 ms	73.8 vid/s
FrameExit [9]	76.1	26.1	102.0 ms	–
Ours	**76.8**	**26.1**	**42.0 ms**	**132.5 vid/s**

Comparison with SOTA on FCVID and Mini-Kinetics. We further evaluate the performance of our method on two large-scale video recognition benchmarks, *i.e.,* FCVID and Mini-Kinetics, with ResNet-50 as the recognizer in Table 4. We have a similar observation that our NSNet can achieve superior mAP with the much lower computational cost, which demonstrate the efficacy of non-saliency suppression (NS) mechanism in both untrimmed video and trimmed video scenarios.

Practical Efficiency. We present the comparison results on inference speed between our NSNet and two SotA methods, FrameExit [9] and AdaFocus [44], in Table 5. Latency and throughput with batch size of 1 and 32 are reported[1]. It can be observed that our method achieves significantly superior latency (42.0 ms) and than two methods (2.4× than FrameExit [9] and 4.3× than AdaFocus [44]), which demonstrate the superiority of our parallel temporal sampling framework over existing methods on practical efficiency.

[1] The latency and throughput results of two SotA methods are obtained by running their official code [9,44] on the same hardware (a NVIDIA 3090 GPU with a Intel Xeon E5-2650 v3 @ 2.30 GHz CPU) as ours.

4.4 Ablation Studies

To comprehensively evaluate our NSNet, we provide extensive ablation studies on ActivityNet in Table 6. Accordingly, the effectiveness of each component in our framework is analyzed as follows. We use ResNet-101 without TSN style training as the recognizer, as the same as in Table 1 and Fig. 3 in Sect. 4.3.

Effectiveness of Non-saliency Suppression. We explore the effectiveness of *non-saliency suppression* (NS) mechanism for two modules. For VGM, "baseline" denotes the variant without $\mathcal{L}_{ns}$. For FSM, "baseline" denotes the variant replacing our NS frame label with video label. As shown in Table 6a, for the VGM, simply adding a *non-salient* class (from C classes to $C+1$ classes) without according supervisions can not elevate performance. In contrast, by applying NS mechanism, the mAP significantly improves by 0.4%. In the FSM, we observe that "baseline" present very low performance, similar to UNIFORM baseline(68.4 *v.s.* 68.6), which is because it imposes many label noises when assigning the label of video to irrelevant or low-quality frames. We also observe that simply adding the *non-salient* class cannot address the issue (68.6 *v.s.* 68.4). NS mechanism elevates the performance significantly with effective and reasonable supervisions (74.7 *v.s.* 68.4). More ablations in supervision signals of FSM are in Table 6d.

Table 6. Ablation studies on ActivityNet with mAP (%) as the evaluation metric. Unless otherwise specified, MobileNetv2 and ResNet-101 are used as the backbone for observation network and recognizer respectively.

(a) Evaluation of the effectiveness of NS mechanism.

Method	VGM	FSM
baseline	73.4	68.4
+ *non-salient* class	73.4	68.6
+ NS	**73.8**	**74.7**

(b) Performance of different number of sampled frames.

#F	VGM	FSM	NSNet
5	72.6	73.9	**74.9**
10	73.8	74.7	**75.5**

(c) Ablation of transformer encoder in feature embedding module.

Network	mAP(%)
1D Conv	73.6
LSTM	74.0
MLP	74.3
Transformer	**75.5**

(d) Results of FS module with different learning objectives

FS Objective	mAP(%)
Baseline	68.4
Regression	72.0
Ranking	72.2
Baseline+	73.7
Ours	**74.7**

Ablations of Transformer Encoder in Feature Embedding Module. Table 6c presents the results of different choice in FEM to passing message among the features from the input frames, including Long short-term memory networks (LSTM) [13], 1-D convolutional networks (1D Conv), multi-layer perceptron (MLP) [48], Transformer Encoder (Transformer) [41]. Among all these choices, the transformer encoder achieves the highest performance.

Different Learning Objectives of the FSM. In Table 6d we compare various objectives of FSM mentioned in Sect. 1 and Sect. 2, including frame classification with video labels ("baseline", as the same one as in Table 6a), ranking [20], and regression [10] with guiding saliency scores. With guiding saliency scores as supervisions, "regression" and "ranking" model saliency sampling as saliency score regression and ranking tasks respectively. They can achieve higher performance than "baseline" (72.0% & 72.2%), whereas they overlook the exploitation of class-specific information, which limits their performance. We modify "baseline" by transforming hard one-hot video label to soft one-hot label using the guiding saliency score, which is denoted as "baseline+". This modification improves the result significantly (**73.7%** *v.s.* 68.4%) by taking into account both the discrimination between salient frames and non-salient frames and the use of category-specific information. With the same setting of guiding saliency score, our NS mechanism based objective outperforms 'baseline+' in a large margin (**74.7%** *v.s.* 73.7%), which verifies the proposed supervisions offer more robust saliency for supplying negative samples.

Different Numbers of Sampled Frames. As shown in Table 6b, we report the performance of different numbers of sampled frames for NSNet. We can see that the fusion of two modules always improves the performance by 0.8% and 1.0% when sampling 10 and 5 frames, respectively. It demonstrates the effectiveness of our fusion strategies, especially when fewer frames are sampled. Besides, when fewer frames are sampled, the performance of FSM degrades more slowly than that of VGM (0.8% *v.s.* 1.2%), which is because FSM can distinguish between salient frames and non-salient frames in finer granularity with the help of frame-level supervisions.

Fig. 4. Visualization of selected frames with different variants of our approach. 1st row: Uniform, 2nd row: Our approach without NS mechanism (Ours w/o NS), 3rd row: Our approach (Ours). Intuitively salient frames are are outlined in aqua while non-salient ones are outlined in red. Please zoom in for best view. (Color figure online)

4.5 Qualitative Analysis

Figure 4 shows frames sampled by different methods. Our NSNet can sample more discriminative salient frames than uniform baseline and the variant without non-saliency suppression. For example, in the 4th column, the 3rd row of this column shows that "ours w/o NS" is mainly attracted by frames with scenes of a cook, which is not discriminative for frequently appearing in other cooking events. In contrast, 4th row shows NSNet can sample more indicative frames.

5 Conclusions

In this paper, we present the Non-saliency Suppression Network (NSNet) to measure the saliency of frames by leveraging both video-level and frame-level supervisions. In Frame Scrutinize module, we propose a pseudo label generation strategy to enable negative sample aware frame-level saliency learning. Meanwhile, in Video Glimpse module, an attention module constrained by dual classification objectives is presented to compensate high-level information. Experiments show that our NSNet outperforms the state-of-the-arts on accuracy-efficiency tradeoff. In the future, we plan to explore non-saliency suppression on both spatial and temporal dimensions to save more redundancy.

Acknowledgment. Wanli Ouyang was supported by the Australian Research Council Grant DP200103223, Australian Medical Research Future Fund MRFAI000085, CRC-P Smart Material Recovery Facility (SMRF) - Curby Soft Plastics, and CRC-P ARIA - Bionic Visual-Spatial Prosthesis for the Blind.

References

1. Bertasius, G., Wang, H., Torresani, L.: Is space-time attention all you need for video understanding? arXiv preprint arXiv:2102.05095 (2021)
2. Caba Heilbron, F., Escorcia, V., Ghanem, B., Carlos Niebles, J.: ActivityNet: a large-scale video benchmark for human activity understanding. In: Proceedings of the IEEE Conference on Computer Vision and Pattern Recognition, pp. 961–970 (2015)
3. Carreira, J., Zisserman, A.: Quo vadis, action recognition? A new model and the kinetics dataset. In: Proceedings of the IEEE Conference on Computer Vision and Pattern Recognition, pp. 6299–6308 (2017)
4. Chen, X., Han, Y., Wang, X., Sun, Y., Yang, Y.: Action keypoint network for efficient video recognition. arXiv preprint arXiv:2201.06304 (2022)
5. Fan, H., Xu, Z., Zhu, L., Yan, C., Ge, J., Yang, Y.: Watching a small portion could be as good as watching all: towards efficient video classification. In: IJCAI International Joint Conference on Artificial Intelligence (2018)
6. Fang, B., Wu, W., Liu, C., Zhou, Y., He, D., Wang, W.: MaMiCo: macro-to-micro semantic correspondence for self-supervised video representation learning. In: Proceedings of the ACMMM (2022)
7. Feichtenhofer, C., Fan, H., Malik, J., He, K.: SlowFast networks for video recognition. In: Proceedings of the IEEE/CVF international conference on computer vision, pp. 6202–6211 (2019)
8. Gao, R., Oh, T.H., Grauman, K., Torresani, L.: Listen to look: action recognition by previewing audio. In: Proceedings of the IEEE/CVF Conference on Computer Vision and Pattern Recognition, pp. 10457–10467 (2020)

9. Ghodrati, A., Bejnordi, B.E., Habibian, A.: FrameExit: conditional early exiting for efficient video recognition. In: Proceedings of the IEEE/CVF Conference on Computer Vision and Pattern Recognition, pp. 15608–15618 (2021)
10. Gowda, S.N., Rohrbach, M., Sevilla-Lara, L.: SMART frame selection for action recognition 35(2), 1451–1459 (2021). https://ojs.aaai.org/index.php/AAAI/article/view/16235
11. Han, Y., Huang, G., Song, S., Yang, L., Wang, H., Wang, Y.: Dynamic neural networks: a survey. IEEE Trans. Pattern Anal. Mach. Intell. **44**, 7436–7456 (2021)
12. He, K., Zhang, X., Ren, S., Sun, J.: Deep residual learning for image recognition. In: Proceedings of the IEEE Conference on Computer Vision and Pattern Recognition, pp. 770–778 (2016)
13. Hochreiter, S., Schmidhuber, J.: Long short-term memory. Neural Comput. **9**(8), 1735–1780 (1997)
14. Huang, D., et al.: ASCNet: self-supervised video representation learning with appearance-speed consistency. In: Proceedings of the IEEE/CVF International Conference on Computer Vision, pp. 8096–8105 (2021)
15. Huang, W., et al.: Toward efficient action recognition: principal backpropagation for training two-stream networks. IEEE Trans. Image Process. **28**(4), 1773–1782 (2018)
16. Ji, Z., Chen, K., Wang, H.: Step-wise hierarchical alignment network for image-text matching. In: Zhou, Z., (ed.) Proceedings of the Thirtieth International Joint Conference on Artificial Intelligence, IJCAI 2021, Virtual Event/Montreal, Canada, 19–27 August 2021, pp. 765–771. ijcai.org (2021). https://doi.org/10.24963/ijcai.2021/106
17. Jiang, Y.G., Wu, Z., Wang, J., Xue, X., Chang, S.F.: Exploiting feature and class relationships in video categorization with regularized deep neural networks. IEEE Trans. Pattern Anal. Mach. Intell. **40**(2), 352–364 (2018). https://doi.org/10.1109/TPAMI.2017.2670560
18. Kay, W., et al.: The kinetics human action video dataset. arXiv preprint arXiv:1705.06950 (2017)
19. Kim, H., Jain, M., Lee, J.T., Yun, S., Porikli, F.: Efficient action recognition via dynamic knowledge propagation. In: Proceedings of the IEEE/CVF International Conference on Computer Vision, pp. 13719–13728 (2021)
20. Korbar, B., Tran, D., Torresani, L.: Scsampler: Sampling salient clips from video for efficient action recognition. In: Proceedings of the IEEE/CVF International Conference on Computer Vision (ICCV) (2019)
21. Li, H., Wu, Z., Shrivastava, A., Davis, L.S.: 2D or not 2D? Adaptive 3D convolution selection for efficient video recognition. In: Proceedings of the IEEE/CVF Conference on Computer Vision and Pattern Recognition, pp. 6155–6164 (2021)
22. Li, Y., Ji, B., Shi, X., Zhang, J., Kang, B., Wang, L.: Tea: temporal excitation and aggregation for action recognition. In: CVPR, pp. 909–918 (2020)
23. Lin, J., Gan, C., Han, S.: TSM: temporal shift module for efficient video understanding. In: Proceedings of the IEEE/CVF International Conference on Computer Vision, pp. 7083–7093 (2019)
24. Lin, J., Duan, H., Chen, K., Lin, D., Wang, L.: OCSampler: compressing videos to one clip with single-step sampling. In: Proceedings of the IEEE/CVF Conference on Computer Vision and Pattern Recognition. pp. 13894–13903 (2022)
25. Liu, Y., Ma, L., Zhang, Y., Liu, W., Chang, S.F.: Multi-granularity generator for temporal action proposal. In: Proceedings of the IEEE/CVF Conference on Computer Vision and Pattern Recognition, pp. 3604–3613 (2019)

26. Liu, Z., et al.: Swin transformer: Hierarchical vision transformer using shifted windows. In: Proceedings of the IEEE/CVF International Conference on Computer Vision, pp. 10012–10022 (2021)
27. Meng, Y., et al.: AR-Net: adaptive frame resolution for efficient action recognition. In: Vedaldi, A., Bischof, H., Brox, T., Frahm, J.-M. (eds.) ECCV 2020. LNCS, vol. 12352, pp. 86–104. Springer, Cham (2020). https://doi.org/10.1007/978-3-030-58571-6_6
28. Meng, Y., et al.: AdaFuse: adaptive temporal fusion network for efficient action recognition. arXiv preprint arXiv:2102.05775 (2021)
29. Nguyen, P.X., Ramanan, D., Fowlkes, C.C.: Weakly-supervised action localization with background modeling. In: Proceedings of the IEEE/CVF International Conference on Computer Vision, pp. 5502–5511 (2019)
30. Panda, R., et al.: AdaMML: adaptive multi-modal learning for efficient video recognition. arXiv preprint arXiv:2105.05165 (2021)
31. Qiu, Z., Yao, T., Mei, T.: Learning spatio-temporal representation with pseudo-3D residual networks. In: Proceedings of the IEEE International Conference on Computer Vision, pp. 5533–5541 (2017)
32. Sandler, M., Howard, A., Zhu, M., Zhmoginov, A., Chen, L.C.: MobileNetV2: inverted residuals and linear bottlenecks. In: Proceedings of the IEEE Conference on Computer Vision and Pattern Recognition, pp. 4510–4520 (2018)
33. Snell, J., Swersky, K., Zemel, R.: Prototypical networks for few-shot learning. In: Advances in Neural Information Processing Systems 30 (2017)
34. Soomro, K., Zamir, A.R., Shah, M.: Ucf101: a dataset of 101 human actions classes from videos in the wild. arXiv preprint arXiv:1212.0402 (2012)
35. Su, R., Ouyang, W., Zhou, L., Xu, D.: Improving action localization by progressive cross-stream cooperation. In: Proceedings of the IEEE/CVF Conference on Computer Vision and Pattern Recognition (CVPR) (2019)
36. Su, R., Yu, Q., Xu, D.: STVGBert: a visual-linguistic transformer based framework for spatio-temporal video grounding. In: Proceedings of the IEEE/CVF International Conference on Computer Vision (ICCV), pp. 1533–1542 (2021)
37. Sun, X., Panda, R., Chen, C.F.R., Oliva, A., Feris, R., Saenko, K.: Dynamic network quantization for efficient video inference. In: Proceedings of the IEEE/CVF International Conference on Computer Vision, pp. 7375–7385 (2021)
38. Szegedy, C., Vanhoucke, V., Ioffe, S., Shlens, J., Wojna, Z.: Rethinking the inception architecture for computer vision. In: Proceedings of the IEEE Conference on Computer Vision and Pattern Recognition, pp. 2818–2826 (2016)
39. Tang, P., Wang, X., Bai, X., Liu, W.: Multiple instance detection network with online instance classifier refinement. In: Proceedings of the IEEE Conference on Computer Vision and Pattern Recognition, pp. 2843–2851 (2017)
40. Tran, D., Wang, H., Torresani, L., Ray, J., LeCun, Y., Paluri, M.: A closer look at spatiotemporal convolutions for action recognition. In: CVPR (2018)
41. Vaswani, A., et al.: Attention is all you need. In: Advances in neural information processing systems, pp. 5998–6008 (2017)
42. Wang, L., et al.: Temporal segment networks: towards good practices for deep action recognition. In: Leibe, B., Matas, J., Sebe, N., Welling, M. (eds.) ECCV 2016. LNCS, vol. 9912, pp. 20–36. Springer, Cham (2016). https://doi.org/10.1007/978-3-319-46484-8_2
43. Wang, X., Zhu, L., Wu, Y., Yang, Y.: Symbiotic attention for egocentric action recognition with object-centric alignment. In: IEEE Transactions on Pattern Analysis and Machine Intelligence (2020)

44. Wang, Y., Chen, Z., Jiang, H., Song, S., Han, Y., Huang, G.: Adaptive focus for efficient video recognition. arXiv preprint arXiv:2105.03245 (2021)
45. Wang, Y., Lv, K., Huang, R., Song, S., Yang, L., Huang, G.: Glance and focus: a dynamic approach to reducing spatial redundancy in image classification. Adv. Neural. Inf. Process. Syst. **33**, 2432–2444 (2020)
46. Wang, Y., et al.: AdaFocus V2: end-to-end training of spatial dynamic networks for video recognition. In: Proceedings of the IEEE/CVF Conference on Computer Vision and Pattern Recognition (CVPR), pp. 20062–20072 (2022)
47. Wei, Y., Feng, J., Liang, X., Cheng, M.M., Zhao, Y., Yan, S.: Object region mining with adversarial erasing: a simple classification to semantic segmentation approach. In: Proceedings of the IEEE Conference on Computer Vision and Pattern Recognition, pp. 1568–1576 (2017)
48. Werbos, P.J.: Applications of advances in nonlinear sensitivity analysis. In: System modeling and optimization, pp. 762–770. Springer, Berlin, Heidelberg (1982). https://doi.org/10.1007/BFb0006203
49. Wu, J., et al.: Weakly-supervised spatio-temporal anomaly detection in surveillance video. IJCAI (2021)
50. Wu, W., He, D., Lin, T., Li, F., Gan, C., Ding, E.: MVFNet: multi-view fusion network for efficient video recognition. In: Proceedings of the AAAI Conference on Artificial Intelligence, vol. 35, pp. 2943–2951 (2021)
51. Wu, W., He, D., Tan, X., Chen, S., Wen, S.: Multi-agent reinforcement learning based frame sampling for effective untrimmed video recognition. In: Proceedings of the IEEE/CVF International Conference on Computer Vision, pp. 6222–6231 (2019)
52. Wu, W., He, D., Tan, X., Chen, S., Yang, Y., Wen, S.: Dynamic inference: a new approach toward efficient video action recognition. In: Proceedings of the IEEE/CVF Conference on Computer Vision and Pattern Recognition Workshops, pp. 676–677 (2020)
53. Wu, W., Sun, Z., Ouyang, W.: Transferring textual knowledge for visual recognition. arXiv e-prints pp. arXiv-2207 (2022)
54. Wu, W., et al.: DSANet: dynamic segment aggregation network for video-level representation learning. In Proceedings of the ACMMM (2021)
55. Wu, Z., Xiong, C., Jiang, Y.G., Davis, L.S.: LiteEval: a coarse-to-fine framework for resource efficient video recognition. arXiv preprint arXiv:1912.01601 (2019)
56. Wu, Z., Xiong, C., Ma, C.Y., Socher, R., Davis, L.S.: AdaFrame: adaptive frame selection for fast video recognition. In: Proceedings of the IEEE/CVF Conference on Computer Vision and Pattern Recognition. pp. 1278–1287 (2019)
57. Xia, B., Wang, Z., Wu, W., Wang, H., Han, J.: Temporal saliency query network for efficient video recognition. In: ECCV (2022)
58. Xie, S., Sun, C., Huang, J., Tu, Z., Murphy, K.: Rethinking spatiotemporal feature learning: speed-accuracy trade-offs in video classification. In: ECCV (2018)
59. Yang, H., et al.: Temporal action proposal generation with background constraint. In: Proceedings of the AAAI Conference on Artificial Intelligence, vol. 36, pp. 3054–3062 (2022)
60. Yeung, S., Russakovsky, O., Mori, G., Fei-Fei, L.: End-to-end learning of action detection from frame glimpses in videos. In: Proceedings of the IEEE Conference on Computer Vision and Pattern Recognition, pp. 2678–2687 (2016)
61. Zhang, M., Song, G., Zhou, H., Liu, Y.: Discriminability distillation in group representation learning. In: Vedaldi, A., Bischof, H., Brox, T., Frahm, J.-M. (eds.) ECCV 2020. LNCS, vol. 12355, pp. 1–19. Springer, Cham (2020). https://doi.org/10.1007/978-3-030-58607-2_1

62. Zheng, Y.D., Liu, Z., Lu, T., Wang, L.: Dynamic sampling networks for efficient action recognition in videos. IEEE Trans. Image Process. **29**, 7970–7983 (2020)
63. Zhu, C., et al.: Fine-grained video categorization with redundancy reduction attention. In: Proceedings of the European Conference on Computer Vision (ECCV), pp. 136–152 (2018)

Video Activity Localisation with Uncertainties in Temporal Boundary

Jiabo Huang[1,4], Hailin Jin[2], Shaogang Gong[1], and Yang Liu[3,5](✉)

[1] Queen Mary University of London, London, UK
{jiabo.huang,s.gong}@qmul.ac.uk
[2] Adobe Research, California, US
hljin@adobe.com
[3] Wangxuan Institute of Computer Technology, Peking University, Beijing, China
yangliu@pku.edu.cn
[4] Vision Semantics Limited, London, UK
[5] Beijing Institute for General Artificial Intelligence, Beijing, China

Abstract. Current methods for video activity localisation over time assume implicitly that activity temporal boundaries labelled for model training are determined and precise. However, in unscripted natural videos, different activities mostly transit smoothly, so that it is intrinsically ambiguous to determine in labelling precisely when an activity starts and ends over time. Such uncertainties in temporal labelling are currently ignored in model training, resulting in learning mis-matched video-text correlation with poor generalisation in test. In this work, we solve this problem by introducing Elastic Moment Bounding (EMB) to accommodate flexible and adaptive activity temporal boundaries towards modelling universally interpretable video-text correlation with tolerance to underlying temporal uncertainties in pre-fixed annotations. Specifically, we construct elastic boundaries adaptively by mining and discovering frame-wise temporal endpoints that can maximise the alignment between video segments and query sentences. To enable both more accurate matching (segment content attention) and more robust localisation (segment elastic boundaries), we optimise the selection of frame-wise endpoints subject to segment-wise contents by a novel Guided Attention mechanism. Extensive experiments on three video activity localisation benchmarks demonstrate compellingly the EMB's advantages over existing methods without modelling uncertainty.

1 Introduction

The goal of video activity localisation is to locate temporally video moments-of-interest (MoIs) of a specific activity described by a natural language query of an untrimmed continuous long video (often unscripted and unstructured) that contains many different activities [21,28,29].

Supplementary Information The online version contains supplementary material available at https://doi.org/10.1007/978-3-031-19830-4_41.

S. Avidan et al. (Eds.): ECCV 2022, LNCS 13694, pp. 724–740, 2022.
https://doi.org/10.1007/978-3-031-19830-4_41

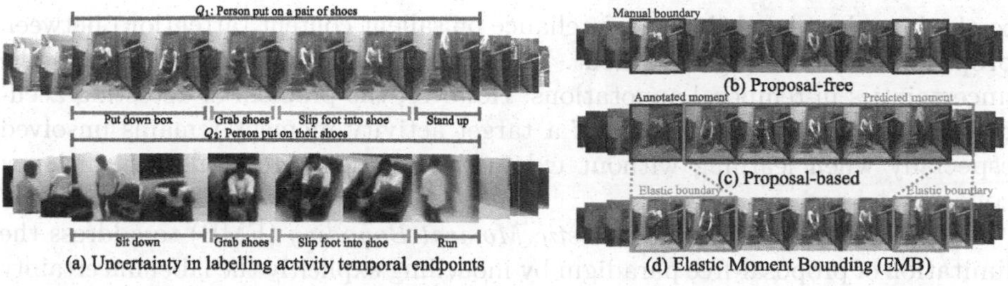

Fig. 1. An illustration of different activity localisation methods. (a) Activity's temporal boundaries are intrinsically uncertain in manual labelling (break-down and highlighted in 'red'). (b) Proposal-free methods learn to identify the frame-wise temporal endpoints. (c) Proposal-based methods learn the holistic alignment of video segments and query sentences between their feature spaces. (d) *Elastic Moment Bounding* (EMB) optimises simultaneously endpoints selection with maximisation of segment content agreement between visual and textual representations. (Color figure online)

One straightforward solution to the task, denoted as proposal-free methods (Fig. 1 (b)), is to predict directly the start and end frames of a target moment that align to the given query [7,14,27,28]. Such paradigm deploys directly the fixed manual activity endpoints labels for model training, implicitly assuming these labels are well-defined and ignoring uncertainties in the labels. However, unlike labelling object spatial bounding-boxes, there is a considerable variation in how activities occur in unconstrained scenarios. There may not even be a precise definition of the exact temporal extent of an activity. Fitting such uncertain temporal endpoints will inevitably lead to semantically mis-matched visual-textual correlations which are not universally interpretable and result in poor generalisation in test. For example, the two queries Q_1 and Q_2 in Fig. 1 (a) are semantically similar in describing 'putting on shoes'. Nonetheless, the annotated activity (gray bars on top) for Q_1 starts from putting down a box while Q_2 begins with sitting down on a sofa. By training a model with such uncertain temporal endpoints (Fig. 1 (b)), the model is trained to match notably different visual features of 'putting down a box' and 'sitting down on a sofa' with the same query on 'putting on shoes'. Clearly, the model suffers from poor learning due to uncertainty in visual cues. Moreover, as observed in [12], *the annotation bias can be inconsistent from different annotators.* Giving the same videos and query sentences to 5 different annotators, only 42% and 35% of their annotated activity boundary are mutually agreed (with at least 50% IoU) on Charades-STA [5] and ActivityNet-Captions [10], respectively. This highlights the extent of activity label uncertainties in model training inherent to the current proposal-free methods, and the potential significant misinformation in training such models. Another solution (Fig. 1 (c)) is to generate many candidate proposals for a target moment and aligns segment-level video features with the query sentences [1,5,29]. By formulating the localisation task as a matching problem, the proposal-based methods consider alignment by the whole moment with less focus on the exact boundary matching [21,22]. By doing so, it can be less sensitive to the boundary labels but more reliance on salient content (attention) between proposals and the target segment. This can make them more tolerant to the uncertainties in temporal annotations. However, the problem of detecting accurately the start- and end-point of a target activity moment remains unsolved especially when learning without exhaustive moment proposals for efficiency concerns.

In this work, we introduce *Elastic Moment Bounding* (EMB) to address the limitation of proposal-free paradigm by modelling explicitly the label uncertainty in the temporal boundaries of an activity moment. Instead of forcing a model to fit manually labelled *rigid* activity endpoints, each MoIs are modelled by an elastic boundary with a set of candidate endpoints. The model then learns to select optimally from consistent visual-textual correlations among semantically similar activities. This introduces model robustness to label uncertainty. Specifically, we conduct a proposal-based segment-wise content alignment in addition to learning of frame-wise boundary identification. As the predicted segment is required to be highly aligned with the query textual description, we represent the gap between the predicted endpoints and the manual labelled endpoints as an elastic boundary (Fig. 1 (d)). This process imposes explictly label uncertainties to model training. To enable activity localisation to be both more attention driven (accurate) and sensitive to an elastic boundary (robust), we introduce an interaction between the segment-wise content representations and frame-wise boundary features by assembling representations through a *Guided Attention* mechanism. The segment-wise boundary-guided attention helps minimise redundant frames in each elastic boundary whilst the frame-wise content-guided attention highlighting transitional frames with apparent visual changes indicating the potential start and end points of an activity.

We make three contributions in this work: (1) We introduce a model to explore collaboratively both proposal-free and proposal-based mechanisms for learning to detect more accurate activity temporal boundary localisation *when training labels are inherently uncertain.* We formulate a new *Elastic Moment Bounding* (EMB) method to expand a manually annotated single pair of fixed activity endpoints to an elastic set. (2) To reinforce directly robust content matching (the spirit of proposal-based) as a condition to accurate endpoints localisation (the spirit of proposal-free) of activities in videos, we introduce a Guided Attention mechanism to explicitly optimise frame-wise boundary visual features subject to segment-wise content representations and vice versa, so to minimise redundant frames in each elastic boundary whilst highlighting frames signalling activity transitions subject to segment content holistically. (3) Our EMB model provides a state-of-the-art performance on three video activity localisation benchmark datasets, improving existing models that suffer from sensitivity to uncertainties in activity training labels.

2 Related Work

Proposal-Based Content Alignment. By aggregating all the frames within a video segment and aligning them holistically with the query sentences, the segment-wise approaches [1,5,6,29,30] are insensitive to the boundary as its most salient and semantically aligned parts are not necessarily at its two ends. The endpoint frames play a significant role to help differentiate video moments from their overlapping counterparts containing redundant frames, hence, critical for video activity localisation. Therefore, we explicitly associate the segment-wise content information with the frame-wise boundary information and complement them by each other through a novel guided attention mechanism.

Proposal-Free Boundary Identification. In contrast, the proposal-free methods learn to directly regress the start and end timestamps of the target moments or predict the per-frame probabilities of being the endpoints [4,7,11,14,27,28,31,33]. In either case, they take the temporal boundaries provided manually as the oracles for learning exactly the same predictions. However, this is prone to be misled by the uncertainty in manual labels and results in less generalisable models. To cope with that, we train our EMB model to identify the target boundary from reliable candidate start and end spans (sets of frames) rather than fitting the single pre-fixed manual endpoints, so as to derive consistent video-text correlations from semantically similar activities that are universally interpretable.

Joint Content-Boundary Learning. There are a few recent attempts [21–23] on locating video activity jointly by the proposal-based and proposal-free strategies. They mostly explored the interaction of frame's and segment's feature representations for better video comprehension. In this work, we study the combination of the two strategies for attention learning of activity temporal boundary conditions beyond feature learning for activity representation. We augment the fixed manual labels by the video segments selected according to their content alignments with query sentences to help improve the robustness of temporal endpoints identification when there is boundary uncertainty.

Temporal Boundary Uncertainty. Recently, Otani *et al.* [12] quantitatively studied the label uncertainty problems on video activity localisation by collecting multiple boundaries for the same activities from different annotators, the results highlighted the extent of uncertainty in the temporal annotations. However, Otani *et al.* [12] did not explicitly propose a solution to the problem. DeNet [33], on the other hand, addressed it w.r.t. the variety of language descriptions, *i.e.*, the same video activity can be described semantically in different ways. They generated different copies of the same query sentences by perturbing the "modified" phrases (adjective, adverb and *etc.*) so to predict diverse boundaries for the same video activities. Rather than studying the uncertainty from the perspective of semantic description, we analyse the uncertainties in activity temporal boundary annotations, which is intrinsically harder to avoid.

3 Learning Localisation with Uncertainty

Given the feature representations of an untrimmed videos $\boldsymbol{F}$ composed of T frames, and that of a natural language sentence $\boldsymbol{Q}$ of L words, the objective of video activity localisation is to identify the temporal boundary of a target

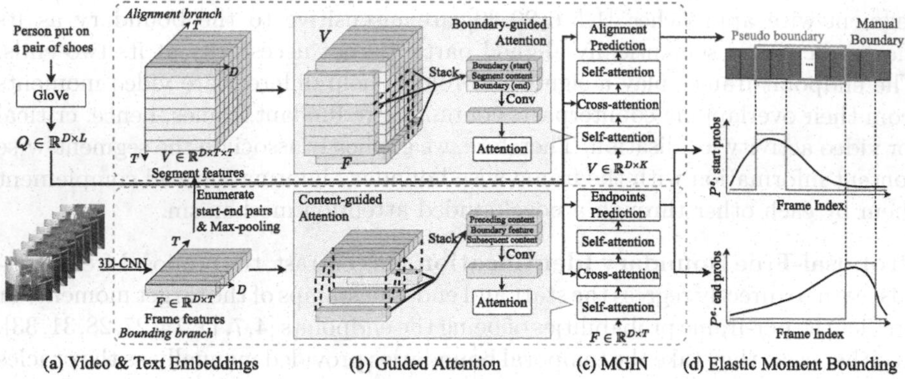

Fig. 2. An overview of *Elastic Moment Bounding* (EMB). **(a)** The EMB model takes the pretrained 3D-CNN features and the GloVe embeddings as inputs. It consists of an 'Alignment branch' (red dashed box) learning the semantic content alignment of video segments and query sentences, and a 'Bounding branch' (green dashed box) to predict the temporal endpoints of target activity moments. Both branches are subject to **(b)** a Guided Attention mechansim with both self- and cross-modalities attention in **(c)** a Multi-grained Interaction Network (MGIN). **(d)** The most confidently aligned video segments predicted by the alignment branch are then selected for constructing the elastic boundary to optimise the endpoints predictions from the bounding branch. (Color figure online)

moment (S, E) – activity endpoints – so that the video segment $\{\boldsymbol{f}_t\}_{t=S}^{E}$ matches with $\boldsymbol{Q}$ in semantics. It is challenging to acquire high-level semantic understandings of either videos or sentences, let alone aligning them to precisely locate the temporal endpoints of a specific activity instance.

In this work, we study the problem of model learning subject to temporal label uncertainty which is inherent to manual video annotation and more importantly not shared in unseen new test videos or language descriptions. To that end, we propose an *Elastic Moment Bounding* (EMB) model (Fig. 2). The EMB model first predicts the per-frame probabilities to be the temporal endpoints of a target moment (Fig. 2's green dashed box) by a *Multi-grained Interaction Network* (MGIN) (Fig. 2 (c)) incorporating with a *Guided Attention* mechanism (Fig. 2 (b)). EMB then optimises the frame-wise probabilities by mining multiple candidate endpoints beyond the manual annotated ones. The candidate endpoints are discovered by an auxiliary alignment branch (Fig. 2's red dashed box). The alignment branch explores the visual-textual content aligment at segment-level, which is less sensitive to exact endpoints annotations so more robust to uncertainty. By doing so, we construct an *elastic boundary* interpretable universally for semantically similar activities with endpoints uncertainty.

3.1 Temporal Endpoints Identification

Our elastic moment bounding is a generic formulation deployable in any multi-modal backbone deep networks. Here, we start with the VSLNet [28] and reconstruct it by introducing a Guided Attention mechanism to form a multi-grained interaction network (MGIN). The overall pipeline of MGIN is shown in Fig. 2 (c) to first encode the video $\boldsymbol{F}$ and the sentence $\boldsymbol{Q}$ by attention both within (self) and across modalities, then predict the frame-wise endpoint probabilities by the joint-modal representations fused by context-query attention [18,24,25].

Adopting the convention [14,22,28], we represent video frames by a pre-trained 3D-CNN model [3] as $\boldsymbol{F} = \{\boldsymbol{f}_t\}_{t=1}^T \in \mathbb{R}^{D^v \times T}$ and the query sentence by the GloVe embeddings [15] of words $\boldsymbol{Q} = \{\boldsymbol{w}_l\}_{l=1}^L \in \mathbb{R}^{D^q \times L}$. To facilitate cross-modal feature interactions, we map both the representations to have the same dimension D by two independent linear projections, *i.e.*, $\boldsymbol{F} \leftarrow \mathrm{FC}(\boldsymbol{F}) \in \mathbb{R}^{D \times T}$ and $\boldsymbol{Q} \leftarrow \mathrm{FC}(\boldsymbol{Q}) \in \mathbb{R}^{D \times L}$.

Vision-Language Attention Representation. We deploy attentive encoding [9,20] for both the visual and textual representations to explore the dependencies among elements in both. In general, to encode a target sequence $\boldsymbol{X}^t \in \mathbb{R}^{D \times L^t}$ of L^t elements with the help of a reference sequence $\boldsymbol{X}^r \in \mathbb{R}^{D \times L^r}$ in size L^r, we first compute an attention matrix $\boldsymbol{A}$ indicating the pairwise target-reference correlations, then represent each target element by its correlated references:

$$\boldsymbol{A} = \mathrm{FC}(\boldsymbol{X}^t)^\top \mathrm{FC}(\boldsymbol{X}^r)/\sqrt{D} \in \mathbb{R}^{L^t \times L^r} \tag{1}$$

$$g(\boldsymbol{X}^t, \boldsymbol{X}^r) = \boldsymbol{X}^t + \mathrm{FC}(\boldsymbol{X}^r)\mathrm{Softmax}(\boldsymbol{A})^\top \in \mathbb{R}^{D \times L^t}. \tag{2}$$

An attention layer formulated in Eq. (2) is parameterised by three independent fully-connected layers. Our MGIN shown in Fig. 2 (c) is constructed by both self-attention within modalities: $\boldsymbol{F} \leftarrow g(\boldsymbol{F}, \boldsymbol{F})$, $\boldsymbol{Q} \leftarrow g(\boldsymbol{Q}, \boldsymbol{Q})$ for context exploration and cross-attention between modalities: $\boldsymbol{F} \leftarrow g(\boldsymbol{F}, \boldsymbol{Q})$, $\boldsymbol{Q} \leftarrow g(\boldsymbol{Q}, \boldsymbol{F})$ to learn the semantic correlations between video frames and query words.

Guided Attention. To effectively locate the temporal endpoints of activities, it is essential for the model to be aware of not only what is shown in each individual frame but also what's different before and after it. As a simple example, the starting point of an activity 'person puts on shoes' should not be arbitrary frames involving shoes-like objects in-between the period but be consistent like when the shoes first appear to interact with the person. Therefore, we propose a content-guided attention module (Fig. 2 (b)'s bottom) to explicitly encode the preceding and subsequent content information of each frame into its representation:

$$\begin{aligned}
\boldsymbol{F}_{\text{pre}} &= \{\mathrm{MaxPool}(\{\boldsymbol{f}_i\}_{i=1}^t)\}_{t=1}^T \in \mathbb{R}^{D \times T}, \\
\boldsymbol{F}_{\text{sub}} &= \{\mathrm{MaxPool}(\{\boldsymbol{f}_i\}_{i=t}^T)\}_{t=1}^T \in \mathbb{R}^{D \times T}, \\
\tilde{\boldsymbol{F}} &= \mathrm{Conv2d}(\{\boldsymbol{F}, \boldsymbol{F}_{\text{pre}}, \boldsymbol{F}_{\text{sub}}\}) \in \mathbb{R}^{D \times T}.
\end{aligned} \tag{3}$$

The feature $\mathrm{MaxPool}(\{\boldsymbol{f}_i\}_{i=1}^t) \in \mathbb{R}^D$ in Eq. 3 aggregate all the frames before $\boldsymbol{f}_t$ by max-pooling as its preceding content representation. Similarly, the subsequent content of the t-th frame is obtained by $\mathrm{MaxPool}(\{\boldsymbol{f}_i\}_{i=t}^T)$. Both the preceding $\boldsymbol{F}_{\text{pre}}$ and subsequent $\boldsymbol{F}_{\text{sub}}$ content features are then stacked and assembled with the frame-wise representations $\boldsymbol{F}$ by a 2D convolution layer. After that, the content-guided representations of video frames $\tilde{\boldsymbol{F}}$ are used for attentive encoding (Eq. (2)) both within $\boldsymbol{F} \leftarrow g(\tilde{\boldsymbol{F}}, \tilde{\boldsymbol{F}})$ and across modalities $\boldsymbol{F} \leftarrow g(\tilde{\boldsymbol{F}}, \boldsymbol{Q})$.

Boundary Prediction. Given a video $\boldsymbol{F} \in \mathbb{R}^{D\times T}$ and sentence $\boldsymbol{Q} \in \mathbb{R}^{D\times L}$ representations, we estimate the frame-wise endpoint probabilities by computing context-query attention [18,24,25], same as the baseline [28]. It is defined as

$$\begin{aligned}
(\boldsymbol{p}^s, \boldsymbol{p}^e) &= \text{Softmax}(\text{LSTM}(\hat{\boldsymbol{F}} \odot \boldsymbol{h})), \text{where } \boldsymbol{h} = \sigma(\text{Conv1d}(\hat{\boldsymbol{F}} \| \boldsymbol{q})) \in \mathbb{R}^{1\times T}, \\
\hat{\boldsymbol{F}} &= H(\boldsymbol{F}, \boldsymbol{Q}) = \text{FC}(\boldsymbol{F} \| \boldsymbol{X}^{v2q} \| \boldsymbol{F} \odot \boldsymbol{X}^{v2q} \| \boldsymbol{F} \odot \boldsymbol{X}^{q2v}) \in \mathbb{R}^{D\times T}; \text{ and} \\
\boldsymbol{A} &= \frac{\text{FC}(\boldsymbol{F})^\top \, \text{FC}(\boldsymbol{Q})}{\sqrt{D}}, \ \boldsymbol{X}^{v2q} = \boldsymbol{Q}\boldsymbol{A}^{r\top}, \ \boldsymbol{X}^{q2v} = \boldsymbol{F}\boldsymbol{A}^{r}\boldsymbol{A}^{c\top}.
\end{aligned} \tag{4}$$

In Eq. (4), we predict the frame-wise endpoint probabilities by two stacked LSTM. This is based on fusing the two modalities $\boldsymbol{F}$ and $\boldsymbol{Q}$ by function H then rescale the per-frame fused feature $\hat{\boldsymbol{F}} \in \mathbb{R}^{D\times T}$ using their estimated likelihood $\boldsymbol{h} \in \mathbb{R}^{1\times T}$ of being foreground to suppress any distractions from redundant frames. Matrix $\boldsymbol{A} \in \mathbb{R}^{T\times L}$ consists of frame-to-word correlation scores; $\boldsymbol{A}^r$ and $\boldsymbol{A}^c$ are its row and column-wise softmax normalised copies. The $\boldsymbol{q}$ are the sentence-level representations from weighted sum of words [2]; $(\cdot\|\cdot)$ stands for concatenation (broadcast if necessary) while $\odot$ is the Hadamard Product.

3.2 Elastic Moment Bounding

Given the uncertainty and ambiguity in manually annotated activity temporal boundaries, it is ineffective to decide heuristically and universally which frames and how many of them should be taken as the candidate endpoints $(\tilde{\boldsymbol{S}}, \tilde{\boldsymbol{E}})$ for different video activities. To address this problem, we formulate an auxiliary alignment branch in the model to learn the visual-textual content mapping per each video segment. It serves as an additional self-learning "annotator" to expand the given single pair of manually annotated boundaries into candidate endpoints proposal sets tailored for individual activities.

Elastic Boundary Construction. As shown in Fig. 2's red dashed box, we first generate a 2D feature map [29] by enumerating pairwise start-end frames to represent $K = T \times T$ video segments $\boldsymbol{V} = \{\boldsymbol{v}_k\}_{k=1}^{K} \in \mathbb{R}^{D\times K}$ as the proposals for a target moment. We flatten the 2D map here for clarity. The k-th proposal with the temporal boundary of (t_k^s, t_k^e) is represented by max-pooling the frames it is composed of $\boldsymbol{v}_k = \text{MaxPool}(\{\boldsymbol{f}_t | \forall t \in [t_k^s, t_k^e]\})$. The segment-wise representations will then be fed into an independent MGIN equipped with *boundary-guided* attention modules (Fig. 2 (b)'s top) for visual encoding. Similar as in the *content-guided* attention for video frames, we explicitly assemble the frame-wise boundary features with the content representations of video segments to encourage boundary-sensitive content alignment:

$$\begin{aligned}
\boldsymbol{V}_{\text{sta}} &= \{\boldsymbol{f}_{t_k^s}\}_{k=1}^{K} \in \mathbb{R}^{D\times K}, \ \boldsymbol{V}_{\text{end}} = \{\boldsymbol{f}_{t_k^e}\}_{k=1}^{K} \in \mathbb{R}^{D\times K}, \\
\tilde{\boldsymbol{V}} &= \text{Conv2d}(\{\boldsymbol{V}, \boldsymbol{V}_{\text{sta}}, \boldsymbol{V}_{\text{end}}\}) \in \mathbb{R}^{D\times K}.
\end{aligned} \tag{5}$$

The features $\boldsymbol{V}_{\text{sta}}$ and $\boldsymbol{V}_{\text{end}}$ in Eq. (5) are the representations of the start and end frames for each of the K proposals. They are stacked and assembled with the segment-wise content features $\boldsymbol{V}$ to derive the boundary guided segment representations $\tilde{\boldsymbol{V}}$ by a 2D convolution layer. Such boundary-guided attention share a similar spirit with temporal pyramid pooling [32], that is to explicitly encode the temporal structure into segment's representation so to be sensitive to its boundary. $\tilde{\boldsymbol{V}}$ is then used for attentive encoding (Eq. (2)) within $\boldsymbol{V} \leftarrow g(\tilde{\boldsymbol{V}}, \tilde{\boldsymbol{V}})$ and across $\boldsymbol{V} \leftarrow g(\tilde{\boldsymbol{V}}, \boldsymbol{Q})$ modalities.

Given the segment-level video representations $\boldsymbol{V}$, we fuse them with the sentence features by H defined in Eq. (4), and re-arrange it to be a 2D feature map then predict the per-proposal alignment scores by a 2D convolution layer:

$$\boldsymbol{p}^a = \sigma(\text{Conv2d}(H(\boldsymbol{V}, \boldsymbol{Q}))) \ \ s.t. \ p_k^a \in (0,1) \ \forall k \in [1, K]. \tag{6}$$

The segment-wise alignment scores $\boldsymbol{p}^a$ activated by the Sigmoid function σ is then supervised by the temporal overlaps between every proposals and the manual boundary:

$$\begin{gathered} \alpha_k = \text{IoU}((t_k^s, t_k^e), (S, E)) \\ y_k^a = \begin{cases} 1, & \text{if } \alpha_k \geq \tau_u \\ 0, & \text{if } \alpha_k < \tau_l \\ \alpha_k, & \text{otherwise} \end{cases} \\ \mathcal{L}_{\text{align}}(\boldsymbol{V}, \boldsymbol{Q}, S, E) = \text{BCE}(\boldsymbol{y}^a, \boldsymbol{p}^a). \end{gathered} \tag{7}$$

The notations τ_u and τ_l are the upper and lower overlap thresholds to control the flexibility of video-text alignment, which are set to 0.7 and 0.3 respectively as in [29]. With the learned segment-wise alignment scores $\boldsymbol{p}^a$, we take the boundary (t_{k*}^s, t_{k*}^e) of the most confident proposal with the greatest predicted score $p_{k*}^a \geq p_k^a \ \forall k \in [1, K]$ as the pseudo boundary and construct the corresponding candidate endpoint sets by:

$$\tilde{\boldsymbol{S}} = [\min(t_{k*}^s, S), \max(t_{k*}^s, S)], \quad \tilde{\boldsymbol{E}} = [\min(t_{k*}^e, E), \max(t_{k*}^e, E)]. \tag{8}$$

We customise the candidate endpoint sets for every individual activity by exploring the content alignments between video segments and query sentences, *i.e.*, elastic boundary. This is intuitively more reliable than applying label smoothing globally [22,23] without considering video context and language semantics.

Reliability *vs.* Flexibility. Introducing too many candidate endpoints that are semantically irrelevant to the query sentences is prone to distracting the model from learning effective visual-textual correlations, especially at the early stage of training a randomly initialised model which is likely to yield inaccurate pseudo boundaries (t_{k*}^s, t_{k*}^e). Therefore, we balance the reliability and flexibility of our elastic boundary by a controllable threshold τ:

$$k* = \arg\max_k \boldsymbol{p}^a \quad s.t. \quad \alpha_k \geq \tau. \tag{9}$$

The α_k in Eq. (9) implies the overlap between the k-th proposal and the manual boundary, whilst the threshold τ serving as a tradeoff between flexibility and reliability so that only the sufficiently overlapped proposals will be selected for constructing the elastic boundary in Eq. (8).

Learning from Elastic Boundary. With the elastic boundary $(\tilde{\boldsymbol{S}}, \tilde{\boldsymbol{E}})$, we formulate the boundary supervision signals to maximise the sum of the candidate endpoint's probabilities obtained in Eq. (4):

$$\mathcal{L}_{\text{bound}}(\boldsymbol{F}, \boldsymbol{Q}, S, E) = -\log(\sum_{t \in \tilde{\boldsymbol{S}}} p_t^s) - \log(\sum_{t \in \tilde{\boldsymbol{E}}} p_t^e). \tag{10}$$

Comparing with the commonly adopted frame-wise supervision which trains $\boldsymbol{p}^s$ and $\boldsymbol{p}^e$ to be one-hot [14,28], we provide in Eq. (10) a more flexible boundary to the target moments so that the model can learn in a data-driven manner to select the endpoints beyond the manual boundary and ignore the unconcerned actions involved.

3.3 Model Training and Inference

Inference. We consider two scenarios when predicting the boundary of video activity: **(a) DET:** following the standard protocol of the task [5,8], we predict a determined boundary enclosed by a single start and end frames according to the outputs of bounding branch in a maximum likelihood manner

$$\hat{S} = \arg\max_t \boldsymbol{p}^s, \quad \hat{E} = \arg\max_t \boldsymbol{p}^e, \tag{11}$$

where $\hat{S}$ and $\hat{E}$ are the predicted start and end frame indices of a video that are corresponding to a given query. **(b) ELA:** considering the uncertain nature of temporal boundary, it is more intuitive to estimate the endpoints of video activity by temporal spans rather than specific frames. Our model is able to predict also an elastic boundary in a similar way as in training:

$$\hat{\boldsymbol{S}} = [\min(t_{k^*}^s, \hat{S}), \max(t_{k^*}^s, \hat{S})], \quad \hat{\boldsymbol{E}} = [\min(t_{k^*}^e, \hat{E}), \max(t_{k^*}^e, \hat{E})]. \tag{12}$$

In Eq. (12), we denote $\hat{\boldsymbol{S}}$ and $\hat{\boldsymbol{E}}$ in bold to indicate a set of candidate endpoints, and differentiate them from the determined boundary in Eq. (11). The (t_{k*}^s, t_{k*}^e) is the boundary of the most confident proposals selected from the alignment branch without constraint on their overlaps to the ground-truth (Eq. (9)).

Training. In addition to $\mathcal{L}_{\text{bound}}$ and $\mathcal{L}_{\text{align}}$, we follow the baseline to learn $\boldsymbol{h}$ in Eq. (4) by a binary cross-entropy loss to highlight foreground video content:

$$\mathcal{L}_{\text{high}}(\boldsymbol{F}, \boldsymbol{Q}, S, E) = \text{BCE}(\boldsymbol{y}^h, \boldsymbol{h}), \quad y_t^h = \mathbb{1}[\min(\tilde{\boldsymbol{S}}) \leq t \leq \max(\tilde{\boldsymbol{E}})]. \tag{13}$$

Note that, the boundary $(\min(\tilde{\boldsymbol{S}}), \max(\tilde{\boldsymbol{E}}))$ is also extended as in [28] to encourage the model to be sensitive to subtle visual changes around the temporal endpoints. The overall loss function of EMB is then formulated as:

$$\mathcal{L} = \lambda_1 \mathcal{L}_{\text{bound}} + \lambda_2 \mathcal{L}_{\text{align}} + \lambda_3 \mathcal{L}_{\text{high}} \tag{14}$$

The EMB model is optimised end-to-end by stochastic gradient descent. Its overall training process is summarised in Algorithm 1.

Algorithm 1. Elastic Moment Bounding

Input: An untrimmed video $\boldsymbol{F}$, a query sentence $\boldsymbol{Q}$, a temporal boundary (S, E).
Output: An updated video activity localisation model.
Encode frames by content-guided attention via Eq. (2)(3);
Fuse frames with query and predict per-frame endpoint probabilities via Eq. (4);
Construct 2D feature map of proposals;
Encode proposals by boundary-guided attention via Eq. (2)(5);
Fuse proposals with query and predict proposal-query alignment scores via Eq. (6);
Construct the elastic boundary via Eq. (8)(9);
Optimise model weights by minimising $\mathcal{L}$ via Eq. (14).

4 Experiments

Datasets. We evaluated the proposed EMB model on three widely adopted video activity localisation benchmark datasets: **(1)** TACoS [16,17], **(3)** Charades-STA [5,19] and **(2)** ActivityNet-Captions [8,10]. Their different data characteristics are summarised in Table 1. Among the three datasets, the raw videos in TACoS have the longest durations while that of its MoIs are shortest in contrast, which means that the video activities are temporally covering less than 2% of the complete videos on average. Therefore, the videos in TACoS contain a lot of redundancy in terms of every MoIs. On the other hand, the ActivityNet-Captions is very different from TACoS whose video activities temporally cover much larger proportions of the videos (~30%) than the other two.

Performance Metrics. We followed the common practices [14,22,28] to measure the quality of our video activity localisation results by their average recall rate at different temporal IoU thresholds (IoU@m). The predicted boundary $(\hat{S}, \hat{E})$ of a MoI is considered correct if its IoU with the manual temporal label (S, E) is greater than the thresholds m which are predefined as $m = \{0.3, 0.5, 0.7\}$. Besides, we also reported the mean IoU (mIoU) of all predictions with their corresponding ground-truth to show the average overlaps between the predicted and manual boundaries. For our elastic boundary, we enumerate all the start-end pairs from $\hat{\boldsymbol{S}}$ and $\hat{\boldsymbol{E}}$ (Eq. (12)) respectively. If a manual boundary's overlap to any of the combinations is greater than the IoU threshold, we consider it is correctly predicted.

Table 1. Statistics of datasets. L^v and L^m are the average lengths of videos and MoIs, respectively. L^q is the average number of words in query sentences.

Datset	#Train	#Val	#Test	L^v	L^q	L^m
TACoS [16]	10,146	4,589	4,083	287.14s	10.1	5.45s
ANet [10]	37,421	17,031	17,505	117.61s	14.8	36.18s
Charades [5]	12,408	–	3,720	30.59s	7.2	8.22s

Implementation Details. We adopted the video features provided by our baseline model [28] and the 300D GloVe [15] embeddings to encode the video and text inputs, respectively. We downsampled videos to have 128 frames at most by max-pooling and zero-padded the shorter ones. The outputs of all the hidden layers were 128D as in [28] and the multi-head variant [20] of the attention layer in Eq. (1) was used with 8 heads followed by layer normalisation and random dropout at 0.2. Cosine positional embeddings were applied to the inputs. The EMB model was trained for 100 epochs with a batch size of 16. It was optimised by an Adam optimiser using a linearly decaying learning rate of $5e-4$ and gradient clipping of 1.0. In the alignment branch, we downsampled the videos to have 16 clips by the max-pooling of every 8 continuous frames for constructing the 2D feature maps of video segments to avoid over-dense proposals. The threshold τ in Eq. (9) was initiated to be 1 and progressively decreased to 0.5. The weights of losses were empirically set to $\lambda_1 = \lambda_2 = 1$ and $\lambda_3 = 5$ in all the datasets.

4.1 Comparisons to the State-of-the-Art

As shown in Table 2, the determined boundary yielded by EMB (DET) outperforms the baseline VSLNet [28] by non-negligble margins on all tests. The more recent IVG [14] shares the same baseline as EMB. The notable performance advantages of EMB over both of them demonstrate its non-trivial improvements. Furthermore, EMB surpasses the state-of-the-art methods on TACoS against all the performance metrics while remaining its competitiveness on the other two datasets. Among the three datasets, TACoS poses the hardest test with the longest average untrimmed videos and the shortest activity moments (see Table 1). That is, TACoS exhibits more realistic scenarios for activity localisation test. In this context, EMB shows its advantage most clearly when the untrimmed videos are longer whilst the video MoIs are sparse and far between.

Moreover, Table 2 shows also the clear performance advantages of the elastic boundary predicted by our EMB (ELA) model over a wide range of the state-of-the-art methods. When constructing the elastic boundaries in inference, over 80% of the predictions pairs yielded by the alignment and bounding branches are consistent with each other (IoU > 0.5). Therefore, the performance improvements we obtained is not due to over-dense sampling of the potential boundaries. For fairer comparisons, we took the adjacent frames before and after the endpoints predicted by VSLNet to generate multiple candidate boundaries for its evaluation. The number of frames is set to be 10% of the moment length so that the density of candidate boundaries is consistent with ours. Although clear performance gains are observed, the improvements from such a *global* shifting strategy are less competitive to our per-sample *adaptive* designs due to missing considerations of sample-dependent bias.

4.2 Ablation Study

We conducted comprehensive ablation studies based on the EMB's determined predictions to provide in-depth analyses and better understandings.

Table 2. Performance comparisons to the state-of-the-art models on three video activity localisation benchmark datasets. The first and second best results are highlighted in red and blue, respectively. The 'DET' modifier of EMB stands for the determined boundary predicted in Eq. (11) while 'ELA' is the elastic boundary (Eq. (12)). The symbol † denotes the reproduced results of our baseline model under the strictly identical setups using the code from authors and ⋆ indicates multi-candidate predictions.

Method	TACoS [16]				Charades-STA [5]				ActivityNet-Captions [10]			
	mIoU	IoU@m			mIoU	IoU@m			mIoU	IoU@m		
		0.3	0.5	0.7		0.3	0.5	0.7		0.3	0.5	0.7
VSLNet [28]	24.11	29.61	24.27	20.03	45.15	64.30	47.31	30.19	43.19	63.16	43.22	26.16
IVG [14]	28.26	38.84	29.07	19.05	48.02	67.63	50.24	32.88	44.21	63.22	43.83	27.10
2D-TAN [29]	–	37.29	25.32	–	–	–	39.70	23.31	–	59.45	44.51	26.54
LGI [13]	–	–	–	–	51.38	72.96	59.46	35.48	41.13	58.52	41.51	23.07
DPIN [21]	–	46.74	32.92	–	–	–	47.98	26.96	–	62.40	47.27	28.31
DRN [27]	–	–	23.17	–	–	–	53.09	31.75	–	–	45.45	24.36
SCDM [26]	–	26.11	21.17	–	–	–	54.44	33.43	–	54.80	36.75	19.86
BPNet [23]	19.53	25.93	20.96	14.08	46.34	65.48	50.75	31.64	42.11	58.98	42.07	24.69
CPNet [11]	28.69	42.61	28.29	–	52.00	–	60.27	38.74	40.65	–	40.56	21.63
CPN [31]	34.63	48.29	36.58	21.25	51.85	72.94	56.70	36.62	45.70	62.81	45.10	28.10
DeNet [33]	–	–	–	–	–	–	59.75	38.52	–	61.93	43.79	–
CBLN [31]	–	38.98	27.65	–	–	–	61.13	38.22	–	66.34	48.12	27.60
SMIN [22]	–	48.01	35.24	–	–	–	64.06	40.75	–	–	48.46	30.34
VSLNet† [28]	28.15	39.07	27.59	16.65	47.33	67.26	50.46	31.53	42.26	57.75	41.10	25.58
EMB (DET)	35.49	50.46	37.82	22.54	53.09	72.50	58.33	39.25	45.59	64.13	44.81	26.07
VSLNet†⋆	30.61	41.14	30.09	18.97	53.88	71.59	57.98	41.64	49.49	65.83	49.68	32.00
EMB⋆ (ELA)	48.36	63.31	52.49	37.02	62.16	79.73	69.22	51.40	56.25	73.72	58.65	40.74

Components Analysis. We investigated the individual contributions of different components in our EMB model to its improvements over the baseline model [28]. As shown in Fig. 3, both our elastic boundary learning objective (Eq. (10)) and the multi-grained interaction network brought clear benefits to the baseline. Such results demonstrate the effectiveness to learn the temporal endpoints of video activities with higher flexibility so to tolerant the uncertainty of manual labels. Besides, they also imply the superiority of our visual encoders which conduct both within and cross-modal attention learning and complement the boundary and content information of video segments mutually.

Candidate Endpoints Mining. We evaluated the advantages of mining candidate endpoints adaptively over several heuristic strategies without the MGIN design: (1) boundary extension [28], (2) smoothing by a gaussian kernel [22,23] and (3) single-frame endpoints (baseline). As shown in Fig. 4, simply improving the boundary's flexibility without considering their reliability ("Extend") tends to degrade the model's performances on both datasets. Boundary smoothing by a gaussian kernel ("Kernel") is sometimes beneficial but less stable than our adaptive designs because their candidates were determined according to only the duration of MoIs without considering the video context and query's unambiguity.

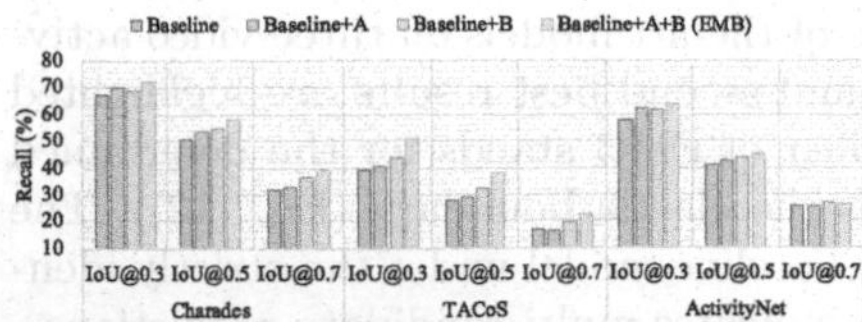

Fig. 3. Effectiveness of different proposed components. The elastic moment bounding formulation is denoted as component "A" while the multi-grained interaction network is component "B".

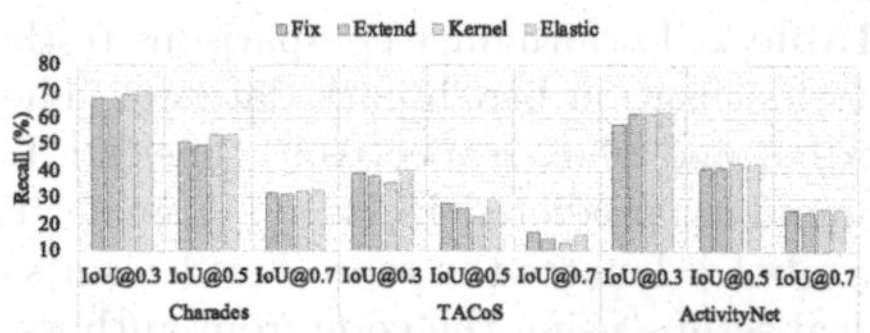

Fig. 4. Effects of multi-candidate mining strategies in training. "Fix": single-frame boundaries. Multiple endpoints are generated by extension (Extend), a gaussian kernel (Kernel), or our elastic bounding.

Evolving Threshold. We studied the effects of threshold's evolving schemes to our elastic boundary constructions (Eq. (9)). Figure 5 shows the curves of schemes and their corresponding performances. The model trained with a constant threshold yielded the worst results in most cases while the 'Sigmoid' scheme is always the best. This is because the 'Sigmoid' scheme maintains a persistently high threshold at the early training stages to avoid introducing distractions when the alignment branch is under-trained, then drops rapidly to involve more diverse candidate endpoints when the alignment branch is reliable.

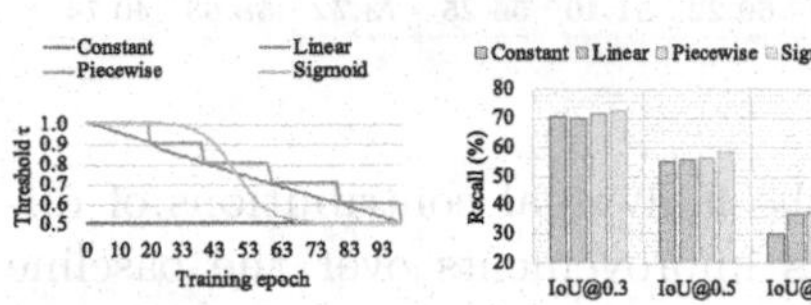

Fig. 5. Effects of constructing elastic boundary subject to an evolving threshold on Charades-STA.

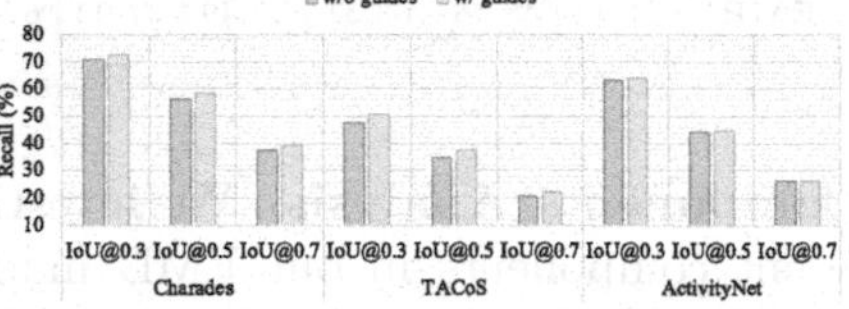

Fig. 6. Effectiveness of guided attention mechanism by comparing with the conventional attention modules [20].

Guided Attention. We validated the effectiveness of our guided attention mechanism by replacing it in our MGIN encoder by the conventional attention modules proposed in [20]. From the comparison results shown in Fig. 6, the models trained with guided attention outperformed their counterparts which learned the video representations without interacting information in multiple granularities. Such results imply the complementary of segment's content and boundary information, which encourage the video feature representations to be sensitive to redundancy and activity transitions.

Qualitative Case Study. We provide several video examples in Fig. 7 which are showing video activities corresponding to semantically similar sentence descriptions. However, their manual boundary are inconsistent, demonstrating

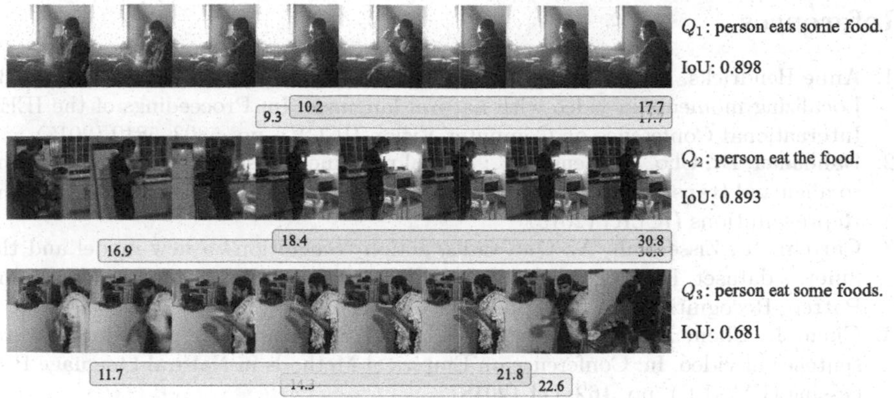

Fig. 7. Cases of video activities with similar semantics but inconsistent manual boundaries. The manual and predicted boundary are shown in red and green, respectively. (Color figure online)

the uncertainty in temporal boundaries. Specifically, the manual boundary for Q_1 starts from grabbing the food right before putting it into the mouth while Q_2 skipping the action of "grabbing" and starts when the person takes a bite. The Q_3 involves even more redundancy which covers the actions of taking a plate from a desk and blending foods by a folk. In contrast, the predictions made by our model are more consistent on interpreting the action of "eat" in different videos, *i.e.*, always starts from delivering food to the mouth. This is accomplished by learning with highly flexible boundaries instead of fitting rigid and ambiguous manual endpoints which are prone to visual-textual miscorrelations.

5 Conclusion

In this work, we introduced a new Elastic Moment Bounding (EMB) approach to learn a more robust model for identifying video activity temporal endpoints with the inherent uncertainty in training labels. EMB is based on modelling elastic boundary tailored to optimise learning more flexibly the endpoints of every target activity moment with the knowledge that the given training labels are uncertain with inconsistency. EMB learns a more accurate and robust visual-textual correlation generalisable to activity moment localisation in more naturally prolonged unseen videos where activity of interests are fractionally small and harder to detect. Comparative evaluations and ablation studies on three activity localisation benchmark datasets demonstrate the competitiveness and unique advantages of EMB over the state-of-the-art models especially when the untrimmed videos are long and activity moments are short.

Acknowledgements. This work was supported by the China Scholarship Council, Vision Semantics Limited, the Alan Turing Institute Turing Fellowship, Adobe Research and Zhejiang Lab (NO. 2022NB0AB05).

References

1. Anne Hendricks, L., Wang, O., Shechtman, E., Sivic, J., Darrell, T., Russell, B.: Localizing moments in video with natural language. In: Proceedings of the IEEE International Conference on Computer Vision (ICCV), pp. 5803–5812 (2017)
2. Bahdanau, D., Cho, K., Bengio, Y.: Neural machine translation by jointly learning to align and translate. In: Proceedings of the International Conference on Learning Representations (ICLR) (2015)
3. Carreira, J., Zisserman, A.: Quo vadis, action recognition? a new model and the kinetics dataset. In: Proceedings of the IEEE Conference on Computer Vision and Pattern Recognition (CVPR), pp. 6299–6308 (2017)
4. Chen, J., Chen, X., Ma, L., Jie, Z., Chua, T.S.: Temporally grounding natural sentence in video. In: Conference on Empirical Methods in Natural Language Processing (EMNLP), pp. 162–171 (2018)
5. Gao, J., Sun, C., Yang, Z., Nevatia, R.: Tall: Temporal activity localization via language query. In: Proceedings of the IEEE International Conference on Computer Vision (ICCV), pp. 5267–5275 (2017)
6. Ge, R., Gao, J., Chen, K., Nevatia, R.: MAC: mining activity concepts for language-based temporal localization. In: Proceedings of the IEEE/CVF Winter Conference on Applications of Computer Vision (WACV), pp. 245–253. IEEE (2019)
7. Ghosh, S., Agarwal, A., Parekh, Z., Hauptmann, A.: ExCL: extractive Clip Localization Using Natural Language Descriptions. In: Proceedings of the 2019 Conference of the North American Chapter of the Association for Computational Linguistics: Human Language Technologies, Volume 1 (Long and Short Papers), pp. 1984–1990. Association for Computational Linguistics, Minneapolis, Minnesota (2019). https://www.aclweb.org/anthology/N19-1198
8. Heilbron, F.C., Escorcia, V., Ghanem, B., Niebles, J.C.: ActivityNet: a large-scale video benchmark for human activity understanding. In: Proceedings of the IEEE Conference on Computer Vision and Pattern Recognition (CVPR), pp. 961–970 (2015). https://doi.org/10.1109/CVPR.2015.7298698
9. Huang, J., Liu, Y., Gong, S., Jin, H.: Cross-sentence temporal and semantic relations in video activity localisation. In: Proceedings of the IEEE/CVF International Conference on Computer Vision, pp. 7199–7208 (2021)
10. Krishna, R., Hata, K., Ren, F., Fei-Fei, L., Niebles, J.C.: Dense-captioning events in videos. In: Proceedings of the IEEE International Conference on Computer Vision (ICCV) (2017)
11. Li, K., Guo, D., Wang, M.: Proposal-free video grounding with contextual pyramid network. In: Proceedings of the AAAI Conference on Artificial Intelligence (AAAI), vol. 35, pp. 1902–1910 (2021)
12. Otani, M., Nakahima, Y., Rahtu, E., Heikkilä, J.: Uncovering hidden challenges in query-based video moment retrieval. In: Proceedings of the British Machine Vision Conference (BMVC) (2020)
13. Mun, J., Cho, M., Han, B.: Local-global video-text interactions for temporal grounding. In: Proceedings of the IEEE Conference on Computer Vision and Pattern Recognition (CVPR), pp. 10810–10819 (2020)
14. Nan, G., et al.: Interventional video grounding with dual contrastive learning. In: Proceedings of the IEEE Conference on Computer Vision and Pattern Recognition (CVPR), pp. 2765–2775 (2021)
15. Pennington, J., Socher, R., Manning, C.D.: Glove: global vectors for word representation. In: Conference on Empirical Methods in Natural Language Processing (EMNLP), pp. 1532–1543 (2014). https://www.aclweb.org/anthology/D14-1162

16. Regneri, M., Rohrbach, M., Wetzel, D., Thater, S., Schiele, B., Pinkal, M.: Grounding action descriptions in videos. Trans. Assoc.Comput. Linguist. **1**, 25–36 (2013)
17. Rohrbach, M., Regneri, M., Andriluka, M., Amin, S., Pinkal, M., Schiele, B.: Script data for attribute-based recognition of composite activities. In: Fitzgibbon, A., Lazebnik, S., Perona, P., Sato, Y., Schmid, C. (eds.) ECCV 2012. LNCS, vol. 7572, pp. 144–157. Springer, Heidelberg (2012). https://doi.org/10.1007/978-3-642-33718-5_11
18. Seo, M., Kembhavi, A., Farhadi, A., Hajishirzi, H.: Bidirectional attention flow for machine comprehension. arXiv preprint arXiv:1611.01603 (2016)
19. Sigurdsson, G.A., Varol, G., Wang, X., Farhadi, A., Laptev, I., Gupta, A.: Hollywood in homes: crowdsourcing data collection for activity understanding. In: Leibe, B., Matas, J., Sebe, N., Welling, M. (eds.) ECCV 2016. LNCS, vol. 9905, pp. 510–526. Springer, Cham (2016). https://doi.org/10.1007/978-3-319-46448-0_31
20. Vaswani, A., et al.: Attention is all you need. In: Proceedings of the Conference on Neural Information Processing Systems (NeurIPS), pp. 5998–6008 (2017)
21. Wang, H., Zha, Z.J., Chen, X., Xiong, Z., Luo, J.: Dual path interaction network for video moment localization. In: Proceedings of the ACM International Conference on Multimedia (MM), pp. 4116–4124 (2020)
22. Wang, H., Zha, Z.J., Li, L., Liu, D., Luo, J.: Structured multi-level interaction network for video moment localization via language query. In: Proceedings of the IEEE Conference on Computer Vision and Pattern Recognition (CVPR), pp. 7026–7035 (2021)
23. Xiao, S., et al.: Boundary proposal network for two-stage natural language video localization. In: Proceedings of the AAAI Conference on Artificial Intelligence (AAAI), vol. 35, pp. 2986–2994 (2021)
24. Xiong, C., Zhong, V., Socher, R.: Dynamic coattention networks for question answering. arXiv preprint arXiv:1611.01604 (2016)
25. Yu, A.W., Dohan, D., Le, Q., Luong, T., Zhao, R., Chen, K.: Fast and accurate reading comprehension by combining self-attention and convolution. In: Proceedings of the International Conference on Learning Representations (ICLR), vol. 2 (2018)
26. Yuan, Y., Ma, L., Wang, J., Liu, W., Zhu, W.: Semantic conditioned dynamic modulation for temporal sentence grounding in videos. In: Proceedings of the Conference on Neural Information Processing Systems (NeurIPS), pp. 534–544 (2019)
27. Zeng, R., Xu, H., Huang, W., Chen, P., Tan, M., Gan, C.: Dense regression network for video grounding. In: Proceedings of the IEEE Conference on Computer Vision and Pattern Recognition (CVPR), pp. 10287–10296 (2020)
28. Zhang, H., Sun, A., Jing, W., Zhou, J.T.: Span-based localizing network for natural language video localization. In: Proceedings of the 58th Annual Meeting of the Association for Computational Linguistics. pp. 6543–6554. Association for Computational Linguistics, Online (2020). https://www.aclweb.org/anthology/2020.acl-main.585
29. Zhang, S., Peng, H., Fu, J., Luo, J.: Learning 2D temporal adjacent networks for moment localization with natural language. In: Proceedings of the AAAI Conference on Artificial Intelligence (AAAI), vol. 34, pp. 12870–12877 (2020)
30. Zhang, S., Su, J., Luo, J.: Exploiting temporal relationships in video moment localization with natural language. In: Proceedings of the ACM International Conference on Multimedia (MM), pp. 1230–1238 (2019)
31. Zhao, Y., Zhao, Z., Zhang, Z., Lin, Z.: Cascaded prediction network via segment tree for temporal video grounding. In: Proceedings of the IEEE Conference on Computer Vision and Pattern Recognition (CVPR), pp. 4197–4206 (2021)

32. Zhao, Y., Xiong, Y., Wang, L., Wu, Z., Tang, X., Lin, D.: Temporal action detection with structured segment networks. In: Proceedings of the IEEE International Conference on Computer Vision, pp. 2914–2923 (2017)
33. Zhou, H., Zhang, C., Luo, Y., Chen, Y., Hu, C.: Embracing uncertainty: decoupling and de-bias for robust temporal grounding. In: Proceedings of the IEEE Conference on Computer Vision and Pattern Recognition (CVPR), pp. 8445–8454 (2021)

Temporal Saliency Query Network for Efficient Video Recognition

Boyang Xia[1,2], Zhihao Wang[1,2], Wenhao Wu[3,4(✉)], Haoran Wang[4], and Jungong Han[5]

[1] Key Lab of Intelligent Information Processing of Chinese Academy of Sciences (CAS), Institute of Computing Technology, CAS, Beijing, China
[2] University of Chinese Academy of Sciences, Beijing, China
[3] The University of Sydney, Sydney, Australia
whwu.ucas@gmail.com
[4] Baidu Inc., Beijing, China
[5] Computer Science Department, Aberystwyth University, Aberystwyth SY23 3FL, UK

Abstract. Efficient video recognition is a hot-spot research topic with the explosive growth of multimedia data on the Internet and mobile devices. Most existing methods select the salient frames without awareness of the class-specific saliency scores, which neglect the implicit association between the saliency of frames and its belonging category. To alleviate this issue, we devise a novel Temporal Saliency Query (TSQ) mechanism, which introduces class-specific information to provide fine-grained cues for saliency measurement. Specifically, we model the class-specific saliency measuring process as a query-response task. For each category, the common pattern of it is employed as a query and the most salient frames are responded to it. Then, the calculated similarities are adopted as the frame saliency scores. To achieve it, we propose a **Temporal Saliency Query Network (TSQNet)** that includes two instantiations of the TSQ mechanism based on visual appearance similarities and textual event-object relations. Afterward, cross-modality interactions are imposed to promote the information exchange between them. Finally, we use the class-specific saliencies of the most confident categories generated by two modalities to perform the selection of salient frames. Extensive experiments demonstrate the effectiveness of our method by achieving state-of-the-art results on ActivityNet, FCVID and Mini-Kinetics datasets. Our project page is at https://lawrencexia2008.github.io/projects/tsqnet.

Keywords: Video recognition · Transformer · Temporal sampling

B. Xia and Z. Wang—Co-first authorship.

Supplementary Information The online version contains supplementary material available at https://doi.org/10.1007/978-3-031-19830-4_42.

S. Avidan et al. (Eds.): ECCV 2022, LNCS 13694, pp. 741–759, 2022.
https://doi.org/10.1007/978-3-031-19830-4_42

1 Introduction

In the recent years, video understanding has drawn considerable attention from the community [9,15,41,45,49,54] for the inexorable increase of video content on the Internet. Much progress has been achieved on the techniques to model complex video events, which can be glimpsed on promising precision on multiple benchmark datasets [18,35]. However, computational costs grow proportionally to the recognition accuracy. This hinders the deployment of video recognition systems in resource-constraint environments, *e.g.* IoT, self-driving and mobile phone applications. Hence, it is imperative to develop efficient video recognition systems to meet the rising demands of resource-efficient applications.

There are many studies that have been conducted on efficient video recognition. One set of approaches focus on designing lightweight architectures [10,38]. At the other end of the spectrum are the dynamic inference-based approaches, which typically utilize a lightweight policy network to preview the video events, and allocate computation resources depending on the saliency of frames. They implant a policy network (or sampler network) inside the reinforce learning paradigm [22,47,51], or adopt attention weight as a proxy of policy under the attention mechanism [11,13]. The sampler networks are optimized under the assumption that the most salient frames/regions contribute most to the video representation, which produces one-size-fits-all, *i.e.*, class-agnostic frame saliency measurements.

Actually, salient patterns are tightly associated with the category semantics. However, one-size-fits-all saliencies are not sensitive to fine-grained semantics. In particular, the sampler may overestimate the saliency of some frames which seem to be representative, but they actually belong to other categories rather than the real one of the current video. By contrast, a human can precisely elect the most informative frames with the aid of prior information about the probable category of the video. Because we can naturally build the logic connection between frame sequences and the common pattern of the predicted category, which can be understood as a query-response manner. For example, in Fig. 1, one can easily select the 3rd, 6th and 7th frames from the video with the assumption that the video may belongs to **Tailgate Party**. By contrast, one-sizes-fit-all sampler may also be inclined to 5th frames besides those three frames for it is quite representative for another category, *e.g.* **Parking Car**.

Inspired by this observation, in this paper, we cast frame saliency measuring as a querying process, to enable discriminative class-specific saliency measurement. To this end, we present a novel **Temporal Saliency Query (TSQ) mechanism**, which can measure saliencies of all semantic categories over frame sequence in parallel, and select the saliency of highly-confident categories as final the result. Concretely, we formulate class-specific saliency measuring as a query-response task. The common patterns of the various categories are adopted as **query**, and frame representations gathered by category-frame similarities are taken as the **response**. Then, the category-frame similarities can be regarded as frame saliencies. A conceptual overview of the TSQ mechanism is shown in Fig. 1. Specifically, we use cross attention in Transformer Decoder [39] to model many-to-many category-frame similarities in parallel. On one hand, we represent the common pattern of a category, namely TSQ embedding, by visual prototypes.

Fig. 1. A conceptual overview of the TSQ mechanism. We cast the saliency estimation task as a query-response task. We ask each category a question: Which frames are the most salient ones for it? As we can see in the above example, we get the answer that frames 3rd, 6th, 7th are most salient for *tailgate party* and the frame 5th is salient for *parking car*. No frame is salient for *playing chess*.

And the query process is performed over the visual feature of the frame sequence. On the other hand, to handle large intra-class variations of visual appearance, we measure saliency by textual event-object relations for complementary information. As we know, the objects in videos are closely associated with the category annotation of video. For instance, **cake, candle and balloon with birthday party**. To model the semantic relationships between object and category, we first employ BERT [7] to represent the object with word embedding of its name. Taking the product as textual embedding, we construct another textual branch in the TSQ mechanism, where the query process is executed over the embedding sequence of object names. Doing so allows us to exploit prior knowledge from off-the-shelf word representations to supply cross-modal complementary clues to saliency measurement.

Our contributions are summarized as: *First*, we propose a novel Temporal Saliency Query mechanism, to alleviate the lack of class-specific information in saliency measuring for temporal sampling frameworks. *Second*, we present an efficient multi-modal salient frame sampler **T**emporal **S**aliency **Q**uery **Net**work **(TSQNet)**, which utilize both visual appearance feature and textual feature obtained by object name embeddings to measure frame saliencies in a unified framework. *Third*, we conduct extensive experiments on three large-scale datasets, *i.e.*, ActivityNet, FCVID and Mini-Kinetics, which show TSQNet significantly outperforms the state-of-the-art approaches on accuracy-efficiency trade-off.

2 Related Work

Efficient Video Recognition. Efficient video recognition approaches can be roughly categorized into two directions. The first focus on elaborating new lightweight architectures by decomposing 3D convolution operations into 2D and

1D ones [38,46,53], channel shifting in 2D CNNs [23], *etc.* The others are based on a dynamic inference mechanism [3,48,52], which allocates computation resources on a per-sample basis based on the saliencies of frames. Wu *et al.* [47] utilizes multi-agent reinforce learning to model parallel frame sampling and Lin *et al.* [24] make one-step decision with holistic view. Meng *et al.* [27] and Wang *et al.* [42,44] focus their attention on spatial redundancy. Panda *et al.* adaptively decide modalities for video segments. Most of the previous works are mainly based on reinforce learning or attention mechanism, which are optimized with video classification objectives. However, this paradigm makes produced adaptive sampling policy class-agnostic and lacks discrimination power in fine-grained semantics. In contrast, our temporal sampling-based framework enables discriminative class-specific frame saliency measuring and shows that class-specific mechanism combined with visual-textual multi-modal complementary measuring can push the envelope of the trade-off between accuracy and computation cost.

Transformer in Vision Tasks. Transformer [39] is initially proposed to solve the long-term dependence problem in machine translation. ViT [8], SwinTransformer [26] and DVT [43] split image to patches as words and bring Transformer Encoder to computer vision classification tasks. Query2label [25] apply Transformer Decoder to multi-label classification task. DETR [2] explore using Transformer Decoder for object detection task. Then Transformer Decoder for segmentation is also developed by MaskFormer [5]. The role of Transformer Encoder in C-Tran [21] and TransVG [6] is to model relations between different modalities.

3 Method

Given a video of T frames $X = \{x_i\}_{i=1}^{T}, x_i \in \mathbb{R}^{3\times H\times W}$, our goal is to estimate the saliency score of frames $S = \{s_i\}_{i=1}^{T}$ and sample top K frames with the highest saliency score to feed into a recognition network to obtain final video prediction P. The overview of our method is shown in Fig. 2. In this section, we first introduce the Temporal Saliency Query (TSQ) mechanism in Sect. 3.1. Then we elaborate on the framework of our TSQNet, including two instantiations of TSQ mechanism with visual and textual modalities and cross-modality interactions of them in Sect. 3.2. Finally, we present the inference procedure of TSQNet in Sect. 3.3.

3.1 Temporal Saliency Query Mechanism

The goal of Temporal Saliency Query (TSQ) mechanism is to perform frame saliency estimation for all categories simultaneously, which is the shared building block for two branches of visual and textual modalities in TSQNet. To expand generic saliency to class-specific version, we are potentially to ask each category a question: which frames are the most similar ones to the common pattern of it? In this way, we can convert saliency estimation task to query-response task: a learnable embedding initialized with the common pattern of each category is set

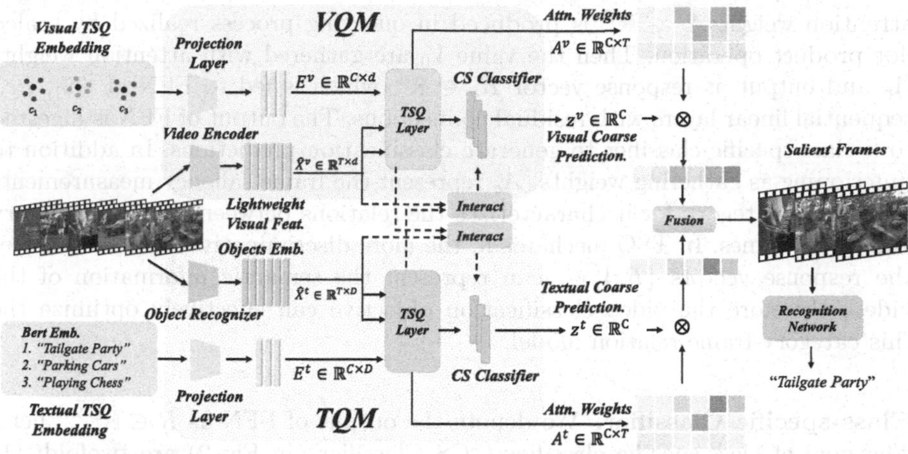

Fig. 2. The overview of the Temporal Saliency Query Networks. Frame sequence is **queried** with visual and textual TSQ embeddings of categories in VQM and TQM, then TSQNet **responded** to the queries by gathering most salient frame representations for each category. And the resultant category-frame similarities are adopted as class-specific saliency measurements for two modalities, which are post-processed and fused for final saliency scores. Top K frames with the highest saliency score are sampled and ingested to an off-the-shelf recognition network for final recognition. Cross-modality interaction ("Interaction") is considered for information exchanging during training. The projection layer is used to reduce the dimension of input features.

as the **query**, and the gathered feature from frame sequence with similarities is the **response**. Then the similarities between each category and frame sequence can be regarded as the saliency scores. We denote the learnable embedding here as **TSQ embedding**. In TSQ mechanism, a TSQ layer is proposed to enable the query-response functionality and a class-specific classifier is designed to generate coarce predictions of video category and enable discriminative learning of TSQ embedding for each category at the same time. The details of TSQ mechanism are described below.

TSQ Layer. The goal of TSQ layer is to model the many-to-many category-frame similarities simultaneously and enable learning of TSQ embeddings, denoted as $\{E_c \in \mathbb{R}^d\}_{c=1}^C$, under the video classification objective. To achieve this, TSQ layer is build on an attention structure in Transformer [39]:

$$A_c = \text{softmax}(\frac{Q_0 {K_0}^{\top}}{\sqrt{d}}), \ R_c = A_c V_0, \tag{1}$$

$Q_0 \in \mathbb{R}^d$ is a query matrix, which is obtained by projecting each TSQ embedding E_c with a parameter matrix $W_q \in \mathbb{R}^{d\times d}$: $Q_0 = E_c W_q$. $K_0 \in \mathbb{R}^{T\times d}$ and $V_0 \in \mathbb{R}^{T\times d}$ are the key and value matrix, which are generated by projecting frame feature sequence $X \in \mathbb{R}^{T\times d}$ with different parameter matrices $W_k, W_v \in \mathbb{R}^{d\times d}$: $K_0 = XW_k, V_0 = XW_v$. Then, for the TSQ embedding of the c-th category E_c, the attention weight $A_c \in \mathbb{R}^T$ is produced in querying process realized by scaled dot product operation. Then the value V_0 are gathered with attention weights A_c and output as response vector $R_c \in \mathbb{R}^d$, which is fed to FFN of [39], *i.e.*, sequential linear layers with residual connections. The output of FFN is ingested to a class-specific classifier to generate classification predictions. In addition to functioning as gathering weights, A_c represent the frame saliency measurements of the c-th category for it characterizes the relations between the c-th category and all T frames. In TSQ mechanism, the more discriminative A_c is, the better the response vectors $\{R_c\}_{c=1}^C$ can represent the semantic information of the video, therefore the video classification objective can effectively optimize the this category-frame relation model.

Class-specific Classifier. We denote the output of FFN as $\hat{R} \in \mathbb{R}^{C\times d}$ here. The goal of class-specific classifier ("CS Classifier" in Fig. 2) are twofold: (1) project $\hat{R} \in \mathbb{R}^{C\times d}$ to a coarse video prediction $z \in \mathbb{R}^C$, (2) enable class-specific learning of TSQ embeddings. In class-specific classifier, instead of directly using projection layer with weight matrix $W \in \mathbb{R}^{1\times d}$ as $z = W\hat{R} + b$, we apply C projection layers with different weight matrices $\{W_c \in \mathbb{R}^{1\times d}\}_{c=1}^C$ to each $\hat{R}_c$ separately. For the c-th category, corresponding element of p is computed as:

$$z_c = W_c\hat{R}_c^{\mathsf{T}} + b_c, \tag{2}$$

where $b_c \in \mathbb{R}^1, b \in \mathbb{R}^C$ are the bias parameters (see Appendix for illustrative examples). This class-specific design endows the response vector of each category with exclusive classifier, which effectively reserves the characteristic of each category and make model converge more easily. z is used for calculating regular cross entropy loss with video labels. Notice here the difference between the coarse video prediction z and the final video prediction P: z is used for saliency measuring while P is the final classification result of the recognition network.

3.2 Temporal Saliency Query Network

Our TSQNet mainly consists of two modules: a Visual Query module and a Textual Query module, which are instantiations of TSQ mechanism with visual and textual representations, respectively. The Visual Query module query the frame appearance sequence with the visual TSQ embedding of each category, and collect the category-frame similarities for class-specific saliency estimation. Textual Query module measures saliencies by modeling event-object (or action-object) relations on the basis of prior knowledge in off-the-shelf language models. Besides, to exchange information between two TSQ modules, cross-modality interactions are performed synchronously during training, which effective compensate scarce scene information for Textual Query module.

Visual Query Module (VQM). The goal of VQM is to generate class-specific saliency measurement from pure visual perspective, which mainly consists of a video encoder, a TSQ layer and a class-specific classifier. The video encoder is a lightweight CNN or transformer backbone, *e.g.,* MobileNetv2 [33] and Mobile-former [4], which extract features from RGB frame sequence $\{x_i\}_{i=1}^T$ to feature sequence $\{\hat{x}_i^v \in \mathbb{R}^d\}_{i=1}^T$. We further use a 1D convolutional layer to reduce the feature dimension from d to d', which we still denote as $\hat{X}^v = \{\hat{x}_i^v\}_{i=1}^T$ for brevity. TSQ layer takes visual TSQ embedding as query, and frame sequence as key and value, to generate saliency measurements $A^v \in \mathbb{R}^{C\times T}$ from visual features. Class-specific classifier produce visual video coarse predictions z^v, which is further used in the post-processing procedure of saliencies. Next we describe how we obtain visual TSQ embedding.

Following the definition in Sect. 3.1, visual TSQ embedding $\{E_c^v \in \mathbb{R}^d\}_{c=1}^C$ here is a set of learnable embeddings initialized with common appearance patterns of categories. We propose a simple prototype based representation for common appearance patterns here. Prior works [34] find that, most of the samples belonging to the same class cluster around a prototype in feature space formed by non-linear mapping of networks. We assume that category prototypes can represent the common patterns of categories. Following definitions in [34], we use the averaged features of videos belonging to each category produced by video encoder in the training set, where a video feature is obtained by top-k pooling of frame features (see Appendix for details). A 1D convolutional layer is also used to project E_c^v to the same d'-dimension space with $\hat{x}_i^v$, which is still represented by E_c^v hereafter.

Textual Query Module (TQM). The goal of TQM is to provide knowledge-aware saliency estimation by mining generic event-object relations in videos with the help of prior knowledge in off-the-shelf language models. As observed by prior works [13,16], the event-object (or action-object) relations are generic in videos. Although this knowledge is typically represented in knowledge graph [40], we exploit it in a much more compact fashion, *i.e.,* pre-trained language models. It is proved that the semantic relationships between words can be effectively captured in pre-trained word representations, *e.g.,* Word2Vec [29] and BERT [7]. To model category-frame relations, we first build a object vocabulary $W \in \mathbb{R}^{C_o\times D}$, on a pre-defined object list, *e.g.,* ImageNet-1K category list ($C_o = 1000$) with word embeddings. Then we introduce a lightweight but precise object recognizer to extract appearing object scores from each frame $\{O_i \in \mathbb{R}^{C_o}\}_{i=1}^T$. The frame-level object embedding based feature can obtained: $\hat{X}^t = \{\hat{x}_i^t\}_{i=1}^T, \hat{x}_i^t = O_i W$. Correspondingly, the textual TSQ embedding $\{E_c^t \in \mathbb{R}^D\}_{c=1}^C$ is initialized by pre-trained word embeddings of the category name, to align with textual feature sequence in embedding space. Similar to VQM, we add a 1D convolutional layer to $\{E_c^t \in \mathbb{R}^D\}_{c=1}^C$ and $\hat{X}^t$ to reduce dimensions, which are fed into a TSQ layer and class-specific classifier for textual frame saliency measurements $A^t \in \mathbb{R}^{C\times T}$ and textual coarse video prediction $z^t \in \mathbb{R}^C$.

Cross-modality Interaction. Here we seek to enable information exchange between TSQ layers of two modalities during training and provide guidance, *e.g.,* scene knowledge, from VQM to TQM. To achieve this, we design a novel *swap-attention* structure, which gather the feature sequence with attention weights of the other modality in both VQM and TQM, to generate two additional response vectors:

$$R^{t\to v} = A^t \hat{X}^v, R^{v\to t} = A^v \hat{X}^t, \tag{3}$$

Then the two response vectors based on visual feature sequence R^v and $R^{t\to v}$ are ingested to subsequent layers and compute loss as $\mathcal{L}_v$ and $\mathcal{L}_{t\to v}$. The same process conducted on textual features sequence renders $\mathcal{L}_t$ and $\mathcal{L}_{v\to t}$. The swap-attention structure is conducive to TQM in two ways: (1) $\mathcal{L}_{t\to v}$ help optimize scene-aware category-frame relation model (2) $\mathcal{L}_{v\to t}$ help optimize scene-aware FFN and classifier. We weighted the existing four losses to obtain the final loss function:

$$\mathcal{L} = \mathcal{L}_v + \mathcal{L}_t + \alpha\mathcal{L}_{t\to v} + \beta\mathcal{L}_{v\to t}, \tag{4}$$

3.3 Inference of TSQNet

During inference, to yield final saliency measurements, we aggregate the generated frame saliency estimation of high-probability predicted categories for two modalities, respectively, and fuse them for final saliency results.

Saliency Aggregation. Here we only describe saliency aggregation for VQM, which is conducted for TQM with the same way. Intuitively, the higher the probability that a video belongs in c-th category, the higher the priority of the c-th row of attention weights in final saliency result. Following this intuition, we aggregate class-specific saliency measurements of VQM, $A^v \in \mathbb{R}^{C\times T}$ with the coarse video prediction $z^v \in \mathbb{R}^C$. For the i-th frame, the measured saliency of VQM is:

$$s_i^v = \sum_{c=1}^{C} z_c^v A_{c,i}^v, \tag{5}$$

In practive, to filter the noise brought about by the low-confidence categories, we only aggregate saliencies of top-5 categories with highest z^v to get final saliency measurements.

Multi-modality Saliency Fusion. We fuse the saliency measurements of VQM and TQM by taking the union of the top s_i^v frames and top s_i^t frames. The number of frames used for union in two modules are controlled by pre-defined proportion λ_v and λ_t, and the budget of selected frames K.

4 Experiments

4.1 Experimental Setup

Datasets. We evaluate our method on three large-scale datasets: ActivityNet, FCVID and Mini-Kinetics. ActivityNet [1] contains 200 categories, it has 10024 videos for training and 4926 videos for validation, where the average duration of videos is 117 s. FCVID [17] includes 91,223 videos which 45,611 for training and 45,612 for validation and divided to 239 classes, where the average duration of the videos is 167 s. Mini-Kinetics is a small version of Kinetics [18], it consists of 121k training videos and 10k validation ones from 200 categories. Different from first two benchmarks, the videos in Mini-Kinetics are trimmed, with a average length of 10 s.

Evaluation Metrics. For all datasets above, we apply the official train-val split to experiment our method. Following the previous work, mean Average Precision (mAP) is used as the main evaluation metric for ActivityNet and FCVID, and Top1 accuracy for Mini-Kinetics. We also evaluate the computation cost with giga floating point operations (GFLOPs).

Table 1. Example of FLOPs computation.

Module	Arch.	Res.	FLOPs/F	#F	FLOPs
Vis.Enc.	MBv2	188	0.220G	16	3.52G
Obj.Rec.	EN-B0	112	0.098G	16	1.56G
Rec.Net.	RN50	224	4.109G	5	20.55G
VQM	–	–	–	–	0.36G
TQM	–	–	–	–	0.10G
Total	–	–	–	–	26.09G

Table 2. Comparisons with simple baselines.

Method	mAP (%)	FLOPs
Uniform	70.9	195.8G
Random	70.2	195.8G
Dense	71.2	930.8G
MaxConf	74.2	930.8G
MaxConf-L	71.2	54.9G
Ours	74.3	55.3G

Implementation Details. We adopt MobileNetv2 [33] trained on target datasets as the video encoder in VQM, and Efficientnet-B0 [37] trained on ImageNet-1K as the object recognizer in TQM, respectively. For fair comparisons with previous works, we adopt three backbones in ResNet [14] series, *e.g.*, ResNet-50, 101, 152 for recognition networks. For resolution of frame processed by recognition networks, we follow previous works to scale the shorter side of frames to 256 and then center cropped them to 224×224 for all datasets. On ActivityNet and FCVID, the resolution of frames processed by VQM is 188×188 and one for TQM is 112×112[1]. On Mini-Kinetics, the resolution is 112×112 for both VQM and TQM. Table 1 shows decomposition of computation cost of TSQNet when adopting ResNet-50 as recognition network. Please refer to Appendix for more implementation details.

[1] Note that the total computation cost of a 188×188 frame processed by MobileNetv2 and a 112×112 frame processed by EfficientNet-B0 equals to the cost of a 224×224 frame processed by MobileNetv2, which is the common setting of previous works [13,42].

4.2 Comparison with Simple Baselines

We compare our TSQNet with some simple baselines with ResNet-101 without TSN-style training as the recognizer in Table 2. There are multiple rule based baselines, "uniform" and "random" stand for uniformly and randomly selecting 10 frames from a video. "Dense" means using all frames of a video. For "Max-Conf", we firstly obtain the maximum confidence among all categories for every frame by applying the model along time axis, then select K frames with highest maximum confidence. We also compare with a simple sampler based baseline, "MaxConf-L", which is a lightweight version of "MaxConf" within a uniformly pre-sampled T frames, as the same as "ours". The T in "MaxConf-L" and "ours" is 50, and K in "MaxConf", "MaxConf-L" and "ours" is 5. Our TSQNet obviously presents the best accuracy with limited FLOPs. In fact, "MaxConf-L" is an ablated baseline for our class-specific motivation, which replaces our TSQ mechanism with direct frame-level classification. Comparison with "MaxConf-L" confirms the efficacy of our TSQ mechanism.

4.3 Comparison with State-of-the-Arts

Results on AcitivtyNet. We compare the proposed method with recent SOTA methods on AcitivtyNet in Table 3: SCSampler [20], AR-Net [27], AdaMML [30], VideoIQ [36], AdaFcous [42], Dynamic-STE [19] and Frame-Exit [12]. Experimental result shows that our method outperforms all existing methods with ResNet50 as the main recognition network. Compared with SCSampler [20] which is also a temporal sampling approach, our method surpass it by 3.7% while using 1.6× less computation overhead, which demonstrates the discrimination power of TSQ mechanism in temporal saliency estimation. Comparing to the state-of-the-art method based on early exiting, FrameExit [12], we still outperforms it by 0.5%, which shows our class-specific sampler can find more discriminative frames than this sequential early exiting framework. For a more fair comparison with above pure visual based methods, we also present the results of the visual variant of TSQNet, *i.e.*, 'VQM-only' with comparable computes. Although without text modality, it still surpass the SotA methods, which verify the superiority of our TSM mechanism.

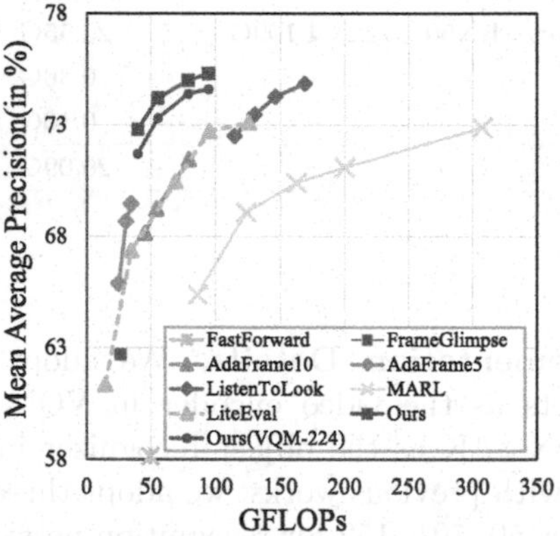

Fig. 3. Comparison of the pure VQM and the whole TSQNet with the state-of-the-art based on ResNet-101 recognition network on ActivityNet.

We further compare TSQNet with SOTA approaches in Fig. 3 based on Res101 backbone. Following previous works [11,47,50,51], ResNet-101 without TSN-style training is used as the recognizer, as the same as in Sect. 4.2. We calculate mAP under different budget K, which varies from 3 to 10. It is shown that our method achieves clearly superior efficiency-accuracy trade-off over all methods. And the result of pure VQM illustrates the efficiency of TSQ Mechanism.

To verify that our TSQNet can collaborate with more backbones, we present experiment results with ResNet-152 and Swin-transformer [26] family as recognition networks in Table 4. It is shown that our method outperforms all method with the same ResNet-152 backbones, and achieves absolute SOTA precision (88.7 Top-1 accuracy and 93.7 mAP) with Swin-Transformer architecture.

Results on FCVID. To verify that performance promotion can be achieved on more untrimmed datasets, we also evaluate our method on FCVID in Table 5,

Table 3. Comparisons with SOTA efficient video recognition methods with ResNet50 as recognition backbone on AcitivtyNet. 188 and 224 here represent resolutions.

Method	Backbone	mAP (%)	FLOPs
SCSampler [20]	ResNet50	72.9	42.0G
AR-Net [27]	ResNet18,34,50	73.8	33.5G
AdaMML [30]	ResNet50	73.9	94.0G
VideoIQ [36]	ResNet50	74.8	28.1G
AdaFocus [42]	ResNet50	75.0	26.6G
Dynamic-STE [19]	ResNet18,50	75.9	30.5G
FrameExit [12]	ResNet50	76.1	26.1G
Ours (VQM-only^{188})	ResNet50	75.7	24.3G
Ours (VQM-only^{224})	ResNet50	76.5	26.1G
Ours	ResNet50	**76.6**	26.1G

Table 4. Comparisons with SOTA video recognition methods using ResNet-152 and more advanced recognition networks on AcitivtyNet.

Method	Backbone	Pretrain	Accuracy (%)	mAP (%)
P3D [32]	ResNet-152	ImageNet	75.1	78.9
RRA [55]	ResNet-152	ImageNet	78.8	83.4
MARL [47]	ResNet-152	ImageNet	79.8	83.8
Ours	ResNet-152	ImageNet	**80.0**	**85.2**
ListenToLook [11]	R(2+1)D-152	Kinetics	–	89.9
MARL [47]	SEResNeXt152	Kinetics	–	90.1
Ours	Swin-B	Kinetics	84.7	91.2
Ours	Swin-L	Kinetics	**88.7**	**93.7**

which shows that our method outperforms competing methods in terms of accuracy while saving much computation cost. Compared with SOTA approach AdaFocus [42], which is motivated by selecting salient spatial regions, we achieve higher mAP with less computation, which implies that our discriminative temporal sampler can capture more salient information of videos.

Results on Mini-Kinetics. We further test the capability of TSQNet on a short trimmed video dataset *i.e.,* Mini-Kinetics, which is more difficult to sample salient frames. Table 6 demonstrates that our method achieves superior Top-1 accuracy (**73.2** *v.s.* 72.9) with 2.0× less FLOPs than the state-of-the-art method [42].

Practical Latency. We further conduct experiments of practical efficiency, which shows that our TSQNet significantly surpasses two state-of-the-art methods in inference latency, *i.e.,* FrameExit [12] (9.8 videos/sec *v.s.* **TSQNet 121.1** videos/sec) and AdaFocus [42] (73.8 videos/sec *v.s.* **TSQNet 121.1** videos/sec)[2]. See Appendix for more details.

4.4 Ablation Study

In this section, we inspect different aspects of our proposed TSQNet. All ablations are completed on AcitivtyNet with ResNet-101 as recognition network.

Table 5. Comparison with SOTA efficient video recognition methods on FCVID. TSQNet achieves the best mAP with significant computation savings. '188' and '224' are resolutions.

Methods	mAP (%)	FLOPs
LiteEval [50]	80.0	94.3G
AdaFrame [51]	80.2	75.1G
SCSampler [20]	81.0	42.0G
AR-Net [27]	81.3	35.1G
AdaFuse [28]	81.6	45.0G
SMART [13]	82.1	-
VideoIQ [36]	82.7	27.0G
AdaFocus [42]	83.4	26.6G
Ours (VQM-only^{188})	82.9	**24.4G**
Ours (VQM-only^{224})	83.3	26.2G
Ours	**83.5**	26.2G

Table 6. Comparison with state-of-the-art methods on Mini-Kinetics. TSQNet achieves the best Top-1 accuracy with comparable computation cost with the most efficient methods.

Methods	Top-1 (%)	FLOPs
LiteEval [50]	61.0	99.0G
SCSampler [20]	70.8	42.0G
AR-Net [27]	71.7	32.0G
AdaFuse [28]	72.3	23.0G
VideoIQ [36]	72.3	20.4G
Dynamic-STE [19]	72.7	18.3G
FrameExit [12]	72.8	19.7G
AdaFocus [42]	72.9	38.6G
Ours (VQM-only)	72.9	**18.1G**
Ours	**73.2**	19.7G

[2] Results are obtained on a NVIDIA 3090 GPU with an Intel Xeon E5-2650 v3 @ 2.30 GHz CPU.

Effectiveness of Class-specific Designs. We investigate the effectiveness of our class-specific designs in TSQ mechanism. Table 7 presents the results of class-specific ("CS") version and class-agnostic ("CA") version of both the attention structure and the classifier in VQM. For attention structure, the class-agnostic version refers to setting the size of visual TSQ embedding set $\{E_c^v\}_{c=1}^C$ to 1. Then generated attention weight $A^v \in \mathbb{R}^{1 \times T}$ is directly used as saliency measurement. For the classifier, the class-agnostic version is to replace existing C-projection-layer classifier with a single-projection-layer one as aforementioned in Sect. 3.1. It is shown that "CS CS" (ours) significantly outperforms "CA CA" choice, which confirms the effectiveness of class-specific information in saliency measurements. Besides, "CS CA" choice presents an unpromising result, which demonstrates that class-specific classifier is critical for TSQ mechanism to function normally in class-specific setting. See Appendix for illustrative examples of these three settings and detailed explanation of comparison of their performance.

Effectiveness of Multi-modal and Fusion and Interactions. To verify the effectiveness of fusion of VQM and TQM and multi-modality interactions, we present experimental results on two individual modalities with different usage of $\mathcal{L}_{t \to v}$ and $\mathcal{L}_{v \to t}$ in Table 8. Without any interactions, fusion of two modules relatively impart improvements on TQM and VQM for 2.9% and 0.3% respectively, which verifies that two modules are complementary. $\mathcal{L}_{t \to v}$ clearly elevate the performance of TQM for better category-frame modelling guided by visual features from VQM. The performance of VQM is also slightly improved by introducing textual-modality attention weights. $\mathcal{L}_{v \to t}$ significantly improves the performance of TQM for better learning of textual FFN and classifier. Finally, when both losses in CIM are added, the results of both TQM and VQM branch are further promoted, and performance of overall TSQNet is obviously improved (**75.3** *v.s.* 74.9). See Appendix for detailed investigations on ratios of two losses.

Table 7. Effectiveness of Class-specific designs.

Attention	Classifier	mAP (%)
CA	CA	74.0
CS	CA	68.7
CS	CS	**74.7**

Table 8. Effectiveness of multi-modality fusion and interactions.

$\mathcal{L}_{t \to v}$	$\mathcal{L}_{v \to t}$	TQM	VQM	Ours
–	–	72.0	74.6	74.9
✓	–	72.5	74.8	75.1
–	✓	72.7	74.6	75.1
✓	✓	**73.1**	**74.8**	**75.3**

Table 9. Results of different textual feature.

Method	Usage	mAP(%)
W2V	Top10	71.2
Glove	Top10	72.0
Bert	All	71.4
Bert	Top10	**72.1**

Table 10. Impacts of initialization of TSQ embedding.

Branch	Init	mAP(%)
Vis	Random	73.8
	Prototype	**74.7**
Text	Random	71.6
	Bert Emb.	**72.1**

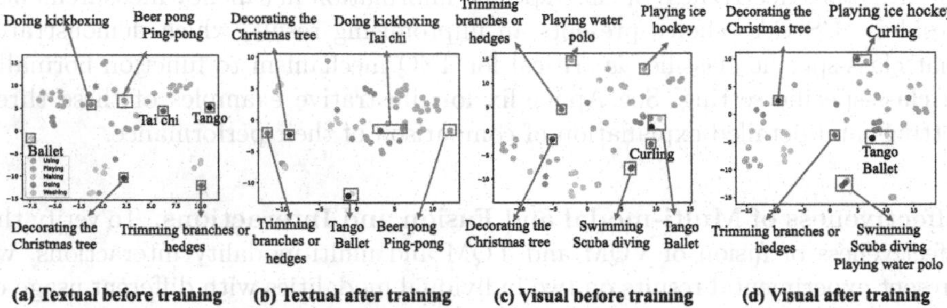

Fig. 4. The visual and textual TSQ embeddings before and after training visualized by t-SNE. The category embeddings with relevant semantics cluster together after training. See Sect. 4.5 for detailed explanation.

Different Textual Feature. In Table 9, we try three commonly used word embeddings, *i.e.*, Bert [7], Glove [31] and Word2Vec [29], as well as two fashions of usage of object scores O_i, *i.e.*, top-10 object categories ("Top10") and all categories ("All"). Experimental result shows that the Bert embedding with top-10 object score gain the best result, which verifies that both the quality of word embedding and noise filtering of object category count for textual instantiation of TSQ mechanism.

Impacts of Initialization of TSQ Embedding. We further explore the initialization of visual and textual TSQ embeddings in Table 10. The comparison with random initialization confirms that proposed prototype based visual TSQ embedding in VQM and word embedding based textual embedding in TQM provide meaningful and effective initialization for TSQ embeddings.

(a) Decorating Christmas tree (b) Golfing

Fig. 5. Qualitative Evaluation of Sampled frames. We visualized the most salient five frames of uniform and our proposed methods with two samples. The frames with golden border represent the identified salient frames by human intuition, and the frames with mask denote the non-salient ones.

4.5 Qualitative Analysis

We visualize visual and textual TSQ embdding by t-SNE in Fig. 4, which shows that our class-specific motivation is highly interpretable in terms of relationships between categories. We also find some categories sharing similar objects are more closer in text TSQ embeddings than in visual ones. For examples, **Decorating the Christmas tree** and **Trimming branches or hedges** share tree or tree-related objects and become closer after training. This may be because TQM measure saliency based on event-object relations, which are more robust against scene variations. In Fig. 5, we exhibit some qualitative examples of **Decorating Christmas tree** and **Golfing** for sampled frames by uniform baseline, TQM, VQM and TSQNet. In the case of **Decorating Christmas tree**, it is shown that TQM and VQM are clearly better than uniform baseline. After fusion, TSQNet can sample further more salient frames. Another qualitative example **Golfing** is quite interesting. VQM captures the action moments of swinging a golf club and scenes of a golf course, while TQM captures the golf balls and a golf cart. After fusion, TSQNet select the frames of these object, actions and scenes, which implies our TQM and VQM can cooperate to build a robust sampler aware of object, scene and action information.

5 Conclusions

This paper investigates efficient video recognition by proposing a novel Temporal Saliency Query mechanism and presents an efficient multi-modal salient frame sampler Temporal Saliency Query Network. Extensive experiments verify the proposed method significantly outperforms the state-of-the-art approaches on accuracy-efficiency trade-off. Our proposed method is model-agnostic and can be used with various network architectures. And since our salient score is class-specific, we can easily extend our method to multi-label efficient video recognition.

References

1. Caba Heilbron, F., Escorcia, V., Ghanem, B., Carlos Niebles, J.: Activitynet: A large-scale video benchmark for human activity understanding. In: Proceedings of the ieee conference on computer vision and pattern recognition, pp. 961–970 (2015)
2. Carion, N., Massa, F., Synnaeve, G., Usunier, N., Kirillov, A., Zagoruyko, S.: End-to-end object detection with transformers. In: Vedaldi, A., Bischof, H., Brox, T., Frahm, J.-M. (eds.) ECCV 2020. LNCS, vol. 12346, pp. 213–229. Springer, Cham (2020). https://doi.org/10.1007/978-3-030-58452-8_13
3. Chen, X., Han, Y., Wang, X., Sun, Y., Yang, Y.: Action keypoint network for efficient video recognition. arXiv preprint arXiv:2201.06304 (2022)
4. Chen, Y., et al.: Mobile-former: Bridging mobilenet and transformer. arXiv preprint arXiv:2108.05895 (2021)
5. Cheng, B., Schwing, A., Kirillov, A.: Per-pixel classification is not all you need for semantic segmentation. In: Advances in Neural Information Processing Systems 34 (2021)
6. Deng, J., Yang, Z., Chen, T., Zhou, W., Li, H.: Transvg: End-to-end visual grounding with transformers. In: Proceedings of the IEEE/CVF International Conference on Computer Vision. pp. 1769–1779 (2021)
7. Devlin, J., Chang, M.W., Lee, K., Toutanova, K.: Bert: Pre-training of deep bidirectional transformers for language understanding. arXiv preprint arXiv:1810.04805 (2018)
8. Dosovitskiy, A., et al.: An image is worth 16x16 words: Transformers for image recognition at scale. arXiv preprint arXiv:2010.11929 (2020)
9. Fang, B., Wu, W., Liu, C., Zhou, Y., He, D., Wang, W.: Mamico: Macro-to-Micro Semantic Correspondence for Self-Supervised Video Representation Learning. In Proc, ACMMM (2022)
10. Feichtenhofer, C.: X3d: Expanding architectures for efficient video recognition. In: Proceedings of the IEEE/CVF Conference on Computer Vision and Pattern Recognition, pp. 203–213 (2020)
11. Gao, R., Oh, T.H., Grauman, K., Torresani, L.: Listen to look: Action recognition by previewing audio. In: Proceedings of the IEEE/CVF Conference on Computer Vision and Pattern Recognition, pp. 10457–10467 (2020)
12. Ghodrati, A., Bejnordi, B.E., Habibian, A.: Frameexit: Conditional early exiting for efficient video recognition. In: Proceedings of the IEEE/CVF Conference on Computer Vision and Pattern Recognition, pp. 15608–15618 (2021)
13. Gowda, S.N., Rohrbach, M., Sevilla-Lara, L.: SMART frame selection for action recognition 35(2), 1451–1459 (2021). https://ojs.aaai.org/index.php/AAAI/article/view/16235
14. He, K., Zhang, X., Ren, S., Sun, J.: Deep residual learning for image recognition. In: Proceedings of the IEEE conference on computer vision and pattern recognition, pp. 770–778 (2016)
15. Huang, D., et al.: Ascnet: Self-supervised video representation learning with appearance-speed consistency. In: Proceedings of the IEEE/CVF International Conference on Computer Vision, pp. 8096–8105 (2021)
16. Jain, M., Van Gemert, J.C., Snoek, C.G.: What do 15,000 object categories tell us about classifying and localizing actions? In: Proceedings of the IEEE conference on computer vision and pattern recognition, pp. 46–55 (2015)

17. Jiang, Y.G., Wu, Z., Wang, J., Xue, X., Chang, S.F.: Exploiting feature and class relationships in video categorization with regularized deep neural networks. IEEE Trans. Pattern Anal. Mach. Intell. **40**(2), 352–364 (2018). https://doi.org/10.1109/TPAMI.2017.2670560
18. Kay, W., et al.: The kinetics human action video dataset. arXiv preprint arXiv:1705.06950 (2017)
19. Kim, H., Jain, M., Lee, J.T., Yun, S., Porikli, F.: Efficient action recognition via dynamic knowledge propagation. In: Proceedings of the IEEE/CVF International Conference on Computer Vision, pp. 13719–13728 (2021)
20. Korbar, B., Tran, D., Torresani, L.: Scsampler: Sampling salient clips from video for efficient action recognition. In: Proceedings of the IEEE/CVF International Conference on Computer Vision (ICCV) (2019)
21. Lanchantin, J., Wang, T., Ordonez, V., Qi, Y.: General multi-label image classification with transformers. In: Proceedings of the IEEE/CVF Conference on Computer Vision and Pattern Recognition, pp. 16478–16488 (2021)
22. Li, H., Wu, Z., Shrivastava, A., Davis, L.S.: 2d or not 2d? adaptive 3d convolution selection for efficient video recognition. In: Proceedings of the IEEE/CVF Conference on Computer Vision and Pattern Recognition, pp. 6155–6164 (2021)
23. Lin, J., Gan, C., Han, S.: Tsm: Temporal shift module for efficient video understanding. In: Proceedings of the IEEE/CVF International Conference on Computer Vision, pp. 7083–7093 (2019)
24. Lin, J., Duan, H., Chen, K., Lin, D., Wang, L.: Ocsampler: Compressing videos to one clip with single-step sampling. arXiv preprint arXiv:2201.04388 (2022)
25. Liu, S., Zhang, L., Yang, X., Su, H., Zhu, J.: Query2label: A simple transformer way to multi-label classification (2021)
26. Liu, Z., et al.: Swin transformer: Hierarchical vision transformer using shifted windows. In: Proceedings of the IEEE/CVF International Conference on Computer Vision, pp. 10012–10022 (2021)
27. Meng, Y., et al.: AR-Net: adaptive frame resolution for efficient action recognition. In: Vedaldi, A., Bischof, H., Brox, T., Frahm, J.-M. (eds.) ECCV 2020. LNCS, vol. 12352, pp. 86–104. Springer, Cham (2020). https://doi.org/10.1007/978-3-030-58571-6_6
28. Meng, Y., et al.: Adafuse: Adaptive temporal fusion network for efficient action recognition. arXiv preprint arXiv:2102.05775 (2021)
29. Mikolov, T., Chen, K., Corrado, G., Dean, J.: Efficient estimation of word representations in vector space. arXiv preprint arXiv:1301.3781 (2013)
30. Panda, R., et al.: Adamml: Adaptive multi-modal learning for efficient video recognition. arXiv preprint arXiv:2105.05165 (2021)
31. Pennington, J., Socher, R., Manning, C.D.: Glove: Global vectors for word representation. In: Proceedings of the 2014 conference on empirical methods in natural language processing (EMNLP), pp. 1532–1543 (2014)
32. Qiu, Z., Yao, T., Mei, T.: Learning spatio-temporal representation with pseudo-3d residual networks. In: proceedings of the IEEE International Conference on Computer Vision, pp. 5533–5541 (2017)
33. Sandler, M., Howard, A., Zhu, M., Zhmoginov, A., Chen, L.C.: Mobilenetv 2: Inverted residuals and linear bottlenecks. In: Proceedings of the IEEE conference on computer vision and pattern recognition, pp. 4510–4520 (2018)
34. Snell, J., Swersky, K., Zemel, R.: Prototypical networks for few-shot learning. In: Advances in neural information processing systems 30 (2017)
35. Soomro, K., Zamir, A.R., Shah, M.: Ucf101: A dataset of 101 human actions classes from videos in the wild. arXiv preprint arXiv:1212.0402 (2012)

36. Sun, X., Panda, R., Chen, C.F.R., Oliva, A., Feris, R., Saenko, K.: Dynamic network quantization for efficient video inference. In: Proceedings of the IEEE/CVF International Conference on Computer Vision, pp. 7375–7385 (2021)
37. Tan, M., Le, Q.: Efficientnet: Rethinking model scaling for convolutional neural networks. In: International Conference on Machine Learning, pp. 6105–6114. PMLR (2019)
38. Tran, D., Wang, H., Torresani, L., Ray, J., LeCun, Y., Paluri, M.: A closer look at spatiotemporal convolutions for action recognition. In: CVPR (2018)
39. Vaswani, A., et al.: Attention is all you need. In: Advances in neural information processing systems, pp. 5998–6008 (2017)
40. Wang, H., Zhang, Y., Ji, Z., Pang, Y., Ma, L.: Consensus-aware visual-semantic embedding for image-text matching. In: Vedaldi, A., Bischof, H., Brox, T., Frahm, J.-M. (eds.) ECCV 2020. LNCS, vol. 12369, pp. 18–34. Springer, Cham (2020). https://doi.org/10.1007/978-3-030-58586-0_2
41. Wang, X., Zhu, L., Wu, Y., Yang, Y.: Symbiotic attention for egocentric action recognition with object-centric alignment. In: IEEE transactions on pattern analysis and machine intelligence (2020)
42. Wang, Y., Chen, Z., Jiang, H., Song, S., Han, Y., Huang, G.: Adaptive focus for efficient video recognition. arXiv preprint arXiv:2105.03245 (2021)
43. Wang, Y., Huang, R., Song, S., Huang, Z., Huang, G.: Not all images are worth 16x16 words: Dynamic transformers for efficient image recognition. Adv. Neural. Inf. Process. Syst. **34**, 11960–11973 (2021)
44. Wang, Y., et al.: Adafocus v2: End-to-end training of spatial dynamic networks for video recognition. arXiv preprint arXiv:2112.14238 (2021)
45. Wu, J., et al.: Weakly-supervised spatio-temporal anomaly detection in surveillance video. IJCAI (2021)
46. Wu, W., He, D., Lin, T., Li, F., Gan, C., Ding, E.: Mvfnet: Multi-view fusion network for efficient video recognition. In: Proceedings of the AAAI Conference on Artificial Intelligence. vol. 35, pp. 2943–2951 (2021)
47. Wu, W., He, D., Tan, X., Chen, S., Wen, S.: Multi-agent reinforcement learning based frame sampling for effective untrimmed video recognition. In: Proceedings of the IEEE/CVF International Conference on Computer Vision, pp. 6222–6231 (2019)
48. Wu, W., He, D., Tan, X., Chen, S., Yang, Y., Wen, S.: Dynamic inference: A new approach toward efficient video action recognition. In: Proceedings of the IEEE/CVF Conference on Computer Vision and Pattern Recognition Workshops, pp. 676–677 (2020)
49. Wu, W., Sun, Z., Ouyang, W.: Transferring textual knowledge for visual recognition. ArXiv abs/2207.01297 (2022)
50. Wu, Z., Xiong, C., Jiang, Y.G., Davis, L.S.: Liteeval: A coarse-to-fine framework for resource efficient video recognition. arXiv preprint arXiv:1912.01601 (2019)
51. Wu, Z., Xiong, C., Ma, C.Y., Socher, R., Davis, L.S.: Adaframe: Adaptive frame selection for fast video recognition. In: Proceedings of the IEEE/CVF Conference on Computer Vision and Pattern Recognition, pp. 1278–1287 (2019)
52. Xia, B., et al.: Nsnet: Non-saliency suppression sampler for efficient video recognition. ECCV (2022)
53. Xie, S., Sun, C., Huang, J., Tu, Z., Murphy, K.: Rethinking spatiotemporal feature learning: speed-accuracy trade-offs in video classification. In: Ferrari, V., Hebert, M., Sminchisescu, C., Weiss, Y. (eds.) ECCV 2018. LNCS, vol. 11219, pp. 318–335. Springer, Cham (2018). https://doi.org/10.1007/978-3-030-01267-0_19

54. Yang, H., et al.: Temporal action proposal generation with background constraint. In: Proceedings of the AAAI Conference on Artificial Intelligence. vol. 36, pp. 3054–3062 (2022)
55. Zhu, C., et al.: Fine-grained video categorization with redundancy reduction attention. In: Ferrari, V., Hebert, M., Sminchisescu, C., Weiss, Y. (eds.) ECCV 2018. LNCS, vol. 11209, pp. 139–155. Springer, Cham (2018). https://doi.org/10.1007/978-3-030-01228-1_9

Author Index

Printed in the United States
by Baker & Taylor Publisher Services